THE NBA'S OFFICIAL ENCYCLOPEDIA OF PRO BASKETBALL

THE NBA'S OFFICIAL ENCYCLOPEDIA OF PRO BASKETBALL

Edited by
ZANDER HOLLANDER

Foreword by LAWRENCE F. O'BRIEN
Commissioner, National Basketball Association

AN ASSOCIATED FEATURES BOOK

NAL BOOKS

NEW AMERICAN LIBRARY

TIMES MIRROR

NEW YORK AND SCARBOROUGH, ONTARIO

PHOTO CREDITS

UPI: ii, 12, 40, 42, 44, 45, 46, 47, 49, 51, 52, 55, 57, 58, 60, 61, 63, 64, 66, 68, 69, 71, 72, 74, 75, 76, 78, 80, 83, 84, 86, 96, 98, 99, 102, 103, 106, 107, 110, 115, 116, 121, 128, 131, 133, 134, 147, 148, 150, 231, 238, 241, 246, 250, 253, 258, 259, 263, 269, 271, 276, 282, 291, 323, 339, 340, 342, 345, 349, 350, 353, 375, 401; Jim Anderson: 129; Cliff Barnard: 284; Paul Bereswill: 286, 293, 294; Boston Celtics: 229; Eric Compton Collection: 41; Chuck Connors Collection: 39; Denver Nuggets: 136, 298; Dudley, Hardin & Yang, Inc.: 274; Dutch Dehnert Collection: 11, 16, 18, 22, 24; Malcolm Emmons: 88, 89, 92, 93, 104, 140, 143, 153, 234, 236, 256, 266, 272, 326; Bert Fox: 296; Steve Fox: 278; George Gojkovich: 122, 130; Eddie Gottlieb Collection: 32; Hall of Fame: 2, 4, 5, 6, 7, 28, 30, 34, 35, 243, 248, 354; Nancy Hogue: 139, 145, 255, 352; George Kalinsky: 264, 268; Kentucky Colonels: 289 (top); Joe Lapchick Collection: 13, 14, 26; Bill Lewis: 279; Peter Mecca: 261; Branch McCracken Collection: 38; Milwaukee Bucks: 108; National Basketball Association: vi, 91, 215·225, 351; Darryl Norenberg: 112, 113; Richard Pilling: 141, 144, 226, 232; Bill Randolph: 289 (left); Ken Regan: 101; Mitchell B. Reibel/Fotosport: 135, 251; Steve Snodgrass: 124, 244, 248; Michael L. Valeri: 118, 125, 239.

JACKET PHOTO CREDITS

Front Cover: All of the photos are by Malcolm Emmons except for Rick Barry (Richard Pilling) and George Mikan (UPI). Back Cover: Richard Pilling.

COLOR INSERT CREDITS

Malcolm Emmons: Elgin Baylor, Bill Russell, Oscar Robertson, Dave Cowens, Rick Barry, Paul Westphal, David Thompson, Moses Malone, George Gervin, Magic Johnson

Walter Iooss, Jr.: John Havlicek

Darryl Norenberg: Wilt Chamberlain, Jerry West

Mickey Palmer/Focus on Sports: Walt Frazier, Willis Reed

Richard Pilling: Larry Bird

Ken Regan/Camera 5: Pete Maravich

Mitchell B. Reibel/Focus on Sports: Bill Walton, Julius Erving

Mitchell B. Reibel/Fotosport: 24-second clock

Carl Skalak: Billy Cunningham, Lenny Wilkens, Calvin Murphy

Jerry Wachter/Focus on Sports: Elvin Hayes

The Original Celtics by Tom Meany, reprinted by permission of *Sport* Magazine © Sport, 1949.

An original edition was published in 1977 as *The Pro Basketball Encyclopedia* © Associated Features, 1977.

NAL BOOKS TRADEMARK REG. U.S. PAT. OFF. AND FOREIGN COUNTRIES
REGISTERED TRADEMARK—MARCA REGISTRADA
HECHO EN HARRISONBURG, VA. U.S.A.

SIGNET, SIGNET CLASSICS, MENTOR, PLUME, MERIDIAN and NAL BOOKS are published by The New American Library, Inc., 1633 Broadway, New York, New York 10019

Library of Congress Catalog Card No. 81-82815

ISBN: 0-453-00407-5

Designed by SOHO Studios

First Printing, October 1981

1 2 3 4 5 6 7 8 9

Printed in the United States of America

For the NBA's All-Time Team and Coach

Kareem Abdul-Jabbar
Elgin Baylor
Wilt Chamberlain
Bob Cousy
Julius Erving
John Havlicek
George Mikan
Bob Pettit
Oscar Robertson
Bill Russell
Jerry West

Red Auerbach

Foreword

You won't find my old knee pads or jersey in the Naismith Hall of Fame in Springfield, Massachusetts, but somewhere in the archives of that city is a certificate attesting to my birth.

I was known as "Gunner" when I played basketball in the schoolyard and at the very YMCA where Dr. Naismith invented the sport. The peach baskets were down by the time I got there. But we were still jumping center after every basket. I loved the sport, although I didn't play it that well.

I guess you might say I made it to the pros, however. And so has Zander Hollander with *The NBA's Official Encyclopedia of Pro Basketball*.

I am fascinated with the material he and his contributors have turned up. I especially enjoyed the photograph of the Original Celtics at the White House in 1925. It makes me wonder whether there was ever a basket at the White House. In my years with President Kennedy, I never saw one. At the rate our sport continues to grow, one day there will be a President whose favorite sport is basketball.

The time is right for a purely pro encyclopedia. I've never seen anything like it. This enormous volume tells us about yesterday and today—in fact and in photo. And it celebrates a landmark—the 35th anniversary of the National Basketball Association.

If I had to sum it up in a word, I'd say it's a "slamdunk."

Lawrence F. O'Brien
Commissioner
National Basketball Association

◄*NBA Commissioner Lawrence O'Brien would be correct in saying that no NBA center measures up to Los Angeles' Kareem Abdul-Jabbar as six-time winner of the league's MVP trophy.*

Acknowledgments

The research, writing and editing of *The NBA's Of- ficial Encyclopedia of Pro Basketball* required a corps of talented, knowledgeable contributors. They came from every level—writers, editors, statisticians, play- ers, coaches, referees, even fans—and all had a com- mon bond: an affection for the game and a desire to faithfully record the history of the professionals.

The editor wishes to thank Leonard Koppett, for- merly with *The New York Times* and now with *The Peninsula Times-Tribune*, for the chapters on the Basketball Association of America and the National Basketball Association; Reid Grosky of the Los An- geles *Times* (The Pioneers, American Basketball Lea- gue, the Rens and National Basketball League); Woody Paige of the *Rocky Mountain News* (American Basketball Association); Bob Ryan of the Boston *Globe* and David Schulz (The Greatest Players); Pete Alfano of *Newsday* (The Officials); Roger Director of the New York *Daily News* (The Globetrotters); and Merv Harris of the San Francisco *Examiner* (The Coaches).

For invaluable copyreading we salute Frank Kelly of the New York *Daily News*, and for the monumental All-Time Player Directory we acknowledge Eric Compton and Lee Stowbridge of the New York *Daily News*, Frank Hellriegel and Bill Himmelman.

To Dennis Lyons, for playing both ends of the court and the middle; Howie Evans for his interviews with the old New York Rens; Nat Holman, Joe Lap- chick, Dutch Dehnert, Benny Borgmann and Eddie Gottlieb, for their total recall of how it was; and Norm Drucker, John Nucatola and Sid Borgia, for the lot of the referee.

To Lee Williams and his staff at the Basketball Hall of Fame, and to *Sport* for permission to reprint Tom Meany's story on the Original Celtics.

To Sandy Padwe, Nat "Feets" Broudy, Med Park, Jim Bukata, Jim Poris, Howard Blatt, John Duxbury, Seymour Siwoff, Steve Hirdt and the Elias Sports Bureau, for filling in some holes.

To NBA Commissioner Lawrence F. O'Brien, Matt Winick, Edgar Falk, Mike Suscavage, Gail Davey, Liz Kupec, Nick Curran and the NBA club publicity directors, for their support and encourage- ment.

To George Monette and Eddie Counter of the Twin Company, for titanic typesetting; to Gerry Burstein and the SoHo Studio, for creative design and exe- cution; to Richard Rossiter of New American Library, for design of the cover; and to Phyllis Hollander, for playing the pivot.

Contents

Introduction

I never got to see the Original Celtics play. But I experienced the next best thing: I saw them through the recollections and scrapbooks of three Celtics who were Originals—Dutch Dehnert, Nat Holman and Joe Lapchick.

I met Dutch for the first time at his beachside apartment in Rockaway Beach, New York. He was in his seventies; the legs that had played a role in the pivot play he invented were hobbled and he had difficulty walking. But Dutch led me to the biggest scrapbook I ever saw, the size of a card table, and I spent the afternoon—and several more—absorbed in the saga of the Celtics and early pro basketball. The scrapbook, teeming with clippings and photos that criss-crossed the United States, represented a labor of love by Mrs. Dehnert, much of whose time during Dutch's barnstorming years was obviously spent at home with a glue pot.

Nat Holman I'd met earlier, much earlier. As a freshman at City College of New York (CCNY) before World War II, I was on the basketball squad, somewhere between the scrubs and the second team. I knew relatively little of the legend of Nat Holman, the City College coach and nonpareil pro, and he had no reason at the time to share it with a callow freshman whose prime interest was in surviving the cut.

As a newspaperman a decade later, I had the trying assignment of interviewing Nat when his CCNY team, 1950 NIT and NCAA champion, was involved in the fix scandal that broke in 1951. It wasn't until many years later, when I began serious research for what would become *The NBA's Official Encyclopedia of Pro Basketball*, that I got to see the side of Nat

Holman that neither player nor public ever saw. At his apartment on Madison Avenue in Manhattan, this proud, debonair gentleman opened up his treasury of photos and scrapbooks, and his heart, to an awed admirer who in many ways became, once again, that callow freshman.

Joe Lapchick was best man at Nat Holman's wedding, and what a man! I knew him as coach of the St. John's University team and as an early coach of the New York Knickerbockers. Joe's lode of memorabilia was tucked away in the attic of his Yonkers, New York, home and he carted it all down, including a priceless 1930-31 contract.

Although I was too young to see these Celtics play, they provided me with the sort of replay that helped inspire this encyclopedia. Through them I lived the old days; in modern times, as a sportswriter and editor, I've been able to follow the pros first-hand and to be involved in book projects with players and coaches like Willis Reed, Jerry West and Tom Meschery. This was all part of my preparation, as it turned out, for my biggest basketball assignment ever—the 35th anniversary edition of *The NBA's Official Encyclopedia of Pro Basketball*.

The goal was to cover the sport from the advent of the first professional player through the earliest leagues and into the modern era—from the American Basketball League and the National Basketball League to the Basketball Association of America, National Basketball Association and the American Basketball Association. Not only the Original Celtics, but such other significant contributors as the New York Rens and the Harlem Globetrotters are included,

INTRODUCTION

along with coaches, officials and members of the Basketball Hall of Fame.

The encyclopedia details every BBA, NBA and ABA season with accompanying statistics. Profiled are ''The Greatest Pros''—the choices of whom will doubtless provoke the kind of controversy that is the lifeblood of any sport.

More than 2,000 players—every man who has ever appeared in BAA, NBA or ABA games—are listed with their year-by-year records in the most complete register of its kind.

Now, once and for all, you can look it up in a single volume.

Zander Hollander
Millerton, New York

PART 1

THE EARLY GAME

BASKET BALL
OUTFITS.

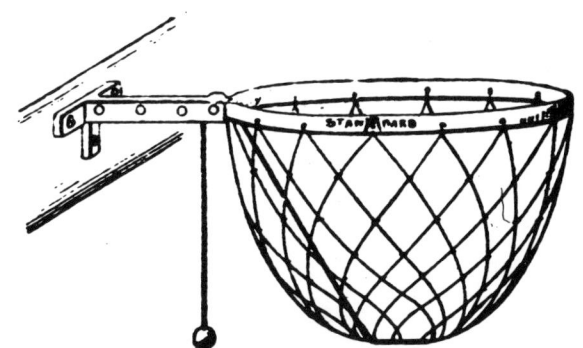

INDOOR BASKET.

The baskets are strong iron hoops, with braided cord netting, arranged to be secured to a gymnasium gallery or wall for indoor use, or on an upright pipe the bottom of which is spiked to be driven into the ground for outdoor use. By means of a cord the ball is easily discharged after a goal is made.

Indoor Goals, per pair,	$15.00
Outdoor Goals, per pair,	30.00
No 10 Association Foot Ball, each,	3.25
American Rubber Foot Ball,	1.25

Prices for Special Portable Baskets for Exhibitions in Halls or low priced outfits given on application.

OUTDOOR BASKET.

Once upon a time there was a peach basket.

CHAPTER 1

The Pioneers

No golden trumpets hailed the arrival of professional basketball in 1896. Few persons, in fact, were even aware of the event in which a team in Trenton, New Jersey, charged admission to one of its games and divided the meager profits among its players. Instead, other happenings were commanding the nation's attention, such as the election of William McKinley as President, the granting of statehood to Utah, the hint of a gold strike in the Canadian Klondike.

Sports were not unknown, of course. Victories that year by Ben Brush in the Kentucky Derby, the Baltimore Orioles in the National Baseball League and the United States in the first modern Olympics in Athens, Greece, all received notice. However, basketball was far from the front of public consciousness.

The game had been invented only five years earlier, in 1891, by Dr. James Naismith, a Canadian-born physical-education training instructor for the Young Men's Christian Association in Springfield, Massachusetts. It had spread to other YMCAs as Naismith's pupils played exhibitions, and set the pace for organized play and leagues at various YMCA branches around the country.

But the YMCA leaders soon concluded that basketball was proving a rough, contact sport that was stealing gym time from the normal YMCA physical training program. Indeed, a Y publication in 1894 editorialized: "The game could never and should never be allowed to take the place of all other exercise in the gymnasium."

Dispossessed but unwilling to give up their newly-discovered sport, many of the Y players sought other facilities—armories, barns, skating rinks and dance halls. They would play for rent money, and leftovers, before their small bands of followers.

Thus was the stage set for the birth of professional basketball on that night in 1896 when the Trenton players rented the local Masonic Hall and gave up their amateur standing for $15 apiece, with a dollar extra going to their captain, Fred Cooper.

By all accounts, the Trenton lads were both colorful and competent. They competed in velvet trunks, long tights and frilled stockings designed by Cooper, a former soccer player, and they were noted for specializing in a new offensive move. Cooper and a teammate, Al Bratton, would pass the ball between them from one end of the court to the other, right to the other team's basket. How daring, indeed, for a time in which plays thought of today as basic were looked upon as innovative. A player named Dutch Wohlfarth, for example, stirred all kinds of talk simply by dribbling without watching the ball. Wohlfarth became known as the "Blind Dribbler" and gained considerable respect, owing to the fact that basketballs, oversized and lopsided and blackened by wear, rarely were controlled with such skill.

By comparison with behind-the-back dribblers and fancy passes, early basketball was almost a football scrimmage. Padded pants, knee guards and elbow pads were standard equipment. And broken noses were the fashion. The rules depended for the most part on whose court the game was held on and who refereed. Crowds were raucously informal, and players and fans often exchanged insults and punches.

The inventor: Dr. James Naismith.

Frank Basloe, an early promoter and manager, remembered a game in Millville, Pennsylvania, in which, as he put it, "a Trenton player was knocked cold on the floor and the Millville fans proceeded to kick him in the face." In tough Pennsylvania coal towns, miners would arrive with pocketsful of nails, heat them with mining lamps and hurl them at referees and opposing free-throw shooters. Refereeing was so hazardous that some officials carried revolvers for protection.

Referees were never very safe among the players, either. A highly dangerous part of the actual game was the center jump, then held after each basket. Honey Russell, an early pro and later a coach at Seton Hall, remembered the play as being nearly homicidal for referees. "The center tap was murderous," Russell said. "We hit real hard. I've seen guys get crippled and I know two or three referees who ended up with broken necks. Their only object was to throw the ball up and try to get out of there."

They could not go far, however, because the courts, usually of 60-by-40-foot bandbox dimen-sions, were enclosed by chicken-wire fences that served to keep the ball continuously in bounds. The enclosure gave the athletes the appearance of being caged in, and led to such terms as "cagers" and "cage game," which are still used today. Similarly, some of the courts were obstructed by pillars, and a player who deftly maneuvered so as to send the man guarding him crashing into one of these obstacles was said to have accomplished the "post play."

The cages remained popular in the East well into the 1920s, although in the West they were used only in such hotbeds as Fond du Lac, Wisconsin, and Red Wing, Minnesota. Netting replaced the dangerous wire in many eastern cities, and players began bouncing off the ropes to change direction. Barney Sedran, one of the great little men, was happy that the safer netting was adopted. "Players would be thrown against the wire," he recalled, "and most of us would get cut. The court was covered with blood." The boisterous fans were unconcerned with safety. One of their favorite pranks was to jab through the cages at players' legs with hatpins and lighted cigarettes.

Another drawback for the players was that games often were merely a sideshow. Dancing was conducted before and after games, and sometimes at the half. The highly waxed floors were fine for the waltz but hardly for a quick move off the ropes toward the basket.

Nonetheless, the object of the game remained the same as today—to score points—although the strategy was quite different. Not only was there a center jump after every basket, but teams could hold the ball indefinitely in the backcourt as a stalling tactic. The players would pursue the ball furiously, much as in hockey or football. Since bruising fouls were one way of breaking the stall, foul shots became an important weapon, and each team used a specialist to take all its free throws.

On offense, following the tip-off, the player who was the best lay-up man moved to the area in front of the basket. There, the opposing team would station a "standing guard," who would try to force the lay-up man out of the slot. The standing guard (a term and not a designated position) usually would remain in the backcourt even when his team was on offense. The objective for the team with the ball was to lure the standing guard away from the basket for an easy lay-up, or to work the ball around for the only other shot of the day, the two-handed set, which sometimes was taken underhand.

Under such strategems, some players would go the entire game without shooting, stalling was common, and so were final scores of 20-15. Yet, the limited facets of the game were developed highly, and many excellent teams and individual players emerged in the years of pro ball leading up to World War I.

The first wonder team was the Buffalo Germans, organized in 1895 as 14-year-olds playing YMCA ball on the east side of their city, where many people of German extraction lived. The team, led by Al Heerdt and Eddie Miller, played for more than two decades, and compiled a remarkable won-lost record of 792-86. As a touring pro club, the Germans once amassed 111 straight victories before losing a game in 1910 to one of Frank Basloe's teams in Herkimer, New York. With stars such as Heerdt, Miller, Ed

The Buffalo Germans, basketball's first wonder team, played more than two decades, compiling a 792-86 record.

Ed Wachter of the Troy (N.Y.) Trojans was the best center of his day at 6-6.

Reimann and Hank Faust, the Germans' reputation grew to where they received $500 guarantees for three-game series against teams as far west as Kansas. Their victims included the Carlisle Indians, featuring the legendary Jim Thorpe. The Germans disbanded in the 1920s but were reunited for an exhibition game in 1931. Averaging 51 years of age, they beat a team from Tonawanda, New York, by one point.

Another successful independent team, and a rival of the Germans, was Basloe's Oswego (N.Y.) Indians. The club won 121 games and lost six in 1914-15 after beating the Germans a year earlier in three of four games. Oswego's big star for the series with the Germans had been Oscar "Swede" Grimstead, whom Basloe lured away from New York City and called "the greatest ball-handler in basketball." The series was expectedly rough and at one point, said Basloe, whose view was not unbiased, "Miller of the Germans had his leg twisted and also got a wallop

in the mouth from an Oswego player. But he deserved it."

Perhaps the best club before World War I, however, was the Troy (N.Y.) Trojans, featuring 6-6 Ed Wachter, the best center of the day, and his brother, Lew, who organized the club and also played. Both had excellent basketball minds and later coached in the Ivy League. Under their direction and with such fine players as Jack Inglis and Andy Suils, the Trojans—also known as the "Wachter Wonders"—claimed to have developed such maneuvers as the fast break and the bounce pass. They also pioneered the idea that each player take his own foul shot, instead of relying on one specialist as was the custom. Still, this rule was not adopted for many more years.

Unlike the independent teams, the Trojans made their reputation in the organized pro leagues, dominating the Hudson River and New York State circuits. The early leagues were loosely structured and short-lived but were showcases for the best teams and talent of the day.

In 1898 the six-team National League was formed for the purpose of protecting players against unscrupulous promoters. It contained Trenton and Camden of New Jersey, Millville of Pennsylvania, the Pennsylvania Bicycle Club, the Hancock Athletic Club and the Germantown Club. Trenton, coached by Fred Cooper, captain of the first pro team, won the first two titles. But after five seasons the league folded.

Many of the former National League players went on to join the new Philadelphia League. Two respected circuits emerged as the Eastern League, which as an expanded version of the Philadelphia League existed from 1909 to 1923, and the Central League, alive from 1906 to 1912. The Eastern League's best teams were the 1904-05 Conshohocken outfit, led by a six-foot center, Bill Keenan, and the 1912-13 Reading Bears, whose star was Andy Sears, a 5-11 guard. Reading won added fame with a post-season victory over the Troy Trojans. The Central League had such franchises as South Side Pittsburgh and East Liverpool, Ohio. Its last title went to Johnstown (Pa.), whose star, Bill Kummer, averaged an amazing 22.6 points a game, more than many teams were scoring.

The leagues were unstable, however, largely because players were not bound by contracts and switched teams nightly, selling their services to the highest bidder. A player might compete for Troy one night and for Johnstown the next. One of these bas-

Carbondale (Pa.) won 35 straight games and the Tri-County League title in 1914–15.

ketball gypsies was Barney Sedran, who had the vivid memories of wire cages and broken noses. Sedran led a superb Carbondale (Pa.) team to 35 straight victories and the 1914-15 Tri-County League title. He somehow found time that same season to play a complete schedule with Utica in the New York State League. Although fast and possessing a deadly shot, Sedran did not look like a star athlete. He was even denied entrance to a game when the ticket-taker mistook him for a boy carrying a player's bag. And little wonder. Sedran, who once scored 17 baskets in a game—without a backboard—and who would make the Hall of Fame, was only 5-4.

About the time Sedran and teams like the Troy

Trojans were at their peak, a tall 15-year-old named Joe Lapchick was just starting to play for pay on teams around New York City. Lapchick, who would develop into the foremost center of the 1920s, remembered the details.

"My first job as a basketball player came in 1915 when I caught on with the Yonkers Bantams. We used to go to Beacon, Wappingers Falls, and Hudson, New York, and were paid $5 a game. Out of this we had to pay our transportation and meals. I netted the grant total of $15 the first year and $18 the second year.

"Slowly but surely I began to improve. Around 1917 and 1918, I began to play with other teams and

was in considerable demand, chiefly because of my height. I had reached 6-5 and was considered exceptionally tall. The Whirlwinds of New York City used me in some of their games, paying $7 per game. My expenses were practically nil, and since I was working as an apprentice machinist at $15 per week, I became affluent.

"By 1919 I was getting $10 per game and was gaining some renown in basketball circles. I was getting $3 per day on my job and $10 per game for playing basketball and could afford to take a day off from work now and then. My experience with the Whirlwinds led to games against the Brooklyn Visitations in the Metropolitan League. Since their games were played on Sunday nights, when other teams were idle, I agreed to play with them. At this time I was playing in four different leagues with four different teams.

"My earnings increased by leaps and bounds. I played one manager against the other and sometimes got as much as $75 a game. I bargained with the managers for every game. The standard rate of pay was a dollar a minute, but the rates were gradually increased until I got up to $90 or $100 a game no matter how many minutes I played. When there was a clash of dates I took the best offer. There was no income tax at that time, and I lived it up."

Lapchick's experience was common to many players of his time. But in the 1920s, the pattern of the pro game would change somewhat with the emergence of the most celebrated team of the early era, the Original Celtics, and of the first league with national aspirations.

Barney Sedran once scored 17 baskets in a game—without a backboard—and he was only 5-4, 118 pounds.

CHAPTER 2

Original Celtics

It was balmy that winter in Miami, perhaps the balmiest winter Florida's great resort city ever was to know, both as to weather and real estate prices. The great hurricane of 1926 was still many months away. In fact, it wasn't until the following September that it came swooshing out of the Caribbean to send buildings and prices tumbling.

The great storm was still in the future, and January and February were months of enjoyment. Every afternoon was the Fourth of July. Jack Dempsey, still the heavyweight king, was building a hotel—as who wasn't in Miami in those days—and looking for an "added attraction." William Jennings Bryan, the Great Commoner, was lending his silver tongue to the sale of lots in Coral Gables, so Dempsey cast about for an antidote. He chose, of all people, the Original Celtics, the greatest basketball team the world had ever seen.

It was a lucrative lark for the Celtics, as were all their basketball junkets in those days. They went Julius Caesar one better, for they came, they saw, they conquered—and they had a rollicking good time. Along with Bryan, with Al Schacht and Nick Altrock, the baseball comedy team, the Celtics made their contribution to the sound and fury of Miami in that hectic season.

Soon it was time for the Celtics to go to work again. Jim Furey, their energetic and industrious manager, had booked them for a game in Chattanooga, Tennessee. There were complications, too, as there so often were in those pioneering days of professional basketball. Nat Holman, one of the most

valued operatives on the Celtics' roster, had to return to New York for business reasons.

Losing a player, even a star like Holman, never bothered the Celtics. One of their members happened to find Benny Borgmann, a high scorer from Paterson, New Jersey, at a dog track one night. So Benny was brought along, like many others before and since, to wear the shamrock jersey and be a member of the Original Celtics, even if only for a one-night stand.

It was characteristic of the Celtics that they neither knew nor cared how many miles it was from Miami to Chattanooga. Furey merely booked a game for them and they went and played it. The next stop was always just around the corner as far as the Celtics were concerned. That Chattanooga was almost as far from Miami as Chicago is from New York came as a distinct surprise to the Celts, the most traveled of all basketball teams but also the most disinterested as to the details of their journeys.

"We were dog-dirty and tired when we got off the train at Chattanooga," recalled Dutch Dehnert. "There were a bunch of guys on the platform, a committee or something, to greet the great Celtics. And there we were, five of us—Johnny Beckman, Pete Barry, Joe Lapchick, Borgmann, and me. And crummy-looking, too, after being on the train about 20 hours.

"Naturally, these guys want to know where the rest of the squad is. So Beckie says, 'This is all there is, there isn't any more.' Then he tells them they can cut out the sightseeing tour they had planned for us, just get us to the hotel, let us get a hot bath, a shave,

and an hour's nap. 'We'll be in the dressing room at eight,' he tells them although it is then nearly five.

"Well, I don't know about the others, but they had a tough time waking me up at 7:30. Beckman is going around whacking us on the soles of our feet with a shoe to get us out of bed.

"We were playing in some auditorium, and they had a good crowd with lots of standees. The club we were playing was the Chattanooga Railites, a local industrial outfit, and rated pretty good. They were already out on the court when we come on, about a dozen of them in nice new uniforms, zipping the ball around and putting on a great show.

"They stopped to watch us when we came out, and I'll never forget how surprised they looked. The crowd started to give us a hand, then stopped almost before it started. There had been no time to get our uniforms laundered, and we looked like five guys who'd just wandered in off the street.

"There was silence when we started to warm up, because we just stood back and took lazy pop shots and lobbed the ball to one another. The crowd didn't know what to make of it. They probably figured they'd been jobbed, and the promoter had run in a lot of stumble-bums. Finally, we broke a sweat and practiced a little faster and then the game got under way.

"Lapchick was a dandy at getting the tap. We had set plays from the tap, which no other club had ever heard of in those days. Beckie went in and took the first tap from Joe, passed over his head to me, and I went under and laid one up, coming up from guard position. Then Lapchick batted the next tap back to Barry, the other guard, and Pete dribbled in to score. We must have scored eight goals in two minutes, and we're in front, 30-1, before there's a time-out.

"The Railites were using a standing guard, something which has long since gone out of basketball. This fellow stood right on his own foul line and never went upcourt, even when his own club had the ball.

"In the time-out, Beckman said, 'we'll have to move that guard out of there. He's breaking up our passes when we cut.' Then I volunteered to stand in front of him, explaining that instead of him breaking

Nat Holman was the Celtics' master faker and passer.

birth of the pivot play, one of the many great contributions the Celtics made to basketball. The Celts knew a good thing when they saw it. They were to basketball what the Baltimore Orioles were to baseball just before the turn of the century. It was the Orioles of John McGraw and Hughey Jennings, of Uncle Wilbert Robinson and Kid Gleason, who brought most of the strategic refinement into baseball—the hit-and-run, the delayed steal, the double steal, the drag bunt, and many more.

The beginnings of the Celtics, who did much the same for the cage game, are lost in what passes for antiquity in basketball. The late Gerry Schmeelk, one of the greatest shots professional basketball ever

Joe Lapchick had to fight for his life as a Celtic until he learned to switch on defense.

up our passes, they could pass to me and I could give it back.

"When play was resumed, I moved up in front of this fellow. Beckman passed to me and I passed to Borgmann, who was coming in from the other side. Then Barry passed to me, kept coming, and I passed right back to him. All of a sudden a great light dawned, and I took time out.

"We all went into a huddle and discussed the possibilities of this maneuver we had accidentally hit on. Beckman was enthusiastic, and we knew if Beckie liked it we had something, because Johnny was the smartest man who ever played basketball.

"This was the pivot play, but we didn't even know it at the time. A couple of minutes later, however, the standing guard, in an effort to bat the ball out of my hands, moved around to my right side. All I had to do was pivot to my left, take one step, and lay the ball up for a basket."

This, then, is the story, among other things, of the

Jim Furey's Original Celtics, circa 1920. Front row (left to right): Jim Furey, Ernie Reich, Johnny Beckman and Tom Furey. Back row: Johnny Witte, Dutch Dehnert, Joe Trippe, Pete Barry and Mike Smolick.

knew, said in 1941 that he didn't think one basketball fan in a thousand could name the Original Celtics. Schmeelk, long since retired from the court by this time, operated a package store on New York's West Side. In the window he had a group picture of the "original" Original Celtics, if you'll overlook the redundancy.

Schmeelk offered any of his customers a case of liquor of their own choosing if they could identify the players. He never had to give up so much as a dram. The players in the photograph were Hart, McCormick, Goggin, Mally, Calhoun, Witte, Barry, and F. McCormick, the latter, judging from the picture, a brother of uninitialed McCormick. Witte and Barry went on with the more famous Celtics but this squad, captioned "New York Celtics, 1914-17," undoubtedly was the original squad. The others

dropped out before the Celtics became nationally known.

It was some five years later before the Celtics began their march to glory. In the winter of 1922-23, Jim Furey, a far-seeing promoter, took the first step that was to bring order out of chaos in basketball. There were hundreds of basketball teams at that time. They were teams in the sense that they were uniformed and had a court on which to play, but not teams in the sense that they played together as such. Their composition was not static. Players were with one team one night and with another, quite possibly their opponents of the night before, on the next.

It was here that the genius of Furey asserted itself. He hired the Seventy-first Regiment Armory in Manhattan for Sunday nights and organized the Original Celtics to play for him and solely for him. There was to be no more wildcat barnstorming, no more playing at so much a night. The Celtics signed contracts with him and were guaranteed straight salaries, instead of having to depend on varying pay scales on a per-game basis. These were the first individual contracts in the history of basketball, although previously promoters had reached the point of signing team contracts when scheduling games.

The members of this first Celtic team were Pete Barry, who appeared in the 1914-17 group picture, Dutch Dehnert, Horse Haggerty, Johnny Beckman, Joe Trippe, and Ernie Reich. The team was coached by another veteran of the 1914 group, Johnny Witte.

These were the Original Celtics as the public came to know them—a squad of six men, although coach Witte could play in a pinch. Later there were important additions—Nat Holman and Chris Leonard from the New York Whirlwinds, Joe Lapchick from the Brooklyn Visitations, Davey Banks, Carl Husta, and Nat Hickey.

Like the professional baseball players of the period preceding World War I, the Celtics were rough, earthy guys—"red necks," as the old-timers fondly refer to the diamond heroes of the second decade of this century.

Most of the Celtics came from a rough, brawling neighborhood which produced racketeers and statesmen, hoodlums and prelates. It also produced basketball players. In an area which ran north from Twenty-third Street to Twenty-ninth Street and west from Eighth Avenue to Tenth Avenue, there sprang up at the same time some of the greatest basketball players the game had ever seen—Pete Barry, Johnny Witte, Ernie Reich, Johnny Beckman, Dutch Dehnert and Nat Hickey.

Of this group, Barry, Witte, Reich, Dehnert and Beckman were with the "original" Original Celtics—the first group organized by Jim Furey to play together as a unit. All, except Reich, who died while still an active player, went on to distinguish themselves as coaches in the game, Witte with his old teammates, Barry with Kate Smith's Celtics, Dehnert with teams in Detroit and Sheboygan, as well as an ex-GI team which won the Hearst Professional Basketball Tournament in Chicago, and Beckman with Baltimore in the American League. All this talent from one section of New York City—an area which a pedestrian could completely cover at a leisurely pace within a half-hour's time.

Little Davey Banks signed this photo for Celtic teammate Joe Lapchick.

The beginnings of the Celtics were rough. The leagues in which they played were rough.

Once, their backer was a mysterious gentleman named Donovan. He had been unearthed somewhere by Witte to bankroll the club. Donovan met the players once and once only. He explained that the pressure of his "outside business" would prevent him from spending much time with them, that he knew little about basketball, but that he had confidence in Witte. Most of the Celtics thought Mr. Donovan an engaging little chap, even though he didn't bother to explain what his "outside business" was.

They were soon to find out. Crossing Tenth Avenue one night, a sedan whizzed by Mr. Donovan, and there was a lot of popping which didn't come from the exhaust. Mr. Donovan was picked up full of lead and very dead. It seems he brewed and sold

Card-playing helped Celtics pass time on the road. Enjoying a game (left to right) are Johnny Beckman, Dutch Dehnert, Pete Barry and Joe Lapchick.

beer, a profession both profitable and precarious in those Volstead days. The gentlemen in the sedan were business rivals. And Witte went scurrying around to find a new backer, preferably one whose bankroll had been acquired in a more conservative business.

Highjinks were the order of the day with the Celts. Their road trips were not only business ventures but fun excursions as well. There was that night in Hudson, New York, when Beckman, on his way back to the hotel after the game, passed a delicatessen where several cases of milk were piled up in the doorway, with a huge cake of ice, which must have weighed 50 pounds. Beckman lugged it into the hotel with him.

"Check this," said Beckman to the night clerk, as he slithered the block of ice along the counter of the desk. Instead of checking in the ice, the clerk checked out the Celtics.

None of the sanitation connected with modern basketball was found among the Shamrocks. They wore their uniforms for weeks on end without laundering them, simply because they never had time to have them laundered. Each man carried his own equipment in a small hand grip. The soiled, sweaty uniforms were stuffed in after each game, never to see daylight or feel fresh air until the following night when they were pulled out of the bag for the next game on the schedule. Eventually somebody would think of ordering a new set, and the old ones would be discarded.

As for medical attention, the Celtics thought physicians were only for the rich. They had their own home remedies for everything, most of them devised by Beckman, who must have had a touch of faith-healer, or witch-doctor in him.

Lapchick recalls being clawed up pretty thoroughly

in one of the rougher games the Celtics played. A day later the scratches developed an infection. Beckman diagnosed, prescribed and treated. He soaked a Turkish towel in steaming hot water and wrapped it tightly around Lapchick's arm. Then he proceeded to rub the scabs from Joe's arm with the towel. The final step was to pour a bottle of bootleg brandy over the open wounds.

"You'll be okay for tomorrow night, kid," said Beckman lightly. After all, it wasn't his arm. The odd part of it was that Lapchick was able to play in the next game, although he didn't get much sleep after Beckie's ministrations.

But these were the Celtics, men among men. Basketball was their religion, and they set up altars in strange and faraway places. They spread the gospel through the Midwest and the South, playing professional, amateur or college teams and, when time permitted, holding clinics after the game. So widespread was their fame that high school coaches sent their squads as far as 150 miles to see the Celts play when the team was in their region.

Because they were so far ahead of most of the contemporaries whom they met on these barnstorming tours, the Celtics had plenty of time in which to experiment. When they enjoyed a comfortable lead, they gave brilliant passing exhibitions without attempting to score. And after games they stayed up far into the night, talking basketball, arguing, discussing the game, working out new tactics.

Most teams of that era used a man-to-man defense. There was no time for teamwork in a sport in which players were constantly changing sides, and the men against whom you played tonight might be on your side tomorrow.

It was the Celtics who brought the "switch" into basketball. Before the advent of the switch, a player, asked how had he fared in the game, was likely to reply, "I got three goals and my man only got one." It was strictly individual with each player being responsible for the player who lined up opposite him at the tap-off.

Not the Celtics, however. They played the game as a team, not as individuals. When the other side had the ball, the Celtic player always guarded the man nearest, whether he was the personal opponent of that particular player or not. Lapchick found this all a little bewildering when he had served his apprenticeship with lesser clubs and was tapped for the Shamrocks.

"The rules for a center in those days," recalled Joe, "were for him to get the tap and then get the hell out of the way, so he wouldn't get hurt. The tap, of course, was important then since the ball was centered for a jump after each score, instead of merely at the beginning of each half.

"I found out it was all different with the Celtics. A center had to work along with the rest of the team. And your defensive duties entailed more than merely guarding the fellow who jumped against you. They were constantly switching on the defense and I couldn't figure out how they did it, except by instinct. Certainly they never practiced it.

"As a result, I was always getting in somebody's way. My teammates were getting picked off right and left. There was a time when the Celtics considered dropping me because of my inability to switch.

"It was Johnny Witte who saved me. I consider Witte one of the greatest psychologists I've ever met, although Johnny would laugh in my face and tell me I was crazy if I told him he was a psychologist.

"All the others on the team were giving me tongue-lashings and telling me what a dope I was not to be able to understand a simple thing like switching. And then Witte would take me aside and tell me what a great basketball player I was going to be, with my physical equipment and my speed, as soon as I mastered the technique.

" 'It isn't how many goals you get, Joe,' Witte used to say, 'or how often you get the tap. We know what you can do with the ball. It's how good you are without the ball that determines how good a basketball player you are.'

"And there, I think, Witte summed up the creed of the Celtics. It's how good you are without the ball that makes you a basketball player."

Basketball, as the Celtics played it, was a science. But their way of preparing for it was hardly scientific. Their summers were lazed away with no attempt to stay in condition. Some of the fellows followed the ponies. One, indeed, made himself a bundle as a bookmaker. He used a couple of his teammates as runners. That was in the days of what was euphemistically known as "oral betting" at the New York tracks. The duties of a runner were to find out what odds rival bookies were quoting and, when necessary, to bet off some of the wagers their bookies had accepted. It was exciting, but hardly a good way to keep in condition.

When the time came to start another season, the

Dutch Dehnert suddenly hit on the pivot play during a game in Chattanooga.

Celtics reported hog fat. They played themselves into shape during their first half-dozen games. Dutch Dehnert, for instance, usually reported at 210 but weighed only 180 pounds when the season ended.

Despite the handicap of not being in shape, plus the disregard many of their members had for training, the Celts averaged better than five victories out of six starts, even when they started going downhill. What made them so truly great was that the Celtics literally won as they pleased most of the time. They rarely poured it on—first, because rolling up the score was bad business and had a weakening effect upon the gate for a return game, and second, because it was exhausting. Some of the few defeats the Celtics

sustained in the season—usually 15 or 20 losses against 100 victories—occurred because a team with which the Shamrocks were toying suddenly got hot in the closing minutes and poured through enough points to erase the Irish margin.

Never, all the Celtic survivors are careful, nay, insistent to point out, was a game lost because the Celts wanted to lose it. Nor was the score ever kept close merely to accomplish a betting coup. There is only one recorded instance of the Celtics betting on a basketball game—and then they bet on themselves to thwart a bookmaker they had reason to believe had double-crossed them. More about that later.

Replacements gradually came to the first Celtic team Furey had organized, but the replacements were carefully screened before acceptance. Horse Haggerty, a giant of a man at 6-2 and 240, had originally come from mining districts around Scranton, Pennsylvania, and he was beginning to wear out. First Joe Trippe, and later Lapchick, were hired as replacements.

Haggerty could be a story in himself, for he was the Paul Bunyan of the courts, a man of surprising speed for one of his height and weight. There were times when Haggerty and the hefty Dehnert were called upon to double-team some obstreperous individual on the opposing team. When they did, he was no longer obstreperous and scarcely an individual.

One of the most gifted of all the Celtic additions was Nat Holman, who came out of New York's teeming East Side to win himself an education and fame through the medium of professional basketball. Smart and glib, the suave Holman also was one of the truly great passers in basketball history. He could thread a needle with his passes, throwing the ball with no spin, making it easy to handle. It was Holman who fed Dehnert in the pivot most of the time, and it was Nat who taught the Dutchman the trick of coming forward to take the pass. When Dehnert stepped forward to take the ball, he was able to return the pass without hindrance from the defensive player.

While much of the magic of Holman's passing went unappreciated, his superb faking did not. Nat could feint basketball players into knots as easily as Willie Pep could tie up opponents in the ring. And when the Celts were in a tight game, where one point meant a great deal, Holman was a master at drawing a foul. Dribbling up the floor, or cutting to take a pass, Nat would recoil from an opposing player like a man who had just been hit by a truck, although actually there may have been no bodily contact at all. Or, if there was, it was Holman who established it.

One night at Madison Square Garden, the Celtics faced the Brooklyn Visitations. Willie Scrill of the visitors was so angry at being made to look foolish by Holman's feints that he blew his top and lit into Nat with the evident intention of taking him apart. The length of the court they went, Willie throwing punches with both hands as fast as he could, Holman back-pedalling like Gene Tunney against Jack Dempsey the night of the long count in Chicago. Nat feinted, bobbed and weaved so coolly that not one of the dozens of punches Scrill threw at him landed. Holman never tried to punch back. When Scrill finally stopped from exhaustion, Nat calmly shot the foul which was awarded him.

Holman, who came to the Celtics from the New York Whirlwinds, was eager to get ahead in the world. He studied at Savage Institute, received a degree as a physical education instructor, and while still playing pro ball, became basketball coach at CCNY. Here he achieved the dignified rating of professor. He was recognized as an authority of the game, precisely as was Lapchick at St. John's University and later among the pros.

Holman took up college coaching early. Lapchick did not do so until 1936, when his playing days were behind him. And, although the rivalry between City and St. John's was among the most intense in the metropolitan area, the two men always remained firm friends. As a matter of fact, when Nat, a bachelor until he was 49, found the charms of Ruth Jackson irresistible, it was Lapchick, his old Celtic teammate, who served as best man.

There was a certain shy aloofness about Holman when he first joined the Celtics. He couldn't quite see their way of playing after the game, but he certainly could appreciate their action during the game. And he added much to it, with his skillful passing and feinting—to say nothing of his accurate shooting.

Later, long after Lapchick had joined Holman with the Celtics, there was another addition to the Shamrocks worth mentioning. That was Davey Banks, a chunky little fellow built like a Shetland pony, who could run all night. Banks, with a barnstorming team featuring Bob McDermott, one of the best of the latter-day professionals to come from New York, and Polly Burch, the great Duquesne center, kept the

name of the Celtics going well into the 1940s touring the country and meeting all comers. Not, however, with the same success as the old Celtics.

There were two phases of Celtic greatness before the team petered out. The first was with Haggerty, Barry, Beckman, Dehnert, Holman and Witte. The second was when Lapchick, Banks, Leonard and Hickey teamed up with Barry, Beckman, Dehnert, and Holman. One team merged into the other, overlapping, as it were. They kept the Celtics booming until the American League split up the team in the late 1920s. And even after that, the barnstorming performances by Holman, Dehnert, Barry, Lapchick and Banks as a unit kept green the memory of the great Shamrock clubs.

Something new was added to basketball in the mid-twenties when George Preston Marshall, the Washington laundry tycoon, decided to take the professionals out of the dance halls and make the sport big-league in every sense of the term.

Marshall was simply ahead of his time with the American Basketball League. The idea was good and the promotion sound, but there was no way to cope with the Original Celtics, who continued to play exhibition games, beating the tar out of the league teams and making more money than any of the ABL players.

A solution was to blacklist the Celtics; no league team would play them. So the Celtics, facing reduced revenues, joined the league and proceeded to win two titles. The Celtics were so superior to the other teams, however, that they were subsequently broken up and their players distributed around the league.

Nonetheless, in those Depression times, the revamped ABL folded, and the old Celtics, like Alexander the Great, had to hit the road, seeking new worlds to conquer.

And hit the road was precisely what the Celtics did. Dehnert, Lapchick, Banks, Hickey and Husta returned to the barnstorming grind. They found it wasn't quite the same, though. Before the Depression, the Celtics used to play road games for a set guarantee of $400 with the privilege of taking a percentage. Invariably, their share of the gross amounted to more than the guarantee. Now, however, the Celtics were playing for $250 per appearance. And they weren't traveling first class any more. It wasn't Pullmans now, but an old jalopy which cost a couple of hundred and had room for seven passengers—provided the passengers were relatives of Singer's Midgets.

World's Basketball Champions
the Original Celtics
paying a visit to President Coolidge at White House
Feb. 16ᵗʰ 1925

A dapper group of Celtics visited President Calvin Coolidge at the White House in 1925: (left to right) Nat Holman, Chris Leonard, Johnny Witte, Pete Barry, Joe Lapchick, Johnny Beckman, Dutch Dehnert and Elmer Ripley.

It made for crowded going. Lapchick not only had to jump center, but also keep the bus moving.

For six years, these remnants of the once great Celtics traveled in this gypsy fashion. It is to their credit that they managed to keep the Shamrock reputation alive, and to win as high a percentage of their games as the old originals had. From 1930 until 1936, when Lapchick quit to become head coach at St. John's, the Celtics kept on the go—and kept the opposition on the go, too.

There was still magic in the Celtic name. Lou O'Neill, sports editor of the *Long Island Star-Journal*

and one of the metropolitan district's finest horse handicappers, discovered ball-promoting at a time when, as he himself expresses it, "a buck was scarce."

O'Neill thought he would go Jim Furey one better in promoting. He lined up a basketball squad, and made it his object to keep the players busy every night in the week and twice on Sundays. But not under the same team name. They represented Long Island City one night, other spots on Long Island other nights, but always as the "home" team. Lou paid them less per game than they had been in the

were at Prospect Hall. You can imagine what the grown-up rooters were like!''

Prospect Hall was a dance hall, and there was dancing before and after the game and between the halves.

''I used to wonder how they could get so many people into the place,'' remarked Dutch Dehnert. ''It seemed as though they were hanging from the rafters. And the guys in the rafters thought nothing of throwing a bottle at you when you were trying to shoot a foul. That was bad enough, but the fellows sitting on the sidelines would trip you up when you were going down the court. They were holy terrors.''

Under such conditions, it isn't remarkable that tempers often ran short and when a fight broke out, whether among the players or the spectators, the management had one set solution. That was for the orchestra leader, Professor John J. Nolan, to break out with a lively dance number. ''I think the number was 'Dardenella,' '' mused Lapchick. ''Believe me, Professor Nolan got a lot of practice playing that one.''

It was not at Prospect Hall but over in Perth Amboy, New Jersey, that the mighty Haggerty met his comeuppance. Arthur Daley, sports columnist of the *New York Times* and an authority on the escapades of the Horse, told the story this way:

''The Horse gave it out, but he could also take it. At Perth Amboy one night, Haggerty was indiscreet enough to put the slug on a local official, to the great indignation of the assembled populace. The game was played in a garage with a sink in the corner serving as a shower room. Last to trudge down toward the waiting automobile was Haggerty. He never made it. Some 30 wild-eyed fans mobbed him. The other Celtics didn't miss him until he showed up a half hour later, his clothes torn and his face bloody. There wasn't a whisper out of him. He dismissed it with a shrug of his broad shoulders.''

One of the idiosyncrasies of the Celtics was that they played a tie game on occasion. A tie game in basketball today is unheard of, unless both teams happen to drop from exhaustion after playing umpty-nine extra periods. Lapchick explained the tie games in the Celtics' record to Dick Young of the *New York Daily News*.

''Tie games weren't uncommon in our barnstorming days,'' said Joe. ''If the game was deadlocked at the end of the regulation time, our manager would enter into hasty negotiations with the local promoter on the sidelines. If the promoter agreed to pay us extra for the overtime, we'd resume. If he refused, the game ended right there with no decision. We had originally contracted only for 40 minutes—and, besides, a tie was good business. It left the fans talking and brought them out in droves when we returned there later that season or the following year.''

It was the aftermath of a tie game which led to the only recorded instance of the Celtics betting on a game. During the season of 1921-22 the Shamrock five played a tie with the Coffee Club in Pittsburgh. The tie wasn't played off and there was great excitement the next winter when the Celts returned to play the Coffee Club again.

The day before the game, Johnny Beckman received a wire from a friend of his in Pittsburgh saying that he could get big odds betting that the Celtics would win by 20 points.

''If we can't beat them by 20 points,'' commented Holman, ''we ought to hang it up.''

Dutch Dehnert nodded in agreement. So did all the others, all except Joe Lapchick, then in his first year with the Celts and getting $50 a game. He liked the idea of getting $300 but he couldn't see risking his week's pay against a team which had held the Celtics even the year before.

''We took it easy on them last year, kid. They just happened to get hot,'' assured Chris Leonard. ''It won't happen again.''

The decision was made to bet the bundle to win by 20 points and the game wasn't very old before Lapchick realized his fears had been groundless. At halftime, the Celtics were in front by more than 20 points and in a position to win as they pleased.

There was a rude awakening before the second half started. Beckman's friend burst into the dressing room with the startling news that the bookie hadn't been able to place all of the $2,000 he had been given to bet—only $250 of it. The Celtics realized immediately that they had been caught in a swindle. Their first reaction was to loaf through the second half and win by fewer than 20 points, but they were hooked there, too, for $250 of their own money was at stake. What happened of course, was that the gambler had placed the bulk of the money for himself. If the Celtics failed to win by 20 points, he was sunk, but so was their $250. It would have cost each of the Celtics about $35 apiece to teach him a lesson.

It was Beckman who finally solved the puzzle. The plan was to take the Coffee Club in stride and protect the $250 and then hang the gambler out to dry the next night, as the Celtics were remaining over in Pittsburgh to play the Loendi Club. Beckie told his friend to tip off the gambler that the Celts wouldn't beat Loendi by more than 11 points. On the basis of this supposedly inside information, the welcher would be a cinch to bet all his previous night's winnings. And the Celtics planned to cover these bets through a middle man. They did, and they walloped Loendi by more than 30 points.

Hackneyed, even corny as it may sound, with the Celtics the game was the thing. In the matter of salaries, they were born too soon. But they averaged $7,500 a season, with the minimum being about $5,000 and with some of the better players getting as much as $10,000.

Like all great athletic groups, the Celtics had to come to the end of the trail some time. After Johnny Witte had abandoned the barnstorming tour with the plain statement that the receipts don't justify dragging the great name of the Celtics into the dust, they made one more stab, in the mid-thirties. They were to play a team of former collegians, kids in their first year of pro ball, at New York's Seventy-first Regiment Armory.

Now, college kids were meat and drink to the Celtics. When Vic Hanson, the Syracuse star, first came into the American League, the Celts made him look silly, although before the season was over, Hanson developed into one of the league's best players. And then there was the case of Homer Stonebreaker, the gangling long shot of Fort Wayne, who had an uncanny eye. Homer made six goals against Chris Leonard the first time he played against the Celtics but the next night Chris blanked Stonebreaker and scored five or six times himself. He had analyzed Homer and discovered that he brought both hands almost to the ground before starting a shot. Leonard played the Fort Wayne ace close and he never got a shot off.

It was always like that with the Celtics. They spotted a weakness in an individual and exploited it to the hilt. Like the time Lapchick scored 17 goals in two successive games against Al Kellett, a player who later became a center of rare ability. Al was new to the game at the time. While guarding Lapchick he couldn't resist turning his head every so often to see what Dehnert was doing with the ball in the pivot. Every time Al turned his head, Joe cut for the basket. He scored eight times the first night and nine times the next. After that Kellett stopped turning his head and kept his eyes on Joe.

Coming up to the game with the ex-collegians, however, Dehnert was a little dubious. He and Lapchick talked over a plan of action. Dutch regarded Ralph Kaplowitz, a former Long Island University player, as a positive menace because of his speed and shooting skill.

"Joe," said the Dutchman to Lapchick, "these kids have too much speed and stamina for us. They'll run us bowlegged before the night is over. Here is what I think we should do. Let's break fast on them and jump into an early lead before they get warmed up and then I'll go into the pivot and hold the ball out on them. That'll save our legs and force them to play our game."

Lapchick listened and thought it sounded all right to him. Once the Celtics got in front, the college boys would be under pressure and would be bound to make mistakes.

"What happened," related Dehnert years later, "was just the reverse. The kids jumped into the early lead instead of us and they went into the pivot, with a big lad from NYU, Irwin "King Kong" Klein, in the bucket. We couldn't get the ball away from them. They made us look silly. We wanted them to play our game and they were playing it, all right, better than we could ourselves at that time!"

It was the last stand of the Celtics. They had not only built well, but too well. They were beaten with weapons they had forged themselves. Once that happened, there was nothing to do but quit. They were left only with memories—but what memories!

◀ *Long before she adopted the Philadelphia Flyers hockey team, singer Kate Smith was a pro basketball owner. Her Celtics, a final rebirth of the Originals, included (left to right) Nat Hickey, Davey Banks and Paul Birch.*

WORLD'S BASKETBALL CHAMPIONS
CLEVELAND ROSENBLUMS
American Basketball League ~
1928 ——— 1929

Max Rosenblum

Carl Husta

Dave Kerr

Pete Barry

Joe Lapchick

Henry (Dutch) Dehnert

J.S. (Nig) Rose

Johnny Beckman

Rich Deighan

*Department store magnate Max Rosenblum brought Celtics
—and ABL titles—to Cleveland.*

CHAPTER 3

American
Basketball League

Pro basketball took its first step toward major-league stature with the formation of the American Basketball League in 1925. Football and baseball were enjoying mass popularity with names such as Red Grange, Babe Ruth and Lou Gehrig in the headlines, and basketball sought its share of the spotlight in the Roaring Twenties.

Joe Carr, also the president of the National Football League, organized the ABL, which unlike previous basketball leagues was concerned with more than a regional operation. It opened with franchises in Washington, Boston, Rochester, Brooklyn, Fort Wayne, Detroit, Buffalo, Chicago and Cleveland.

The league took several measures that helped shape the modern game. To end the roster jumping that characterized former leagues, ABL teams signed their players to exclusive contracts for as much as $1,500 a month, a then handsome sum. Also, rules were standardized to accommodate teams of all regions. Cages were banned, backboards were made mandatory and the foul-out rule and three-second lane violation were later implemented. Further, the ABL adopted a collegiate rule in eliminating the two-handed dribble. This opened the pro game to college-trained players for the first time, although most teams preferred to stick with the veteran pros.

The ABL included several prominent owners and teams, among them the Washington Palace Five, run by George Preston Marshall, a laundry-business tycoon, and the Chicago Bruins, owned by George Halas of football fame. Another strong team was the

Cleveland Rosenblums, sponsored by a successful department-store owner, Max Rosenblum.

The owners were upset, however, by their inability to draw the game's top attraction, the Original Celtics, into the league for the first season. The Celtics preferred to play independently, and added further insult by trouncing ABL clubs in exhibitions.

Nevertheless, the league got through its opening year, although the Boston franchise dropped out at the halfway mark. The schedule was divided into two half-seasons, with the champions of each half, Cleveland and Brooklyn, meeting in the playoffs. Honey Russell, whose 7.4 scoring average was second highest in the league, paced Cleveland to a sweep of the 1925-26 series for the first ABL title. Playoff crowds at Cleveland averaged 10,000, but at Brooklyn only 2,000 turned out for the final game.

1925-26

STANDINGS

First Half

	W	L	PCT	GB
Brooklyn	12	4	.750	—
Washington	11	5	.688	1
Cleveland	10	6	.625	2
Rochester	9	7	.563	3
Fort Wayne	7	9	.438	5
Boston	6	10	.375	6
Chicago	6	10	.375	6
Detroit	6	10	.375	6
Buffalo	5	11	.313	7

Second Half

	W	L	PCT	GB
Cleveland	13	1	.929	—
Washington	11	3	.786	2
Rochester	9	5	.643	4
Brooklyn	7	7	.500	6
Fort Wayne	6	8	.429	7
Buffalo	5	9	.357	8
Chicago	3	11	.214	10
Detroit	2	12	.143	11

Playoffs—Cleveland beat Brooklyn, 3 games to 0
Note: Boston dropped out after first half.

SCORING LEADERS

	G	FG	FT	PTS	PPG
Russell (Rusty) Saunders, Brooklyn-Washington	34	74	93	241	7.4
John (Honey) Russell, Cleveland	30	69	83	221	7.4
Ray Kennedy, Washington	27	67	86	220	8.1
Elmer Ripley, Brooklyn	30	58	84	200	6.7
Matthew (Nat) Hickey, Cleveland	30	66	64	196	6.5
George Glasco, Brooklyn-Washington	35	64	67	195	6.0
Marty Barry, Rochester	26	51	77	179	6.0
Teddy Feldt, Buffalo	29	57	50	164	5.7
Carl Husta, Cleveland	30	47	70	164	5.5
Francis (Red) Conaty, Washington Brooklyn	25	64	34	162	6.5

Cleveland lost the 1926–1927 title after its star, John "Honey" Russell, feuded with management and was sold to Chicago.

With the inaugural season behind it, the ABL turned full attention toward the Celtic problem and came up with a solution: The club owners voted to prohibit their teams from playing the New Yorkers in exhibition games. This left the Celtics with the choice of joining the league or doing without top competition needed to draw large crowds. The Celtics opted for the larger crowds (and more money). They signed with the ABL in 1926 and proceeded to win two straight titles, representing first Brooklyn and then New York.

The year the Celtics joined up, the ABL lost a franchise, Buffalo, and added the Philadelphia Warriors and the Baltimore Orioles. The Warriors were run by Eddie Gottlieb, whose Philadelphia Sphas had beaten the Celtics a year earlier in a non-league series. Gottlieb brought to the Warriors several Sphas stars, among them 6-7 Stretch Meehan and rugged Chick Passon, but the team failed to make the ABL playoffs.

The Celtics took the 1926-27 title by sweeping the playoff series from the Cleveland Rosenblums, the defending champions. Cleveland was not the same without Honey Russell, who had been sold to Chicago after a dispute with owner Max Rosenblum. The

Rosenblums also had lost Vic Hanson, a top college recruit from Syracuse who had become disillusioned with the rough style of pro ball, as well as with his lack of playing time. Hanson was playing for an independent team when the Celtics rolled over the Rosenblums in the playoffs by such typical scores of the era as 29-21, 28-20 and 35-22.

1926-27

STANDINGS

First Half

	W	L	PCT	GB
Cleveland	17	4	.810	—
Washington	16	5	.762	1
Philadelphia	14	7	.667	3
Brooklyn	13	8	.619	4
Fort Wayne	8	13	.381	9
Rochester	8	13	.381	9
Chicago	7	14	.333	10
Baltimore	1	20	.048	16

Second Half

	W	L	PCT	GB
Brooklyn	19	2	.905	—
Fort Wayne	15	6	.714	4
Washington	14	7	.667	5
Philadelphia	10	11	.476	9
Cleveland	9	12	.429	10
Chicago	6	15	.286	13
Rochester	6	15	.286	13
Baltimore	5	16	.238	14

Playoffs—Brooklyn beat Cleveland, 3 games to 0
Note: Detroit dropped out in middle of first half with 0-6 record; games struck from standings. Brooklyn Arcadians dropped out during the first half with 0-5 record; Celtics replaced Arcadians, assuming their record.

SCORING LEADERS

	G	FG	FT	PTS	PPG
Russell (Rusty) Saunders, Washington	42	119	161	399	9.5
Bernhardt (Benny) Borgmann, Fort Wayne	34	87	206	380	11.2
Herman (Chicky) Passon, Philadelphia	41	93	181	367	9.0
Matthew (Nat) Hickey, Cleveland	41	103	137	343	8.4
Carl Husta, Cleveland	41	84	162	330	8.0
Johnny Beckman, Brooklyn-Baltimore	37	91	141	323	8.7
Ray Kennedy, Washington	40	69	172	308	7.7
Nat Holman, Brooklyn	34	82	135	299	8.8
John (Honey) Russell, Cleveland-Chicago	40	61	134	256	6.4
Harry Topel, Rochester	37	81	91	253	6.9

The next season, 1927-28, Joe Lapchick, Nat Holman, Pete Barry, Dutch Dehnert and Davey Banks were in their usual superb form for the Celtics. Their snappy passing game and defense took the team to a 40-9 won-lost record and into the playoffs against Fort Wayne. The Hoosiers' top shooter, Benny Borgmann, hurt his ankle six minutes into the opening game, but Homer Stonebreaker was always a threat for Fort Wayne with his long, accurate underhand

shots, which he took from nearly the length of the court.

After winning the opener, the Celtics lost the second game, 28-21, when they were held without a basket in the second half. Then, rallying behind Banks, the league scoring champion with an 8.3 average, the Celtics won the next two games and their second title.

The Celtics were the only ones smiling. Their one-team domination had hurt the rest of the league. Fan interest and attendance sagged, and owners like George Preston Marshall of Washington had spent huge sums on players they vainly hoped could beat the New Yorkers. Watching his Palace Five get routed before a sparse crowd one night, Marshall winced when the Celts' Dutch Dehnert yelled at him, "We'll break you yet, George." Before the Celtics' second straight title, Marshall sold his players and folded his franchise, to be followed shortly by Detroit and Philadelphia, the latter having lost $60,000 over two years.

1927-28

STANDINGS

Eastern Division

	W	L	PCT	GB
New York	40	9	.899	—
Philadelphia	30	21	.588	11
Washington-Brooklyn	25	26	.490	16
Rochester	24	28	.462	17½

Western Division

	W	L	PCT	GB
Fort Wayne	27	24	.529	—
Cleveland	22	29	.431	5
Detroit	5	13	.278	11
Chicago	13	36	.265	13

Playoffs—Fort Wayne beat Cleveland, 2 games to 0
New York beat Philadelphia, 2 games to 0
New York beat Fort Wayne, 3 games to 1
Note: Detroit franchise disbanded on January 3; Washington franchise shifted to Brooklyn on January 3; Washington record was 6-14.

SCORING LEADERS

	G	FG	FT	PTS	PPG
Davey Banks, New York	49	—	—	406	8.3
Harry Topel, Rochester	52	—	—	402	7.7
Bernhardt (Benny) Borgmann, Fort Wayne	50	125	141	391	7.8
Matthew (Nat) Hickey, Cleveland	44	146	64	356	8.1
John (Honey) Russell, Chicago	46	129	81	339	7.4
Al Kellett, Philadelphia	43	129	80	338	7.9

Clearly, the league was in trouble, and the cry, ''Break up the Celtics,'' was soon heeded. The ABL disbanded the great team and distributed the players to other clubs. This was done not only to restore competitive balance. It also was necessary because Madison Square Garden threatened to evict the Celtics, who curiously had never drawn well at home. The Celtics' organizer, Jim Furey, was in no position to protest, having been imprisoned on an embezzlement charge in a separate venture.

Another man no longer around was Joe Carr. He resigned as league president to devote full time to football and was replaced by John O'Brien, the operator of a respected eastern regional circuit, the Metropolitan League. O'Brien incorporated two strong Metro teams, Paterson and Trenton, into the revamped ABL for the start of the 1928-29 season.

The Cleveland Rosenblums, having acquired Lapchick, Barry and Dehnert when the Celtic players were dispersed, were now the team to beat. The Rosenblums already had two one-time Celtics, Nat Hickey and Carl Husta, but the league was wary of one-team control and made them sell Hickey to Chicago. Undaunted, the Rosenblums bought ex-Celtic great Johnny Beckman from Rochester, and an old pattern was repeated: The ''Rosenblum-Celtics'' ran away with the league, sweeping the playoff series against Fort Wayne in four games despite Benny Borgmann's 40 points.

Following the series, a sports column in the *Cleveland Plain Dealer* credited the team with bringing the city ''its first 100-percent-pure cage title. The championship of three years ago was registered before the Celtic stars entered the circuit. While they marched on to an almost endless victory string outside the fold of organized basketball, a league championship hardly could be accepted as being a genuine world honor. Cleveland now has the greatest basketball combination in existence.''

Fort Wayne's Benny Borgmann, one of the ABL's leading players, wound up in the Hall of Fame.

1928-29

STANDINGS

First Half

	W	L	PCT	GB
Cleveland	19	9	.679	—
Fort Wayne	18	10	.643	1
Brooklyn	15	12	.556	3½
Chicago	15	12	.556	3½
New York	13	16	.448	6½
Trenton	12	16	.429	7
Rochester	11	15	.423	7
Paterson	6	19	.240	11½

Second Half

	W	L	PCT	GB
Fort Wayne	11	3	.786	—
Brooklyn	10	4	.714	1
Cleveland	10	4	.714	1
Rochester	7	7	.500	4
New York	5	9	.357	6
Trenton	4	8	.333	6
Chicago	4	10	.286	7
Paterson	3	9	.250	7

Playoffs—Cleveland beat Fort Wayne, 4 games to 0

SCORING LEADERS

	G	FG	FT	PTS	PPG
Bernhardt (Benny) Borgman, Fort Wayne	42	100	125	325	7.7
Matthew (Nat) Hickey, Cleveland-Chicago	46	124	74	322	7.0
Carl Husta, Cleveland	42	101	83	285	6.8
Lou Rabin, Rochester	40	110	54	274	6.9
Tom Barlow, Trenton	38	120	34	274	7.3
Johnny Beckman, Rochester-Cleveland	38	101	67	269	7.1
Russell (Rusty) Saunders, Fort Wayne	42	104	50	258	6.1
Francis (Red) Conaty, Brooklyn	39	107	37	251	6.4
Davey Banks, New York	42	98	48	244	5.8
Al Kellett, Trenton-Chicago	38	79	79	237	6.2

1929-30

STANDINGS

First Half

	W	L	PCT	GB
Cleveland	17	7	.738	—
Brooklyn	15	9	.625	2
Rochester	14	10	.583	3
Fort Wayne	12	12	.500	5
Chicago	12	12	.500	5
Paterson	10	14	.417	7
Syracuse	4	20	.167	13

Second Half

	W	L	PCT	GB
Rochester	19	11	.633	—
Cleveland	18	12	.600	1
Chicago	17	13	.567	2
Brooklyn	15	15	.500	4
Fort Wayne	13	17	.433	6
Paterson	8	22	.267	11

Playoffs—Cleveland beat Rochester, 4 games to 1
Note: New York dropped out on December 10 with a 5-5 record deleted from records; Syracuse dropped out on January 6; forfeited 4 remaining games.

SCORING LEADERS

	G	FG	FT	PTS	PPG
Bernhardt (Benny) Borgmann, Fort Wayne-Paterson	50	149	118	416	8.3
Gaza (Jazz) Chizmadia, Rochester .	55	113	117	343	6.2
Carl Husta, Cleveland	56	135	61	331	5.9
Matthew (Nat) Hickey, Chicago	53	133	51	317	6.0
Davey Banks, Fort Wayne	50	122	63	307	6.1
Joe Brennan, Brooklyn	43	108	61	277	6.4
Francis (Red) Conaty, Brooklyn	54	109	40	258	4.7
Pat Herlihy, Brooklyn	53	101	37	239	4.5
Lloyd (Lefty) Kintzing, Rochester ..	52	100	32	232	4.5
Nat Holman, Syracuse-Chicago	47	88	51	227	4.8

Perhaps true. But it was unlikely this achievement comforted Clevelanders after the stock market crashed on October 29, 1929. The ABL accepted the optimistic view that the Depression would end shortly, however, and conducted business as usual. Jim Furey, paroled from prison, reorganized for the 1929-30 season a Celtic team consisting of Nat Holman, Davey Banks and Johnny Beckman. Lapchick, Dehnert and Barry were still under contract to the Rosenblums, so Furey brought in big Stretch Meehan. However, the team never measured up to the old Celtics. Meehan didn't play up to his 6-7 height, and age had eroded Beckman's skills. Holman was unable to make the Saturday games because of a coaching job at City College of New York. Disappointed, Furey sold his high-priced veterans (Holman and Beckman were making close to $10,000) and folded the team after only 12 games.

The Rosenblums again went on to make the playoffs easily. They were matched in the final series against Rochester, whose 6-9 rookie center from Georgia Tech, Tiny Hearn, was a demon on center taps. Lapchick, bothered by a sore knee, had been switched to forward and replaced at center by Cookie Cunningham, a former all-around athlete at Ohio State. Cunningham was notable because he was one of the few players who could palm a basketball, and also because he played pro football for the Chicago Bears. Undoubtedly using some of his gridiron techniques, he outplayed—and outmuscled—Hearn despite giving away nearly five inches in height, and the Rosenblums swept the four games for their second straight title.

Notions of a Cleveland dynasty proved to be short-lived. The Depression wasn't going away, and salaries and attendance became severe problems. Basketball still had not achieved wide popularity, and the ABL clubs, who averaged two games a week, had to play exhibitions along the way to meet traveling expenses.

Before the start of the next season, Joe Lapchick received his contract, along with a letter from Nig Rose, who ran the Cleveland team for Max Rosenblum. The letter, dated August 30, 1930, said in part:

I am enclosing your contract for $1,000 per month, which is less than last year, but will guarantee you four months of play. While I am

THE AMERICAN BASKETBALL LEAGUE
UNIFORM PLAYERS' CONTRACT

The **Cleveland Rosenblum's** herein called the club and... **Joe Lapchick**

of **Yonkers, New York** herein called the player.

The club is a member of the AMERICAN BASKETBALL LEAGUE and as such, and jointly with the other members of the league, is obligated to insure to the public wholesome and high-class professional basketball by defining the relations between the club and the player and between club and club.

In view of the facts above recited, the parties to this contract agree as follows:

(1)   The club shall pay the player a salary for his skilled services during the playing season of 19**30-31** at the rate of $**1,000.00** per **month**..... The salary above provided for shall be paid as follows: **$500.00 on the 1st and 15th of each month.** 90 per cent at the close of each and the remaining 10 per cent at the close of the season, or upon the release of the player by the club.

(2)   The player agrees that during the playing season he will faithfully serve the club and pledges himself to the American public to conform to the highest standards of fair play and good sportsmanship.

(3)   The player will not play basketball during the season of 19**30-31** other than for the club, except in case the club shall have released the player and such release has been approved by the president of the AMERICAN BASKETBALL LEAGUE.

(4)   The player accepts as part of this contract such reasonable regulations as the club may announce from time to time.

(5)   This contract may be terminated at any time by the club upon six (6) days notice given in writing to the player.

(6)   The player submits himself to the discipline of the AMERICAN BASKETBALL LEAGUE and agrees to accept its decision pursuant to its Constitutions and By-laws.

(7)   Any time prior to September 1, 19**31**., by written notice to the player, the club may renew this contract for the term of that year, except that the salary rate shall be such as the parties may then agree upon, or in default of agreement, such as the club may fix.

(8)   The player may be fined or suspended for violation of this contract, but in all cases, the player shall have the right of appeal to the president of the AMERICAN BASKETBALL LEAGUE, whose decision in the matter shall be final.

(9)   In the event of disagreement between the club and the player in regard to the salary rate, the player shall accept the rate set by the club and the player may appeal for readjustment to the president of the AMERICAN BASKETBALL LEAGUE. The decision of the president shall be final and binding on both the club and the player.

(10)   The reservation by the club of the valuable right to contract and fix the salary for the succeeding year and the promise of the player not to play during said year other than with the club to whom he is under contract, have been taken under consideration in the fixing of the salary stated herein and the guarantee by the club to pay said salary, is in consideration for playing, the right to reserve the player for the succeeding season and the player's agreement to submit to other agreements as stated above.

(11)   In case of any dispute between the player and the club, the same shall be referred to the president of the AMERICAN BASKETBALL LEAGUE and his decision shall be accepted by both parties as final.

(12)   In the absence of a regular league contract, agreements in writing which may be executed in an emergency, shall be as binding as a contract, providing a copy is on file with the secretary; however, such agreements must be placed in regular contract form as soon as possible. Verbal contracts and agreements between the club and player will not be considered by the league in the event of a dispute.

Signed this ... **11th** day of **August** A. D. 19**30**.

....   **CLEVELAND ROSENBLUM'S INC.**..............
                                                                                                        Club

....
Witnesses   Player

This copy to be forwarded to Secretary's office.

sorry that this cannot be the same as last year, still it is a whole lot more money than what the other clubs can afford to, or intend, to pay. Everyone intends to make drastic cuts in salary, as the salaries all along the line were entirely too high for the income that can be attained out of basketball.

Under these ominous conditions, the 1930-31 season signaled the start of a new decade and what would be the end of the ABL as a national circuit. Max Rosenblum shocked the league by folding his franchise in December, unable to fulfill the terms of a full season expressed in the contract letter to Lapchick. Dehnert, Barry and Lapchick signed as free agents with the league's second-year Toledo franchise, but the aging stars could not lift the club to a winning record. The Paterson team, although it had acquired sharpshooting Benny Borgmann from Fort Wayne and Honey Russell from Chicago, also disbanded.

The rest of the league soon followed into oblivion. In Chicago, George Halas had obtained Nat Holman the year before from a fading Syracuse club, paying him $6,000 for half a season. But the Bruins now were forced to abandon the high-rent Chicago Stadium for lesser quarters, and Halas had decided this would be his last year.

For once, the old Celtic faces were not in the playoffs. A rookie out of the University of Indiana named Branch McCracken led Fort Wayne into the final series. Brooklyn, though, used a tough, switching defense, held Fort Wayne to under 20 points and surprisingly won the title, four games to two.

1930-31

STANDINGS

First Half

	W	L	PCT	GB
Brooklyn	14	7	.667	—
Fort Wayne	13	9	.591	1½
Rochester	10	9	.526	3
Paterson	9	9	.500	3½
Cleveland	6	6	.500	3½
Toledo	8	13	.381	6
Chicago	7	14	.333	7

Second Half

	W	L	PCT	GB
Fort Wayne	11	5	.688	—
Chicago	11	5	.688	—
Brooklyn	8	8	.500	3
Rochester	5	10	.333	5
Toledo	4	11	.274	6½

Playoffs—Fort Wayne beat Chicago, 1 game to 0; Brooklyn beat Fort Wayne, 4 games to 2
Note: Cleveland dropped out on December 8; Paterson dropped out on December 30

SCORING LEADERS

	G	FG	FT	PTS	PPG
Bernhardt (Benny) Borgmann, Paterson-Chicago	33	111	68	290	8.8
Davey Banks, Toledo	34	94	66	254	7.5
Manuel (Manny) Hirsch, Rochester	28	81	49	211	7.6
Willie Scrill, Brooklyn	37	87	29	203	5.5
Frank Shimek, Fort Wayne	37	78	47	203	5.5
Al Kellett, Brooklyn	36	59	55	173	4.8
Carl Husta, Cleveland-Fort Wayne	35	64	42	170	4.9
Russell (Rusty) Saunders, Fort Wayne	38	66	34	166	4.4
Harold (Cookie) Cunningham, Toledo	33	53	44	150	4.5
Lou Spindell, Cleveland-Toledo	35	58	28	144	4.1

Brooklyn never got to defend its crown. During the summer, O'Brien, the league president, reviewed the losses sustained the previous two years and suspended operations. The Depression was accepted as a major cause, but Eddie Gottlieb, who had gone down in the league with the Philadelphia Warriors, cited another. ''We had big buildings and players on monthly salaries and we stretched from New York to Chicago,'' Gottlieb said of the ABL, ''but we were just three or four years ahead of our time.''

O'Brien reorganized the league for the 1933-34 season and it survived until after World War II. But O'Brien's new ABL was strictly a regional operation in the East. The dominant team in the new setup was Gottlieb's Philadelphia Sphas, who won seven titles in 13 years.

Featuring an all-Jewish lineup of such stars as Harry Litwack, Cy Kaselman, Red Wolfe, Moe Goldman, Shikey Gotthoffer and Inky Lautman, the Sphas played at the Broadwood Hotel, where fans had to climb three flights of marble stairs to reach the ballroom. But once there, they could relax in luxury, for every seat in the reserved section was individual, with plush green upholstery.

Gottlieb liked to contrast this setting with the days

Eddie Gottlieb (far right, second row) liked to contrast playing conditions in the ABL with those his earlier Philadelphia Sphas (above) encountered in a city league.

when the Sphas played in a city league. "In one of those games 1,700 persons paid admission," he said. "Half of those people never saw the game. They were standing on the long stairway leading down to the street, and all they got for their money was a relay of the score handed down from mouth to mouth."

But at the Broadwood it was different. The seating capacity was 3,000, and there was dancing afterward. One of the Sphas' players, Gil Fitch, would change into a tuxedo and lead his band in the postgame festivities. Gottlieb, no purist, would also promise a fight in every game.

So, for the time, pro basketball had returned to the armories and the dance halls, to the local leagues and the barnstorming circuit. The concept of major-league ball was temporarily forgotten, and the college game began to surpass the pros in popularity. By now the collegians were playing at Madison Square Garden, ushering in a new era for the sport. A crowd of 16,188 had turned out for the first regularly scheduled doubleheader there on December 29, 1934.

Still, the 1930s saw the blossoming of yet another super pro team, the New York Rens, and of a robust pro league in the Midwest which would one day play a significant role in the establishment of big-league basketball.

CHAPTER 4

The Rens

On a night of snow and bitter cold in 1934, a bus carrying a professional basketball team ground to a halt in front of a restaurant in a midwestern city.

The players, hungry and weary after a ride of several hours following their game, filed off the bus and walked toward the restaurant door. But before they could enter, the proprietor owner blocked their path.

"Waddya want?" he snapped.

"Something to eat," said a player.

"Sorry," the owner said. "We don't serve niggers."

So familiar was this phrase to them that the players showed no anger, no emotion at all. They turned to reboard their bus, knowing they might drive all night without finding a place to eat; knowing, too, they likely would sleep on the bus because no hotel would admit them.

These were facts of life for the players of the New York Renaissance, the best basketball team of the 1930s. They were spat upon by some fans, insulted by others, and often they slept on cold floors and dined on cold cuts in their bus.

All this because they were black.

The saga of the New York Renaissance was one of pride and excellence amid the searing, open prejudice of the 1920s and '30s. The Rens, as they were known to their fans, began playing in 1922, before anyone had heard of the Harlem Globetrotters, and before anyone suspected that a Negro team would succeed the Original Celtics as the kingpins of basketball.

Bob Douglas, a West Indian native and an ardent fan, founded the Rens and named them after the Renaissance Casino ballroom in Harlem, which he rented out as the team's home court. In the dance-hall era of basketball, the Rens shared the ballroom with such bands as Count Basie's and Jimmy Lunsford's. And the basketball became as good as the music.

In the mid-1920s, Douglas captured public attention by signing James "Pappy" Ricks, Clarence "Fat" Jenkins and Eyre "Bruiser" Saitch. Jenkins starred in the Negro Baseball League and Saitch was a superb tennis player, but discrimination prevented both from competing against the top white athletes in the two sports.

In basketball, which was still growing, things were different. The Rens competed against the best white clubs and usually won. They were, in fact, capable of playing the fabulous Celtics eyeball-to-eyeball, and not blinking. The two teams battled like Kilkenny cats before packed houses of black and white fans. Tickets for the Rens-Celtics clashes sold for a dollar in New York, 25 cents more than for a normal game.

The Rens vaulted to prominence when they split a six-game series with the Celtics in 1926-27, and also added more excellent players in Bill Yancey, Charles "Tarzan" Cooper and John "Casey" Holt. In 1932, Douglas signed a Cleveland lad named Wee Willie Smith, who stood 6-5, and the glory years began. Over the next four seasons, the Rens' won-lost record was an amazing 473-49, which included an 88-game winning streak. The Celtics, having peaked years earlier, now had trouble staying with the strong, young Rens. A group of Celtic players

The Rens, lined up according to height (left to right): Clarence "Fat" Jenkins, Bill Yancey, John Holt, James "Pappy" Ricks, Eyre "Bruiser" Saitch, Charles "Tarzan" Cooper and Wee Willie Smith. Inset: founder Bob Douglas.

lost seven of eight games to the Rens in 1933.

At the time, the Rens were barnstorming from Boston to Kansas City, the Depression having taken its toll on the Renaissance Casino. Denied hotels in which to stay on the road, the Rens set up command posts in such cities as Chicago and Indianapolis. The players traveled 200 miles for a game, returned at night to sleep and then would set out on another long journey for a game the next night. "It was so unfair," recalled Bob Douglas. "We had to ride miles to get somewhere to sleep and had to play the Celtics in a town right near another town where they had slept all night." Under these arduous conditions, the Rens were playing almost every night, and twice on Sundays. Their record was nearly unbelievable, espe-

cially since all the games were on foreign courts, where referees often were partial to the home teams.

What made the Rens so difficult to beat was their teamwork, a benefit of their close association. Not a single player joined or left the team during the four-year span starting in 1932. The Rens consisted only of the magnificent seven—Cooper, Smith, Jenkins, Yancey, Holt, Ricks and Saitch—and each was a star in his own right.

Each also possessed remarkable stamina. The Rens would never call a time-out first, feeling this would be a sign of weakness. They would keep playing to the point of exhaustion, often hoping the other team would ask for the temporary halt to the action.

Smith and the 6-4 Cooper gave the team good

height for its day. And the 5-7 Jenkins, billed as "the fastest man in basketball," would lead a devastating fast break. The little men—Jenkins, Saitch and Yancey—scored from the outside, and whatever they missed would be put in by Cooper and Smith.

Smith remembered some of the Rens' strategy: "The thing they stressed was not to miss a man. And they said if you dribble the ball and the ball is on the floor and a man went to cut, you couldn't get it to him, so that was our theory of not dribbling. To get the ball to the backboard sometimes, you had to dribble. But most of the time we would come up with the ball off the backboard and pass it to an outlet man and we would keep the ball up off the floor, keep it moving all the time."

Perfecting their teamwork to a greater degree each time they played, the Rens took on the best opponents anybody could offer. In a game against the Celtics in Kansas City, they held the ball for the last six minutes and won by a point. They might play in Cincinnati one night and Indianapolis the next against strong league teams. They played the first basketball game between blacks and whites in the South, meeting the Celtics in Louisville, Kentucky. Then afterward, as they always were to do in the South, they went to an all-Negro college, the only place they could secure food and lodging.

Through their bitter rivalry on the court, the Rens and Celtics developed a mutual respect. The great Celtic center, Joe Lapchick, often said Tarzan Cooper was the best center he ever saw. And many of the white players were appalled by the discrimination the Rens had to endure. Lapchick was once interviewed with Eric Illidge, the Rens' road secretary, on an Alabama radio station. The Celtic center learned that Illidge had been told to use the service elevator in the building. Stunned, Lapchick refused to use the regular elevator after the interview, electing instead to ride down with Illidge in the service car.

The Rens and Celtics drew huge crowds when playing one another—as many as 15,000 in Kansas City and in Cleveland. But then, the Rens usually drew well against all opponents. Promoters everywhere were eager to land the team, although some were not as eager to pay. Illidge carried a tabulator and personally counted the fans, for teams then were paid a percentage of the gate. He also carried a pistol, but never used it. "Eric would tell the guys," said Wee Willie Smith, "not to come out on the court until he

Tarzan Cooper was the best center he ever saw, said Original Celtic Joe Lapchick.

had the money. It was the only way we could survive.''

Survival was always an issue for the Rens in a white man's society. Douglas made sure his players were well paid, and he bought them a $10,000 custom-made bus in which, as was often necessary, they could sleep in some comfort. On one occasion the bus broke down in Wisconsin, and the Rens pushed it 10 miles in below-freezing weather to the next town with a railroad station. There, unable to get food or sleeping quarters, they waited until morning to catch a train for Chicago, where they played that same night. Ironically, the Rens lost the game in Chicago and had to escape through a back door because angry fans, unaware of how weary the players were, thought the team had been paid to lose on purpose.

In some instances, such irate fans were the Rens' biggest threat. During a game in Akron, Ohio, Wee Willie Smith got into a skirmish with an opposing white player, and the crowd became so incensed it attacked Smith and the rest of the Rens. Gathering together in a circle, the Rens fought off the mob until someone reached the light switch, darkening the building and ending the brawl. A similar outburst occurred in Cicero, Illinois, this time provoked by a biased referee. In both cases the Rens were given

a police escort out of the city for their own safety.

Such incidents were rare, however, considering the number of games and the mood of the times in which the Rens played. Honey Russell, a respected early pro who played against the Rens many times, remembered them as ''one of the cleanest teams I ever played against. They just played basketball that was so good they didn't have to resort to any of the rough stuff.''

The Rens received many such tributes, and more acclaim. In 1939 they won 112 games, lost only seven and captured the indisputable world title in a tournament of the best pro teams held in Chicago. The Rens beat the Harlem Globetrotters and in the final downed the Oshkosh All-Stars, a top league club.

Adding such players as Puggy Bell and John Isaacs, the Rens played well into the 1940s and disbanded with a record of 2,588 games won and 529 lost.

Often asked later how the team had endured so many abuses in its basketball odyssey. Eric Illidge said simply, ''We would not let anyone deny us our right to make a living.''

No one would deny the Rens their pinnacle in the game, either. And in 1963 another tribute was added. The team was inducted into the Hall of Fame.

CHAPTER 5

National Basketball League

The Midwest came into focus as fertile ground for pro basketball with the formation of the National Basketball League in 1937. Formerly, the East had produced the best players, and even the clubs in the Midwest in the old American Basketball League had been stocked liberally with veteran eastern pros.

A change in this pattern was signaled when three large corporations chose to enter the pro arena. Goodyear and Firestone, both of Akron, Ohio, and General Electric of Fort Wayne, Indiana, had been powers in the Midwest Industrial League and decided to match their clubs against pro teams for the 1937-38 season. To form the NBL, they were joined by 10 predominantly midwestern independent clubs. This brought into the spotlight of organized ball such outfits as the Indianapolis Kautskys and the Whiting Ciesar All-Americans of Indiana, the Kankakee Gallagher Trojans of Illinois, and the Oshkosh All-Stars and Sheboygan Redskins of Wisconsin. Franchises soon sprang up in Chicago, Detroit and Cleveland, and the league added a smattering of eastern teams, such as the Pittsburgh Pirates and Buffalo Bisons.

Lon Darling, the founder of the Oshkosh club, was instrumental in organizing the new league, which over a 10-year period emerged as the cream of the pro game—this despite the ever-present problem of unstable and shifting franchises. The league began with 13 teams, shrank to seven, and during the roster-depleting years of World War II operated with only four, each of which made the playoffs. Yet, after a decade the NBL boasted such strong franchises as the Minneapolis Lakers, Syracuse Nationals and

Rochester Royals, and proved to be a hardy link to the inception of the current National Basketball Association.

One of the keystones of the NBL's prominence was its intense and successful pursuit of college players. Aware of the popularity of the cleaner and faster college game, the NBL altered its rules to incorporate such collegiate measures as the elimination of the center jump after each basket. This made it easier for popular college players to enter the pro game, and many signed with the NBL, among them George Mikan, Red Holzman, Johnny Wooden, Buddy Jeannette, Jim Pollard and Bob Davies. The league also landed two players who would go on to fame in baseball and football, respectively, Lou Boudreau and Otto Graham.

Several old faces appeared, too. Dutch Dehnert of the Original Celtics and Benny Borgmann, a top scorer in the American Basketball League of the 1920s, became coaches in the NBL. Another respected pro, Bobby McDermott, starred for the NBL's Fort Wayne Pistons, and George Halas brought his Chicago Bruins into the league for several seasons before the war. The resourceful Halas built his club around two young men out of Loyola University, Wibs Kautz and 6-9 Mike Novak, and used as reserve forwards two of his Chicago Bear football players, end George Wilson and halfback Bob MacLeod.

One of the best players in the league was Leroy Edwards of Oshkosh. A center who took hook shots with either hand, Edwards scored 30 points in a game

One of the NBL's organizers was Lon Darling, whose earlier Oshkosh All-Stars included Hall of Famer Branch McCracken (back row, far right).

against Kankakee and averaged 16.2 points a game for the 1937-38 season. In later years Oshkosh employed the 6-4 Edwards and 6-5 Bob Carpenter, out of East Texas State, in the then-unusual double-pivot offense. Carpenter, a deadly shooter, scored 40 points in a game against Cleveland.

Oshkosh took the league title two years in a row beginning in 1940-41, after a championship by Goodyear in 1937-38 and two straight by Firestone. But with several of its players, including Carpenter, lost to military service, Oshkosh surrendered the crown to the Sheboygan Redskins in 1942-43. The Fort Wayne Pistons then won two straight titles in 1943-44 and 1944-45 with a strong team paced by the backcourt combination of McDermott and Jeannette.

The Pistons combined their two NBL crowns with successive championships in the World Tournament, which brought together in Chicago the nation's best pro teams. In the 1943-44 tourney, before crowds ranging from 7,200 to 14,116, the Pistons defeated the Dayton Aviators, 59-34; the New York Rens, 42-38; and the Brooklyn Eagles, 50-33, for the title. The next year, they downed the Dayton Acmes in the final, 78-52, before a crowd of 15,119.

The Pistons' string of impressive victories had not ended. In the fall of 1945, they beat the College All-Stars, 63-55, before 23,912 fans at Chicago Stadium. The Pistons could not produce a third straight NBL crown, however. In the ensuing season, they were ousted by the Rochester Royals in the platoff semifinals. Rochester, a new franchise drawing mostly

from the college ranks (except for old pro Al Cervi), had such young stars as Bob (Seton Hall) Davies, Red (CCNY) Holzman, George (North Carolina) Glamack and Fuzzy (St. John's) Levane. Football's Otto Graham, Del Rice, a St. Louis Cardinal catcher, and Chuck Connors, who would play major-league baseball briefly before making it as a television and movie actor, were also on the Royals squad which, once past Fort Wayne, swept the championship series from Sheboygan.

At this point, basketball was growing in popularity, as the war's end brought a rise in the nation's spirits and in its interest in sports events. In 1946, Ward Lambert left Purdue to become commissioner of the NBL, and the league achieved further acclaim by signing the most popular college player of the day, George Mikan.

The 6-10 Mikan, out of DePaul University, stimulated the pro game. Fans followed him on the streets and often kept him on the court giving autographs after games. Famous for his hook shots, his thick glasses and his No. 99, Mikan commanded a $60,000, five-year contract from the Chicago Gears. And to be sure he would get it, he sat out the first six weeks of his first season in a contract dispute.

But Mikan proved to be worth waiting for, leading the Gears into the playoffs against the defending champion Rochester Royals. The Royals, who had added rookie Arnie Johnson and veteran Dolly King to their club, held Mikan to 14 points the first game and got 23 points from Bob Davies to win, 71-65.

The Brooklyn Eagles, runner-up in the 1943–44 World Tournament, with some of their young fans. Chuck Connors (left), went on to play for the Brooklyn Dodgers and star in television and the movies. Other players (left to right) are Bernie Okker, Dutch Garfinkel, and Red Tough. Old Celtic Dutch Dehnert (rear) was the coach.

Rochester Royals, 1945–46 NBL champs. Front row (left to right): Bernie Voorheis, Red Holzman, Otto Graham, Dutch Garfinkel, Al Cervi, Bob Davies. Back: Fuzzy Levane, Tom Rich, Al Negratti, John Mahnken, assistant coach Ed Malanowicz, Chuck Connors, George Glamack and Bob Fitzgerald. Coach and co-owner Lester Harrison is not pictured.

George Mikan led Minneapolis to the World Tournament title in 1948, and received MVP honors.

The NBL added clubs in Flint, Michigan, and in Minneapolis and prepared to go on without Mikan as its big drawing card in 1947-48. But it did not have to do without him for long. The PBLA collapsed after just two weeks, and Mikan and his former Chicago teammates returned to the NBL, where they were parceled out among the other clubs.

Mikan wound up teaming with another outstanding player, Jim Pollard, on the new Minneapolis Lakers, and, naturally, the Lakers landed in the NBL playoffs. Their opponent in the finals, Rochester, was riddled with injuries, one of which put 6-9 center Arnie Risen on the sidelines with a broken jaw, and the Royals provided only small resistance. Without Risen to guard him, Mikan had games of 26, 25, 32 and 27 points as Minneapolis won three of four games for the title. Then, in the final of what would be the last World Tournament, Mikan scored 40 points in a 75-71 victory over the New York Rens.

In a poll to decide the NBL's Most Valuable Player, Mikan received all 240 votes. He had, after all, led Minneapolis to the league crown and World Tournament title in the team's first year. But, as it turned out, the Lakers' first year was also their last in the NBL.

The team that Mikan and Pollard had made famous jumped to the Basketball Association of America for the 1948-49 season, as did three other NBL teams: Rochester, Fort Wayne and Indianapolis. The suddenly-decimated NBL still had Anderson, Oshkosh, Syracuse, Tri-Cities and Sheboygan, and to these were added Denver, Detroit, Hammond and Waterloo. Detroit didn't last long; after winning only two of 19 games, it folded. A collection of New York Rens, past their prime as a team, came in as a replacement, representing Dayton. The Anderson Packers took the title in three straight games over Oshkosh and its Alex (Southern California) Hannum, who was a prize rookie along with Dolph (New York University) Schayes of Syracuse.

The NBL, still trying to recover from the loss of Mikan and four good teams, girded for 1949-50 with an initial show of strength. It signed, for an Indianapolis franchise, the graduating starters of the University of Kentucky team that had won the national collegiate title. This coup, in effect, helped end the war between the leagues and pave the way for a merger with the BAA before that 1949-50 season got under way.

But Mikan scored 27 and 23 points in the next two games, and the Gears won three straight to capture the 1946-47 title.

The Gears never tried for two straight crowns. They instead stunned the league by joining the 24-team Professional Basketball League of America, one of two new circuits in operation; the other, the Basketball Association of America, already had lured away two players from the Fort Wayne Pistons, Buddy Jeannette and Ed Sadowski, and one from the Oshkosh All-Stars, Bob Feerick.

This was the cover of the program for the opening game of the Basketball ▶
Association of America at Madison Square Garden in 1946.

PART 2

THE MAJOR LEAGUES

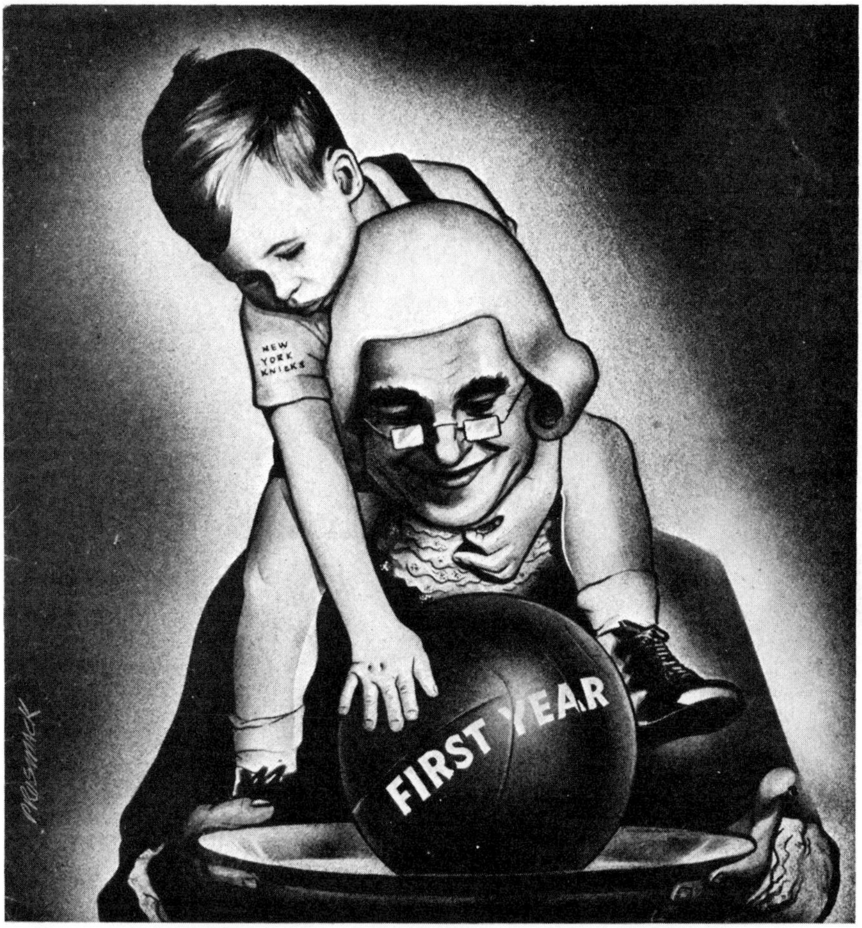

NEW YORK KNICKERBOCKERS
vs.
CHICAGO STAGS

MADISON SQUARE GARDEN   NOVEMBER 11, 1946

25c

24c, N. Y. C. SALES TAX 1c

St. Louis' Red Rocha and Philadelphia's Chuck Halbert were 6-9 pioneers in the BAA.

CHAPTER 6

Basketball
Association of America

It was the spring of 1946. The Atomic Age was only 10 months old. World War II had formally ended in September of 1945. In the United States that spring, the conversion to peacetime life was still incomplete, with millions of people just settling back into civilian jobs or schools, and billions of dollars waiting to be spent on products and entertainment that hadn't been available through the war years. Anyone could see that for spectator sports, boom times were coming.

Basketball, in those days, meant college basketball. Professional players and teams existed, and had existed for nearly half a century, but they had virtually no impact on the general public beyond their immediate small circles of followers. Schedules, rosters, playing rules and playing sites shifted with bewildering speed in the pro world, and there was an air of disreputability about it—and relatively little money available for everyone involved.

The college game, however, had blossomed into a commercial bonanza, through the promotion of Ned Irish and Madison Square Garden in New York. In a space of 10 years, college basketball had jumped from small gyms to big business, and the doubleheader programs at the Garden during the 1945-46 season had drawn more than half-a-million customers, who bought up 98 percent of the available seats.

It was this success of the college doubleheaders, paralleled in other large city arenas in Chicago, Buffalo, Boston and Philadelphia, that made the next step inevitable. The very fact that 98 percent of seating capacity represented saturation made it clear that

a larger audience could be tapped, or that the existing audience could be attracted more often.

And the shape, as well as the needs, of the future seemed plain: large-city arenas had open dates and lots of seats to fill; these were being partially filled by big-league hockey teams, often owned by the arena in question; why wouldn't a professional basketball team, also owned by the arena, do just as well? The public obviously liked the college game, but college players necessarily left their teams (by graduation) at the peak of their fame but long before the peak of their abilities. Wouldn't the public pay to see the same players continue in a college-type game under pro auspices?

It sounds so simple in retrospect, but it took nerve and foresight to act on the idea then. The leaders were Walter Brown of Boston and Al Sutphin of Cleveland, both deeply involved in hockey and arena businesses. But it also took money, and the inclusion of New York was essential, so Irish and the Garden joined the project with no particular eagerness, but for self-protection as much as for hope of reward. If it did succeed, it wouldn't do to let someone else be using the unequalled facilities and prestige of Madison Square Garden.

So they met to organize. For everyone else, it was a historic date: June 6, 1946, was the second anniversary of D-Day—the day the Allies landed on Normandy beaches and began the defeat of Hitler and a changed course in the history of the world. For a little more than a dozen men at the Commodore Hotel on New York's East Forty-second Street (next to

Newly-signed coach Harold Olsen goes over plans for the BAA's Chicago Stags with owner Judge John A. Sbarbaro (right) as league president Maurice Podoloff (center) looks on.

Grand Central Station), it was less cosmic but more personal history: the birth of a professional league that could, in time, be truly called "major league."

They named it the Basketball Association of America—the BAA. There were 11 members, all operators or prime tenants of large arenas. Five were connected with National Hockey League clubs (with only Montreal not represented among the six cities that comprised hockey's major league). Five others were tied to the American Hockey League, that sport's top minor league. The eleventh was Mike Uline, who ran an arena but not a hockey team in Washington, D.C.

They modeled their new league on hockey experience in almost every respect. There would be two divisions: New York, Boston, Providence, Philadelphia, Washington and Toronto in the East; Chicago, St. Louis, Cleveland, Pittsburgh and Detroit in the West. There would be a 60-game schedule with post-season championship playoffs involving the top three teams in each division.

The playing rules, style of operation and atmosphere would be based as closely as possible on the college game that was so successful. The games would have to be 48 minutes long instead of 40, to bring an evening's entertainment up to the two-hour period ticket buyers were used to, and a player would be allowed six personal fouls instead of five in proportion to the longer playing time; otherwise, it was intended to reproduce the college game. However, no zone defense would be permitted, since it tended to slow games down.

As president of the league, they chose someone almost all of them knew—Maurice Podoloff, a New

Haven (Conn.) lawyer whose family operated the arena there, and who was serving as president of the American Hockey League.

The existing professional leagues, and their players, would not be touched seriously by the BAA as it was conceived: the whole idea was to cash in on new college talent and the college-game image. They had less than five months to get set up for their first game, scheduled for November 1, but that proved to be time enough. They chose their coaches, and their players, and when the first season of the BAA began, this was the line-up:

TEAM	COACH	ARENA
New York Knickerbockers	Neil Cohalan	Madison Square Garden
Boston Celtics	Honey Russell	Boston Garden
Providence Steamrollers	Robert Morris	Providence Arena
Philadelphia Warriors	Eddie Gottlieb	Philadelphia Arena
Washington Capitols	Red Auerbach	Uline Arena
Toronto Huskies	Ed Sadowski	Maple Leaf Gardens
Chicago Stags	Harold Olsen	Chicago Stadium
St. Louis Bombers	Ken Loeffler	St. Louis Arena
Cleveland Rebels	Dutch Dehnert	Cleveland Arena
Detroit Falcons	Glenn Curtis	Olympia
Pittsburgh Ironmen	Paul Birch	Pittsburgh Arena

Of the 11, only three were to succeed.

1946-47

The first season of the BAA got little public attention. Crowds were small. There was no television yet, and radio broadcasts were not universal. Newspapers gave little space to the games, except for home teams. The existence of the new league was being acknowledged, but not much more.

Yet, several items of permanent significance were established within the first couple of months. One was that the traditional, experienced-pro techniques (of physical toughness, drawing fouls, deliberate offense) were better suited to winning games than the college style, however well-intentioned. Another was that a pro league was capable of producing and showcasing an individual scoring star to a degree college play could never match. A third was that results within the league would quickly create star players regardless of their college credentials, and that col-

Chicago's Don Carlson tries to stop Philadelphia's George Senesky in the fifth game of 1946–47 BAA playoffs. Warriors won, 83–80, to take the league's first title.

Washington's Bones McKinney shoots during 1947 playoff game against Chicago. Stags upset regular-season champions in six-game semifinal.

lege stars who didn't continue to perform brilliantly among the pros weren't going to be worth much.

The teams with pro experience, or pro outlook, quickly took charge: Washington, Chicago, St. Louis, Philadelphia. The scoring star turned out to be a 6-5 Philadelphia forward from Kentucky named Joe Fulks, who *averaged* more than 20 points a game at a time when 20 points in one game was still considered an outstanding achievement. But neither Fulks nor Bob Feerick of Washington nor Stan Miasek of Detroit nor Max Zaslofsky of Chicago (who made the all-league first team along with Bones McKinney of Washington) had been "big names" as college players. McKinney was the exception.

Then, in the spring of 1947, the most important point of all was established conclusively: in this league, in this sport, the playoffs would always overshadow the regular season.

During the regular season, Washington ran away from everyone else. Red Auerbach, the coach with no credentials, still in his twenties, had put together an outstanding team including several players he knew from the Navy. McKinney, John Mahnken and John Norlander played up front, with Feerick and Fred Scolari in backcourt, with Irv Torgoff. The backcourt did the scoring, the frontcourt got the ball, and the team led the league in defense—a pattern that would bring Auerbach much success in other contexts. In this context, the Capitols posted a 49-11 record and finished 14 games ahead of Philadelphia in the East, with 11 more victories than anyone in the West. The Caps were 29-1 at home, which was remarkable because the rest of the league produced only a 57 percent home-court winning average.

In the Western Division, Chicago and St. Louis finished in a tie for first, and the Stags won the tiebreaker playoff game in overtime. Their chief backcourt scorer was Zaslofsky, their center Chuck Halbert. And because the post-season playoff system was modeled on hockey's, the two division leaders had to play each other in the first round, while second played second and third played third.

The Stags shocked Washington by winning the first two games of a best-of-seven series in Washington—where the Caps had lost only once all season. Chicago went on to win the series, four games to two, to qualify for the final round.

The other series, meanwhile, were two-of-three affairs. New York eliminated Cleveland, and Philadelphia eliminated St. Louis, in lopsided third games. Then the Warriors polished off the Knicks in two straight, and prepared to take on Chicago for the first BAA championship.

Eddie Gottlieb, the Warrior coach, had the most extensive old-pro background of anyone in the BAA. In Fulks, who had averaged 23.1 points a game during the regular season, he had the league's outstanding player. In the other corner, he had Howie Dallmar,

Jumpin' Joe Fulks of Philadelphia soars over St. Louis' Don Martin in a 1947 BAA playoff game. Fulks was the league scoring champ with 1,389 points and the Warriors wound up with the championship.

a former Stanford star of exceptional size for those days (6-5) to have such well-rounded skills. The guards included a terrific shooter in Angelo Musi, and fine drivers and passers in Jerry Fleishman, George Senesky and Ralph Kaplowitz. The center was Art Hillhouse, big and experienced and a college star.

This group turned out to be too strong for the Stags in every respect, winning the final series, four games to one. Fulks scored 37 in the first game and 34 in the last. The games in Philadelphia sold out. The winning team collected about $2,000 a man in prize money, which was almost half-a-season's pay in many cases. And the fact that the Caps, who hadn't made it to the final round, had beaten the Warriors five out of six times during the season didn't seem to bother anyone but the Caps.

So the illogical element of major-league basketball showed itself right at the start.

1946-47

STANDINGS

Eastern Division

	W.	L.	Pct.
Washington	49	11	.817
Philadelphia	35	25	.583
New York	33	27	.550
Providence	28	32	.467
Toronto	22	38	.367
Boston	22	38	.367

Western Division

	W.	L.	Pct.
Chicago	39	22	.639
St. Louis	38	23	.623
Cleveland	30	30	.500
Detroit	20	40	.333
Pittsburgh	15	45	.250

First Round

April 2—Chicago 81, Washington 65
April 3—Chicago 69, Washington 53
April 8—Chicago 67, Washington 55
April 10—Washington 76, Chicago 69
April 12—Washington 67, Chicago 55
April 13—Chicago 66, Washington 61

April 2—Philadelphia 73, St. Louis 68
April 5—St. Louis 73, Philadelphia 51
April 6—Philadelphia 75, St. Louis 59

April 2—Cleveland 77, New York 51
April 5—New York 86, Cleveland 74
April 9—New York 93, Cleveland 71

Second Round

April 12—Philadelphia 82, New York 70
April 14—Philadelphia 72, New York 53

Championship Series

April 16—Philadelphia 84, Chicago 71
April 17—Philadelphia 85, Chicago 74
April 19—Philadelphia 75, Chicago 72
April 20—Chicago 74, Philadelphia 73
April 22—Philadelphia 83, Chicago 80

TOP SCORERS

	Pts.	Ave.
Joe Fulks, Philadelphia	1389	23.2
Bob Feerick, Washington	926	16.8
Stan Miasek, Detroit	895	14.9
Ed Sadowski, Toronto-Cleveland	877	16.5
Max Zaslofsky, Chicago	877	14.4

LEADERS IN ASSISTS

	No.	Ave.
Ernie Calverley, Providence	202	3.4
Ken Sailors, Cleveland	134	2.3
Ossie Schectman, New York	109	2.0
Howie Dallmar, Philadelphia	104	1.7
Marv Rottner, Chicago	93	1.7

1947-48

The second year of the BAA was a disaster, from every point of view. Four of the original teams—Detroit, Cleveland, Toronto and Pittsburgh—had folded. That left seven, which wasn't enough for a balanced schedule, so a team from one of the older professional leagues, the Baltimore Bullets, was brought in. That the Bullets emerged as champions, beating Philadelphia, four games to two, in the final round, emphasized to everyone that the original BAA idea—arena-owned teams playing college-style basketball—had not taken root. Philadelphia, the first champion, had been the only team to come into the BAA from a previous league, the American; now the Bullets, another transfer from that circuit, were champions. Those who feared that the BAA would go the way of previous stillborn pro leagues had reason for their apprehension.

Other aspects of the second season were damaging, too. In an attempt to save on travel expense, the

League assists leader Howie Dallmar of Philadelphia drives against Dick Holub of the Knicks.

league had cut the schedule to 48 games, and that proved to be too few economically and even artistically. On the one hand, it wasn't enough to sort out contending teams at the top. On the other, it didn't display the league's stars often enough, so that the benefits that should flow from close races in the standings couldn't be translated into dollars.

A further complication was geographic. Chicago and St. Louis were the only teams left off the Atlantic seaboard, so Baltimore and Washington were placed in the Western Division. In 1948, this was perceived by the public as ridiculous, and was a blow to prestige and credibility. Since then, sports fans have learned

to accept arbitrary division designations, but in the context of that time, a division name was taken seriously and the incongruity hurt.

The actual season bore out the troublesome possibilities inherent in the arrangements. In the Eastern Division, New York and Philadelphia—the two soundest franchises—had a fine race, with the Warriors finishing one game ahead of the Knicks; but the playoff pattern prevented them from meeting because Baltimore knocked out the Knicks in the first round. At the bottom of the Eastern Division, Providence had a 6-42 record, from which the franchise would never recover.

The Western Division was a complete tangle. St. Louis finished first, by a one-game margin—and the other three teams tied for second. In a pair of one-game playoffs, Chicago beat Washington and Baltimore beat Chicago—which meant that Washington, with a better record than the Eastern Division winner and the best two-year record in the league, was out altogether, Chicago was third, and Baltimore second. Once Baltimore beat the Knicks, and Chicago beat a weak Boston team (the third-place finisher in the East), Baltimore had to beat Chicago again to get to the final—where Philadelphia was waiting on the strength of surviving a seven-game series with St. Louis.

The Baltimore champions had a player-coach (another old-pro feature that lessened the college image) in Buddy Jeannette. It had an old-pro backcourt shooter in Chick Reiser and a rugged rookie named Paul Hoffman. Its top scorer and center was Cleggie Hermsen, who had midwest pro experience after coming out of Minnesota. The other big men were Connie Simmons and Grady Lewis. It was a smart, tough, deliberate-style team, aggressive and efficient—but hardly what the college audience was being turned on by.

It wasn't all negative, of course. The Knicks had a new coach, Joe Lapchick, who had played with the Original Celtics and had coached championship college teams at St. John's, in the heart of the Madison Square Garden excitement. His personal prestige and selling ability would do much for the league in the next few years. The Knicks also picked up Carl Braun, a 19-year-old Colgate dropout, who set a record by pouring in 47 points in a single game. Fulks, averaging 22.1 points a game, didn't win the scoring championship because he missed five games, and

Zaslofsky, the only man to reach 1,000 points in the shortened schedule, was ranked first on total points with a 20.9 average.

But all the events of the 1948 season could be summed up in one sentence: things could not go on this way if the BAA was going to survive.

1947-48

STANDINGS

Eastern Division

	W.	L.	Pct.
Philadelphia	27	21	.563
New York	26	22	.542
Boston	20	28	.417
Providence	6	42	.125

Western Division

	W.	L.	Pct.
St. Louis	29	19	.604
Baltimore	28	20	.583
Chicago	28	20	.583
Washington	28	20	.583

First Round

March 23—St. Louis 60, Philadelphia 58
March 25—Philadelphia 65, St. Louis 64
March 27—Philadelphia 84, St. Louis 56
March 30—St. Louis 56, Philadelphia 51
April 1—St. Louis 69, Philadelphia 62
April 3—Philadelphia 84, St. Louis 61
April 6—Philadelphia 85, St. Louis 46

March 27—Baltimore 85, New York 81
March 28—New York 79, Baltimore 69
April 1—Baltimore 84, New York 77

March 28—Chicago 79, Boston 72
March 31—Boston 81, Chicago 77
April 2—Chicago 81, Boston 74

Second Round

April 7—Baltimore 73, Chicago 67
April 8—Baltimore 89, Chicago 72

Championship Series

April 10—Philadelphia 71, Baltimore 60
April 13—Baltimore 66, Philadelphia 63
April 15—Baltimore 72, Philadelphia 70
April 17—Baltimore 78, Philadelphia 75
April 20—Philadelphia 91, Baltimore 82
April 21—Baltimore 88, Philadelphia 73

TOP SCORERS

	Pts.	Ave.
Max Zaslofsky, Chicago	1007	21.0
Joe Fulks, Philadelphia	949	22.1
Ed Sadowski, Boston	910	19.4
Bob Feerick, Washington	775	16.1
Stan Miasek, Chicago	716	14.9

LEADERS IN ASSISTS

	No.	Ave.
Howie Dallmar, Philadelphia	120	2.5
Ernie Calverley, Providence	119	2.5
Jim Seminoff, Chicago	89	1.8
Chuck Gilmur, Chicago	77	1.6
Ed Sadowski, Boston	74	1.6

1948-49

It was clear to that minority of sports fans who followed basketball in 1948 that the competitive level of the National Basketball League—which operated basically in the Midwest—was higher than that of the BAA. The National not only had most of the established older pros (like the ones who had won for Baltimore in 1948), it also had the most glamorous and important younger player: George Mikan, the 6-10 giant center who had dominated college basketball out of DePaul in Chicago. He was with the Minneapolis team, a new entry in a league whose traiditional powers were Fort Wayne, Rochester (N.Y.) and Indianapolis.

Just before the 1948-49 season was to begin, those four teams abandoned the National League and joined the BAA.

Overnight, the best players and the biggest arenas, in the biggest publicity outlets, were brought together. The possibility of a true major league had been created.

The four new teams joined Chicago and St. Louis in a Western Division, while Baltimore and Washington moved into the Eastern Division, where they belonged. Now the playoff system could be rearranged, too. Four of the six teams in each division qualified, and No. 1 would play No. 4 while No. 2 would play No. 3. In the semifinal round, the winners within each division would meet, so that the best-of-seven final would always pit an Eastern team against a Western team.

With the schedule back to 60 games, the revitalized

Rochester's Bob Davies, hitting layup against the Knicks, led the BAA in assists in 1948–49.

league had an encouraging year. Mikan's Minneapolis Lakers, coached by John Kundla, battled the older and slicker Rochester Royals all year—but Rochester finished first by one game as both posted the best records in the league by a sizeable margin. In the Eastern Division, Washington—still coached by Red Auerbach, still featuring Bob Feerick and Bones McKinney—returned to first place with a six-game margin over New York.

In the playoffs, however, the Lakers knocked out Rochester, and went on to face Washington in the final. Mikan proved to be the difference as the Lakers won in six games, and the league's first "dynasty" was on its way.

Mikan drew large crowds wherever he went, and his scoring from the pivot was the element that excited everyone. He was wide-shouldered and agile. He averaged 28.3 points a game (an unimaginable figure in those days) during the regular season—and 30.3 in 10 playoff games. Joe Fulks, scoring more than ever with a 26.0 average, had to settle for second place and Max Zaslofsky, at 20.6, was third. But

Senator Hubert Humphrey autographs George Mikan's wrist bandage as two Minnesotans met at White House during 1948–49 BAA finals. Despite injury, Mikan led the Lakers to the title, averaging 30.3 points a game in playoffs.

Fulks produced the most incredible individual feat: 63 points in one game, against Indianapolis.

The Lakers, of course, had more than Mikan. There were Jim Pollard, a 6-5 forward from Stanford, and Herman Schaefer, Don Carlson, Arnie Ferrin and Tony Jaros. The Lakers were big, strong and featured a deliberate style.

To basketball purists, however, the Rochester Royals were more appealing. Their backcourt had Bob Davies, Bobby Wanzer and Red Holzman, the ulti-

mate in savvy, quickness and the combination of shooting and ball-handling that guards were expected to have in those days. Arnie Risen, the center, was a relatively skinny 6-9—at least, compared to Mikan—but a big scorer and all-around operator. Andy Duncan and Arnie Johnson were big, rugged cornermen who blended well with the others. The coach was the owner, Lester Harrison.

When it came time to choose the all-league team, there wasn't much room for argument: Mikan in the middle, Fulks and Pollard up front, Zaslofsky and Davies in the backcourt.

The remnants of the National Basketball League, meanwhile, played out their year with eight teams. The Anderson (Ind.) Duffy Packers posted the best record and also swept through the playoffs, polishing off Oshkosh (Wis.) in three straight in a best-of-five final. One statistic reveals how different a style and level of play this league had: the scoring champion, Don Otten of the Tri-City Blackhawks, averaged 13.8 points a game.

1948-49

STANDINGS

Eastern Division

	W.	L.	Pct.
Washington	38	22	.633
New York	32	28	.533
Baltimore	29	31	.483
Philadelphia	28	32	.467
Boston	25	35	.417
Providence	12	48	.200

Western Division

	W.	L.	Pct.
Rochester	45	15	.750
Minneapolis	44	16	.733
Chicago	38	22	.633
St. Louis	29	31	.483
Fort Wayne	22	38	.367
Indianapolis	18	42	.300

Eastern Division Semifinal Series

March 23—Washington 92, Philadelphia 70
March 24—Washington 80, Philadelphia 78

March 23—Baltimore 82, New York 81
March 24—New York 84, Baltimore 74
March 26—New York 103, Baltimore 99 (OT)

Eastern Division Final Series

March 29—Washington 77, New York 71
March 31—New York 86, Washington 84 (OT)
April 2—Washington 84, New York 76

Western Division Semifinal Series

March 22—Rochester 93, St. Louis 64
March 23—Rochester 66, St. Louis 64

March 23—Minneapolis 84, Chicago 77
March 24—Minneapolis 101, Chicago 85

Western Division Final Series

March 27—Minneapolis 80, Rochester 79
March 29—Minneapolis 67, Rochester 55

Championship Series

April 4—Minneapolis 88, Washington 84
April 6—Minneapolis 76, Washington 62
April 8—Minneapolis 94, Washington 74
April 9—Washington 83, Minneapolis 71
April 11—Washington 74, Minneapolis 66
April 13—Minneapolis 77, Washington 56

TOP SCORERS

	Pts.	Ave.
George Mikan, Minneapolis	1698	28.3
Joe Fulks, Philadelphia	1560	26.0
Max Zaslofsky, Chicago	1197	20.6
Arnie Risen, Rochester	995	16.6
Ed Sadowski, Philadelphia	920	15.3

LEADERS IN ASSISTS

	No.	Ave.
Bob Davies, Rochester	321	5.4
Andy Phillip, Chicago	319	5.3
John Logan, St. Louis	276	4.8
Ernie Calverley, Providence	251	4.3
George Senesky, Philadelphia	233	3.9

CHAPTER 7

National Basketball Association

1949-50

The survivors of the NBL were brought into the BAA after the 1948-49 season, and the name of the unified league became the National Basketball Association.

There were now 17 teams, an unwieldly number under any circumstances, but especially so because of the conditions of the merger. The old BAA teams did not want to play the NBL leftovers—names like Sheboygan and Waterloo and Anderson that were further than ever from the big-league image that had launched the BAA, and with no Mikans on them to make them palatable. The compromise reached was neither logical nor appealing to the public: three divisions, with some teams playing more games than others, and with the new entries more or less segregated from the older ones.

It worked this way:

In the Eastern Division were New York, Washington, Philadelphia and Boston, the remaining core of the original league, with Baltimore and one new team, Syracuse. In memory of its origin, the Syracuse team was called the Nationals. Providence had disappeared.

In the Central Division were Minneapolis, Rochester, Fort Wayne, Chicago and St. Louis—from the previous year's Western Division. The Indianapolis team, which had been called the Jets, was gone.

In the Western Division was a brand-new Indianapolis team, called the Olympians, composed of (and owned jointly by) the Kentucky University stars of recent years: Alex Groza, Ralph Beard, Wallace "Wah-Wah" Jones, Cliff Barker.

The rest of the Western Division contained the Anderson Packers (the last NBL champions); the Tri-Cities Blackhawks (representing Moline and Rock Island, Illinois, and Davenport, Iowa); the Sheboygan (Wisconsin) Redskins, the Waterloo (Iowa) Hawks and the Denver Nuggets.

But it was even more complicated than that. The new clubs would play the old clubs (the 10 left from the 1948-49 BAA season) only twice each and each other seven times each. That meant 62 games. The Eastern and Central teams would play each other six times each, which meant 68 games. But Syracuse, Anderson, Tri-Cities and Indianapolis added a couple among themselves, giving them 64-game slates.

Furthermore, Syracuse, even though playing a western schedule, would be listed in the Eastern Division standings—a division in which it would play only 10 games.

The results, when play began, were appropriately confusing. Syracuse whipped through its schedule with a 51-13 record and finished 13 games ahead of New York, which had the best legitimate Eastern Division mark. Rochester and Minneapolis finished in a flat tie, with 51-17 marks (against tougher opposition than Syracuse had). And the Olympians of Indianapolis won their division by two games over Anderson.

Then the untangling process began in the playoffs. The Lakers beat Rochester in a playoff for first place, and went on to the final round by sweeping Chicago, Fort Wayne and Anderson in six straight games (of best-of-three series). Fort Wayne had eliminated the disappointed Rochester team, and Anderson had

The NBA was born on August 3, 1949, when the BAA and NBL merged. Celebrating are (left to right) NBL President Ike Duffy, Leo Ferris of the Syracuse Nats, BAA President Maurice Podoloff, Ned Irish of the New York Knicks and Walter Brown of the Boston Celtics.

Knicks' Dick McGuire, fouled here by Lakers' Slater Martin, led the NBA in assists its first year.

knocked off Indianapolis by two points in the third game of the second-round series in that division.

Syracuse, meanwhile, progressed to the final round beating Philadelphia in two games and the Knicks two out of three.

Because it had the better regular-season record, regardless of inequities, Syracuse was entitled to the odd home game in the final round. And this was no minor item: the Nats, at that point, were 34-1 at home. (The Lakers were 33-1, and the Royals had been 33-1 until the Lakers beat them in that first-place playoff). To retain their title, then, the Lakers would have to win at least one game in Syracuse.

They made it the first one, on a 40-foot shot by Bob Harrison at the buzzer, after George Mikan had already scored 37 points. The Nats won the second game, and the fifth when it was played back at Syracuse, but the Lakers won the other three at home and had their second straight championship.

Mikan, during the regular season, averaged 27.4 points a game, and Groza 23.4, with no one else over 20. In the playoffs, Big George averaged 31.3. His dominance was beyond question.

1949-50

STANDINGS

Eastern Division

	W.	L.	Pct.
Syracuse	51	13	.797
New York	40	28	.588
Washington	32	36	.471
Philadelphia	26	42	.382
Baltimore	25	43	.368
Boston	22	46	.324

Western Division

	W.	L.	Pct.
Indianapolis	39	25	.609
Anderson	37	27	.578
Tri-Cities	29	35	.453
Sheboygan	22	40	.355
Waterloo	19	43	.306
Denver	11	51	.177

Central Division

	W.	L.	Pct.
Minneapolis*	51	17	.750
Rochester	51	17	.750
Fort Wayne*	40	28	.588
Chicago	40	28	.588
St. Louis	26	42	.382

*Won playoff to break tie

Eastern Division Semifinal Series

March 22—Syracuse 93, Philadelphia 76
March 23—Syracuse 59, Philadelphia 53

March 21—New York 90, Washington 87
March 22—New York 103, Washington 83

Eastern Division Final Series

March 26—Syracuse 91, New York 83 (OT)
March 30—New York 80, Syracuse 76
April 2—Syracuse 91, New York 80

Central Division Semifinal Series

March 22—Minneapolis 85, Chicago 75
March 25—Minneapolis 75, Chicago 67

March 23—Fort Wayne 90, Rochester 84
March 25—Fort Wayne 79, Rochester 78 (OT)

Central Division Final Series

March 27—Minneapolis 93, Fort Wayne 79
March 28—Minneapolis 89, Fort Wayne 82

Western Division Semifinal Series

March 21—Indianapolis 86, Sheboygan 85
March 23—Sheboygan 95, Indianapolis 85
March 25—Indianapolis 91, Sheboygan 84

March 21—Anderson 89, Tri-Cities 77
March 23—Tri-Cities 76, Anderson 75
March 24—Anderson 94, Tri-Cities 71

Western Division Final Series

March 28—Indianapolis 77, Anderson 74
March 30—Anderson 84, Indianapolis 67
April 1—Anderson 67, Indianapolis 65

Championship Semifinal Series

Syracuse, bye
April 5—Minneapolis 75, Anderson 50
April 6—Minneapolis 90, Anderson 71

Championship Series

April 8—Minneapolis 68, Syracuse 66
April 9—Syracuse 91, Minneapolis 85
April 14—Minneapolis 91, Syracuse 77
April 16—Minneapolis 77, Syracuse 69
April 20—Syracuse 83, Minneapolis 76
April 23—Minneapolis 110, Syracuse 95

TOP SCORERS

	Pts.	Ave.
George Mikan, Minneapolis	1865	27.4
Alex Groza, Indianapolis	1496	23.4
Frank Brian, Anderson	1138	17.8
Max Zaslofsky, Chicago	1115	16.4
Ed Macauley, St. Louis	1081	16.1

LEADERS IN ASSISTS

	No.	Ave.
Dick McGuire, New York	386	5.7
Andy Phillip, Chicago	377	5.8
Bob Davies, Rochester	294	4.6
George Senesky, Philadelphia	264	3.9
Al Cervi, Syracuse	264	4.7

1950-51

The 17-team league had been obviously unstable. For the fifth season of what had started as the BAA, the league was down to 11 teams and—more importantly—there were no rival leagues competing for college stars. The result was a tighter operation, with much stronger teams, and a pattern that could make sense to its followers.

Six teams comprised the East: New York, Philadelphia, Boston, Syracuse, Baltimore and Washington. The West had five: Minneapolis, Rochester, Indianapolis, Fort Wayne and (rather surprisingly) Tri-Cities.

But Washington couldn't make it through the sea-son. Red Auerbach had left the year before, to coach Tri-Cities, and had now been hired by Walter Brown to coach his Boston Celtics. The players who had made the Caps strong had scattered, and Uline Arena wasn't big enough to cash in on occasional visits by drawing cards like Mikan or other winners. Early in January, with a 10-25 record, the Caps folded.

The games already played against Washington remained in the standings of the other teams.

The other failures had far-reaching consequences. One of the star rookies of 1950 was Ed Macauley of St. Louis, a smooth center. When the Bombers went out of business, the Knicks wanted to buy the whole franchise (for $50,000) to bring Macauley to New York—but the league wouldn't approve such a move, and Macauley was awarded to Boston in an attempt to strengthen that persistently weak franchise. A complicated redistribution of Chicago players resulted in Max Zaslofsky going to New York, Andy Phillip to Philadelphia and a rookie named Bob Cousy to Boston. When Washington folded, the Celtics also got Bones McKinney, and suddenly they were one of the most exciting offensive teams in the league.

When the regular season was over, Philadelphia

Globetrotter star Nat ''Sweetwater'' Clifton joined coach Joe Lapchick's Knicks and helped lead them to playoff finals.

had finished first in the East, with Boston second and New York third, while the Lakers finally won more games than the Royals over the regular schedule. But the won-lost records were less lopsided than in the past two years, indicating the greater balance in the league: 44-24 for Minneapolis, 41-27 for Rochester, 40-26 for Philadelphia.

The playoffs, however, were a strikingly different story. Fourth-place Syracuse knocked off Philadelphia, and the Knicks knocked off Boston, in straight games, while Rochester needed three to get past Fort Wayne and the Lakers needed three to just barely get by the Olympians. Then the Knicks survived a savage five-game set with Syracuse while the Royals, reversing their experience of the past two years, whipped the Lakers three games to one.

By the time the final round began in April, the NBA suddenly had national attention for two reasons. Two months before, the college fix scandals had erupted, wiping out the credibility and glamor (for the moment) of the college game. And now, for the first time, the pro final involved New York, un-

Rochester's Red Holzman (16) battles two Lakers for rebound in Western Division playoff final. Royals won, 80–75, and went on to win the 1950–51 title.

questioned and unparalleled at that time as the capital of the sports world and of all forms of communication.

It was of great significance, therefore, that the Knicks and Royals put on the most spectacular final round so far, at a moment when the league had the public eye. The Royals, heavily favored, won the first three games, with their old pros clearly giving lessons to the eager college-style Knicks. But the Knicks managed to pull out the fourth game, in New York, and succeeded in winning at Rochester as well. Back in New York (where the games were being played in a 5,000-seat armory because the Garden was occupied by the circus), the Knicks won again, and for the first time in the league's history the championship came down to a seventh and deciding game.

It was played on April 21 in Rochester, and it wasn't settled until the final minute. Down by 16 points during the first half, the Knicks battled back and led by two with two minutes to go. With 40 seconds left, the score was tied, and the title still undecided. Then Bob Davies, fouled on a drive for the basket, sank two free throws, and the Royals won, 79-75.

The exciting final wasn't the only element that increased the league's recognition factor. In March, Walter Brown had staged the league's first All-Star Game in Boston, the most glamorous event pro basketball had ever known up to then, and the East won, 111-94, even though the West had George Mikan and Alex Groza. And Mikan, leading the league again with a 28.4 scoring average, had become a national sports figure transcending his sport.

That year's all-league team of Mikan, Groza, Macauley, Davies and Ralph Beard marked the transition, in star quality, to exactly that college image the BAA had intended. Only Davies was a prewar collegian in this group, and he was a "finesse" player too.

So in the spring of 1951, the NBA moved into the mainstream of major-league sports for the first time. It had unchallenged access to all college stars since the merger; it had reached a suitable size and schedule pattern; it had benefitted from the blow dealt college basketball by the scandals; and it had developed its own galaxy of stars, led by Mikan. In five years, it had developed along lines its founders hadn't foreseen or intended, but it had become viable in its own way.

1950-51

STANDINGS

Eastern Division

	W.	L.	Pct.
Philadelphia	40	26	.606
Boston	39	30	.565
New York	36	30	.545
Syracuse	32	34	.485
Baltimore	24	42	.364
Washington*	10	25	.286

*Disbanded Jan. 10, 1951

Western Division

	W.	L.	Pct.
Minneapolis	44	24	.647
Rochester	41	27	.603
Fort Wayne	32	36	.471
Indianapolis	31	37	.456
Tri-Cities	25	43	.368

Eastern Division Semifinal Series

March 20—New York 83, Boston 69
March 22—New York 92, Boston 78

March 20—Syracuse 91, Philadelphia 89 (OT)
March 22—Syracuse 90, Philadelphia 78

Eastern Division Final Series

March 28—New York 103, Syracuse 92
March 29—Syracuse 102, New York 80
March 31—New York 97, Syracuse 75
April 1—Syracuse 90, New York 83
April 4—New York 83, Syracuse 81

Western Division Semifinal Series

March 20—Rochester 110, Fort Wayne 81
March 22—Fort Wayne 83, Rochester 78
March 24—Rochester 97, Fort Wayne 78

March 21—Minneapolis 95, Indianapolis 81
March 23—Indianapolis 108, Minneapolis 88
March 25—Minneapolis 85, Indianapolis 80

Western Division Final Series

March 29—Minneapolis 76, Rochester 73
March 31—Rochester 70, Minneapolis 66
April 1—Rochester 83, Minneapolis 70
April 3—Rochester 80, Minneapolis 75

Championship Series

April 7—Rochester 92, New York 65
April 8—Rochester 99, New York 84
April 11—Rochester 78, New York 77
April 13—New York 79, Rochester 73
April 15—New York 92, Rochester 89
April 18—New York 80, Rochester 73
April 21—Rochester 79, New York 75

TOP SCORERS

	Pts.	Ave.
George Mikan, Minneapolis	1932	28.4
Alex Groza, Indianapolis	1429	21.7
Ed Macauley, Boston	1384	20.4
Joe Fulks, Philadelphia	1236	18.7
Frank Brian, Tri-Cities	1144	16.8

TOP REBOUNDERS

	No.	Ave.
Dolph Schayes, Syracuse	1080	16.4
George Mikan, Minneapolis	958	14.1
Harry Gallatin, New York	800	12.1
Arnie Risen, Rochester	795	12.0
Alex Groza, Indianapolis	709	10.7

LEADERS IN ASSISTS

	No.	Ave.
Andy Phillip, Philadelphia	414	6.3
Dick McGuire, New York	400	6.3
George Senesky, Philadelphia	342	5.3
Bob Cousy, Boston	341	4.9
Ralph Beard, Indianapolis	318	4.8

1951-52

The most important statistic about the 1951-52 NBA season was that the same 10 teams that finished 1951 started and finished 1952. This was unprecedented stability for the pro basketball world.

Still, there were changes, one positive, one negative. The Tri-Cities team, owned by Ben Kerner (who was to become a major force in league affairs), had moved to Milwaukee, a big city with a brand new 10,000-seat downtown arena. That was the positive development. The negative one was that Ralph Beard and Alex Groza, backbone of the Indianapolis Olympians, were implicated in the college scandals as investigations proceeded, and were taken into custody just as the NBA season was to start. Their pro careers were over, and eventually the Indianapolis franchise would not survive; but there was still no hint that the pro games themselves had been fixed, so the damage was limited to that one team.

Oddly enough, the Olympians went on to win more games than the year before, but they were no factor in the races that, at last, were getting day-to-day coverage throughout the country. The East had another fine three-team battle, which wound up Syracuse-Boston-New York, in that order, just three games apart. In the West, Rochester did it again, nosing out Minneapolis by one game and posting the best record in the league (but it was only 41-25 now, with league-wide talent getting thicker every year).

And the second season—the playoffs—proved wilder than ever. Syracuse needed three games to get past Philadelphia, and the Knicks eliminated Boston in a double-overtime third game at Boston. Then they wiped out Syracuse's home-court advantage by winning the first game there, and made it to the final again by winning the third and fourth at home. In the western half, in the semifinals, the Lakers picked up the necessary road victory in the second game at Rochester, and closed out the series by winning two at home.

So it was the Knicks and Lakers in the final, with the odd home game belonging to the Lakers because of their better regular-season record.

The year before, it had been Knick youth against

This shot wasn't easy for Ed Macauley, as Milwaukee's Mel Hutchins defends, but the Boston center breezed to all-league honors.

Rochester's more seasoned skills. Now it would be Knick speed and a persistent running game against Laker size. To George Mikan and Jim Pollard, the Lakers had added a 6-7 giant named Vern Mikkelsen, and that overpowering frontcourt was ably guided by a backcourt that contained Bob Harrison, Pep Saul (a former Royal) and Slater Martin, a little Texan who was barely 5-10 but who knew how to move the ball.

This time, the most dramatic game was the first one, played in St. Paul. Everyone's attention was on the home-away situation—and the Knicks almost got what they needed before losing in overtime. Then, astonishingly, they got it by winning the second game—but lost it by losing the third at New York. The series went seven games again, but the seventh was all Lakers, 82-65.

But although the league was stabilizing itself structurally, and its activities were getting more recognition, a different sort of problem had been growing to alarming proportions: the game itself was deteriorating, the way it had so often in earlier pro leagues, because roughness and deliberate fouling (for tactical advantage) were the key to victory.

The problem was built into the rules, and heightened by two old-pro qualities: confidence in ball-handling ability, and quick thinking. Every time you scored, the other team was given possession of the ball. Once you had a sizeable lead, therefore, it was foolish to try to score any more: simply hanging on to the ball would let the clock run out. That meant, in turn, that if you were behind, and the other team tried to hold the ball out, you had to foul to get it. That way, at least you'd have the chance that the free throw would be missed (which didn't happen often among the pros), or that a one-shot foul could be answered by a two-point basket.

But that meant, naturally, that the leading team's answer was to foul right back.

And the fouling problem was all tied up with the big-man problem, of which Mikan was the symbol but by no means the only practitioner. A smaller man trying to guard or rebound against a much bigger man had to either risk fouling or leave the big man unhindered. If the bigger team wanted to play a waiting game, sooner or later it would get fouled.

The first approach to adjusting the rules was made in the 1951 season: in the last three minutes of play, after a free throw was good, there would be a jump

Paul Arizin, shown with Warriors' boss Eddie Gottlieb, beat out George Mikan for the scoring title.

ball instead of automatic possession for the team scored upon. That way, the team committing the foul couldn't be sure it would get the ball afterwards.

In 1952, an attempt was made to counteract size by widening the foul lane (where the three-second rule prevents an offensive player from taking a stationary position) to 12 feet instead of six. This was aimed directly at Mikan, who did most of his scoring by setting up his pivot play as close to the basket as possible.

This rule didn't hurt Mikan much, even though his scoring average did drop to 23.8 a game and the scoring title went to a young Philadelphia jump-shooter, Paul Arizin. It did open up the middle for more driving—but that only encouraged more fouling.

And more fouls meant more pressure on referees, and more complaints about uncalled fouls, and a bigger edge than ever for home teams. In 1951 and 1952 fouls averaged 54 a game (against both teams), so neither rule change was helping much.

The league's stars now had the college look: Mikan, Ed Macauley, Bob Cousy and Arizin were the first-team all-stars in 1952, with Bob Davies sharing the fifth spot with Dolph Schayes of Syracuse; but the game itself was getting more and more of an old-pro look, and this had emerged as the fundamental problem in league conclaves.

1951-52

STANDINGS

Eastern Division

	W.	L.	Pct.
Syracuse	40	26	.606
Boston	39	27	.591
New York	37	29	.561
Philadelphia	33	33	.500
Baltimore	20	46	.303

Western Division

	W.	L.	Pct.
Rochester	41	25	.621
Minneapolis	40	26	.606
Indianapolis	34	32	.515
Fort Wayne	29	37	.439
Milwaukee	17	49	.258

Eastern Division Semifinal Series

March 20—Syracuse 102, Philadelphia 83
March 22—Philadelphia 100, Syracuse 95
March 23—Syracuse 84, Philadelphia 78

March 19—Boston 105, New York 94
March 23—New York 101, Boston 97
March 26—New York 88, Boston 87 (2 OT)

Eastern Division Final Series

April 2—New York 87, Syracuse 85
April 3—Syracuse 102, New York 92
April 4—New York 99, Syracuse 92
April 8—New York 100, Syracuse 93

Western Division Semifinal Series

March 23—Minneapolis 78, Indianapolis 70
March 25—Minneapolis 94, Indianapolis 87

March 18—Rochester 95, Fort Wayne 78
March 20—Rochester 92, Fort Wayne 86

Western Division Final Series

March 29—Rochester 88, Minneapolis 78
March 30—Minneapolis 83, Rochester 78
April 5—Minneapolis 77, Rochester 67
April 6—Minneapolis 82, Rochester 80

Championship Series

April 12—Minneapolis 83, New York 79 (OT)
April 13—New York 80, Minneapolis 72
April 16—Minneapolis 82, New York 77
April 18—New York 90, Minneapolis 89 (OT)
April 20—Minneapolis 102, New York 89
April 23—New York 76, Minneapolis 68
April 25—Minneapolis 82, New York 65

TOP SCORERS

	Pts.	Ave.
Paul Arizin, Philadelphia	1674	25.4
George Mikan, Minneapolis	1523	23.8
Bob Cousy, Boston	1433	21.7
Ed Macauley, Boston	1264	19.2
Bob Davies, Rochester	1052	16.2

TOP REBOUNDERS

	No.	Ave.
Mel Hutchins, Milwaukee	880	13.3
Larry Foust, Fort Wayne	880	13.3
George Mikan, Minneapolis	866	13.5
Arnie Risen, Rochester	841	12.7
Dolph Schayes, Syracuse	773	12.3

LEADERS IN ASSISTS

	No.	Ave.
Andy Phillip, Philadelphia	539	8.2
Bob Cousy, Boston	441	6.7
Bob Davies, Rochester	390	6.0
Dick McGuire, New York	388	6.1
Fred Scolari, Baltimore	303	4.7

1952-53

The same 10 teams were back for the 1952-53 season, with a new rule adjustment. The jump-ball-after-a-free-throw rule had been quickly nullified by pro imaginations: all you had to do was make sure that it was one of your big men who fouled one of their little men. So the game-end, free-throw rule now required the jump ball to take place between the man who was fouled and ''the player whom the fouled player was playing immediately prior thereto''—that is, his ''normal'' match-up. (And the answer to that was formulated before the ink in the rulebook was dry: get four big men out there to the other team's three, and create a ''natural'' mismatch before you foul.)

Anyhow, the whole concept of a special rule in the closing minutes (it was two minutes now, instead of three) was doomed to failure. All it did was push up the foul-trading tactic into the minutes immediately preceding the last two minutes.

So through a rugged 1952-53 campaign, the fouls per game rose to 58, George Mikan's individual statistical dominance was reduced—and his Lakers went on to their most decisive triumph of all.

For the first time, the two division leaders made it to the final round. The Knicks emerged from a blanket finish in the East, one game ahead of Boston and Syracuse, who had to play off for second place. The Lakers wound up four games ahead of Rochester—the largest margin between those two in the four years they had been in the league. And the won-lost records indicated how equal in strength the two divisions had become: the Lakers won 48 games (in a 70-game schedule), the Knicks 47, the Celtics and Nats 46 each and the Royals 44.

The Knicks, always lacking a big center, had built their success on remarkable rebounding by Harry Gallatin (who was to set records for durability) and Sweetwater Clifton, once one of the most famous Harlem Globetrotters, both in the 6-6 range; on an outstanding backcourt that included Max Zaslofsky, Carl Braun, and Dick McGuire, a superb playmaker; and on Connie Simmons (who had come from Baltimore), Vince Boryla and Ernie Vandeweghe, the medical student who commuted to most of their games.

The Celtics, though, had become even more attractive to fans as Red Auerbach put together Ed Macauley, Bob Cousy and Bill Sharman, a great shooter acquired when Washington folded, with Chuck Cooper, Bob Donham and Bob Harris. The Celtics had terrific offense, but not quite enough board strength and defense.

Syracuse, like Rochester, had the old-pro virtues even with younger players. Al Cervi, the player-coach, was a former Royal who excelled at toughness and backcourt skill; Dolph Schayes, the 6-8 corner man, was an exceptional shooter and ball-handler for one his size. Red Rocha, Earl Lloyd and Noble Jorgensen were the other big men, and Paul Seymour, George King and Billy Gabor the other guards. The Nats emphasized defense, ball-handling and balanced team flow—and court brains—to the highest degree.

On ability, these three teams were really a tossup, and the first playoff round produced a remarkable game. The Celtics, having won the first game at Syracuse, won the second at home—in four overtime

Philadelphia's Neil Johnston, grabbing rebound against the Knicks, won the scoring title and was second in rebounding.

periods. As well as anything, this game demonstrated how inadequate the rules were when professionals played for high stakes: there were 107 fouls called; Cousy, scoring 50 points, got 30 of them at the free-throw line; no player but Cousy scored more than five baskets, in 68 minutes of action; and each team took 65 free throws while making only 27 field goals.

The Knicks were then able to get by Boston in four games, while the Lakers needed all five to eliminate

Knicks' Harry Gallatin fouls Lakers' Jim Pollard in the fifth game of playoff final. Minneapolis won, 91–84, to retain title.

Fort Wayne, which had upset the Royals in the first round.

So it was the Lakers and Knicks in the final again, not only the first true final in the sense of divisional champions meeting, but the first rematch of previous year's finalists.

This time, the schedule was slightly different, although the Lakers did have the odd home game again: it would be two in Minneapolis, then three in New York, and the last two back in Minneapolis. Again the emphasis lay on New York's need to win at least one away game.

The Knicks won it right away, and almost won the second. But the Lakers put the full stamp of authority on their dynasty when the series moved to New York:

they won three straight on that armory court and wrapped up the title, four games to one.

With four titles in five years, the Lakers truly seemed invincible as long as George Mikan lasted.

New stars were being produced, however. The scoring champion was a 6-8, hook-shooting center at Philadelphia, Neil Johnston. The 12-foot lane didn't seem to bother him, as he averaged 22.3 points a game (to Mikan's 20.6, Macauley's 20.3 and Cousy's 19.8).

Since there were no rules about voting by position, the all-league team wound up with Mikan, Neil Johnston and Macauley—three centers—on it with Schayes and Cousy, while the second team had the guards: Sharman, Andy Phillip, Bob Davies and Bobby Wanzer, along with Vern Mikkelsen. This little absurdity was a trivial symptom of a deeper difficulty: the game itself needed repair.

1952-53

STANDINGS

Eastern Division

	W.	L.	Pct.
New York	47	23	.671
Syracuse	47	24	.662
Boston	46	25	.648
Baltimore	16	54	.229
Philadelphia	12	57	.174

Western Division

	W.	L.	Pct.
Minneapolis	48	22	.686
Rochester	44	26	.629
Fort Wayne	36	33	.522
Indianpolis	28	43	.394
Milwaukee	27	44	.380

Eastern Division Semifinal Series

March 17—New York 80, Baltimore 62
March 20—New York 90, Baltimore 81

March 19—Boston 87, Syracuse 81
March 21—Boston 111, Syracuse 105 (4 OT)

Eastern Division Final Series

March 25—New York 95, Boston 91
March 26—Boston 86, New York 70
March 28—New York 101, Boston 82
March 29—New York 82, Boston 75

Western Division Semifinal Series

March 20—Fort Wayne 84, Rochester 77
March 22—Rochester 83, Fort Wayne 71
March 24—Fort Wayne 67, Rochester 65

March 22—Minneapolis 85, Indianpolis 69
March 23—Minneapolis 81, Indianpolis 79

Western Division Final Series

March 26—Minneapolis 83, Fort Wayne 73
March 28—Minneapolis 82, Fort Wayne 75
March 30—Fort Wayne 98, Minneapolis 95
April 1—Fort Wayne 85, Minneapolis 82
April 2—Minneapolis 74, Fort Wayne 58

Championship Series

April 4—New York 96, Minneapolis 88
April 5—Minneapolis 73, New York 71
April 7—Minneapolis 90, New York 75
April 8—Minneapolis 71, New York 69
April 10—Minneapolis 91, New York 84

TOP SCORERS

	Pts.	Ave.
Neil Johnston, Philadelphia	1564	22.3
George Mikan, Minneapolis	1442	20.6
Bob Cousy, Boston	1407	19.8
Ed Macauley, Boston	1402	20.3
Dolph Schayes, Syracuse	1262	17.8

TOP REBOUNDERS

	No.	Ave.
George Mikan, Minneapolis	1007	14.4
Neil Johnston, Philadelphia	976	13.9
Dolph Schayes, Syracuse	920	13.0
Harry Gallatin, New York	916	13.1
Mel Hutchins, Milwaukee	793	11.2

LEADERS IN ASSISTS

	No.	Ave.
Bob Cousy, Boston	547	7.7
Andy Phillip, Fort Wayne	397	5.7
George King, Syracuse	364	5.1
Dick McGuire, New York	296	4.9
Paul Seymour, Syracuse	294	4.4

1953-54

The attempt to cope with fouls took a new form for this season. Each player would be limited to two fouls per quarter; if he committed a third, he would be disqualified for the remainder of that period, and, of course, his game limit of six remained in force.

It didn't do any good at all. The number of fouls did decrease (to 51 a game), but not their prevalence in game-end situations.

Now there were only nine teams, Indianapolis having finally given up, so the Western Division contained only four teams, three of which would make the playoffs. Since the fourth team, Milwaukee, embarked on a 21-51 season, and the fifth team in the East, Baltimore, was to go 16-56, the whole regular season (now 72 games) was reduced to jockeying for home-court advantage in the playoffs.

During that season, it seemed like business as usual. The Knicks finished first again, while Boston and Syracuse tied for second, only two games behind. The Lakers finished first again, two games ahead of Rochester with Fort Wayne only four games further back. Neil Johnston was the scoring champion again, at 24.4, with George Mikan slipping to fourth behind Bob Cousy and Ed Macauley, but that was largely

Driving Dolph Schayes led Syracuse to playoff final, but Lakers won again.

because Big George, approaching the age of 30, was playing fewer minutes.

But a new playoff system had been devised, and it was less than a rousing success.

The first round, instead of elimination, would be a round robin among the top three teams, with two to survive. As an attempt to lessen the home-court advantage, this was theoretically desirable—but it also took away that advantage from whichever team earned it by getting a better record over 72 games, and created the possibility of a game that would be meaningless for one team but not the other.

Both things happened. The Knicks, losing to Boston at home and to Syracuse there, were out of business when they lost a three-hour, foul-filled televised game in Boston. But they still had to play a fourth game against Syracuse, to help determine whether

Boston or Syracuse would have the odd home game in the next round. They lost. And in the other round robin, the Lakers won three straight and Rochester beat Fort Wayne twice, so the final scheduled Minneapolis-Rochester game was unnecessary, and canceled.

Now the Nats beat Boston two straight, reaching the finals, and the Lakers took out Rochester in three. At that point, Minneapolis and Rochester had played each other 15 times, with the Lakers winning nine of the games; Boston and Syracuse had met 14 times, with Syracuse winning nine.

The final, then, was Minneapolis-Syracuse, a rematch of 1950 for Al Cervi and Dolph Schayes and George Mikan and Jim Pollard, but with quite different supporting casts.

The series went the distance. Syracuse managed

to win the second game, at Minneapolis, but the Lakers countered by winning two of the next three at Syracuse. Syracuse prolonged it with a 65-63 upset in Minneapolis in the sixth game, but the Lakers wrapped up their fifth title in six years with an 87-80 victory in the final game.

But conditions were becoming impossible. Throughout the playoffs, fouls averaged 59 a game. Over the regular season, the average team score dipped below 80 points for the first time in six years, despite the obvious fact that shooters were more talented and more plentiful than ever—a reflection of how the foul patterns destroyed the rhythm of play. The very skills the spectators were paying to see were being nullified by the grab-and-hold tactics that paid off on the scoreboard. Attendance fell.

Something drastic would have to be done.

1953-54

STANDINGS

Eastern Division

	W.	L.	Pct.
New York	44	28	.611
Boston	42	30	.583
Syracuse	42	30	.583
Philadelphia	29	43	.403
Baltimore	16	56	.222

Western Division

	W.	L.	Pct.
Minneapolis	46	26	.639
Rochester	44	28	.611
Fort Wayne	40	32	.556
Milwaukee	21	51	.292

Eastern Division First Round

March 16—Boston 93, New York 71
March 17—Syracuse 96, Boston 95 (OT)
March 18—Syracuse 75, New York 68
March 20—Boston 79, New York 78
March 21—Syracuse 103, New York 99
March 22—Syracuse 98, Boston 85

Eastern Division Final Series

March 25—Syracuse 109, Boston 94
March 27—Syracuse 83, Boston 76

Western Division First Round

March 16—Rochester 82, Fort Wayne 75
March 17—Minneapolis 109, Rochester 88
March 18—Minneapolis 90, Fort Wayne 85
March 20—Minneapolis 78, Fort Wayne 73
March 21—Rochester 89, Fort Wayne 71
March 23—Minneapolis at Rochester (cancelled)

Western Division Final Series

March 24—Minneapolis 89, Rochester 76
March 27—Rochester 74, Minneapolis 73
March 28—Minneapolis 82, Rochester 72

Championship Series

March 31—Minneapolis 79, Syracuse 68
April 3—Syracuse 62, Minneapolis 60
April 4—Minneapolis 81, Syracuse 67
April 8—Syracuse 80, Minneapolis 69
April 10—Minneapolis 84, Syracuse 73
April 11—Syracuse 65, Minneapolis 63
April 12—Minneapolis 87, Syracuse 80

TOP SCORERS

	Pts.	Ave.
Neil Johnston, Philadelphia	1759	24.4
Bob Cousy, Boston	1383	19.2
Ed Macauley, Boston	1344	18.9
George Mikan, Minneapolis	1306	18.1
Ray Felix, Baltimore	1269	17.6

LEADERS IN ASSISTS

	No.	Ave.
Bob Cousy, Boston	578	7.2
Andy Phillip, Fort Wayne	449	6.3
Paul Seymour, Syracuse	364	5.1
Dick McGuire, New York	354	5.2
Bob Davies, Rochester	323	4.5

TOP REBOUNDERS

	No.	Ave.
Harry Gallatin, New York	1098	15.3
George Mikan, Minneapolis	1028	14.3
Larry Foust, Fort Wayne	967	13.4
Ray Felix, Baltimore	958	13.3
Dolph Schayes, Syracuse	879	12.3

1954-55

Only a few days after the 1954 season ended, unsatisfactorily for everyone but the Lakers, the world of pro basketball changed radically.

The owners of the nine NBA clubs adopted two revolutionary playing-rule concepts: a time limit on ball possession without trying a shot at the basket, and a limit on the number of fouls a team (rather than an individual player) could commit in any one quarter.

This combination—and both rules have to be taken together to make them work—created the basketball we know today.

The time limit was set at 24 seconds, essentially

Milwaukee's Bob Pettit made the all-league team as a rookie.

by rule-of-thumb estimate of what would be good. The team fouls were set at six per quarter.

If a team exceeded the foul limit, it was penalized by a "bonus" free throw. That is, every ordinary foul became a two-shot foul, costing two points (if made), and if the foul called for two shots anyhow, the shooter was given three chances to make the two points. If a team didn't take a shot that hit the rim within 24 seconds after getting possession, it was a

violation and the other team put the ball in play from out of bounds.

Rarely has a problem been solved more completely. The time limit made it unnecessary (and unproductive) for the trailing team to foul deliberately: it would get its chance at the ball within 24 seconds, on a missed shot or on some defensive maneuver against the leading team's legitimate attempt to score. At the same time, the limit on fouls made it too costly to foul to prevent a basket. (Without this element, and just a time limit, it would pay to foul as soon as possible, before a shot could be attempted, to give up only one point on a free throw).

And two other refinements became possible in this format. A backcourt foul—on the far side of the center line—could be presumed to be tactical and deliberate, and its value nullified by making it a two-shot foul (and three-for-two if you were over the limit). An offensive foul on the other hand—charging or going for an offensive rebound—could safely be assumed to be accidental, since no tactical advantage could be gained by giving up a single free throw when your team already had the ball. So it wasn't necessary to award a free throw at all for this infraction: it could be treated as a violation, with loss of possession a sufficient penalty. However, to avoid indiscriminate roughness by the offense, the foul would still count as a personal against the man, towards his game limit of six.

In those strokes of the pen, the pro game was transformed into a fair contest right down to the last 24 seconds of every game. With no way to benefit from tactical fouling, both coaches and players could concentrate on legitimate play, and the impossible tasks of the referees were made at least a little less impossible.

Other consequences were immediately foreseen. The 24-second clock would mean a running game, a higher-scoring game—but this was exactly what had made the college game so popular a decade before, and exactly what the founders of the league had in mind anyhow.

What would this do to a championship team built around George Mikan? Would he (and others like him) be able to run back and forth all night, especially in his thirties? That question wouldn't have to be faced, it turned out, because Mikan retired after the 1953-54 season.

While it would take a few years for teams to master all the implications of the new game, its improved

Boston's Bob Cousy paced the league in assists for the third consecutive season.

nature was evident immediately. One-hundred-point games became so commonplace that the Celtics averaged 101.4 a game over the 72-game schedule, and the league as a whole averaged 93.1 per team per game. More important, although the new rule meant much more action content in every game—a leisurely move up the floor was not possible—the number of fouls actually went down (to less than 50 a game for both teams).

Yet, the higher scores did not send individual scoring through the roof; they seemed to promote team balance. Neil Johnston, scoring champion again, won that title with a 22.7 average, while Paul Arizin (back

from military service) had 21.0 and Bob Cousy 21.2.

Without Mikan, the Lakers finished second behind Fort Wayne, with Rochester's aging team unable to cope with the new conditions and losing more than half its games. Syracuse, on the other hand, was well equipped for the new style and won the Eastern Division by five games.

Early in the season, the Baltimore franchise folded, leaving the league with eight teams and the possibility of a better playoff system. With only four teams in each division, three would still qualify for the playoffs; but the leader would be given a first-round bye, and then play the survivor of a best-of-three set between the second and third teams in that division. Under this setup, Fort Wayne and Syracuse moved smoothly to the final round, and Syracuse finally won the championship it had been unable to get when Mikan was around.

But the way that title was won was significant. The final game, at Syracuse, was close right down to the wire—and completely unspoiled by the foul-trading that would have been mandatory under the old rules. In the last few seconds, George King sank a free throw for a 92-91 lead, then stole the ball to preserve the victory.

The Fort Wayne team, coming so close, was remarkable in itself. Fred Zollner, its owner, had startled everyone by making Charlie Eckman the coach—the same Charlie Eckman who had been refereeing in the NBA for years. That he succeeded was taken as something of an insult by the experienced professional coaches; but that he had a backcourt of Max Zaslofsky, Andy Phillip and Frankie Brian to guide a strong frontcourt of George Yardley, Larry Foust, Mel Hutchins and Bob Houbregs didn't hurt.

Another feature of this eventful year was the arrival of two spectacular rookies. Bob Pettit, a 6-9 shooter and rebounder from Louisiana State, was an immediate hit with the Milwaukee Hawks. Frank Selvy, a 6-4 shooter who had once scored 100 points in a college game for Furman, was drafted by Baltimore but wound up with the Hawks after the Bullets disappeared (on November 27 with a 3-11 record). Pettit wound up averaging 20.4 points a game and Selvy 19.0, but they couldn't lift the Hawks out of last place.

And the all-league team underlined the start of a new era; Johnston, Dolph Schayes, Pettit, Bob Cousy and Larry Foust, the Fort Wayne center.

1954-55

STANDINGS

Eastern Division

	W.	L.	Pct.
Syracuse	43	29	.597
New York	38	34	.528
Boston	36	36	.500
Philadelphia	33	39	.458

Western Division

	W.	L.	Pct.
Fort Wayne	43	29	.597
Minneapolis	40	32	.556
Rochester	29	43	.403
Milwaukee	29	46	.361

Eastern Division Semifinal Series

March 15—Boston 122, New York 101
March 16—New York 102, Boston 95
March 19—Boston 116, New York 109

Eastern Division Final Series

March 22—Syracuse 110, Boston 100
March 24—Syracuse 116, Boston 110
March 26—Boston 100, Syracuse 97 (OT)
March 27—Syracuse 110, Boston 94

Western Division Semifinal Series

March 16—Minneapolis 82, Rochester 78
March 18—Rochester 94, Minneapolis 92
March 19—Minneapolis 119, Rochester 110

Western Division Final Series

March 20—Fort Wayne 96, Minneapolis 79
March 22—Fort Wayne 98, Minneapolis 97 (OT)
March 23—Minneapolis 99, Fort Wayne 91 (OT)
March 27—Fort Wayne 105, Minneapolis 96

Championship Series

March 31—Syracuse 86, Fort Wayne 82
April 2—Syracuse 87, Fort Wayne 84
April 3—Fort Wayne 98, Syracuse 89
April 5—Fort Wayne 109, Syracuse 102
April 7—Fort Wayne 74, Syracuse 71
April 9—Syracuse 109, Fort Wayne 104
April 10—Syracuse 92, Fort Wayne 91

TOP SCORERS

	Pts.	Ave.
Neil Johnston, Philadelphia	1631	22.7
Paul Arizin, Philadelphia	1512	21.0
Bob Cousy, Boston	1504	21.2
Bob Pettit, Milwaukee	1466	20.4
Frank Selvy, Milwaukee	1348	19.0

TOP REBOUNDERS

	No.	Ave.
Neil Johnston, Philadelphia	1085	15.1
Harry Gallatin, New York	995	13.8
Bob Pettit, Milwaukee	994	13.8
Dolph Schayes, Syracuse	887	12.3
Ray Felix, New York	818	11.4

LEADERS IN ASSISTS

	No.	Ave.
Bob Cousy, Boston	557	7.8
Dick McGuire, New York	542	7.6
Andy Phillip, Fort Wayne	491	7.7
Paul Seymour, Syracuse	483	6.7
Slater Martin, Minneapolis	427	5.9

Rookie Tom Gola, on the ball, and Paul Arizin (11), helped Warriors win the title.

1955-56

The 10th season of the NBA (counting the BAA years) was a continuation of the ninth.

The new rules continued to work well. The league scoring average soared to 99 points per team per game. Bob Pettit, as a second-year player, beat out Paul Arizin and Neil Johnston for the scoring title, averaging 25.7 to Arizin's 24.2 and Johnston's 22.1. Fouls dropped to 47 a game.

But Pettit was operating in a new setting now. Ben Kerner had moved his Hawks from Milwaukee to St. Louis. In Milwaukee, the Hawks had become completely over-shadowed by the baseball Braves, who moved there from Boston in 1953; in St. Louis, there was something of a sports vacuum because the baseball Browns had moved to Baltimore in 1954. It turned out to be a productive move for Kerner and for the league.

All the Hawks could do was to tie Minneapolis for second place in the West, with a 33-39 record, but by beating the Lakers in the first round and pushing

Fort Wayne to the limit in five games in the semifinals, the Hawks established what was to be the most profitable franchise in the league for the next few years.

For Wayne, however, was the strongest team in the West again, with Charlie Eckman still coaching and trying an innovation that soon became universal: a "four big man" alignment by having Mel Hutchins, a 6-5 forward, play one of the guard positions with three regular forwards. It turned out that in the helter-skelter, run-and-shoot 24-second-rule game, the added rebounding gained more than the lessened ball-handling skills lost.

And in the other division, the Philadelphia Warriors—dead last the year before—had come to a similar alignment more naturally. Flanking Johnston and Arizin, their great scorers, they had Joe Graboski and Walt Davis to provide strong rebounding in the other corner—and their prize rookie, Tom Gola, was a full-fledged backcourt man who was nearly 6-6. Jack George, Ernie Beck and George Dempsey filled out

Celtics' Bill Sharman drove his way onto the all-league team.

a fine and versatile set of guards. The Warriors got off to a fine start (12-4) and never stopped, beating the Celtics by six games. All this was under the direction of George Senesky, made coach by Eddie Gottlieb, who moved upstairs as owner.

The defending champion Syracuse Nats had a poor year, and made the playoffs only by beating the Knicks in a tiebreaker game after the teams had tied for last in the East with 35-37 records—only two games worse than Fort Wayne's first-place record in

the West. The Nats did knock off Boston, but couldn't get past the Warriors, although they forced them to five games.

The Warriors then proved simply too good for the Pistons, and took the final, four games to one.

The all-league team was not open to argument, and, for once, a true team that could play: Johnston at center, Arizin and Pettit as forwards, Bob Cousy and Bill Sharman as guards. But the most exciting new player of all was Maurice Stokes, of Rochester, a 6-7 broad-shouldered center with incredibly smooth all-around skills. He had joined a deteriorating team, but his quality was appreciated on all sides.

1955-56

STANDINGS

Eastern Division

	W.	L.	Pct.
Philadelphia	45	27	.625
Boston	39	33	.542
Syracuse*	35	37	.486
New York	35	37	.486

Western Division

	W.	L.	Pct.
Fort Wayne	37	35	.514
Minneapolis*	33	39	.458
St. Louis	33	39	.458
Rochester	31	41	.431

*Won playoff to break tie

Eastern Division third-place tie
March 15—Syracuse 82, New York 77

Western Division second-place tie
March 16—Minneapolis 103, St. Louis 97

Eastern Division Semifinal Series

March 17—Boston 110, Syracuse 92
March 19—Syracuse 101, Boston 98
March 21—Syracuse 102, Boston 97

Eastern Division Final Series

March 23—Philadelphia 109, Syracuse 87
March 25—Syracuse 122, Philadelphia 118
March 27—Philadelphia 119, Syracuse 96
March 28—Syracuse 108, Philadelphia 104
March 29—Philadelphia 109, Syracuse 104

Western Division Semifinal Series

March 17—St. Louis 116, Minneapolis 115
March 19—Minneapolis 133, St. Louis 75
March 21—St. Louis 116, Minneapolis 115

Western Division Final Series

March 22—St. Louis 86, Fort Wayne 85
March 24—St. Louis 84, Fort Wayne 74
March 25—Fort Wayne 107, St. Louis 84
March 27—Fort Wayne 93, St. Louis 84
March 29—Fort Wayne 102, St. Louis 97

Championship Series

March 31—Philadelphia 98, Fort Wayne 94
April 1—Fort Wayne 84, Philadelphia 83
April 3—Philadelphia 100, Fort Wayne 96
April 5—Philadelphia 107, Fort Wayne 105
April 7—Philadelphia 99, Fort Wayne 88

TOP SCORERS

	Pts.	Ave.
Bob Pettit, St. Louis	1849	25.7
Paul Arizin, Philadelphia	1741	24.2
Neil Johnston, Philadelphia	1547	22.1
Clyde Lovellette, Minneapolis	1526	21.5
Dolph Schayes, Syracuse	1472	20.4

TOP REBOUNDERS

	No.	Ave.
Bob Pettit, St. Louis	1164	16.2
Maurice Stokes, Rochester	1094	16.3
Clyde Lovellette, Minneapolis	992	14.0
Neil Johnston, Philadelphia	872	12.5
Dolph Schayes, Syracuse	872	12.4

LEADERS IN ASSISTS

	No.	Ave.
Bob Cousy, Boston	642	8.9
Jack George, Philadelphia	457	6.3
Slater Martin, Minneapolis	445	6.2
Andy Phillip, Fort Wayne	410	5.9
George King, Syracuse	410	5.7

1956-57

As the NBA entered its 11th year, there was more talk about what would be than about what was. Coming out of college was Bill Russell, a 6-9 center of extraordinary defensive skills, who had led the University of San Francisco through two unbeaten seasons. There was a sophomore at Kansas named Wilt Chamberlain—a Philadelphian who was seven feet tall by the time he left high school (with 100 colleges bidding for his services), whose draft rights were already held by the Warriors. And insiders were aware of a high school kid in Indiana who was so good you couldn't believe it—a kid named Oscar Robertson, who was headed for the University of Cincinnati.

But Russell was the one who was going to have the most profound effect on basketball history, although even his boosters didn't realize how much.

Red Auerbach's and Walter Brown's frustration in Boston had reached breaking point. They had a spectacular scoring machine, but never enough rebounding. Yet they won too many games each year to get a high draft choice. On the other hand, losing teams, choosing earlier, might not be able to pay what Russell would want (about $25,000 as a bonus, considered a huge sum then). Auerbach made a deal

Boston gave up a lot to get Olympian Bill Russell from St. Louis, but the rookie center was well worth it, helping Celtics to the championship.

with Kerner, whose team had second pick in the draft: Ed Macauley (who was eager to return to St. Louis) and Cliff Hagan, a prize rookie, for Russell.

Furthermore, as their regular draft pick, the Celtics got Tom Heinsohn, a 6-7 high-scoring center from Holy Cross.

Henceforth, the Celtics would be able to get the ball—for years and years and years.

Russell didn't join the team until December, because he was on the Olympic team and the 1956 Olympics, in Australia, were being held in November-December. By the time he got to Boston, Heinsohn had helped get the Celtics off to a 13-3 start. When Russell did arrive, he needed a few weeks to fit in. But by the time the regular season was over, the Celtics were clearly the best team in the league, with a 44-28 record. Not only did they have the all-star pair of Bob Cousy and Bill Sharman now driving a front line of Russell, Heinsohn and the muscular Jim Loscutoff; they had as reserves such distinguished veterans as Arnie Risen, Andy Phillip and Jack Nichols, and an invaluable young sixth man in Frank Ramsey, who had been Hagan's teammate on an unbeaten Kentucky college team.

As clear as things were in the East, they were muddled in the West. Kerner, in St. Louis, changed coaches in midseason, dropping Red Holzman and installing Alex Hannum—one of his reserve forwards. He had acquired Slater Martin in a trade, to play alongside Jack McMahon in backcourt, and between Bob Pettit and Ed Macauley he had a seven-foot center in Chuck Share—with Jack Coleman and Hagan in reserve. Yet the best the Hawks could do was finish in a three-way tie for first with Fort Wayne and Minneapolis—all of them four games under .500 at 34-38, three games ahead of Rochester.

In other words, the entire Eastern Division finished ahead of the entire Western Division.

What all this led up to was the first nationally-recognized truly great championship playoff series.

The Hawks had to beat Fort Wayne and Minneapolis in special playoff games to get that first-place bye, then beat the Lakers in three straight (the third in double overtime) in the regular playoffs. The Celtics beat Syracuse in three straight, by margins of 18, 15 and 3. Boston was heavily favored to beat the Hawks almost as easily.

Instead, the Hawks won the opener in Boston, in double overtime. They lost the second game by 20 points, but took the third game, at St. Louis, by 100-

Rookie Tom Heinsohn can't bear to watch, but coach Red Auerbach does, as final seconds tick off in the Celtics' 125–123 double-overtime victory over St. Louis for their first championship. Heinsohn fouled out after scoring 37 points.

98. Boston won the fourth game, there, and the fifth at home, but the Hawks stayed alive with a 96-94 decision in St. Louis.

So there had to be a seventh game, on April 13, a Saturday afternoon, in Boston.

It was one of the most dramatic basketball games ever played, and became one of the most retold. Six times the Celtics seemed to take command; each time the Hawks caught up. In the closing seconds, two free throws by Pettit sent the game into overtime. In the closing seconds of the extra period, a basket by Coleman forced another overtime. In the last two seconds of the second overtime, a free throw by Loscutoff increased Boston's lead to 125-123—and a final shot by Pettit, which could have meant another overtime, went off the rim.

A large television audience saw this game, on the eve of a baseball season, and the visibility of the NBA took a quantum jump.

So Brown and Auerbach, at long last, had a title. The new rules had been vindicated again, under the

greatest pressure. The all-league team—Cousy, Sharman, Paul Arizin, Pettit and Dolph Schayes—now was fully staffed by names recognizable to all sports fans, not just a minority of basketball buffs. Never again would there be questions about the league's ability to survive.

1956-57

STANDINGS

Eastern Division

	W.	L.	Pct.
Boston	44	28	.611
Syracuse	38	34	.528
Philadelphia	37	35	.524
New York	36	36	.500

Western Division

	W.	L.	Pct.
St. Louis**	34	38	.472
Minneapolis	34	38	.472
Fort Wayne	34	38	.472
Rochester	31	41	.431

*Won playoff with Minneapolis and Fort Wayne to break tie

Western Division three-way 1st place tie
March 14—St. Louis 115, Fort Wayne 103
March 16—St. Louis 114, Minneapolis 111

Eastern Division Semifinal Series

March 16—Syracuse 103, Philadelphia 96
March 18—Syracuse 91, Philadelphia 80

Eastern Division Final Series

March 21—Boston 108, Syracuse 90
March 23—Boston 120, Syracuse 105
March 24—Boston 83, Syracuse 80

Western Division Semifinal Series

March 17—Minneapolis 131, Fort Wayne 127
March 19—Minneapolis 110, Fort Wayne 108

Western Division Final Series

March 21—St. Louis 118, Minneapolis 109
March 24—St. Louis 106, Minneapolis 104
March 25—St. Louis 143, Minneapolis 135 (2 OT)

Championship Series

March 30—St. Louis 125, Boston 123 (OT)
March 31—Boston 119, St. Louis 99
April 6—St. Louis 106, Boston 98
April 7—Boston 123, St. Louis 118
April 9—Boston 124, St. Louis 109
April 11—St. Louis 96, Boston 94
April 13—Boston 125, St. Louis 123 (2 OT)

TOP SCORERS

	Pts.	Ave.
Paul Arizin, Philadelphia	1817	25.6
Bob Pettit, St. Louis	1755	24.7
Dolph Schayes, Syracuse	1617	22.5
Neil Johnston, Philadelphia	1575	22.8
George Yardley, Fort Wayne	1547	21.5

TOP REBOUNDERS

	No.	Ave.
Maurice Stokes, Rochester	1256	17.4
Bob Pettit, St. Louis	1037	14.6
Dolph Schayes, Syracuse	1008	14.0
Bill Russell, Boston	943	19.6
Clyde Lovellette, Minneapolis	932	13.5

LEADERS IN ASSISTS

	No.	Ave.
Bob Cousy, Boston	478	7.4
Jack McMahon, St. Louis	367	5.1
Maurice Stokes, Rochester	331	4.6
Jack George, Philadelphia	307	4.6
Slater Martin, St. Louis	269	4.1

ankle, and that changed the equation. Back in Boston for the fifth game, the Hawks had a great rebounding advantage, and used it to pull out a 102-100 victory. Now they could end the series by winning at home—and they did, with Bob Pettit pouring in 50 points, 19 of them in the last quarter, and needing every one for a 110-109 victory.

This made the Hawks the fifth different champion in five years, in an eight-team league, quite an antidote to the dynasty George Mikan's Lakers had enjoyed.

The fourth year of the 24-second rule saw scoring rise to unprecedented heights. Teams were now scoring an average of 106.6 points a game, even though the field goal percentage (.383) wasn't any different than it had been when the average was 13 points lower, and not much different than in pre-24-second days.

George Yardley, the high-jumping Piston forward, had become the first player to score 2,000 points in

1957-58

The big-league image and population potential of the NBA got two more boosts going into the season. The Fort Wayne Pistons moved to Detroit and the Rochester Royals to Cincinnati. Only three years before, half the league's members were based in metropolitan areas of less than a million people; now only Syracuse was in that category.

Boston, St. Louis and Syracuse were clearly the strongest teams in the league, as the Celtics won 49 games and the other two 41 each. That meant Boston finished eight games ahead of Syracuse; the Hawks won their division by the same margin over Detroit.

But Philadelphia upset Syracuse in the first round of the playoffs, so no Boston-Syracuse confrontation took place. The semifinal round had now been increased to a four-of-seven series, and both the Celtics and Hawks swept through it in five games, setting up their rematch.

It started like a replay of the previous year. Again, St. Louis got the jump with a two-point victory at Boston before the Celtics evened the series with a one-sided decision. Again the Hawks eked out a victory at home, and again the Celtics evened the series by winning a road game.

But in the third game, Bill Russell had injured his

Detroit's George Yardley (left) became the first NBA player to score 2,000 points in a season. Here he drives past Cliff Hagan, who helped St. Louis win the title.

a season, taking the scoring title with a 27.8-point average to Dolph Schayes' 24.9 and Bob Pettit's 24.6. (Mikan, of course, still held the record at 28.4 in a 68-game schedule in 1951, when he had scored 1,932). But now there were five other players who averaged more than 19 a game—Paul Arizin, Neil Johnston and Bill Sharman, perennial leaders; Clyde Lovellette, who had been Mikan's replacement at Minneapolis but who had moved on to Cincinnati; and Cliff Hagan, who had blossomed into a new type of small forward, a quick, strong 6-4 who could operate near the basket.

Harry Gallatin, who had wound up his career in Detroit (where his rebounding helped free Yardley for his scoring), finished with an iron-man streak of 746 consecutive games played.

Yardley's performance enabled him to crack the all-star team, which again contained Bob Cousy, Sharman, Pettit and Schayes.

1957-58

STANDINGS

Eastern Division

	W.	L.	Pct.
Boston	49	23	.681
Syracuse	41	31	.569
Philadelphia	37	35	.514
New York	35	37	.486

Western Division

	W.	L.	Pct.
St. Louis	41	31	.569
Detroit	33	39	.458
Cincinnati	33	39	.458
Minneapolis	19	53	.264

Eastern Division Semifinal Series

March 15—Syracuse 86, Philadelphia 82
March 16—Philadelphia 95, Syracuse 93
March 18—Philadelphia 101, Syracuse 88

Eastern Division Final Series

March 19—Boston 107, Philadelphia 98
March 22—Boston 109, Philadelphia 87
March 23—Boston 106, Philadelphia 92
March 26—Philadelphia 111, Boston 98
March 27—Boston 93, Philadelphia 88

Western Division Semifinal Series

March 15—Detroit 100, Cincinnati 93
March 16—Detroit 124, Cincinnati 104

Western Division Final Series

March 19—St. Louis 114, Detroit 111
March 22—St. Louis 99, Detroit 96
March 23—Detroit 109, St. Louis 89
March 25—St. Louis 145, Detroit 101
March 27—St. Louis 120, Detroit 96

Championship Series

March 29—St. Louis 104, Boston 102
March 30—Boston 136, St. Louis 112
April 2—St. Louis 111, Boston 107
April 5—Boston 109, St. Louis 98
April 9—St. Louis 102, Boston 100
April 12—St. Louis 110, Boston 109

TOP SCORERS

	Pts.	Ave.
George Yardley, Detroit	2001	27.8
Dolph Schayes, Syracuse	1791	24.9
Bob Pettit, St. Louis	1719	24.6
Clyde Lovellette, Cincinnati	1659	23.4
Paul Arizin, Philadelphia	1406	20.7

TOP REBOUNDERS

	No.	Ave.
Bill Russell, Boston	1564	22.7
Bob Pettit, St. Louis	1216	17.4
Maurice Stokes, Cincinnati	1142	18.1
Dolph Schayes, Syracuse	1022	14.2
John Kerr, Syracuse	963	13.4

LEADERS IN ASSISTS

	No.	Ave.
Bob Cousy, Boston	463	7.1
Dick McGuire, Detroit	454	6.6
Maurice Stokes, Cincinnati	403	6.4
Carl Braun, New York	393	5.5
George King, Cincinnati	337	5.3

1958-59

A new superstar burst on the NBA horizon in the 1959 season—Elgin Baylor, joining a weak Laker team—and one of the results was a short-circuiting of the anticipated rubber match between the Celtics and Hawks.

Boston and St. Louis did overwhelm everyone in the regular season. Stronger than ever, the Celtics won 52 games and averaged 116.4 points a game; the Hawks, picking up Clyde Lovellette in a trade as Ed Macauley became a coach, won 49 and Bob Pettit broke all individual records by averaging 29.2

Rookie of the Year Elgin Baylor of Minneapolis is guarded by MVP Bob Pettit of St. Louis. Pettit was first in scoring, Baylor fourth.

a game. Boston won the eastern race by 12 games, St. Louis the western by 16.

Baylor, however, had scored 24.9 (placing fourth in the league behind Pettit, Jack Twyman of Cincinnati and Paul Arizin of Philadelphia). He had made the all-star team as a rookie (something only Pettit and Alex Groza had accomplished before him) along with Pettit and (inevitably) the three chief Celtics: Bill Russell, Bob Cousy and Bill Sharman. The honors system was better organized now: the all-stars were chosen by position, and a Player of the Year was chosen by the players themselves. It had been Pettit in 1956, Cousy in 1957, Russell in 1958 and Pettit again this time—with Baylor third behind Russell.

Though only 6-5, Baylor was strong, and quick, and a great rebounder as well as scorer and passer. In one game he scored 55 points, the third highest on record (after the 63 Joe Fulks posted back in 1949, and a 61 George Mikan had scored in a double-overtime game in 1952). Through Baylor's efforts, an otherwise helpless Laker team was able to win 33 games, finish second, and make the playoffs.

The Lakers got by Detroit in the first round of the playoffs—and shocked everyone by eliminating the Hawks in six games, winning the fifth in overtime at St. Louis and the sixth at home by two points.

Meanwhile, a late-season trade altered the situation in the East. Syracuse acquired George Yardley from Detroit, and now the Nats had a team capable of challenging Boston seriously. Coach Paul Seymour had a front line of Dolph Schayes, Yardley and John Kerr, and two young whirlwind guards, Hal Greer and Larry Costello. And they lived up to their potential, forcing the Celtics (who had a deeper squad than ever, with Sam Jones, K. C. Jones and Gene Conley as reserves) to the limit. The seven-game series was finally won by the Celtics at home in a hard-fought 130-125 game.

That made the final round something of an anti-climax, since the Lakers obviously weren't in a class with Syracuse or St. Louis in terms of personnel. Besides, the Celtics had a string of 18 straight victories over the Lakers, the last a 173-139 rout which was the highest regular-season score ever achieved by a team—a record that still stands.

Form held. The Celtics scored the first four-game sweep in the history of the final round, and regained the title that Russell's injury (they felt) had cost them the year before.

1958-59

STANDINGS

Eastern Division

	W.	L.	Pct.
Boston	52	20	.722
New York	40	32	.556
Syracuse	35	37	.486
Philadelphia	32	40	.444

Western Division

	W.	L.	Pct.
St. Louis	49	23	.681
Minneapolis	33	39	.458
Detroit	28	44	.389
Cincinnati	19	53	.264

Eastern Division Semifinal Series

March 13—Syracuse 129, New York 123
March 15—Syracuse 131, New York 115

Eastern Division Final Series

March 18—Boston 131, Syracuse 109
March 21—Syracuse 120, Boston 118
March 22—Boston 133, Syracuse 111
March 25—Syracuse 119, Boston 107
March 28—Boston 129, Syracuse 108
March 29—Syracuse 133, Boston 121
April 1—Boston 130, Syracuse 125

Western Division Semifinal Series

March 14—Minneapolis 92, Detroit 89
March 15—Detroit 117, Minneapolis 103
March 18—Minneapolis 129, Detroit 102

Western Division Final Series

March 21—St. Louis 124, Minneapolis 90
March 22—Minneapolis 106, St. Louis 98
March 24—St. Louis 127, Minneapolis 97
March 26—Minneapolis 108, St. Louis 98
March 28—Minneapolis 98, St. Louis 97 (OT)
March 29—Minneapolis 106, St. Louis 104

Championship Series

April 4—Boston 118, Minneapolis 115
April 5—Boston 128, Minneapolis 108
April 7—Boston 123, Minneapolis 120
April 9—Boston 118, Minneapolis 113

TOP SCORERS

	Pts.	Ave.
Bob Pettit, St. Louis	2105	29.2
Jack Twyman, Cincinnati	1857	25.8
Paul Arizin, Philadelphia	1851	26.4
Elgin Baylor, Minneapolis	1742	24.9
Cliff Hagan, St. Louis	1707	23.7

TOP REBOUNDERS

	No.	Ave.
Bill Russell, Boston	1612	23.0
Bob Pettit, St. Louis	1182	16.4
Elgin Baylor, Minneapolis	1050	15.0
John Kerr, Syracuse	1008	13.4
Dolph Schayes, Syracuse	962	13.4

LEADERS IN ASSISTS

	No.	Ave.
Bob Cousy, Boston	557	8.6
Dick McGuire, Detroit	443	6.2
Larry Costello, Syracuse	379	5.4
Richie Guerin, New York	364	5.1
Carl Braun, New York	349	4.8

1959-60

Wilt Chamberlain arrived this season, and the NBA immediately moved to a higher level in three areas: player salaries, gate receipts and individual scoring.

Wilt had passed up his last year of college eligibility to tour the world with the Globetrotters, since the NBA wouldn't accept a player until his entering college class had graduated, but there was no question that he was going to go to work for Eddie Gottlieb

in his home town of Philadelphia. He was about seven feet, two inches tall (which was about five inches taller than Bill Russell and Bob Pettit), with thicker arms and shoulders than George Mikan ever had.

His pay was supposed to be $65,000—about twice as much as Bob Cousy was getting as the highest paid member of the champion Celtics.

And he was expected to pull in a capacity crowd wherever he played.

He was joining a Warrior team that had Paul Arizin, Tom Gola and Joe Graboski from the championship team of 1956, and a young playmaker in Guy Rodgers. Neil Johnston, his career ended by a knee injury but scheduled to be replaced anyhow, was made coach.

Such a team certainly seemed capable of challenging Boston, but Gottlieb—who always believed in feeding the best scorer, from Joe Fulks through Johnston—was also determined that the paying customers would get their money's worth when they came to see Wilt. He would play 48 minutes of every game, and he would concentrate on scoring.

He did. He averaged 37.6 points a game. As a rookie. He scored 50 or more in seven different games. And he outrebounded everybody, averaging 27 a game to Russell's 24 and Pettit's 17.

People had seriously wondered whether this giant, once he started to play, would wreck the league. What he really proved, however, was that basketball is a team game, foremost and always, no matter how overwhelming an individual player is—because the Warriors couldn't match Boston. The Celtics won 59 games and finished 10 ahead of the Warriors, who posted the best record in the history of their club.

The Hawks won their division by a 16-game margin, and this time they kept their final-round appointment with the Celtics. Boston eliminated the Warriors in six games in their semifinal, while St. Louis needed all seven to get by Minneapolis, and the rematch of 1957 and 1958 was on.

Once again, the Hawks got a split in the first two games at Boston, although this time they lost the opener and won the second. The same sequence occurred in St. Louis. Boston won the fifth at home, handily, but the Hawks took the sixth, in a struggle, at St. Louis.

That brought it down to another seventh game at the Boston Garden—but this one wasn't close. Russell grabbed 35 rebounds (and scored 22 points) and the Celtics won, 122-103.

The league was now into an era of runaway offense. Behind Chamberlain, who could be accepted as an exception, Jack Twyman, a 6-6 cornerman, averaged 31.2 points a game for Cincinnati, now a last-place club with only 19 victories. Elgin Baylor averaged 29.6, Pettit 26.1, Cliff Hagan 24.8. All told, 15 players in an eight-team league averaged more than 19. Clyde Lovellette, with 20.8, gave the Hawks a front line that averaged 71.7 points a game—almost as much as entire championship teams were scoring in the early years. Baylor raised the single-game record to 64 early in the season.

The Celtics, with their balance, averaged an incredible 124.5. The whole league was up to 115.3, with the league's shooting percentage up to .402. The 24-second clock had done its work, but this was almost too much of a good thing.

Chamberlain, inevitably, was both Rookie of the Year and Most Valuable Player, the first to score such a double. Since the all-league team was now chosen by positions, Wilt relegated Russell to the second team. Pettit, Baylor and Cousy were there again, of course, but Gene Shue of the Pistons displaced Bill Sharman as the other guard.

◀ *Rookie Wilt Chamberlain won the scoring title and beat out Bill Russell (right) in rebounding, but Russell's Celtics ousted Wilt's Warriors en route to championship.*

1959-60

STANDINGS

Eastern Division

	W.	L.	Pct.
Boston	59	16	.787
Philadelphia	49	26	.653
Syracuse	45	30	.600
New York	27	48	.360

Western Division

	W.	L.	Pct.
St. Louis	46	29	.613
Detroit	30	45	.400
Minneapolis	25	50	.333
Cincinnati	19	56	.253

Eastern Division Semifinal Series

March 11—Philadelphia 115, Syracuse 92
March 13—Syracuse 125, Philadelphia 119
March 14—Philadelphia 132, Syracuse 112

Eastern Division Final Series

March 16—Boston 111, Philadelphia 105
March 18—Philadelphia 115, Boston 110
March 19—Boston 120, Philadelphia 90
March 20—Boston 112, Philadelphia 104
March 22—Philadelphia 128, Boston 107
March 24—Boston 119, Philadolphia 117

Western Division Semifinal Series

March 12—Minneapolis 113, Detroit 112
March 13—Minneapolis 114, Detroit 99

Western Division Final Series

March 16—St. Louis 112, Minneapolis 99
March 17—Minneapolis 120, St. Louis 113
March 19—St. Louis 93, Minneapolis 89
March 20—Minneapolis 103, St. Louis 101
March 22—Minneapolis 117, St. Louis 110 (OT)
March 24—St. Louis 117, Minneapolis 96
March 26—St. Louis 97, Minneapolis 86

Championship Series

March 27—Boston 140, St. Louis 122
March 29—St. Louis 113, Boston 103
April 2—Boston 102, St. Louis 86
April 3—St. Louis 104, Boston 96
April 5—Boston 127, St. Louis 102
April 7—St. Louis 105, Boston 102
April 9—Boston 122, St. Louis 103

TOP SCORERS

	Pts.	Ave.
Wilt Chamberlain, Philadelphia	2707	37.6
Jack Twyman, Cincinnati	2338	31.2
Elgin Baylor, Minneapolis	2074	29.6
Bob Pettit, St. Louis	1882	26.1
Cliff Hagan, St. Louis	1858	24.8

TOP REBOUNDERS

	No.	Ave.
Wilt Chamberlain, Philadelphia	1941	26.9
Bill Russell, Boston	1778	24.0
Bob Pettit, St. Louis	1221	16.9
Elgin Baylor, Minneapolis	1150	16.4
Dolph Schayes, Syracuse	959	12.8

LEADERS IN ASSISTS

	No.	Ave.
Bob Cousy, Boston	715	9.5
Guy Rodgers, Philadelphia	482	7.1
Richie Guerin, New York	468	6.3
Larry Costello, Syracuse	446	6.3
Tom Gola, Philadelphia	409	5.4

1960-61

Oscar Robertson, Jerry West, the Los Angeles Lakers—three names that would become unsurpassed in distinction, glamor, familiarity and prestige in the basketball world—cntcrcd the NBA this season.

Robertson and West, both backcourt men, had been compared constantly throughout their All-American college careers at Cincinnati and West Virginia. They had played together on the U.S. Olympic team in Rome in the summer of 1960. They were fantastic scorers, great passers, terrific ball-handlers and strong on defense. Oscar was about two inches taller, at 6-5, and somewhat more consistent, so he was rated a little higher by most of the pro observers; but there were plenty of supporters for West, and no one else could be mentioned in the same breath.

Under the territorial rule, the Cincinnati Royals were entitled to claim Oscar, but that was a technicality since they had finished last anyhow, and would have had first choice in any case. The last-place team in the Eastern Division, and the only other team not to make the 1960 playoffs, was the Knicks; but the Lakers, finishing third ahead of Cincinnati, had won fewer games than New York—so the Lakers got second pick: West. (The Knicks had to settle for Darrall Imhoff, a center from California.)

Meanwhile, the Lakers themselves were on the move. They had been acquired, two years before, by Bob Short, a young Minneapolis businessman, who was well aware that Elgin Baylor and West would be coming.

He was also aware that basketball in Minnesota was in bad shape. The crowds that had come out to enjoy championship teams built around George Mikan were not interested in also-rans, even with a Baylor present. Besides, major-league baseball was on its way into Minneapolis (to start in the spring of 1961), and a National Football League franchise

Prize rookies Jerry West (left) and Oscar Robertson met in the college all-star game before beginning their NBA careers.

would be starting there in the fall of 1961. The largest building in the area could seat about 10,000; a Mikan team, without competition for the entertainment dollar, could fill that; but even filling it wouldn't help in the coming salary structure triggered by Wilt Chamberlain—and Baylor and West would certainly become high-bracket stars.

On top of all this, there was the shining example of the baseball Dodgers, who had moved from Brooklyn to Los Angeles in 1958, and prospered mightily. Transportation coast-to-coast, while expensive, was no longer a time problem because jet planes had come into use. And Los Angeles had a new city-built arena seating 14,500. It was time to go.

So the Minneapolis Lakers, dominant power of the league in the preceding decade, became the Los Angeles Lakers, a potential economic equal of the Knicks.

Short hired Fred Schaus, who was West's coach at West Virginia, to coach his new Lakers. It took West about half a season to find himself, but by the time it was over he had emerged as a spectacular "Mr. Outside" to go with Baylor's "Mr. Inside." (And "Mr. Inside," in an early-season game at Mad-

ison Square Garden, raised the single-game record to 71 points).

It took Robertson no time at all to find himself: he shone from the start, averaging 30.5 points a game and leading the league in assists with 9.7. But although he was teamed with Jack Twyman, his supporting cast was not quite equal to the Lakers.

Nevertheless, St. Louis was still the class of the Western Division. The Hawks got 72 points a game from their Pettit-Lovellette-Hagan front line, and magnificent backcourt play from an underpublicized rookie from Providence, Lenny Wilkens. Paul Seymour was their coach now, and the Hawks finished 15 games ahead of the Lakers. The Royals, winning almost twice as many games as the year before, still missed the playoffs by one game.

And in the East, Boston won again handily, chased by Philadelphia. Chamberlain, in his second season, raised the scoring record to 38.4 (with Baylor averaging 34.8 and Robertson placing third), and Syracuse, now coached by Alex Hannum, also won more games than the Lakers.

As might be expected, the scoring had now gone through the roof. The whole league averaged 118.1

Clyde Lovellette (34) and the Hawks were in control in the third game of playoff finals, but the Celtics breezed to the title in five.

points a game—38.6 points *more* than in the last season before the 24-second rule. Fourteen players averaged more than 20 a game. And the lowest-scoring team in the league—the Knicks, last again—averaged 113.7.

The change now, however, was no longer a matter of rules. A new generation of shooters was coming into the game, with Oscar (the ''Big O'') and West simply the vanguard. The league's shooting accuracy was up to .415; when the league began, it had been .279.

So even though Chamberlain, Bob Pettit, Bob Cousy, Baylor and Robertson made up the all-star first team, the second-team members—Bill Russell, Dolph Schayes, Tommy Heinsohn, Gene Shue and Larry Costello—were more familiar to the public than the first-stringers of a decade before had been.

The Celtics, however, were at their peak, in a class by themselves. Russell's defensive play was revo-

lutionizing the game: his ability to block shots made the lay-up a poor-percentage shot if he was anywhere near, and all other centers began acquiring this technique to the limits of their own abilities. Boston's offense, usually a fast break triggered by a Russell rebound and guided by a Cousy pass, was incredibly well balanced: Heinsohn scored 21.3 points a game, Cousy 18.1, Russell 16.9, Bill Sharman 16.0, Frank Ramsey 15.1, Sam Jones 15.0.

Such a team simply wasn't going to be stopped. They didn't have to confront Chamberlain directly, because Syracuse won the first-round series, two games to one; but the Celtics brushed aside Syracuse, four games to one, and did the same to the Hawks in what was becoming an annual final-round match-up.

In fact, the feature of the playoffs was a semifinal series between the Hawks and Lakers. It went seven games, and the Lakers, tying it at 3-3 with an overtime victory in Los Angeles, established their hold on that city's fans through that game, even though they lost the seventh game by two points when they got back to St. Louis.

1960-61

STANDINGS

Eastern Division

	W.	L.	Pct.
Boston	57	22	.722
Philadelphia	46	33	.582
Syracuse	38	41	.481
New York	21	58	.266

Western Division

	W.	L.	Pct.
St. Louis	51	28	.646
Los Angeles	36	43	.456
Detroit	34	45	.430
Cincinnati	33	46	.418

Eastern Division Semifinal Series

March 14—Syracuse 115, Philadelphia 107
March 16—Syracuse 115, Philadelphia 114
March 18—Syracuse 106, Philadelphia 103

Eastern Division Final Series

March 19—Boston 128, Syracuse 115
March 21—Syracuse 115, Boston 98
March 23—Boston 133, Syracuse 110
March 25—Boston 120, Syracuse 107
March 26—Boston 123, Syracuse 101

Western Division Semifinal Series

March 14—Los Angeles 120, Detroit 102
March 15—Los Angeles 120, Detroit 118
March 17—Detroit 124, Los Angeles 113
March 18—Detroit 123, Los Angeles 114
March 19—Los Angeles 137, Detroit 120

Western Division Final Series

March 21—Los Angeles 122, St. Louis 118
March 22—St. Louis 121, Los Angeles 106
March 24—Los Angeles 118, St. Louis 112
March 25—St. Louis 118, Los Angeles 117
March 27—Los Angeles 121, St. Louis 112
March 29—St. Louis 114, Los Angeles 113 (OT)
April 1—St. Louis 105, Los Angeles 103

Championship Series

April 2—Boston 129, St. Louis 95
April 5—Boston 116, St. Louis 108
April 8—St. Louis 124, Boston 120
April 9—Boston 119, St. Louis 104
April 11—Boston 121, St. Louis 112

TOP SCORERS

	Pts.	Ave.
Wilt Chamberlain, Philadelphia	3033	38.4
Elgin Baylor, Los Angeles	2538	34.8
Oscar Robertson, Cincinnati	2165	30.5
Bob Pettit, St. Louis	2120	27.9
Jack Twyman, Cincinnati	1997	25.3

TOP REBOUNDERS

	No.	Ave.
Wilt Chamberlain, Philadelphia	2149	27.2
Bob Pettit, St. Louis	1540	20.3
Elgin Baylor, Los Angeles	1447	19.8
Bailey Howell, Detroit	1111	14.4
Willie Naulls, New York	1055	13.4

LEADERS IN ASSISTS

	No.	Ave.
Oscar Robertson, Cincinnati	690	9.7
Guy Rodgers, Philadelphia	677	8.9
Bob Cousy, Boston	591	7.8
Gene Shue, Detroit	530	6.8
Richie Guerin, New York	503	6.4

1961-62

The new stars had helped make the 1960-61 season so successful that the NBA went into the next campaign with a new team, an imitator, and more new stars. The results were spectacular.

The new team was Chicago, called the Packers because it was playing in the Amphitheater, near the stockyards. It was the first new franchise added to the league since the merger of 1950, and it raised the membership of the Western Division to five without altering the playoff structure (although the first round was expanded to a three-of-five series and the semifinals to four-of-seven).

The imitator was another league, a new American Basketball League, started by Abe Saperstein, who ran the Harlem Globetrotters. It had eight teams (Chicago, Los Angeles, Kansas City, San Francisco, Cleveland, Washington, Pittsburgh and Hawaii), five coached by familiar NBA names: Bill Sharman in Los Angeles, Neil Johnston in Pittsburgh, Red Rocha in Hawaii, Andy Phillip in Chicago, Jack McMahon in Kansas City.

But few of the top-name collegians were willing to try the new league, and it lasted only a season and a half.

The biggest newcomer, in size and reputation, was

Syracuse's durable Dolph Schayes donned face mask and kept playing.

on March 2, 1962. He also had a 78, a 73, a pair of 67s and a 65. In January, he had three 62-point games in one eight-day stretch.

That performance, once and for all, made individual scoring meaningless. Until this time, the basketball public had marvelled at one-game highs, but what Chamberlain did not only put the record out of reach, it made the very idea of exceptional scoring commonplace. His incredible totals, combined with the fact that Boston was winning the titles, shifted attention to team values in judging an offense, and scoring champions have never since been considered such marvels, nor big drawing cards simply as scorers.

As fantastic as Chamberlain was, the supremacy of the offense was universal. The nine-team league averaged 118.9 (which turned out to be a peak never reached again). Along with Chamberlain and Bellamy, Oscar Robertson, Bob Pettit and Jerry West averaged 30 or more over the full season, and Elgin Baylor, who spent much of the year commuting to weekend games while doing military service, averaged 38.3 for 48 games. The Knicks, finishing last in their division again, had the sixth and seventh highest scorers in the league, Richie Guerin (29.5) and Willie Naulls (25.0).

The message was getting through: team balance, not individual scorers or physical giants, won basketball games. Boston, having added a strong defensive forward named Tom "Satch" Sanders, was better than ever. The Lakers, with an experienced Frank Selvy alongside West in backcourt, and strong, skilled forwards like Rudy LaRusso and Tom Hawkins to go with Baylor, were terrific even without a dominating center. The Warriors, now coached by Frank McGuire, of college fame, had Tom Gola, Guy Rodgers and Al Attles to feed Chamberlain and Paul Arizin, and another strong forward in Tom Meschery.

These were clearly the dominant teams. The Hawks lost their quarterback when Len Wilkens went into the Army, and with Clyde Lovellette out for half a season, dropped out of the playoffs. Cincinnati, without enough frontcourt power to supplement Robertson, could win more than half its games, but not much more.

During the regular season, then, the usual one-sided races played themselves out: Boston, winning a record 60 games, by 11 over Philadelphia; Los

Walt Bellamy, a 6-11 center from Indiana. In stocking the new Chicago team, it was decided to assign first draft rights to the Packers, so that's where Bellamy wound up—and he produced a 31.6 scoring average, second only to Wilt Chamberlain.

But what a second! Chamberlain had 50.4. This defied imagination, and still does. Chamberlain scored 4,029 points in 3,882 minutes of playing time over 80 games. Once he scored 100 in one game—against the Knicks at Hershey, Pennsylvania,

Willis Reed was forced by injury to leave the fifth game of the championship series against the Lakers, but he returned in the seventh game to give the Knicks a psychological lift that carried them to their first title.

overtime first game won by New York), and then contained Alcindor while beating Milwaukee in five, but not without some difficulty.

The Lakers, with Chamberlain just back in action, found themselves trailing Phoenix and Hawkins, three to one, in the first round. But they pulled themselves together, won the next three in a row and then swept Atlanta in four straight, setting a league record of seven straight playoff game victories.

That created a New York-Los Angeles final, in two big new arenas, in the two largest cities, with several games on national television. For prestige, dollars, attention and big-league aura, this could not be surpassed.

Neither could the drama. The first four games were split, each team winning one in the other city. The fifth game, in New York, seemed to belong to the Lakers, who opened a big lead and then saw Reed

leave the game with a leg injury. But in a scrambling fourth quarter, the Knicks pulled it out. In Los Angeles, without Reed, Chamberlain overwhelmed them (with 45 points and 27 rebounds while Jerry West scored 33 and got 13 assists). But in the seventh game, at New York, Reed hobbled out on a bandaged leg just at game time, and played long enough to trigger a devastating 113-99 victory.

After 24 years of trying, the Knicks had finally won a championship.

And West and Elgin Baylor had come up short in the final round for the seventh time in nine years.

The excitement of that series couldn't blot out other important events. When the ABA began, it had filed an antitrust suit against the NBA. By 1970, the two leagues agreed on a merger plan—only to have the players block it by filing an antitrust suit of their own (under the guidance of Larry Fleisher, their counsel

Oscar Robertson (1) teamed with Lew Alcindor to lead the Bucks to a 66–16 record and four-game sweep of Baltimore in the finals.

and chief negotiator, and Robertson, their president). So the competition for players would have to continue.

West, averaging 31.2 a game, was the league's high scorer, now that this title was determined on average, but he had missed eight games and Alcindor, who averaged 28.8, actually scored more points. The rest of the top ten showed how completely new stars had moved in: Elvin Hayes, Billy Cunningham, Lou Hudson, Connie Hawkins, Bob Rule (Seattle), John Havlicek, Earl Monroe, Dave Bing.

Final rule adjustments reduced the number of permissable team fouls to four a quarter, and made a loose-ball foul the same as an offensive foul—possession, no free throw.

Reed, as MVP, was joined on the all-star team by Frazier, Hawkins, West and Cunningham. Bob Cousy had returned to the league as Cincinnati's coach. Tommy Heinsohn had returned as Boston's coach. Len Wilkens was a playing coach in Seattle, Alex Hannum had returned to the NBA in midseason to take over San Diego.

The wheel was turning faster and faster.

1969-70

STANDINGS

Eastern Division

	W.	L.	Pct.
New York	60	22	.732
Milwaukee	56	26	.683
Baltimore	50	32	.610
Philadelphia	42	40	.512
Cincinnati	36	46	.439
Boston	34	48	.415
Detroit	31	41	.378

Western Division

	W.	L.	Pct.
Atlanta	48	34	.585
Los Angeles	46	36	.561
Chicago	39	43	.476
Phoenix	39	43	.476
Seattle	36	46	.439
San Francisco	30	52	.366
San Diego	27	55	.329

Eastern Division Semifinal Series

March 25—Milwaukee 125, Philadelphia 118
March 27—Philadelphia 112, Milwaukee 105
March 30—Milwaukee 156, Philadelphia 120
April 1—Milwaukee 118, Philadelphia 111
April 3—Milwaukee 115, Philadelphia 106

March 26—New York 120, Baltimore 117 (2 OT)
March 27—New York 106, Baltimore 99
March 29—Baltimore 127, New York 113
March 31—Baltimore 102, New York 92
April 2—New York 101, Baltimore 80
April 5—Baltimore 96, New York 87
April 6—New York 127, Baltimore 114

Eastern Division Final Series

April 11—New York 110, Milwaukee 102
April 13—New York 112, Milwaukee 111
April 17—Milwaukee 101, New York 96
April 19—New York 117, Milwaukee 105
April 20—New York 132, Milwaukee 96

Western Division Semifinal Series

March 25—Atlanta 129, Chicago 111
March 28—Atlanta 124, Chicago 104
March 31—Atlanta 106, Chicago 101
April 3—Chicago 131, Atlanta 120
April 5—Atlanta 113, Chicago 107

March 25—Los Angeles 128, Phoenix 112
March 29—Phoenix 114, Los Angeles 101
April 2—Phoenix 112, Los Angeles 98
April 4—Phoenix 112, Los Angeles 102
April 5—Los Angeles 138, Phoenix 121
April 7—Los Angeles 104, Phoenix 93
April 9—Los Angeles 129, Phoenix 94

Western Division Final Series

April 12—Los Angeles 119, Atlanta 115
April 14—Los Angeles 105, Atlanta 94
April 16—Los Angeles 115, Atalanta 114 (OT)
April 19—Los Angeles 133, Atlanta 114

Championship Series

April 24—New York 124, Los Angeles 112
April 27—Los Angeles 105, New York 103
April 29—New York 111, Los Angeles 108 (OT)
May 1—Los Angeles 121, New York 115 (OT)
May 4—New York 107, Los Angeles 100
May 6—Los Angeles 135, New York 113
May 8—New York 113, Los Angeles 99

TOP SCORERS

	Pts.	Ave.
Jerry West, Los Angeles	2309	31.2
Lew Alcindor, Milwaukee	2361	28.8
Elvin Hayes, San Diego	2256	27.5
Billy Cunningham, Philadelphia	2114	26.1
Lou Hudson, Atlanta	2031	25.4

TOP REBOUNDERS

	No.	Ave.
Elvin Hayes, San Diego	1386	16.9
Wes Unseld, Baltimore	1370	16.7
Lew Alcindor, Milwaukee	1190	14.5
Bill Bridges, Atlanta	1181	14.4
Gus Johnson, Baltimore	1086	13.9

LEADERS IN ASSISTS

	No.	Ave.
Lenny Wilkens, Seattle	683	9.1
Walt Frazier, New York	629	8.2
Clem Haskins, Chicago	624	7.6
Gail Goodrich, Phoenix	605	7.5
Jerry West, Los Angeles	554	7.5

1970-71

The 25th year of the NBA started with 17 teams in action and ended with one unquestionably supreme: the Milwaukee Bucks, with Lew Alcindor in the middle and Oscar Robertson, no less, in backcourt.

Buffalo, Cleveland and Portland were the new entries. Back in 1950, the league had tried 17 teams in three divisions. Now there was a more sensible plan: four divisions, the westernmost containing five teams, the others four. They were grouped this way:

Atlantic—New York, Boston, Philadelphia, Buffalo.

Central—Atlanta, Baltimore, Cincinnati, Cleveland.

Midwest—Milwaukee, Chicago, Phoenix, Detroit.

Pacific—Los Angeles, San Francisco, San Diego, Portland and Seattle.

Only five years before, there had been nine teams playing 360 games with 108 men on their rosters. Now there would be 697 scheduled games and 204 roster places.

The top two teams in each division would make the playoffs.

But there was nothing complicated about the competition itself. Pairing the most mobile of the seven-foot centers with the supreme high-scoring quarterback, in a league with the talent spread around, made Milwaukee almost invincible.

The Bucks won 66, lost 16. They had a 20-game winning streak, wiping out the Knick record of a year before. Alcindor was scoring champion (31.9), and MVP, flanked by two mobile forwards, Bob Dandridge and Greg Smith. Robertson, aided in backcourt by Jon McGlocklin and Lucius Allen, ran this machine like the world's greatest racing driver at the wheel of the world's greatest car.

In their half of the playoffs, the Bucks brushed aside San Francisco in five games and Los Angeles

Seattle's signing of Spencer Haywood (24) had repercussions on the court and in the courts.

in the same number. In the East, Baltimore won a spectacular seven-game semifinal from the Knicks, taking the seventh game at New York.

But the Bucks blasted the Bullets in four straight, a final-round sweep accomplished only once before (by Boston in 1959).

This time, though, the sweep would not launch a dynasty, and it was evident why. The all-rookie team was the most distinguished the league had ever seen: Pete Maravich, Dave Cowens, Bob Lanier, Calvin Murphy, Geoff Petrie.

There was also Jim McMillian, a 6-5 forward of the Bradley type, from Columbia, who took Baylor's

place when Elgin retired. And Seattle, in midseason, had acquired Spencer Haywood in what developed into another landmark legal decision.

Haywood had been an Olympic star in 1968, while still a college sophomore. He decided to turn pro with the ABA, which didn't have a stringent rule (as the NBA had had from the beginning) against using a player before his entering class graduated. But Haywood decided, after playing for Denver, to switch to Seattle of the NBA, in the face of a big offer from Sam Schulman, the Seattle owner.

Haywood had not yet gone through an NBA draft, and other league members objected. In the court case that resulted, a federal judge ruled that the draft rules were improper if they didn't provide some way for a player to turn pro whenever he wanted to. Haywood stayed with Seattle, and the NBA had to institute a hardship draft for underclassmen.

Through all this, both leagues were seeking the permission of Congress to merge—and the players were lobbying successfully against it. Things were much too volatile for anyone to be thinking of dynasties.

1970-71

STANDINGS

Eastern Conference
Atlantic Division

	W.	L.	Pct.
New York	52	30	.634
Philadelphia	47	35	.573
Boston	44	38	.537
Buffalo	22	60	.268

Central Division

	W.	L.	Pct.
Baltimore	42	40	.512
Atlanta	36	46	.439
Cincinnati	33	49	.402
Cleveland	15	67	.183

Western Conference
Midwest Division

	W.	L.	Pct.
Milwaukee	66	16	.805
Chicago	51	31	.622
Phoenix	48	34	.585
Detroit	45	37	.549

Pacific Division

	W.	L.	Pct.
Los Angeles	48	34	.585
San Francisco	41	41	.500
San Diego	40	42	.488
Seattle	38	44	.463
Portland	29	53	.354

Atlantic Division
March 25—New York 112, Atlanta 101
March 27—Atlanta 113, New York 104
March 28—New York 110, Atlanta 95
March 30—New York 113, Atlanta 107
April 1—New York 111, Atlanta 107

Central Division
March 24—Philadelphia 126, Baltimore 112
March 26—Baltimore 119, Philadelphia 107
March 28—Baltimore 111, Philadelphia 103
March 30—Baltimore 120, Philadelphia 105
April 1—Philadelphia 104, Baltimore 103
April 3—Philadelphia 98, Baltimore 94
April 4—Baltimore 128, Philadelphia 120

Eastern Conference Final Series
April 6—New York 112, Baltimore 111
April 9—New York 107, Baltimore 88
April 11—Baltimore 114, New York 88
April 14—Baltimore 101, New York 80
April 16—New York 89, Baltimore 84
April 18—Baltimore 113, New York 96
April 19—Baltimore 93, New York 91

Midwest Division
March 27—Milwaukee 107, San Francisco 96
March 29—Milwaukee 104, San Francisco 90
March 30—Milwaukee 114, San Francisco 102
April 1—San Francisco 106, Milwaukee 104
April 4—Milwaukee 136, San Francisco 86

Pacific Division
March 24—Los Angeles 100, Chicago 99
March 26—Los Angeles 105, Chicago 95
March 28—Chicago 106, Los Angeles 98
March 30—Chicago 112, Los Angeles 102
April 1—Los Angeles 115, Chicago 86
April 4—Chicago 113, Los Angeles 99
April 6—Los Angeles 109, Chicago 98

Western Conference Final Series
April 9—Milwaukee 106, Los Angeles 85
April 11—Milwaukee 91, Los Angeles 73
April 14—Los Angeles 118, Milwaukee 107
April 16—Milwaukee 117, Los Angeles 94
April 18—Milwaukee 116, Los Angeles 98

Championship Series
April 21—Milwaukee 98, Baltimore 88
April 25—Milwaukee 102, Baltimore 83
April 28—Milwaukee 107, Baltimore 99
April 30—Milwaukee 118, Baltimore 106

TOP SCORERS

	Pts.	Ave.
Lew Alcindor, Milwaukee	2596	31.7
John Havlicek, Boston	2338	28.9
Elvin Hayes, San Diego	2350	28.7
Dave Bing, Detroit	2213	27.0
Lou Hudson, Atlanta	2039	26.8

TOP REBOUNDERS

	No.	Ave.
Wilt Chamberlain, Los Angeles	1493	18.2
Wes Unseld, Baltimore	1253	16.9
Elvin Hayes, San Diego	1362	16.6
Lew Alcindor, Milwaukee	1311	16.0
Jerry Lucas, San Francisco	1265	15.8

LEADERS IN ASSISTS

	No.	Ave.
Norm Van Lier, Cincinnati	832	10.1
Len Wilkens, Seattle	654	9.2
Oscar Robertson, Milwaukee	668	8.2
John Havlicek, Boston	607	7.5
Walt Frazier, New York	536	6.7

1971-72

In the center of uncertainty—the two leagues trying to merge, the players preventing it, franchises moving, players switching from one league to the other—the one thing that had long ago seemed certain but had never come to pass finally did. The Lakers won—big.

Cooke had changed coaches again, bringing in Bill Sharman. Wilt Chamberlain was physically sound, Jim McMillian no longer a rookie, Happy Hairston a strong and experienced forward. Alongside Jerry West was Gail Goodrich, once a UCLA star and promising Laker, back from a couple of years in Phoenix. (Elgin Baylor tried to play briefly, but couldn't; his legs were gone.) And Sharman, a Los Angeles hero since his college days at USC, excelled at three things: organizing, conditioning and motivating.

The Knicks had launched a championship drive in 1970 by winning a record 18 straight. The Bucks had topped that the next year with 20 straight, and made it their springboard.

Now the Lakers won 33 in a row.

They went two full months, from November 5 to January 9, without losing a game. At that point, their season record was 39-3. They finished 69-13, breaking the record Wilt's Philadelphia team had set five years before for victories and winning percentage.

And they simply never stopped. They swept Chicago in four games when the playoffs began, brushed aside Milwaukee in six, and the Knicks in five, winning four straight after losing the opener. Their total performance even surpassed the incredible records

of the 76ers and the Bucks. Counting playoff games, the Lakers wound up 81-16.

It had taken them eight tries in the final round, since moving to Los Angeles, to win it.

Even so, the season's MVP could not be denied to Kareem Abdul-Jabbar, the name Lew Alcindor had adopted. He had led the league in scoring again, at 34.8; his team, with much less supporting talent than Wilt had, had won 63 games. Oscar Robertson, slowing down, had never completely shaken off leg injuries. The rest of the Bucks were ordinary major-league talent. Yet, in three seasons with Kareem at center, this team had won 185 games and lost 61. He had lived up to his promise.

The second-highest scorer in the league was a new kind of star—Nate Archibald, a Cincinnati guard barely six feet tall, playing his second pro season.

Sparked by Jerry West, the Lakers fast-breaked to 33 straight victories and won the championship in a walk.

The Royals' little Nate Archibald averaged 28.2 points a game, second only to MVP Kareem Abdul-Jabbar.

He averaged 28.2, and there wasn't any fan who could fail to identify with his speed and skill. Among the other NBA players, he was truly a "little guy." And also among the top ten scorers were other guards: West, Goodrich, Archie Clark, and that all-around man, John Havlicek.

And Chamberlain? In his finest season, he averaged 14.8 points a game, less than a third of what used to be normal. He took only 764 shots, less than 10 a game. But he led the league in rebounding for the 10th time, and his defensive play, less agile in style than Bill Russell's had been, was just as effective because he denied the offense more space. That, of course, gave West and Goodrich and McMillian free reign. It was something to see.

Elsewhere in the league, there were changes of significance. The Rockets had moved from San Diego to Houston. The Warriors playing a few games in San Diego and almost all their home games in the Oakland Coliseum, changed their name from San Francisco to Golden State. The Celtics, built around Dave Cowens, Havlicek and Jo Jo White, had returned to first place in their division (but the Knicks, who now had Jerry Lucas and Earl Monroe but no Willis Reed because of injury, knocked them out of the playoffs).

Walt Frazier, and West, Kareem, Spencer Haywood and Havlicek were the all-star team. Sidney Wicks, the latest UCLA star, was Rookie of the Year for Portland.

And league attendance reached a new high: 5.6 million.

1971-72

STANDINGS

Eastern Conference
Atlantic Division

	W.	L.	Pct.
Boston	56	26	.683
New York	48	34	.585
Philadelphia	30	52	.366
Buffalo	22	60	.268

Central Division

	W.	L.	Pct.
Baltimore	38	44	.463
Atlanta	36	46	.439
Cincinnati	30	52	.366
Cleveland	23	59	.280

Western Conference
Midwest Division

	W.	L.	Pct.
Milwaukee	63	19	.768
Chicago	57	25	.695
Phoenix	49	33	.598
Detroit	26	56	.317

Pacific Division

	W.	L.	Pct.
Los Angeles	69	13	.841
Golden State	51	31	.622
Seattle	47	35	.573
Houston	34	48	.415
Portland	18	64	.220

Eastern Conference Semifinal Series

March 29—Boston 126, Atlanta 108
March 31—Atlanta 113, Boston 104
April 2—Boston 136, Atlanta 113
April 4—Atlanta 112, Boston 110
April 7—Boston 124, Atlanta 114
April 9—Boston 127, Atlanta 118

March 31—Baltimore 108, New York 105 (OT)
April 2—New York 110, Baltimore 88
April 4—Baltimore 104, New York 103
April 6—New York 104, Baltimore 98
April 9—New York 106, Baltimore 82
April 11—New York 107, Baltimore 101

Eastern Conference Final Series

April 13—New York 116, Boston 94
April 16—New York 106, Boston 105
April 19—Boston 115, New York 109
April 21—New York 116, Boston 98
April 23—New York 111, Boston 103

Western Conference Semifinal Series

March 28—Los Angeles 95, Chicago 80
March 30—Los Angeles 131, Chicago 124
April 2—Los Angeles 108, Chicago 101
April 4—Los Angeles 108, Chicago 97

March 28—Golden State 117, Milwaukee 106
March 30—Milwaukee 118, Golden State 93
April 1—Milwaukee 122, Golden State 94
April 4—Milwaukee 106, Golden State 99
April 6—Milwaukee 108, Golden State 100

Western Conference Final Series

April 9—Milwaukee 93, Los Angeles 72
April 12—Los Angeles 135, Milwaukee 134
April 14—Los Angeles 108, Milwaukee 105
April 16—Milwaukee 114, Los Angeles 88
April 18—Los Angeles 115, Milwaukee 90
April 22—Los Angeles 104, Milwaukee 100

Championship Series

April 26—New York 114, Los Angeles 92
April 30—Los Angeles 106, New York 92
May 3—Los Angeles 107, New York 96
May 5—Los Angeles 116, New York 111 (OT)
May 7—Los Angeles 114, New York 100

TOP SCORERS

	Pts.	Ave.
Kareem Abdul-Jabbar, Milwaukee	2822	34.8
Nate Archibald, Cincinnati	2145	28.2
John Havlicek, Boston	2252	27.5
Spencer Haywood, Seattle	1914	26.2
Gail Goodrich, Los Angeles	2127	25.9

TOP REBOUNDERS

	No.	Ave.
Wilt Chamberlain, Los Angeles	1572	19.2
Wes Unseld, Baltimore	1336	17.6
Kareem Abdul-Jabbar, Milwaukee	1346	16.6
Nate Thurmond, Golden State	1252	16.1
Dave Cowens, Boston	1203	15.2

LEADERS IN ASSISTS

	No.	Ave.
Jerry West, Los Angeles	747	9.7
Lenny Wilkens, Seattle	766	9.6
Nate Archibald, Cincinnati	701	9.2
Archie Clark, Phila.-Balt.	613	8.0
John Havlicek, Boston	614	7.5

1972-73

Now the Knicks had Willis Reed back, a partially hobbled Reed, but able to share duty with Jerry Lucas. Walt Frazier and Earl Monroe had learned better

Even Wilt Chamberlain couldn't stop Walt Frazier (10) and the Knicks in the playoff finals.

how to play together. They were again the kind of team they had been in 1970.

But the Lakers were what they were the previous year, and the Celtics had developed a devastating fast break strengthened by Paul Silas as a rebounder. Oscar Robertson, at 34, was going to give it another try with Kareem Abdul-Jabbar at Milwaukee. And Rick Barry was back with the Warriors, after an eventful few years in the ABA, reunited with Nate Thurmond on a team that also had Cazzie Russell.

Baltimore had acquired Elvin Hayes and a back-court of Archie Clark and Phil Chenier, to go with Wes Unseld. Chicago, stressing defense under coach Dick Motta, had won 57 games the year before.

Every one of these teams seemed a potential champion.

During the regular season, the running Celtics were most successful: 68-14, only one game worse than the dazzling performance of the Lakers in 1972. The Lakers and Bucks won 60 apiece, the Knicks 57, Baltimore 52, Chicago 51.

And in a league with such winners, there naturally had to be some losers. Portland and Buffalo lost 61 games apiece, Seattle 56. But the superloser of all time was Philadelphia. With Billy Cunningham gone to the ABA, the 76ers lacked size, experience and skill, and started out with a college coach inexperienced in the pros, Roy Rubin. When their record reached 4-47, they switched to Kevin Loughery—and finished 9-73, a .110 percentage that was even worse than the 6-42-.125 Providence had in 1948. The Cincinnati Royals had moved, becoming the Kansas

City-Omaha Kings (sharing home games with the two cities), but at least they had Nate Archibald, who emerged as the smallest (6-1) scoring champion in the league's history, averaging 34.9 to Kareem's 30.2. They were now in the Midwest Division, with Phoenix in the Pacific and Houston in the Central, which was better geography but not significant competitively.

So the second season arrived with all the playoff teams (Atlanta was the eighth) dreaming more legitimately than usual of eventual triumph.

Right away, there were surprises. Golden State knocked out Milwaukee in six games, and the Knicks had an unexpectedly easy time with Baltimore, winning in five. Boston had to go six to beat Atlanta, and the Lakers just did survive a seven-game war with Chicago, winning the last game at home by only 95-92.

Thereupon, the Lakers turned on the Warriors and beat them in five. After winning the first two in Los Angeles, the Lakers applied a 126-70 crusher in Oakland, and the Warriors never recovered. It was the most one-sided playoff game on record.

The Knicks and Celtics, meanwhile, put on a seven-game thriller. The Knicks, with the best defensive team in the league, knew how to stop the Boston fast break. They lost the opener at Boston, but won the next three, the third a double-overtime victory at New York. But Boston won the fifth game by a point at home, and the sixth rather decisively in New York. In the seventh, however, with Havlicek partially disabled, the Celtics were held to 78 points and the Knicks, scoring 94, were on their way to another final against the Lakers, the third such pairing in four years.

This one turned out to be the reverse of 1972. The Knicks lost the first game, but swept the next four, all close and low-scoring games. Willis Reed played enough of a key role to become the first repeat winner of the car awarded to the outstanding player in the playoffs.

The season-long MVP, however, was Dave Cowens, beating out Kareem for that honor, but not for an all-star berth. Archibald was the first player ever to lead the league in scoring and assists the same year (he had 11.4 assists a game), so he wound up with Jerry West on the first team, while Spencer Haywood and John Havlicek claimed the forward positions.

Yet it was possible to argue that the second team—Cowens, Hayes, Barry, Frazier and Pete Maravich—might well beat that first team in an actual game.

With stylish Walt ''Clyde'' Frazier in the driver's seat, the Knicks rolled to their second championship in four years.

But there was no doubt about the hot rookie: Bob McAdoo, out of North Carolina, a 6-9 center-forward with impressive shooting skills, who averaged 18 points a game for Buffalo, and looked as if he could go much higher.

1972-73

STANDINGS

Eastern Conference
Atlantic Division

	W.	L.	Pct.
Boston	68	14	.829
New York	57	25	.695
Buffalo	21	61	.256
Philadelphia	9	73	.110

Central Division

	W.	L.	Pct.
Baltimore	52	30	.634
Atlanta	46	36	.561
Houston	33	49	.402
Cleveland	32	50	.390

Western Conference
Midwest Division

	W.	L.	Pct.
Milwaukee	60	22	.732
Chicago	51	31	.622
Detroit	40	42	.488
KC-Omaha	36	46	.439

Pacific Division

	W.	L.	Pct.
Los Angeles	60	22	.732
Golden State	47	35	.573
Phoenix	38	44	.463
Seattle	26	56	.317
Portland	21	61	.256

Eastern Conference Semifinal Series

April 1—Boston 134, Atlanta 109
April 4—Boston 126, Atlanta 113
April 6—Atlanta 118, Boston 105
April 8—Atlanta 97, Boston 94
April 11—Boston 108, Atlanta 101
April 13—Boston 121, Atlanta 103

March 30—New York 95, Baltimore 83
April 1—New York 123, Baltimore 103
April 4—New York 103, Baltimore 96
April 6—Baltimore 97, New York 89
April 8—New York 109, Baltimore 99

Eastern Conference Finals

April 15—Boston 134, New York 108
April 18—New York 129, Boston 96
April 20—New York 98, Boston 91
April 22—New York 117, Boston 110 (2 OT)
April 25—Boston 98, New York 97
April 27—Boston 110, New York 100
April 29—New York 94, Boston 78

Western Conference Semifinal Series

March 30—Milwaukee 110, Golden State 90
April 1—Golden State 95, Milwaukee 92
April 5—Milwaukee 113, Golden State 93
April 7—Golden State 102, Milwaukee 97
April 10—Golden State 100, Milwaukee 97
April 13—Golden State 100, Milwaukee 86

March 30—Los Angeles 107, Chicago 104
April 1—Los Angeles 108, Chicago 93
April 6—Chicago 96, Los Angeles 86
April 8—Chicago 98, Los Angeles 94
April 10—Los Angeles 123, Chicago 102
April 13—Chicago 101, Los Angeles 93
April 15—Los Angeles 95, Chicago 92

Western Conference Final Series

April 17—Los Angeles 101, Golden State 99
April 19—Los Angeles 104, Golden State 93
April 21—Los Angeles 126, Golden State 70
April 23—Golden State 117, Los Angeles 109
April 25—Los Angeles 128, Golden State 118

Championship Series

May 1—Los Angeles 115, New York 112
May 3—New York 99, Los Angeles 95
May 6—New York 87, Los Angeles 83
May 8—New York 103, Los Angeles 98
May 10—New York 102, Los Angeles 93

TOP SCORERS

	Pts.	Ave.
Nate Archibald, KC-Omaha	2719	34.9
Kareem Abdul-Jabbar, Milwaukee	2292	30.2
Spencer Haywood, Seattle	2251	29.2
Lou Hudson, Atlanta	2029	27.1
Pete Maravich, Atlanta	2063	26.1

TOP REBOUNDERS

	No.	Ave.
Wilt Chamberlain, Los Angeles	1526	18.6
Nate Thurmond, Golden State	1349	17.1
Dave Cowens, Boston	1329	16.2
Kareem Abdul-Jabbar, Milwaukee	1224	16.1
Wes Unseld, Baltimore	1260	15.9

LEADERS IN ASSISTS

	No.	Ave.
Nate Archibald, KC-Omaha	910	11.4
Lenny Wilkens, Cleveland	628	8.4
Dave Bing, Detroit	637	7.8
Oscar Robertson, Milwaukee	551	7.5
Norm Van Lier, Chicago	567	7.1

Buffalo's Bob McAdoo won the scoring title, but Dave Cowens (left) helped make the Celtics champions once more.

1973-74

The theme of the season was: the old order passeth, once and for all.

Wilt Chamberlain was gone, to coach the San Diego team in the ABA. Over a 14-year period, he had scored more than 31,000 points and pulled in more than 23,000 rebounds. He had averaged 45.8 minutes played through 1,045 regular-season games, and had played in 160 playoff games—and had never fouled out. In regular-season play he had averaged 30.1 points a game—*averaged* it, over more than 1,000 games. In the record book, where the top single-game scoring performances were listed, Chamberlain's name occupied 49 of the top 57 lines (down through 58 points in a game). He was 37 years old.

Jerry West, now 35, wasn't ready to quit, but his battered legs limited him to 31 games during the campaign. It was his last.

Hoping to rebuild, the Lakers traded Jim McMillian to Buffalo for Elmore Smith, a defensive center, and got Connie Hawkins from Phoenix to build up their offense—and they did manage to beat out the Warriors by two games for first place in the Pacific Division.

Willis Reed, too, was playing out the string, out of action almost all year until shortly before the playoffs. Dave DeBusschere and Jerry Lucas were playing their last year. The Knicks managed to come in second again, seven games behind Boston, but they faced a complete rebuilding job, too.

Kareem Abdul-Jabbar still had Robertson, but

Oscar, like so many older players, was having persistent leg problems and was no longer a fixed quantity.

On the other hand, new teams were on the rise. The Celtics, except for John Havlicek and Don Nelson, were a young team. Buffalo, with a sparkling little man, Ernie DiGregorio, had something to work with in Bob McAdoo and McMillian. Chicago had been getting steadily better, with a shooter like Bob Love and the experienced Walker up front, and an aggressive pair of guards in Norm Van Lier and Jerry Sloan. Detroit was building a new team around Bob Lanier.

Bill Russell had returned to basketball, as coach and general manager of the Seattle Sonics, and some rebuilding could be expected there. Len Wilkens was now with Cleveland, which also had Austin Carr (of Notre Dame), no longer held back by injuries.

Phoenix had another recent ABA star, Charley Scott, and Houston had three fine young players in Rudy Tomjanovich, Mike Newlin and the sensational ''little man,'' Calvin Murphy.

New names, new emphasis, new conditions.

The owners of the Baltimore Bullets had completed building a large arena on the outskirts of Washington, and the team was now known as the Capitol Bullets. Houston was still playing on the campus of Houston University, but a new arena, the Summit, was being built.

The regular season went more or less according to form, but with a much narrower gap between the top and bottom. Milwaukee wound up with the best record, 59-23; Boston was 56-26, seven games ahead of the Knicks; the Bullets, at 47-35, were the only team in their division over .500, and the Lakers, with the same record, won a close race from Golden State. But Chicago and Detroit, chasing Milwaukee in the Midwest Division, won 54 and 52 games, respectively.

And no team won fewer than 25 games, the total posted by the 76ers as they began to regroup under Gene Shue. The new coach of the Bullets was K. C. Jones.

In the playoffs, though youth began to tell. Boston got respectable but not alarming opposition in a six-game set with Buffalo, then ran over the Knicks in five games, after the Knicks had eliminated the Bullets in another of the eventful seven-game series those teams played. Milwaukee cruised through the Lakers

in five games, while Detroit and Chicago battered each other in a seven-game set that the Bulls won by two points at home; then the Bucks polished off Chicago in four straight.

Milwaukee seemed on the verge of repeating its 1971 triumph, just as the Knicks had repeated 1970 in 1973; and because of Kareem (the 1974 MVP), the Bucks were favored.

But in one of the great final rounds of NBA history, the Celtics prevailed. It went seven games, with Boston winning the opener at Milwaukee and losing the second only in overtime. The next two at Boston were also split, but the Celtics won the fifth game on the road, and had a chance to wrap up the title at home. Instead, the Bucks won a double-overtime game (on a hook shot by Kareem in the last three seconds), and went into the seventh with a home-court advantage. However, the Celtics altered their pattern, fed Dave Cowens instead of John Havlicek, and won the title, 102-87.

Actually, the young Boston guards—Jo Jo White, Don Chaney and Paul Westphal—had proved too much for the aging Robertson. But Cowens had proved something else, even more forcefully than Reed had against Chamberlain. It had been axiomatic that a championship could not be won without a dominating force in the middle, and the long string of titles won by Mikan, Russell, Chamberlain and Kareem had borne this out. Yet Cowens was only 6-8, excelling on mobility and drive rather than on bulk and height. The triumph of the newer total-balance style was complete.

1973-74

STANDINGS

Eastern Conference
Atlantic Division

	W.	L.	Pct.
Boston	56	26	.683
New York	49	33	.598
Buffalo	42	40	.512
Philadelphia	25	57	.305

Central Division

	W.	L.	Pct.
Capital	47	35	.573
Atlanta	35	47	.427
Houston	32	50	.390
Cleveland	29	53	.354

Western Conference

Midwest Division

	W.	L.	Pct.
Milwaukee	59	23	.720
Chicago	54	28	.659
Detroit	52	30	.604
KC-Omaha	33	49	.402

Pacific Division

	W.	L.	Pct.
Los Angeles	47	35	.573
Golden State	44	38	.537
Seattle	36	46	.439
Phoenix	30	52	.366
Portland	27	55	.329

Eastern Conference Semifinal Series

March 30—Boston 107, Buffalo 97
April 2—Buffalo 115, Boston 105
April 3—Boston 120, Buffalo 107
April 6—Buffalo 104, Boston 102
April 9—Boston 100, Buffalo 97
April 12—Boston 106, Buffalo 104

March 29—New York 102, Capital 91
March 31—Capital 99, New York 87
April 2—Capital 88, New York 79
April 5—New York 101, Capital 93 (OT)
April 7—New York 106, Capital 105
April 10—Capital 109, New York 92
April 12—New York 91, Capital 81

Eastern Conference Final Series

April 14—Boston 113, New York 88
April 16—Boston 111, New York 99
April 19—New York 103, Boston 100
April 21—Boston 98, New York 91
April 24—Boston 105, New York 94

Western Conference Semifinal Series

March 29—Milwaukee 99, Los Angeles 95
March 31—Milwaukee 109, Los Angeles 90
April 2—Los Angeles 98, Milwaukee 96
April 4—Milwaukee 112, Los Angeles 90
April 7—Milwaukee 114, Los Angeles 92

March 30—Detroit 97, Chicago 88
April 1—Chicago 108, Detroit 103
April 5—Chicago 84, Detroit 83
April 7—Detroit 102, Chicago 87
April 9—Chicago 98, Detroit 94
April 11—Detroit 92, Chicago 88
April 13—Chicago 96, Detroit 94

Western Conference Final Series

April 16—Milwaukee 101, Chicago 85
April 18—Milwaukee 113, Chicago 111
April 20—Milwaukee 113, Chicago 90
April 22—Milwaukee 115, Chicago 99

Championship Series

April 28—Boston 98, Milwaukee 83
April 30—Milwaukee 105, Boston 96 (OT)
May 3—Boston 95, Milwaukee 83
May 5—Milwaukee 97, Boston 89
May 7—Boston 96, Milwaukee 87
May 10—Milwaukee 102, Boston 101 (2 OT)
May 12—Boston 102, Milwaukee 87

TOP SCORERS

	Pts.	Ave.
Bob McAdoo, Buffalo	2261	30.6
Pete Maravich, Atlanta	2107	27.7
Kareem Abdul-Jabbar, Milwaukee	2191	27.0
Gail Goodrich, Los Angeles	2076	25.3
Rick Barry, Golden State	2009	25.1

TOP REBOUNDERS

	No.	Ave.
Elvin Hayes, Capital	1463	18.1
Dave Cowens, Boston	1257	15.7
Bob McAdoo, Buffalo	1117	15.1
Kareem Abdul-Jabbar, Milwaukee	1178	14.5
Nate Thurmond, Golden State	878	14.2

LEADERS IN ASSISTS

	No.	Ave.
Ernie DiGregorio, Buffalo	663	8.2
Calvin Murphy, Houston	603	7.4
Lenny Wilkens, Cleveland	522	7.1
Walt Frazier, New York	551	6.9
Dave Bing, Detroit	555	6.9

1974-75

Total team balance, with emphasis on aggressive defense—this had become the prevailing religion in the NBA, which added an 18th team, New Orleans.

The Celtics, in their legendary streak of championships, had been ahead of the rest in perfecting that style. But the Knicks had shown it could be done without a Bill Russell, and the Celtics had just shown they could do it again with a totally new cast. Now every team pursued that goal. The watchword had been, for more than 20 years, that you had to have ''a big guy in the middle,'' to cope with Mikan, or Russell, or Wilt, or now Kareem. Now the formula was integrating the big men—who were still essential, of course—into a team pattern.

This season bore this out in the most vivid manner. The most-sought rookie, 6-11 Bill Walton—the most recent UCLA superstar, compared favorably to Ka-

Portland rookie Bill Walton, beset with injuries, had his hands full when confronted by his fellow UCLA alumnus, Kareem Abdul-Jabbar (right).

reem—went to Portland; but he was injured most of the time, and no unified team developed there.

But the Golden State Warriors, coached by Al Attles, had finally faced up to the need for dismantling. Nate Thurmond was traded to Chicago for Cliff Ray, a young defensive center, and lots of money, which was used to sign Keith Wilkes, still another of those glittering UCLA products. Another prize rookie, of less reputation, was Phil Smith, of San Francisco. Cazzie Russell had played out his option and moved on to Los Angeles. Only Rick Barry was left of their big names.

Attles responded to the nature of his material by embarking on a team-unit program that involved at least 10 men in every game. Aside from Barry, who was the acknowledged leader, the others shared time and produced maximum speed pressure on the op-

position right through 48 minutes. They would, in effect, win by attrition, hustling on defense and finding the open man on offense.

It took half a season for this system to really take hold, and the rest of the league didn't pay too much attention. Through the regular season, the Celtics and the Bullets (now frankly called Washington) posted the best records, 60-22, and they would obviously settle the title between them in a semifinal round (as the Celtics and 76ers used to do nearly a decade before). Washington had added backcourt speed in Kevin Porter, and with Unseld playing, in effect, defensive center and Hayes offensive center, was very much a balanced team.

The third-best record in the league, 49 victories, belonged to Buffalo. McAdoo, who had won the scoring championship in 1974 with 30.6 points a

Elvin Hayes couldn't believe the way Golden State destroyed his Bullets in the championship series.

game, now won it again with 34.5. He also won the MVP award and was the all-star center (over Kareem, who was injured part of the year, and whose team fell to last place in its division, and over Dave Cowens). Barry, Elvin Hayes, Nate Archibald and Walt Frazier were the rest of the honor lineup.

The Warriors, with 48 victories, won their division race by five games (over Seattle) while Chicago, with 47, won its race by three (over Kansas City-Omaha).

The addition of an 18th team—New Orleans had become the fifth team in the Central Division, giving the league two nine-team conferences, east and west—produced an adjustment in the playoffs. A preliminary round was added which gave a fifth team in each conference a shot at the fourth team, before the familiar pattern got under way. In this two-of-three round, Houston beat New York, and Seattle beat Detroit, but that was like marking time.

Only the Celtics had an easy time in the regular first round, beating Houston in five. The Warriors had a struggle on their hands, in a very physical series, getting by Russell's Seattle team in six, and Chicago fought through a low-scoring six-game series with the Kings. As for the Bullets, they had to go

through a seven-game shootout with Buffalo in order to reach the anticipated showdown with Boston.

And Washington won it, in six games, getting the jump by winning the first game at Boston and "holding service" the rest of the way.

Relatively little attention was paid, while that was going on, to the Golden State-Chicago struggle, which developed into a seven-game set of low-scoring games. With the series tied at 2-2, the Bulls seemed to take command by winning an 89-79 game at Oakland—but the Warriors bounced back with an 86-72 decision at Chicago. By the time the seventh game came up, at Oakland on May 14, the Boston-Washington series was over, and everyone became aware of the Golden State trademark: endless hustle that provided one come-from-behind victory after another. The Warriors won this one, 83-79, and were identified as appropriate cannon fodder for the Bullets, who would, of course, win the championship, having got past Boston.

Instead, the Warriors won—in four straight, only the third final-round sweep in the history of the league.

For the sixth year in a row, a defending champion had failed to repeat. That had never happened before, in a league that had now completed 29 seasons. The days of dynasties, built on supercenters, were indeed ended. The total-team-play era had arrived, and the Warriors, with their endless flow of substitutions, were its prophet.

1974-75

STANDINGS

Eastern Conference
Atlantic Division

	W.	L.	Pct.
Boston	60	22	.732
Buffalo	49	33	.598
New York	40	42	.488
Philadelphia	34	48	.415

Central Division

	W.	L.	Pct.
Washington	60	22	.732
Houston	41	41	.500
Cleveland	40	42	.488
Atlanta	31	51	.378
New Orleans	23	59	.280

Western Conference

Midwest Division

	W.	L.	Pct.
Chicago	47	35	.573
KC-Omaha	44	38	.537
Detroit	40	42	.488
Milwaukee	38	44	.463

Pacific Division

	W.	L.	Pct.
Golden State	48	34	.585
Seattle	43	39	.524
Portland	38	44	.463
Phoenix	32	50	.390
Los Angeles	30	52	.366

Eastern Conference Qualifying Round

April 8—Houston 99, New York 84
April 10—New York 106, Houston 96
April 12—Houston 118, New York 86

Western Conference Qualifying Round

April 8—Seattle 90, Detroit 77
April 10—Detroit 122, Seattle 106
April 12—Seattle 100, Detroit 93

Eastern Conference Semifinal Series

April 14—Boston 123, Houston 106
April 16—Boston 112, Houston 100
April 19—Houston 117, Boston 102
April 22—Boston 122, Houston 117
April 24—Boston 128, Houston 115

April 10—Buffalo 113, Washington 102
April 12—Washington 120, Buffalo 106
April 16—Washington 111, Buffalo 96
April 18—Buffalo 108, Washington 102
April 20—Washington 97, Buffalo 93
April 23—Buffalo 102, Washington 96
April 25—Washington 115, Buffalo 96

Eastern Conference Finals

April 27—Washington 100, Boston 95
April 30—Washington 117, Boston 92
May 3—Boston 101, Washington 90
May 7—Washington 119, Boston 108
May 9—Boston 103, Washington 99
May 11—Washington 98, Boston 92

Western Conference Semifinal Series

April 14—Golden State 123, Seattle 96
April 16—Seattle 100, Golden State 99
April 17—Golden State 105, Seattle 96
April 19—Seattle 111, Golden State 94
April 22—Golden State 124, Seattle 100
April 24—Golden State 105, Seattle 96

April 9—Chicago 95, Kansas City-Omaha 89
April 13—Kansas City-Omaha 102, Chicago 95
April 16—Chicago 93, Kansas City-Omaha 90
April 18—Kansas City-Omaha 104, Chicago 100 (OT)
April 20—Chicago 104, Kansas City-Omaha 77
April 23—Chicago 101, Kansas City-Omaha 89

Western Conference Final Series

April 27—Golden State 107, Chicago 89
April 30—Chicago 90, Golden State 89
May 4—Chicago 108, Golden State 101
May 6—Golden State 111, Chicago 106
May 8—Chicago 89, Golden State 79
May 11—Golden State 86, Chicago 72
May 14—Golden State 83, Chicago 79

Championship Series

May 18—Golden State 101, Washington 95
May 20—Golden State 92, Washington 91
May 23—Golden State 109, Washington 101
May 25—Golden State 96, Washington 95

TOP SCORERS

	Pts.	Ave.
Bob McAdoo, Buffalo	2831	34.5
Rick Barry, Golden State	2450	30.6
Kareem Abdul-Jabbar, Milwaukee	1949	30.0
Nate Archibald, KC-Omaha	2170	26.5
Charlie Scott, Phoenix	1680	24.3

TOP REBOUNDERS

	No.	Ave.
Wes Unseld, Washington	1077	14.8
Dave Cowens, Boston	958	14.7
Sam Lacey, KC-Omaha	1149	14.2
Bob McAdoo, Buffalo	1155	14.1
Kareem Abdul-Jabbar, Milwaukee	912	14.0

LEADERS IN ASSISTS

	No.	Ave.
Kevin Porter, Washington	650	8.0
Dave Bing, Detroit	610	7.7
Nate Archibald, KC-Omaha	557	6.8
Randy Smith, Buffalo	534	6.5
Pete Maravich, New Orleans	488	6.2

1975-76

Just as the season was about to start, the two strongest teams in the ABA—New York and Denver—applied for entry into the NBA.

This couldn't be acted upon, because the antitrust suit of the players had not been finally settled yet, although all the step-by-step decisions were going in

Jazzy Pete Maravich went from Atlanta to New Orleans and made the all-league team.

their favor. But that decision by Denver and the Nets made inevitable the eventual demise of the ABA as an independent entity, and the eventual acceptance of a merger in some form.

That, as it turned out, was a year away. For 1976, the NBA was still a swollen 18-team circuit, without a complete monopoly on all the most glamorous players (notably Julius Erving).

There was, however, a major change at the top. Walter Kennedy retired, and the new commissioner was Lawrence O'Brien, the prominent political figure whose associations went back to the late President Kennedy, and whose office had been the scene of the burglary that started the Watergate chapter of American history. He had exceptional administrative credentials, but no basketball background other than as a fan, a schoolyard player and as a native of Springfield, Massachusetts, birthplace of basketball.

On the player front, there were happenings as well. George McGinnis, for four years an ABA star second only to Erving, had cast his lot with the Philadelphia 76ers (after yielding to league objections when he tried to sign with the Knicks). Doug Collins, whose first couple of years were slowed by injury, had developed into a high-scoring guard. The 76ers were competitive again.

The Celtics had acquired Charley Scott from Phoenix, for Paul Westphal, adding to their already potent offense. The Warriors came up with a flashy backcourt rookie too, Gus Williams, from USC.

Phoenix had two rookies, neither fully appreciated at first: Alvan Adams, a center from Oklahoma, and Rick Sobers, a backcourt man from Nevada-Las Vegas. Adams wound up Rookie of the Year.

In fact, the flow of new young stars seemed endless. Atlanta's John Drew, in his second year, was the team's top scorer (Pete Maravich having gone to New Orleans); Buffalo came up with Randy Smith; Cleveland's Campy Russell, in his second season, found himself; another second-year blossomer was Eric Money, in Detroit; and Seattle's Fred Brown was coming into his own.

The big changes, however, were made by big names moving, partially at their own request in the freer negotiating atmosphere created by the accumulation of court cases.

Kareem Abdul-Jabbar decided he was no longer interested in Milwaukee, where he had played out his contract. A trade was arranged with Los Angeles (where he had played in college), and Milwaukee got four players in exchange.

The Knicks, unsuccessful in landing McGinnis or Abdul-Jabbar, bought Spencer Haywood from Seattle for $1 million.

Dave Bing, like Kareem, was tired of the place he had always played, and wanted to go home. In his case, that was Washington, and Kevin Porter was traded for him.

And Cleveland, which had picked up a fine young center from the ABA in Jim Chones the year before, got Nate Thurmond from Chicago to back him up shortly after the season began.

After all that shifting and inflow of new talent, the regular-season races produced a couple of surprises.

The Warriors, maintaining the style that had brought them a title, won 59 games, more than anyone, and led their division by 16 games. Boston won 54 and led the Atlantic by eight. There was nothing in the least surprising about those two.

But Cleveland, a laughing stock only a few years back, beat out the Bullets by one game for first place in the Central Division—and Milwaukee, which had finished last with Kareem the year before, finished first without him—while the Lakers, with him, failed to make the playoffs.

That last weird situation had an explanation, however. Although the Bucks finished two games ahead of Detroit, they did so with a 38-44 record: it happened that the whole division had teams with losing records. The year before they had posted the identical record, and been last. As for the Lakers, they won 40 games, but lost out to Phoenix by two games for third place and the last playoff berth in the tougher Pacific Division.

The playoffs had their twists, too. Buffalo and Philadelphia had tied for second in the Atlantic Division, and played each other in the preliminary round. Buffalo won, by one point in overtime, in the third game at Philadelphia. Detroit got by Milwaukee by three points in the third game at Milwaukee. But that just gave the winners the privilege of losing to Boston and Golden State in a pair of six-game series.

Phoenix, however, had found its pattern in midseason under coach John MacLeod: tough defense, team offense, the textbook stuff with great motivation. The Suns upset Seattle in six games, while Cleveland outlasted the Bullets in an 87-85 seventh game at Cleveland.

Rookie of the Year Alvan Adams led Phoenix into the championship finals against Boston.

The Cleveland-Boston semifinal followed home court for five games before Boston won it in the sixth, 94-87 at Cleveland.

But the Warriors stumbled in the second game at home, and even though they won the next at Phoenix, they missed a chance to take command in a double-overtime loss there in the fourth game. They won at home, lost by one point back at Phoenix—and found themselves eliminated when the Suns ran all over them in the second half of the seventh game, at Oakland.

So it was Phoenix, not the Warriors, facing Boston, and for the seventh year in a row the defending champion would not repeat.

The Celtics were overwhelming favorites, but the Suns gave them all they could handle. They lost two at Boston, won two at home, and the fifth, in Boston, turned out to be one of the league's historic games: a triple-overtime, the longest final-round game ever, which the Celtics won, 128-126. Less than 48 hours later, more than 2,000 miles away, they wrapped up another title, 87-80.

Thus ended the 30th season of the NBA. Abdul-Jabbar was the Most Valuable Player again, and center of an all-league team that included McGinnis, Rick Barry, Nate Archibald and Pete Maravich. Four of them had not yet been born when the league began, and Barry had been just two years old.

Bob McAdoo had won his third straight scoring title, at 31.1, but other statistics were more interesting. Over the last four years, scoring had been stabilized at about 104 points per team per game. About 46 percent of all shots taken were good. The average game contained 49 personal fouls, but only about 52 free throws attempted (by both teams). Back before the 24-second rule, there used to be 58 fouls in an average game, with free throws totalling almost half as many as field goal attempts; now that proportion was less than one to three.

And once again, at the top of the heap, were the Boston Celtics—champions for the 13th time in the last 20 years, beaten only once in 14 final rounds. Red Auerbach, who had coached when the league started, was still in action as president and general manager—the only one left from the beginning (except for Eddie Gottlieb, who was still making the schedules for the league office although long since unconnected with any one team).

Soon after the season ended, the merger was worked out, and for the 1977 season the league would have 22 teams.

1975-76

STANDINGS

Eastern Conference

Atlantic Division

	W.	L.	Pct.
Boston	54	28	.659
Buffalo	46	36	.561
Philadelphia	46	36	.561
New York	38	44	.463

Central Division

	W.	L.	Pct.
Cleveland	49	33	.598
Washington	48	34	.585
Houston	40	42	.488
New Orleans	38	44	.463
Atlanta	29	53	.354

Western Conference

Midwest Division

	W.	L.	Pct.
Milwaukee	38	44	.463
Detroit	36	46	.439
Kansas City	31	51	.378
Chicago	24	58	.293

Pacific Division

	W.	L.	Pct.
Golden State	59	23	.720
Seattle	43	39	.524
Phoenix	42	40	.512
Los Angeles	40	42	.488
Portland	37	45	.451

Eastern Conference Qualifying Round

April 15—Buffalo 95, Philadelphia 89
April 16—Philadelphia 131, Buffalo 106
April 18—Buffalo 124, Philadelphia 123 (OT)

Eastern Conference Semifinal Series

April 21—Boston 107, Buffalo 98
April 23—Boston 101, Buffalo 96
April 25—Buffalo 98, Boston 93
April 28—Buffalo 124, Boston 122
April 30—Boston 99, Buffalo 88
May 2—Boston 104, Buffalo 100

April 13—Washington 100, Cleveland 95
April 15—Cleveland 80, Washington 79
April 17—Cleveland 88, Washington 76
April 21—Washington 109, Cleveland 98
April 22—Cleveland 92, Washington 91
April 26—Washington 102, Cleveland 98 (OT)
April 29—Cleveland 87, Washington 85

Eastern Conference Final Series

May 6—Boston 111, Cleveland 99
May 9—Boston 94, Cleveland 89
May 11—Cleveland 83, Boston 78
May 14—Cleveland 106, Boston 87
May 16—Boston 99, Cleveland 94
May 18—Boston 94, Cleveland 87

Western Conference Qualifying Round

April 13—Milwaukee 110, Detroit 107
April 15—Detroit 126, Milwaukee 123
April 18—Detroit 107, Milwaukee 104

Western Conference Semifinal Series

April 20—Golden State 127, Detroit 103
April 22—Detroit 123, Golden State 111
April 24—Golden State 113, Detroit 96
April 26—Detroit 106, Golden State 102
April 28—Golden State 128, Detroit 109
April 30—Golden State 118, Detroit 116 (OT)

April 13—Seattle 102, Phoenix 99
April 15—Phoenix 116, Seattle 111
April 18—Phoenix 103, Seattle 91
April 20—Phoenix 130, Seattle 114
April 25—Seattle 114, Phoenix 108
April 27—Phoenix 123, Seattle 112

Western Conference Final Series

May 2—Golden State 128, Phoenix 103
May 5—Phoenix 108, Golden State 101
May 7—Golden State 99, Phoenix 91
May 9—Phoenix 133, Golden State 129 (2 OT)
May 12—Golden State 111, Phoenix 95
May 14—Phoenix 105, Golden State 104
May 16—Phoenix 94, Golden State 86

Championship Series

May 23—Boston 98, Phoenix 87
May 27—Boston 105, Phoenix 90
May 30—Phoenix 105, Boston 98
June 2—Phoenix 109, Boston 107
June 4—Boston 128, Phoenix 126 (3 OT)
June 6—Boston 87, Phoenix 80

TOP SCORERS

	Pts.	Ave.
Bob McAdoo, Buffalo	2427	31.1
Kareem Abdul-Jabbar, Los Angeles	2275	27.7
Pete Maravich, New Orleans	1604	25.9
Nate Archibald, Kansas City	1935	24.8
Fred Brown, Seattle	1757	23.1

TOP REBOUNDERS

	No.	Ave.
Kareem Abdul-Jabbar, Los Angeles	1383	16.9
Dave Cowens, Boston	1246	16.0
Wes Unseld, Washington	1036	13.3
Paul Silas, Boston	1025	12.7
Sam Lacey, Kansas City	1024	12.6

LEADERS IN ASSISTS

	No.	Ave.
Slick Watts, Seattle	661	8.1
Nate Archibald, Kansas City	615	7.9
Calvin Murphy, Houston	596	7.3
Norm Van Lier, Chicago	500	6.6
Rick Barry, Golden State	496	6.1

1976-77

The league's 31st season began with a fantastic transaction, Fitz Eugene Dixon, who had just bought control of the Philadelphia 76ers, made a $6 million deal to get Julius Erving, who refused to continue with the New York Nets because of a dispute with Roy Boe, owner of the Nets, about promised salary increases. Dixon paid $3 million to the Nets—the last champions of the ABA and one of the four teams brought into the NBA in the merger—and $3 million to Erving for a five-year commitment.

That deal, many people thought, would guarantee the 76ers the league championship.

But nine months later, as a shot by Erving failed to tie the sixth playoff game of the final round in its closing seconds, the Portland Trail Blazers, built around Bill Walton, emerged as champions.

It was, once again, a triumph for well-integrated team play over a collection of more brilliant individual talents. This was completely in line with the pattern of the 1970s: the Knicks, Lakers, Celtics, Warriors had won titles on cohesion rather than individual brilliance.

But in all other respects, the 1977 season was a distinct break with the NBA past.

With Denver, the New York Nets, Indiana and San Antonio brought in under the merger agreement, the NBA now had 22 teams, and the divisions had to be realigned. More important, the schedule had to be rearranged, and it came out in a highly undesirable form: each team would play every other team four times—twice at home and twice away—except that each team would face two of its opponents only three times each. That was to keep within the limit of 82 games that the players insisted on.

The Atlantic Division now had both New York teams, Boston, Philadelphia and Buffalo. The Pacific Division remained the same, with Portland, Seattle, Golden State, Los Angeles and Phoenix.

Bill Walton had the winning touch as Portland's Trail Blazers won their first NBA title in 1976–77. Beneath the Walton palm is coach Jack Ramsay, coveting the new championship trophy, a $10,000 sterling silver Tiffany piece finished with 22-carat gold. Commissioner Lawrence O'Brien is at the right.

But the two middle divisions had six teams each: Washington, Cleveland, Houston, San Antonio, Atlanta and New Orleans made up the Central, which was part of the Eastern Conference; Denver, Detroit, Chicago, Milwaukee, Kansas City and Indiana made up the Midwest, which was paired with the Pacific in the Western Conference.

The playoff system, then, had to be changed too. The four division leaders would get a first-round bye; but the remaining four qualifiers in each conference would be ranked by won-lost record, regardless of division. They would play a two-of-three round (No. 1 vs. No. 4, No. 2 vs. No. 3) to produce four survivors to take on the four first-place teams in the next round. Again, all teams would be ranked by won-lost record within each half of the league, and a four-of-seven series would lead to a four-of-seven semifinal (called a "Conference championship"), and a four-of-seven East-West final.

The merger also meant a tremendous reshuffle of star players. It had been made possible by the fact that the Players Association and the NBA had finally reached agreement on a new reserve system, which gave all players much greater freedom of movement

between contracts. As a result, many instances arose where a star (like Erving) had to be satisfied or traded. But in addition, there were players on the rosters of the three ABA teams to whom the NBA teams had no clear title. So a "dispersal draft" was held, in which teams could choose players for stipulated sums (to be used as part of the settlement made with the teams that decided to go out of business quietly). And that, in turn, led to a flurry of trades that scrambled the roster still further.

When the dust had settled, Moses Malone was in Houston, Maurice Lucas was in Portland, Sidney Wicks was in Boston, Paul Silas was in Denver, Artis Gilmore was in Chicago, Gail Goodrich was in New Orleans, Nate Archibald was with the Nets, Brian Taylor was in Kansas City and Erving was in Philadelphia, alongside McGinnis.

For the first time in nine years, therefore, all the best players were operating in a single league.

This had implications for the Golden State Warriors and similar teams. In the past two years, they had succeeded by running the opposition into the ground by rotating players off a "deeper" bench; but now every bench was deeper, and with that factor equalized, the pendulum swung back to the importance of a dominating center.

The most dominating center was in Los Angeles, Kareem Abdul-Jabbar, at the peak of his powers. The Lakers hired Jerry West as coach, with Bill Sharman moving into the front office, and West hired two outstanding assistants, Stan Albeck and Jack McCloskey, to form an unusual staff system. It turned out to be a fine combination: the Lakers won 53 games, the best record in the league, and Kareem was named Most Valuable Player for the fifth time in his career, tying him with Bill Russell and putting him two ahead of Wilt Chamberlain in that respect.

Behind the Lakers came Portland, with Walton and Lucas sweeping the boards and running a fine offense under another new coach, Jack Ramsay, who had left Buffalo. The Warriors were third in that division and Phoenix, the glamor team of the year before, was crippled early and finished last.

The Midwest Division was dominated by Denver, which did a lot of lineup shuffling but settled on Dan Issel at center, and had its superstar, David Thompson, play both front and backcourt. Detroit might have done better if Bob Lanier hadn't been injured half the season and Chicago, off to a terrible start, finished with a rush as Gilmore earned more and more appreciation.

Houston, with Malone at center, beat out Washington for the Central Division title, and the 76ers had little real trouble winning in the Atlantic, although their play was inconsistent. Only they, among the top teams, didn't have a dominating center quite yet; but Caldwell Jones, from the ABA, and Darryl Dawkins, a 19-year-old in his second season, were seven-footers who did dominate the non-star centers.

During the season, Buffalo traded Bob McAdoo to the Knicks, and his reign as scoring champion ended. The new scoring leader was Pete Maravich, fully mature and every bit as spectacular at the age of 28 as had been predicted in his college days. He averaged 31.1 points a game and had a 68-point game against the Knicks, a performance surpassed only by

New Orleans' Pete Maravich had a spectacular year, winning the NBA scoring crown. He scored 68 points in one game against the Knicks.

Even Kareem Abdul-Jabbar, the league's regular-season MVP for the fourth time, could not keep the Trail Blazers from sweeping the Lakers in the playoffs.

Chamberlain (six times) and Elgin Baylor (once) in league history.

The enlarged league produced another set of new statistics: home victories at a rate not seen in the NBA for 20 years. Not one of the 22 teams was able to win as many as half its road games (Philadelphia was best at 18-23). Only the Nets, stripped by trades and injuries, and Atlanta failed to win half their games at home. The Lakers set a record by winning 37 games at home (including 21 straight in midseason), while Denver won 36, Portland 35 and Houston 34. This may have helped attendance (which reached record levels, of course, with more teams and with the monopoly restored), but it also heightened complaining about the referees. (Before the season, the club owners had voted down a proposal to add a third official to the game.)

By late season, there was another problem with referees: they had a union now, and, while negotiating a new contract for the following year, called a strike that began on the last day of the regular season—just before the playoffs began. Play continued with substitute officials (except for Richie Powers and Earl Strom, who withdrew from the union and continued to work), and there was surprisingly little visible difference. Halfway through the playoffs, a settlement was reached and the experienced referees worked the rest of the way without incident.

One question that fans had asked for years was settled conclusively in 1977: the caliber of the two leagues, by the time they merged, was equal. Of the four ABA teams brought in, Denver was outstanding, San Antonio above average, Indiana below average and the dismantled Nets terrible; yet their combined record of 152-156 certainly represented par value. Even more striking was the performance of former ABA players who went to established NBA teams. In the final round, four of the 10 starting players were former ABA stars, and ABA alumni were also prominent on the two semifinal losers, L.A. and Houston.

The playoffs built to an unusual climax. Boston, Washington, Golden State and Portland came through the first round. Then Philadelphia had to go to a seventh game to get past Boston, while the Lakers were similarly extended by Golden State (in a series in which the home team won every game). Houston got by Washington, and Portland past Denver, in six.

In the semifinal, the Blazers really hit their stride and eliminated Kareem and the Lakers in four straight, bringing Walton (whose first two seasons had been injury-ridden) into full prominence. Philadelphia needed six games to get by Houston, but only because the 76ers blew a big lead at home when they could have ended the series in Game No. 5.

Still, the 76ers were favored in the final. Erving, all year long, had lived up to expectations, even while subordinating some of his sensational abilities to team interests. McGinnis had been as effective as ever, but had gone into a terrible shooting slump at the start of the playoffs. Portland's teamwork would be overwhelmed by superior individual talents, many felt.

And that's how it seemed as Philadelphia won the first two games at home. But when the series shifted to Portland, everything changed. Moving at top speed against a deteriorating Philadelphia defense, and with McGinnis still totally ineffective, the Blazers won by

22 and 32 points, and went back to Philadelphia all even and high in confidence.

And they won there, running up a big lead in the third quarter and fighting off a belated 76er rally.

So on Sunday, June 5, back in Portland, they were able to end it. McGinnis, at last, played his normal game, and Erving scored 40. But the Blazers took command with a 19-4 spurt in the second period, and with Walton at his most brilliant, just did hang on. Ahead by 12 with five minutes to go, they saw their margin cut to 109-107 with 18 seconds left, and Philadelphia got the ball; but both Erving and McGinnis missed medium-range shots that could have tied it, and the Blazers were champions.

They were only seven years old, having entered the league in the expansion of 1970-71. Their original front-office team—owners Larry Weinberg and Herman Sarkowski, general manager Harry Glickman and player personnel director Stu Inman—was intact. And so was an indomitable redhead named Walton. Fittingly, he rode his bicycle in the victory parade.

Their way of winning was unprecedented. Only once before had a team lost the first two games of a final round and still won; the Celtics of 1969, in Russell's last year, had done it to Los Angeles, but they had needed all seven games to do it. The Blazers were the first to win four straight after losing the first two.

And Walton, chosen outstanding player of the series, was also directly in line with a great tradition. When Mikan had come into the league (with a year of experience in another league), he had taken his team to a championship right away. When the Celtics acquired Russell, they became champions immediately—and when Chamberlan arrived, his Philadelphia teams didn't win only because Russell and the Celtics were in the way. (Wilt had to wait until his eighth year for a title.) Then, when Milwaukee was able to draft Lew Alcindor (before he changed his name to Abdul-Jabbar), it took just two seasons to turn a last-place expansion team into a champion. Now Walton, in his third year but actually his first free of serious injury, took his team to a title on its first shot at the playoffs, a team that had never been higher than last until the 1976 season.

So the lesson, now three decades old, was taught again: you can spend $6 million on the best forward in the world, but the title goes to the team that can control the middle.

Bill Walton wound up as MVP of the playoffs despite heroics by the inimitable Julius Erving (left).

1976-77

STANDINGS

Eastern Conference
Atlantic Division

	W.	L.	Pct.
Philadelphia	50	32	.610
Boston	44	38	.537
New York Knicks	40	42	.488
Buffalo	30	52	.366
New York Nets	22	60	.288

Central Division

	W.	L.	Pct.
Houston	49	33	.598
Washington	48	34	.585
San Antonio	44	38	.537
Cleveland	43	39	.524
New Orleans	35	47	.427
Atlanta	31	51	.378

Western Conference

Midwest Division

	W.	L.	Pct.
Denver	50	32	.610
Detroit	44	38	.537
Chicago	44	38	.537
Kansas City	40	42	.488
Indiana	36	46	.439
Milwaukee	30	52	.366

Pacific Division

	W.	L.	Pct.
Los Angeles	53	29	.646
Portland	49	33	.598
Golden State	46	36	.561
Seattle	40	42	.488
Phoenix	34	48	.415

Eastern Conference First Round

April 12—Boston 104, San Antonio 94
April 15—Boston 115, San Antonio 109

April 13—Washington 109, Cleveland 100
April 15—Cleveland 91, Washington 83
April 17—Washington 104, Cleveland 98

Eastern Conference Semifinal Series

April 17—Boston 113, Philadelphia 111
April 20—Philadelphia 113, Boston 101
April 22—Philadelphia 109, Boston 100
April 24—Boston 124, Philadelphia 119
April 25—Philadelphia 110, Boston 91
April 29—Boston 113, Philadelphia 108
May 1—Philadelphia 83, Boston 77

April 10—Washington 111, Houston 101
April 21—Houston 124, Washington 118 (OT)
April 24—Washington 93, Houston 90
April 26—Houston 107, Washington 103
April 29—Houston 123, Washington 115
May 1—Houston 108, Washington 103

Eastern Conference Final Series

May 5—Philadelphia 128, Houston 117
May 8—Philadelphia 106, Houston 97
May 11—Houston 118, Philadelphia 94
May 13—Philadelphia 107, Houston 95
May 15—Houston 118, Philadelphia 115
May 17—Philadelphia 112, Houston 109

Western Conference First Round

April 12—Detroit 95, Golden State 90
April 14—Golden State 138, Detroit 108
April 17—Golden State 109, Detroit 101

April 12—Portland 96, Chicago 83
April 15—Chicago 107, Portland 104
April 17—Portland 106, Chicago 98

Western Conference Semifinal Series

April 20—Los Angeles 115, Golden State 106
April 22—Los Angeles 95, Golden State 86
April 24—Golden State 109, Los Angeles 105
April 26—Golden State 114, Los Angeles 103
April 29—Los Angeles 112, Golden State 105
May 1—Golden State 115, Los Angeles 106
May 4—Los Angeles 97, Golden State 84

April 20—Portland 101, Denver 100
April 22—Denver 121, Portland 110
April 24—Portland 110, Denver 106
April 26—Portland 105, Denver 96
May 1—Denver 114, Portland 105 (OT)
May 2—Portland 108, Denver 92

Western Conference Final Series

May 6—Portland 121, Los Angeles 109
May 8—Portland 99, Los Angeles 97
May 10—Portland 102, Los Angeles 97
May 13—Portland 105, Los Angeles 101

World Championship Series

May 22—Philadelphia 107, Portland 101
May 26—Philadelphia 107, Portland 89
May 29—Portland 129, Philadelphia 107
May 31—Portland 130, Philadelphia 98
June 3—Portland 110, Philadelphia 104
June 5—Portland 109, Philadelphia 107

TOP SCORERS

	Pts.	Ave.
Pete Maravich, New Orleans	2273	31.1
Billy Knight, Indiana	2075	26.6
Kareem Abdul-Jabbar, Los Angeles	2152	26.2
David Thompson, Denver	2125	25.9
Bob McAdoo, New York Knicks	1861	25.8

TOP REBOUNDERS

	No.	Ave.
Bill Walton, Portland	934	14.4
Kareem Abdul-Jabbar, Los Angeles	1090	13.3
Moses Malone, Houston	1072	13.1
Artis Gilmore, Chicago	1070	13.0
Bob McAdoo, New York Knicks	926	12.9

LEADERS IN ASSISTS

	No.	Ave.
Don Buse, Indiana	685	8.5
Slick Watts, Seattle	630	8.0
Norm Van Lier, Chicago	636	7.8
Kevin Porter, Detroit	592	7.3
Tom Henderson, Washington	598	6.9

1977-78

The league's 32nd season started in violence and controversy and ended in one of the most harmonious and happy final rounds it had ever enjoyed. Two Cinderella teams, the Washington Bullets and the Seattle Sonics, wound up playing for the championship in what was officially the longest season—lasting until June 7, and comprising 104 games for the Sonics, 103 for the Bullets. When Washington won the seventh game, 105-99, at Seattle, the popularity of the triumph of the Bullets (within the NBA family) did not diminish the appreciation of what the Sonics had accomplished.

The Bullets were a team that had been to the final round twice before—without winning a game. They were swept by Milwaukee in 1971 and Golden State in 1975, and when they started their second season under coach Dick Motta, they weren't expected to get that far. When they suffered a series of crippling injuries in midseason, it seemed doubtful they could make the playoffs at all.

But they wound up as champions because of Wes Unseld, the center who had been with them 10 years and who emerged as the Most Valuable Player of the playoffs; Elvin Hayes, the great power forward who had been sometimes lionized, sometimes criticized, but always overshadowed through nine pro years—and a college career—by Kareem Abdul-Jabbar; Bob Dandridge, the smooth forward who was signed as a free agent and who had been part of the 1971 Milwaukee team that had overwhelmed the Bullets (with Kareem and Oscar Robertson); and Charley Johnson, picked up in midseason after being cut by Golden State, only because the Bullets had to have an eighth player when the injuries piled up. These four made the key contributions to as evenly matched and as hard-fought—if not quite as spectacular—a final round as any of the previous 31.

Seattle's success was even more startling. Opening the season with Bob Hopkins as coach, the Sonics lost 17 of their first 22 games. Lenny Wilkens, director of player personnel, replaced Hopkins as coach on November 30, and promptly changed the entire

Elvin Hayes and the Washington Bullets finally went all the way . . . and the Big E looks as though he'll never give up the NBA championship trophy.

President Carter greets the champion Bullets as proud owner, Abe Pollin, looks on from the right.

startling lineup. Marvin Webster, obtained in a be-tween-season trade with Denver, where his two years of predicted stardom were ruined by illness, became the center. Dennis Johnson, a second-year man who had been unable to make his high school varsity team half a dozen years before, and Gus Williams, signed as a free agent, became the guards; John Johnson, discarded by Houston and Boston early in the season, and Jack Sikma, a spectacular rookie, played the corners. And the two veterans, Fred Brown and Paul Silas, became devastating regulars coming off the bench.

This group, then, produced the best record in the league for the rest of the regular season—42-18. It made the playoffs, beating out the Lakers (with a whole new cast of supporting stars around Kareem), but didn't challenge Portland, the defending champion and early-season runaway leader.

But late in the season Bill Walton got hurt, and so did several other Portland players, and the Sonics were able to eliminate the Blazers in the second round. They got by Denver, too, and reached the final against the Bullets—who had scored a big upset by eliminating the star-studded 76ers in the semifinal.

Because of previous commitments, Seattle's home court in the 14,000-seat Coliseum was not available for Game No. 4 of the final, so it was played in the Kingdome, the domed stadium built for football and baseball, in a temporary basketball setup. The result was a crowd of 39,457, the largest ever to attend an NBA playoff game. In 1978-79, the Sonics planned to move into the Kingdome in a more permanent configuration, which would give them 28,000 seats for every game.

Washington, however, won that game, in over-time. The Sonics won the fifth, to take a 3-2 lead, but the Bullets struck back with a 117-82 victory at home, the 35-point margin constituting a final-round record, and won the title on the road—only the third time that had happened in the 12 finals that went the full seven games.

The copious praise for both teams, and the absence of any friction about officiating or anything else, was in marked contrast to the first half of the season.

Right at the season's start, Kareem unfurled a right to the face of Milwaukee rookie Kent Benson and broke his hand. Commissioner Larry O'Brien, trying to impress the public with the league's intolerance of violence, fined Kareem $5,000—but didn't suspend him, because Kareem's broken hand kept him from playing for two months anyhow. His absence prompted the Lakers to begin a series of trades, and although he eventually came back and played with full effectiveness, the Lakers never did find the right combination.

In December, there was an even more serious incident: Kermit Washington of the Lakers got into a fight with Kevin Kunnert of Houston. As Houston's Rudy Tomjanovich ran over to be a peacemaker, Washington turned and swung his fist, inflicting massive injuries to Tomjanovich's jaw, eye and cheek. Tomjanovich was out for the season, his career in jeopardy, and required a series of operations.

Washington was fined and suspended for 60 days—which amounted to more than a $50,000 fine in terms of lost salary.

Even though the Tomjanovich incident was more accident than aggression—he wasn't the man Washington was fighting—the enormously publicized event had a sobering effect. Washington, later in the season, was traded to Boston and played with the Celtics after serving his suspension. Houston, a strong team the year before, finished last in its division.

Other turmoil was financial. Roy Boe, owner of the Nets, moved his team from the Nassau Coliseum on Long Island to New Jersey, where a new arena was planned for the Meadowlands, opposite Manhattan Island. The arena was years away, however, so Boe got permission to play at Rutgers University,

Injuries again befell Bill Walton and killed Portland's chances of repeating as champion, but Walton's play brought him regular-season MVP honors.

Denver's David Thompson scored 73 points in one game and wound up with a $4-million contract.

some 40 miles from New York. There was a court squabble between the Nets and the Knicks about the indemnity the Nets had promised to pay as a condition for entering the NBA, and Boe's financial difficulties mounted. By the end of the season, the Nets had the worst record in the league and Boe was on the verge of being forced out.

But the other three ABA imports had successful seasons in their second year inside the merged league. Indiana had severe financial difficulties between seasons, but managed to resolve them and seemed stable by the end of the year, even though the team didn't make the playoffs. Denver finished first in its division for the second time and San Antonio was the unexpected leader of the Central Division with a 52-30 record, a victory total surpassed only by Portland and Philadelphia. (But in the playoffs, San Antonio was one of Washington's victims.)

Denver with David Thompson and San Antonio with George Gervin had two of the most spectacular stars. They fought it out for the scoring title in the most remarkable finish in league history. On the final afternoon of the season, Thompson scored 73 points—and Gervin came back that night and scored 63, winding up as scoring champion with 27.21 per game to Thompson's 27.15.

Thompson and Gervin—players of ''in between'' height who were neither natural forwards nor natural guards—were part of the new wave of stars. In addition to his all-around skills, Thompson was particularly amazing as a leaper; Gervin, as a fantastic marskman. Taking more than 1,600 shots, many from outside, Gervin sank 53.6 percent of them.

Leaders in other categories also drove home the change in generations: the leader in rebounding was Truck Robinson of New Orleans; in assists, Kevin Porter of the Nets; in field-goal percentage, Bobby Jones of Denver; and in offensive rebounds, Moses Malone of Houston. In general, players and teams whose careers had begun in the ABA settled old (and forgotten) arguments by proving conclusively their parity with the older NBA members.

Rick Barry with Golden State was still going strong, and led the league in free-throw accuracy (.924); but the old order was passing: John Havlicek retired from the Celtics at the end of the season, and the deterioration of the team (which finished 32-50) underscored the new balances of power.

In midseason the Celtics, still run by Red Auerbach, dropped Tom Heinsohn as coach and replaced him with Satch Sanders, another of their one-time championship players. The Knicks were coached by Willis Reed, one of their former stars, who took over when Red Holzman retired at the end of the 1977 season. The 76ers, early in the season, fired Gene Shue and made Billy Cunningham the coach—but they came no closer to the championship as the team's basic individualism remained uncured. Detroit fired coach Herb Brown and let the general manager, Bob Kauffman, handle the rest of the season before hiring Dick Vitale. Kansas City followed the same route, dropping Phil Johnson, using Larry Staverman, and signing Cotton Fitzsimmons, who had spent the 1978 season coaching Buffalo.

Don Nelson, as a rookie Milwaukee coach replacing Larry Costello early in the season, received recognition for getting a young team into the playoffs and knocking off favored Phoenix, and San Antonio's fine showing brought attention to coach Doug Moe. But Coach-of-the-Year honors were voted to Hubie Brown of Atlanta, whose low-rated squad made the playoffs—a choice disputed by West Coasters conscious of what Wilkens had done. Bill Walton was named the regular-season Most Valuable Player. And Walter Davis of Phoenix was Rookie of the Year.

A new four-year television contract with CBS promised each club $1 million in income in the fourth year, and attendance was up again. All in all, despite the incredible player salaries (which put several players in the $500,000-a-year-and-up class), it was a prosperous year in which the 22-team structure was stabilized.

1977-78

STANDINGS

Eastern Conference

Atlantic Division

	W.	L.	Pct.
Philadelphia	55	27	.671
New York	43	39	.524
Boston	32	50	.390
Buffalo	27	55	.329
New Jersey	24	58	.293

Central Division

	W.	L.	Pct.
San Antonio	52	30	.634
Washington	44	38	.537
Cleveland	43	39	.524
Atlanta	41	41	.500
New Orleans	39	43	.476
Houston	28	54	.341

Western Conference

Midwest Division

	W.	L.	Pct.
Denver	48	34	.585
Milwaukee	44	38	.537
Chicago	40	42	.488
Detroit	38	44	.463
Indiana	31	51	.378
Kansas City	31	51	.378

Pacific Division

	W.	L.	Pct.
Portland	58	24	.707
Phoenix	49	33	.598
Seattle	47	35	.573
Los Angeles	45	37	.549
Golden State	43	39	.524

Eastern Conference First Round

April 12—New York 132, Cleveland 114
April 14—New York 109, Cleveland 107

April 12—Washington 103, Atlanta 94
April 14—Washington 107, Atlanta 103 (OT)

Eastern Conference Semifinal Series

April 16—Philadelphia 130, New York 90
April 18—Philadelphia 119, New York 100
April 20—Philadelphia 137, New York 126
April 23—Philadelphia 112, New York 107

April 16—San Antonio 114, Washington 103
April 18—Washington 121, San Antonio 117
April 21—Washington 118, San Antonio 105
April 23—Washington 98, San Antonio 95
April 25—San Antonio 116, Washington 105
April 28—Washington 103, San Antonio 100

Eastern Conference Final Series

April 30—Washington 122, Philadelphia 117
May 3—Philadelphia 110, Washington 104
May 5—Washington 123, Philadelphia 108
May 7—Washington 121, Philadelphia 104
May 10—Philadelphia 107, Washington 94
May 12—Washington 101, Philadelphia 99

Western Conference First Round

April 11—Milwaukee 111, Phoenix 103
April 14—Milwaukee 94, Phoenix 90

April 12—Seattle 102, Los Angeles 90
April 14—Los Angeles 105, Seattle 99
April 16—Seattle 111, Los Angeles 102

Western Conference Semifinal Series

April 18—Seattle 104, Portland 95
April 21—Portland 96, Seattle 93
April 23—Seattle 99, Portland 84
April 26—Seattle 100, Portland 98
April 30—Portland 113, Seattle 89
May 1—Seattle 105, Portland 94

April 18—Denver 119, Milwaukee 103
April 21—Denver 127, Milwaukee 111
April 23—Milwaukee 143, Denver 112
April 25—Denver 118, Milwaukee 104
April 28—Milwaukee 117, Denver 112
April 30—Milwaukee 119, Denver 91
May 3—Denver 116, Milwaukee 110

Western Conference Final Series

May 5—Denver 116, Seattle 107
May 7—Seattle 121, Denver 111
May 10—Seattle 105, Denver 91
May 12—Seattle 100, Denver 94
May 14—Denver 123, Seattle 114
May 17—Seattle 123, Denver 108

World Championship Series

May 21—Seattle 106, Washington 102
May 25—Washington 106, Seattle 98
May 28—Seattle 93, Washington 92
May 30—Washington 120, Seattle 116 (OT)
June 2—Seattle 98, Washington 94
June 4—Washington 117, Seattle 82
June 7—Washington 105, Seattle 99

TOP SCORERS

	Pts.	Ave.
George Gervin, San Antonio	2232	27.21
David Thompson, Denver	2172	27.15
Bob McAdoo, New York	2097	26.5
Kareem Abdul-Jabbar, Los Angeles	1600	25.8
Calvin Murphy, Houston	1949	25.6

TOP REBOUNDERS

	No.	Ave.
Truck Robinson, New Orleans	1288	15.7
Moses Malone, Houston	886	15.0
Dave Cowens, Boston	1078	14.0
Elvin Hayes, Washington	1075	13.3
Swen Nater, Buffalo	1029	13.2

LEADERS IN ASSISTS

	No.	Ave.
Kevin Porter, New Jersey	837	10.2
John Lucas, Houston	768	9.4
Ricky Sobers, Indiana	584	7.4
Norm Nixon, Los Angeles	553	6.8
Norm Van Lier, Chicago	531	6.8

1978-79

The most exciting part of the 1978-79 NBA season involved a couple of collegians.

At Indiana State, there was a remarkably versatile 6-9 forward named Larry Bird. He had been eligible for the 1978 draft, and had been chosen by the Boston Celtics, but had decided to continue his college career.

At Michigan State, there was a 6-9 sophomore named Earvin "Magic" Johnson—a guard, no less. He had the right to declare himself eligible for the 1979 draft if he wanted to.

To keep the rights to Bird, the Celtics would have to sign him before the 1979 draft began (in late June). Would they? And would Magic turn pro? As it turned out, their teams wound up in the final game of the NCAA tournament, and Johnson's Michigan State Spartans won.

The excitement generated by these two players had a lot to do with an outbreak of criticism directed at the NBA "product", because its television ratings went down. Their power would be exhibited the following year, when they did enter the league, and brought that excitement with them. But they actually overshadowed, to a degree, what the pros of 1978-79 were doing in their own right.

And the pros were doing plenty.

There was a franchise move. The Buffalo Braves became the San Diego Clippers, in a complex shift of ownerships that left Irving Levin and Hal Lipton in Southern California, where they operated, instead of in the northeast, where they had owned the Boston Celtics. They swapped with the owners of the Braves, then moved out of Buffalo.

And there was a more significant ownership change. Jack Kent Cooke, who had bought the Lakers when they moved from Minneapolis to Los Angeles back in 1961, and built the Forum to house them and his other sports enterprises, sold the whole package to Dr. Jerry Buss. That removed Cooke's influential voice from league councils.

Meanwhile, managements played musical chairs with coaches. The 1978-79 season began with four new situations: Larry Costello (formerly of Milwaukee) in Chicago; Gene Shue (formerly of Philadelphia) in San Diego; Cotton Fitzsimmons (formerly of Buffalo) in Kansas City; and Dick Vitale, a newcomer to the pros, in Detroit.

Houston's Moses Malone snared 400 more rebounds than anyone else in the league and was awarded regular-season MVP honors.

But by December, Dave Cowens was made playing-coach of the Celtics, replacing Tom Sanders; by February, Costello was gone, in favor of Scotty Robertson, and in Denver, Donnie Walsh had replaced Larry Brown. And before any of that happened, Red Holzman had returned to the helm of the New York Knicks, replacing Willis Reed when the team's record was 6-8.

The regular-season races generated less excitement than they used to, and not just because of the college competition. The league was now too diffuse. With 22 teams facing each other only four times a year, fans in any city got to see any particular opponent only twice in a six-month period. And with 12 teams qualifying for the playoffs, the regular schedule (which now encompassed a total of 902 games) simply lacked urgency.

And this was true despite close races in three divisions. Kansas City, last the year before, finished a game ahead of Denver in the Midwest, a triumph for Fitzsimmons; San Antonio fought off Houston by one game in the Central, stirring up Texas; Atlanta wound up only one game behind Houston, and Seattle held off Phoenix by two games in the Pacific. Only Washington, the defending champion, had an easier time, winning the Atlantic Division by seven games and posting the best record in the league, 54-28.

The second-best record, 52-30, belonged to Seattle, and the 1978 finalists made it to the finals again. This time, however, the result was different: the Sonics lost the first game but swept the next four, and Seattle had its first major-league title.

Coach Lenny Wilkens had an unusually flexible and cohesive seven-man unit, with John Johnson and

George Gervin netted his second straight scoring title with a 29.6 average.

Lonnie Shelton up front, Jack Sikma at center, Dennis Johnson and Gus Williams in backcourt, and Paul Silas and Fred Brown coming off the bench. And Shelton's presence was part of an issue that became the chief topic of the league's business activity, the "compensation" question.

Under the agreements reached in 1976, when a free agent signed with a new club, that club had to "arrange" a mutually satisfactory compensation to his former club—or, if agreement wasn't reached, accept the Commissioner's decision on what would "make whole" the original team.

Marvin Webster, a mainstay of Seattle's near-miss championship team of 1978, signed with the Knicks. Commissioner Lawrence O'Brien's compensation award was Shelton, $400,000 and a top draft choice. The Knicks claimed this was unfair. The Players Association claimed this was a "punitive" award to discourage teams from making offers to free agents. It led to appeals, hearings and legal judgments that were still unsettled more than a year later.

The individual scoring champion was George Gervin again, averaging 29.6 points a game. Houston's Moses Malone, the rebounding leader, won the Most Valuable Player award, and Kansas City's Phil Ford was Rookie of the Year. The All-Star Game, in Detroit, was won by the West, 134-129, and the home-court advantage, which had become alarmingly high the two preceding years, subsided a bit to 66.5 percent.

Three referees were used, as part of a program to curb violence, but at the end of the season the club owners decided it was too expensive and returned to a two-man system.

1978-79

STANDINGS

Eastern Conference
Atlantic Division

	W.	L.	Pct.
Washington	54	28	.659
Philadelphia	47	35	.573
New Jersey	37	45	.451
New York	31	51	.378
Boston	29	53	.354

Central Division

	W.	L.	Pct.
San Antonio	48	34	.585
Houston	47	35	.573
Atlanta	46	36	.561
Cleveland	30	52	.366
Detroit	30	52	.366
New Orleans	26	56	.317

Western Conference

Midwest Division

	W.	L.	Pct.
Kansas City	48	34	.585
Denver	47	35	.573
Indiana	38	44	.463
Milwaukee	38	44	.463
Chicago	31	51	.378

Pacific Division

	W.	L.	Pct.
Seattle	52	30	.634
Phoenix	50	32	.610
Los Angeles	47	35	.573
Portland	45	37	.549
San Diego	43	39	.524
Golden State	38	44	.463

Eastern Conference First Round

April 11—Philadelphia 122, New Jersey 114
April 13—Philadelphia 111, New Jersey 101

April 11—Atlanta 109, Houston 106
April 13—Atlanta 100, Houston 91

Eastern Conference Semifinal Series

April 15—Washington 103, Atlanta 89
April 17—Atlanta 107, Washington 99
April 20—Washington 89, Atlanta 77
April 22—Washington 120, Atlanta 118 (OT)
April 24—Atlanta 107, Washington 103
April 26—Atlanta 104, Washington 86
April 29—Washington 100, Atlanta 94

April 15—San Antonio 119, Philadelphia 106
April 17—San Antonio 121, Philadelphia 120
April 20—Philadelphia 123, San Antonio 115
April 22—San Antonio 115, Philadelphia 112
April 26—Philadelphia 120, San Antonio 97
April 29—Philadelphia 92, San Antonio 90
May 2—San Antonio 111, Philadelphia 108

Eastern Conference Final Series

May 4—San Antonio 118, Washington 97
May 6—Washington 115, San Antonio 95
May 9—San Antonio 116, Washington 114
May 11—San Antonio 118, Washington 102
May 13—Washington 107, San Antonio 103
May 16—Washington 108, San Antonio 100
May 18—Washington 107, San Antonio 105

Dennis Johnson's play at both ends of the court led the underdog SuperSonics to the NBA championship.

Western Conference First Round

April 10—Phoenix 107, Portland 103
April 13—Portland 96, Phoenix 92
April 15—Phoenix 101, Portland 91

April 10—Denver 110, Los Angeles 105
April 13—Los Angeles 121, Denver 109
April 15—Los Angeles 112, Denver 111

Western Conference Semifinal Series

April 17—Seattle 112, Los Angeles 101
April 18—Seattle 108 (OT), Los Angeles 103
April 20—Los Angeles 118 (OT), Seattle 112
April 22—Seattle 117, Los Angeles 115
April 25—Seattle 106, Los Angeles 100

April 17—Phoenix 102, Kansas City 99
April 20—Kansas City 111, Phoenix 91
April 22—Phoenix 108, Kansas City 93
April 25—Phoenix 108, Kansas City 94
April 27—Phoenix 120, Kansas City 99

Western Conference Final Series

May 1—Seattle 108, Phoenix 93
May 4—Seattle 103, Phoenix 97
May 6—Phoenix 113, Seattle 103
May 8—Phoenix 100, Seattle 91
May 11—Phoenix 99, Seattle 93
May 13—Seattle 106, Phoenix 105
May 17—Seattle 114, Phoenix 110

World Championship Series

May 20—Washington 99, Seattle 97
May 24—Seattle 92, Washington 82
May 27—Seattle 105, Washington 95
May 29—Seattle 114, Washington 112 (OT)
June 1—Seattle 97, Washington 93

TOP SCORERS

	Pts.	Ave.
George Gervin, San Antonio	2365	29.6
Lloyd Free, San Diego	2244	28.8
Marques Johnson, Milwaukee	1972	25.6
Bob McAdoo, Boston	1487	24.8
Moses Malone, Houston	2031	24.8

TOP REBOUNDERS

	No.	Ave.
Moses Malone, Houston	1444	17.6
Rich Kelley, New Orleans	1026	12.8
Kareem Abdul-Jabbar, Los Angeles	1025	12.8
Artis Gilmore, Chicago	1043	12.7
Jack Sikma, Seattle	1013	12.4

LEADERS IN ASSISTS

	No.	Ave.
Kevin Porter, Detroit	1099	13.4
John Lucas, Golden State	762	9.3
Norm Nixon, Los Angeles	737	9.0
Phil Ford, Kansas City	681	8.6
Paul Westphal, Phoenix	529	6.5

1979-80

Reacting to criticism, not always well-founded, that their game was stagnating, the NBA owners made several changes for the 1979-80 season.

They adopted the three-point basket, for shots from beyond 23 feet 9 inches, that had been used by the ABA with much fan approval.

They altered the schedule, so that teams faced rivals in their own division more often than others.

They approved a shift of the New Orleans Jazz to Salt Lake City, a former ABA site, where the team took the unlikely name of Utah Jazz.

And they made a production out of the signings of Larry Bird and Magic Johnson.

The Celtics did sign Bird before the draft, exercising their 1978 rights. And the Lakers, who had acquired Utah's right to the No. 1 pick, picked Johnson.

Rarely in the league's history did two top choices have such an immediate effect.

With Bird, the Celtics made the greatest turnaround on record, from 29-53 to 61-21, the season's best. That swing of 32 games came under the leadership of Bill Fitch, who had been Cleveland's only coach until he left to take charge of the Celtics after the ill-advised player-coach experiment with Dave Cowens.

And with Johnson, who was not only spectacular himself but seemed to bring new enthusiasm to Kareem Abdul-Jabbar, the Lakers went all the way to the championship. They won an exceptionally dramatic six-game final from the Philadelphia 76ers, who had eliminated Boston in the semifinals.

But the whole Los Angeles season was dramatic. They started with a new coach, Jack McKinney, a long-time assistant to Jack Ramsay at Portland, taking over from Jerry West. A bicycle accident which caused a brain injury put McKinney out of action when the team was 10-4, and his close friend and assistant, Paul Westhead, took over. With Kareem playing the best ball of his illustrious career, the Lakers kept rolling, and wound up 60-22.

As the playoffs approached, McKinney had recovered and was ready to go back to work—but it was decided to keep Westhead in command, and when it was over, no one could argue with the result. Westhead remained as coach for 1980-81, and McKinney moved on to become coach at Indiana.

In the final round, the Lakers and 76ers played a

The Lakers found a touch of magic as Earvin Johnson guided them to the title.

furious set of games, worthy of the most memorable finals. They split in Los Angeles, and split in Philadelphia, with Julius Erving spectacular for the 76ers. In Game No. 5 at Los Angeles, Kareem injured his ankle in the third quarter but came back to play and scored 40 points in a 108-103 decision. He couldn't play the next game, though, at Philadelphia—and Johnson, who had been playing guard, took his place at center and scored 42 (with seven assists and 15 rebounds) during a 123-107 victory, the only non-cliff-hanger finish of the series.

The divisional races weren't quite as close this time, but the coaching turnover picked up even more steam. Six teams opened the season with new head coaches: Fitch in Boston, McKinney in Los Angeles, Jerry Sloan (as a rookie) in Chicago, Tom Nissalke (from Houston) in Utah, Del Harris (also a rookie coach) in Houston and Stan Albeck (a former top Laker assistant under West) in Cleveland.

Twelve games into the season, Detroit changed from Dick Vitale to Richie Adubato, and Doug Moe, who had been San Antonio's coach ever since the team came in from the ABA, was replaced by Bob Bass late in the season.

The revived Celtics finished two games ahead of the 76ers, who proved able to handle them in the playoffs. Atlanta, the surprise team, caught and passed Houston and San Antonio, beating both by a nine-game margin. Don Nelson's Milwaukee team took the Midwest Division title by two games over Kansas City, and the Lakers wound up with a respectable margin of four games over Seattle and five over Phoenix in a division of exceptional power.

Portland and San Diego finished far back, both because of Bill Walton's absence. After leading the Blazers to their 1977 championship, the injury-prone center had been hurt again late in the 1978 season and his team fell out of contention. He couldn't play

In the most shattering performances of the season, Philadelphia's Darryl Dawkins smashed two backboards with slam dunks.

at all in 1978-79, charged Portland with mishandling his ailment and forcing him to play hurt, and declared his free agency. He signed with San Diego (causing another complex compensation wrangle which cost San Diego three regulars) but was able to play only 14 games before hurting his leg again.

George Gervin, averaging 33.1 points a game, was scoring champion for the third straight year, a feat never before accomplished by a backcourt player. Only Wilt Chamberlain (who had a seven-year streak), George Mikan and Neil Johnston, all centers, and Bob McAdoo, who played both center and forward, had previously had three-year strings. And Lloyd Free, who placed second with 30.2 points, was one of the few players ever to reach such a level without leading the league.

But Kareem was clearly the MVP, winning that honor for the sixth time, matching the record total of Bill Russell.

When Bird was named Rookie of the Year over Johnson, it caused great controversy, but the balloting is done on the basis of the regular season, without taking playoff events into account, and Bird, leading a team that didn't have Abdul-Jabbar, made a greater impression in that span.

The All-Star Game, on Washington's home court at Capital Centre, went into overtime for only the second time in the 30-year history of the gala, and the East won, 144-136.

After the season, the league voted to admit Dallas as a 23rd team for 1980-81, setting the entry fee at $12 million—more than the entire league was worth 20 years before, and more than any major-league baseball team ever had to pay for an expansion franchise.

1979-80

STANDINGS

Eastern Conference
Atlantic Division

	W.	L.	Pct.
Boston	61	21	.744
Philadelphia	59	23	.720
Washington	39	43	.476
New York	39	43	.476
New Jersey	34	48	.415

Central Division

	W.	L.	Pct.
Atlanta	50	32	.610
Houston	41	41	.500
San Antonio	41	41	.500
Indiana	37	45	.451
Cleveland	37	45	.451
Detroit	16	66	.195

Western Conference
Midwest Division

	W.	L.	Pct.
Milwaukee	49	33	.598
Kansas City	47	35	.573
Denver	30	52	.366
Chicago	30	52	.366
Utah	24	58	.293

Pacific Division

	W.	L.	Pct.
Los Angeles	60	22	.732
Seattle	56	26	.683
Phoenix	55	27	.671
Portland	38	44	.463
San Diego	35	47	.427
Golden State	24	58	.293

Eastern Conference First Round

April 2—Philadelphia 111, Washington 96
April 4—Philadelphia 112, Washington 104

April 2—Houston 95, San Antonio 85
April 4—San Antonio 106, Houston 101
April 6—Houston 141, San Antonio 120

Eastern Conference Semifinal Series

April 9—Boston 119, Houston 101
April 11—Boston 95, Houston 75
April 13—Boston 100, Houston 81
April 14—Boston 138, Houston 121

April 6—Philadelphia 107, Atlanta 104
April 9—Philadelphia 99, Atlanta 92
April 10—Atlanta 105, Philadelphia 93
April 13—Philadelphia 107, Atlanta 83
April 15—Philadelphia 105, Atlanta 100

Eastern Conference Final Series

April 18—Philadelphia 96, Boston 93
April 20—Boston 96, Philadelphia 90
April 23—Philadelphia 99, Boston 97
April 24—Philadelphia 102, Boston 90
April 27—Philadelphia 105, Boston 94

Larry Bird soared in his first NBA season, leading the Celtics in scoring, rebounds and steals.

Western Conference First Round

April 2—Phoenix 96, Kansas City 93
April 4—Kansas City, 106, Phoenix 96
April 6—Phoenix 114, Kansas City 99

April 2—Seattle 120, Portland 110
April 4—Portland 105, Seattle 95
April 6—Seattle 103, Portland 86

Western Conference Semifinal Series

April 8—Los Angeles 119, Phoenix 110
April 9—Los Angeles 131, Phoenix 128
April 11—Los Angeles 108, Phoenix 105
April 13—Phoenix 127, Los Angeles 101
April 15—Los Angeles 126, Phoenix 101

April 8—Seattle 114, Milwaukee 113
April 9—Milwaukee 114, Seattle 112
April 11—Milwaukee 95, Seattle 91
April 13—Seattle 112, Milwaukee 107
April 15—Milwaukee 108, Seattle 97
April 18—Seattle 86, Milwaukee 85
April 20—Seattle 98, Milwaukee 94

Western Conference Final Series

April 22—Seattle 108, Los Angeles 107
April 23—Los Angeles 108, Seattle 99
April 25—Los Angeles 104, Seattle 100
April 27—Los Angeles 98, Seattle 93
April 30—Los Angeles 111, Seattle 105

World Championship Series

May 4—Los Angeles 109, Philadelphia 102
May 7—Philadelphia 107, Los Angeles 104
May 10—Los Angeles 111, Philadelphia 101
May 11—Philadelphia 105, Los Angeles 102
May 14—Los Angeles 108, Philadelphia 103
May 16—Los Angeles 123, Philadelphia 107

TOP SCORERS

	Pts.	Ave.
George Gervin, San Antonio	1585	33.1
Lloyd Free, San Diego	2055	30.2
Adrian Dantley, Utah	1903	28.0
Julius Erving, Philadelphia	2100	26.9
Moses Malone, Houston	2119	25.8

TOP REBOUNDERS

	No.	Ave.
Swen Nater, San Diego	1216	15.0
Moses Malone, Houston	1190	14.5
Wes Unseld, Washington	1094	13.3
Caldwell Jones, Philadelphia	950	11.9
Jack Sikma, Seattle	908	11.1

LEADERS IN ASSISTS

	No.	Ave.
Michael Richardson, New York	832	10.1
Nate Archibald, Boston	671	8.4
Foots Walker, Cleveland	607	8.0
Norm Nixon, Los Angeles	642	7.8
John Lucas, Golden State	602	7.5

1980-81

This time it was Larry Bird's turn. The one thing left undone in his rookie season was accomplished in his second: another championship for the Boston Celtics.

Magic Johnson had little chance to repeat his 1980 heroics because of an early-season injury and, although he rejoined Kareem Abdul-Jabbar in the Los Angeles Laker lineup in time for the playoffs, neither he nor the team ever regained full stride. The Lakers were eliminated in the opening mini-round, 2-1, losing both games at home to a Houston team that had barely qualified for the playoffs after a 40-42 season.

And the Rockets, led by Moses Malone, wound up in the final round, pushing Boston hard before yielding in six games.

But it was all much more complicated than that, and the story should start at the beginning.

First of all, there was a new team. The Dallas Mavericks took an expansion franchise for a record $12-million entry fee, and this required reshuffling the divisions. The two extremes, Atlantic and Pacific, stayed the same, but Houston, in the Central Division of the Eastern Conference since 1973, wound up in the Western Conference.

In the new alignment, Atlanta, Cleveland, Detroit and Indiana, joined by Chicago and Milwaukee from the Western half, made up the new Central; San Antonio, Kansas City, Denver, Utah, transplanted Houston and new Dallas comprised the Midwest Division of the Western Conference.

As things turned out, all six Eastern playoff qualifiers finished well over .500, while Houston and Kansas City got the last two playoff berths in the West, beating out Golden State by one game in the final weekend of the regular schedule.

Nor was that a routine development. The Warriors, committed to total reconstruction, had traded Robert Parish, their starting center for several years, to the Celtics for the No. 1 draft turn (which Boston had acquired from Detroit). They took Purdue's Joe Barry Carroll, the highest-rated center, and got a good rookie season out of him. But on the final weekend, when they needed two victories to make the playoffs, their veteran back-up center, Clifford Ray, suddenly quit, leaving Carroll to try to play the full game on successive nights. He faded in the closing stages of both, the Warriors lost both—and Houston stayed alive.

The Celtics, meanwhile, found a perfect blend in Parish at center, backed up by Rick Robey; Bird in one corner, displaying his remarkable all-court and rise-to-the-occasion skills; playoff MVP Cedric Maxwell in the other corner; and Kevin McHale, No. 3 man in the draft (with the pick obtained from Golden State with Parish) spelling them all.

With Nate Archibald physically sound and Chris

Utah's Adrian Dantley won the scoring championship.

Ford and M.L. Carr operating in the backcourt, the Celtics were once again deep enough and unified enough to play the best-integrated, fast-break, team-defense game that had brought so many previous titles to Red Auerbach's teams.

And Auerbach, fully in command in the front office after a succession of ownership changes that had interfered with his autonomy at various times, celebrated his 35th year in the league with his 14th championship. For Bill Fitch, in his second year as Celtic coach, the thrill was even bigger.

As had happened before, the real power showdown was in the semifinal round, when the Celtics had to face the Philadelphia 76ers. Philadelphia, with Julius Erving heading its powerful lineup, was again more one-on-one oriented. The 76ers took a 3-1 lead in games, but the Celtics pulled out the next three, winning the seventh in the closing moments on a series of interceptions and a deciding basket by Bird. It was widely taken for granted that either team would go on to beat Houston, and the surprising thing about the final round was the extent of the resistance put up by the Rockets, coached by Del Harris.

During the regular season, the Celtics and 76ers had finished with 62-20 records, best in the league, but the Celtics took first place in the Atlantic Division (and a mini-round bye) by winning the final game on the schedule from the 76ers, thus prevailing in tiebreaking procedures. The next best record in the league, 60-22, belonged to Milwaukee, the Central Division winner, and the 76ers just did get by the Bucks in a fierce, seven-game series to reach Boston.

Julius Erving took the season's MVP laurels, but he couldn't get the 76ers past the Celtics in the playoffs.

Houston, meanwhile, followed its upset of the Lakers by beating San Antonio, the Midwest champion, in seven games, while Kansas City, after knocking off Portland, eliminated Phoenix, the Pacific leader, also in seven games. But the Rockets needed only five games to dispose of the Kings.

On the individual level, the tilt of the Johnson-Bird pendulum was not the only change.

Adrian Dantley, playing for Utah, ended George Gervin's three-year reign as scoring champion. Hitting a league high of 55 points in one game and going over 40 in nine others, Dantley finished with a 30.7

points-per-game average, while San Antonio's Gervin, at 27.1, fell to third place behind Malone.

Malone, who scored 27.8, was also the league leader in rebounding, averaging 14.8, or 2.4 a game more than the runner-up, Swen Nater of San Diego. In all, Malone, who turned pro right out of high school in 1974 with the American Basketball Association, had been slowly gaining full recognition (this was his second straight rebounding title), and by the end of the playoffs was being hailed as the league's best center.

Another factor in Houston's late success was an older player, Calvin Murphy, for years the smallest in the league at 5-9, now 33 years old and an 11-year veteran. He set two remarkable records for free throws. Early in the season, Murphy sank 78 consecutive free throws, surpassing the record of 60 Rick Barry had set in 1976. When it was over, Murphy had posted a .957 record of accuracy (206 of 215), erasing the mark of .947 Barry had set in 1979 as a teammate of Murphy's.

The 76ers, winning 37 of their 41 road games, equalled a league record set by the 1977 Lakers and matched by Philadelphia in 1978 and by Los Angeles again in 1980. Denver, limping through a 37-45 campaign, nevertheless had the distinction of having three full-time players average more than 20 points a game: David Thompson (25.5), Alex English (23.8) and Dan Issel (21.9). That hadn't happened since 1972, when three Warriors (Jeff Mullins, Nate Thurmond and Cazzie Russell) all averaged between 21 and 22.

The All-Star Game, with Cleveland the host, featured Nate Archibald's playmaking as the East topped the West, 123-120.

Julius Erving was the Most Valuable Player, Utah's Darrell Griffith the Rookie of the Year and Indiana's Jack McKinney the Coach of the Year.

1980-81

Eastern Conference

Atlantic Division

	W.	L.	Pct.
Boston	62	20	.756
Philadelphia	62	20	.756
New York	50	32	.610
Washington	39	43	.476
New Jersey	24	58	.293

Central Division

	W.	L.	Pct.
Milwaukee	60	22	.732
Chicago	45	37	.549
Indiana	44	38	.537
Atlanta	31	51	.378
Cleveland	28	54	.341
Detroit	21	61	.256

Western Conference

Midwest Division

	W.	L.	Pct.
San Antonio	52	30	.634
Kansas City	40	42	.488
Houston	40	42	.488
Denver	37	45	.451
Utah	28	54	.341
Dallas	15	67	.183

Pacific Division

	W.	L.	Pct.
Phoenix	57	25	.695
Los Angeles	54	28	.659
Portland	45	37	.549
Golden State	39	43	.476
San Diego	36	46	.439
Seattle	34	48	.415

Eastern Conference First Round

March 31—Philadelphia 124, Indiana 108
April 2—Philadelphia 96, Indiana 85

March 31—Chicago 90, New York 80
April 3—Chicago 115, New York 114 (OT)

Eastern Conference Semifinal Series

April 5—Boston 121, Chicago 109
April 7—Boston 106, Chicago 97
April 10—Boston 113, Chicago 107
April 12—Boston 109, Chicago 103

April 5—Philadelphia 125, Milwaukee 122
April 7—Milwaukee 109, Philadelphia 99
April 10—Philadelphia 108, Milwaukee 103
April 12—Milwaukee 109, Philadelphia 98
April 15—Philadelphia 116, Milwaukee 99
April 17—Milwaukee 109, Philadelphia 86
April 19—Philadelphia 99, Milwaukee 98

Eastern Conference Final Series

April 21—Philadelphia 105, Boston 104
April 22—Boston 118, Philadelphia 99
April 24—Philadelphia 110, Boston 100
April 26—Philadelphia 107, Boston 105
April 29—Boston 111, Philadelphia 109
May 1—Boston 100, Philadelphia 98
May 3—Boston 91, Philadelphia 90

Larry Bird celebrates the championship season with one of Red Auerbach's cigars.

Western Conference First Round

April 1—Kansas City 98, Portland 97 (OT)
April 3—Portland 124, Kansas City 119 (OT)
April 5—Kansas City 104, Portland 95

April 1—Houston 111, Los Angeles 107
April 3—Los Angeles 111, Houston 106
April 5—Houston 89, Los Angeles 86

Western Conference Semifinal Series

April 7—Phoenix 102, Kansas City 80
April 8—Kansas City 88, Phoenix 83
April 10—Kansas City 93, Phoenix 92
April 12—Kansas City 102, Phoenix 95
April 15—Phoenix 101, Kansas City 89
April 17—Phoenix 81, Kansas City 76
April 19—Kansas City 95, Phoenix 88

April 7—Houston 107, San Antonio 98
April 8—San Antonio 125, Houston 113
April 10—Houston 112, San Antonio 99
April 12—San Antonio 114, Houston 112
April 14—Houston 123, San Antonio 117
April 15—San Antonio 101, Houston 96
April 17—Houston 105, San Antonio 100

Western Conference Final Series

April 21—Houston 97, Kansas City 78
April 22—Kansas City 88, Houston 79
April 24—Houston 92, Kansas City 88
April 26—Houston 100, Kansas City 89
April 29—Houston 97, Kansas City 88

World Championship Series

May 5—Boston 98, Houston 95
May 7—Houston 92, Boston 90
May 9—Boston 94, Houston 71
May 10—Houston 91, Boston 86
May 12—Boston 109, Houston 80
May 14—Boston 102, Houston 91

TOP SCORERS

	Pts.	Ave.
Adrian Dantley, Utah	2452	30.7
Moses Malone, Houston	2222	27.8
George Gervin, San Antonio	2221	27.1
Kareem Abdul-Jabbar, Los Angeles	2095	26.2
David Thompson, Denver	1967	25.5

TOP REBOUNDERS

	No.	Ave.
Moses Malone, Houston	1180	14.8
Swen Nater, San Diego	1017	12.4
Larry Smith, Golden State	994	12.1
Larry Bird, Boston	895	10.9
Jack Sikma, Seattle	852	10.4

LEADERS IN ASSISTS

	No.	Ave.
Kevin Porter, Washington	734	9.1
Norm Nixon, Los Angeles	696	8.8
Phil Ford, Kansas City	580	8.8
Michael Richardson, New York	627	7.9
Nate Archibald, Boston	618	7.7

MOST VALUABLE PLAYER

Podoloff Cup

(By vote of players)

Year	Player	Team
1955-56	Bob Pettit	St. Louis
1956-57	Bob Cousy	Boston
1957-58	Bill Russell	Boston
1958-59	Bob Pettit	St. Louis
1959-60	Wilt Chamberlain	Philadelphia
1960-61	Bill Russell	Boston
1961-62	Bill Russell	Boston
1962-63	Bill Russell	Boston
1963-64	Oscar Robertson	Cincinnati
1964-65	Bill Russell	Boston
1965-66	Wilt Chamberlain	Philadelphia
1966-67	Wilt Chamberlain	Philadelphia
1967-68	Wilt Chamberlain	Philadelphia
1968-69	Wes Unseld	Baltimore
1969-70	Willis Reed	New York
1970-71	Lew Alcindor	Milwaukee
1971-72	Kareem Abdul-Jabbar	Milwaukee
1972-73	Dave Cowens	Boston
1973-74	Kareem Abdul-Jabbar	Milwaukee
1974-75	Bob McAdoo	Buffalo
1975-76	Kareem Abdul-Jabbar	Los Angeles
1976-77	Kareem Abdul-Jabbar	Los Angeles
1977-78	Bill Walton	Portland
1978-79	Moses Malone	Houston
1979-80	Kareem Abdul-Jabbar	Los Angeles
1980-81	Julius Erving	Philadelphia

ROOKIE OF THE YEAR

Year	Player	Team
1952-53	Don Meineke	Fort Wayne
1953-54	Ray Felix	Baltimore
1954-55	Bob Pettit	Milwaukee
1955-56	Maurice Stokes	Rochester
1956-57	Tom Heinsohn	Boston
1957-58	Woody Sauldsberry	Philadelphia
1958-59	Elgin Baylor	Minneapolis
1959-60	Wilt Chamberlain	Philadelphia
1960-61	Oscar Robertson	Cincinnati
1961-62	Walt Bellamy	Chicago
1962-63	Terry Dischinger	Chicago
1963-64	Jerry Lucas	Cincinnati
1964-65	Willis Reed	New York
1965-66	Rick Barry	San Francisco
1966-67	Dave Bing	Detroit
1967-68	Earl Monroe	Baltimore
1968-69	Wes Unseld	Baltimore
1969-70	Lew Alcindor	Milwaukee
1970-71	Dave Cowens	Boston
	Geoff Petrie	Portland
1971-72	Sidney Wicks	Portland
1972-73	Bob McAdoo	Buffalo
1973-74	Ernie DiGregorio	Buffalo
1974-75	Keith Wilkes	Golden State
1975-76	Alvan Adams	Phoenix
1976-77	Adrian Dantley	Buffalo
1977-78	Walter Davis	Phoenix
1978-79	Phil Ford	Kansas City
1979-80	Larry Bird	Boston
1980-81	Darrell Griffith	Utah

COACH OF THE YEAR

1963	Harry Gallatin	St. Louis
1964	Alex Hannum	San Francisco
1965	Red Auerbach	Boston
1966	Dolph Schayes	Philadelphia
1967	Johnny Kerr	Chicago
1968	Richie Guerin	St. Louis
1969	Gene Shue	Baltimore
1970	Red Holzman	New York
1971	Dick Motta	Chicago
1972	Bill Sharman	Los Angeles
1973	Tom Heinsohn	Boston
1974	Ray Scott	Detroit
1975	Phil Johnson	Kansas City-Omaha
1976	Bill Fitch	Cleveland
1977	Tom Nissalke	Houston
1978	Hubie Brown	Atlanta
1979	Cotton Fitzsimmons	Kansas City
1980	Bill Fitch	Boston
1981	Jack McKinney	Indiana

ALL-NBA TEAMS

1946-47

First	Second
Joe Fulks, Philadelphia	Ernie Calverley, Providence
Bob Feerick, Washington	Frank Baumholtz, Cleveland
Stan Miasek, Detroit	John Logan, St. Louis
Bones McKinney, Washington	Chuck Halbert, Chicago
Max Zaslofsky, Chicago	Fred Scolari, Washington

1947-48

Joe Fulks, Philadelphia	John Logan, St. Louis
Max Zaslofsky, Chicago	Carl Braun, New York
Ed Sadowski, Boston	Stan Miasek, Chicago
Howie Dallmar, Philadelphia	Fred Scolari, Washington
Bob Feerick, Washington	Buddy Jeannette, Baltimore

1948-49

George Mikan, Minneapolis	Arnie Risen, Rochester
Joe Fulks, Philadelphia	Bob Feerick, Washington
Bob Davies, Rochester	Bones McKinney, Washington
Max Zaslofsky, Chicago	Ken Sailors, Providence
Jim Pollard, Minneapolis	John Logan, St. Louis

1949-50

George Mikan, Minneapolis	Frank Brian, Anderson
Jim Pollard, Minneapolis	Fred Schaus, Fort Wayne
Alex Groza, Indianapolis	Dolph Schayes, Syracuse
Bob Davies, Rochester	Al Cervi, Syracuse
Max Zaslofsky, Chicago	Ralph Beard, Indianapolis

1950-51

George Mikan, Minneapolis	Dolph Schayes, Syracuse
Alex Groza, Indianapolis	Frank Brian, Tri-Cities
Ed Macauley, Boston	Vern Mikkelsen, Minneapolis
Bob Davies, Rochester	Joe Fulks, Philadelphia
Ralph Beard, Indianapolis	Dick McGuire, New York

1951-52

First	Second
George Mikan, Minneapolis	Larry Foust, Fort Wayne
Ed Macauley, Boston	Vern Mikkelsen, Minneapolis
Paul Arizin, Philadelphia	Jim Pollard, Minneapolis
Bob Cousy, Boston	Bob Wanzer, Rochester
Bob Davies, Rochester	Andy Phillip, Philadelphia
Dolph Schayes, Syracuse	

1952-53

George Mikan, Minneapolis	Bill Sharman, Boston
Bob Cousy, Boston	Vern Mikkelsen, Minneapolis
Neil Johnston, Philadelphia	Bob Wanzer, Rochester
Ed Macauley, Boston	Bob Davies, Rochester
Dolph Schayes, Syracuse	Andy Phillip, Philadelphia

1953-54

Bob Cousy, Boston	Ed Macauley, Boston
Neil Johnston, Philadelphia	Jim Pollard, Minneapolis
George Mikan, Minneapolis	Carl Braun, New York
Dolph Schayes, Syracuse	Bob Wanzer, Rochester
Harry Gallatin, New York	Paul Seymour, Syracuse

1954-55

Neil Johnston, Philadelphia	Vern Mikkelsen, Minneapolis
Bob Cousy, Boston	Harry Gallatin, New York
Dolph Schayes, Syracuse	Paul Seymour, Syracuse
Bob Pettit, Milwaukee	Slater Martin, Minneapolis
Larry Foust, Fort Wayne	Bill Sharman, Boston

1955-56

Bob Pettit, St. Louis	Dolph Schayes, Syracuse
Paul Arizin, Philadelphia	Maurice Stokes, Rochester
Neil Johnston, Philadelphia	Clyde Lovellette, Minneapolis
Bob Cousy, Boston	Slater Martin, Minneapolis
Bill Sharman, Boston	Jack George, Philadelphia

1956-57

Paul Arizin, Philadelphia	George Yardley, Fort Wayne
Dolph Schayes, Syracuse	Maurice Stokes, Rochester
Bob Pettit, St. Louis	Neil Johnston, Philadelphia
Bob Cousy, Boston	Dick Garmaker, Minneapolis
Bill Sharman, Boston	Slater Martin, St. Louis

1957-58

Dolph Schayes, Syracuse	Cliff Hagan, St. Louis
George Yardley, Detroit	Maurice Stokes, Cincinnati
Bob Pettit, St. Louis	Bill Russell, Boston
Bob Cousy, Boston	Tom Gola, Philadelphia
Bill Sharman, Boston	Slater Martin, St. Louis

1958-59

Bob Pettit, St. Louis	Paul Arizin, Philadelphia
Elgin Baylor, Minneapolis	Cliff Hagan, St. Louis
Bill Russell, Boston	Dolph Schayes, Syracuse
Bob Cousy, Boston	Slater Martin, St. Louis
Bill Sharman, Boston	Richie Guerin, New York

1959-60

First	Second
Bob Pettit, St. Louis	Jack Twyman, Cincinnati
Elgin Baylor, Minneapolis	Dolph Schayes, Syracuse
Wilt Chamberlain, Philadelphia	Bill Russell, Boston
Bob Cousy, Boston	Richie Guerin, New York
Gene Shue, Detroit	Bill Sharman, Boston

1960-61

Elgin Baylor, Los Angeles	Dolph Schayes, Syracuse
Bob Pettit, St. Louis	Tom Heinsohn, Boston
Wilt Chamberlain, Philadelphia	Bill Russell, Boston
Bob Cousy, Boston	Larry Costello, Syracuse
Oscar Robertson, Cincinnati	Gene Shue, Detroit

1961-62

Bob Pettit, St. Louis	Tom Heinsohn, Boston
Elgin Baylor, Los Angeles	Jack Twyman, Cincinnati
Wilt Chamberlain, Philadelphia	Bill Russell, Boston
Jerry West, Los Angeles	Richie Guerin, New York
Oscar Robertson, Cincinnati	Bob Cousy, Boston

1962-63

Elgin Baylor, Los Angeles	Tom Heinsohn, Boston
Bob Pettit, St. Louis	Bailey Howell, Detroit
Bill Russell, Boston	Wilt Chamberlain, San Francisco
Oscar Robertson, Cincinnati	Bob Cousy, Boston
Jerry West, Los Angeles	Hal Greer, Syracuse

1963-64

Bob Pettit, St. Louis	Tom Heinsohn, Boston
Elgin Baylor, Los Angeles	Jerry Lucas, Cincinnati
Wilt Chamberlain, San Francisco	Bill Russell, Boston
Oscar Robertson, Cincinnati	John Havlicek, Boston
Jerry West, Los Angeles	Hal Greer, Philadelphia

1964-65

Elgin Baylor, Los Angeles	Bob Pettit, St. Louis
Jerry Lucas Cincinnati	Gus Johnson, Baltimore
Bill Russell, Boston	Wilt Chamberlain, S.F.-Phila.
Oscar Robertson, Cincinnati	Sam Jones, Boston
Jerry West, Los Angeles	Hal Greer, Philadelphia

1965-66

Rick Barry, San Francisco	John Havlicek, Boston
Jerry Lucas, Cincinnati	Gus Johnson, Baltimore
Wilt Chamberlain, Philadelphia	Bill Russell, Boston
Oscar Robertson, Cincinnati	Sam Jones, Boston
Jerry West, Los Angeles	Hal Greer, Philadelphia

1966-67

Rick Barry, San Francisco	Willis Reed, New York
Elgin Baylor, Los Angeles	Jerry Lucas, Cincinnati
Wilt Chamberlain, Philadelphia	Bill Russell, Boston
Jerry West, Los Angeles	Hal Greer, Philadelphia
Oscar Robertson, Cincinnati	Sam Jones, Boston

Paul Westphal made the All-NBA first team three times with the Phoenix Suns.

1967-68

First
Elgin Baylor, Los Angeles
Jerry Lucas, Cincinnati
Wilt Chamberlain, Philadelphia
Dave Bing, Detroit
Oscar Robertson, Cincinnati

Second
Willis Reed, New York
John Havlicek, Boston
Bill Russell, Boston
Hal Greer, Philadelphia
Jerry West, Los Angeles

1968-69

Billy Cunningham, Philadelphia
Elgin Baylor, Los Angeles
Wes Unseld, Baltimore
Earl Monroe, Baltimore
Oscar Robertson, Cincinnati

John Havlicek, Boston
Dave DeBusschere, Det.-N.Y.
Willis Reed, New York
Hal Greer, Philadelphia
Jerry West, Los Angeles

1969-70

Billy Cunningham, Philadelphia
Connie Hawkins, Phoenix
Willis Reed, New York
Jerry West, Los Angeles
Walt Frazier, New York

John Havlicek, Boston
Gus Johnson, Baltimore
Lew Alcindor, Milwaukee
Lou Hudson, Atlanta
Oscar Robertson, Cincinnati

1970-71

First
John Havlicek, Boston
Billy Cunningham, Philadelphia
Lew Alcindor, Milwaukee
Jerry West, Los Angeles
Dave Bing, Detroit

Second
Gus Johnson, Baltimore
Bob Love, Chicago
Willis Reed, New York
Walt Frazier, New York
Oscar Robertson, Milwaukee

1971-72

John Havlicek, Boston
Spencer Haywood, Seattle
Kareem Abdul-Jabbar, Milwaukee
Jerry West, Los Angeles
Walt Frazier, New York

Bob Love, Chicago
Billy Cunningham, Philadelphia
Wilt Chamberlain, Los Angeles
Nate Archibald, Cincinnati
Archie Clark, Phila.-Balt.

1972-73

John Havlicek, Boston
Spencer Haywood, Seattle
Kareem Abdul-Jabbar, Milwaukee
Nate Archibald, KC-Omaha
Jerry West, Los Angeles

Elvin Hayes, Baltimore
Rick Barry, Golden State
Dave Cowens, Boston
Walt Frazier, New York
Pete Maravich, Atlanta

1973-74

First	Second
John Havlicek, Boston	Elvin Hayes, Capital
Rick Barry, Golden State	Spencer Haywood, Seattle
Kareem Abdul-Jabbar, Milwaukee	Bob McAdoo, Buffalo
Walt Frazier, New York	Dave Bing, Detroit
Gail Goodrich, Los Angeles	Norm Van Lier, Chicago

1974-75

Rick Barry, Golden State	John Havlicek, Boston
Elvin Hayes, Washington	Spencer Haywood, Seattle
Bob McAdoo, Buffalo	Dave Cowens, Boston
Nate Archibald, KC-Omaha	Phil Chenier, Washington
Walt Frazier, New York	Jo Jo White, Boston

1975-76

Rick Barry, Golden State	Elvin Hayes, Washington
George McGinnis, Philadelphia	John Havlicek, Boston
Kareem Abdul-Jabbar, L.A.	Dave Cowens, Boston
Nate Archibald, Kansas City	Randy Smith, Buffalo
Pete Maravich, New Orleans	Phil Smith, Golden State

1976-77

Kareem Abdul-Jabbar, L.A.	Bill Walton, Portland
Pete Maravich, New Orleans	George Gervin, San Antonio
Paul Westphal, Phoenix	Jo Jo White, Boston
Elvin Hayes, Washington	Julius Erving, Philadelphia
David Thompson, Denver	George McGinnis, Philadelphia

1977-78

Truck Robinson, New Orleans	Walter Davis, Phoenix
Julius Erving, Philadelphia	Maurice Lucas, Portland
Bill Walton, Portland	Kareem Abdul-Jabbar, L.A.
George Gervin, San Antonio	Paul Westphal, Phoenix
David Thompson, Denver	Pete Maravich, New Orleans

1978-79

Marques Johnson, Milwaukee	Walter Davis, Phoenix
Elvin Hayes, Washington	Bobby Dandridge, Washington
Moses Malone, Houston	Kareem Abdul-Jabbar, L.A.
George Gervin, San Antonio	Lloyd Free, San Diego
Paul Westphal, Phoenix	Phil Ford, Kansas City

1979-80

Julius Erving, Philadelphia	Dan Roundfield, Atlanta
Larry Bird, Boston	Marques Johnson, Milwaukee
Kareem Abdul-Jabbar, L.A.	Moses Malone, Houston
George Gervin, San Antonio	Dennis Johnson, Seattle
Paul Westphal, Phoenix	Gus Williams, Seattle

1980-81

Julius Erving, Philadelphia	Adrian Dantley, Utah
Larry Bird, Boston	Marques Johnson, Milwaukee
Kareem Abdul-Jabbar, L.A.	Moses Malone, Houston
George Gervin, San Antonio	Nate Archibald, Boston
Dennis Johnson, Phoenix	Otis Birdsong, Kansas City

ALL-ROOKIE TEAMS

1963-64
Jerry Lucas, Cincinnati
Gus Johnson, Baltimore
Nate Thurmond, San Francisco
Art Heyman, New York
Rod Thorn, Baltimore

1964-65
Willis Reed, New York
Jim Barnes, New York
Howie Komives, New York
Luke Jackson, Philadelphia
Wally Jones, Baltimore
Joe Caldwell, Detroit

1965-66
Rick Barry, San Francisco
Bill Cunningham, Philadelphia
Tom Van Arsdale, Detroit
Dick Van Arsdale, New York
Fred Hetzel, San Francisco

1966-67
Lou Hudson, St. Louis
Jack Marin, Baltimore
Erwin Mueller, Chicago
Cazzie Russell, New York
Dave Bing, Detroit

1967-68
Earl Monroe, Baltimore
Bob Rule, Seattle
Al Tucker, Seattle
Walt Frazier, New York
Phil Jackson, New York

1968-69
Wes Unseld, Baltimore
Elvin Hayes, San Diego
Bill Hewitt, Los Angeles
Art Harris, Seattle
Gary Gregor, Phoenix

1969-70
Lew Alcindor, Milwaukee
Bob Dandridge, Milwaukee
Jo Jo White, Boston
Mike Davis, Baltimore
Dick Garrett, Los Angeles

1970-71
Geoff Petrie, Portland
Dave Cowens, Boston
Pete Maravich, Atlanta
Calvin Murphy, San Diego
Bob Lanier, Detroit

1971-72
Elmore Smith, Buffalo
Phil Chenier, Baltimore
Sidney Wicks, Portland
Austin Carr, Cleveland
Clifford Ray, Chicago

1972-73
Bob McAdoo, Buffalo
Lloyd Neal, Portland
Fred Boyd, Philadelphia
Dwight Davis, Cleveland
Jim Price, Los Angeles

1973-74
Ernie DiGregorio, Buffalo
Ron Behagen, KC-Omaha
Mike Bantom, Phoenix
John Brown, Atlanta
Nick Weatherspoon, Capital

1974-75
Keith Wilkes, Golden State
John Drew, Atlanta
Scott Wedman, KC-Omaha
Tom Burleson, Seattle
Brian Winters, Los Angeles

1975-76
Alvan Adams, Phoenix
Gus Williams, Golden State
Joe Meriweather, Houston
John Shumate, Phoenix-Buffalo
Lionel Hollins, Portland

1976-77
Adrian Dantley, Buffalo
Scott May, Chicago
Mitch Kupchak, Washington
John Lucas, Houston
Ron Lee, Phoenix

1977-78
Walter Davis, Phoenix
Marques Johnson, Milwaukee
Jack Sikma, Seattle
Bernard King, New Jersey
Norm Nixon, Los Angeles

1978-79
Phil Ford, Kansas City
Mychal Thompson, Portland
Ron Brewer, Portland
Reggie Theus, Chicago
Terry Tyler, Detroit

1979-80
Larry Bird, Boston
Earvin Johnson, Los Angeles
Bill Cartwright, New York
Calvin Natt, N.J.-Portland
David Greenwood, Chicago

1980-81
Joe Barry Carroll, Golden State
Larry Smith, Golden State
Kevin McHale, Boston
Darrell Griffith, Utah
Kelvin Ransey, Portland

NBA ALL-STAR GAME

It was 1951 and virtually nobody except the late Walter Brown, owner of the Boston Celtics, thought it had a chance.

"It was at the time of the college scandals and basketball had a black eye," Brown would recall later. "Things were going so bad that even my wife wanted me to get out of the business. But I thought the All-Star Game would be a good thing. The league didn't want it because they felt it would be a financial flop. But I told them I would take care of all the expenses and all the losses if there were any.

"Even up until the last week, the game was in doubt. A few days before the game, Maurice Podoloff, the commissioner, called me on the phone and asked me to call it off. He said that everyone he had talked to said it would be a flop, and that the league would look bad."

The indomitable Brown refused to back down. The game went on, and the rest is history.

1951 First Game

A crowd of 10,094 flocked to Boston Garden to watch 20 of the NBA's finest compete in the first All-Star Game. The East had little trouble taking it, 111-94, as Easy Ed Macauley of the Boston Celtics won the MVP trophy. Macauley not only scored a game high of 20 points, he held George Mikan of the Minneapolis Lakers to just four field goals.

Top man for the West was Alex Groza of the Indianapolis Olympians with 17 points and 13 rebounds. Joe Fulks of the Philadelphia Warriors contributed 19 points for the winners.

MARCH 2, 1951, AT BOSTON

East Coach—Joe Lapchick   **West Coach**—John Kundla

EAST ALL-STARS (111)

Player and Team	FGA	FGM	FTA	FTM	Reb.	Ast.	PF	Pts.
Joe Fulks, Philadelphia	15	6	9	7	7	3	5	19
Paul Arizin, Philadelphia	12	7	2	1	7	0	2	15
Dolph Schayes, Syracuse	10	7	2	1	14	3	1	15
Vince Boryla, New York	6	4	1	1	2	2	3	9
Ed Macauley, Boston	12	7	7	6	6	1	3	20
Harry Gallatin, New York	4	2	1	1	5	2	4	5
Bob Cousy, Boston	12	2	5	4	9	8	3	8
Red Rocha, Baltimore	10	2	4	4	2	3	2	8
Dick McGuire, New York	4	3	0	0	5	10	2	6
Andy Phillip, Philadelphia	8	3	0	0	10	8	1	6
Totals	93	43	31	25	67	40	26	111

WEST ALL-STARS (94)

Player and Team	FGA	FGM	FTA	FTM	Reb.	Ast.	PF	Pts.
Alex Groza, Indianapolis	16	8	1	1	13	1	4	17
Dike Eddleman, Tri-Cities	9	2	5	3	0	3	3	7
Jim Pollard, Minneapolis	11	2	0	0	4	5	1	4
Vern Mikkelsen, Minneapolis	11	4	4	3	9	1	3	11
George Mikan, Minneapolis	17	4	6	4	11	3	2	12
Larry Foust, Fort Wayne	6	1	0	0	5	2	3	2
Bob Davies, Rochester	6	4	5	5	5	5	3	13
Frank Brian, Tri-Cities	14	5	5	4	6	3	2	14
Ralph Beard, Indianapolis	8	3	3	0	3	2	1	6
Fred Schaus, Fort Wayne	9	2	4	4	4	2	3	8
Totals	107	35	33	24	60	27	25	94

Score by Periods:	1st	2nd	3rd	4th	Totals
East	31	22	30	28	111
West	22	20	22	30	94

Referees—Pat Kennedy and Charley Eckman. Attendance—10,094.

1952 Second Game

Paul Arizin of the Philadelphia Warriors connected on nine of 13 shots and wound up with 26 points and the MVP award as the East made it two in a row over the West by a score of 108-91.

The game, played again in Boston Garden, was close until the five-minute mark of the fourth quarter when the East went on a scoring spree, outshooting the West, 16-3.

George Mikan of the Minneapolis Lakers was high for the West with 26 points and a game-leading 15 rebounds.

FEBRUARY 11, 1952, AT BOSTON

East Coach—Al Cervi   West Coach—John Kundla

EAST ALL-STARS (108)

Player and Team	Min.	FGA	FGM	FTA	FTM	Reb.	Ast.	PF	Pts.
Paul Arizin, Philadelphia	32	13	9	8	8	6	0	1	26
Joe Fulks, Philadelphia	9	7	3	1	0	5	2	2	6
Red Rocha, Syracuse	28	11	5	2	2	5	2	4	12
Max Zaslofsky, New York	25	7	3	5	5	4	2	0	11
Ed Macauley, Boston	28	7	3	9	9	7	3	2	15
Harry Gallatin, New York	22	5	3	4	1	9	3	3	7
Bob Cousy, Boston	33	14	4	2	1	4	13	3	9
Dick McGuire, New York	18	0	0	3	1	1	4	0	1
Andy Phillip, Philadelphia	30	6	4	3	3	3	6	1	11
Fred Scolari, Baltimore	15	9	5	0	0	0	2	0	10
Dolph Schayes, Syracuse									
Totals	240	79	39	37	30	53	37	16	108

WEST ALL-STARS (91)

Player and Team	Min.	FGA	FGM	FTA	FTM	Reb.	Ast.	PF	Pts.
Vern Mikkelsen, Minneapolis	23	8	5	2	2	10	0	2	12
Dike Eddleman, Milwaukee	26	3	1	0	0	2	2	2	2
Jim Pollard, Minneapolis	29	17	2	0	0	11	5	3	4
Leo Barnhorst, Indianapolis	23	16	7	1	0	2	2	4	14
George Mikan, Minneapolis	29	19	9	9	8	15	1	5	26
Arnie Risen, Rochester	19	7	3	1	0	5	1	3	6
Bobby Davies, Rochester	27	11	4	0	0	0	5	4	8
Paul Walther, Indianapolis	17	4	1	0	0	2	2	1	2
Bobby Wanzer, Rochester	22	8	1	2	2	5	5	2	4
Frank Brian, Fort Wayne	25	10	4	6	5	7	4	2	13
Larry Foust, Fort Wayne									
Totals	240	103	37	21	17	64	27	28	91

Score by Periods:	1st	2nd	3rd	4th	Totals
East	26	23	33	26	108
West	22	22	27	20	91

Referees—Sid Borgia and Stan Stutz. Attendance—10,211.

1953 Third Game

The West finally broke the East's two-year domination of the series by coming up with a 79-75 victory in the third All-Star Game, played in Fort Wayne.

Bob Davies, Rochester's master floorman, put on a dazzling demonstration late in the fourth period, scoring eight points and giving the West a lead it never relinquished.

But MVP honors went to Davies' teammate of the night, Minneapolis' George Mikan, who poured in 22 points and dominated the boards with 16 rebounds. Boston's Ed Macauley led the East with 18 points.

JANUARY 13, 1953, AT FORT WAYNE, IND.

East Coach—Joe Lapchick

West Coach—John Kundla

EAST ALL-STARS (75)

Player and Team	Min.	FGA	FGM	FTA	FTM	Reb.	Ast.	PF	Pts.
Harry Gallatin, New York	19	4	1	2	1	3	2	1	3
Don Barksdale, Boston	11	1	0	3	1	3	2	0	1
Dolph Schayes, Syracuse	26	7	2	4	4	13	3	3	8
Carl Braun, New York	21	4	1	1	1	3	2	2	3
Ed Macauley, Boston	35	12	5	8	8	7	3	2	18
Neil Johnston, Philadelphia	27	13	5	2	1	12	0	2	11
Bob Cousy, Boston	36	11	4	7	7	5	3	1	15
Paul Seymour, Syracuse	14	3	2	2	1	3	2	1	5
Bill Sharman, Boston	26	8	5	1	1	4	0	2	11
Billy Gabor, Syracuse	25	3	0	1	0	5	2	1	0
Totals	240	66	25	31	25	66	19	15	75

Team rebounds—8.

WEST ALL-STARS (79)

Player and Team	Min.	FGA	FGM	FTA	FTM	Reb.	Ast.	PF	Pts.
Mel Hutchins, Milwaukee	30	8	1	1	0	6	5	2	2
Leo Barnhorst, Indianapolis	13	2	0	3	1	3	2	0	1
Vern Mikkelsen, Minneapolis	19	13	3	0	0	6	3	3	6
Larry Foust, Fort Wayne	18	7	5	0	0	6	0	4	10
George Mikan, Minneapolis	40	26	9	4	4	16	2	2	22
Arnie Risen, Rochester	19	7	2	3	1	9	2	3	5
Andy Phillip, Fort Wayne	36	9	4	1	1	6	8	2	9
Bob Davies, Rochester	17	7	3	6	3	3	2	2	9
Bob Wanzer, Rochester	22	7	4	1	1	2	2	1	9
Slater Martin, Minneapolis	26	10	2	1	1	2	1	2	5
Totals	240	97	33	18	11	62	26	23	79

Team rebounds—3.

Score by Periods:	1st	2nd	3rd	4th	Totals
East	20	14	21	20	75
West	20	15	22	22	79

Referees—Sid Borgia and Bud Lowell. Attendance—10,322.

1954 Fourth Game

Overtime, an amazing Bob Cousy performance and an SRO crowd at New York's Madison Square Garden made the fourth All-Star Game a thriller for 16,487 eyewitnesses.

Featuring the ball-handling of Boston's Bob Cousy and the Knicks' Dick McGuire, the East held an 84-82 edge with seconds remaining in the game. Then George Mikan of Minneapolis was fouled. He sank both free throws, sending the game into overtime.

In the extra period Cousy went on a tear, bewildering and bewitching the West as he scored 10 points to lead a 98-93 victory. The losers' Jim Pollard of Minneapolis, the game's high scorer with 23 points, had been named MVP in a vote taken, as is custom, before regulation time had run out. But after Cousy's overtime show, another ballot was taken, and the Boston star became the MVP.

Apart from being the first such overtime contest, this marked the first time that the 24-second clock was used in the All-Star Game.

JANUARY 21, 1954, AT NEW YORK

East Coach—Joe Lapchick

West Coach—John Kundla

EAST ALL-STARS (98)

Player and Team	Min.	FGA	FGM	FTA	FTM	Reb.	Ast.	PF	Pts.
Dolph Schayes, Syracue	24	3	1	6	4	12	1	1	6
Carl Braun, New York	29	8	4	1	1	4	2	3	9
Ed Macauley, Boston	25	11	4	6	5	1	3	2	13
Harry Gallatin, New York	28	2	0	6	5	18	3	0	5
Ray Felix, Baltimore	32	8	4	5	5	11	1	4	13
Neil Johnston, Philadelphia	20	9	2	4	2	7	2	1	6
Bob Cousy, Boston	34	15	6	8	8	11	4	1	20
Bill Sharman, Boston	30	9	6	4	2	2	3	3	14
Dick McGuire, New York	24	5	2	0	0	4	2	1	4
Paul Seymour, Syracuse	19	6	2	4	4	1	3	2	8
Totals	265	76	31	44	36	78	24	20	98

Team rebounds—7.

WEST ALL-STARS (93)

Player and Team	Min.	FGA	FGM	FTA	FTM	Reb.	Ast.	PF	Pts.
Mel Hutchins, Milwaukee	31	8	1	2	1	4	2	5	3
Don Sunderlage, Milwaukee	6	2	1	2	2	0	1	1	4
Jim Pollard, Minneapolis	41	22	10	5	3	3	3	3	23
Larry Foust, Fort Wayne	27	9	1	1	1	15	0	1	3
George Mikan, Minneapolis	31	18	6	8	6	9	1	5	18
Arnie Risen, Rochester	20	10	4	1	0	7	0	5	8
Bobby Davies, Rochester	31	16	8	3	2	5	5	4	18
Slater Martin, Minneapolis	23	5	1	0	0	0	3	3	2
Bobby Wanzer, Rochester	36	13	5	3	2	2	6	6	12
Andy Phillip, Fort Wayne	19	4	1	1	0	3	3	1	2
Totals	265	97	38	25	17	53	24	24	93

Team rebounds—5.

Score by periods:	1st	2nd	3rd	4th	5th	Totals
East	28	20	17	19	14	98
West	25	19	23	17	9	93

Referees—Mendy Rudolph and Sid Borgia. Attendance—16,487.

1955 Fifth Game

Boston's Bill Sharman uncorked a scoring rampage to give the East a 100-91 victory over the West at Madison Square Garden.

Sharman scored 10 points in the fourth quarter and 15 overall to win the game for the East and the MVP award for himself. Before Sharman went on his spree, the lead had exchanged hands no less than 20 times.

Bob Cousy, Sharman's Boston backcourt mate, was high scorer for the East with 20 points. Minneapolis' Jim Pollard topped the West with 17 points.

JANUARY 18, 1955, AT NEW YORK

East Coach—Al Cervi

West Coach—Charley Eckman

EAST ALL-STARS (100)

Player and Team	Min.	FGA	FGM	FTA	FTM	Reb.	Ast.	PF	Pts.
Harry Gallatin, New York	36	7	4	5	5	14	3	2	13
Paul Arizin, Philadelphia	23	9	4	2	1	2	2	5	9
Dolph Schayes, Syracuse	29	12	6	3	3	13	1	4	15
Carl Braun, New York	16	6	4	0	0	2	2	2	8
Ed Macauley, Boston	27	5	1	5	4	4	2	1	6
Neil Johnston, Philadelphia	15	7	1	1	1	6	1	0	3
Bob Cousy, Boston	35	14	7	7	6	9	5	1	20
Dick McGuire, New York	25	2	1	2	1	3	6	1	3
Paul Seymour, Syracuse	16	8	3	2	2	3	1	1	8
Bill Sharman, Boston	18	10	5	5	5	4	2	4	15
Totals	240	80	36	32	28	67	25	21	100

WEST ALL-STARS (91)

Player and Team	Min.	FGA	FGM	FTA	FTM	Reb.	Ast.	PF	Pts.
Jim Pollard, Minneapolis	27	19	7	3	3	4	0	1	17
Bob Pettit, Milwaukee	27	14	3	4	2	9	2	0	8
George Yardley, Fort Wayne	22	11	4	4	3	4	2	2	11
Jack Coleman, Rochester	19	8	2	3	2	6	1	0	6
Larry Foust, Fort Wayne	24	10	3	1	1	7	1	1	7
Vern Mikkelsen, Minneapolis	25	15	7	3	2	9	1	5	16
Andy Phillip, Fort Wayne	28	4	3	0	0	3	6	3	6
Slater Martin, Minneapolis	23	5	2	2	1	2	5	3	5
Bobby Wanzer, Rochester	26	7	3	2	2	3	2	4	8
Frank Selvy, Milwaukee	19	7	2	4	3	3	1	4	7
Totals	240	100	36	26	19	50	21	23	91

Score by Periods:	1st	2nd	3rd	4th	Totals
East	21	28	21	30	100
West	21	29	21	20	91

Referees—Phil Fox and Joe Serafin. Attendance—15,564.

1956 Sixth Game

The West, led by Bob Pettit of the St. Louis Hawks, breezed to a 108-94 victory over the East, in the sixth annual meeting of the stars.

Marking the second victory for the West, Pettit chalked up a game-high 20 points and 24 rebounds. Vern Mikkelsen of Minneapolis scored 16 points to help the winning cause.

For the East, Philadelphia's Neil Johnston led the way with 17 points and New York's Harry Gallatin added 16.

JANUARY 24, 1956, AT ROCHESTER

East Coach—George Senesky   **West Coach**—Charley Eckman

WEST ALL-STARS (108)

Player and Team	Min.	FGA	FGM	FTA	FTM	Reb.	Ast.	PF	Pts.
Mel Hutchins, Fort Wayne	27	11	5	2	1	4	0	0	11
Bob Pettit, St. Louis	31	17	7	7	6	24	7	4	20
George Yardley, Fort Wayne	19	7	3	3	2	6	1	1	8
Maurice Stokes, Rochester	20	11	4	5	2	16	2	5	10
Larry Foust, Fort Wayne	20	9	3	4	3	4	0	1	9
Vern Mikkelsen, Minneapolis	22	13	5	7	6	9	2	4	16
Clyde Lovellette, Minneapolis	20	10	3	3	1	10	0	4	7
Slater Martin, Minneapolis	29	7	3	3	3	1	7	5	9
Bob Harrison, St. Louis	25	7	2	2	1	0	1	4	5
Bobby Wanzer, Rochester	25	8	4	6	5	5	2	4	13
Totals	240	100	39	42	30	79	22	32	108

EAST ALL-STARS (94)

Player and Team	Min.	FGA	FGM	FTA	FTM	Reb.	Ast.	PF	Pts.
Paul Arizin, Philadelphia	28	13	5	5	3	7	1	6	13
John Kerr, Syracuse	16	4	2	1	0	8	0	2	4
Harry Gallatin, New York	30	12	5	7	6	5	2	4	16
Ed Macauley, Boston	20	9	1	4	2	2	3	3	4
Dolph Schayes, Syracuse	25	8	4	10	6	4	2	2	14
Neil Johnston, Philadelphia	25	9	5	11	7	10	1	3	17
Bob Cousy, Boston	24	8	2	4	3	7	2	6	7
Dick McGuire, New York	29	9	2	5	2	0	3	1	6
Jack George, Philadelphia	21	7	2	2	2	3	2	1	6
Bill Sharman, Boston	24	8	2	4	3	7	2	6	7
Totals	240	87	30	53	34	53	18	34	94

Score by Periods:	1st	2nd	3rd	4th	Totals
West	17	26	41	24	108
East	24	16	24	30	94

Referees—Arnie Heft and Lou Eisenstein. Attendance—8,517.

1957 Seventh Game

They played the regulation 48 minutes of the All-Star Game at Boston Garden, but for all intents and purposes it was won in the waning moments of the first half.

With just seconds remaining before half time, the West led, 43-39. Bill Sharman threw a length-of-the-floor pass to fellow Celtic Bob Cousy from under his own basket. The pass was too high for Cousy to pull down. Instead, it landed in the basket for the longest field goal, a 70-footer, in All-Star Game history. The incredible shot took the wind out of the West, and the East went on to win, 109-97.

Cousy's brilliant playmaking and 10 points earned him his second MVP award. Bob Pettit led the West with 21 points.

JANUARY 15, 1957, AT BOSTON

East Coach—Red Auerbach

West Coach—Bobby Wanzer

EAST ALL-STARS (109)

Player and Team	Min.	FGA	FGM	FTA	FTM	Reb.	Ast.	PF	Pts.
Paul Arizin, Philadelphia	26	13	6	2	1	5	0	2	13
Harry Gallatin, New York	24	7	4	2	0	11	1	3	8
Tom Heinsohn, Boston	23	17	5	2	2	7	0	3	12
Dolph Schayes, Syracuse	25	6	4	1	1	10	1	1	9
Neil Johnston, Philadelphia	23	12	8	3	3	9	1	2	19
Nat Clifton, New York	23	11	4	0	0	11	3	1	8
Bob Cousy, Boston	28	14	4	2	2	5	7	0	10
Jack George, Philadelphia	21	6	3	2	2	1	5	1	8
Bill Sharman, Boston	23	17	5	2	2	6	5	1	12
Carl Braun, New York	24	9	4	2	2	3	2	2	10
Totals	240	112	47	18	15	70	25	16	109

Teams rebounds—2.

WEST ALL-STARS (97)

Player and Team	Min.	FGA	FGM	FTA	FTM	Reb.	Ast.	PF	Pts.
George Yardley, Fort Wayne	25	10	4	1	1	9	0	2	9
Ed Macauley, St. Louis	19	6	3	2	1	5	3	0	7
Bob Pettit, St. Louis	31	18	8	6	5	11	2	2	21
Jack Twyman, Rochester	17	8	1	3	1	0	1	1	3
Mel Hutchins, Fort Wayne	26	12	4	3	2	7	0	0	10
Vern Mikkelsen, Minneapolis	21	10	3	4	0	9	1	3	6
Slater Martin, St. Louis	31	11	4	0	0	2	3	1	8
Maurice Stokes, Rochester	31	19	8	3	3	12	7	1	19
Richie Regan, Rochester	21	7	2	0	0	4	1	0	4
Dick Garmaker, Minneapolis	18	10	5	0	0	7	1	2	10
Totals	240	111	42	22	13	70	19	12	97

Team rebounds—4.

Score by Periods:	1st	2nd	3rd	4th	Totals
East	18	23	33	35	109
West	26	17	23	31	97

Referees—Mendy Rudolph and Sid Borgia. Attendance—11,178.

1958 Eighth Game

Bob Pettit's 28 points and 26 rebounds were not enough to keep the West from falling at the hands of the East, 130-118, at the Arena in St. Louis. However, it was enough to win him the game's MVP award, the first member of a losing team to do so in the eight-year history of the event.

Leading the East were Philadelphia's Paul Arizin with 24 points and Boston's Bob Cousy with 20. Arizin established an All-Star Game record by hitting 11 field goals.

For Pettit, of the St. Louis Hawks, it was the second time he had been named MVP.

JANUARY 21, 1958, AT ST. LOUIS

East Coach—Red Auerbach   **West Coach**—Alex Hannum

EAST ALL-STARS (130)

Player and Team	Min.	FGA	FGM	FTA	FTM	Reb.	Ast.	PF	Pts.
Dolph Schayes, Syracuse	39	15	6	6	6	9	2	4	18
Ken Sears, New York	14	8	4	5	4	1	0	1	12
Willie Naulls, New York	15	9	3	2	2	3	0	0	8
Paul Arizin, Philadelphia	29	17	11	2	2	8	2	3	24
Bill Russell, Boston	26	12	5	3	1	11	2	5	11
Neil Johnston, Philadelphia	22	13	6	2	2	8	1	5	14
Bob Cousy, Boston	31	20	8	6	4	5	10	0	20
Richie Guerin, New York	22	10	2	4	3	8	7	3	7
Bill Sharman, Boston	25	19	6	3	3	4	3	2	15
Larry Costello, Syracuse	17	6	0	1	1	1	4	2	1
Totals	240	129	51	34	28	67	31	25	130

Team rebounds—9.

WEST ALL-STARS (118)

Player and Team	Min.	FGA	FGM	FTA	FTM	Reb.	Ast.	PF	Pts.
George Yardley, Detroit	32	15	8	5	3	9	1	1	19
Maurice Stokes, Cincinnati	36	13	3	7	4	14	3	2	10
Jack Twyman, Cincinnati	25	13	8	2	2	3	0	3	18
Bob Pettit, St. Louis	38	21	10	10	8	26	1	1	28
Larry Foust, Minneapolis	13	4	1	8	8	3	0	3	10
Slater Martin, St. Louis	26	9	2	4	2	2	8	3	6
Gene Shue, Detroit	25	11	8	3	2	2	0	3	18
Dick Garmaker, Minneapolis	13	9	1	3	3	6	1	4	5
Dick McGuire, Detroit	31	4	2	0	0	7	10	4	4
Totals	240	99	43	42	32	79	24	24	118

Team rebounds—7.

Score by Periods:	1st	2nd	3rd	4th	Totals
East	30	31	31	38	130
West	31	35	25	27	118

Referees—Jim Duffy and Arnie Heft. Attendance—12.854.

1959 Ninth Game

St. Louis' veteran Bob Pettit and Minneapolis' rookie Elgin Baylor became the first players ever to tie for MVP honors as they led the West to a 124-108 triumph over the East at Detroit's Cobo Arena.

Pettit outscored Baylor by one, 25-24, and out-rebounded the rookie forward, 16-11, but the two divided the MVP ballots equally. Cincinnati's Jack Twyman also contributed 18 points as the West won for the third time in nine games.

Paul Arizin of Philadelphia led the East with 16 points, one more than Ken Sears of the New York Knicks.

JANUARY 23, 1959, AT DETROIT

East Coach—Red Auerbach   **West Coach**—Ed Macauley

WEST ALL-STARS (124)

Player and Team	Min.	FGA	FGM	FTA	FTM	Reb.	Ast.	PF	Pts.
Cliff Hagan, St. Louis	22	12	6	3	3	8	3	5	15
George Yardley, Detroit	17	8	2	2	2	4	0	3	6
Elgin Baylor, Minneapolis	32	20	10	5	4	11	1	3	24
Jack Twyman, Cincinnati	23	12	8	4	2	8	3	4	18
Bob Pettit, St. Louis	34	21	8	9	9	16	5	1	25
Larry Foust, Minneapolis	16	9	3	2	2	9	0	3	8
Gene Shue, Detroit	31	11	6	2	1	4	3	4	13
Dick McGuire, Detroit	24	7	2	2	1	3	3	2	5
Slater Martin, St. Louis	22	6	2	2	1	6	1	2	5
Dick Garmaker, Minneapolis	19	6	2	1	1	2	1	2	5
Totals	240	112	49	32	26	80	20	29	124

Team rebounds—9.

EAST ALL-STARS (108)

Player and Team	Min.	FGA	FGM	FTA	FTM	Reb.	Ast.	PF	Pts.
Ken Sears, New York	26	9	5	5	5	8	1	4	15
Dolph Schayes, Syracuse	22	11	3	8	7	13	1	6	13
Paul Arizin, Philadelphia	30	15	4	9	8	8	0	2	16
Woody Sauldsberry, Philadelphia	18	11	5	4	4	2	3	2	14
Bill Russell, Boston	27	10	3	1	1	9	1	4	7
John Kerr, Syracuse	21	14	3	2	1	9	2	0	7
Bill Sharman, Boston	24	12	3	6	5	2	0	1	11
Larry Costello, Syracuse	18	8	3	1	1	3	3	1	7
Bob Cousy, Boston	32	8	4	6	5	5	4	0	13
Richie Guerin, New York	22	7	1	5	3	3	3	1	5
Totals	240	108	34	47	40	70	18	21	108

Team rebounds—8.

Score by Periods:	1st	2nd	3rd	4th	Totals
West	27	34	30	33	124
East	31	21	32	24	108

Referees—Jim Duffy and Mendy Rudolph. Attendance—10,541.

1960 Tenth Game

Philadelphia's Wilt Chamberlain celebrated his rookie season in the NBA by scoring 23 points and pulling down 23 rebounds to lead the East to a 125-115 victory over the West in his home arena, Convention Hall.

Chamberlain was the East's high scorer and was voted MVP. Dolph Schayes of Syracuse was the second-leading scorer for the East with 19 points.

The West's and the game's top scorer was Jack Twyman of Cincinnati with 27 points. Minneapolis' Elgin Baylor added 25.

JANUARY 22, 1960, AT PHILADELPHIA

East Coach—Red Auerbach   **West Coach**—Ed Macauley

EAST ALL-STARS (125)

Player and Team	Min.	FGA	FGM	FTA	FTM	Reb.	Ast.	PF	Pts.
Dolph Schayes, Syracuse	27	19	8	3	3	10	0	3	19
George Yardley, Syracuse	16	9	5	2	1	3	0	4	11
Bill Russell, Boston	27	7	3	2	0	8	3	1	6
Tom Gola, Philadelphia	20	13	5	3	2	4	2	3	12
Wilt Chamberlain, Philadelphia	30	20	9	7	5	25	2	1	23
Willie Naulls, New York	26	19	5	4	3	10	0	1	13
Bob Cousy, Boston	26	7	1	0	0	5	8	2	2
Bill Sharman, Boston	26	21	8	1	1	6	2	1	17
Richie Guerin, New York	22	11	5	2	2	4	4	4	12
Larry Costello, Syracuse	20	9	5	0	0	4	2	1	10
Totals	240	135	54	24	17	79	23	21	125

Team rebounds—7.

WEST ALL-STARS (115)

Player and Team	Min.	FGA	FGM	FTA	FTM	Reb.	Ast.	PF	Pts.
Bob Pettit, St. Louis	28	15	4	6	3	14	2	2	11
Cliff Hagan, St. Louis	21	9	1	0	0	3	2	1	1
Jack Twyman, Cincinnati	28	17	11	8	5	5	1	4	27
Chuck Noble, Detroit	11	5	0	0	0	1	3	1	0
Walter Dukes, Detroit	26	10	2	1	0	15	1	3	4
Clyde Lovellette, St. Louis	18	11	6	0	0	8	1	1	12
Gene Shue, Detroit	34	13	6	2	1	6	6	0	13
Rod Hundley, Minneapolis	23	12	5	0	0	3	2	2	10
Elgin Baylor, Minneapolis	28	18	10	7	5	13	3	4	25
Dick Garmaker, Minneapolis	23	11	5	2	1	4	3	1	11
Totals	240	121	50	26	15	72	24	19	115

Team rebounds—12.

Score by Periods:	1st	2nd	3rd	4th	Totals
East	25	33	33	34	125
West	26	25	30	34	115

Referees—Arnie Heft and Sid Borgia. Attendance—10,421.

1961 Eleventh Game

Rookie sensation Oscar Robertson of Cincinnati upstaged the veterans and led the West to an overwhelming 153-131 triumph over the East in Syracuse.

Robertson had 23 points and 14 assists on his way to the game's MVP award. The 14 assists broke Bob Cousy's old mark of 13. St. Louis' Bob Pettit set a then single-game high of 29 points as the West had the most torrid first quarter in the classic's history, running up a 49-19 lead in the first twelve minutes.

Boston's Bill Russell led the East with 24 points and Syracuse's Dolph Schayes posted 21.

JANUARY 17, 1961, AT SYRACUSE

East Coach—Red Auerbach   **West Coach**—Paul Seymour

EAST ALL-STARS (131)

Player and Team	Pos.	Min.	FGA	FGA	FTA	FTM	Reb.	Ast.	PF	Pts.
Tom Heinsohn, Boston	F	19	16	2	0	0	6	1	4	4
Paul Arizin, Philadelphia	F	17	12	6	6	5	2	1	4	17
Dolph Schayes, Syracuse	F	27	15	7	7	7	6	3	4	21
Willie Naulls, New York	F	16	6	4	1	0	6	2	2	8
Wilt Chamberlain, Philadelphia	C	38	8	2	15	8	18	5	1	12
Bill Russell, Boston	C	28	15	9	8	6	11	1	2	24
Bob Cousy, Boston	G	33	11	2	0	0	3	8	6	4
Larry Costello, Syracuse	G	5	2	1	0	0	0	0	2	2
Richie Guerin, New York	G	15	8	3	6	5	0	2	2	11
Tom Gola, Philadelphia	G	25	13	6	4	2	5	3	2	14
Hal Greer, Syracuse	G	18	11	7	0	0	6	2	2	14
Totals		204	117	49	47	33	78	28	30	131

Team rebounds—15.

WEST ALL-STARS (153)

Player and Team	Pos.	Min.	FGA	FGM	FTA	FTM	Reb.	Ast.	PF	Pts.
Elgin Baylor, Los Angeles	F	27	11	3	10	9	10	4	5	15
Bailey Howell, Detroit	F	16	10	5	4	3	3	3	4	13
Bob Pettit, St. Louis	F	32	22	13	7	3	9	0	2	29
Cliff Hagan, St. Louis	F	13	2	0	2	2	2	0	1	2
Clyde Lovellette, St. Louis	C	31	19	10	1	1	10	3	4	21
Wayne Embry, Cincinnati	C	8	4	2	0	0	3	0	0	4
Walt Dukes, Detroit	C	17	6	3	2	2	4	1	4	8
Gene Shue, Detroit	G	23	10	6	4	3	3	6	1	15
Oscar Robertson, Cincinnati	G	34	13	8	9	7	9	14	5	23
Jerry West, Los Angeles	G	25	8	2	6	5	2	4	3	9
Rod Hundley, Los Angeles	G	14	10	6	2	2	0	2	1	14
Totals		240	115	58	47	37	71	37	30	153

Team rebounds—16.

Score by Periods:	1st	2nd	3rd	4th	Totals
East	19	43	35	34	131
West	47	37	31	38	153

Referees—Norm Drucker and Richie Powers. Attendance—8,016.

1962 Twelfth Game

For the second year in a row, the West overpowered the East by means of awesome shooting in a 150-130 victory at St. Louis.

Los Angeles' Elgin Baylor led the winners' attack with 32 points, but it was St. Louis' Bob Pettit, with 25 points and 27 rebounds, who took the MVP award, his fourth. Cincinnati's Oscar Robertson and Chicago's Walt Bellamy also had 25 points apiece.

But the game's high scorer was Philadelphia's Wilt Chamberlain, who set an All-Star Game scoring record of 42 points.

JANUARY 16, 1962, AT ST. LOUIS

East Coach—Red Auerbach   **West Coach**—Fred Schaus

WEST ALL-STARS (150)

Player and Team	Pos.	Min.	FGA	FGM	FTA	FTM	Reb.	Ast.	PF	Pts.
Elgin Baylor, Los Angeles	F	37	23	10	14	12	9	4	2	32
Cliff Hagan, St. Louis		9	3	1	0	0	2	1	1	2
Bob Pettit, St. Louis	F	37	20	10	5	5	27	2	5	25
Bailey Howell, Detroit		8	2	1	0	0	0	1	1	2
Jack Twyman, Cincinnati		8	6	4	3	3	1	2	0	11
Walt Bellamy, Chicago	C	29	18	10	8	3	17	1	6	23
Wayne Embry, Cincinnati		16	6	2	0	0	4	1	4	4
Oscar Robertson, Cincinnati	G	37	20	9	14	8	7	13	3	26
Frank Selvy, Los Angeles		11	3	0	0	0	4	1	1	0
Jerry West, Los Angeles	G	31	14	7	6	4	3	1	2	18
Gene Shue, Detroit		17	6	3	1	1	5	4	3	7
Totals		240	121	57	51	36	95	31	28	150

Team rebounds—16.

EAST ALL-STARS (130)

Player and Team	Pos.	Min.	FGA	FGM	FTA	FTM	Reb.	Ast.	PF	Pts.
Dolph Schayes, Syracuse	F	4	0	0	0	0	1	0	3	0
Paul Arizin, Philadelphia		21	12	2	0	0	2	0	4	4
Tom Heinsohn, Boston	F	13	11	4	2	2	2	1	4	10
John Green, New York		21	4	2	3	3	2	0	1	7
Willie Naulls, New York		21	16	5	1	1	7	0	5	11
Wilt Chamberlain, Philadelphia	C	37	23	17	16	8	24	1	4	42
Bill Russell, Boston		27	12	5	3	2	12	2	2	12
Bob Cousy, Boston	G	31	13	4	4	3	6	8	2	11
Hal Greer, Syracuse		24	14	3	7	2	10	9	3	8
Richie Guerin, New York	G	27	17	10	6	3	3	1	6	23
Sam Jones, Boston		14	8	1	1	0	1	0	1	2
Totals		240	130	53	43	24	80	22	35	130

Team rebounds—10.

Score by Periods:	1st	2nd	3rd	4th	Totals
West	35	29	41	45	150
East	32	28	34	36	130

Referees—Sid Borgia and Willie Smith. Attendance—15,112.

1963 Thirteenth Game

Franchise shifts put Wilt Chamberlain in San Francisco on the West team and set up the initial head-to-head All-Star Game confrontation between Wilt and Bill Russell of the Boston Celtics.

When the buzzer sounded in Los Angeles, the East had taken the West, 115-108, and Russell had won the battle of the boards 24-19. As a final touch, Russell, who scored two points more than Chamberlain, 19-17, was named the game's MVP. His 10 rebounds in the first quarter set an All-Star Game record.

Oscar Robertson's 21 points was tops for the East. The West's Bob Pettit led all scorers with 25 points.

JANUARY 16, 1963, AT LOS ANGELES

East Coach—Red Auerbach   West Coach—Fred Schaus

EAST ALL-STARS (115)

Player and Team	Pos.	Min.	FGA	FGM	FTA	FTM	Reb.	Ast.	PF	Pts.
Jack Twyman, Cincinnati	F	16	12	6	0	0	4	1	2	12
Lee Shaffer, Syracuse		19	13	6	0	0	1	1	3	12
Tom Heinsohn, Boston	F	21	11	6	4	3	2	1	4	15
John Green, New York		27	8	6	1	1	5	0	1	13
Bill Russell, Boston	C	37	14	8	4	3	24	5	3	19
John Kerr, Syracuse		11	4	0	2	2	2	1	3	2
Oscar Robertson, Cincinnati	G	37	15	9	4	3	3	6	5	21
Tom Gola, New York		18	3	1	0	0	2	1	3	2
Bob Cousy, Boston	G	25	11	4	0	0	4	6	2	8
Hal Greer, Syracuse		15	7	3	0	0	3	2	4	6
Richie Guerin, New York		14	3	2	3	1	1	1	2	5
Totals		240	101	51	18	13	51	25	32	115

WEST ALL-STARS (108)

Player and Team	Pos.	Min.	FGA	FGM	FTA	FTM	Reb.	Ast.	PF	Pts.
Walt Bellamy, Chicago	F	14	4	1	2	0	1	2	3	2
Rudy LaRusso, Los Angeles		11	3	3	0	0	1	2	1	6
Tom Meschery, San Francisco		8	3	1	2	1	1	1	1	3
Bob Pettit, St. Louis	F	32	16	7	12	11	13	0	1	25
Bailey Howell, Detroit		11	3	2	0	0	1	1	2	4
Wilt Chamberlain, San Francisco	C	35	11	7	7	3	19	0	2	17
Jerry West, Los Angeles	G	32	15	5	4	3	7	5	1	13
Don Ohl, Detroit		12	4	1	1	1	0	2	2	3
Len Wilkens, St. Louis		25	7	2	1	0	2	3	0	4
Elgin Baylor, Los Angeles	G	36	15	4	13	9	14	7	0	17
Terry Dischinger, Chicago		7	3	3	1	1	1	0	0	7
Guy Rodgers, San Francisco		17	6	3	2	1	2	4	2	7
Totals		240	90	39	45	30	62	27	15	108

Score by Periods:	1st	2nd	3rd	4th	Totals
East	32	24	24	35	115
West	25	25	23	35	108

Referees—Sid Borgia and Earl Strom. Attendance—14,838.

1964 Fourteenth Game

The All-Star Game returned to Boston, its birthplace in 1951, and was threatened by a possible players' strike until close to game time. But they played it, and the winners' total was the same as it was 13 years ago as the East topped the West, 111-107.

Cincinnati's Oscar Robertson, who scored 26 points and was named MVP for the second time in four years, and Boston's Bill Russell, who produced 13 points and 21 rebounds, were an unbeatable combination.

St. Louis' Bob Pettit and San Francisco's Wilt Chamberlain tied for West scoring honors with 19 points in a game that gave the East a 9-5 margin in the series.

JANUARY 14, 1964, AT BOSTON

East Coach—Red Auerbach   **West Coach**—Fred Schaus

EAST ALL-STARS (111)

Player and Team	Pos.	Min.	FGA	FGM	FTA	FTM	Reb.	Ast.	PF	Pts.
Jerry Lucas, Cincinnati	F	36	6	3	6	5	8	0	5	11
Len Chappell, New York		12	5	1	2	2	1	2	2	4
Tom Heinsohn, Boston	F	21	12	5	0	0	3	0	5	10
Tom Gola, New York		7	0	0	2	1	0	1	2	1
Bill Russell, Boston	C	42	13	6	2	1	21	2	4	13
Wayne Embry, Cincinnati		21	14	6	1	1	7	1	1	13
Oscar Robertson, Cincinnati	G	42	23	10	10	6	14	8	4	26
Chet Walker, Philadelphia		12	5	2	0	0	0	0	1	4
Hal Greer, Philadelphia	G	20	10	5	4	3	3	4	1	13
Sam Jones, Boston		27	20	8	0	0	4	3	2	16
Totals		240	108	46	27	19	77	21	27	111

Team rebounds—16.

WEST ALL-STARS (107)

Player and Team	Pos.	Min.	FGA	FGM	FTA	FTM	Reb.	Ast.	PF	Pts.
Bob Pettit, St. Louis	F	36	15	6	9	7	17	2	3	19
Terry Dischinger, Baltimore		13	4	2	3	3	2	1	1	7
Elgin Baylor, Los Angeles	F	29	15	5	11	5	8	5	1	15
Bailey Howell, Detroit		6	3	1	0	0	2	0	0	2
Walt Bellamy, Baltimore	C	23	11	4	5	3	7	0	3	11
Wilt Chamberlain, San Francisco		37	14	4	14	11	20	1	2	19
Jerry West, Los Angeles	G	42	20	8	1	1	4	5	3	17
Don Ohl, Detroit		18	9	3	2	2	2	0	2	8
Guy Rodgers, San Francisco	G	22	6	3	0	0	2	2	4	6
Len Wilkens, St. Louis		14	5	1	1	1	0	0	3	3
Totals		240	102	37	46	33	75	16	22	107

Team rebounds—11.

Score by Periods:	1st	2nd	3rd	4th	Totals
East	25	34	27	25	111
West	22	27	28	30	107

Referees—Sid Borgia and Mendy Rudolph. Attendance—13,464.

1965 Fifteenth Game

On the night the San Francisco Warriors shocked the basketball world by trading superstar center Wilt Chamberlain to the Philadelphia 76ers, Jerry Lucas of the Cincinnati Royals scored 25 points and was named the game's MVP as the East nipped the West, 124-123, in St. Louis.

Cincinnati's Oscar Robertson led the East with 28 points. High for the West was Baltimore's Gus Johnson with 25. Chamberlain, playing his third and last All-Star Game as a representative of the western Warriors, scored 20 points and took down a game-high 16 rebounds.

JANUARY 13, 1965, AT ST. LOUIS

East Coach—Red Auerbach   **West Coach**—Alex Hannum

WEST ALL-STARS (123)

Player and Team	Pos.	Min.	FGA	FGM	FTA	FTM	Reb.	Ast.	PF	Pts.
Elgin Baylor, Los Angeles	F	27	13	5	8	8	7	0	4	18
Gus Johnson, Baltimore		25	13	7	13	11	8	2	2	25
Bob Pettit, St. Louis	F	34	14	5	5	3	12	0	4	13
Nate Thurmond, San Francisco		10	2	0	0	0	3	0	1	0
Wilt Chamberlain, San Francisco	C	31	15	9	8	2	16	1	4	20
Walt Bellamy, Baltimore		17	5	4	4	4	5	1	3	12
Jerry West, Los Angeles	G	40	16	8	6	4	5	6	2	20
Don Ohl, Baltimore		12	1	0	2	2	2	1	1	2
Len Wilkens, St. Louis	G	20	6	2	4	4	3	3	3	8
Terry Dischinger, Detroit		24	8	2	2	1	5	1	4	5
Totals		240	93	42	52	39	78	15	28	123

Team rebounds—12.

EAST ALL-STARS (124)

Player and Team	Pos.	Min.	FGA	FGM	FTA	FTM	Reb.	Ast.	PF	Pts.
Jerry Lucas, Cincinnati	F	35	19	12	1	1	10	1	2	25
John Green, New York		17	4	3	3	2	0	0	6	8
Lucious Jackson, Philadelphia	F	15	5	2	2	1	1	1	4	5
Willis Reed, New York		25	11	3	2	1	5	1	2	7
Bill Russell, Boston	C	33	12	7	9	3	13	5	6	17
Wayne Embry, Cincinnati		19	10	5	1	1	4	0	5	11
Oscar Robertson, Cincinnati	G	40	18	8	13	12	6	8	5	28
Hal Greer, Philadelphia		21	11	5	4	3	4	1	2	13
Sam Jones, Boston	G	24	12	2	2	2	5	3	2	6
Larry Costello, Philadelphia		11	7	2	0	0	1	2	2	4
Totals		240	109	49	37	26	57	22	36	124

Team rebounds—8.

Score by Periods:	1st	2nd	3rd	4th	Totals
West	27	34	30	32	123
East	36	39	32	17	124

Referees—Mendy Rudolph and Joe Gushue. Attendance—16,713.

1966 Sixteenth Game

The MVP award in the sixteenth All-Star Game would mean, for the first time, a new car for the winner. Of the 20 players on the two squads, none was a less-heralded candidate to drive off in it than the Cincinnati Royals' guard, Adrian Smith. Yet that is precisely what he did. A late addition to the East team, Smith scored 25 points and generally sparked the 137-94 triumph over the West in Cincinnati.

Wilt Chamberlain, once again a Philadelphian, excelled for the East with 21 points. For the West, top scorer was Detroit's Eddie Miles with 17 points.

JANUARY 11, 1966, AT CINCINNATI

East Coach—Red Auerbach

West Coach—Fred Schaus

EAST ALL-STARS (137)

Player and Team	Pos.	Min.	FGA	FGM	FTA	FTM	Reb.	Ast.	PF	Pts.
Jerry Lucas, Cincinnati	F	23	11	4	2	2	19	0	2	10
Chet Walker, Philadelphia		25	10	3	3	2	6	4	2	8
John Havlicek, Boston	F	25	16	6	6	6	6	1	2	18
Willis Reed, New York		23	11	7	2	2	8	1	3	16
Wilt Chamberlain, Philadelphia	C	25	11	8	9	5	9	3	2	21
Bill Russell, Boston		23	6	1	0	0	10	2	2	2
Sam Jones, Boston	G	22	11	5	2	2	2	5	0	12
Hal Greer, Philadelphia		23	13	4	1	1	5	1	4	9
Oscar Robertson, Cincinnati	G	25	12	6	6	5	10	8	0	17
Adrian Smith, Cincinnati		26	18	9	6	6	8	3	5	24
Totals		240	118	53	37	31	95	28	22	137

Team rebounds—12

WEST ALL-STARS (94)

Player and Team	Pos.	Min.	FGA	FGM	FTA	FTM	Reb.	Ast.	PF	Pts.
Rick Barry, San Francisco	F	17	10	4	4	2	2	2	6	10
Dave DeBusschere, Detroit		22	14	1	2	2	6	1	1	4
Bailey Howell, Baltimore	F	26	11	3	2	1	2	2	4	7
Rudy LaRusso, Los Angeles		22	10	4	7	3	3	2	2	11
Nate Thurmond, San Francisco	C	33	16	3	3	1	16	1	1	7
Zelmo Beaty, St. Louis		24	11	0	13	10	18	1	2	10
Guy Rodgers, San Francisco	G	34	11	3	0	0	7	11	4	8
Eddie Miles, Detroit		28	16	8	5	1	1	0	1	17
Jerry West, Los Angeles	G	11	5	1	2	2	1	0	2	4
Don Ohl, Baltimore		23	16	7	3	2	4	2	2	16
Totals		240	120	35	41	24	78	22	25	94

Team rebounds—18.

Score by Periods:	1st	2nd	3rd	4th	Totals
East	33	30	38	36	137
West	18	18	32	26	94

Referees—Norm Drucker and John Vanak. Attendance—13,653.

1967 Seventeenth Game

The West ended five years of frustration as San Francisco's Rick Barry scored 38 points in 34 minutes to lead a 135-120 victory over the East at the Cow Palace in San Francisco.

Barry, whose performance won him the MVP award, was followed in scoring by Detroit's Dave DeBusschere, 22 points, and Los Angeles' Elgin Baylor, 20.

Cincinnati's Oscar Robertson led the East with 26 points while Philadelphia's Wilt Chamberlain played a game-high 39 minutes, scoring 14 points and pulling down 14 rebounds.

JANUARY 10, 1967, AT SAN FRANCISCO

East Coach—Red Auerbach   **West Coach**—Fred Schaus

EAST ALL-STARS (120)

Player and Team	Pos.	Min.	FGA	FGM	FTA	FTM	Reb.	Ast.	PF	Pts.
Bailey Howell, Boston	F	14	4	1	2	2	2	1	1	4
John Havlicek, Boston		17	14	7	0	0	2	1	1	14
Willis Reed, New York	F	17	6	2	0	0	9	1	0	4
Chet Walker, Philadelphia		22	9	6	4	3	4	2	2	15
Jerry Lucas, Cincinnati		22	5	3	1	1	7	2	3	7
Wilt Chamberlain, Philadelphia	C	39	7	6	5	2	22	4	1	14
Bill Russell, Boston		22	2	1	0	0	5	5	2	2
Hal Greer, Philadelphia	G	31	16	5	8	7	4	1	5	17
Don Ohl, Baltimore		22	13	5	7	7	1	2	3	17
Oscar Robertson, Cincinnati	G	34	20	9	10	8	2	5	4	26
Totals		240	96	45	37	30	64	24	22	120

Team rebounds—6.

WEST ALL-STARS (135)

Player and Team	Pos.	Min.	FGA	FGM	FTA	FTM	Reb.	Ast.	PF	Pts.
Rick Barry, San Francisco	F	34	27	16	8	6	6	3	5	38
Bill Bridges, St. Louis		17	5	4	2	0	3	3	1	8
Elgin Baylor, Los Angeles	F	20	14	8	4	4	5	5	2	20
Dave DeBusschere, Detroit		25	17	11	0	0	6	0	1	22
Nate Thurmond, San Francisco	C	42	16	7	4	2	18	0	1	16
Darrall Imhoff, Los Angeles		6	7	0	0	0	7	1	1	0
Guy Rodgers, Chicago	G	28	4	0	1	1	2	8	3	1
Jerry Sloan, Chicago		22	9	4	0	0	4	4	5	8
Jerry West, Los Angeles	G	30	11	6	4	4	3	6	3	16
Len Wilkens, St. Louis		16	6	2	3	2	2	6	2	6
Totals		240	116	58	26	19	61	36	24	135

Team rebounds—5.

Score by Periods:	1st	2nd	3rd	4th	Totals
East	33	34	28	25	120
West	39	38	27	31	135

Referees—Willie Smith and Earl Strom. Attendance—13,972.

1968 Eighteenth Game

Philadelphia's Hal Greer played only 17 minutes, but it was long enough for the smallest man on the East squad to hit eight field goals without a miss in the All-Star Game. His perfect performance from the field—plus five of seven foul shots for a 21-point harvest—brought Greer the MVP award and led the East to a 144-124 victory at Madison Square Garden.

Boston's John Havlicek also turned in a big effort with 26 points in 22 minutes. All told, it was the East's best offensive output ever.

Los Angeles' Jerry West was the top performer on the losing side with 17 points, six rebounds and six assists. High scorer for the West was the Lakers' Elgin Baylor, 22 points.

JANUARY 23, 1968, AT NEW YORK

East Coach—Alex Hannum   **West Coach**—Bill Sharman

WEST ALL-STARS (124)

Player and Team	Pos.	Min.	FGA	FGM	FTA	FTM	Reb.	Ast.	PF	Pts.
Bob Boozer, Chicago	F	19	5	2	0	0	5	0	0	4
Don Kojis, San Diego		10	5	2	0	0	2	1	0	4
Elgin Baylor, Los Angeles	F	27	13	8	7	6	6	1	5	22
Bill Bridges, St. Louis		21	9	7	4	1	7	1	4	15
Rudy LaRusso, San Francisco		19	8	3	2	0	7	0	0	6
Zelmo Beaty, St. Louis	C	30	11	2	2	2	10	1	4	6
Clyde Lee, San Francisco		18	8	2	4	2	11	2	3	6
Jerry West, Los Angeles	G	32	17	7	4	3	6	6	4	17
Archie Clark, Los Angeles		15	8	5	7	7	0	3	2	17
Len Wilkens, St. Louis	G	22	10	4	8	6	3	3	1	14
Walt Hazzard, Seattle		20	12	4	1	1	3	3	3	9
Jim King, San Francisco		7	4	1	3	2	1	2	3	4
Totals		240	110	47	42	30	68	23	29	124

Team rebounds—7.

EAST ALL-STARS (144)

Player and Team	Pos.	Min.	FGA	FGM	FTA	FTM	Reb.	Ast.	PF	Pts.
Jerry Lucas, Cincinnati	F	21	9	6	4	4	5	4	3	16
Gus Johnson, Baltimore		16	9	3	2	1	6	1	2	7
Willis Reed, New York	F	25	14	7	3	2	8	1	4	16
Dave DeBusschere, Detroit		12	3	0	0	0	4	0	1	0
John Havlicek, Boston		22	15	9	11	8	5	4	0	26
Wilt Chamberlain, Philadelphia	C	25	4	3	4	1	7	6	2	7
Bill Russell, Boston		23	4	2	0	0	9	8	5	4
Dave Bing, Detroit	G	20	7	4	1	1	2	4	3	9
Dick Barnett, New York		22	12	7	2	1	1	0	2	15
Oscar Robertson, Cincinnati	G	22	9	7	7	4	1	5	2	18
Sam Jones, Boston		15	5	2	1	1	2	4	1	5
Hal Greer, Philadelphia		17	8	8	7	5	3	3	2	21
Totals		240	99	58	42	28	62	40	27	144

Team rebounds—9.

Score by Periods:	1st	2nd	3rd	4th	Totals
West	25	34	32	33	124
East	37	27	37	43	144

Referees—Mendy Rudolph and Don Murphy. Attendance—18,422.

1969 Nineteenth Game

Cincinnati's Oscar Robertson, who has played on a losing team only once in his nine years in the All-Star Game, walked off with his third MVP trophy by scoring 24 points and leading the East to a 123-112 victory over the West at the Baltimore Civic Center.

Sharing the spotlight with ''Big O'' was Baltimore's Earl Monroe, who scored 21 points and worked his customary magic.

For the West, Los Angeles' Elgin Baylor was the main man, coming up with 21 points and taking five MVP votes from Robertson.

JANUARY 14, 1969, AT BALTIMORE

East Coach—Gene Shue   **West Coach**—Richie Guerin

EAST ALL-STARS (123)

Player and Team	Pos.	Min.	FGA	FGM	FTA	FTM	Reb.	Ast.	PF	Pts.
John Havlicek, Boston	F	31	14	6	2	2	7	2	2	14
Gus Johnson, Baltimore		18	10	4	8	5	10	0	3	13
Jerry Lucas, Cincinnati	F	17	5	2	5	4	6	1	3	8
Billy Cunningham, Philadelphia		22	10	5	0	0	5	1	3	10
Willis Reed, New York		14	8	5	0	0	4	2	2	10
Bill Russell, Boston	C	28	4	1	2	1	6	3	1	3
Wes Unseld, Baltimore		14	7	5	3	1	8	1	3	11
Oscar Robertson, Cincinnati	G	32	16	8	8	8	6	5	3	24
Dave Bing, Detroit		13	3	1	1	1	0	3	0	3
Earl Monroe, Baltimore	G	27	15	6	12	9	4	4	4	21
Hal Greer, Philadelphia		17	1	0	5	4	3	2	2	4
Jon McGlocklin, Milwaukee		7	2	1	0	0	1	0	0	2
Totals		240	95	44	46	35	60	24	26	123

Team rebounds—6.

WEST ALL-STARS (112)

Player and Team	Pos.	Min.	FGA	FGM	FTA	FTM	Reb.	Ast.	PF	Pts.
Elgin Baylor, Los Angeles	F	32	13	5	12	11	9	5	2	21
Rudy LaRusso, San Francisco		18	6	3	0	0	6	2	3	6
Dick Van Arsdale, Phoenix		10	4	2	0	0	1	0	0	4
Don Kojis, San Diego	F	16	7	2	5	4	5	3	1	8
Lou Hudson, Atlanta		20	13	6	1	1	1	1	0	13
Elvin Hayes, San Diego	C	21	9	4	3	3	5	0	4	11
Wilt Chamberlain, Los Angeles		27	3	2	1	0	12	2	2	4
Len Wilkens, Seattle	G	24	15	3	5	4	7	5	3	10
Jeff Mullins, San Francisco		25	14	7	0	0	4	5	4	14
Jerry Sloan, Chicago	G	18	8	2	1	0	3	0	5	4
Joe Caldwell, Atlanta		23	9	6	1	0	4	3	5	12
Gail Goodrich, Phoenix		6	4	2	2	1	1	1	1	5
Totals		240	105	44	31	24	58	27	30	112

Team rebounds—6.

Score by Periods:	1st	2nd	3rd	4th	Totals
East	35	25	26	37	123
West	19	34	30	29	112

Referees—Joe Gushue and Norm Drucker. Attendance—12,348.

1970 Twentieth Game

New York's Willis Reed and Cincinnati's Oscar Robertson collaborated to bring the East a 142-135 triumph in the twentieth All-Star Game at Philadelphia's Spectrum.

The barrel-chested Knickerbocker center toted up 21 points and 11 rebounds for MVP honors, and the redoubtable Royal, in his tenth All-Star Game, scored 21 points to break Bob Pettit's All-Star Game career record of 224 by six points.

It was a game which saw the East twice dissipate large leads before preserving its fourteenth victory in the series. Biggest contributors to the West were San Diego's Elvin Hayes, with 24 points for game high, and Los Angeles' Jerry West, 22.

JANUARY 20, 1970, AT PHILADELPHIA

East Coach—Red Holzman   **West Coach**—Richie Guerin

EAST ALL-STARS (142)

Player and Team	Pos.	Min.	FGA	FGM	FTA	FTM	Reb.	Ast.	PF	Pts.
Billy Cunningham, Phila.	F	28	13	7	5	5	4	2	3	19
Dave DeBusschere, New York		14	10	5	0	0	7	2	1	10
John Havlicek, Boston	F	29	15	7	3	3	5	7	2	17
Gus Johnson, Baltimore		17	12	5	0	0	7	1	2	10
Tom Van Arsdale, Cincinnati		8	7	2	1	1	0	1	2	5
Willis Reed, New York	C	30	18	9	3	3	11	0	6	21
Lew Alcindor, Milwaukee		18	8	4	2	2	11	4	6	10
Oscar Robertson, Cincinnati	G	29	11	9	4	3	6	4	3	21
Hal Greer, Philadelphia		21	11	7	1	1	4	3	4	15
Walt Frazier, New York	G	24	7	3	2	1	3	4	2	7
Jimmy Walker, Detroit		14	3	0	1	1	1	0	2	1
Flynn Robinson, Milwaukee		8	4	3	0	0	1	2	2	6
Totals		240	119	61	22	20	60	30	35	142

Team rebounds—5.

WEST ALL-STARS (135)

Player and Team	Pos.	Min.	FGA	FGM	FTA	FTM	Reb.	Ast.	PF	Pts.
Elgin Baylor, Los Angeles	F	26	9	2	7	5	7	3	3	9
Bill Bridges, Atlanta		15	2	2	5	1	4	2	1	5
Connie Hawkins, Phoenix	F	19	4	2	6	6	4	2	3	10
Joe Caldwell, Atlanta		19	11	5	4	3	7	1	2	13
Chet Walker, Chicago		17	3	1	2	2	2	1	2	4
Elvin Hayes, San Diego	C	35	21	9	12	6	15	1	1	24
Bob Rule, Seattle		13	6	2	1	1	4	0	2	5
Jerry West, Los Angeles	G	31	12	7	12	8	5	5	3	22
Jeff Mullins, San Francisco		14	6	4	0	0	1	1	2	8
Lou Hudson, Atlanta	G	18	12	5	5	5	1	0	1	15
Dick Van Arsdale, Phoenix		16	8	4	0	0	2	2	0	8
Lenny Wilkens, Seattle		17	7	5	3	2	2	4	1	12
Totals		240	101	48	57	39	54	22	21	135

Team rebounds—12.

Score by Periods:	1st	2nd	3rd	4th	Totals
East	36	35	35	36	142
West	21	38	26	50	135

Referees—Richie Powers and Jack Madden. Attendance—15,244.

1971 Twenty-First Game

There were 48 seconds to play when Lew Alcindor (before he was Kareem Abdul-Jabbar) scored on a five-foot jumper and converted a foul to give the West a 108-107 victory over the East at the San Diego Sports Arena.

MVP honors, however, went to Lenny Wilkens, player-coach of the Seattle SuperSonics, the leading scorer with 21 points on eight of 11 from the floor and a stellar all-around performer. Milwaukee's Alcindor tallied 19 points for the winners and Atlanta's Lou Hudson topped the losers with 14.

JANUARY 12, 1971, AT SAN DIEGO

East Coach—Red Holzman

West Coach—Larry Costello

WEST ALL-STARS (108)

Player and Team	Pos.	Min.	FGA	FGM	FTA	FTM	Reb.	Ast.	PF	Pts.
Lew Alcindor, Milwaukee	C	30	16	8	4	3	14	1	2	19
Dave Bing, Detroit	G	19	7	2	0	0	2	2	1	4
Wilt Chamberlain, Los Angeles		18	1	1	0	0	8	5	0	2
Connie Hawkins, Phoenix	F	1	0	0	0	0	0	0	0	0
Elvin Hayes, San Diego		19	13	4	3	2	4	2	1	10
Bob Love, Chicago		21	12	6	5	4	4	0	2	16
Jerry Lucas, San Francisco	F	29	9	5	2	2	9	4	2	12
Jeff Mullins, San Francisco		3	0	0	0	0	0	0	0	0
Geoff Petrie, Portland		5	3	0	0	0	0	1	0	0
Oscar Robinson, Milwaukee		24	6	2	3	1	2	2	3	5
Dick Van Arsdale, Phoenix		12	4	2	1	0	5	3	1	4
Chet Walker, Chicago		19	9	3	5	4	3	1	1	10
Jerry West, Los Angeles	G	20	4	2	3	1	1	9	1	5
Lenny Wilkens, Seattle		20	11	8	5	5	1	1	1	21
Totals		240	95	43	31	22	53	31	15	108

EAST ALL-STARS (107)

Player and Team	Pos.	Min.	FGA	FGM	FTA	FTM	Reb.	Ast.	PF	Pts.
Billy Cunningham, Phila.	F	19	8	2	2	1	4	3	1	5
Dave DeBusschere, New York		19	7	4	0	0	7	3	3	8
Walt Frazier, New York	G	26	9	3	0	0	6	5	2	6
Johnny Green, Cincinnati		7	3	2	1	0	2	0	1	4
John Havlicek, Boston	F	24	12	6	2	0	3	2	3	12
Lou Hudson, Atlanta		17	13	6	3	2	3	1	3	14
Gus Johnson, Baltimore		23	12	5	2	2	4	2	3	12
John Johnson, Cleveland		2	0	0	0	0	0	1	0	0
Bob Kauffman, Buffalo		4	2	0	0	0	0	0	0	0
Earl Monroe, Baltimore	G	18	9	3	0	0	5	2	3	6
Willis Reed, New York	C	27	16	5	6	4	13	1	3	14
Wes Unseld, Baltimore		21	9	4	0	0	10	2	2	8
Tom Van Arsdale, Cincinnati		11	8	4	2	0	2	1	1	8
Jo Jo White, Boston		22	10	5	0	0	9	2	2	10
Totals		240	118	49	18	9	68	25	27	107

Score by Periods:	1st	2nd	3rd	4th	Totals
West	30	32	20	26	108
East	26	34	23	24	107

Referees—Mendy Rudolph And Ed Rush. Attendance—14,378.

1972 Twenty-Second Game

The Lakers' Jerry West thrilled the hometown fans at the Los Angeles Forum with a last-second 20-foot jump shot on the run to give the West an exciting 112-110 victory over the East.

West's end-of-the-game heroics won him the MVP award, the first time he has achieved that honor. West led his team in scoring with 13 points.

Outstanding for the East was Boston's Dave Cowens, outplaying giants Kareem Abdul-Jabbar and Wilt Chamberlain under the boards and scoring a jump shot that climaxed a rally that tied the game, 110-110, with 11 seconds remaining. Cowens wound up with 14 points, one less than his Celtic teammate, John Havlicek.

JANUARY 18, 1972, AT LOS ANGELES

East Coach—Tom Heinsohn   **West Coach**—Bill Sharman

WEST ALL-STARS (112)

Player and Team	Pos.	Min.	FGA	FGM	FTA	FTM	Reb.	Ast.	PF	Pts.
Kareem Abdul-Jabbar, Milw.	C	19	10	5	2	2	7	2	0	12
Wilt Chamberlain, Los Angeles		24	3	3	8	2	10	3	2	8
Gail Goodrich, Los Angeles	G	14	7	2	0	0	1	2	2	4
Connie Hawkins, Phoenix		14	7	5	4	3	4	0	1	13
Elvin Hayes, Houston		11	6	1	2	2	2	0	2	4
Spencer Haywood, Seattle	F	25	10	4	4	3	7	1	2	11
Bob Lanier, Detroit		5	2	0	3	2	3	0	0	2
Bob Love, Chicago	F	16	11	4	2	0	6	0	1	8
Oscar Robertson, Milwaukee		24	9	3	10	5	3	3	4	11
Cazzie Russell, Golden State		20	13	4	2	2	1	0	1	10
Paul Silas, Phoenix		15	6	0	3	2	9	1	1	2
Jimmy Walker, Detroit		16	9	4	5	2	2	1	1	10
Jerry West, Los Angeles	G	27	9	6	2	1	6	5	2	13
Sidney Wicks, Portland		10	5	2	0	0	2	0	3	4
Totals		240	107	43	47	26	63	18	22	112

EAST ALL-STARS (110)

Player and Team	Pos.	Min.	FGA	FGM	FTA	FTM	Reb.	Ast.	PF	Pts.
Butch Beard, Cleveland		7	4	1	1	1	1	0	0	3
Archie Clark, Baltimore		21	5	2	4	4	1	6	1	8
Dave Cowens, Boston	C	32	12	5	5	4	20	1	4	14
Billy Cunningham, Philadelphia	F	24	13	4	8	6	10	3	4	14
Dave DeBusschere, New York		26	8	4	0	0	11	0	2	8
Walt Frazier, New York	G	25	11	7	2	1	3	5	2	15
John Havlicek, Boston	F	24	13	5	5	5	3	2	2	15
Lou Hudson, Atlanta	G	18	7	2	2	2	3	3	3	6
John Johnson, Cleveland		3	2	0	0	0	1	0	1	0
Bob Kauffman, Buffalo		7	1	1	0	0	1	1	3	2
Jack Marin, Baltimore		15	8	5	1	1	0	1	2	11
Wes Unseld, Baltimore		16	5	1	0	0	7	1	3	2
Tom Van Arsdale, Cincinnati		4	1	0	0	0	1	0	0	0
Jo Jo White, Boston		18	15	6	2	0	4	3	1	12
Totals		240	105	43	30	24	66	26	28	110

Score by periods:	1st	2nd	3rd	4th	Totals
West	27	27	33	25	112
East	33	31	20	26	110

Referees—Darell Garretson and Manny Sokol. Attendance—17,214.

1973 Twenty-Third Game

The West, forced to play without its two biggest guns, Kareem Abdul-Jabbar and Rick Barry, scored the lowest number of points since the addition of the 24-second clock in 1954 as the East prevailed, 104-84, in Chicago.

Boston's Dave Cowens scored 15 points and took down 13 rebounds in winning the MVP award. Elvin Hayes of the Bullets also stood out for the East, scoring 10 points and pulling down 12 rebounds.

Bright spots for the West were Kansas City-Omaha's Nate Archibald, who scored 17 points, and Portland's Sidney Wicks, Barry's replacement, who talled 13 points.

JANUARY 23, 1973, AT CHICAGO

East Coach—Tom Heinsohn   **West Coach**—Bill Sharman

EAST ALL-STARS (104)

Player and Team	Pos.	Min.	FGA	FGM	FTA	FTM	Reb.	Ast.	PF	Pts.
John Block, Philadelphia		5	4	2	0	0	2	0	1	4
Bill Bradley, New York		12	5	2	0	0	1	0	2	4
Dave Cowens, Boston	C	30	15	7	1	1	13	1	2	15
Dave DeBusschere, New York	F	25	8	4	2	1	7	2	1	9
Walt Frazier, New York	G	26	15	5	0	0	6	2	1	10
John Havlicek, Boston	F	22	10	6	5	2	3	5	1	14
Elvin Hayes, Baltimore		16	13	4	2	2	12	0	0	10
Lou Hudson, Atlanta		9	8	2	2	2	2	0	2	6
Bob Kauffman, Buffalo		9	2	1	2	1	1	1	1	3
Pete Maravich, Atlanta	G	22	8	4	0	0	3	5	4	8
Jack Marin, Houston		11	6	2	0	0	4	1	0	4
Wes Unseld, Baltimore		11	4	2	0	0	5	1	0	4
Jo Jo White, Boston		18	7	3	0	0	5	5	0	6
Len Wilkens, Cleveland		24	8	3	2	1	2	1	1	7
Totals		240	113	47	16	10	66	24	16	104

WEST ALL-STARS (84)

Player and Team	Pos.	Min.	FGA	FGM	FTA	FTM	Reb.	Ast.	PF	Pts.
Nate Archibald, K.C.-Omaha	G	27	12	6	5	5	1	5	1	17
Dave Bing, Detroit		19	4	0	2	2	3	0	1	2
Wilt Chamberlain, Los Angeles	C	22	2	1	0	0	7	3	0	2
Bob Dandridge, Milwaukee		11	4	2	0	0	3	0	0	4
Gail Goodrich, Los Angeles		16	7	1	0	0	2	1	2	2
Connie Hawkins, Phoenix		11	5	1	0	0	2	3	1	2
Spencer Haywood, Seattle	F	22	10	5	2	2	10	0	5	12
Bob Lanier, Detroit		12	9	5	0	0	6	0	1	10
Bob Love, Chicago		12	4	2	2	2	3	0	1	6
Charlie Scott, Phoenix		14	5	0	0	0	2	2	1	0
Nate Thurmond, Golden State		14	5	2	0	0	4	1	2	4
Chet Walker, Chicago		16	5	1	2	2	1	0	2	4
Jerry West, Los Angeles	G	20	6	3	0	0	4	3	2	6
Sidney Wicks, Portland	F	24	10	4	5	5	5	1	2	13
Totals		240	88	33	18	18	53	19	21	84

Score by Periods:	1st	2nd	3rd	4th	Totals
East	27	23	26	28	104
West	27	18	20	19	84

Referees—Richie Powers and Jake O'Donnell. Attendance—17,527.

1974 Twenty-Fourth Game

The combination of Bob Lanier and Spencer Haywood enabled the West to put down the East, 134-123, in the Seattle Coliseum before 14,360 spectators, the largest crowd at that time ever to watch a basketball game in the Pacific Northwest.

Detroit's Lanier, edging Seattle's Haywood for MVP honors, cinched the award in the fourth quarter when he scored 12 of his 24 points. Haywood wound up with 23 and was a leading force throughout the game. He was visibly and audibly disappointed that he wasn't named MVP. ''I thought I played up to the capacity to be selected,'' asserted Haywood.

New York's Dave DeBusschere, 16 points, and Atlanta's Pete Maravich, 15, were the losers' leading scorers.

JANUARY 15, 1974, AT SEATTLE

East Coach—Tom Heinsohn   **West Coach**—Larry Costello

EAST ALL-STARS (123)

Player and Team	Pos.	Min.	FGM	FGA	FTM	FTA	Reb.	Ast.	PF	Pts.
John Havlicek, Boston	F	18	5	10	0	2	0	2	2	10
Lou Hudson, Atlanta	F	17	5	8	2	2	3	1	2	12
Dave Cowens, Boston	C	26	5	10	1	3	12	1	3	11
Walt Frazier, New York	G	28	5	12	2	2	2	5	1	12
Pete Maravich, Atlanta	G	22	4	15	7	9	3	4	2	15
Elvin Hayes, Capital		35	5	13	2	3	15	6	4	12
Bob McAdoo, Buffalo		13	3	4	5	8	3	1	4	11
Jo Jo White, Boston		22	6	12	1	3	6	4	1	13
Dave DeBusschere, New York		24	8	14	0	0	3	3	2	16
Phil Chenier, Capital		13	3	6	1	2	2	1	0	7
Rudy Tomjanovich, Houston		17	2	5	0	0	5	0	1	4
Austin Carr, Cleveland		5	0	4	0	0	1	0	1	0
Totals		240	51	113	21	34	55	28	23	123

WEST ALL-STARS (134)

Player and Team	Pos.	Min.	FGM	FGA	FTM	FTA	Reb.	Ast.	PF	Pts.
Rick Barry, Golden State	F	19	3	6	2	2	4	3	3	8
Chet Walker, Chicago	F	14	4	5	4	4	2	1	1	12
Kareem Abdul-Jabbar, Milwaukee	C	23	7	11	0	0	8	6	2	14
Gail Goodrich, Los Angeles	G	26	9	16	0	0	4	6	2	18
Geoff Petrie, Portland	G	26	3	11	2	2	2	4	1	8
Sidney Wicks, Portland		24	5	6	6	10	1	1	4	16
Charlie Scott, Phoenix		19	0	4	2	2	1	4	2	2
Bob Lanier, Detroit		26	11	15	2	2	10	2	1	24
Spencer Haywood, Seattle		33	10	17	3	3	11	5	5	23
Dave Bing, Detroit		16	2	9	1	1	6	2	1	5
Norm Van Lier, Chicago		9	0	0	0	0	1	2	1	0
Nate Thurmond, Golden State		5	2	4	0	1	3	0	0	4
Totals		240	56	104	22	27	53	36	23	134

Score by Periods:	1st	2nd	3rd	4th	Totals
East	29	18	38	38	123
West	39	27	35	33	134

Blocked shots: Haywood 3, Lanier 2, Abdul-Jabbar, Cowens, Hayes, Hudson, McAdoo, Scott, White. Referees—Don Murphy and Bob Raskel. Attendance—14,360.

1975 Twenty-Fifth Game

The New York Knicks' Walt Frazier led all scorers with 30 points and dribbled off with the MVP award as the East topped the West, 108-102, at the Veterans' Memorial Coliseum in Phoenix.

Boston's John Havlicek was the winners' second-leading scorer with 16. For the West, Kansas City-Omaha's Nate Archibald led with 27 points, but it was Golden State's Rick Barry, with 22 points, eight steals and eight assists, who helped keep the losers close.

For his night's work, Frazier collected $500.25, which was 25 cents more than his fellow winning-team members. The extra quarter was the result of a "fun bet" Frazier made on the outcome of the game with the 12-year-old ballboy for the East, who didn't think his team would win.

JANUARY 14, 1975, AT PHOENIX

East Coach—K. C. Jones   **West Coach**—Al Attles

EAST ALL-STARS (108)

Player and Team	Pos.	Min.	FGM	FGA	FTM	FTA	Reb.	Ast.	PF	Pts.
John Havlicek, Boston	F	31	7	12	2	2	6	1	2	16
Elvin Hayes, Washington	F	17	2	6	0	0	5	2	1	4
Bob McAdoo, Buffalo	C	26	4	9	3	3	6	2	4	11
Walt Frazier, New York	G	35	10	17	10	11	5	2	2	30
Earl Monroe, New York	G	25	3	8	3	5	3	2	2	9
Rudy Tomjanovich, Houston		14	0	3	0	0	3	0	3	0
West Unseld, Washington		15	2	3	2	2	6	1	2	6
Phil Chenier, Washington		23	4	8	1	2	2	1	0	9
Dave Cowens, Boston		15	3	7	0	0	6	3	4	6
Steve Mix, Philadelphia		11	2	5	0	0	2	0	2	4
Jo Jo White, Boston		13	1	2	5	6	1	4	1	7
Paul Silas, Boston		15	2	4	2	2	2	2	2	6
Totals		240	40	84	28	33	47	20	25	108

WEST ALL-STARS (102)

Player and Team	Pos.	Min.	FGM	FTM	FTA	Reb.	Ast.	PF	Pts.
Rick Barry, Golden State	F	38	20	0	0	5	8	4	22
Spencer Haywood, Seattle	F	17	9	0	0	3	0	1	2
Kareem Abdul-Jabbar, Milwaukee	C	19	10	1	2	10	3	2	7
Nate Archibald, K.C. Omaha	G	36	15	7	8	2	6	2	27
Gail Goodrich, Los Angeles	G	15	4	0	0	1	4	1	4
Sidney Wicks, Portland		23	19	2	3	9	1	1	16
Bob Lanier, Detroit		12	4	0	0	7	2	3	2
Charlie Scott, Phoenix		16	6	0	0	2	1	3	2
Dave Bing, Detroit		12	2	2	2	0	1	0	2
Bob Dandridge, Milwaukee		18	6	0	0	2	1	3	4
Sam Lacey, K.C.-Omaha		17	6	2	2	7	1	2	6
Jim Price, Milwaukee		17	9	2	2	2	0	4	8
Totals		240	110	16	19	50	28	26	102

Score by Periods:	1st	2nd	3rd	4th	Totals
East	29	22	32	25	108
West	29	17	27	29	102

Blocked Shots: Barry, Abdul-Jabbar, Archibald, Wicks, Lacey.
Referees: Mendy Rudolph and Jerry Loeber. Attendance: 12,885.

1976 Twenty-Sixth Game

All-Star Game veteran Dave Bing, who had been having a tough time in his first season with the Washington Bullets, showed his old form in leading the East to a 123-109 victory over the West at Philadelphia's Spectrum.

Bing scored 16 points, had four assists and was named the game's MVP. Buffalo's Bob McAdoo led the East in scoring with 22. Boston's Dave Cowens chipped in with 16 points and 16 rebounds. Starring for the West were Los Angeles' Kareem Abdul-Jabbar, 22 points and 15 rebounds, and Golden State's Rick Barry, 17 points. The game was played before 17,511, the largest crowd in All-Star Game history.

FEBRUARY 3, 1976, AT PHILADELPHIA

East Coach—Tom Heinsohn   **West Coach**—Al Attles

EAST ALL-STARS (123)

Player and Team	Pos.	Min.	FGM	FGA	FTM	FTA	Reb.	Ast.	PF	Pts.
John Havlicek, Boston	F	21	3	10	3	3	2	2	0	9
Elvin Hayes, Washington	F	31	6	14	0	2	10	1	5	12
Bob McAdoo, Buffalo	C	29	10	14	2	4	7	1	5	22
Walt Frazier, New York	G	19	2	7	4	4	2	3	0	8
Dave Bing, Washington	G	26	7	11	2	2	3	4	1	16
Dave Cowens, Boston		23	6	13	4	5	16	1	3	16
George McGinnis, Philadelphia		19	4	9	2	4	7	2	2	10
Rudy Tomjanovich, Houston		12	1	2	0	0	3	0	2	2
John Drew, Atlanta		9	1	3	0	0	3	0	2	2
Jo Jo White, Boston		16	3	7	0	0	1	1	1	6
Doug Collins, Philadelphia		20	5	10	2	2	6	3	3	12
Randy Smith, Buffalo		15	4	7	0	0	1	3	0	8
Totals		240	52	107	19	26	61	21	24	123

WEST ALL-STARS (109)

Player and Team	Pos.	Min.	FGM	FGA	FTM	FTA	Reb.	Ast.	PF	Pts.
Rick Barry, Golden State	F	28	6	15	5	5	4	2	5	17
Bob Dandridge, Milwaukee	F	27	5	10	0	0	6	0	4	10
Kareem Abdul-Jabbar, Los Angeles	C	36	9	16	4	4	15	3	3	22
Nate Archibald, Kansas City	G	30	5	13	3	3	5	7	0	13
Brian Winters, Milwaukee	G	16	1	5	0	0	2	1	2	2
Alvan Adams, Phoenix		11	2	4	0	0	3	0	1	4
Jamaal Wilkes, Golden St.		14	3	9	2	2	4	2	0	8
Curtis Rowe, Detroit		8	0	2	1	2	2	0	2	1
Scott Wedman, Kansas City		20	4	5	0	0	6	2	2	8
Norm Van Lier, Chicago		14	1	4	1	2	1	0	2	3
Fred Brown, Seattle		24	7	13	0	0	0	1	3	14
Phil Smith, Golden State		12	3	7	1	4	1	0	1	7
Totals		240	46	103	17	22	49	18	25	109

Score by Periods:	1st	2nd	3rd	4th	Totals
East	28	17	38	40	123
West	23	27	30	29	109

Blocked Shots: Abdul-Jabbar 3, Van Lier, R. Smith.
Referees: Paul Mihalak and Darrell Garretson. Attendance: 17,511.

1977 Twenty-Seventh Game

It was as though Julius Erving had waited for the NBA All-Star Game to display the artistry that had made him the most exciting player in the ABA. As a first-year man in the NBA, with the Philadelphia 76ers, Dr. J had been less than sensational. He made up for it all at Milwaukee Arena when he threw in 30 points and posted a game-high 13 rebounds as his East team lost to the West, 125-124.

In this first year of the merged NBA-ABA, Erving did something he never did in his five appearances in the ABA All-Star Game: he won the MVP award.

There was also support for Paul Westphal of Phoenix, best man for the winners, and for the Knicks' Bob McAdoo, who scored 14 of his 30 points for the losers in the fourth quarter. It was Westphal who, in the closing seconds, stole the ball from New Orleans' Pete Maravich to preserve the one-point verdict. But it was, notwithstanding, the day of Dr. J.

FEBRUARY 13, 1977, AT MILWAUKEE

East Coach—Gene Shue   **West Coach**—Larry Brown

EAST ALL-STARS (124)

Player and Team	Pos.	Min.	FGM	FGA	FTM	FTA	Reb.	Ast.	PF	Pts.
Julius Erving, Philadelphia	F	30	12	20	6	6	12	3	2	30
George McGinnis, Philadelphia	F	26	2	9	0	2	7	2	3	4
Bob McAdoo, Knicks	C	38	13	23	4	4	10	2	3	30
Doug Collins, Philadelphia	G	21	3	6	2	2	2	6	2	8
Pete Maravich, New Orleans	G	21	5	13	0	0	0	4	1	10
John Havlicek, Boston		17	2	5	0	0	1	1	1	4
Earl Monroe, Knicks		15	2	7	0	0	0	3	1	4
Jo Jo White, Boston		15	5	7	0	0	1	2	0	10
Elvin Hayes, Washington		11	6	6	0	0	2	1	5	12
Rudy Tomjanovich, Houston		22	3	9	0	0	10	1	1	6
Phil Chenier, Washington		12	3	6	0	0	1	1	0	6
George Gervin, San Antonio		12	0	6	0	0	1	0	1	0
Totals		240	56	117	12	14	47	26	20	124

WEST ALL-STARS (125)

Player and Team	Pos.	Min.	FGM	FGA	FTM	FTA	Reb.	Ast.	PF	Pts.
Bobby Jones, Denver	F	14	1	4	0	0	0	3	0	2
David Thompson, Denver	F	29	7	9	4	6	7	3	3	18
Dan Issel, Denver	C	10	0	3	0	0	1	0	0	0
Paul Westphal, Phoenix	G	31	10	16	0	0	1	6	2	20
Norm Van Lier, Chicago	G	14	1	3	0	0	1	1	2	2
Kareem Abdul-Jabbar, Los Angeles		23	8	14	5	6	4	2	1	21
Rick Barry, Golden State		29	7	16	4	4	4	8	1	18
Phil Smith, Golden State		28	6	13	1	2	6	8	3	13
Don Buse, Indiana		19	2	4	0	0	2	5	0	4
Billy Knight, Indiana		12	1	5	2	2	5	0	0	4
Bob Lanier, Detroit		20	7	8	3	3	10	4	3	17
Maurice Lucas, Portland		11	3	9	0	0	4	2	2	6
Totals		240	53	104	19	23	45	42	17	125

Score by Periods:	1st	2nd	3rd	4th	Totals
East	34	34	21	35	124
West	23	35	39	28	125

Blocked Shots: Westphal 2, Erving, Gervin, McAdoo, Tomjanovich, Abdul-Jabbar, Jones, Lanier, Lucas.
Referees—Earl Strom and Lee Jones. Attendance—10,938.

1978 Twenty-Eighth Game

Buffalo's Randy Smith was a dandy as he threw two first-half bombs and dominated the fourth quarter to pace the East to a 133-125 victory over the West in the All-Star Game at Atlanta.

The quickest guard in the NBA, who went 11-for-14 from the field, connected on 30- and 40-foot jumpers at the buzzers ending the first and second quarters, but it was in the final period that he propelled the East into the lead when he connected for eight consecutive points. His 27-point performance clearly made him MVP of a game that saw the West leading, 66-57, at halftime.

For the 6-3 Smith, who was not among the first 10 guards in the fans' All-Star voting, this was his second All-Star Game appearance. For 37-year-old John Havlicek, a last-minute replacement for the injured Pete Maravich, this marked his 13th straight—and final—appearance in this annual classic. And the Celtic hero went out on a happy note, scoring six of the East's first eight points.

David Thompson of Denver and Paul Westphal of Phoenix were high men for the losers with 22 and 20 points, respectively.

FEBRUARY 5, 1978, AT ATLANTA

East Coach—Billy Cunningham   **West Coach**—Jack Ramsay

WEST ALL-STARS (125)

Player and Team	Pos.	Min.	FGM	FGA	FTM	FTA	Reb.	Ast.	PF	Pts.
Rick Barry, Golden State	F	30	7	17	1	1	4	5	6	15
Maurice Lucas, Portland	F	33	6	13	0	0	13	4	2	12
Bill Walton, Portland	C	31	6	14	3	3	10	2	3	15
David Thompson, Denver	G	35	10	16	2	4	3	3	4	22
Paul Westphal, Phoenix	G	24	9	14	2	5	0	5	4	20
Walter Davis, Phoenix		15	3	6	4	4	1	6	1	10
Artis Gilmore, Chicago		13	2	4	6	8	2	0	1	10
Lionel Hollins, Portland		23	3	8	4	5	0	8	2	10
Bobby Jones, Denver		18	1	3	0	0	6	2	4	2
Brian Winters, Milwaukee		14	4	7	0	0	4	1	2	8
Bob Lanier, Detroit		4	0	0	1	2	2	0	0	1
Totals		240	51	102	23	32	45	36	29	125

Turnovers: Barry 5, Walton 4, Thompson 4, Westphal 3, Gilmore 1, Hollins 1, Jones 1, Winters 3. Lanier 1. Total—23.

EAST ALL-STARS (133)

Player and Teams	Pos.	Min.	FGM	FGA	FTM	FTA	Reb.	Ast.	PF	Pts.
Julius Erving, Philaadelphia	F	27	3	14	10	12	8	3	1	16
Larry Kenon, San Antonio	F	20	8	15	0	0	4	0	0	16
Dave Cowens, Boston	C	28	7	9	0	0	14	5	5	14
George Gervin, San Antonio	G	18	4	11	1	3	2	1	2	9
John Havlicek, Boston	G	22	5	8	0	0	3	1	2	10
Doug Collins, Philadelphia		27	3	8	8	11	5	8	3	14
Truck Robinson, New Orleans		24	3	7	1	2	6	1	2	7
Bob McAdoo, New York		20	7	14	0	0	4	0	2	14
Randy Smith, Buffalo		29	11	14	5	6	7	6	5	27
Elvin Hayes, Washington		11	1	7	0	0	4	0	4	2
Moses Malone, Houston		14	1	1	2	4	4	1	1	4
Totals		240	53	108	27	38	61	26	27	133

Turnovers: Erving 2, Kenon 2, Cowens 2, Gervin 2, Havlicek 4, Collins 4, Robinson 3, McAdoo 3, Smith 3, Hayes 1. Total—26.

Score by Periods:	1st	2nd	3rd	4th	Totals
West	39	27	34	25	125
East	28	29	35	41	133

Blocked Shots: Walton 2, Gilmore 2, Jones, Westphal, Erving, Gervin.
Referees—Jake O'Donnell and Jim Capers. Attendance—15,491

1979 Twenty-Ninth Game

Veterans of the old ABA had a field day as the West held off the East, 134-129, in Detroit's Silverdome before a crowd of 31,745, the largest ever to witness an All-Star Game.

Denver's David Thompson was voted the game's MVP with a 25-point effort but he had to battle ex-ABA stars Julius Erving and George Gervin for the award. Philadelphia's Erving had 29 points and San Antonio's Gervin 26 for the East.

The West blew away to an 80-58 lead in the first half but Erving and Gervin led an East charge in a 40-point third quarter. Another ABA veteran, George McGinnis of Denver, added 16 points for the winners.

FEBRUARY 4, 1979, AT DETROIT

East Coach—Dick Motta

West Coach—Lenny Wilkens

WEST ALL-STARS (134)

Player and Team	Pos.	Min.	FGM	FGA	FTM	FTA	Reb.	Ast.	PF	Pts.
Marques Johnson, Milwaukee	F	20	3	11	4	6	6	2	1	10
George McGinnis, Denver	F	25	5	12	6	11	6	3	4	16
Kareem Abdul-Jabbr, Los Angeles	C	28	5	12	1	2	8	3	4	11
David Thompson, Denver	G	34	11	17	3	7	5	2	4	25
Paul Westphal, Phoenix	G	21	8	12	1	2	1	5	0	17
Otis Birdsong, Kansas City		14	4	6	1	2	2	0	1	9
Walter Davis, Phoenix		19	4	9	0	0	4	4	0	8
Artis Gilmore, Chicago		15	3	4	2	2	1	2	1	8
Dennis Johnson, Seattle		27	5	7	2	2	1	3	3	12
Maurice Lucas, Portland		19	4	10	2	2	7	1	5	10
Jack Sikma, Seattle		18	4	5	0	0	4	0	1	8
Totals		240	56	105	33	36	45	25	24	134

Turnovers: Abdul-Jabbar 3, Lucas 3, Davis 2, Thompson 1, Westphal 1, Birdsong 1, Gilmore 1, Dennis Johnson 1. Total—13.

EAST ALL-STARS (129)

Player and Team	Pos.	Min.	FGM	FGA	FTM	FTA	Reb.	Ast.	PF	Pts.
Julius Erving, Philadelphia	F	39	10	22	9	12	8	5	4	29
Rudy Tomjanovich, Houston	F	24	6	13	0	0	6	1	2	12
Moses Malone, Houston	C	17	2	2	4	5	7	1	0	8
Pete Maravich, New Orleans	G	14	5	8	0	0	2	2	1	10
George Gervin, San Antonio	G	34	8	16	10	11	6	2	4	26
Bob Dandridge, Washington		18	3	5	2	3	3	1	2	8
Elvin Hayes, Washington		28	5	11	3	5	13	0	5	13
Larry Kenon, San Antonio		7	1	3	1	2	2	1	0	3
Bob Lanier, Detroit		31	5	10	0	0	4	4	4	10
Calvin Murphy, Houston		15	3	5	0	0	1	5	4	6
Campy Russell, Cleveland		13	2	8	0	0	1	0	0	4
Totals		240	50	103	29	38	53	22	26	129

Turnovers: Maravich 4, Murphy 4, Gervin 3, Erving 1, Malone 1, Dandridge 1, Hayes 1, Russell 1. Total—16.

Score by Periods:	1st	2nd	3rd	4th	Totals
West	36	44	24	30	134
East	27	31	40	31	129

Blocked Shots: Abdul-Jabbar 1, Thompson 1, Dennis Johnson 1, Gervin 1, Hayes 1, Lanier 1.
Referees: John Vanak, Jack Madden and Hugh Evans. Attendance: 31,745.

1980 Thirtieth Game

In what was only the second overtime game in the 30-year history of the event, George Gervin of San Antonio led the East to a 144-136 victory over the West at Landover, Md.

Voted MVP after a 34-point performance, Gervin scored 18 in the third quarter, when the East broke loose from a 64-64 halftime tally.

The game was tied, 128-128, at the end of regulation time, and it was decided largely by the overtime heroics of Boston's Larry Bird and Houston's Moses Malone.

Atlanta's Eddie Johnson tallied 22 points and Malone 20 for the East, while Utah's Adrian Dantley topped the West with 23 before a capacity crowd at the Capital Centre.

FEBRUARY 4, 1980, AT LANDOVER, MD.

East Coach—Billy Cunningham   **West Coach**—Lenny Wilkens

WEST ALL-STARS (136)

Player and Team	Pos.	Min.	FGM	FGA	FTM	FTA	Reb.	Ast.	PF	Pts.
Adrian Dantley, Utah	F	30	8	15	7	8	5	2	1	23
M. Johnson, Milwaukee	F	34	1	6	2	2	4	1	2	4
Kareem Abdul-Jabbar, Los Angeles	C	30	6	17	5	6	16	9	5	17
Lloyd Free, San Diego	G	21	7	13	0	1	3	5	1	14
Earvin Johnson, Los Angeles	G	24	5	8	2	2	2	4	3	12
Dennis Johnson, Seattle		20	7	13	5	6	4	1	3	19
Walter Davis, Phoenix		23	5	10	2	2	4	2	2	12
Jack Sikma, Seattle		28	4	10	0	0	8	4	5	8
Paul Westphal, Phoenix		27	8	14	5	6	1	5	5	21
K. Washington, Portland		14	1	6	2	4	8	1	4	4
Otis Birdsong, Kansas City		14	1	2	0	0	0	0	1	2
Totals		265	53	114	30	37	55	34	32	136

FG Pct.: .465. FT Pct.: .811. Turnovers: Dantley 2, Abdul-Jabbar 9, Free 5, Johnson, Earvin 2, Johnson, Dennis 2, Davis 3, Sikma 1, Westphal 3, Washington 1, Birdsong 1. Total—29. Team Rebounds: 14.

EAST ALL-STARS (144)

Player and Team	Pos.	Min.	FGM	FGA	FTM	FTA	Reb.	Ast.	PF	Pts.
John Drew, Atlanta	F	15	0	4	4	5	3	0	5	4
Julius Erving, Philadelphia	F	20	4	12	3	4	5	2	5	11
Moses Malone, Houston	C	31	7	12	6	12	12	2	4	20
George Gervin, San Antonio	G	40	14	26	6	9	10	3	2	34
Eddie Johnson, Atlanta	G	32	11	16	0	0	1	7	2	22
Dan Roundfield, Atlanta		27	7	15	4	9	13	0	2	18
Nate Archibald, Boston		21	0	8	2	3	3	6	1	2
Elvin Hayes, Washington		29	5	10	2	2	5	4	5	12
M. Richardson, New York		13	3	7	0	0	1	2	2	6
Bill Cartwright, New York		14	4	8	0	0	3	1	1	8
Larry Bird, Boston		23	3	6	0	0	6	7	1	7
Totals		265	58	124	27	44	62	34	30	144

FG Pct.: .468. FT Pct.: .614. Turnovers: Drew 3, Erving 2, Malone 5, Gervin 3, Johnson, Eddie 2, Roundfield 3, Archibald 2, Hayes 3, Richardson 2, Cartwright 3, Bird 3. Total—30. Team Rebounds: 20.

Score by periods:	2st	2nd	3rd	4th	5th	Totals
West	37	27	27	37	8	136
East	28	36	44	20	16	144

Blocked Shots: Abdul-Jabbar 6, Johnson, Dennis 1, Sikma 3, Washington 1, Johnson, Earvin 2, Johnson, Marques 1, Westphal 1, Free 1, Erving 1, Malone 2, Hayes 4, Roundfield 2. 3-Pt. Field Goals: Johnson, Earvin 0-1, Sikma 0-1, Bird 1-2.

Officials: Joe Gushue and Ed Rush, Alt. Wally Rooney. Attendance: 19,035.

1981 Thirty-First Game

Barely 6-1 and the smallest man on the court, Nate (Tiny) Archibald was the master playmaker for the East in its 123-120 triumph over the West at The Coliseum in Richfield (Ohio).

The Boston Celtic floorman scored only nine points, but he contributed nine assists and, as Philadelphia's Bobby Jones, a teammate, put it, "You just knew wherever you went, you'd get the ball from Tiny if you were open."

The 32-year-old Archibald, whose team led, 61-58, at the half, was especially effective in the closing minutes of the game when the West had drawn within three points.

The sellout crowd of 20,239 saw Philadelphia's Julius Erving score 18 points, two more than Celtic Robert Parish, whose 10 rebounds led all players. Seattle's Paul Westphal and Phoenix's Dennis Johnson tallied a game-high 19 points each in a losing cause.

FEBRUARY 1, 1981, AT RICHFIELD, OHIO

East Coach—Billy Cunningham, Philadelphia   **West Coach**—John MacLeod, Phoenix

WEST ALL-STARS (120)

Player and Team	Pos.	Min.	FGM	FGA	FTM	FTA	Reb.	Ast.	PF	Pts.
Walter Davis, Phoenix	F	22	5	9	2	2	7	1	2	12
Adrian Dantley, Utah	F	21	3	9	2	2	5	0	1	8
Kareem Abdul-Jabbar, Los Angeles	C	23	6	9	3	3	6	4	3	15
Paul Westphal, Seattle	G	25	8	12	3	3	4	3	3	19
George Gervin, San Antonio	G	24	5	9	1	2	3	0	3	11
Jamaal Wilkes, Los Angeles		25	6	12	3	3	8	3	3	15
Moses Malone, Houston		22	3	8	2	4	6	3	3	8
Len Robinson, Phoenix		21	3	6	0	0	5	2	4	6
Jack Sikma, Seattle		21	2	6	2	2	4	4	5	6
Dennis Johnson, Phoenix		24	5	8	9	10	2	1	1	19
Otis Birdsong, Houston		12	0	3	1	2	1	1	0	1
Totals		240	46	91	28	33	51	22	28	120

Turnovers: Davis 1, Abdul-Jabbar 3, Westphal 4, Gervin 2, Wilkes 2, Malone 1, Robinson 4, Sikma 2, D. Johnson 2, Birdsong 1. Total—22.

EAST ALL-STARS (123)

Player and Team	Pos.	Min.	FGM	FGA	FTM	FTA	Reb.	Ast.	PF	Pts.
Larry Bird, Boston	F	18	1	5	0	0	4	3	1	2
Julius Erving, Philadelphia	F	29	6	15	6	7	3	2	2	18
Artis Gilmore, Chicago	C	22	5	7	1	2	6	2	4	11
Eddie Johnson, Atlanta	G	28	7	12	2	3	2	2	1	16
Reggie Theus, Chicago	G	19	4	7	0	0	1	3	0	8
Nate Archibald, Boston		25	4	7	1	3	5	9	3	9
Robert Parish, Boston		25	5	18	6	6	10	2	3	16
Bobby Jones, Philadelphia		16	5	11	1	1	4	0	2	11
Marques Johnson, Milwaukee		19	1	2	5	6	4	2	2	7
M. R. Richardson, New York		24	5	8	1	2	5	3	3	11
Mike Mitchell, Cleveland		15	6	12	2	2	4	2	2	14
Totals		240	49	104	25	32	48	30	23	123

Turnovers: Bird 2, Erving 2, E. Johnson 3, Theus 4, Archibald 2, Parish 1, Richardson 2, Mitchell 1. Total—17.

Score by Periods:	1st	2nd	3rd	4th	Totals
West	27	31	30	32	120
East	23	38	36	26	123

Blocked Shots: Abdul-Jabbar 4, Parish 2, Gervin, Sikma, Westphal, Erving, Gilmore, Jones.
Referees—Paul Mihalik and Darell Garretson. Attendance—20,239.

ALL-TIME NBA RECORDS

Season

Individual

Single Game

Most Points	100	Wilt Chamberlain, Philadelphia vs New York, at Hershey, Pa., Mar. 2, 1962
Most F.G. Attempted	63	Wilt Chamberlain, Philadelphia vs New York, at Hershey, Pa., Mar. 2, 1962
Most F.G. Made	36	Wilt Chamberlain, Philadelphia vs New York, at Hershey, Pa., Mar. 2, 1962
Most Consecutive F.G. Made	18	Wilt Chamberlain, San Francisco vs New York, at Boston, Nov. 27, 1963
	18	Wilt Chamberlain, Philadelphia vs Baltimore, at Pittsburgh, Feb. 24, 1967
Most F.T. Attempted	34	Wilt Chamberlain, Philadelphia vs St. Louis, at Philadelphia, Feb. 22, 1962
Most F.T. Made	28	Wilt Chamberlain, Philadelphia vs New York, at Hershey, Pa., Mar. 2, 1962
Most Consecutive F.T. Made	19	Bob Pettit, St. Louis vs Boston, at Boston, Nov. 22, 1961
Most F.T. Missed	22	Wilt Chamberlain, Philadelphia vs Seattle, at Boston, Dec. 1, 1967
Most Consecutive Points	15	Wilt Chamberlain, Philadelphia vs Baltimore, at Baltimore, Mar. 20, 1966
Most Assists	29	Kevin Porter, New Jersey vs Houston at New Jersey, Feb. 24, 1978
Most Personal Fouls	8	Don Otten, Tri-Cities, at Sheboygan, Nov. 24, 1949

Season

Most Points	4,029	Wilt Chamberlain, Philadelphia, 1961-62
Highest Average	50.4	Wilt Chamberlain, Philadelphia, 1961-62
Most F.G. Attempted	3,159	Wilt Chamberlain, Philadelphia, 1961-62
Most 3-Pt. F.G. Attempted	239	Brian Taylor, San Diego 1979-80
Most F.G. Made	1,597	Wilt Chamberlain, Philadelphia, 1961-62
Most 3-Pt. F.G. Made	73	Rick Barry, 1979-80
Highest F.G. Percentage	.727	Wilt Chamberlain, Los Angeles, 1972-73
Highest 3-Pt. F.G. Pct.	.443	Fred Brown, Seattle, 1979-80
Most F.T. Attempted	1,363	Wilt Chamberlain, Philadelphia, 1961-62
Most F.T. Made	840	Jerry West, Los Angeles, 1965-66
Highest F.T. Percentage	.958	Calvin Murphy, Houston, 1980-81
Most Rebounds	2,149	Wilt Chamberlain, Philadelphia, 1960-61
Most Assists	1,099	Kevin Porter, Detroit, 1978-79
Most Personal Fouls	367	Bill Robinzine, Kansas City, 1978-79
Most Disqualifications	26	Don Meineke, Fort Wayne, 1952-53

Career

Most Points Scored	31,419	Wilt Chamberlain, Philadelphia Warriors, San Francisco Warriors, Philadelphia 76ers and Los Angeles Lakers, 1960-73
Highest Scoring Average	30.1	Wilt Chamberlain, 1960-73
Most F.G. Attempted	23,900	John Havlicek, Boston, 1962-78
Most F.G. Made	12,681	Wilt Chamberlain, 1960-73
Highest F.G. Percentage	.577	Artis Gilmore, Chicago, 1976-81
Most F.T. Attempted	11,862	Wilt Chamberlain, 1960-73
Most F.T. Made	7,694	Oscar Robertson, Cincinnati and Milwaukee, 1961-74
Highest F.T. Percentage	.900	Rick Barry, San Francisco and Golden State Warriors, Houston Rockets, 1965-67, 1972-80
Most Rebounds	23,924	Wilt Chamberlain, 1960-73
Most Assists	9,887	Oscar Robertson, 1961-74
Most Minutes	47,859	Wilt Chamberlain, 1960-73
Most Games	1,270	John Havlicek, 1962-78
Most Personal Fouls	3,885	Hal Greer, 1959-73
Most Times Disqualified	127	Vern Mikkelsen, Minneapolis 1950-59

Team records

Single Game

Most Points, One Team	173	Boston vs Minneapolis at Boston, Feb. 27, 1959
Most Points, Two Teams	316	Philadelphia 169, New York 147 at Hershey, Pa., Mar. 2, 1962
	316	Cincinnati 165, San Diego 151, at Cincinnati, Mar. 12, 1970
Most F.G. Attempted, One Team	153	Philadelphia vs Los Angeles at Philadelphia (3 OT), Dec. 8, 1961

Most F.G. Attempted, Two Teams	291	Philadelphia 153, Los Angeles 138 at Philadelphia, (3 OT), Dec. 8, 1961
Most F.G. Made, One Team	72	Boston vs Minneapolis at Boston, Feb. 27, 1959
Most F.G. Made, Two Teams	134	Cincinnati 67, San Diego 67 at Cincinnati, Mar. 12, 1970
Most F.T. Attempted, One Team	86	Syracuse vs Anderson at Syracuse (5 OT), Nov. 24, 1949
Most F.T. Attempted, Two Teams	160	Syracuse 86, Anderson 74 at Syracuse (5 OT), Nov. 24, 1949
Most F.T. Made, One Team	59	Syracuse vs Anderson at Syracuse (5 OT), Nov. 24, 1949
Most F.T. Made, Two Teams	116	Syracuse 59, Anderson 57 at Syracuse (5 OT), Nov. 24, 1949
Most Rebounds, One Team	112	Philadelphia vs Cincinnati at Philadelphia, Nov. 8, 1959
	112	Boston vs Detroit at Boston, Dec. 24, 1960
Most Rebounds, Two Teams	215	Philadelphia 110, Los Angeles 105 at Philadelphia (3 OT), Dec. 8, 1961
Most Assists, One Team	60	Syracuse vs Baltimore at Syracuse (OT), Nov. 15, 1952
Most Assists, Two Teams	89	Detroit 48, Cleveland 41 at Cleveland (OT), Mar. 28, 1973
Most Personal Fouls, One Team	66	Anderson at Syracuse (5 OT), Nov. 24, 1949
Most Personal Fouls, Two Teams	122	Anderson 66, Syracuse 56 at Syracuse (5 OT), Nov. 24, 1949
Most Disqualifications, One Team	8	Syracuse vs Baltimore at Syracuse (OT), Nov. 15, 1952
Most Disqualifications, Two Teams	13	Syracuse 8, Baltimore 5 at Syracuse (OT), Nov. 15, 1952
Most Points in a Losing Game	151	San Diego, at Cincinnati, Mar. 12, 1970
Widest Point Spread	63	Los Angeles 162, Golden State 99 at Los Angeles, Mar. 19, 1972
Most Consecutive Points in a Game	24	Philadelphia vs Baltimore at Baltimore, Mar. 20, 1966

Season

Most Games Won	69	Los Angeles, 1971-72
Most Games Lost	73	Philadelphia, 1972-73
Longest Winning Streak	33	Los Angeles, Nov. 5, 1971 to Jan. 7, 1972
Longest Losing Streak	20	Philadelphia, Jan. 9, 1973 to Feb. 11, 1973
Most Points Scored	10,143	Philadelphia, 1966-67
Most Points Allowed	10,261	Seattle, 1967-68
Highest Scoring Average	125.4	Philadelphia, 1961-62
Highest Average, Points Allowed	125.1	Seattle, 1967-68
Most F.G. Attempted	9,295	Boston, 1960-61

Most 3-Pt. F.G. Attempted	543	San Diego, 1979-80
Most F.G. Made	3,972	Milwaukee, 1970-71
Most 3-Pt. F.G. Made	177	San Diego, 1979-80
Highest F.G. Percentage	.529	Los Angeles, 1979-80
Highest 3-Pt. F.G. Percentage	.384	Boston, 1979-80
Most F.T. Attempted	3,411	Philadelphia, 1966-67
Most F.T. Made	2,434	Phoenix, 1969-70
Highest F.T. Percentage	.821	KC-Omaha, 1974-75
Most Rebounds	6,131	Boston, 1960-61
Most Assists	2,562	Milwaukee, 1978-79

Playoffs
CHAMPIONSHIP PLAYOFF SERIES

Player

Full Game

Most Points	61	Elgin Baylor, Los Angeles at Boston, Apr. 14, 1962
Most F.G.A.	48	Rick Barry, San Francisco vs. Philadelphia at San Francisco, Apr. 18, 1967
Most F.G.M.	22	Elgin Baylor, Los Angeles at Boston, Apr. 14, 1962
Most F.T.A.	24	Bob Pettit, St. Louis at Boston, Apr. 9, 1958
Most F.T.M.	19	Bob Pettit, St. Louis at Boston, Apr. 9, 1958
Most Rebounds	40	Bill Russell, Boston vs. St. Louis at Boston, Mar. 29, 1960
	40	Bill Russell, Boston vs. Los Angeles at Boston, Apr. 18, 1962 (OT)
Most Assists	19	Bob Cousy, Boston vs. St. Louis at Boston, Apr. 9, 1958
	19	Bob Cousy, Boston vs. Minneapolis at St. Paul, Apr. 7, 1959
	19	Walt Frazier, New York vs. Los Angeles at N.Y., May 8, 1970

One Half

Most Points	33	Elgin Baylor, Los Angeles at Boston, Apr. 14, 1962
Most F.G.A.	25	Elgin Baylor, Los Angeles at Boston, Apr. 14, 1962
Most F.G.M.	13	Bob Pettit, St. Louis at Boston, Apr. 9, 1957
Most F.T.A.	15	Bill Russell, Boston vs. St. Louis at Boston, Apr. 11, 1961
Most F.T.M.	12	Rick Barry, San Francisco vs. Philadelphia at San Francisco, Apr. 24, 1967
Most Rebounds	26	Wilt Chamberlain, Philadelphia vs. San Francisco at Philadelphia, Apr. 16, 1967

Most Assists	10	Bob Cousy, Boston vs. St. Louis at Boston, Apr. 9, 1957
	10	Bob Cousy, Boston vs. Minneapolis at Boston, Apr. 9, 1959
	10	Bob Cousy, Boston vs. Minneapolis at St. Paul, Apr. 9, 1959
	10	Walt Frazier, New York vs. Los Angeles at New York, May 8, 1970
Most Personals	5	Jack McMahon, St. Louis vs. Boston at Boston, Apr. 13, 1957
	5	Jim Krebs, Los Angeles vs. Boston at Boston, Apr. 21, 1963
	5	Bob Dandridge, Milwaukee vs. Boston at Milwaukee, Apr. 30, 1974
	5	Dave Cowens, Boston vs. Milwaukee at Boston, May 5, 1974

One Quarter

Most Points	21	Joe Fulks, Philadelphia vs. Chicago at Philadelphia, Apr. 16, 1947
Most Points in Overtime Period	9	John Havlicek, Boston vs. Milwaukee at Boston, May 10, 1974
Most F.G.A.	17	Rick Barry, San Francisco vs. Philadelphia at Philadelphia, Apr. 14, 1967 (OT)
Most F.G.M.	8	Bob Pettit, St. Louis vs. Boston at St. Louis, Apr. 12, 1958
	8	John Havlicek, Boston vs. San Francisco at Boston, Apr. 18, 1964
Most F.T.A.	11	Bob Pettit, St. Louis vs. Boston at Boston, Apr. 9, 1958
	11	Wilt Chamberlain, Philadelphia vs. San Francisco at Philadelphia, Apr. 16, 1967
Most F.T.M.	9	Frank Ramsey, Boston vs. Minneapolis at Boston, Apr. 4, 1959
Most Rebounds	19	Bill Russell, Boston vs. Los Angeles at Boston, Apr. 18, 1962 (OT)
Most Assists	8	Bob Cousy, Boston vs. St. Louis at Boston, Apr. 9, 1957
Most Personals	5	Jim Krebs, Los Angeles vs. Boston at Boston, Apr. 21, 1963

One Team

Full Game

Most Points	142	Boston vs. Los Angeles at Boston, Apr. 18, 1965

Most F.G.A.	140	San Francisco vs. Philadelphia at Philadelphia, Apr. 14, 1967
Most F.G.M.	61	Boston vs. St. Louis at Boston, Mar. 27, 1968
Most F.T.A.	64	Philadelphia at San Francisco, Apr. 24, 1967
Most F.T.M.	41	Philadelphia at San Francisco, Apr. 24, 1967
Most Rebounds	101	Philadelphia vs. San Francisco at Philadelphia, Apr. 16, 1967
Most Assists	44	Los Angeles vs. New York at Los Angeles, May 6, 1970
Most Personals	40	Portland vs. Philadelphia at Portland, May 31, 1977

One Half

Most Points	79	Boston vs. Philadelphia at Boston, Mar. 28, 1969
Most F.G.A.	70	Boston vs. St. Louis at Boston, Mar. 27, 1960
Most F.G.M.	32	Boston vs. St. Louis at Boston, Mar. 27, 1960
Most F.T.A.	32	St. Louis at Boston, Apr. 9, 1957
Most F.T.M.	26	Phoenix vs. Boston, Jun. 2, 1976
Most Rebounds	60	Philadelphia vs. San Francisco at Philadelphia, Apr. 16, 1967
Most Assists	22	Los Angeles vs. New York at Los Angeles, May 6, 1970
Most Personals	22	Golden State vs. Washington, May 23, 1975
	22	Portland vs. Philadelphia at Portland, May 31, 1977
Most Disqualifications	3	Boston vs. Los Angeles at Boston, Apr. 18, 1962 (OT)

One Quarter

Most Points	46	Boston vs. St. Louis at Boston, Mar. 27, 1960
Most F.G.A.	38	Minneapolis at Boston, Apr. 5, 1959
	38	St. Louis at Boston, Apr. 5, 1961
Most F.G.M.	21	Boston vs. Los Angeles at Boston, Apr. 18, 1965
Most F.T.A.	20	Phoenix vs. Boston at Phoenix, June 2, 1977
Most F.T.M.	19	Phoenix vs. Boston at Phoenix, June 2, 1977
Most Rebounds	31	Philadelphia vs. San Francisco at Philadelphia, Apr. 16, 1967
Most Assists	12	Philadelphia vs. San Francisco at Philadelphia, Apr. 16, 1967
	12	Los Angeles vs. New York at Los Angeles, May 6, 1970

Most Personals	13	Golden State vs. Washington at Golden State, May 23, 1975
	13	Boston vs. Phoenix at Phoenix, June 2, 1976
Most Disqualifications	3	Boston vs. Los Angeles at Boston, Apr. 18, 1962 (OT)
	3	Los Angeles vs. Boston at Boston, Apr. 18, 1962 (OT)

Two Teams

Full Game

Most Points	276	(Philadelphia 141, San Francisco 135) at Philadelphia, Apr. 14, 1967 (OT)
Most F.G.A.	256	(San Francisco 140, Philadelphia 116) at Philadelphia, Apr. 14, 1967 (OT)
Most F.G.M.	112	(Philadelphia 57, San Francisco 55) at Philadelphia, Apr. 14, 1967 (OT)
Most F.T.A.	107	(St. Louis 57, Boston 50) at Boston, Apr. 9, 1958
Most F.T.M.	80	(St. Louis 44, Boston 36) at Boston, Apr. 9, 1958
Most Rebounds	173	(Boston 95, Minnesota 78) at Boston, Apr. 4, 1959
	173	(Boston 92, Los Angeles 81) at Boston, Apr. 7, 1962
Most Assists	73	(Los Angeles 44, New York 29) at Los Angeles, May 6, 1970
Most Personals	74	(Portland 40, Philadelphia 34) at Portland, May 31, 1977
Most Disqualifications	7	(Boston 4, Los Angeles 3) at Boston, Apr. 18, 1962 (OT)

One Half

Most Points	140	(San Francisco 72, Philadelphia 68) at San Francisco, Apr. 24, 1967
Most F.G.A.	127	(Boston 68, Minneapolis 59) at Boston, Apr. 4, 1959
Most F.G.M.	58	(Boston 29, St. Louis 29) at Boston, Mar. 27, 1960
Most F.T.A.	60	(Boston 30, St. Louis 30) at Boston, Apr. 9, 1958
Most F.T.M.	45	(Phoenix 26, Boston 19) at Phoenix, June 2, 1976
Most Rebounds	104	(Philadelphia 60, San Francisco 44) at Philadelphia, Apr. 16, 1967

Most Assists	37	(Los Angeles 22, New York 15) at Los Angeles, May 6, 1970
Most Personals	38	(Boston 20, Phoenix 18) at Phoenix, June 2, 1976
	38	(Portland 22, Philadelphia 16) at Portland, May 31, 1977
	38	(Philadelphia 22, Portland 16) at Philadelphia, June 3, 1977
Most Disqualifications	3	(Boston 3, Los Angeles 0) at Boston, Apr. 18, 1962 (OT)

One Quarter

Most Points	84	(Philadelphia 43, San Francisco 41) at San Francisco, Apr. 24, 1967
Most F.G.A.	69	(Minnesota 39, Boston 30) at Boston, Apr. 5, 1959
Most F.G.M.	49	(Boston 26, Minneapolis 23) at Boston, Apr. 5, 1959
Most F.T.A.	34	(Phoenix 20, Boston 14) at Phoenix, June 2, 1976
Most F.T.M.	31	(Phoenix 19, Boston 12) at Phoenix, June 2, 1976
Most Rebounds	56	(Boston 38, Los Angeles 18) at Boston, Apr. 18, 1962 (OT)
Most Assists	20	(Los Angeles 11, New York 9) at Los Angeles, May 6, 1970
Most Personals	24	(Boston 13, Phoenix 11) at Phoenix, June 2, 1976

PRELIMINARY PLAYOFF SERIES

Player

Full Game

Most Points	56	Wilt Chamberlain, Philadelphia vs. Syracuse at Philadelphia, Mar. 22, 1962
Most F.G.A.	48	Wilt Chamberlain, Philadelphia vs. Syracuse at Philadelphia, Mar. 22, 1962
Most F.G.M.	24	Wilt Chamberlain, Philadelphia vs. Syracuse at Philadelphia, Mar. 14, 1960
	24	John Havlicek, Boston vs. Atlanta at Boston, Apr. 1, 1960
Most F.T.A.	32	Bob Cousy, Boston vs. Syracuse at Boston, Mar. 21, 1953 (4 OT)
	23	Jerry West, Los Angeles at Detroit, Apr. 3, 1962
	23	Wilt Chamberlain, Philadelphia at Boston, Apr. 17, 1968

Most F.T.M.	30	Bob Cousy, Boston vs. Syracuse at Boston, Mar. 21, 1953 (4 OT)
	21	Oscar Robertson, Cincinnati at Boston, Apr. 10, 1963
Most Successive F.T.M.	18	Bob Cousy, Boston vs. Syracuse at Boston, Mar. 21, 1953 (4 OT)
Most Rebounds	41	Wilt Chamberlain, Philadelphia vs. Boston at Philadelphia, Apr. 5, 1967
Most Assists	19	Wilt Chamberlain, Philadelphia vs. Cincinnati at Philadelphia, Mar. 24, 1967
	19	Jerry West, Los Angeles vs. Chicago at Los Angeles, Apr. 1, 1973
	19	Norm Nixon, Los Angeles vs. Seattle at Los Angeles, Apr. 22, 1979
Most Personals	8	Jack Toomay, Baltimore at New York, Mar. 26, 1949 (OT)

One Half

Most Points	32	Elgin Baylor, Los Angeles vs. Detroit at Los Angeles, Mar. 15, 1961
	32	Jerry West, Los Angeles vs. Baltimore at Los Angeles, Apr. 5, 1965
Most F.G.A.	25	Wilt Chamberlain, Philadelphia vs. Syracuse at Philadelphia, Mar. 22, 1962
Most F.G.M.	14	John Havlicek, Boston vs. Atlanta at Boston, Apr. 1, 1973
Most F.T.A.	14	Wilt Chamberlain, Philadelphia at Boston, Mar. 22, 1960
	14	Jerry West, Los Angeles at Detroit, Apr. 3, 1962
	14	Jerry West, Los Angeles vs. Baltimore at Los Angeles, Apr. 5, 1965
Most F.T.M.	14	Jerry West, Los Angeles vs. Baltimore at Los Angeles, Apr. 5, 1965
Most Rebounds	25	Wilt Chamberlain, Philadelphia vs. Boston at Philadelphia, Apr. 5, 1967
Most Assists	12	Wilt Chamberlain, Philadelphia vs. Cincinnati at Philadelphia, Mar. 2, 1967
Most Personals	6	Jack Toomay, Baltimore at New York, Mar. 26, 1949 (OT)
	6	Gene Conley, Boston vs. Syracuse at Boston, Mar. 22, 1959

One Quarter

Most Points	22	Elgin Baylor, Los Angeles vs. Detroit at Los Angeles, Mar. 15, 1961
Most Points in Overtime period	12	Bob Cousy, Boston at Syracuse, Mar. 17, 1954
Most F.G.A.	14	Wilt Chamberlain, Philadelphia vs. Syracuse at Philadelphia, Mar. 22, 1962
	14	Hal Greer, Philadelphia vs. Boston at Philadelphia, Mar. 11, 1968
Most F.G.M	10	Gail Goodrich, Los Angeles vs. Golden State at Los Angeles, Mar. 25, 1973
Most F.T.A.	12	Jerry West, Los Angeles at Detroit, Apr. 3, 1962
Most F.T.M.	10	Dolph Schayes, Syracuse at Boston, Mar. 17, 1956
	10	Elgin Baylor, Los Angeles vs. Detroit at Los Angeles, Mar. 15, 1961
	10	Jerry West, Lost Angeles at Detroit, Apr. 3, 1962
Most Rebounds	14	Wilt Chamberlain, Philadelphia vs. Boston at Philadelphia, Mar. 20, 1960
	14	Wilt Chamberlain, Philadelphia vs. Boston at Philadelphia, Mar. 22, 1962
	14	Wilt Chamberlain, Philadelphia vs. Boston at Philadelphia, Mar. 27, 1962
Most Assists	9	Lloyd Walton, Milwaukee vs. Denver at Milwaukee, Apr. 23, 1978
Most Personals	5	Arnie Risen, Boston vs. Syracuse at Boston, Mar. 21, 1957
	5	Brian Winters, Milwaukee vs. Philadelphia at Milwaukee, Apr. 10, 1981

	6	Frank Ramsey, Boston vs. Syracuse at Boston, Apr. 1, 1959
	6	Ernie Grunfeld, Kansas City at Portland, Apr. 1, 1981

One Team

Full Game

Most Points	156	Milwaukee at Philadelphia, Mar. 30, 1970
Most F.G.A.	140	Boston vs. Syracuse at Boston, Mar. 18, 1959

Most F.G.M.	67	Milwaukee at Philadelphia, Mar. 30, 1970
Most F.T.A.	66	Philadelphia at New York, Mar. 30, 1968
Most F.T.M.	57	Boston vs. Syracuse at Boston, Mar. 21, 1953 (4 OT)
	56	St. Louis at Minneapolis, Mar. 25, 1957 (2 OT)
	45	Milwaukee at Philadelphia, Apr. 7, 1981
Most Rebounds	107	Boston vs. Philadelphia at Boston, Mar. 19, 1960
Most Assists	46	Milwaukee at Philadelphia, Mar. 30, 1970
	46	Milwaukee vs. Denver at Milwaukee, Apr. 23, 1978
Most Personals	55	Syracuse at Boston, Mar. 21, 1953 (4 OT)
	53	Baltimore at New York, Mar. 26, 1949 (OT)
	40	Los Angeles at Detroit, Apr. 3, 1962
Most Disqualifications	7	Syracuse at Boston, Mar. 21, 1953 (4 OT)

One Half

Most Points	87	Milwaukee vs. Denver at Milwaukee, Apr. 23, 1978
Most F.G.A.	77	Boston vs. Philadelphia at Boston, Mar. 22, 1960
Most F.G.M.	38	Milwaukee vs. Denver at Milwaukee, Apr. 23, 1978
Most F.T.A.	40	Baltimore at Philadelphia, Mar. 30, 1971
Most F.T.M.	34	Baltimore at Philadelphia, Mar. 30, 1971
Most Rebounds	60	Boston vs. Philadelphia at Boston, Mar. 19, 1960
Most Assists	28	Milwaukee vs. Denver at Milwaukee, Apr. 23, 1978
Most Personals	32	Baltimore at New York, Mar. 26, 1949 (OT)
Most Disqualifications	5	Minneapolis vs. St. Louis at Minneapolis, Mar. 25, 1957 (2 OT)
	5	Baltimore at New York, Mar. 26, 1949 (OT)
	5	New York vs. Baltimore at New York, Mar. 26, 1949 (OT)

One Quarter

Most Points	51	Los Angeles vs. Detroit at Los Angeles, Mar. 31, 1962
Most F.G.A.	42	Boston vs. Philadelphia at Boston, Mar. 22, 1960
Most F.G.M.	24	Syracuse at Boston, Mar. 27, 1955
Most F.T.A.	23	Philadelphia vs. Syracuse at Philadelphia, Mar. 22, 1962
	23	Philadelphia at Boston, Apr. 1, 1962
	21	Los Angeles at Detroit, Apr. 3, 1962
Most F.T.M.		
Most Rebounds	31	Boston vs. Philadelphia at Boston, Mar. 19, 1960
	31	Boston vs. Syracuse at Boston, Mar. 23, 1961
	31	Atlanta vs. Washington at Atlanta, Apr. 20, 1979
Most Assists	16	Milwaukee vs. Denver at Milwaukee, Apr. 23, 1978
Most Personals	17	Baltimore at New York, Mar. 26, 1949 (OT)
Most Disqualifications	4	Baltimore at New York, Mar. 26, 1949 (OT)

Two Teams

Full Game

Most Points	278	(St. Louis 143, Minneapolis 135) at Minneapolis, Mar. 25, 1957 (2 OT)
	276	(Milwaukee 156, Philadelphia 120) at Philadelphia, Mar. 30, 1970
Most F.G.A.	257	(Boston 135, Philadelphia 122) at Boston, Mar. 22, 1960
Most F.G.M.	119	(Milwaukee 67, Philadelphia 52) at Philadelphia, Mar. 30, 1970
Most F.T.A.	128	(Boston 64, Syracuse 64) at Boston, Mar. 21, 1953 (4 OT)
	105	(Los Angeles 58, Detroit 47) at Detroit, Apr. 3, 1962
Most F.T.M.	108	(Boston 57, Syracuse 51) at Boston, Mar. 21, 1953 (4 OT)
Most Rebounds	184	(Boston 94, Philadelphia 90) at Boston, Mar. 16, 1960
Most Assists	76	(Milwaukee 46, Denver 30) at Milwaukee, Apr. 23, 1978
Most Personals	106	(Syracuse 55, Boston 51) at Boston, Mar. 21, 1953 (4 OT)
	78	(Detroit 40, Los Angeles 38) at Detroit, Apr. 3, 1962
Most Disqualifications	12	(Syracuse 7, Boston 5) at Boston, Mar. 21, 1953 (4 OT)
	11	(Baltimore 6, New York 5) at New York, Mar. 26, 1949 (OT)
	7	(Los Angeles 4, Detroit 3) at Detroit, Apr. 3, 1962

One Half

Most Points	158	(Milwaukee 79, Philadelphia 79) at Philadelphia, Mar. 30, 1970
Most F.G.A.	138	(Boston 77, Philadelphia 61) at Boston, Mar. 22, 1960
Most F.G.M.	69	(Milwaukee 35, Philadelphia 34) at Philadelphia, Mar. 30, 1970
Most F.T.A.	68	(New York 36, Baltimore 32) at New York, Mar. 26, 1949 (OT)
	67	(Baltimore 40, Philadelphia 27) at Philadelphia, Mar. 30, 1971
Most F.T.M.	56	(New York 29, Baltimore 27) at New York, Mar. 26, 1949 (OT)
	52	(Baltimore 34, Philadelphia 18) at Philadelphia, Mar. 30, 1971
Most Rebounds	102	(Boston 52, Philadelphia 50) at Boston, Mar. 22, 1960
Most Assists	47	(Milwaukee 28, Denver 19) at Milwaukee, Apr. 23, 1978
Most Personals	61	(Baltimore 32, New York 29) at New York, Mar. 26, 1949 (OT)
Most Disqualifications	11	(Baltimore 6, New York 5) at New York, Mar. 26, 1949 (OT)

One Quarter

Most Points	83	(Milwaukee 47, Denver 36) at Milwaukee, Apr. 23, 1978
Most F.G.A.	70	(Boston 35, Philadelphia 35) at Boston, Mar. 22, 1960
Most F.G.M.	36	(Philadelphia 20, Milwaukee 16) at Philadelphia, Mar. 30, 1970
Most F.T.A.	39	(Philadelphia 23, Boston 16) at Boston, Apr. 1, 1962
Most F.T.M.	29	(New York 15, Baltimore 14) at New York, Mar. 26, 1949 (OT)
Most Rebounds	53	(Boston 30, Philadelphia 23) at Boston, Mar. 24, 1962
Most Assists	28	(Milwaukee 16, Denver 12) at Milwaukee, Apr. 23, 1978
Most Personals	36	(Baltimore 19, New York 17) at New York, Mar. 26, 1949 (OT)

NBA COLLEGE DRAFT

The NBA held its first draft of college players prior to the start of the 1947-48 season. It was not until 1952, however, that the league began to keep complete records of team-by-team draft lists.

Draft choices are listed by team and in the order in which they were selected, starting with 1956. In some cases, choices were traded before the draft actually took place. Listed here are the teams with original rights to each pick.

1952

Baltimore
Jim Baechtold, Eastern Kentucky; Blaine Denning, Lawrence Tech; Chuck Grigsby, Dayton; Frank Guisness, Washington; Bill Lea, Southwest Missouri; Art Press, Western Maryland; Bud Priddy, New Mexico A&M; Benny Purcell, Murray State; Bud Penwell, Oklahoma City; Mike Magula, Youngstown; Bud Peterson, Oregon; Jim Walsh, Stanford.

Boston
Bill Stauffer, Missouri; Jim Iverson, Kansas State; J.C. Maze, Southwest Texas; Bob Hedderick, Canisius; Don Johnson, Oklahoma State; Jim Buchanan, Nebraska; Fred Eydt, Cornell (N.Y.); Gordon Mungier, Spring Hill; Jim Dilling, Holy Cross; Gene Conley, Washington State.

Fort Wayne
Bill Carlson, Fordham; Hal Cerra, Duquesne; Bob Clifton, Iowa; Leo Corkery, St. Bonaventure; Dick Groat, Duke; Don Meineke, Dayton; Lee Terrill, North Carolina State; Jim Ramstead, Stanford.

Indianapolis
Joe Dean, Louisiana State; Jay Handlan, Washington & Lee; Bill Harrell, Siena; Jim Hoverder, Central Missouri State; Gene Rhodes, Western Kentucky; Dale Toft, Denver; Lucian Whitaker, Kentucky; Bob Zawoluk, St. John's (N.Y.); Gordon Stauffer, Michigan State.

Milwaukee
Pete Brewster, Purdue; Roger Johnson, Arizona; Ed Miller, Syracuse; George McLeod, TCU; Ab Nicholas, Wisconsin; Dick Retherford, Baldwin-Wallace; John Snee, Clemson; Jim Tackett, New Mexico; Coyt Vance, Mississippi State; Bob Watson, Kentucky; Mark Workman, West Virginia.

Minneapolis
Tom Ackerman, West Liberty; Jim Bishop, Mississippi Southern; Rod Fletcher, Illinois; Cliff Haag, Wyoming; Jim Holstein, Cincinnati; Bob Holt, Tulane; Tom Katsimpalis, Eastern Illinois; Clyde Lovellette, Kansas; Dick Means, Minnesota; Dwight Morrison, Southern California; Carl McNulty, Purdue; Ed Ramiraz, Centenary; Don Schneider, Arizona; Gene Smith, Xavier (O.); Gene Smith, Huron; Homer Spain, Union (Tenn.); John Wallesea, Memphis State.

New York
Ray Belliveau, Seton Hall; Dick Bunt, New York U.; Bert Cook, Utah State; Ben Gibson, St. Mary's (Calif.); Bud Julian, Southwest Missouri State; Ralph Polson, Whitworth; Paul Sullivan, Alabama; Dick Surhoff, Long Island.

Philadelphia
Tom Brennan, Villanova; Bob Brown, Louisville; Burr Carlson, Connecticut; Walter Davis, Texas A&M; Nick Kladis, Loyola (Ill.); Bill Mlkvy, Temple; Newt Jones, LaSalle; Moe Radovich, Wyoming; Don Scanlon, Pennsylvania; Glenn Smith, Utah; Ben Stewart, Villanova.

Rochester
Chuck Darling, Iowa; Bryant Ivey, Alabama; Leroy Leslie, Notre Dame; Ronnie MacGilvray, St. John's (N.Y.); Jewell McDowell, Texas A&M; Jack McMahon, St. John's (N.Y.); Sam Miranda, Indiana; Jerry Romney; Brigham Young; Ray Royce, Houston; Arnold Smith, CCNY; Ray Sonnenberg, St. Louis; Ray Steiner, St. Louis; Bob Whitmer, Florida State.

Syracuse
Jim Brasco, New York U.; Bud Donnelly, LaSalle; Jim Kennedy, Duquesne; Bob Luchmueller, Louisville; Ken McBride, Maryland State; Harry Moore, West Virginia; Bob Roche, Syracuse.

1953

Baltimore
Ray Felix, Long Island; Bob Speight, North Carolina State; Bob Peterson, Illinois; Bill Schyman, DePaul; Paul Nolen, Texas Tech; Elmer Tolson, Eastern Kentucky; Herman Sledzik, Penn State; Connie Rea, Centenary; Dennis Murphy, Georgetown (D.C.); Jack Carby, Kansas State, Bob Emmerick, Clarion State; Russ Johnson; Don Stemmerich; Bob Kraback; Joe Piorkowski; Edward Walsh.

Boston
Frank Ramsey, Kentucky; Chet Noe, Oregon; Cliff Hagan, Kentucky; Earle Markey, Holy Cross; John Holup, George Washington; Vernon Stokes, St. Francis (N.Y.); Lou Tsiotopoulos, Kentucky; Ted Lallier, Colby; Lewis Gilcrease, Southwest Texas; Tom Lillis, St. Louis; Gil Reich, Kansas; Jim Dogerty, Whitworth.

Ford Wayne
Jack Molinas, Columbia; George Glasgow, Fairleigh Dickinson; Jim Bredar, Illinois; Jim Bingham, Eastern Kentucky; Mike Bodnar, St. Bonaventure; Norb Lewinski, Notre Dame; William Hagan, Siena; Dean Kelley, Kansas; Dick White, Eastern Kentucky.

Milwaukee
Bob Houbregs, Washington; Bill Bolger, Georgetown (D.C.); Irv Bemoras, Illinois; Gene Dyker, DePaul; Joe Cipriano, Washington; John O'Brien, Seattle; Eddie O'Brien, Seattle; Darrell Tucker, Utah State; Paul Brandt, Columbia; Bob Rousey, Kansas State.

Minneapolis
Jim Fritsche, Hamline; Ron Feiereisel, DePaul; Hartly Kruger, Idaho; Ken Flowers, USC; Zippy Morocco, Georgia; Pete Silas, Georgia Tech; Lloyd Olmstead, Cornell (Iowa); Joe Richey, Brigham Young; Hank Budde, Xavier (O.); Walt Kearns, Arkansas; Bill Chambers, William & Mary; Harold Christensen, Brigham Young; Bob Gelle, Minnesota; Lloyd Thorgaard, Hamline; Bob Gussner, Hamline; Chuck Wolfe, North Dakota; Doug Atkins, Tennessee; Roger Kuss, River Falls State.

New York
Walter Dukes, Seton Hall; Donald Ackerman, Long Island; Neil Gordon, Furman; Joe Smyth, Niagara; Allan Schutts, Springfield; Richard Atha, Indiana State; Forrest Hamilton, Southwest Missouri State; Robert Santini, Iona; Thomas Bishop, Mississippi Southern; Richard Prater, Kentucky; Bob Matheny, California; Larry O'Connor, Canisius; Delmar Diercks, Iowa State.

Philadelphia
Ernie Beck, Pennsylvania; Larry Hennessey, Villanova; Norm Grekin, LaSalle; Fred Ihle, LaSalle; Eddie Solomon, West Virginia Tech; Don Eby, USC; Bob Marske, South Dakota; Bill Dodd, Colgate; Bob Sassone, St. Bonaventure; Toar Hester, Centenary; John Doogan, St. Joseph's (Pa.); Charles Duffley, St. Anselm's.

Rochester
Richie Regan, Seton Hall; Norman Swanson, Detroit; Frank Reddout, Syracuse; Will Walls, Miami (O.); Hugh Beins, Georgetown (D.C.); Kendall Sheets, Oklahoma A&M; Jim Sottile, West Virginia; Dick Gross, Wheaton; Jim Gerber, Bowling Green; Will Bales, Eastern Kentucky; Bill Edwards, St. Bonaventure; Bob Goss, North Carolina State; Paul Smaagard, Hamline; Ken Sears, Santa Clara; John Kurz, Loyola (Calif.); Ed Kohl, Regis; Gene Lambert Jr., Arkansas; Tex Silverman, Nick McGuire.

Syracuse
James Neal, Wofford; Dick Knostman, Kansas State; Bill Kenville, St. Bonaventure; Andy McGowan, Manhattan; Warren Shackelford, Tulsa; Bill Jenkins, LeMoyne; Bill Hull, Utah State; Joe Hughes, Denver; Gerald Nappy, Georgetown (D.C.); Al Bailey, Duquesne; Glen Dille, Tulsa; Garrett Beshear, Murray State.

1954

Baltimore
Frank Selvy, Furman; Bob Leonard, Indiana; Werner Killen, Lawrence Tech; Burt Spice, Toledo; Lou Scott, Indiana; Bob Heim, Xavier (O.); Joe Pehanick, Seattle; Harry Brooks, Seton Hall; Ron Goerrs, Concordia (St. Louis, Mo.); Don Shivers, Houston; Elliott Karver, George Washington.

Boston
Togo Palazzi, Holy Cross; Duane Morrison, Idaho; Henry Daubenschmidt, St. Francis (N.Y.); Ron Perry, Holy Cross; Troy Burris, West Texas; Otto Krieghauser, Washington (Mo.); Paul Estergaard, Bradley; Jim Young, Santa Clara; Tony Daukas, Boston College; Bill Johnson, Nebraska.

Fort Wayne
Dick Rosenthal, Notre Dame; Arnold Short, Oklahoma City; B. H. Born, Kansas; Mel Thompson, North Carolina State; Dutch Burch, Pittsburgh; Charles Kraak, Indiana; Bernie Janicki, Duke; Don Bielke, Valparaiso; Joel Hittleman, Loyola (Md.); Phil Larson, Brigham Young; Forrest Jackson, Taylor.

Milwaukee
Bob Pettit, LSU; Bob Mattick, Oklahoma State; Walt Walowac, Marshall; Phil Martin, Toledo; Paul Ebert, Ohio State; Bob Carney, Bradley; Alan Kelley, Kansas; Dick Nunneley, Tulsa; Hal Cervini, Tulane; Joe Bertrand, Notre Dame; Jerry Domerschick, CCNY; Ron Weisner, Wisconsin.

Minneapolis
Ed Kalafat, Minnesota; Al Bianchi, Bowling Green; Don Lance, Rice; Gene Schwinger, Rice; Buzz Bennett, Minnesota; Nick Revon, Mississippi Southern; Dan Finch, Vanderbilt; Bob Hopkins, Pasadena; Dick Garmaker, Minnesota; John Biever, Northwestern.

New York
Jack Turner, Western Kentucky; Richie Guerin, Iona; Don Anielak, Southwest Missouri; Don Lange, Navy; Jesse Priscock, Kansas State; Ron Rivers, Wyoming; Solly Walker, St. John's (N.Y.); Cob Jarvis, Mississippi State; Henry Duckham, Brooklyn Poly; John Clune, Navy; Bob Waller, Oklahoma; Bill Stickel, Hastings.

Philadelphia
Gene Shue, Maryland; Larry Costello, Niagara; Ben Peters, St. Benedict; Chuck Noble, Louisville; Rudy D'Emilio, Duke; Len Winograd, Brandeis; Bob Brady, San Diego State; Bob Hodges, East Carolina; Vince Leta, Lycoming; Bill Sullivan, Notre Dame; Frank O'Hara, LaSalle; John Glinski; John Holup, George Washington.

Rochester
Tom Marshall, Western Kentucky; Boris Nachamkin, New York U.; Lee Morton, Cornell (N.Y.); Art Spoelstra, Western Kentucky; Bo Erias, Niagara; Jim Davis, St. John's (N.Y.); Bill Hull, Utah State; Paul Morrow, Wisconsin; Roy Irvin, USC; Ed Parchinski, Fordham; John Paxson, Dayton.

Syracuse
John Kerr, Illinois; Dick Farley, Indiana; Jim Tucker, Duquesne; Don McLane, Duquesne; Paul Pottenburgh, Siena; Norman Pott, Wheaton; Gus Levett, Franklin & Marshall; Mel Besdin, Syracuse; Fletcher Johnson, Duquesne; Jack Davidson, UCLA.

1955

Boston
Jim Ahearn, Connecticut; Mark Davis, Marietta; Henry Dooley, Wiley; Carl Hartman, Alderson-Broaddus; Dick Hemric, Wake Forest; Bart Leach, Pennsylvania; Jim Loscutoff, Oregon; John Mahoney, William & Mary; John Moore, UCLA; Bob Patterson, Tulsa; Dean Parsons, Washington; Nick Romanoff, College of Pacific; Bob Scuddelari, Cooper Union; Buzz Wilkinson, Virginia.

Fort Wayne
Jesse Arnelle, Penn State; Don Belcher, LSU; Ron Bennink, Washington State; Tom Harrold, Colorado; John Horan, Dayton; Dick Howard, Western Reserve; Cleo Littleton, Wichita State; Happy Mahfouz, Spring Hill; Tom Mock, Colorado; Tom Mixon, Mercer; Bob Reiter, Missouri; Ray Warren, TCU.

Milwaukee
Harvey Babetch, Bradley; Dick Cable, Wisconsin; Lynn Cole, Creighton; Al Ferrari, Michigan State; Joe Fitt; Burdette Haldorson, Colorado; Charles Hoxie, Niagara; Ed O'Connor, Manhattan; Bill Reigel, McNeese; Dick Ricketts, Duquesne; Jack Stephens, Notre Dame; Dick Welsh, USC.

Minneapolis
Bill Banks, Southwest Texas; Don Boldebuck, Houston; Dick Boushka, St. Louis; Don Bragg, UCLA; Dick Garmaker, Minnesota; K.C. Jones, San Francisco; Chuck Mencel, Minnesota; John Miller, Ohio State; Jim Scott, West Texas; Bill Warden, North Central (Ill.); O'Neal Weaver, Midwestern (Tex.).

New York
Joe Beck, Northeast Missouri; Denver Brackeen, Mississippi; Ed Cole, Creighton; Joe Fay, St. Ambrose; Mickey Harrington, Southern Mississippi; Wally McCarvill, Iona; Jerry Mullen, San Francisco; Don Payne, Adelphi; Ken Sears, Santa Clara; Howard Sessums, Mississippi College; Guy Sparrow, Detroit; Charles Stickels, Hastings.

Philadelphia
Jack Devine, Villanova; Walt Devlin, George Washington; Al Didriksen, Temple; Tom Gola, LaSalle; Jerry Koch, St. Louis; Lester Lane, Oklahoma; Bob Schafer, Villanova; Harry Silcox, Temple; George Swyers, West Virginia Tech; Ed Wiener, Tennessee.

Rochester
Bob Armstrong, Michigan State; Bill Evans, Kentucky; Ed Fleming, Niagara; Harry Jorgensen, Wyoming; Jerry Jung, Kansas State; Jim McConnell, Niagara; Bob McKeen, California; John Prudhoe, Louisville; Art Quimby, Connecticut; Maurice Stokes, St. Francis (Pa.); Jack Twyman, Cincinnati; Tony Vlastelica, Oregon State.

Syracuse
Ed Conlin, Forham; Mal Duffy, St. Bonaventure; Frank Ehmann, Northwestern; Cliff Dwyer, North Carolina State; Ed Galvin, Loyola (La.); Stan Glowaski, Seattle; Russ Lawler, Stanford; Jack Sallee, Dayton; Don Schlundt, Indiana; Marty Satalino, St. John's (N.Y.); Ron Tomsic, Stanford.

1956

Boston
Tom Heinsohn, Holy Cross; K.C. Jones, San Francisco; George Linn, Alabama; Dan Swartz, Morehead State; Bill Logan, Iowa; Don Boldebuck, Houston; O'Neal Weaver, Midwestern (Tex.); Vic Molodei, North Carolina State; Jim Houston, Brandeis; Theophileus Lloyd, Maryland State.

Fort Wayne
Rob Sobieszczyk, DePaul; Bob Kessler, Maryland; Bill Thieben, Hofstra; Charles Slack, Marshall; Joe Lieber, Holy Cross; John Schlimm, John Carroll; Bruce Harris, Tennessee Poly.

Minneapolis
Jim Paxson, Dayton; Terry Rand, Marquette; Jerry Bird, Kentucky; Lloyd Aubrey, Notre Dame; Bill Reigel, McNeese State; Phil Jordon, Whitworth; John Barber, Los Angeles State; Sam Jones, North Carolina College; Jim Springer, Gustavus Adolphus; Phil Grawmeyer, Kentucky; Robert Hodgson, Wichita; Carl Widseth, Tennessee; John Patzwald, Gustavus Adolphus; Elgin Baylor, Seattle.

New York
Ronnie Shavlik, North Carolina State; Gary Bergen, Utah; Jerry Harper, Alabama; Ronnie Mayer, Duke; Joe Sexton, Purdue; Pat Dunn, Utah State; Jack Adams, Eastern Kentucky; Art Bunte, Utah; Dick Miller, Wisconsin; Howard Crittendon, Murray State Teachers; Dick Miani, Miami; Ed Petrie, Seton Hall; Tony Roybal, New Mexico.

Philadelphia
Hal Lear, Temple; Phil Rollins, Louisville; Bevo Francis, Rio Grande; Phil Wheeler, Cincinnati; Joe Belmont, Duke; Mickey Winograd, Duquesne; John Fannon, Notre Dame; Max Anderson, Oregon; Ronald Clark, Springfield.

Rochester

Si Green, Duquesne; Bob Burrow, Kentucky; Dave Piontek, Xavier (O.); John McCarthy, Canisius; Bill Uhl, Dayton; Kevin Thomas, Boston; Carl Cain, Iowa; Clayton Carter, Oklahoma A&M; Dan Minnix, St. Francis (N.Y.); Jerry Moreman, Louisville; Gene Carpenter, Texas Tech.

St. Louis

Bill Russell, San Francisco; Willie Naulls, UCLA; Darrell Floyd, Furman; Robin Freeman, Ohio State; Norman Stewart, Missouri; Dave Plunkett, Cincinnati; Julius McCoy, Michigan State; Morris Taft, UCLA; Jim Reed, Texas Tech; Hershel Pederson, Brigham Young; Wally Choice, Indiana; Ed Huse, Wyoming; Arthur Helms, Houston; Junior Morgan, Duke.

Syracuse

Joe Holup, George Washington; Paul Judson, Illinois; Forest Able, Western Kentucky; Wade Halbrook, Oregon State; Jim Ray, Toledo; Jim McLaughlin, St. Louis; Jess Roh, Idaho State; Chester Webb, Georgia State Teachers; Dick Julio, New Bedford State; Bob Hopkins, Grambling; Willie Bergines, West Virginia; Dick Kenyon, LeMoyne; Milt Graham, Colgate; Chuck Rolles, Cornell.

1957

Boston

Sam Jones, North Carolina College; Dick O'Neal, Texas Christian; Chuck Schramm, Western Illinois; Jim Ashmore, Mississippi State; Grady Wallace, South Carolina; Maurice King, Kansas; Dick Brott, Denver; Bill Von Weyhe, Rhode Island; Joe Gibbon, Mississippi; Jack Butcher, Memphis State; Dick Neal, Indiana; Don Tobin, Florida Southern.

Cincinnati

Rod Hundley, West Virginia; Dick Duckett, St. John's (N.Y.); Gerry Paulson, Manhattan; Jed Dommeyer, Minnesota; Stuart Murray, Lafayette; John Maglio, North Carolina State; Chet Forte, Columbia; Bob Daniels, Western Kentucky; Dick Heise, DePaul; Mel Wright, Oklahoma A&M; Cliff Hafer, North Carolina State; Jim Boothe, Xavier (O.).

Detroit

Charles Tyra, Louisville; Bob McCoy, Grambling; Bill Ebben, Detroit; Kurt Englebert, St. Joseph's (Pa.), Ron Kramer, Michigan; Walt Adamushko, St. Francis (N.Y.); Carl Boldt, San Francisco; Doug Bolstorff, Minnesota; Bob Lazor, Pittsburgh.

Minneapolis

Jim Krebs, Southern Methodist; Harvey Schmidt, Illinois; Jim Spivey, Southeast Oklahoma; George Brown, Wayne State (Mich.); Gary Thompson, Iowa State; Phil Murrell, Drake; George Ferguson, Michigan; Jon Haaven, North Dakota; Jim Sutton, North Dakota State; Gordon Fosness, Dakota Wesleyan.

New York

Brendan McCann, St. Bonaventure; Larry Friend, California; Gary Clark, Syracuse; Raeford Wells, Lenoir Rhyne; Lee Marshall, Washington & Lee; Jim Humphries, St. Michael's.

Philadelphia

Len Rosenbluth, North Carolina; Jack Sullivan, Mount St. Mary's; Angelo Lombardo, Manhattan; Ray Radziszewski, St. Joseph's (Pa.); Jim Radcliff, Lafayette; Alonzo Lewis, LaSalle; Max Jamieson, Kentucky State; Woodrow Sauldsberry, Texas Southern; Steve Hamilton, Morehead State; Jerry Calvert, Kentucky; Jerry Gibson.

St. Louis

Win Wilfong, Memphis State; Jim Palmer, Dayton; John Smyth, Notre Dame; Hank Nowak, Canisius; Al Rochelle, Vanderbilt; Raymond Downs, Texas; Mason Cope, Kentucky Wesleyan; Bill Darragh, Louisville; Calvin Grosscup, Tulane; Bobby Mills, Southern Methodist; Drier, Macalester; Bob Seitz, North Carolina State; Ed Romanoff; Lavelle Langston, Northwestern State.

Syracuse

George BonSalle, Illinois; Jim Morgan, Louisville; Vince Cohen, Syracuse; Jerry Mallett, Baylor; Frank Nimmo, Cincinnati; Lyndon Lee, Oklahoma City; Dick Gaines, Seton Hall; Cebe Prince, Marshall; Jim Brown, Syracuse; Jack Nichols, Colgate; Jim Weeks, New York Tech.

1958

Boston

Ben Swain, Texas Southern; Jimmy Smith, Steubenville; Joe Cunningham, Fordham; Dom Flora, Washington & Lee; Gene Brown, San Francisco; Dave Keleher, Morehead State; Rudy Fenderson, Brandeis.

Cincinnati

Archie Dees, Indiana; Vern Hatton, Kentucky; Arlen Bockhorn, Dayton; Phil Murrell, Drake, Jim Fulmer, Alabama; Jim McClellan, St. Francis (Pa.); Wayne Stephens, Cincinnati; Bob Mantz, Lafayette; Larry Staverman, Villa Madonna; Jack Parr, Kansas State; Frank Tartaron, Xavier (O.); Don Medsker, Iowa State; Jerry DuPont, Louisville; Jim Newcomb, Duke; Bill Smith, Kentucky; Jack McCarthy, Dayton; John Powell, Miami (O.).

Detroit

Mike Farmer, San Francisco; Barney Cable, Bradley; Roy Dewitz, Kansas State; Ralph Crosthwaite, Western Kentucky; Hank Morano, St. Peter's; Shelly McMillon, Bradley; Ed Blair, Western Michigan; Jack Quiggle, Michigan State; Harry Marske, North Dakota State; Pete Gaudin, Loyola (La.); Herb Merritt, Tennessee Tech; Jim Dew, Alabama State.

Minneapolis

Elgin Baylor, Seattle; Steve Hamilton, Morehead State; Alex Ellis, Niagara; George Kline, Minnesota; Quitman Sullins, Murray State; Al Inniss, St. Francis (N.Y.); Jim Bond, Pasadena; Ed Brinkley, Clemson; Joe Hobbs, Florida; Shorty Paterson, Gustavus Adolphus; Hal Duffy, Oregon; Gary Simmons, Idaho; Jerry Alcorn, Fresno State.

New York

Pete Brennan, North Carolina; Joe Quigg, North Carolina; John Lee, Yale; John Cox, Kentucky; Don Lane, Dayton; Joe King, Oklahoma; Owen Lawson, Western Kentucky; Milt Kane, Utah; John McCarthy, Notre Dame.

Philadelphia

Guy Rodgers, Temple; Lloyd Sharrar, West Virginia; Frank Howard, Ohio State; Temple Tucker, Rice; Don Ohl, Illinois; Bucky Allen, Duke; Jay Norman, Temple; Tom Brennan, Villanova; Nick Davis, Maryland; Larry Hedden, Michigan State.

St. Louis

Dave Gambee, Oregon State; Hub Reed, Oklahoma City; Wayne Embry, Miami (O.); Julius Pegues, Pittsburgh; Rick Herrscher, Southern Methodist; John Crawford, Iowa State; Ken Sidle, Ohio State; Bruno Boin, Washington; Tink Van Patton, Temple; James Purcell, Coe; Don Klein, Rockhurst; Joe Buckhalter, Tennessee A&I.

Syracuse

Connie Dierking, Cincinnati; Hal Greer, Marshall; John Nacincik, Maryland; Tommy Kearns, North Carolina; Fred Grim, Arkansas; Jack Mimlitz, St. Louis; Pete Tillotson, Michigan; Ruel Tucker, Rockhurst.

1959

Boston

John Richter, North Carolina State; Gene Guarilia, George Washington; Ralph Crosthwaite, Western Kentucky; Ed Kazakavich, Scranton; Don Lange, William & Mary; Bob Cumings, Boston U.

Cincinnati

Bob Boozer, Kansas State; Tom Robitaille, Rice; Mike Mendenhall, Cincinnati; Leo Byrd, Marshall; Harry Kirchner, Texas Christian; Don Hennon, Pittsburgh; Dale Moore, Eastern Kentucky; Don Matuszak, Kansas State; Joe Billy McDade, Bradley; Joe Vivano, Xavier (O.); Charley Brown, Seattle; Roger Wendel, Tulsa.

Detroit

Bailey Howell, Mississippi State; Don Goldstein, Louisville; Gary Alcorn, Fresno State; George Lee, Michigan; Tony Windis, Wyoming; Lou Jordan, Cornell (N.Y.); Doug Smart, Washington; Chuck Curtis, Pacific Lutheran; Doyle Edmiston, Hardin-Simmons; Bruno Boin, Washington; M.C. Burton, Michigan.

Minneapolis

Tom Hawkins, Notre Dame; Rudy LaRusso, Dartmouth; Bob Smith, West Virginia; Wilson Eison, Purdue; Bobby Joe Mason, Bradley; Jim Henry, Vanderbilt; Charley Grote, Georgetown (Ky.); Leon Hill, Texas Tech; Jim Mudd, North Texas State; Roger Johnson, Minnesota; Jack Evans, Superior State; Vern Baggenstoss, St. Cloud State; Dwayne Smith, Gustavus Adolphus.

New York

John Green, Michigan State; Alan Seiden, St. John's (N.Y.); Bob Anderegg, Michigan State; John Cox, Kentucky; Herb Busch, Virginia; Bucky McDonald, George Washington; Russ Robinson, Southwest Missouri; Walt Torrence, UCLA; Jerry Shipp, Southeast Oklahoma; Paul Wilcox, Davis & Elkins; Paul Benes, Hope; Ed Blair, Western Michigan; John Nicoll, Brigham Young; Jack Israel, Southwest Missouri.

Philadelphia

Wilt Chamberlain, Kansas; Joe Ruklick, Northwestern; Jim Hockaday, Memphis State; Ron Stevenson, Texas Christian; Bill Telasky, George Washington; Joe Spratt, St. Joseph's (Pa.); Joe Ryan, Villanova; Dave Gunther, Iowa; Carl Belz, Princeton; Tony Sellari, Lenoir Rhyne; Phil Warren, Northwestern.

St. Louis

Bob Ferry, St. Louis; Cal Ramsey, New York University; Hank Stein, Xavier (O); Lee Harman, Oregon State; Nick Mantis, Northwestern; Mike Moran, Marquette; Orby Arnold, Memphis State; Willie Merriweather, Purdue; Lou Pucillo, North Carolina State; Ron Loneski, Kansas; John Barnhill, Tennessee State.

Syracuse

Dick Barnett, Tennessee State; Gene Tormohlen, Tennessee; John Cincebox, Syracuse; Paul Neumann, Stanford; Roger Taylor, Illinois; Bob Dalton, California; Darnell Haney, U.S. Navy.

1960

Boston

Tom Sanders, New York U.; Leroy Wright, College of the Pacific; Mike Graney, Notre Dame; Sid Cohen, Kentucky; Wayne Lawrence, Texas A&M; George Newman, Kentucky.

Cincinnati

Oscar Robertson, Cincinnati; Jay Arnette, Texas; Ralph Davis, Cincinnati; Dalen Showaiter, Tennessee; Don Ogorek, Seattle; Bobby Joe Mason, Bradley; Fred Sobrero, Santa Clara; Sam Stith, St. Bonaventure; Al Nealey, Arizona State; Lon Sizemore, West Virginia Tech; Dennis Moore, Regis; Ron Attenberg, Cornell (Iowa); John Milhoan, Marshall; Larry Chaney, Montana State; Ducky Potter, Moravian; Gene Jordan, Northwest Missouri; Ernie McCray, Arizona; Don Mills, Kentucky; Larry Willey, Cincinnati; Tony Wilcox, Wittenberg; Jim McDonald, West Virginia Wesleyan.

Detroit

Jack Moreland, Louisiana Tech; Ron Johnson, Minnesota; Frank Case, Dayton; Ken Remley, West Virginia Wesleyan; Willie Jones, Northwestern; Bill Lowry, Christian Brothers; Doug Moe, North Carolina; Mike Yugovich, Youngstown; Martin Holland, Kentucky Wesleyan; Mel Peterson, Wheaton; Don Dobbert, Wheaton; Lee Hopfenspirger, Hamline.

Minneapolis

Jerry West, West Virginia; Dave Budd, Wake Forest; Jim Hagan, Tennessee Tech; Wally Frank, Kansas State; George Farley, Cornell (N.Y.); Bobby Goodall, Tulsa; Howard Joliff, Ohio; John Werhas, Southern California; Claude Lefevre, Gonzaga; Dick Harvey, Creighton; Sterling Forbes, Pepperdine; Willie Jones, American.

New York

Darrall Imhoff, California; Kelly Coleman, Kentucky Wesleyan; Bob McNeill, St. Joseph's (Pa.); Ben Warley, Tennessee A&I; Charley McNeil, Maryland; David Denton, Georgia Tech; Dick Doughty, California; George Price, Memphis State; Tony Davis, Hawaii; Walter Mangham, Marquette; Howard Willis, Grambling; Henry Hart, Auburn; Dick Furry, Ohio State; Jim Hanna, Southern California; Jerry Bechtal, Maryland; Jerry Schofield, Utah State; Tandy Gillis, California; George Krajack, Clemson.

Philadelphia

Al Bunge, Maryland; Bill Kennedy, Temple; Bob Mealy, Manhattan; Charley Sharp, Southwest Texas; Al Attles, North Carolina A&T; Jim Brangan, Princeton; Bob Clarke, St. Joseph's (Pa.); George Raveling, Villanova.

St. Louis

Fred LaCour, San Francisco; Horace Walker, Michigan State; Jimmie Darrow, Bowling Green; Bob Sims, Pepperdine; Don Curry, Mississippi Southern; Bob Castaneda, Rockhurst; Americus John-Lewis, Iowa; Dick Davies, Louisiana State; Bob Wilkinson, Indiana; Ed Smallwood, Evansville.

Syracuse

Lee Shaffer, North Carolina; Wilbur Trosch, St. Francis (Pa.); Joe

Roberts, Ohio State; Carl Cole, Eastern Kentucky; Jim Mudd, North Texas State; Herschell Tucker, Nebraska; Bernie Coffman, Kentucky; Don Lynch, LeMoyne; Bernie Findlay, San Diego State.

1961

Boston

Gary Phillips, Houston; Al Butler, Niagara; Bill Depp, Vanderbilt; Carl Cole, Eastern Kentucky; Bob DiStefano, North Carolina State; Ned Twyman, Duquesne; Mel Klein, Northern State (S.D.).

Chicago

Walter Bellamy, Indiana; John Turner, Louisville; Jerry Graves, Mississippi State; York Larese, North Carolina; Don Kojis, Marquette; Doug Moe, North Carolina; Jeff Cohen, William & Mary; Bill Bridges, Kansas; Roger Kaiser, Georgia Tech; Howie Carl, DePaul; Dave Voss, Tulsa; Ron Heller, Wichita; John Wessels, Illinois; Steve Strange, Southern Methodist; Larry Comley, Kansas State.

Cincinnati

Larry Siegfried, Ohio State; Bob Wiesenhan, Cincinnati; Bob Nordmann, St. Louis; Lowery Kirk, Memphis State; Rossie Johnson, Tennessee A&I; Bob Slobodnik, Duquesne; Dave Zeller, Miami (O.); Jerry Thelen, Villa Madonna; Larry Krueger, Ohio; Jack Waters, Mississippi; Carl Short, Newberry; George Patterson, Toledo; Clair McRoberts, Monmouth (Ill.); Carl Bouldin, Cincinnati.

Detroit

Ray Scott, Portland; John Egan, Providence; Doug Kistler, Duke; George Finley, Tennessee A&I; Dan Doyle, Belmont Abbey; Lee Patrone, West Virginia; Burt Price, Wittenberg; Walter Ward, Hampton; Peter Baltic, Penn State; Wayne Monson, Northern Michigan; Richard Kraft, Brockport.

Los Angeles

Wayne Yates, Memphis State; Fred Sawyer, Louisville; Frank Burgess, Gonzaga; Charles Henke, Missouri; Bill Lickert, Kentucky; Bill McClintock, California; Albert Alamanza, Texas; Bill Ellis, UCLA; Carl Anderson, Oregon State; Robert Williams, Hancock; Howard Hurt, Duke.

New York

Tom Stith, St. Bonaventure; Whitey Martin, St. Bonaventure; Tony Jackson, St. John's (N.Y.); George Blaney, Holy Cross; Bill Smith, St. Peter's; Cleveland Buckner, Jackson State; Donnis Butcher, Pikeville; Cedrick Price, Kansas State; Charles Bowman, Wabash; Ron Dibelius, Wisconsin State Teachers-Oshkosh; Kevin Loughery, St. John's (N.Y.); Earl Shultz, California; Ned Jennings, Kentucky; Bill Engressor, Louisiana State; Vince Kempton, St. John's (N.Y.).

Philadelphia

Tom Meschery, St. Mary's (Calif.); Ted Luckenbill, Houston; Jack Egan, St. Joseph's (Pa.); John Tidwell, Michigan; Bruce Spraggins, Virginia Union; Dick Goldberg, Mississippi Southern; Charles McNeil, Maryland; Larry Swift, Northeast Missouri State; Leo Hill, Los Angeles State; Corky Whitrow, Georgetown (Ky.).

St. Louis

Cleo Hill, Winston-Salem; Ron Horn, Indiana; Tom Chilton, Eastern Tennessee; Gus Guydon, Drake; John Berberich, UCLA; Bob McDonald, Maryland; Charles Riley, Winston-Salem; Gene Velloff, Doane; Herbert Gray, North Carolina A&T; Tom Faszholz, Concordia (St. Louis, Mo.); Dick Kepley, North Carolina; Jackie Crawford, Centenary; Howard Stacey, Louisville.

Syracuse

Ben Warley, Tennessee A&L; Chris Smith, Virginia Tech; Charles Osbourne, Western Kentucky; Henry Whitney, Iowa State; Don Jacobson, South Dakota; Billy Joe Price, New Mexico State; Roger Newman, Kentucky; Dave Mills, Seattle; Rex Tippitt, Grambling; Pete Chudy, Syracuse; Chuck Sammons, LeMoyne.

1962

Boston

John Havlicek, Ohio State; Jack Foley, Holy Cross; Jim Hadnot, Providence; Roger Strickland, Jacksonville; Gary Daniels, Citadel; Jim Hooley, Boston College; Clyde Arnold, Duquesne; Chuck Chevalier, Boston College; Mike Cingiser, Brown.

Chicago

Billy McGill, Utah; Terry Dischinger, Purdue; Don Nelson, Iowa; Charles Vaughn, Southern Illinois; Cornell Green, Utah State; Bill Hanson, Washington; Jack Ardon, Tulane; Larry Pursiful, Kentucky; Carroll Broussard, Texas A&M; Pete Campbell, Princeton; Jeff Slade, Kenyon; Mel Nowell, Ohio State; Tom Kennedy, Lewis; Bob Mahland, Williams; Pat McKenzie, Kansas State; Norman Majors, Rockhurst.

Cincinnati

Jerry Lucas, Ohio State; Bud Olsen, Louisville; Chris Appel, USC; Jack Thobe, Xavier (O.); Mike Wroblewski, Kansas State; Jerry Foster, Drake; Gary Cunningham, UCLA; Ed Bento, Loyola (Calif.); Chris Jones, Carson-Newman; George Knighton, New Mexico State; Frank Pinchback, Xavier (O.).

Detroit

Dave DeBusschere, Detroit; Kevin Loughery, St. John's (N.Y.); Harold Hudgens, Texas Tech; Reggie Harding, none; Lindbergh Moody, South Carolina; Ed Noe, Morehead State; John Bradley, Lawrence Tech; Mike Rice, Duquesne; Bill Nelson, Hamline; Glenn Moore, Oregon.

Los Angeles

Leroy Ellis, St. John's (N.Y.); Gene Wiley, Wichita; John Green, UCLA; Jan Loudermilk, Southern Methodist; Art Whisnant, South Carolina; Bucky Keller, Virginia Tech; Bill Garner, Portland; Bill Matson, Minnesota.

New York

Paul Hogue, Cincinnati; John Rudometkin, Southern California; Bobby Rascoe, Western Kentucky; Cliff Luyk, Florida; Bob Burgess, Marshall; Ken Stanley, Pacific (Calif.); Richie Swarz, Hofstra; Warren Fouts, Oklahoma; Paul Benec, Duquesne; Ralph Richardson, Eastern Kentucky; Ed Mazria, Pratt.

Philadelphia

Wayne Hightower, Kansas; Hubie White, Villanova; Dave Fedor, Florida State; Garry Roggenburk, Dayton; Jack Jackson, Virginia Union; Jim Hudock, North Carolina; Howard Montgomery, Pan American; Bill Kirvin, Xavier (O.); Tom Kieffer, St. Louis; Ken McComb, North Carolina; Don Walsh, North Carolina; Charles Warren, Oregon.

St. Louis

Zelmo Beaty, Prairie View; Bob Duffy, Colgate; Charles Hardnett, Grambling; Jerry Grote, Loyola (Calif.); Tom Hatton, Dayton; Jay Carty, Oregon State; Bob McAteer, LaSalle; Terry Ball, Washington State; Marvin Trotman, Elizabeth City; Charlie Sells, Washington State;

Tom Chappele, Maine; John Caveny, LeMoyne; Jerry Carlton, Arkansas; Wilky Gilmore, Colorado; Dave Ricerto, Rhode Island; Wally Roundsville, California Tech.

Syracuse
Len Chappell, Wake Forest; Chet Walker, Bradley; Porter Merriweather, Tennessee State; Bob McCully, St. Bonaventure; John Windsor, Stanford; Len Van Eman, Wichita; Bob Sharpenter, Georgetown (D.C.); Jerry Harkness, Loyola (III.); Vince Brewer, Iowa State.

1963

Baltimore
Rod Thorn, West Virginia; Gus Johnson, Idaho; Tom Bolyard, Indiana; Nolen Ellison, Kansas; Ron Glaser, Marquette; Ken Siebel, Wisconsin; Larry Brown, North Carolina; Dick Riesback, Iowa State; Ron Jackson, Wisconsin; M.C. Thompson, DePaul.

Boston
Bill Green, Colorado State; Ken Saylors, Arkansas Tech; Chuck Kriston, Valparaiso; Connie McGuire, Southeast Oklahoma; W.D. Stroud, Mississippi State; Vinnie Ernst, Providence; Herb Magee, Philadelphia Textile.

Cincinnati
Tom Thacker, Cincinnati; Jim King, Tulsa; Jimmy Rayl, Indiana; Ken Charlton, Colorado; Mac Herndon, Bradley; Jim McCormack, West Virginia; Hunter Beckman, Memphis State.

Detroit
Eddie Miles, Seattle; Jerry Smith, Furman; Mike McCoy, Miami; Dave Erickson, Marquette; Bill Small, Illinois; Reggie Harding, none; Ira Harge, New Mexico; Gary Silc, Northern Michigan; Ernie Durston, Seattle.

Los Angeles
Roger Strickland, Jacksonville; Mel Gibson, Western Carolina; Lyle Harger, Houston; Layton Johns, Auburn; Larry Jones, Toledo; Warren Salade, Westminster (Pa.); Gordie Martin, Southern California.

New York
Art Heyman, Duke; Jerry Harkness, Loyola (III.); Bill O'Connor, Canisius; Nate Cloud, Delaware; Joe McDermott, Belmont Abbey; Jim Kerwin, Tulane; Bob Woolard, Wake Forest; Fred Crawford, St. Bonaventure; Ray Cronk, Lakeland; Gerald Glur, Furman; Orb Bowling, Tennessee; Bob Walters, Baldwin Wallace; Jerry Szachara, Cornell (N.Y.); Bill Raftery, LaSalle; Ron Pickett, Eastern Kentucky.

St. Louis
Jerry Ward, Boston College; Leland Mitchell, Mississippi State; Bill Burwell, Illinois; Waite Bellamy, Florida A&M; Tony Yates, Cincinnati; Ron Santio, Maryland State; Ken Rohloff, North Carolina State; Harold Strothers, Texas A&M; Frank Davis, Oklahoma Christian; Carl Ritter, Southeast Missouri State; Marv Straw, Iowa State; Hugh Evans, North Carolina A&T; Gordon McFarland, Central Missouri State.

San Francisco
Nate Thurmond, Bowling Green; Gary Hill, Oklahoma City; Steve Gray, St. Mary's (Calif.); Dave Downey, Illinois; Don Turner, Southwestern (Kan.); Gene Shields, Santa Clara; Don Clemetson, Stanford; Harry Dinnel, Pepperdine; Chuck White, Idaho.

Syracuse
Tom Hoover, Villanova; Hershell West, Grambling; Jerry Greenspan, Maryland; Ray Flynn, Providence; Tony Cerkvenik, Arizona State; Vince Brewer, Iowa State; Bill Brown, Howard Payne.

1964

Baltimore
Gary Bradds, Ohio State; Paul Silas, Creighton; Jerry Sloan, Evansville; Pete Spoden, State Coll. of Iowa; Bennie Lennox, Texas A&M; Bob Edmonds, Tennessee State; Ron Miller, Loyola (III.); Danny Schultz, Tennessee; Tom Black, South Dakota State; Bill Kusleika, Tulsa; Fred Glover, Winston-Salem; Frank Kamiaski, Randolph-Macon; Doug Moon, Utah; Pete Gent, Michigan State; Sandy Williams, St. Francis (Pa.).

Boston
Mel Counts, Oregon State; Ron Bonham, Cincinnati; John Thompson, Providence; Joe Strawder, Bradley; Nick Werkman, Seton Hall; LaVern Tart, Bradley; Rich Falk, Northwestern; Jeff Blue, Butler; Charles Kelley, West Virginia Tech; Duane Corribeau, Clark.

Cincinnati
George Wilson, Cincinnati; Bill Chmielewski, Dayton; Steve Courtin, St. Joseph's (Pa.); Harold Hairston, New York University; George Kirk, Memphis State; Al Thrasher, Wittenberg; Vic Rouse, Loyola (III.); Joe Gieger, Xavier (O.); Scotty Pierce, West Texas State; Bob Neumann, Memphis State; Jim Reynolds, Abilene Christian; Fred Jones, Youngstown.

Detroit
Joe Caldwell, Arizona State; Les Hunter, Loyola (III.); Wally Jones, Villanova; Jim Davis, Colorado; Ray Wolford, Toledo; Larry Phillips, Rice; Jerry Jackson, Ohio; Ralph Telken, Rockhurst.

Los Angeles
Walt Hazzard, UCLA; Cotton Nash, Kentucky; Tom Dose, Stanford; Henry Finkel, Dayton; John Savage, North Texas State; Troy Collier, Utah State; Steve Anstett, Portland; Jay Buckley, Duke.

New York
Jim Barnes, Texas Western; Willis Reed, Grambling; Brian Generalovich, Pittsburgh; Fred Crawford, St. Bonaventure; Tony Gennari, Canisius; Tom Lavelle, Western Carolina; Emmette Bryant, DePaul; Jim Boutin, Lewis & Clark; Jack Brens, Wisconsin; Jim Christie, Georgetown (D.C.); Dennis Lynch, Yale.

Philadelphia
Lucious Jackson, Pan American; Ira Harge, New Mexico; Larry Jones, Toledo; Frank Corace, LaSalle; Lou Skurcenski, Westminster (Pa.); Ricky Kaminsky, Yale; Gordon Hatton, Dayton; Bob Pelkington, Xavier (O.); Jim Brennan, Clemson; Wally Briggs, North Carolina A&T; Thomas Lowry, West Virginia; Julius Myers, Morris Brown.

St. Louis
Jeff Mullins, Duke; Howard Komives, Bowling Green; Art Becker, Arizona State; Willie Murrell, Kansas State; John Tresvant, Seattle; Ernest Block, Virginia State; Maurice McHartley, North Carolina A&T; Kendall Rhine, Rice; Darrell Carrier, Western Kentucky; Frank Stephens, Virginia State; Gerry Govan, St. Mary's (Kan.); Warren Sutton, George Williams; Rich Spears, Acadia; Bill Blair, Virginia Military; Al Cech, Detroit.

San Francisco

Barry Kramer, New York University; Bob Koper, Oklahoma City; McCoy McLemore, Drake; Gene Elmore, Southern Methodist; Roger Suttner, Kansas State; Ray Carey, Missouri; Dave Lee, San Francisco; Bob Garabaldi, Santa Clara; Camden Wall, California; Jeff Cartwright, Chapman.

1965

Baltimore

Jerry Sloan, Evansville; Tal Brody, Illinois; Joe Newton, Auburn; Skip Thoren, Illinois; Charles Dinkens, Miami (O.); Lavonne LeFlore, Jackson State; Willie Somerset, Duquesne; Jim Murphy, DePaul; John Wendelken, Holy Cross; Bogie Redmon, Illinois; Thales McReynolds, Miles; Walt Sahm, Notre Dame; Joe Ramsey, Southern Illinois; Jerry Rook, Arkansas; Dave Hicks, none; Bunk Adams, Ohio; Roger Taylor, Illinois.

Boston

Ollie Johnson, San Francisco; Ronnie Watts, Wake Forest; Toby Kimball, Connecticut; Richie Tarrant, St. Michael's; Don Davidson, Davidson; Haskell Tison, Duke; George Deehan, Lenoir Rhyne.

Cincinnati

Nate Bowman, Wichita; Flynn Robinson, Wyoming; Jon McGlocklin, Indiana; Robert Love, Southern (La.); Warren Issac, Iona; Leon Clements, Ouachita Baptist; Jeff Gehring, Miami (O.); Jim Fox, South Carolina; Ron Krick, Cincinnati; Richie Dec, Seton Hall; Dick Maile, Louisiana State; Robert McCullough, Benedict; Oliver Jones, Albany State (Ga.); Larry Franks, Texas; Ronald Scharf, Georgia Tech; Willie Porter, Tennessee State.

Detroit

Bill Buntin, Michigan; Tom Van Arsdale, Indiana; Ron Reed, Notre Dame; Jim King, Oklahoma State; Ted Manning, North Carolina College; Barry Smith, High Point.

Los Angeles

Gail Goodrich, UCLA; John Fairchild, Brigham Young; Jim Caldwell, Georgia Tech; Brooks Henderson, Florida; A.W. Davis, Tennessee; Theo Cruz, Seattle; Dwayne Cruze, Idaho State; George Unseld, Kansas; Marlbert Pradd, Dillard; Don Rae, Montana; Bob Andrews, Alabama.

New York

Bill Bradley, Princeton; Dave Stallworth, Wichita; Dick Van Arsdale, Indiana; Barry Clemens, Ohio Wesleyan; Larry Lembo, Michigan; Steve Nisenson, Hofstra; Warren Davis, North Carolina A&T; Dale Neel, High Point; Frank Granat, Alliance; Ray Neary, Wilmington; Wayne Molis, Lewis; Bill Meyer, Hiram; Steve Trupin, Yale; Dennis McGovern, Rhode Island.

Philadelphia

Bill Cunningham, North Carolina; Jesse Branson, Elon; Bob Weiss, Penn State; Henry Finkel, Dayton; Richie Moore, Villanova; Mitch Edwards, Pan American; John Young, Midwestern (Tex.); Bob Barnek, St. Bonaventure; Gene West, Drake; Dean Church, Southwest Louisiana; Curt Fromal, LaSalle; Dan Anderson, Augsburg; Rich Parks, Tulsa; Jack Margenthaler, Houston; James Pitts, Georgia; Larry Rafferty, Fairfield.

St. Louis

Jim Washington, Villanova; Hal Blevins, Arkansas A&M; Ken Mc-

Intyre, St. John's (N.Y.); Lynn Nance, Washington; Theodore Werner, Washington State; John Rambo, Long Beach; Terry Kunze, Minnesota; Cincinnatus Powell, Portland; Leroy Walker, Utah State; Spencer Carlson, Baylor; Weldon Kytle, Fenn; Elton McGriff, Creighton; Mel Northway, Minnesota; Terry Page, Detroit; George Pomey, Michigan; Bob Tolan, Eastern Kentucky.

San Francisco

Fred Hetzel, Davidson; Rick Barry, Miami (Fla.); Wilbur Frazier, Grambling; Keith Erickson, UCLA; Warren Rustand, Arizona; Eddie Jackson, Oklahoma City; Jim Jarvis, Oregon State; Dan Wolters, California; Willie Cotton, Central State (Okla.).

1966

Baltimore

Jack Marin, Duke; Neil Johnson, Creighton; Dave Wagnon, Idaho State; George Peeples, Iowa; John Beasley, Texas A&M; John Jones, Los Angeles State; Jeff Neuman, Pennsylvania; Dave Mills, DePaul; Roland West, Cincinnati; Chuck Gardner, Colorado; Guy Manning, Prairie View; Stan McKenzie, New York University; Grant Simmons, Nebraska; Al Lopes, Kansas; Jim Harter, Pan American; Howard Bayne, Tennessee; Ken Barnes, Wisconsin; Chris Pervall, Iowa; Jerry Trice, Weber State; Gene Visscher, Weber State.

Boston

Jim Barnett, Oregon; Leon Clark, Wyoming; Gary Turner, Texas Christian; John Austin, Boston College; Charlie Hunter, Oklahoma City; Jerry Ward, Maryland; Russ Gumina, San Francisco.

Chicago

Dave Schellhase, Purdue; Irwin Mueller, San Francisco; Eddie Bodkin, Eastern Kentucky; Jim Williams, Temple; Larry Humes, Evansville; John Comeaux, Grambling; Stan Curtis, Michigan State; Gene Summers, Northern Michigan; Don Swanson, DePaul; Carver Clinton, Penn State.

Cincinnati

Walt Wesley, Kansas; Jerry Lee Wells, Oklahoma City; James Ware, Oklahoma City; Charles Schmaus, Virginia Military Institute; Rich Parks, St. Louis; Steve Cunningham, Western Kentucky; Gary Schull, Florida State; Ron Krick, Cincinnati; Billy Smith, Loyola (Ill.); Freddie Lewis, Arizona State; R.B. Lynam, Oklahoma Baptist.

Detroit

Dave Bing, Syracuse; Dorrie Murrey, Detroit; Oliver Darden, Michigan; Jeff Congdon, Brigham Young; William Pickens, Georgia Southern; Carroll Hooser, Southern Methodist; Ted Manning, North Carolina College; George McNeil, Southern Illinois.

Los Angeles

Jerry Chambers, Utah; Henry Finkel, Dayton; John Block, Southern California; Archie Clark, Minnesota; Stan Washington, Michigan State; Keith Thomas, Vanderbilt; Tab Jackson, Idaho College; John Wetzel, Virginia Tech; Julian Hammond, Tulsa; Mike Rooney, Oklahoma; George Grams, Purdue.

New York

Cazzie Russell, Michigan; Henry Akin, Morehead State; Stewart Johnson, Murray State; Lee DeFore, Auburn; Ron Jackson, Clark; George Fisher, Utah; Mike Dabich, New Mexico State; Mike Silliman, Army; Bill Turner, Akron; Rich Moore, Hiram Scott; Rich Dyer, New York U.; Dave Deutsch, Rochester; Bob Bennett, North Carolina.

Philadelphia

Matt Guokas, St. Joseph's (Pa.); Bill Melchionni, Villanova; Don Freeman, Illinois; Ken Wilburn, Central State (O.); Tom Duff, St. Joseph's (Pa.); Austin Robbins, Tennessee; Pat Caldwell, Rockhurst; Bob Bedell, Stanford.

St. Louis

Lou Hudson, Minnesota; Dick Snyder, Davidson; Tommy Kron, Kentucky; Bob McIntyre, St. John's (N.Y.); Dick Nemelka, Brigham Young; Lonnie Wright, Colorado State; Ray Neary, Wilmington; Brian Williams, Xavier (O.); Al Grant, Long Island U.; Don Yates, Minnesota; Curt Gammell, Pacific Lutheran; Lonnie Lynn, Wilberforce; Nick Aloi, Bowling Green; Ollie Carter, San Francisco; Paul Long, Wake Forest; Eddie Jackson, Bradley.

San Francisco

Clyde Lee, Vanderbilt; Joe Ellis, San Francisco; Steve Chubin, Rhode Island; Steve Vacendak, Duke; Tom Kerwin, Centenary; Jim Pitts, Northwestern; Lon Hughey, Fresno State; Ken Washington, UCLA.

1967

Baltimore

Earl Monroe, Winston-Salem; James Jones, Grambling; Malkin Strong, Seattle; Al Salvadori, South Carolina; Dexter Westbrook, Providence; Bob Reidy, Duke; Ron Perry, Virginia Tech; Ed Manning, Jackson State; Ron Allen, Arkansas A&M; Bill Gillespie, Montana State; Bubba Smith, Michigan State; Tony Eatmon, Pan American; Lyn Burkholder, South Carolina; Paul Mickey, Penn State; Rich Peck, Louisiana Tech; Gary Williams, Oklahoma; Loy Peterson, Oregon State; Jerry Southwood, Vanderbilt; George Spencer, Washington; Roland West, Cincinnati.

Boston

Mal Graham, New York University; Sam Smith, Kentucky Wesleyan; Neville Shed, Texas Western; Mike Redd, Kentucky Wesleyan; Ed Hummer, Princeton; Edgar Lacey, UCLA; Andy Anderson, Canisius; Henry Brown, Lowell Tech; Ricky Weitzman, Northeastern; Joe Harrington, Maryland.

Chicago

Clem Haskins, Western Kentucky; Byron Beck, Denver; John Dickson, Arkansas State; Jim Burns, Northwestern; Dick Pruet, Jacksonville; Marlbert Pradd, Dillard; Bob Wolf, Marquette; Leon Simon, Santa Fe; Ernie Laurant, Albuquerque; Jim Boshart, Wake Forest; Jim Andros, New Haven; Ron Widby, Tennessee; Tom Storm, Montana State; Don Whitehead, Erskine; Jim Garza, Detroit Tech; Jim Dawson, Illinois.

Cincinnati

Mel Daniels, New Mexico; Gary Gray, Oklahoma City; Louie Dampier, Kentucky; Tom Washington, Cheyney State; Frank Stronczek, American International; Charley Beasley, Southern Methodist; Frank Hollendoner, Georgetown (D.C.); Ron Sepic, Ohio State; Willie Davis, North Texas State; Ken Callway, Cincinnati; Frank Gadjunas, Villanova; John Moates, Richmond; Jerry Pettway, Northwood; Earl Beechum, Midwestern (Tex.); John Vermelyea, Morningside; Darryl Meachem, Edinboro State.

Detroit

Jimmy Walker, Providence; Steve Sullivan, Georgetown (D.C.); Darrell Hardy, Baylor; Ron Franz, Kansas; Paul Long, Wake Forest; Bob Lloyd, Rutgers; George Carter, St. Bonaventure; George Dalzell, Colgate; Matthew Aitch, Michigan State.

Los Angeles

Sonny Dove, St. John's (N.Y.); Randy Mahaffey, Clemson; Dwight Smith, Western Kentucky; Cliff Anderson, St. Joseph's (Pa.); Joe Allen, Bradley; Gary Keller, Florida; Jamie Thompson, Wichita; Don Carlos, Otterbein; Jay McMillen, Maryland; Don Kruse, Houston; Nick Pino, Kansas State; Ben Monroe, New Mexico; Gary Jones, Iowa.

New York

Walt Frazier, Southern Illinois; Phil Jackson, North Dakota; Gary Gregor, South Carolina; Keith Swagerty, Pacific (Calif.); Barry Leibowitz, Long Island University; Ben Benfield, West Virginia; Butch Wade, Indiana State; Gil Radday, St. Francis (N.Y.); Ray Smith, Kansas State; Bruce Kaplan, New York U.; Mark Merkin, North Carolina; Mike Riordan, Providence.

Philadelphia

Craig Raymond, Brigham Young; Richie Moore, Hiram Scott; Ron Kozlicki, Northwestern; James Reid, Winston-Salem; Tim Powers, Creighton; Frank Card, South Carolina State; Jim Conley, Virginia; Ron Filipek, Tennessee Tech; Butch Erwin, Niagara; Ted Campbell, North Carolina A&T; Hubie Marshall, LaSalle; George Mack, North Carolina A&T; Wayne Brabender, Minnesota-Morris; Sherman Dillard, Tulsa; Warren Chapman, Western Kentucky; Charlie Paulk, Northeast Oklahoma.

St. Louis

Tom Workman, Seattle; Bob Verga, Duke; Wes Bialosuknia, Connecticut; Mike Wittman, Miami (Fla.); John Morrison, Canisius; Carl Fuller, Bethune-Cookman; Arvesta Kelly, Lincoln (Mo.); Ed Biedenbach, North Carolina State; Rich Falkenbush, St. Michael's.

San Diego

Pat Riley, Kentucky; Bob Netolicky, Drake; Nick Jones, Oregon; Craig Dill, Michigan; Robert Cole, St. Louis; Elbert Miller, Nevada Southern; Al Grundy, St. Joseph's (Pa.); John Duncan, Murray State; Al Razutis, California Western; Bob Chlupsa, Manhattan; John Tolbert, South Carolina Trade School.

San Francisco

Dave Lattin, Texas Western; Bill Turner, Akron; Bob Lewis, North Carolina; Mike Lynn, UCLA; Dale Schlueter, Colorado State; Sonny Bustion, Colorado State; Bob Krulish, Pacific (Calif.); Richard Dean, Syracuse; Joe Calbo, San Francisco State; Bill Morgan, New Mexico; Dave Fox, Pacific (Calif.)

Seattle

Al Tucker, Oklahoma Baptist; Bob Rule, Colorado State; Sam Singleton, Omaha; Larry Bunce, Utah State; Plummer Lott, Seattle; Craig Dill, Michigan; Gordon Harris, Washington; Dick Kolbert, Santa Barbara; Willie Wolters, Boston College; Rod McDonald, Whitworth; Gary Lechman, Gonzaga; Randy Matson, Texas A&M; Rubin Russell, North Texas State; Jim Sutherland, Wake Forest; Willie Campbell, Nebraska.

1968

Atlanta

Skip Harlicka, South Carolina; Jack Thompson, South Carolina; Bob Warren, Vanderbilt; Rusty Parker, Miami (Fla.); Phil Wagner, Georgia Tech; Oscar Smith, Elizabeth City; Martin Baietti, Manhattan; Mac Daughty, Albany State (Ga.); Dwight Walker, Tennessee State; Henry Watkins, Tennessee State; Bill Harris, Texas Western; Frank Standard, South Carolina; George Hicker, Syracuse; Bernie Foster, Pasadena; Terry Allerton, Baldwin-Wallace.

Baltimore

Wes Unseld, Louisville; Bob Quick, Xavier (O.); Ron Nelson, New Mexico; Dallas Thornton, Kentucky Wesleyan; Ed Chaplin, Voorhees; Joe Heiser, Princeton; Jasper Wilson, Southern (La.); Barry Orms, St. Louis; Wayne Chapman, Western Kentucky; Steve Adelman, Boston College; Al Dixon, Bowling Green; Willie Cager, Texas Western; Rudy Bogad, St. John's (N.Y.); Ernest Sims, East Tennessee; Joe Allen, Bradley; Dennis Black, San Francisco; Greg Morris, Cornell (N.Y.); Art Kenny, Fairfield; Jim LaCour, Seattle; Ron Woodruff, Midwestern (Tex.).

Boston

Don Chaney, Houston; Garfield Smith, Eastern Kentucky; Rich Johnson, Grambling; Thad Jaracz, Kentucky; Jerry Newsom, Indiana State; Mike Lewis, Duke; Julius Keyes, Alcorn; Bill Butler, St. Bonaventure; Ivan Leschinsky, Long Island University; Tom Neimeir, Evansville; Jim Langheld, Fordham; Art Stephenson, Rhode Island; Keith Hochstein, Holy Cross.

Chicago

Tom Boerwinkle, Tennessee; Lloyd Peterson, Oregon State; Don Dee, St. Mary's (Kan.); Mike Lynn, UCLA; Jim Tillman, Loyola (Ill.); Ken Barnett, Delaware; Willie Davis, North Texas State; Lloyd Higgins, Pasadena College; Corky Bell, Loyola (Ill.); Mike Weaver, Northwestern; Jim McGonigle, Iowa State; John Lallensack, Oshkosh State; Herman Gilliam, Purdue; Dave Carr, Washington; Mickey McCarthy, Texas Christian; Fred Holden, Louisville; Tom Benedict, Central Washington State; Bob Zoretich, DePaul; Rich Mason, Indiana State; Rich Rirkendal, Norfolk State; Willie Horton, Delaware.

Cincinnati

Don Smith, Iowa State; Pat Frink, Colorado; Dan Sparks, Weber State; Jim Kissane, Boston College; Calvin Martin, Texas Southern; Dick Dumas, Northeast Oklahoma; Dave Williams, Mississippi State; Butch Joyner, Indiana; Robert Wyenandt, Vanderbilt; James Robinson, Rochester Institute; Glynn Saulters, Northeast Louisiana; Jim Tindall, Massachusetts; Charles Core, Southeastern Louisiana; Mike Drespling, Westminster (Pa.); Dick Harris, unavailable; John Howard, Cincinnati; Larry Humes, Evansville; Jay Reffords, unavailable.

Detroit

Otto Moore, Pan American; Manny Leaks, Niagara; Fred Foster, Miami (O.); Rich Niemann, St. Louis; Carl Fuller, Bethune-Cookman; Wally Anderzunas, Creighton; Larry Newbold, Long Island University; Harry Laurie, St. Peter's; Vaughn Harper, Syracuse; Tom Baack, Nebraska.

Los Angeles

Bill Hewitt, Southern California; Dave Newmark, Columbia; Ed Biedenbach, North Carolina State; Lou Shepherd, Southwest Missouri State; Nick Pino, Kansas State; Dennis Hrcka, Hillsdale; John Smith, Southern Colorado; George Stone, Marshall; Charles Alford, East Carolina; Harry Singletary, Presbyterian; Reggie Lacefield, Western Michigan; Harvey Mumford, Montana State; John Godfrey, Abilene Christian; John Baum, Temple; Mike Eberle, Wyoming.

Milwaukee

Charles Paulk, Northeast Oklahoma; Eugene Moore, St. Louis; Sam Williams, Iowa; Greg Smith, Western Kentucky; Joe Franklin, Wisconsin; Fred Smith, Hawaii; Tom Kondla, Minnesota; Elbert Miller, Nevada Southern; Cliff Berger, Kentucky; Eugene Jones, Missouri; Brad Luchini, Marquette; Dave Miller, Florida.

New York

Bill Hosket, Ohio State; Don May, Dayton; Warren Armstrong, Wichita; Hal Booker, Cheyney State; Brian Brunkhorst, Marquette; Bob Waldal,

Dickinson State; Bob Hooper, Dayton; Roger Bohnenstiehl, Kansas; Sylvester Adams, North Carolina A&T; Bob Redd, Marshall; Pat Moriarty, Guilford; Ken Moorehead, Hillsdale; John Haarlow, Princeton; Ed Fellers, Guilford; Bob Ferguson, Tennessee Wesleyan; Milton Williams, Lincoln (Mo.).

Philadelphia

Shaler Halimon, Utah State; Ed Johnson, Tennessee State; Larry Miller, North Carolina; Chuck Williams, Colorado; Bill Jones, Fairfield; Melvin Jones, Albany State (Ga.); Clarence Brookins, Temple; Greg Cisson, Rider; Bill Soens, Miami (Fla.); Ted Campbell, North Carolina A&T; Earl Seyfert, Kansas State; Tom Youngdale, Davidson; George Mack, North Carolina A&T; Joe Crews, Villanova; Nate Ware, Tennessee State.

Phoenix

Gary Gregor, South Carolina; Dick Cunningham, Murray State; Art Beatty, American; Rich Jones, Memphis State; Harry Hollines, Denver; Rodney Knowles, Davidson; Charles Parks, Idaho State; Brian Clare, Denver; Merv Jackson, Utah; Lee Davis, North Carolina College; Ron Boone, Idaho State; Bill Davis, Arizona; Pat Hobard, California State.

San Diego

Elvin Hayes, Houston; John Trapp, Nevada Southern; Stuart Lantz, Nebraska; Harry Barnes, Northeastern; Glen Combs, Virginia Tech; Eldridge Webb, Tulsa; Rick Adelman, Loyola (Calif.); Aaron Sellers, Jackson State; John Schetzsle, Ashland; Mike Butler, Memphis State; Leonardo Epps, Clark; Roy Manning, Lane; Marshall Evans, Lincoln; Bobby Lewis, North Carolina State; Bill Gaines, East Texas State; Chuck Caldwell, Missouri-St. Louis; Dave Miller, South Dakota State; Harold Grant, Pepperdine; Bill Corley, Connecticut.

San Francisco

Ron Williams, West Virginia; Don Sidle, Oklahoma; Edgar Lacey, UCLA; Jim Eakins, Brigham Young; Bob Allen, Marshall; Dave Reasor, West Virginia; Walt Piatkowski, Bowling Green; Art Wilmore, San Francisco; Bob Heaney, Santa Clara; Jerry Chandler, Nevada Southern; Bob Wolfe, California.

Seattle

Bob Kauffman, Guilford; Art Harris, Stanford; Jeff Ockel, Utah; Henry Logan, Western Carolina; Al Hairston, Bowling Green; Ron Guziak, Duquesne; Jim McKean, Washington State; Willie Rogers, Oklahoma; Jimmy Smith, Utah State; Joe Kennedy, Duke; Jim Marsh, Southern California; Walt Simon, Utah; Bud Ogden, Santa Clara; Mike Warren, UCLA.

1969

Atlanta

Butch Beard, Louisville; Wally Anderzunas, Creighton; Lloyd Kerr, Colorado State; Billy Hann, Tennessee; Mike Mitchell, West Texas State; Guy Mackner, South Dakota; Bob Bundy, Vanderbilt; Bob Christian, Grambling; Pete Gayeska, Massachusetts; Dick Stewart, Rutgers; Loran Bracci, San Fernando Valley State; Dave Jones, LaVerne; Dick Barton, Riverside; Mike Dahl, Oglethorpe; Norm Carmichael, Virginia; Buddy Cornelius, Jacksonville State (Ala.); John Tolmie, Navy; Cliff Parsons, Air Force; Grady O'Malley, Manhattan; Carl Rodwell, California.

Baltimore

Mike Davis, Virginia Union; Willie Scott, Alabama State; Fred Carter, Mount St. Mary; Gene Ford, Western Michigan; Willie Jackson, Morehead State; Paul Loveday, California; Jeff Claypool, Grove City; Barry White, Hofstra; Gary Major, Duquesne; Frank Bartleson, Tennessee Tech; Gerald McKee, Ohio; Bob Washington, Tulsa; Bill Thompson, Shepard; Perry Johnson, Robert Morris JC; Jodie Harrison, Illinois; Phil Harris, Texas A&M; Tom Haggert, Brandeis; Chip Case, Virginia; Brian Heaney, Acadia; Stan McKain, Southern.

Boston
Jo Jo White, Kansas; Gene Williams, Kansas State; Julius Keye, Alcorn A&M; Steve Kuberski, Bradley; George Thompson, Marquette; Dolph Pulliam, Drake; Jim Johnson, Wisconsin; Bob Whitmore, Notre Dame; Gordon Smith, Cincinnati; Jim Picka, High Point; Larry Finstrom, Kenyon; Rod Forbes, Boston State; Billy Evans, Boston College.

Chicago
Larry Cannon, LaSalle; Ken Spain, Houston; Norm Van Lier, St. Francis (Pa.); Dave Nash, Kansas; Chris Ellis, Virginia Tech; George Tinsley, Kentucky Wesleyan; Frank Judge, Houston; Roger Moller, Westmar; Sterling Burke, Northwestern; Al Smith, Bradley; Larry Bergh, Weber State; Harry Hall, Wyoming; Rich Kirkland, Norfolk State; Bill Voight, Southern Methodist.

Cincinnati
Herman Gilliam, Purdue; John Baum, Temple; Luther Rackley, Xavier (O.); Ron Sanford, New Mexico; Jake Ford, Maryland State; Mel Coleman, Stout State; L.C. Bowen, Bradley; Merlon Bancroft, Southwest Missouri State; James Hurley, Transylvania; Bill Bowes, Elon; Jim Supple, Georgetown (D.C.); Mike Davis, Colorado State; Ted Johnson, Baldwin-Wallace.

Detroit
Terry Driscoll, Boston College; Willie Norwood, Alcorn A&M; Lamar Green, Morehead State; Ted Wierman, Washington State; Steve Mix, Toledo; Larry Jeffries, Trinity (Tex.); Steve Vandenberg, Duke; Bob Arnzen, Notre Dame; George Reynolds, Houston; Bill English, Winston-Salem; Rusty Clark, North Carolina.

Los Angeles
Willie McCarter, Drake; Rick Roberson, Cincinnati; Dick Garrett, Southern Illinois; Luther Green, Long Island U.; Don Griffin, Stanford; Wilbur Jones, Albany State (Ga.); Dick Grubar, North Carolina; Kari Liimo, Brigham Young; Joe Smith, Oklahoma State; Jim Smith, Northern Illinois; Phil Argento, Kentucky; Ron Peret, Texas A&M; Jack Gillespie, Montana State; Mallory Chestnutt, Tuskegee; Mack Calvin, USC.

Milwaukee
Lew Alcindor, UCLA; Bob Greacen, Rutgers; Harley Smith, East Tennessee State; Bob Dandridge, Norfolk State; Ken Heitz, UCLA; John Arthurs, Tulane; Bill Keller, Purdue; John Schell, Wisconsin; Jim Satalin, St. Bonaventure; Willie Brown, Middle Tennessee; Bob Presley, California; Jack Lutz, Carthage; Lee Osgood, Northeastern; Waymon Stewart, Lakeland; Stan Wlodarczyk, LaSalle; Bill Voight, Southern Methodist; Lynn Phillips, Southern Methodist; Ken Hall, Westminster (Utah).

New York
John Warren, St. John's (N.Y.); Bill Bunting, North Carolina; Ed Mast, Temple; Elnardo Webster, St. Peter's; Gene Littles, High Point; Dwight Durante, Catawba; Chris Thomforde, Princeton; Jim Healey, Rockhurst; Roger Walaszak, Columbia; Mike McLaughlin, Fordham; Marvin Lewis, Southampton; Bill O'Rourke, St. John Fisher; James Wyatt, Northwestern State (La.); Rich Travis, Oklahoma City.

Philadelphia
Bud Ogden, Santa Clara; Willie Taylor, LeMoyne; Mike Grosso, Louisville; Dave Scholz, Illinois; Joe Cromer, Temple; John Jones, Villanova; Dave Hamilton, West Virginia State; Jim Bowles, Trinity (Tex.); Larry Lewis, St. Francis (Pa.); Bill Justus, Tennessee; Bruce Sloan, Kansas; Roland Taylor, LaSalle.

Phoenix
Neal Walk, Florida; Sim Hill, West Texas State; Floyd Kerr, Colorado State; Dennis Stewart, Michigan; Rich Jones, Memphis State; Dan Sadlier, Dayton; Bill Sweet, UCLA; Bob Edwards, Arizona State; Steve Jennings, USC; Rich Abrahamson, Oregon; Fred Lind, Duke; Bob Miller, Toledo; Andy White, Texas-El Paso; Marv Schmidt, Western New Mexico; Bob Beamon, Texas-El Paso; Wayne Huckel, Davidson; Howie Dickerman, Central Connecticut; Al Nuness, Minnesota; Solomon Davis, Kentucky State; Jim Plump, Northern Arizona.

San Diego
Bobby Smith, Tulsa; Bernie Williams, LaSalle; Charles Bonaparte, Norfolk State; Charles Hentz, Arkansas A&M; Bob Tallent, George Washington; Lynn Shackelford, UCLA; Bill DeHeer, Indiana; Larry Cheatham, Tulsa; Lee Sims, Ashland; Justus Thigpen, Weber State; Paul Duarte, South Dakota State; Joe McBride, Augusta; Mike Heckman, California-Irvine; Jerry Nickens, Tougaloo; Dick Groves, San Jose State; Steve Howell, Ohio State; Joe Pridgen, North Carolina College; Blaine Royer, Illinois State.

San Francisco
Bob Portman, Creighton; Ed Siudut, Holy Cross; Tom Hagan, Vanderbilt; Lee Lafayette, Michigan State; Willie Wise, Drake; Dan Obrovac, Dayton; Pat Foley, Pacific (Calif.); Steve Rippe, Santa Barbara; Greg Reed, Sacramento State; Dick Chapman, San Francisco State; Rich Holmberg, St. Mary's (Calif.); Joe Callahan, San Francisco State.

Seattle
Lucius Allen, UCLA; Ron Taylor, USC; Leroy Winfield, North Texas State; Hal Booker, Cheyney State; Jerry King, Louisville; Ben McGilmer, Iowa; Greg Wittman, Western Carolina; Theartis Wallace, Central Washington; Vince Fritz, Oregon State; Al Cueto, Tulsa; Jim Connolly, Bowling Green; John Smith, Puget Sound; Bob Burrow, Seattle Pacific; Jerry Conley, Morehead State; Ernie Powell, Southern California; Danny Cornett, Morehead State; Steve Honeycutt, Kansas State.

1970

Atlanta
John Vallely, UCLA; Dan Hester, Louisiana State; Van Williford, North Carolina State; Fred Davis, Howard Payne; Bob Riley, Mount St. Mary's; Dave Parker, Windham; John Shinall, Jackson State; Herb White, Georgia; Larry Jackson, Sul Ross College; Manuel Raga, Mexican National Team; Deno Mengham, Italian National Team.

Baltimore
John Hummer, Princeton; Ken Warzynski, DePaul; Seaburn Hill, Arizona State; Billy Jones, Louisiana College; Gary Zeller, Drake; Marvin Polnick, Stephen F. Austin; Charlie Wallace, Oklahoma City; Tom Dykstra, Wheaton; Will Hetzel, Maryland; Ron Becker, New Mexico; Mel Bell, Houston; Ben McGilmer, Iowa; Dan Debardelaben, Northern Arizona; Mike Williams, Northern Arizona; Ted Rose, Northern Michigan; Don Rather, Northern Arizona; Vince Fritz, Oregon State.

Boston
Dave Cowens, Florida State; Rex Morgan, Jacksonville; Willie Williams, Florida State; Jon McKinney, Norfolk State; Tom Carter, Paul Quinn; Rod McIntyre, Jacksonville; Charlie Scott, North Carolina; Bob Croft, Tennessee; Tom Little, Seattle; Mike Maloy, Davidson.

Buffalo
George Johnson, Stephen F. Austin; Cornell Warner, Jackson State; Chip Case, Virginia; Erwin Polnick, Stephen F. Austin; Robert Moore, Central Ohio State; Cliff Shegogg, Colorado State; Doug Hess, Toledo; Larry Woods, West Virginia; Larry Duckworth, Henderson State; Joe Taylor, Dillard; Dick Walker, Wake Forest.

Chicago
Jimmy Collins, New Mexico State; Paul Ruffner, Brigham Young; Lou Herndon, Jackson State; Jimmy Wilson, Cheyney State; George Johnson, Dillard; Lonny Kluttz, North Carolina A&T; Lou West, Seattle; Mike Casey, Kentucky; Glen Johnson, Jackson State; Dale Blaut, West Texas State; Doug Howard, Brigham Young; Booker Brown, Middle Tennessee; Charles Bloodworth, Northwest Louisiana; Paul Funkhouser, McKendree; Paul Otay, Boise State.

Cincinnati
Sam Lacey, New Mexico State; Doug Cook, Davidson; Greg Hyder, Eastern New Mexico; Wade Fuller, Loyola (Ill.); Uluss Thompson, Wiley; Charles Bishop, Louisiana Tech; Mike Bernard, Kentucky State; Joel McBride, Augusta; Bob Mabry, Rio Grande; Carl Johnson, Gustavus Adolphus; Ted Hillary, St. Joseph's (Ind.); Reggie Roach, Virginia State; Larry Gray, Huston-Tillotson; Andy Jennings, Alderson-Broaddus; Mike Neer, Washington & Lee; Paul Favorite, Georgetown (D.C.).

Cleveland
John Johnson, Iowa; Dave Sorenson, Ohio State; Surry Oliver, Stephen F. Austin; Glen Vidnovic, Iowa; Wayne Sokolowski, Ashland; Joe Cooke, Indiana; Narvis Anderson, Stephen F. Austin; Walter Robertson, Loyola (Ill.); Tom Lagodich, Kent State; Ken Johnson, Indiana; Dave Schneider, Wayne State (Neb.); Ollie Taylor, Houston; Kevin Wilson, Ashland; Don Tomilson, Missouri; Steve Wanamaker, Drake; Steve Wilson, Hanover; Bob Peterson, Concordia; John Cannon, Grambling; Allen Waller, St. Mary's (Kan.).

Detroit
Bob Lanier, St. Bonaventure; Jake Ford, Maryland State; Bob St. Pierre, Hanover; Bill Stricker, Pacific (Calif.); Bill Jankans, Long Beach State; Sevira Brown, DePaul; Marv Copeland, Michigan Lutheran; Dan Issel, Kentucky; Alex Wynn, Dartmouth; Bruce Chapman, Nevada; Rick Anheuser, North Carolina State; Don Ogletree, Cincinnati; Ernest Hardy, Harvard; Randy Smith, Buffalo State; Dennis Clark, Springfield; Harvey Marlatt, Eastern Michigan.

Los Angeles
Jim McMillian, Columbia; Ernest Killium, Stetson; Jim Hayes, Boston U.; Larry Mikan, Minnesota; John Fultz, Rhode Island; Jerry Kroll, Davidson; Willie Woods, Eastern Kentucky; Rick Mount, Purdue; Bobby Sands, Pepperdine; Kindell Stephens, Fisk; Bob Dukiet, Boston College; Dewey Varner, Tuskegee; Gary Elliott, Washington; Ron Sanford, New Mexico State; Will Teague, Youngstown; Pete Walthour, Fort Valley; Bob Thate, Occidental.

Milwaukee
Gary Freeman, Oregon State; Bill Zopf, Duquesne; Marvin Winkler, Southwestern Louisiana; Virgle Fredrick, Drury College; Mike Grosso, Louisville; Willy Watson, Oklahoma City; John Rinka, Kenyon; Jim

Sarno, Northwestern; Joe Hamilton, North Texas State; Bob Seemer, Georgia Tech.

New York
Mike Price, Illinois; Howie Wright, Austin Peay; Al Williams, Drake; John Marren, Manhattan; Jim Oxley, Army; Jim Signorile, New York U.; Roy Hodge, Wagner; Greg Filmore, Cheyney State; Walter Banks, Western Kentucky; Don Curnutt, Miami (Fla.).

Philadelphia
Al Henry, Wisconsin; Joe DePre, St. John's (N.Y.); Dennis Awtrey, Santa Clara; Dan Crenshaw, Alabama State; Perry Wallace, Vanderbilt; Jerry Venable, Kansas State; Carlton Poole, Philadelphia Textile; Fred O'Hanlon, Villanova; Mike Haur, St. Joseph's (Pa.); Gordon Stiles, American; David Whitley, Tufts.

Phoenix
Greg Howard, New Mexico; Fred Taylor, Pan American; Greg McDivitt, Ohio; Bob Lienhard, Georgia; John Canine, Ohio; Joe Thomas, Marquette; Heyward Dotson, Columbia; Steve Patterson, UCLA; Carl Ashley, Wyoming; Gerhardus Antonius Schreur, Jr., Arizona State; Jim Walls, Clark College; Ric Cobb, Marquette; Fred Carpenter, Hawaii; Chad Calabria, Iowa; Walt Williams, Miami (O.).

Portland
Jeff Petrie, Princeton; Walt Gilmore, Fort Valley State; Bill Cain, Iowa State; Jim Penix, Bowling Green; Ron Knight, Los Angeles State; George Janky, Dayton; Claude English, Rhode Island; Doug Boyd, Texas Christian; Billy Gaskins, Oregon; Israel Oliver, Elizabeth City; Don McClemore, Bowling Green; Paul Adams, Central Washington; Alex Boyd, Nevada-Reno; Frank Lotheridge, Pan American; Wayne Canady, Miami (Fla.); Doug Williams, St. Mary's (Tex.); Borollas, Trinity; Butch Butchko, Southern Illinois; Mark Gabriel, Hanover College.

San Diego
Rudy Tomjanovich, Michigan; Calvin Murphy, Niagara; Curtis Perry, Southwest Missouri; Jody Finney, Ohio State; James Gilbert, Adams State; Mike Kretzer, East Tennessee; Bill Paultz, St. John's; Don Adams, Northwestern; Jim Gottschall, Dayton; Toke Coleman, Eastern Kentucky; Ron Belton, Bellarmine; Jim Brooks, Nebraska; Harry Lozon, Old Dominion; Clyde Oatis, Aurora; Jay Bond, Washington; Dean Olofson, Wayne State; Dennis Dickens, Azusa; Jeff Cunningham, California-Irvine; Rick Erickson, Washington State.

San Francisco
Pete Maravich, Louisiana State; Nate Archibald, Texas-El Paso; Earl Higgins, Eastern Michigan; Ralph Ogden, Santa Clara; Levi Fontaine, Maryland State; Vic Bartolome, Oregon State; Joe Bergman, Creighton; Jeff Sewell, Marquette; Lou Small, Nevada; Coby Dietrick, San Jose State.

Seattle
Jim Ard, Cincinnati; Pete Cross, San Francisco; Garfield Heard, Oklahoma; John Davis, Alabama State; Boyd Lynch, Eastern Kentucky; Sam Robinson, Long Beach State; James Morgan, Maryland State; George Irvine, Washington; Claude Virden, Murray State; Chuck Lloyd, Yankton College; Andy Owens, Florida; John Brunson, Furman; Allen McManus, Winston-Salem; Don Beenson, Linfield.

1971

Atlanta
George Trapp, Long Beach State; Ted McClain, Tennessee State; Jeff Halliburton, Drake; Jim Welch, Houston; Tyrone Marionneaux, Loyola (La.); Willie Humes, Idaho State; Mike Jordan, Savannah State; Jim Smith, Kentucky Wesleyan; Ernie Fleming, Jacksonville; Ron Rippitoe, David Lipscomb; Levi Wyatt, Alcorn A&M; Roger Moore, Columbus; Ed Jenkins, Michigan Lutheran.

Baltimore
Stan Love, Oregon; Rick Fisher, Colorado State; Rich Rinaldi, St. Peter's; Willie Allen, Miami (Fla.); Don Johnson, Tennessee; John Novey, Mount St. Mary's; Dennis Hogg, Washington State; Russell Golden, Jackson State; Ron Johnston, Murray State; Eddie Myers, Arizona; Chuck Olowski, Baltimore; Bob Connor, Loyola (Md.); Ron Crosswhite, Dayton; Rudolph Peele, Norfolk State; James Morrell, Norfolk State.

Boston
Clarence Glover, Western Kentucky; Jim Rose, Western Kentucky; Dave Robisch, Kansas; Randy Denton, Duke; Greg Nelson, Jacksonville; Thorpe Weber, Vanderbilt; Skip Young, Florida State; John Ribock, South Carolina; Ray Green, California State (Pa.); Dale Dover, Harvard; Reggie Brooks, New Hampshire College; John Dalton, Suffolk; Leroy Chalk, Nebraska.

Buffalo
Elmore Smith, Kentucky State; Fred Hilton, Grambling; Amos Thomas, Southwest Oklahoma State; Jim O'Brien, Boston College; Garry Nelson, Duquesne; Glenn Summors, Gannon; Randy Smith, Buffalo State; Craig Love, Ohio; Gary Stewart, Canisius; Don Ward, Colgate; Bill Warner, Arizona; Butch Webster, Louisiana State; Pete Smith, Valdosta State; Ray Lavender, Drury; William Chatmon, Baylor; James Douglas, Memphis State; Nelson Isley, Louisiana State; Joe Meyer, DePaul.

Chicago
Kennedy McIntosh, Eastern Michigan; Marvin Stewart, Nebraska; Dick Gibbs, Texas-El Paso; Jim Irving, St. Louis; Larry Weatherford, Purdue; Jim England, Tennessee; Artis Gilmore, Jacksonville; Clarence Sherrod, Wisconsin; Jackie Dinkins, Voorhees State; David Withers, Delaware State; Al Smith, Bradley; Ken Riley, Middle Tennessee; Ed Goode, DePaul; Richard Dixon, Loyola (Calif.); Liscio Thomas, Furman; Bob Bissant, Loyola (La.).

Cincinnati
Ken Durrett, LaSalle; John Mengelt, Auburn; Rich Yunkus, Georgia Tech; Sid Catlett, Notre Dame; Jim Guymon, Eastern New Mexico; Gil McGregor, Wake Forest; Ollie Shannon, Minnesota; Frank Fitzgerald, Boston College.

Cleveland
Austin Carr, Notre Dame; Steve Patterson, UCLA; Gerald Lockett, Arkansas A&M; Cliff Harris, Hardin-Simmons; Brian Mahoney, Manhattan; Mike Childress, Colorado State; Tom Bush, Drake; Charlie Davis, Wake Forest; Rich Walker, Bowling Green; Jim Meredith, Washington State; Mike Casey, Kentucky; Doug Hess, Toledo; Bobby Jones, Drake; Bubbles Harris, Indiana; Larry Baker, Wittenberg; Vance Tyree, Wisconsin State.

Detroit
Curtis Rowe, UCLA; Bunny Wilson, Baltimore; Marv Roberts, Utah State; Jarrett Durham, Duquesne; Vincent White, Savannah State; Jim

Larranga, Providence; Steve Kelly, Brigham Young; Wayne Jones, Niagara; Paul Botts, Central Michigan; Steve Butcher, Pikeville; Larry Saunders, Duke; Bob Horn, Drake; Willie Roberson, Wyoming; Art Davis, Johnson C. Smith; James Fleming, Alcorn A&M; Fred Smiley, Detroit College; Leroy Jenkins, Detroit College; Ike Bundy, Detroit Tech; Ed Jenkins, Shaw (Mich.).

Los Angeles
Jim Cleamons, Ohio State; Joe Bergman, Creighton; Mike Gale, Elizabeth City; Roger Brown, Kansas; Lee Dedmon, North Carolina; Bill Brickhouse, Montana State; Gene Gathers, Bradley; Luke Adams, Lamar Tech; Bob Cheeks, Whittier College; Cliff Mosely, Quinnipiac.

Milwaukee
Collis Jones, Notre Dame; Willie Long, New Mexico; Gary Brell, Marquette; Henry Smith, Missouri; Barry Nelson, Duquesne; Ed Kemp, Adams State; Gene Phillips, Southern Methodist; Felix Thruston, Trinity (Tex.); Rick Howat, Illinois; Dan Fife, Michigan; Blaine Henry, Marshall; Gene Mumford, Scranton; Pierre Russell, Kansas; George Jackson, Dayton; Loyd King, Virginia Tech.

New York
Dean Meminger, Marquette; Gregg Northington, Alabama State; Ken Mayfield, Tuskegee; Steve Niles, Texas A&M; Bob Kissane, Holy Cross; Bill Mainor, Fordham; Danny Davis, Henderson State; Leroy Eldridge, Cheyney State; Andy Toth, Cheyney State; Ken Davis, Georgetown (Ky.); Carl Greenfield, Eastern Kentucky; Larry Duckworth, Henderson State; Jack O'Connor, Grant Falls.

Philadelphia
Dana Lewis, Tulsa; Spencer Haywood, Detroit; Dave Wohl, Pennsylvania; Erwin Johnson, Augusta; Richard Hood, Phillips; Jake Jones, Assumption College; Curtis Ford, Northeast Oklahoma State; Barry Yates, Maryland; Tom Lee, Arizona; Jim Dinwiddie, Kentucky; Dana Padgett, Southern California; Ken Kowall, Ohio; Hank Commodore, Northwest Oklahoma.

Phoenix
John Roche, South Carolina; Howard Porter, Villanova; Dennis Layton, USC; Walt Szczerbiak, George Washington; Ken Gardner, Utah; Bob Kissane, Holy Cross; William Graham, Kentucky State; Ralph Brateris, Trenton State; Vernell Elizy, Florida State; Mike Johnson, Kansas State; Tom Newell, Hawaii; Paul Leitz, Western Carolina; Floyd Mason, Alcorn A&M; Ron Dorsey, DePaul; Curtis Carter, Bishop.

Portland
Sidney Wicks, UCLA; Willie Sojourner, Weber State; Larry Steele, Kentucky; Bobby Fields, LaSalle; Hector Blondet, Murray State; Jim Day, Morehead; Gene Knolle, Buffalo State; John Sutter, Tulane; Gene Kennedy, Texas Christian; Greg Starrick, Southern Illinois; Howard Burford, Gonzaga; Don Sechler, Delaware Valley.

San Diego
Cliff Meely, Colorado; Mike Newlin, Utah; Jackie Ridgle, California; Tom Owens, South Carolina; Rudy Blondet, Murray State; Rudy Benjamin, Michigan State; Garry Reist, Rice; Eric Hill, Minnesota; Rick Katherman, Duke; Willie Cherry, Denver; Calvin Oliver, Pan American; Doug Rex, California-Santa Barbara; Chris Schrobilgen, USC; Lee McCullough, Indiana State (Pa.); Gene Roberson, Canisius; Terry Quigg, Gonzaga; Leonard Jackson, Oregon; Steve Sims, Pepperdine; Carlos Quintinar, U. of Mexico; Gary Schneider, San Diego State.

San Francisco
Darnell Hillman, San Jose State; Charles Yelverton, Fordham; Bill

Smith, Syracuse; Greg Gary, St. Bonaventure; Odis Allison, Nevada-Las Vegas; Charlie Johnson, California; Ken May, Dayton; Jim Haderlein, Loyola (Calif.); Clarence Smith, Villanova; Bill Drozdiak, Oregon.

Seattle

Fred Brown, Iowa; Jim McDaniels, Western Kentucky; Clifford Ray, Oklahoma; Pembroke Burrows, Jacksonville; Jeff Smith, New Mexico State; Mike Necaise, William Carey; John Duncan, Kentucky Wesleyan; Chuck Lowery, Puget Sound; Larry Holliday, Oregon; Ed Huston, Puget Sound; Jerome Perry, Western Kentucky.

1971 NBA HARDSHIP DRAFT

Atlanta
Tom Payne, Kentucky.

Baltimore
Phil Chenier, California.

Cincinnati
Nate Williams, Utah State.

Golden State
Cyril Baptiste, Creighton.

Los Angeles
Joe Hammond, none.

1972

Atlanta
Steve Bracey, Tulsa; Ron Riley, USC; Reggie Bird, Princeton; Bob Lackey, Marquette; Randy Knoll, Marshall; Billy Pleas, Detroit; Oscar Evans, Butler; Larry Strozier, Morehouse; Jim Clesson, Tulsa; Charles Allen, Texas Southern; James Green, Paine.

Baltimore
Kevin Porter, St. Francis (Pa.); Al Saunders, Louisiana State; Walter Jones, Long Island U.; Wayne Dillard, Eastern Michigan; Marvin Brown, Jackson State; Jim Floyd, Shaw; Ruppert Breedlove, Oglethorpe; Will Loftin, Southwestern Louisiana; Marvin Wadkins, Jackson State; Lloyd Adams, Rhode Island; Mike Krawzyk, Loyola (Md.); Aubrey Nash, Kansas; Garry Handelman, Hopkins.

Boston
Paul Westphal, USC; Dennis Wuycik, North Carolina; Wayne Grabiec, Michigan; Nate Stephens, Long Beach State; Bryan Adrian, Davidson; Doug Holcomb, Memphis; Steve Previs, North Carolina; Sam McCarney, Cheyney; Marty Hunt, Kenyon; Mark Minor, Ohio State; Phil Stephens, South Carolina State.

Buffalo
Bob McAdoo, North Carolina; Harold Fox, Jacksonville; Bob Morse, Pennsylvania; George Bryant, Eastern Kentucky State; Arnie Berman, Brown; Ed Czernota, Sacred Heart; Greg Kohls, Syracuse; Andy Denny, South Alabama State; John Collins, Brockport State; Jim Prokell, Edinboro State; Frank Dewitt, Virginia; Kim Huband, North Carolina; Greg Corson, North Carolina; Paul Hoffman, St. Bonaventure; Norman Bounds, Brockport State.

Chicago
Ralph Simpson, Michigan State; Mike Ratliff, Eau Claire State; Chuck Jura, Nebraska; Ted Martiniuk, St. Peter's; Rowland Garrett, Florida State; Mike Stewart, Santa Clara; Jerry Pender, Fresno State; Gavin Anderson, Valley City; Ralph Houston, West Texas State; Chuck Taylor, West Liberty State; Jackie Young, Rocky Mountain; Al Cotler, Pennsylvania; Mike Barr, Duquesne; Andrew Pettes, Oklahoma; Greg Lowery, Texas Tech; Charles Hall, Western Montana; John Thorton, South Carolina State; Ron Manning, Manhattan.

Cincinnati
Sam Sibert, Kentucky State; Frank Russell, Detroit; Frank Schade, Wisconsin-Eau Claire; Dave Bustion, Denver; Jerry Crocker, Guilford; Mike Sneed, Fayetteville; Jerry Clack, Oklahoma; Steve McMahon, Merrimack College; David Hall, Kansas State; Floyd Mathew, Northern Arizona; Len Baltimore, George Washington; Kent Scott, Pittsburgh; Bob Allen, Missouri; Mike Jeffries, Oklahoma State; Mike Peterson, Nebraska.

Cleveland
Dwight Davis, Houston; Jim Price, Louisville; Scott English, Texas-El Paso; Hank Siemiontkowski, Villanova; Sam Cash, California-Riverside; Tom Parker, Kentucky; Steve Davidson, West Texas State; Roger Evans, Kent State; Greg Starrick, Southern Illinois; Kent Martens, Abilene Christian.

Detroit
Corky Calhoun, Pennsylvania; Chris Ford, Villanova; Don Buse, Evansville; Ernie Fleming, Jacksonville; Ernest Pettis, Western Michigan; Terry Benton, Wichita State; Bruce Anderson, Arizona; Ben Kelso, Central Michigan; Kessie Mangam, Ferris State; Kent Hollenbeck, Kentucky.

Golden State
Dave Twardzik, Old Dominion; Bill Chamberlain, North Carolina; John Tschogl, Santa Barbara; Charles Dudley, Washington; Henry Bacon, Louisville; William Franklin, Purdue; Joe Burks, San Francisco; Bill Duey, California.

Houston
Russell Lee, Marshall; John Gianelli, Pacific (Calif.); Eric McWilliams, Long Beach State; Wil Robinson, West Virginia; James Silas, Stephen F. Austin; Mike Collins, Seattle; Mike Jackson, Los Angeles State; Henry Harris, Auburn.

Los Angeles
Travis Grant, Kentucky State; Ollie Johnson, Temple; Gregg Northington, Alabama State; Glen Summors, Gannon; Sam Simmons, Bradley.

Milwaukee
Julius Erving, Massachusetts; Chuck Terry, Long Beach State; George Adams, Gardner-Webb; Art White, Georgetown (D.C.); Wally Wright, Penn Military College; Mickey Davis, Duquesne; Ron Harris, Wichita State; Charles Kirkland, Cheyney; Jim Regenold, Ball State; Jolly Spight, Santa Clara.

New York
Tom Riker, South Carolina; Steven Hawes, Washington; Ansley Truitt, California; Henry Bibby, UCLA; Bob Ford, Purdue; Greg Cluess, St. John's (N.Y.); Tracy Tripucka, Lafayette; Tom Corde, Ohio; Tom Sullivan, Fordham; Richie Garner, Manhattan; Chic Downing, Benedictine.

Philadelphia
Fred Boyd, Oregon State; Joby Wright, Indiana; Charlie Tharp, Bel-

haven; Marshall Wingate, Niagara; Joe Bynes, Arkansas AM&N; John Glover, Wiley; Curtis Pritchard, St. Augustine's; Jim Kopp, Rockhurst; Rod Murray, Los Angeles State; Gary Watson, Wisconsin.

Phoenix
Bob Nash, Hawaii; Tom Patterson, Ouachita Baptist; Claude Terry, Stanford; Matt Gantt, St. Bonaventure; Wardell Dyson, Shaw; Charles Edge, LeMoyne-Owen; Bernie Fryer, Brigham Young; Russell Golden, Jackson State; Bill Kennedy, Arizona; Al Vilcheck, Louisville; John Belcher, Arkansas State; Mark Soderberg, Utah; Kelly Utley, Shaw; Ray Golson, West Texas State.

Portland
LaRue Martin, Loyola (Ill.); Bob Davis, Weber State; Lloyd Neal, Tennessee State; Gary Stewart, Canisius; Mike Reid, California-Riverside; Joe Gaines, Belmont; Bob Lynn, Long Beach State; Ruben Vance, Kent State; Jimmy Wilkins, San Diego State; Larry Morris, Tulsa; Paul Kelley, Shaw; Rich Habegger, Wake Forest.

Seattle
Bud Stallworth, Kansas; Brian Taylor, Princeton; Jim Creighton, Colorado; Joe Mackey, USC; Gary Ladd, Seattle; Ron Thomas, Louisville; Jerry Dunn, Western Kentucky; Willy Stoudamire, Portland State; Dwight Holliday, Hawaii; Dan Stewart, Washington; Steve Turner, Vanderbilt; Gregg Daust, Missouri-St. Louis.

1973

Atlanta
John Brown, Missouri; Pat McFarland, St. Joseph's (Pa.); Leonard Gray, Long Beach State; James Brown, Harvard; Dave Winfield, Minnesota; John Williamson, New Mexico State; Pete Harris, Stephen F. Austin; Tim Dominey, Valdosta State.

Boston
Steve Downing, Indiana; Phil Hankinson, Pennsylvania; Martinez Denmon, Iowa State; Richie Fuqua, Oral Roberts; Byron Jones, San Francisco; Joe Cafferky, North Carolina State; Mike Stewart, Santa Clara; Robert White, Sam Houston State; Corky Taylor, Minnesota; Steve Turner, Vanderbilt; Ed Hastings, Villanova; Bruce Winkler, Santa Clara; Scott Koelzer, Montana State; Rick Williams, Iowa; James Gilchrist, Florida Southern; Sam Barber, Bethune-Cookman; Lamont King, Long Beach State; Peter Gavitt, Maine; Tom Austin, Massachusetts.

Buffalo
Ernie DiGregorio, Providence; Mike D'Antoni, Marshall; Ken Charles, Fordham; Doug Little, Oregon; Randy Knoll, Marshall; Mike Macaluso, Canisius; Tim Bassett, Georgia; Carl Jackson, St. Bonaventure; Bob Fullarton, Xavier (O.); Nick Conner, Illinois; Mike Lee, Syracuse; Aaron Covington, Canisius; Bob Vartanian, Buffalo; Ron Gilliam, Brockport; John Fraley, Georgia; John Green, Oregon; James Garvin, Boston University; Don Johnston, North Carolina; Ron Thornson, British Columbia; Phil Tollestrup, Brigham Young.

Capital
Nick Weatherspoon, Illinois; Jim Chones, Marquette; Tom Kozelko, Toledo; Aron Stewart, Richmond; Danny Traylor, South Carolina; Mike Allocco, Stonehill; Ronnie Hogue, Georgia; Mike Jellison, Northeastern; Mike Boylan, Assumption; Dick Kelly, Bay College; Dale Adams, St. Mary's; Mike Battle, George Washington; Chester Davis, Morgan State; Howard White, Maryland; Shorty Williams, St. Mary's.

Chicago
Kevin Kunnert, Iowa; Wendell Hudson, Alabama; Steve Newsome, Houston; Mark Sibley, Northwestern; Roy Simpson, Furman; John Neumann, Mississippi; Billy Harris, Northern Illinois; J.G. Brosterhous, Texas; Rubin Montanez, Duquesne; Ross Hunt, Furman.

Cleveland
Kermit Washington, American; Bill Schaeffer, St. John's (N.Y.); Ozzie Edwards, Oklahoma City; Luke Witte, Ohio State; John Coughran, California; Willie Calvert, Abilene Christian; Larry Farmer, UCLA; John Ritter, Indiana; Les Taylor, Murray State; Dean Martin, Baldwin-Wallace; Floyd Lewis, Harvard; Chris McMurray, San Diego State; John Pennebacker, Hawaii; Charles Mitchell, Eastern Kentucky; Reese Stovall, Pan American; Tom O'Connor, Iowa; Phil Elderkin, Boston.

Detroit
Dwight Jones, Houston; Tom Inglesby, Villanova; Dwight Lamar, Southwest Louisiana State; Ken Brady, Michigan; Dennis Johnson, Ferris State; Fred Smiley, Northwood Michigan Institute; Ben Kelso, Central Michigan; Bill Kilgore, Michigan State; Bob Solomon, Wayne State (Mich.); Len Paul, Akron; Clarence Carlisle, Ferris State.

Golden State
Kevin Joyce, South Carolina; Derrek Dickey, Cincinnati; Jim Retseck, Auburn; Ron King, Florida State; Nate Stephens, Long Beach State; Bob Lauriski, Utah State; Steve Smith, Loyola; Jeff Dawson, Illinois; Everett Fopma, Idaho State; Fred Lavoroni, Santa Clara.

Houston
Ed Ratleff, Long Beach State; Kevin Stacom, Providence; James Lister, Sam Houston; Lee Colborn, South Dakota State; Gary Rhoades, Colorado State; Tom Peck, Wisconsin-Eau Claire; Fred DeVaughn, Westmont; John Thomas, Missouri Southern.

Kansas City-Omaha
Ron Behagen, Minnesota; Larry McNeill, Marquette; Joe Reeves, Bethel (Tenn.); Clyde Turner, Minnesota; M.L. Carr, Guilford; Mike Quick, San Francisco; Mike Jeffries, Missouri; Mike Williams, Kentucky Wesleyan; James Brown, Dartmouth; Ernie Kusyner, Kansas State.

Los Angeles
Barry Parkhill, Virginia; John Perry, Pan American; Larry Kenon, Memphis State; Larry Finch, Memphis State; Kresimir Cosic, Brigham Young; David Brent, Jacksonville; Nate Hawthorne, Southern Illinois; Roy McPipe, Eastern Montana.

Milwaukee
Swen Nater, UCLA; Gary Melchionni, Duke; E.C. Coleman, Houston Baptist; Harry Rogers, St. Louis; Larry Jackson, Northern Illinois; James Floyd, Shaw; Eddie Childress, Austin Peay; Walt McGary, Tennessee-Chattanooga; Bob Bocca, Quinnipiac; Ron Battle, Sam Houston State.

New York
Mel Davis, St. John's (N.Y.); Caldwell Jones, Albany State (Ga.); Allie McGuire, Marquette; George Karl, North Carolina; Dennis Bell, Drake; Lawrence Lilly, Alabama State; Mike Moore, Manhattan; Steve Rowell, Rhode Island; Joe Wise, Bridgewater State; Ed Fields, C.W. Post; Charles Edge, LeMoyne-Owen.

Philadelphia
Doug Collins, Illinois State; Louis Nelson, Washington; Ted Manakas, Princeton; Darrell Minniefield, New Mexico; Reggie Royals, Florida

State; Sterling Wright, Lincoln (Pa.); James Greene, Kentucky Wesleyan; Dave Langston, Drake; Harvey Catchings, Hardin-Simmons; Abe Steward, Jacksonville; Rod Freeman, Vanderbilt; Connie Warren, Xavier (O.); Jim Crawford, LaSalle; Ernie Johnson, Michigan; Lionel Harris, Cincinnati; Larry Robinson, Tennessee; Tony Prince, St. John's (N.Y.).

Phoenix
Mike Bantom, St. Joseph's (Pa.); Allan Hornyak, Ohio State; Steve Mitchell, Kansas State; Ron Robinson, Memphis State; Clinton Harris, Iowa State; Gene Doyle, Holy Cross; Jerry Bisbano, Southwestern Louisiana; Jim Owens, Oregon State; Sandy Smith, Winston-Salem; Claude White, Elmhurst; Lynn Greer, Virginia State; Lyman Williamson, Samford; Kalevi Sarkalahti, Brigham Young.

Portland
Jim Brewer, Minnesota; Allan Bristow, Virginia Tech; Jim O'Brien, Maryland; William Averitt, Pepperdine; Fran Costello, Providence; Neal Jurgenson, Oregon State; Larry Hollyfield, UCLA; Lindell Reason, Eastern Michigan; Mike Contreras, Arizona State; Sam Whitehead, Oregon State; Ed Payne, Wake Forest; Rick Holdt, North Carolina State.

Seattle
Mike Green, Louisiana Tech; George McGinnis, Indiana; Martin Terry, Arkansas; William Harris, North Carolina A&T; Chuck Iverson, South Dakota; Bill McCoy, Northern Iowa; Jim Andrews, Kentucky; Wardell Jeffries, Oklahoma Baptist; Greg Williams, Seattle; Bob Bodell, Maryland.

1974

Atlanta
Tom Henderson, Hawaii; John Drew, Gardner-Webb; Darrell Elston, North Carolina; Ed Palubinskas, Louisiana State; Tyrone Medley, Utah; Sammy Hervey, Southern Methodist; Greg Lee, UCLA; Bill Butler, Louisville; Lon Kruger, Kansas State; Brendy Lee, Nebraska.

Boston
Glenn McDonald, Long Beach State; Kevin Stacom, Providence; Roscoe Pondexter, Long Beach State; Lerman Battle, Fairmont State; Ben Clyde, Florida State; Gene Harmon, Creighton; Ron Brown, Pennsylvania State; Richard Wallace, Georgia Southern; Al Skinner, Massachusetts; Phil Rogers, Fairfield.

Buffalo
Tom McMillen, Maryland; Leon Benbow, Jacksonville; Kim Hughes, Wisconsin; Bernard Harris, Virginia Commonwealth; Tony Byers, Wake Forest; Gary Link, Missouri; Tom Curtis, UCLA; Glenn Price, St. Bonaventure; John Falconi, Davidson; Andy Rimol, Princeton.

Chicago
Cliff Pondexter, Long Beach State; Phil Lumpkin, Miami (O.); Bob Wilson, Wichita State; Jim Forbes, Texas-El Paso; Randy Knowles, Texas A&M; Robert Rosier, St. Thomas; Geoff Roberts, Missouri Western; Sam McCants, Oral Roberts; Jerry Davenport, Cameron; Rick Hockenos, St. Francis (Pa.).

Cleveland
Tom Burleson, North Carolina State; Bill Knight, Pittsburgh; Kevin Restani, San Francisco; Jim Foster, Connecticut; Gary Novak, Notre Dame; Aron Stewart, Richmond; Mike Robinson, Michigan State; Kerry Hughes, Wisconsin; Jim Buskofsky, Upper Iowa; Jim Kelly, Loras.

Detroit
Al Eberhard, Missouri; Eric Money, Arizona; Roland Grant, New Mexico State; Mickey Martin, Pittsburgh; Joe Newman, Temple; Mike Sylvester, Dayton; Sammy High, Tulsa; Greg Newman, Drexel; Gary Deitelhoff, Milliken; Bill Ligon, Vanderbilt.

Golden State
Keith Wilkes, UCLA; Phil Smith, San Francisco; Frank Kendrick, Purdue; Willie Biles, Tulsa; Steve Erickson, Oregon; John Errecart, Pacific (Calif.); Brady Allen, California; Clarence Allen, Santa Barbara; Carl Meier, California; Marvin Buckley, Nevada-Reno.

Houston
Bob Jones, North Carolina; Gus Bailey, Texas-El Paso; Robert Wilson, Iowa State; Larry Robinson, Texas; Owen Wells, Detroit; Lawrence Johnson, Prairie View; Kevin Fitzgerald, Oklahoma; Steve Brooks, Arkansas State; Ken Stalling, Missouri-Rolla; Marcus Washington, Marquette.

Kansas City-Omaha
Scott Wedman, Colorado; Len Kosmalski, Tennessee; Harvey Catchings, Hardin-Simmons; Lloyd Batts, Cincinnati; Terry Compton, Vanderbilt; Ron Kennedy, Arizona; Mark Browne, Missouri Western; Richie O'Connor, Fairfield; Jeff Dawson, Illinois; Dennis White, Arizona.

Los Angeles
Brian Winters, South Carolina; Fred Saunders, Syracuse; Jim Bradley, Northern Illinois; Ron de Vries, Illinois State; Seymour Reed, Bradley; Billy Morris, St. Louis; Dennis Vanzant, Azusa Pacific; Bob Florence, Nevada-Las Vegas.

Milwaukee
Gary Brokaw, Notre Dame; Rubin Collins, Maryland-Eastern Shore; Greg McDonald, Oral Roberts; Lionell Billingy, Duquesne; John Johnson, Denver; Larry Williams, Kansas State; Ralph Palomar, Cameron; Mike Deane, Potsdam State; Bruce Featherston, Southwest Texas State.

New Orleans
Mike Sojourner, Utah; Aaron James, Grambling; Bruce King, Pan American; Ray Price, Washington; Ed Searcy, St. John's (N.Y.); Lawrence McCray, Florida State; Joel Copeland, California; Jay Piccola, Roanoke; Ken Boyd, Boston University; Walt McGary, Tennessee-Chattanooga.

New York
Maurice Lucas, Marquette; Jesse Dark, Virginia Commonwealth; Rudy Jackson, Hutchinson Junior College; Roy Ebron, Southwestern Louisiana; Greg Jackson, Guilford; Billy Smith, Mercer; Dennis McDermott, St. Francis (N.Y.); Earl Brown, Lafayette; John O'Donnell, North Carolina.

Philadelphia
Marvin Barnes, Providence; Don Smith, Dayton; Coniel Norman, Arizona; Butch Taylor, Jacksonville; Gary Crowthers, Hardin-Simmons; Mark Westra, USC; Dave Stoczynski, Gannon; Jimmy Powell, Middle Tennessee; Perry Warbington, Georgia Southern; Larry Witherspoon, Towson State.

Phoenix
John Shumate, Notre Dame; Leonard Robinson, Tennessee State; George Gervin, Eastern Michigan; Randy Allen, Indiana (Pa.); Ralph Bobik, Creighton; Collis Temple, Louisiana State; Clyde Dickey, Boise State; Tom Holland, Oklahoma; Ted Evans, Oklahoma; Mark Wasley, Arizona State.

Portland
Bill Walton, UCLA; Jan van Breda Kolff, Vanderbilt; Clarence Walker, West Georgia; Mickey Jackson, Aurora; Bernard Hardin, New Mexico; Dan Anderson, Southern California; Doug Richards, Brigham Young; Eldridge Broussard, Pacific (Ore.); Lee Haven, Colorado; Ron Jones, Oregon State.

Seattle
Campy Russell, Michigan; Leonard Gray, Long Beach State; Talvin Skinner, Maryland-Eastern Shore; Willie Gordon, Maryland-Eastern Shore; Dean Tolson, Arkansas; Wardell Jackson, Ohio State; Jerry Faulkner, West Georgia; Leonard Coulter, Morehead State; Bertrand du Pont, Dillard; Rod Derline, Seattle.

Washington
Len Elmore, Maryland; Dennis DuVal, Syracuse; Earl Williams, Winston-Salem; Stan Washington, San Diego; Gary Anderson, Wisconsin; Roy McPipe, Eastern Michigan; Tom Turner, West Georgia; Steve Platt, Huntington (Ind.); Mark Raterink, Boston College; Pete Collins, High Point.

1975

Atlanta
Marvin Webster, Morgan State; Bruce Seals, Xavier (La.); Jim Baker, Hawaii; Monte Towe, North Carolina State; Wilbur Holland, New Orleans; Danny Williams, Mississippi; Gus Johnson, Winona State; Oscar Jackson, Duquesne; Dave Schlesser, Morningside; Vic Kelly, Hawaii.

Boston
Tom Boswell, South Carolina; Jimmy Dan Conner, Kentucky; Jerome Anderson, West Virginia; Cyrus Mann, Illinois State; Darryl Brown, Fordham; Rick Coleman, Jacksonville; Al Boswell, Oral Roberts; Roger Morningstar, Kansas; Robert Rhodes, Creighton; Bill Endicott, Massachusetts.

Buffalo
Ricky Sobers, Nevada-Las Vegas; Larry Fogle, Canisius; George Bucci, Manhattan; Bob Fleischer, Duke; Sam Berry, Armstrong; Larry Jackson, North Carolina-Charlotte; Mike Franklin, Cincinnati; Allen Jones, Pepperdine; Art Allen, Pepperdine.

Chicago
Joe Bryant, LaSalle; John Laskowski, Indiana; Gus Gerard, Virginia; Ron Haigler, Pennsylvania; Bob Iverson, North Texas State; Bill Andreas, Ohio State; John Grochowalski, Assumption; John Murphy, Massachusetts; Gary Tomaszewski, St. Mary's (Tex.).

Cleveland
Junior Bridgeman, Louisville; Dan Roundfield, Central Michigan; Ted Hathaway, Cleveland State; Eric Fernsten, San Francisco; Mike Odemns, Western Kentucky; Henry Ward, Jackson State; Shawn Leftwich, Jacksonville; Andre McCarter, UCLA; Skip Howard, Bowling Green; Eric Anderson, Macalester.

Detroit
Bill Robinzine, DePaul; Walter Luckett, Ohio; Pete Trgovich, UCLA; Lindsey Hairston, Michigan State; Cliff Pratt, Shaw (Mich.); Allen Spruill, North Carolina A&T; Ike Williams, Armstrong State; John Kelley, Dillard; Terry Thomas, Detroit; Mickey Fox, St. Mary's (Nova Scotia).

Golden State
John Lambert, USC; Mel Utley, St. John's (N.Y.); Robert Hawkins, Illinois State; Billy Taylor, LaSalle; Larry Pounds, Washington; Tony Styles, San Francisco; Stan Boyer, Wyoming; Mike Rozenski, St. Mary's (Calif.); Scott Trobbe, Stanford; Maurice Harper, St. Mary's (Calif.).

Houston
Joe Meriweather, Southern Illinois; Jim Blanks, Gardner-Webb; Rudy White, Arizona State; Ken Smith, Tulsa; Rick Whitlow, Illinois State; William Johnson, Texas Tech; Nate Barnett, Akron; Leon Johnson, Centenary; Steve Strother, Providence.

Kansas City-Omaha
Bob Bigelow, Pennsylvania; Glen Hanson, Louisiana State; Bob Guyette, Kentucky; Kevin Cluess, St. John's (N.Y.); Ed Stahl, North Carolina; Clint Chapman, USC; Wayne Croft, Clemson; Jim Bostic, New Mexico State.

Los Angeles
David Meyers, UCLA; Gus Williams, Southern California; Jim McElroy, Central Michigan; C.J. Kupec, Michigan; Charles Russell, Alabama; Don Ford, Santa Barbara; Rick Suttle, Kansas; Mike Cashman, Willamette.

Milwaukee
Rich Kelley, Stanford; Cornelius Cash, Bowling Green; Brian Hammel, Bentley; Bill Campion, Manhattan; Jim Lee, Syracuse; Oliver Purnell, Old Dominion; Wilbur Thomas, American; Bob McCurdy, Richmond; Eric Hays, Montana; Romy Thomas, Wisconsin-Eau Claire.

New Orleans
David Thompson, North Carolina State; William Willoughby, none; Rudy Hackett, Syracuse; Mack Coleman, Houston Baptist; Andre Hampton, Kentucky State; Rick Schmidt, Illinois; Bill Higgins, Ashland; Harvey Carmichael, Kentucky State; Fred Stokes, Barber Scotia; Aleksander Belov, Leningrad, Russia.

New York
Eugene Short, Jackson State; Luther Burden, Utah; John Ramsey, Seton Hall; David Vaughn, Oral Roberts; Don Washington, North Carolina; Henry Williams, Jacksonville; Peter Davis, Michigan State; Jerry Homan, Marquette; Tim Van Blommesteyn, Princeton; Mo Rivers, North Carolina State.

Philadelphia
Darryl Dawkins, none; Lloyd Free, Guilford; Charles Cleveland, Alabama; Louis Dunbar, Houston; Ken Tyler, Gonzaga; Ken Alston, Valdosta State; Mike Flynn, Kentucky; Freeman Blade, Eastern Montana; Larry Haralson, Drake; Rick Reed, Azusa Pacific.

Phoenix
Alvan Adams, Oklahoma; Clyde Mayes, Furman; Otis Johnson, Stetson; Sam McCants, Oral Roberts; Joe Pace, Coppin State; Biff Burrell, USC; Dave Edmunds, West Georgia; Jack Schrader, Arizona State; Owen Brown, Maryland; Mike Moon, Arizona State.

Portland
Lionel Hollins, Arizona State; Bob Gross, Long Beach State; Tom Roy, Maryland; Phil Hicks, Tulane; Maurice Presley, Houston; Gerald Willett, Oregon; Steve Fields, Miami (O.); Charley Neal, Oregon State; Quentin Braxton, Portland; Tyree Foster, Portland.

Seattle
Frank Oleynick, Seattle; Steve Green, Indiana; Tom Kropp, Kearney State; Jim Moore, Utah State; Dwain Govan, Bishop; Larry Smith, North Carolina A&T; Hollis Miller, Drury; Ken McKenzie, Montana; Rich Haws, Utah State; Jerry Bellotti, Santa Clara.

Washington
Kevin Grevey, Kentucky; Allen Murphy, Louisville; Bayard Forrest, Grand Canyon; Fessor Leonard, Furman; Rich Jones, Virginia Commonwealth; John Garrett, Purdue; Fletcher Johnson, Randolph-Macon; Bruce Hamming, Augustana; Doug Brookins, Creighton; Mike Fahey, Brandeis.

1976

Atlanta
John Lucas, Maryland; Bayard Forrest, Garand Canyon; Mike Dabney, Rutgers; Tom Barker, Hawaii; Ron Davis, Washington State; Pete Padgett, Nevada-Reno; Carl Gerlach, Kansas State; Doug Terry, Utah; Bob Kovach, San Diego State; Mike Dickerson, South Florida.

Boston
Norman Cook, Kansas; Butch Feher, Vanderbilt; Jerry Fort, Nebraska; Lewis Linder, Kentucky State; Lewis McKinney, St. Louis; Art Collins, Biscayne; Ralph Drollinger, UCLA; John Clark, Northeastern; Bill Collins, Boston College; Otho Tucker, Illinois.

Buffalo
Mitch Kupchak, North Carolina; Al Fleming, Arizona; Gary Brewster, Texas-El Paso; Connie White, California; Danny Odums, Fairfield; Frank Jones, Tennessee Tech; Mark McAndrew, Providence; Bob Rozyczko, St. Bonaventure; Tim Stokes, Canisius.

Chicago
Scott May , Indiana; Willie Smith, Missouri; Dallas Smith, West Texas State; Keith Starr, Pittsburgh; Nate Williams, Illinois; Tom Paulin, Winston-Salem; Barry McLeod, Centenary; Dave Koehler, Wisconsin; John Thomas, Connecticut; John Hudson, Concord.

Cleveland
Chuckie Williams, Kansas State; Mo Howard, Maryland; Gary Cole, Wisconsin-Pakrkside; John Engles, Pennsylvania; Ed Lawrence, McNeese State; Johnny Britt, UCLA; Tim Sisneros, Middle Tennessee; Bruce Parkinson, Purdue; Elisha McSweeney, Mankato State.

Detroit
Leon Douglas, Alabama; Earl Tatum, Marquette; Phil Sellers, Rutgers; Scott Thompson, Iowa; Jim Hearns, Marymount; Russell Davis, Virginia Tech; Curt Peterson, Puget Sound; Randy Henry, Illinois State; Bill Martin, Hartwick; Bob Johnson, Wisconsin.

Golden State
Sonny Parker, Texas A&M; Marshall Rogers, Pan American; Jeff Fosnes, Vanderbilt; Carl Bird, California; Gene Cunningham, Norfolk State; Jesse Campbell, Mercyhurst; Stan Boskovich, West Virginia; Howard Smith, San Francisco; Ken Smith, San Diego State.

Houston
Armond Hill, Princeton; Phil Hicks, Tulane; Barnes Hauptfuhrer, Princeton ; David Marsrs, Houston; Robert Paige, Houston Baptist; Barry Davis, Texas A&M; Dan Krueger, Texas.

Kansas City
Richard Washington, UCLA; Major Jones, Albany State (Ga.); Lars Hansen, Washington; Clarence Ramsey, Washington; Willie Hodge, Duke; Andre McCarter, UCLA; Craig Prosser, Canisius; Mike Davis, Bradley; Dave Logan, Colorado; Harry Bailey, North Texas State.

Los Angeles
Robert Parish, Centenary; Jack Dorsey, Georgia; Tom Abernethy, Indiana; Waymon Britt, Michigan; James Rappis, Arizona; Ed Schweitzer, Stanford; Tommy Lipsey, Los Angeles State; Ed Gregg, Utah State; David Pickett, Northeast Louisiana.

Milwaukee
Quinn Buckner, Indiana; Scott Lloyd, Arizona State; Lloyd Walton, Marquette; Don Frost, Iowa; Tom Lockhart, Manhattan; Phil Spence, North Carolina State; Ron Barrow, Southern; Bob Warner, Maine; Benny Shaw, Florida Tech; Hugo Cabrera, East Texas State.

New Orleans
Adrian Dantley, Notre Dame; Alex English, South Carolina; Steve Copp, San Diego State; John Service, California-Santa Barbara; Paul Griffin, Western Michigan; Bernard Tomlin, Hofstra; Andy Walker, Niagara; Richard Bryant, Southwest Texas State; Calvin Robinson, Mississippi Valley; Art Johnson, Iowa State.

New York
Lonnie Shelton, Oregon State; John McGill, Alcorn State; Rich Bullock, Texas Tech; Beaver Smith, St. John's (N.Y.); Joe Jones, Grambling; Boyd Batts, Nevada-Las Vegas; Rich McCutcheon, Arizona State; Archie Talley, Salem; Eugene Shy, Florida.

Philadelphia
Terry Furlow, Michigan State; Ron Norwood, DePaul; Freeman Blade, Eastern Montana; Jeff Browne, Missouri Western; Mike Dunleavy, South Carolina; Phil Walker, Millersville; Lee Dixon, Hardin-Simmons; Fly Williams, Austin Peay; Ed Stefanski, Pennsylvania.

Phoenix
Ron Lee, Oregon; Bob Carrington, Boston College; Ira Terrell, Southern Methodist; Paul Miller, Oregon State; Ralph Walker, St. Mary's; Carl Brown, Eastern Kentucky; Brad Warble, Eastern Illinois; Tom DeBerry, Northern Arizona; John Irving, Hofstra; Gary Jackson, Arizona State.

Portland
Wally Walker, Virginia; Johnny Davis, Dayton; Jeff Tyson, Western Michigan; David Everett, Grand Canyon; Gary Redding, Auburn; Dwaine Barnett, Stanford; Al DeWitt, Weber State; Brant Gibler, Puget Sound; Rob Torresdal, Linfield; Marcos Leite, Pepperdine.

Seattle
Bob Wilkerson, Indiana; Dennis Johnson, Pepperdine; Larry Cooke, Virginia Tech; Willie Parr, LeMoyne-Owen; Robert Gray, Wichita State; Daryl Peterson, Wake Forest; Mark Klein, Malone; Norton Barnhill, Washington State; Ron Johnson, North Carolina A&T; Ricky Lewis, Alcorn State.

Washington
Larry Wright, Grambling; Joe Pace, Coppin State; Bill Cook, Memphis

State; Marion Hillard, Memphis State; L.C. Mason, Alabama State; Pat Tallent, George Washington; Ralph Vallott, Loyola (Ill.); Merlin Wilson, Georgetown (D.C.); Clyde Agnew, Newberry; Mike Beuscher, Seton Hall.

1976 DISPERSAL DRAFT OF ABA PLAYERS

Atlanta
Maurice Lucas, Kentucky Colonels.

Chicago
Artis Gilmore, Kentucky Colonels.

Detroit
Marvin Barnes, St. Louis Spirits.

Houston
Ron Thomas, Kentucky Colonels.

Indiana
Wil Jones, Kentucky Colonels.

Kansas City
Ron Boone, St. Louis Spirits; Mike Barr, St. Louis Spirits.

Buffalo
William Averitt, Kentucky Colonels.

New York Knicks
Randy Denton, St. Louis Spirits.

New York Nets
Jan van Breda Kolff, Kentucky Colonels.

Portland
Moses Malone, St. Louis Spirits.

San Antonio
Louis Dampier, Kentucky Colonels.

1977

Atlanta
Wayne Rollins, Clemson; Sam Smith, Nevada-Las Vegas; Eddie Johnson, Auburn; Dave Bormann, Gardner-Webb; Bill Gordon, Tennessee-Chattanooga; Calvin Crews, Southwestern Louisiana; James Holliman, Arizona State; Vern Thompson, Brigham Young.

Boston
Cedric Maxwell, North Carolina-Charlotte; Skip Brown, Wake Forest; Jeff Cummings, Tulane; Bill Langloh, Virginia; Roy Pace, Rutgers-Camden; Dave Kyle, Cleveland State; Tom Harris, Bowling Green.

Buffalo
Larry Johnson, Kentucky; Melvin Watkins, North Carolina-Charlotte; Mike Hanley, Niagara; Curvan Lewis, Virginia Union; Mike Jackson, Tennessee; Emery Sammons, Philadelphia Textile.

Chicago
Tate Armstrong, Duke; Mike Glenn, Southern Illinois; Steve Sheppard, Maryland; Mark Landsberger, Arizona State; Mike McConalthy, Louisiana Tech; Nate Davis, South Carolina; Jay Chessman, Brigham Young; Mike Smith, Evansville; Rich Rhodes, Eastern Illinois.

Cleveland
Ed Jordan, Rutgers; Steve Grote, Michigan; Melvin Jones, West Texas State; Al Smith, Jackson State; Ron Cox, East Washington State; Bob Riddle, Eastern Michigan; Tom Cutter, Western Michigan.

Denver
Tom LaGarde, North Carolina; Anthony Roberts, Oral Roberts; Robert Smith, Nevada-Las Vegas; John Billups, Mississippi; Jim Town, Massachusetts; Willie High, Alabama State; Len Saunders, Florida.

Detroit
Ben Poquette, Central Michigan; John Irving, Hofstra; Bruce King, Iowa; Jim Kennedy, Missouri; Herb Nobles, Kansas; Robert Lewis, Johnson C. Smith; Tim Appleton, Kenyon.

Golden State
Rickey Green, Michigan; Wesley Cox, Louisville; Ricky Love, Alabama-Huntsville; Marlon Redmond, San Francisco; Roy Smith, Kentucky State; Leartha Scott, Wisconsin-Parkside; Ray Epps, Norfolk State; Jack Phelan, St. Francis (Pa.); Jerry Thruston, Mercer; Ricky Marsh, Manhattan.

Houston
Larry Moffett, Nevada-Las Vegas; Robert Reid, St. Mary's (Tex.); Phil Bond, Louisville; Rocky Smith, Oregon State; Ed Thompson, Idaho State.

Indiana
Alonzo Bradley, Texas Southern; Stan Mayhew, Weber State; George Pendleton, Georgia State; Marvin Jackson, Prairie View A&M; Tom Scheffler, Purdue.

Kansas City
Otis Birdsong, Houston; Eddie Owens, Nevada-Las Vegas; Bill Paterno, Notre Dame; John Kuester, North Carolina; Larry Williams, Texas Southern; Bob Chapman, Michigan State; Bob Cooper, Providence; Bruce Jenner, Graceland.

Los Angeles
Kenny Carr, North Carolina State; Brad Davis, Maryland; Norm Nixon, Duquesne; James Edwards, Washington; Tony Robertson, West Virginia; John Robinson, Michigan; Grover Woolard, Murray State; Lars Hansen, Washington; Art Allen Pepperdine.

Milwaukee
Kent Benson, Indiana; Marques Johnson, UCLA; Ernie Grunfeld, Tennessee; Glen Williams, St. John's (N.Y.); Gary Yoder, Cincinnati; Lewis Brown, Nevada-Las Vegas; Ron Norwood, DePaul; Chuck Goodyear, Miami (O.); Ron Bostic, Detroit; Larry Pikes, Wisconsin-Milwaukee.

New Jersey
Bernard King, Tennessee; Bob Elmore, Wichita State; Gerald Cunningham, Kentucky State; Mark Crow, Duke; Scott Conant, Newberry; Ralph Drollinger, UCLA.

New Orleans
Essie Hollis, St. Bonaventure; Tony Hanson, Connecticut; Dennis

Boyd, Detroit; Jim Grady, Gonzaga; Wayne Golden, Tennessee-Chattanooga; Lucy Harris, Delta State; Dave Speicher, Toledo.

New York
Ray Williams, Minnesota; Glen Gondrezick, Nevada-Las Vegas; Toby Knight, Notre Dame; Lloyd McMillian, Long Beach State; Steve Hayes, Idaho State; Bill Terry, Monmouth (N.J.); Jerry Graycraft, Milligan; Tom Weadock, St. John's (N.Y.); Ken Slappy, St. Peter's.

Philadelphia
Glenn Mosley, Seton Hall; Wilson Washington, Old Dominion; Bob Elliott, Arizona; Herm Harris, Arizona; Arnold Dugger, Oral Roberts; Jeff Jonas, Utah; Teko Wynder, Tulsa; George Gibson, Winston-Salem; Dennis Forest, Nebraska-Omaha; John Olive, Villanova.

Phoenix
Walter Davis, North Carolina; Mike Bratz, Stanford; Greg Griffin, Idaho State; Cecil Rellford, St. John's (N.Y.); Billy McKinney, Northwestern; Alvin Scott, Oral Roberts; Alvin Joseph, California-Riverside.

Portland
Rich Laurel, Hofstra; Kim Anderson, Missouri; T.R. Dunn, Alabama; Ricky Brown, Alabama; Greg White, USC; Donn Wilber, LaSalle; Myron Jordan, Pacific (Calif.); Harold Rhodes, Washington State.

San Antonio
Jeff Wilkins, Illinois State; Dan Henderson, Arkansas State; Matt Hicks, Northern Illinois; Scott Sims, Missouri; Bruce Buckley, North Carolina; Richard Robinson, New Mexico; Jerome Gladney, Arizona.

Seattle
Jack Sikma, Illinois Wesleyan; Joe Hassett, Providence; Jim Cooper, Alabama State; Dale Haverman, McKendree; Bucky O'Brien, Seattle; Billy Reynolds, Northwest Louisiana; Jeff Frey, Evansville.

Washington
Greg Ballard, Oregon; Bo Ellis, Marquette; Phil Walker, Millersville (Pa.); Steve Puidokas, Washington State; Jerry Schellenberg, Wake Forest; David Reavis, Georgia; Bruce Parkinson, Purdue; Ernie Wansley, Virginia Tech; Calvin Brown, American; Pat McKinley, Towson State.

1978

Atlanta
Butch Lee, Marquette; Jack Givens, Kentucky; Rick Wilson, Louisville; Steve Grant, Manhattan; Chris Potter, Holy Cross; Gerald Glover, Howard; Jim DeWeese, Gonzaga; Ed Murphy, Merrimack; Maurice Robinson, West Virginia; Marshall Lester, Florida Southern.

Boston
Larry Bird, Indiana State; Freeman Williams, Portland State; Jeff Judkins, Utah; Dana Skinner, Merrimack; Dave Nelson, Bloomfield; Greg Tynes, Seton Hall; Dave Winey, Minnesota; Steve Balkun, Fairfield; Kim Fisher, Fairfield; Les Anderson, George Washington; Walter Harrigan, Brandeis.

Buffalo
Jerome Whitehead, Marquette; Mike Santos, Utah State; Ricky Gallon, Louisville; Marvin Delph, Arkansas; Jim Boylan, Marquette; Larry

Harris, Pittsburgh; Leroy McDonald, Wake Forest; David Thompson, Florida State; Bob Miscevicious, Providence; Stan Pietkiewicz, Auburn; Felton Young, Jacksonville; Bobby White, Centenary.

Chicago
Reggie Theus, Nevada-Las Vegas; Marvin Johnson, New Mexico; Randy Ayers, Miami (O.); Ron Anthony, Jacksonville; John Shoemaker, Miami (O.); Jarvis Reynolds, West Georgia; Chubby Cox, San Francisco; Joe Ponsetto, DePaul; Mark Tucker, Oklahoma.

Cleveland
Mike Mitchell, Auburn; Harry Davis, Florida State; Ken Higgs, Louisiana State; Stan Rome, Clemson; Ken Koenigs, Kansas; Ron Bell, Virginia Tech; Tony Smith, Nevada-Las Vegas; Roland Martin, Missouri Southern; Steve Bayless, Central State (O.); Gary Winton, Army.

Denver
Rod Griffin, Wake Forest; Mike Evans, Kansas State; Hollis Copeland, Rutgers; Michael Edwards, Pan American; Robert Heard, Columbus (Ga.); Jack Gilloon, South Carolina; Larry Vaculik, Colorado; Tom Schneeberger, Air Force; Phil Taylor, Arizona.

Detroit
Terry Tyler, Detroit; John Long, Detroit; Dave Caligaris, Northeastern; Audie Matthews, Illinois; Herb Entzminger, Johnson C. Smith; Earl Evans, Nevada-Las Vegas; Ulice Payne, Marquette; Dave Grauzer, Central Michigan.

Golden State
Purvis Short, Jackson State; Ray Townsend, UCLA; Wayne Cooper, New Orleans; Steve Neff, Bethany Nazarene; Derrick Jackson, Georgetown (D.C.); Bubba Wilson, Western Carolina; Buzz Hartnett, San Diego; Rick Bernard, St. Mary's (Calif.); Tony Searcy, Appalachian State; Bobby Humbles, Bradley; Mike Muff, Murray State.

Houston
Buster Matheney, Utah; Billy Ray Bates, Kentucky State; Jackie Robinson. Nevada-Las Vegas; Joel Thompson, Michigan; Gary Goodner, Texas; Eddie Joe Chavez, Santa Clara; Stan Stewart, Loyola (Calif.).

Indiana
Rick Robey, Kentucky; Wayne Radford, Indiana; Ricky Lee, Oregon State; James Sparrow, North Carolina A&T; Sherman Dillard, James Madison; Ollie Matson, Jr., Pepperdine.

Kansas City
Phil Ford, North Carolina; Jeff Cook, Idaho State; Mike Russell, Texas Tech; Geoff Crompton, North Carolina; Derick Clayborne, Massachusetts; Jim Krivacs, Texas; Charles McMillian, North Texas State; Ron Hammye, Bowling Green.

Los Angeles
Ron Carter, Virginia Military; Lew Massey, North Carolina-Charlotte; Michael Cooper, New Mexico; Harold Robertson, Lincoln (Mo.); Carlos Terry, Winston-Salem; Kim Stewart, Washington; Larry Paige, Colorado State.

Milwaukee
George Johnson, St. John's (N.Y.); Pat Cummings, Cincinnati; Otis Howard, Austin Peay; Russ Coleman, Pacific (Calif.); Dave Kyle, Cleveland State; Kim Anderson, Missouri; Tom Zaligaris, North Carolina; Gary Rosenberger, Marquette; Tom Anderson, Wisconsin-Green Bay.

New Jersey

Winford Boynes, San Francisco; Mike Phillips, Kentucky; Dave Batton, Notre Dame; Walter Jordan, Purdue; Cecile Rose, Houston; Golie Augustus, South Carolina; Doug Jemison, San Francisco; Bruce Campbell, Providence; Frank Sowinski, Princeton; Michael Vicens, Holy Cross.

New Orleans

James Hardy, San Francisco; Tom Green, Southern (La.); Mel Davis, North Texas State; Jeff Covington, Youngstown State; Don Williams, Notre Dame; John Douglas, Kansas; Willie Howard, New Mexico; Carl Kirkpatrick, Northeast Louisiana; Chad Nelson, Drake; Ricky Williams, Long Beach State.

New York

Michael Ray Richardson, Montana; John Rudd, McNeese State; Greg Bunch, California-Fullerton; Marc Iavaroni, Virginia; Erving Giddings, Dayton; Greg Green, Southern (La.); Ed Warren, Briarcliff; Gary Pember, Nasson; Greg Sanders, St. Bonaventure; Danny Fields, North Carolina-Wilmington; Ernest Simons, Pace.

Philadelphia

Maurice Cheeks, West Texas State; Glenn Hagan, St. Bonaventure; Brett Vroman, Nevada-Las Vegas; Mark Haymore, Massachusetts; Osborne Lockhart, Minnesota; Anthony Murray, Alabama; Alan Cunningham, Colorado State; Dennis James, Widener.

Phoenix

Marty Byrnes, Syracuse; Joel Kramer, San Diego State; Bob Miller, Cincinnati; Wayne Smith, California-Irvine; Andre Wakefield, Loyola (Ill.); Charles Thompson, Houston; Steve Malovic, San Diego State; George Fowler, Pacific (Calif.); Nate Stokes, Grand Canyon; Lewis Cohen, Cal Poly-San Luis Obispo.

Portland

Mychal Thompson, Minnesota; Ron Brewer, Arkansas; Keith Herron, Villanova; Clemon Johnson, Florida A&M; Sterling Edmonds, Dartmouth; Clay Johnson, Missouri; Tim Evans, Puget Sound; Walter Reason, Pacific (Ore.); Mark Wickman, Linfield; Paul Cozens, George Fox; Tim Warkentin, Biola.

San Antonio

Frankie Sanders, Southern (La.); Gerald Henderson, Virginia Commonwealth; Rich Adams, Illinois; Eugene Parker, Purdue; Harry Morgan, Indiana State; Hector Olivencia, Sacred Heart; Henry Taylor, Pan American; Rick Taylor, Arizona State; Larry Brewster, Florida.

Seattle

James Lee, Kentucky; Keven McDonald, Pennsylvania; Dave Baxter, Michigan; Billy Lewis, Illinois State; Ralph Drollinger, UCLA.

Washington

Roger Phegley, Bradley; Dave Corzine, DePaul; Terry Sykes, Grambling; Rick Apke, Creighton; Larry Boston, Maryland; Roger Dickens, Towson State; Archie Aldridge, Miami (O.); Ed Hopkins, Georgetown; Nestor Cora, St. Francis (N.Y.); Tim Claxton, Temple; Steve Connor, Boise State.

1979

Atlanta

James Bradley, Memphis State; Larry Wilson, Nicholls State; Don Marsh, Franklin & Marshall; Tiny Pinder, North Carolina State; Dwight Williams, Gardner-Webb; Tim Waterman, St. Bonaventure; John Goedeke, Maryland Baltimore Co.; Cedric Oliver, Hamilton (N.Y.); Chad Nelson, Drake.

Boston

Wayne Kreklow, Drake; Ernesto Malcolm, Briar Cliff; Nick Galis, Seton Hall; Jimmy Allen, New Haven; Marvin Delph, Arkansas; Steve Castellan, Virginia; Glenn Sudhop, North Carolina State; Kevin Sinnett, Navy; Alton Byrd, Columbia.

Chicago

David Greenwood, UCLA; Lawrence Butler, Idaho State; Calvin Garrett, Oral Roberts; Cedric Hordges, South Carolina; George Maynor, East Carolina; Larry Washington, Drury; Steve Smith, USC; Mike Eversley, Chicago State; Tony Warren, North Carolina State; James Jackson, Minnesota; Marvin Thomas, UCLA.

Cleveland

Bruce Flowers, Notre Dame; Bill Laimbeer, Notre Dame; Rick Swing, Citadel; Matt Simpkins, Georgia Southern; Jon Manning, North Texas State; Steve Skaggs, Ohio University; Mark Haymore, Massachusetts; Tim Joyce, Ohio University; Terry Peavy, Point Park (Pa.).

Denver

Gary Garland, DePaul; Larry Williams, Louisville; Odell Ball, Marquette; John Johnson, Creighton; Matt Teahan, Denver; Emmett Lewis, Colorado.

Detroit

Greg Kelser, Michigan State; Roy Hamilton, UCLA; Phil Hubbard, Michigan; Tony Price, Pennsylvania; Terry Duerod, Detroit; Flintie Ray Williams, Nevada-Las Vegas; Truman Claytor, Kentucky; Ken Jones, St. Mary's (Calif.); Rodney Lee, Memphis State; Val Bracey, Central Michigan; Willie Polk, Grand Canyon.

Golden State

Danny Salisbery, Pan American; Lynbert Johnson, Wichita State; Ron Ripley, Wisconsin-Green Bay; Jerry Sichting, Purdue; George Lett, Centenary; Jim Mitchem, DePaul; Ren Watson, Virginia Commonwealth; Mario Butler, Briarcliff; Gene Ransom, California; Kevin Heenan, California-Fullerton.

Houston

Lee Johnson, East Texas State; Paul Mokeski, Kansas; Ricardo Brown, Pepperdine; Sammy Drummer, Georgia Tech; Lionel Green, LSU; Allen Leavell, Oklahoma City; Collie Davis, Southern (B.R.); Rich Valivicius, Auburn; Delbert Watson, East Tennessee State.

Indiana

Dudley Bradley, North Carolina; Tony Zeno, Arizona State; Don Newman, Idaho; Billy Reid, San Francisco; Greg Guye, Stetson; Dirk Ewing, Stetson; Brian Magid, George Washington.

Kansas City

Reggie King, Alabama; Terry Crosby, Tennessee; John McCullough, Oklahoma; Curtis Watkins, DePaul; Bob Roma, Princeton; Nick Daniels, Xavier (O.); Tony Vann, Alabama-Huntsville; Gary Wilson, Southern Illinois; Russell Saunders, New Mexico.

Los Angeles

Earvin Johnson, Michigan State; Brad Holland, UCLA; Oliver Mack, East Carolina; Victor King, Louisiana Tech; Mark Young, Fairfield; Walter Daniels, Georgia; Ray White, Mississippi State; Ricky Reed, Temple.

Milwaukee

Sidney Moncrief, Arkansas; Edgar Jones, Nevada-Reno; Larry Gibson, Maryland; Eugene Robinson, Northeast Louisiana; James Tillman, Eastern Kentucky; Derrick Mayes, Illinois State; Stan Ray, California-Fullerton; Larry Spicer, Alabama-Birmingham; Roger Lapham, Maine; Chris Fahrbach, North Dakota.

New Jersey

Calvin Natt, Northeast Louisiana; Cliff Robinson, USC; John Gerdy, Davidson; Jim Abramaitis, Connecticut; Tony Smith, Nevada-Las Vegas; Jim Strickland, South Carolina; Henry Hollingsworth, Hofstra; Ricky Free, Columbia; Eric Fleisher, Tulane.

New York

Bill Cartwright, San Francisco; Larry Demic, Arizona; Sylvester Williams, Rhode Island; Reggie Carter, St. John's (N.Y.); Kim Goetz, San Diego State; Geoff Huston, Texas Tech; Larry Rogers, Southeast Missouri State; Johnny Green, California-Riverside; Phil Abney, New Mexico; Marc Coleman, Seton Hall; Billy Tucker, Tennessee State; Brett Wyatt, Jersey City State; Gordon Thomas, St. John's (N.Y.).

Philadelphia

Jim Spanarkel, Duke; Clint Richardson, Seattle; Bernard Toone, Marquette; Earl Cureton, Detroit; Mike Niles, California-Fullerton; Carl McPipe, Nebraska; Dan Hartshorne, Oregon; Bobby Willis, Pennsylvania; Rick Raivio, Portland; Coby Leavitt, Utah; Keith McCord, Alabama-Birmingham.

Phoenix

Kyle Macy, Kentucky; Johnny High, Nevada-Reno; Al Green, LSU; Malcolm Cesare, Florida; Mark Eaton, Cypress Junior College; Dale Shackelford, Syracuse; Ollie Matson, Jr., Pepperdine; Charlie Jones, Albany State (Ga.); Hosea Champine, Robert Morris (Pa.); Korky Nelson, Santa Clara.

Portland

Jim Paxson, Dayton; Andrew Fields, Cheyney State; Mickey Fox, St. Mary's (B.C.); Daryll Robinson, Appalachian State; Matt White, Pennsylvania; Ray Ellis, Pepperdine; Jeff Tropf, Central Michigan; Willie Pounds, Chaminade; Stan Eckwood, Harding College; Kelvin Small, Oregon.

San Antonio

Wiley Peck, Mississippi State; Sylvester Norris, Jackson State; Al Daniel, Furman; Steve Schall, Arkansas; Terry Knight, Pittsburgh; Tyrone Branyan, Texas; Eddie McLeod, Nevada-Las Vegas; Glen Fine, Harvard.

San Diego

Tom Channel, Boston University; Lionel Garrett, Southern (La.); Greg Joyner, Middle Tennessee State; Bob Bender, Duke; Jene Grey, LeMoyne; Renaldo Lawrence, Appalachian State; Mike Dodd, San Diego State; Greg Hunter, Loyola-Marymount.

Seattle

James Bailey, Rutgers; Vinnie Johnson, Baylor; John Moore, Texas; James Donaldson, Washington State; Richie Allen, Cal State-Dominguez Hills.

Utah

Larry Knight, Loyola (Ill.); Tico Brown, Georgia Tech; Arvid Kramer, Augustana (S.D.); Greg Deane, Utah; Perry Wolfe, Stanford; Ernie Cobb, Boston College; Paul Poe, Louisiana College; Keith McDonald, Utah State; Milt Huggins, Southern Illinois; Paul Dawkins, Northern Illinois.

Washington

Joe DeSantis, Fairfield; Andrew Parker, Iowa State; Charles Floyd, High Point; Lamont Reid, Oral Roberts; Marshall Ashford, Virginia Tech; Garcia Hopkins, Morgan State; Jo Jo Walters, Manhattan; Ray Hooker, Murray State; Steve Martin, Georgetown (D.C.).

1980

Atlanta

Don Collins, Washington State; Craig Shelton, Georgetown (D.C.); Mike Doyle, South Carolina; Mike Zagardo, George Washington; Charles Hightower, Dillard; Stanley Lamb, Steubenville.

Boston

Kevin McHale, Minnesota; Arnette Hallman, Purdue; Ron Perry, Holy Cross; Donald Newman, Idaho; Kevin Hamilton, Iona; Rufus Harris, Maine; Kenny Evans, Norfolk State; Les Henson, Virginia Tech; Steve Wright, Boston University; Brian Jung, Northwestern; John Nolan, Providence.

Chicago

Kelvin Ransey, Ohio State; Sam Worthen, Marquette; James Wilkes, UCLA; Ron Charles, Michigan State; Mike Campbell, Northwestern; Bernard Rencher, St. John's (N.Y.); Robert Byrd, Marquette; Modzel Greer, North Park; Jay Shidler, Kentucky; Billy Foster, Eastern Montana.

Cleveland

Chad Kinch, North Carolina-Charlotte; Stuart House, Washington State; Wayne Abrams, Southern Illinois; Ron Jones, Illinois State; Murray Brown, Florida State; LeVon Williams, Kentucky; Antonio Martin, Oral Roberts; Leroy Berry, Wilmington (O.); Jim Ellinghausen, Ohio State; Marvin Crafter, Central State.

Dallas

Kiki Vandeweghe, UCLA; Roosevelt Bouie, Syracuse; Dave Britton, Texas A&M; Dave Johnson, Weber State; Darrell Allums, UCLA; Leroy Jackson, Cameron; Tony Forch, Midwestern (Tex.); Clarence Kea, Lamar; Ken Williams, Houston; Tom Morgan, California State-Fullerton.

Denver

James Ray, Jacksonville; Carl Nicks, Indiana State; Jawaan Oldham, Seattle; Curt Nimphius, Arizona State; Eddie Lee, Cincinnati; Ron Valentine, Old Dominion; Sammie Ellis, Pittsburgh; James Patrick, Southwest Texas State; Ernie Hill, Oklahoma City; Tommy Springer, Vanderbilt; Jim Graziano, South Carolina; Earl Sango, Regis.

Detroit

Larry Drew, Missouri; Brad Branson, Southern Methodist; Jonathan Moore, Furman; Darwin Cook, Portland; Tony Fuller, Pepperdine; Tony Turner, Alaska-Anchorage; Carl Pierce, Gonzaga; Leroy Loggins, Fairmont State; Terry Dupris, Huron.

Golden State

Joe Barry Carroll, Purdue; Rickey Brown, Mississippi State; Larry Smith, Alcorn; Jeff Ruland, North Carolina; John Virgil, North Carolina; Robert Scott, Alabama; Don Carfino, USC; Neil Bresnahan, Illinois; Lorenzo Romar, Washington; Kurt Kanaskie, LaSalle; Billy Reid, San Francisco; Tim Higgins, Kearney State.

Houston
John Stroud, Mississippi; Terry Stotts, Oklahoma; Billy Williams, Clemson; Dean Hunger, Utah State; Albert Jones, New Mexico; Everette Jefferson, New Mexico; Joe Nehls, Arizona; Rosie Barnes, Bowling Green.

Indiana
Louis Orr, Syracuse; Kenny Natt, Northeast Louisiana; Dick Miller, Toledo; Rich Branning, Notre Dame; Joe Galvin, Illinois State; Randy Owens, Philadelphia Textile; Charles Naddaff, Lafayette; Steve Stielper, James Madison; Scott Rogers, Kenyon; John Bates, West Virginia Wesleyan.

Kansas City
Hawkeye Whitney, North Carolina State; Tony Murphy, Southern (La.); Kelvin Blakely, Eastern Michigan; Trent Grooms, Kent State; Arnold McDowell, Montana State; Charley Cole, Delta State.

Los Angeles
Wayne Robinson, Virginia Tech; Butch Carter, Indiana; Tony Jackson, Florida State; Ron Baxter, Texas; Rick Raivio, Portland; Odis Boddie, North Carolina; Melvin Hooker, Edinboro State.

Milwaukee
Al Beal, Oklahoma; Jeff Wolff, North Carolina; Ken Jones, Virginia Commonwealth; Alex Gilbert, Indiana State; Ron White, Furman; Keith Valentine, Virginia Union; Del Yarbrough, Illinois State; Melvin Crayton, Alabama State.

New Jersey
Mike O'Koren, North Carolina; Mike Gminski, Duke; Lowes Moore, West Virginia; Rory Sparrow, Villanova; Aaron Curry, Oklahoma; Rick Mattick, Louisiana State; Larry Spicer, Alabama-Birmingham; Lloyd Terry, New Orleans; Barry Young, Colorado State.

New York
Mike Woodson, Indiana; DeWayne Scales, Louisiana State; Kurt Rambis, Santa Clara; Joseph Chrnelich, Wisconsin; William Carey, Albright; Kelvin Hicks, New York Tech; Bobby Turner, Louisville; James Salters, Pennsylvania; Don Wiley, Monmouth (N.J.); Gerald Ross, Grand Canyon.

Philadelphia
Andrew Toney, Southwest Louisiana; Monti Davis, Tennessee State; Clyde Austin, North Carolina State; Reggie Gaines, Winston-Salem; Harold Hubbard, Savannah State; Jim Swaney, Toledo; Donald Cooper, St. Augustine's; Richard Smith, Weber State; Martin Lemelle, Grambling; Luke Griffin, St. Joseph's (Pa.); Joe Hand, Kings (Pa.).

Phoenix
Kimberly Belton, Stanford; John Campbell, Clemson; Doug True, California; Leroy Stampley, Loyola (Ill.); Mark Stevens, Northern Arizona; Coby Leavitt, Utah; Ron Williams, Western Montana; Jim Connolly, LaSalle; Keith French, North Park; Randy Carroll, Kansas.

Portland
Ronnie Lester, Iowa; David Lawrence, McNeese State; Bruce Collins, Weber State; Mike Harper, North Park; Kelvin Henderson, St. Louis; Larry Belin, New Mexico; Perry Mirkovich, Lethbridge; Gig Sims, UCLA; John Stroeder, Montana; Rick Boucher, Maine; Dave Kufeld, Yeshiva (N.Y.).

San Antonio
Reggie Johnson, Tennessee; Michael Wiley, Long Beach State; Lavon Mercer, Georgia; Rich Yonakor, North Carolina; Calvin Roberts, California-Fullerton; Gib Hinz, Wisconsin-Eau Claire; Dean Uthoff, Iowa State; Alan Zahn, Arkansas; Bill Bailey, Pan American; Al Williams, North Texas State; Steve Schall, Arkansas.

San Diego
Michael Brooks, LaSalle; Ed Odom, Oklahoma State; Wally Rank, San Jose State; Londale Theus, Santa Clara; Paul Anderson, Southern California College.

Seattle
Bill Hanzlik, Notre Dame; Carl Bailey, Tuskegee; Gary Hooker, Murray State; Lenny Horton, Georgia Tech; Jim Strickland, South Carolina; Carl Ervin, Seattle; Al Dutch, Georgetown (D.C.); James Tillman, Eastern Kentucky; Kent Williams, Texas Tech.

Utah
Darrell Griffith, Louisville; John Duren, Georgetown (D.C.); Alan Taylor, Brigham Young; Wally West, Boston University; Ken Cunningham, Western Michigan; Dave Colescott, North Carolina; Jim Brandon, St. Peter's; Paul Renfro, Texas-Arlington; Leroy Coleman, Middle Tennessee.

Washington
Wes Matthews, Wisconsin; Ricky Mahorn, Hampton Institute; Francois Wise, Long Beach State; Daryl Strickland, Rutgers; Ken Dancy, Chicago State; Karl Godine, Stephen F. Austin; Rich Valivicius, Auburn; Clinton Wyatt, Alcorn State; Don Youman, Oklahoma State.

NBA CHAMPIONS

1946–47 PHILADELPHIA WARRIORS

Seated (left to right): Jerry Rullo, Angelo Musi, General Manager Peter Tyrell, Pete Rosenberg, Jerry Fleishman. Standing: Assistant Coach Cy Kaselman, George Senesky, Ralph Kaplowitz, Howard Dallmar, Art Hillhouse, Joe Fulks, Matt Guokas, Coach Ed Gottlieb.

1947–48 BALTIMORE BULLETS

Left to right: Connie Simmons, Clarence Hermsen, Grady Lewis, Carl Meinhold, Paul Hoffman, Dick Schulz, Herman Feutsch, Chick Reiser, Herman Klotz, Player-Coach Buddy Jeannette.

1948–49 MINNEAPOLIS LAKERS

Left to right: Don Forman, Herman Schaefer, Don Carlson, Don Smith, Tony Jaros, John Jorgensen, Earl Gardner, Arnie Ferrin, Jack Dwan, Jim Pollard, George Mikan.

1949–50 MINNEAPOLIS LAKERS

Left to right: Slater Martin, Billy Hassett, Don Carlson, Herm Schaefer, Bob Harrison, Tony Jaros, Coach John Kundla, Bud Grant, Arnie Ferrin, Jim Pollard, Vern Mikkelsen, George Mikan.

1950–51 ROCHESTER ROYALS

Front row (left to right): Bob Davies, Bob Wanzer, William "Red" Holzman, Paul Noel, Frank Saul. Back row: Bill Calhoun, Joe McNamee, Arnold Risen, Jack Coleman, Arnold Johnson.

1951–52 MINNEAPOLIS LAKERS

Left to right: Slater Martin, Joe Hutton, Frank Saul, Bob Harrison, Jim Pollard, Howie Schultz, Vern Mikkelsen, Lew Hitch, George Mikan.

1952–53 MINNEAPOLIS LAKERS

Left to right: Coach John Kundla, Slater Martin, Frank Saul, Jim Holstein, Vern Mikkelsen, Lew Hitch, George Mikan, Jim Pollard, Bob Harrison, Whitey Skoog, Assistant Coach Dave Mc-Millan.

1953–54 MINNEAPOLIS LAKERS

Left to right: Slater Martin, Frank Saul, Jim Holstein, Jim Pollard, Clyde Lovellette, George Mikan, Vern Mikkelsen, Dick Schnittker, Whitey Skoog, Coach John Kundla.

1954–55 SYRACUSE NATIONALS

Front Row (left to right): Dick Farley, Billy Kenville. Center Row: Earl Lloyd, Captain Paul Seymour, Coach Al Cervi, George King, Jim Tucker. Standing: President Daniel Biasone, Wally Osterkorn, Business Manager Bob Sexton, Dolph Schayes, John Kerr, Billy Gabor, Red Rocha, Trainer Art Van Auken.

1955–56 PHILADELPHIA WARRIORS

Seated (left to right): Coach George Senesky, Larry Hennessy, Paul Arizin, Jack George, George Dempsey, President Eddie Gottlieb. Standing: Ernie Beck, Neil Johnston, Joe Graboski, Walter Davis, Tom Gola, Jackie Moore.

1956–57 BOSTON CELTICS

Seated (left to right): Lou Tsioropoulos, Andy Phillip, Frank Ramsey, Coach Arnold "Red" Auerbach, Captain Bob Cousy, Bill Sharman, Jim Loscutoff. Standing: President Walter A. Brown, Dick Hemric, Jack Nichols, Bill Russell, Arnold Risen, Tom Heinsohn, Trainer Harvey Cohn, Treasurer Lou Pieri.

1957–58 ST. LOUIS HAWKS

Seated (left to right): Coach Alex Hannum, Cliff Hagan, Jack Coleman, Captain Charley Share, Bob Pettit, Walt Davis, Ed Macauley. Standing: Ball Boy Max Shapiro, Slater Martin, Win Wilfong, Jack McMahon, Med Park, Frank Selvy, Trainer Bernie Ebert.

1958–59 BOSTON CELTICS

Seated (left to right): Gene Conley, Bob Cousy, Coach Arnold "Red" Auerbach, President Walter A. Brown, Bill Sharman, Bill Russell. Standing: Trainer Buddy LeRoux, K.C. Jones, Lou Tsioropoulos, Tommy Heinsohn, Ben Swain, Jim Loscutoff, Sam Jones, Frank Ramsey. Inset: Treasurer Lou Pieri.

1959–60 BOSTON CELTICS

Seated (left to right): Frank Ramsey, Bob Cousy, Coach Arnold "Red" Auerbach, President Walter Brown, Treasurer Lou Pieri, K.C. Jones, Bill Sharman. Standing: Gene Guarilia, Tom Heinsohn, John Richter, Bill Russell, Gene Conley, Jim Loscutoff, Sam Jones, Trainer Buddy LeRoux.

1960–61 BOSTON CELTICS

Seated (left to right): K.C. Jones, Bob Cousy, Coach Arnold "Red" Auerbach, President Walter A. Brown, Bill Sharman, Frank Ramsey. Standing: Trainer Buddy LeRoux, Tom Sanders, Tom Heinsohn, Gene Conley, Bill Russell, Gene Guarilia, Jim Loscutoff, Sam Jones. Inset: Treasurer Lou Pieri.

1961–62 BOSTON CELTICS

Seated (left to right): K.C. Jones, Gary Phillips, President Walter A. Brown, Coach Arnold "Red" Auerbach, Treasurer Lou Pieri, Captain Bob Cousy, Sam Jones. Standing: Frank Ramsey, Tom Sanders, Tom Heinsohn, Bill Russell, Gene Guarilia, Jim Loscutoff, Carl Braun, Trainer Buddy LeRoux.

1962–63 BOSTON CELTICS

Seated (left to right): K.C. Jones, Bill Russell, President Walter A. Brown, Coach Arnold "Red" Auerbach, Treasurer Lou Pieri, Captain Bob Cousy, Sam Jones. Standing: Frank Ramsey, Gene Guarilia, Tom Sanders, Tom Heinsohn, Clyde Lovellette, John Havlicek, Jim Loscutoff, Dan Swartz, Trainer Buddy LeRoux.

1963–64 BOSTON CELTICS

Seated (left to right): Sam Jones, Frank Ramsey, K.C. Jones, Coach Arnold "Red" Auerbach, President Walter A. Brown, Bill Russell, John Havlicek. Standing: Jack McCarthy, Tom Sanders. Tom Heinsohn, Clyde Lovellette, Willie Naulls, Jim Loscutoff, Larry Siegfried, Trainer Buddy LeRoux. Inset: Vice-President Lou Pieri.

1964–65 BOSTON CELTICS

Seated (left to right): K.C. Jones, Tom Heinsohn, President Louis Pieri, Coach Arnold "Red" Auerbach, Bill Russell, Sam Jones. Standing: Ron Bonham, Larry Siegfried, Willie Naulls, Mel Counts, John Thompson, Tom Sanders. John Havlicek, Trainer Buddy LeRoux.

1965–66 BOSTON CELTICS

Seated (left to right): John Havlicek, K.C. Jones, Chairman of the Board Marvin Kratter, Coach Arnold "Red Auerbach, President John Waldron, Bill Russell. Standing: Ron Bonham, Don Nelson, Tom Sanders, Mel Counts, John Thompson, Woody Sauldsberry, Willie Naulls, Sam Jones, Larry Siegfried, Trainer Buddy LeRoux.

1966–67 PHILADELPHIA 76ERS

Seated (left to right): Wilt Chamberlain, Dave Gambee, Luke Jackson, Billy Cunningham, Chet Walker. Standing: Trainer Al Domenico, Coach Alex Hannum, Wally Jones, Bill Melchionni, Matt Guokas, Hal Greer, Larry Costello, Owner Irv Kosloff, General Manager Jack Ramsay.

221

1967–68 BOSTON CELTICS

Seated (left to right): Sam Jones, Larry Siegfried, General Manager Arnold "Red" Auerbach, Chairman of the Board Marvin Kratter, President Clarence Adams, Coach Bill Russell, John Havlicek. Standing: Trainer Joe DeLauri, Rick Weitzman, Tom Thacker, Tom Sanders, Bailey Howell, Wayne Embry, Don Nelson, John Jones, Mal Graham.

1968–69 BOSTON CELTICS

Seated (left to right): Don Nelson, Sam Jones, Coach Bill Russell, President Jack Waldron, General Manager Arnold "Red" Auerbach, John Havlicek, Team Physician Dr. Thomas Silva, Larry Siegfried. Standing: Trainer Joe DeLauri, Emmette Bryant, Don Chaney, Tom Sanders, Rich Johnson, Jim Barnes, Bailey Howell, Mal Graham.

1969–70 NEW YORK KNICKERBOCKERS

Seated (left to right): John Warren, Don May, Walt Frazier, President Ned Irish, Chairman of the Board Irving M. Felt, General Manager Eddie Donovan, Dick Barnett, Mike Riordan, Cazzie Russell. Standing: Coach William "Red" Holzman, Phil Jackson, Dave Stallworth, Dave DeBusschere, Captain Willis Reed, Bill Hosket, Nate Bowman, Bill Bradley.

1970–71 MILWAUKEE BUCKS

Seated (left to right): Bob Boozer, Greg Smith, Bob Dandridge, Oscar Robertson, Lew Alcindor, Jon McGlocklin, Lucius Allen, Coach Larry Costello. Standing: Trainer Arnie Garber, Jeff Webb, Marvin Winkler, Dick Cunningham, Bob Greacen, McCoy McLemore, Assistant Coach Tom Nissalke.

1971–72 LOS ANGELES LAKERS

Seated (left to right): Keith Erickson, Happy Hairston, Leory Ellis, Coach Bill Sharman, Chairman of the Board and President Jack Kent Cooke, General Manager Fred Schaus, Wilt Chamberlain, John Q. Trapp, Elgin Baylor. Standing: Assistant Coach K.C. Jones, Gail Goodrich, Jim Cleamons, Pat Riley, Jim Mc-Millian, Jerry West, Flynn Robinson, Trainer Frank O'Neill.

1972–73 NEW YORK KNICKERBOCKERS

Seated (left to right): Henry Bibby, Walt Frazier, President Ned Irish, Chairman of the Board Irving M. Felt, General Manager and Coach William "Red" Holzman, Earl Monroe, Dick Barnett. Standing: Bill Bradley, Phil Jackson, John Gianelli, Dave DeBusschere, Willis Reed, Jerry Lucas, Tom Riker, Dean Meminger, Trainer Danny Whalen.

1973-74 BOSTON CELTICS

Seated (left to right): Jo Jo White, Don Chaney, John Havlicek, Pres. and GM Arnold "Red" Auerbach, Chairman Robert Schmertz, Coach Tom Heinsohn, Dave Cowens, Paul Silas, Asst. Coach John Kililea. Standing: Asst. Trainer Mark Volk, Team Dentist Dr. Sam Kane, Paul Westphal, Phil Hankinson, Steve Downing, Don Nelson, Hank Finkel, Steve Kuberski, Art Williams, Team Physician Dr. Tom Silva, Trainer Frank Challant.

1974–75 GOLDEN STATE WARRIORS

Front Row (left to right): Charles Johnson, Jeff Mullins, Assistant Coach Joe Roberts, Coach Al Attles, Owner Frank Mieuli, Captain Rick Barry, Butch Beard, Phil Smith, Trainer Dick D'Oliva. Back Row: Assistant General Manager Hal Childs, Charles Dudley, Bill Bridges, Clifford Ray, George Johnson, Derrek Dickey, Keith Wilkes, Steve Bracey, Director of Player Personnel Bob Feerick, General Manager Dick Vertlieb.

1975-76 BOSTON CELTICS

Seated (left to right): Charlie Scott, Paul Silas, Dave Cowens, Chairman Irvin Levin, Coach Tom Heinsohn, President Arnold "Red" Auerbach, John Havlicek, Jo Jo White, Don Nelson. Standing: Dr. Tom Silva, Asst. Trainer Mark Volk, Kevin Stacom, Glenn McDonald, Tom Boswell, Jim Ard, Steve Kuberski, Jerome Anderson. Trainer Frank Challant, Dr. Sam Kane.

1976-77 PORTLAND TRAIL BLAZERS

Seated (left to right): Pres. Larry Weinberg, GM Harry Glickman, Herm Gilliam, Dave Twardzik, Johnny Davis, Lionel Hollins, Coach Jack Ramsay, Asst. Coach Jack McKinney. Second row: Lloyd Neal, Larry Steele, Corky Calhoun, Bill Walton, Maurice Lucas, Wally Walker, Robin Jones, Bob Gross. Back row: Radio Announcer Bill Schonely, Team Physician Dr. Bob Cook, Trainer Ron Culp, Promotions Dir. Wallace Scales, Team Dentist Dr. Larry Mudrick, Bus. Mgr. George Rickles, Adm. Asst. Berlyn Hodges.

224

1977–78 WASHINGTON BULLETS

Front row (left to right): General Manager Bob Ferry, Coach Dick Motta, Larry Wright, Phil Chenier, Tom Henderson, Phil Walker, President Abe Pollin, Executive Vice President Jerry Sachs. Back row: Assistant Coach Bernie Bickerstaff, Kevin Grevey, Greg Ballard, Elvin Hayes, Wes Unseld, Mitch Kupchak, Joe Pace, Bob Dandrige, Trainer John Lally.

1978–79 SEATTLE SUPERSONICS

Front row (left to right): Trainer Frank Furtardo, Dick Snyder, Jackie Robinson, Fred Brown, Joe Hassett, Dennis Johnson, Gus Williams. Second row: Coach Lenny Wilkens, Dennis Awtrey, Tom LaGarde, John Johnson, Lonnie Shelton, Paul Silas, Scout Mike Uporsky, Assistant Coach Les Habegger. Back row: Jack Sikma, General Manager Zollie Volchok. Missing: Wally Walker.

1979–80 LOS ANGELES LAKERS

Seated (left to right): Chairman of the Board Dr. Jerry Buss, Spencer Haywood, Jamaal Wilkes, Kareem Abdul-Jabbar, Earvin Johnson, Jim Chones, General Manager Bill Sharman. Standing: Coach Paul Westhead, Butch Lee, Brad Holland, Mark Landsberger, Marty Byrnes, Michael Cooper, Norm Nixon, Trainer Jack Curran, Assistant Coach Pat Riley.

1980–81 BOSTON CELTICS

Seated (left to right): Chris Ford, Cedric Maxwell, President Arnold "Red" Auerbach, Coach Bill Fitch, Chairman of the Board Harry Mangurian, Larry Bird, Nate Archibald. Standing: Assistant Coach K.C. Jones, Wayne Kreklow, M.L. Carr, Rick Robey, Robert Parish, Kevin McHale, Eric Fernsten, Gerald Henderson, Assistant Coach Jimmy Rodgers, Trainer Ray Melchiorre.

Kareem Abdul-Jabbar shoots patented sky hook against the Knicks.

CHAPTER 8

The Greatest Players

The selection of greatest players in any sport is a subjective thing that inevitably breeds debate. The editor of *The NBA's Official Encyclopedia of Pro Basketball* had this confirmed when he sought the opinion of coaches, players and writers in determining who would make up the list of THE GREATEST PLAYERS. The only stipulation was that the players, to be eligible, had to have played after World War II, which marked the advent of the new era of pro basketball. This was not intended as a slight of the great early players, but it was felt there was no way to select between the Nat Holmans and the Dutch Dehnerts of the Original Celtic days and the Bob Cousys and Dr. J.'s of the last three decades. But what a team they would have made!

KAREEM ABDUL-JABBAR

Graceful Power

Mikan's game was ruggedness and determination. Chamberlain's was raw power. Russell's was timing, instinct and competitiveness. Kareem Abdul-Jabbar's is one of grace and elegance.

It is almost as though this gifted basketball machine views the game from a different perspective than others. The pushing, shoving, clutching, grabbing and even maiming which marks the strategy of some opponents simply does not appeal to him. Occasionally he flares up on the court and he has been known

to floor opponents with punches, but generally he answers the stray elbow with another patented sky hook which, to him, is the preferred way of dealing with nasty opponents.

Thoughtful and withdrawn, almost reclusive, Kareem Abdul-Jabbar is not well understood by fans, teammates or even coaches, all of whom want him to be more aggressive on the floor. He takes this all in stride; he is accustomed to being misunderstood.

By any standards, however, Kareem (born Ferdinand Lewis Alcindor in New York City April 16, 1947) is among the most renowned basketball players who has ever lived. As a high school player at Power Memorial in New York, he was as famous as many professional players. He had a national reputation by the time he enrolled at UCLA in the fall of 1965.

At UCLA he lived up to all expectations, leading the Bruins to three consecutive NCAA titles. None of the championship games was even remotely competitive. Rivals were at a loss to deal with him. Said Notre Dame coach Johnny Dee, "The only way to beat Alcindor is to hope for the three F's—foreign court, friendly officials and foul out Alcindor."

Early in his sophomore year, Washington State played him in a straight man-to-man defense and he responded with 61 points. The next time he saw a straight man-to-man was three years later when he was wearing the uniform of the Milwaukee Bucks in the NBA. His 28.8-point scoring average, 1,190 rebounds, 337 assists and superior defense assured him Rookie of the Year honors as he powered the second-year expansion Bucks to a second-place finish and the Eastern Division finals against eventual champion New York.

In his second season as a pro, Abdul-Jabbar was a runaway choice as the league's Most Valuable Player. More significantly, he teamed with Oscar Robertson to lead the Bucks to a 66-16 regular-season record and to 12 playoff victories in 14 games, including a four-game sweep of the Baltimore Bullets in the final round.

The Bucks and Kareem were in the playoffs three more times, and reached the final round again in 1974 only to lose to the Boston Celtics, as Abdul-Jabbar raised his scoring average to 30 points a game and steadily increased his rebounding and playmaking skills. He was rewarded with two more MVP trophies for his efforts during this period.

Nearing the end of his first multi-year contract, Abdul-Jabbar expressed a desire to be traded, not being totally satisfied with the coaching style of Larry Costello or the *gemutlichkeit* of Milwaukee. The club accommodated him; he was traded to Los Angeles prior to the 1975-76 season.

By this time Abdul-Jabbar had developed a full arsenal of offensive weapons and was equally adept at shooting hook shots, drop jumpers, artful driving layups and stuff shots coming off ballet-like inside moves. He most preferred, however, the celebrated sky hook, the nickname given to his altitudinous hook shot by Milwaukee play-by-play announcer Eddie Doucette.

In his first season at Los Angeles, Abdul-Jabbar averaged 27.7 points a game and 16.9 rebounds, leading the league in rebounds for the first time as he won his fourth MVP award in seven seasons in the NBA. To his disappointment, however, the Lakers failed to make the playoffs for the second straight year. With Jerry West as new head coach in 1976-77, and Abdul-Jabbar earning his fifth MVP trophy, Los Angeles was in contention again, with one of the best records in the league and a spot in the playoffs.

In 1979-80, at 33, he led the Lakers to their second NBA championship. He averaged 24.8 points and re-established himself as a dominating force in the game. "I know the game a lot better," Kareem said. "I'm physically stronger . . . and I'm still quicker than most centers in the league."

There was little disagreement. Kareem won his sixth MVP trophy.

Kareem Abdul-Jabbar had all the physical skills any basketball player could ever want, and he could use them as well as anybody. But often, especially in recent years, he seemed to play with a lack of intensity and concentration. He had been the subject of a number of death threats, and as a member of a small, strict Islamic sect, he was often the target of publicity-seeking fanatics. Throughout it all, Abdul-Jabbar maintained an outward calm. And when he was able to put his mind entirely on basketball, he was beautiful to watch—one so tall moving with such fluid grace and awesome power.

NATE ARCHIBALD

Little Big Man

Skillful big men win ball games and, ultimately, championships, but skillful little men win fans. It happened in the 1950s with Bob Cousy and the phenomenon was repeated in the 1970s with Nate "Tiny" Archibald.

From coast to coast, basketball fans pay to see this undersized (6-1, 150 pounds) demon slide and slither his way over, under, around and through the redwoods of the game. He enables spectators to identify more closely with the sport when they realize it isn't solely a game of size, but one of speed and quickness, as Bob Cousy always says. Combine those attributes with body control and one beholds one of the most exciting little men ever to play basketball—Nate Archibald.

Curiously, Cousy had a lot to do with Archibald's emergence as a star. As coach of the Kansas City-Omaha Kings in 1972-73, Cousy turned over full direction of the team to Tiny, who responded with one of the most amazing seasons any player has ever had. He led the league in scoring with 34.9 points and in assists with 11.4, an unprecedented statistical double. He also became the first guard since Slater Martin nearly 20 years earlier to lead the league in minutes played.

The eldest of seven children, Nate was born in New York on April 18, 1948. He picked up his nickname from his father, who was called Big Tiny after Nate was born, and his son was called Little Tiny. Nate learned to play basketball on the playgrounds and schoolyards of the Bronx before attending DeWitt

Clinton High School, Arizona Western Junior College and the University of Texas at El Paso. UTEP coach Don Haskins preferred a controlled game and used Tiny primarily as a playmaker. When Archibald scored over 40 points in an all-star match after his senior year, a pro scout remarked to Haskins that he hadn't realized Tiny could score like that. ''Don't feel badly,'' Haskins answered, ''I had him for three years and didn't know it either.''

At the end of the 1969-70 season, when Cousy and the Royals were still in Cincinnati, the team was looking for a quarterback to replace the legendary Oscar Robertson. On the second round of the college draft, Archibald was selected and three weeks later Robertson was headed for Milwaukee.

The gutsy little Archibald became an immediate starter, playing every game and averaging 16.0 points. He started well the following season and felt he earned a spot in the All-Star Game. He wasn't selected to the squad either by the vote or by the coaches filling out the teams, and it was a decision which aroused Tiny.

Furious over what he considered a snub. Archibald dedicated himself to proving the coaches wrong. He achieved new performing heights and by the end of the season he had succeeded in raising his scoring average to 28.2 points.

The next season with the team now playing in Kansas City as the Kings, was the breakthrough. Cousy simply gave Tiny carte blanche and Archibald responded by tearing the league apart. They couldn't keep him out of the All-Star Game this time, and he made the most of his opportunity. He threw passes between his legs and around his back and he drove to the basket in his inimitable style. Although the East won by 20 points, Archibald had acquitted himself admirably. After the game he criticized his teammates for their lackadaisical play.

Archibald is a very difficult man to guard because of his versatility. Few players of any size have quickness to match his, and nobody anywhere has more body control. Because Archibald can do so much while driving to the basket, most opponents choose to drop back, conceding him the outside shot. Unfortunately for them, Tiny has worked on improving the accuracy and range of his outside shot.

Double-teaming him is no solution, either, because he is an absolute master at finding and hitting the open man. Teams employing gimmick strategies are

Nate ''Tiny'' Archibald made remarkable comeback with the Celtics.

doomed to failure. Once the Celtics tried a thinly disguised zone on him and he responded with 35 points and 15 assists. ''I don't think that's the way to play him,'' Celtic coach Tommy Heinsohn lamented afterward.

The little southpaw had no sooner established himself as one of the league's brightest young stars with the Kings than he had to battle back from serious injury. Early in the 1973-74 season, he was accidentally stepped on by Chicago's massive Tom Boerwinkle, who outweighed Tiny by at least 120 pounds. He suffered a leg injury and was out of action for 47 games.

But he rebounded the following year to score 26.5 points and hand out 6.8 assists a game, ranking high among the league leaders in both categories. He returned to New York for the 1976-77 season to play for the Nets after the ABA champions came into the NBA. He was just fitting in with his new team when a broken ankle sidelined him for the rest of the season. He was then traded to Buffalo.

After sitting out the entire 1977-78 campaign with a torn Achilles tendon, Archibald was traded to Boston, where he has enjoyed a rebirth. His playmaking and steady guidance led the Celtics into the 1979-80 playoffs and to the 1980-81 championship. He added another accomplishment when he was named Most Valuable Player in the 1981 All-Star Game.

In addition to his speed, quickness and finesse, Tiny possesses an attribute which could never be taught or transferred. That quality is fearlessness. Even given all his skills, he could not accomplish what he does on the court were he afraid to drive to the basket and challenge much taller and stronger men. He is tiny in size, but big in heart.

PAUL ARIZIN

The Philadelphia Story

The nickname was Pitchin' Paul, and the image was that of a slightly undersized forward huffing and puffing his way down-court shaking and flapping his hands until the ball came his way. Then he would stop, jump and in a flash launch the ball toward the basket. Paul Arizin, they said, was the only player you could hear running in sneakers.

The cause of his heavy breathing was thought to be a mild asthmatic condition, but Arizin denied this and explained it was due to a sinus condition which doctors said was not serious and which acted up only when he ran without getting sufficient oxygen. "That's the only time it bothers me," he said, but opponents had it in their heads that it bothered him every night despite the fact that he averaged over 40 minutes of playing time per game throughout his career.

One thing in certain: he bothered his foes every night, since he had an uncanny ability for sensing when a defender was relaxed or leaning in the wrong direction, and he would go right up for a jump shot.

Arizin's was a bizarre success story. Born April 9, 1928, in Philadelphia, he attended LaSalle High School, adjacent to LaSalle College, but didn't even play for the school team, preferring to demonstrate his talent in several of the recreational leagues around the city.

When he enrolled at Villanova, as a chemistry major with his family paying the bills, nobody in the athletic department even knew his name. He continued his play in the independent leagues, scoring his usual 30 or more points a game, and before long Philadelphia Warriors' owner Eddie Gottlieb heard about him. But before Gottlieb could sign him up, Villanova coach Al Severance got wind of the recreational league hotshot who was supposed to be better than anyone on the Wildcat varsity. Arizin joined the team. In his sophomore year he was a bench warmer for seven games, but then became a starter, and a star, leading the Wildcats in scoring. In his junior season he averaged 25 points a game and led Villanova into the NCAA tournament, only to lose to eventual national champion Kentucky.

The following year Arizin's 26-point average led the nation's major college scorers and in one game he poured in 85 points, although this was later scrubbed from the record book since it came against the Philadelphia Navy Air Materials Center and not an accredited four-year college. Eddie Gottlieb was impressed enough, however, and made Arizin the first-round draft choice of the Warriors.

Thus began a 12-year career which elevated Arizin to the top of his profession. Though only 6-4 and 210 pounds at his heaviest, Arizin was able to get away with playing up front with the big boys because of his intelligence, superior jumping ability, and the fact that he was one of the few practitioners of the jump shot. It was the jumper that offset his defender's height advantage and eventually propelled Arizin into the basketball Hall of Fame.

As a rookie he was sixth in league scoring with 17.2 points a game, and he was eighth in the league in rebounding. In his second season he topped all scorers with a 25.4 average and improved his rebounding to 11.3 a game. He then served a two-year hitch with the Marines, one of the few pro basketball players to have his career interrupted by military service, but he returned in 1954-55 to show he had lost none of his skills by finishing second to teammate Neil Johnston in the scoring race.

Arizin reached the 10,000-point club faster than any man before him, and when he retired prema-

Even the long arm of Laker Walter Dukes couldn't stop Paul Arizin from scoring for the Warriors in this 1956 game.

turely, he had a career total of 16,266 points and a per-game average of 22.8 points. When the Warriors left Philadelphia for San Francisco for the 1962-63 season, Arizin decided he would rather stay in Philadelphia. He had played in nine All-Star Games in his 10 seasons, was named to the All-NBA team three times and played on the Warriors' championship club of 1956, which he rated as his biggest thrill in the NBA.

After the Warriors left town, Arizin showed he still could live up to his Pitchin' Paul nickname by playing in the Eastern Basketball League, where he earned MVP honors, thanks mostly to his unique jump shot. Many observers assumed he had developed the shot by watching Joe Fulks, an early Philadelphia standout, but Arizin said that expediency was the real source of the shot. "When I began playing basketball in 1946," he once explained, "our team, St. Monica's in the Catholic league, played on a narrow floor which was also used for dances. They would wax the floor and it would be very slippery. When I tried to shoot a hook shot or drive, I would slide. One day I tried jumping and shooting. I didn't slip, and I was having success with the shots. That's how I developed my jumper."

However, it came about, Pitchin' Paul's jump shot—accompanied by wheezing, breathing, huffing, puffing—found its mark.

RICK BARRY

A Nose for the Basket

There is an undefinable ability certain players have for manufacturing two points. There have been pure shooters, and there have been scorers. Rick Barry

231

was one of the latter, with an unquenchable desire to take the basketball and somehow get it through the hoop.

The record book provides ample proof that Barry has been in the basket and around the hoop world. He is the only man to have led both the ABA and NBA in scoring. Four times he averaged more than 30 points a game, including an impressive 35.6 a game as a skinny 22-year-old kid during his second season in the NBA in 1966-67. He has scored as many as 64 points in a regular-season game and 55 in a playoff game.

The curious thing about Barry is that there were

Rick Barry, scoring over Knicks' Bill Bradley, has nose for the basket.

so many doubters when he broke into professional ball with the San Francisco Warriors. Born March 28, 1944, in Elizabeth, New Jersey, he was a standout high school athlete at Roselle (N.J.) High, where he actually preferred baseball to basketball. His uniform number, 24, was selected because it was the number of his boyhood hero, a baseball player known as Willie Mays. Barry attended the University of Miami in Florida where he was a big scorer despite his slight build—less than 200 pounds packed on a 6-7 frame. Many questioned whether he could take the kind of punishment dealt out in the pros.

Barry fooled the critics by scoring 25.7 points a game and earning Rookie of the Year honors. The next season, when he scored at a 35.6-point clip, he teamed with Nate Thurmond to lead the Warriors to the NBA finals where they extended the mighty Philadelphia 76ers—winners of 68 regular-season games—to a six-game series for the championship.

After that, the Warriors and their fans were looking forward to a dynasty with Barry, but he had other plans. Rick accepted a lucrative offer to jump across the Bay and play under his father-in-law and college coach, Bruce Hale, for the Oakland Oaks of the ABA. In order to do that, however, the courts said he had to sit out the entire 1967-68 season, which he spent playing in a local league. When he did join the Oaks, however, he showed he had lost none of his ability, as he led the team to the ABA title with a 34.0 scoring average.

He might have remained in the new league had not the Oaks encountered gate troubles and decided to move across the continent, first to Washington, D.C., then to Virginia. This was not exactly what Barry had in mind when he left the Warriors. He had become financially and emotionally tied to the Bay Area, and he didn't relish playing in Richmond and Norfolk. He forced a trade, which landed him in New York with the Nets. It wasn't San Francisco, but it was better than Virginia.

The Warriors, meanwhile, never stopped trying to get Barry back. Owner Franklin Mieuli considered Barry a prodigal son, and even had Barry's No. 24 hanging in his office. Barry finally did sign a contract to return to the NBA, and was back for the 1973-74 season.

It was a different Barry in his second NBA career. He had undergone knee surgery while in the ABA, and he had been robbed of some quickness. But he had also filled out to a sturdy 220 pounds, and he had the benefit of experience. He didn't drive to the basket as much as in the old days, but when he did drive, he did so with more control and with more of an eye to pass than shoot. At the same time, he had improved his outside shooting to the point where he could score 30 points with minimal driving. His rebounding and defense had also improved.

Rick put all his skills together in the spectacular season of 1974-75 after the Warriors had lost several players through trades, expansion and front office bungling. Most experts felt the team would be lucky to escape the cellar.

Putting underrated center Clifford Ray and rookie guard Phil Smith to good use, and utilizing the leadership and all-around brilliance of Barry, the Warriors swept to the Pacific Division championship. In the playoffs, they stunned heavily favored Chicago in seven games, winning the deciding contest on the Bulls' home court. Then they astounded everyone by sweeping the Washington Bullets in four straight games.

Barry was the key. Though he finished only fourth in the all-star balloting, he had enjoyed the best season of any player in the league, leading his team in scoring, assists, foul shooting and minutes played. He was second in the league in scoring, sixth in assists and first in steals. He continued his outstanding play in the playoffs, where he was named MVP for such feats as scoring 36 and 38 points in back-to-back efforts against Washington.

Barry always was a controversial figure who did not always get along with teammates. After leading the Warriors to the title, he spent two more years in the Bay Area before playing out his contract and signing with the Houston Rockets. Age finally began to erode his talent, however, and Barry's performance slipped dramatically in the 1978-79 and 1979-80 seasons.

One aspect of his game did not suffer, however, and that was free-throw shooting. With his two-handed underhand style, he always led his team, and often the whole league in free throw accuracy. Early in the 1976-77 season, he set a league record by making 60 consecutive free throws.

But a player cannot prolong his career indefinitely, even if he still can make free throws. Prior to the start of the 1980-81 season, Barry announced his retirement and became a television commentator.

ELGIN BAYLOR

Poetry in Motion

For 12 seasons Elgin Baylor was the highest-scoring forward in the game, providing leadership for the Laker franchise he had saved from extinction and leading the team to the playoffs every year. Then, in the 1970-71 season, his playing time was reduced to two games, not because of chronically ailing knees but due to a pulled Achilles tendon. He came back for the 1971-72 season, then stepped down for good after nine games.

"I was depriving Jim McMillian of playing time," Baylor explained at the time, "and I knew the same would be true when Keith Erickson [injured] comes back."

It was a noble gesture, stepping aside for the younger men, but Baylor was also giving up a chance at the one thing he never won—an NBA championship ring. Indeed the Lakers went on to win the title that year for the first time since the days of George Mikan back in Minneapolis.

Baylor burst upon the basketball world at Seattle University in the mid-1950s. Born September 16, 1934, he had come out of Washington, D.C., where he had drawn attention at Springarn High School with his basketball talents, but less than rave notices as a student either there or at Phelps Vocational. He even dropped out of school for a while to work as a checker in a furniture store and play basketball in recreational leagues.

His poor school habits kept him out of most colleges, but a friend named Warren Williams arranged a scholarship for Baylor at the College of Idaho, where Elgin was expected to play football as well as basketball. After one season, the school dismissed the head coach and restricted the scholarships. A Seattle car dealer named Ralph Malone interested Baylor in Seattle University, and while Elgin was sitting out the required year after transferring, he played for an amateur team sponsored by Malone.

He became eligible for the 1956-57 season and with Baylor as the fulcrum, the Chieftains went all the way to the NCAA finals in 1958 before losing to Kentucky. Though Baylor had a year of college eligibility left, he was available in the NBA draft, and was selected and signed by the Minneapolis Lak-

Master driver Elgin Baylor glides around Cincinnati's Jerry Lucas.

ers, the worst team in the league. Owner Bob Short later said if Baylor hadn't signed or had returned to college he would have had to sell, or even fold, the franchise. As it was, Baylor took a team which had finished 19-53 the season before and turned it into a playoff team which defeated Detroit, and upset defending champion St. Louis before bowing to Boston in the championship series.

In just one season Baylor established himself as one of the outstanding players in the league. He averaged 24.9 points, 15 rebounds and 4.1 assists a game, and was named to the All-NBA first team for seven consecutive years—starting with his rookie season—and three times thereafter.

Before he had come into the league, nobody spoke of body control, but after watching this extremely powerful 6-5, 225-pound man hang in the air, drift

laterally and somehow squeeze up a shot while appearing to be off-balance, the term became a permanent part of basketball's lexicon. Where most men drove directly to the basket, Baylor took a more circuitous route which sometimes meant changing direction in mid-air.

Of course, there was more to Baylor than simply an exceptional driving ability. When his soft, medium-range jumper was on, he was capable of scoring 50 points and upward because to play him tight in hopes of stopping his jumper was to invite almost certain disaster by allowing him to drive past. On the occasions he missed, Baylor was usually there to grab his own rebound and make the score. Before his knees gave out completely, Baylor performed awesome feats underneath the boards.

After his remarkable rookie season, he increased

234

his scoring average to 29.6 points in his second season and broke Joe Fulks' one-game scoring mark of 63 points with a 64-point outburst against Boston on November 8, 1959. The following season he became the first man to break the 70-point barrier by scoring 71 points against the Knicks.

His scoring averages kept rising. From 29.6 to 34.8 and 38.3. In 1962-63, he became the first NBA player ever to finish in the top five of four different statistical categories when he placed among the leaders in scoring, rebounding, assists and free throw accuracy. Once he played a month with a steel plate on a finger of his shooting hand, and still averaged 30 points a game.

Knee troubles began plaguing him in the 1963-64 season and although he still had five more first team all-star seasons ahead of him, he was never quite the same ballplayer again. From that point on it was always a case of how well he felt on a given night, how much pain he could stand. During one playoff, when Baylor was being held to eight and 10 points a game, teammate Jerry West said, "I'm just sick about it. This is a hard thing to watch. Elg is one of the finest men in the world and the best player I ever saw. To see him scoring less than some of tne subs on the other team makes you want to cry."

When Baylor finally did call it quits, he was the third leading scorer in NBA history with 23,149 points, the number two rebounding forward with 11,463, and the most graceful cornerman ever to play the game.

WILT CHAMBERLAIN

Nobody Loves Goliath

Wilton Norman Chamberlain has been called by some experts "the best basketball player who ever lived." By some detractors he was often called the worst.

It was always this way for this archetypal giant. He understood the situation. At 7-1 1/16 and weighing between 275 and 325 pounds depending upon what kind of condition he was in, Chamberlain could never hide. Whatever he did, good or bad, the actions were always visible. Many expected him to perform superhuman feats, simply because of his size, ignoring

the fact that other big men (such as 7-3 Swede Halbrook) played the game without much success. Wilt himself summed it up best when he said on more than one occasion, "Nobody loves Goliath."

Loved or hated, Wilt made a lasting impact on the game of basketball. On an individual basis, he stands alone as the most awesome force in the history of the sport. He is the all-time NBA scoring leader, and is likely to remain so, having scored 31,419 points. One season he averaged 50.4 points per game, breaking not only the 3,000-point barrier but 4,000 as well. He averaged as many as 27 rebounds a game and once grabbed 55 in a single game. On the night of March 2, 1962, he threw in 36 or 63 shots from the floor and 28 of 32 free throws to score 100 points against the New York Knicks at Hershey, Pennsylvania. Nobody else has come within 27 points of that in the professional ranks.

Angered at charges that he was a selfish ballplayer, he dedicated himself to passing in the middle of his career and became the first center ever to lead the league in assists. In his later years, he wanted to lead the league in field goal accuracy and, during the 1972-73 season, he achieved that goal by connecting on a record 72.7 percent of his shots. It was one of the many times that it appeared Chamberlain could do anything he wanted.

The Philadelphia native, born August 21, 1936, first attracted national attention while playing at Overbrook High School. When he was a senior, he became the object of what was then the biggest recruiting scramble in the history of college basketball. After sifting through hundreds of offers, he selected the University of Kansas, a school with a rich basketball tradition.

At Kansas, Chamberlain was so intimidating as a freshman that he scared the rulemakers. He had concocted a favorite out-of-bounds play underneath his own basket in which a teammate would lob the ball in-bounds over the top of the backboard where Chamberlain would grab it and stuff it through the hoop. Accordingly, a rule was passed prohibiting anyone from throwing the ball in-bounds from directly underneath the basket. That was only the beginning of Chamberlain's impact.

Though he was college basketball's most dominant player, Chamberlain failed to lead the Jayhawks to the NCAA championship during his two varsity seasons. Wilt began to acquire the reputation as a

Wilt Chamberlain soars above Kareem Abdul-Jabbar in meeting of Goliaths.

"loser." Kansas couldn't have come much closer in 1957, however, losing to North Carolina in triple overtime, 54-53. After his junior season, Chamberlain decided he wasn't going to benefit any more from playing in college, so he quit school to join the Harlem Globetrotters and await his chance to play in the NBA.

There was never any question of where he would play. Owner Eddie Gottlieb of the Philadelphia Warriors had long before made his pitch to the league fathers to broaden the scope of the "territorial draft pick" which gave teams first crack at local college players. Gottlieb had the provision extended to high school in Chamberlain's case.

Wilt joined the Warriors in 1959-60 and proceeded to lead the league in scoring and become its MVP. But no championships were forthcoming as a Warrior. The team went to San Francisco in 1962, and in the middle of the 1964-65 season Chamberlain was traded to the Philadelphia 76ers. By the 1966-67 season, his time had come. He enjoyed perhaps the finest all-around season of any NBA center ever, averaging 24 points, 24 rebounds and 8 assists a game. He topped the league in field goal accuracy, played outstanding defense and led the 76ers to the NBA title. In the deciding game of the Eastern finals against defending champion Boston, Wilt had 29 points, 36 rebounds and 13 assists.

Traded because of salary demands to Los Angeles in 1968, he overcame serious knee surgery to regain his form and earn his second championship ring in 1972. He had reduced his offensive role and concentrated on defense and rebounding. With the Big Dipper, as he liked to call himself, controlling the middle, the Lakers won a record 33 straight games, compiling a 69-13 record and won the title easily. One year later Chamberlain retired to take a short-lived position as coach of the San Diego Conquistadors in the rival ABA. Although often rumored to be contemplating a return, Chamberlain remained retired and was named to the Hall of Fame.

Critics frequently harped on his alleged shortcomings and disagreements with coaches, and the fact that he appeared to cherish his status of never having fouled out of a game at the expense of all-out play in close games. They said he always did things in extremes, either shooting too much or too little. In some eyes he suffered in comparison to his contemporary, Bill Russell, but those who understood the game knew their roles were different.

Wilt was forever shrouded in controversy, but friends and foes alike agreed on one thing: you always knew the Big Fella was around.

BOB COUSY

One of a Kind

"The image of the Celtics is the image of Cousy."

The speaker was Bill Russell. The date was March 17, 1963—St. Patrick's Day to the rest of the world, but Bob Cousy Day inside Boston Garden.

One by one, teammates and friends had their say. When it was coach Red Auerbach's turn, Arnold shrugged and said, "What can you say when you know you're going to lose the greatest backcourt man who ever lived?"

This was quite a turnaround for Auerbach, who 13 years earlier wanted no part of the 6-1, 170-pound Holy Cross guard despite his All-America credentials.

Cousy, born August 9, 1928, shortly after his parents emigrated from France to the United States, learned basketball on the playgrounds of St. Albans, Queens, a section of New York City. He was an all-city performer at Andrew Jackson High before going on to national honors at Holy Cross.

Though the Boston press was clamoring for the Celtics to exercise their territorial rights and draft Cousy in 1950, Auerbach decided the Celts needed a big man and went for 6-11 Charley Share out of Bowling Green. Cousy was taken by the Tri-Cities Black Hawks, signed with them and was traded to the Chicago Stags before the season started. The Chicago franchise collapsed and its players were up for grabs in a dispersal draft. Everything went smoothly until there were only three players left: Cousy and veterans Max Zaslofsky and Andy Phillip. There was haggling among New York, Philadelphia and Boston over the players because no one wanted the rookie Cousy. The names were tossed into a hat and the Knicks got Zaslofsky, the Warriors landed Phillip and Boston was stuck with Cousy. All Auer-

Bob Cousy flips one in backhanded against the Knicks.

bach could say at the time was "Cousy will have to make the team."

He did, by showing he was an electrifying player who could more than anyone keep the franchise operating in Boston until the simultaneous arrival of Bill Russell and Tom Heinsohn six years later. Cousy

showed he was the best playmaker and floor leader in the game, and the kind of man who became one of the most popular ballplayers in the history of the game.

Cousy came out of college with a reputation for dazzling audiences with his unique style of play. Never before had anyone passed the way Cousy did, looking one way while sending the ball in another direction, nor had anyone before him dared to attempt the most intricate shots or passes in the tensest moments of ball games. It took a long time for Auerbach to get used to this flamboyant style. He had always thought that the best pass was the simplest pass, and that Cousy was making a basically simple game excessively complicated. Red's feeling was strengthened when he watched Cousy fire passes which bounced off hands, knees, chests and even heads of his teammates in practice.

But this was the only way Cousy knew how to play, and soon his mates learned that he was actually very easy to play with. They found out that if they worked to get open, he would reward them with the ball. In his second season, Cousy was voted to the All-NBA team, an honor he would receive nine more times, to go along with two second-team selections. Moreover, he had given the Celtics an identity with the fast break that they would maintain for the next quarter of a century. There are those who would even go so far as to say Cousy invented fast-break basketball, at least on the professional level. Before Cousy came along, teams had only to worry about playing defense when the offense crossed midcourt. But in the face of Cousy's ability to throw the long pass (helped in large part by his long arms and large hands as well as his peripheral vision and innate daring) the opposition never could relax.

Cousy developed into basketball's top quarterback, one who could direct and inspire a team like nobody else. Big game or not, he was something to behold. In the 1954 All-Star Game in New York, he excelled in the overtime period to such an extent that he was given the MVP award after it had been voted to someone else. In the 1953 playoffs against Syracuse, he scored 50 points, including 17 of the Celtics' last 21 in a four-overtime game which eliminated the Nationals.

When Russell came along to get the ball so Cousy could dispense it more often, the Celtics put together the best team yet assembled, winning with almost monotonous regularity, as the Cooz led the league in assists eight consecutive times. He was in the middle of the Celtic juggernaut, directing the attack.

His finale was typically dramatic. In the sixth game of the 1963 finals against Los Angeles, he sprained his left ankle with the Celtics comfortably ahead in the final period. Suddenly, the Lakers rallied and Boston's 14-point lead was evaporating. The 34-year-old Cousy, bad ankle and all, was rushed back into the game to settle the team. Though he didn't score after his return, his presence was magnetic and the Celts held on to win the game, and the championship, with Cousy flinging the ball toward the ceiling triumphantly as the buzzer sounded.

Auerbach, of course, had long since became Cousy's biggest booster. And one of his frequent remarks at dinners and banquets would go something like this: "I'm getting awfully tired of this baloney. Every kid who can dribble a basketball gets called another Cousy. Well, I've got news for you. There ain't nobody as good as Cooz. There never was."

DAVE COWENS

His Own Man

For what will Dave Cowens be most remembered? That he sparked a minor revolution in basketball by taking the conventional pivot and moving it some 20 feet from the basket? Or that he let a little of his Huck Finn attitude toward life show through and walked away from the game for a large part of a season at the peak of his career?

Suffice it to say, all normal yardsticks of athletic behavior are totally useless when evaluating Cowens. The mercurial 6-8½, 230-pound, red-haired center from Newport, Kentucky, by way of Florida State University, came into the NBA relatively unheralded and proceeded to lead the Boston Celtics to a pair of league titles. Then he stunned the sports world by asking for, and receiving, a "leave of absence" following the eighth game of the 1976-77 season. He eventually returned, helping the Celts into the playoffs, but such heresy in sport made headlines, something he didn't seek, nor really care about.

Dave Cowens' rebounding triggers the Celtics' fast-break offense.

Dave Cowens has always been his own man. He made his presence known from the minute he began his professional career. That came in August 1970 during the annual Maurice Stokes Benefit Game, a preseason affair played in Monticello, New York. Cowens, the 1970 first-round draft choice of the Celtics, inaugurated his pro career by dominating a game which involved some of the biggest names in basketball. He dunked a rebound almost immediately after the game started, and went on to score 32 points and grab 12 rebounds en route to being named the game's MVP. That dynamic display, combined with the rave notices he had drawn while playing summer ball in Harlem's Rucker Tournament, put the NBA on notice that Boston had more than just another rookie.

He moved into the league and averaged 17 points and 15 rebounds a game, sharing Rookie of the Year honors with Portland's Geoff Petrie. But there was more to Cowens' accomplishment. He helped transform the Celtics from a dull, lifeless team basking in reflected glory into a suitable replica of the fast-breaking juggernaut of the late 1950s and early 1960s.

Recognizing that in Cowens he had a strange hybrid—a muscular center with great foot speed and a decent outside shot—Celtic coach Tom Heinsohn built an entire new offense geared at putting the somewhat undersized young center in an advantageous position vis-a-vis his opponents. Heinsohn and Cowens scrapped the notion of the traditional and strictly back-to-the-basket pivotman. Against some defenders, Cowens took the conventional low post, but against taller, slower men, he roamed outside, shooting relatively soft jumpers or driving to the basket from a well-conceived spread offense.

In addition, Cowens improved the Celtics' fast break by providing not only the rebounding to trigger it, but the speed to get down court and become an extra scoring threat. Cowens was able to get the ball off the boards, pitch it out, then outrun or outhustle opponents down the floor to become a wing man or trailer.

Cowens' running ability turned 3-on-2 fast breaks into 4-on-2s, making for easy baskets. And just by running up and down the court throughout a game, he wore out less physically fit opponents and was able to make attrition a Celtic ally late in ball games.

Even greater assets were his rebounding and defense. He displayed an aggressiveness underneath that was frightening to behold. Because of his determination and ability to move laterally in the air, he grabbed rebounds that, in a sense, did not belong to him. Defensively, he again was an innovator. Because he was quicker than most forwards and many guards, he was not reluctant to switch out on opponents. Alleged mismatches became pluses for the Celtics because Cowens was not afraid to cover any forward or guard. This dimension tied together Boston's defense and helped make it one of the best in the league for several years running.

Cowens' game showed continuous improvement. In areas such as passing, shot variety and shot selection, he was on a steady upswing. In time, he became the league's most complete center. He was always, of course, its most competitive.

Honors came his way. In his third season, he was elected MVP by the players as Boston won 68 games. He was the MVP in the 1973 All-Star Game as well, and was named to the All-Defensive first team in 1975-76. But the most important achievements came in 1974 and 1976 when he was the driving force behind two more Celtic championships.

A product of the 1960s (he was born in Newport, Kentucky, on October 25, 1948), Cowens adopted a counterculture lifestyle, very modest considering his income, and he was stamped as a supreme individualist. Whatever forces motivated him to play with such intensity were part of the same personality which made him stop playing for a while when he felt he couldn't give his best.

It came as somewhat of a surprise when the Celtics' Red Auerbach made Cowens player-coach after Satch Sanders was fired early in 1978-79. Auerbach hoped the challenge would keep Cowens' competitive fires burning. The coaching role didn't really fit, and in 1979-80 he was just a player again. But not for long. Prior to the 1980-81 season, he made a decision.

Injuries had taken their toll over the years and Cowens felt he could no longer play the game with the same energy and enthusiasm. He composed a letter in his hotel room detailing his reasons for retiring and mailed a copy to the *Boston Globe*. He then telephoned Celtics' President Red Auerbach and told him of his intention to quit.

Cowens' final act was to board the team bus and tell his teammates personally. Few athletes are as complicated as he was; few as honest in evaluating themselves. Cowens was unique.

BILLY CUNNINGHAM

The Kangaroo Kid

Some players get the job done with quiet efficiency, but others give the crowd a jolt, no matter what they do. Such a player was Billy Cunningham.

There was a spark, an electricity, in Cunningham's game whether he was outleaping taller opponents for a key rebound or uncorking a left-handed jump shot fired from somewhere behind his ear.

Born June 3, 1943, in Brooklyn, New York, he sharpened his skills on the playgrounds of Manhattan Beach and the courts at Erasmus Hall High School where he led an undefeated team to the New York City title in 1961. Frank McGuire lured the 6-5, 215-pound youth to North Carolina, where he earned the nickname "Kangaroo Kid" for his unusual leaping ability, which he combined with superb body control to become a devastating inside player.

His outside shooting was spotty, but he worked on it continuously so that it was at least passable by the time he was a senior. The Philadelphia 76ers made him their first draft choice in 1965 with a specific purpose in mind. The club was searching for a "big" guard at the time, when it was customary to make all players under 6-6 operate in the backcourt no matter what their individual skills or personal inclination. So Cunningham, too, had the traditional consideration at guard. As a Philadelphia writer later observed, "The 76ers thought they were getting a big guard to feed Wilt Chamberlain, but what they really had was a forward to feed Billy Cunningham."

The guard experiment was soon abandoned and Cunningham became a sixth man who would impress all observers with his explosiveness coming off the bench. He served as a perfect complement to the Philadelphia starting forwards, bruising Luke Jackson and clever Chet Walker. He scored 14.3 points a game for the 76ers as they ended the Celtics' nine-year strangle-hold on the Eastern Division title.

By his second season, Cunningham had established himself as one of the league's top players and helped the 76ers to the NBA championship. His outside shot had improved to the point where he was capable of hot streaks. On some nights he was able to score in the 30s, because he was as good a driver as any forward in the league. Given a choice between con-

ceding Cunningham the jumper and risking the drive, a defender had to give him the outside shot because at least that avoided the risk of a foul and three-point play.

Cunningham was also an exceptional rebounder, where his "Kangaroo Kid" label was fully justified. Twice he grabbed more than 1,000 rebounds, which is the hallmark of a topflight boardman. He was especially effective on the offensive boards because of his leaping ability and resourcefulness at tapping the ball through the hoop.

Cunningham had become such an integral member of the 76ers' cast by his third season that when he suffered a broken arm during Philadelphia's third playoff game, it was generally conceded that his absence cost the team a chance to repeat as champion.

Cunningham rebounded from that physical setback to enter the real glory part of his career. He made the first team All-NBA squad in each of the next three seasons, and earned a second team berth in the fourth. During this stage he added an important new

Billy Cunningham lets out a howl as his kangaroo leap fails to snare the ball.

dimension to his game—passing. It got so that Cunningham was the key to the entire Philadelphia offense. He did, in fact, lead the team in assists in the 1971-72 season, and finished sixth in the league in that category.

He had already signed an ABA contract, however, and for the next two seasons he showcased his game to old fans in Carolina as a member of the Cougars, and to new fans in other ABA cities. He stormed into the league, capturing MVP honors in his first season while leading Carolina to the best regular-season record in the league.

After two years in the ABA, Cunningham returned to the 76ers, but in a weakened physical condition. He had been suffering with a serious kidney ailment, and there was some question about his ever playing again. Through medication and determination he did return, but he didn't have his old zip. Nevertheless, he scored 19.5 points a game and led the team in assists in 1974-75, and he personally sent exciting young guard Doug Collins in for about 100 back-door lay-ups with well-timed bounce passes from the perimeter.

The kidney situation had stabilized somewhat when he sustained a serious knee injury in December 1975. That was the final blow and he never played another regular-season game, although he attempted a comeback for 1976-77 and played in some preseason games before retiring for good.

The fans had not seen the last of him, however. Just six games into the 1977-78 season, the 76ers fired coach Gene Shue and the popular Cunningham was persuaded to take the job. Although he had never coached before, capable assistants and good players enabled him to take the 76ers to the playoffs. As he did as a player, Cunningham learned from his mistakes, and as the NBA entered the decade of the '80s, he was becoming one of its better coaches.

BOB DAVIES

Harrisburg Houdini

"He was what we called a 'fancy Dan,' and it is meant in the most complimentary way," said Eddie Gottlieb, who saw them all as an owner and coach. "He was one of the first truly great guards to play what we call present-day basketball. He was an excellent shooter, an exceptional passer and team player."

Bob Davies was—before Bob Cousy—a master of the behind-the-back dribble, imitated by countless youngsters and collegians after he introduced the technique during his college days at Seton Hall University in South Orange, New Jersey.

His spectacular performances at Seton Hall—where he was the magnetic force and stylist on a team that won 43 straight games in the early 1940s—served as a springboard to a pro career with the Rochester Royals that landed him in the Basketball Hall of Fame.

Early in life it was thought that Robert Edris Davies—born in Harrisburg, Pennsylvania, on January 5, 1920—would have a future in marbles. When he was 11 he won the Pennsylvania state marbles championship. "I was top-seeded in a national tourney," he once recalled, "but I wound up third."

It was one of the few occasions in which Bob Davies didn't land on top. Blond and good-looking, he was literally an All-American boy. He might have been a big league baseball player if he had chosen that route. In fact, the Boston Red Sox arranged a scholarship at Seton Hall for Davies, an outstanding second baseman. But basketball won out.

The 6-1, 175-pound Davies, on everybody's All-America team in college, enlisted in the Navy after graduation. He starred for the Great Lakes Naval Training Station before shipping out on a sub chaser for combat duty in World War II.

When he got out of the Navy, owner Les Harrison of the Rochester Royals signed Davies to his first pro contract. Thus began a dynamic 10-year stretch, all with the Royals, in the NBL, BAA and NBA.

In his rookie season, Davies, whose teammates included such notables as Red Holzman, Al Cervi, George Glamack, Otto Graham and Chuck Connors, figured prominently in Rochester's winning the NBL championship.

Holzman and Bobby Wanzer, who joined the team in 1947-48, were backcourt mates of Davies, and the trio was, in the view of Eddie Gottlieb and all who saw them, "hell on wheels."

Davies led the Royals to the NBA championship in 1951 when he climaxed the seven-game series against the New York Knicks by making two foul shots with the score 75-75 and 40 seconds remaining.

He won first-team All-NBA honors four times and

Bob Davies drives around Knicks' Harry Gallatin. His two foul shots in closing seconds enabled Rochester to beat New York for the 1951 title.

played in the first four All-Star Games. At Fort Wayne in 1953, Davies captivated onlookers by scoring eight quick points in the final period to win it for the West.

"He had no weakness," declared Bob Cousy, the Boston Celtic who was a rookie in 1950-51 when Davies was nearing the end of his career. "He had such imagination and control—the perfect playmaker."

The Harrisburg Houdini, as he was known because of his magical feats, had coached at his alma mater in 1946-47. When he retired from the pros at the end of the 1954-55 season, he became the coach at Gettysburg College for two years. Then he joined the Converse Rubber Co. to promote the sale of sneakers. Nobody would ever be able to fill Bob Davies' sneakers.

DAVE DeBUSSCHERE

Big D for Defense

At 6-6 and 220 pounds, he wasn't exceptionally graceful. His game was very basic. He set picks. He moved to open spots. He banged the boards at both ends. Most importantly, he worked diligently on defense.

The true professionals were well aware of his greatness, but the message was never transmitted effectively to the league's sportswriters and broadcasters. They wrote and said "DeBusschere this" and "DeBusschere that," but when it came time to sit down and vote for postseason honors, they reverted

243

to their basic instincts and went with flashier players, usually scorers.

As a result, Dave DeBusschere was named to an NBA postseason all-star team exactly once in his 12-year career—when he made the second team in 1968-69, the year he played for both the Detroit Pistons and the New York Knicks.

In one area, at least, he was recognized. The league's All-Defensive team, voted by the coaches, was instituted in 1968-69. DeBusschere made the first team in each of his six remaining seasons. In the last four he was the leading vote-getter. The coaches knew how valuable DeBusschere was.

Had he not been traded in the middle of his career, he would have been recognized even less, for it wasn't until he became a New York Knick that he began to acquire a reputation outside of Detroit, where he was born on October 16, 1940.

He was a high school star who attended the University of Detroit, where he was not only a standout basketball player, but a talented baseball pitcher who signed a contract with the Chicago White Sox and actually reached the major leagues. He was undecided between a career in baseball and one in basketball, and initially pursued both. He abandoned baseball when the Detroit Pistons asked him to become a player-coach at the age of 24, the youngest in NBA history.

He played and coached for two-and-a-half seasons before giving up coaching. "I was too young to handle men and I soon found out that playing and coaching can't be done," he later observed.

He appeared to be destined solely for local heroics until the fateful day of December 19, 1968. He was home hanging ornaments on the Christmas tree when he was informed he had been traded to the New York Knicks. New York had been looking for a bruising power forward. Detroit needed a center. The Pistons surrendered DeBusschere and received center Walt Bellamy and guard Howard Komives in return.

That deal was the making of the Knicks. De-

Busschere stepped in at forward. Willis Reed, meanwhile, moved from an unnatural spot in the corner to the pivot. DeBusschere fit perfectly into coach Red Holzman's offensive and defensive scheme of things. He and the cerebral Bill Bradley proved to be complementary forwards.

By the following season the unit was ready to accomplish big things. DeBusschere supplied perimeter shooting, inside strength, rebounding power and excellent defense, as well as an inbred instinct for doing the right thing at the right time. He had been playing the same way all those years in Detroit, except that nobody was paying any attention. Now with the benefit of the New York press, radio and TV, as well as the network coverage emanating from the nation's media capital, the message was getting across. Dave DeBusschere was the basketball world's newest overnight sensation.

Rivals marveled at DeBusschere's basketball ability, because he didn't fit everyone's physical conception of an NBA star. For one thing, he had what the players like to refer to as "beer legs," due to his overly heavy thighs. The fact is that he was a legendary beer drinker. He lost so much fluid during a game that he had a postgame ritual of downing up to a six-pack in the locker room in order to replenish the lost liquids. The beer didn't affect him at all.

Though he wasn't what anyone would call speedy, he was quick for the first few vital steps. And, of course, he was never out of position on defense or offense. He was a great success because he could think the game, as well as execute it.

Offensively, he was amazingly versatile. He was a streak-shooter with phenomenal range. Rivals were fascinated by how deep the Knicks would set picks for both DeBusschere and Bradley. Ironically, the New York forwards had more shooting range at the time than the starting guards.

Injuries eventually slowed him down, and a stomach muscle pull in the 1973-74 season finally ended his career. He retired to accept a job as general manager of the ABA New York Nets, but after one year he left to become the last commissioner of the ABA.

He retired with a healthy total of 14,053 points. But points, or any other statistic, will never tell the full story of his sagacity and competitiveness on the court. He may very well have been the least recognized NBA superstar of all time.

JULIUS ERVING

Dr. J

He's the most famous doctor since Kildare and the most celebrated player of the 1970s. He is, of course, the fabulous Julius Erving, alias Dr. J.

He is credited with almost single-handedly creating the 1976 merger between the ABA and NBA. As ABA commissioner Dave DeBusschere observed, "You've heard of guys carrying ball clubs? Well Dr. J. carries our league!" And after the merger, Erving provided the box office transfusion that the NBA sorely needed.

Even in an age of crowd-pleasing ballplayers, Julius Erving is in a class by himself. He looks like just another 6-6, 200-pound forward in his sweatshirt, but upon closer examination the difference between him and mere mortals is more apparent. He has a powerful build, with shoulders and arms bordering on the massive. His legs are sleek and powerful. And his hands—the key to his whole act—are positively enormous, as big as Kareem Abdul-Jabbar's.

Nobody was quite prepared for the emergence of Dr. J. or the way he operates when he left the University of Massachusetts in 1971 after his junior year to join the ABA Virginia Squires. Born February 22, 1950, in Roosevelt, New York, he was not widely recruited as a high school player and chose UMass, a school with no basketball tradition, because he liked assistant coach Ray Wilson and the campus atmosphere in bucolic Amherst.

Erving was impressive but not overpowering as a freshman. The school didn't let on that it had anything special in its midst, one reason probably being that few aside from coach Jack Leaman knew how good Erving was. Still, he played well enough to join the exclusive 20-20 club by averaging both 20 points and 20 rebounds a game for his college career.

When he signed a four-year, $500,000 contract in 1971 with the Squires, it was considered only a minor coup, just another building block for a mediocre team. Instead, it turned out to be the launching of a meteoric career. He immediately teamed with Charlie Scott to make Virginia a strong club, as he averaged 27.3 points a game and was the third leading rebounder in the league with 15.7 per game.

Julius Erving makes his NBA debut as a very wealthy Philadelphian.

Freed of the restrictions of the college game and at long last able to indulge in his specialty, dunking, Erving captivated ABA fans with his unique style of play, which could best be described at the time as an updating of vintage Connie Hawkins, with rebounding and defense thrown in to a far greater degree.

It was also readily apparent that Erving was a fast-break player. As a wing man on the fast break, Erving has no peer, for he can take off from as far out as the foul line and dunk the basketball. When the game pace is fast, Erving can be unstoppable, for he possesses just about every offensive weapon imaginable. One of his favorites is the "finger roll," a drive to the basket in which he scoops the ball underhanded toward the basket and ladles it into the net. It is not the hard, decisive motion of a slamdunk, and the softness of the shot gives him flexibility in its execution should a defender try to block it.

Unlike many other flamboyant players, Erving has never been accused of not being a team player. He always looks for teammates, and he has repeatedly finished among the leaders in assists. Nor can they say he won't mix it up under the boards, or take on the tough defensive assignment.

It was obviously no accident that championships began to follow him around, especially after he reached the New York Nets in 1973. The Nets paid more than $1 million to two clubs to acquire Erving, then gave him an eight-year package that amounted to nearly $3 million. Dr. J. reciprocated by leading them to the ABA title, averaging 27.4 points, 10.7 rebounds and 5.2 assists a game.

Trades significantly altered the Nets going into the 1975-76 season, and they weren't favored to win the title. Erving did everything he could, leading the league in scoring with 29.3 points a game, ranking third in steals and finishing seventh or better in rebounds, blocked shots and assists. The Nets went on to defeat the powerful Denver Nuggets in the finals as Dr. J. put on what might possibly be the finest sustained one-man show in professional playoff history in the seven-game series.

After that triumph, the Dr. J. legend reached its zenith, and when the merger was consummated in the summer of 1976, the Nets and their fans prepared for a successful entrance into the NBA. But a financial dispute arose between Erving and the club. The Nets solved it by peddling him to the Philadelphia 76ers for $3 million. The 76ers then signed him to a $3.5 million contract.

The price for Dr. J. was spectacular, even in this age of millionaire basketball players. The Knicks' resident philosopher, Bill Bradley, was asked if Erving or any athlete was worth more than $6 million. "Do I feel an athlete is worth more than a scientist or a doctor? My feeling is no. But you live in America and under our economic system Erving submitted his services to the marketplace. If you say that is wrong, you're suggesting a totally different system, one in which the state would set the salaries for all professions. I'm not for that. It would be giving up a freedom."

Although he was in the NBA at last, Erving showed only glimpses of the form that made him such an exciting player. One such glimpse came in the midseason All-Star Game in which Dr. J was named MVP. But although the 76ers won the Eastern Conference title and went to the final against Portland, Erving remained in his shell, aware he had to share the ball with George McGinnis, Lloyd Free and Doug Collins.

Before the start of the 1978-79 season, McGinnis and Free were traded by the talent-rich 76ers and fans waited breathlessly for the emergence of the real Dr. J. Knee injuries, however, limited him and skeptics implied he was never that good in the first place.

Erving underwent therapy for his knees during the summer of 1979 and, the following season, played without braces. The Doctor was back as he averaged 26.9 points and was the unquestioned leader of the 76ers. He led the team to the finals where it was beaten by the Lakers. But the skeptics had been convinced.

"I have talents," Erving says. "I have a job because of those talents. I do want to be the greatest."

WALT FRAZIER

Clyde's Game

When Walt Frazier was "on" and that often happened in the fourth quarter of a game, he was a devastating offensive force. Otherwise, he was simply one of the best defensive players in the league.

One problem in discussing Frazier, the man who was a key component of two New York Knick championship teams, is that the basketball player must be separated from "Clyde," the swinging man-about-town with his Rolls Royce and expensively decorated bachelor apartment on Manhattan's East Side.

He was capable of playing with extreme skill at either end of the floor—and there are statistics and honors enough to attest to that. But he was also capable of going into his "cool" act, standing around and watching all the action, as though he had slipped into his swinging alter ego.

Though he didn't enter the NBA as an unknown, neither did he come into the professional ranks as a widely heralded college player. The 6-4, 200-pounder was born March 29, 1945, in Atlanta and attended Southern Illinois University. He first attracted attention in the 1967 National Invitation Tournament where he earned MVP honors in leading the Salukis to the championship. Off the strength of this performance in Madison Square Garden, he was a popular first-round draft choice of the Knickerbockers.

The Knicks at that time were a stumbling, confused team with a losing attitude and a steady turnover in personnel. Nobody seemed to know who was in charge, and Frazier was just one of several guards sharing playing time in 1967-68 rather than a highly-prized prospect being developed as quickly as possible. He averaged only 9.0 points a game in that

Clever "Clyde" Frazier choreographed Knicks' attack in title years.

rookie season, but showed flashes of brilliance. He increased his scoring to 17.5 points a game in 1968-69, while nearly doubling his playing time. The Celtics, especially, found out how good Frazier could be when he scored 43 points against them in a playoff game. But he suffered an injury in that series and had to miss some games. Without him, the Knicks, who had lost only one game to Boston during the regular season, dropped a six-game series to the Celts.

In his third year, Frazier saw all the pieces fall into place both for him personally and for the team. Knick coach Red Holzman had his dream unit of Willis Reed at center, Bill Bradley and Dave DeBusschere at forward and Frazier and Dick Barnett in the backcourt. On offense, Frazier choreographed a beautiful attack. The ball danced when New York advanced into the forecourt. Frazier sensed who had the hot hand and he parceled out the passes accordingly. He maintained a neat balance between being a scorer and playmaker, and in that season of 1969-70, no one could have asked for a better lead guard than Walt Frazier.

On defense, the Knicks were even more devastating. They employed a clever, sagging, "helping out" defense, and Frazier was the key. He grew all the more proficient at leaving his man and doubling upon an unsuspecting opponent. He was an ideal "floater," with his superb instinct for playing the passing lanes. His quick hands resulted in countless steals and easy baskets for the Knicks.

Frazier's single greatest moment of glory came in the final game of the playoffs. New York had lost Reed early in the fifth game of the finals against Los Angeles, but had hung on to win. They were routed in the sixth game in Los Angeles, and appeared to be in bad shape in the deciding game if Reed couldn't play.

The Knick captain limped onto the floor and hit his first two shots, giving the team an incalcuable psychological lift. Then Frazier took over. He put the capper on a great year by scoring 36 points and handing out 19 assists as New York won its first NBA title ever by the surprisingly easy score of 113-99.

That was the season "Clyde" was born. Frazier

had shown a taste for the good life, as reflected in his wardrobe, car and apartment. He was nicknamed Clyde by teammate Reed after the title character in the then popular film ''Bonnie and Clyde.'' Clyde wore wide-brimmed hats, and Frazier had adopted the fashion. He carefully cultivated the ''Clyde'' image over the next several years, offering advice to anyone on good grooming as easily as he talked about his jump shot.

On the court, Frazier continued to enjoy success as the Knicks remained one of the best teams in basketball, winning a second championship in 1973 after losing to Los Angeles the season before. Moreover, Frazier was solidifying his reputation as a clutch shooter and tough defender, being named to the NBA's All-Defensive first team for seven years. And he roused himself for the 1975 All-Star Game in Phoenix when he scored 30 points and walked off with the MVP award.

But those who achieve great heights, also have the farthest to fall. Age and retirement had taken their toll of the Knicks' championship teams and Frazier found himself trying to shoulder an added burden. His incentive was questioned and he became injury-prone. Finally, at the start of the 1977-78 season, he was traded to the Cleveland Cavaliers.

He seemed stunned and disappointed. And his career nosedived after the trade. Finally, after playing in only three games in 1979-80, he retired. The fans had seen the last of Clyde.

He will be remembered, though, not for the end, but for those outstanding seasons when he blended talent and style so well. He was one of the game's great guards and one of its more irrepressible personalities. In his prime, Walt Frazier could always back his talk with action. As Willis Reed once said, ''It's Clyde's ball. He just lets us play with it once in a while.''

JOE FULKS

The Jumper

Throughout the 1950s it appeared to be an unassailable record. George Mikan had once come within two points of tying it, but he never again came close.

It stood until a space-age product named Elgin Baylor shattered it by a single point.

If modern fans have heard of Joe Fulks at all, it's because for 10 years he held the NBA one-game scoring record. On the night of February 10, 1949, the skinny 6-5 cornerman pumped in an unheard-of 63 points to lead the Philadelphia Warriors over the Indianapolis Jets at the Philadelphia Arena. At the time, 20 points a game made a high scorer.

Jumpin' Joe Fulks had his jump shot working to perfection that evening, canning 27 field goals to go with nine free throws. Indianapolis coach Burl Friddie, exasperated over his team's inability to stop the Warrior scoring machine, finally inserted a substitute named Leo Mogus, with these instructions: ''Go to the official scorer and report for Fulks. Maybe we'll get rid of him that way.''

Many years later, Fulks would say, ''I know now you can't teach a boy to shoot. It's something that comes naturally. You either have the knack or you don't.''

Fulks had the knack from his earliest days in Kutawa, Kentucky where he was born on October 26, 1921. But he was a relative unknown when he began playing pro ball in 1946-47. He had starred for Murray State Teachers College in Kentucky, then far from the mainstream of major college competition. Then he joined the Marines for a four-year hitch which included a lot of service ball.

''I played against a number of so-called All-Americans overseas,'' Joe said, ''and I wasn't very impressed with them. Their press clippings couldn't buy them a basket or a rebound. When I was approached about playing pro ball, I knew I could play.''

Eddie Gottlieb, who ran the Philadelphia franchise, heard about Fulks from Petey Rosenberg, one of Gottlieb's players on the old Sphas. Rosenberg had seen Fulks in basketball action at Pearl Harbor and recommended him so enthusiastically that Gottlieb signed up the Kentuckian.

Fulks scored 25 points in the Warriors' first game, a victory over Pittsburgh. Within a week Ned Irish, president of the New York Knickerbockers, told Gottlieb, ''You've got the best player in the country.''

Fulks became the Basketball Association of America's first scoring champion and his team won the title. Fulks' 23.2 points a game gave him a nearly seven-point edge over runner-up Bob Feerick of

Philadelphia's Joe Fulks was a pioneer of the jump shot.

Washington. In one game against Toronto, Jumpin' Joe scored 41 points, high for the BAA season.

His stock in trade was the jump shot, which some called the ''ear shot'' because Joe seemed to toss it off his ear. He came back to score 22.1 points a game the following season before peaking with a 26.0 in 1948-49. But George Mikan had come along to revolutionize the game and in that same season the Minneapolis giant averaged 28.3 to win the scoring title.

Fulks' entire eight-year career was spent with Philadelphia. This member of the Hall of Fame doesn't show up on many career record charts because he was already 26 when he began in the pros. But as the BAA's (NBA) first big scorer, as a pioneer of the jump shot and as the author of that unforgettable 63-

point game, he qualifies as a basketball immortal.

He died in his home state in a shooting incident in 1976.

GEORGE GERVIN

The Iceman Cometh

When the Virginia Squires of the old American Basketball Association found him, George Gervin was playing for a semipro team in Pontiac, Michigan, hardly a showcase for a future star. His collegiate career was in ruins, his dream of playing professionally apparently reduced to a fleeting thought now and then. But the Squires, like most ABA teams, had to follow every lead in search of talent and scout John Kerr often traveled to the most unlikely places. When he saw Gervin, he wasted no time in offering him a contract.

Not for big money—because a semipro player doesn't have the opportunity to dictate terms. He doesn't get to bask in the glare of hot television lights as he answers question during a press conference following his ceremonial signing. Gervin signed a modest contract and took a seat on the bench where he watched Julius Erving perform for the Squires.

But also like most ABA teams, the Squires had financial problems. Erving was traded and in 1973-74 the Iceman came into his own. Nicknamed by teammate Fatty Taylor, Gervin averaged 25 points and played with the polish and poise that belied his age. Gervin was only 20 and Taylor was impressed with how unflappable he was on the court. "I don't know if I'm cool or not," Gervin said then, "but that's what others have taken it to mean."

Gervin did not try to imitate Erving, but sitting and watching Dr. J proved to be a valuable lesson. It helped on the court, where Gervin became the new darling of the few but devoted Squires' fans, and it helped get him through the shock of being traded the next season. The Squires were in desperate need of money and Gervin was their most valuable commodity. He was sent to San Antonio.

"I couldn't figure out the trade because I was playing so well," he said. "I guess I really didn't understand the financial problems of the team. If they could trade the Doctor, they could trade anyone."

If only the Squires could have held on to players like Gervin a while longer. In 1976, when the ABA consolidated with the NBA, San Antonio was one of the four teams admitted into the established league. The Spurs were attractive not only because of the sizeable crowds they drew, but because Gervin had become one of the best young players in either league, a prolific scorer with a variety of shots from all angles and distances.

And perhaps the best move former San Antonio coach Doug Moe made was when he switched the lanky Gervin from forward to guard. At 6-7 and 185 pounds, Gervin was too tall and too quick for most backcourt players to contain. The inside game that developed from years of playing forward enabled him

George Gervin had a three-year reign as NBA scoring champ.

to take smaller players down low. He was virtually unstoppable.

"I think he's the best scorer I've ever seen," Moe said. "Ice has such a tremendous variety of shots. Inside, outside, it doesn't matter. Nobody can score with him."

Gervin became only the fourth player in the NBA to win three or more consecutive scoring titles. It began in 1977-78 when he averaged 27.2. He won the title the following year with a 29.6 average and in 1979-80 he scored at a 33.1 point clip. Only Wilt Chamberlain, George Mikan, Neil Johnston and Bob McAdoo had dominated the pro game as Gervin had and all were centers, picking up several points a game from close range.

Refining these skills was a lonely endeavor for Gervin. As a youth in Detroit, where he was born on April 27, 1952, he was befriended by a high school janitor who allowed George to use the gym until midnight. First, Gervin had to earn the court time by sweeping the floor. Then he would practice, often shooting between 500 and 1,000 times a night. "It gave me solitude," he said. "That constant practice has to be the key to my success. I was alone in the gym for hours. There was nothing but me and my imagination. There's no telling what kind of shots I used to try in there."

Those hours spent in the gym also served Gervin another way. He was one of six children living in a Detroit ghetto and supported by his mother. He often thought of how much trouble he might have encountered if it were not for basketball. "It was my outlet," Gervin noted. "That's where my heart was. A lot of people didn't have that and they got into drugs and into trouble. I'm a lucky guy. I thank God every day for it."

Gervin did have a problem or two, though. He was recruited and went to Long Beach State in California, where the change in lifestyle made him homesick. He transferred to Eastern Michigan and was averaging 29.5 points in his sophomore year (1971-72) when in a rare outburst he punched an opposing player in a playoff game. He was permanently suspended by Eastern Michigan and an invitation to try out for the 1972 Olympic team was withdrawn. Gervin was an outcast. But basketball remained his outlet and he joined the semipro team in Pontiac.

Rarely has a modern-day NBA superstar emerged from such obscure beginnings. Gervin has proven, however, that his accomplishments were no fluke. "I'm just glad that it's working, that I'm able to show my skills now, to show what I've spent the majority of my life doing."

HAL GREER
Middle-Range Gunner

He was known for consistency, longevity and uncanny ability for popping in jump shots from 12 to 20 feet. For 15 years, from the 1960s into the 1970s, there was no better middle distance shooter than Hal Greer. He had so much confidence in his jump shot that he even used it in free throw situations.

Greer spent his entire career with one organization, and ranks along with Dolph Schayes as one of the two keystones of the Syracuse National-Philadelphia 76ers franchise. When he retired at the end of the 1972-73 season, Greer held the all-time NBA record for games played, with 1,122, a figure since eclipsed, but still eloquent testimony to his skills and durability. His consistency was attested to by the fact that he played in 70 games every season save his rookie and final years. Along the way, he averaged nearly 20 points a game, earned MVP honors in the All-Star Game, and was a vital figure—with a cast of Wilt Chamberlain, Luke Jackson, Chet Walker, Larry Costello and Billy Cunningham—on Philadelphia's 1967 championship team that ended Boston's long string of titles.

Born in Huntington, West Virginia, June 26, 1936, Greer was one of nine children. His father, William Garfield Greer, was a diesel engineer on the Chesapeake & Ohio Railway. Under the influence of his older brother Jim, Hal took to basketball and became a star, leading Douglas High to the Negro state championship.

One of the colleges interested in him was the hometown state school, Marshall. The coach, Cam Henderson, "recruited" Hal's stepmother and she was a strong influence in his decision to attend Marshall. This was no easy choice, for it made Greer a pioneer, the first black to play for a major college team in West Virginia.

After an outstanding college career, where he was among the top scorers in the country, the 6-2, 170-

Determined Hal Greer drives around John Havlicek.

pound Greer was drafted in the second round in 1958 by Syracuse. Club officials wondered if he could make the adjustment to the professional ranks after spending a lot of time in the forecourt at Marshall. Since he was so slight, there was no way he could play up front in the NBA.

Then, too, Greer had played only zone defense while in college, but this did not prove to be a handicap. With his speed and athletic ability, he adjusted to the pro man-to-man very quickly. Defense was never a problem. Very little was, in fact, as Greer stepped into a starting role by the second half of his rookie season. He and Larry Costello made up the league's fastest backcourt, and right there in his first season Greer found himself involved in an epic playoff series between the Nats and the Celtics—the 1958-59 Eastern finals, won by Boston in seven games.

By his fourth season, Greer was in the 20-points-a-game category, and by 1962-63 he was considered

to be one of the league's top guards. After that season, he was named to the second-team All-NBA squad, the first of seven consecutive second-team nominations he would receive. No other player in NBA history received so many second-team selections without ever being named to the first squad. Not that it's any disgrace to finish behind Oscar Robertson and Jerry West, who were his chief rivals for the first-team spot.

Greer also appeared in 10 All-Star Games, at least one of which, in 1968, will always be remembered. It was the last one in the old Madison Square Garden. The East prevailed, 144-124, as Greer carted home the MVP award. In just 17 minutes of play, he scored 21 points, grabbed three rebounds and made three assists. He shot 8-for-8 from the floor.

When the 76ers rolled to the league title in 1966-67, Greer was at the top of his game, scoring 22.1 points a game, and was even more productive the following season—when the 76ers again won more than 60 games—averaging 24.1 points and 4.5 assists a game.

Though always an outstanding player, Greer was most dangerous in a fast-breaking game, because then he had ample opportunity to launch his medium-range jumpers. At his peak, he practically wore out the vocal cords of Philadelphia public address announcer Dave Zinkoff, who yelled ''Greeeeeeeeeeeeer!'' whenever Hal made a basket.

Greer closed out his distinguished career in 1973 as one of only eight men in league annals to have scored 20,000 points. He also had the record for games played (1,122), and to show he was in the thick of the action, he had committed more fouls, 3,855, than any player before him. It's little wonder that his uniform number (15) has been retired and now hangs in the Spectrum where he gave thousands of fans so many great moments.

JOHN HAVLICEK

Hondo

There was no way anyone could have forecast such a brilliant career for this mild-mannered son of a Czechoslovakian immigrant when he broke into the NBA in 1962. Though an All-American, John Havlicek was considered only the number two man on his college team, Ohio State. The big star on those fabulous 1960-62 Buckeye teams was center Jerry Lucas, who had been a national figure since high school. Havlicek was noted for his industry on defense and his constant movement on offense, but in the eyes of many he was a questionable commodity as a pro. One Big Ten rival even went so far as to call him a ''butcher'' and suggested that if he could make the NBA, things were pretty bad in the league.

The 6-5, 205-pound Havlicek, who was born on April 8, 1940, in Martins Ferry, Ohio, admits that he might not have made it had he not been drafted by the right team. ''I am not, and never have been, a one-on-one player,'' he points out. ''The Celtics were the perfect team for me. The only other teams I might have been comfortable with would have been Syracuse, which ran a lot, and possibly Los Angeles.''

The Celtics had taken him as the last choice in the first round. Celtic maestro Red Auerbach debated between Havlicek and Bradley's Chet Walker, who, while an outstanding player, proved to be no Havlicek. First, however, the Celtics had to await the results of Havlicek's summer trial with the Cleveland Browns in the National Football League. Despite the fact that Havlicek had not played football since high school (where he was an all-state quarterback), the Browns made him their seventh-round draft pick. He tried out for the team as a wide receiver, but was beaten out by eventual all-pro Gary Collins.

He was an instant smash with the Celtics, however, averaging 14 points a game as a rookie simply by running on the fast break and moving without the ball. ''I made a living off Bob Cousy,'' Havlicek recalls. He played mostly forward that rookie season, primarily because he was not yet an accomplished ball-handler.

He went home in the summer of 1963 to work on two phases of his game, ball-handling and outside shooting. When he came back in the fall, he was ready. He demonstrated to Auerbach that he had sufficient ball-handling skills to be a guard, and was, therefore, a logical heir to Frank Ramsey as the all-important Celtics' sixth man. For the next six seasons he was renowned as the best non-starter in the game, a man who could be relied upon to come into the game at either guard or forward and remain in there until the job was done. Along the way he usually accumulated more playing time than anyone on the team except Bill Russell, and he developed a reputation for being a clutch player who would respond with a 35- or 40-point effort in a ''must win'' ball game.

By the 1969-70 season Havlicek, or ''Hondo,'' as he became known, was firmly fixed in the public eye as a vastly skilled player, a winning player and a true Celtic. But it wasn't until then that people realized his total value. For that was the Celtics' first season without Russell. Tom Heinsohn was the new coach, and he determined that he could not afford the luxury of having Havlicek in reserve. John became a 48-

John Havlicek became one of the best all-around performers in NBA history.

minute man, and he led the team in scoring, assists and even, at 6-5, rebounding.

This marked the launching of a six-year stretch during which Havlicek cemented his reputation as perhaps the best all-around player ever in the NBA. He strung together back-to-back seasons in 1970-71 and 1971-72 in which he played 45 minutes a game and scored more points than ever before, averaging 28.9 and 27.5, respectively. In addition, he performed all those tasks which win games but don't show up in the statistics. He was proficient at making the right pass, drawing the charging foul, settling the team down in tense situations, grabbing the clutch rebound and making the key basket.

Havlicek gradually improved his passing to the point where he qualified as one of the game's legitimate playmakers, as opposed to being one who was simply good at hitting the open man. Most of all, he represented movement, a trait which accounted for the fact that only Wilt Chamberlain ever took more shots. Though not what could be called a ''pure'' shooter, he was a great scorer, with rare instinct.

His trump card was his unparalleled ability to play two positions. There have been other swing men, but never in the NBA had a man played at the first-team all-star level at two different positions in the manner of John Havlicek.

SAM JONES

Out of Nowhere

Without a doubt, the most unlikely of all the Celtic greats was a mild-mannered small-college star from North Carolina.

Red Auerbach never made a more startling first-round draft pick than he did in 1957 when he chose Sam Jones, a 6-4 guard from unknown North Carolina College.

In those low-budget days of the NBA, few teams had extensive scouting networks, assistant coaches were unheard of, and nobody had scouts, as such, on the payroll. It was easy enough to keep track of the All-Americans, and to see the heralded players in postseason tournaments.

But Auerbach had all the angles covered. Nobody in the pros had more contacts around the country.

Clutch shooting and speed marked Sam Jones, looking for the shot here as Bill Russell picks off the Royals' Odie Smith.

Red knew he could never keep track of all the prospects on his own, so he had a loose network of "scouts," friends who gave him tips on players they had seen.

One of those he trusted was Horace "Bones" McKinney, who had played for Auerbach on the old BAA Washington Capitals. Bones was coaching at Wake Forest, and his attention was drawn to the star of North Carolina College, a school that played mostly other Negro colleges. Bones alerted Auerbach to his potential. And when it was Red's turn to draft in 1957, he selected Sam Jones, a Carolina native born on June 24, 1933.

Red had a definite spot for Sam in the 1957-58 season—right next to him on the bench. This has been the traditional Celtic way of doing things. Jones saw about as little playing time his first season as an average Celtic rookie, averaging about 10 minutes and 4.6 points a game.

At first Sam hardly had an identity of his own. He and K.C. Jones were known strictly as "the Jones boys," hard-working kids who often entered the game in tandem to press and upgrade the tempo. They played behind aging stars Bob Cousy and Bill Sharman, and they simply had to wait their turn.

Sam's came first, Sharman retired following the 1960-61 season, and Sam was well-schooled by this time as he looked ahead to his fourth pro season. He had scored 15 points a game the previous season coming off the bench, and he increased that to 18.4 as a starter.

It was soon evident that Sam was the best clutch shooter on the squad, and the team began to look to him more and more in tight situations. His patented bank shot defeated Philadelphia, 109-107, in the seventh game of a tough playoff series in 1962. That was only the first of many heroic shots Sam Jones would make.

Speed was the key to Sam's game. At 6-4 he was faster than most opponents, large or small, and the combination of size and speed made him difficult to guard. He was an excellent middle distance shooter who could also explode to the basket with a variety of acrobatic drives if the defender played too close. Sam became noted for his ability to use the backboard. An accomplished bank shooter, he even used the backboard on the two-handed set shots which he occasionally employed.

Defensively, he knew very little when he broke in with the Celtics, but his superior physical equipment and devotion to duty helped him become a sound defensive guard.

It wasn't until the 1964-65 season that Sam joined the league's elite. After averaging 18.4 and 19.4 points the two previous seasons, Sam exploded for 25.9 points a game, setting a club record (since broken). That was the first of four straight 20-point seasons for Sam.

At age 36, in the 1968-69 season, Jones saw his scoring slip to 16.3 points a game as the Celtics finished fourth in the division race. In championship fashion, though, Boston upset Philadelphia and New York to earn the right to meet Los Angeles for the championship.

Then Sam had as much to do as anyone with the Celtics gaining their 11th crown in 13 years, because he made one of the most memorable shots in playoff history. It came when Los Angeles was leading in games, 2-1, and held a one-point lead in the waning seconds of the pivotal fourth game of the finals. Sam came off a pick, slipped and, off-balance, threw in a jump shot which evened the series. Had the Lakers won, they would have been ahead in games, 3-1, heading back home, and they might very well have won the series.

When he retired after that championship season, the Celtics gave Sam the highest tribute—they retired his number, 24.

SLATER MARTIN

Glue on Guard

He stood 5-10—maybe. But it never occurred to Slater Martin that his size would keep him from achieving success on the basketball court. "No famous coach or talent scout discovered any hidden genius in me when I was a boy," he once explained. "The person who was always sure I could be a great basketball player was my grandmother. She felt that if I worked hard enough at it, there was no good reason why I shouldn't be."

The little grandson, born on October 22, 1925, in El Mina, Texas, played at Jefferson Davis High School in Houston, where he and neighbor Jamie Owens led the school to a pair of Texas state titles in 1942 and 1943. Though he was to make his mark as a professional via defense and playmaking, he was quite a scorer at the University of Texas. He left there as the school's all-time scorer, and he set the Southwest Conference scoring record of 49 points in a single game. "I was a gunner in college," he admitted.

By this time he was used to the jokes about his size, so the prospect of playing professional ball against the biggest competition of all didn't faze him. "I played without worrying about how big I wasn't," he said.

Martin's professional role was dictated immediately by the nature of the team which drafted him. The Minneapolis Lakers were famous for their powerful frontcourt of 6-10 George Mikan, 6-7 Vern Mikkelsen and 6-3 Jim Pollard. It was the prototype of the modern professional frontcourt, with an intimidating center in Mikan, a legitimate power forward in Mikkelsen and a sleek, clever "small" forward in Pollard. The last thing the Lakers needed was a 5-10 gunner throwing them up from 20 feet and beyond.

What the Lakers did need was a guard who could bring the ball upcourt, make the good pass and, most importantly, play tough defense against some of the league's top guards, men such as Max Zaslofsky, Frankie Brian, Bob Davies, Carl Braun and Bobby Wanzer.

And so Martin, always adaptable, began to concentrate his efforts on defense and playmaking. The most points he would ever average as a pro would be 13, which he did twice in Minneapolis. But he remained a dangerous scoring threat whenever the defense concentrated too much of its attention on the Laker big men.

He established himself as a standout defensive guard as a rookie, but his reputation really took hold the following season when a flashy rookie named Bob Cousy entered the league. It was Bob Cousy,

Slater Martin shows offensive skills as he sidesteps the Knicks' Ernie Vandeweghe.

more than anyone else, who helped foster the idea that Martin was a terrific force, because Bob Cousy was the unpaid president of the Slater Martin Fan Club. Their duels highlighted NBA competition for the next decade. Alone among the league's top players, Slater "Dugie" Martin was capable of driving The Cooz to distraction.

"I always preferred to give away height, rather than speed," Cousy explained. "If an opponent had more speed than I did, he was taking away one of my strengths. In Martin's case, he had the speed, but, far more importantly, he had the ability to sustain his concentration as long as he had to. The only two men I ever played against who were capable of sustaining their concentration on defense for 48 minutes were Martin and Larry Costello.

"Often, I found that I could score more easily in the second half, when my opponent was tired of fighting through picks, or was just getting bored. That

never happened with Martin. He was the toughest man I ever played against."

After seven seasons in Minneapolis, Martin made a brief stop in New York before finding another team in desperate need of the services he could provide. That club was the St. Louis Hawks. After obtaining Martin from the Knicks during the 1956-57 season, the Hawks turned themselves around and made it to the championship finals, where they lost to Boston in the second overtime of the seventh game. The next season, Martin and the Hawks went all the way, winning the championship in six games over the Celtics.

One night in a game against Fort Wayne, Martin was slammed to the floor by 6-11 Chuck Share while driving to the basket. He appeared to be seriously hurt, and his teammates hovered over him, anxiously. Finally, he slowly opened an eye and inquired, "Did it go in?" That was Slater Martin.

GEORGE MIKAN

Giant in His Time

He was outsized in an era when excessive size was thought to be more a detriment to success on the basketball floor than an asset. He was myopic. And he didn't appear to have much of an athletic temperament. Yet a competitive spirit and a capacity for hard work enabled him to become the first truly outstanding big man in professional basketball history.

George Mikan, who would be voted ''The Greatest Basketball Player of the First Half Century,'' put professional basketball on the map. Oh, they'll say in New York that the sport didn't move the national spirit until the Knicks became a superior team. And in Boston, of course, they will point out that it was the Celtics who became the nation's favorite basketball team through their team play and countless appearances on television in the fifties and sixties.

But long before the Knicks got straightened out, and shortly before Bill Russell made the Celtics an item, the Minneapolis Lakers were all that kept the NBA (and its two immediate ancestors, the BAA and the NBL) from sharing half a column in the papers with local bowling news.

As five-time champions of the professional basketball world, the Lakers of the late forties and early fifties were lumped with the Yankees when one thought of dynasties in sport.

Could Mikan play at the same level today? By current standards he would be considered slow and awkward. His shooting range was limited. Despite that, he was resourceful enough to make the most of what he did have, and that included being a tough competitor.

The Mikan story began on a small farm outside of Joliet, Illinois. Born on June 18, 1924, he originally enrolled in the Quigley Preparatory Seminary in Chicago, but transferred to Joliet Catholic High School. He was tall (6-4 at age 13), and uncoordinated. His high school career was marred by a broken leg which laid him up for a protracted period, and he is said to have grown approximately six inches while in traction. He enrolled at DePaul University on his own.

There a young coach named Ray Meyer proceeded to ''make'' George Mikan. Meyer put the gangling youngster through special drills to improve his quick-

Big George Mikan, battling Knicks underneath, was dominant force in NBA's early years.

ness and coordination. He skipped rope. He shadow-boxed. He learned modern dance and ballet from a coed Meyer hired for the purpose.

On the basketball side, he worked out with smaller men. He diligently practiced his shooting, taking 200 right-hand hooks and 200 left-hand hooks a day. From a 6-9 freshman forward with no redeeming athletic value ("We just wanted him to go into a corner and get lost," Meyer said) he turned into an aggressive 6-10, 250-pound center who led DePaul to the NIT title.

He turned professional with the Chicago team of the National Basketball League, and he quickly became the fulcrum of both the team and the league. When the league merged with the Basketball Association of America in 1949, Mikan, now with Minneapolis, was suddenly the most influential basketball player in the world.

Mikan at his peak was unstoppable. The Lakers eschewed the fast break, preferring, instead, to bring the ball upcourt deliberately and wait for Mikan to get into position. Ol' number 99 would set up low, just outside the then six-foot foul lanes, and call for the ball. Once he got it, he would wheel in, clearing out a path with his free hand and take his hook or some other inside shot. There were few players who could handle his bulk inside.

He was, of course, a skillful rebounder and a decent enough passer. Moreover, he was a fine free throw shooter, so fouling him deliberately wasn't the answer, either. In an era when hardly anybody even thought of averaging 20 points a game for a season, Mikan flirted with the 30-point mark. In 1948-49, when only three men averaged 20, Mikan averaged 28.3. The next year two men averaged 20, with Mikan scoring 27.4. The following year three men averaged 20, and Mikan popped in 28.4. He once scored 61 points in a game.

Because he was so vital to the success of his team, he was subjected to a succession of physical beatings. He played with the requisite number of broken bones and bruises, but he never complained, and he never retaliated with dirty play, either.

By the 1954-55 season, he recognized that he was through. An abortive comeback a year later did little for his reputation, except establish that he still was as competitive as ever. But he really had nothing to prove. Pioneers never do.

There is a great danger that moderns will downgrade his statistics and his contribution to the sport.

But his legacy remains. The fact remains that only one player was ever accorded the following treatment by the old Madison Square Garden, then basketball's mecca. On a night the Knicks were hosting the Lakers, the marquee said:

> **TONIGHT**
> **GEORGE MIKAN**
> **VS.**
> **KNICKS**

EARL MONROE

The Magic Show

Helplessness was being the lone defensive man back on a 2-on-1 fast break when Earl Monroe was the man with the ball.

No matter what the defensive man did, Monroe would usually circumvent it with his "now-you-see-it-now-you-don't" legerdemain before going into his spinning, twisting magic act which results in a simple lay-up, a short jumper or a funny little shot with both feet on the floor and the defender faked into the first row of seats.

Vernon Earl Monroe had been working his magic act ever since bursting into basketball prominence at Winston-Salem College, where he averaged 41.5 points a game and scored an NCAA record 1,329 points in his senior year of 1966-67.

Strangely enough, Monroe, who was born November 21, 1944, in Philadelphia, wasn't all that interested in basketball as a youngster. Soccer was his first love, but since all his friends preferred basketball, the 6-3 Monroe would usually join in at center in pickup games after soccer practice. He showed an aptitude for the game, but instead of heading for college he worked as a shipping clerk for a year before finishing his high school requirements and attending Winston-Salem.

Under the tutelage of Clarence Gaines, Monroe gained a national reputation even though not many people had actually seen him play. The gyms in his conference weren't very big and his school didn't do much traveling. His fame was spread mostly by pro scouts and the few nationally-oriented writers who were able to cover Winston-Salem on special assignment. So the basketball world at large knew little of Monroe when he entered the NBA as the first draft choice of the Baltimore Bullets in 1967.

Any doubts that Monroe's collegiate scoring feats were attributable to "small-college" opposition were soon erased as he showed his shooting touch in the pros. He wound up averaging 24.3 points a game, a high figure for a rookie guard. On February 13, 1968, he poured in 20 field goals and 16 free throws for a club record 56 points against Los Angeles. The Bullets, then in Baltimore, won 16 more games than they had the previous season and Monroe was named Rookie of the Year and along the way became familiarly known as "The Pearl." Or "Earl the Pearl."

But it wasn't simply Monroe's scoring ability that won him admiration and respect. It was how he did it. He played with an unmatched flair. Monroe incorporated spinning movements into many situations, thereby expanding his offensive options and creating confusion among his opponents.

He shot with a soft touch that belied the furious activity he employed to get free for the shot. Arthritic knees and bone spurs on his left foot limited his jumping ability, forcing Monroe to develop a repertoire of moves unmatched by anyone in the league. Even more spectacular, however, were his passes, whether behind the back, around the shoulder or be-

tween the legs. A defender confronted by Monroe couldn't tell if he was going to shoot one of his 1,001 shots or make one of his 1,002 types of passes.

When the Bullets picked up muscular center Westley Unseld in Monroe's second season, the team jelled and went on to win the Eastern Conference regular-season title, with Earl increasing his scoring average to 25.8 points a game and earning All-NBA first-team honors. The Bullets returned to the playoffs each season, with Monroe getting his more than 20 points a game. In 1971 they made it all the way to the championship finals before bowing to the Milwaukee Bucks. Early the next season, Monroe joined the New York Knicks, but saw only limited action as he underwent the first of two bone spur operations. He returned in 1972-73 not as The Pearl of old, but as an integral part of the Knicks' team offense concept, averaging just 15.5 points and helping New York to its second NBA championship.

He missed 40 games the following season for more surgery, but by 1975-76 he was back in peak form, resurrecting his old Magic Show. Night after night Monroe went out and gave 100 percent effort against overwhelming odds and personal pain. He has had his critics, but no one ever accused him of not hustling.

Monroe had two more productive seasons before

Earl Monroe mystified defenders with his many moves.

a combination of age and the Knicks' youth movement forced him to spend more time on the bench. Like an old soldier, Earl eventually faded away. Prior to the start of the 1979-80 season, he held out for a better contract and the Knicks went on without him. Soon, however, they realized that a young team needs the guiding hand of experience and Monroe was signed to play in the final 51 games.

He averaged 7.4 points and once again found himself unsigned when 1980-81 rolled around. This time there were no takers. Monroe had played his last game and never had the opportunity to formally announce his retirement. He disappeared like Magic.

BOB PETTIT

In Record Numbers

As a teen-ager Robert E. Lee Pettit couldn't make the high school basketball team until his junior year. And though he was an All-American in college, he played for a school with no basketball tradition and his potential as a pro was suspect. His size, with only a little more than 200 pounds stretched over his 6-9 frame, and limited jumping ability mitigated against a long stay in the NBA.

Yet he recorded these accomplishments:

In the first 10 of his 11 years in pro basketball, Pettit placed no lower than fifth in the league as either a rebounder or scorer. It wasn't until his final season, when injury kept him out of 30 games, that he fell out of the top five in scoring, and then it was only down to seventh. Twice he led the league in scoring, and in 1955-56 he was tops in scoring and rebounding. He was the league's Most Valuable Player twice, and in six other seasons he placed no lower than fourth in the voting. He was chosen to the all-league first team for 10 consecutive seasons before winding up on the second unit in his last year. He was the first man to score 20,000 points, finishing with 20,880, and grabbed 12,849 rebounds, which meant that in his 792 NBA games he averaged 26.4 points and 16.1 rebounds.

The statistics give an indication, but don't begin to tell how he did it. It all began in Baton Rouge, Louisiana, where Bob was born on December 12, 1932. After being cut from the high school team in his sophomore year, the uncoordinated youngster went into his backyard and shot thousands of times at a basket hanging over the family garage. His only playing experience was in a three-team church league. Bob's family was well-to-do, but he still possessed the self discipline and desire to succeed, and the will to put in the countless hours needed to achieve his goal.

He made his high school team as a gangly junior, and at 6-4 he was the tallest player on the team. He played well enough in his senior year to draw attention from a few colleges, but he had little problem in choosing. He had always wanted to attend Louisiana State in his hometown. The backyard shooting practice paid off, for as a 6-7 collegian, he had a repertoire of hook shots, jump shots and inside moves which enabled him to score 30 points a game his senior year when he was selected an All-American.

The Milwaukee Hawks made him their first draft choice in 1954, but with 6-11, 270-pound Chuck Share in the pivot, Pettit was going to have to learn how to play forward. Again, it took long hours of practice, supplemented by a weight-training program prescribed by Alvin Roy, trainer of the 1952 U.S. Olympic team. The result: Pettit averaged 20.4 points and 13.8 rebounds in winning Rookie-of-the-Year honors and a berth on the All-NBA first team for the 1954-55 season.

The team moved to St. Louis the following year, and Pettit captivated a new set of fans by leading the league in both scoring, with 25.7 points a game, and rebounding, 16.2 average. He was chosen the league MVP and was hailed as the best forward in the league.

Pettit was always the consummate professional. "He doesn't make a lot of noise," Ed Macauley, one of Bob's coaches, once said. "He always knows exactly what he wants to do and how to go about doing it. That goes for ballplaying, cardplaying or anything else. This is a guy who knows his business. You don't have to tell him anything."

Pettit compensated for limited physical abilities by mastering position play, timing and keeping his mind on the game at all times. But he was also physically tough. Twice he continued to play with broken bones that required casts on his shooting hand. By the end of his playing days, he had endured 125 stitches in his face, four broken bones in his back, a torn-up knee and a chronic dispeptic stomach. None of this

Fouling was one of the few sure ways to stop high-scoring Bob Pettit.

kept him from helping the Hawks or from getting into the All-Star Game.

He thrived on competition, averaging 25.5 points per game in 88 playoff contests, and led the Hawks to many memorable championship encounters with the Boston Celtics. In 1958, he brought the team its only NBA championship by scoring 50 points, including 19 of the Hawks' last 21, in the sixth and deciding game.

The All-Star Game was his special domain. He won three MVP awards and shared a fourth with Elgin Baylor. In 1956 he had 20 points and 24 rebounds; in 1958 it was 28 points and 26 rebounds with a cast on his hand, and in 1962 his totals were 25 points and 27 rebounds in just 37 minutes of play.

When he retired in 1965 to become a full-time banker, he was the league's leading scorer. He left

for all time an example of how a player could combine toughness with finesse, and be the perfect southern gentleman in a sport that doesn't breed etiquette.

WILLIS REED

Pride of the Knicks

What made young Willis Reed spend hours in his backyard skipping rope?

What made second-round draft choice Willis Reed work hard enough to earn a spot in the 1965 All-Star Game and Rookie-of-the-Year honors?

What made New York Knick captain Willis Reed hobble on to the court May 8, 1970, to confront Wilt

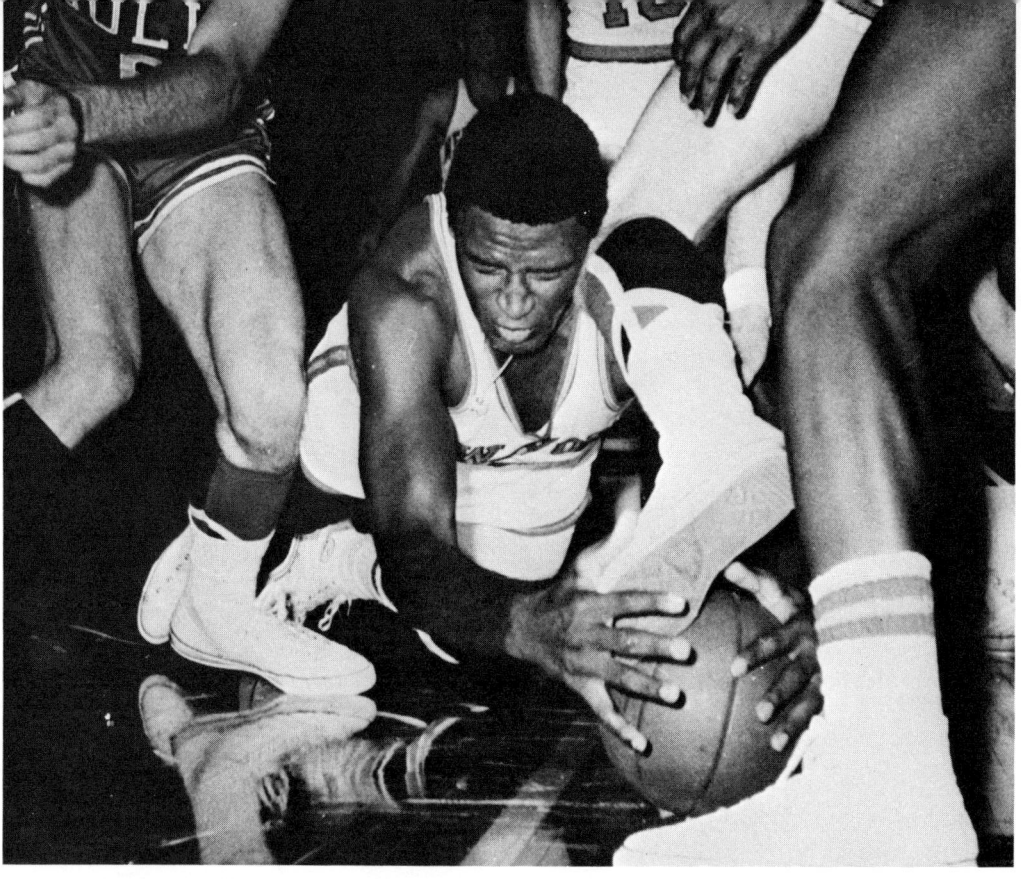

Pain was no stranger to the Knicks' gallant captain, Willis Reed.

Chamberlain, the most awesome force basketball has ever seen?

Pride. Pride. Pride.

Born on June 25, 1942, in Hico, Louisiana, Reed grew up in nearby Bernice where he attended segregated West Side High. Even though he was 6-5 and enthusiastic, he was clumsy and coach Lendon Stone told him he would have to spend hours jumping rope if he expected enough coordination to play basketball. Work Reed did, and he developed to the point where two colleges were interested in him.

Willis chose Grambling over Southern University, and proceeded to lead the Tigers to a 110-17 record in the next four years, as well as three Southwest Athletic Conference titles, an NAIA championship and, for himself, three Little All-American selections while scoring 2,335 points.

That might sound impressive, but it didn't earn Reed a spot on the 1964 U.S. Olympic team which went to Tokyo. And in the NBA draft, eight players were selected before he was. This double affront spurred Reed to outperform everyone else. He became the Knicks' starting center, was the lone New York representative in the All-Star Game, was the fifth-best rebounder in the league with 14.7 per game, led the Knicks in scoring with 19.5 points a game and earned that Rookie-of-the-Year designation over those eight men chosen ahead of him in the draft.

In Reed's second season, he was asked to play forward after New York acquired Walt Bellamy. Reed, who had been a center all his life, took a while to adjust and his scoring fell off four points a game and his rebound total dipped below 900. But the following season, he regained his form and for two years earned both a berth in the All-Star Game and a spot on the All-NBA second team while miscast as a forward.

Filling out to his full height of just under 6-10 and bulk of 240 pounds, Reed seemed destined to be simply just another very fine power forward. Then on December 19, 1968, came the trade which brought Dave DeBusschere to the Knicks, sent Bellamy to Detroit, and allowed Reed to return to center. The experience he gained at forward helped his maneuverability and improved his play while facing the basket, including medium-range jump shots. He was a joy for pivot purists to behold, using hooks, underhanded shots, reverse lay-ups and short jumpers to get the ball in the basket. He could pass and set picks as well as any big man who ever played the game. And he had the muscle to play against much taller centers like Wilt Chamberlain and Kareem Abdul-Jabbar.

Reed reached his peak in 1969-70, being named to the All-Defensive team, winning the MVP award and leading the Knicks to their first NBA championship ever. He also earned MVP honors in the annual All-Star Game. He was the fulcrum of a well-coordinated New York offense and the anchor of a devastating defense. He was 27 years old, and should have had several more productive seasons ahead of him.

But even before the end of that season, Reed's seemingly indestructible body was beginning to fall apart. Like so many players, he had long suffered from knee trouble. But he learned to cope with pain and play hurt. Then, in the 1970 playoffs, his luck ran out. In the fifth game of the final series against Los Angeles, Reed went up for a shot, but never made it. Instead, he crumpled to the floor with a torn muscle in his thigh. The crowd in Madison Square Garden sat in stunned silence. His teammates rallied to win the game without him, 107-100.

The Lakers blew the Knicks out in game number six, with Chamberlain exploding for 45 points and 27 rebounds without Reed in the lineup to stop him.

No one knew whether Reed would play in the seventh game back in the Garden. The Knicks took the floor without him. Finally, after the start of the game had been delayed a few minutes and Reed had been given some pain-killer, he hobbled out of the locker room directly on to the playing floor. The normally boisterous crowd of 19,500-plus was positively deafening as the game began. It grew louder—if that was possible—as Reed hit on his first two shots. The Lakers never knew what hit them. Reed played 27 minutes and didn't score another point. But he provided the lift the team needed to easily defeat Los Angeles, 113-99, for the championship.

Reed came back to enjoy another fine season in 1970-71, but the end was already in sight. He was able to play only 11 games the following season. Determinedly, he came back in 1972-73 and led the Knicks to another championship, earning playoff MVP honors as well.

He suffered through a 19-game season the next year, and when he realized he would never be able to again perform up to his own standards, he stepped down as a player at the age of 31.

It was not the end of Reed's relationship with the Knicks, however. In the closing stages of the 1976-77 season, it was announced that Red Holzman would retire as coach and that Willis Reed, the prideful, popular captain, would replace him, effective 1977-78. Willis was ready for his newest challenge.

Reed led the Knicks to a winning season in 1977-78 and a playoff berth. But the man who had heard only applause as a player, began to hear boos as a coach. He complained publicly about the poor mix of rookies, aging veterans and high-priced superstars that were purchased by management and this rankled the Garden brass.

After getting off to a poor start in 1978-79, Reed was fired as coach. He returned to hunting and fishing while the Knicks fulfilled their contractual agreement with him. But clearly, Reed was depressed by events which led to his firing. He vowed to return to coaching and show management it had made a mistake. Toward that end, he signed as head coach at Creighton University in the spring of 1981.

OSCAR ROBERTSON

Big O

Oscar Robertson is probably the only player who ever gave a clinic in basketball technique every time he stepped onto the floor.

The "Big O," as he was known from his college days at the University of Cincinnati, was the consummate stylist, a walking instruction book on the dos and don'ts of basketball. It was this facet of his game which continually fascinated opponents. "Robertson," observed Red Auerbach, "wastes the least amount of motion of any player I've ever seen. Every move has a purpose."

There was greatness written all over this well-built 6-5 product of Crispus Attucks High in Indianapolis, Indiana. Oscar was born on November 24, 1938, in Charlotte, Tennessee, shortly before his mother and two older brothers moved north. When he first entered high school he was known as Bailey Robertson's little brother since Bailey had set an Indiana state scoring record. But when Oscar led his high school to 45 straight victories and consecutive state titles in basketball-mad Hoosierland, the natives forgot all about Bailey.

The local colleges let Oscar get away, and he entered Cincinnati, never before a national basketball power. Once Robertson got on the varsity, the Bearcats ripped off records of 25-3, 26-4 and 28-2, with Oscar leading the nation in scoring each season and capturing All-America honors. About the only thing which eluded Oscar's grasp was a national championship.

While Robertson was performing his miracles on the college courts, the NBA's Rochester Royals left upstate New York for the Rhineland, where they figured to make Oscar their territorial draft selection when he was a senior. They hoped he would pack the Cincinnati Garden, and while that dream was never fully realized, Robertson did have a significant impact on the fortunes of the team. The Royals still finished last in the Western Conference, but they won 14 more games in Oscar's rookie season of 1960-61 than they had the year before, and by the following season they were solid contenders for the league title.

Robertson had played forward exclusively as a collegian, but he took immediately to the guard position and was named Rookie of the Year after av-

Oscar Robertson always tried to make the defenders give ground.

eraging 30.5 points and 9.7 assists a game, setting an NBA playmaking record he would exceed six times. He also demonstrated a remarkable capacity for controlling a game by himself.

He was amazingly consistent, averaging more than 30 points a game in six of his first seven seasons, "slipping" to 28.3 points in the seventh. Unlike other players who might score 42 points one night and 18 the next, Robertson could be counted on to score near his average each and every game and still get his eight to 12 assists. This remarkable consistency, in addition to all else, enabled him to earn a place in basketball's Hall of Fame.

"You can't stereotype him," teammate Jack Twyman once said. "Whatever is needed at the time, against particular opposition, comes out because he has complete physical control of his body. It's not any one thing; it's his completeness that amazes you."

Indeed, he was complete enough to lead the Royals in rebounding until Jerry Lucas came along.

The Royals had several good playoff confrontations with the Celtics in the mid-sixties, but somehow Cincinnati always came out on the short end. It appeared as though Oscar was destined never to play on a championship team.

The situation changed, however, when Bob Cousy became coach of the Royals in 1969. He was interested in a running attack, and he felt that Robertson didn't particularly fit into a fast-break offense since he was accustomed to controlling the tempo of the game by handling the ball all by himself. After one season, Robertson was traded to the Milwaukee Bucks, where Lew Alcindor had been waiting for a playmaker. It was the perfect marriage of a talented young center and a wily guard.

Robertson met his new role with enthusiasm, and the Bucks steamrollered their way to a 66-16 regular-season record in 1970-71. And then they went all the way to the championship, losing just two games. Robertson didn't lead the league in any statistical categories, but he supplied the necessary floor direction and veteran leadership for an otherwise young Milwaukee team.

Technically, Robertson was virtually flawless. His shooting form was perfect, and his shot selection was impeccable. There was a saying around the NBA that if you gave Oscar a 15-footer, he'd want a 14-footer, if you gave him a 10-footer, he'd want it from nine,

and if you gave him a shot from a foot away from the basket, he'd try to move six inches closer. He had a great deal of patience, and, of course, the confidence to implement his ideas. He was capable of thinking two or three steps ahead of his opponents.

BILL RUSSELL

Man on the Block

He was a professional basketball player for 13 seasons, all with the Boston Celtics. He played on 11 championship teams. In one of the two "off" years a severely sprained ankle kept him out of the deciding playoff games. And in the playoffs of 1967, he was burdened with the dual role of starting center and rookie head coach.

Bill Russell truly revolutionized basketball, placing an emphasis on defense which has influenced the play of countless others. He made the blocked shot a feared and valued weapon. As his coach Red Auerbach described it, "Nobody had ever blocked shots on the pros before Russell came along. He upset everybody. The only defense they could think of was to dish out a physical beating and hope he couldn't take it."

He did. Though at 6-9, 220 pounds, he wasn't the biggest center around, his long arms, leaping ability and timing allowed him to play defense as no man before him had ever done. It was tantamount to discovering a secret weapon whose effectiveness became more apparent with each passing season.

Because Russell also brought an intellectual approach to the game, his foes were immediately in for trouble. Rather than running around indiscriminately trying to block every shot attempted, Russell kept his deadly weapon in reserve.

"I've always said," he once explained, "that I can block only around eight to ten percent of the shots taken against me—if I'm lucky. The secret is in knowing which eight or ten percent I'm going after. To put it another way, if I can block only eight percent of the shots you take, but 90 percent of the ones I go after, whose shooting is going to be affected?"

One of the early victims of Russell's strategy was Neil Johnston, a three-time NBA scoring champ before Russell entered the league. Bill knew he could block nine out of ten Johnston shots because they had an exceedingly low trajectory. But if he blocked all the ones he could, Johnston would eventually change his shot, which Russell didn't want him to do.

Russell's value as a player was established before he entered the professional ranks. Born on February 12, 1935, in Monroe, Louisiana, Russell moved with his family to Oakland, California, when he was nine. He never developed a great shooting touch, and as a 6-5 senior at McClymonds High School the most points he ever scored was 14, in his last game. But

Despite his size, Bill Russell played with balletic grace.

he displayed enough defensive ability to attract the attention of people at the University of San Francisco, where head coach Phil Woolpert stressed defense. As a 6-9 sophomore, William Felton Russell played on a 14-7 Don team. In his junior year, the team won its first two games, lost to UCLA, then went unbeaten the rest of the way while winning the NCAA title. The following season, the Dons didn't lose a game at all, and repeated as national champions. They established a collegiate record of 55 victories in a row.

Russell capped the 1955-56 season by making the Olympic basketball team, and in the fall of 1956, he led the U.S. to a gold medal at Melbourne, Australia.

His defensive abilities were unquestioned, but the pros were still looking for big men in the George Mikan mold—scorers. So Auerbach was able to engineer a trade in which the St. Louis Hawks got hometown hero Ed Macauley and the draft rights to Cliff Hagan, while the Celtics received the rights to Russell, who didn't report to the team until December because of the Olympics.

Russell immediately established himself as a nonpareil rebounder and defensive player, but his team value did not end there. Few players, and almost no other big men, have viewed the entire playing area the way Russell did. His awareness of the other nine men on the floor bordered on the psychic. He was a superb passing center, whether grabbing a defensive rebound and keying the vaunted Celtic fast break with an outlet pass, or on the offensive end of the court where the Celtic offense was predicated on his ability to perceive situations and make the right decision. He set countless picks and was a master at salvaging broken plays. He was always a threat to grab a missed shot and make a tap-in. Though not called upon to be a big scorer, he was capable of scoring if the situation demanded, and his lifetime average of 15.1 points a game could easily have been expanded by five points if he felt that would have helped the team.

He was at his best in clutch situations, as is attested by his record 165 appearances in playoff games, 4,104 rebounds, and 7,497 minutes played. For recognizing what it took to win, and for being able to adapt himself to changing auxiliary personnel and changing times, Russell had no peer. In a sport where many participants stand above the norm, Russell stood a little taller than everyone else.

And he brought this same stature to his coaching posts with the Celtics and the Seattle SuperSonics.

As further evidence of the respect he commanded, Russell was voted the NBA's outstanding player for its first 35 years.

DOLPH SCHAYES

Three-Point Specialist

If the three-point play did not exist, Dolph Schayes would undoubtedly have invented it. This 6-8, 220-pound forward probably converted more free throws after making a basket than any of his contemporaries in a career which extended from the 1948-49 season through 1963-64 when he retired as a player-coach. Schayes was a driver who combined strength, agility, ambidexterity and determination in an unparalleled package which allowed him to excel in the pre-24-second-clock era, and thereafter as well.

There was no more versatile player during the early days of the NBA. Schayes could score from inside, or he could move out and dazzle onlookers, as well as opponents, with a high, arching two-hand set. He rebounded well, and he was the best-passing big man of his time. He was durable and he was a clutch performer. He was also one of the very best foul shooters of all time.

Schayes played his entire career with the Syracuse National-Philadelphia 76er franchise. A native of the Bronx, New York, where he was born on May 19, 1928, he attended DeWitt Clinton High School before starring for New York University. Schayes had two offers to turn pro when he left college at age 20. One was from the New York Knicks of the Basketball Association of America and the other from the Nats who belonged to the National Basketball League. The two leagues later merged to form the present NBA. Schayes elected to bypass the more glamorous home-town team for a shot with Syracuse for a very ordinary reason, money. The BAA had a $6,000 ceiling on salaries for rookies and the Knicks offered that. The Nats were able to go higher, so Schayes signed with them. In addition to the money, it was a tremendous break the way he figured it.

"The Nats were a young team," he later explained, "and they needed a big man. As a result, I got to play a lot. If I had been with the Knicks, I wouldn't

have had the chance to develop. Also, there was the inspiration of Al Cervi, the coach of the Nats. Howard Cann taught me many things at NYU, but Cervi really showed me the need for, and the results of, aggressiveness.''

He learned his lessons well, for there was probably no more aggressive and determined player than Schayes. Twice he broke a wrist while playing, and neither injury kept him out of the lineup for long. In fact, he was able to turn the first fracture into a benefit.

"My first wrist fracture," he said, "helped me to become a better shooter. I had always admired Bobby Wanzer's finger-tip set shot. The cast on my wrist forced me to shoot with my finger tips. It gave me better control. Then, too, the cast made me work on my left-handed shots, which soon improved. Later, when the left wrist was cracked, the right-hand shots improved.''

A great driver, Dolph Schayes was a master at drawing fouls—and making free throws.

During the two seasons in which he fractured his wrists, he missed a total of just nine games, playing with an old-fashioned heavy plaster cast in each instance. And if the casts gave Schayes a bit of an edge under the boards, well . . .

Years before it became a routine training aid, Schayes conceived the idea of improving his shooting and rebounding by practicing with a ring inside the regular basketball rim. This was typical of his career-long desire to excel and improve himself. He was a perfectionist at one of the most taken-for-granted parts of basketball, free throw shooting. With his soft, two-handed touch, he led his team in foul shooting percentage 11 straight years, and was the league leader three times. He shot .904 from the line in both the 1956-57 and 1957-58 seasons, and were it not for the amazing Bill Sharman, he would have led the league several more times. But Schayes was always being one-upped. When he retired he had scored more points than anyone else in the league, yet never led the league in scoring. He made more than 3,000 assists, but never led the league in that category, and despite his lifetime 10.9 rebounds-per-game average, he was tops in the league only once.

When Schayes ended his 16-year career (still the longest in league history) he went out as the first man to score 15,000 points in a career, and was just 751 points short of the exclusive 20,000-point club. He also held the mark for playing in the most games (1,035). But though his records may have been surpassed, his legacy as one of the league's most noble pioneers has remained firmly entrenched in basketball annals.

BILL SHARMAN

Fit to Be Tough

Bill Sharman's number 21 hangs atop the Boston Garden, and sometimes young fans want to know why.

You don't hear much about Sharman, what with all the flashy, spectacular guards who have come along since he retired in 1961. Yet it's a good thing for some of the newcomers that Sharman isn't around.

Ask Hal Greer, who found himself shut out—shut out!—in a 1959 playoff game by Sharman's tenacious

guarding. Ask Tom Heinsohn, who has seen all the Celtics come and go for more than 20 years. "Sharman," Heinsohn says, "was the best competitor of all the Celtics. I never saw a tougher guy."

The word "toughness" comes up in many discussions of Sharman, for he was the embodiment of it, both physically and mentally. An avowed physical-fitness nut, Sharman was always in perfect shape, in or out of season. Born in Abilene, Texas, on May 25, 1926, he and his family moved to California, where he became a 15-letter man at Porterville High School. He was captain and fullback of the football team, a first baseman in baseball and a track star, as well as a standout basketball player. He also was a weightlifter and amateur boxer. Later on, he would add tennis and golf to his athletic repertoire.

Sharman tried to combine a baseball career with one in basketball, but he had the misfortune of being in the strong Dodger chain of the late forties and early fifties. He was a promising Triple A prospect for several years, and he was even called up late in 1951. He never got into a game, but he did sit in on history. He was in the Dodger dugout when Bobby Thomson hit the Shot Heard Round the World in the 1951 National League playoffs to give the pennant to the Giants. Sharman finally gave up trying to crack the Brooklyn lineup and concentrated exclusively on basketball.

He had been an All-American at Southern California, and he joined the Washington franchise of the NBA in 1950. That team disbanded, and the following year he joined the Celtics, where he was to forge a successful partnership with a playmaker named Bob Cousy. They went on to be the premier backcourt of the fifties, and, some say, of all time.

Sharman complemented Cousy in every way. He was a superb shooter who knew how to get to open spots and how to shoot coming off a pick. As one teammate said, "Sharman shoots between their finger tips." Sharman couldn't have asked for a better man to get him the ball than Cousy, and the Cooz couldn't have asked for a better recipient for his passes than Sharman.

Sharman was also as dogged a defender as ever graced the NBA. Due to his amazing physical conditioning, he was always ready to go 48 minutes, although he seldom had to. Whereas some good offensive ballplayers would seek a rest on defense, Sharman got mentally tougher when his team didn't have the ball. Cousy liked to gamble and try for steals. Sharman, meanwhile, was the ''stay-at-home'' guard. So even on defense the pair complemented each other.

Sharman's aggressiveness bordered on pugnaciousness, and he had his share of fights during his career. He always drew the toughest opposing guard, and occasionally there arose a difference of opinion that, apparently, could only be settled by fists.

But fans remember Sharman most for his shooting. Attempting almost nothing except jumpers from 15 feet and beyond, Sharman was hailed as the shooter of the fifties. ''Sharman,'' Red Auerbach explained, ''has the ability to hold an object such as a basketball in his hand and judge instantaneously its weight, the distance to the target and the arc needed to get that object through the target. This judgment is a gift, and Sharman has it, much more so than do most shooters. His hard work turns this potential into achievement.''

Everyone associated with Sharman thinks of him as a meticulous person and incessant worker. They recall how he always had a cup of tea and a chocolate bar before each game, no matter what the circumstances, and they tell of his unshakeable daily if-this-is-noon-I-must-be-hungry routine. On a day trip to New York for a game, Sharman would pack a valise and then empty the contents into a dresser drawer, even if the stay in the hotel room was only a few hours. His entire life was organized, and this approach was considered to be the key to his success, for in terms of sheer physical attributes he was not as gifted as some other players.

Nowhere did his habit of repetition and powers of concentration reveal themselves better than at the foul line, where he was the greatest marksman of his time. Seven seasons he led the league in free throw percentage, and his 1958-59 record of 93.2 was the single season mark for a decade and a half. In one stretch he made 79 out of 80 free throws. And at one time he held the regular season and playoff marks for consecutive free throws made.

Sharman was the first NBA guard to average as many as 22 points a game in the pre-24 second clock days, with his scoring coming in the context of Boston's emphasis on team play.

He learned his lessons well, and combined them with his personal philosophy when he turned to coaching. He is the only man ever to win championships in three major professional leagues.

Celtics' Bill Sharman always stayed in peak condition.

Jerry West thrived on pressure and finally won a championship ring.

JERRY WEST

In the Clutch

,Like most great players, Jerry West thrived on pressure situations. "I learned," he once explained, "that no matter what happens in a game, the last four minutes seem to decide it. So when it comes, I'm ready."

So ready was he on so many occasions that he earned the nickname, "Mr. Clutch," which became the title of his autobiography. Nobody could deny him that description, for he won countless regular-season games, playoff games and the 1972 All-Star Game with clutch shots. He also earned the affection and respect of his opponents.

In the 1969 playoff finals, West's Los Angeles team was battling the aging but proud Boston Celtics for the sixth time in eight seasons. The previous five series had ended in defeat for L.A., although certainly through no fault of West's. Again the Lakers found themselves in a tough series, and it came down to a seventh game.

But the Celtics again prevailed, despite West's 42 points, 13 rebounds and 12 assists. No man could have done more for his team. When the game was over, Boston captain John Havlicek put his arm around Jerry and told him, on behalf of all the Celtics, how much they respected him and how they hoped he would win a championship one day. It illustrated the reverence his fellow pros had for the brilliant guard of the Lakers.

He was born Jerry Alan West on May 28, 1938, in Cheylan, West Virginia, but the post office was in Cabin Creek and that's how he came to be called "Zeke from Cabin Creek."

He was an All-American at West Virginia University and he played on the 1960 Olympic team, regarded as the strongest ever to represent the United States. His teammates included Oscar Robertson, Jerry Lucas, Walt Bellamy and Terry Dischinger.

When West turned pro in 1960 with the Lakers, he was considered an adjunct to Elgin Baylor, who had already established himself as the star of the team. He had played a lot of forward in college, but at 6-3, 175 pounds, there was no way he could play up front in the pros. Many doubted that he could stand the punishment dealt out in the rough money game. Yet, countless broken noses and all, he would last 14 years.

West took only his first season, when he averaged 17.6 points a game, to acclimate himself in the NBA. He never again averaged under 20 points, including his aborted final season, 1973-74, when injuries limited him to 35 games. He lasted long enough and played often enough to retire as the third-leading scorer in NBA history with 25,192 points, a per-game average of 27.0. He set an all-time one-game scoring record for a guard when he pumped in 63 points against New York on January 17, 1963—a record broken 14 years later by New Orleans' Pete Maravich, who tallied 68 points against New York on February 25, 1977.

However, West was known as more than just a scoring guard. He became a playmaker of the highest order, retiring as the fifth-leading assists man in the league.

Defense was another West specialty. Perhaps only Boston's John Havlicek played both ends of the court as consistently hard as West, who never relaxed on the court. As he got older, he became particularly adept at anticipating opponents' passes. His reputation as the master at playing the passing lanes and coming up with stray passes was unchallenged.

The one continuing frustration of West's career was the inability of the Lakers to win the championship. Something always seemed to happen to his team in the finals. Either it was an injury to Baylor or to West (sometimes both), or perhaps it was just the presence of Bill Russell on the other team.

However, in the 1971-72 season Los Angeles finally jelled. Bill Sharman came in as coach and exerted influence on Wilt Chamberlain, selling him on the merits of a fast-breaking game. L.A. went off on a 33-game winning streak and won 69 games overall. This time when the playoffs came, somebody other than West was ready. The Lakers dispatched the Knicks in five games, and West finally had his championship ring.

In 1976, Jerry West entered a new phase of his basketball career when he became coach of the Lakers. He led them to the Pacific Division title before they were upset by the Portland Trail Blazers in the playoffs. West took the Lakers to the playoffs the next two years as well, although the championship remained elusive. Constant bickering with owner

Jack Kent Cooke finally took its toll, however, and following the 1978-79 season, West resigned. His coaching experience did not detract from his achievements as a player, though. West was named to the Hall of Fame soon thereafter.

LEN WILKENS

Cool Stylist

Behind the mild-mannered disposition and angelic facial expression lay just what you would expect—a nice guy who just happened to be one of the best guards ever to play in the NBA.

Lenny Wilkens was slightly built at 6-1 and 170 pounds, and didn't put on a menacing front in an attempt to intimidate opponents. Rather, he would dazzle foes with his fluid moves, deft passing and thinking man's quarterbacking in the backcourt.

Playing with an emotionless expression on his face, Wilkens was always concentrating deeply while he glided up and down the court bringing the ball up, calling a play, penetrating for a lay-up, arching a soft push shot or racing back on defense. Game in, game out, the smooth left-hander out of Providence College played with a masked intensity which earned him a spot on the All-Star squad in nine of his 14 seasons.

Born October 28, 1937, Lenny gave little evidence during his youth that he might one day play in the NBA. He wasn't a big name scholastic ballplayer, preferring instead to play the game on the CYO level in his native Brooklyn. After his father died when Wilkens was still very young, the most important man in his life was Father Thomas Mannion of Holy Rosary Church. He introduced Lenny to basketball, and soon the CYO league became the center of his life.

Wilkens attended Boys High, but for his first three years he didn't want to play on the school team. A shy teenager, he wasn't happy with the aggressive coaching methods of the school's coach, Mickey Fisher. It wasn't until Lenny was a senior that he went out for the varsity, where his backcourt mate was future big-league baseball star Tommy Davis.

Lenny went on to Providence, which at that time had no great basketball tradition. He found himself

Stylish Len Wilkens (right) was a folk hero in Seattle after joining the Sonics late in his career.

in the middle of a building process which included another standout guard, Johnny Egan. The Friars received national publicity by getting into the National Invitation Tournament, and Wilkens attracted attention for his slick passing and brilliant defense. He didn't worry too much about scoring, although he shot enough to average 14.9 points a game during his three-year varsity career.

His lack of height and bulk, low scoring average and lack of an effective jump shot made him an uncertain pro prospect, and there were many who figured he wouldn't make it, despite college credentials which included an MVP award when he led the Friars to the NIT finals in 1960.

Still, the St. Louis Hawks made him their first-round draft choice, and they found an immediate use for him. Lenny moved in as a starting guard for a team which advanced all the way to the championship finals. Hawks' coach Harry Gallatin had an intricate offense which included 25 plays, plus numerous options. None of this mattered much to Wilkens, however, for he understood perfectly that his role was to feed the big men: Bob Pettit, Cliff Hagan and Clyde Lovellette.

"I never even looked at the playbook," he said. "I knew I was supposed to get the ball to Bob and Cliff. What did I need plays for?" Yet he still managed to score 11.7 points a game himself.

He missed most of the 1961-62 season while serving in the Army, and when he returned the following season, he again settled into his feeding role. By 1964-65, however, Hagan was slowing down and Wilkens upped his scoring to 16 points a game. Pettit retired before the 1965-66 campaign, and Lenny was ready to do whatever was necessary to help the team. He scored at an 18-point clip and began to be recognized as a top-flight guard.

The second phase of Wilkens' career came prior to the 1968-69 season when he was traded to the expansion Seattle team, which was a break for him, as he showed his floor generalship with the inexperienced SuperSonics and increased his scoring to 22.4 points per game. Off the court and on, he was the most popular player on the team, and in 1969 he became player-coach at Seattle.

Three years later, when he was 35 years old and the team traded him to Cleveland, the fans were outraged. When Cleveland made its initial appearance of the 1972-73 season in Seattle, the Sonics had their first sellout as the crowd turned out to welcome Lenny. They gave him a standing ovation and proceeded to root the Cavaliers to victory as Wilkens played a key role.

He closed out his player-coach career in 1974-75 with the Portland Trail Blazers, where he played 60 minutes in a four-overtime game on opening night against Cleveland. He limited his playing time and appeared in only 65 games, scoring just 6.5 points a game, the first time in his career that he failed to average double figures. He stepped down as second only to Oscar Robertson in assists, with 7,211.

He accomplished his feats with a cool demeanor which concealed the competitiveness within his meager frame. He operated with the stealth of a cat burglar. "You turn around," his college coach, Joe Mullaney, once said, "and all of a sudden you say, 'Where did he come from?' And everybody is sweating, while Lenny is dry."

But Lenny wasn't dry on June 1, 1979. That was the night in Washington, D.C., when Lenny and the team he'd return to coach, the SuperSonics, defeated the Bullets for their first NBA championship.

GEORGE YARDLEY

Breaking the Barrier

Times change, but barriers can only fall once. Roger Bannister was the first to run a four-minute mile; Cornelius Warmerdam was the first 15-foot pole vaulter; Beattie Feathers was the first NFL player to gain 1,000 yards in one year, and George Yardley was the first NBA player to score 2,000 points in a season.

That achievement probably didn't look like much when Wilt Chamberlain came along four years later and scored over *twice* as many points, but no matter. George Mikan wasn't able to score 2,000 points, and neither were Dolph Schayes, Paul Arizin, Neil Johnston, Bob Cousy or any of the other top NBA scorers of the day. Yet in the 1957-58 season there came an unlikely-looking 29-year-old forward from the Detroit Pistons named George Yardley to score 2,001 points and earn a permanent spot in basketball annals.

George Yardley was not an unknown. In fact, the year before he had scored 21.5 points per game and made the all-league second team. The 6-5 cornerman had been improving steadily since coming into the league in 1953-54. He had increased his scoring yearly, going from 9.0 in his rookie season to 17.3, 17.4, 21.5 and, finally, to 27.8 in his big year. He had clearly established himself as one of the league's more inventive scorers by his fifth year as a professional.

The problem was that people were never ready to accept Yardley as a basketball player after looking at him in uniform. Born November 3, 1928, he was built like a human flamingo, and was, in fact, nicknamed "The Bird," with 190 pounds, at best, stretched over a 6-5 frame. He was bald, had knobby knees and ran with a deceptive loping style which made him look more like a guy picking up some exercise during lunch hour at the YMCA than a serious professional.

He had been a civil engineering major at Stanford and when his college career was over in 1950 he passed up the Fort Wayne Pistons' offer and went into AAU ball instead. Playing for the Stewart Chevrolet team of San Francisco, he led his team to the title twice and earned the Most Valuable Player award in the National AAU tournament. He spent the 1952-53 season in the Naval Air Corps and his team won

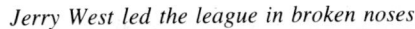

Jerry West led the league in broken noses.

Elgin Baylor was one of the greatest offensive players imaginable.

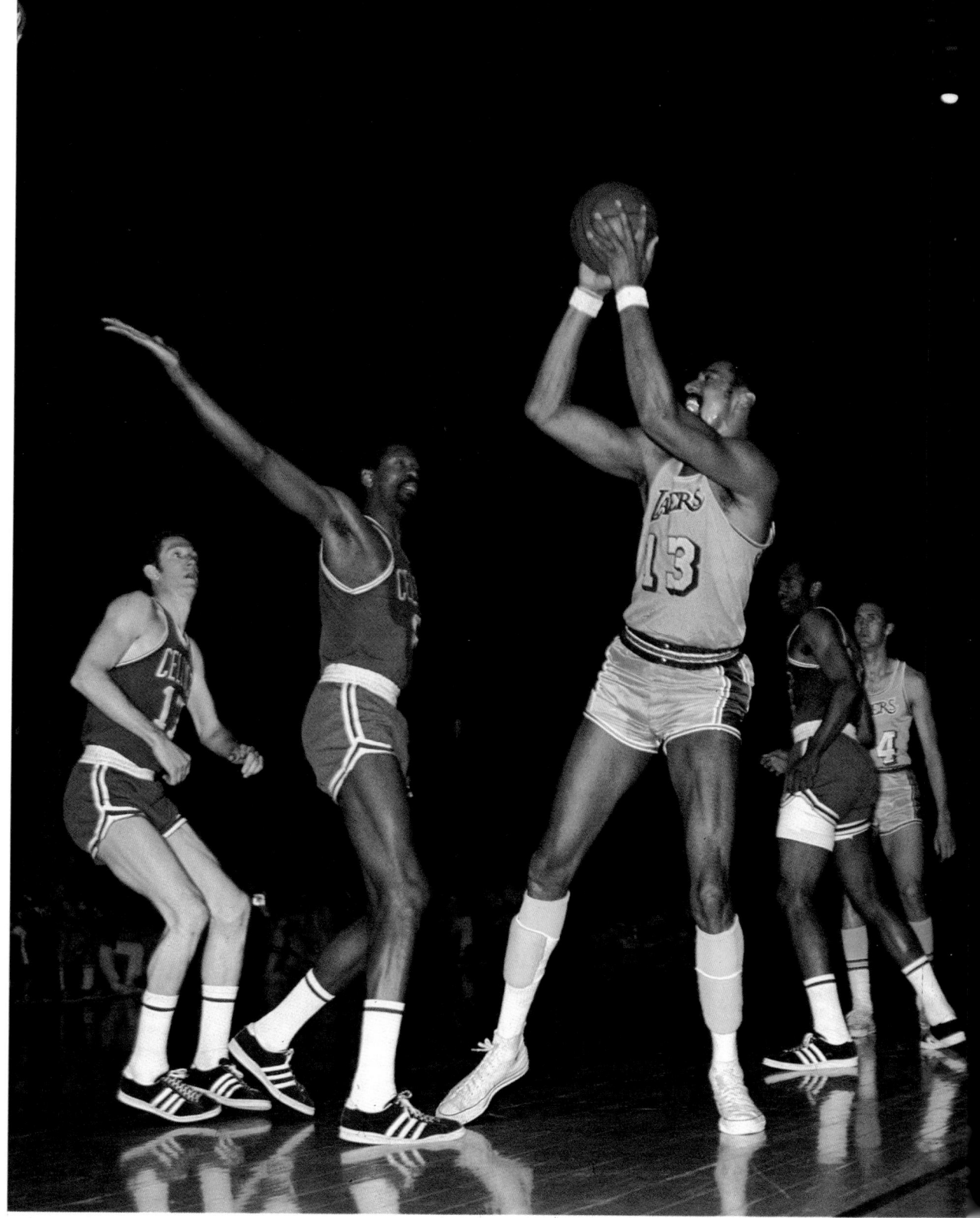

Wilt Chamberlain stood as a colossus over all.

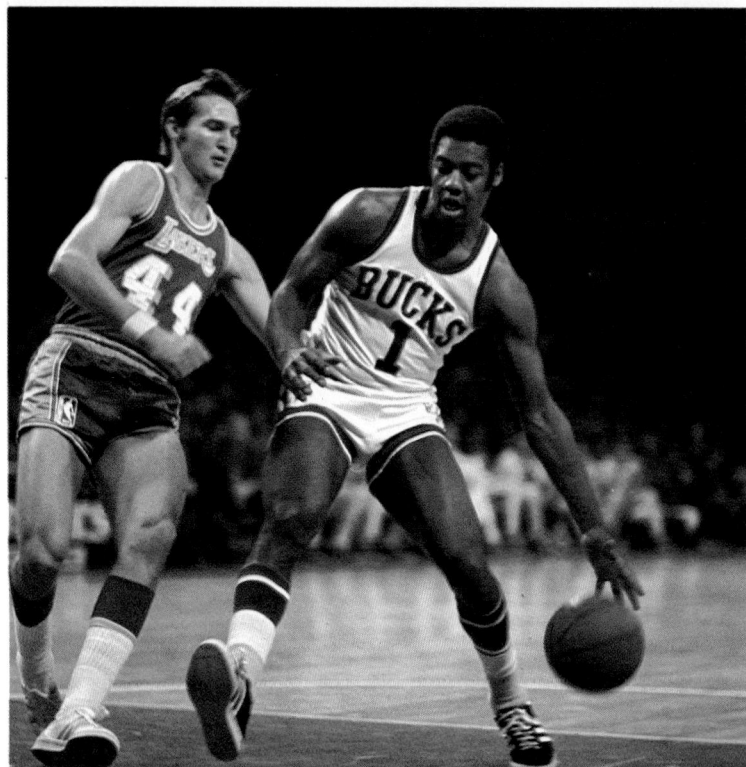

Bill Russell revolutionized the game.

As scorer, feeder, rebounder (except for the giants of course), defender, foul-shooter, driver, Oscar Robertson was the complete superstar.

Bill Bradley described Walt Frazier as an artist who took an artistic approach to the game.

Billy Cunningham's unusual leaping ability, coupled with superb body control, made him a devastating inside player.

Willis Reed was more mobile than most giants ▶
and a competitor to the core.

*Len Wilkens displayed the stealth of a
cat burglar.*

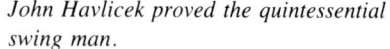

*John Havlicek proved the quintessential
swing man.*

Pete Maravich came with his pistol.

Dave Cowens played with intensity on the court and had a flair for the unusual off it.

Elvin Hayes, a center with the ▶ range of a guard, demonstrated that he was more than a floor show.

Calvin Murphy proved there will always be a place for the little man.

Rick Barry's nomadic travels brought him back to San Francisco and an NBA championship with Golden State.

Bill Walton's world went beyond the baskets, and the tragedy of it all was that he had to leave so soon.

Skywalker David Thompson came out of a hamlet in North Carolina to find a home in the Rockies.

Body balance and bull's-eye shooting up to 20 feet made Paul Westphal one of the best guards in the game.

◀ *Always a sight to behold, Julius Erving is Baryshnikov with a basketball.*

Facing page:

Left: Magic Johnson's sleight of hand led the Lakers to a crown.

Right: Schoolboy Moses Malone came of age as a pro.

Cool George Gervin is the ultimate scoring machine.

CHAPTER 9

American Basketball Association

On February 1, 1967, the American Basketball Association was officially born.

On June 17, 1976, the American Basketball Association officially died.

In between, during nine crazy years, the ABA experienced incredible times, memorable moments and costly occurrences. But the ABA did leave its impression on basketball.

The ABA was an idea whose time had come, according to a group of California entrepreneurs, businessmen and lawyers who met in 1966 and tried to organize a new professional basketball league. The American Football League had proven that a young upstart could challenge the establishment and succeed when it finally merged with the National Football League.

The ABA founders—including young, enterprising attorney Gary Davidson, who would go on to help form new leagues in hockey and football—were primarily intrigued by the spiraling size of the entertainment and advertising dollar. As they early on noted, a minute of commercial time on a nationally-televised football game sold for $75,000, and it had been estimated in 1966 that ''personal spending for consumption'' was a record $455 million in this country.

A number of markets and men were approached, with franchises selling initially for $650,000, and, after several hits and misses, the ABA settled on and in 11 territories—New Jersey, Indianapolis, Louisville, New Orleans, Anaheim, Denver, Pittsburgh, Minneapolis-St. Paul, Dallas, Houston and Oakland.

Before the ABA eventually was amalgamated—in abbreviated form—with the National Basketball Association, the locales added to the list included: Miami (and other cities in Florida), Memphis, New York, Los Angeles, Salt Lake City, St. Louis, Hampton (and other cities in Virginia), San Antonio, Washington, San Diego, and, briefly, Baltimore. At least the ABA touched a lot of lives.

Even when a team stayed in the same city, more often than not, the ownership, player personnel, coaches and nicknames underwent drastic revisions. For example, during a five-year tenure in Memphis, the franchise was known as Pros, Tams and then Sounds, had four coaches, 28 players on the roster in one year alone and four owners (in addition to being taken over by the league twice). Only the Kentucky, Denver and Indiana clubs remained in the same spot throughout the league's existence.

There were seven commissioners—George Mikan, Jim Gardner, Jack Dolph, Robert Carlson, Mike Storen, Tedd Munchak and Dave DeBusschere.

There were bad debts and good players, new owners and old faces, tight games and loose organizations, a three-point shot from 25 feet, a 30-second clock and a red, white and blue ball.

There were very few concrete plans for the future, and there was never a major national television contract. Attendance increased yearly and the teams moved into new, big buildings, but, no matter what, small crowds remained common.

But the game is supposed to be for the players, and more than a few good ones passed through the

Indiana's Mel Daniels (left) and George McGinnis (teammate in white) were two of the ABA's outstanding players.

ABA's portals. Among the great, near-great and exciting were Julius Erving, George McGinnis, Rick Barry, Spencer Haywood, Billy Cunningham, David Thompson, Connie Hawkins, Artis Gilmore, Mel Daniels, Roger Brown, Jimmy Jones, Mack Calvin, Charlie Scott, George Gervin, Doug Moe, Dan Issel, Warren Jabali, James Silas, Bobby Jones, Marvin Barnes, Ralph Simpson and Moses Malone.

Only three players played from the league's inception until it joined with the NBA. Byron Beck stuck with Denver; Louie Dampier, the league's all-time leading scorer, played nine years with Kentucky and then went to San Antonio when the leagues merged, and Freddie Lewis bounced from Indiana to two other teams and back.

No one can, or will, estimate how much the ABA lost in its "war" with the NBA, but it must have been in excess of $50 million. Only a couple of teams ever went through a season on the profitable side.

And, at last, the NBA and the ABA agreed to come together and return a monopolistic atmosphere to professional basketball. Just four teams—the New York Nets, the Denver Nuggets, the Indiana Pacers and the San Antonio Spurs—were accepted in June of 1976, and each had to pay $3.2 million (plus assorted other fees to take care of those left behind).

The ABA tombstone might best read:
1967-1976. After a nine-year war, may it rest in peace.

1967-68

The red, white and blue ball moved from the nose of a seal, where a coach named Alex Hannum said it belonged, to the basketball court, where the American Basketball Association decided it belonged, in 1967.

Ironically, the first official bounce was made on a Friday the 13th, providing an indicator of the unluckiness of the ABA over the years. On the night of October 13 in Oakland Coliseum, the Oakland Oaks beat the Anaheim Amigos, 134-129, and the league was off and, if not running, at least standing up.

The league's two biggest names didn't participate in a game that first season. George Mikan, the former collegiate and NBA great, was in the commissioner's chair, and Rick Barry was in an arena chair, sitting out. The Oaks were owned by singer Pat Boone, and the coach was Bruce Hale, who, conveniently enough, had been Barry's coach at the University of Miami and was the 6-7 forward's father-in-law. So Barry became the first to jump from the old to the new league, but couldn't play during his contractual option season (1967-68).

Thus, the ABA had to develop its own standout players. Foremost was Connie Hawkins, who had been a legend on the playgrounds of New York City, then in the old American Basketball League and with the Harlem Globetrotters. He was banned from the NBA because of sketchy involvement with the college betting scandals of the early 1960s. Two others who were tainted (but were not involved), Roger Brown and Doug Moe, also hooked up with the infant league and were among its best performers.

Moe's little playmaker friend from the University of North Carolina, Larry Brown, joined him at New Orleans, and the 5-9 Brown even won the Most Valuable Player award at the league's first All-Star Game, played before a creditably-sized crowd of 10,872 at Butler Field House in Indianapolis, and won by the East, 126-120.

Some of the other top players in the league's initial season were centers Mel Daniels, who finished first

Connie Hawkins, banned from the NBA, led Pittsburgh to ABA title.

in rebounding; pencil-thin Red Robbins and Bob Netolicky; forwards Cincy Powell, Art Heyman and Cliff Hagan, the Dallas player-coach who had only a few moves left from when he was at the pinnacle in the NBA, and guards Louie Dampier, Larry Jones, "Sweet" Charlie Williams and Chico Vaughn.

The league was constructed around, mainly, the long-range three-point bombs (an ABL leftover) and roughhouse tactics around the basket. Finesse was a seldom-heard word.

Despite minimal attendance, and resulting financial problems (which would always haunt the ABA), the league did finish the season with the 11 teams it started with—New Orleans, Dallas, Denver, Houston, Anaheim and Oakland in the West and Pittsburgh, Minnesota, Indiana, Kentucky and New Jersey in the East.

The Pittsburgh Pipers—led by Hawkins down low and Vaughn and Williams gunning from the perimeters—ended up with the best regular-season record (54-24) and won the East, while New Orleans, with an Auburn shuffle offense, took the West with a 48-30 mark.

Even though Kentucky and New Jersey tied for fourth (the final playoff spot) in the East, the southern Colonels went on to postseason play because of a forfeit that fairly reflected the ABA's early image. A one-game playoff was set for New Jersey, but was shifted to Commack (Long Island) because of arena scheduling problems. When the teams arrived they found a patched-up court with loose boards and unscrewed bolts. Commissioner Mikan declared the conditions unplayable and awarded the triumph to Kentucky.

The rest of the playoffs weren't as disastrous. Pittsburgh and New Orleans waded through the opposition and met for the championship. Surprisingly, the Buccaneers took the first two games in Pittsburgh, but, just as shocking, lost in their home opener. The fourth game, in New Orleans, probably was the best of the entire season, with Pittsburgh winning in overtime, 106-105. That tied the series at 2-2, and, typically, New Orleans won the next contest in Pittsburgh. But the Pipers came right back in New Orleans, and it went down to the final game in Pittsburgh on May 4, 1968.

A crowd of 11,427—some induced by reduced ticket prices—turned out and saw the Pipers take a 21-point lead in the third quarter. The Bucs, under coach James "Babe" McCarthy, rallied to within five points twice late in the fourth quarter, but Pittsburgh, coached by Vince Cazetta, hung on for a 122-113 victory.

In that first season the ABA attracted just over 1.2 million fans (an average of 2,804), not a startlingly successful figure, but enough to convince the masterminds behind the league to keep going. Losses were about $3 million.

Dampier, a six-foot guard, scored 54 points in one game, Les Selvage of Anaheim tried 26 three-pointers in a contest, making 10, and Hawkins averaged 26.8 points to lead the league. A shot was attempted and made from one end of the court to the other (for three points); a protest was upheld because a court was too short, and a coach was demoted to public relations man.

It was that kind of strange beginning for the ABA.

1967-68

STANDINGS

Eastern Division

	W.	L.	Pct.
Pittsburgh	54	24	.692
Minnesota	50	28	.641
Indiana	38	40	.487
Kentucky	36	42	.462
New Jersey	36	42	.462

Western Division

	W.	L.	Pct.
New Orleans	48	30	.615
Dallas	46	32	.590
Denver	45	33	.577
Houston	29	49	.372
Anaheim	25	53	.321
Oakland	22	56	.282

Eastern Division Semifinal Series

March 25—Pittsburgh 146, Indiana 127
March 26—Pittsburgh 121, Indiana 108
March 27—Pittsburgh 133, Indiana 114

March 24—Minnesota 115, Kentucky 102
March 26—Kentucky 100, Minnesota 95
March 27—Minnesota 116, Kentucky 107
March 29—Kentucky 94, Minnesota 86
March 30—Minnesota 114, Kentucky 108

Eastern Division Final Series

April 4—Pittsburgh 125, Minnesota 117
April 6—Minnesota 137, Pittsburgh 123
April 10—Pittsburgh 107, Minnesota 99
April 13—Pittsburgh 117, Minnesota 108
April 14—Pittsburgh 114, Minnesota 105

Western Division Semifinal Series

March 26—New Orleans 130, Denver 104
March 27—New Orleans 105, Denver 93
March 30—Denver 105, New Orleans 98
March 31—Denver 108, New Orleans 100
April 3—New Orleans 102, Denver 97

March 23—Dallas 111, Houston 110
March 25—Dallas 115, Houston 97
March 26—Dallas 116, Houston 103

Western Division Final Series

April 5—New Orleans 104, Dallas 99
April 9—Dallas 112, New Orleans 109
April 10—New Orleans 110, Dallas 107
April 11—New Orleans 119, Dallas 103
April 13—New Orleans 108, Dallas 107

Championship Series

April 18—Pittsburgh 120, New Orleans 112
April 20—New Orleans 109, Pittsburgh 100
April 24—New Orleans 109, Pittsburgh 101
April 25—Pittsburgh 106, New Orleans 105 (OT)
April 27—New Orleans 111, Pittsburgh 108
May 1—Pittsburgh 118, New Orleans 112
May 4—Pittsburgh 122, New Orleans 113

TOP SCORERS

	Pts.	Ave.
Connie Hawkins, Pittsburgh	1875	26.8
Doug Moe, New Orleans	1884	24.2
Levern Tart, Oakland-New Jersey	1718	23.5
Darel Carrier, Kentucky	1765	22.9
Larry Jones, Denver	1742	22.9

TOP REBOUNDERS

	No.	Ave.
Mel Daniels, Minnesota	1213	15.6
Connie Hawkins, Pittsburgh	945	13.5
John Beasley, Dallas	982	12.8
Ira Harge, Pittsburgh-Oakland	1038	12.7
Red Robbins, New Orleans	894	12.2

LEADERS IN ASSISTS

	No.	Ave.
Larry Brown, New Orleans	506	6.5
Cliff Hagan, Dallas	276	4.9
Steve Chubin, Anaheim	364	4.7
Connie Hawkins, Pittsburgh	320	4.6
Roger Brown, Indiana	327	4.3

1968-69

The ABA began a franchise shuffle, moving four of the 11. The Anaheim team shifted from across the street from Disneyland to Los Angeles; the New Jersey Americans went to Commack (Long Island, N.Y.) and became the New York Nets; the Minnesota Muskies traveled to Miami and were transformed into the Floridians, and the defending champions, the Pittsburgh Pipers, apparently knowing something that the Muskies didn't, moved into Minneapolis-St. Paul.

When the movement ended, Oakland was recognized as a dominant force. Alex Hannum, who had coached two NBA championship teams, brought in his bald and intelligent head, and was able to work with Rick Barry, his year's layoff over after leaping leagues; the duo of Larry Brown and Doug Moe, who had been traded from New Orleans, and rookie jump king, guard Warren Armstrong.

The Oaks, as predicted, ran away with the Western Division by a massive 14 games (with a 60-18 mark) over the previous division champions, the New Orleans Buccaneers, even though Barry injured a knee and played in just 35 games. In the East the Indiana Pacers had picked up Mel Daniels from Minnesota and edged out Daniels' old team (now the Floridians) by one game with a 44-34 record. The 6-9 center definitely was the difference and would be a significant factor for Indiana in years to come. He averaged 24 points and 16.5 rebounds and was picked the league's MVP.

The Pacers and the Oaks advanced to the ABA title series with no undue stress. Indiana popped Miami in five games, and Oakland defeated New Orleans in four straight.

Both the Pacers and the Oaks were high-scoring units—Oakland averaging 126 points a game while Indiana was accounting for 119—so an explosive series was expected, and produced. But it took the Oaks just five games to establish their complete superiority—winning 123-114, 134-126 (in overtime), 144-117 and finally 135-131 (in another extra-period contest). Indiana's only victory was in the second game when the Pacers, for once, overwhelmed the Oaks, 150-122.

Still, the ABA was having troubles opening eyes in America. Few paid any heed to the antics of the young league. No national television existed, and sports pages in most cities didn't run the league standings.

Attendance did improve slightly, however, over the first season, with the total at 1.275 million, an average of 2,981 per game. For the second consecutive year, Indiana—a hotbed of high school and college basketball and once a member of the NBA—took top honors by drawing 2,888,678—more than 100,000 above any of the other 10 teams. At

Rick Barry (right) sparked Oakland to the title and became the first player to lead two pro leagues in scoring.

the other end of the scale were Houston and the New York Nets, each under 50,000. The Nets couldn't attract audiences no matter where they played in the vicinity of New York City.

The All-Star Game in Louisville brought in a lowly 5,407, and the escapade of the year developed there. Minnesota coach Jim Harding was supposed to coach in the game, but got into a fist fight with one of his owners at a cocktail party and was immediately dismissed. Kentucky's Gene Rhodes took over, and his East squad lost, 133-127. John Beasley, a journeyman center, had his fleeting moment of fame by being named the game's MVP. The coach of the winning West was Oakland's Hannum, who only the year before had been the victorious coach in the NBA All-Star Game.

Despite playing in less than half the games, Oakland's Barry became the first pro ever to lead two leagues in scoring. He averaged 34 points. The all-league team consisted of Barry, Connie Hawkins, Daniels and guards Larry Jones and Jimmy Jones. The all-rookie team included three with potential—Oakland's Armstrong, Larry Miller (a

scorer from the University of North Carolina) and Ron Boone, who would never miss a game during his ABA career.

The caliber of play had improved over the first season, with emphasis on big scores and wide-open games. But financial losses were still in the millions; a few owners were getting restless; and the world was keeping a death watch over the ABA.

It wasn't through, though.

1968-69

STANDINGS

Eastern Division

	W.	L.	Pct.
Indiana	44	34	.564
Miami	43	35	.551
Kentucky	42	36	.538
Minnesota	36	42	.462
New York	17	61	.218

Western Division

	W.	L.	Pct.
Oakland	60	18	.769
New Orleans	46	32	.590
Denver	44	34	.564
Dallas	41	37	.526
Los Angeles	33	45	.423
Houston	23	55	.295

Eastern Division Semifinals

April 8—Kentucky 128, Indiana 118
April 9—Indiana 120, Kentucky 115
April 10—Kentucky 130, Indiana 111
April 13—Kentucky 105, Indiana 104 (OT)
April 14—Indiana 116, Kentucky 97
April 15—Indiana 107, Kentucky 89
April 17—Indiana 120, Kentucky 111

April 7—Miami 119, Minnesota 110
April 9—Minnesota 106, Miami 99
April 10—Minnesota 109, Miami 93
April 12—Miami 116, Minnesota 109
April 13—Miami 122, Minnesota 107
April 15—Minnesota 105, Miami 100
April 19—Miami 137, Minnesota 128

Eastern Division Final Series

April 20—Indiana 126, Miami 110
April 22—Indiana 131, Miami 116
April 23—Indiana 119, Miami 105
April 25—Miami 114, Indiana 110
April 26—Indiana 127, Miami 105

Western Division Semifinal Series

April 5—Oakland 129, Denver 99
April 6—Denver 122, Oakland 119
April 8—Oakland 121, Denver 99
April 10—Denver 109, Oakland 108
April 12—Oakland 128, Denver 118
April 13—Denver 126, Oakland 115
April 16—Oakland 115, Denver 102

April 5—New Orleans 129, Dallas 106
April 7—New Orleans 122, Dallas 108
April 10—Dallas 130, New Orleans 106
April 12—New Orleans 114, Dallas 107
April 14—Dallas 123, New Orleans 112
April 15—Dallas 136, New Orleans 118
April 17—New Orleans 101, Dallas 95

Western Division Final Series

April 19—Oakland 128, New Orleans 118
April 21—Oakland 135, New Orleans 124
April 23—Oakland 113, New Orleans 107
April 25—Oakland 128, New Orleans 114

Championship Series

April 30—Oakland 123, Indiana 114
May 2—Indiana 150, Oakland 122
May 3—Oakland 134, Indiana 126 (OT)
May 5—Oakland 144, Indiana 117
May 7—Oakland 135, Indiana 131 (OT)

TOP SCORERS

	Pts.	Ave.
Rick Barry, Oakland	1190	34.0
Connie Hawkins, Minnesota	1420	30.2
Larry Jones, Denver	2133	28.4
Jim Jones, New Orleans	2050	26.6
Louie Dampier, Kentucky	1933	24.8

TOP REBOUNDERS

	No.	Ave.
Mel Daniels, Indiana	1256	16.5
Red Robbins, New Orleans	1024	13.5
Skip Thoren, Miami	1046	13.4
Tom Washington, Minnesota	868	12.6
Connie Hawkins, Minnesota	534	11.4

LEADERS IN ASSISTS

	No.	Ave.
Larry Brown, Oakland	544	7.1
Don Freeman, Miami	501	6.4
Louie Dampier, Kentucky	456	5.8
Jim Jones, New Orleans	437	5.7
Roger Brown, Indiana	345	4.6
Steve Chubin, New York	354	4.6

1969-70

The ABA suffered its worst defeat in three years even before the season began. The league failed to sign Lew Alcindor, the greatest big man headed for the pros in years. He could have been an early savior for a league starving for attention.

Alcindor's rights were given to the New York Nets (because the seven-foot-plus center had grown up in the city, and the league badly needed a hype in its prime market). Alcindor, who had carried UCLA to three straight collegiate championships, said he would accept one sealed bid from each league. By winning a coin toss, Milwaukee naturally picked him in the NBA. Although all the ABA franchises were to share in the cost of Alcindor's contract and had agreed to an incredible offer, Nets' owner Art Brown and commissioner George Mikan submitted a lower bid. When Alcindor said Milwaukee's was the higher, the ABA representatives rushed back with a better deal, but Alcindor stuck to his prearranged promise. The ABA failed, and years later when executive assistant Thurlo McCrady retired, he hung onto the sole reminder of the episode—a worthless cashier's check made out to Alcindor for $1 million.

Alcindor—who later changed his name to Kareem Abdul-Jabbar—became a one-man wrecking crew in

Denver phenom Spencer Haywood led the league in scoring and rebounding, and won Rookie of the Year and MVP honors.

the NBA, and Mikan came to his end in professional basketball. He resigned, and Jim Gardner became head of the league as president.

Meanwhile, Connie Hawkins, one of the few genuine ABA stars, jumped to Phoenix of the NBA. The Oakland Oaks went under and were purchased by Earl Foreman, who moved the club to Washington. Coach Alex Hannum resigned, and Rick Barry announced he didn't want to leave the West Coast. He signed a new contract with his former team, Golden State, but was forced to remain in the ABA while the legal entanglements were argued for years.

The ABA was teetering on the brink of extinction again. The Houston Mavericks had finally given up and shifted to Carolina (as a regional franchise), and

the Minnesota Pipers returned from whence they came, Pittsburgh.

Amid the negatives, a few positives did suddenly surface. The Denver Rockets signed Spencer Haywood, who had played only two years of college ball, but was considered a blooming superstar. His signing established a new mood in the ABA. The league, from then on, would feel free to sign any player no matter how much college eligibility remained. The Los Angeles Stars had gotten Zelmo Beaty, a good NBA center, to agree to a contract that would take effect in two seasons. The Nets were sold to millionaire clothier Roy Boe, who promised to push for a new Long Island arena, and fresh capital, from somewhere, was being pumped into other teams.

Shortly into the season Jack Dolph was hired as commissioner. He came from the CBS Television Network, where he had been an executive in sports, and the ABA's goal, a major national TV package, was no secret.

On the court the Indiana Pacers were dominant, winning 59 games while losing just 25. Denver, behind young Haywood, rallied from a poor beginning—at just about the juncture Joe Belmont took over as coach—to finish first in the West with a 51-33 mark. The All-Star Game returned to Indianapolis, drew 11,000-plus and was televised to a nationwide audience which saw Haywood drive off with the MVP automobile as the West made it two in a row, 128-98. The game almost didn't come off. A threatened strike by the ABA Players' Association, which was seeking recognition by the league, was averted less than an hour before game time.

Attendance in the league took a jump to 1.75 million, with an average that climbed 1,000 over the previous season to 3,950. Indiana went past the 380,000 mark after drawing 58,000 in the playoffs.

Indiana swept past Carolina and Kentucky in Eastern Division postseason play, losing but one game, while Denver and Los Angeles (which had been taken over by the league after funds ran out) met in the Western finals. The Stars—who had placed fourth in the division during the regular season—came on strong to beat the Rockets. The Stars' coach was Bill Sharman, who would become a Hall of Famer after being all-league in the NBA and coaching in three different pro leagues (NBA, ABA and the defunct American Basketball League).

Although forced to play two of their home contests

in the championship series at Anaheim, the Stars carried the Pacers to six games before finally fading, 111-107.

Haywood, 6-10 and with talent to burn, averaged 30 points and 19.5 rebounds and was voted both Rookie of the Year and MVP. He was joined on the all-league team by Barry, Mel Daniels, Bob Verga and Larry Jones.

The competition in the ABA was still not close to the equal of the NBA, but it was coming. Franchises in Indiana, Kentucky, New York and Denver (which had 23 sellouts in a 7,000-seat building) were getting stronger, and attempts were already being made at season's end to improve the others soon.

1969-70

STANDINGS

Eastern Division

	W.	L.	Pct.
Indiana	59	25	.702
Kentucky	45	39	.536
Carolina	42	42	.500
New York	39	45	.464
Pittsburgh	29	55	.345
Miami	23	61	.274

Western Division

	W.	L.	Pct.
Denver	51	33	.607
Dallas	45	39	.536
Washington	44	40	.524
Los Angeles	43	41	.512
New Orleans	42	42	.500

Eastern Division Semifinal Series

April 18—Indiana 123, Carolina 105
April 19—Indiana 103, Carolina 98
April 22—Indiana 117, Carolina 106
April 24—Indiana 110, Carolina 106

April 17—New York 122, Kentucky 118 (OT)
April 18—Kentucky 113, New York 111
April 19—New York 107, Kentucky 99
April 22—Kentucky 128, New York 101
April 26—New York 127, Kentucky 112
April 28—Kentucky 116, New York 113
April 29—Kentucky 112, New York 101

Eastern Division Final Series

May 1—Kentucky 114, Indiana 110
May 2—Indiana 121, Kentucky 110
May 3—Indiana 114, Kentucky 110
May 5—Indiana 111, Kentucky 103
May 6—Indiana 117, Kentucky 103

Western Division Semifinal Series

April 17—Denver 130, Washington 111
April 18—Denver 143, Washington 135
April 19—Washington 125, Denver 120
April 22—Washington 131, Denver 114
April 23—Denver 132, Washington 110
April 25—Washington 116, Denver 111
April 28—Denver 143, Washington 119

April 17—Los Angeles 115, Dallas 103
April 18—Dallas 129, Los Angeles 121
April 20—Dallas 116, Los Angeles 104
April 22—Los Angeles 144, Dallas 138
April 24—Los Angeles 146, Dallas 139
April 26—Los Angeles 124, Dallas 123

Western Division Final Series

April 30—Denver 123, Los Angeles 113 (OT)
May 1—Los Angeles 114, Denver 105
May 4—Los Angeles 119, Denver 113
May 5—Los Angeles 114, Denver 110
May 9—Los Angeles 109, Denver 107

Championship Series

May 15—Indiana 109, Los Angeles 93
May 17—Indiana 114, Los Angeles 111
May 18—Los Angeles 109, Indiana 106
May 23—Los Angeles 117, Indiana 113
May 25—Indiana 111, Los Angeles 107

TOP SCORERS

	Pts.	Ave.
Spencer Haywood, Denver	2519	30.0
Rick Barry, Washington	1442	27.7
Bob Verga, Carolina	2258	27.5
Don Freeman, Miami	2163	27.4
Louie Dampier, Kentucky	2125	25.9

TOP REBOUNDERS

	No.	Ave.
Spencer Haywood, Denver	1637	19.5
Mel Daniels, Indiana	1462	17.6
Red Robbins, New Orleans	1332	16.2
Gerald Govan, New Orleans	1217	14.5
Ira Harge, Washington	1177	14.0

LEADERS IN ASSISTS

	No.	Ave.
Larry Brown, Washington	580	7.1
Bill Melchionni, New York	457	5.7
Mack Calvin, Los Angeles	478	5.7
Larry Jones, Denver	426	5.7
Louie Dampier, Kentucky	447	5.5

1970-71

The ABA finally managed a miniscule TV alignment with CBS (calling for six games a season and few

Rick Barry was traded to the New York Nets, giving the league a big name in the Big Apple for the first time.

dollars); it moved franchises to new bases (New Orleans to Memphis, Los Angeles to Salt Lake City, Washington to Virginia as a regional franchise, and both the Floridians and the Dallas—nee Texas—Chapparrals became regional teams), and it brought in the best crop of rookies thus far.

While the league was giving up some of its biggest markets, choosing to go into untapped areas, it finally made a financial commitment to compete heavily against the NBA for collegiate stars.

Dan Issel of the University of Kentucky signed with the home-state Kentucky Colonels, and Purdue guard Rick Mount stayed in Indiana with the Pacers. Charlie Scott went to Virginia, Jim Ard to New York, and Ralph Simpson came out of college early to join his friend Spencer Haywood at Denver. After Rick Barry made disparaging remarks about his children being raised with Southern accents in Virginia (he did it to force a trade), he was sent to the Nets, and the league finally had a big-name performer in its biggest town.

The ABA stole four of the NBA's finest referees—Norm Drucker, Joe Gushue, John Vanak and Earl Strom. Alex Hannum returned as coach and general manager at Denver; Atlanta's Joe Caldwell leaped to Carolina for $225,000 a year, and Zelmo Beaty was in Salt Lake City awaiting the end of his option year so he could play with the Stars. Big salaries also had been offered to NBA stickouts such as John Havlicek and Billy Cunningham. The NBA was forced to sit up and take notice of its rival, at last. The NBA had been hoping the ABA would give up and go away. Indications were that it wouldn't.

In fact, NBA owners voted favorably to seek a merger approval in Congress. However, Washington legislators were slow to act, and the issue died down.

As always, the ABA had its diverse ups and downs. The owner of the new Memphis franchise pulled out after only two months of operation. Yet, to the positive, 6,500 Memphians purchased $750,000 in stock at $5 a share) to keep the team going until new owners could be found. Haywood, the sensation a year before, had contractual disputes with the Denver owner and bolted—eventually signing with Seattle of the NBA. The ABA took a doubleheader to Madison Square Garden—appearing in the showcase spot of basketball for the first time—and drew 12,500 while giving out the league's top promotional item—the multicolored ball.

The All-Star Game in Greensboro drew a record 14,407 and was on national television that Saturday afternoon. But the game became secondary when a reporter discovered Commissioner Dolph's opened briefcase and happened upon league contracts signed by seven-foot center Jim McDaniels and Howard Porter, both All-Americans whose collegiate seasons weren't over. Their colleges were penalized; Mc-Daniels came to the ABA the next year, and Porter had his contract voided and went into the NBA.

The All-Star Game itself was settled in the final minute when Barry scored four points for the East in a come-from-behind upset, 126-122. Indiana's Mel Daniels was MVP, marking the fourth straight year that a member of the West All-Stars had won that distinction.

The regular season produced a few interesting battles. Barry and Issel fought for the scoring leadership, with the rookie center emerging ahead with a 29.9 average to Barry's 29.4. Virginia, behind first-year guard Scott, glided to the Eastern Division crown, while Indiana and Utah, developing a spirited rivalry, were nip-and-tuck all year. The Pacers, with a 58-26 record, finished one game ahead. In the playoffs Utah and Indiana cast aside opponents to meet in the Western finals, and Virginia was bumped off by Kentucky in the Eastern finals. Utah bested Indiana, four games to three, advancing against Kentucky with a 108-101 triumph in Indianapolis before a full house. The Utah-Kentucky series also went the complete distance, with the Stars winning, 131-121, in the finale.

Attendance climbed past the two-million mark for the first time in the league's history, and five teams, with playoff crowds included, ended up with at least 200,000. Nobody drew under 100,000, which was a first, of sorts.

The ABA was still not on solid ground, but it had made strides in 1970-71 and was beginning to act major league.

1970-71

STANDINGS

Eastern Division

	W.	L.	Pct.
Virginia	55	29	.655
Kentucky	44	40	.524
New York	40	44	.476
Floridians	37	47	.440
Pittsburgh	36	48	.429
Carolina	34	50	.405

Western Division

	W.	L.	Pct.
Indiana	58	26	.690
Utah	57	27	.679
Memphis	41	43	.488
Texas	30	54	.357
Denver	30	54	.357

Eastern Division Semifinal Series

April 2—Kentucky 116, Floridians 112
April 4—Kentucky 120, Floridians 110
April 6—Floridians 120, Kentucky 102
April 8—Floridians 129, Kentucky 117
April 10—Kentucky 118, Floridians 101
April 12—Kentucky 112, Floridians 103

April 2—Virginia 113, New York 105
April 4—Virginia 114, New York 108
April 6—New York 135, Virginia 131
April 7—New York 130, Virginia 127
April 9—Virginia 127, New York 124
April 10—Virginia 118, New York 114

Eastern Division Final Series

April 15—Kentucky 136, Virginia 132
April 17—Virginia 142, Kentucky 122
April 19—Virginia 150, Kentucky 137
April 21—Kentucky 128, Virginia 110
April 23—Kentucky 115, Virginia 107
April 24—Kentucky 129, Virginia 117

Western Division Semifinal Series

April 2—Indiana 114, Memphis 98
April 3—Indiana 106, Memphis 104
April 5—Indiana 91, Memphis 90
April 7—Indiana 102, Memphis 101

April 2—Utah 125, Texas 115
April 3—Utah 137, Texas 107
April 4—Utah 113, Texas 101
April 6—Utah 128, Texas 107

Western Division Final Series

April 12—Utah 120, Indiana 118
April 14—Indiana 120, Utah 107
April 17—Utah 121, Indiana 108
April 20—Utah 126, Indiana 99
April 22—Indiana 127, Utah 109
April 24—Indiana 105, Utah 102
April 28—Utah 108, Indiana 101

Championship Series

May 3—Utah 136, Kentucky 117
May 5—Utah 138, Kentucky 125
May 7—Kentucky 116, Utah 110
May 8—Kentucky 129, Utah 125 (OT)
May 12—Utah 137, Kentucky 127
May 15—Kentucky 105, Utah 102
May 18—Utah 131, Kentucky 121

TOP SCORERS

	Pts.	Ave.
Dan Issel, Kentucky	2480	29.9
Rick Barry, New York	1734	29.4
John Brisker, Pittsburgh	2315	29.3
Mack Calvin, Floridians	2201	27.2
Charlie Scott, Virginia	2276	27.1

TOP REBOUNDERS

	No.	Ave.
Mel Daniels, Indiana	1475	18.0
Julius Keye, Denver	1454	17.5
Zelmo Beaty, Utah	1190	15.7
Mike Lewis, Pittsburgh	1213	14.6
Gerald Govan, Memphis	1138	13.6

LEADERS IN ASSISTS

	No.	Ave.
Bill Melchionni, New York	672	8.3
Mack Calvin, Floridians	619	7.6
Jim Jones, Memphis	468	5.9
Charlie Scott, Virginia	472	5.6
George Lehmann, Carolina	464	5.6

1971-72

The oddest aspect at the outset of the ABA's fifth season was that all 11 franchises remained in the same places they were the year before.

Plus, the ABA owners became downright loose with their money—readily giving million-dollar-type contracts to such people as 7-2 center Artis Gilmore (Kentucky), Johnny Neumann (Memphis), John Roche (New York), Jim McDaniels (Carolina), Collis Jones (Dallas) and a few assorted others. However, two of the assorted others, with the least accompanying publicity, would have more impact on the ABA and pro basketball as a whole than anyone before their careers in the league were out.

Julius Erving, nicknamed "Dr. J," joined the Virginia Squires after the New York Nets decided (as they would later regret) not to tamper with college undergraduates. Erving had spent two seasons with the University of Massachusetts and was an unknown talent. Even though he was signed to a lucrative pact, neither the owner, the coach and the general manager of the Squires nor his own agent, Bob Woolf, had ever seen Erving play.

They would.

Indiana convinced George McGinnis, called "The Baby Bull," to drop out of Indiana University two years early, and even though he had averaged 28 points a game for the Hoosiers, he was still unknown.

He wouldn't be for long.

Erving quickly became noted as a wizard with a basketball, able to perform aerial acts never before witnessed. The 6-8 McGinnis, some believed, was one of the strongest players ever, but with the finesse of a guard.

With that dynamic duo and the other young players being groomed by the ABA, the league was attracting attention because it had the stars of tomorrow while many of the superheroes of the NBA were retiring or thinking seriously about it.

The two leagues were still attempting—with the NBA serious at times and hesitant at others—to get merger off dead-center, and exhibitions were arranged between the ABA and the NBA for the first time. The Kentucky Colonels met and lost to the Milwaukee Bucks and the New York Knicks during one weekend, but were close enough to establish respect among the opponents.

The Colonels were considered the class of the ABA after luring Gilmore and moving scoring champ Dan Issel to forward. Veteran college and pro coach Joe Mullaney was brought in as overseer. As expected, Kentucky went off and hid from the rest of the Eastern Division teams—finishing with a league record 68 victories (against just 18 setbacks) and placing ahead of Virginia, the runner-up, by a whopping 23 games. In the West it was Utah and Indiana once again, but the Stars were regular-season titlists by a rather lengthy 13 games. At the other end of the spectrum were Pittsburgh and Memphis. The Condors were 43 games back in the East, Memphis 34 in the West. One night those two teams played after a pregame exhibition bout featuring Muhammad Ali. When he left the arena, more than half the crowd of 5,000 left with him.

The midseason All-Star Game revealed how far the league had progressed since the previous time the game was held in Louisville. Attendance was up to 15,738 (as compared to 5,407 before), and Issel won the MVP trophy by one vote over Jim McDaniels as the East overwhelmed the West, 142-115.

A few days later McDaniels pulled a disappearing act and wound up in Seattle. Before season's end, Charlie Scott, the ABA's top scorer, jumped to Phoenix, and Erving was threatening to leave.

The Pittsburgh, Miami, Memphis and Dallas franchises were having severe problems, but the ABA, nevertheless, went into the playoffs with spirits high. They sank rapidly for the strong Colonels, who were ousted in the first round by surprising New York (and Rick Barry). The Nets went on to face the Indiana Pacers, who had defeated Utah in the West. Under coach Bobby Leonard, Indiana became the first two-time titlist in league history. However, New York

![Artis Gilmore receiving jersey]

Artis Gilmore gets Kentucky Colonels' jersey from team president Mike Storen. The 7–2 center filled it well, leading Kentucky to a league-record 68 victories.

The Doctor, Julius Erving, began operations with the Virginia Squires.

had moved into a new arena at last—Nassau Coliseum—after playing in the depressing, bowling alley-like atmosphere of Island Garden and averaged more than 12,000 for the playoffs. Two games with Indiana drew 15,000-plus, and the six games were played in front of 70,000—a high-water mark for the league. Plus, New York had announced the signing of Marquette's All-American center, Jim Chones.

Commissioner Jack Dolph was talking merger, and the ABA was talking about its newest collegiate target, the center who had taken Lew Alcindor's place at UCLA and filled the shoes well. Bill Walton was the name.

1971-72

STANDINGS

Eastern Division

	W.	L.	Pct.
Kentucky	68	16	.810
Virginia	45	39	.536
New York	44	40	.524
Floridians	36	48	.429
Carolina	35	49	.417
Pittsburgh	25	59	.298

Western Division

	W.	L.	Pct.
Utah	60	24	.714
Indiana	47	37	.560
Dallas	42	42	.500
Denver	34	50	.405
Memphis	26	58	.310

Eastern Division Semifinal Series

April 1—New York 122, Kentucky 108
April 4—New York 105, Kentucky 90
April 5—Kentucky 105, New York 99
April 7—New York 100, Kentucky 92
April 8—Kentucky 109, New York 103
April 10—New York 101, Kentucky 96

March 31—Virginia 114, Floridians 107 (OT)
April 1—Virginia 125, Floridians 100
April 4—Virginia 118, Floridians 113
April 6—Virginia 115, Floridians 106

Eastern Division Final Series

April 13—Virginia 138, New York 91
April 15—Virginia 115, New York 106
April 24—New York 119, Virginia 117
April 26—New York 118, Virginia 107
April 29—Virginia 116, New York 107
May 1—New York 146, Virginia 136
May 4—New York 94, Virginia 88

Western Division Semifinal Series

April 1—Utah 106, Dallas 96
April 3—Utah 113, Dallas 107
April 5—Utah 96, Dallas 89
April 7—Utah 103, Dallas 99

March 31—Indiana 102, Denver 95
April 1—Denver 106, Indiana 105
April 4—Indiana 122, Denver 120 (OT)
April 6—Denver 112, Indiana 105
April 8—Indiana 91, Denver 79
April 9—Denver 106, Indiana 99
April 13—Indiana 91, Denver 89

Western Division Final Series

April 15—Utah 108, Indiana 100
April 17—Utah 117, Indiana 109
April 19—Indiana 116, Utah 111
April 22—Indiana 118, Utah 108
April 24—Utah 139, Indiana 130
April 26—Indiana 105, Utah 99
May 1—Indiana 117, Utah 113

Championship Series

May 6—Indiana 124, New York 103
May 9—New York 117, Indiana 115
May 12—Indiana 114, New York 108
May 15—New York 110, Indiana 105
May 18—Indiana 100, New York 99
May 20—Indiana 108, New York 105

TOP SCORERS

	Pts.	Ave.
Charlie Scott, Virginia	2524	34.6
Rick Barry, New York	2518	31.5
Dan Issel, Kentucky	2538	30.6
John Brisker, Pittsburgh	1417	28.9
Ralph Simpson, Denver	2300	27.4

TOP REBOUNDERS

	No.	Ave.
Artis Gilmore, Kentucky	1491	17.6
Mel Daniels, Indiana	1297	16.4
Julius Erving, Virginia	1319	15.7
Gerald Govan, Memphis	1182	14.2
Jim McDaniels, Carolina	814	14.0

LEADERS IN ASSISTS

	No.	Ave.
Bill Melchionni, New York	669	8.4
George Lehmann, Memphis	411	7.8
Larry Brown, Denver	549	7.2
Jim Jones, Utah	485	6.2
Louie Dampier, Kentucky	515	6.2

1972-73

The ABA went through an exchange process in 1972-73—exchanging two weak franchises for another weak franchise, one star for another, one commissioner for another.

But one thing was constant—the Indiana Pacers.

For the second year in a row, and the third time in six years, the Pacers took the league championship.

But, first, a few other developments occurred. The league felt the proper method to solve some of the franchise problems was to eliminate them—the franchises. So Pittsburgh and Miami, which had never been very successful at the gate or on the floor, were struck from the league, and their players were dispersed among the remaining nine teams. Soon after, a rich San Diego dentist, Leonard Bloom, petitioned the league for a franchise in his city (which had lost an NBA team to Houston, which, oddly enough, was an old ABA city) and was accepted.

The San Diego Conquistadors ended up with a bunch of marginal players, but had an aggressive coach in K.C. Jones, the former Boston Celtic guard, and finished credibly enough in fourth place in the West with a 30-54 mark. However, when negotiations to play in the spacious San Diego Sports Arena fell through, the club was forced into the 3,200-seat San Diego State gymnasium.

The Memphis franchise, meanwhile, was saved from sudden death when the Oakland A's controversial owner, Charles O. Finley, stepped in with cash at the last moment. He now owned teams in three sports—baseball, hockey (Golden Seals) and basketball (Memphis Tams). He named Bob Bass (late of Denver and Miami) as coach and brought 28 players through town during the season. Still, Finley's gimmickry wasn't enough to swing the franchise around.

Dallas continued, as always, to struggle. Toward the end of the season a New Jersey group agreed to buy the team, and coach Babe McCarthy departed for a college job. Whatever crowds there had been vanished, and the club finished a dismal last. Then the New Jersey deal fell through.

Most of the other teams were doing fairly well, though.

Utah and Indiana carried on their annual West Division chase, and Carolina and Kentucky battled for first in the East. Carolina had a new player in Billy Cunningham, who had dropped in from the NBA, and a new coach in Larry Brown, the little guard who had played in the ABA five years.

However, the ABA finally lost Rick Barry, who had become comfortable in New York, but was forced by a court decision to return to Golden State. Jack Dolph stepped down as commissioner, failing to provide the major TV contract or merger with the elder circuit. His replacement was Robert Carlson, who had been the Nets' counsel and was working in behalf of the league toward merger.

The caliber of play was on the incline significantly, as exemplified by the fact that the Kentucky Colonels,

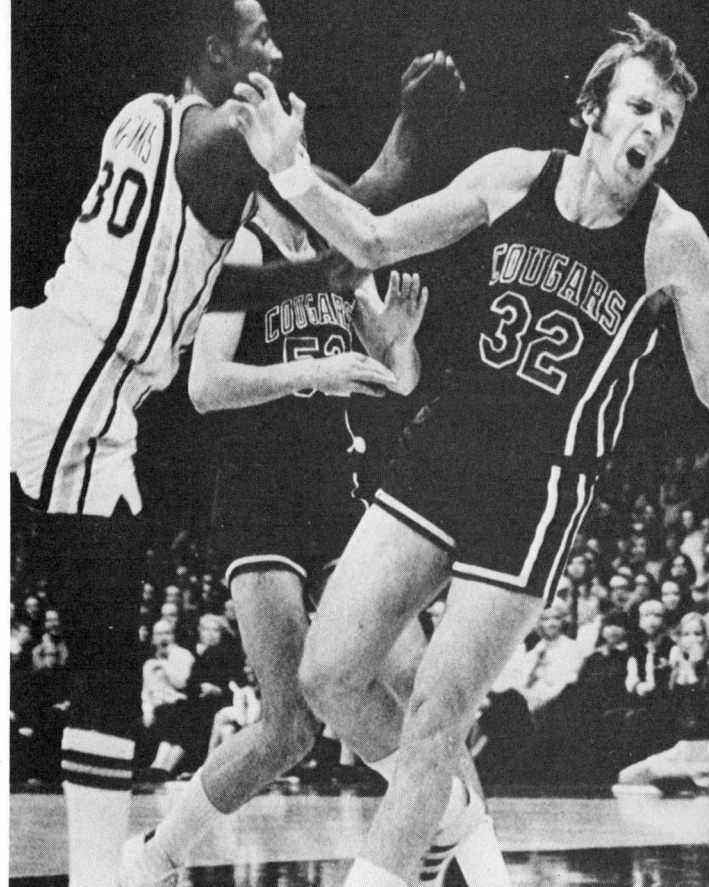

NBA refugee Billy Cunningham of Carolina won MVP honors, but George McGinnis (left) led Indiana to its second straight league crown.

who had won 68 games the previous season, fell to 57 in 1972-73 despite being a better team. The Colonels dropped to second, one game behind Carolina, and Cunningham, the Kangaroo Kid, was named the league's MVP with a 24.1 average, fourth to Julius Erving of Virginia at 32 per game. Utah ended up four games ahead of Indiana in the West.

Indiana, however, reached the championship finals against the Colonels, and packed arenas in both nearby cities were the norm. The series was extended to a full seven games—with Indiana taking the opener in Kentucky before dropping the next two. Indiana tied the series at 2-2, and it was still knotted two games later. The Pacers had to take the championship the hard way, winning on a foreign floor, 88-81, before 16,597 in Freedom Hall.

The all-league first and second teams were the strongest ever—with Cunningham and Erving at forwards, Artis Gilmore at center and James Jones and Warren Jabali at guards on the first five, with George McGinnis and Dan Issel at forwards, Mel Daniels the center and Ralph Simpson and Mack Calvin at guards on the second team. Jabali (formerly Warren Armstrong) was named the MVP in the All-Star Game with a super second-half performance that enabled the West to top the East, 123-111, before a sellout crowd at Utah's Salt Palace.

The ABA was fortunate to still have Erving around. He had jumped to the Atlanta Hawks before the season began, but a court order forced his return to Virginia four games into the season.

Merger remained foremost in the minds of the ABA owners, who were continuing to lose millions because of climbing salaries. Overall, though, 1972-73 was a quiet season in the ABA, one without major trauma.

1972-73

STANDINGS

Eastern Division

	W.	L.	Pct.
Carolina	57	27	.679
Kentucky	56	28	.667
Virginia	42	42	.500
New York	30	54	.357
Memphis	24	60	.286

Western Division

	W.	L.	Pct.
Utah	55	29	.655
Indiana	51	33	.607
Denver	47	37	.560
San Diego	30	54	.357
Dallas	28	56	.333

Eastern Division Semifinal Series

March 30—Carolina 104, New York 96
March 31—New York 114, Carolina 111
April 3—Carolina 101, New York 91
April 5—Carolina 112, New York 108
April 6—Carolina 136, New York 113

March 30—Kentucky 129, Virginia 101
April 1—Virginia 109, Kentucky 94
April 3—Kentucky 115, Virginia 113
April 6—Kentucky 108, Virginia 90
April 7—Kentucky 114, Virginia 93

Eastern Division Final Series

April 11—Kentucky 113, Carolina 103
April 14—Carolina 125, Kentucky 105
April 16—Kentucky 108, Carolina 94
April 18—Carolina 102, Kentucky 91
April 20—Carolina 112, Kentucky 107
April 21—Kentucky 119, Carolina 100
April 24—Kentucky 107, Carolina 96

Western Division Semifinal Series

April 2—Utah 107, San Diego 93
April 4—Utah 103, San Diego 92
April 7—Utah 97, San Diego 96
April 8—Utah 120, San Diego 98

March 31—Indiana 114, Denver 91
April 1—Indiana 106, Denver 93
April 3—Denver 105, Indiana 94
April 5—Indiana 97, Denver 95
April 7—Indiana 121, Denver 107

Western Division Final Series

April 12—Utah 124, Indiana 107
April 14—Indiana 116, Utah 110
April 16—Indiana 118, Utah 108
April 18—Utah 104, Indiana 103
April 19—Indiana 104, Utah 102
April 21—Indiana 107, Utah 98

Championship Series

April 28—Indiana 111, Kentucky 107
April 30—Kentucky 114, Indiana 102
May 3—Kentucky 92, Indiana 88
May 5—Indiana 90, Kentucky 86
May 8—Indiana 89, Kentucky 86
May 10—Kentucky 109, Indiana 93
May 12—Indiana 88, Kentucky 81

TOP SCORERS

	Pts.	Ave.
Julius Erving, Virginia	2268	31.9
George McGinnis, Indiana	2261	27.6
Dan Issel, Kentucky	2292	27.3
Billy Cunningham, Carolina	2028	24.1
Ralph Simpson, Denver	1890	23.3

TOP REBOUNDERS

	No.	Ave.
Artis Gilmore, Kentucky	1476	17.5
Mel Daniels, Indiana	1247	15.4
Billy Paultz, New York	1015	12.5
George McGinnis, Indiana	1022	12.4
Randy Denton, Memphis	820	12.4

LEADERS IN ASSISTS

	No.	Ave.
Billy Melchionni, New York	453	7.5
Chuck Williams, San Diego	582	7.0
Warren Jabali, Denver	539	6.6
Louie Dampier, Kentucky	521	6.5
Billy Cunningham, Carolina	530	6.3

1973-74

In 1973 Julius Erving moved his aerial act to New York, and the ABA, as a result, moved to great heights itself.

The league had failed miserably in attempts to sign the two biggest stars of its seven-year era—UCLA centers Lew Alcindor (Kareem Abdul-Jabbar) and Bill Walton—but it had developed one of its own in Erving, the fabulous Dr. J. However, Erving had been playing in Virginia, not a media mecca, and was attempting to leap to the NBA. In one fell swoop, the ABA prevented the departure of Erving and placed him in the spotlight. The New York Nets purchased Erving from the Squires, paid off the Atlanta Hawks (who had his future contract rights) and presented him to the press of New York. Not since Joe Namath had signed with New York in the old American Football League had so much attention been focused on a "second" league.

Erving paid royal dividends to the Nets, catapulting them to their first ABA championship.

However, prior to that accomplishment, the league went through more of the ever-present changes. Mike Storen was hired as commissioner, replacing Robert Carlson, who had not succeeded in getting merger passed through Congress. Storen had, as general manager, built the Indiana and Kentucky franchises into perennial contenders. The Colonels' franchise became the first to be owned by a woman, Ellie Brown, wife of chicken entrepreneur John Y. Brown. The San Diego Conquistadors shifted from one small home to another (still unable to gain a contract for the Sports Arena), and the Dallas franchise finally gave up and surfaced in San Antonio.

The league signed five first-round selections, pulled two more established referees from the NBA and attracted possibly the biggest name (if not body) in basketball—Wilt Chamberlain—to San Diego. Because of an option year in his NBA contract, Chamberlain was unable to play for the Conquistadors, but did coach the team.

In addition to Erving, the Nets took on rookies Larry Kenon and John Williamson, both college dropouts who would step into starting roles. To show which direction the ABA had taken, not a one of the five Nets' starters had completed his college eligibility. Erving had come out of Massachusetts after his sophomore year, and the other two—guard Brian

Julius Erving hooked on with the Nets and led them to their first title, winning the scoring crown and MVP honors along the way.

Taylor and center Billy Paultz—had bypassed senior seasons. Kevin Loughery, long-time guard in the NBA, was brought in to guide the young troop.

Despite the presence of powerful Kentucky, the Nets racked up a 55-29 record and won the Eastern Division by two games. Carolina was third, Virginia fourth and annual tail-ender Memphis fifth.

In the West the skirmish revolved around Utah and Indiana, as usual. The Stars, at 51-33, beat the Pacers by five games, followed by San Antonio. Denver and San Diego tied for fourth with identical 37-47 records, and the Conquistadors, behind rookie coach Chamberlain, won the special one-game playoff in Denver.

Possibly the most pleasant surprise of the season,

Wilt Chamberlain was unable to play for the San Diego Conquistadors, but he did coach them to a playoff berth.

though, was San Antonio. The city had never possessed a major-league franchise, and the people came out in droves to watch an exciting club. Eventually, the men who had brought the club in on a unique two-year basis would purchase the franchise outright because of the early success.

Erving ended the season as the top scorer, 27.4, and MVP, and George McGinnis was next at 25.9.

New York and Erving took Virginia in five playoff games, then wiped out Kentucky in four in a row and awaited the Western Division representative. This season it was Utah, but the Stars were not much of a challenge for the Nets. New York won the first three, lost by eight points in Salt Lake City and then completed a whirlwind season with a 111-100 triumph at Nassau Coliseum, watched by 15,935.

In the All-Star Game, played at Norfolk, the Kentucky combination of Artis Gilmore, MVP, and Dan Issel led the East's 128-112 victory over the West and its outstanding rookie, San Antonio's Swen Nater.

Erving, McGinnis, Gilmore, Jimmy Jones and Mack Calvin were named to the all-league team. And, just as before, the ABA had both satisfying moments and disappointments. San Diego, even with Chamberlain, was a losing proposition. Charles O. Finley

had made a shambles out of the Memphis franchise. Virginia owner Earl Foreman—who had sold Rick Barry and Julius Erving, and lost Charlie Scott to the NBA previously—had kept up his fire sale by sending the two remaining stickouts on the roster, Nater and George Gervin, to San Antonio for cash. Stars' owner Bill Daniels wanted out, and Carolina was suffering in attendance.

But, at least, Julius Erving had made things all right in New York. Some players are referred to as the franchise. He was beginning to be called the league.

1973-74

STANDINGS

Eastern Division

	W.	L.	Pct.
New York	55	29	.655
Kentucky	53	31	.631
Carolina	47	37	.560
Virginia	28	56	.333
Memphis	21	63	.250

Western Division

	W.	L.	Pct.
Utah	51	33	.607
Indiana	46	38	.548
San Antonio	45	39	.536
Denver	37	47	.440
San Diego	37	47	.440

Eastern Division Semifinal Series

March 29—New York 108, Virginia 96
April 1—New York 129, Virginia 110
April 4—Virginia 116, New York 115
April 7—New York 116, Virginia 88
April 8—New York 108, Virginia 96

April 1—Kentucky 118, Carolina 102
April 5—Kentucky 99, Carolina 96
April 6—Kentucky 120, Carolina 110
April 8—Kentucky 128, Carolina 119

Eastern Division Final Series

April 13—New York 119, Kentucky 106
April 15—New York 99, Kentucky 80
April 17—New York 89, Kentucky 87
April 20—New York 103, Kentucky 90

Western Division Semifinal Series

March 30—Utah 114, San Diego 99
April 1—Utah 119, San Diego 105
April 3—San Diego 97, Utah 96
April 4—San Diego 100, Utah 98
April 6—Utah 100, San Diego 93
April 8—Utah 110, San Diego 99

March 30—San Antonio 113, Indiana 109
April 1—Indiana 128, San Antonio 101
April 3—San Antonio 115, Indiana 96
April 4—Indiana 91, San Antonio 89
April 6—Indiana 105, San Antonio 100
April 10—San Antonio 102, Indiana 86
April 12—Indiana 97, San Antonio 86

Western Division Final Series

April 13—Utah 105, Indiana 96
April 15—Utah 106, Indiana 102
April 17—Utah 99, Indiana 90
April 18—Indiana 118, Utah 107
April 22—Indiana 110, Utah 101
April 25—Indiana 91, Utah 89
April 27—Utah 109, Indiana 87

Championship Series

April 30—New York 89, Utah 85
May 4—New York 118, Utah 94
May 6—New York 103, Utah 100 (OT)
May 8—Utah 97, New York 89
May 10—New York 111, Utah 100

TOP SCORERS

	Pts.	Ave.
Julius Erving, New York	2299	27.4
George McGinnis, Indiana	2071	25.9
Dan Issel, Kentucky	2118	25.5
George Gervin, San Antonio	1730	23.4
Willie Wise, Utah	1826	22.3

TOP REBOUNDERS

	No.	Ave.
Artis Gilmore, Kentucky	1538	18.3
George McGinnis, Indiana	1187	15.0
Caldwell Jones, San Diego	1095	13.9
Swen Nater, San Antonio	998	12.6
Mel Daniels, Indiana	885	11.6

LEADERS IN ASSISTS

	No.	Ave.
Al Smith, Denver	619	8.2
Chuck Williams, Kentucky	557	6.2
Louie Dampier, Kentucky	473	5.6
Roland Taylor, Virginia	416	5.2
James Jones, Utah	429	5.2

1974-75

The ABA's eighth season was purely a case of same song, new verse. More viable young players were being signed to outrageous contracts, and the league was on the incline in play, attendance and credibility. But franchises were still having problems; another new commissioner was named, and merger was the only sane answer, according to the league owners who had gotten themselves into the mess.

They had hoped during the summer of 1973 that the NBA would finally seriously consider the proposition, but ABA trustees sat in a day-long session in Louisville awaiting a telephone call that never came from the NBA meetings.

In Virginia, Earl Foreman sold out to a group of businessmen, who called the team the New Virginia Squires. But it was the same old team, failing to get big crowds or big results on the court. Carolina owner Tedd Munchak sold his team to a group of New Yorkers, who transferred the franchise to St. Louis (a former NBA town), and Charles O. Finley sold his Memphis team to a group headed by ABA commissioner Mike Storen, who stepped down. Ironically, Munchak became sort of a commissioner-in-waiting (waiting for someone else to take over). Carl Scheer, Carolina's general manager, went to Denver,

Moses Malone, fresh out of high school, averaged 18.8 points and 14.6 rebounds for Utah, Artis Gilmore, defending here against Malone, helped Kentucky win title.

taking with him coach Larry Brown. Between the two, the franchise was revitalized on and off the floor. San Diego still had troubles, particularly after Chamberlain declined to return. Indiana did move into a new building (17,000) and the other franchises were solid for the moment.

The most prominent announcement by the league was the signing of high school player Moses Malone by the Utah Stars. Players had left college to join the ABA, but none had ever totally bypassed college before. The 6-11 Malone proved he could make the transition, averaging 18.8 points and 14.6 rebounds. St. Louis also pulled off a tidy coup, signing the

NBA's second choice, All-American Marvin Barnes, and two other solid young players, Gus Gerard and Maurice Lucas (dropouts). Billy Knight, Bobby Jones, Len Elmore and Jan van Breda Kolff (son of Butch van Breda Kolff, who coached in both leagues) also sided with the ABA.

The rebuilt Denver team (called the Nuggets) played before nothing but SRO crowds and raced to 65 victories while losing only 19 to top San Antonio by 14 games in the West. Utah and Indiana, kingpins of the past, dropped considerably. And San Diego brought up the rear.

Kentucky and New York were at it again in the Eastern Division, and on the final day of the season they ended up dead even at 58-26. A playoff (for the home-court advantage) was held in Louisville, with the Colonels winning, 108-99.

Kentucky proceeded to walk over Memphis, but New York, the defending champion, was stunned by the upstart Spirits of St. Louis. The Nets won the opener, but then fell in four straight. Weird things happened in the West, too, as Indiana, led by George McGinnis, knocked off Denver, four games to three.

So the closely-situated bitter rivals, Kentucky and Indiana, were placed together again. And Kentucky was just too much, winning in five games during a series that averaged 15,000 in attendance.

Erving and McGinnis tied for the MVP award, and George got the best of Julius in the scoring race this season, 29.8 to 27.9. Artis Gilmore remained the all-league center, but he lost his rebounding title for the first time—to Swen Nater, 16.4 to 16.2. Ron Boone and Mack Calvin were the all-league guards.

Ownership of the Memphis and San Diego teams had to be picked up in midseason by the league, but, at the All-Star Game in San Antonio (won by the East, 151-124), an NBC sports executive said his network was considering hooking up with the ABA the next season (replacing National Hockey League telecasts). Something like the hype a TV package would provide was needed in a hurry. Once more several franchises had severe troubles, and merger was not even being whispered about any more.

And that's what Dave DeBusschere, the outstanding New York Knicks' forward, inherited when he took command of the commissioner's position at season's end. He had been the Nets' general manager for a season after retiring.

About the best aspect of the ABA was that it had lasted eight years.

1974-75

STANDINGS

Eastern Division

	W.	L.	Pct.
Kentucky	58	26	.690
New York	58	26	.690
St. Louis	32	52	.381
Memphis	27	57	.321
Virginia	15	69	.179

Western Division

	W.	L.	Pct.
Denver	65	19	.774
San Antonio	51	33	.607
Indiana	45	39	.536
Utah	38	46	.452
San Diego	31	53	.369

Eastern Division Semifinal Series

April 6—Kentucky 98, Memphis 91
April 8—Kentucky 119, Memphis 105
April 10—Kentucky 101, Memphis 80
April 11—Memphis 107, Kentucky 93
April 13—Kentucky 111, Memphis 99

April 6—New York 111, St. Louis 105
April 9—St. Louis 115, New York 97
April 11—St. Louis 113, New York 108
April 13—St. Louis 100, New York 89
April 15—St. Louis 108, New York 107

Eastern Division Final Series

April 21—Kentucky 112, St. Louis 109
April 23—Kentucky 108, St. Louis 103
April 25—St. Louis 103, Kentucky 97
April 27—Kentucky 117, St. Louis 98
April 28—Kentucky 123, St. Louis 103

Western Division Semifinal Series

April 5—Indiana 122, San Antonio 119 (OT)
April 7—Indiana 98, San Antonio 93
April 10—Indiana 113, San Antonio 103
April 12—San Antonio 110, Indiana 109
April 14—San Antonio 123, Indiana 117
April 16—Indiana 115, San Antonio 100

April 6—Denver 122, Utah 107
April 7—Denver 126, Utah 120
April 9—Utah 122, Denver 108
April 11—Utah 132, Denver 110
April 12—Denver 130, Utah 119
April 14—Denver 115, Utah 113

Western Division Final Series

April 20—Denver 131, Indiana 128
April 22—Indiana 131, Denver 124
April 24—Indiana 118, Denver 112
April 25—Denver 126, Indiana 109
April 27—Indiana 109, Denver 90
April 30—Denver 104, Indiana 99
May 3—Indiana 104, Denver 96

Championship Series

May 13—Kentucky 120, Indiana 94
May 15—Kentucky 95, Indiana 93
May 17—Kentucky 109, Indiana 101
May 19—Indiana 94, Kentucky 86
May 22—Kentucky 110, Indiana 105

TOP SCORERS

	Pts.	Ave.
George McGinnis, Indiana	2353	29.8
Julius Erving, New York	2343	27.9
Ron Boone, Utah	2117	25.2
Travis Grant, San Diego	1335	25.2
Marvin Barnes, St. Louis	1849	24.0

TOP REBOUNDERS

	No.	Ave.
Swen Nater, San Antonio	1279	16.4
Artis Gilmore, Kentucky	1361	16.2
Marvin Barnes, St. Louis	1202	15.6
Moses Malone, Utah	1209	14.6
George McGinnis, Indiana	1126	14.3

LEADERS IN ASSISTS

	No.	Ave.
Mack Calvin, Denver	570	7.7
Chuck Williams, Memphis	576	7.1
George McGinnis, Indiana	495	6.3
Jim O'Brien, San Diego	443	5.6
Warren Jabali, San Diego	358	5.7

1975-76

The last season.

It was starting to look more and more like the ABA would just fold up in the night and disappear.

To begin with, the Memphis team was sold to Baltimore interests, but, before the first game was played in the ninth season, the team (Baltimore Claws) went under.

Shortly into the schedule the San Diego Sails (renamed from Conquistadors) went belly up—despite grand promise. The team had finally moved into the large San Diego Sports Arena and had new ownership in Frank Goldberg, who had sold off his Denver team to take over his hometown franchise. Minnesota's Bill Musselman was brought in as coach, and several trades were made. But the citizenry of that southern California city could care less, and the Sails sailed off.

Then it was Utah's turn. The on-again, off-again sale by owner Bill Daniels never fully materialized, and he finally gave in. That dropped the ABA to just seven teams, so the two divisions were combined.

But public relations were bad, and the troubles hadn't even ended. The Virginia owners struggled to meet each payroll, and that franchise threatened to sink at any time. It managed, barely, to hang on till season's end. In St. Louis, despite the injection of new strength with four standouts from the Utah roster, the club did poorly on the floor and even worse at the gate—drawing less than a thousand on more than one occasion. Commissioner Dave DeBusschere said: "Every day was a crisis."

Three things held the league together, however. New York and Julius Erving were playing well again; Denver was one of the most viable franchises in all of basketball, and the NBA had settled its lawsuit with the Players' Association.

Erving had brought the Nets back to the front, but, in the West, the Nuggets were even more amazing. Denver had moved into a new 17,000-seat arena and was averaging 13,000. Also, the club had signed the two most coveted college players—forward David Thompson and center Marvin Webster. Thompson was a two-time College Player of the Year and became the first No. 1 choice of the NBA ever to sign with the other league. Webster, like Thompson, was picked by the Atlanta Hawks (also in the first round, the third selection in the draft), but went to Denver instead. He had a recurrence of hepatitis, though, and was no factor during his rookie season. However, Denver also had come up with center Dan Issel, acquired from Baltimore.

The Oscar Robertson Suit, as the players' action against the NBA was commonly called, came to an end at the NBA All-Star Game in Philadelphia. The players dropped the suit in return for far-ranging personal freedoms. Even though the NBA announced publicly that merger was not imminent—the judge had not allowed merger discussions while the suit was in litigation—the ABA began to formulate a plan to present to the elder circuit.

The ABA's own All-Star Game may have been the crowning glory in the league's history. A standing room-only crowd of 17,798 was on hand in Denver for a game matching the Nuggets (the first-place team at the break) against the All-Stars from the rest of the league. At half time the league put on a spectacular Slam-Dunk contest, won by Erving, and the Nuggets won the game, 144-138, as Thompson scored 29 points and walked off with the MVP award.

Denver went on to take the regular-season crown,

Denver's high-flying David Thompson averaged 26 points and won Rookie of the Year honors.

winning at least 60 games for the second straight year. New York was second, San Antonio third, and Virginia won just 15 games, finishing 44½ back. San Diego had been 3-8 before folding, and Utah was 4-12.

New York and Denver reached the final round of the playoffs, and Erving, MVP for the third time, hit a jumper at the buzzer of the opener to give New York the victory. The Nuggets came back in the second game, but lost the next pair in New York. Denver won at home and returned to Long Island for the sixth contest, which attracted the fifth sellout of the series. Denver was up by as many as 22 points in the third period, but, behind the mastery of Erving, the Nets rallied to beat the collapsing Nuggets, 112-106, and own their second title in three years—and last in the league.

"If this is going to be it, I wanted to go out in style," Erving said. He did. Erving's major adversary, George McGinnis, had jumped to the NBA, but Dr. J got a new foe in young Thompson, who averaged 26 points a game and was named Rookie of the Year.

A fog shrouded the future of the ABA. Most believed that it couldn't go on to a tenth season. So, behind the scenes, ABA executives met with NBA owners to draw up a settlement. An end to the war was finally reached on Treaty Day, June 17, 1976.

But only four ABA teams—New York, Denver, Indiana and San Antonio—survived.

The ABA's nine years had been a full roller-coaster ride, up and down continuously. But just like a roller coaster, it had been a fun—albeit costly—ride.

1975-76

STANDINGS

	W.	L.	Pct.
Denver	60	24	.714
New York	55	29	.665
San Antonio	50	34	.595
Kentucky	46	38	.548
Indiana	39	45	.464
St. Louis	35	49	.417
Virginia	15	68	.181

First Round

April 8—Kentucky 120, Indiana 109
April 10—Indiana 109, Kentucky 95
April 12—Kentucky 100, Indiana 99

Semifinal Series

April 9—New York 116, San Antonio 101
April 11—San Antonio 105, New York 79
April 14—San Antonio 111, New York 103
April 18—New York 110, San Antonio 108
April 19—New York 110, San Antonio 108
April 21—San Antonio 106, New York 105
April 24—New York 121, San Antonio 114

April 15—Denver 110, Kentucky 107
April 17—Kentucky 138, Denver 119
April 19—Kentucky 126, Denver 114
April 21—Denver 108, Kentucky 106
April 22—Denver 127, Kentucky 117
April 25—Kentucky 119, Denver 115
April 28—Denver 133, Kentucky 110

Championship Series

May 1—New York 120, Denver 118
May 4—Denver 127, New York 121
May 6—New York 117, Denver 111
May 8—New York 121, Denver 112
May 11—Denver 118, New York 110
May 13—New York 112, Denver 106

TOP SCORERS

	Pts.	Ave.
Julius Erving, New York	2462	29.3
Billy Knight, Indiana	1969	28.1
David Thompson, Denver	2158	26.0
Artis Gilmore, Kentucky	2067	24.6
Marvin Barnes, St. Louis	1616	24.1

TOP REBOUNDERS

	No.	Ave.
Artis Gilmore, Kentucky	1303	15.5
Maurice Lucas, St. Louis-Kentucky	970	11.3
Caldwell Jones, St. Louis	853	11.2
Larry Kenon, San Antonio	897	11.1
Julius Erving, New York	925	11.0

LEADERS IN ASSISTS

	No.	Ave.
Don Buse, Indiana	689	8.2
Ralph Simpson, Denver	597	7.1
Mack Calvin, Virginia	271	6.0
Louie Dampier, Kentucky	467	5.7
Jim Silas, San Antonio	452	5.4

MOST VALUABLE PLAYER

1968	Connie Hawkins	Pittsburgh
1969	Mel Daniels	Indiana
1970	Spencer Haywood	Denver
1971	Mel Daniels	Indiana
1972	Artis Gilmore	Kentucky
1973	Billy Cunningham	Carolina
1974	Julius Erving	New York
1975	Julius Erving	New York
	George McGinnis	Indiana
1976	Julius Erving	New York

ROOKIE OF THE YEAR

1968	Mel Daniels	Minnesota
1969	Warren Armstrong	Oakland
1970	Spencer Haywood	Denver
1971	Charlie Scott	Virginia
	Dan Issel	Kentucky
1972	Artis Gilmore	Kentucky
1973	Brian Taylor	New York
1974	Swen Nater	San Antonio
1975	Marvin Barnes	St. Louis
1976	David Thompson	Denver

COACH OF THE YEAR

1967-68	Vince Cazetta	Pittsburgh
1968-69	Alex Hannum	Oakland
1969-70	Bill Sharman	Los Angeles
	Joe Belmont	Denver
1970-71	Al Bianchi	Virginia
1971-72	Tom Nissalke	Dallas
1972-73	Larry Brown	Carolina
1973-74	Babe McCarthy	Kentucky
	Joe Mullaney	Utah
1974-75	Larry Brown	Denver
1975-76	Larry Brown	Denver

ALL-ABA TEAMS

1967-68

First	Second
Connie Hawkins, Pittsburgh	Roger Brown, Indiana
Doug Moe, New Orleans	Cincy Powell, Dallas
Mel Daniels, Minnesota	John Beasley, Dallas
Larry Jones, Denver	Larry Brown, New Orleans
Charlie Williams, Pittsburgh	Louie Dampier, Kentucky

1968-69

Connie Hawkins, Minnesota	John Beasley, Dallas
Rick Barry, Oakland	Doug Moe, Oakland
Mel Daniels, Indiana	Red Robbins, New Orleans
James Jones, New Orleans	Don Freeman, Miami
Larry Jones, Denver	Louie Dampier, Kentucky

1969-70

Rick Barry, Washington	Roger Brown, Indiana
Spencer Haywood, Denver	Bob Netolicky, Indiana
Mel Daniels, Indiana	Red Robbins, New Orleans
Bob Verga, Carolina	Louie Dampier, Kentucky
Larry Jones, Denver	Don Freeman, Miami

1970-71

Roger Brown, Indiana	John Brisker, Pittsburgh
Rick Barry, New York	Joe Caldwell, Carolina
Mel Daniels, Indiana	Zelmo Beaty, Utah
Mack Calvin, Floridians	Dan Issel, Kentucky
Charlie Scott, Virginia	Don Freeman, Texas
	Larry Cannon, Denver

1971-72

Rick Barry, New York	Willie Wise, Utah
Dan Issel, Kentucky	Julius Erving, Virginia
Artis Gilmore, Kentucky	Zelmo Beaty, Utah
Don Freeman, Dallas	Ralph Simpson, Denver
Bill Melchionni, New York	Charlie Scott, Virginia

1972-73

Billy Cunningham, Carolina	George McGinnis, Indiana
Julius Erving, Virginia	Dan Issel, Kentucky
Artis Gilmore, Kentucky	Mel Daniels, Indiana
James Jones, Utah	Ralph Simpson, Denver
Warren Jabali, Denver	Mack Calvin, Carolina

1973-74

Julius Erving, New York	Dan Issel, Kentucky
George McGinnis, Indiana	Willie Wise, Utah
Artis Gilmore, Kentucky	Swen Nater, San Antonio
James Jones, Utah	Ron Boone, Utah
Mack Calvin, Carolina	Louie Dampier, Kentucky

1974-75

Julius Erving, New York	Marvin Barnes, St. Louis
George McGinnis, Indiana	George Gervin, San Antonio
Artis Gilmore, Kentucky	Swen Nater, San Antonio
Mack Calvin, Denver	Brian Taylor, New York
Ron Boone, Utah	James Silas, San Antonio

1975-76

Julius Erving, New York	David Thompson, Denver
Billy Knight, Indiana	Bobby Jones, Denver
Artis Gilmore, Kentucky	Dan Issel, Denver
James Silas, San Antonio	Don Buse, Indiana
Ralph Simpson, Denver	George Gervin, San Antonio

ALL-ROOKIE TEAMS

1968	1973
Tom Washington, Pittsburgh	George Gervin, Virginia
Bob Netolicky, Indiana	Dennis Wuycik, Carolina
Mel Daniels, Minnesota	Jim Chones, New York
Louie Dampier, Kentucky	Brian Taylor, New York
James Jones, New Orleans	James Silas, Dallas

1969

Larry Miller, Los Angeles
Walt Piatkowski, Denver
Gene Moore, Kentucky
Warren Armstrong, Oakland
Ron Boone, Dallas

1970

Willie Wise, Los Angeles
John Brisker, Pittsburgh
Spencer Haywood, Denver
Mike Barrett, Washington
Mack Calvin, Los Angeles

1971

Wendell Ladner, Memphis
Sam Robinson, Floridians
Dan Issel, Kentucky
Charlie Scott, Virginia
Joe Hamilton, Texas

1972

Julius Erving, Virginia
George McGinnis, Indiana
Artis Gilmore, Kentucky
John Roche, New York
Johnny Neumann, Memphis

1974

Larry Kenon, New York
Mike Green, Denver
Swen Nater, San Antonio
Dwight Lamar, San Antonio
John Williamson, New York

1975

Bobby Jones, Denver
Marvin Barnes, St. Louis
Moses Malone, Utah
Billy Knight, Indiana
Gus Gerard, St. Louis

1976

David Thompson, Denver
Mark Olberding, San Antonio
Kim Hughes, New York
M. L. Carr, St. Louis
Ticky Burden, Virginia

ABA CHAMPIONS

1968	Pittsburgh
1969	Oakland
1970	Indiana
1971	Utah
1972	Indiana
1973	Indiana
1974	New York
1975	Kentucky
1976	New York

ALL-TIME ABA RECORDS

Individual

Single Game

Most Points	67	Larry Miller, Carolina, vs Memphis at Greensboro, N.C., Mar. 18, 1972
Most 2-Point F.G. Attempted	46	Julius Erving, New York, vs San Diego at San Diego, Feb. 14, 1975 (4 OT)
Most 2-Point F.G. Made	25	Mel Daniels, Indiana, vs New York at Indianapolis, April 18, 1969
	25	Larry Miller, Carolina, vs Memphis at Greensboro, N.C., Mar. 18, 1972
	25	Julius Erving, New York, vs San Diego at San Diego, Feb. 14, 1975 (4 OT)
	25	Marvin Barnes, St. Louis, vs Memphis at St. Louis, Mar. 16, 1975 (OT)
Most 3-Point F.G. Attempted	26	Les Selvage, Anaheim, vs Denver at Denver, Feb. 15, 1968
Most 3-Point F.G. Made	10	Les Selvage, Anaheim, vs Denver at Denver, Feb. 15, 1968
Most F.T. Attempted	30	George Thompson, Memphis, vs San Diego at San Diego, Oct. 14, 1972
Most F.T. Made	24	Tony Jackson, New Jersey, vs Kentucky at Louisville, Nov. 27, 1967
Most Rebounds	40	Artis Gilmore, Kentucky, vs New York at New York, Feb. 3, 1974
Most Assists	23	Larry Brown, Denver, vs Pittsburgh at Denver, Feb. 20, 1972
Most Consecutive F.T.	23	Rick Barry, Oakland, vs Kentucky at Louisville, Feb. 7, 1969

Season

Most Points	2,538	Dan Issel, Kentucky, 1971-72
Highest Average	34.58	Charlie Scott, Virginia, 1971-72
Most 2-Point F.G. Attempted	2,082	Charlie Scott, Virginia, 1971-72
Most 2-Point F.G. Made	986	Spencer Haywood, Denver, 1969-70
Highest 2-Point F.G. Percentage	.605	Bobby Jones, Denver, 1974-75
Most 3-Point F.G. Attempted	552	Louie Dampier, Kentucky, 1968-69
Most 3-Point F.G. Made	199	Louie Dampier, Kentucky, 1968-69
Highest 3-Point F.G. Percentage	.420	Billy Shepherd, Memphis, 1974-75
Most F.T. Attempted	805	Mack Calvin, Floridians, 1970-71
Most F.T. Made	696	Mack Calvin, Floridians, 1970-71
Highest F.T. Percentage	.896	Mack Calvin, Denver, 1974-75
Most Rebounds	1,637	Spencer Haywood, Denver, 1969-70
Most Assists	689	Don Buse, Indiana, 1975-76
Most Personal Fouls	382	Gene Moore, Kentucky, 1969-70
Most Times Disqualified	25	Gene Moore, Kentucky, 1969-70

Career

Most Points Scored	13,726	Louie Dampier, Kentucky, 1968-76
Highest Scoring Average (Minimum 250 Games)	28.7	Julius Erving, Virginia and New York, 1971-76
Most 2-Point F.G. Attempted	9,886	Mel Daniels, Minnesota, Indiana and Memphis, 1967-75
Most 2-Point F.G. Made	4,692	Mel Daniels, Minnesota, Indiana and Memphis, 1967-75
Most 3-Point F.G. Attempted	2,217	Louie Dampier, Kentucky, 1968-76
Most 3-Point F.G. Made	794	Louie Dampier, Kentucky, 1968-76
Most F.T. Attempted	4,105	Mack Calvin, Los Angeles, Miami, Carolina, Denver and Virginia, 1969-76
Most F.T. Made	3,554	Mack Calvin, Los Angeles, Miami, Carolina, Denver and Virginia, 1969-76
Most Rebounds	9,494	Mel Daniels, Minnesota, Indiana and Memphis, 1967-75
Most Assists	4,084	Louie Dampier, Kentucky, 1968-76
Most Minutes Played	27,770	Louie Dampier, Kentucky, 1968-76
Most Personal Fouls	1,689	Jim Ligon, Kentucky, Pittsburgh and Virginia, 1967-74
Most Times Disqualified	43	Gene Moore, Kentucky, Texas, Dallas, New York, San Diego and St. Louis, 1968-74
Most Games Played	728	Louie Dampier, Kentucky, 1968-76

Team

Single Game

Most Points, One Team	177	Indiana vs Pittsburgh at Indianapolis, April 12, 1970
Most Points, Two Teams	342	San Diego (176) vs New York (166) at San Diego, Feb. 14, 1975 (4 OT)
Fewest Points, One Team	66	Indiana vs San Antonio at San Antonio, Oct. 20, 1973
Largest Winning Margin	57	Utah 150, Carolina 93 at Salt Lake City, Oct. 19, 1971
Most 2-Point F.G. Attempted	131	Minnesota vs New Orleans at New Orleans (overtime) Dec. 6, 1967
	131	Miami vs Dallas at Dallas, Feb. 10, 1970
Most 2-Point F.G. Made	66	San Diego vs New York at San Diego, Feb. 14, 1975 (4 OT)
Most 3-Point F.G. Attempted	32	Anaheim vs Denver at Denver, Feb. 15, 1968
Most 3-Point F.G. Made	12	Kentucky vs Miami at Louisville, March 1, 1969
Most F.T. Attempted	73	Miami vs New York at Miami Beach, Fla., Nov. 20, 1968
Most F.T. Made	60	Indiana vs Los Angeles at Indianapolis, Feb. 1, 1969
Most Rebounds	93	Denver vs Dallas at Denver, April 8, 1970
Most Assists	51	Virginia vs Memphis at Virginia, Feb. 3, 1973
Most Personal Fouls	46	New York vs Washington at New York, Dec. 26, 1969
	46	Carolina vs Indiana at Greensboro, N.C., Dec. 11, 1970

Season

Most Games Won	68	Kentucky, 1971-72
Most Games Lost	69	Virginia, 1974-75
Highest Winning Percentage	.810	Kentucky, 1971-72
Most Points	10,355	Virginia, 1970-71
Highest Scoring Average	126.49	Oakland, 1968-69
Most 2-Point F.G. Attempted	8,375	Denver, 1970-71
Most 2-Point F.G. Made	3,960	Virginia, 1970-71
Most 3-Point F.G. Attempted	1,024	Indiana, 1970-71
Most 3-Point F.G. Made	335	Kentucky, 1968-69
Most F.T. Attempted	3,434	Oakland, 1968-69
Most F.T. Made	2,607	Oakland, 1968-69
Most Rebounds	4,866	Utah, 1970-71
Most Assists	2,231	Virginia, 1970-71

ABA ALL-STAR GAME

FIRST GAME

JANUARY 9, 1968 AT INDIANAPOLIS, IND.

EAST (126)

PLAYER	Min.	2-Pt. FG-A	3-Pt. FG-A	FT-A	Reb.	A	PF	TP
Roger Brown, Indiana	27	5-14	0-1	2-2	4	2	3	12
Connie Hawkins, Pittsburgh	26	3-6	0-0	1-3	9	2	3	7
Mel Daniels, Minnesota	29	9-18	0-0	4-11	15	0	1	22
Roger Lewis, Indiana	18	3-9	0-0	0-0	0	3	1	6
Don Freeman, Minnesota	24	8-13	0-0	4-6	4	2	3	20
Les Hunter, Minnesota	21	2-7	0-0	3-5	8	1	4	7
Darel Carrier, Kentucky	21	3-7	0-3	2-2	2	1	3	8
Randy Mahaffey, Kentucky	7	1-2	0-0	2-6	4	0	0	4
Louie Dampier, Kentucky	29	8-17	0-1	2-2	3	3	1	18
Bob Netolicky, Indiana	19	4-8	0-0	4-4	11	1	1	12
Tony Jackson, New Jersey	15	2-3	0-3	0-0	2	1	0	4
Chico Vaughn, Pittsburgh	4	0-0	2-2	0-0	0	0	0	6
Totals	240	48-104	2-10	24-41	62	16	20	125

WEST (120)

PLAYER	Min.	2-Pt. FG-A	3-Pt. FG-A	FT-A	Reb.	A	PF	TP
Cliff Hagan, Dallas	24	4-11	0-0	2-2	0	5	2	10
Doug Moe, New Orleans	29	7-12	0-1	3-5	7	5	4	17
Red Robbins, New Orleans	18	2-5	0-0	0-0	4	0	1	4
Levern Tart, Oakland	27	4-12	0-0	5-5	3	3	0	13
Larry Jones, Denver	28	6-10	0-0	2-3	13	2	3	14
Art Becker, Houston	19	5-13	0-0	1-1	5	0	1	11
Larry Brown, New Orleans	22	5-7	2-2	1-1	3	5	2	17
Dewitt Menyard, Houston	6	2-4	0-0	0-1	2	0	2	4
James Jones, New Orleans	19	4-9	0-0	2-4	1	3	1	10
Ben Warley, Anaheim	17	2-4	0-3	4-4	1	3	2	8
John Beasley, Dallas	24	4-9	0-0	1-1	4	0	5	9
Larry Bunse, Anaheim	7	1-2	0-0	1-1	0	0	0	3
Totals	240	46-98	2-6	22-28	43	26	23	120

Score by Quarters

West All-Stars	29	30	32	29	120
East All-Stars	30	31	31	34	126

Officials—Belmont and Feiereisel
Attendance—10,872

SECOND GAME

JANUARY 28, 1969, AT LOUISVILLE, KY.

EAST (127)

PLAYER	Min.	2-Pt. FG-A	3-Pt. FG-A	FT-A	Reb.	A	PF	TP
Bob Netolicky, Indiana	26	5-9	0-0	3-5	12	1	2	13
Walt Simon, New York	21	8-11	0-0	2-3	4	1	3	18
Les Hunter, Miami	22	5-10	0-0	2-2	6	0	3	12
Jim Ligon, Kentucky	12	0-2	0-0	3-4	3	0	2	3
Tom Washington, Minnesota	15	2-5	0-0	2-2	5	1	3	6
Mel Daniels, Indiana	31	5-16	0-0	7-10	10	2	3	17
Duane Thoren, Miami	17	1-4	0-0	0-0	5	2	3	2
Louie Dampier, Kentucky	38	4-10	1-4	3-3	2	6	2	14
Darel Carrier, Kentucky	26	4-8	1-4	8-10	4	5	3	19
Don Freeman, Miami	27	7 13	0-0	7-7	6	7	6	21
Charlie Williams, Minnesota	5	0-2	0-0	2-2	0	1	0	2
Totals	240	41-90	2-8	39-48	57	26	30	127

WEST (133)

PLAYER	Min.	2-Pt. FG-A	3-Pt. FG-A	FT-A	Reb.	A	PF	TP
Wayne Hightower, Denver	9	1-2	0-0	4-4	5	0	2	6
Rick Barry, Oakland	12	3-9	0-0	4-5	3	1	2	10
Doug Moe, Oakland	25	6-13	0-0	5-8	6	6	3	17
John Beasley, Dallas	29	8-12	0-0	3-3	14	2	5	19
Warren Davis, Los Angeles	20	3-8	0-0	0-0	7	2	2	6
Byron Beck, Denver	27	7-13	0-0	0-0	10	1	3	14
Austin Robbins, New Orleans	21	8-14	0-0	3-4	5	1	2	19
James Jones, New Orleans	18	4-11	0-0	6-6	1	2	1	14
Larry Jones, Denver	25	3-8	1-1	5-8	5	9	3	14
Willie Somerset, Houston	17	2-7	0-0	2-2	3	3	3	6
Larry Brown, Oakland	25	1-6	0-1	3-5	0	7	2	5
Merv Jackson, Los Angeles	11	1-3	0-0	1-1	2	1	1	3
Totals	240	47-106	1-2	36-46	61	35	29	133

Score by Quarters

West All-Stars	38	26	37	32	133
East All-Stars	33	27	30	37	127

Officials—Hershock and Rakel
Attendance—5,407

THIRD GAME

JANUARY 24, 1970, AT INDIANAPOLIS, IND.

EAST (98)

PLAYER	Min.	2-Pt. FT-A	3-Pt. FG-A	FG-A	Reb.	A	PF	TP
Doug Moe, Carolina	36	0-5	0-0	2-3	8	6	1	2
Bob Netolicky, Indiana	33	7-18	0-0	1-4	8	2	2	15
Mel Daniels, Indiana	26	6-14	0-0	1-3	12	1	4	13
Louie Dampier, Kentucky	26	7-16	1-6	2-3	3	1	2	17
Don Freeman, Miami	24	4-16	0-0	2-3	4	5	2	10
Bob Verga, Carolina	16	6-14	1-3	1-2	5	2	1	14
Fred Lewis, Indiana	9	0-5	0-0	1-2	6	1	1	1
Levern Tart, New York	13	1-8	1-2	0-0	3	1	2	3
Darel Carrier, Kentucky	10	0-4	0-2	2-3	1	0	2	3
Roger Brown, Indiana	28	5-10	0-0	5-6	6	2	4	15
Charlie Williams, Pittsburgh	7	1-5	0-2	0-0	0	1	2	2
Gene Moore, Kentucky	12	2-6	0-1	0-0	4	0	1	4
Totals	240	39-121	3-16	17-29	64*	22	24	98

*—Includes four team rebounds.

WEST (128)

PLAYER	Min.	2-Pt. FG-A	3-Pt. FG-A	FT-A	Reb.	A	PF	TP
Warren Armstrong, Washington	15	1-3	0-0	2-2	2	1	2	4
Cincy Powell, Dallas	26	5-9	0-0	2-2	7	0	1	12
Spencer Haywood, Denver	39	10-19	0-0	3-4	19	2	4	23
Larry Jones, Denver	36	10-20	0-2	10-13	6	5	3	30
James Jones, New Orleans	14	0-3	0-0	0-0	3	0	1	0
Glen Combs, Dallas	12	4-6	2-4	0-0	3	1	2	10
Larry Brown, Washington	15	0-2	0-0	3-3	3	3	1	3
Gerald Govan, New Orleans	11	1-2	0-0	0-0	4	0	0	2
Steve Jones, New Orleans	18	4-9	0-0	6-6	5	1	2	14
Rick Barry, Washington	27	7-12	0-0	2-2	7	7	0	16
John Beasley, Dallas	18	5-7	1-1	0-0	8	0	5	11
Lee Davis, New Orleans	9	1-3	0-1	1-1	2	0	1	3
Totals	240	48-95	3-8	29-33	75*	20	22	128

*—Includes six team rebounds.

Score by Quarters

West All-Stars	34	27	25	42	128
East All-Stars	18	23	33	24	98

Officials—Strom and Vanak
Attendance—11,932

FOURTH GAME

JANUARY 23, 1971 AT GREENSBORO, N.C.

EAST (126)

PLAYER	Min.	2-Pt. FG-A	3-Pt. FG-A	FT-A	Reb.	A	PF	TP
Joe Caldwell, Carolina	32	10-19	0-0	1-3	8	3	3	21
John Brisker, Pittsburgh	27	5-18	0-1	5-7	17	1	3	15
Dan Issel, Kentucky	34	8-15	0-0	5-8	11	0	2	21
Mack Calvin, Floridians	20	1-5	1-2	3-7	4	4	2	8
Charlie Scott, Virginia	21	2-6	0-0	3-6	2	3	4	7
Neil Johnson, Virginia	4	0-3	0-0	0-0	1	0	1	0
Rick Barry, New York	17	4-6	0-0	6-6	2	2	3	14
Cincy Powell, Kentucky	21	4-6	0-0	3-3	10	0	2	11
George Carter, Virginia	8	2-3	0-0	0-2	2	0	2	4
Mike Lewis, Pittsburgh	14	3-7	0-0	1-1	5	1	4	7
Larry Jones, Floridians	18	2-3	0-0	2-2	2	1	2	6
Bill Melchionni, New York	24	5-10	0-0	2-3	1	4	2	12
Totals	240	46-101	1-3	31-48	65	19	30	126

WEST (122)

PLAYER	Min.	2-Pt. FG-A	3-Pt. FG-A	FT-A	Reb.	A	PF	TP
Roger Brown, Indiana	28	3-9	0-2	6-8	3	3	4	12
Bob Netolicky, Indiana	22	3-4	0-0	0-2	4	1	2	6
Zelmo Beaty, Utah	27	5-11	0-0	2-3	8	3	4	12
Glen Combs, Utah	17	1-5	0-2	0-2	1	2	2	2
Don Freeman, Texas	27	6-12	0-0	5-8	7	3	3	17
Red Robbins, Utah	14	2-6	0-0	0-0	2	1	2	4
Wendell Ladner, Memphis	20	6-11	0-0	0-0	7	0	3	12
Ron Boone, Utah	4	2-4	0-0	2-3	2	0	0	6
Mel Daniels, Indiana	30	12-19	0-0	5-7	13	3	3	29
Jimmy Jones, Memphis	27	3-5	0-0	7-9	0	4	5	13
Steve Jones, Memphis	21	4-8	0-1	1-1	3	0	4	9
Julius Keye, Denver	7	0-1	0-0	0-0	4	0	1	0
Totals	240	47-95	0-5	28-43	54	20	33	122

Score by Quarters

West All-Stars	29	40	28	25	122
East All-Stars	33	26	33	34	126

Officials—Drucker and Gushue
Attendance—14,407

FIFTH GAME

JANUARY 29, 1972 AT LOUISVILLE, KY.

EAST (142)

PLAYER	Min.	2-Pt. FG-A	3-Pt. FG-A	FT-A	Reb.	A	PF	TP
Dan Issel, Kentucky	23	9-13	0-0	3-4	9	5	2	21
Rick Barry, New York	26	2-10	0-0	0-1	12	8	2	4
Artis Gilmore, Kentucky	27	4-5	0-0	6-10	10	2	5	14
Bill Melchionni, New York	18	2-4	0-0	1-1	2	2	1	5
Charlie Scott, Virginia	23	9-20	0-1	2-3	4	3	2	20
Julius Erving, Virginia	25	9-15	0-0	2-2	6	3	3	20
John Brisker, Pittsburgh	21	3-9	0-1	2-3	5	3	1	8
Jim McDaniels, Carolina	20	11-15	0-0	2-3	11	1	3	24
George Thompson, Pittsburgh	17	5-7	0-2	0-0	0	2	1	10
Mack Calvin, Floridians	14	4-7	0-0	2-2	2	4	4	10
Warren Jabali, Floridians	17	2-7	0-1	0-0	9	1	4	4
Louie Dampier, Kentucky	9	1-2	0-2	0-0	1	3	0	2
Totals	240	61-114	0-7	20-29	71	37	28	142

WEST (115)

PLAYER	Min.	2-Pt. FG-A	3-Pt. FG-A	FT-A	Reb.	A	PF	TP
Roger Brown, Indiana	25	2-5	0-2	0-1	6	2	3	4
Willie Wise, Utah	33	5-8	0-0	5-7	9	3	2	15
Zelmo Beaty, Utah	27	7-11	0-0	1-1	7	0	4	15
Glen Combs, Utah	18	1-5	0-3	0-0	0	3	0	2
Ralph Simpson, Denver	20	6-13	0-1	0-1	1	0	1	12
Wilbert Jones, Memphis	10	1-3	0-0	0-0	3	0	2	2
Wendell Ladner, Memphis	14	2-4	0-1	0-0	6	1	2	4
Art Becker, Denver	9	0-2	0-0	0-0	0	1	0	0
Mel Daniels, Indiana	26	8-14	0-0	5-8	9	1	4	21
Steve Jones, Dallas	19	2-6	1-1	2-2	2	3	0	9
Donnie Freeman, Dallas	21	3-8	0-0	7-8	5	2	1	13
Freddie Lewis, Indiana	18	6-11	1-2	3-4	1	1	2	18
Totals	240	43-90	2-10	23-32	49	17	21	115

Score by Quarters					
West All-Stars	31	35	23	26	115
East All-Stars	36	29	32	45	142

Officials—Vanak and Serafin.
Attendance—15,738.

SIXTH GAME

FEBRUARY 6, 1973 AT SALT LAKE CITY, UTAH

EAST (111)

PLAYER	Min.	2-Pt. FG-A	3-Pt. FG-A	FT-A	Reb.	A	PF	TP
Julius Erving, Virginia	30	8-16	0-0	6-8	5	1	4	22
Billy Cunningham, Carolina	20	9-11	0-1	0-0	6	4	6	18
Artis Gilmore, Kentucky	31	3-8	0-0	4-8	16	0	5	10
Mack Calvin, Carolina	23	3-8	0-0	7-7	2	8	5	13
George Thompson, Memphis	22	4-10	0-0	2-2	1	0	1	10
Dan Issel, Kentucky	29	6-14	0-0	2-2	7	4	0·	14
Joe Caldwell, Carolina	23	3-5	0-0	1-1	5	2	2	7
Billy Paultz, New York	15	1-3	0-0	1-1	5	3	2	3
Louie Dampier, Kentucky	23	5-12	0-1	0-0	1	0	3	10
Bill Melchionni, New York	24	1-6	0-0	2-2	8	2	1	4
Totals	240	43-93	0-2	25-31	56	24	29	111

WEST (123)

PLAYER	Min.	2-Pt. FG-A	3-Pt. FG-A	FT-A	Reb.	A	PF	TP
George McGinnis, Indiana	34	10-14	0-1	3-6	15	2	5	23
Willie Wise, Utah	37	11-20	0-0	4-4	6	4	3	26
Mel Daniels, Indiana	33	8-19	0-0	9-12	11	1	3	25
James Jones, Utah	36	6-10	0-0	2-2	5	4	2	14
Ralph Simpson, Denver	13	2-6	0-0	2-3	3	2	1	6
Rich Jones, Dallas	14	0-6	0-2	0-0	4	1	1	0
Stew Johnson, San Diego	11	1-3	0-0	0-0	1	0	2	2
Zelmo Beaty, Utah	15	3-6	0-0	0-0	4	1	1	6
Chuck Williams, San Diego	16	2-3	0-0	1-3	0	2	2	5
Warren Jabali, Denver	31	6-11	1-1	1-3	4	7	2	16
Totals	240	49-98	1-4	22-33	53	24	22	123

Score by Quarters

West All-Stars	28	24	32	39	123
East All-Stars	28	37	27	19	111

Officials—Drucker and Middleton.
Attendance—12,556.

SEVENTH GAME

JANUARY 30, 1974 AT NORFOLK, VA.

EAST (128)

PLAYER	Min.	2-Pt. FG-A	3-Pt. FG-A	FT-A	Reb.	A	PF	TP
Julius Erving, New York	27	6-15	0-0	2-2	11	8	1	14
Dan Issel, Kentucky	26	10-15	0-0	1-1	4	1	1	21
Artis Gilmore, Kentucky	27	8-12	0-0	2-3	13	1	4	18
Louie Dampier, Kentucky	23	8-12	0-0	0-0	2	1	0	16
Mack Calvin, Carolina	27	3-10	0-0	2-3	2	11	3	8
George Gervin, Virginia	21	3-8	0-1	3-4	5	3	1	9
Larry Kenon, New York	22	8-12	0-0	2-3	6	0	1	18
Jim Eakins, Virginia	21	1-4	0-0	0-0	4	4	2	2
Ted McClain, Carolina	25	6-8	0-0	0-0	3	4	3	12
George Thompson, Memphis	21	5-8	0-0	0-0	2	3	1	10
Totals	240	58-104	0-1	12-16	52	36	17	128

WEST (112)

PLAYER	Min.	2-Pt. FG-A	3-Pt. FG-A	FT-A	Reb.	A	PF	TP
Willie Wise, Utah	25	4-12	0-0	0-0	7	0	1	8
George McGinnis, Indiana	30	7-21	0-0	0-0	11	1	3	14
Mel Daniels, Indiana	20	2-11	0-0	1-2	7	0	2	5
James Jones, Utah	25	4-6	0-0	3-5	4	2	1	11
Warren Jabali, Denver	24	3-10	0-5	0-1	2	3	2	6
Stew Johnston, San Diego	22	3-7	0-2	2-2	4	0	2	8
Rich Jones, San Antonio	19	2-10	0-1	0-0	8	2	4	4
Swen Nater, San Antonio	28	13-24	0-0	3-4	22	0	2	29
Ron Boone, Utah	24	6-11	1-2	0-0	3	5	1	15
Ralph Simpson, Denver	23	6-17	0-0	0-0	1	0	0	12
Totals	240	50-129	1-10	9-14	69	13	18	112

Score by Quarters					
West All-Stars	25	30	28	29	112
East All-Stars	35	27	37	29	128

Officials—Vanak and Rooney.
Attendance—10,624.

EIGHTH GAME

JANUARY 28, 1975 AT SAN ANTONIO, TEX.

EAST (151)

PLAYER	Min.	2-Pt. FG-A	3-Pt. FG-A	FT-A	Reb.	A	PF	TP
Marvin Barnes, St. Louis	21	6-13	0-0	4-4	1	1	2	16
Julius Erving, New York	27	5-11	1-1	8-10	7	7	4	21
Artis Gilmore, Kentucky	28	4-8	0-0	3-7	13	2	3	11
Freddie Lewis, St. Louis	33	10-14	1-1	3-3	5	10	3	26
Louie Dampier, Kentucky	27	4-6	1-2	0-0	3	1	4	11
Billy Paultz, New York	18	2-7	0-0	0-0	4	4	2	4
Stew Johnson, Memphis	14	4-10	0-1	0-0	3	2	2	8
Dave Twardzik, Virginia	15	4-4	0-0	6-7	1	3	6	14
Brian Taylor, New York	21	9-13	0-0	3-5	1	3	4	21
Larry Kenon, New York	16	6-11	0-0	0-0	4	1	0	12
Dan Issel, Kentucky	20	3-6	0-0	1-2	7	1	4	7
Totals	240	57-103	3-5	28-38	49	35	34	151

WEST (124)

PLAYER	Min.	2-Pt. FG-A	3-Pt. FG-A	FT-A	Reb.	A	PF	TP
George McGinnis, Indiana	32	6-13	0-1	6-11	12	5	5	18
George Gervin, San Antonio	30	8-14	0-1	7-8	6	3	2	23
Swen Nater, San Antonio	26	5-13	0-0	2-2	5	1	3	12
Mack Calvin, Denver	28	4-15	0-1	9-10	3	7	2	17
Ron Boone, Utah	23	4-8	0-0	2-2	2	2	4	10
Caldwell Jones, San Diego	15	2-4	0-0	1-1	4	0	4	5
James Silas, San Antonio	23	5-7	0-0	11-11	3	5	3	21
Mike Green, Denver	18	3-6	0-0	0-0	3	0	4	6
Moses Malone, Utah	20	2-3	0-0	2-5	10	0	1	6
Ralph Simpson, Denver	25	3-10	0-0	0-0	3	0	1	6
Totals	240	42-93	0-3	40-50	51	23	29	124

Score by Quarters					
West All-Stars	22	28	30	34	124
East All-Stars	32	38	39	42	151

Officials—Madden and Kersey.
Attendance—10,449.

FINAL GAME

JANUARY 27, 1976 AT DENVER, COL.

DENVER (144)

PLAYER	Min.	2-Pt. FG-A	3-Pt. FG-A	FT-A	Reb.	A	PF	TP
Bobby Jones	29	8-12	0-0	8-11	10	3	2	24
David Thompson	34	9-18	0-0	11-13	8	2	4	29
Dan Issel	31	6-16	0-0	7-9	9	5	3	19
Chuck Williams	22	2-6	0-0	3-5	1	4	2	7
Ralph Simpson	37	8-15	0-0	3-3	7	5	0	19
Monty Towe	11	1-3	0-0	0-0	0	2	0	2
Jimmy Foster	5	0-3	0-0	0-0	1	0	1	0
Roger Brown	9	2-2	0-0	0-0	3	3	1	4
Claude Terry	25	5-12	1-3	3-5	3	3	2	14
Gus Gerard	17	5-14	0-0	2-2	9	1	5	12
Byron Beck	20	6-11	0-0	2-2	4	0	3	14
Totals	240	52-112	1-3	39-50	55	28	23	144

ALL-STARS (138)

PLAYER	Min.	2-Pt. FG-A	3-Pt. FG-A	FT-A	Reb.	A	PF	TP
Billy Knight, Indiana	23	9-14	0-1	2-2	10	2	3	20
Julius Erving, New York	25	9-12	0-1	5-7	7	5	4	23
Artis Gilmore, Kentucky	27	5-7	0-0	4-6	7	1	6	14
James Silas, San Antonio	23	6-10	0-0	8-8	0	5	6	20
Brian Taylor, New York	29	3-9	0-1	0-0	4	8	3	6
Ron Boone, St. Louis	16	5-11	0-0	0-0	3	2	1	10
Billy Paultz, San Antonio	20	4-6	0-0	2-2	2	1	1	10
Don Buse, Indiana	14	2-4	1-2	0-0	1	3	0	5
Maurice Lucas, St. Louis	14	2-5	0-0	1-1	5	3	1	5
Marvin Barnes, St. Louis	13	3-5	0-0	1-1	0	1	3	7
Larry Kenon, San Antonio	20	5-7	0-0	0-0	6	2	5	10
George Gervin, San Antonio	16	3-13	1-2	1-2	6	1	1	8
Totals	240	56-103	2-7	24-29	51	34	34	138

Score by Quarters

Denver	32	23	37	52	144
All-Stars	31	25	41	41	138

Officials—Drucker and Middleton.
Attendance—17,798

ABA COLLEGE DRAFT

1967

Anaheim

FIRST FIVE ROUNDS—Darrel Hardy, Baylor; Bob Krulish, Pacific; Bob Lewis, North Carolina; Mike Lynn, UCLA; Tom Workman, Seattle.
ADDITIONAL ROUNDS—Jim Connolly, Virginia; Denny Holman, Southern Methodist; Edgar Lacy, UCLA; Les Powell, Utah State; Malcolm Strong, Seattle; Gary Williams, Oklahoma State; Mike Wittman, Miami (Fla.)

Dallas

FIRST FIVE ROUNDS—Matt Aitch, Michigan State; Jim Burns, Northwestern; Gary Gray, Oklahoma City; Pat Riley, Kentucky; Jamie Thompson, Wichita State.
ADDITIONAL ROUNDS—Paul Brateris, Tennessee Wesleyan; Jeff Fitch, East Texas State; Ted Manning, North Carolina A&T; Duane Heckman, Dickinson; Gilbert McDowell, Tennessee Wesleyan; Jerry Southwood, Vanderbilt; Tom Storm, Montana State.

Denver

FIRST FIVE ROUNDS—Byron Beck, Denver; Walt Frazier, Southern Illinois; Gary Keller, Florida; Bob Rule, Colorado State University; Neville Shed, Texas Western.
ADDITIONAL ROUNDS—Vaughn Harper, Syracuse; Rick Dean, Syracuse; Neil Heskin, Georgetown; Dave Lattin, Texas Western; John Morrison, Canisius; Neil Roberts, Brigham Young; Bill Turner, Akron.

Houston

FIRST FIVE ROUNDS—Bob Benfield, West Virginia; Tony Eatmon, Pan-American; Bob Reidy, Duke; Frank Stronzek, American International; Keith Swagerty, Pacific.
ADDITIONAL ROUNDS—Don Carlos, Otterbein; Hal Hale, Utah State; Guy Manning, Prairie View; Jim Monahan, Notre Dame; Mike Nau, Oregon State; Jerry Pettway, Northwood, Mich.; Dale Schlueter, Colorado State University.

Indiana

FIRST FIVE ROUNDS—Charles Beasley, Southern Methodist; Jim Dawson, Illinois; Craig Dill, Michigan; Bob Netolicky, Drake; Jim Walker, Providence.
ADDITIONAL ROUNDS—Frank Gaidjunes, Villanova; Jerry Jones, Iowa; Ron Kozlicky, Northwestern; Hubie Marshall, LaSalle; Ed McKee, Rockhurst; Bill Russell, Indiana; Gene Washington, Michigan State.

Kentucky

FIRST FIVE ROUNDS—Louie Dampier, Kentucky; Clem Haskins, Western Kentucky; Dwight Smith, Western Kentucky; Willie Wolters, Boston College; Bob Verga, Duke.
ADDITIONAL ROUNDS—Earl Beecham, Midwest University; Mel Cox, Central Washington; Ken Gibbs, Vanderbilt; Pres Judy, Georgia Tech; Gwendell MacSwain, Valdosta State; Randy Mahaffey, Clemson; John Smith, Kent State.

Minnesota

FIRST FIVE ROUNDS—Mel Daniels, New Mexico; Phil Jackson, North Dakota; Bob Lloyd, Rutgers; Tim Powers, Creighton; Sam Smith, Kentucky Wesleyan.
ADDITIONAL ROUNDS—Al Clark, Eastern Kentucky; Gary Gregor, South Carolina; Irv Inniger, Indiana; Rich Jones, Illinois; Lindberg

Moody, South Carolina State; Earl Palmer, DePaul; Ron Perry, Virginia Poly Institute.

New Orleans

FIRST FIVE ROUNDS—Robert Allen, Arkansas AM&N; John Dickson, Arkansas State; James Jones, Grambling; Paul Long, Wake Forest; Ron Widby, Tennessee.
ADDITIONAL ROUNDS—Al Andrews, Tulane; George Carter, St. Bonaventure; Carl Head, West Virginia; Allan Parris, Utah; Jeff Ramsey, Florida; Bob Seagren, Southern California; Dexter Westbrook, Laurinberg Institute.

New York

FIRST FIVE ROUNDS—Sonny Dove, St. John's; Mal Graham, New York University; George Stone, Marshall; Dick Pruett, Jacksonville; Bob Wolfe, Marquette.
ADDITIONAL ROUNDS—Tim Edwards, Amherst; Dan Hansard, St. Thomas, Minn.; Frank Hoflendoner, Georgetown; Harry Laurie, St. Peters, N.J.

Oakland

FIRST FIVE ROUNDS—Wes Bialosuknia, Connecticut; Gordy Harris, Washington; Richie Moore, Hiram Scott; Al Salvadori, South Carolina; Al Tucker, Oklahoma Baptist.
ADDITIONAL ROUNDS—Art Allen, Bethune-Cookman; Nate Branch, Nebraska; Mike Davis, Virginia Union; Dave Fox, Pacific; Ron Franz, Kansas; Bill Morgan, New Mexico; Malbert Pradd, Dillard.

Pittsburgh

FIRST FIVE ROUNDS—Cliff Anderson, St. Joseph's (Pa.); Barry Liebowitz, Long Island; Earl Monroe, Winston-Salem; Craig Raymond, Brigham Young; Tom Washington, Cheyney State.
ADDITIONAL ROUNDS—Frank Card, North Carolina A&T; Ron Coleman, Missouri; Chris Kefalos, Temple; Mike Riordan, Providence; John Schroeder, Ohio University; Steve Sullivan, Georgetown; Jim Southerland, Clemson.

1968

Dallas

FIRST FIVE ROUNDS—Shaler Halimon, Utah State; Rich Jones, Memphis State; Bob Lewis, South Carolina State; John Smith, Southern Colorado State; Jo Jo White, Kansas.
SECOND FIVE ROUNDS—Wally Anderzunas, Creighton; Ron Bonne, Idaho State; Glen Combs, Virginia Tech; C. A. Core, Southeastern Louisiana; Roy Manning, Lane College.
THIRD FIVE ROUNDS—Billy Arnold, Texas; Gene Jones, Missouri; Gene Littles, High Point (N.C.); Mickey McCarty, Texas Christian; Calvin Pettit, Central Missouri.
ADDITIONAL ROUNDS—Willie Worsley, Texas-El Paso.

Denver

FIRST FIVE ROUNDS—Tom Boerwinkle, Tennessee; Hal Booker, Cheyney State; Bill Hewitt, Southern California; Walt Piatkowski, Bowling Green.
SECOND FIVE ROUNDS—Harry Hollines, Denver; Charley Parks, Idaho State; Vernon Payne, Indiana; Willie Rogers, Oklahoma; Glynn Saulters, Northeast Louisiana.
THIRD FIVE ROUNDS—Ken Hall, Westminster (Utah); Melvin Jones, Albany (Ga.) State; Julius Keye, Alcorn A&M; Mickey Smith, Memphis State; Oscar Smith, Elizabeth City (N.C.).

Houston

FIRST FIVE ROUNDS—Art Beatty, American University; Don Chaney,

Houston; John Godfrey, Abilene Christian; Elvin Hayes, Houston; Aaron Sellers, Jackson State.
SECOND FIVE ROUNDS—Martin Baietti, Manhattan; Rich Dumas, Northeast Oklahoma; Calvin Martin, Texas Southern; Mike Nordholz, Alabama; Dan Smith, Howard-Payne.
THIRD FIVE ROUNDS—Sam Butler, Southern University; Warren Chapman, Duke; Bill Gaines, East Texas State; Jim Jones, Beloit; Frank Standard, South Carolina.

Indiana
FIRST FIVE ROUNDS—Don Dee, St. Mary's of the Plains; Mike Lewis, Duke; Don May, Dayton; Bob Quick, Xavier; Phil Wagner, Georgia Tech.
SECOND FIVE ROUNDS—Dave Benedict, Central Washington; Rudy Bogad, St. John's; Jerry Newsom, Indiana State; Rich Nieman, St. Louis; Jack Thompson, South Carolina.
THIRD FIVE ROUNDS—Greg Cisson, Rider; Bob Hooper, Dayton; Harry Joyner, Indiana; Tom Niemier, Evansville.

Kentucky
FIRST FIVE ROUNDS—Wayne Chapman, Western Kentucky; Willie Davis, North Texas State; Al Dixon, Bowling Green; Fred Foster, Miami (Ohio); Westley Unseld, Louisville.
SECOND FIVE ROUNDS—Joe Gallagher, Pembroke; Joe Kennedy, Duke; Manny Leaks, Niagara; Gene Moore, St. Louis; Greg Smith, Western Kentucky.
THIRD FIVE ROUNDS—Booker Brown, Middle Tennessee; Al Hairston, Bowling Green; Thad Jaracz, Kentucky; Reggie Lacefield, Western Michigan; Bob Zoretich, DePaul.
ADDITIONAL ROUNDS—Kermit Meystedt, Southeast Missouri; John Snipes, Elizabeth City (N.C.); Butch Kaufman, Western Kentucky; Bo Wyenandt, Vanderbilt.

Los Angeles
FIRST FIVE ROUNDS—Mervin Jackson, Utah; Ed Johnston, Tennessee State; Larry Miller, North Carolina; George Stone, Marshall; Mike Warren, UCLA.
SECOND FIVE ROUNDS—Carl Fuller, Bethune-Cookman; Ed Leggett, Rocky Mountain; Lou Shepherd, Southwest Missouri State; Bob Warren, Vanderbilt; Eldridge Webb, Tulsa.
THIRD FIVE ROUNDS—Rick Adelman, Loyola (Los Angeles); Brian Brunkhorst, Marquette; Ben Foster, Pasadena; Phil Harris, Texas-El Paso; Lloyd Higgins, Pasadena.
ADDITIONAL ROUNDS—Mike LaRoche, Cal Poly (San Luis Obispo); Cary Smith, California State (Los Angeles).

Miami
FIRST FIVE ROUNDS—Tom Kondla, Minnesota; Ron Nelson, New Mexico; Don Sidle, Oklahoma; Dan Sparks, Weber State; Dallas Thornton, Kentucky Wesleyan.
SECOND FIVE ROUNDS—Ken Barnett, Delaware; Joe Franklin, Wisconsin; Darryl Jones, St. Benedict (Kan.); Al Knott, Cedarville (Ohio); Jerry Waugh, Northern Iowa.
THIRD FIVE ROUNDS—Lyndall Conway, Albuquerque; Jim Barza, Detroit Tech; Willey Iverson, Central Michigan; Terry Porter, St. Cloud (Minn.); Jim Sterkin, Detroit.

Minnesota
FIRST FIVE ROUNDS—Bill Hosket, Ohio State; Larry Newbold, Long Island; Dave Newmark, Columbia; Nick Pino, Kansas State; Sam Williams, Iowa.
SECOND FIVE ROUNDS—Roger Bohnenstiehl, Kansas; Clarence Brookins, Temple; John Haarlow, Princeton; Keith Hochstein, Holy Cross; Jeff Ockel, Utah.
THIRD FIVE ROUNDS—Willie Betts, Bradley; Greg Morris, Cornell; Billy Jones, Fairfield; Bob Redd, Marshall; Bill Tindall, Massachusetts

New Orleans
FIRST FIVE ROUNDS—Mike Butler, Memphis State; Richard Johnson, Grambling; Mark LaMoreaux, Lenoir-Rhyne; Charles Paulk, Northeast Oklahoma; Ron Williams, West Virginia.
SECOND FIVE ROUNDS—Charles Alford, Eastern Carolina; Ted Campbell, North Carolina A&T; Lee Davis, Carolina College; Dave Williams, Mississippi State; Jasper Wilson, Southern University.
THIRD FIVE ROUNDS—Passed.

New York
FIRST FIVE ROUNDS—Joe Allen, Bradley; Dick Cunningham, Murray State; Rodney Knowles, Davidson; Don Smith, Iowa State.
SECOND FIVE ROUNDS—Steve Adelman, Boston College; Eddie Biedenbach, North Carolina State; Ron Gruziak, Duquesne; Pete O'Dea, St. Peter's; Bill Soens, Miami (Fla.)
THIRD FIVE ROUNDS—Bill Butler, St. Bonaventure; John Chamberlain, C. W. Post; Anthony Koski, Providence; Bill Langheld, Fordham; Art Stephenson, Rhode Island.
ADDITIONAL ROUNDS—Harry Laurie, St. Peter's.

Oakland
FIRST FIVE ROUNDS—Warren Armstrong, Wichita; Jim Eakins, Brigham Young; Skip Harlicka, South Carolina; Bob Kauffman, Guilford; Stuart Lantz, Nebraska; Henry Logan, Western Carolina; Garfield Smith, Eastern Kentucky.
SECOND FIVE ROUNDS—Jim McKean, Washington State; Bud Ogden, Santa Clara; Rusty Parker, Miami (Fla.); Lloyd Peterson, Oregon State; John Trapp, Nevada Southern.
THIRD FIVE ROUNDS—Russ Critchfield, California; Hal Grant, Pepperdine; Art Harris, Stanford; Bryan Phillips, Valdosta; Tony Sapit, Carroll (Mont.).

1969

Carolina
FIRST FIVE ROUNDS—L. C. Bowen, Bradley; Mel Coleman, Stout (Wis.); Steve Kuberski, Bradley; Steve Mix, Toledo; Jesse Price, Milliken; Neal Walk. Florida.
SECOND FIVE ROUNDS—Howie Dickerman, Central Connecticut; Gene Ford, Western Michigan; Gene Littles, High Point (N.C.); Jack Stenner, Missouri at St. Louis; Justus Thigpen, Weber State.
ADDITIONAL ROUNDS—Phil Argento, Kentucky; Rudy Bennett, New York Tech.

Dallas
FIRST FIVE ROUNDS—Willie Brown, Middle Tennessee; Bobby Christian, Grambling; Tom Hagan, Vanderbilt, A. W. Holt, Jackson (Miss.); Cliff Shegogg, Colorado State University.
SECOND FIVE ROUNDS—Butch Beard, Louisville; Jake Ford, Maryland State; Jud Roberts, Mercer (Ga.); Ron Sanford, New Mexico; Willie Scott, Troy (Ala.) State.

Denver
FIRST FIVE ROUNDS—Isiah King, Hiram Scott; Jerry King, Louisville; Bob Portman, Creighton; Bob Presley, California; Bob Tallent, George Washington; Greg Whitman, Western Carolina.
SECOND FIVE ROUNDS—Harry Hall, Wyoming; Jim Healey, Rockhurst (Mo.); Larry Jeffries, Trinity (Tex.); Bill Justus, Tennessee; Elnardo Webster, St. Peter's (N.J.).

Indiana
FIRST FIVE ROUNDS—Bob Arnzen, Notre Dame; Dick Grubar, North Carolina; Tony Masiello, Canisius; Willie McCarter, Drake.
SECOND FIVE ROUNDS—Bill Deher, Indiana; Dave Golden, Duke; Bill

Keller, Purdue; Gerald McKee, Ohio; Ron Peret, Texas A&M.
ADDITIONAL ROUNDS—John Jamerson, Fairmont (W. Va.) State; Jim Stephenson, Maine.

Kentucky
FIRST FIVE ROUNDS—Bob Dandridge, Norfolk (Va.) State; Herm Gilliam, Purdue; Mike Grosso, Louisville; Dave Scholz, Illinois; Gene Williams, Kansas State.
SECOND FIVE ROUNDS—Chris Ellis, Virginia Tech; Dick Garrett, Southern Illinois; Willie Norwood, Alcorn A&M; Dan Saddlier, Dayton; Bobby Washington, Eastern Kentucky.
ADDITIONAL ROUNDS—Doug Brittelle, Rutgers; Gary Major, Duquesne.

Los Angeles
FIRST FIVE ROUNDS—John Baum, Temple; Simmie Hill, West Texas State; Bobby Smith, Tulsa; Dennis Stewart, Michigan; Ted Weirman, Washington State.
SECOND FIVE ROUNDS—Mack Calvin, Southern California; Mike Davis, Colorado State University; Roger Moeler, Westmar (Iowa); Dan Obrovac, Dayton; Leroy Winfield, North Texas State.
ADDITIONAL ROUNDS—Vince Fritz, Oregon State; Floyd Kerr, Colorado State University.

Miami
FIRST FIVE ROUNDS—Bill Bunting, North Carolina; Larry Cannon, LaSalle; Bob Greacen, Rutgers; John Jones, Villanova; Wilbert Jones, Albany (Ga.) State; Jim Smith, Northern Illinois.
SECOND FIVE ROUNDS—Johnny Allen, Bethune-Cookman; John Faircloth, Biscayne (Fla.); Luther Green, Long Island; Larry Lewis, St. Francis (Pa.); Lynn Shackleford, UCLA.
ADDITIONAL ROUNDS—Ed Szczesny, LaSalle.

Minnesota
FIRST FIVE ROUNDS—Luther Rackley, Xavier (Ohio); George Thompson, Marquette; Bob Whitmore, Notre Dame.
SECOND FIVE ROUNDS—Charley Bonaparte, Norfolk (Va.) State; Charles Hentz, Arkansas; Wilbur Kirkland, Cheyney (Pa.) State; Lee Lafayette, Michigan State; Kerri Limo, Brigham Young.
ADDITIONAL ROUNDS—Mike Davis, Virginia Union; Bill English, Winston-Salem; Rich Tyler, Cheyney (Pa.) State.

New Orleans
FIRST FIVE ROUNDS—John Arthurs, Tulane; Rusty Clark, North Carolina; Dave Nash, Kansas; Harley Swift, Eastern Tennessee State; Willie Taylor, Temple.
SECOND FIVE ROUNDS—Sammy Little, Delta (Miss.) State) Charley Powell, Loyola of New Orleans; James Wyatt, Northwestern Louisiana. Passed in ninth and 10th rounds.

New York
FIRST FIVE ROUNDS—Lew Alcindor, UCLA; Terry Driscoll, Boston College; Rick Roberson, Cincinnati; Ed Siudut, Holy Cross; Chris Thomford, Princeton; Norm Van Lier, St. Francis (Pa.).
SECOND FIVE ROUNDS—Bill Evans, Boston College; Tom Haggerty, Brandeis; Rob Washington, New York.
ADDITIONAL ROUNDS—Jess Claypool, Grove City (Pa.); Marv Lewis, Southampton (N.Y.).

Oakland
FIRST FIVE ROUNDS—Jack Gillespie, Montana State; Lamar Green, Morehead (Ky.) State; Don Griffin, Stanford; Edward Mast, Temple; Ron Taylor, Southern California.
SECOND FIVE ROUNDS—Bill Bowes, Elon; Joe Comer, Temple; Lloyd

Kerr, Colorado State University; Ken Spain, Houston; George Tinsley, Kentucky Wesleyan.
ADDITIONAL ROUNDS—Jim Johnson, Wisconsin; Ron Teixeria, Holy Cross.

1970

Carolina
FIRST FIVE ROUNDS—Bob Leinhard, Georgia; Pete Maravich, Louisiana State; Greg McDivit, Ohio University; Vann Wiliford, North Carolina State.
SECOND FIVE ROUNDS—Paul Adams, Central Washington; Carl Johnson, Gustavus Adolphus; Ernest Killum, Stetson; Wayne Sokolowski, Ashland State.
THIRD FIVE ROUNDS—Don Adams, Northwestern; Norvis Anderson, Stephen F. Austin; John Fultz, Rhode Island; Chuck Lloyd, Yankton; Jim Signorile, New York University.

Denver
FIRST FIVE ROUND—Greg Daust, Missouri at St. Louis; Spencer Haywood, Detroit; Dan Hester, Louisiana State; Greg Hyder, East New Mexico; John Marren, Manhattan; Ron St. Pierre, Hanover; John Vallely, UCLA.
SECOND FIVE ROUNDS—Ron Becker, New Mexico; Joe McBride, Augusta; Larry Mikan, Minnesota; Jim Penix, Bowling Green; Mike Price, Illinois.
THIRD FIVE ROUNDS—Fred Taylor, Pan American; Ken Warzyski, DePaul.

Floridians
FIRST FIVE ROUNDS—John Hummer, Princeton; Sam Robinson, Long Beach State.
SECOND FIVE ROUNDS—Clarence Ellis, Albany (Ga.) State; Levi Fontaine, Maryland State; Walt Gilmore, Ft. Valley (Ga.); John McKinney, Norfolk State; Fran O'Hanlon, Villanova; Dan Sager, Kentucky State; Gary Zeller, Drake.
THIRD FIVE ROUNDS—Rubin Daniels, Cheyney State.

Indiana
FIRST FIVE ROUNDS—Dennis Awtrey, Santa Clara; Vince Fritz, Oregon State; Rick Mount, Purdue; Surry Oliver, Stephen F. Austin.
SECOND FIVE ROUNDS—Don Curnutt, Miami; Rick Erickson, Washington State; Billy Jones, Louisiana College; Jerry Kroll, Davidson; Bob Reily, Mt. St. Mary's.
THIRD FIVE ROUNDS—Heywood Dotson, Columbia; Mickey Foster, Arizona; Seabern Hill, Arizona State; Ted Hillery, St. Joseph's (Ind.); Jeff Sewell, Marquette.

Kentucky
FIRST FIVE ROUNDS—Pete Cross, San Francisco U.; Dan Issel, Kentucky; Mike Pratt, Kentucky; Claude Virden, Murray State; Howard Wright, Austin Peay.
SECOND FIVE ROUNDS—Joe Bergman, Creighton; Mike Casey, Kentucky; Ted Rose, Northern Michigan; Charles Wallace, Oklahoma City; Al Williams, Drake.
THIRD FIVE ROUNDS—Skip Hess, Toledo; Perry Wallace, Vanderbilt; Lou West, Seattle; Willie Woods, Eastern Kentucky.

Memphis
FIRST FIVE ROUNDS—Garfield Heard, Oklahoma; George Johnson, Stephen F. Austin; Sam Lacey, New Mexico; Wendell Ladner, Mississippi Southern.
SECOND FIVE ROUNDS—Charles Bishop, Louisiana Tech; Coby Die-

trick, San Jose State; George Johnson, Dillard; Robert Mabry, Rio Grande; Marvin Winkler, Southwestern Louisiana.
THIRD FIVE ROUNDS—Ron Coleman, Mississippi; Frank Lothridge, Pan American; Andy Owens, Florida.

New York
FIRST FIVE ROUNDS—Jim Ard, Cincinnati; Doug Cook, Davidson; Jim Hayes, Boston University; Bob Lanier, St. Bonaventure; Geoff Petrie, Princeton.
SECOND FIVE ROUNDS—Joe DePre, St. John's; Harvey Marlatt, Eastern Michigan; Rod McIntyre, Jacksonville; Carleton Poole, Philadelphia Textile; Ollie Taylor, Houston.
THIRD FIVE ROUNDS—Dale Kelley, Northwestern; Carl Macklin, Florida State; Erwin Polnick, Stephen F. Austin; Mike Switzer, Texas-El Paso; John Venerable, Kansas State.

Pittsburgh
FIRST FIVE ROUNDS—Vic Bartolome, Oregon State; George Janky, Dayton; Mike Maloy, Davidson; Rex Morgan, Jacksonville; Calvin Murphy, Niagara; Doug Ogletree, Cincinnati; Cornell Warner, Jackson State.
SECOND FIVE ROUNDS—Lou Herndon, Jackson State; Lavern Howard, Grambling; Bill Jankins, Long Beach State.
THIRD FIVE ROUNDS—Robert Kornegay, Hampton Institute; Boyd Lynch, Eastern Kentucky; Willie Watson, Oklahoma City; Jimmy Wilson, Cheyney State; Billy Zopf, Duquesne.

Texas
FIRST FIVE ROUNDS—Nate Archibald, Texas-El Paso; Immanual Cannon, Grambling; Bob Croft, Tennessee; Joe Hamilton, North Texas State; John Johnson, Iowa; Stan Love, Oregon.
SECOND FIVE ROUNDS—Michael Bernard, Kentucky State; Bill Cain, Iowa State; Randall Causey, McMurry College; Al Henry, Wisconsin; Steve Patterson, UCLA; Glen Vidnovic, Iowa.
THIRD FIVE ROUNDS—Paul Brown, Arkansas Tech; Ron Pitts, Wiley.

Utah
FIRST FIVE ROUNDS—Carl Ashley, Wyoming; Jim Collins, New Mexico; Dave Cowens, Florida State; Fred Davis, Howard Payne; Jim McMillan, Columbia; Dave Sorensen, Ohio State; Rudy Tomjanovich, Michigan.
SECOND FIVE ROUNDS—Stan Dodds, Wyoming; Virgil Frederick, Drury; Ralph Ogden, Santa Clara; Israel Oliver, Elizabeth City (N.C.); Bill Stricker, Pacific; Kevin Wilson, Ashland (Colo.).
THIRD FIVE ROUNDS—Bruce Chapman, Nevada-Las Vegas; Dennis Clark, Springfield; Ron Knight, California State (L.A.); Robert Moore, Central State (Ohio); Lou Small, Nevada-Las Vegas.

Virginia
FIRST FIVE ROUNDS—Gary Freeman, Oregon State; James Gilbert, Adams State (Colo.); Gregg Howard, New Mexico; George Irvine, Washington; Bill Paultz, St. John's; Charlie Scott, North Carolina.
SECOND FIVE ROUNDS—Tommy Carter, Paul Quinn; Tom Everette, Carson-Newman; Curtis Perry, Southwest Missouri State; Paul Ruffner, Brigham Young; Will Teague, Youngstown.
THIRD FIVE ROUNDS—Charles Bloodworth, Northwest Louisiana State; Leon Edmund, Portland; Andy Jennings, Alderson-Broaddus; George Jerman, West New England; Scott Warner, Brigham Young.

1971

Carolina
FIRST THREE ROUNDS—Ted McClain, Tennessee State; Gregg Nor-

thington, Alabama State; Elmore Smith, Kentucky State (redshirt); Rich Yunkus, Georgia Tech.
ADDITIONAL ROUNDS—Luke Adams (5), Lamar Tech; Ron Rippetoe (6), David Lipscomb; Ed Kemp (7), Adams State; Kenny Davis (8), Georgetown (Ky.); Dave Wohl (9), Pennsylvania; Kendall Mayfield (10), Tuskegee; Robert McKenney (11), Pepperdine; Gregg Love (12), Ohio University; Bob Wenczel (13), Rutgers; Ron Dorsey (14), Tennessee State; Hank Commodore (15), Northwest Oklahoma; Frank Lorthridge (16), Pan American; Dan Fife (17), Michigan; Cliff Harris (18), Hardin-Simmons; Steve Bilsky (19), Pennsylvania.

Dallas
FIRST THREE ROUNDS—Roger Brown, Kansas; Stan Love, Oregon; Gary Nelson, Duquesne; Walt Szczerbiak, George Washington; Sidney Wicks, UCLA.
ADDITIONAL ROUNDS—Gene Phillips (4), SMU; Collis Jones (5), Notre Dame; George Trapp (6), Long Beach State; Sterling Quant (7), Central State (Ohio); Curtis Rowe (8), UCLA; Jimmy Guymon (9), E. New Mexico State; Gene Knolle (10), Texas Tech; Al Shumate (11), No. Texas State; Willie Hart (12), Grambling; Eugene Kennedy (13), TCU; Bill Brickhouse (14), Montana State; William Chatman (15), Baylor; Harry Taylor (16), Los Angeles Baptist; Dan McGhee (17), Howard Payne.

Denver
FIRST THREE ROUNDS—Cliff Meely, Colorado; Mike Newlin, Utah; Marv Roberts, Utah State.
ADDITIONAL ROUNDS—Al Smith (4), Bradley; Dave Robisch (5), Kansas; William Graham (6), Kentucky State; Ken Gardner (7), Utah; Tyron Marioneaux (8), Loyola of New Orleans; Mike Childress (9), Colorado State University; George Fasber (10), Purdue; John Ribock (11), South Carolina; Gary Brell (12), Marquette; Glen Richels (13), Wisconsin; Jerry Hyder (14), East New Mexico; Richard Dixon (16), Loyola of Los Angeles; David Walls (17), Jackson State; Paul Botts (18), Central Michigan; Ron Smith (19), Wichita; Bobby Jones (20), Drake.

Floridians
FIRST THREE ROUNDS—Willie Long, New Mexico.
ADDITIONAL ROUNDS—Rich Rinaldi (5), St. Peters (N.J.); Larry Holliday (6), Oregon; Gregg Starrick (7), Southern Illinois; Tom Lee (8), Arizona; Jim Haderlein (9), Loyola of Los Angeles; Doug Rex (10), Santa Barbara; Gerald Lockett (11) Arkansas AM&N; Willie Allen (12), Miami (Fla.); Jackie Ridgle (13), California; Pembroke Burroughs (14), Jacksonville; Ken May (15), Dayton; Wayman Terrell (16), Oklahoma Baptist; Bill Drozdiak (17), Oregon; Eddie Myers (18), Arizona; Steve Sims (19), Pepperdine; Pat Biber (20), Tampa.

Indiana
FIRST THREE ROUNDS—Darnell Hillman, San Jose State; John Mengelt, Auburn.
ADDITIONAL ROUNDS—Jim Cleamons (4), Ohio State; Clarence Glover (5), Western Kentucky; Jeff Haliburton (6), Drake; Dean Meminger (7), Marquette; Ken Booker (8), UCLA; Tom Crosswhite (9), Dayton; Larry Weatherford (10), Purdue; James England (11), Tennessee; Jeff Smith (12), New Mexico State; Rick Katherman (13), Duke; Clarence Smith (14), Villanova; Rich Walker (15), Bowling Green; Tom Bush (16), Drake; Jim Irving (17), St. Louis; Bob Bissant (18), Loyola of New Orleans; Rudy Benjamin (19), Michigan State; Slick Pinkham (20), DePauw (redshirt).

Kentucky
FIRST THREE ROUNDS—Artis Gilmore, Jacksonville; John Roche, South Carolina.
ADDITIONAL ROUNDS—Fred Brown (4), Iowa; Mike Gale (5), Eliz-

abeth Cith (N.C.); James Welch (6), Houston; Larry Steele (7), Kentucky; Clarence Sherrod (8), Wisconsin; Mike O'Brien (9), St. Leo College (Fla.); Larry Sanders (10), Duke; Sid Catlett (11), Notre Dame; James Dinwiddle (12), Kentucky; Pierre Russell (13), Kansas; Jerome Perry (14), Western Kentucky; Willie Cherry (15), Denver.

Memphis
FIRST THREE ROUNDS—Randy Denton, Duke; Jim Rose, Western Kentucky; Thorpe Weber, Vanderbilt.
ADDITIONAL ROUNDS—Tom Owens (4), South Carolina; Amos Thomas (4), Southwest Oklahoma; Ken McIntosh (5), Eastern Michigan; Fred Hilton (6), Grambling; Loyd King (7), Virginia Tech; James Douglas (8), Memphis State; Henry Smith (9), Missouri; Jim Gregory (10), E. Carolina; Danny Davis (11), Henderson; Gary Reist (12), Rice; Edward Hoskins (13), Lemoyne; Ken Riley (14), Middle Tennessee State; Rod Behrens (15), Stanford; Don Johnson (16), Tennessee; Haywood Hill (17), Oral Roberts; Reggie Wood (18), Steubenville; Billy Barnes (19), Southern State; Alan Dalton (20), Suffolk (Mass.).

New York
FIRST THREE ROUNDS—Charles Davis, Wake Forest; Bob Kissane, Holy Cross; Marvin Stewart, Nebraska.
ADDITIONAL ROUNDS—Dick Gibbs (4), Texas-El Paso; Glen Sommers (5), Gannon; Mike Necaise (6), William Carey; Otis Allison (7), Nevada; John Duncan (8), Kentucky Wesleyan; Jarrett Durham (9), Duquesne; Bill Warner (11), Arizona; Blain Henry (12), Marshall; Don Ward (13), Colgate; Skip Young (14), Florida State; George Sisk (15), Georgia Southern; Brian Mahoney (16), Manhattan; Ollie Sherman (17), Minnesota; Bobby Doyle (18), Texas-El Paso; Calvin Oliver (19), Pan American; Greg Cluess (20), St. John's (redshirt).

Pittsburgh
FIRST THREE ROUNDS—Jim O'Brien, Boston College; Howard Porter, Villanova; Levi Wyatt, Alcorn A&M.
ADDITIONAL ROUNDS—Bubba Jones (4), Ashland; Bill Smith (4), Syracuse; Mike Jordan (5), Savannah State; Barry Nelson (6), Duquesne; John Sutter (7), Tulane; Charles Yelverton (8), Fordham; Vincent White (9), Savannah State; James Fleming (10), Alcorn A&M; Eric Hill (10), Minnesota; Rayford McCambray (11), Miles; Bunny Wilson (12), Baltimore; Ray Green (13), California (Pa.) State; Gene Mumford (14), Scranton; Lee McCullough (15), Indiana (Pa.) State; Russell Golden (16), Jackson State (redshirt); Harry James (17), Montclair State; Stan Novey (18), Mt. St. Mary's.

Utah
FIRST FIVE ROUNDS—Rick Fisher, Colorado State University (redshirt); Jim McDaniels, Western Kentucky.
ADDITIONAL ROUNDS—Dennis Layton (4), Southern California; Lee Dedmon (5), North Carolina; Bobby Fields (6), LaSalle; Erwin (Chip) Johnson (7), Augusta; Jim Day (8), Morehead State; Willy Humes (9), Idaho State; Jake Jones (10), Assumption (Mass.)

Virginia
FIRST THREE ROUNDS—Austin Carr, Notre Dame; Ken Durrett, LaSalle; Dana Lewis, Tulsa (redshirt); Willie Sojourner, Weber State.
ADDITIONAL ROUNDS—Dana Pagett (4), Southern California; Clifford Ray (7), Oklahoma; Bill Gerry (8), Virginia; Gilbert McGregor (10), Wake Forest; Hector Blondet (11), Murray State; Lou Grillo (12), Mt. St. Mary's.

1971 SPECIAL CIRCUMSTANCE DRAFT

Denver
SECOND ROUND—Mickey Davis, Duquesne.

Carolina
FOURTH ROUND—Phil Chenier, California.

New York
FOURTH ROUND—Ed Leftwich, North Carolina State.

1972

Carolina
FIRST FIVE ROUNDS—Tom Riker, South Carolina; Dennis Wuycik, North Carolina; Dill Chamberlain, North Carolina; Freddie Boyd, Oregon State.
ADDITIONAL ROUNDS—Steve Bracey, Tulsa; Don Holcomb, Memphis State; Henry Bibby, UCLA; Jerry Crocker, Guilford; Mike Collins, Seattle; Wilbur Loftin, Southwestern Louisiana; Charles Dudley, Washington; Mike Sneed, Fayetteville State; Steve Previs, North Carolina; Kent Martens, Abilene Christian; Nathan Cannady, Virginia Union; David Smith, Western Carolina; Curtis Pritchett, St. Augustine; Paul Coder, North Carolina State.

Dallas
FIRST FIVE ROUNDS—LaRue Martin, Chicago Loyola; Mike Ratliff, Eau Claire State; Bob Morse, Penn; Bill Walton, UCLA; Steve Hawes, Washington.
ADDITIONAL ROUNDS—Jim Creighton, Colorado; Frank Schade, Eau Claire State; Ansley Truitt, California; Wayne Grabiec, Michigan; Jerry Zelinski, Northern Illinois; Jeff Hickman, Houston; Stan Key, Kentucky; Don Wiese, Ripon; Rhea Taylor, Arizona State; Ron Williams, Murray State (Ky.); Joe Reddick, Albany (Ga.) State; Al Vilchek, Louisville.

Denver
FIRST FIVE ROUNDS—Bud Stallworth, Kansas; Paul Stovall, Arizona State; Paul Westphal, Southern California; Claude Terry, Stanford; Doug Collins, Illinois State; Dave Bustion, Denver.
ADDITIONAL ROUNDS—Sam Siebert, Kentucky State; Ron Riley, Southern California; Ted Martiniuk, St. Peter's (N.J.); Bernie Fryer, Brigham Young; Paul Pender, Fresno State; Gary Stewart, Canisius; Mike Reid, California-Riverside; John Burks, San Francisco; John Tschogl, Santa Barbara; Leon Huff, Drake; Larry Morris, Tulsa; Dave Hullman, Arizona State; Harold Little, New Mexico; Andy Knowles, Louisiana Tech; John Belcher, Arkansas State.

Floridians
FIRST FIVE ROUNDS—Dwight Davis, Houston; Mike Stewart, Santa Clara (redshirt); Scott English, Texas-El Paso; Greg Starrick, Southern Illinois.
ADDITIONAL ROUNDS—Charles Tharp, Belhaven; Swen Nater, UCLA (redshirt); Ron Thomas, Louisville; Ernie Fleming, Jacksonville; Sam Cash, California-Riverside; Tracy Tripucka, Lafayette; Jerry Brucks, Wyoming; Bobby Jack, Oklahoma; Gregg Flaker, Missouri; Ray Golson, West Texas State (redshirt); Gregg Lowery, Texas Tech; Arnie Berman, Brown; Fred Devaughn, Westmont (redshirt); Bob Zinder, Kansas State; Al Davis, Hawaii.

Indiana

FIRST FIVE ROUNDS—Ed Ratleff, Long Beach State; Nate Stephens, Long Beach State; Oscar Evans, Butler.
ADDITIONAL ROUNDS—George Adams, Gardner-Webb; Rich Garner, Manhattan; Cavin Anderson, Valley City; Wardell Dyson, Shaw; Jolly Spight, Santa Clara; Bill Burton, Eastern Kentucky; Wally Rice, Penn Military; Lee Sims, Morehead State; Nate Williams, Utah State.

Kentucky

FIRST FIVE ROUNDS—Corky Calhoun, Penn.
ADDITIONAL ROUNDS—Matt Gantt, St. Bonaventure; Bill Kennedy, Arizona State; Terry Benton, Wichita State; Ernest Pettis, Western Michigan; Cleveland Hill, Nicholls State; Andrew Pettes, Oklahoma; David Hall, Kansas State; Jerry Clack, Oklahoma State; Tom Parker, Kentucky; Jerry Dunn, Western Kentucky; Mike Bowling, Arizona State.

Memphis

FIRST FIVE ROUNDS—David Brent, Jacksonville; Russell Lee, Marshall; Jim Price, Louisville; Rusty Blair, Oregon.
ADDITIONAL ROUNDS—Bob Ford, Purdue; Rowland Garrett, Florida State; Sam Simmons, Bradley; Steve Davidson, West Texas State; Jackie Young, Rocky Mountain; Steve Turner, Vanderbilt (redshirt); Henry Bacon, Louisville; Rupert Breedlove, Oglethorpe; Sam Mc-Carney, Oral Roberts; Gene Mack, Iowa State; Tom Arnholt, Vanderbilt; Steve Schmidt, South Alabama; Terry Hankton, Arkansas Tech.

New York

FIRST FIVE ROUNDS—Jim Chones, Marquette; Brian Taylor, Princeton; Joby Wright, Indiana; Bob Lackey, Marquette; Dwayne Dillard, Eastern Michigan; Art White, Georgetown.
ADDITIONAL ROUNDS—Ron Harris, Wichita State; Hank Siemiontkowski, Villanova; Wally Jones, Long Island; Ed Czernota, Sacred Heart; Randy Noll, Marshall (redshirt); Quinas Brower, Hofstra; Bill Phillips, St. John's; Kelly Utley, Shaw; Paul Hoffman, St. Bonaventure; Ken Bradley, Nazarene.

Pittsburgh

FIRST FIVE ROUNDS—John Gianelli, Pacific; Chuck Terry, Long Beach State; Bob Davis, Weber State; Will Robinson, West Virginia; Harold Fox, Jacksonville.
ADDITIONAL ROUNDS—James Silas, Stephen F. Austin; Joe Mackey, Southern California; Marshall Wingate, Niagara; Charles Edge, Lemoyne-Owen; Bryan Adrian, Davidson; Joe Gaines, Belmont; Chick Downing, St. Benedict's; Bill Pleas, Detroit; Dave Werthman, West Virginia; Henry Seawright, Manhattan (redshirt); Steve McMahon, Merrimac; Harry Andersen, St. Peter's (N.J.); Manual Raga, Mexico.

Utah

FIRST FIVE ROUNDS—Chris Ford, Villanova; Travis Grant, Kentucky State; Chuck Jura, Nebraska; Bob Nash, Hawaii.
ADDITIONAL ROUNDS—Tommy Patterson, Ouachita Baptist; Eric McWilliams, Long Beach State; Frank Russell, Detroit; Mike Jackson, Colorado State; Kevin Porter, St. Francis (Pa.); Willie Hart, Grambling; Lloyd Neal, Tennessee State; Simpson DeGrate, Texas Christian; Mose Adolph, California State; Harvey Catchings, Hardin-Simmons (redshirt); Gary Ladd, Seattle; Henry Speele, Northeast Louisiana; Dwight Holliday, Hawaii; George Price, Colorado State U.; George Bryant, Eastern Kentucky.

Virginia

FIRST FIVE ROUNDS—Bill Franklin, Purdue.
ADDITIONAL ROUNDS—Reggie Bird, Princeton; Al Saunders, Louisiana State; Billy Shepherd, Butler; Mike Barr, Duquesne; Rick Aydlett,

South Carolina; Kent Hollenbeck, Kentucky; Milton Adams, Portland; Ralph Houston, West Texas; Rudy Peele, Norfolk State; Scott Mc-Candlish, Virginia; Jay Mottola, Lafayette.

1972 DISPERSAL DRAFT

Following is the list of veteran and rookies drafted on June 13, 1972, following the resolution of the Floridians and Pittsburgh franchises.

First Round

Memphis—George Thompson, Pittsburgh; Denver—Warren Jabali, Floridians; Carolina—Mike Lewis, Pittsburgh; Dallas—John Brisker, Pittsburgh; Dallas—Harley Swift, Pittsburgh; Carolina—Mack Calvin, Floridians; Denver—Willie Long, Floridians; Memphis—Ron Franz, Floridians; Virginia—Swen Nater (UCLA) (redshirt), Floridians; Utah—Larry Jones, Floridians; Kentucky—Walt Szczerbiak, Pittsburgh; New York—Chuck Terry (Long Beach State), Pittsburgh; Indiana—Dwight Davis (Houston), Floridians.

Second Round

Memphis—Dave Lattin, Pittsburgh; Denver—Scott English (Texas-El Paso), Floridians; Carolina—Mike Stewart (Santa Clara) (redshirt), Floridians; Dallas—John Gianelli (Pacific), Pittsburgh; Virginia—Joe Mackey (Southern California), Pittsburgh; Utah—Chick Downing (St. Benedicts), Pittsburgh; Kentucky—Ernie Fleming (Jacksonville), Floridians; Indiana—Dwight Jones (Houston), Floridians.

Third Round

Memphis—Sam Cash (California Riverside), Floridians; Denver—Al Tucker, Floridians; Carolina—Mike Grosso, Pittsburgh; Dallas—Jerry Brucks (Wyoming), Floridians; Virginia—Craig Raymond, Floridians; Utah—Wil Robinson (West Virginia), Pittsburgh; Kentucky—Lonnie Wright, Floridians; New York—George Tinsley, Floridians; Indiana—Tracy Tripucka (Lafayette), Floridians.

Fourth Round

Memphis—Ron Thomas (Louisville), Floridians; Carolina—Greg Starrick (Southern Illinois), Floridians; Dallas—Bobby Jack (Oklahoma), Floridians; Virginia—Jim Ligon, Pittsburgh; Utah—Henry Seawright (Manhattan) (redshirt), Pittsburgh; Kentucky—Gregg Flaker (Missouri), Floridians; Indiana—Bryan Adrian (Davidson), Pittsburgh.

Fifth Round

Memphis—Charles Edge (Lemoyne-Owen), Pittsburgh; Virginia—Greg Lowery (Texas Tech), Floridians; Utah—Bill Pleas (Detroit), Pittsburgh.

Sixth Round

Memphis—Ray Golson (West Texas State) (redshirt), Floridians; Virginia—Al Davis (Hawaii), Floridians.

1972 EXPANSION DRAFT

San Diego

FIRST ROUND—Stew Johnson, Carolina; George Johnson, Dallas; Art Becker, Denver; George Peeples, Indiana; Les Hunter, Kentucky; Don Sidle, Memphis; Ollie Taylor, New York; Red Robbins, Utah; Mike Barrett, Virginia.
SECOND ROUND—Larry Miller, Carolina; Simmie Hill, Dallas; Chuck

Williams, Denver; rights to Dwight Jones (Houston), Indiana; Lonnie Wright, Kentucky; Charlie Williams, Memphis; Gene Moore, New York; Mike Butler, Utah; Craig Raymond, Virginia.

1973 SPECIAL CIRCUMSTANCE DRAFT

(Teams Listed Alphabetically)

First Round

Denver—Mike Bantom, St. Joseph's (Pa.); Indiana—Mike Green, Louisiana Tech; Kentucky—Ernie DiGregorio, Providence; Memphis—Larry Kenon, Memphis State; New York—Jim Brewer, Minnesota; San Antonio—Kevin Kunnert, Iowa; San Diego—David Vaughan, Oral Roberts; Utah—Robert Parrish, Centenary, and Jim Baker, Nevada; Virginia—George Gervin, Eastern Michigan.

Second Round

Carolina—Bobby Jones, North Carolina, and Tom Burleson, North Carolina State; Denver—Clyde Turner, Minnesota; Indiana—Louis Dunbar, Houston; Memphis—Ray Lewis, L.A. State; New York—Bill Schaeffer, St. John's; San Antonio—John Brown, Missouri; San Diego—Bird Averitt, Pepperdine; Utah—Alvan Adams, Oklahoma; Virginia—Barry Parkhill, Virginia.

1973 SENIOR DRAFT

First Round

San Diego—Dwight Lamar, Southwest Louisiana; Memphis—Larry Finch, Memphis State; San Antonio—Mike D'Antoni, Marshall; New York—Doug Collins, Illinois State; Virginia—Allen Bristow, V.P.I.; Denver—Ed Ratleff, Long Beach State; Indiana—Steve Downing, Indiana; Utah—Ronnie Robinson, Memphis State; Kentucky—Louis Nelson, Washington; Carolina—Mel Davis, St. John's.

Second Round

Memphis—Wendell Hudson, Alabama; San Antonio—Kevin Joyce, South Carolina; San Diego—Tim Bassett, Georgia; Kentucky (from Utah-N.Y.)—Derek Dickey, Cincinnati; Virginia—Allie McGuire, Marquette; Denver—Steve Mitchell, Kansas State; Indiana—Jim O'Brien, Maryland; Utah—Leonard Gray, Long Beach State; Kentucky—Ron King, Florida State; Carolina—Nick Weatherspoon, Illinois.

Third Round

Memphis—David Langston, Drake; San Antonio—Tom Kozelko, Toledo; New York—Tom Ingelsby, Villanova; San Diego—Jim Lister, Sam Houston State; Virginia—Caldwell Jones, Albany (Ga.) State; Denver—Kevin Stacom, Providence; Indiana—Jim Retseck, Auburn; Utah—Steve Newsome, Houston; Kentucky—M. L. Carr, Guilford State; Utah (from Car.)—Ted Manakas, Princeton.

Fourth Round

Memphis—Harry Rogers, St. Louis; New York (from S.A.)—Phil Hankinson, Penn.; San Diego—Darryl Minniefield, New Mexico; New York—Kermit Washington, American; Virginia—Bob Lauriski, Utah State; Denver—Pat McFarland, St. Joseph's (Pa.); Indiana—John Ritter, Indiana; Utah—Martin Terry, Arkansas; Kentucky—Ron Behagen, Minnesota; Carolina—Kresimir Cosic, Brigham Young.

Fifth Round

Memphis—Dennis Bell, Drake; San Antonio—Luke Witte, Ohio State; New York—Reggie Royals, Florida State; San Diego—Ken Brady, Michigan; Virginia—John Perry, Pan American; Denver—Larry Farmer, UCLA; Indiana—Alan Hornyak, Ohio State; Utah—Pete Harris, Stephen F. Austin; Kentucky—William Harris, North Carolina State; Carolina—Larry Hollyfield, UCLA.

Sixth Round

Memphis—George Karl, North Carolina; San Antonio—Gary Melchionni, Duke; San Diego—Jim Owens, Arizona State; New York—Neal Jorgenson, Oregon State; Virginia—Aaron Stewart, Richmond; Denver—Martinez Denmon, Iowa State; Indiana—Joe Wallace, Denver; Utah—David Winfield, Minnesota; Kentucky—Mike Boylan, Assumption (Mass.); Carolina—Joe Reaves, Bethel.

Seventh Round

Memphis—E. C. Coleman, Houston Baptist; San Antonio—Richie Fuqua, Oral Roberts; New York—Kenny Charles, Fordham; San Diego—Nate Stevens, Long Beach State; Virginia—Rubin Montanez, Duquesne; Denver—James Brown, Harvard; Indiana—Jim Andrews, Kentucky; Utah—B. G. Brosterhaus, Texas; Kentucky—Les Taylor, Murray State; Carolina—Ozzie Edwards, Oklahoma City.

Eighth Round

Memphis—Rod Freeman, Vanderbilt; San Antonio—Henry Wilmore, Michigan; San Diego—Chris McMurray, San Diego State; New York—Gene Doyle, Holy Cross; Virginia—Walter McGary, Tennessee at Chattanooga; Denver—Gary Rhoades, Colorado State; Indiana—Mike Edwards, Tennessee; Utah—Mike Williams, Kentucky Wesleyan; Kentucky—James Greene, Kentucky Wesleyan; Carolina—Steve Becker, Yankton (S.D.)

Ninth Round

Memphis—Charles Mitchell, Eastern Kentucky; San Antonio—Mark Sidley, Northwestern; New York—Russ Hunt, Furman; San Diego—Clint Harris, Iowa State; Virginia—Phil Chenier, California (Balt.-NBA); Denver—Connie Warren, Xavier; Indiana—Robert Wilson (redshirt), Wichita State; Utah—Roy McPipe, Eastern Montana; Kentucky—John Johnson (redshirt), Denver; Carolina—Abe Stewart, Jacksonville.

Tenth Round

Memphis—Chuck Iverson, South Dakota; San Antonio—Larry Lilly, Alabama State; San Diego—Nick Connor, Illinois; New York—Gene Armstead, Rutgers; Virginia—Joe Cafferky, North Carolina State; Denver—Jeff Dawson (redshirt), Illinois; Indiana—Byron Jones, San Francisco; Utah—Melvin Russell, Centenary; Kentucky—Mike Macaluso, Canisius; Carolina—Gerald Smith, Detroit.

1973 UNDERGRADUATE DRAFT

Round One

San Diego—Bill Walton, UCLA; Memphis—David Thompson, North Carolina State; San Antonio—Dwight Jones, Houston; New York—Henry Williams, Jacksonville; Virginia—Phil Smith, San Francisco; Denver—Marvin Barnes, Providence; Indiana—Len Elmore, Maryland; Utah—Bruce Seals, Xavier (La.); Kentucky—Don Smith, Dayton; Carolina—Maurice Lucas, Marquette.

Round Two

Memphis—Larry Robinson, Texas; San Antonio—Tom Henderson, Hawaii; San Diego—Jim Bradley, Northern Illinois; New York—Campy

Russell, Michigan; Virginia—John Shumate, Notre Dame; Denver—Dennis DuVal, Syracuse; Indiana—Rudy Jackson, Hutchinson JC; Utah—Marvin Webster, Morgan State; Kentucky—James Forbes, Texas-El Paso; Carolina—Kevin Restani, San Francisco.

1973 SUPPLEMENTARY DRAFT

(Teams Listed Alphabetically)

First Round
Carolina—Cal Tatum, Southern Colorado State; Denver—Lamont King, Long Beach State; Kentucky—Steve Rowell, Rhode Island; Memphis—Wardell Jeffries, Oklahoma Baptist; San Antonio—Craig Littlepage, Penn.; San Diego—Larry Moore, Texas-Arlington; Utah—Dennis Johnson, Ferris State; Virginia—Willie Calvert, Abilene Christian.

Second Round
Carolina—Steve Smith, Loyola (Calif.); Denver—Tom Peck, Eau Claire; Kentucky—James Garvin, Boston U.; Memphis—Don Watts, Xavier (La.); San Antonio—Tom Coughran, California; San Diego—Mike Contreras, Arizona State; Utah—Bill McCoy, North Iowa; Virginia—Don Johnson, Lebanon Valley.

Third Round
Carolina—Bill Bailey, Catawba; Denver—Lindell Reason, Eastern Michigan; Kentucky—Chuck Witt, Western Kentucky; Memphis—Roy Simpson, Furman; San Antonio—Bob Fullerton, Xavier; San Diego—Doug Little, Oregon; Utah—James Floyd, Shaw; Virginia—Gregg Hawkins, North Carolina State.

Fourth Round
Carolina—David Angel, Clemson; Kentucky—Fran Costello, Providence; Memphis—Norman Russell, Oklahoma; San Antonio—Bob Kilgore, Michigan State; San Diego—Ernie Kusyner, Kansas State; Utah—Charles Golson, Col. of Emporia; Virginia—Mike Allocco, Stonehill (Mass.)

Fifth Round
Carolina—Carl Jackson, St. Bonaventure; Kentucky—Ed Childress, Austin Peay; Memphis—Aaron Covington, Canisius; Utah—Mike Quick, San Francisco; San Antonio—Ron Hogue, Georgia; Virginia—Allan Shaw, Duke.

Sixth Round
Carolina—Lynn Greer, Virginia State; Kentucky—Jerry Clark, Skagit Valley JC (Wash.); Memphis—Fred Laboroni, Santa Clara; San Antonio—John Lang, Augustana; San Diego—Jerry Brisbano, S.W. Louisiana; Utah—Lee Colburn, South Dakota State; Virginia—Howard White, Sam Houston State.

Seventh Round
Carolina—Dale Adams, Mount St. Mary's; Memphis—John Wolfenberg, Valparaiso; San Antonio—Jeff Overhouse, Texas A&M; San Diego—Mark Beckwith, Montana State; Utah—Robert White, Sam Houston State; Virginia—Darryl Brown, Maryland.

Eighth Round
Carolina—Terrance Murchinson, Fayetteville; Memphis—Jim Crawford, LaSalle; San Antonio—Tim Dominiz, Valdosta; San Diego—Wayne Pack, Tennessee Tech; Utah—Gary Watson, Wisconsin; Virginia—Linwood Johnson, Virginia State (redshirt).

Ninth Round
Memphis—Rick Williams, Iowa; San Antonio—Bill Harris, No. Illinois; San Diego—Fred DeVaughn, Western Montana; Utah—Larry Davis, Centenary.

Tenth Round
Memphis—Joe Wise, Bridgewater (Mass.) St.; San Antonio—Bob Bodell, Maryland; Utah—Ben Kelso, Central Michigan

Eleventh Round
Memphis—Reed Johnson, Oklahoma Christian; San Antonio—Leon Howard, Wisconsin; Utah—Nate Hawthorne, So. Illinois.

Twelfth Round
Memphis—Greg Juricisin, Cincinnati; San Antonio—Jeff Jellison, N.E. Massachusetts; Utah—John Thomas, Mississippi Southern.

Fourteenth Round
Utah—Gary Black, Rocky Mountain; Utah—Sam Whitehead, Sam Houston State.

Fifteenth Round
Utah—Harvey Catchings, Hardin-Simmons.

1974 COLLEGE DRAFT

First Round
Virginia—Tom McMillen, Maryland; Memphis—Scott Wedman, Colorado; San Diego—Major Jones, Albany (Ga.) State; Denver—James "Fly" Williams, Austin Peay; Virginia (from S.A.)—Jan Van Breda Kolff, Vanderbilt; Indiana—Billy Knight, Pittsburgh; Carolina—John Lucas, Maryland; San Diego (from Ky.)—Cliff Pondexter, Long Beach State; New York—Brian Winters, South Carolina; Utah—Joe Meriweather, Southern Illinois.

Second Round
Memphis—Clarence "Foots" Walker, West Georgia State; Virginia—Jesse Dark, Virginia Commonwealth; San Diego—Gus Bailey, Texas-El Paso; Denver—Frank Kendrick, Purdue; San Antonio—Leonard Robinson, Tennessee State; Indiana—Bruce King, Pan American; New York (from Car.)—Rich Kelley, Stanford; Kentucky—Al Eberhard, Missouri; Carolina (from N.Y.)—Gus Gerard, Virginia; Utah—Len Kosmalski, Tennessee.

Third Round
Memphis—Bob Wilson, Iowa State; Utah (from Va.)—Moses Malone, Petersburg (Va.) H.S.; Denver—Mike Sojourner, Utah; Virginia (from S.D.)—Lionel Billingy, Duquesne; Utah (from S.A.)—Aaron James, Grambling; Indiana—Roland Grant, New Mexico State; Utah (from Car.)—Tom Barker, Southern Idaho; Kentucky (from Utah)—Sammy High, Tulsa; San Antonio (from Ky.)—Colis Temple, Louisiana State; New York—Tom Boswell, South Carolina.

Fourth Round
Memphis—Glenn McDonald, Long Beach State; Virginia—Lermon Battle, Fairmont State; San Diego—Richie O'Connor, Fairfield; Denver—Coniel Norman, Arizona; San Antonio—Fred Saunders, Syracuse; San Antonio (from Ind.)—Kim Hughes, Wisconsin; Carolina—Darrell Elston, North Carolina; Utah—Sam McCants, Oral Roberts; Kentucky—Lloyd Batts, Cincinnati; New York—Talvin Skinner, Maryland Eastern Shore.

Fifth Round

Memphis—Tyrone Medley, Utah; Virginia—Bernard Harris, Virginia Commonwealth; Denver—Bernard Hardin, New Mexico; San Diego—Greg Lee, UCLA; San Antonio—Eugene Short, Jackson State; Indiana—Eddie Woods, Oral Roberts; Carolina—Mickey Johnson, Aurora Illinois; Utah—Steve Brooks, Arkansas State; Kentucky—Seymour Reed, Bradley; New York—Eric Fernsten, San Francisco.

Sixth Round

Memphis—Wolfgang Fengler, Delaware; Virginia—Phil Lumpkin, Miami of Ohio; San Diego—Richard Wallace, Georgia Southern; Denver—Luther Burden, Utah; San Antonio—Gary Anderson, Wisconsin; Indiana—Ron De Vries, Illinois State; Carolina—Gary Novak, Notre Dame; Carolina (from Utah)—Harvey Catchings, Hardin Simmons; Kentucky—Bill Ligon, Vanderbilt; New York—Gary Brokaw, Notre Dame.

Seventh Round

Memphis—Lawrence Johnson, Prairie View; Virginia—Earl Williams, Winston Salem; Denver—Eric Money, Arizona; San Diego—Leon Benbow, Jacksonville; San Antonio—Gerald Cunningham, Kentucky State; Indiana—Alex English, South Carolina; Carolina—Jim Foster, Connecticut; Utah—Ron Lee, Oregon; Kentucky—Bill Butler, Louisville; New York—Dean Tolson, Arkansas.

Eighth Round

Memphis—Willie Biles, Tulsa; Virginia—John Drew, Gardner Webb; San Diego—Dan Anderson, Southern California; Denver—Larry Fogle, Canisius; San Antonio—Hercle Ivy, Iowa State; Indiana—Bobby Florence, Nevada Las Vegas; Carolina—Tom Kivisto, Kansas; Utah—Ed Palubinskas, Louisiana State; Kentucky—Len Coulter, Morehead State; New York—Al Skinner, Massachusetts.

Ninth Round

Memphis—Ron Brown, Penn State; Virginia—Bill Campion, Manhattan; Denver—Tony Byers, Wake Forest; San Diego—Stan Washington, San Diego; San Antonio—Walter Luckett, Ohio; Indiana—Kevin Fitzgerald, Oklahoma State; Carolina—Marcus Washington, Marquette; Utah—Lionel Hollins, Arizona State; Kentucky—Glen Hansen, Louisiana State; New York—Bob Fleisher, Duke.

Tenth Round

Memphis—Candy LaPrince, Iowa; Virginia—Mark Cartwright, Bowling Green; San Diego—Marques Johnson, UCLA; Denver—Roscoe Pondexter, Long Beach State; San Antonio—Charles McKinney, Baylor; Indiana—Mark Browne, Missouri Western; Carolina—Mike Sylvester, Dayton; Utah—Mike Westra, Southern California; Kentucky—Steve Walker, Kentucky Wesleyan; San Antonio (from N.Y.)—Mike Ogan, Carson Newman.

1974 DRAFT OF NBA PLAYERS

First Round

Virginia—Bob Kauffman, Buffalo; Memphis—Rick Roberson, Portland; Denver—Nate Thurmond, Golden State; San Diego—Cazzie Russell, Golden State; San Antonio—Tom Boerwinkle, Chicago; Indiana—Clifford Ray, Chicago; Carolina—Pete Maravich, Atlanta; Utah—Bob Christian, Phoenix; Kentucky—Jim Price, Los Angeles; New York—Phil Chenier, Capitol.

Second Round

Memphis—Norm Van Lier, Chicago; Virginia—George Johnson,

Golden State; San Diego—Sidney Wicks, Portland; Denver—Tom Van Arsdale, Philadelphia; San Antonio—Clyde Lee, Golden State; Indiana—Bill Bradley, New York; Carolina—Henry Bibby, New York; Utah—Geoff Petrie, Portland; Kentucky—Greg Smith, Portland; New York—Dave Cowens, Boston.

Third Round

Virginia—Dick Snyder, Seattle; Memphis—Len Wilkens, Cleveland; Denver—Don Adams, Detroit; San Diego—Curtis Rowe, Detroit; San Antonio—Neal Walk, Phoenix; Indiana—Mel Counts, Los Angeles; Carolina—Phil Jackson, New York; Utah—Howard Porter, Chicago; Kentucky—Rowland Garrett, Chicago; New York—Jerry Sloan, Chicago.

Fourth Round

Memphis—Paul Silas, Boston; Virginia—Calvin Murphy, Houston; San Diego—Gale Goodrich, Los Angeles; Denver—Rick Adelman, Chicago; San Antonio—Steve Kuberski, Boston; Indiana—Pat Riley, Los Angeles; Carolina—Paul Westphal, Boston; Utah—Rudy Tomjanovich, Houston; Kentucky—Herm Gilliam, Atlanta; New York—Jim Fox, Seattle.

Fifth Round

Virginia—Barry Clemens, Cleveland; Memphis—Dave DeBusschere, New York; Denver—Lou Hudson, Atlanta; San Diego—Connie Hawkins, Los Angeles; San Antonio—Lloyd Neal, Portland; Indiana—Jim Davis, Detroit; Carolina—Jeff Mullins, Golden State; Utah—Bob McAdoo, Buffalo; Kentucky—Larry Steele, Portland; New York—Garfield Heard, Buffalo.

1975 COLLEGE DRAFT

Bonus Choice

Denver—Marvin Webster, Morgan State; St. Louis, pass.

First Round

Virginia—David Thompson, North Carolina State; Memphis—Lonnie Shelton, Oregon State; San Diego—Kevin Grevey, Kentucky; St. Louis—Gus Williams, Southern California; Utah—Steve Green, Indiana; Indiana—Dan Roundfield, Central Michigan; San Antonio—Mark Olberding, Minnesota; New York—John Lucas, Maryland; Virginia (from Denver)—Melvin Bennett, Pittsburgh; Kentucky—Jim Baker, Hawaii.

Second Round

Virginia—Jim Dan Conner, Kentucky; Memphis—Rich Kelley, Stanford; San Diego—Cornelius Cash, Bowling Green; St. Louis—Rudy White, Arizona State; Utah—Norman Cook, Kansas; Indiana—Charles Jordan, Canisius; Indiana (from San Antonio)—Jim Lee, Syracuse; New York—George Bucci, Manhattan; Denver—Bill Willoughby (high school player); San Antonio (from Kentucky)—Rich Suttle, Kansas.

Third Round

Kentucky (from Virginia)—Allen Murphy, Kentucky; Memphis—Ron Haigler, Pennsylvania; San Diego—Bob Gross, Long Beach State; St. Louis—Rudy Hackett, Syracuse; Denver (from Utah)—Tom Kropp, Kearney State; Indiana—Ken Tyler, Gonzaga; San Antonio—Billy Taylor, LaSalle; New York—Leon Douglas, Alabama; Denver—Monte Towe, North Carolina State; Kentucky—Eric Fernsten, San Francisco.

Fourth Round

Virginia—Ticky Burden, Utah; Memphis—Glenn Hansen, Louisiana State; San Diego—Pete Trgovich, UCLA; St. Louis—Tom Roy, Maryland; Virginia (from Utah)—Fessor Leonard (Furman); Indiana—Brian Hammel, Bentley; San Antonio—Ken Smith, Tulsa; New York—Bob Guyette, Kenucky; Denver—Bob Fleischer, Duke; Kentucky—John Laskowski, Indiana.

Fifth Round
Virginia—Rich Jones, Virginia Commonwealth; Memphis—Walter Luckett, Ohio U.; San Diego—Biff Burrell, Southern California; St. Louis—Larry Fogle, Canisius; St. Louis (from Utah through Denver)—C. J. Kupec, Michigan; Indiana—John Ramsey, Seton Hall; San Antonio—Robert Parrish, Centenary; New York—Darryl Brown, Fordham; Denver—Jim Moore, Utah State; Kentucky—Charles Cleveland, Alabama.

Sixth Round
Virginia—Fletcher Johnson, Randolph-Macon; Memphis—Terry Furlow, Michigan State; San Diego—Louis Dunbar, Houston; St. Louis—Al Jones, Univ. of San Diego; Utah—Otis Johnson, Stetson; Indiana—Mike Flynn, Kentucky; San Antonio—Bayard Forrest, Grand Canyon; New York—Mike Mitchell, Auburn; Denver—Charles Russell, Alabama; Kentucky—Mike Rozenski, St. Mary's (Calif.).

Seventh Round
Virginia—Bill Bunton, Louisville; Memphis—Rich Whitlow, Illinois State; San Diego—Jerome Anderson, West Virginia; St. Louis—Al Spruill, North Carolina A&T; Utah—Tim Van Blommesteyn, Princeton; Indiana—Cliff Pratt, Shaw; San Antonio—Henry Ward, Jackson State; New York—Wayne Croft, Clemson; Denver—Mike Odems, Western Kentucky; Kentucky—Randy Meister, Penn State.

Eighth Round
Virginia—Ricky Coleman, Jacksonville; Memphis—John Murphy, Massachusetts; San Diego—Mack Coleman, Houston Baptist; St. Louis—Ted Hathaway, Cleveland State; Utah—Kirk Bruce, Pittsburgh; Indiana—Bill Andreas, Ohio State; San Antonio—Gary Tomaszewski, St. Mary's (Texas); New York—John Lambert, Southern California; Denver—Owen Brown, Maryland; Kentucky—Lou Silver, Harvard.

CHAPTER 10

The Coaches

The Boston Celtics already were 18 points up on the Los Angeles Lakers, and 13,909 fans at old and musty Boston Garden sensed the kill. On the home-team bench, so did a pudgy, balding man named Arnold "Red" Auerbach. He clutched a rolled-up game program in his left hand and his right was clenched in concentration as he sent his team out for the fourth period of the fifth game of the 1964-65 NBA championship playoffs.

K.C. Jones cut across the key, took a pass from Bill Russell, and tossed up an arching hook shot which fell cleanly through the hoop. The Lakers came upcourt, desperate to prolong a best-of-seven series in which they'd won only once. Boston's Willie Naulls cut in front of Gail Goodrich to steal the dribble, however, and continued unmolested for an easy lay-up.

The crowd roared as crowds must have roared in ancient Roman arenas when lions hungrily approached fallen, bleeding Christians.

Eight times more in succession the Celtics raced to field goals against the dazed Lakers. Finally, Naulls had the ball again, Auerbach on his feet and waving him forward with that program, and the soon-to-retire veteran responded with an off-balance hook which flew crisply through the basket. The Celtics had run off 20 consecutive points!

It was the most one-sided, most cruelly homicidal destruction of one team by another in playoff history, and it demonstrated anew the mastery which Auerbach, Russell and the Celtics had come to epitomize.

This was the moment the coach chose, then, to observe what had become so often his personal moment of glory. He reached ino his plaid sportcoat for one of his "Red Auerbach" monogrammed cigars.

With exaggerated care and great puffs of blue smoke which prompted a burst of raucous approval from the crowd, he lit up in affirmation of triumph assured.

In the glory and sheer frenzy of the 20-point spree and the impending championship, just one victory cigar seemed insufficient. Auerbach reached into his pocket again, whirled dramatically as though he were an Olympic discus thrower, and flung a handful of his private stock panatellas upward toward the adoring fans in a grand, emotion-rich gesture of joy.

The 129-96 victory, the series triumph and still another world championship after a then-record 62 regular season victories was the capstone of Auerbach's coaching career, ultimate success for his greatest team yet—Russell, the Jones Boys (Sam and K.C.), Tom Sanders and Naulls and strong reserves.

A year later, the Celtics and the Lakers were playing for the crown again. Auerbach had announced he would retire from the bench after the playoffs to devote himself to the increasingly demanding role of executive vice-president and general manager. His ferocious will to succeed demanded that his final game be a victory.

On April 28, 1966, after three decisions by each team in an epic series, the Celtics dominated play from the opening tip-off. The score was 95-93, but the numbers were mere formality. The Lakers had gotten their last six points meaninglessly in the final

Lighting a victory cigar became a yearly ritual for Red Auerbach, who coached the Celtics to eight straight NBA titles. Here, he does the honors after winning the 1965 East crown. Helping him celebrate are Massachusetts Governor John A. Volpe and (left to right) Tom Sanders, Bill Russell, John Havlicek and Sam Jones.

90 seconds amid chaos on the sidelines. Governor John Volpe of the Commonwealth of Massachusetts jubilantly was offering a match to Auerbach's final victory cigar, and players and fans overflowed out onto the court near the Celtics' bench in celebration of the man's 1,037th coaching victory (compared to 548 losses).

In 1971, on the 25th anniversary of the founding of what would become the NBA, Auerbach was elected overwhelmingly by a blue ribbon panel as ''Silver Anniversary Coach.'' Quarrelsome, pugnacious, conniving and argumentative as he may have been on the court, and cunning as he had continued to be in the gathering and nurturing of basketball players since 1946, he clearly had been master of his craft to a greater degree than any rival for the honor could claim in any other professional sport.

In his autobiography, *Go Up for Glory*, all-time all-star Russell attempted to explain Auerbach's suc-

cess—10 NBA championships in 11 seasons. ''He knows exactly the right way to select a player—rookie or old pro—and move him onto a squad without disrupting the fluidity of the team,'' said Russell. ''A tough kid who fought his way up from the streets of Brooklyn, he never deluded himself.

''Auerbach has a reason for everything—from yelling at a referee, to selling out Boston Garden with a promotion, to bringing in a player who, on the surface, appears to be useless.

''Auerbach cannot stand the thought of losing. Neither can I. Anyone who has ever come to the Celtics has immediately been instilled with this philosophy. If you don't play to win, Auerbach has no place for you.''

And the gruff-talking, excitable, one-time George Washington University guard said himself, ''I found players who wanted to win. They didn't have what we like to call 'Celtic pride' or tradition when they got here. They acquired it. It rubbed off on them.

"The learning was there if you wanted it. First and foremost, I considered myself a teacher. I taught basketball. If you were a Celtic, you learned to motivate and communicate."

For Auerbach, basketball is essentially a simple game governed by time-tested fundamentals. He sought out players willing to observe those fundamentals, willing to follow his stringent, physical-conditioning regimen, willing to play with constant intensity. These things were true when he brashly talked himself into the job of recruiting the Washington Capitals for arena owner Mike Uline following his discharge from the Navy in 1946, true when he went on to a job coaching the Tri-Cities Hawks of the Midwest for Ben Kerner in 1949, true when he was hired by Walter Brown to coach the Celtics in 1950. They remain true of Celtics today.

Auerbach's gypsying from team to team, his credentials as a former college and pro player without sufficient reputation to have landed one of the important coaching jobs at a major university . . . his brawling, no-quarter-given personality . . . these were traits he held in common with a number of his fellow coaches in the pioneer days.

Most players were ex-servicemen glad to accept the $4,000 and $5,000 salaries which prevailed during the quest for national attention.

A coach's job in those days was a challenge to endurance and versatility. First, there was the task of helping the owner sign the best players he could hire—free agents at first, from the draft later, through trades and by picking up other teams' discards. Next was the essential job of establishing a playing system which, ideally, combined his own concept of how to play the game with the skills his personnel could contribute.

During games, the need was to provide strategy and to conduct the vital job of substitution, seeking to establish size, strength and speed mismatches in his team's favor, seeking to counteract rivals' ploys.

Between games, especially for games away from home, the job was toughest of all. The coach was responsible for shepherding his men from town to town by auto, rail and occasional airliner. He was teacher, trainer, traveling secretary and public relations man all in one, and no player or coach without abiding affection for the pure sport of playing basketball and the special give-and-take, goad-and-re-spond of the locker room stayed with this harsh life for long.

The trade with the St. Louis Hawks which he engineered to land Russell for the Celtics in 1956 was the step which catapulted Auerbach to the head of his profession.

The union of the coach's benevolent despot manner with Russell's revolutionary shot-blocking ability and rebounding skills—along with the demands they made on themselves and the rest of the Celtics—resulted in their succession of championships. Two additional titles were won under Russell's player-coach direction in 1967-68 and 1968-69. When Russell retired, Auerbach turned the coaching job over to another ex-Celtic of the glory years, Tom Heinsohn, and another pair of NBA crowns was earned with new players in 1973-74 and 1975-76.

The years between Auerbach's arrival in Boston and the team's 13th championship were marked by growth, expansion, merger and, finally, maturity for pro basketball. Another demonstration of evolution was the changing role of the coach.

By the 1970s, teams were traveling with their own full-time trainers. Charter buses whisked teams comfortably from airport to hotel and from hotel to arena. Travel was usually by air—first class, of course.

In these nonbasketball respects, a coach's job was simpler. In the handling of players, the job had become far more difficult.

"The coach loses games and the players win 'em, that's the way they look at it," said Johnny Kerr not long after he was discharged as coach of the Phoenix Suns in 1970. "That's the way they look at it. But as I see it, the coach doesn't win or lose more than four or five games a season. The players are responsible for the rest."

Kerr, a 6-10 redhead from the University of Illinois whose playing career was marked by his superb passing out of the pivot as well as by his sense of humor, reflected further, "I guess I should have given 'em more pep talks, inspired them more, laid into them more. All they talk about in coaching today is how you motivate the players. Why do you have to motivate players? Shouldn't they motivate themselves? Isn't the chance to play with the best in their profession motivation enough?

"I came in during the early days of the NBA. We didn't make the money the players make today, and we didn't have the comforts or the prominence. We played basketball because we loved it or because it was what we did best and could make a living at it. We weren't as good as the players that have come along since, but we gave it a hell of a lot more. The coaches I played under—Al Cervi, Alex Hannum, Dolph Schayes, Paul Seymour—didn't have to motivate players. We lived and talked basketball all the time.

"Today, I don't think half the players know who they're playing that night until they look at the tickets they're leaving at the box office for their friends. They know the latest dance steps, but they don't know the plays. The more money they make, the less they care about it."

Auerbach's selection of Russell as his successor, of Heinsohn as Russell's, Russell's return to the league after four years in broadcasting to become general manager-coach of the Seattle Sonics, and Kerr's tenure as coach of the Chicago Bulls before going to Phoenix all reflected a tradition. They were aging or briefly-retired players who had exhibited leadership traits and they had been hired to coach.

Was it that Auerbach trained future coaches? Or, rather that he selected men to play for him who had the special aptitude for the game that led them into coaching? The record shows that Bob Cousy, Bill Sharman, K.C. Jones, Frank Ramsey, Dave Cowens, Paul Silas and Don Nelson, in addition to Heinsohn and Russell, all became pro coaches at one time or another. At least a dozen other ex-Celtics, including Sanders and Sam Jones, left the NBA to become college coaches.

In the mid-sixties, another pattern became sufficiently prevalent to be called a trend—selection of men directly from college ranks for NBA jobs whether they had played in the league themselves or not.

West Virginia's Fred Schaus, a journeyman pro, earlier took over the Minneapolis Lakers the season they transferred to Los Angeles. North Carolina's Frank McGuire coached the Philadelphia Warriors in 1961-62 before returning to the college ranks. Dr. Jack Ramsay, highly successful St. Joseph's of Pennsylvania coach, began a long tenure by accepting the general managership of the champion Philadelphia 76ers in 1966-67 and became their coach two years later. And there was Dick Motta, hired from little Weber State University of Ogden, Utah, by the Chicago Bulls in 1968 even though he'd failed to make

either his junior or senior high school teams, much less the varsity as an undergraduate physical education major at Utah State.

By early 1977, in the first season after absorption by the NBA of four teams from the American Basketball Association, there were 10 men coaching teams—including Ramsay by now at Portland and Motta at Washington—whose backgrounds were primarily collegiate. Twelve others were retired former players.

The collegians learned from the pros the realities of dealing with demanding owners and the inquiring news media, the problems of coping with prima donna players. The pros, in turn, absorbed and built upon tactical ideas the collegians introduced.

Another source of coaches came to be developed, in a sense, by the league's expansion and financial growth. When there were as few as eight teams in the league, clubs opposed each other frequently and quickly learned each others' plays and individual traits. As teams were added, schedules were expanded, too, and by the time of merger in 1976 opponents met as infrequently as two or three times a season.

Personnel changes and injuries altered styles, and coaches needed assistants as well, often as chief scouts to get advance looks at opponents they'd not seen, sometimes for several months. Some of these men were ex-pros, others exclusively college trained. Financial stability meant there was money available to hire them.

When a change was to be made, an owner could look to ex-players, to college ranks . . . or to the ranks of pro assistant coaches, or scouts, for a replacement. Sophistication of that sort might have mystified the men who played the game in its earliest years.

Such a man was 6-5 Joe Lapchick, whose dedication made him a star in the early 1920s, and who later was an outstanding coach at St. John's University in New York and led the New York Knicks in their early NBA years.

In his book, *50 Years of Basketball*, the late Hall of Fame honoree noted: "Coaching, organization, discipline and regular practices are routine today. But in the early days they were fairly loose. The 'coach' was either the oldest man on the club or the club owner, who kept his office in his inside coat pocket. Just before the start of the game the club owner would

An ex-Princeton player and coach who played professionally with the Knicks, Butch van Breda Kolff has expressed his emotions as a pro coach with four NBA teams and one in the ABA.

stick his head in the dressing room and say, 'This is no baloney, you guys. You gotta win!' Then he would slam the door for emphasis and go out to count the house. There was no coaching. Trial and error and advice from better players was the method used to improve.''

From 1923 to 1936, Lapchick was a member of that great touring team, the Original Celtics. ''The Celtics had no coach,'' Lapchick wrote about the organization founded by promoters Jim and Tom Furey of New York in 1918, ''but they had great leaders—Johnny Beckman, Dutch Dehnert and Nat Holman. They were the best teachers a player could possibly find. They taught me everything I knew.''

The Furey brothers' special contribution was their signing of their group of brilliant players to exclusive contracts.

Two other men who were called coaches, but whose special gifts were more truly organization and promotion, were New Yorker Bob Douglas with his Renaissance Ballroom Big Five, an all-black independent team which dominated the mid-thirties, and

Philadelphia's Eddie Gottlieb, known affectionately as ''The Mogul.'' Gottlieb was involved in a variety of sports activities, including organization of his Philadelphia Sphas (South Philadelphia Hebrew Association), one of the most successful pro teams in the mid-thirties.

Gottlieb's involvement in basketball continued through World War II, and he was one of the men sought out by Ned Irish of Madison Square Garden in 1946 when he joined a group of arena operators and promoters in founding the Basketball Association of America. Gottlieb became owner-coach of the Philadelphia Warriors, one of the men who worked out the merger with the Midwest-based National Basketball League to form the NBA two years later.

The powers in these early seasons were the Minneapolis Lakers, coached for a total of 11 seasons by scholarly John Kundla and starring massive George Mikan, and the Rochester Royals, owned and coached by the flamboyant Lester Harrison.

The Royals emphasized slick-passing Eastern backcourt play as mastered by Bob Davies, Bobby Wanzer, Pep Saul and, among others, a player named Red Holzman.

Power prevailed over finesse, and the Lakers won five titles between 1949 and 1954, earning Kundla runner-up status to Auerbach in the 1971 Silver Anniversary poll, 19 votes to four. Lapchick earned three votes, Hannum and Harrison, two each. Gottlieb and Holzman, in a remarkable span of eras, received single votes.

Among the Royals who played for Harrison in upstate New York before he moved his franchise to Cincinnati in 1959 were Holzman and another ex-New York City player, Fuzzy Levane. Levane was one of a succession of coaches hired by Kerner for his Milwaukee (and later St. Louis) Hawks. When Holzman, gray hair mingling more and more with the crimson, was released by Rochester, Levane picked up his friend on waivers. Then, when Kerner decided in 1954 that Levane wasn't his man, it was Holzman who was designated to succeed him.

Holzman learned 13 years later he was about to be elevated from college scout for the New York Knicks to head coach in an exchange of positions with Dick McGuire. Holzman, in *The Knicks*, his story of the team's first NBA title, spoke of the sympathy he felt for general manager Eddie Donovan.

''Eddie knew how I felt,'' Holzman recalled about

his reluctance to leave the security of his scouting role. "He also knew how McGuire felt. He was in the middle of a tough predicament. Nobody likes to tell a nice guy like Dick McGuire he is finished as the coach.

"I know how I felt when Ben Kerner told me I was out in 1957. It was the only thing he could do because the team was losing. He had Bob Pettit and he had just moved from Milwaukee. He was struggling for his existence and had to come up with a winner. You expect to get fired, but it hurts when it happens. It hurts your pride. You always feel you did a good job, and things would get better if they just gave you time.

"Alex Hannum insists to this day he cried when he heard Kerner fired me. I believe him when he says he was upset. Alex is a good-natured, sensitive human being and I had gotten him a job as a player with the Hawks. He had been dropped by Syracuse and had no place to go but home to California."

It is one of those classic NBA stories, what happened in St. Louis. Kerner turned first to Slater Martin, nearing the end of his playing career after earlier stardom as the clever backcourt man whose job it had been to feed the ball to Mikan in Minneapolis. "Martin didn't want to coach," Holzman recounts. "Kerner persisted, and Martin coached, but not for long. He convinced Kerner he didn't want the job. 'Get another coach or I go home to Texas,' he told Ben."

So, Holzman continued, Kerner prodded Martin for a suggestion. " 'Get Hannum,' volunteered Slater. 'He's been sitting on the bench and doing the coaching while I've been playing.' Hannum, who felt so badly when I was fired, wound up with my job!"

The elevation of Hannum helped the league in its struggle to escape its "bush" image. The 6-7, bald, one-time University of Southern California star proved not only an inspirational and innovative coach, but also one of the game's most eloquent spokesmen.

He coached St. Louis to victory over Boston in the 1958 playoffs, and that was the only championship Russell and Auerbach were to lose until Hannum's Wilt Chamberlain-led Philadelphia 76ers defeated the Celts in the Eastern Division finals of 1967. He had coached, in the interim, at Syracuse and San Francisco, and his career continued in startling zigzags afterward when he coached Rick Barry and the Oak-

land Oaks to the American Basketball Association championship in 1969. Hannum returned to the NBA with San Diego in 1970 and '71 and then went back to the ABA for a brief stay as part-owner, president, general manager and coach of the Denver Rockets.

It was Hannum, then with the 76ers, who had sneered about the fledgling ABA's red, white and blue basketball, "It looks like it belongs in the circus—on the nose of a seal."

The extent to which the Celtics and Hannum have influenced contemporary pro basketball—or, at the least, been at the core of its development—is demonstrated by the evolution of the NBA title in the seasons following 1967.

After Hannum's and Chamberlain's victory, it was player-coach Russell who prevailed the next two seasons. The 1969-70 campaign marked culmination of Holzman's transformation of the Knicks and their first title. The following season, the new champion was the Milwaukee Bucks, led by their brilliant second-year center, Lew Alcindor (later Kareem Abdul-Jabbar) and coached by Larry Costello, who had played for Hannum on his Syracuse teams and with his world champions in Philadelphia.

By 1971-72, Chamberlain was in his fourth season with the Los Angeles Lakers and already playing for his third coach there—ex-Celtic Sharman, succeeding Butch van Breda Kolff, and Joe Mullaney. Sharman had been, to maintain this remarkable chain of circumstances, a teammate of Hannum's at USC. Sharman etched two incredible statistics with the champion Lakers that year—a run of 33 consecutive victories from November 5, 1971, to January 7, 1972, and 69 wins overall with only 13 losses.

New York regained the title from Los Angeles the following season, and Heinsohn's Celtics and their fine young center, Dave Cowens, won the crown in 1973-74.

The most surprising championship team of all, perhaps, emerged the following season—the Golden State Warriors. Their coach, Alvin Attles, had been drafted and hired originally in Philadelphia by Gottlieb. He played his rookie season under Frank McGuire. Then the Warriors transferred to San Francisco, and Attles played and learned under Hannum for three seasons, Sharman for two more.

Hannum's career touched the American Basketball Association, too. In addition to his personal role, he had given 5-9 Larry Brown the chance to play with his Oakland team, opening a pro career for the ex-North Carolina backcourt star from Long Beach, New York, which led to coaching jobs in Carolina and as Hannum's successor in 1974 when new ownership took over at Denver.

Auerbach and Heinsohn were incendiary personalities, men quick to shout at referees, opponents or their own players. Holzman was a patient, defense-stressing philosopher who kept his ideas fresh through three decades in the sport. Hannum was an affectionate big brother, ready to physically stand up even to a Chamberlain in order to assert authority, but a cheerleader on the sidelines as well as a crafty tactician.

Sharman manifested an entirely different coaching personality in his command of the Los Angeles Jets and Cleveland Pipers of the short-lived American Basketball League of 1961 and 1962, later with the San Francisco Warriors, the Los Angeles (and later Utah) Stars of the American Basketball Association and finally with the Lakers.

As a player, he had studied the mechanics of shooting so thoroughly that he became the most accurate free-throw maker of his time, an absolutely textbook-pure technician. As a coach, he was equally meticulous, establishing elaborate systems of fines and bonuses for on-court transgressions and accomplishments, conducting precisely-scheduled workouts, scouting extensively and attempting to anticipate situations rather than be forced to improvise experimentally under the pressure of the clock.

"I have observed," said Sharman, "that critical games turn on a single steal, shot, pass or rebound at the right time and that championships often are decided by a point or two somewhere along the way. In seeking every advantage for our side, I do not believe any detail is too small not to be worth pursuing. Shooting is 'muscle memory.' Just as you rehearse during the day a speech you must give that night, I believe you should practice during the day for shots you must take that night."

Attles incorporated some of Hannum's techniques and some of Sharman's, including day-of-game "shoot-arounds," light drills consisting of muscle-loosening exercises and shooting. Unlike Sharman, Attles did not hesitate to experiment with strategies and combinations of players during games, and when his Warriors won the championship in four straight games over K.C. Jones' Washington Bullets, his use of nine, ten or even eleven men in a game was hailed as an innovation.

The evolution in pro basketball from its all-white days to its later showcasing of black players was another aspect of Attles' success. The huzzahs were for his accomplishments and for his leadership, and sportswriters left to their concluding paragraphs or ignored altogether the fact that he had become the first black other than Russell to coach a league champion.

The first black to coach in a pro league—first to coach a team in any major league sport—had been John McLendon at the founding of the Cleveland Pipers of the ABL in 1961. He had come to the league with outstanding credentials in all-black college conferences of the South and had guided Tennessee A&I to three consecutive National Association for Intercollegiate Athletics (NAIA) titles. He was dismissed after half a season for reasons which had nothing to do with race, and Sharman took over the Pipers to take them to the only ABL championship ever decided (titles in the ABA with Utah and in the NBA with the Lakers, incidentally, give Sharman the distinction of being the only man ever to win championships in three leagues).

When Auerbach turned his Celtics over to Russell in 1966, it was because, he insisted, Russell was the best man he could find for the assignment. Three seasons later, the Seattle Sonics named Len Wilkens as their coach, and other black players were hired in subsequent years, including Earl Lloyd and Ray Scott at Detroit, Elgin Baylor at New Orleans, Al Attles and K.C. Jones.

Scott had coached at Virginia of the ABA and Jones with San Diego before going to the NBA, and Zelmo Beaty had coached Virginia in the last season prior to the merger.

The acceptance of these men as coaches first, black men secondarily, was proven more by their dismissals when they came, than by acclaim when they'd been hired. They were coaches, subject therefore to the whims and frustrations of team owners.

Even Sharman was deposed in time, following two seasons in which the Lakers failed to reach the playoffs. He was politely elevated to general manager, and owner Jack Kent Cooke turned the task over to the team's former "Mr. Clutch," Jerry West.

This was a fascinating selection in two regards. First, West as a player had been a superstar—with

Oscar Robertson the consensus all-time guard. Such specially-gifted men, it had always been said, would be too impatient with lesser talents to remain on the job for long. Second, West introduced a further level of sophistication by selection of not just a single assistant coach, but two—ex-Portland and ex-collegiate coach Jack McCloskey to concentrate on defense, and former ABA aide Stan Albeck to work with the offense. West, himself, worked with individual players during workouts while supervising the overview, and during games he concentrated on substitutions and strategy.

"There's no way one guy or even two can coach a basketball team," West said after three months in which the Lakers began a strong comeback to eminence. "How can you scout and prepare and condition and run practices without constant disruptions if you don't have at least three? I don't think it was such a brilliant idea, just practical."

Said Albeck, "Jerry has a sixth sense about when things begin to turn sour. He senses when the momentum is about to change, and he knows how to use his players to their best advantage. He trusts Jack and me, and we confer on a lot of decisions, but he is the boss."

It was ironic that, within months of West's return to the league from uncomfortable retirement, his 11-year teammate and fellow superstar, Baylor, came to become a head coach, too. Futher irony was that Baylor's elevation from an assistant role came when one of their former coaches in Los Angeles, van Breda Kolff, was dismissed because of friction with management. The Louisiana fans were angered because the volatile van Breda Kolff seemed to be doing well, and because his explosions of temper had been so entertaining.

The reaction of one player, star guard Pete Maravich, stands as a classic commentary on the transitory nature of the coaching profession. He was asked if van Breda Kolff's firing, or Baylor's hiring had surprised him. "I wasn't shocked by the change," responded the player. "The last time I was shocked was when I found out ice cream cones were hollow."

CHAPTER 11

All-Time Team Records

(National Basketball Association teams
unless otherwise noted)

Season	Coach	W.	L.
ANAHEIM AMIGOS (ABA)			
See Utah Stars, 1967-68			
ANDERSON PACKERS			
1949-50	Howard Schultz (21-14)		
	Ike Duffey (1-2)		
	Doxie Moore (15-11)	37	27
	Totals	37	27
ATLANTA HAWKS			
1949-50	Roger Potter (1-6)		
	Arnold Auerbach (28-29)	29	35
1950-51	Dave McMillan (9-14)		
	John Logan (2-1)		
	Marko Todorovich (14-28)	25	43
1951-52*	Doxie Moore	17	49
1952-53	Andrew Levane	27	44
1953-54	Andrew Levane (11-35)		
	William Holzman (10-16)	21	51
1954-55	William Holzman	26	46
1955-56**	William Holzman	33	39
1956-57	William Holzman (14-19)		
	Slater Martin (5-3)		
	Alex Hannum (15-16)	34	38
1957-58	Alex Hannum	41	31
1958-59	Andy Phillip (6-4)		
	Ed Macauley (43-19)	49	23
1959-60	Ed Macauley	46	29
1960-61	Paul Seymour	51	28
1961-62	Paul Seymour (5-9)		
	Andrew Levane (20-40)		
	Bob Pettit (4-2)	29	51

*Team moved from Tri-Cities to Milwaukee
**Team moved from Milwaukee to St. Louis

Season	Coach	W.	L.
1962-63	Harry Gallatin	48	32
1963-64	Harry Gallatin	46	34
1964-65	Harry Gallatin (17-16)		
	Richie Guerin (28-19)	45	35
1965-66	Richie Guerin	36	44
1966-67	Richie Guerin	39	42
1967-68	Richie Guerin	56	26
1968-69***	Richie Guerin	48	34
1969-70	Richie Guerin	48	34
1970-71	Richie Guerin	36	46
1971-72	Richie Guerin	36	46
1972-73	Lowell Fitzsimmons	46	36
1973-74	Lowell Fitzsimmons	35	47
1974-75	Lowell Fitzsimmons	31	51
1975-76	Lowell Fitzsimmons (28-46)		
1976-77	Gene Tormohlen (1-7)	29	53
1977-78	Hubert Brown	31	51
1978-79	Hubert Brown	41	41
1979-80	Hubert Brown	46	36
1980-81	Hubert Brown	50	32
	Hubert Brown (31-48)		
	Mike Fratello/Brendan Suhr (0-3)	31	51
	Totals	1206	1278

***Team moved from St. Louis to Atlanta

Season	Coach	W.	L.
BALTIMORE BULLETS			
1947-48	Buddy Jeannette	28	20
1948-49	Buddy Jeannette	29	31
1949-50	Buddy Jeannette	25	43
1950-51	Buddy Jeannette (14-23)		
	Walt Budko (10-19)	24	42
1951-52	Fred Scolari (12-27)		
1952-53	John Reiser (8-19)	20	46
	John Reiser (0-3)		
1953-54	Clair Bee (16-51)	16	54

Season	Coach		W.	L.
1954-55*	Clair Bee		16	56
	Clair Bee (2-9)			
	Al Barthelme (1-2)		3	11
		Totals	161	303

*Team disbanded Nov. 27, 1954

BALTIMORE BULLETS
See Washington Bullets, 1972-73

BOSTON CELTICS

Season	Coach		W.	L.
1946-47	John Russell		22	38
1947-48	John Russell		20	28
1948-49	Alvin Julian		25	35
1949-50	Alvin Julian		22	46
1950-51	Arnold Auerbach		39	30
1951-52	Arnold Auerbach		39	27
19 2-53	Arnold Auerbach		46	25
1953-54	Arnold Auerbach		42	30
1954-55	Arnold Auerbach		36	36
1955-56	Arnold Auerbach		39	33
1956-57	Arnold Auerbach		44	28
1957-58	Arnold Auerbach		49	23
1958-59	Arnold Auerbach		52	20
1959-60	Arnold Auerbach		59	16
1960-61	Arnold Auerbach		57	22
1961-62	Arnold Auerbach		60	20
1962-63	Arnold Auerbach		58	22
1963-64	Arnold Auerbach		59	21
1964-65	Arnold Auerbach		62	18
1965-66	Arnold Auerbach		54	26
1966-67	Bill Russell		60	21
1967-68	Bill Russell		54	28
1968-69	Bill Russell		48	34
1969-70	Tom Heinsohn		34	48
1970-71	Tom Heinsohn		44	38
1971-72	Tom Heinsohn		56	26
1972-73	Tom Heinsohn		68	14
1973-74	Tom Heinsohn		56	26
1974-75	Tom Heinsohn		60	22
1975-76	Tom Heinsohn		54	28
1976-77	Tom Heinsohn		44	38
1977-78	Tom Heinsohn (11-23)			
	Tom Sanders (21-27)		32	50
1978-79	Tom Sanders (1-12)			
	Dave Cowens (27-41)		29	53
1979-80	Bill Fitch		61	21
1980-81	Bill Fitch		62	20
		Totals	1646	1011

BUFFALO BRAVES
See San Diego Clippers, 1978-79

CAPITAL BULLETS
See Washington Bullets, 1973-74

CAROLINA COUGARS (ABA)
See St. Louis Spirits, 1969-74

CHICAGO BULLS

Season	Coach		W.	L.
1966-67	John Kerr		33	48
1967-68	John Kerr		29	53
1968-69	Dick Motta		33	49
1969-70	Dick Motta		39	43
1970-71	Dick Motta		51	31
1971-72	Dick Motta		57	25
1972-73	Dick Motta		51	31
1973-74	Dick Motta		54	28
1974-75	Dick Motta		47	35
1975-76	Dick Motta		24	58
1976-77	Ed Badger		44	38
1977-78	Ed Badger		40	42
	Larry Costello (20-36)			
1978-79	Scotty Robertson (11-15)		31	51
1979-80	Jerry Sloan		30	52
1980-81	Jerry Sloan		45	37
		Totals	608	621

CHICAGO PACKERS
See Baltimore Bullets, 1961-62

CHICAGO STAGS

Season	Coach		W.	L.
1946-47	Harold Olsen		39	22
1947-48	Harold Olsen		28	20
1948-49	Harold Olsen (28-21)			
	Philip Brownstein (10-1)		38	22
1949-50	Philip Brownstein		40	28
		Totals	145	92

CHICAGO ZEPHYRS
See Baltimore Bullets, 1962-63

CINCINNATI ROYALS
See Kansas City Kings, 1971-72

CLEVELAND CAVALIERS

Season	Coach		W.	L.
1970-71	Bill Fitch		15	67
1971-72	Bill Fitch		23	59
1972-73	Bill Fitch		32	50
1973-74	Bill Fitch		29	53
1974-75	Bill Fitch		40	42
1975-76	Bill Fitch		49	33
1976-77	Bill Fitch		43	39
1977-78	Bill Fitch		43	39
1978-79	Bill Fitch		30	52
1979-80	Stan Albeck		37	45
1980-81	Bill Musselman (25-46)			
	Don Delaney (3-80)		28	54
		Totals	369	533

CLEVELAND REBELS

Season	Coach		W.	L.
1946-47	Dutch Dehnert (17-20)			
	Roy Clifford (13-10)		30	30
		Totals	30	30

Season	Coach	W.	L.
DALLAS CHAPARRALS (ABA)			
See San Antonio Spurs, 1972-73			
DALLAS MAVERICKS			
1980-81	Dick Motta	15	67
DENVER ROCKETS (ABA)			
See Denver Nuggets 1974-75			
DENVER NUGGETS			
1949-50	James Darden	11	51
DENVER NUGGETS (ABA-NBA)			
1967-68	Bob Bass	45	33
1968-69	Bob Bass	44	34
1969-70	John McLendon (9-19)		
	Joe Belmont (42-14)	51	33
1970-71	Joe Belmont (3-10)		
	Stan Albeck (27-44)	30	54
1971-72	Alex Hannum	34	50
1972-73	Alex Hannum	47	37
1973-74	Alex Hannum	37	47
1974-75*	Larry Brown	65	19
1975-76	Larry Brown	60	24
1976-77**	Larry Brown	50	32
1977-78	Larry Brown	48	34
1978-79	Larry Brown (28-25)		
	Donnie Walsh (19-10)	47	35
1979-80	Donnie Walsh	30	52
1980-81	Donnie Walsh (11-20)		
	Doug Moe (26-25)	37	45
	Totals	625	529

*Changed name from Rockets to Nuggets
**Joined NBA

Season	Coach	W.	L.
DETROIT FALCONS			
1946-47	Glen Curtis (12-22)		
	Philip Sachs (8-18)	20	40
	Totals	20	40
DETROIT PISTONS			
1948-49	Carl Bennett (0-6)		
	Paul Armstrong (22-32)	22	38
1949-50	Murray Mendenhall	40	28
1950-51	Murray Mendenhall	32	36
1951-52	Paul Birch	29	37
1952-53	Paul Birch	36	33
1953-54	Paul Birch	40	32
1954-55	Charles Eckman	43	29
1955-56	Charles Eckman	37	35
1956-57	Charles Eckman	34	38
1957-58*	Charles Eckman (9-16)		
	Ephraim Rocha (24-23)	33	39
1958-59	Ephraim Rocha	28	44
1959-60	Ephraim Rocha (13-21)		
	Dick McGuire (17-24)	30	45
1960-61	Dick McGuire	34	45
1961-62	Dick McGuire	37	43

Season	Coach	W.	L.
1962-63	Dick McGuire	34	46
1963-64	Charles Wolf	23	57
1964-65	Charles Wolf (2-9)		
	Dave DeBusschere (29-40)	31	49
1965-66	Dave DeBusschere	22	58
1966-67	Dave DeBusschere (28-45)		
	Donnis Butcher (2-6)	30	51
1967-68	Donnis Butcher	40	42
1968-69	Donnis Butcher (10-12)		
	Paul Seymour (22-38)	32	50
1969-70	Bill van Breda Kolff	31	51
1970-71	Bill van Breda Kolff	45	37
1971-72	Bill van Breda Kolff (6-6)		
	Terry Dischinger (0-2)		
	Earl Lloyd (20-50)	26	58
1972-73	Earl Lloyd (2-5)		
	Ray Scott (38-37)	40	42
1973-74	Ray Scott	52	30
1974-75	Ray Scott	40	42
1975-76	Ray Scott (17-25)		
	Herb Brown (19-21)	36	46
1976-77	Herb Brown	44	38
1977-78	Herb Brown (9-15)		
	Bob Kauffman (29-29)	38	44
1978-79	Dick Vitale	30	52
1979-80	Dick Vitale (4-8)		
	Richie Adubato (12-58)	16	66
1980-81	Scotty Robertson		
		21	61
	Totals	1106	1440

*Team moved from Fort Wayne to Detroit

Season	Coach	W.	L.
FORT WAYNE PISTONS			
See Detroit Pistons, 1957-58			
GOLDEN STATE WARRIORS			
1946-47	Edward Gottlieb	35	25
1947-48	Edward Gottlieb	27	21
1948-49	Edward Gottlieb	28	32
1949-50	Edward Gottlieb	26	42
1950-51	Edward Gottlieb	40	26
1951-52	Edward Gottlieb	33	33
1952-53	Edward Gottlieb	12	57
1953-54	Edward Rottlieb	29	43
1954-55	Edward Gottlieb	33	39
1955-56	George Senesky	45	27
1956-57	George Senesky	37	35
1957-58	George Senesky	37	35
1958-59	Al Cervi	32	40
1959-60	Neil Johnston	49	26
1960-61	Neil Johnston	46	33
1961-62	Frank McGuire	49	31
1962-63*	Bob Feerick	31	49
1963-64	Alex Hannum	48	32
1964-65	Alex Hannum	17	63
1965-66	Alex Hannum	35	45
1966-67	Bill Sharman	44	37
1967-68	Bill Sharman	43	39
1968-69	George Lee	41	41
1969-70	George Lee (22-30)		
	Al Attles (8-22)	30	52
1970-71	Al Attles	41	41

Season	Coach	W.	L.
1971-72	Al Attles	51	31
1972-73	Al Attles	51	31
1973-74	Al Attle	44	38
1974-75	Al Attles	48	34
1975-76	Al Attles	59	23
1976-77	Al Attles	46	36
1977-78	Al Attles	43	39
1978-79	Al Attles	38	44
1979-80	Al Attles (18-43)		
	John Bach (6-15)	24	58
1980-81	Al Attles	39	43
	Totals	1327	1324

*Team moved from Philadelphia to San Francisco
**Became Golden State Warriors

HOUSTON MAVERICKS (ABA)

See St. Louis Spirits, 1967-69

HOUSTON ROCKETS

Season	Coach	W.	L.
1967-68	Jack McMahon	15	67
1968-69	Jack McMahon	37	45
1969-70	Jack McMahon (9-17)		
	Alex Hannum (18-38)	27	55
1970-71	Alex Hannum	40	42
1971-72*	Tex Winter	34	48
1972-73	Tex Winter (17-30)		
	John Egan (16-19)	33	49
1973-74	John Egan	32	50
1974-75	John Egan	41	41
1975-76	John Egan	40	42
1976-77	Tom Nissalke	49	33
1977-78	Tom Nissalke	28	54
1978-79	Tom Nissalke	47	35
1979-80	Del Harris	41	41
1980-81	Del Harris	40	42
	Totals	446	644

*Team moved from San Diego to Houston

INDIANA PACERS (ABA-NBA)

Season	Coach	W.	L.
1967-68	Larry Staverman	38	40
1968-69	Larry Staverman (2-7)		
	Bob Leonard (42-27)	44	34
1969-70	Bob Leonard	59	25
1970-71	Bob Leonard	58	26
1971-72	Bob Leonard	47	37
1972-73	Bob Leonard	51	33
1973-74	Bob Leonard	46	38
1974-75	Bob Leonard	45	39
1975-76	Bob Leonard	39	45
1976-77*	Bob Leonard	36	46
1977-78	Bob Leonard	31	51
1978-79	Bob Leonard	38	44
1979-80	Bob Leonard	37	45
1980-81	Jack McKinney	44	38
	Totals	613	541

*Joined NBA

INDIANAPOLIS JETS

Season	Coach	W.	L.
1948-49	Bruce Hale (4-13)		
	Burl Friddle (14-29)	18	42

INDIANAPOLIS OLYMPIANS

Season	Coach	W.	L.
1949-50	Clifford Barker	39	25
1950-51	Clifford Barker (24-32)		
	Wallace Jones (7-5)	31	37
1951-52	Herman Schaefer	34	32
1952-53	Herman Schaefer	28	43
	Totals	132	137

KANSAS CITY KINGS

Season	Coach	W.	L.
1948-49	Les Harrison	45	15
1949-50	Les Harrison	51	17
1950-51	Les Harrison	41	27
1951-52	Les Harrison	41	25
1952-53	Les Harrison	44	26
1953-54	Les Harrison	44	28
1954-55	Les Harrison	29	43
1955-56	Bob Wanzer	31	41
1956-57	Bob Wanzer	31	41
1957-58*	Bob Wanzer	33	39
1958-59	Bob Wanzer (3-15)		
	Tom Marshall (16-38)	19	53
1959-60	Tom Marshall	19	56
1960-61	Charles Wolf	33	46
1961-62	Charles Wolf	43	37
1962-63	Charles Wolf	42	38
1963-64	Jack McMahon	55	25
1964-65	Jack McMahon	48	32
1965-66	Jack McMahon	45	35
1966-67	Jack McMahon	39	42
1967-68	Ed Jucker	39	43
1968-69	Ed Jucker	41	41
1969-70	Bob Cousy	36	46
1970-71	Bob Cousy	33	49
1971-72**	Bob Cousy	30	52
1972-73	Bob Cousy	36	46
1973-74	Bob Cousy (6-14)		
	Draff Young (0-4)	33	
	Phil Johnson (27-31)	44	49
1974-75	Phil Johnson	31	38
1975-76	Phil Johnson	40	51
1976-77	Phil Johnson		42
1977-78	Phil Johnson (13-24)	31	
	Larry Staverman (18-27)	48	51
1978-79	Cotton Fitzsimmons	47	34
1979-80	Cotton Fitzsimmons	40	35
1980-81	Cotton Fitzsimmons		42
	Totals	1262	1285

*Team moved from Rochester to Cincinnati
**Team moved from Cincinnati to Kansas City at end of season and changed name to Kings

KENTUCKY COLONELS (ABA)

Season	Coach	W.	L.
1967-68	John Givens (5-12)		
	Gene Rhodes (31-30)	36	42
1968-69	Gene Rhodes	42	36
1969-70	Gene Rhodes	45	39
1970-71	Gene Rhodes (10-5)		
	Alex Groza (2-0)		
	Frank Ramsey (32-35)	44	40
1971-72	Joe Mullaney	68	16
1972-73	Joe Mullaney	56	28
1973-74	Babe McCarthy	53	31

Season	Coach	W.	L.
1974-75	Hubie Brown	58	26
1975-76*	Hubie Brown	46	38
	Totals	448	296

*Franchise folded, 1976

LOS ANGELES LAKERS

Season	Coach	W.	L.
1948-49	John Kundla	44	16
1949-50	John Kundla	51	17
1950-51	John Kundla	44	24
1951-52	John Kundla	46	26
1952-53	John Kundla	48	22
1953-54	John Kundla	40	26
1954-55	John Kundla	40	32
1955-56	John Kundla	33	39
1956-57	John Kundla	34	38
1957-58	George Mikan (9-30)		
	John Kundla (10-23)	19	53
1958-59	John Kundla	33	39
1959-60	John Castellani (11-25)		
	Jim Pollard (14-25)	25	50
1960-61*	Fred Schaus	36	43
1961-62	Fred Schaus	54	26
1962-63	Fred Schaus	53	27
1963-64	Fred Schaus	42	38
1964-65	Fred Schaus	49	31
1965-66	Fred Schaus	45	35
1966-67	Fred Schaus	36	45
1967-68	Bill van Breda Kolff	52	30
1968-69	Bill van Breda Kolff	55	27
1969-70	Joe Mullaney	46	36
1970-71	Joe Mullaney	48	34
1971-72	Bill Sharman	69	13
1972-73	Bill Sharman	60	22
1973-74	Bill Sharman	47	35
1974-75	Bill Sharman	30	52
1975-76	Bill Sharman	40	42
1976-77	Jerry West	53	29
1977-78	Jerry West	45	37
1978-79	Jerry West	47	35
1979-80	Jack McKinney (10-4)		
	Paul Westhead (50-18)	60	22
1980-81	Paul Westhead	54	28
	Totals	1478	1069

*Team moved from Minneapolis to Los Angeles

LOS ANGELES STARS (ABA)
See Utah Stars, 1968-69

MEMPHIS PROS (ABA)
See Memphis Sounds, 1970-71

MEMPHIS SOUNDS (ABA)

Season	Coach	W.	L.
1967-68	James (Babe) McCarthy	48	30
1968-69	James (Babe) McCarthy	46	32
1969-70	James (Babe) McCarthy	42	42
1970-71*	James (Babe) McCarthy	41	43
1971-72	James (Babe) McCarthy	26	58
1972-73**	Bob Bass	24	60

  *Team moved from New Orleans to Memphis changed name to Pros
**Changed name to Tams

Season	Coach	W.	L.
1973-74	Butch van Breda Kolff	21	63
1974-75***	Joe Mullaney	27	57
	Totals	275	385

***Changed name to Sounds; folded, 1975

MEMPHIS TAMS (ABA)
See Memphis Sounds, 1972-73

MIAMI FLORIDIANS (ABA)

Season	Coach	W.	L.
1967-68	Jim Pollard	50	28
1968-69*	Jim Pollard	43	35
1969-70	Jim Pollard (5-15)		
	Hal Blitman (18-46)	23	61
1970-71	Hal Blitman (18-30)		
	Bob Bass (19-17)	37	47
1971-72**	Bob Bass	36	48
	Totals	189	219

 *Team moved from Minnesota to Miami, changed name to Floridians
**Team folded, 1972

MILWAUKEE HAWKS
See Atlanta Hawks, 1951-52

MILWAUKEE BUCKS

Season	Coach	W.	L.
1968-69	Larry Costello	27	55
1969-70	Larry Costello	56	26
1970-71	Larry Costello	66	16
1971-72	Larry Costello	63	19
1972-73	Larry Costello	60	22
1973-74	Larry Costello	59	23
1974-75	Larry Costello	38	44
1975-76	Larry Costello	38	44
1976-77	Larry Costello (3-15)		
	Don Nelson (27-37)	30	52
1977-78	Don Nelson	44	38
1978-79	Don Nelson	38	44
1979-80	Don Nelson	49	33
1980-81	Don Nelson	60	22
	Totals	628	438

MINNEAPOLIS LAKERS
See Los Angeles Lakers, 1960-61

MINNESOTA MUSKIES (ABA)
See Miami Floridians, 1968-69

MINNESOTA PIPERS (ABA)
See Pittsburgh Condors, 1968-69

NEW JERSEY AMERICANS (ABA)
See New Jersey Nets, 1967-68

NEW JERSEY NETS (ABA-NBA)

Season	Coach	W.	L.
1967-68	Max Zaslofsky	36	42
1968-69*	Max Zaslofsky	17	61
1969-70	York Larese	39	45
1970-71	Lou Carnesecca	40	44

Season	Coach	W.	L.
1971-72	Lou Carnesecca	44	40
1972-73	Lou Carnesecca	30	54
1973-74	Kevin Loughery	55	29
1974-75	Kevin Loughery	58	26
1975-76	Kevin Loughery	55	29
1976-77**	Kevin Loughery	22	60
1977-78***	Kevin Loughery	24	58
1978-79	Kevin Loughery	37	45
1979-80	Kevin Loughery	34	48
1980-81	Kevin Loughery (12-23)		
	Bob MacKinnon (12-35)	24	58
	Totals	503	639

*Moved from New Jersey to New York, changed name to Nets
**Joined NBA
***Moved to New Jersey

NEW ORLEANS BUCCANEERS (ABA)
See Memphis Sounds, 1970-71

NEW ORLEANS JAZZ
See Utah Jazz, 1979-80

NEW YORK KNICKERBOCKERS

Season	Coach	W.	L.
1946-47	Neil Cohalan	33	27
1947-48	Joe Lapchick	26	22
1948-49	Joe Lapchick	32	28
1949-50	Joe Lapchick	40	28
1950-51	Joe Lapchick	36	30
1951-52	Joe Lapchick	37	29
1952-53	Joe Lapchick	47	23
1953-54	Joe Lapchick	44	28
1954-55	Joe Lapchick	34	38
1955-56	Joe Lapchick (26-25)		
	Vince Boryla (9-12)	35	37
1956-57	Vince Boryla	36	36
1957-58	Vince Boryla	35	37
1958-59	Andrew Levane	40	32
1959-60	Andrew Levane (8-19)		
	Carl Braun (19-29)	27	48
1960-61	Carl Braun	21	58
1961-62	Eddie Donovan	29	51
1962-63	Eddie Donovan	21	59
1963-64	Eddie Donovan	22	58
1964-65	Eddie Donovan (12-26)		
	Harry Gallatin (19-23)	31	49
1965-66	Harry Gallatin (6-15)		
	Dick McGuire (24-35)	30	50
1966-67	Dick McGuire	36	45
1967-68	Dick McGuire (15-22)		
	William Holzman (28-17)	43	39
1968-69	William Holzman	54	28
1969-70	William Holzman	60	22
1970-71	William Holzman	52	30
1971-72	William Holzman	48	34
1972-73	William Holzman	57	25
1973-74	William Holzman	49	33
1974-75	William Holzman	40	42
1975-76	William Holzman	38	44
1976-77	William Holzman	40	42
1977-78	Willis Reed	43	39
1978-79	Willis Reed (6-8)		
	William Holzman (25-43)	31	51
1979-80	William Holzman	39	43
1980-81	William Holzman	50	32
	Totals	1340	1313

NEW YORK NETS
See New Jersey Nets, 1968-69

OAKLAND OAKS (ABA)
See Virginia Squires, 1968-69

PHILADELPHIA WARRIORS
See Golden State Warriors, 1962-63

PHILADELPHIA 76ERS

Season	Coach	W.	L.
1949-50	Al Cervi	51	13
1950-51	Al Cervi	32	34
1951-52	Al Cervi	40	26
1952-53	Al Cervi	47	24
1953-54	Al Cervi	42	30
1954-55	Al Cervi	43	29
1955-56	Al Cervi	35	37
1956-57	Al Cervi (4-8)		
	Paul Seymour (34-26)	38	34
1957-58	Paul Seymour	41	31
1958-59	Paul Seymour	35	37
1959-60	Paul Seymour	45	30
1960-61	Alex Hannum	38	41
1961-62	Alex Hannum	41	39
1962-63	Alex Hannum	48	32
1963-64*	Dolph Schayes	34	46
1964-65	Dolph Schayes	40	40
1965-66	Dolph Schayes	55	25
1966-67	Alex Hannum	68	13
1967-68	Alex Hannum	62	20
1968-69	Jack Ramsay	55	27
1969-70	Jack Ramsay	42	40
1970-71	Jack Ramsay	47	35
1971-72	Jack Ramsay	30	52
1972-73	Roy Rubin (4-47)		
	Kevin Loughery (5-26)	9	73
1973-74	Gene Shue	25	57
1974-75	Gene Shue	34	48
1975-76	Gene Shue	46	36
1976-77	Gene Shue	50	32
1977-78	Gene Shue (2-4)		
	Billy Cunningham (53-23)	55	27
1978-79	Billy Cunningham	47	35
1979-80	Billy Cunningham	59	23
1980-81	Billy Cunningham	62	20
	Totals	1396	1086

*Team moved from Syracuse to Philadelphia, changed name to 76ers

PHOENIX SUNS

Season	Coach	W.	L.
1968-69	Johnny Kerr	16	66
1969-70	Johnny Kerr (15-23)		
	Jerry Colangelo (24-20)	39	43
1970-71	Cotton Fitzsimmons	48	34
1971-72	Cotton Fitzsimmons	49	33
1972-73	Bill van Breda Kolff (3-4)		
	Jerry Colangelo 335-40)	38	44
1973-74	John MacLeod	30	52
1974-75	John MacLeod	32	50
1975-76	John MacLeod	42	40
1976-77	John MacLeod	34	48
1977-78	John MacLeod	49	33

career in eastern professional leagues before joining Original Celtics in 1920 . . . Credited with developing pivot play . . . Became famous for its execution and success . . . Celtics and Cleveland Rosenblums won 1,900 games when he was in lineup . . . Coached Detroit Eagles to pro titles in 1940 and 1941 . . . Also coached Sheboygan (Wis.) team.

Ed Diddle

Elected as coach 1971 . . . Born: Gradyville, Ky., March 12, 1895 . . . Died: Jan. 2, 1970 . . . Graduate of Centre College 1920 . . . Started at Western Kentucky in 1922 and for the next 42 years he had one of the nation's most consistent teams . . . Fast-breaking Hilltoppers won or shared in 32 conference titles, participated in three NCAA, eight NIT tournaments . . . Had 759 wins.

Robert Douglas

Elected as contributor 1971 . . . Born: St. Kitts, B.W.I., Nov. 4, 1884 . . . Died: July 16, 1979 . . . Came to America at age four . . . First black elected to Hall of Fame . . . Organized the famed New York Rennaissance Five in 1922 . . . Played mostly touring games . . . In 22 years the team won 2,318, including 88 straight in 1933 . . . Won 128 in 1934 . . . 1939 World Pro champions . . . Coached Rens throughout their golden era.

Bruce Drake

Elected as coach 1973 . . . Born: Gentry, Tex., Dec. 5, 1905 . . . Though much of his fame came through coaching, he also made the Helms All-America team in 1929 when he was the captain at the University of Oklahoma . . . Later became head coach at Oklahoma for 17 seasons and invented the "Drake Shuffle" . . . His teams won 200 games and captured or tied for the conference championship six times . . . Oklahoma lost the national championship game to Holy Cross in 1947 . . . A former president of the National Collegiate Coaches' Association . . . Assistant coach of 1956 U.S. Olympic team.

Paul Endacott

Elected as player 1971 . . . Born: Lawrence, Kan.,

July 13, 1902 . . . Played at University of Kansas . . . Phog Allen called him "the greatest player I ever coached" . . . Led Jayhawks to mythical national title 1923 . . . Helms Foundation Player of Year 1923 . . . His abilities withstood the passing of the years and in 1969 Dr. Allen selected him for the national all-time college team.

Jim Enright

Elected as referee 1978 . . . Born: Chicago, April 3, 1910 . . . Key official in the Big Ten, Big Eight and Missouri Valley Conferences for 24 years, including assignments to two NCAA regionals and the Final Four in 1954 . . . Rockne Club of Kansas City named him Referee of the Year in 1956 . . . Widely-recognized sports writer, too . . . Conducted officiating clinics in Europe in 1958 and 1968 . . . President of U.S. Basketball Writers in 1967.

Harry Fisher

Elected as contributor 1973 . . . Born: New York City, Feb. 6, 1882 . . . Died: Dec. 29, 1967 . . . Scoring leader at Columbia 1902-05 . . . Lions won two Ivy League titles during that time . . . Established school single-game field goal record of 13 which stood for next 48 years . . . Member of committee which rewrote collegiate basketball rules . . . First full-time coach at Columbia in 1906 . . . Led his teams to three Ivy crowns and 101-39 record during 10-year stay . . . Columbia graduate manager of athletics 1911-1917 . . . Editor of *Collegiate Guide* until 1915.

Harold "Bud" Foster

Elected as player 1964 . . . Born: Newton, Kan., May 30, 1906 . . . All-American for University of Wisconsin 1930 . . . Center and forward . . . All-Western Conference 1929 and 1930 . . . Captain 1930 Wisconsin team . . . During his three varsity years Wisconsin lost only seven games . . . Later coached at Wisconsin . . . Pro career with Duffy Florals of Chicago.

Marty Friedman

Elected as player 1971 . . . Born: New York City, July 12, 1889 . . . Played for University Settlement

House Metropolitan A.A.U. champs 1906-08 . . . Turned pro in 1909 with New York Roosevelts . . . Considered one of first defensive stars of early pro leagues in East . . . Finished career as captain and coach of Cleveland Rosenblums 1923-27 . . . Only 5-8, but helped win many championships.

Joe Fulks

Elected as player 1977 . . . Born: Marshall County, Ky., March 21, 1921 . . . Died: March 21, 1976 . . . "Jumpin' Joe" was one of the first great jump shooters, scoring 1,560 NBA points for 26-point average after starring for Murray State . . . Scored 63 points for Philadelphia Warriors against Indianapolis Jets 1949, a record that stood for 10 years . . . Led Philadelphia Warriors to BAA title in 1947 . . . Hit 49 consecutive free throws twice . . . Unanimous All-NBA first team three times in eight-year career . . . Member of NBA's Silver Anniversary Team.

Lauren Gale

Elected as player 1976 . . . Born: Grants Pass, Ore., April 22, 1917 . . . All-State at Oakridge (Ore.) High School . . . Went on to lead Oregon U. to first Pacific Coast and NCAA titles in 1939 . . . All-Pacific Coast 1938 and 1939 . . . All-American 1939 . . . Played pro ball with Detroit and Salt Lake City . . . Selected to Oregon Hall of Fame 1964.

Amory "Slats" Gill

Elected as coach 1967 . . . Born: Salem, Ore., May 1, 1901 . . . Died: April 5, 1966 . . . All-American guard Oregon State University 1924 . . . Later head coach Oregon State, beginning 1924 . . . Coached 36 years, compiling 599-392 record . . . Five Pacific Coast Conference champions . . . Past president National Association Basketball Coaches . . . Helms Foundation Hall of Fame . . . Tournament director NCAA championships 1965.

Tom Gola

Elected as player 1965 . . . Born: Philadelphia, Jan. 13, 1933 . . . Scored 2,222 points as high school star at LaSalle . . . Became only second player to achieve All-America honors all four years at LaSalle University . . . MVP in 1952 NIT and 1954 NCAA, leading LaSalle to both titles . . . Compiled 2,461 points and 2,201 rebounds in four years . . . Spent outstanding 10-year NBA career with Philadelphia and San Francisco Warriors and New York Knicks . . . All-NBA in 1958 . . . Always among league leaders in scoring, rebounds, assists and steals . . . Selected to *Sport* magazine all-time All-America team 1960.

Eddie Gottlieb

Elected as contributor 1971 . . . Born: Kiev, Russia, Sept. 15, 1898 . . . Died: Dec. 7, 1979 . . . One of early organizers of pro game . . . Coached the famed Philadelphia Sphas beginning 1918 . . . Team's achievements included beating Original Celtics and New York Rens . . . Later dominated Eastern and American Basketball Leagues . . . Eddie helped organize the Basketball Association of America in 1946 . . . His Philadelphia Warriors won the first BAA title . . . BAA later became NBA and Warriors joined . . . He coached through 1954-55, then became owner . . . Subsequently sold out and assumed functions as NBA consultant and schedule-maker.

Robert "Ace" Gruenig

Elected as player 1963 . . . Born: Chicago, March 12, 1913 . . . Died: Aug. 11, 1958 . . . Outstanding AAU player with Rosenberg-Arvey of Chicago, Denver Safeways, Denver Nuggets, Denver American Legion, Denver Ambrose and Murphy-Mahoney, 1933-48 . . . First team AAU All-American 10 times . . . One of game's early big men at 6-8, 220.

Dr. Luther Gulick

Elected as contributor 1959 . . . Born: Honolulu, Hawaii, Dec. 4, 1865 . . . Died: Aug. 13, 1918 . . . Met Dr. James Naismith while teaching at Springfield College, helped in development of the game . . . Profound influence on Naismith as director of physical education at Springfield . . . Later became director of physical education for New York Public School system . . . Set up New York's Public Schools Athletic League . . . One of the game's first boosters . . . Former chairman AAU basketball committee.

Cliff Hagan

Elected as player 1977 . . . Born: Owensboro, Ky., Sept. 12, 1931 . . . Led Owensboro (Ky.) H.S. to state title in 1949 . . . One of Kentucky's all-time top collegiate players . . . His University of Kentucky teams won NCAA title in 1951 and went undefeated (25-0) in 1954 . . . After 10 seasons with St. Louis Hawks in which he averaged 18.5 per game, he completed 13-year pro career as player-coach of ABA Dallas Chapparals . . . Wound up with 14,908 points . . . One of the great all-time hook shooters . . . Played in five All-Star Games and was MVP in 1968 . . . Was a vital performer as the Hawks won six Western Division titles and NBA crown in 1958.

Victor Hanson

Elected as player 1960 . . . Born: Watertown, N.Y., July 30, 1903 . . . Great all-around athlete at Syracuse University . . . Earned nine varsity letters . . . Basketball All-American 1925, 1926 and 1927 . . . Player of the Year, Helms Athletic Foundation 1927 . . . Led 1925-26 team to national championship with 19-1 record . . . Syracuse 48-7 during his career . . . Scored 25 of Syracuse's 30 points in victory over Pennsylvania in 1926 . . . All-time All-American as selected by Grantland Rice . . . Played professionally with Cleveland Rosenblums . . . Former head football coach at Syracuse . . . Signed with New York Yankees in baseball.

Lester Harrison

Elected as contributor 1979 . . . Born: Rochester, N.Y., Aug. 20, 1904 . . . Organized teams and games throughout 1930s and Rochester Pros in 1945 . . . As owner-coach, he changed name to Royals, won NBL title in 1946 and NBA title in 1951 . . . Won 394 games before selling team in 1958 . . . Served as member of Board of Directors of three leagues (NBL, BAA, NBA) . . . Early proponent of time clock . . . Organized Kodak Classic Tournament in 1963.

George Hepbron

Elected as referee 1960 . . . Born: Still Pond, Md., Aug. 27, 1863 . . . Died: April 30, 1946 . . . First basketball official in New York area . . . Organized Brooklyn YMCA league . . . Editor of AAU basketball guide 1901-14 . . . Member AAU rules committee 1896-1915 . . . Member and secretary, joint rules committee 1915-36 . . . Traveled extensively encouraging game and referees . . . in 1904 wrote first book on how to play the game.

Ferenc Hepp

Elected as contributor 1980 . . . Born: Bekes, Hungary, Nov. 3, 1909 . . . Died: Nov. 27, 1980 . . . Considered the "Father of Basketball" in Hungary, he was first Director of National School of P.E. and Sports in Hungary and longtime president of Hungarian Basketball Federation . . . Member of FIBA Technical Commitee and FIBA Central Board . . . Made contribution to administration of amateur ball around the world.

Ed Hickey

Elected as coach 1978 . . . Born: Reynolds, Neb. . . . Died: December 1980 . . . Commenced 35-year coaching career at Creighton Prep . . . Coached Creighton U., St. Louis U. and Marquette U. to seven Missouri Valley titles, five NCAA tourney berths and nine NIT selections . . . Won NIT crown with 1948 St. Louis unit . . . Coach of the Year in 1959 . . . President of NABC . . . 436 career victories.

Edward J. Hickox

Elected as contributor 1959 . . . Born: Cleveland, Ohio, April 10, 1878 . . . Died: Jan. 28, 1966 . . . Coached Springfield College basketball team for 16 years and American International College for one season . . . First executive secretary of Hall of Fame . . . President National Association of Basketball Coaches 1944-46 . . . Introduced basketball at Lycoming College in 1907 . . . Eaton (Colo.) high school team won 1911 high school championship of Colorado, Wyoming and Northern New Mexico . . . His 1912 high school team defeated five college teams, including Rocky Mountain champion, Colorado School of Mines.

Paul "Tony" Hinkle

Elected as contributor 1965 . . . Born: Logansport, Ind., Dec. 19, 1899 . . . Began coaching basketball at Butler University, Indianapolis 1924 . . . 534-366 through 39 seasons . . . Member, NCAA rules committee 1953-54; chairman, 1955-56 . . . President National Association Basketball Coaches 1954-55 . . . All Western Conference for University of Chicago . . . Helms All-American 1920 . . . Coached Butler to national championship in 1929 . . . During World War II coached Great Lakes team to 98 victories . . . Football and baseball coach at Butler . . . Also director of athletics . . . Professor and director of Physical Education department.

Howard Hobson

Elected as coach 1965 . . . Born: Portland, Ore., July 4, 1903 . . . Coach at Kelso (Wash.) High School, Benson (Ore.) High School, Southern Oregon College, University of Oregon, Yale University 1927-53 . . . Had 495-291 record . . . 1939 Oregon team won first NCAA tournament . . . Oregon teams were among first from West to travel East for intersectional games . . . Conducted numerous basketball clinics in U.S. and foreign countries . . . President, National Association Basketball Coaches 1947 . . . Served twelve years on U.S. Olympic Basketball Committee . . . Record at Oregon, 211-124.

Nat Holman

Elected as player 1964 . . . Born: New York City, Oct. 18, 1896 . . . Star of the Original Celtics . . . Coach CCNY 38 years . . . Coached National Collegiate champion and National Invitation Tournament champion 1950 . . . President National Association Basketball Coaches 1941 . . . *Sport* magazine Coach of the Year 1950 . . . Professor, Department Physical Education CCNY . . . Graduate Savage School of Physical Education.

George Hoyt

Elected as referee 1961 . . . Born: South Boston, Mass., Aug. 9, 1883 . . . Died: Nov. 11, 1962 . . . First listed in directory of registered officials 1911 . . . One of best-known referees in New England . . . Organized first official referees' board in eastern Massachusetts . . . One of the pioneers in officiating the game and introducing the job of the referee to others.

Charles "Chuck" Hyatt

Elected as player 1959 . . . Born: Syracuse, N.Y., Feb. 28, 1908 . . . Died: May 9, 1978 . . . All-American forward, University of Pittsburgh 1929-30 . . . Led Pitt to first national title in 1927-28, scoring 266 points . . . Scored 314 points in 1929-30 . . . Hit an even 300 as a junior . . . Played in only six losing games in three years . . . One of great scorers of his time . . . Later an AAU All-American for nine years.

Henry "Hank" Iba

Elected as coach 1968 . . . Born: Easton, Mo., Aug. 6, 1904 . . . Coaching success from beginning at Classen (Okla.) High School . . . Maryville (Mo.) Teachers runner-up for national title in 1932 . . . Moved to Oklahoma A&M, now Oklahoma State, where he won 14 conference titles . . . In 1945 and 1946 his teams won consecutive national collegiate titles . . . Only coach to guide two U.S. Olympic teams, 1964 and 1968, to gold medals . . . President National Association Basketball Coaches 1968.

Edward Simmons "Ned" Irish

Elected as contributor 1964 . . . Born: Lake George, N.Y., May 6, 1905 . . . Introduced the basketball doubleheader to Madison Square Garden on large-scale basis in 1934 . . . That move credited with making basketball a major sport . . . New York and the Garden became mecca of basketball as the game, because of Irish, went intersectional . . . Founded New York Knickerbockers 1946.

William Johnson

Elected as player 1976 . . . Born: Oklahoma City, Okla., Aug. 16, 1911 . . . Died: Feb. 5, 1980 . . . All-American at Oklahoma City Central High in 1929 . . . Three-year standout at Kansas U. . . . All-Big Six 1932-33 . . . Conference MVP and All-American as a senior in 1933 . . . Led Jayhawks to three straight Big Six titles and 42-11 record . . . AAU All-American with Kansas Stage Line as Missouri Valley leading scorer . . . Selected as "All-Time Great in Oklahoma" in 1975.

R. William Jones

Elected as contributor 1964 . . . Born: Rome, Italy, Oct. 5, 1906 . . . Co-founder International Basketball Federation 1932 . . . Introduced basketball in Olympics 1936 . . . Executive Secretary, F.I.B.A., since 1932 . . . Organized international tournaments . . . Director, UNESCO Youth Institute, Munich, Germany.

Alvin "Doggie" Julian

Elected as coach 1967 . . . Born: Reading, Pa., April 5, 1901 . . . Died: July 28, 1967 . . . The coach who brought about a renaissance of basketball in Boston and Worcester, Mass. . . . Coached at Muhlenberg College, Allentown, Pa., before coming to Holy Cross 1945-46 . . . 1947 Holy Cross team won NCAA title . . . Later coached at Dartmouth College . . . Coached Bob Cousy, Joe Mullaney, George Kaftan, Frank Oftring and Bob Curran at Holy Cross . . . 65-10 record in three years there . . . More than 400 lifetime victories . . . His teams participated in five NCAA tournaments and two National Invitation Tournaments . . . 1966 president of Coaches Association.

Frank Keaney

Elected as coach 1960 . . . Born: Boston, Mass., June 5, 1886 . . . Died: Oct. 10, 1967 . . . Coach Putnam, Conn., High School; Woonsocket, R.I., High School; Everett (Mass.) High School . . . University of Rhode Island 1920-48 . . . Record at Rhode Island 401-124 . . . Coached four NIT entrants . . . Athletic director University of Rhode Island . . . Graduate Bates College 1911 . . . Set college record in baseball with .410 average and 38 stolen bases.

Matthew "Pat" Kennedy

Elected as referee 1959 . . . Born: Hoboken, N.J., Jan. 28, 1908 . . . Died: June 16, 1957 . . . Most famous referee in game's history . . . High school, college and professional official 1928-46 . . . Supervisor of officials in NBA 1946-50 . . . Toured with Harlem Globetrotters from 1950 through 1957 . . . Often worked ten games a week, 125 per season . . . A gate attraction in his own right because of his colorful mannerisms on the court.

Walter Kennedy

Elected as contributor 1980 . . . Born: Stamford, Conn., June 8, 1912 . . . Died: June 26, 1977 . . . Commissioner of NBA from 1963-75, presiding over expansion, national TV contract . . . A Notre Dame alumnus, he served there as publicity man, then became BAA's (later NBA) first PR director . . . Toured world as consultant to Harlem Globetrotters . . . Became mayor of Stamford, resigning in second term when named NBA Commissioner in 1963.

George Keogan

Elected as coach 1961 . . . Born: Minnesota Lakes, Minn., March 8, 1890 . . . Died: Feb. 17, 1943 . . . Successful coach at St. Louis University, Valparaiso University, Notre Dame . . . Record at Notre Dame 1923-43, 327-96 . . . Created "shifting man-to-man" defense . . . From 1935 through 1937 season, Fighting Irish won 42 of 47 and were one of nation's best teams.

Ed "Moose" Krause

Elected as player 1975 . . . Born: Chicago, Feb. 2, 1913 . . . Three-sport star at DeLaSalle High, Chicago . . . Three-time All-American in both football and basketball at Notre Dame . . . Before graduating in 1934, established all-time game, season and three-season scoring marks . . . Team captain in 1934 . . . "Moose" came from 6-3, 215-pound frame . . . Coach and athletic director at St. Mary's, Minnesota, 1934-39 . . . Went on to coach Irish five 1946-51 . . . Was athletic director at Notre Dame 1951-80.

Bob Kurland

Elected as player 1961 . . . Born: St. Louis, Mo., Dec. 23, 1924 . . . Led Oklahoma A&M to successive national collegiate titles in 1945, '46 . . . Played for 1948 and 1952 U.S. Olympic teams . . . Most Valuable Player NCAA tournament 1945, 1946 . . . Consensus All-American, 1944-46 . . . National scoring champion 1946 . . . AAU standout with Phillips Oilers . . . One of first really talented big men at seven foot . . . Made AAU All-America team 1947-52.

Ward "Piggy" Lambert

Elected as coach 1960 . . . Born: Deadwood, S.D., May 28, 1888 . . . Died: Jan. 20, 1958 . . . Head coach Purdue University 1916-46 . . . His Purdue teams won or shared 11 Western Conference Big Ten championships . . . Overall record 371-152 . . . Pioneered fast-break game . . . Coached many All-Americans including Hall of Famer John Wooden . . . Commissioner National Professional Basketball League 1946-49.

Joe Lapchick

Elected as player 1966 . . . Born: Yonkers, N.Y., April 12, 1900 . . . Died: August 10, 1970 . . . Gained fame as first legitimate "star" center in game when he played for Original Celtics . . . Also played briefly with Cleveland Rosenblums . . . Played pro ball from 1917 to 1936 . . . Later coached at St. John's University, where his teams won four National Invitation Tournament titles . . . Also coached New York Knickerbockers of NBA . . . Twice national college Coach of Year.

Emil Liston

Elected as contributor 1974 . . . Born: Stockton, Mo., Aug. 21, 1890 . . . Died: Oct. 26, 1949 . . . Coached Baldwin High to Kansas state title while still attending Baker University in 1912 . . . Coached at Fort Scott, Kemper Military, Michigan College and Connecticut Wesleyan before embarking on 25-year career as head coach at Baker . . . Pioneered Kansas Coaches Association . . . Founded National Association of Intercollegiate Basketball 1938 . . . Served as first Executive Director of NAIB 1940-49 . . . Small college organization grew into 500-plus-member NAIA (National Association of Intercollegiate Athletics).

Harry Litwack

Elected as coach 1975 . . . Born: Austria, Sept. 20, 1907 . . . High school all-star at South Philadelphia . . . Captained Temple University two years, graduating in 1930 . . . A pro for seven years with Philadelphia Sphas in Eastern and American Leagues . . . Began coaching career at Gatz High in 1930 . . . Went on to coach Temple frosh and amass

182-32 mark while doubling as assistant with Philadelphia Warriors . . . Twenty-one years as head coach at Temple followed, with 373-193 record . . . Led Owls to 13 post-season tournaments including NIT championship in 1969 and third place in the NCAA in 1956 and 1958 . . . New York Writers' Coach of the Year in 1958.

Ken Loeffler

Elected as coach 1964 . . . Born: Beaver Falls, Pa., April 14, 1902 . . . Died: Jan. 1, 1974 . . . Coached at Geneva College 1928-34; Yale 1934-42; St. Louis Bombers professional team 1946-49; LaSalle College 1949-55; Texas A&M 1955-57 . . . Coached 1954 LaSalle team to national championship . . . Had his greatest years with Explorers, 145-27 . . . Coached Tom Gola, rated as one of best collegiate players of all time . . . Professor of law . . . Also worked as a newspaper columnist in Pittsburgh 1924-29.

Dutch Lonborg

Elected as coach 1973 . . . Born: Gardner, Ill., March 16, 1898 . . . Spent 29 years coaching college basketball teams . . . Started with McPherson College, moved to Washburn University and then spent 23 seasons at Northwestern . . . In 1925, his Washburn team won the AAU championship, the last time a college was able to win the crown . . . In 1931, he coached Northwestern to its first Big Ten championship . . . Served as president of the Coaches' Association in 1935 and as manager of the U.S. Olympic team in 1960.

Jerry Lucas

Elected as player 1979 . . . Born: Middletown, Ohio, March 30, 1940 . . . Ohio Player of the Year at Middletown H.S. in 1957 and 1958 . . . Collegiate Player of the Year at Ohio State in 1961 and 1962 . . . His Buckeyes were 78-6, won three Big Ten titles and NCAA crown in 1960 . . . Member of U.S. Olympic champs in 1960 . . . NBA Rookie of the Year with Cincinnati in 1964, NBA All-Star seven times, including MVP performance in 1965 . . . Scored 14,053 points in 11-year career with Cincinnati, San Francisco and New York, which he helped to NBA title in 1973 . . . At time of election, he was sixth-leading NBA career rebounder with 12,942.

Angelo "Hank" Luisetti

Elected as player 1959 . . . Born: San Francisco, California, June 16, 1916 . . . Revolutionized the game with one-hand shot . . . Led Stanford to three consecutive Pacific Coast titles 1936-38 . . . Three-time All-American . . . Recognized as greatest player in coast history . . . Scored 1,596 points in four-year career . . . Scored 50 points against Duquesne in his senior year.

Ed "Easy Ed" Macauley

Elected as player 1960 . . . Born: St. Louis, Mo., March 22, 1928 . . . Youngest person elected to Hall of Fame . . . Two-time All-American St. Louis University . . . Player of the Year 1947, 1948 . . . Most Valuable Player National Invitation Tournament 1948 . . . Led nation in field-goal percentage with .524 average in 1946-47 . . . Led St. Louis to NIT title 1948; Sugar Bowl title following season . . . Played professionally with St. Louis, Boston . . . Played in eight NBA All-Star games . . . Career high of 46 vs. George Mikan and Minneapolis Lakers, March 6, 1953 . . . Coached St. Louis Hawks to Western Division titles 1958-60.

Branch McCracken

Elected as player 1960 . . . Born: Monrovia, Ind., June 9, 1908 . . . Died: June 4, 1970 . . . Played three years at Indiana University under Everett Dean . . . Led team in scoring all three years . . . In senior year set Western Conference record of 147 points . . . Consensus All-American 1929-30 . . . Scored 525 career points . . . That was 32 percent of points scored by Indiana during the three-year period . . . Later coached at Indiana during the three-year period . . . Later coached at Indiana 1938-65 . . . Teams won 275, lost 119 . . . Won national titles in 1940 and 1953 . . . Coach of the Year 1940, 1953.

Jumpin' Jack McCracken

Elected as player 1962 . . . Born: Chickasha, Okla., June 11, 1911 . . . Died: Jan. 5, 1958 . . . Played high school and college basketball for Henry Iba . . . All-American at Northwest Missouri Teachers College . . . Considered by Iba one of finest players he coached . . . Consistently named to AAU All-American teams between 1932 and 1942, when he played for Denver teams and Phillips 66ers.

Arad McCutchan

Elected as coach 1980 . . . Born: Evansville, Ind., July 4, 1912 . . . Coached at his alma mater, Evansville, for 31 years and retired in 1977 as one of two coaches in NCAA history to win at least five national championships . . . Won 14 Indiana Conference titles and posted 514 career wins . . . NCAA Coach of the Year in 1964 and 1965, when team was 29-0 . . . "Mac" coached Pan Am team in 1971.

Frank McGuire

Elected as coach 1976 . . . Born: New York City, Nov. 8, 1916 . . . All-star at Xavier High and St. John's U. in New York . . . Coached at Xavier for 11 years after brief career in American League . . . First coach to win 100 games at three colleges . . . Won 103 at St. John's and 164 at North Carolina before moving to South Carolina where he won 283 games . . . First coach with NCAA finalists at two colleges, St. John's and North Carolina . . . Undefeated North Carolina squad (32-0) won 1957 NCAA title . . . Three-time Coach of the Year . . . Coached NBA Philadelphia Warriors to 49-31 mark in 1962 . . . Has won over 70 percent of his games as a coach.

John McLendon

Elected as contributor 1978 . . . Born: Hiawatha, Kan., April 5, 1915 . . . Began coaching career at Lawrence (Kan.) H.S. . . . Won 522 (three-quarters) of the games he coached at the collegiate level at North Carolina College, Hampton Institute, Tennessee A&I State, Kentucky State and Cleveland State . . . First coach to win three straight national titles, with Tennessee A&I State in NAIA 1957-59 . . . NAIA Coach of the Year in 1958 . . . Also won titles in CIAA (1949-52), NIBL and AAU (Cleveland Pipers in 1961) and ABL Eastern Division (1962) . . . Coached Denver Nuggets in ABA (1969-70) . . . Acknowledged leader in the emergence of the black colleges.

Walter Meanwell

Elected as coach 1959 . . . Born: Leeds, England, Jan. 26, 1884 . . . Died: Dec. 2, 1953 . . . Coached at University of Wisconsin . . . University of Missouri . . . Record 290-101 . . . Eleven conference championships . . . Helms Hall of Fame; Wisconsin Hall of Fame . . . Developed valve for laceless basketball . . . Also developed the basketball shoe that bore his name . . . One of pioneers in giving clinics . . . Traveled all over United States . . . Author on basketball and conditioning.

Ray Meyer

Elected as coach 1978 . . . Born: Chicago, Dec. 18, 1913 . . . When elected, Ray was nation's winningest active major-college coach with 596 wins . . . Had led 16 teams to NCAA and NIT Tournaments and won NIT title in 1945 . . . Captained Notre Dame during playing days (1934-38) . . . Assistant at Notre Dame before taking only head coaching job he has ever had—at DePaul—in 1942 . . . Coached College All-Americans for 15 years on Harlem Globetrotters' tour . . . USBWA Coach of the Year in 1978 and NABC Coach of the Year in 1979.

George Mikan

Elected as player 1960 . . . Born: Joliet, Ill., June 18, 1924 . . . Three-time All-American center at DePaul . . . Scored 1,870 points in four years . . . Fifty-three in NIT game against Rhode Island, 1945 . . . Player of the Year 1944-45 and 1945-46 . . . Associated Press' Player of the Half Century . . . One of all-time pro greats with Minneapolis Lakers . . . First commissioner of the American Basketball Association, 1967.

William Mokray

Elected as contributor 1965 . . . Born: Passaic, N.J., June 6, 1907 . . . Died: March 22, 1974 . . . Editor *Official NBA Guide* . . . Author *Basketball Encyclopedia* 1963 . . . Wrote history of basketball for *Encyclopedia Brittanica* 1957 . . . First chairman, Hall of Fame Honors Committee 1959-64 . . . Scout and promotion director, Boston Celtics . . . Basketball director Boston Garden.

Ralph Morgan

Elected as contributor 1959 . . . Born: Philadelphia, Pa., March 9, 1884 . . . Died: Jan. 5, 1965 . . . Founded collegiate basketball rules committee 1905 . . . Secretary-Treasurer, Eastern Intercollegiate Basketball League . . . Founded Eastern Collegiate Basketball League, now Ivy League, in 1910.

Frank "Pop" Morgenweck

Elected as contributor 1962 . . . Born: Egg Harbor, N.J., July 15, 1875 . . . Died: Dec. 8, 1941 . . . Spent 32 years managing, financing and promoting early professional games . . . Coached Kingston, N.Y., to New York State and world's pro championship 1922-23 . . . Coached Rochester Centrals to American League title 1929-30 . . . Discovered Original Celtic stars Benny Borgmann and Johnny Beckman . . . Coached Chicago Bruins for George Halas.

Charles "Stretch" Murphy

Elected as player 1960 . . . Born: Marion, Ind., April 10, 1907 . . . Purdue University All-American at 6-9 under Ward Lambert . . . Played from 1926 through 1930 . . . Set Western Conference record of 143 points in 1929 . . . Captained 1930 conference championship team . . . Teamed with Johnny Wooden in 1930 . . . Helms Foundation All-American three years.

Dr. James Naismith

Elected as contributor 1959 . . . Born: Almonte, Ontario, Nov. 6, 1861 . . . Died: Nov. 28, 1939 . . . Invented basketball at Springfield College, December 1891, then promoted the game all over country . . . M.A. Physical Education 1910 . . . Studied for ministry at Presbyterian College, Montreal . . . Director of Physical Education McGill University 1887 . . . Instructor YMCA Training School, Springfield, Mass. . . . Ordained Presbyterian minister 1915 . . . Received medical degree Gross Medical School 1898 . . . Physical Education Denver YMCA 1895 . . . Head of Physical Education Department, University of Kansas 1898-1925 . . . Retired from teaching 1937 . . . Little-known fact is that while at Springfield he tested and wore first football helmet.

Pete Newell

Elected as contributor 1978 . . . Born: Vancouver, B.C., Aug. 31, 1913 . . . Won unprecedented triple as head coach—took NIT title in 1949 with University of San Francisco, NCAA crown in 1959 with California-Berkeley and won Olympic goal medal in 1960 . . . Added four straight Pac-8 championships (1956-60) . . . Coach of the Year in 1960 . . . Coaching stops included USF, Michigan State and Cal-Berkeley after graduating from Loyola (L.A.) in 1939 . . . Won respect and recognition as college administrator, pro general manager and coaching clinician overseas . . . Co-authored "Basketball Methods."

John Nucatola

Elected as referee 1977 . . . Born: New York City, Nov. 17, 1907 . . . After playing as a pro, he began officiating career that spanned more than 2,000 games, many of them while still a coach at his alma mater, Newtown H.S. (N.Y.) . . . Worked collegiate games in ECAC, ACC, Southern, Big 8, NCAA and NIT tourneys . . . Ref in pros in ABL, BAA and NBA until he hung up whistle in 1959 to concentrate on administrative supervisor's career . . . Retired as NBA's Supervisor of Officials in 1977 . . . Early proponent of three-man officiating . . . Author of "Officiating Basketball."

John J. O'Brien

Elected as contributor 1961 . . . Born: Brooklyn, N.Y., Nov. 4, 1888 . . . Died: Dec. 9, 1967 . . . Organized Metropolitan Basketball League 1921 . . . President, American Basketball League, 25 years . . . Leading professional and college official . . . Assisted in organizing interstate Pro Basketball League in 1914 . . . Served as its president 1915-17 . . . Officiated many early pro games around New York, city and state.

Harold G. Olsen

Elected as contributor 1959 . . . Born: Rice Lake, Wis., May 12, 1895 . . . Died: Oct. 29, 1953 . . . Basketball coach at Ohio State 1922-46 . . . Won conference titles 1925, 1939, 1944 and 1946 . . . Past president, Coaches Association . . . Former chairman NCAA rules committee, NCAA tournament committee . . . Member of 1948 Olympic basketball committee . . . Helped introduce the 10-second rule . . . Coached Chicago Stags pro team 1946-49.

H.O. "Pat" Page

Elected as player 1962 . . . Born: Chicago, March 20, 1887 . . . Died: Nov. 23, 1965 . . . Player of the Year 1910 while at Chicago U. . . . Led team to national title in 1908, undefeated season in 1909 . . . Western Conference titles in 1907, 1909, 1910 . . . Played guard . . . Effective left-handed shooter . . . Later basketball coach at Chicago U. 1911-20 . . . Also coached at Butler, 1930-33.

Bob Pettit

Elected as player 1970 . . . Born: Dec. 12, 1932, Baton Rouge, La. . . . All-American at LSU 1952-54 . . . NBA Rookie of Year, 1954-55 . . . Played forward . . . All-league first team 10 straight years for Milwaukee and St. Louis Hawks . . . NBA MVP 1956, '59 . . . All-Star game MVP four times . . . Retired in 1965 as highest scorer in NBA history with 20,880 points . . . One of the league's all-time rebounders.

Andy Phillip

Elected as player 1961 . . . Born: Granite City, Ill., March 7, 1922 . . . Leader of famed "Whiz Kids" team at University of Illinois . . . Two-time All-American . . . Elected to Associated Press' all-time All-America team . . . Set Western Conference records for most points season (255), most field goals (16) and most points (40) in a single game . . . Played 1941-42, 1942-43, then entered service and returned for 1946-47 season . . . Later played pro ball with Chicago Stags, Philadelphia Warriors, Fort Wayne Pistons and Boston Celtics.

Maurice Podoloff

Elected as contributor 1973 . . . Born: Elizabethgrad, Russia, Aug. 18, 1890 . . . Graduated from Yale 1913 and from Yale Law School two years later . . . Because of strong legal and administrative background was asked to assume leadership of Basketball Association of America . . . Led BAA into merger with NBA in 1949 . . . Guided NBA through early years and secured first TV contract 1954 . . . Did much to bring NBA to national prominence before retiring after 17 years as commissioner in 1963.

Jim Pollard

Elected as player 1977 . . . Born: Oakland, Cal., July 9, 1922 . . . Stanford All-American as soph as team won NCAA championship in 1942 . . . Three-year Service All-Star, two year AAU All-Star and MVP in 1947 and 1948 . . . Smooth player with great finesse . . . Started in four NBA All-Star Games during career with Minneapolis Lakers from 1949-55 . . . Totalled 6,522 points, 1,417 assists and 2,487 rebounds and Lakers won two NBL titles and five NBA crowns as that era's dynasty . . . Chosen All-Time Pacific Coast forward in 1955.

Henry Porter

Elected as contributor 1960 . . . Born: Oct. 2, 1891 . . . As director of the National Federation of State High School Athletic Associations he helped organize the National Basketball Committee of U.S. and Canada . . . First representative of high schools on NABC, member 30 years . . . Codified rules of basketball with Oswald Tower . . . Pioneered invention and adoption of molded ball and use of films for rules study . . . Author of basketball books . . . His player handbook and other books sold 10 million copies.

Ernest Quigley

Elected as referee 1961 . . . Born: New Castle, New Brunswick, Canada, March 22, 1880 . . . Died: Dec. 10, 1968 . . . College and AAU basketball official for 40 years 1904-44 . . . Supervisor, NCAA tournament officials 1940-42 . . . Also a baseball umpire in National League . . . Umpired at many World Series . . . Played basketball under Dr. James Naismith at Kansas.

William Reid

Elected as contributor 1963 . . . Born: Detroit, Sept. 26, 1893 . . . Died: Oct. 30, 1955 . . . Basketball coach and director of athletics Colgate University . . . Coached ten years, director 36 years . . . President Eastern Collegiate Athletic Conference 1944-45 . . . Vice-president National Collegiate Athletic Association 1942-46 . . . Record as coach at Colgate, 151-56 . . . Also famous for his play during military days with American Expeditionary Force team which won AEF title in 1919 . . . Averaged 17.3 points per game in AEF ball, unheard of in that era.

Elmer Ripley

Elected as player 1973 . . . Born: Staten Island, N.Y., July 21, 1891 . . . A 20-year career with a number of championship teams . . . His pro career started with the Carbondale, Pa., team . . . Also played for Scranton, the Original Celtics, Fort Wayne K. of C., Brooklyn and Cleveland . . . Later turned to coaching at Georgetown, Yale, Columbia, Notre Dame, Army and Regis . . . Conducted many clinics and toured Israel for the U.S. State Department . . . Coached the 1960 Canadian Olympic team . . . Had a three-year stint as coach of the Harlem Globetrotters.

Oscar Robertson

Elected as player 1979 . . . Born: Charlotte, Tenn., Nov. 24, 1938 . . . Player of the Year twice and All-American three times at University of Cincinnati . . . Major-college scoring leader three years and set 14 NCAA records . . . Co-captained 1960 Olympic champs . . . In 14 NBA years with Cincinnati and Milwaukee, "The Big O" was Rookie of the Year (1961), league MVP (1964), All-Star MVP (1961, 1964, 1969) . . . Scored 26,710 points for a 25.7 average in 1,035 games with 9,887 assists and 7,694 free throws . . . Scored 246 points in 12 All-Star Games.

John Roosma

Elected as player 1961 . . . Born: Passaic, N.J., Sept. 3, 1900 . . . Led West Point through unbeaten season (31 games) in 1922-23 . . . Received All-America notice . . . On all-time New Jersey team . . . One of Ernest Blood's favorites at Passaic High School . . . Outstanding athlete class of 1926, West Point . . . Later coached and played for many military teams both in the United States and overseas . . . Also refereed major-college games.

Adolph Rupp

Elected as coach 1968 . . . Born: Halstead, Kan., Sept. 2, 1901 . . . Died: Dec. 10, 1977 . . . Played for Phog Allen at University of Kansas . . . Member of 1923 national-championship team . . . Allen's protege became most successful college coach in history, winning his 800th game during the 1968-69 season at University of Kentucky, where he began coaching in 1930 . . . Kentucky teams winners of 24 Southeastern Conference titles, four NCAA titles, one NIT championship . . . Co-coach 1948 U.S. Olympic team. Four times Coach of Year.

Bill Russell

Elected as player 1974 . . . Born: Monroe, La., Feb. 12, 1934 . . . All-California high school player at McClymonds . . . Led University of San Francisco to two national titles and 56-game winning streak . . . Named College Player of the Year as a senior in 1956 . . . Two-time All-American . . . Key to 1956 U.S. Olympic championship at Melbourne . . . Revolutionized NBA defensive concepts and brought Boston Celtics eight straight titles, 11 in 13 seasons . . . Amassed 21,721 career rebounds and 15.1 scoring average . . . Appeared in 11 All-Star games, winning MVP in 1963 . . . Five-time NBA MVP . . . Player-coach with Celtics 1966-69, winning two championships . . . Named Athlete of the Decade by *Sporting News* 1970 . . . Coach-GM of Seattle SuperSonics 1973-77.

John "Honey" Russell

Elected as player 1964 . . . Born: Brooklyn, N.Y., May 31, 1903 . . . Died: Nov. 15, 1973 . . . Played in more than 3,200 professional basketball games with Brooklyn Visitations, Cleveland Rosenblums, Chicago Bruins, Rochester Centrals . . . Also coached Chicago franchise . . . One of best scoring guards in early days of pro game . . . Once held early pro scoring record of 22 points in one game . . . Successful coach at Seton Hall University in New Jersey after retiring as player . . . Big-league baseball scout.

Leonard Sachs

Elected as coach 1961 . . . Born: Chicago, Aug. 7, 1897 . . . Died: Oct. 27, 1942 . . . Had 224-129 record at Loyola of Chicago from 1924-42 . . . Noted for his defensive strategy . . . His 1927-28, 1928-29 teams won 32 straight games . . . 1938-39 team lost only one game, to LIU in NIT finals . . . Member of Illinois Athletic Club team that won AAU title in 1918.

Lynn St. John

Elected as contributor 1962 . . . Born: Union City, Pa., Nov. 18, 1876 . . . Died: Sept. 30, 1950 . . . Served on NCAA rules committee 1912-37 . . . Chairman rules committee 1919-37 . . . At time of first basketball competition in Olympics, prevented a split in ranks of separate factions in U.S. amateur basketball . . . Helped organize National Basketball Committee of U.S. and Canada . . . Director of Athletics, Ohio State University, 1915-47 . . . Basketball coach, Ohio State 1912-19.

Abe Saperstein

Elected 1970 as contributor . . . Born: London, England, July 4, 1902 . . . Died: March 15, 1966 . . . Settled in Chicago . . . Formed famed touring comedy team called Harlem Globetrotters . . . Played before millions of fans around the world, and on TV . . . Team won World Pro title in 1940 . . . Credited with making basketball a truly international game.

Arthur Schabinger

Elected as contributor 1961 . . . Born: Sabetha, Kan., Aug. 6, 1889 . . . Died: Oct 13, 1972 . . . Basketball coach at Creighton University for thirteen years (169-67), Ottawa University, Emporia Teachers College . . . Co-founder of National Association Basketball Coaches . . . Member of rules committee 1935-36 . . . Founder and director of Official Sports Film Service . . . NABC president 1931-32 . . . Early advocate of intersectional scheduling . . . Basketball official in Midwest . . . Conducted tryouts for first U.S. Olympic team . . . Graduate of Emporia Teachers and Springfield College.

Dolph Schayes

Elected as player 1973 . . . Born: New York City, May 19, 1928 . . . Entered NYU when only 16 and finished career as All-American . . . Joined the Syracuse Nationals in 1948 and for the next decade he was one of the top scorers in professional basketball and the Nats were one of the best teams . . . A member of the NBA all-star team 12 times as a forward, with an exciting outside touch . . . Scored 19,249 points and played in a one-time record 1,059 games . . . Later coached the Philadelphia 76ers—formerly the Nats—and Buffalo Braves . . . He was Coach of the Year with the 76ers in 1965-66 . . . Also served as supervisor of NBA officials.

Ernest Schmidt

Elected as player 1973 . . . Born: Nashville, Kan., Feb. 12, 1911 . . . Led Winfield (Kan.) High to three state championships . . . Continued winning ways at Kansas State by leading Wildcats to a record 47 straight wins and four conference titles . . . Conference high scorer three times before graduating in 1933 . . . Won All-American recognition in 1932 . . . Voted Greatest College Player in Missouri Valley same year . . . All-Central Conference center four years.

John Schommer

Elected as player 1959 . . . Born: Chicago, Jan. 29, 1884 . . . Died: Jan. 11, 1960 . . . All-time All-America selection by Helms Athletic Foundation . . . 12-letterman at University of Chicago 1906-09 . . . Four-time All-America center in basketball . . . His 80-foot goal gave Chicago a last-second victory for the national title over Pennsylvania in 1908 . . . Once scored 15 field goals in game against University of Illinois . . . During 1908-09 season he had an amazing defensive string of nine games when he held the opposing centers to a total of four baskets.

Barney Sedran

Elected as player 1962 . . . Born: New York City, Jan. 28, 1891 . . . Died: Jan. 14, 1969 . . . Played professional basketball in eastern United States for 15 seasons, 1912-26 . . . Teamed with such other immortals as Nat Holman, John Beckman, Dutch Dehnert, Elmer Ripley, Honey Russell, Marty Friedman . . . Ended career with Fort Wayne and Cleveland Rosenblums . . . Selected on many all-time all-pro teams . . . Played at 118 pounds, 5-4 . . . Coached a number of well-known teams including Brooklyn Jewels, Kate Smith Celtics, New York Whirlwinds.

Bill Sharman

Elected as player 1975 . . . Born: Abilene, Tex., May 25, 1926 . . . Scoring star and captain three years at Porterville H.S. . . . Two years conference MVP, All-Pacific Coast and All-American before graduating from USC in 1950 . . . Broke into NBA with Washington in 1951, then on to 10 seasons with Boston Celtics . . . All-NBA seven years . . . 1955 NBA All-Star Game MVP . . . Scored 12,665 career points and ranks as one of top all-time foul shooters with 89 percent lifetime mark . . . Selected to NBA Silver Anniversary Team 1971 . . . Only coach to win championships in three professional leagues . . . Won ABL title with Cleveland Pipers 1962, ABA crown with Utah 1971 and NBA championship with Los Angeles 1972 . . . Became Lakers' GM in 1976.

Everett Shelton

Elected as coach 1979 . . . Born: Cunningham, Kan., May 12, 1898 . . . Died: April 16, 1974 . . . Began 46-year coaching career at alma mater, Phillips College, in 1924 . . . Won 850 games and two national titles (AAU in 1937 with Denver Safeways and NCAA in 1943 with University of Wyoming) . . . Won eight conference crowns with Wyoming . . . As NABC President in 1960, he was crusader for National Rules Interpreter . . . West Team coach in 1967 NABC All-Star Game . . . Commissioner of Far West Conference 1969-74.

J. Dallas Shirley

Elected as referee 1979 . . . Born: Washington, D.C., June 7, 1913 . . . Worked games in Southern, ACC, ECAC, CBOA, Mason-Dixon Conferences as well as NIT, NCAA tourneys, Sugar Bowl and Olympic Playoffs during 32-year refereeing career . . . Alumnus of George Washington . . . Officiated 1959 Pan-Am Games and 1960 Olympic Games, national games in Columbia, Iceland, Puerto Rico and Libya . . . IAABO president in 1953, CBOA president in 1954 . . . Chief of Mission to China in 1979 . . . Supervisor of Southern Conference refs . . . Received FIBA Award 1979 for devoting lifetime to officiating development.

Amos Alonzo Stagg

Elected as contributor 1959 . . . Born: West Orange, N.J., Aug. 16, 1862 . . . Died: March 17, 1965 . . . Helped James Naismith in early development of game when both were students and instructors at Springfield College . . . Introduced sport at University of Chicago . . . Coached seven Western Conference basketball champions . . . Conducted National Interscholastic Basketball Tournament in Chicago for 13 years . . . Football immortal . . . Hall of Famer in that sport as well.

Christian Steinmetz

Elected as player 1961 . . . Born: Milwaukee, June 28, 1881 . . . Died: June 11, 1963 . . . "Father" of Wisconsin basketball . . . One of game's earliest scoring greats at University of Wisconsin 1903-05 . . . His following Wisconsin records were standing in 1954: most points single game (50), most field goals single game (20), most free throws single game (26), most points single season (462) . . . Helms Hall of Fame . . . Member of Wisconsin Hall of Fame.

Charles "Chuck" Taylor

Elected as contributor 1968 . . . Born: Brown County, Indiana, June 24, 1901 . . . Died: June 23, 1969 . . . Developed basketball shoe in 1921 . . . What began as business promotion developed into career of selling basketball . . . Gave first basketball clinic in 1922 at North Carolina State . . . Clinics took him to every major American city as well as Puerto Rico, Mexico, Hawaii, Canada, South America, Africa and Europe . . . Began Converse Rubber Co. *Yearbook* in 1922 . . . Selected All-American teams from 1932 . . . Coached Air Force basketball team in World War II . . . Eleven-year pro career.

John "Cat" Thompson

Elected as player 1962 . . . Born: St. George, Utah, Feb. 10, 1906 . . . All-Rocky Mountain Conference selection at Montana State 1927-30 . . . 1928-29 team, 36-2, led by Thompson . . . Named Player of the Year by Helms Foundation . . . The first real "name" player to come out of Montana area . . . Also in Helms Hall of Fame.

David Tobey

Elected as referee 1961 . . . Born: New York City, May 1, 1898 . . . Professional official, New York City, 1918-25 . . . Eastern intercollegiate official 1926-46 . . . Wrote *Basketball Officiating* 1944 . . . Officiated in traditional games for many years in Madison Square Garden and Philadelphia's Convention Hall . . . Also a fine professional player with the early New York Knickerbockers and Philadelphia Sphas.

Oswald Tower

Elected as contributor 1959 . . . Born: North Adams, Mass., Nov. 23, 1883 . . . Died: May 28, 1968 . . . Best known for contributions made in interpretation of rules . . . Member of rules committee 1910-59 . . . Editor of *Basketball Guide* and official rules interpreter 1915-59 . . . Officiated for 35 years.

Arthur Trester

Elected as contributor 1961 . . . Born: Pecksburg, Ind., June 10, 1878 . . . Died: Sept. 18, 1944 . . . Commissioner of Indiana High School Athletic Association 22 years . . . This association served as model for many state organizations . . . Organized tournament system to play for state championship 1911.

Robert Vandiver

Elected as player 1974 . . . Born: Franklin, Ind., Dec. 26, 1903 . . . Regarded as one of greatest high school players in Indiana history . . . Led Franklin H.S. to state championship three straight years 1920-22 . . . All-state and captain of "Franklin Wonder Five" . . . Entire team entered Franklin College . . . Led Grizzlies to their greatest record between 1922-26 . . . Member of Indiana's All-Time All-Star Five.

Edward Wachter

Elected as player 1961 . . . Born: Troy, N.Y., June 30, 1883 . . . Died: March 12, 1966 . . . One of the earliest professionals with Ware, Mass., team in Western Professional Basketball League 1900-02 . . . Played for many other pro teams in Massachusetts, Pennsylvania and New York including Haverhill and Pittsfield, Mass., Schenectady, N.Y., McKeesport, Pa. . . . Key man on teams that carried basketball to the hinterlands, where sport was bidding for recognition . . . Played center for Troy team that barnstormed across country to Billings, Mont. . . . Team won 37 games on this tour . . . Played on more championship teams than any other player of his generation . . . Leading scorer Hudson River and New York State leagues for five years.

David Walsh

Elected as referee 1961 . . . Born: Hoboken, N.J., Oct. 5, 1889 . . . Died: June 2, 1975 . . . High school, college, professional official 1911-33 . . . Associate director, Collegiate Basketball Officials Bureau 1941-56 . . . Secretary-treasurer international Association Approved Basketball Officials 1948-56 . . . Coached and taught physical education in New Jersey school system for 45 years.

W. R. Clifford Wells

Elected as contributor 1971 . . . Born: Indianapolis, March 17, 1896 . . . Died: Aug. 15, 1977 . . . Indiana U graduate 1920 . . . Began coaching career in Indiana high schools . . . His teams at Bloomington, Columbus and Logansport won 617 games, including 50 district, regional and invitational titles . . . Coached at Tulane, 1945-63 . . . Finished with combined high-school college record of 885-418 . . . Conducted clinics and wrote articles about the game . . . Member of national rules committee.

Jerry West

Elected as player 1979 . . . Born: Cabin Creek, W. Va., May 28, 1938 . . . West Virginia Player of the Year at University of West Virginia in 1956 . . . Two-time All-American . . . Member Pan Am champs of 1959 and co-captain of Olympic titlists in 1960 . . . In 14-year career with Los Angeles Lakers, he was the greatest shooting guard in NBA history . . . Scored 63 points in one game, totalled 25,192 points for an average of 27 in 932 games . . . Scored record 4,457 playoff points (29.1 in 153 games), including 40.6 average in 1965 . . . MVP in 1969 . . . All-Defensive Team 1969-73, All-NBA 12 times, played in 13 All-Star Games . . . "Mr. Clutch." . . . After playing career, he coached Lakers for three seasons.

John Wooden

Elected as player 1960 . . . Rehonored as coach 1972 . . . Born: Martinsville, Ind., Oct. 14, 1910 . . . Three-time All-America guard at Purdue 1930-32 . . . Captained 1931-32 national-championship team . . . Later became one of most successful college coaches at UCLA . . . First coach to win five national titles and six straight from 1967 through 1972 . . . UCLA teams won 10 national titles in 12 years, '64-75 . . . Credited with developing and perfecting zone-press defense.

THE FIRST TEAM

Eighteen students from Dr. James Naismith's physical-education class participated in the first basketball game in December 1891, at Springfield Armory YMCA, Springfield, Mass. . . . Nine players competed for each team at the same time . . . In 1897, rules stipulated that only five men could compete on one team at the same time . . . Yale defeated Pennsylvania, 32-10, in first game played with five on side, March 20, 1897 . . . Players in the first game were: William Davis, Eugene Libby, John Thompson, George Weller, Wilbert Carey, Ernest Hildner, Lyman Archibald, T. Duncan Patton, Finley MacDonald, Raymond Kaighn, Genzabaro Ishikawa, Franklin Barnes, Edwin Ruggles, Frank Mahan, William Chase, Benjamin French, George Day and Henri Gelan.

BUFFALO GERMANS

Organized during season of 1895-96 by Frederick Burkhardt, physical director of Buffalo German YMCA . . . Won Pan-American Exposition in June 1901 in Buffalo on 40 × 60 grass court . . . Players wore cleats . . . During season, Germans defeated Hobart College, 134-0 . . . In 1904, won "exhibition" tournament at Olympic Games in St. Louis . . . Center Alfred Heerdt, William Rhode, George Redlein, Alfred Manweiler and Edward Miller were stars of that team . . . Though no official AAU tournaments were held between 1904 and 1910, Germans were considered best team of period . . . Heerdt later became team manager and guided the Germans until squad disbanded in 1929.

ORIGINAL CELTICS

Organized as the New York Celtics in 1914 by Frank McCormack . . . Represented a settlement house on the city's West Side . . . Pete Barry and John Witte only members of original team that eventually played for namesake, which gained national and international fame . . . New York Celtics broke up before World War I . . . Jim and Tom Furey reorganized it after the war, but McCormack owned rights to name "New York Celtics," so Furey team became known as Original Celtics . . . The Celtics barnstormed the country in addition to playing in the American Pro League . . . Dutch Dehnert, Nat Holman, Chris Leonard, Johnny Beckman, Horse Haggerty, Ernie Reich, Eddie Burke, Joe Trippe, Joe Lapchick, Eddie White, Benny Borgmann and Dave Banks played for the team during its greatest days . . . Johnny Witte coached . . . From 1921 through 1929, Celtics averaged 120 victories and 10

losses . . . Won American League title twice in row, 1926-27, 1927-28, and then league broke up team, with players going to other franchises . . . Team reorganized for barnstorming purposes again in 1930s, but never attained success of earlier clubs.

NEW YORK RENS

Not until Jackie Robinson broke the color line in baseball in 1946 were black athletes accepted in organized professional sport . . . They organized their own teams, often playing the top teams of the time in exhibition games . . . The New York Rens were regarded as the best basketball team in the United States from 1932 to 1936 . . . They had an 88-game winning streak in 1933-34 . . . Organized in 1922 by Bob Douglas . . . Lasted 27 years . . . Frequently played two or three games in a day . . . Between 1932 and 1936 won 473 and lost 49 . . . Some outstanding players included Clarence Jenkins, Bill Yancey, John Holt, Pappy Ricks, Eyre Saitch, Charles "Tarzan" Cooper, Wee Willie Smith.

PART 4

OFFICIAL NBA RULES

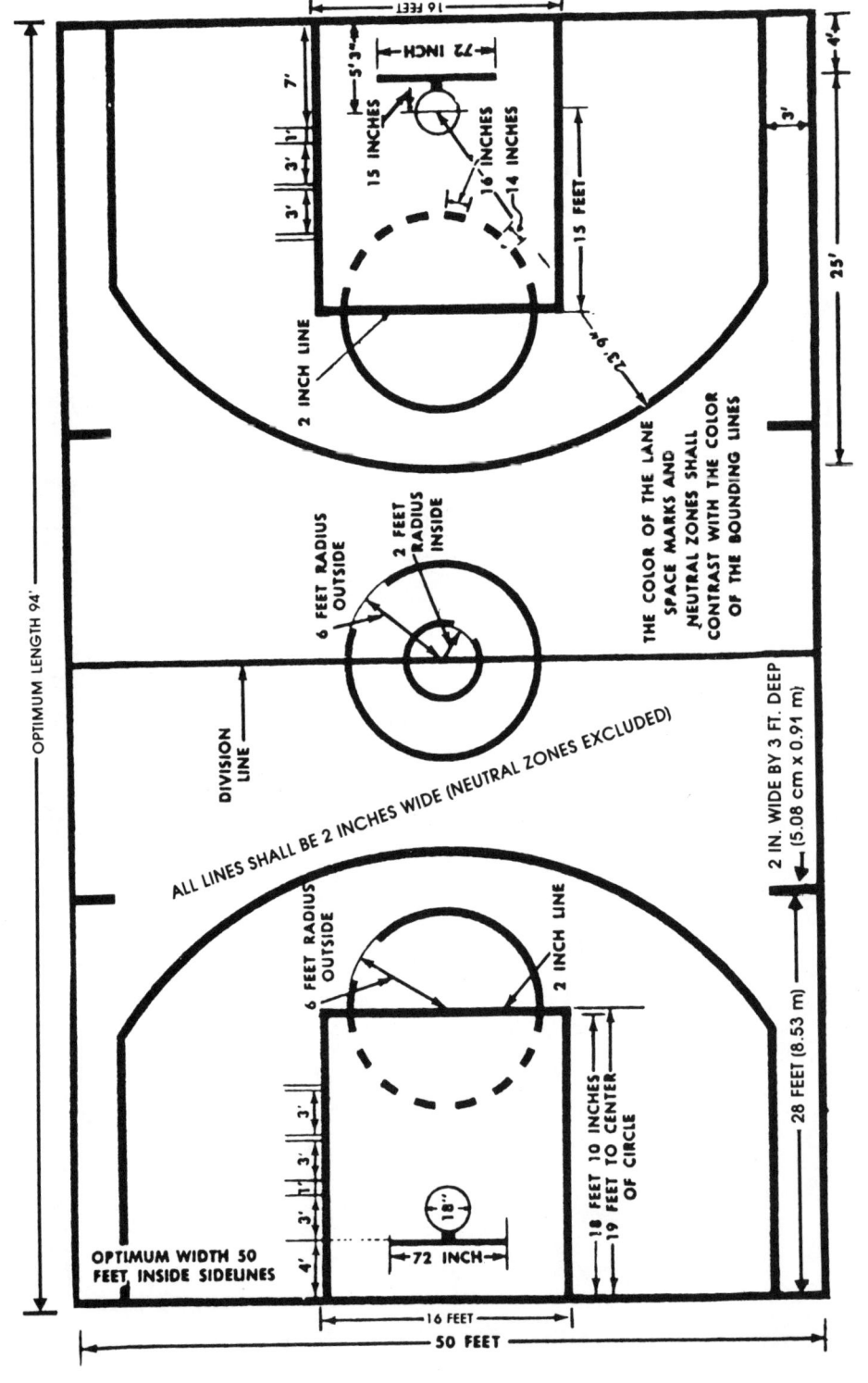

16 FEET

72 INCH

7'

5' 3"

15 INCHES

16 INCHES

14 INCHES

3' 3' 1'

3'

2 INCH LINE

15 FEET

2' 9" 3' 6"

4'

3'

25'

THE COLOR OF THE LANE SPACE MARKS AND NEUTRAL ZONES SHALL CONTRAST WITH THE COLOR OF THE BOUNDING LINES

OPTIMUM LENGTH 94'

6 FEET RADIUS OUTSIDE

2 FEET RADIUS INSIDE

DIVISION LINE

ALL LINES SHALL BE 2 INCHES WIDE (NEUTRAL ZONES EXCLUDED)

2 IN. WIDE BY 3 FT. DEEP (5.08 cm x 0.91 m)

28 FEET (8.53 m)

6 FEET RADIUS OUTSIDE

2 INCH LINE

3'

3' 1'

3'

18"

72 INCH

18 FEET 10 INCHES
19 FEET TO CENTER OF CIRCLE

OPTIMUM WIDTH 50 FEET INSIDE SIDELINES

4'

16 FEET

50 FEET

RULE NO. 1—COURT DIMENSIONS—EQUIPMENT

Section I—Court and Dimensions

a. The playing court shall be measured and marked as shown in court diagram.

b. A free throw lane shall be marked at each end of the court with dimensions and markings as shown on court diagram. All boundary lines are part of the lane; lane space marks and neutral zone marks are **not**. The color of the lane space marks and neutral zones shall contrast with the color of the boundary lines. The areas identified by the lane space markings are two inches by thirty-six and the neutral zone marks are twelve inches by thirty-six inches.

c. A free throw line, 2 inches wide, shall be drawn across each of the circles indicated in court diagram. It shall be parallel to the end line and shall be 15 feet from the plane of the face of the backboard.

d. Three-point field goal area which has parallel lines three feet from the sidelines, extending from the baseline, and an arc of 23 feet-nine inches from the middle of the basket which intersects the parallel lines.

e. Four hash marks shall be drawn (two inches wide) perpendicular to the side line on each side of the court and 28 feet from the base line. The hash mark shall extend three feet onto the court.

Section II—Equipment

a. The backboard shall be a rectangle measuring 6 feet horizontally and 4 feet vertically. The front surface shall be flat and transparent.

b. A transparent backboard shall be marked as follows: a rectangle marked by a 2″ white line shall be centered behind the ring. This rectangle shall have outside dimensions of 24″ horizontally and 18″ vertically.

NOTE: (1) Home management is required to have a spare board with supporting unit on hand for emergencies, and a steel tape or extension ruler and a level for use if necessary.

c. Each basket shall consist of a metal ring 18″ in inside diameter with white cord net 15 to 18 inches in length. The cord of the net shall not be less than 30 thread nor more than 120 thread and shall be constructed as to check the ball momentarily as it passes through the basket.

d. Each basket ring shall be securely attached to the backboard with its upper edge 10 feet above and parallel to the floor and equidistant from the vertical edges of the board. The nearest point of the inside edge of the ring shall be 6″ from the plane of the face of the board. The ring shall be painted orange.

e. (1) The ball shall be an officially approved NBA ball between 7½ and 8½ lbs. pressure.

(2) Six balls must be made available to each team for pre-game warmup.

f. At least one electric light is to be placed behind the backboard, obvious to officials and synchronized to light up when the horn sounds at the expiration of time for each period. The electric light is to be ''red.''

RULE NO. 2—OFFICIALS AND THEIR DUTIES

Section I—The Officials

a. The officials shall be a lead official and a referee, assisted by two trained timers, one to operate the game clock, the other to operate the 24 second timer and by a scorer who will compile the statistics of the game. All officials shall be approved by the Commissioner.

b. The officials shall wear the uniform prescribed by the NBA.

Section II—Duties of the Officials

a. The officials shall, prior to start of game, inspect and approve all equipment, including court, baskets, balls, backboards, timers and scorer's equipment.

b. The officials shall not permit players to play with any type of hand, arm, face, nose, ear, head or neck jewelry.

c. The officials shall not permit any player to wear equipment which, in his judgment is dangerous to other players. Any equipment which is of hard substance (casts, splints, guards and braces) must be padded or foam covered and have no exposed sharp or cutting edge. All face masks and eye or nose protectors must conform to the contour of the face and have no sharp or protruding edges. Approval is on a game to game basis.

d. All equipment used must be appropriate for basketball and equipment that is unnatural and designed to increase a players height or reach, or to gain an advantage shall not be used.

e. The officials must check the three game balls to see they are properly inflated to a pressure between 7½ and 8½ pounds, if necessary.

f. The senior official shall be the referee in charge.

NOTE: (1) If a coach desires to discuss a rule or interpretation of a rule prior to the start of a game, it will be mandatory for the officials to ask the other coach to be present during the discussion. The same procedure shall be followed for requests made at the start of a period.

g. The designated official shall toss the ball at the start of the game; the lead official shall decide whether or not a goal shall count if the officials disagree; he shall decide matters upon which scorers and timers disagree.

h. All officials shall be present during the 20-minute pre-game warm-up period to observe and report to the Commissioner any infractions of Rule 12-VII i—hanging on the rim and to review scoring and timing procedures with table personnel if necessary.

i. Meet with team captains to discuss rules & interpretations, prior to start of game.

Section III—Elastic Power

The referees shall have power to make decisions on any point not specifically covered in the rules. The Commissioner will be advised of all such decisions at the earliest possible moment.

Section IV—Different Decisions By Officials

The lead official shall have the authority to set aside or question decisions made by the other within the limits of his respective outlined duties.

Question (1)—A violation and personal contact occur at same time. Both are observed by the same official, or the violation by one and foul by the other. What is the proper procedure?

Answer—The foul takes precedence over any violation.

Question (2)—Ball in flight on try for field goal by A1, A2 pushes B1. After personal foul while ball is rolling around the ring B2 bats ball away from ring. Which infraction of the rules shall be penalized?

Answer—Both. Two points to Team A, the penalty for personal foul.

NOTE: (1) It is the primary duty of the trail official to signal if goals count. If for any reason he does not know if goal is made he should ask the other official. If neither saw the goal made they should refer to the timer. If the timer saw the goal scored it shall count. Exception: The drive-in or quick down court shot shall be the responsibility of the lead official.

Section V—Time and Place for Decisions

a. The officials shall have power to have decisions for infractions of rules committed either within or outside the boundary lines. This includes periods when the game may be stopped for any reason.

b. When a foul occurs, an official shall signal the timer to stop his watch and if it is a personal foul, he shall also designate the number of the offender to the scorer and indicate with his fingers the number of free throws to be attempted.

c. When a team is entitled to a throw-in, an official

shall clearly signal the act which caused the ball to become dead, the throw-in spot and the team entitled to the throw-in; unless it follows a successful goal or an awarded goal.

Section VI—Correcting Errors

a. Officials may correct an error if a rule is inadvertently set aside and results in:

(1) A team not shooting a merited penalty shot.

(2) A team shooting an unmerited penalty shot.

(3) Permitting the wrong player to attempt a free throw.

NOTE: (1) Officials should be notified of error at first dead ball. All errors must be rectified before the start of the next quarter. Ball is not in play on corrected foul and whether foul shot is made or missed, play shall be resumed at the same spot where referee declared the ball dead and under the same conditions as would have prevailed had play not been stopped to correct error. If the officials are notified of error within 24 seconds, any play action that occurs during that time period is to be nullified. This nullifies scoring and fouls committed by either team. However, if a player or coach is ejected during this period he is not permitted to return to the game. The official shall also reset the game clock so that the time left to play shall be the same as it was when the error occurred. However, any acts of unsportsmanlike conduct or points scored there from are not nullified.

NOTE: (2) Errors in the fourth quarter and overtimes, in order to be rectified, must be discovered before the end of the period.

NOTE: (3) If any period begins with teams lined up improperly and scores result from this error all points will be deleted and the period re-started unless 24 seconds have elapsed from the game clock. If 24 seconds have elapsed, all points count and teams shoot for the same baskets. Example: 12:00 to 11:36—do not restart.

Section VII—Duties of Scorers

a. The scorers shall record the field goals made, the free throws made and missed, and shall keep a running summary of the points scored. They shall record the personal and technical fouls called on each player and shall notify the official immediately when a sixth personal foul is called on any player. They shall record the time-outs charged to each team, shall notify a team and its coach through an official whenever that team takes a sixth and seventh charged time-out and shall notify the nearest official each time a team is granted a charged time-out in excess of the legal number. In case there is a question about an error in the scoring, the scorer shall check with the official at once to find the discrepancy. If the error cannot be found, the official shall accept the record of the official scorer, unless he has knowledge that forces him to decide otherwise.

b. The scorers shall keep a record of the names, numbers and positions of players who are to start the game and of all substitutes who enter the game. When there is an infraction of the rules pertaining to submission of line-up, substitutions or numbers of players, they shall notify the nearer official immediately if the ball is dead, or as soon as it becomes dead if it is in play when the infraction is discovered. Scorer shall mark the time at which players are disqualified by reason of receiving six personal fouls so that it may be easy to ascertain the order in which the players are eligible to go back in the game in accordance with Rule 3-1.

c. The scorers shall use a horn or other device unlike that used by the officials or timers to signal the officials. This may be used when the ball is dead or in certain specified situations when the ball is in control of a given team. Scorer shall signal coach on the bench on every personal foul, designating number of personal fouls a player has, and number of team.

NOTE: White paddles—team fouls; Red paddles—personal fouls.

d. When a player is disqualified from the game, or whenever a penalty shot is being awarded, a buzzer, a siren or some other clear audible sound must be used by the scorer or timer to notify the game officials. It is the duty of the scorekeeper to be certain the officials have acknowledged the 6th personal foul buzzer and the penalty shot buzzer.

Question (1)—The scorers fail to notify the official that a player has committed his 6th personal foul and he remains in the game. What should be done?

Answer—Playing time consumed, if any, and points scored count. The offending player must be removed as soon as the official discovers the error. Scorers should notify an official as soon as a player commits his 6th personal foul, but if play is resumed before such notification, they should signal when the ball is next dead or is in control of the offending team.

Question (2)—What should be done if the scorer's horn sounds, while the ball is in play?

Answer—Players should ignore the horn since it does not make the ball dead. The scorers should not signal while the ball is in play except in certain cases such as are noted in the first question above. The officials must use their judgment in blowing the ball dead to consult the scorers.

Question (3)—If the scorers fail to notify a team or its coach when it takes its 7th charged time-out, should the team be penalized if it takes an 8th time-out?

Answer—Yes.

e. Scorers shall record on scoreboard the number of team fouls to a total of five—which will indicate that the team is in a penalty situation.

Section VIII—Duties of Timers

a. The timers shall note when each half is to start and shall notify the referee and coach five minutes before this time, or cause them to be notified at least five minutes before the half is to start. They shall signal the scorers two minutes before starting time They shall record playing time and time of stoppages as provided in the rules. The timer shall be provided with an extra stop watch to be used in time outs, etc., other than the official game clock or watch. Official clock or scoreboard should show 12 minute quarters.

b. At the beginning of each quarter or extra period or whenever play is resumed by a jump ball the game clock shall be started when the ball has been legally tapped by either of the jumpers. If, after time has been out, the ball is put in play by a throw-in from out of bounds or by a free throw, the game watch shall be started when the official gives the time-in signal as the ball is touched by a player in the court.

NOTE: (1) During a jump ball time may not be reduced from the 24 second clock or game clock if there is an illegal tap.

c. The game clock shall be stopped: at the expiration of time for each period and when an official signals time-out. For a charged time-out, the timer shall start a time-out watch and shall signal the official when it is time to resume play.

d. The timers shall indicate with a controlled game horn the expiration of playing time. If the timer's signal fails to sound, or not heard, the timer shall use other means to notify the official immediately. If, in the meantime, a goal has been made or a foul has occurred, the official shall consult the timer. If the timer agrees that time expired before the ball was in

flight, the goal shall not count. If they agree that the period ended before the foul occurred, the foul shall be disregarded unless it was unsportsmanlike. If there is disagreement the goal shall count or the foul shall be penalized unless the official has other knowledge.

NOTE: (2) However, in a dead ball situation, if the clock shows :00 the period or game is considered to have ended although the buzzer may not have sounded.

e. Record only actual playing time in the last two minutes of the fourth period and the last two minutes of any overtime period or periods.

NOTE: (3) Clock will be stopped immediately without signal from official, on all violations.

RULE NO. 3—PLAYERS, SUBSTITUTES AND COACHES

Section I—Team

Each team shall consist of five players, one of whom shall be designated as the captain. No team may be reduced to less than five players. If and when a player in the game receives his sixth personal foul and all substitutes have already been disqualified, said player remains in the game and is charged with a personal and team foul. A technical foul also is assessed against his team. All subsequent personal fouls, including offensive fouls, shall be treated similarly. All players who have six or more personal fouls and remain in game shall be treated similarly.

In the event a player is injured and must leave the game, he must be replaced by the last player who was disqualified by reason of receiving six personal fouls. Each subsequent requirement to replace an injured player will be treated in this inverse order. Any such re-entry in a game by a disqualified player shall be penalized by a technical foul.

Section II—Starting Line-Ups

At least ten minutes before the game is scheduled to begin the scorers shall be supplied with the name and number of each player who may participate in the game. Starting line-ups will be indicated. Failure to comply with this provision should be reported to the Commissioner.

Section III—The Captain

a. Only the designated captain may talk to an official during a time out charged to his team.

b. He may discuss a rule interpretation but not a judgment play.

c. If the captain and the official are not in agreement, the coach may then enter an official protest and the game continues to completion. The official will then inform the official scorer and have it entered into the official score-book with time, score and rule quoted. The public address announcer will be instructed to inform the spectators that the game is being played under protest.

Section IV—The Coach and Others

a. The coaches position is directly in front of his bench and during the game all coaches and trainers must always remain within the 28-foot designated area between the base line and hash mark 19 feet from the mid-court line and they may not leave this area unless specifically requested to do so by the referees. Coaches and trainers are not permitted to go to the scorers tables, for any reason, except during time-out or between periods and only to check statistical information. The penalty for violation of this rule is a technical foul.

b. Coaches are not permitted to talk to an official during any time-out. (See Sec. 3(a) for captain's rights.)

c. A playing coach will have no special privileges. He is to conduct himself in the same manner as any other player.

d. Any club personnel not seated on the bench must conduct themselves so as not to reflect unfavorably on the dignity of the game or that of the officials. Violations by any of the personnel indicated shall require a written report to the Commissioner for subsequent action.

e. The bench shall be occupied only by league-approved coach, assistant coaches, players and trainer.

NOTE: (2) If a player, coach or assistant coach is ejected from a game or games, he shall not at any time before, during or after such game or games appear in any part of the auditorium or stands where his team is playing, during such ejection. A player, coach or assistant coach may only remain in the dressing room of his team during such suspension.

A violation of this rule shall call for an automatic fine of $500.

Section V—Substitutes

a. A substitute shall report to the scorer, giving his name, number and who he is to replace. The scorer shall sound the horn as soon as the ball is dead to indicate a substitution. The horn does not have to be sounded between quarters and halves. No substitute may enter a game after a field goal by either team, unless the ball is dead due to a technical foul. He may enter after the 1st of 2 or more free throws, whether made or missed.

b. The substitute shall remain outside the boundary lines until he is beckoned on by an official. If the ball is about to become alive, the beckoning signal shall be withheld.

NOTE: (1) A substitute must be ready to enter when beckoned. He must have discarded any articles of clothing he will not wear on the playing floor. No delays for removal of sweat clothes will be permitted.

c. The substitute shall not replace a free throw shooter or a player involved in a jump ball.

d. Once the substitute has been beckoned onto court, he must enter the game and cannot be removed until the next dead ball.

NOTE: (2) A substitute **can be** recalled from the scorer's table prior to being beckoned in the game.

e. Any player who fails to properly report to the scorer as shown in (a) above shall be subject to a $25 fine on recommendation of the official scorer. Any player who doesn't wait until he is properly beckoned on the floor by the referee as in (b) above shall be charged with a technical foul.

NOTE: (3) Notification of all above infractions and ensuing procedures shall be in accordance with Rule II, Section 7.

Question: May a substitution be made during an official's time-out?

Answer: No.

Section VI—Uniforms (Players' Jerseys)

a. Each player shall be numbered on the front and back of his jersey with a number of solid color contrasting with the color of the shirt.

b. Each number must be not less than ¾" in width and not less than 6" in height on both front and back. Each player shall have his surname affixed to the back of his game jersey in letters at least 2" in height.

c. The home team shall wear light color jerseys with the visitors dressed in dark jerseys. For neutral court games and doubleheaders the 2nd team named in the official schedule shall be regarded as the home team and shall wear the light colored jerseys.

RULE NO. 4—DEFINITIONS

Section I—Basket

A team's own basket is the ring and net through

which its players try to throw the ball. The visiting team has the choice of basket for the first half.

The teams change baskets for the second half.

NOTE: (1) The basket selected by the visiting team when **first entering upon the court** shall be their basket for the first half.

Section II—Blocking

Blocking is personal contact which impedes the progress of an opponent.

Section II—Dribble

A dribble is ball movement caused by a player IN CONTROL who throws or taps the ball in the air or to the floor and then touches it once before the dribble ends. The dribble ends when the dribbler: (a) touches the ball with both hands simultaneously, or (b) permits it to come to rest while he is in contact with it, or (c) tries for goal, or (d) otherwise loses control, or when ball becomes dead.

Question (1)—Is a player dribbling while tapping the ball during a jump, or when a pass rebounds from his hand or when he fumbles or when he taps a rebound or a pass away from other players who are attempting to get it?

Answer—No, the player is not in control under these conditions.

Question (2)—Is it a dribble when a player stands still and: (a) bounces the ball; or (b) holds the ball and touches it to the floor once or more?

Answer—(a) Yes; (b) No.

Question (3)—May a dribbler alternate hands?

Answer—Yes.

Question (4)—May a player touch the ball more than once while dribbling before it touches the floor?

Answer—No.

Section IV—Fouls

a. A personal foul is a foul which involves contact with an opponent.

b. A technical foul is a foul which does not involve contact with an opponent and can be assessed against player and against non-player who is on the bench.

c. A double foul is a situation in which two opponents commit personal or technical fouls against each other at approximately the same time.

d. Offensive foul is a foul committed by a player while he or a teammate is in control of the ball.

Section V—Free Throw

A free throw is the privilege given a player to score one point by an unhindered throw for goal from a position directly behind the free throw line.

Section VI—Front/Back Court

a. A team's front court consists of that part of the court between its end line and the nearer edge of the center line, including its basket and inbounds part of backboard. A team's back court consists of the entire division line and the rest of the court to include opponent's basket and inbounds part of backboard.

NOTE: (1) A ball which is in contact with a player or with the court is in the back court if either the ball or the player is touching the back court. It is in the front court if neither the ball nor the player is touching the back court.

A ball which is not in contact with a player or the court retains the same status as when it was last in contact with a player or the court.

Question—From the front court, a player passes the ball across the division line, it touches a teammate who is in the air after leaping from the back court or it touches an official in the back court. Is the ball in the back court?

Answer—Yes. The location of a player is determined by the point where his foot is touching the floor. When he is in the air from a leap, he retains the same status as when he last touched the floor as far as the boundary or the division line or the free throw line is connected. The location of an official is determined in the same manner as that of a player. Hence, if the official is touching the back court of the team in control, he is in the back court. When the ball touches an official it is the same as touching the floor at the official's location.

b. The team on the offense must bring the ball across the center or division line within 10 seconds. No additional 10 second count is permitted in the backcourt. Exception: Kicked ball violation or punched ball violation.

NOTE: (2) Ball is considered in frontcourt once it has broken the plane of the mid-court line.

Section VII—Held Ball

Held ball occurs when two opponents have one or both hands firmly on the ball.

NOTE: (1) Held ball should not be called until

both players have both hands so firmly on the ball that neither can gain sole possession without undue roughness. If a player is lying or sitting on the floor while in possession, he should have opportunity to throw the ball, but held ball should be called if there is danger of injury.

Section VIII—Pivot

A pivot takes place when a player who is holding the ball steps once or more than once in any direction with the same foot, the other foot, called the pivot foot, being kept at its point of contact with the floor.

Section IX—Traveling

Running with ball is progressing in any direction in excess of prescribed limits while holding the ball. The limits follow: (a.) A player who receives the ball while standing still may pivot, using either foot as the pivot foot. (b.) A player who receives the ball while he is progressing or upon completion of a dribble may use a two-count rhythm in coming to a stop or in getting rid of the ball. The first count occurs:

(1) As he receives the ball if either foot is touching the floor at the time he receives it;

(2) As the foot touches the floor or as both feet touch the floor simultaneously after he receives the ball if both feet are off the floor when he receives it.

The second count occurs when, after the count of one, either foot touches the floor or both feet touch the floor simultaneously.

When a player comes to a stop on the count of one he may pivot and may use either foot as the pivot foot.

When a player comes to a stop on the count of two, if one foot is in advance of the other he may pivot but the rear foot only may be used as the pivot foot; however, if neither foot is in advance of the other he may use either foot as the pivot foot.

c. (1) A player who receives the ball while standing still, or who comes to a legal stop while holding the ball, may lift the pivot foot or jump when he throws for goal or passes, but the ball must leave his hands before the pivot foot again touches the floor, or before either foot again touches the floor if the player has jumped;

(2) In starting a dribble after receiving the ball while standing still, or after coming to a legal

stop, a player may not jump before the ball leaves his hands, nor may he lift the pivot from the floor before the ball leaves his hands.

(3) If a player does not pass or shoot when leaving floor with ball, he is guilty of traveling.

Question (1)—Is it traveling if a player falls to the floor while holding the ball?

Answer—No. Unless he makes progress by sliding.

Question (2)—A1 jumps to throw the ball. B1 prevents the throw by placing one or both hands firmly on the ball so that (a) A1; or (b) A1 and B1 both return to the floor holding it.

Answer—Held ball. However, if A1 voluntarily drops the ball before he returns to the floor and he then touches the ball before it is touched by another player, A1 has committed a traveling violation.

Section X—Screen

A screen is legal action of a player who, without causing undue contact, delays or prevents an opponent from reaching a desired position.

Section XI—Try for Goal

A try for field goal is a player's attempt to throw the ball into his basket for a field goal. The try starts when the player begins the motion which habitually precedes the actual throw. It continues until the throwing effort ceases. The term is also used to include the movement of the ball in flight until it has become dead or has been touched by a player.

NOTE: (1) A player may not assist himself to score by using the ring or backboard to lift, hold or raise his body.

Section XII—Throw-In

A throw-in is a method of putting ball in play from out of bounds in accordance with Rule No. 6. The throw-in begins when the ball is at the disposal of the team or player entitled to it and ends when the passed ball touches or is touched by an inbounds player other than the thrower in.

RULE NO. 5—SCORING AND TIMING

Section I—Scoring

a. A legal goal is made when a live ball enters the basket from above and remains in or passes through.

b. A goal from the field counts 2 points unless attempted from beyond the 3 pt. line which counts 3 points.

c. A goal from the free throw line counts one point for the thrower's team.

NOTE: (1) If a free throw attempt is unsuccessful and while the ball is in the air it is tapped into the basket by a player who has not obtained complete control of the ball with both feet touching the floor, the basket, if scored, shall count two points and shall be credited to the player tapping the ball in.

Question—A player makes a free throw in his opponent's basket. Does the point count for his opponent?

Answer—No. If the mistake is discovered before time is in, the error should be corrected and player required to make attempt at his own basket.

NOTE: (2) Goals from the field, thrown in an opponent's basket shall be credited to the opponent's score and mentioned in a footnote. Basket is credited to opponent nearest the shooter. Any field goal that, in the opinion of the officials, is intentionally scored in the wrong basket shall be disallowed.

NOTE: (3) If a discrepancy in the score cannot be resolved, the running score shall be official.

NOTE: (4) For successful 3 point field goal player must be beyond 3 point line when he attempts shot. After release of ball he may land on line or in 2 point area.

Section II—Timing

a. All periods of regulation play in the NBA will be twelve minutes.

b. All overtime periods of play will be five minutes.

c. Fifteen minutes will be permitted between halves of all games.

d. Ninety seconds will be permitted between all periods and for time-outs except one 20-second time-out per half.

EXCEPTION: Disqualification (30 seconds).

NOTE: (1) The game is considered to be in the 2:00 minute part when the game clock shows 2:00 or less time remaining in the period.

NOTE: (2) The public address operator is required to announce the fact that there are two minutes remaining in regulation or overtime periods.

Section III—End of Period

a. Each period ends when time expires.

Exceptions:

(1) If a live ball is in flight, the period ends when the goal is made or missed.

(2) If a foul occurs at approximately the instant time expires for a period, the period officially ends after the free throw or throws are attempted.

NOTE: (1) No line-up of players will be permitted in conditions outlined in (2) above.

(3) If the ball is in the air when the buzzer sounds ending a period and it subsequently is touched by a defensive player, the goal, if successful, shall count.

(4) If a time-out request is made at approximately the instant time expires for a period, the period ends and the time-out shall not be granted.

NOTE: (2) If the ball is dead and the game clock shows :00, the period has ended even though the buzzer may not have sounded.

Section IV—Tie Score—Overtime

If the score is tied at the end of the 4th period, play shall resume in 90 seconds without change of baskets for one or more periods whichever is needed to determine a winner. (See Rule 5, Sec II (d) for amount of time between overtime periods.)

Question—With score tied, a foul is committed near the expiration of time in the fourth period. If free throw is successful, should an extra period be played?

Answer—If the foul occurs before the ball becomes dead and the fourth period is ended, no extra period is played. However, if the foul occurs after the fourth period has ended, the extra period must be played whether the foul shot is made or not.

Section V—Time-Out

a. Time-out occurs and the timing instruments shall be stopped when:

(1) A foul is called.

(2) A jump ball is called.

(3) Granting of a player's request for a time-out, such request being granted only when the ball is dead or in control of the requesting player's team. The scoring team cannot stop play immediately after scoring, by calling a time-out or making a substitution. The team scored upon shall have the opportunity to put the ball in play.

(4) An unusual delay in getting the ball into play after a field goal.

(5) On all floor violations (whenever official's whistle sounds, goal tending included).

(6) Time-out for any other emergency. (Official's time.)

NOTE: (1) When a defensive player is injured, the officials shall not stop play **under any circumstances** until after a goal is scored or the ball becomes dead.

NOTE: (2) If on a jump ball or foul shot situation a player is injured or ejected and must be removed from the game, the opposing coach selects his replacement. The injured player cannot return to the game. Exception: If the player is injured due to a flagrant foul he may reenter the game at any time and the offended player's coach may choose any player on his squad to attempt the free throw(s).

(7) During the last two minutes of the regulation game or any overtime period, a field goal is scored.

NOTE: (3) Whenever a team is granted a time-out, play shall not resume until the full 90 seconds have elapsed. Unless it is a 20-second time-out.

(8) No time-out will be charged if it is called to correct a wrong interpretation of a call and correction is sustained.

(9) A coach shall have 30 seconds to replace a disqualified player.

b. Time-out shall not be granted:

(1) After a score of any kind to the team that has scored.

(2) Unless the team has possession of the ball.

(3) When a player of the team not in possession is injured, until a goal is scored or the ball becomes dead or his team gains possession.

NOTE: (4) If a request for time-out is made it should be ignored. However, if an official upon receiving a time-out request, inadvertently blows his whistle, play shall be suspended and the team in possession shall put the ball into play immediately at the sideline nearest where the ball was when the time-out was called. The team in possession shall have only the time remaining of the original ten seconds in which to move the ball to front court. The 24 second clock shall remain the same.

Section VI—Twenty (20) Second Time-Out

a. Each team is entitled to one (1) 20-second time-out per half for a total of two (2) per game, including overtimes.

b. During a 20-second time-out a team may only subsitute for one player. If the team calling the 20-second time-out replaces a player the opposing team may also replace one player.

c. Only one player per team may be replaced during a 20-second time-out. If two players on the same team are injured at the same time and must be replaced the coach must call a regular (90-second) time-out.

d. If a second 20-second time-out is called during a half, it automatically becomes a regular charged time-out. An overtime is considered to be an extension of the second half.

e. The official shall instruct the timer to record the 20 seconds and to inform him when the time has expired.

f. This rule may be used for any reason.

NOTE: (1) No time-out will be permitted to allow any player to adjust his clothing or equipment (shoes, laces, glasses, etc.).

g. Players should say "20-second time-out" when requesting this time.

Section VII—Time-In

a. After time has been out, the game clock shall be started when the official signals time-in; the timer is authorized to start game clock if officials neglect to signal.

b. On a free throw that is unsuccessful and the ball is to continue in play, the clock shall be started when the missed free throw is touched by any player.

c. If play is resumed by a throw-in from out of bounds, the clock shall be started when the ball touches a player within the playing area of the court.

d. Time-out during the last two minutes of regulation play or overtimes (See 5, VIII-d.). The last two minutes begin when the clock shows 2:00 minutes to play.

Section VIII—Regular Time-Outs—90 Seconds

Time-outs are considered regular unless called, "20-second time-out."

a. Each team may be granted seven (7) charged time-outs during regulation play. Each team is limited to no more than four (4) time-outs in the fourth period and no more than three (3) time-outs in the last two minutes of regulation play. (This is in addition to one 20-second time-out per half.)

b. In overtime periods each team shall be allowed two (2) time-outs regardless of the number of time-outs called or remaining during the regulation play or previous overtimes. There is no restriction as to when a team must call its time-outs during any overtime period.

NOTE: (1) Additional time-outs may be granted at the expense of a technical foul and all privileges apply. (Exception: see Rule 12A, II)

c. Each team must take at least one time-out per period. If neither team has taken a time-out during the first five minutes of each of the four regulation periods, it shall be mandatory for the official scorer to take a time-out before the sixth minute of play is completed. Time-out is charged to the home team. If neither team has taken a second time-out before the ninth minute of play, it shall be mandatory for the official scorer to take a time-out before the tenth minute of play has elapsed. Time-out is charged to the visiting team. If one team takes two time-outs during any single period, it is not mandatory for the official scorer to take a time-out.

d. Time-out in back court: during the last two minutes of regulation play or overtimes, if a team requests a time-out after the ball is out-of-bounds or after getting the ball from a rebound or change of possession, time-out shall be granted, and upon resumption of play, they shall have the option of putting the ball into play at midcourt or at the out of bounds spot.

However, once the ball is thrown in from out-of-bounds or the ball is dribbled or passed after receiving it from a rebound or change of possession and a time-out request is granted—upon resumption of play, the ball shall be put into play at the spot nearest where the ball was when time-out was called, and the time shall remain as it was when the time-out was called.

Question—During the last two minutes of regulation play, team A attempts a field goal. The ball rebounds to the corner of team B's backcourt where B secures possession and immediately requests a timeout. Where is the ball put into play?

Answer—The team calling the time-out, upon resumption of play, shall have the **option** of putting the ball into play on that side of the court where the ball was when time-out was called or moving the ball to midcourt on that side of the court. However, if the time-out request was made immediately after a score, the team scored upon would have the **option** of putting the ball into play at the division line on either side of the court or at the endline.

NOTE: (2) In both situations, time-out is granted.

Question—A player receives the ball from a throw-in in the backcourt or from a rebound or change of possession and a time-out request is granted, where is the ball put into play after the resumption of time?

Answer—Ball is put into play, after the time-out, at the spot nearest where the ball was when time-out was called.

In the case where possession may change, with the ball still in play, the team now in possession may call a time-out without penalty.

If a regular time-out is called in the backcourt in the last two minutes of regulation play or overtimes, the team shall have the option of moving the ball to mid-court. At all other times, the ball shall be passed in from a point out-of-bounds nearest to where the ball was when the time-out was called.

NOTE: (3) The official scorer shall notify a team when it has been charged with a time-out.

e. A time-out shall not be called by the official scorer after a score of any kind, except after a free throw that is to be followed by another free throw attempt.

f. When the clock shows 2:00 remaining in regulation play or overtimes, the game is considered to be in the 2:00 minute period.

RULE NO. 6—PUTTING BALL IN PLAY—LIVE/DEAD BALL

Section I—Start of Games/Quarters and Others

a. The game and overtimes shall be started with a jump ball in the center circle.

b. The team which gains possession after the opening tap will put the ball into play at their opponent's end line to begin the fourth period. The team losing the opening tap will put the ball into play at their opponent's end line at the beginning of the second and third quarters.

NOTE: (1) In putting the ball into play, the thrower-in may run along the end line or pass it to a teammate who is also out-of-bounds at the end line—as after a score.

c. After any dead ball, play shall be resumed by a jump, a throw-in or by placing ball at the disposal of a free-thrower.

d. On any *floor* violation except where the ball goes out-of-bounds at the end-line or defensive goaltending is called, the ball shall be put into play at the sideline.

Section II—Live Ball

a. The ball becomes alive when:

(1) Tossed by an official on any jump ball.

NOTE: (1) Clock starts only when tapped. (See Rule 5)

(2) Ball is placed at the disposal of designated player for throw-in.

(3) Ball is placed at the disposal of a free-throw shooter.

Section III—Jump Balls in Center Circle

a. The ball shall be put in play in the center circle by a jump between two opponents:

(1) at the start of the game.

(2) at the start of each overtime period.

(3) double foul on ball by both involved players.

Section IV—Other Jump Balls

a. The ball shall be put in play by a jump ball at the circle which is closest to the spot where:

(1) a held ball occurs.

(2) a ball out of bounds caused by both teams.

(3) a double free-throw violation occurs.

(4) the ball lodges in a basket support.

(5) the ball becomes dead when neither team is in control and no goal or infraction is involved.

(6) unless both officials have conflicting possession decisions.

NOTE: (1) In (1) or (2) the jump ball shall be between the two involved players unless injury or ejection, precludes one of the jumpers from participation. If injured player must leave the game, the coach of the opposing team shall select from his opponent's bench a player who will replace the injured player. The injured player will not be permitted to re-enter the game.

Section V—Restrictions Governing Jump Balls

a. Each jumper must have one, but may have both feet on or inside that half of the jumping circle which is farthest from his own basket.

b. The ball must be tapped by one or both of the players participating in jump ball after it reaches its highest point. If ball falls to floor without being tapped by at least one of the jumpers, the official off the ball shall whistle the ball dead and signal another toss.

c. Neither jumper may tap the tossed ball before it reaches its highest point.

d. Neither jumper may leave the circle until the ball has been tapped.

e. Neither jumper may catch the tossed ball nor tapped ball until such time as it has been touched by one of the eight non-jumpers, the floor, the basket or the backboard.

f. Neither jumper is permitted to tap ball more than twice on any jump ball.

g. The eight non-jumpers will remain outside the restraining circle until the ball has been tapped. Teammates may not occupy adjacent positions around the restraining circle if an opponent desires one of the positions.

Penalty for c., d., e., f., g.: Ball awarded out of bounds to opponent.

Question—During a jump ball is a jumper required to (a) face his own basket; (b) jump and attempt to tap ball?

Answer—(a) No specific facing is required, (b) No. But if neither jumper taps the ball, it must be tossed again with both jumpers being ordered to jump.

NOTE: (1) During any jump ball situation officials shall sound whistle only if an infraction that occurs benefits offending team.

Section VI—Dead Ball

a. The ball becomes dead or remains dead when:

(1) held ball occurs or ball lodges between the basket and backboard.

(2) time expires for a period, half or extra period.

(3) there is an unsuccessful attempt: (a) on a free throw for technical foul or (b) a free throw which is to be followed by another throw.

(4) a foul occurs.

(5) a floor violation (traveling, 3 secs, 24 secs, 10 secs, etc.) occurs or there is basket interference or a free throw violation by the thrower's team.

(6) Any goal is made in the last two minutes of the fourth quarter.

EXCEPTION: The ball does not become dead when (2), occurs after a live ball is in flight.

Question—If the ball is in flight and on its downward path on a field goal try by Team A and the period expires, does the goal count if the ball is touched by: Team A or Team B?

Answer—It is basket interference when touched by Team B. No points scored if touched by Team A.

RULE NO. 7—24-SECOND CLOCK

Section I—Definition

For the purpose of clarification the 24-second device shall be referred to as ''the 24-second clock.''

Section II—Starting and Stopping of 24-Second Clock

a. The 24-second clock will start when a team gains possession of the ball.

b. A team in possession of the ball must attempt a shot to score within 24 seconds after gaining possession of the ball. To constitute a legal shot to score, the following conditions must be complied with:

(1) The ball must leave the player's hand prior to the expiration of 24 seconds.

(2) After leaving the player's hand the ball must hit the rim or a legal surface of the backboard. If it does not and the 24 seconds expires there has been a violation committed.

c. A team is considered in possession of the ball when holding, passing or dribbling.

NOTE: (1) In the case of passing or dribbling, the team is considered in possession of the ball even though the ball has been batted away but the opponent has not gained possession. No three second violation can occur under these conditions.

d. Team control ends when:

(1) there is a try for field goal.

(2) opponent gains possession.

(3) ball becomes dead.

e. If a ball is touched by a defensive player who does not gain possession of the ball, the 24-second clock shall continue to run.

f. If a defensive player causes the ball to go out of bounds, the 24-second clock is stopped and the offensive team shall, on regaining the ball for throw-in, have the unexpired time or 5 seconds, whichever is longer, to attempt a shot.

g. If during any period there are 24 seconds OR LESS left to play in the period, the 24-second clock shall not function.

NOTE: (2) If an official inadvertently blows his whistle and the 24-second clock buzzer sounds while the ball is in air, play shall be suspended and play resumed by a jump ball between any two opponents in the nearest free throw circle if shot is unsuccessful. If the shot is successful, the goal shall count and the whistle is ignored. It should be noted that even though the official blows his whistle, all provisions of the above rule apply.

h. If there is a question whether or not an attempt to score has been made within the 24 seconds allowed the final decision shall be made by the referee.

i. On a throw-in, the 24-second clock shall start when the ball touches a player on the court.

j. Any time a personal foul is called the clock is to be re-set to 24 seconds.

k. Any time a technical foul is called on the defensive team, the clock shall remain as is or be re-set to 10 seconds, whichever is greater. If the technical is called on the offensive team the 24-second clock is never re-set.

l. Whenever the 24-second clock shows 0, and the ball is dead, 24-second time is considered expired even though the horn may not have sounded.

m. On any deliberate kicked ball or punching the ball with the fist violation the 24-second clock will be re-set to 24 seconds.

Section III—Putting Ball In Play After Violation

If a team fails to attempt a shot within the time allotted, the ball shall be taken out of bounds on the side of the court nearest to the spot where the play was suspended and handed to the thrower-in.

Section IV—Resetting 24-Second Clock

An official shall have the power to reset the 24-second clock to cover any special situation that he thinks warrants such action. On all technical fouls, on the defensive team, the 24-second clock shall remain the same as when play was stopped or re-set to 10 seconds, whichever is greater. The 24-second clock shall be re-set to 24 seconds on all violations.

RULE NO. 8—OUT OF BOUNDS AND THROW-IN

Section I—Player

a. The player is out of bounds when he touches the floor or any object on or outside a boundary. For location of a player in the air his position is that from which he last touched the floor.

Section II—Ball

a. The ball is out of bounds when it touches a player who is out of bounds or any other person, the floor, or any object on, above or outside of a boundary or the supports or back of the backboard.

NOTE: (1) Any ball that rebounds or passes behind or over the backboard from any point is considered out of bounds.

Question—Ball glances off face of backboard and across boundary line, but before it touches the floor or any obstruction out of bounds it is caught by a player who is inbounds. Is the ball inbounds or out of bounds?

Answer—Inbounds.

b. The ball is caused to go out of bounds by the last player to touch it before it goes out, provided it is out of bounds because of touching something other than a player. If the ball is out of bounds because of touching a player who is on or outside a boundary, such player caused it to go out.

c. If the ball goes out of bounds and was last touched simultaneously by two opponents, both of whom are inbounds or out of bounds, or if the official is in doubt as to who last touched the ball, or if the officials disagree, play shall be resumed by a jump ball between the two involved players in the nearest restraining circle.

d. After the ball is out of bounds the official shall designate a **nearby opponent of the player who committed the violation** and he shall make the throw-in a the spot out of bounds nearest where the ball crossed the boundary.

e. After any playing court violation, the ball is to be put into play at the sideline.

Section III—The Throw-In

a. The throw-in starts when the ball is at the disposal of a player entitled to the throw-in. He shall pass it inbounds within 5 seconds from the time the throw-in starts. Until the passed ball has crossed the plane of the boundary no player shall have any part of his person over the boundary line and teammates shall not occupy adjacent positions near the boundary if an opponent desires one of the positions.

b. On out of bound plays the ball shall be put in play at the point where the ball crossed a boundary line and not from original throw-in spot.

c. After a score, field goal or free throw, the latter coming as the result of a personal foul, any player of the team not credited with the score shall put the ball into play from any point out of bounds at the end line of the court where the goal was made. He may pass the ball to a teammate behind the end line; however, the 5 second pass-in rule applies.

d. After a free throw violation by the throwing team, the throw-in is made from out of bounds at either end of the free throw line extended.

e. Any ball out of bounds in a team's front court cannot be passed into the back court. On all back-court rule violations, the ball shall be given to opposing team at center court and must be passed into the front court.

NOTE: (1) Penalty for violating this rule is loss of ball to opposing team at point of infraction.

RULE NO. 9—FREE THROW

Section I—Positions

When a free throw is awarded, an official shall take the ball to the free throw line of the offended team. After allowing reasonable time for the players to take their positions, he shall put the ball in play by placing it at the disposal of the free throw shooter. The same procedure shall be followed for each free throw of a multiple throw. During a free throw for personal foul, each of the spaces perpendicular to the end line must be occupied by an opponent of the free thrower. Teammates of the free thrower must occupy the next adjacent spaces on each side. It is not mandatory for the defensive team to occupy the third adjacent space. However, no teammates of the free thrower are permitted in these spaces. No more than three defensive team players are allowed on the free throw lanes. All other players not stationed on the free throw lanes must be at least six feet from the foul shooter and/or the free throw lanes or foul circle.

NOTE: (1) If the ball is to become dead after the last free throw, players shall not take positions along the free-throw lane.

EXAMPLE: All technical foul attempts and any fouls which will be attempted with game clock showing :00.

Section II—Shooting of Free Throw

a. The free throw or throws awarded because of a personal foul shall be attempted by the offended player. Exception: If a player is fouled and is subsequently ejected from the game, before shooting the awarded free throw(s), he must immediately leave the court and another of the four players on the court will be designated by the opposing coach to shoot such free throw(s).

NOTE: (1) If a player is fouled and injured on the same play and cannot shoot the awarded shots, the opposing coach shall select from his opponent's bench the player who will replace the injured player and this player will attempt the shot(s). The injured player will not be permitted to re-enter the game, unless such injury is a result of a flagrant act of an opponent. If a flagrant foul is called and the offended player is unable to attempt the free throws his coach may designate any member of the squad to attempt the free throw(s).

b. A foul try, personal or technical, shall neither be legal nor count unless an official handles the ball and is also in the free throw area when foul try is attempted.

c. When a player is allowed three attempts to make two points, if the shooter or a member of his team causes a violation to occur on one of the two attempts, and a foul goal is nullified, the third shot must be taken.

Section III—Time Limit

The try for goal shall be made within 10 seconds after the ball has been placed at the disposal of the free thrower at the free throw line; this applies to each free throw.

Section IV—Next Play

After a successful free throw which is not followed by another free throw, the ball shall be put in play by a throw-in: as after a field goal if the try is successful.

EXCEPTION: After a free throw for a foul which occurs during a dead ball which immediately precedes any period, the ball shall be put into play by the team entitled to the throw-in in the period which follows. (See Rule 6, Section I (b)).

RULE NO. 10—VIOLATIONS AND PENALTIES

Section I—A Player Shall Not:

A. Violate the free throw provisions:

(1) After the ball is placed at the disposal of a free thrower, he shall throw within 10 seconds in such a way that the ball enters the basket or touches the ring before it is touched by a player.

(2) Touch the ball or basket while the ball is on or within the basket.

(3) Touch the floor on or across the free throw line or lanes.

NOTE: (1) The restriction in (3) above applies until the ball leaves the free thrower's hands, except for the free thrower who may not cross the free throw line until the ball touches the ring or backboard or the free throw ends.

(4) Disconcert the free thrower in any way once the ball has been placed at the disposal of the free-throw shooter.

(5) Deflect or catch ball before it reaches the basket.

PENALTY:

a. In (1), (2), (3), (4), (5), if violations by offense, no point can be scored. Ball is awarded out of bounds to opponents opposite free throw line extended.

b. In (1), (2), (3), (4), if violation is by defense and throw is successful, disregard violation; if throw is unsuccessful, substitute throw shall be attempted.

c. In (5), if the violation is by the defensive team the point is scored and the same player receives another free throw attempt. The additional free throw is considered a new play.

NOTE: (2)

a. If there is a violation by each team, ball becomes dead, no point can be scored, play shall be resumed by a jump ball between any two opponents in nearest free throw circle.

b. The out of bounds in "a" under Penalty and the jump ball provision in "a" above do not apply if the free throw is to be followed by another free throw or if there are free throws by both teams.

B. Cause the ball to go out of bounds.

Question—Dribbler in control steps on or outside a boundary, but does not touch the ball while he is out of bounds, returns in-bounds and continues dribbling. Is this a violation?

Answer—Yes.

C. Violate provisions of putting ball in play from out of bounds.

(1) Thrower-in shall not carry ball into the court nor fail to pass it within 5 seconds, nor touch it in the court before it has touched another player.

(2) No player shall have any part of his person over the boundary line before the ball has been passed across the line.

(3) After an official has designated a player to throw ball in, there shall be no change of player unless a time-out by either team has subsequently been called.

(4) A player shall not step or run over any

boundary line while putting ball in play.

PENALTY: Loss of ball (The ball is put into play at the point of infraction).

D. Run with ball, kick it, or strike it with the fist.

NOTE: (3) Kicking the ball or blocking it with any part of a players' leg is a violation when it is a positive act; accidentally striking the ball with the foot or leg is not a violation.

E. Dribble a second time after his first dribble has ended, unless it is after he has lost control: (a) through a try for field goal at his own basket; or (b) through a bat by an opponent; or (c) through a pass or fumble which has then touched another player.

F. Violate provisions governing jump ball situations:

(1) If both teams violate the jumping rule, or if the official makes a bad toss, the toss should be repeated;

(2) If a foul is committed on any jump ball, it shall result in the loss of the ball for the offending team and the offended team shall be awarded the ball at the sideline nearest the jumping circle.

NOTE: (4) To be treated as a loose ball foul.

G. Remain for more than 3 seconds in that part of his free throw lane between the end line and the farther edge of the free throw line while the ball is in control of his team.

NOTE: (5) Allowance may be made for a player who, having been in the restricted area for less than 3 seconds is in the act of shooting at the end of the third second.

NOTE: (6) Three second count shall not begin until the ball is in control in the offensive team's front court.

Question—Does the 3-second restriction apply: (a) to a player who has only one foot touching the lane boundary; or (b) while the ball is dead or is in flight on a try or while the ball is loose?

Answer—(a) Yes, the line is part of the lane. (b) No, the team is not in control.

H. Be in continuous control of a ball which is in his back court for more than 10 consecutive seconds.

I. Be the first to touch a ball which he or a teammate caused to go from front court to back court while his team was in control of the ball.

EXCEPTION: This restriction does not apply if, after a jump ball in the center circle, the player who first secures control of the tapped ball is in his front court at the time he secures such control and causes

the ball to go to his back court, not later than the first loss of control by him and provided it is the first time the ball is in his back court following the jump ball. Once said player establishes a positive offensive position this exception does not apply.

NOTE: (7) During a jump ball, a try for goal or a situation in which a player taps the ball away from congested area, as during rebounding, in an attempt to get the ball out where player control may be secured, the ball is not in control of either team. Hence the restriction on first touching does not apply.

Question—Player A receives pass in his front court and throws ball to his back court where ball: (a) is touched by a teammate; or (b) goes directly out of bounds; or (c) lies or bounces with all players hesitating to touch it.

Answer—Violation when touched in (a). In (b) it is a violation for going out of bounds. In (c) ball is alive so that B may secure control. If A touches ball first, it is a violation. In either case, 24 second clock continues to run and rules apply.

PENALTY: Items D. thru G. Ball becomes dead when violation occurs. Ball is awarded to opponent at out of bounds spot nearest violation.

J. Use "STICK-UM" or any similar substance.

PENALTY: Fine of $25 for first violation, doubled for each subsequent violation upon notification to Commissioner by either official.

K. Excessive and/or vigorous swinging of the elbows in a swinging motion (no contact necessary) and when a defensive player is nearby and the offensive player has the ball—is considered a violation (loss of ball).

L. If the ball enters the basket from below, a violation has occurred.

RULE NO. 11—BASKETBALL INTERFERENCE—GOAL-TENDING

Section I—A Player Shall Not:

a. Touch the ball or basket when the ball is on or within either basket.

b. Touch the ball when it is touching the cylinder having the ring as its lower base.

EXCEPTION: In a or b if a player near his own basket has his hand legally in contact with the ball, it is not a violation if his contact with the ball continues after the ball enters the cylinder, or if, in such action, he touches the basket.

NOTE: (1) Impetus factor by offensive player!

c. Touch the ball when it is not touching the cylinder but is in downward flight during a try for field goal while the entire ball is above the basket ring level and before the ball has touched the ring or the try has ended.

NOTE: (2) For goal-tending to occur, the ball, in the judgment of the official, must have a chance to score. This section is not intended to conflict with paragraph (d) or (e) of Rule 11, Section I.

d. During a field goal attempt, touch a ball after it has touched any part of the backboard above ring level whether ball is considered on its upward or downward flight.

e. During a field goal attempt, touch a ball after it has touched the backboard below ring level and while ball is on its upward flight.

f. Trap ball against face of backboard.

NOTE: (3) To be a trapped ball three elements must exist simultaneously. The hand, the ball and the backboard must all occur at the same time. A batted ball against the backboard is not a trapped ball.

NOTE: (4) Any live ball from within the playing area that is in flight is considered to be a ''field goal attempt'' or trying for a goal.

PENALTY FOR ABOVE. If violation is at the opponent's basket, offended team is awarded two points, if attempt is from the two point zone and three points if from the three point zone. The crediting of the score and subsequent procedure is the same as if the awarded score has resulted from the ball having gone through the basket except that the official shall hand the ball to a player of the team entitled to the throw-in. If violation is at a team's own basket, no points can be scored and the ball is awarded to the offended team at the out of bounds spot on the side at either end of the free throw line extended. If there is a violation by both teams, play shall be resumed by a jump ball between any two opponents in the nearest circle.

RULE NO. 12—FOULS AND PENALTIES
A. TECHNICAL FOUL

Section I—Zone Defenses

a. A zone defense is not permitted in NBA games. If an official is of the opinion that a team is guilty of violating this rule, he shall impose a technical foul on the team and, for the second violation, two technical fouls shall be imposed. Any recurrence of this violation will be penalized by two technical fouls and action by the Commissioner.

NOTE: (1) Three basic principles govern the use of defensive alignments permitted in the NBA games:

1. Any type of pressing defense is legal, whether it is a front court press or a back court press, and by any number of defensive players.

2. After the offensive team has advanced the ball into its front court, a defensive player may not station himself in the 16-foot key area, longer than three (3) seconds, if it is apparent he is making no effort to play an opponent. Three-second count starts when the offensive team is in clear control of the ball in its front court. Penalty—technical foul, and for every recurrence of the violation, two technical fouls shall be imposed.

3. When ball has passed center court, no defensive player can guard an area of the court, instead of guarding an opponent. Penalty—technical foul, and for every recurrence of the infraction, two technical fouls shall be imposed.

NOTE: (2) The first two violations are charged to the bench. On the third such infraction, coach is ejected. On the fourth violation the assistant coach is ejected. On the fifth violation an assistant coach or the captain is ejected. Lead official reports by Telex if more than 2 zone violations are called on any team.

Section II—Excessive Time-Outs

a. Requests for time out in excess of authorized number shall be granted. However, a technical foul penalty shall be assessed. A team is entitled to all regular time out privileges.

EXCEPTION: During the last two minutes of play and/or overtimes, if a team calls an excessive time out, the ball shall remain at the out-of-bounds spot where the ball was when the excessive time out was called.

Section III—Delay of Game

a. A player shall not delay the game by preventing ball from being promptly put into play such as:

(1) attempt to gain an advantage by interfering with ball after a goal.

(2) failing to immediately pass ball to the nearest official when a violation is called.

(3) bat ball away from an opponent before the player has the opportunity to in-bounds the ball.

Section IV—Substitution

a. A substitute shall not enter the court without reporting to the scorer and being beckoned by an official.

b. A substitute shall not enter after having been disqualified.

c. It is the responsibility of each team to have the proper number of players on the court at all times.

NOTE: (1) Penalty for failure to report to the scorer is $25 fine. No technical foul.

Section V—Basket Ring

a. Any player, who in the opinion of the officials, has deliberately hung on the basket ring shall be assessed a technical foul and a $100 fine.

Section VI—Conduct

An official may assess a technical foul without prior warning at any time.

a. Officials may penalize, without prior warning, any act of unsportsmanlike conduct by anyone seated on the bench which, in the opinion of the officials, is detrimental to the game.

b. The first infraction shall be penalized by a technical foul and a $100 fine. The second infraction shall be penalized by a technical foul with violator expelled from the game and an additional $150 fine.

NOTE: (1) Technical fouls called for: delay of game, or illegal defensive alignments are not considered acts of unsportsmanlike conduct in this case.

c. A technical foul shall be assessed for unsportsmanlike tactics such as:

(1) disrespectfully addressing an official.

(2) physically contacting an official.

(3) overt actions indicating resentment to a call.

(4) use of profanity.

(5) a coach entering onto the court without permission of an official.

NOTE: (2) Cursing or blaspheming an official shall not be considered the only cause for imposing technical fouls. Running tirade, continuous criticism or griping may be sufficient cause to assess a technical. Flagrant misconduct shall result in ejection from the game.

NOTE: (3) Assessment of technical foul shall be avoided whenever and wherever possible, but when necessary they are to be applied without delay or procrastination.

NOTE: (4) If a personal foul and a technical foul are called against the same team at the same time, the technical foul shall be attempted first.

NOTE: (5) On technical foul attempts, whether the attempt has been successful or not, the ball shall be returned to the team having possession at the time the foul was called and play shall be resumed from a point out of bounds where play ended.

NOTE: (6) A foul which occurs when the ball is dead is a technical foul and must be unsportsmanlike in order to be penalized. Exception: fighting foul.

NOTE: (7) The shooter of a technical must be in the game when the technical is called. If called during time-out, shooter of technical must have been in game during last live ball. If technical is called before start of game anyone noted in the scorebook as a starter may attempt the technical.

NOTE: (8) A referee may eject a player or a coach with only one technical.

Question—May a player or a coach be ejected without the assessment of a technical foul?

Answer—No, ejection calls for the assessment of a technical foul. Exception: A player may be ejected after a flagrant foul.

NOTE: (9) Only 2 technicals for unsportsmanlike conduct may be called on a player, coach, trainer. Additional unsportsmanlike behavior is to be reported by Telex immediately to the commissioner.

NOTE: (10) Eye guarding (placing hands in front of opponent's eyes when guarding from the rear) is unsportsmanlike and is a technical foul.

NOTE: (11) Fighting or punching fouls (technicals) may be called on opponents. Foul tries are not attempted.

Section VII—Fines

a. Technical foul for unsportsmanlike conduct, violators are assessed a $100 fine for the first offense, and an additional $150 for the second offense in any one given game, for a total of $250 in fines. For ejection after the first technical foul, violators are assessed a $250 fine. If a player is ejected for a punching or fighting foul he shall be fined $250.

NOTE: (1) Whether or not said player(s) are ejected, a fine not exceeding $10,000 and/or suspension may be imposed upon such player(s) by the Commissioner at his sole discretion.

b. During a fight all players not involved must remain in vicinity of their bench. Violators will be assessed a $150 fine.

c. A player, coach or assistant coach, upon being notified by an official that he has been ejected from the game, must leave the playing area IMMEDIATELY and remain in the dressing room of his team during such suspension until completion of the game. Violation of this rule shall call for an automatic fine of $500. A fine not to exceed $10,000 and possible forfeiture of the game may be imposed for any violation of this rule.

d. Any player who in the opinion of the officials has deliberately hung on the basket shall be assessed a technical foul and a fine of $100.

e. Penalty for the use of "stickum" is a fine of $25 for the first violation, doubled for each subsequent violation.

f. Any player who fails to properly report to the scorer (Rule 3, V a.) shall be subject to a $25 fine on recommendation of the official scorer.

g. At half-time and the end of each game, the coach and his players are to leave the court and go directly to their dressing room, without pause or delay. There is to be **absolutely** no talking to game officials.

PENALTY—$100 fine to be doubled for any additional violation.

h. Each player, when introduced prior to the start of the game, must be uniformly dressed.

PENALTY—$100 fine.

i. A $250 fine shall be assessed to any player(s) hanging on the rim during pre-game warm-up. Officials shall be present during warm-up to observe violations.

j. Any player who is guilty of contact with the rim or backboard which causes the backboard to shatter is ejected from the game. (See Comment on Rules—I Guides for Administration and Application of the Rules.)

k. If a flagrant foul is called it must be reported to the commissioner by Telex.

B. PERSONAL FOUL

Section I—Types

a. A player shall not hold, push, charge into, impede the progress of an opponent by extended arm, knee or by bending the body into a position that is not normal.

b. Contact caused by a defensive player approaching the ball holder from the rear is a form of pushing or holding.

c. Excessive use of elbows (2 shots if contact is made by elbows).

NOTE: (1) A defensive player is not permitted to retain hand contact with an offensive player when the player is in his "sights."

Hand checking will be eliminated by rigid enforcement of this rule by both officials. The illegal use of hands will not be permitted.

Section II—By Dribbler

A dribbler shall not charge into nor contact an opponent in his path nor attempt to dribble between two opponents or between an opponent and a boundary, unless the space is such as to provide a reasonable chance for him to go through without contact. If a dribbler, without contact, passes an opponent sufficiently to have head and shoulders in advance of him, the greater responsibility for subsequent contact is on the opponent. If a dribbler in his progress has established a straight line path, he may not be crowded out of that path but, if an opponent is able legally to establish a defensive position in that path, the dribbler must avoid contact by changing direction or ending his dribble. After an official blows his whistle, for a foul, a player may not legally dribble again.

Section III—By Screening

a. A player who screens shall not: (1) when he is behind a stationary opponent, take a position closer than a normal step from him; (2) when he assumes a position at the side or in front of a stationary opponent, make contact with him; (3) take a position so close to a moving opponent that this opponent cannot avoid contact by stopping or changing direction. In (3) the speed of the player to be screened will determine where the screener may take his stationary position. This position will vary and may be one to two normal steps or strides from his opponent. (4) **Move after assuming his screening position, except in the same direction and path of his opponent.**

b. If the screener violates any of these provisions and contact results, he has committed a personal foul.

I. PENALTIES FOR SECTIONS I, II, III

Offender is charged with one foul and if it is his sixth personal foul he is disqualified. Offended player is awarded one free throw providing it is not an offensive foul. A second free throw shall be awarded if the foul is:

a. Flagrant (fouls are to be attempted whether the ball is dead, in possession or loose).

b. Against a field goal shooter whose attempt was not successful.

c. Swinging of elbows (contact must be made. Fouls are to be attempted whether the ball is dead, in possession or loose).

d. Back court (if team is in control of the ball in its back court and a foul is committed against a member of the team, it is a two shot foul. Once the ball passes over the mid-court line from back-court to front-court, it shall then be considered to be **front-court control**).

e. Committed by a player whose team has exceeded the limit for team fouls per quarter. (See 2 below.)

f. Committed by a defensive player before ball is thrown in from out of bounds.

g. Against any offensive player who has a clear path to the basket thereby being deprived of the opportunity of scoring.

h. Undercutting an opponent.

NOTE: (1) If a player is fouled and is subsequently ejected from the game before shooting the awarded free throw(s), he must immediately leave the court and another of the four players on the floor will be designated by the opposing coach to shoot such free throw(s).

NOTE: (2) When a foul is committed by an opponent of a player who as part of a continuous motion which started before the foul occurred, succeeds in making a goal, the goal shall count even if the ball leaves the player's hands after the whistle blows. The player must, in the opinion of the officials be throwing for a goal or starting an effort at the time the foul occurs. The goal does not count if the time expires before the ball leaves the player's hand.

2. FREE THROW PENALTY SITUATIONS

a. Each team shall be limited to four team fouls per quarter. Team fouls charged to a team in excess of four will be penalized by an additional free throw except as hereinafter provided.

(1) The first four team fouls committed by a team in each quarter—no shots will be taken—the opponents shall put the ball into play at the sideline nearest where the foul occurred. (Not closer to end-line than foul line extended.) The first three team fouls committed each over-time period—the ball shall be put into play in the same manner as in the first four quarters. Shooting, backcourt, elbowing and fighting (punching) fouls will carry their own penalties and are included in the team totals.

(2) During each over-time period the limitation shall be three personal fouls per team with an additional free throw for each foul in excess of three.

(3) If a team has not committed its quota of four team fouls during the first ten minutes of each quarter or its three team fouls in the first three minutes of any overtime period it shall be permitted to incur one team foul during the last two minutes of each regular quarter and the last two minutes of any overtime period without penalty.

(4) If the excess foul calls for two free throws (flagrant, back court, unsuccessful field goal attempt, swinging of elbows) the penalty free throw shall be permitted if either of the two is unsuccessful.

(5) If the foul committed by a player calls for a single free throw after a successful field goal, one additional free throw is allowed if the shot is missed.

NOTE: (1) The highest number of points that may be scored by the same team in one play is three. Exception: On a successful 3 point field goal 4 points may be scored.

NOTE: (2) Penalty free throws must be attempted by the player who attempted the original free throws.

Section IV—Double Fouls

a. On all double fouls, personal or technical, no free throws are attempted. Where double fouls are personal fouls a personal foul is charged to each player but not to team totals.

NOTE: (1) If the double foul is "on" the ball, play resumes with a jump ball between the involved players at the center jump ball circle. There can be no scoring in this situation.

NOTE: (2) If the double foul is "off" the ball, the team that had possession of the ball at the time of the call retains possession. Play is resumed at a point out of bounds nearest where the play was interrupted and the 24-second clock is reset to 24 seconds.

NOTE: (3) If the ball is in the air when a double off the ball foul occurs and the field goal is unsuccessful, there will be a jump ball at the nearest free throw circle between the two players involved. If the goal is successful, the team that has been scored upon will put the ball into play at the end line, as after any score.

Section V—Offensive Fouls

All personal fouls by players of the offensive team shall be penalized as follows: Personal foul charged against the offensive player, ball awarded to the opponent out of bounds at a point nearest to where foul occurred. Official must handle ball. No charge is made to team total.

Section VI—Loose Ball Fouls

A personal foul committed while the ball is in the air for a shot or during rebounding and where there is no ball possession will be treated in the following manner: The offending team will be charged with a team foul, the offending player with a personal foul, no shot will be taken and the team fouled will retain possession. All other loose balls will be treated in a similar manner. If such foul occurs during a penalty situation all shots that apply on the personal will be attempted.

NOTE: (1) When a "loose ball" foul is called against the defensive team that is then followed by a successful field goal (or successful foul try), the foul shot will be attempted, allowing for the 3 point or 4 point play. This applies regardless which offensive player is fouled. If a foul is called against the offensive team during this type of situation, the original rule applies (no shot and possession).

Section VII—Fighting Fouls

A foul called against a player for punching or fighting is to be charged as a team foul and a personal foul where only one player is involved. However, the penalty situation does not apply and whether the foul try is made or missed, the ball shall be given to the team shooting the attempt at mid-court. If **two players** are involved the fouls are technical and no shots will be attempted as in any other double foul situation. It is the official's decision whether or not the offending player or players shall be ejected. Whether or not said player or players are ejected, a fine not exceeding $10,000 and/or suspension may be imposed upon such player(s) by the Commissioner at his sole discretion. (See Rule 12A—Section VII—page 31.)

NOTE: (1) This rule applies whether the play is in progress or ball is dead.

NOTE: (2) In the case where one punching foul is followed by another, all aspects of the rule are applied in both cases, and the team last offended is awarded possession.

Section VIII—Away From Play Foul

During the last two minutes of the game, when ball is in play, and any overtime period, all deliberate defensive fouls away from the play, except loose ball fouls will be treated as follows:

The foul is charged to the player and the team but is treated as a technical, with no fine. Anyone in the game may attempt the free throw and the ball remains in the possession of the offended team.

Question—During the last two minutes of the fourth period, player A1 is out of bounds and attempting to inbounds the ball. Player B1 reaches across the out-of-bounds line and fouls player A1. How is this treated?

Answer—This is considered a deliberate away-from-the-play foul, and is a one (1) shot foul attempt, which is treated as a technical. (If this occurred during the game, at a time other than the last two minutes of the fourth period or overtime, it would be a two-shot foul attempt.)

COMMENTS ON THE RULES

I. GUIDES FOR ADMINISTRATION AND APPLICATION OF THE RULES

Each official should have a definite and clear conception of his overall responsibility to include the intent and purpose of each rule. If all officials possess the same conception there will be a guaranteed uniformity in the administration of all contests.

The restrictions placed upon the player by the rules are intended to create a balance of play; equal opportunity for the defense and the offense; to provide reasonable safety and protection; and to emphasize cleverness and skill without unduly limiting freedom of action of player or team.

The primary purpose of penalties is to compensate a player who has been placed at a disadvantage through an illegal act of an opponent. A secondary purpose is to restrain players from committing acts which, if ignored, might lead to roughness even though they do not affect the immediate play. To implement this philosophy, many of the rules are written in general terms while the need for the rule may have been created by specific play situations. This practice eliminates the necessity for many additional rules and provides the officials the latitude and authority to adapt application of the rules to fit conditions of play in any particular game.

II. BASIC PRINCIPLES

A. CONTACT SITUATIONS

1. Incidental Contact:

a. The mere fact that contact occurs does not necessarily constitute a foul. Contact which is incidental to an effort by a player to play an opponent, reach a loose ball, or perform normal defensive or offensive movements, should not be considered illegal. If, however, a player attempts to play an opponent from a position where he has no reasonable chance to perform without making contact with his opponent, the responsibility is on the player in this position.

2. Guarding an Opponent.

In all guarding situations, a player is entitled to any spot on the court which he desires provided he gets to that spot first and without contact with an opponent.

a. In most guarding situations, the guard must be facing his opponent at the moment he assumes a guarding position after which no particular facing is required.

b. A player may continue to move after gaining a guarding position in the path of an opponent provided he is not moving directly or obliquely toward his opponent when contact occurs. A player is never permitted to move into the path of an opponent after the opponent has jumped into the air.

c. A player who extends an arm, shoulder, hip or leg into the path of an opponent and thereby causes contact is not considered to have a legal position in the path of an opponent.

d. A player is entitled to an erect (vertical) position even to the extent of holding his arms above his shoulders, as in post play or when double teaming in pressing tactics.

e. A player is not required to maintain any specific distance from an opponent.

f. Any player who conforms to the above is ab-

solved from responsibility for any contact by an opponent which may dislodge or tend to dislodge such player from the position which he has attained and is maintaining legally. If contact occurs, the official must decide whether the contact is incidental or a foul has been committed.

The following are the usual situations to which the foregoing principles apply:

   a. Guarding a player with the ball.
   b. Guarding a player who is trying for goal.
   c. Switching to a player with the ball.
   d. Guarding a dribbler.
   e. Guarding a player without the ball.
   f. Guarding a post player with or without the ball.
   g. Guarding a rebounder.

3. Screening.

When a player screens in front or at the side of a stationary opponent, he may be as close as he desires providing he does not make contact. His opponent can see him and, therefore, is expected to detour around the screen.

If he screens behind a stationary opponent, the opponent must be able to take a normal step backward without contact. Because the opponent is not expected to see a screener behind him, the player screened is given latitude of movement.

To screen a moving opponent, the player must stop soon enough to permit his opponent to stop or change direction. The distance between the player screening and his opponent will depend upon the speed at which the players are moving.

If two opponents are moving in the same direction and path, the player who is behind is responsible for contact. The player in front may stop or slow his pace, but he may not move backward or sidewards into his opponent. The player in front may or may not have the ball. This situation assumes the two players have been moving in identically the same direction and path before contact.

4. The Dribble.

If the dribbler's path is blocked, he is expected to pass or shoot; that is, he should not try to dribble by an opponent unless there is a reasonable chance of getting by without contact.

B. THE ACT OF TRYING FOR GOAL

A player is trying for goal when he has the ball

and (in the judgment of the official) is throwing, or attempting to throw for goal. It is not essential that the ball leave the player's hand. His arm might be held so that he cannot throw yet he may be making an attempt. He is thus deprived of his opportunity to score, and is entitled to two free throws.

If a player is fouled when tapping a tossed ball or a rebound toward or into the basket, he is not considered to be "trying for goal." If a live ball is in flight when time expires, the goal, if made, shall count.

C. FOULS: FLAGRANT—UNSPORTSMANLIKE

To be unsportsmanlike is to act in a manner unbecoming to the image of professional basketball. It consists of acts of deceit, such as accepting a personal foul charge which should be credited to a teammate or willfully accepting a free throw which belongs to a teammate, disrespect of officials, vulgarity such as the use of profanity. The penalty for acts of unsportsmanlike conduct is a technical foul. Repeated unsportsmanlike acts shall result in expulsion from the game and a total of $250 in fines.

A flagrant foul is defined as attempting to hurt an opponent and involves violent or savage contact such as kicking, kneeing or running under a player while this player is in the air as the result of attempting a shot or otherwise. A flagrant foul always carries a penalty of two free throws, is charged as a personal foul and a team foul. The shots are attempted whether the ball is in possession or loose. The player is ejected. A fine not exceeding $10,000 and/or suspension may be imposed upon such player(s) by the Commissioner at his sole discretion.

If the offended player is unable to shoot the foul (flagrant) his coach may choose any player on or off the floor to attempt the foul shots.

D. DEFENSIVE ALIGNMENTS

It is legal for a defensive player(s) to double-team an opponent, and thereby leave an offensive player supposedly free. The other defensive players, not double-teaming, must be guarding an opponent. This applies to all areas of the court, as well as the pivot and post play, when the ball is in the front court.

Although it is the responsibility of the offensive team to demonstrate the defensive violation by their movement, it is also the responsibility of the defensive team to demonstrate they are not playing a zone defense.

E. CHARGING-BLOCKING

A player is never permitted to move into the path of an opponent who has become airborne.

If contact occurs on this play, and it is anything but negligible and/or incidental, the personal is charged to the player who moved into the airborne player's path.

The opposite is also true. If an airborne player causes contact with a **stationary** opponent, and it is anything but negligible and/or incidental, the personal is charged to the airborne player.

On a drive-in shot, if the defensive player has established his defending position **legally** and the offensive player (the shooter) causes contact either prior to the release of the ball or immediately after release of the ball, the personal is on the shooter—an offensive foul.

In this type of play situation—where the shooter is responsible for contact—no points can be scored and the goal, if successful, is wiped out. This interpretation is consistent with the one that protects the shooter prior to his release of the ball while in a "shooting motion" as well as protecting him after release—until he "regains a normal playing position."

With this interpretation, not only is the defensive player held responsible for his position and movement before and after release of the ball on an attempted shot—but the offensive player is held responsible for his position and movement as well. Consistency on this play places neither player at a disadvantage nor accords him an undue advantage. Both are equally responsible for their position and movement that precedes and follows release of the ball on an attempted shot. Of course, if the personal is on the defensive player, it is a "shooting" foul and if on the offensive player, it is an offensive foul, and again—the goal, if successful, is wiped out.

In summary, the mere fact that contact occurs on this play or any other similar play, does not mean that a personal foul has been committed. The officials must decide whether the contact is negligible and/or incidental, judging each situation separately. In judging this play, the officials must be aware that if either player has been placed at a disadvantage by the contact that has occurred, then a personal foul should be called on the responsible player. A defensive player may not submarine an offensive player at any time. A player taking a charge may protect himself but may not submarine an opponent.

Official Signals

TECHNICAL FOUL

Form T

**CANCEL SCORE
CANCEL PLAY**

Shift arms across body

**3 SECOND RULE
INFRACTION**

Fingers sidewards

**24-SECOND
VIOLATION**

Tap head

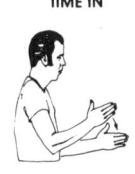

TIME IN

Chop with hand
or finger

TIME-OUT

Open palm

TRAVELLING

Rotate fists

JUMP BALL

Thumbs up

BASKET INTERFERENCE

Rotate finger

**GOAL TENDING
TWO POINTS**

"Flag" from wrist

PERSONAL FOUL

Clenched fist

**TO DESIGNATE
OFFENDER**

Hold up number
of player

FOR 3 PT. FIELD GOAL

Official will raise one
arm on attempt

If goal is successful
raise the other arm.

ILLEGAL DRIBBLE

Patting
motion

DIRECTION OF PLAY

Point-Direction
call team
color

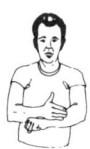

**ILLEGAL USE
OF HANDS**

Signal foul:
strike wrist

HOLDING

Signal foul:
grasp wrist

LOOSE BALL FOUL

Extend arms
to shoulder level

PUSHING

Signal foul:
imitate push

CHARGING

Clenched fist striking

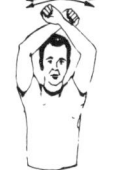

DOUBLE FOUL

Waving clenched
fists

BLOCKING

Hands on hips

NOTE: (1) When an offensive player is driving to the basket a defensive player will not benefit for the setting of a block directly under the basket with no intent to play defense. The official will permit the play to continue unless it is a blocking foul.

F. GAME CANCELLATION

For the purpose of game cancellation, the officials' jurisdiction begins with the opening tipoff. Prior to this, it shall be the decision of the home management whether or not playing conditions are such to warrant postponement.

However, once the game begins, if because of extremely hazardous playing conditions the question arises whether or not the game should be cancelled, the lead official shall see that EVERY effort is made to continue the game before making the decision to terminate it.

G. PHYSICAL CONTACT—SUSPENSION

''Any player or coach guilty of intentional physical contact with an official, shall automatically be suspended without pay for one game. A fine and/or longer period of suspension will result if circumstances so dictate.''

H. PROTEST

In order to protest against or appeal from the result of a game, notice thereof must be given to the Commissioner within forty-eight (48) hours after the conclusion of said game, by telegram, stating therein the grounds for such protest. No protest may be filed in connection with any game played during the regular season after midnight of the day of the last game of the regular schedule. A protest in connection with a playoff game must be filed not later than midnight of the day of the game protested. A game may be protested only by a Governor, Alternate Governor or Head Coach. The right of protest shall inure not only to the immediately allegedly aggrieved contestants, but to any other member who can show an interest in the grounds of protest and the results that might be attained if the protest were allowed. Each telegram of protest shall be immediately confirmed by letter and no protest shall be valid unless the letter of confirmation is accompanied by a check in the sum of $1,500 payable to the Association. If the member filing the protest prevails, the $1,500 is to be refunded. If the member does not prevail, the $1,500 is to be forfeited and retained in the Association treasury.

If during the course of a game, a Governor, Alternate Governor, Head Coach or other representative of a member states to an official, the scorer's table or the press or broadcast announcers that the result of such game is, will, or may be protested, then such member shall immediately become obligated to forward to the Commissioner $500 of the Protest Fee. If a notice of protest is thereafter filed, the letter of confirmation shall be accompanied by a check in the sum of the remaining $1,000 of the Protest Fee. If no notice of protest and confirming letter are subsequently filed within the applicable period stated above, such $500 shall not be refunded to such member.

Upon receipt of a protest, the Commissioner shall at once notify the member operating the opposing team in the game protested and require both of said members within five (5) days to file with him such evidence as he may desire bearing upon the issue. The Commissioner shall decide the question raised within five (5) days after receipt of such evidence.

I. SHATTERING BACKBOARDS

Any player whose contact with the rim or backboard causes the backboard to shatter will be penalized in the following manner:

Pre-game warm-up: $250 fine and suspended from game.

During game: $100 fine, technical foul and suspension for the remainder of the game and next regularly-scheduled game.

Halftime warm-up: $250 fine and suspension for the remainder of the game and next regularly-scheduled game.

The Commissioner will review all actions and plays involved in shattering backboards.

PART 5

ALL-TIME PLAYER DIRECTORY

ACTIVE PLAYERS

This section contains the season-by-season records of every player who was active in the National Basketball Association through the 1980-81 season.

Each player's individual record lists his team, games played (G), field goals made (FG), free throws made (FT), total points (TP) and average (Avg.). The number in parenthesis following field goals totals indicates the number of three-point field goals scored. Each player's date of birth, height, weight and college are listed wherever available.

Yr.	Team	G	FG	FT	TP	Avg.
ABDUL-JABBAR, KAREEM (Lew Alcindor)						
b. April 16, 1947 Ht. 6-2 Wt. 225 College—UCLA						
1969-70	Milwaukee	82	938	485	2361	28.8
1970-71	Milwaukee	82	1063	470	2596	31.7
1971-72	Milwaukee	81	1159	504	2822	34.8
1972-73	Milwaukee	76	982	328	2922	30.2
1973-74	Milwaukee	81	948	295	2191	27.0
1974-75	Milwaukee	65	812	325	1949	30.0
1975-76	Los Angeles	82	914	447	2275	27.7
1976-77	Los Angeles	82	888	376	2152	26.2
1977-78	Los Angeles	62	663	274	1600	25.8
1978-79	Los Angeles	80	777	349	1903	23.8
1979-80	Los Angeles	82	835	364	2034	24.8
1980-81	Los Angeles	80	836	423	2095	26.2
	Totals	935	10815	4640	26270	28.1
ABERNETHY, TOM						
b. May 6, 1954 Ht. 6-7 Wt. 220 College—Indiana						
1976-77	Los Angeles	70	169	101	439	6.3
1977-78	Los Angeles	73	201	91	493	6.8
1978-79	Gold. St.	70	176	70	422	6.0
1979-80	Gold. St.	67	153	56	362	5.4
1980-81	G.S.-Ind.	39	25	13	63	1.6
	Totals	319	724	331	1779	5.6
ADAMS, ALVAN						
b. July 19, 1954 Ht. 6-9 Wt. 220 College—Oklahoma						
1975-76	Phoenix	80	629	261	1519	19.0
1976-77	Phoenix	72	522	252	1296	18.0
1977-78	Phoenix	70	434	214	1082	15.5
1978-79	Phoenix	77	569	231	1369	17.8
1979-80	Phoenix	75	465	188	1118	14.9
1980-81	Phoenix	75	458	199	1115	14.9
	Totals	449	3077	1345	7499	16.7
ALLUMS, DARRELL						
b. Sept. 12, 1958 Ht. 6-8 Wt. 220 College—UCLA						
1980-81	Dallas	22	23	13	59	2.7

Yr.	Team	G	FG	FT	TP	Avg.
ARCHIBALD, NATE						
b. April 18, 1948 Ht. 6-1 Wt. 160 College—Texas-El Paso						
1970-71	Cincinnati	82	486	336	1308	16.0
1971-72	Cincinnati	76	734	677	2145	28.2
1972-73	K.C.-Omaha	80	1028	663	2719	34.0
1973-74	K.C.-Omaha	35	222	173	617	17.6
1974-75	K.C.-Omaha	82	759	652	2170	26.5
1975-76	Kansas City	78	717	501	1935	24.8
1976-77	N.Y. Nets	34	250	197	697	20.5
1977-78	Buffalo		(Injured)			
1978-79	Boston	69	259	242	760	11.0
1979-80	Boston	80	383(4)	361	1131	14.1
1980-81	Boston	80	382	342	1106	13.8
	Totals	705	5220(4)	4144	14588	20.7
AWTREY, DENNIS						
b. Feb. 22, 1948 Ht. 6-10 Wt. 250 College—Santa Clara						
1970-71	Philadelphia	70	200	104	504	7.2
1971-72	Philadelphia	58	98	49	245	4.2
1972-73	Phila.-Chi.	82	146	86	378	4.6
1973-74	Chicago	68	65	54	184	2.7
1974-75	Phoenix	82	339	132	810	9.9
1975-76	Phoenix	74	142	75	359	4.9
1976-77	Phoenix	72	160	91	411	5.7
1977-78	Phoenix	81	112	69	293	3.6
1978-79	Bost.-Seattle	63	44	41	129	2.0
1979-80	Chicago	26	27	32	86	3.3
1980-81	Seattle	47	44	14	102	2.2
	Totals	723	1377	747	3501	4.8
BAILEY, JAMES						
b. May 21, 1957 Ht. 6-9 Wt. 220 College—Rutgers						
1979-80	Seattle	67	122	68	312	4.4
1980-81	Seattle	82	444(1)	256	1145	14.0
	Totals	149	566(1)	324	1457	9.8
BALLARD, GREG						
b. Jan. 29, 1955 Ht. 6-7 Wt. 215 College—Oregon						
1977-78	Washington	76	142	88	372	4.9
1978-79	Washington	82	260	119	639	7.8
1979-80	Washington	82	545(16)	171	1277	15.6
1980-81	Washington	82	549(7)	166	1271	15.5
	Totals	233	1496(23)	544	3559	11.1

Yr.	Team		G	FG	FT	TP	Avg.

BANTOM, MIKE
b. Dec. 3, 1951 Ht. 6-9 Wt. 220 College—St. Joseph's (Pa.)

Yr.	Team		G	FG	FT	TP	Avg.
1973-74	Phoenix		76	314	141	769	10.1
1974-75	Phoenix		82	418	185	1021	12.5
1975-76	Pho.-Sea.		73	220	136	576	7.9
1976-77	Sea.-N.Y. Nets		77	361	224	946	12.3
1977-78	Indiana		82	502	254	1258	15.3
1978-79	Indiana		81	482	227	1191	14.7
1979-80	Indiana		77	384(1)	139	908	11.8
1980-81	Indiana		76	431	199	1061	14.0
	Totals		624	3112(1)	1505	7730	12.4

BATES, BILLY RAY
b. May 31, 1956 Ht. 6-4 Wt. 210 College—Kentucky St.

1979-80	Portland		16	72(8)	28	180	11.3
1980-81	Portaand		77	439(14)	170	1062	13.8
	Totals		93	511(22)	198	1242	13.4

BENNETT, MEL
b. Jan. 4, 1955 Ht. 6-7 Wt. 220 College—Pittsburgh

1975-76	Virginia	(ABA)	75	329	246	904	12.1
1976-77	Indiana		67	101	112	314	4.7
1977-78	Indiana		31	23	28	74	2.4
1980-81	Utah		28	26	53	105	3.8
	Totals		201	479	439	1397	7.0

BENSON, M. KENT
b. Dec. 27, 1954 Ht. 6-11 Wt. 245 College—Indiana

1977-78	Milwaukee		69	220	92	532	7.7
1978-79	Milwaukee		82	413	180	1006	12.3
1979-80	Milw.-Det.		73	299(1)	99	698	9.6
1980-81	Detroit		59	364	196	924	15.7
	Totals		283	1296(1)	567	3160	11.2

BIBBY, C. HENRY
b. Nov. 24, 1949 Ht. 6-1 Wt. 185 College—UCLA

1972-73	New York		55	78	73	229	4.2
1973-74	New York		66	210	73	493	7.5
1974-75	N.Y.-N.O.		75	270	137	677	9.0
1975-76	New Orleans		79	266	200	732	9.3
1976-77	Philadelphia		81	302	221	825	10.2
1977-78	Philadelphia		82	286	171	743	9.1
1978-79	Philadelphia		82	368	266	1002	12.2
1979-80	Philadelphia		82	251(11)	226	739	9.0
1980-81	San Diego		73	118(32)	67	335	4.6
	Totals		675	2149(43)	1434	5775	8.6

BIRD, LARRY
b. Dec. 7, 1956 Ht. 6-10 Wt. 220 College—Indiana State

1979-80	Boston		82	693(58)	301	1745	21.3
1980-81	Boston		82	719(20)	283	1741	21.2
	Totals		164	1412(78)	584	3486	21.3

BIRDSONG, OTIS
b. Dec. 9, 1955 Ht. 6-4 Wt. 190 College—Houston

1977-78	Kansas City		73	470	216	1156	15.8
1978-79	Kansas City		82	741	296	1778	21.7
1979-80	Kansas City		82	781(10)	286	1858	22.7
1980-81	Kansas City		71	710(10)	317	1747	24.6
	Totals		308	2702(20)	115	6539	21.2

BLACK, NORMAN
b. Nov. 12, 1957 Ht. 6-5 Wt. 190 College—St. Joseph's (Pa.)

1980-81	Detroit		3	3	2	8	2.7

BOONE, RON
b. Sept. 6, 1946 Ht. 6-2 Wt. 200 College—Idaho State

1968-69	Dallas	(ABA)	78	520(2)	436	1478	18.9
1969-70	Dallas	(ABA)	84	423(17)	300	1163	13.9
1970-71	Dall.-Utah	(ABA)	86	510(49)	278	1547	18.0
1971-72	Utah	(ABA)	84	404(13)	271	1092	13.0
1972-73	Utah	(ABA)	84	566(10)	415	1557	18.5
1973-74	Utah	(ABA)	84	587(6)	300	1480	17.6
1974-75	Utah	(ABA)	84	872(10)	363	2117	25.2
1975-76	Utah-St. L	(ABA)	78	713(16)	277	1719	22.0
1976-77	Kansas City		82	747	324	1818	22.2
1977-78	Kansas City		82	563	322	1448	17.7
1978-79	Los Angeles		82	259	90	608	7.4
1979-80	L.A.-Utah		81	405(19)	175	1004	12.4
1980-81	Utah		52	160(11)	75	406	7.8
	Totals		1041	6829(153)	3626	17437	16.8

BOYNES, WINFORD
b. May 17, 1957 Ht. 6-6½ Wt. 186 College—San Francisco

1978-79	New Jersey		69	256	133	645	9.3
1979-80	New Jersey		64	221	104	546	8.5
1980-81	Dallas		44	121	45	287	6.5
	Totals		177	598	282	1478	8.4

BRADLEY, DUDLEY
b. Mar. 19, 1957 Ht. 6-6 Wt. 195 College—North Carolina

1979-80	Indiana		82	275(2)	136	688	8.4
1980-81	Indiana		82	265(2)	125	657	8.0
	Totals		164	540(4)	261	1345	8.2

BRATZ, MIKE
b. Oct. 17, 1955 Ht. 6-2 Wt. 185 College—Stanford

1977-78	Phoenix		80	159	56	374	4.7
1978-79	Phoenix		77	242	139	623	8.1
1979-80	Phoenix		82	269(21)	141	700	8.5
1980-81	Cleveland		80	319(57)	107	802	10.0
	Totals		319	989(78)	443	2499	7.8

BREWER, JIM
b. Dec. 3, 1951 Ht. 6-9 Wt. 220 College—Minnesota

1973-74	Cleveland		82	210	80	500	3.1
1974-75	Cleveland		82	291	103	685	8.4
1975-76	Cleveland		82	400	140	940	11.5
1976-77	Cleveland		81	296	97	689	8.5
1977-78	Cleveland		80	175	46	396	5.0
1978-79	Cleve.-Det.		80	141	26	308	3.9
1979-80	Portland		67	90	14	194	2.9
1980-81	Los Angeles		78	101	15	217	2.8
	Totals		632	1704	521	3929	6.2

BREWER, RON
b. Sept. 16, 1955 Ht. 180 College—Arkansas

1978-79	Portland		81	434	210	1078	13.3
1979-80	Portland		82	548(6)	184	1286	15.7
1980-81	Port-S.A.		75	275(1)	91	642	8.6
	Totals		238	1257(7)	485	3006	12.6

Yr.	Team		G	FG	FT	TP	Avg.
BRIDGEMAN, ULYSSES (Junior)							
b. Sept. 17, 1953 Ht. 6-5 Wt. 210 College—Louisville							
1975-76 Milwaukee		81	286	128	700	8.6	
1976-77 Milwaukee		82	491	197	1179	14.4	
1977-78 Milwaukee		82	476	166	1118	13.6	
1978-79 Milwaukee		82	540	189	1269	15.5	
1979-80 Milwaukee		81	594(5)	230	1423	17.6	
1980-81 Milwaukee		77	537(3)	213	1290	16.8	
Totals		485	2924(8)	1123	6979	14.4	
BRISTOW, ALLAN							
b. Aug. 23, 1951 Ht. 6-7 Wt. 227 College—Toledo							
1973-74 Philadelphia		55	108	42	258	4.7	
1974-75 Philadelphia		72	163	121	447	6.2	
1975-76 San Antonio	(ABA)	47	125	78	328	6.0	
1976-77 San Antonio		82	365	206	936	11.4	
1977-78 San Antonio		82	257	152	666	8.1	
1978-79 San Antonio		74	174	124	472	6.4	
1979-80 Utah		82	377(2)	197	953	11.6	
1980 81 Utah		82	271(5)	166	713	8.7	
Totals		576	18740(7)	1086	4773	8.3	
BRITTON, DAVE							
b. Aug. 29, 1958 Ht. 6-4 Wt. 202 College—Texas A&M							
1980-81 Washington		2	2	0	4	2.0	
BROOKS, MICHAEL							
b. Aug. 17, 1958 Ht. 6-7 Wt. 220 College—LaSalle							
1980-81 San Diego		82	488	226	1202	14.7	
BROWN, FRED							
b. July 7, 1948 Ht. 6-3 Wt. 185 College—Iowa							
1971-72 Seattle		33	59	22	140	4.2	
1972-73 Seattle		79	471	121	1063	13.5	
1973-74 Seattle		82	578	195	1351	16.5	
1974-75 Seattle		81	737	226	1700	21.0	
1975-76 Seattle		76	742	273	1757	23.1	
1976-77 Seattle		72	534	168	1236	17.2	
1977-78 Seattle		72	508	176	1192	16.6	
1978-79 Seattle		77	446	183	1075	14.0	
1979-80 Seattle		80	404(39)	113	960	12.0	
1980-81 Seattle		78	505(23)	173	1206	15.5	
Totals		730	4984(62)	1650	11680	16.0	
BROWN, LEWIS							
b. Feb. 19, 1955 Ht. 6-11 Wt. 235 College—Nevada Las Vegas							
1980-81 Washington		2	0	2	2	1.0	
BROWN, RICKEY							
b. Aug. 20, 1958 Ht. 6-10 Wt. 215 College—Mississippi State							
1980-81 Golden State		45	83	16	182	4.0	
BRYANT, JOE							
b. Oct. 19, 1954 Ht. 6-9 Wt. 215 College—LaSalle							
1975-76 Philadelphia		75	233	92	558	7.4	
1976-77 Philadelphia		61	107	53	267	4.4	
1977-78 Philadelphia		81	190	111	491	6.1	
1978-79 Philadelphia		70	205	123	533	7.6	
1979-80 San Diego		81	294(5)	161	854	9.3	
1980-81 San Diego		82	379(2)	193	953	11.6	
Totals		450	1408(7)	733	3556	7.9	

Yr.	Team		G	FG	FT	TP	Avg.
BUCKNER, QUINN							
b. Aug. 20, 1954 Ht. 6-3 Wt. 205 College—Indiana							
1976-77 Milwaukee		79	299	83	681	8.6	
1977-78 Milwaukee		82	314	131	759	9.3	
1978-79 Milwaukee		81	251	79	581	7.2	
1979-80 Milwaukee		67	306(2)	105	719	10.7	
1980-81 Milwaukee		82	471(1)	149	1092	13.3	
Totals		391	1641(3)	547	3832	9.8	
BURLESON, TOM							
b. Feb. 24, 1952 Ht. 7-2 Wt. 228 College—North Carolina State							
1974-75 Seattle		82	322	182	826	10.1	
1975-76 Seattle		82	496	291	1283	15.6	
1976-77 Seattle		82	288	220	796	9.7	
1977-78 Kansas City		76	228	197	653	8.6	
1978-79 Kansas City		56	157	121	435	7.8	
1979-80 Kansas City		37	36	23	95	2.6	
1980-81 Atlanta		31	41	20	102	3.3	
Totals		446	1568	1054	4190	9.4	
BUSE, DON							
b. Aug. 10, 1950 Ht. 6-4 Wt. 195 College—Evansville							
1972-73 Indiana	(ABA)	77	163(5)	82	413	5.4	
1973-74 Indiana	(ABA)	77	170(36)	48	424	5.5	
1974-75 Indiana	(ABA)	80	216(38)	47	517	6.5	
1975-76 Indiana	(ABA)	84	400(72)	179	1051	12.5	
1976-77 Indiana		81	266	114	646	8.0	
1977-78 Phoenix		82	287	112	686	8.4	
1978-79 Phoenix		82	285	70	640	7.8	
1979-80 Phoenix		81	261(19)	85	626	7.7	
1980-81 Indiana		58	114(19)	50	297	5.1	
Totals		702	2162(189)	787	5300	7.5	
BYRNES, MARTY							
b. April 30, 1956 Ht. 6-7 Wt. 218 College—Syracuse							
1978-79 Phoenix-N.O.		79	187	106	480	6.1	
1979-80 Los Angeles		32	25	13	63	2.0	
1980-81 Dallas		72	216(9)	120	561	7.8	
Totals		183	428(9)	239	1104	6.0	
CALVIN, MACK							
b. July 27, 1949 Ht. 6-0 Wt. 165 College—So. California							
1969-70 Los Angeles	(ABA)	84	441(3)	529	1414	16.8	
1970-71 Floridians	(ABA)	81	744(17)	696	2201	27.2	
1971-72 Floridians	(ABA)	82	552(11)	611	1726	21.0	
1972-73 Carolina	(ABA)	84	478(11)	500	1467	17.5	
1973-74 Carolina	(ABA)	83	498(10)	490	1496	18.0	
1974-75 Denver	(ABA)	74	483(3)	475	1444	19.5	
1975-76 Virginia	(ABA)	45	306(7)	253	872	19.4	
1976-77 L.A.-S.A.-Den.		76	220	287	727	9.6	
1977-78 Denver		77	147	173	467	6.1	
1979-80 Utah		48	100(1)	105	306	6.4	
1980-81 Cleveland		21	13(1)	25	52	2.5	
Totals		755	3982(64)	4144	12172	16.1	
CARR, AUSTIN							
b. March 10, 1948 Ht. 6-4 Wt. 200 College—Notre Dame							
1971-72 Cleveland		43	381	149	911	21.2	
1972-73 Cleveland		82	702	281	1685	20.5	
1973-74 Cleveland		81	748	279	1775	21.9	
1974-75 Cleveland		41	252	89	593	14.5	
1975-76 Cleveland		65	276	106	658	10.1	

Yr.	Team	G	FG	FT	TP	Avg.
1976-77	Cleveland	82	558	213	1329	16.2
1977-78	Cleveland	82	414	183	1011	12.3
1978-79	Cleveland	82	551	292	1394	17.0
1979-80	Cleveland	77	390(2)	127	909	11.8
1980-81	Dallas-Wash.	47	87	34	208	4.4
	Totals	682	4359(2)	1753	10473	15.4

CARR, KEN
b. Aug. 15, 1955 Ht. 6-7 Wt. 215 College—North Carolina State

Yr.	Team	G	FG	FT	TP	Avg.
1977-78	Los Angeles	52	134	55	323	6.2
1978-79	Los Angeles	72	225	83	533	7.4
1979-80	L.A.-Clev.	79	378	173	929	11.8
1980-81	Cleveland	81	469	292	1230	15.2
	Totals	284	1206	603	3015	10.6

CARR, MICHAEL LEON (M.L.)
b. Jan. 9, 1951 Ht. 6-6 Wt. 205 College—Guilford

Yr.	Team		G	FG	FT	TP	Avg.
1975-76	St. Louis	(ABA)	74	380(9)	137	906	12.2
1976-77	Detroit		82	443	205	1091	13.3
1977-78	Detroit		79	390	200	980	12.4
1978-79	Detroit		80	587	323	1497	18.7
1979-80	Boston		80	362(12)	178	914	11.1
1980-81	Boston		41	97(1)	53	248	6.0
	Totals		436	2259(22)	1096	5636	12.9

CARROLL, JOE BARRY
b. July 24, 1958 Ht. 7-0 Wt. 225 College—Purdue

Yr.	Team	G	FG	FT	TP	Avg.
1980-81	Golden State	82	616	315	1547	18.9

CARTER, CLARENCE (Butch)
b. June 11, 1958 Ht. 6-5 Wt. 180 College—Indiana

Yr.	Team	G	FG	FT	TP	Avg.
1980-81	Los Angeles	54	114(3)	70	301	5.6

CARTER, REGGIE
b. Oct. 10, 1957 Ht. 6-3 Wt. 175 College—Hawaii and St. John's

Yr.	Team	G	FG	FT	TP	Avg.
1980-81	New York	60	59	51	169	2.8

CARTWRIGHT, BILL
b. July 30, 1957 Ht. 7-1 Wt. 255 College—San Francisco

Yr.	Team	G	FG	FT	TP	Avg.
1979-80	New York	82	665	451	1781	21.7
1980-81	New York	82	619	408	1646	20.1
	Totals	164	1284	859	3427	20.9

CATCHINGS, HARVEY
b. Sept. 2, 1951 Ht. 6-9 Wt. 218 College—Hardin-Simmons

Yr.	Team	G	FG	FT	TP	Avg.
1974-75	Philadelphia	37	41	16	98	2.6
1975-76	Philadelphia	75	103	58	264	3.5
1976-77	Philadelphia	53	62	33	157	3.0
1977-78	Philadelphia	61	70	34	174	2.9
1978-79	Phila.-N.J.	56	102	60	264	4.7
1979-80	Milwaukee	72	97	39	233	3.2
1980-81	Milwaukee	77	134	59	327	4.2
	Totals	431	609	299	1517	3.5

CHEEKS, MAURICE
b. Sept. 8, 1956 Ht. 6-1 Wt. 180 College—W. Texas St.

Yr.	Team	G	FG	FT	TP	Avg.
1978-79	Philadelphia	82	292	101	685	8.4
1979-80	Philadelphia	79	357(4)	180	898	11.4
1980-81	Philadelphia	81	310(3)	140	763	9.4
	Totals	242	959(7)	421	2346	9.7

CHENIER, PHIL
b. Oct. 30, 1950 Ht. 6-3 Wt. 180 College—California

Yr.	Team	G	FG	FT	TP	Avg.
1971-72	Baltimore	81	407	182	996	12.3
1972-73	Baltimore	71	602	194	1398	19.7
1973-74	Capital	76	697	274	1668	21.9
1974-75	Washington	77	690	301	1681	21.8
1975-76	Washington	80	654	282	1590	19.9
1976-77	Washington	78	654	270	1578	20.2
1977-78	Washington	36	200	109	509	14.1
1978-79	Washington	27	69	18	156	5.8
1979-80	Wash.-Ind.	43	136(5)	49	326	7.6
1980-81	Golden State	9	11(1)	6	29	3.2
	Totals	578	4120(6)	1685	9931	17.2

CHONES, JIM
b. Nov. 30, 1949 Ht. 6-11 Wt. 220 College—Marquette

Yr.	Team		G	FG	FT	TP	Avg.
1972-73	New York	(ABA)	82	395	142	932	11.4
1973-74	Carolina	(ABA)	83	535	155	1225	14.7
1974-75	Cleveland		76	446	152	1044	14.5
1975-76	Cleveland		82	563	172	1298	15.8
1976-77	Cleveland		82	450	155	1055	12.9
1977-78	Cleveland		82	525	180	1230	15.0
1978-79	Cleveland		82	472	158	1102	13.4
1979-80	Los Angeles		82	372	125	869	10.6
1980-81	Los Angeles		82	378	126	882	10.8
	Totals		733	4136	1365	9637	13.1

COLLINS, ART
Ht. 6-5 Wt. 170 College—Biscayne

Yr.	Team	G	FG	FT	TP	Avg.
1980-81	Atlanta	29	35	24	94	3.2

COLLINS, DON
b. Nov. 28, 1958 Ht. 6-6 Wt. 190 College—Washington State

Yr.	Team	G	FG	FT	TP	Avg.
1980-81	Atl.-Wash.	81	360	211	931	11.5

COLLINS, DOUG
b. July 28, 1951 Ht. 6-6 Wt. 180 College—Illinois State

Yr.	Team	G	FG	FT	TP	Avg.
1973-74	Philadelphia	25	72	55	199	8.0
1974-75	Philadelphia	81	561	331	1453	17.9
1975-76	Philadelphia	77	614	372	1600	20.8
1976-77	Philadelphia	58	426	210	1062	18.3
1977-78	Philadelphia	79	643	267	1553	19.7
1978-79	Philadelphia	47	358	201	914	19.5
1979-80	Philadelphia	36	191	113	495	13.8
1980-81	Philadelphia	12	62	24	148	12.3
	Totals	415	2927	1573	7427	17.9

COOK, DARWIN
b. Aug. 6, 1956 Ht. 6-3 Wt. 184 College—Portland

Yr.	Team	G	FG	FT	TP	Avg.
1980-81	New Jersey	81	383(6)	132	904	11.2

COOK, JEFF
b. Oct. 21, 1956 Ht. 6-10 Wt. 215 College—Idaho State

Yr.	Team	G	FG	FT	TP	Avg.
1979-80	Phoenix	66	129	104	362	5.5
1980-81	Phoenix	79	286	100	672	8.5
	Totals	145	415	204	1034	7.1

COOPER, MIKE
b. April 15, 1956 Ht. 6-5 Wt. 170 College—New Mexico

Yr.	Team	G	FG	FT	TP	Avg.
1978-79	Los Angeles	3	3	0	6	2.0
1979-80	Los Angeles	82	303(5)	111	722	8.8
1980-81	Los Angeles	81	321(4)	117	763	9.4
	Totals	166	627(9)	228	1491	9.0

Yr.	Team	G	FG	FT	TP	Avg.

COOPER, WAYNE
b. Nov. 16, 1956 Ht. 6-10 Wt. 220 College—New Orleans

Yr.	Team	G	FG	FT	TP	Avg.
1978-79	Golden State	65	128	41	297	4.6
1979-80	Golden State	79	367(1)	136	871	11.0
1980-81	Utah	71	213(1)	62	489	6.9
	Totals	215	708(2)	239	1657	7.7

CORZINE, DAVE
b. April 25, 1956 Ht. 6-11 Wt. 250 College—DePaul

Yr.	Team	G	FG	FT	TP	Avg.
1978-79	Washington	59	63	49	175	3.0
1979-80	Washington	78	90	45	225	2.9
1980-81	San Antonio	82	366	125	857	10.5
	Totals	219	519	219	1257	5.7

CRISS, CHARLES
b. Nov. 6, 1949 Ht. 5-8 Wt. 165 College—New Mexico St.

Yr.	Team	G	FG	FT	TP	Avg.
1977-78	Atlanta	77	319	236	874	11.4
1978-79	Atlanta	54	109	67	285	5.3
1979-80	Atlanta	81	249(1)	172	671	8.3
1980-81	Atlanta	66	220(1)	185	626	9.5
	Totals	278	897(2)	660	2456	8.8

CROMPTON, GEOFF
b. July 4, 1955 Ht. 6-11 Wt. 270 College—No. Carolina

Yr.	Team	G	FG	FT	TP	Avg.
1978-79	Denver	20	10	6	26	1.3
1980-81	Portland	6	4	1	9	1.5
	Totals	26	14	7	35	1.3

CUMMINGS, PAT
b. July 11, 1956 Ht. 6-9½ Wt. 235 College—Cincinnati

Yr.	Team	G	FG	FT	TP	Avg.
1979-80	Milwaukee	71	187	94	468	6.6
1980-81	Milwaukee	74	248	99	595	8.0
	Totals	145	435	193	1063	7.3

CURETON, EARL
b. Sept. 3, 1957 Ht. 6-9 Wt. 210 College—Detroit

Yr.	Team	G	FG	FT	TP	Avg.
1980-81	Philadelphia	52	93	33	219	4.2

DANDRIDGE, BOB
b. Nov. 15, 1947 Ht. 6-6 Wt. 195 College—Norfolk State

Yr.	Team	G	FG	FT	TP	Avg.
1969-70	Milwaukee	81	434	199	1067	13.2
1970-71	Milwaukee	79	594	264	1452	18.4
1971-72	Milwaukee	80	630	215	1475	18.4
1972-73	Milwaukee	73	638	198	1474	20.2
1973-74	Milwaukee	71	583	175	1341	18.9
1974-75	Milwaukee	80	691	211	1593	19.9
1975-76	Milwaukee	73	650	271	1571	21.5
1976-77	Milwaukee	70	585	283	1453	20.8
1977-78	Washington	75	560	330	1450	19.3
1978-79	Washington	78	629	331	1589	20.4
1979-80	Washington	45	329(2)	123	783	17.4
1980-81	Washington	23	101	28	230	10.0
	Totals	828	6424(2)	2628	15478	18.7

DANTLEY, ADRIAN
b. Feb. 26, 1956 Ht. 6-5 Wt. 208 College—Notre Dame

Yr.	Team	G	FG	FT	TP	Avg.
1976-77	Buffalo	77	544	476	1564	20.3
1977-78	Ind.-L.A.	79	578	541	1697	21.5
1978-79	Los Angeles	60	374	292	1040	17.3
1979-80	Utah	68	730	443	1903	28.0
1980-81	Utah	80	909(2)	632	2452	30.7
	Totals	364	3135(2)	2384	8656	23.8

DAVIS, BRAD
b. Dec. 17, 1955 Ht. 6-3 Wt. 180 College—Maryland

Yr.	Team	G	FG	FT	TP	Avg.
1977-78	Los Angeles	33	30	22	82	2.5
1978-79	L.A.-Ind.	27	31	16	78	2.9
1979-80	Ind.-Utah	18	35	13	83	4.6
1980-81	Dallas	56	230(3)	163	626	11.2
	Totals	134	326(3)	214	869	6.5

DAVIS, JOHNNY
b. Oct. 21, 1955 Ht. 6-1 Wt. 170 College—Dayton

Yr.	Team	G	FG	FT	TP	Avg.
1976-77	Portland	79	234	166	634	8.0
1977-78	Portland	82	343	188	874	10.7
1978-79	Indiana	79	565	314	1444	18.3
1979-80	Indiana	82	496(4)	304	1300	15.9
1980-81	Indiana	76	426(4)	238	1094	14.4
	Totals	398	2064(8)	1210	5346	13.4

DAVIS, MONTI
b. July 26, 1958 Ht. 6-7 Wt. 205 College—Tennessee State

Yr.	Team	G	FG	FT	TP	Avg.
1980-81	Phil.-Dallas	2	1	1	3	1.5

DAVIS, RON
b. April 1, 1954 Ht. 6-7 Wt. 205 College—Washington State

Yr.	Team	G	FG	FT	TP	Avg.
1980-81	San Diego	64	139(2)	94	374	5.8

DAVIS, WALTER
b. Sept. 9, 1954 Ht. 6-6 Wt. 193 College—North Carolina

Yr.	Team	G	FG	FT	TP	Avg.
1977-78	Phoenix	81	786	387	1959	24.2
1978-79	Phoenix	79	764	340	1868	23.6
1979-80	Phoenix	75	657	299	1613	21.5
1980-81	Phoenix	78	593(7)	209	1402	18.0
	Totals	313	2800(7)	1235	6842	21.9

DAWKINS, DARRYL
b. Jan. 11, 1957 Ht. 6-11 Wt. 252 College—None

Yr.	Team	G	FG	FT	TP	Avg.
1975-76	Philadelphia	37	41	8	90	2.4
1976-77	Philadelphia	59	135	40	310	5.3
1977-78	Philadelphia	70	332	156	820	11.7
1978-79	Philadelphia	78	430	158	1018	13.1
1979-80	Philadelphia	80	494	190	1178	14.7
1980-81	Philadelphia	76	423	219	1065	14.0
	Totals	400	1855	771	4481	11.2

DEMIC, LARRY
b. June 27, 1957 Ht. 6-9 Wt. 225 College—Arizona

Yr.	Team	G	FG	FT	TP	Avg.
1979-80	New York	82	230	110	570	7.0
1980-81	New York	76	128	58	314	4.1
	Totals	158	358	168	884	5.6

DIETRICK, COBY
b. July 23, 1948 Ht. 6-10½ Wt. 230 College—San Jose St.

Yr.	Team		G	FG	FT	TP	Avg.
1970-71	Memphis	(ABA)	37	61	21	143	3.8
1971-72	Memphis	(ABA)	1	1	0	2	2.0
1972-73	Dallas	(ABA)	77	205	96	506	6.6
1973-74	San Antonio	(ABA)	84	251	81	583	6.9
1974-75	San Antonio	(ABA)	82	222(2)	76	522	6.4
1975-76	San Antonio	(ABA)	81	200(1)	68	469	5.8
1976-77	San Antonio		82	285	119	689	8.4
1977-78	San Antonio		79	250	89	589	7.5
1978-79	San Antonio		76	209	79	497	6.5
1979-80	Chicago		79	227(1)	90	545	6.9
1980-81	Chicago		82	146(2)	77	371	4.5
	Totals		760	2057(6)	796	4916	6.5

Yr.	Team	G	FG	FT	TP	Avg.

DONALDSON, JAMES
b. Aug. 16, 1957 Ht. 7-2 Wt. 270 College—Washington State

Yr.	Team	G	FG	FT	TP	Avg.
1980-81	Seattle	68	129	101	359	5.3

DORSEY, JACKY
b. Dec. 18, 1954 Ht. 6-7 Wt. 230 College—Georgia

Yr.	Team	G	FG	FT	TP	Avg.
1977-78	Denv.-Port.	11	12	10	34	3.1
1978-79	Houston	20	24	8	56	2.8
1980-81	Seattle	29	20	13	53	1.8
	Totals	60	56	31	143	2.4

DOUGLAS, LEON
b. Aug. 26, 1954 Ht. 6-10 Wt. 230 College—Alabama

Yr.	Team	G	FG	FT	TP	Avg.
1976-77	Detroit	82	245	127	617	7.5
1977-78	Detroit	79	321	221	863	10.9
1978-79	Detroit	78	342	208	892	11.4
1979-80	Detroit	70	221	125	567	8.1
1980-81	Kansas City	79	185	102	472	6.0
	Totals	388	1314	783	3411	8.8

DREW, JOHN
b. Sept. 30, 1954 Ht. 6-6 Wt. 205 College—Gardner-Webb

Yr.	Team	G	FG	FT	TP	Avg.
1974-75	Atlanta	78	527	388	1442	18.5
1975-76	Atlanta	77	586	488	1660	21.6
1976-77	Atlanta	74	689	412	1790	24.2
1977-78	Atlanta	70	593	437	1623	23.2
1978-79	Atlanta	79	650	495	1795	22.7
1979-80	Atlanta	80	535	489	1559	19.5
1980-81	Atlanta	67	500	454	1454	21.7
	Totals	525	4080	3163	11323	21.6

DREW, LARRY
b. April 2, 1958 Ht. 6-1 Wt. 170 College—Missouri

Yr.	Team	G	FG	FT	TP	Avg.
1980-81	Detroit	76	197(4)	106	504	6.6

DROLLINGER, RALPH
b. April 20, 1954 Ht. 7-2 Wt. 250 College—UCLA

Yr.	Team	G	FG	FT	TP	Avg.
1980-81	Dallas	6	7	1	15	2.5

DUEROD, TERRY
b. July 29, 1956 Ht. 6-2 Wt. 180 College—Detroit

Yr.	Team	G	FG	FT	TP	Avg.
1979-80	Detroit	67	282(15)	45	624	9.3
1980-81	Dal.-Bos.	50	104(8)	31	247	4.9
	Totals	117	386(23)	76	871	7.4

DUNLEAVY, MIKE
b. March 21, 1954 Ht. 6-3 Wt. 180 College—South Carolina

Yr.	Team	G	FG	FT	TP	Avg.
1976-77	Philadelphia	32	60	34	154	4.8
1977-78	Phil.-Hou.	15	20	13	53	3.5
1978-79	Houston	74	215	159	589	8.0
1979-80	Houston	51	148(3)	111	410	8.0
1980-81	Houston	74	310(1)	156	777	10.5
	Totals	246	753(4)	473	1983	8.1

DUNN, THEODORE ROOSEVELT (T.R.)
b. Feb. 1, 1955 Ht. 6-4 Wt. 192 College—Alabama

Yr.	Team	G	FG	FT	TP	Avg.
1977-78	Portland	63	100	37	237	3.8
1978-79	Portland	80	246	122	614	7.7
1979-80	Portland	82	240	84	564	6.9
1980-81	Denver	82	146	79	371	4.5
	Totals	299	732	322	1786	6.0

DUREN, JOHN
b. Oct. 30, 1958 Ht. 6-3 Wt. 195 College—Georgetown

Yr.	Team	G	FG	FT	TP	Avg.
1980-81	Utah	40	33	5	71	1.8

EDWARDS, JAMES
b. Nov. 22, 1955 Ht. 7-0 Wt. 225 College—Washington

Yr.	Team	G	FG	FT	TP	Avg.
1977-78	L.A.-Ind.	83	495	272	1262	15.2
1978-79	Indiana	82	534	298	1366	16.7
1979-80	Indiana	82	528	231	1287	15.7
1980-81	Indiana	81	511	244	1266	15.6
	Totals	328	2068	1045	5181	15.8

ELLIOTT, BOB
b. Aug. 18, 1955 Ht. 6-9½ Wt. 225 College—Arizona

Yr.	Team	G	FG	FT	TP	Avg.
1978-79	New Jersey	14	41	41	123	8.8
1979-80	New Jersey	54	101(1)	104	307	5.7
1980-81	New Jersey	73	214(1)	121	550	7.5
	Totals	141	356(2)	266	980	7.0

ELMORE, LEN
b. March 28, 1952 Ht. 6-10 Wt. 230 College—Maryland

Yr.	Team		G	FG	FT	TP	Avg.
1974-75	Indiana	(ABA)	77	218(1)	72	509	6.6
1975-76	Indiana	(ABA)	76	480	152	1112	14.6
1976-77	Indiana		6	7	4	18	3.0
1977-78	Indiana		69	142	88	372	5.4
1978-79	Indiana		80	139	56	334	4.2
1979-80	Kansas City		58	104	51	259	4.5
1980-81	Milwaukee		72	76	54	206	2.9
	Totals		438	1166(1)	477	2810	6.4

ENGLISH, ALEX
b. Jan. 5, 1954 Ht. 6-7 Wt. 190 College—South Carolina

Yr.	Team	G	FG	FT	TP	Avg.
1976-77	Milwaukee	60	132	46	310	5.2
1977-78	Milwaukee	82	343	104	790	9.6
1978-79	Indiana	81	563	173	1299	16.0
1979-80	Ind.-Denv.	78	553(2)	210	1318	16.9
1980-81	Denver	81	768(3)	390	1929	23.8
	Totals	382	2359(5)	923	5646	14.8

ERVING, JULIUS
b. Feb. 22, 1950 Ht. 6-6 Wt. 200 College—Massachusetts

Yr.	Team		G	FG	FT	TP	Avg.
1971-72	Virginia	(ABA)	84	910(3)	467	2290	27.3
1972-73	Virginia	(ABA)	71	894(5)	475	2268	31.9
1973-74	New York	(ABA)	84	914(17)	454	2299	27.4
1974-75	New York	(ABA)	84	914(29)	486	2343	27.9
1975-76	New York	(ABA)	84	949(34)	530	2462	29.3
1976-77	Philadelphia		82	685	400	1770	21.6
1977-78	Philadelphia		74	611	306	1528	20.6
1978-79	Philadelphia		78	715	373	1803	23.1
1979-80	Philadelphia		78	838(4)	420	2100	26.9
1980-81	Philadelphia		82	794(4)	422	2014	24.6
	Totals		801	8224(96)	4333	20877	26.1

EVANS, MIKE
b. Apr. 19, 1955 Ht. 6-1 Wt. 170 College—Kansas State

Yr.	Team	G	FG	FT	TP	Avg.
1979-80	San Antonio	79	208(12)	58	486	6.2
1980-81	Milwaukee	71	134(2)	50	320	4.5
	Totals	150	342(14)	108	806	5.4

Yr.	Team	G	FG	FT	TP	Avg.

FERNSTEN, ERIC
b. Nov. 1, 1953 Ht. 6-10 Wt. 205 College—San Francisco

Yr.	Team	G	FG	FT	TP	Avg.
1975-76	Cleve.-Chi.	37	33	26	92	2.5
1976-77	Chicago	5	3	8	14	2.8
1979-80	Boston	56	71	33	175	3.1
1980-81	Boston	45	38	20	96	2.1
	Totals	143	145	87	377	2.6

FORD, CHRIS
b. Jan. 11, 1949 Ht. 6-5 Wt. 190 College—Villanova

Yr.	Team	G	FG	FT	TP	Avg.
1972-73	Detroit	74	208	60	476	6.4
1973-74	Detroit	82	264	57	585	7.1
1974-75	Detroit	80	206	63	475	5.9
1975-76	Detroit	82	301	83	685	8.4
1976-77	Detroit	82	437	131	1005	12.3
1977-78	Detroit	82	374	113	861	10.5
1978-79	Det.-Bost.	81	538	172	1248	15.4
1979-80	Boston	73	330(70)	86	816	11.2
1980-81	Boston	82	314(36)	64	728	8.9
	Totals	718	2972(106)	829	6879	9.6

FORD, DON
b. Dec. 31, 1952 Ht. 6-8 Wt. 215 College—N. Mex./S. Barbara

Yr.	Team	G	FG	FT	TP	Avg.
1975-76	Los Angeles	76	311	104	726	9.6
1976-77	Los Angeles	82	262	73	597	7.3
1977-78	Los Angeles	79	272	68	612	7.7
1978-79	Los Angeles	79	228	72	528	6.7
1979-80	L.A.-Clev.	73	131(1)	45	308	4.2
1980-81	Cleveland	64	100	22	222	3.5
	Totals	453	1304(1)	384	2993	6.6

FORD, PHIL
b. Feb. 9, 1956 Ht. 6-2 Wt. 176 College—North Carolina

Yr.	Team	G	FG	FT	TP	Avg.
1978-79	Kansas City	79	467	326	1260	15.9
1979-80	Kansas City	82	489(4)	346	1328	16.2
1980-81	Kansas City	66	424(11)	294	1153	17.5
	Totals	227	1380(15)	966	3741	16.5

FREE, LLOYD
b. Dec. 9, 1953 Ht. 6-1 Wt. 185 College—Guilford

Yr.	Team	G	FG	FT	TP	Avg.
1975-76	Philadelphia	71	239	112	590	8.3
1976-77	Philadelphia	78	467	334	1268	16.3
1977-78	Philadelphia	76	390	411	1191	15.7
1978-79	San Diego	78	795	654	2244	28.8
1979-80	San Diego	68	737(9)	572	2055	30.2
1980-81	Golden State	65	516(5)	528	1565	24.1
	Totals	436	3144(14)	2611	8913	20.4

FULLER, TONY
b. Sept. 4, 1958 Ht. 6-4 Wt. 185 College—Pepperdine

Yr.	Team	G	FG	FT	TP	Avg.
1980-81	Detroit	15	24	12	60	4.0

GALE, MIKE
b. July 18, 1950 Ht. 6-1 Wt. 190 College—Elizabeth City

Yr.	Team		G	FG	FT	TP	Avg.
1971-72	Kentucky	(ABA)	78	201	95	497	6.4
1972-73	Kentucky	(ABA)	81	218(1)	100	537	6.6
1973-74	Ken.-N.Y.	(ABA)	80	314(2)	105	735	9.2
1974-75	New York	(ABA)	72	228(7)	72	535	7.4
1975-76	San Antonio	(ABA)	78	230(3)	64	527	6.8
1976-77	San Antonio		82	353	137	843	10.3
1977-78	San Antonio		70	275	87	637	9.1
1978-79	San Antonio		82	284	91	659	8.0
1979-80	San Antonio		67	171(2)	97	441	6.6
1980-81	S.A.-Port.		77	157(2)	55	371	4.8
	Totals		767	2431(17)	903	5782	7.5

GARRETT, CALVIN
b. July 11, 1956 Ht. 6-7 Wt. 190 College—Aust. Peay/Oral Rbts

Yr.	Team	G	FG	FT	TP	Avg.
1980-81	Houston	70	188(1)	50	427	6.1

GERARD, GUS
b. July 27, 1953 Ht. 6-8 Wt. 200 College—Virginia

Yr.	Team		G	FG	FT	TP	Avg.
1974-75	St. Louis	(ABA)	84	554(1)	206	1315	15.7
1975-76	St. L.-Den.	(ABA)	82	332(4)	175	843	10.3
1976-77	Den.-Buf.		65	201	78	480	7.4
1977-78	Buf.-Det.		57	170	75	415	7.3
1978-79	Det.-K.C.		58	84	50	218	3.8
1979-80	Kansas City		73	159(1)	66	385	5.3
1980-81	K.C.-S.A.		27	41	27	109	4.0
	Totals		446	1541(6)	677	3765	8.4

GERVIN, GEORGE
b. April 27, 1952 Ht. 6-7 Wt. 185 College—Long Beach State /E. Mich.

Yr.	Team		G	FG	FT	TP	Avg.
1972-73	Virginia	(ABA)	30	155(6)	96	424	14.1
1973-74	Virg.-S.A.	(ABA)	74	672(8)	378	1730	23.4
1974-75	San Antonio	(ABA)	84	784(17)	380	1965	23.4
1975-76	San Antonio	(ABA)	81	706(14)	342	1768	21.8
1976-77	San Antonio		82	726	443	1895	23.1
1977-78	San Antonio		82	864	504	2232	27.2
1978-79	San Antonio		80	947	471	2365	29.6
1979-80	San Antonio		78	1024(32)	505	2585	33.1
1980-81	San Antonio		82	850(9)	512	2221	27.1
	Totals		673	6734(86)	3631	17185	25.5

GILMORE, ARTIS
b. Sept. 21, 1949 Ht. 7-2 Wt. 240 College—Jacksonville

Yr.	Team		G	FG	FT	TP	Avg.
1971-72	Kentucky	(ABA)	84	806	391	2003	23.9
1972-73	Kentucky	(ABA)	84	687(1)	368	1743	20.9
1973-74	Kentucky	(ABA)	84	621	326	1568	18.7
1974-75	Kentucky	(ABA)	84	784(1)	412	1981	23.6
1975-76	Kentucky	(ABA)	84	773	521	2067	24.6
1976-77	Chicago		82	570	387	1527	18.6
1977-78	Chicago		82	704	471	1879	22.9
1978-79	Chicago		82	753	434	1940	23.7
1979-80	Chicago		48	305	245	855	17.8
1980-81	Chicago		82	547	375	1469	17.9
	Totals		796	6550(2)	3930	17032	21.4

GLENN, MIKE
b. Sept. 10, 1955 Ht. 6-3 Wt. 175 College—Southern Illinois

Yr.	Team	G	FG	FT	TP	Avg.
1977-78	Buffalo	56	195	51	441	7.9
1978-79	New York	75	263	57	583	7.8
1979-80	New York	75	188(2)	63	441	5.9
1980-81	New York	82	285(4)	98	672	8.2
	Totals	288	931(6)	269	2137	7.4

GMINSKI, MIKE
b. Aug. 3, 1959 Ht. 6-11 Wt. 250 College—Duke

Yr.	Team	G	FG	FT	TP	Avg.
1980-81	New Jersey	56	291	155	737	13.2

Yr.	Team	G	FG	FT	TP	Avg.

GONDREZICK, GLEN
b. Aug. 30, 1955 Ht. 6-6 Wt. 218 College—NV Las Vegas

Yr.	Team	G	FG	FT	TP	Avg.
1977-78	New York	72	131	83	345	4.8
1978-79	New York	75	161	55	377	5.0
1979-80	Denver	59	148(2)	92	390	6.6
1980-81	Denver	73	155	112	422	5.8
	Totals	279	595(2)	342	1534	5.5

GREEN, RICKEY
b. Aug. 18, 1954 Ht. 6-2 Wt. 170 College—Michigan

Yr.	Team	G	FG	FT	TP	Avg.
1977-78	Golden State	76	143	54	340	4.5
1978-79	Detroit	27	67	45	179	6.6
1980-81	Utah	47	176	70	422	9.0
	Totals	150	386	169	941	6.3

GREENWOOD, DAVID
b. May 27, 1957 Ht. 6-9½ Wt. 222 College—UCLA

Yr.	Team	G	FG	FT	TP	Avg.
1979-80	Chicago	82	498(1)	337	1334	16.3
1980-81	Chicago	82	481	217	1179	14.4
	Totals	164	979(1)	554	2513	15.3

GREVEY, KEVIN
b. May 12, 1953 Ht. 6-5 Wt. 210 College—Kentucky

Yr.	Team	G	FG	FT	TP	Avg.
1975-76	Washington	56	79	52	210	3.8
1976-77	Washington	76	224	79	527	6.9
1977-78	Washington	81	505	243	1253	15.5
1978-79	Washington	65	418	173	1009	15.5
1979-80	Washington	65	331(34)	216	912	14.0
1980-81	Washington	75	500(45)	244	1289	17.2
	Totals	418	2057(79)	1007	5200	12.4

GRIFFIN, PAUL
b. Jan. 1, 1954 Ht. 6-9 Wt. 205 College—W. Michigan

Yr.	Team	G	FG	FT	TP	Avg.
1976-77	New Orleans	81	140	145	425	5.2
1977-78	New Orleans	82	160	112	432	5.3
1978-79	New Orleans	77	106	91	303	3.9
1979-80	San Antonio	82	173	174	520	6.3
1980-81	San Antonio	82	166	170	502	6.1
	Totals	404	745	692	2182	5.4

GRIFFITH, DARRELL
b. June 16, 1958 Ht. 6-4 Wt. 190 College—Louisville

Yr.	Team	G	FG	FT	TP	Avg.
1980-81	Utah	81	716(10)	229	1671	20.6

GROSS, BOB
b. Aug. 3, 1953 Ht. 6-6 Wt. 200 College—Long Beach St.

Yr.	Team	G	FG	FT	TP	Avg.
1975-76	Portland	76	209	97	515	6.8
1976-77	Portland	82	376	183	935	11.4
1977-78	Portland	72	381	152	914	12.7
1978-79	Portland	53	209	96	514	9.7
1979-80	Portland	62	221(1)	95	538	8.7
1980-81	Portland	82	253	135	641	7.8
	Totals	427	1649(1)	758	4057	9.5

GRUNFELD, ERNIE
b. April 24, 1955 Ht. 6-6 Wt. 215 College—Tennessee

Yr.	Team	G	FG	FT	TP	Avg.
1977-78	Milwaukee	73	204	94	502	6.9
1978-79	Milwaukee	82	326	191	843	10.3
1979-80	Kansas City	80	186(1)	101	474	5.9
1980-81	Kansas City	79	260	75	595	7.5
	Totals	314	976(1)	461	2414	7.7

HAMILTON, ROY
b. July 20, 1957 Ht. 6-2 Wt. 180 College—UCLA

Yr.	Team	G	FG	FT	TP	Avg.
1979-80	Detroit	72	115	103	333	4.6
1980-81	Portland	1	1	1	3	3.0
	Totals	73	116	104	336	4.6

HANZLIK, BILL
b. Dec. 6, 1957 Ht. 6-7 Wt. 185 College—Notre Dame

Yr.	Team	G	FG	FT	TP	Avg.
1980-81	Seattle	74	138(1)	119	396	5.4

HARDY, ALAN
b. May 25, 1957 Ht. 6-7 Wt. 195 College—Michigan

Yr.	Team	G	FG	FT	TP	Avg.
1980-81	Los Angeles	22	22	7	51	2.3

HARDY, JAMES
b. Dec. 1, 1956 Ht. 6-8 Wt. 220 College—San Fran.

Yr.	Team	G	FG	FT	TP	Avg.
1978-79	New Orleans	68	196	61	453	6.7
1979-80	Utah	76	184(1)	51	420	5.5
1980-81	Utah	23	52	11	115	5.0
	Totals	167	432(1)	123	988	5.9

HARPER, MIKE
b. Dec. 9, 1957 Ht. 6-10 Wt. 195 College—North Park

Yr.	Team	G	FG	FT	TP	Avg.
1980-81	Portland	55	56	37	149	2.7

HASSETT, JOE
b. Sept. 11, 1955 Ht. 6-5 Wt. 180 College—Providence

Yr.	Team	G	FG	FT	TP	Avg.
1977-78	Seattle	48	91	10	192	4.0
1978-79	Seattle	55	100	23	223	4.1
1979-80	Indiana	74	215(69)	24	523	7.1
1980-81	Dallas-G.S.	41	143(53)	17	356	8.7
	Totals	218	549(122)	74	1294	5.9

HAWES, STEVE
b. May 26, 1950 Ht. 6-9 Wt. 220 College—Washington

Yr.	Team	G	FG	FT	TP	Avg.
1974-75	Houston	55	140	45	325	5.9
1975-76	Hou.-Port.	72	199	87	485	6.7
1976-77	Atlanta	44	147	67	361	8.2
1977-78	Atlanta	75	387	175	949	12.7
1978-79	Atlanta	81	372	108	852	10.5
1979-80	Atlanta	82	304(3)	150	761	9.3
1980-81	Atlanta	74	333(1)	222	889	12.0
	Totals	483	1882(4)	854	4622	9.6

HAYES, ELVIN
b. Nov. 17, 1945 Ht. 6-9 Wt. 235 College—Houston

Yr.	Team	G	FG	FT	TP	Avg.
1968-69	San Diego	82	930	467	2327	28.4
1969-70	San Diego	82	914	428	2256	27.5
1970-71	San Diego	82	948	454	2350	28.7
1971-72	Houston	82	832	399	2063	25.2
1972-73	Baltimore	81	713	291	1717	21.2
1973-74	Capital	81	689	357	1735	21.4
1974-75	Washington	82	739	409	1887	23.0
1975-76	Washington	80	649	287	1585	19.8
1976-77	Washington	82	760	422	1942	23.7
1977-78	Washington	81	636	326	1598	19.7
1978-79	Washington	82	720	349	1789	21.8
1979-80	Washington	81	761(3)	334	1859	23.0
1980-81	Washington	81	584	271	1439	17.8
	Totals	1059	9875(3)	4797	24547	23.2

Yr.	Team	G	FG	FT	TP	Avg.

HEARD, GARFIELD
b. May 3, 1948 Ht. 6-8 Wt. 220 College—Oklahoma

Yr.	Team	G	FG	FT	TP	Avg.
1970-71	Seattle	65	152	82	386	5.9
1971-72	Seattle	58	190	79	459	7.9
1972-73	Sea.-Chi.	81	350	116	816	10.1
1973-74	Buffalo	81	524	191	1239	15.3
1974-75	Buffalo	67	318	106	742	11.1
1975-76	Phoenix	86	392	158	942	11.0
1976-77	Phoenix	46	173	100	446	9.7
1977-78	Phoenix	80	265	90	620	7.8
1978-79	Phoenix	63	162	71	395	6.3
1979-80	Phoenix	82	171	64	406	5.0
1980-81	San Diego	78	149	79	377	4.8
	Totals	787	2846	1136	6828	8.7

HENDERSON, GERALD
b. Jan. 16, 1956 Ht. 6-2 Wt. 175 College—Va. Commonwealth

Yr.	Team	G	FG	FT	TP	Avg.
1979-80	Boston	76	191(2)	89	473	6.2
1980-81	Boston	82	261(1)	113	636	7.8
	Totals	158	452(3)	202	1109	7.0

HENDERSON, TOM
b. Jan. 26, 1952 Ht. 6-3 Wt. 190 College—Hawaii

Yr.	Team	G	FG	FT	TP	Avg.
1974-75	Atlanta	79	367	168	902	11.4
1975-76	Atlanta	81	469	216	1154	14.2
1976-77	Atl.-Wash.	87	371	233	975	11.2
1977-78	Washington	75	339	179	857	11.4
1978-79	Washington	70	299	156	754	10.8
1979-80	Houston	66	154	56	364	5.5
1980-81	Houston	66	137	78	352	5.3
	Totals	524	2136	1086	5358	10.2

HERRON, KEITH
b. June 14, 1956 Ht. 6-6 Wt. 195 College—Villanova

Yr.	Team	G	FG	FT	TP	Avg.
1978-79	Atlanta	14	14	12	40	2.9
1980-81	Detroit	80	432(2)	228	1094	13.7
	Totals	94	446(2)	240	1134	12.1

HIGGS, KEN
b. Jan. 31, 1955 Ht. 6-0 Wt. 185 College—Louisiana St.

Yr.	Team	G	FG	FT	TP	Avg.
1978-79	Cleveland	68	127	85	339	5.0
1980-81	Denver	72	209(4)	140	562	7.8
	Totals	140	336(4)	225	901	6.4

HIGH, JOHNNY
b. Apr. 25, 1957 Ht. 6-3 Wt. 185 College—Nevada-Reno

Yr.	Team	G	FG	FT	TP	Avg.
1979-80	Phoenix	82	144(1)	120	409	5.0
1980-81	Phoenix	81	246(2)	183	677	8.4
	Totals	163	390(3)	303	1086	6.7

HILL, ARMOND
b. March 31, 1953 Ht. 6-4 Wt. 190 College—Princeton

Yr.	Team	G	FG	FT	TP	Avg.
1976-77	Atlanta	81	175	139	489	6.0
1977-78	Atlanta	82	304	189	797	9.7
1978-79	Atlanta	82	296	246	838	10.2
1979-80	Atlanta	79	177(1)	124	479	6.1
1980-81	Atl.-Seattle	75	117	141	375	5.0
	Totals	399	1069(1)	839	2978	7.5

Yr.	Team	G	FG	FT	TP	Avg.

HOLLAND, J. BRADLEY (Brad)
b. Dec. 6, 1956 Ht. 6-3 Wt. 185 College—UCLA

Yr.	Team	G	FG	FT	TP	Avg.
1979-80	Los Angeles	38	44(3)	15	106	2.8
1980-81	Los Angeles	41	47(1)	35	130	3.2
	Totals	79	91(4)	50	236	3.0

HOLLINS, LIONEL
b. Oct. 19, 1953 Ht. 6-3 Wt. 185 College—Arizona St.

Yr.	Team	G	FG	FT	TP	Avg.
1975-76	Portland	74	311	178	800	10.8
1976-77	Portland	76	452	215	1119	14.7
1977-78	Portland	81	531	223	1285	15.9
1978-79	Portland	64	402	172	976	15.3
1979-80	Port.-Phil.	47	212(3)	101	528	11.2
1980-81	Philadelphia	82	327(2)	125	781	9.5
	Totals	424	2235(5)	1014	5489	12.9

HORDGES, CEDRICK
b. Jan. 8, 1957 Ht. 6-8 Wt. 220 College—South Carolina

Yr.	Team	G	FG	FT	TP	Avg.
1980-81	Denver	68	221	130	572	8.4

HUBBARD, PHIL
b. Dec. 13, 1956 Ht. 6-8 Wt. 215 College—Michigan

Yr.	Team	G	FG	FT	TP	Avg.
1979-80	Detroit	64	210	165	585	9.1
1980-81	Detroit	80	433(1)	294	1161	14.5
	Totals	144	643(1)	459	1746	12.1

HUGHES, KIM
b. June 4, 1952 Ht. 6-11 Wt. 220 College—Wisconsin

Yr.	Team		G	FG	FT	TP	Avg.
1975-76	New York	(ABA)	84	300	92	692	8.2
1976-77	N.Y. Nets		81	151	19	321	4.0
1977-78	New Jersey		56	57	9	123	2.2
1978-79	Denver		81	98	18	214	2.6
1979-80	Denver		70	102	15	219	3.1
1980-81	Den.-Clev.		53	27	1	55	1.0
	Totals		425	735	154	1624	3.8

HUSTON, GEOFF
b. Nov. 8, 1957 Ht. 6-2 Wt. 175 College—Texas Tech

Yr.	Team	G	FG	FT	TP	Avg.
1979-80	New York	71	94(3)	28	219	3.1
1980-81	Dal.-Clev.	81	461(1)	150	1073	13.2
	Totals	152	555(4)	178	1292	8.5

ISSEL, DAN
b. Oct. 25, 1948 Ht. 6-9 Wt. 240 College—Kentucky

Yr.	Team		G	FG	FT	TP	Avg.
1970-71	Kentucky	(ABA)	83	938	604	2480	29.9
1971-72	Kentucky	(ABA)	83	972(3)	591	2538	30.6
1972-73	Kentucky	(ABA)	84	902(3)	485	2292	27.3
1973-74	Kentucky	(ABA)	83	829(3)	457	2118	25.5
1974-75	Kentucky	(ABA)	83	614	237	1465	17.7
1975-76	Denver	(ABA)	84	752(1)	425	1930	23.0
1976-77	Denver		79	660	445	1765	22.3
1977-78	Denver		82	659	428	1746	21.3
1978-79	Denver		81	532	316	1380	17.0
1979-80	Denver		82	715(4)	517	1951	23.8
1980-81	Denver		80	614(2)	519	1749	21.9
	Totals		904	8187(16)	5024	21414	23.7

JACKSON, TONY
b. Jan. 17, 1958 Ht. 6-0 Wt. 175 College—Florida State

Yr.	Team	G	FG	FT	TP	Avg.
1980-81	Los Angeles	2	1	0	2	1.0

Yr.	Team		G	FG	FT	TP	Avg.
JEELANI, ABDUL							
b. Feb. 10, 1954 Ht. 6-8 Wt. 210 College—Wisc.-Parkside							
1979-80	Portland		77	288	161	737	9.6
1980-81	Dallas		66	187	179	553	8.4
		Totals	143	475	340	1290	9.0
JOHNSON, CLEMON							
b. Sept. 12, 1956 Ht. 6-10 Wt. 240 College—Fla. A&M							
1978-79	Portland		74	102	36	240	3.2
1979-80	Indiana		79	199	74	472	6.0
1980-81	Indiana		81	235	112	582	7.2
		Totals	234	536	222	1294	5.5
JOHNSON, DENNIS							
b. Sept. 18, 1954 Ht. 6-4 Wt. 210 College—Pepperdine							
1976-77	Seattle		81	285	179	749	9.2
1977-78	Seattle		81	367	297	1031	12.7
1978-79	Seattle		80	482	306	1270	15.9
1979-80	Seattle		81	574(12)	380	1540	19.0
1980-81	Phoenix		79	532(11)	411	1486	18.8
		Totals	402	2240(23)	1573	6076	15.1
JOHNSON, EARVIN (Magic)							
b. Aug. 14, 1959 Ht. 6-8 Wt. 215 College—Michigan State							
1979-80	Los Angeles		77	503(7)	374	1387	18.0
1980-81	Los Angeles		37	312(3)	171	798	21.6
		Totals	114	815(10)	545	2185	19.2
JOHNSON, EDDIE							
b. Feb. 24, 1955 Ht. 6-2 Wt. 175 College—Auburn							
1977-78	Atlanta		79	332	164	828	10.5
1978-79	Atlanta		78	501	243	1245	16.0
1979-80	Atlanta		79	590(5)	280	1465	18.5
1980-81	Atlanta		75	573(6)	279	1431	19.1
		Totals	291	1996(11)	966	4969	17.1
JOHNSON, GEORGE							
b. Dec. 8, 1956 Ht. 6-7 Wt. 205 College—St. John's (NY)							
1978-79	Milwaukee		67	165	84	414	6.2
1979-80	Denver		75	309(2)	148	768	10.2
1980-81	Indiana		43	182	93	457	10.6
		Totals	185	656(2)	325	1639	8.9
JOHNSON, GEORGE T.							
b. Dec. 18, 1948 Ht. 6-11 Wt. 205 College—Dillard							
1972-73	Golden State		56	41	7	89	1.6
1973-74	Golden State		66	173	59	405	6.1
1974-75	Golden State		82	152	60	364	4.4
1975-76	Golden State		82	165	70	400	4.9
1976-77	G.S.-Buf.		78	198	71	467	6.0
1977-78	New Jersey		81	285	133	703	8.7
1978-79	New Jersey		78	206	105	517	6.6
1979-80	New Jersey		81	248	89	585	7.2
1980-81	San Antonio		82	164	80	408	5.0
		Totals	686	1362	674	3938	5.7

Yr.	Team		G	FG	FT	TP	Avg.
JOHNSON, JOHN							
b. Oct. 18, 1947 Ht. 6-7 Wt. 200 College—Iowa							
1970-71	Cleveland		67	435	240	1110	16.6
1971-72	Cleveland		82	557	277	1391	17.0
1972-73	Cleveland		82	492	199	1183	14.4
1973-74	Portland		69	459	212	1130	16.4
1974-75	Portland		80	527	236	1290	16.1
1975-76	Port.-Hou.		76	316	120	752	9.9
1976-77	Houston		79	319	94	732	9.3
1977-78	Hou.-Sea.		77	342	133	817	10.6
1978-79	Seattle		82	356	190	902	11.0
1979-80	Seattle		81	377	161	915	11.3
1980-81	Seattle		80	373	173	919	11.5
		Totals	855	4553	2035	11141	13.0
JOHNSON, LEE							
b. June 16, 1957 Ht. 6-11 Wt. 210 College—Montana/E. Tex. St.							
1980-81	Hou.-Det.		12	7	3	17	1.4
JOHNSON, MARQUES							
b. Feb. 8, 1956 Ht. 6-7 Wt. 218 College—UCLA							
1977-78	Milwaukee		80	628	301	1557	19.5
1978-79	Milwaukee		77	820	332	1972	25.6
1979-80	Milwaukee		77	689(2)	291	1671	21.7
1980-81	Milwaukee		76	636	269	1541	20.3
		Totals	310	2773(2)	1193	6741	21.7
JOHNSON, OLLIE							
b. April 11, 1949 Ht. 6-6 Wt. 200 College—Temple							
1972-73	Portland		78	308	156	772	9.9
1973-74	Portland		79	209	77	495	6.3
1974-75	N.O.-K.C.-O.		73	203	95	501	6.9
1975-76	Kansas City		81	348	125	821	10.1
1976-77	Kansas City		81	218	101	537	6.6
1977-78	Atlanta		82	292	111	695	8.5
1978-79	Chicago		71	281	88	650	9.2
1979-80	Chicago		79	262(1)	82	607	7.7
1980-81	Philadelphia		40	87(1)	27	202	5.1
		Totals	664	2208(2)	862	5280	8.0
JOHNSON, REGGIE							
b. June 25, 1957 Ht. 6-9 Wt. 205 College—Tennessee							
1980-81	San Antonio		79	340	128	808	10.2
JOHNSON, VINNIE							
b. Sept. 1, 1956 Ht. 6-2 Wt. 200 College—Baylor							
1979-80	Seattle		38	45	31	121	3.2
1980-81	Seattle		81	419(1)	214	1053	13.0
		Totals	119	464(1)	245	1174	9.9
JOHNSON, WALLACE (Mickey)							
b. Aug. 31, 1952 Ht. 6-10 Wt. 190 College—Aurora							
1974-75	Chicago		38	53	37	143	3.8
1975-76	Chicago		81	478	283	1239	15.3
1976-77	Chicago		81	538	324	1400	17.3
1977-78	Chicago		81	561	362	1484	18.3
1978-79	Chicago		82	496	273	1265	15.4
1979-80	Indiana		82	588(5)	385	1566	19.1
1980-81	Milwaukee		82	379(3)	262	1023	12.5
		Totals	527	3093(8)	1926	8120	15.4

Yr.	Team		G	FG	FT	TP	Avg.

JONES, BOBBY
b. Dec. 18, 1951 Ht. 6-9 Wt. 210 College—No. Carolina

Yr.	Team		G	FG	FT	TP	Avg.
1974-75	Denver	(ABA)	84	529	187	1245	14.8
1975-76	Denver	(ABA)	83	510	215	1235	14.9
1976-77	Denver		82	501	236	1238	15.1
1977-78	Denver		75	440	208	1088	14.5
1978-79	Philadelphia		80	378	209	965	12.1
1979-80	Philadelphia		81	398	257	1053	13.0
1980-81	Philadelphia		81	407	282	1096	13.5
	Totals		566	3163	1594	7920	14.0

JONES, CALDWELL
b. Aug. 4, 1950 Ht. 6-11 Wt. 213 Coll.—Albany St. (Ga.)

Yr.	Team		G	FG	FT	TP	Avg.
1973-74	San Diego	(ABA)	79	507(2)	171	1187	15.0
1974-75	San Diego	(ABA)	76	606(3)	264	1479	19.5
1975-76	S.D.-Ken.-St. L.	(ABA)	76	423	140	986	13.0
1976-77	Philadelphia		82	215	64	494	6.0
1977-78	Philadelphia		81	169	96	434	5.4
1978-79	Philadelphia		78	302	121	725	9.3
1979-80	Philadelphia		80	232	124	588	7.4
1980-81	Philadelphia		81	218	148	584	7.2
	Totals		633	2672(5)	1128	6477	10.2

JONES, DWIGHT
b. Feb. 27, 1952 Ht. 6-10 Wt. 210 College—Houston

Yr.	Team	G	FG	FT	TP	Avg.
1973-74	Atlanta	74	238	116	592	8.0
1974-75	Atlanta	75	323	132	778	10.4
1975-76	Atlanta	66	251	163	665	10.1
1976-77	Houston	74	167	101	435	5.9
1977-78	Houston	82	346	181	873	10.6
1978-79	Houston	81	181	96	458	5.7
1979-80	Hous.-Chic.	74	257	146	660	8.9
1980-81	Chicago	81	245	125	615	7.6
	Totals	607	2008	1060	5076	8.4

JONES, EDGAR
b. June 17, 1956 Ht. 6-10 Wt. 225 College—Nevada-Reno

Yr.	Team	G	FG	FT	TP	Avg.
1980-81	New Jersey	60	189	146	524	8.7

JONES, MAJOR
b. July 9, 1953 Ht. 6-9 Wt. 225 College—Albany State

Yr.	Team	G	FG	FT	TP	Avg.
1979-80	Houston	82	188(1)	61	438	5.3
1980-81	Houston	68	117	64	298	4.4
	Totals	150	305(1)	125	736	4.9

JORDAN, ED
b. Jan. 29, 1955 Ht. 6-1 Wt. 170 College—Rutgers

Yr.	Team	G	FG	FT	TP	Avg.
1977-78	Cleve.-N.J.	73	215	131	561	7.7
1978-79	New Jersey	82	401	213	1015	12.4
1979-80	New Jersey	82	437(12)	201	1087	13.3
1980-81	N.J.-L.A.	74	150(6)	87	393	5.3
	Totals	311	1203(18)	632	3056	9.8

JORDAN, WALTER
b. Feb. 19, 1956 Ht. 6-8 Wt. 210 College—Purdue

Yr.	Team	G	FG	FT	TP	Avg.
1980-81	Cleveland	30	29	10	68	2.3

JUDKINS, JEFF
b. March 23, 1956 Ht. 6-6 Wt. 185 College—Utah

Yr.	Team	G	FG	FT	TP	Avg.
1978-79	Boston	81	295	119	709	8.8
1979-80	Boston	65	139(11)	62	351	5.4
1980-81	Utah	62	92(9)	45	238	3.8
	Totals	208	526(20)	226	1298	6.2

KEA, CLARENCE
b. Feb. 12, 1959 Ht. 6-7 Wt. 220 College—Lamar

Yr.	Team	G	FG	FT	TP	Avg.
1980-81	Dallas	16	37	43	117	7.3

KELLEY, RICH
b. March 23, 1953 Ht. 7-0 Wt. 230 College—Stanford

Yr.	Team	G	FG	FT	TP	Avg.
1975-76	New Orleans	75	184	159	527	7.0
1976-77	New Orleans	76	184	156	524	6.9
1977-78	New Orleans	82	304	225	833	10.2
1978-79	New Orleans	80	440	373	1253	15.7
1979-80	N.J.-Phoe.	80	229	244	702	8.8
1980-81	Phoenix	81	196	175	567	7.0
	Totals	474	1537	1332	4406	9.3

KELSER, GREG
b. Sept. 17, 1957 Ht. 6-7 Wt. 190 College—Michigan State

Yr.	Team	G	FG	FT	TP	Avg.
1979-80	Detroit	50	280(3)	146	709	14.2
1980-81	Detroit	25	120	68	308	12.3
	Totals	75	400(3)	214	1017	13.6

KENON, LARRY
b. Dec. 13, 1952 Ht. 6-9 Wt. 205 College—Memphis St.

Yr.	Team		G	FG	FT	TP	Avg.
1973-74	New York	(ABA)	84	589	156	1334	15.9
1974-75	New York	(ABA)	84	676(1)	217	1570	18.7
1975-76	San Antonio	(ABA)	81	647	221	1515	18.7
1976-77	San Antonio		78	706	293	1705	21.9
1977-78	San Antonio		81	698	276	1672	20.6
1978-79	San Antonio		81	748	295	1791	22.1
1979-80	San Antonio		78	647(1)	270	1565	20.1
1980-81	Chicago		77	454	180	1088	14.1
	Totals		644	5165(2)	1908	12240	19.0

KINCH, CHAD
b. May 22, 1958 Ht. 6-4 Wt. 190 College—No. Carolina-Charlotte

Yr.	Team	G	FG	FT	TP	Avg.
1980-81	Clev.-Dal.	41	52	14	118	2.9

KING, BERNARD
b. Dec. 4, 1956 Ht. 6-7 Wt. 205 College—Tennessee

Yr.	Team	G	FG	FT	TP	Avg.
1977-78	New Jersey	79	798	313	1909	24.2
1978-79	New Jersey	82	710	349	1769	21.6
1979-80	Utah	19	71	34	176	9.3
1980-81	Golden State	81	731(2)	307	1771	21.9
	Totals	261	2310(2)	1003	5625	21.6

KING, REGGIE
b. Feb. 14, 1957 Ht. 6-6 Wt. 235 College—Alabama

Yr.	Team	G	FG	FT	TP	Avg.
1979-80	Kansas City	82	257	159	673	8.2
1980-81	Kansas City	81	472	264	1208	14.9
	Totals	163	729	423	1881	11.5

Yr.	Team		G	FG	FT	TP	Avg.
KNIGHT, BILLY							
b. June 9, 1952 Ht. 6-7 Wt. 200 College—Pittsburgh							
1974-75 Indiana	(ABA)		80	580(4)	207	1371	17.1
1975-76 Indiana	(ABA)		70	774(6)	415	1969	28.1
1976-77 Indiana			78	831	413	2075	26.6
1977-78 Buffalo			53	457	301	1215	22.9
1978-79 Indiana			79	441	249	1131	14.3
1979-80 Indiana			75	385(4)	212	986	13.1
1980-81 Indiana			82	546(3)	341	1436	17.5
	Totals		517	4014(17)	2138	10183	19.7
KNIGHT, TOBY							
b. May 3, 1955 Ht. 6-9 Wt. 210 College—Notre Dame							
1977-78 New York			80	222	63	507	6.3
1978-79 New York			82	609	145	1363	16.6
1979-80 New York			81	669	211	1549	19.1
1980-81 New York				(Injured)			
	Totals		243	1500	419	3419	14.1
KRAMER, JOEL							
b. Oct. 30, 1955 Ht. 6-7 Wt. 203 College—San Diego St.							
1978-79 Phoenix			82	181	125	487	5.9
1979-80 Phoenix			54	67	56	190	3.5
1980-81 Phoenix			82	136	63	335	4.1
	Totals		218	384	244	1012	4.6
KREKLOW, WAYNE							
b. Jan. 4, 1957 Ht. 6-4 Wt. 182 College—Drake							
1980-81 Boston			25	11(1)	7	30	1.2
KUNNERT, KEVIN							
b. Nov. 11, 1951 Ht. 7-0 Wt. 231 College—Iowa							
1973-74 Buf.-Hou.			64	105	21	231	3.6
1974-75 Houston			75	346	116	808	10.8
1975-76 Houston			80	465	102	1032	12.9
1976-77 Houston			81	333	93	759	9.4
1977-78 Houston			80	368	93	829	10.4
1978-79 San Diego			81	234	56	524	6.5
1979-80 Portland			18	50	26	126	7.0
1980-81 Portland			55	101	42	244	4.4
	Totals		534	2002	549	4553	8.5
KUPCHAK, MITCH							
b. May 24, 1954 Ht. 6-10 Wt. 230 College—North Carolina							
1976-77 Washington			82	341	170	852	10.4
1977-78 Washington			67	393	280	1066	15.9
1978-79 Washington			66	369	223	961	14.6
1979-80 Washington			40	67	52	186	4.7
1980-81 Washington			82	392	240	1024	12.5
	Totals		337	1562	965	4089	12.1
LACEY, SAM							
b. March 28, 1948 Ht. 6-10 Wt. 235 College—N.Mex.St.							
1970-71 Cincinnati			81	467	156	1090	13.5
1971-72 Cincinnati			81	410	119	939	11.6
1972-73 K.C.-Omaha			79	471	126	1068	13.5
1973-74 K.C.-Omaha			79	467	185	1119	14.2
1974-75 K.C.-Omaha			81	392	144	928	11.5
1975-76 Kansas City			81	409	217	1035	12.8
1976-77 Kansas City			82	327	215	869	10.6

Yr.	Team	G	FG	FT	TP	Avg.
1977-78 Kansas City		77	265	134	664	8.6
1978-79 Kansas City		82	350	167	867	10.6
1979-80 Kansas City		81	303	137	743	9.2
1980-81 Kansas City		82	237(1)	92	567	6.9
	Totals	886	4098(1)	1692	9889	11.2
LAGARDE, TOM						
b. Feb. 10, 1955 Ht. 6-10 Wt. 220 College—No. Carolina						
1977-78 Denver		77	96	114	306	4.0
1978-79 Seattle		23	98	57	253	11.0
1979-80 Seattle		82	146	90	382	4.7
1980-81 Dallas		82	417	288	1122	13.7
	Totals	264	757	549	2063	7.8
LAIMBEER, BILL						
b. May 19, 1957 Ht. 6-11 Wt. 245 College—Notre Dame						
1980-81 Cleveland		81	337	117	791	9.8
LAMBERT, JOHN						
b. Jan. 14, 1953 Ht. 6-10 Wt. 225 College—USC						
1975-76 Cleveland		54	49	25	123	2.3
1976-77 Cleveland		63	67	25	159	2.5
1977-78 Cleveland		76	142	27	311	4.1
1978-79 Cleveland		70	148	35	331	4.7
1979-80 Cleveland		74	165	73	403	5.4
1980-81 Clev.-K.C.		46	68	18	154	3.3
	Totals	383	639	203	1481	3.9
LANDSBERGER, MARK						
b. May 21, 1955 Ht. 6-8 Wt. 215 College—Minnesota and Arizona St.						
1977-78 Chicago		62	127	91	345	5.6
1978-79 Chicago		80	278	91	647	8.1
1979-80 Chic.-L.A.		77	249	116	614	8.0
1980-81 Los Angeles		69	164	62	390	5.7
	Totals	288	818	360	1996	6.9
LANIER, BOB						
b. Sept. 10, 1948 Ht. 6-11 Wt. 265 College—St. Bonaventure						
1970-71 Detroit		82	504	273	1281	15.6
1971-72 Detroit		80	834	388	2056	25.7
1972-73 Detroit		81	810	307	1927	23.8
1973-74 Detroit		81	748	326	1822	22.5
1974-75 Detroit		76	731	361	1823	24.0
1975-76 Detroit		64	541	284	1366	21.3
1976-77 Detroit		64	678	260	1616	25.3
1977-78 Detroit		63	622	298	1542	24.5
1978-79 Detroit		53	489	275	1253	23.6
1979-80 Detr.-Milw.		63	466(1)	277	1210	19.2
1980-81 Milwaukee		67	376(1)	208	961	14.3
	Totals	774	6799(2)	3257	16857	21.8
LAWRENCE, ED						
b. Dec. 8, 1952 Ht. 6-11 Wt. 247 College—McNeese State						
1980-81 Detroit		3	5	2	12	4.0
LEAVELL, ALLEN						
b. May 27, 1957 Ht. 6-1 Wt. 170 College—Oklahoma City						
1979-80 Houston		77	330(3)	180	843	10.9
1980-81 Houston		79	258(2)	124	642	8.1
	Totals	156	588(5)	304	1485	9.5

Yr.	Team		G	FG	FT	TP	Avg.

LEE, RON
b. Nov. 2, 1952 Ht. 6-3 Wt. 193 College—Oregon

Yr.	Team		G	FG	FT	TP	Avg.
1976-77	Phoenix		82	347	142	836	10.2
1977-78	Phoenix		82	417	170	1004	12.2
1978-79	Phoenix-N.O.		60	218	98	534	8.9
1979-80	Atl.-Detr.		61	113(22)	44	292	4.8
1980-81	Detroit		82	113(2)	113	341	4.2
		Totals	367	1208(24)	567	3007	8.2

LESTER, RONNIE
b. Jan. 1, 1959 Ht. 6-2 Wt. 175 College—Iowa

Yr.	Team	G	FG	FT	TP	Avg.
1980-81	Chicago	8	10	10	30	3.8

LLOYD, SCOTT
b. Dec. 19, 1952 Ht. 6-10 Wt. 230 College— Arizona St.

Yr.	Team		G	FG	FT	TP	Avg.
1976-77	Milwaukee		69	153	95	401	5.8
1977-78	Mil.-Buff.		70	80	49	209	3.0
1978-79	S.D.-Chi		72	42	27	111	1.5
1980-81	Dallas		72	245	147	637	8.8
		Totals	283	520	318	1358	4.8

LONG, JOHN
b. Aug. 28, 1956 Ht. 6-5 Wt. 210 College—Detroit

Yr.	Team		G	FG	FT	TP	Avg.
1978-79	Detroit		82	581	157	1319	16.1
1979-80	Detroit		69	588(1)	160	1337	19.4
1980-81	Detroit		59	441(2)	160	1044	17.7
		Totals	210	1610(3)	477	3700	17.6

LUCAS, JOHN
b. Oct. 31, 1953 Ht. 6-2 Wt. 180 College—Maryland

Yr.	Team		G	FG	FT	TP	Avg.
1976-77	Houston		82	388	135	911	11.1
1977-78	Houston		82	412	193	1017	12.4
1978-79	Golden State		82	530	264	1324	16.1
1979-80	Golden State		80	388(12)	222	1010	12.6
1980-81	Golden State		66	222(4)	107	555	8.4
		Totals	392	1940(16)	921	4817	12.3

LUCAS, MAURICE
b. Feb. 18, 1952 Ht. 6-9 Wt. 215 College—Marquette

Yr.	Team		G	FG	FT	TP	Avg.
1974-75	St. Louis	(ABA)	83	591	375	1557	18.8
1975-76	St. L.-Ken.	(ABA)	86	620(3)	217	1460	17.0
1976-77	Portland		79	632	335	1599	20.2
1977-78	Portland		68	453	207	1113	16.4
1978-79	Portland		69	568	270	1406	20.4
1979-80	Port.-N.J.		63	371(2)	179	923	14.7
1980-81	New Jersey		68	404	191	999	14.7
		Totals	516	3639(5)	1774	9057	17.6

MACK, OLIVER
b. June 6, 1957 Ht. 6-3 Wt. 195 College—East Carolina

Yr.	Team		G	FG	FT	TP	Avg.
1979-80	L.A.-Chic.		50	98	38	234	4.7
1980-81	Chi.-Dal.		65	279	80	638	9.8
		Totals	115	377	118	872	7.6

MACY, KYLE
b. Apr. 9, 1957 Ht. 6-3 Wt. 175 College—Purdue and Kentucky

Yr.	Team	G	FG	FT	TP	Avg.
1980-81	Phoenix	82	272(12)	107	663	8.1

MAHORN, RICKY
b. Sept. 21, 1958 Ht. 6-10 Wt. 240 College—Hampton

Yr.	Team	G	FG	FT	TP	Avg.
1980-81	Washington	52	111	27	249	4.8

MALONE, MOSES
b. March 23, 1954 Ht. 6-10 Wt. 215 College—None

Yr.	Team		G	FG	FT	TP	Avg.
1974-75	Utah	(ABA)	83	591	375	1557	18.8
1975-76	St. Louis	(ABA)	43	251	112	614	14.3
1976-77	Buf.-Hou.		82	389	305	1083	13.5
1977-78	Houston		59	413	318	1144	19.4
1978-79	Houston		82	716	599	2031	24.8
1979-80	Houston		82	778	563	2119	25.8
1980-81	Houston		80	806(1)	609	2222	27.8
		Totals	511	3944(1)	2881	10770	21.1

MATTHEWS, WES
b. Aug. 24, 1959 Ht. 6-1 Wt. 170 College—Wisconsin

Yr.	Team	G	FG	FT	TP	Avg.
1980-81	Wash.-Atl.	79	385(5)	202	977	12.4

MAXWELL, CEDRIC (Cornbread)
b. Nov. 21, 1955 Ht. 6-8 Wt. 205 College—N.C. Charlotte

Yr.	Team		G	FG	FT	TP	Avg.
1977-78	Boston		72	170	188	528	7.3
1978-79	Boston		80	472	574	1518	19.0
1979-80	Boston		80	457	436	1350	16.9
1980-81	Boston		81	441	352	1234	15.2
		Totals	313	1540	1550	4630	14.8

MAY, SCOTT
b. March 19, 1954 Ht. 6-7 Wt. 215 College—Indiana

Yr.	Team		G	FG	FT	TP	Avg.
1976-77	Chicago		72	431	188	1050	14.6
1977-78	Chicago		55	280	175	735	13.4
1978-79	Chicago		37	59	30	148	4.0
1979-80	Chicago		54	264	144	672	12.4
1980-81	Chicago		63	165	113	443	7.0
		Totals	281	1199	650	3048	10.8

MAYFIELD, WILLIAM
b. Oct. 17, 1957 Ht. 6-7 Wt. 210 College—Iowa

Yr.	Team	G	FG	FT	TP	Avg.
1980-81	Golden State	7	8	1	17	2.4

McADOO, BOB
b. Sept. 25, 1951 Ht. 6-9 Wt. 210 College—North Carolina

Yr.	Team		G	FG	FT	TP	Avg.
1972-73	Buffalo		80	585	271	1441	18.0
1973-74	Buffalo		74	901	459	2261	30.6
1974-75	Buffalo		82	1095	641	2831	34.5
1975-76	Buffalo		78	934	559	2427	31.1
1976-77	Buf.-NYK		72	740	381	1861	25.8
1977-78	New York		79	814	469	2097	26.5
1978-79	N.Y.-Bos.		60	596	295	1487	24.8
1979-80	Detroit		58	492(3)	235	1222	21.1
1980-81	Det.-N.J.		16	68	29	165	10.3
		Totals	599	6225(3)	3339	15792	26.4

McCARTER, ANDRE
b. Aug. 25, 1953 Ht. 6-3 Wt. 190 College—UCLA

Yr.	Team		G	FG	FT	TP	Avg.
1976-77	Kansas City		59	119	32	270	4.6
1977-78	Kansas City		1	0	0	0	0.0
1980-81	Washington		43	51(2)	18	122	2.8
		Totals	103	170(2)	50	392	3.8

Yr.	Team		G	FG	FT	TP	Avg.
McCORD, KEITH							

b. June 22, 1957 Ht. 6-7 Wt. 210 College—Alabama (Birmingham)

Yr.	Team		G	FG	FT	TP	Avg.
1980-81	Washington		2	2	0	4	2.0

McELROY, JIM

b. Oct. 4, 1953 Ht. 6-3 Wt. 190 College—Central Mich.

Yr.	Team		G	FG	FT	TP	Avg.
1975-76	New Orleans		51	151	81	383	7.5
1976-77	New Orleans		73	301	169	771	10.6
1977-78	New Orleans		74	287	123	697	9.4
1978-79	New Orleans		79	539	259	1337	16.9
1979-80	Detr.-Atla.		67	228(5)	132	593	8.9
1980-81	Atlanta		54	78(1)	48	205	3.8
	Totals		400	1584(6)	812	3986	10.0

McGINNIS, GEORGE

b. Aug. 12, 1950 Ht. 6-8 Wt. 235 College—Indiana

Yr.	Team		G	FG	FT	TP	Avg.
1971-72	Indiana	(ABA)	73	465(6)	298	1234	16.9
1972-73	Indiana	(ABA)	82	868(8)	517	2261	27.6
1973-74	Indiana	(ABA)	80	789(5)	488	2071	25.9
1974-75	Indiana	(ABA)	79	873(62)	545	2353	29.8
1975-76	Philadelphia		77	647	475	1769	23.0
1976-77	Philadelphia		79	659	372	1690	21.4
1977-78	Philadelphia		78	588	411	1587	20.3
1978-79	Denver		76	603	509	1715	22.6
1979-80	Denv.-Ind.		73	400(2)	270	1072	14.7
1980-81	Indiana		69	348	207	903	13.1
	Totals		766	6240(83)	4092	16655	21.7

McHALE, KEVIN

b. Dec. 19, 1957 Ht. 6-10 Wt. 210 College—Minnesota

Yr.	Team		G	FG	FT	TP	Avg.
1980-81	Boston		82	355	108	818	10.0

McKINNEY, BILLY

b. June 5, 1955 Ht. 6-0 Wt. 162 College—Northwestern

Yr.	Team		G	FG	FT	TP	Avg.
1978-79	Kansas City		78	240	129	609	7.8
1979-80	Kansas City		76	206(1)	107	520	6.8
1980-81	Utah-Denver		84	327(2)	162	818	9.7
	Totals		238	773(3)	398	1947	8.2

McMILLEN, C. THOMAS

b. May 26, 1952 Ht. 6-11 Wt. 215 College—Maryland

Yr.	Team		G	FG	FT	TP	Avg.
1975-76	Buffalo		50	96	41	233	4.7
1976-77	Buf.-NYK		76	274	96	644	8.5
1977-78	Atlanta		68	280	116	676	9.9
1978-79	Atlanta		82	232	106	570	7.0
1979-80	Atlanta		53	191	81	463	8.7
1980-81	Atlanta		79	253(1)	80	587	7.4
	Totals		408	1326(1)	520	3173	7.8

MENGELT, JOHN

b. Oct. 16, 1949 Ht. 6-2½ Wt. 195 College—Auburn

Yr.	Team		G	FG	FT	TP	Avg.
1971-72	Cincinnati		78	287	208	782	10.0
1972-73	K.C.-O.-Det.		79	320	127	767	9.7
1973-74	Detroit		77	249	182	680	8.8
1974-75	Detroit		80	336	211	8833	11.0
1975-76	Detroit		67	264	192	720	10.7
1976-77	Chicago		61	209	89	507	8.3
1977-78	Chicago		81	325	184	834	11.0
1978-79	Chicago		75	338	150	826	6.1
1979-80	Chicago		36	90	39	219	0.0
1980-81	Golden State		2	0	0	0	0.0
	Totals		636	2418	1382	6218	9.8

MERIWEATHER, JOE C.

b. Oct. 26, 1953 Ht. 6-10 Wt. 215 College—So. Illinois

Yr.	Team		G	FG	FT	TP	Avg.
1975-76	Houston		81	338	154	830	10.2
1976-77	Atlanta		74	319	182	820	11.1
1977-78	New Orleans		54	194	87	475	8.8
1978-79	N.O.-NYK		77	242	126	610	7.9
1979-80	New York		65	252	78	582	9.0
1980-81	Kansas City		74	206	148	560	7.6
	Totals		425	1551	775	3877	9.1

MILLER, DICK

b. April 26, 1958 Ht. 6-7 Wt. 223 College—Toledo

Yr.	Team		G	FG	FT	TP	Avg.
1980-81	Indiana-Utah		8	4	0	8	1.0

MITCHELL, MIKE

b. Jan. 1, 1956 Ht. 6-7½ Wt. 215 College—Auburn

Yr.	Team		G	FG	FT	TP	Avg.
1978-79	Cleveland		80	362	131	855	10.7
1979-80	Cleveland		82	775	270	1820	22.2
1980-81	Cleveland		82	853(4)	302	2012	24.5
	Totals		244	1990(4)	703	4687	19.2

MIX, STEVE

b. Dec. 30, 1947 Ht. 6-7 Wt. 215 College—Toledo

Yr.	Team		G	FG	FT	TP	Avg.
1969-70	Detroit		18	48	23	119	6.6
1970-71	Detroit		35	111	68	290	8.3
1971-72	Detroit		8	15	7	37	4.6
1971-72	Denver	(ABA)	1	1	0	2	2.0
1973-74	Philadelphia		82	495	228	1218	14.9
1974-75	Philadelphia		46	280	159	719	15.6
1975-76	Philadelphia		81	421	287	1129	13.9
1976-77	Philadelphia		75	288	215	791	10.5
1977-78	Philadelphia		82	291	175	757	9.2
1978-79	Philadelphia		74	265	161	691	9.3
1979-80	Philadelphia		81	363(4)	207	937	11.6
1980-81	Philadelphia		72	288	200	776	10.8
	Totals		655	2866(4)	1730	7466	11.4

MOKESKI, PAUL

b. Jan. 3, 1957 Ht. 7-0 Wt. 250 College—Kansas

Yr.	Team		G	FG	FT	TP	Avg.
1979-80	Houston		12	11	7	29	2.4
1980-81	Detroit		80	224	120	568	7.1
	Totals		92	235	127	597	6.5

MONCRIEF, SIDNEY

b. Sept. 21, 1957 Ht. 6-4 Wt. 190 College—Arkansas

Yr.	Team		G	FG	FT	TP	Avg.
1979-80	Milwaukee		77	211	232	654	8.5
1980-81	Milwaukee		80	400(2)	320	1122	14.0
	Totals		157	611(2)	552	1776	11.3

MOORE, JOHNNY

b. March 3, 1958 Ht. 6-1 Wt. 175 College—Texas

Yr.	Team		G	FG	FT	TP	Avg.
1980-81	San Antonio		82	249(1)	105	604	7.4

MOORE, LOWES

b. May 5, 1957 Ht. 6-1 Wt. 170 College—West Virginia

Yr.	Team		G	FG	FT	TP	Avg.
1980-81	New Jersey		71	212(4)	69	497	7.0

Yr.	Team		G	FG	FT	TP	Avg.

MURPHY, CALVIN
b. May 9, 1948 Ht. 5-9 Wt. 165 College—Niagara

Yr.	Team		G	FG	FT	TP	Avg.
1970-71	San Diego		82	471	356	1298	15.8
1971-72	Houston		82	571	349	1491	18.2
1972-73	Houston		77	381	239	1001	13.0
1973-74	Houston		81	671	310	1652	20.4
1974-75	Houston		78	557	341	1455	18.7
1975-76	Houston		82	675	372	1722	21.0
1976-77	Houston		82	596	272	1464	17.9
1977-78	Houston		76	852	245	1949	25.6
1978-79	Houston		82	707	246	1660	20.2
1979-80	Houston		76	624(1)	271	1520	20.0
1980-81	Houston		76	528(4)	206	1266	16.7
	Totals		874	6633(5)	3207	16478	18.9

NATER, SWEN
b. Jan. 14, 1950 Ht. 6-11 Wt. 250 College—UCLA

Yr.	Team		G	FG	FT	TP	Avg.
1973-74	Vir.-S.A.	(ABA)	79	467	180	1114	14.1
1974-75	San Antonio	(ABA)	78	495	185	1175	15.1
1975-76	N.Y.-Vir.	(ABA)	76	320	108	748	9.8
1976-77	Milwaukee		72	383	172	938	13.0
1977-78	Buffalo		78	501	208	1210	15.5
1978-79	San Diego		79	357	132	846	10.7
1979-80	San Diego		81	443	196	1082	13.4
1980-81	San Diego		82	517	244	1278	15.6
	Totals		625	3483	1425	8391	13.4

NATT, CALVIN
b. Jan. 8, 1957 Ht. 6-6 Wt. 220 College—N.E. Louisiana

Yr.	Team		G	FG	FT	TP	Avg.
1979-80	N.J.-Port.		78	622(3)	306	1553	19.9
1980-81	Portland		74	395(4)	200	994	13.4
	Totals		152	1017(7)	506	2547	16.8

NATT, KENNY
b. Oct. 5, 1958 Ht. 6-3 Wt. 185 College—Northeast Louisiana

Yr.	Team		G	FG	FT	TP	Avg.
1980-81	Indiana		19	25(2)	7	59	3.1

NEWLIN, MIKE
b. Jan. 2, 1949 Ht. 6-4 Wt. 200 College—Utah

Yr.	Team		G	FG	FT	TP	Avg.
1971-72	Houston		82	256	108	620	7.6
1972-73	Houston		82	534	327	1395	17.0
1973-74	Houston		76	510	380	1400	18.4
1974-75	Houston		79	436	265	1137	14.4
1975-76	Houston		82	569	385	1523	18.6
1976-77	Houston		82	387	269	1043	12.7
1977-78	Houston		45	216	152	584	13.0
1978-79	Houston		76	283	212	778	10.2
1979-80	New Jersey		78	611(45)	367	1634	20.9
1980-81	New Jersey		79	632(10)	414	1688	21.4
	Totals		761	4434(55)	2879	11802	15.5

NICKS, CARL
b. Oct. 6, 1958 Ht. 6-1 Wt. 175 College—Indiana State

Yr.	Team		G	FG	FT	TP	Avg.
1980-81	Denver-Utah		67	172	71	415	6.2

NILES, MIKE
b. March 31, 1955 Ht. 6-6 Wt. 225 College—Cal. State Fullerton

Yr.	Team		G	FG	FT	TP	Avg.
1980-81	Phoenix		44	48(2)	17	115	2.6

NIXON, NORM
b. Oct. 10, 1955 Ht. 6-2 Wt. 175 College—Duquesne

Yr.	Team		G	FG	FT	TP	Avg.
1977-78	Los Angeles		81	496	115	1107	13.7
1978-79	Los Angeles		82	623	158	1404	17.1
1979-80	Los Angeles		82	624(1)	197	1446	17.6
1980-81	Los Angeles		79	576(2)	196	1350	17.1
	Totals		324	2319(3)	666	5307	16.4

O'KOREN, MIKE
b. Feb. 7, 1958 Ht. 6-7 Wt. 207 College—North Carolina

Yr.	Team		G	FG	FT	TP	Avg.
1980-81	New Jersey		79	365(5)	135	870	11.0

OLBERDING, MARK
b. April 21, 1956 Ht. 6-8 Wt. 230 College—Minnesota

Yr.	Team		G	FG	FT	TP	Avg.
1975-76	S.D.-S.A.	(ABA)	81	302	191	795	9.8
1976-77	San Antonio		82	301	251	853	10.4
1977-78	San Antonio		79	231	184	646	8.2
1978-79	San Antonio		80	261	233	755	9.4
1979-80	San Antonio		75	291	210	792	10.6
1980-81	San Antonio		82	348(1)	315	1012	12.3
	Totals		479	1734(1)	1384	4853	10.1

OLDHAM, JAWANN
b. July 4, 1957 Ht. 7-0 Wt. 215 College—Seattle

Yr.	Team		G	FG	FT	TP	Avg.
1980-81	Denver		4	2	0	4	1.0

ORR, LOUIS
b. May 7, 1958 Ht. 6-8 Wt. 175 College—Syracuse

Yr.	Team		G	FG	FT	TP	Avg.
1980-81	Indiana		82	348	163	859	10.5

OWENS, TOM
b. June 28, 1949 Ht. 6-10 Wt. 223 College—So. Carolina

Yr.	Team		G	FG	FT	TP	Avg.
1971-72	Mem.-Carolina	(ABA)	69	197(1)	109	504	7.3
1972-73	Carolina	(ABA)	83	393	193	979	11.8
1973-74	Carolina	(ABA)	81	444(2)	226	1116	13.8
1974-75	St.L.-Mem.	(ABA)	82	511	217	1239	15.1
1975-76	Ken.-S.A.	(ABA)	74	178	92	448	6.1
1976-77	Houston		46	68	52	188	4.1
1977-78	Portland		82	313	206	832	10.1
1978-79	Portland		82	600	320	1520	18.5
1979-80	Portland		76	518(1)	213	1250	16.4
1980-81	Portland		79	322	191	835	10.6
	Totals		754	3544(4)	1819	8911	11.8

PARISH, ROBERT
b. Aug. 30, 1953 Ht. 7-0 Wt. 235 College—Centenary

Yr.	Team		G	FG	FT	TP	Avg.
1976-77	Golden State		77	288	121	697	9.1
1977-78	Golden State		82	430	165	1025	12.5
1978-79	Golden State		76	554	196	1304	17.2
1979-80	Golden State		72	510	203	1223	17.0
1980-81	Boston		82	635	282	1552	18.9
	Totals		389	2417	967	5801	14.9

PARKER, SONNY
b. March 22, 1955 Ht. 6-7 Wt. 215 College—Texas A & M

Yr.	Team		G	FG	FT	TP	Avg.
1976-77	Golden State		65	154	71	379	5.8
1977-78	Golden State		82	406	122	934	11.4
1978-79	Golden State		79	512	175	1199	15.2
1979-80	Golden State		82	483	237	1203	14.7
1980-81	Golden State		73	191	94	476	6.5
	Totals		381	1746	699	4191	11.0

Yr.	Team		G	FG	FT	TP	Avg.

PATRICK, MYLES
b. Nov. 19, 1954 Ht. 6-8 Wt. 220 College—Auburn

Yr.	Team		G	FG	FT	TP	Avg.
1980-81 Los Angeles			3	2	1	5	1.7

PAULTZ, BILLY (The Whopper)
b. July 30, 1948 Ht. 6-11 Wt. 240 College— Cameron and St. John's

Yr.	Team		G	FG	FT	TP	Avg.
1970-71 New York	(ABA)		83	510	201	1221	14.7
1971-72 New York	(ABA)		83	498	207	1203	14.5
1972-73 New York	(ABA)		81	532	287	1351	16.7
1973-74 New York	(ABA)		77	519	222	1260	16.4
1974-75 New York	(ABA)		80	524	214	1262	15.8
1975-76 San Antonio	(ABA)		83	566	238	1370	16.5
1976-77 San Antonio			82	521	238	1280	15.6
1977-78 San Antonio			80	518	230	1266	15.8
1978-79 San Antonio			79	399	114	912	11.5
1979-80 S.A.-Hous.			84	327	109	763	9.1
1980-81 Houston			81	262	75	599	7.4
	Totals		893	5176	2135	12487	14.0

PAXSON, JIM
b. July 9, 1957 Ht. 6-6 Wt. 200 College—Dayton

Yr.	Team		G	FG	FT	TP	Avg.
1979-80 Portland			72	189(1)	64	443	6.2
1980-81 Portland			79	585(2)	182	1354	17.1
	Totals		151	774(3)	246	1797	11.9

PELLOM, SAM
b. Oct. 2, 1951 Ht. 6-9 Wt. 225 College—SUNY Buffalo

Yr.	Team		G	FG	FT	TP	Avg.
1979-80 Atlanta			44	44	21	109	2.5
1980-81 Atlanta			77	186	81	453	5.9
	Totals		121	230	102	562	4.6

PHEGLEY, ROGER
b. Oct. 16, 1956 Ht. 6-6 Wt. 205 College—Bradley

Yr.	Team		G	FG	FT	TP	Avg.
1978-79 Washington			29	28	24	80	2.8
1979-80 Wash.-N.J.			78	350(4)	177	881	11.3
1980-81 Cleveland			82	474(8)	224	1180	14.4
	Totals		189	852(12)	425	2141	11.3

PIETKIEWICZ, STAN
b. July 14, 1956 Ht. 6-5 Wt. 200 College—Auburn

Yr.	Team		G	FG	FT	TP	Avg.
1978-79 San Diego			4	1	2	4	1.0
1979-80 San Diego			50	91(9)	37	228	4.6
1980-81 S.D.-Dallas			42	57(19)	11	144	3.4
	Totals		96	149(28)	50	376	3.9

POQUETTE, BEN
b. May 7, 1955 Ht. 6-9 Wt. 235 College—Central Mich.

Yr.	Team		G	FG	FT	TP	Avg.
1977-78 Detroit			52	95	42	232	4.5
1978-79 Detroit			76	198	111	507	6.7
1979-80 Utah			82	296	139	731	8.9
1980-81 Utah			82	324(3)	126	777	9.5
	Totals		292	913(3)	418	2247	7.7

PORTER, KEVIN
b. April 17, 1950 Ht. 6-0 Wt. 175 College—St. Francis (Pa.)

Yr.	Team		G	FG	FT	TP	Avg.
1972-73 Baltimore			71	205	62	472	6.6
1973-74 Capital			81	477	180	1134	14.0
1974-75 Washington			81	406	131	943	11.6
1975-76 Detroit			19	99	42	240	12.6
1976-77 Detroit			81	310	97	717	8.9
1977-78 Det.-N.J.			82	495	244	1234	15.0
1978-79 Detroit			82	534	192	1260	15.4
1979-80 Washington			70	201	110	512	7.3
1980-81 Washington			81	446(3)	191	1086	13.4
	Totals		648	3173(3)	1249	7598	11.7

PRICE, TONY
b. Jan. 5, 1957 Ht. 6-6 Wt. 210 College—Pennsylvania

Yr.	Team		G	FG	FT	TP	Avg.
1980-81 San Diego			5	2	0	4	0.8

RANK, WALLY
b. March 1, 1958 Ht. 6-6½ Wt. 220 College—San Jose State

Yr.	Team		G	FG	FT	TP	Avg.
1980-81 San Diego			25	21	13	55	2.2

RANSEY, KELVIN
b. May 3, 1958 Ht. 6-1 Wt. 170 College—Ohio State

Yr.	Team		G	FG	FT	TP	Avg.
1980-81 Portland			80	525(3)	164	1217	15.2

RAY, CLIFFORD
b. Jan. 21, 1949 Ht. 6-9 Wt. 235 College—Oklahoma

Yr.	Team		G	FG	FT	TP	Avg.
1971-72 Chicago			82	222	134	578	7.0
1972-73 Chicago			73	254	117	625	8.6
1973-74 Chicago			80	313	121	747	9.3
1974-75 Golden State			82	299	171	769	9.4
1975-76 Golden State			82	212	140	564	6.9
1976-77 Golden State			77	263	105	631	8.2
1977-78 Golden State			79	272	148	692	8.8
1978-79 Golden State			82	231	106	568	6.9
1979-80 Golden State			81	203	84	490	6.0
1980-81 Golden State			66	64	29	157	2.4
	Totals		784	2333	1155	5821	7.4

RAY, JAMES
b. July 27, 1957 Ht. 6-8 Wt. 215 College—Jacksonville

Yr.	Team		G	FG	FT	TP	Avg.
1980-81 Denver			18	15	7	37	2.1

REID, BILLY
b. Sept. 10, 1957 Ht. 6-5 Wt. 190 College—San Francisco

Yr.	Team		G	FG	FT	TP	Avg.
1980-81 Golden State			59	84	22	190	3.2

REID, ROBERT
b. Aug. 30, 1955 Ht. 6-8 Wt. 205 College—St. Mary's (Tex.)

Yr.	Team		G	FG	FT	TP	Avg.
1977-78 Houston			80	261	63	585	7.3
1978-79 Houston			82	382	131	895	10.9
1979-80 Houston			76	419	153	991	13.0
1980-81 Houston			82	536	229	1301	15.9
	Totals		320	1598	576	3772	11.8

RESTANI, KEVIN
b. Dec. 23, 1951 Ht. 6-9 Wt. 225 College—San Francisco

Yr.	Team		G	FG	FT	TP	Avg.
1974-75 Milwaukee			76	188	35	411	5.4
1975-76 Milwaukee			82	234	24	492	6.0
1976-77 Milwaukee			64	173	12	358	5.6
1977-78 Mil.-K.C.			54	72	9	153	2.8
1978-79 Milwaukee			81	262	51	575	7.1
1979-80 San Antonio			82	369(5)	131	874	10.7
1980-81 San Antonio			64	192(3)	62	449	7.0
	Totals		503	1490(8)	324	3312	6.6

Yr.	Team	G	FG	FT	TP	Avg.

RICHARDSON, CLINT
b. Aug. 7, 1956 Ht. 6-3 Wt. 195 College—Seattle

Yr.	Team	G	FG	FT	TP	Avg.
1979-80	Philadelphia	52	159(1)	28	347	6.7
1980-81	Philadelphia	77	227	84	538	7.0
	Totals	129	386(1)	112	885	6.9

RICHARDSON, MICHAEL RAY
b. April 11, 1955 Ht. 6-5 Wt. 189 College—Montana

Yr.	Team	G	FG	FT	TP	Avg.
1978-79	New York	72	200	69	469	6.5
1979-80	New York	82	502(27)	223	1254	15.3
1980-81	New York	79	523(23)	224	1293	16.4
	Totals	233	1225(50)	516	3016	12.9

ROBERTS, ANTHONY
b. April 15, 1955 Ht. 6-5 Wt. 185 College—Oral Roberts U.

Yr.	Team	G	FG	FT	TP	Avg.
1977-78	Denver	82	311	153	775	9.5
1978-79	Denver	63	211	76	498	7.9
1979-80	Denver	23	69	39	177	7.7
1980-81	Washington	26	54	19	127	4.9
	Totals	194	645	287	1577	8.1

ROBEY, RICK
b. Jan. 30, 1956 Ht. 6-11 Wt. 230 College—Kentucky

Yr.	Team	G	FG	FT	TP	Avg.
1978-79	Ind.-Boston	79	322	174	818	10.4
1979-80	Boston	82	379	184	942	11.5
1980-81	Boston	82	298	144	740	9.0
	Totals	243	999	502	2500	10.3

ROBINSON, CLIFF
b. Mar. 13, 1960 Ht. 6-9½ Wt. 220 College—So. California

Yr.	Team	G	FG	FT	TP	Avg.
1979-80	New Jersey	70	391(1)	168	951	13.6
1980-81	New Jersey	63	525(1)	178	1229	19.5
	Totals	133	916(2)	346	2180	16.4

ROBINSON, LEN (Truck)
b. Oct. 4, 1951 Ht. 6-7 Wt. 225 College—Tenn. State

Yr.	Team	G	FG	FT	TP	Avg.
1974-75	Washington	76	191	60	442	5.8
1975-76	Washington	82	354	211	919	11.2
1976-77	Wash.-Atl.	77	574	314	1462	19.0
1977-78	New Orleans	82	748	366	1862	22.7
1978-79	N.O.-Phoe.	69	566	324	1456	21.1
1979-80	Phoenix	82	545	325	1415	17.3
1980-81	Phoenix	82	647	249	1543	18.8
	Totals	550	3625	1849	9099	16.5

ROBINSON, WAYNE
b. April 19, 1958 Ht. 6-8 Wt. 217 College—Virginia Tech

Yr.	Team	G	FG	FT	TP	Avg.
1980-81	Detroit	81	234	175	643	7.9

ROBINZINE, BILL
b. Jan. 20, 1953 Ht. 6-7 Wt. 230 College—DePaul

Yr.	Team	G	FG	FT	TP	Avg.
1975-76	Kansas City	75	229	145	603	8.0
1976-77	Kansas City	75	307	159	773	10.3
1977-78	Kansas City	82	305	206	816	10.0
1978-79	Kansas City	82	459	180	1098	13.4
1979-80	Kansas City	81	362(1)	200	925	11.4
1980-81	Clev.-Dallas	78	392(1)	218	1003	12.9
	Totals	473	2054(2)	1108	5218	11.0

ROBISCH, DAVE
b. Dec. 22, 1949 Ht. 6-10 Wt. 235 College—Kansas

Yr.	Team		G	FG	FT	TP	Avg.
1971-72	Denver	(ABA)	84	505	294	1304	15.5
1972-73	Denver	(ABA)	83	521	309	1351	16.3
1973-74	Denver	(ABA)	84	449	318	1216	14.5
1974-75	Denver	(ABA)	84	392	304	1088	13.0
1975-76	S.D.-Ind.	(ABA)	87	436	324	1196	13.7
1976-77	Indiana		80	369	213	951	11.9
1977-78	Ind.-L.A.		78	177	100	454	5.8
1978-79	Los Angeles		80	150	86	386	4.8
1979-80	Cleveland		82	489	277	1255	15.3
1980-81	Clev.-Denver		84	330	200	860	10.2
	Totals		826	3818	2425	10061	12.2

ROCHE, JOHN
b. Sept. 26, 1949 Ht. 6-3 Wt. 170 College—So. Carolina

Yr.	Team		G	FG	FT	TP	Avg.
1971-72	New York	(ABA)	82	403(12)	240	1058	12.9
1972-73	New York	(ABA)	77	404(34)	265	1107	14.4
1973-74	N.Y.-Ken.	(ABA)	84	397(36)	148	978	11.6
1974-75	Ken.-Utah	(ABA)	58	241(13)	85	580	10.0
1975-76	Utah	(ABA)	16	112(9)	31	264	16.5
1975-76	Los Angeles		15	3	2	8	0.5
1979-80	Denver		82	354(49)	175	932	11.4
1980-81	Denver		26	82(9)	58	231	8.9
	Totals		440	1996(162)	1004	5158	11.7

ROLLINS, WAYNE (Tree)
b. June 16, 1955 Ht. 7-1 Wt. 235 College—Clemson

Yr.	Team	G	FG	FT	TP	Avg.
1977-78	Atlanta	80	253	104	610	7.6
1978-79	Atlanta	81	297	89	683	8.4
1979-80	Atlanta	82	287	157	731	8.9
1980-81	Atlanta	40	116	46	278	7.0
	Totals	283	953	396	2302	8.1

ROMAR, LORENZO
b. Nov. 13, 1958 Ht. 6-2 Wt. 175 College—Washington

Yr.	Team	G	FG	FT	TP	Avg.
1980-81	Golden State	53	87(2)	43	219	4.1

ROUNDFIELD, DAN
b. May 26, 1953 Ht. 6-8 Wt. 205 College—Cent. Michigan

Yr.	Team		G	FG	FT	TP	Avg.
1975-76	Indiana	(ABA)	67	131	77	339	5.1
1976-77	Indiana		61	342	164	848	13.9
1977-78	Indiana		79	421	218	1060	13.4
1978-79	Atlanta		80	462	300	1224	15.3
1979-80	Atlanta		81	502	330	1334	16.5
1980-81	Atlanta		63	426	256	1108	17.6
	Totals		431	2284	1345	5913	13.7

RUSSELL, M. CAMPANELLA (Campy)
b. Jan. 12, 1952 Ht. 6-8 Wt. 215 College—Michigan

Yr.	Team	G	FG	FT	TP	Avg.
1974-75	Cleveland	68	150	124	424	6.2
1975-76	Cleveland	82	483	266	1232	15.0
1976-77	Cleveland	70	435	288	1158	16.5
1977-78	Cleveland	72	523	352	1398	19.4
1978-79	Cleveland	74	603	417	1623	21.9
1979-80	Cleveland	41	284(1)	178	747	18.2
1980-81	New York	79	508(8)	268	1292	16.4
	Totals	486	2986(9)	1893	7874	16.2

SANDERS, FRANK
b. Jan. 23, 1957 Ht. 6-6 Wt. 200 College—Southern

Yr.	Team	G	FG	FT	TP	Avg.
1978-79	S.A.-Boston	46	105	54	264	5.7
1980-81	Kansas City	23	34	20	88	3.8
	Totals	69	139	74	352	5.1

Yr.	Team	G	FG	FT	TP	Avg.

SCALES, DeWAYNE
b. Dec. 28, 1958 Ht. 6-8 Wt. 208 College—Louisiana State

Yr.	Team	G	FG	FT	TP	Avg.
1980-81	New York	44	94(1)	26	215	4.9

SCOTT, ALVIN
b. Sept. 14, 1955 Ht. 6-7 Wt. 185 College—Oral Roberts

Yr.	Team	G	FG	FT	TP	Avg.
1977-78	Phoenix	81	180	132	492	6.1
1978-79	Phoenix	81	212	120	544	6.7
1979-80	Phoenix	79	127(1)	95	350	4.4
1980-81	Phoenix	82	173(1)	97	444	5.4
	Totals	323	692(2)	444	1830	5.7

SHELTON, CRAIG
b. May 1, 1957 Ht. 6-7 Wt. 210 College—Georgetown

Yr.	Team	G	FG	FT	TP	Avg.
1980-81	Atlanta	55	100	35	235	4.3

SHELTON, LONNIE
b. Oct. 19, 1955 Ht. 6-9 Wt. 235 College—Oregon St.

Yr.	Team	G	FG	FT	TP	Avg.
1976-77	N.Y. Knicks	82	398	159	955	11.6
1977-78	New York	82	508	203	1219	14.9
1978-79	Seattle	76	446	131	1023	13.5
1979-80	Seattle	76	425(1)	184	1035	13.6
1980-81	Seattle	14	73	36	182	13.0
	Totals	330	1850(1)	713	4414	13.4

SHORT, PURVIS
b. July 2, 1957 Ht. 6-7 Wt. 210 College—Jackson St.

Yr.	Team	G	FG	FT	TP	Avg.
1978-79	Golden State	75	369	57	795	10.6
1979-80	Golden State	62	461	134	1056	17.0
1980-81	Golden State	79	549(3)	168	1269	16.1
	Totals	216	1379(3)	359	3120	14.4

SHUMATE, JOHN
b. April 6, 1952 Ht. 6-9 Wt. 235 College—Notre Dame

Yr.	Team	G	FG	FT	TP	Avg.
1974-75	Phoenix		(Injured)			
1975-76	Pho.-Buf.	75	332	212	876	11.7
1976-77	Buffalo	74	407	302	1116	15.1
1977-78	Buf.-Det.	80	391	400	1182	14.8
1978-79	Detroit		(Injured)			
1979-80	Hous.-S.A.	65	207	165	579	8.9
1980-81	S.A.-Seattle	24	56	55	167	7.0
	Totals	318	1393	1134	3920	12.3

SICHTING, JERRY
b. Nov. 29, 1956 Ht. 6-1½ Wt. 180 College—Purdue

Yr.	Team	G	FG	FT	TP	Avg.
1980-81	Indiana	47	34	25	93	2.0

SIKMA, JACK
b. Nov. 14, 1955 Ht. 6-11 Wt. 230 College— Ill. Wesleyan

Yr.	Team	G	FG	FT	TP	Avg.
1977-78	Seattle	82	342	192	865	10.7
1978-79	Seattle	82	476	329	1281	15.6
1979-80	Seattle	82	470	235	1175	14.3
1980-81	Seattle	82	595	340	1530	18.7
	Totals	328	1883	1096	4862	14.8

SILAS, JAMES
b. Feb. 11, 1949 Ht. 6-1 Wt. 185 College—S.F. Austin

Yr.	Team		G	FG	FT	TP	Avg.
1972-73	Dallas	(ABA)	78	341	389	1071	13.7
1973-74	San Antonio	(ABA)	84	486	349	1321	15.7
1974-75	San Antonio	(ABA)	82	578	430	1586	19.3
1975-76	San Antonio	(ABA)	84	718	564	2000	23.8
1976-77	San Antonio		22	61	87	209	9.5
1977-78	San Antonio		37	43	60	146	3.9
1978-79	San Antonio		79	466	334	1266	16.0
1979-80	San Antonio		77	513	339	1365	17.7
1980-81	San Antonio		75	476	374	1326	17.7
	Totals		618	3682	2926	10290	16.7

SMITH, ELMORE
b. May 9, 1949 Ht. 7-1 Wt. 250 College—Kentucky State

Yr.	Team	G	FG	FT	TP	Avg.
1971-72	Buffalo	78	579	194	1352	17.3
1972-73	Buffalo	76	600	188	1388	18.3
1973-74	Los Angeles	81	434	147	1015	12.5
1974-75	Los Angeles	74	346	112	804	10.9
1975-76	Milwaukee	78	498	222	1218	15.6
1976-77	Mil.-Cleve.	70	241	117	599	8.6
1977-78	Cleveland	81	402	205	1009	12.5
1978-79	Cleveland	24	69	18	156	6.5
1979-80	Cleveland		(Injured)			
1980-81	Cleveland		(Injured)			
	Totals	562	3169	1203	7541	13.4

SMITH, LARRY
b. Jan. 18, 1958 Ht. 6-8 Wt. 215 College—Alcorn State

Yr.	Team	G	FG	FT	TP	Avg.
1980-81	Golden State	82	304	177	785	9.6

SMITH, PHIL
b. April 22, 1952 Ht. 6-4 Wt. 187 College—San Francisco

Yr.	Team	G	FG	FT	TP	Avg.
1974-75	Golden State	74	221	127	569	7.7
1975-76	Golden State	82	659	323	1641	20.0
1976-77	Golden State	82	631	295	1557	19.0
1977-78	Golden State	82	648	316	1612	19.7
1978-79	Golden State	59	489	194	1172	19.9
1979-80	Golden State	51	325(7)	135	792	15.5
1980-81	San Diego	76	519(4)	237	1279	16.8
	Totals	506	3492(11)	1627	8622	17.0

SMITH, RANDY
b. Dec. 12, 1948 Ht. 6-3 Wt. 180 College—Buffalo St.

Yr.	Team	G	FG	FT	TP	Avg.
1971-72	Buffalo	76	432	158	1022	13.4
1972-73	Buffalo	82	511	192	1214	14.8
1973-74	Buffalo	82	531	205	1267	15.5
1974-75	Buffalo	82	610	236	1456	17.8
1975-76	Buffalo	82	702	383	1787	21.8
1976-77	Buffalo	82	702	294	1698	20.7
1977-78	Buffalo	82	789	443	2021	24.6
1978-79	San Diego	82	693	292	1678	20.5
1979-80	Cleveland	82	599(10)	233	1441	17.6
1980-81	Cleveland	82	486(1)	221	1194	14.6
	Totals	814	6055(11)	2657	14778	18.2

SOBERS, RICKY
b. Jan. 15, 1953 Ht. 6-3 Wt. 198 College—Nev.-Las Vegas

Yr.	Team	G	FG	FT	TP	Avg.
1975-76	Phoenix	78	280	158	718	9.2
1976-77	Phoenix	79	414	243	1071	13.6
1977-78	Indiana	79	553	330	1436	18.2
1978-79	Indiana	81	553	298	1404	17.3
1979-80	Chicago	82	470(21)	200	1161	14.2
1980-81	Chicago	71	355(17)	231	958	13.5
	Totals	470	2625(38)	1460	6748	14.4

Yr.	Team		G	FG	FT	TP	Avg.

SPANARKEL, JIM
b. June 28, 1957 Ht. 6-5 Wt. 190 College—Duke

Yr.	Team		G	FG	FT	TP	Avg.
1979-80	Philadelphia		40	72	54	198	5.0
1980-81	Dallas		82	404(1)	375	1184	14.4
	Totals		122	476(1)	429	1382	11.3

SPARROW, RORY
b. June 12, 1958 Ht. 6-2 Wt. 192 College—Villanova

Yr.	Team		G	FG	FT	TP	Avg.
1980-81	New Jersey		15	22	12	56	3.7

STROUD, JOHN
b. Oct. 29, 1957 Ht. 6-7 Wt. 215 College—Mississippi

Yr.	Team		G	FG	FT	TP	Avg.
1980-81	Houston		9	11	3	25	2.8

TAYLOR, BRIAN
b. June 9, 1951 Ht. 6-2 Wt. 185 College—Princeton

Yr.	Team		G	FG	FT	TP	Avg.
1972-73	New York	(ABA)	63	395(4)	168	962	15.3
1973-74	New York	(ABA)	75	363(8)	100	834	11.1
1974-75	New York	(ADA)	79	472(10)	150	1104	14.0
1975-76	New York	(ABA)	54	354(32)	164	904	16.7
1976-77	Kansas City		72	501	225	1227	17.0
1977-78	Denver		39	182	88	452	11.6
1978-79	San Diego		20	30	16	76	3.8
1979-80	San Diego		78	418(90)	130	1056	13.5
1980-81	San Diego		80	310(44)	146	810	10.1
	Totals		560	3025(188)	1187	7425	13.3

TERRY, CARLOS
b. June 22, 1956 Ht. 6-5 Wt. 220 College—Winston-Salem

Yr.	Team		G	FG	FT	TP	Avg.
1980-81	Washington		26	80	28	188	7.2

THEUS, REGGIE
b. Oct. 13, 1957 Ht. 6-7 Wt. 205 College—NV.-Ls.Vgs.

Yr.	Team		G	FG	FT	TP	Avg.
1978-79	Chicago		82	537	264	1338	16.3
1979-80	Chicago		82	566(28)	500	1660	20.2
1980-81	Chicago		82	543(18)	445	1549	18.9
	Totals		246	1646(46)	1209	4547	18.5

THOMPSON, DAVID
b. July 13, 1954 Ht. 6-5 Wt. 195 College—No.Carolina St.

Yr.	Team		G	FG	FT	TP	Avg.
1975-76	Denver	(ABA)	83	807(3)	541	2158	26.0
1976-77	Denver		82	824	477	2125	25.9
1977-78	Denver		80	826	520	2172	27.2
1978-79	Denver		76	693	439	1825	24.0
1979-80	Denver		39	289(7)	254	839	21.5
1980-81	Denver		77	734(10)	489	1967	25.5
	Totals		437	4173(20)	2720	11086	25.4

THOMPSON, MYCHAL
b. Jan. 30, 1955 Ht. 6-10 Wt. 226 College—Minnesota

Yr.	Team		G	FG	FT	TP	Avg.
1978-79	Portland		73	460	154	1074	14.7
1979-80	Portland			(Injured)			
1980-81	Portland		79	569	207	1345	17.0
	Totals		152	1029	361	2419	15.9

TOMJANOVICH, RUDY
b. Nov. 24, 1948 Ht. 6-8 Wt. 218 College—Michigan

Yr.	Team		G	FG	FT	TP	Avg.
1970-71	San Diego		77	168	73	409	5.3
1971-72	Houston		78	500	172	1172	15.0
1972-73	Houston		81	655	250	1560	19.3
1973-74	Houston		80	788	385	1961	24.5
1974-75	Houston		81	694	289	1677	20.7
1975-76	Houston		79	622	221	1465	18.5
1976-77	Houston		81	733	287	1753	21.6
1977-78	Houston		23	217	61	495	21.5
1978-79	Houston		74	620	168	1408	19.0
1979-80	Houston		62	370(22)	118	880	14.2
1980-81	Houston		52	263(12)	65	603	11.6
	Totals		768	5630(34)	2089	13383	17.4

TONEY, ANDREW
b. Nov. 23, 1957 Ht. 6-3 Wt. 178 College—Southwestern Louisiana

Yr.	Team		G	FG	FT	TP	Avg.
1980-81	Philadelphia		75	399(9)	161	968	12.9

TWARDZIK, DAVE
b. Sept. 20, 1950 Ht. 6-1 Wt. 180 College—Old Dominion

Yr.	Team		G	FG	FT	TP	Avg.
1972-73	Virginia	(ABA)	80	141(2)	178	462	5.8
1973-74	Virginia	(ABA)	57	163(3)	168	497	8.7
1974-75	Virginia	(ABA)	76	359(1)	317	1036	13.6
1975-76	Virginia	(ABA)	43	100(3)	113	316	7.4
1976-77	Portland		74	263	239	765	10.3
1977-78	Portland		75	242	183	667	8.9
1978-79	Portland		64	203	261	667	10.4
1979-80	Portland		67	183(4)	197	567	8.5
1980-81	Portland			(Injured)			
	Totals		536	1654(13)	1656	4977	9.3

TYLER, TERRY
b. Oct. 30, 1956 Ht. 6-7 Wt. 215 College—Detroit

Yr.	Team		G	FG	FT	TP	Avg.
1978-79	Detroit		82	456	144	1056	12.9
1979-80	Detroit		82	430(2)	143	1005	12.3
1980-81	Detroit		82	476	148	1100	13.4
	Totals		246	1362(2)	435	3161	12.8

UNSELD, WESTLEY
b. March 14, 1946 Ht. 6-8 Wt. 245 College—Louisville

Yr.	Team		G	FG	FT	TP	Avg.
1968-69	Baltimore		82	427	277	1131	13.8
1969-70	Baltimore		82	526	273	1325	16.2
1970-71	Baltimore		74	424	199	1047	14.1
1971-72	Baltimore		76	409	171	989	13.0
1972-73	Baltimore		79	421	149	991	12.5
1973-74	Capital		56	146	36	328	5.9
1974-75	Washington		73	273	126	672	9.2
1975-76	Washington		78	318	114	750	9.6
1976-77	Washington		82	270	100	640	7.8
1977-78	Washington		80	257	93	607	7.6
1978-79	Washington		77	346	151	843	10.9
1979-80	Washington		82	327(1)	139	794	9.7
1980-81	Washington		63	225(2)	55	507	8.0
	Totals		984	4369(3)	1883	10624	10.8

VALENTINE, RONNIE
b. Nov. 27, 1957 Ht. 6-7 Wt. 210 College—Old Dominion

Yr.	Team		G	FG	FT	TP	Avg.
1980-81	Denver		24	37(1)	9	84	3.5

VAN BREDA KOLFF, JAN
b. Dec. 16, 1951 Ht. 6-7 Wt. 200 College—Vanderbilt

Yr.	Team		G	FG	FT	TP	Avg.
1974-75	Denver	(ABA)	84	155	177	487	5.8
1975-76	Vir.-Ken.	(ABA)	80	223(2)	165	613	7.7
1976-77	N.Y. Nets		72	271	195	737	10.2
1977-78	New Jersey		68	107	87	301	4.4
1978-79	New Jersey		80	196	146	538	6.7

Yr.	Team	G	FG	FT	TP	Avg.
1979-80	New Jersey	82	212(7)	130	561	6.8
1980-81	New Jersey	78	100(2)	98	300	3.8
	Totals	544	1264(11)	998	3537	6.5

VANDEWEGHE, ERNEST (Kiki)
b. Aug. 1, 1958 Ht. 6-8 Wt. 220 College—UCLA

Yr.	Team	G	FG	FT	TP	Avg.
1980-81	Denver	51	229	130	588	11.5

VROMAN, BRETT
b. Dec. 25, 1955 Ht. 7-0 Wt. 225 College—UCLA/NV Las Vegas

Yr.	Team	G	FG	FT	TP	Avg.
1980-81	Utah	11	10	14	34	3.1

WALKER, CLARENCE (Foots)
b. May 21, 1951 Ht. 6-1 Wt. 172 College—W. Georgia

Yr.	Team	G	FG	FT	TP	Avg.
1974-75	Cleveland	72	111	80	302	4.2
1975-76	Cleveland	81	143	84	370	4.6
1976-77	Cleveland	62	157	89	403	6.5
1977-78	Cleveland	81	287	159	733	9.0
1978-79	Cleveland	55	208	137	553	10.1
1979-80	Cleveland	76	258(1)	195	712	9.4
1980-81	New Jersey	41	72(2)	88	234	5.7
	Totals	468	1236(3)	832	3307	7.1

WALKER, WALLY
b. July 18, 1954 Ht. 6-6 Wt. 200 College—Virginia

Yr.	Team	G	FG	FT	TP	Avg.
1976-77	Portland	66	137	67	341	5.2
1977-78	Port.-Sea.	77	204	75	483	6.3
1978-79	Seattle	60	168	58	394	6.6
1979-80	Seattle	70	139	48	326	4.7
1980-81	Seattle	82	290	109	689	8.4
	Totals	355	938	357	2233	6.3

WALTON, LLOYD
b. Nov. 23, 1953 Ht. 6-1 Wt. 160 College—Marquette

Yr.	Team	G	FG	FT	TP	Avg.
1976-77	Milwaukee	53	88	53	229	4.3
1977-78	Milwaukee	76	154	54	362	4.8
1978-79	Milwaukee	75	157	61	375	5.0
1979-80	Milwaukee	76	110(1)	49	270	3.6
1980-81	Kansas City	61	90	26	206	3.4
	Totals	341	599(1)	243	1442	4.2

WASHINGTON, KERMIT
b. Sept. 17, 1951 Ht. 6-8 Wt. 230 College—American

Yr.	Team	G	FG	FT	TP	Avg.
1973-74	Los Angeles	45	73	26	172	3.8
1974-75	Los Angeles	55	87	72	246	4.5
1975-76	Los Angeles	36	39	45	123	3.4
1976-77	Los Angeles	53	191	132	514	9.7
1977-78	L.A.-Bos.	57	247	170	664	11.6
1978-79	San Diego	82	350	227	927	11.3
1979-80	Portland	80	421	231	1073	13.4
1980-81	Portland	73	325	181	831	11.4
	Totals	481	1733	1084	4550	9.5

WASHINGTON, RICHARD
b. July 15, 1955 Ht. 6-10 Wt. 220 College—UCLA

Yr.	Team	G	FG	FT	TP	Avg.
1976-77	Kansas City	82	446	177	1069	13.0
1977-78	Kansas City	78	425	150	1000	12.8
1978-79	Kansas City	18	14	10	38	2.1
1979-80	Milwaukee	75	197	46	440	5.9
1980-81	Dal.-Clev.	80	340(1)	119	800	10.0
	Totals	333	1422(1)	502	3347	10.1

WEBSTER, MARVIN
b. April 13, 1952 Ht. 7-1 Wt. 230 College—Morgan St.

Yr.	Team	G	FG	FT	TP	Avg.
1975-76	Denver (ABA)	38	55	55	165	4.3
1976-77	Denver	80	198	143	539	6.7
1977-78	Seattle	82	427	290	1144	14.0
1978-79	New York	60	264	150	678	11.3
1979-80	New York	20	38	12	88	4.4
1980-81	New York	82	159(1)	104	423	5.2
	Totals	362	1141(1)	754	3037	8.4

WEDMAN, SCOTT
b. July 29, 1952 Ht. 6-7 Wt. 215 College—Colorado

Yr.	Team	G	FG	FT	TP	Avg.
1974-75	K.C.-O.	80	375	139	889	11.1
1975-76	Kansas City	82	538	191	1267	15.5
1976-77	Kansas City	81	521	206	1248	15.4
1977-78	Kansas City	81	607	221	1435	17.7
1978-79	Kansas City	73	561	216	1338	18.3
1979-80	Kansas City	68	569(7)	145	1290	19.0
1980-81	Kansas City	81	685(25)	140	1535	19.0
	Totals	546	3856(32)	1258	9002	16.5

WESTPHAL, PAUL
b. Nov. 30, 1950 Ht. 6-4 Wt. 195 College—USC

Yr.	Team	G	FG	FT	TP	Avg.
1972-73	Boston	60	89	67	245	4.1
1973-74	Boston	82	238	112	588	7.2
1974-75	Boston	82	342	119	803	9.8
1975-76	Phoenix	82	657	365	1679	20.5
1976-77	Phoenix	81	682	362	1726	21.3
1977-78	Phoenix	80	809	396	2014	25.2
1978-79	Phoenix	81	801	339	1941	24.0
1979-80	Phoenix	82	692(26)	382	1792	21.9
1980-81	Seattle	36	221(6)	153	601	16.7
	Totals	666	4531(32)	2295	11389	17.1

WHITE, RUDY
b. June 23, 1953 Ht. 6-2 Wt. 195 College—Arizona St.

Yr.	Team	G	FG	FT	TP	Avg.
1975-76	Houston	32	42	18	102	3.2
1976-77	Houston	46	47	15	109	2.4
1977-78	Houston	21	31	14	76	3.6
1978-79	Houston	(Injured)				
1979-80	Houston	9	13	10	36	4.0
1980-81	G.S.-Sea.	16	23	15	61	3.8
	Totals	124	156	72	384	3.1

WHITEHEAD, JEROME
b. Sept. 30, 1956 Ht. 6-10 Wt. 220 College—Marquette

Yr.	Team	G	FG	FT	TP	Avg.
1978-79	San Diego	31	15	8	38	1.2
1979-80	S.D.-Utah	50	58	10	126	2.5
1980-81	Dal.-Clev.-S.D.	48	83	28	194	4.0
	Totals	129	156	46	358	2.8

WHITNEY, CHARLES (Hawkeye)
b. June 22, 1957 Ht. 6-5 Wt. 235 College—North Carolina State

Yr.	Team	G	FG	FT	TP	Avg.
1980-81	Kansas City	47	149(2)	50	350	7.4

WICKS, SIDNEY
b. Sept. 19, 1949 Ht. 6-9 Wt. 225 College—UCLA

Yr.	Team	G	FG	FT	TP	Avg.
1971-72	Portland	82	784	441	2009	24.5
1972-73	Portland	80	761	384	1906	23.8
1973-74	Portland	75	685	314	1684	22.5
1974-75	Portland	82	692	394	1778	21.7

Yr.	Team	G	FG	FT	TP	Avg.
1975-76	Portland	79	580	345	1505	19.7
1976-77	Boston	82	464	310	1238	15.1
1977-78	Boston	81	433	217	1083	13.4
1978-79	San Diego	79	312	147	771	9.8
1979-80	San Diego	71	210	83	503	7.1
1980-81	San Diego	49	125	76	326	6.7
	Totals	760	5046	2711	12803	16.8

WILEY, MICHAEL
b. Oct. 16, 1957 Ht. 6-9 Wt. 200 College—Long Beach State

Yr.	Team	G	FG	FT	TP	Avg.
1980-81	San Antonio	33	76	36	188	5.7

WILKERSON, BOB
b. Aug. 15, 1954 Ht. 6-7 Wt. 195 College—Indiana

Yr.	Team	G	FG	FT	TP	Avg.
1976-77	Seattle	78	221	84	526	6.7
1977-78	Denver	81	382	157	921	11.4
1978-79	Denver	80	396	119	911	11.4
1979-80	Denver	75	430(7)	166	1033	13.8
1980-81	Chicago	80	330(1)	137	798	10.0
	Totals	394	1759(8)	663	4189	10.6

WILKES, JAMAAL (Silk)
b. May 2, 1953 Ht. 6-7 Wt. 190 College—UCLA

Yr.	Team	G	FG	FT	TP	Avg.
1974-75	Golden State	82	502	160	1164	14.2
1975-76	Golden State	82	617	227	1461	17.8
1976-77	Golden State	76	548	247	1343	17.7
1977-78	Los Angeles	51	277	106	660	12.9
1978-79	Los Angeles	82	626	272	1524	18.6
1979-80	Los Angeles	82	726(3)	189	1644	20.0
1980-81	Los Angeles	81	786(1)	254	1827	22.6
	Totals	536	4082(4)	1455	9623	18.0

WILKES, JAMES
b. March 12, 1958 Ht. 6-7 Wt. 195 College—UCLA

Yr.	Team	G	FG	FT	TP	Avg.
1980-81	Chicago	48	85	29	199	4.1

WILKINS, JEFF
b. March 9, 1955 Ht. 7-0 Wt. 225 College—Illinois State

Yr.	Team	G	FG	FT	TP	Avg.
1980-81	Utah	56	117	27	261	4.7

WILLIAMS, FREEMAN
b. May 15, 1956 Ht. 6-4 Wt. 195 College—Portland St.

Yr.	Team	G	FG	FT	TP	Avg.
1978-79	San Diego	72	335	76	746	10.4
1979-80	San Diego	82	645(42)	194	1526	18.6
1980-81	San Diego	82	642(48)	253	1585	19.3
	Totals	236	1622(90)	523	3857	16.3

WILLIAMS, GUS
b. Oct. 10, 1953 Ht. 6-2 Wt. 175 College—USC

Yr.	Team	G	FG	FT	TP	Avg.
1975-76	Golden State	77	365	173	903	11.7
1976-77	Golden State	82	325	112	762	9.3
1977-78	Seattle	79	602	227	1431	18.1
1978-79	Seattle	76	606	245	1457	19.2
1979-80	Seattle	82	739(7)	331	1816	22.1
1980-81	Seattle		(Did not play)			
	Totals	396	2637(7)	1088	6369	16.1

WILLIAMS, RAY
b. Oct. 14, 1954 Ht. 6-2 Wt. 188 College—Minnesota

Yr.	Team	G	FG	FT	TP	Avg.
1977-78	New York	81	305	146	756	9.3
1978-79	New York	81	575	251	1401	17.3
1979-80	New York	82	687(7)	333	1714	20.9
1980-81	New York	79	616(16)	312	1560	19.7
	Totals	323	2183(23)	1042	5431	16.8

WILLIAMS, SYLVESTER (Sly)
b. Jan. 26, 1958 Ht. 6-7 Wt. 210 College—Rhode Island

Yr.	Team	G	FG	FT	TP	Avg.
1979-80	New York	57	104	58	266	4.7
1980-81	New York	67	349(2)	185	885	13.2
	Totals	124	453(2)	243	1151	9.3

WILLIAMSON, JOHN
b. Nov. 10, 1952 Ht. 6-2 Wt. 185 College—N. Mex. St.

Yr.	Team		G	FG	FT	TP	Avg.
1973-74	New York	(ABA)	77	482(2)	150	1116	14.5
1974-75	New York	(ABA)	75	370(3)	123	866	11.5
1975-76	New York	(ABA)	76	519(8)	187	1233	16.2
1976-77	NYN-Ind.		72	618	250	1495	20.8
1977-78	Ind.-N.J.		75	723	331	1777	23.7
1978-79	New Jersey		74	635	373	1643	22.5
1979-80	N.J.-Wash.		58	359(11)	116	845	14.6
1980-81	Washington		9	18(1)	5	42	4.7
	Totals		516	3724(25)	1544	9017	17.5

WILLOUGHBY, BILL
b. May 20, 1957 Ht. 6-8 Wt. 205 College—None

Yr.	Team	G	FG	FT	TP	Avg.
1975-76	Atlanta	62	113	66	292	4.7
1976-77	Atlanta	39	75	43	193	4.9
1977-78	Buffalo	56	156	64	376	6.7
1979-80	Cleveland	78	219(1)	96	535	6.9
1980-81	Houston	55	150	49	349	6.3
	Totals	290	713(1)	318	1745	6.0

WINTERS, BRIAN
b. March 1, 1952 Ht. 6-4 Wt. 185 College—S. Carolina

Yr.	Team	G	FG	FT	TP	Avg.
1974-75	Los Angeles	68	359	76	794	11.7
1975-76	Milwaukee	78	618	180	1416	18.2
1976-77	Milwaukee	78	652	205	1509	19.3
1977-78	Milwaukee	80	674	246	1594	19.9
1978-79	Milwaukee	79	662	237	1561	19.8
1979-80	Milwaukee	80	535(38)	184	1292	16.2
1980-81	Milwaukee	69	331(18)	119	799	11.6
	Totals	532	3831(56)	1247	8965	16.9

WOODSON, MIKE
b. March 24, 1958 Ht. 6-5 Wt. 195 College—Indiana

Yr.	Team	G	FG	FT	TP	Avg.
1980-81	New York	81	165(1)	49	380	4.7

WORTHEN, SAM
b. Jan. 17, 1958 Ht. 6-6 Wt. 195 College—Marquette

Yr.	Team	G	FG	FT	TP	Avg.
1980-81	Chicago	64	95	45	235	3.7

WRIGHT, LARRY
b. Nov. 23, 1954 Ht. 6-0 Wt. 175 College—Grambling

Yr.	Team	G	FG	FT	TP	Avg.
1976-77	Washington	78	262	88	612	7.8
1977-78	Washington	70	283	76	642	9.2
1978-79	Washington	73	276	125	677	9.3
1979-80	Washington	76	229(4)	96	558	7.3
1980-81	Detroit	45	140(2)	53	335	7.4
	Totals	342	1190(6)	438	2824	8.3

RETIRED PLAYERS

The lifetime summaries and year-by-year records of every player who played in the Basketball Association of America, National Basketball Association and the American Basketball Association and retired prior to the 1981-1982 season are contained in this section. Also included are yearly statistics for all National Basketball League players who later showed up in the BAA or NBA.

Each player's individual record lists his team, games played (G), field goals made (FG), free throws made (FT), total points (TP) and average (Avg.). The number in parenthesis following field goal totals indicates the number of three-point field goals scored. Each player's date of birth, height, weight and college are listed wherever available.

Yr.	Team		G	FG	FT	TP	Avg.
ABDUL-AZIZ, ZAID (Don Smith)							
b. April 7, 1946 Ht. 6-9 Wt. 235 College—Iowa							
1968-69	Cin.-Mil.		49	144	70	352	7.3
1969-70	Milwaukee		80	237	119	593	7.4
1970-71	Seattle		61	263	139	665	10.9
1971-72	Seattle		58	322	154	798	13.8
1972-73	Houston		48	149	119	413	8.7
1973-74	Houston		79	336	193	865	10.9
1974-75	Houston		65	235	159	629	9.7
1975-76	Seattle		27	35	16	96	3.2
1976-77	Buffalo		22	25	33	83	3.8
1977-78	Bos.-Hou.		16	23	17	63	3.9
	Totals		505	1769	1019	4557	9.0
ABDUL-RAHMAD, MAHDI (Walt Hazzard)							
b. April 15, 1942 Ht. 6-2 Wt. 190 College—UCLA							
1964-65	Los Angeles		66	117	46	280	4.2
1965-66	Los Angeles		80	458	182	1098	13.7
1966-67	Los Angeles		79	301	129	731	9.3
1967-68	Seattle		79	733	428	1894	23.9
1968-69	Atlanta		80	345	208	898	11.2
1969-70	Atlanta		82	493	267	1253	15.3
1970-71	Atlanta		82	517	315	1349	16.5
1971-72	Buffalo		72	450	237	1137	15.8
1972-73	Buf.-G.S.		55	107	47	261	4.7
1973-74	Seattle		49	76	34	186	3.8
	Totals		724	3597	1893	9087	12.6
ABLE, FOREST							
b. July 17, 1932 Ht. 6-3 Wt. 180 College—Western Ky.							
1956-57	Syracuse		1	0	0	0	0.0
ABRAMOVIC, JOHN (Brooms)							
b. Feb. 9, 1919 Ht. 6-3 Wt. 196 College—Salem							
1946-47	Pittsburgh		47	202	123	527	11.2
1947-48	St. L.-Balt.		9	1	4	6	0.7
1947-48	Syracuse	(NL)	35	72	42	186	5.3
	Totals		91	275	169	719	7.9
ACKERMAN, DONALD (Buddy)							
b. Sept. 4, 1930 Ht. 6-0 Wt. 183 College—Long Island Univ.							
1953-54	New York		28	14	15	43	1.5

Yr.	Team		G	FG	FT	TP	Avg.
ACTON, CHARLES (Bud)							
Ht. 6-6 Wt. 210 College—Alma and Hillsdale							
1967-68	San Diego		23	29	19	77	3.3
ADAMS, DON							
b. Nov. 27, 1947 Ht. 6-7 Wt. 210 College—Northwestern							
1970-71	San Diego		82	391	155	937	11.4
1971-72	Houston-Atl.		73	313	205	831	11.4
1972-73	Atl.-Det.		74	265	145	675	9.1
1973-74	Detroit		74	303	153	759	10.3
1974-75	Detroit		51	127	45	299	5.9
1974-75	St. Louis	(ABA)	16	42	17	101	6.3
1975-76	St. Louis	(ABA)	20	99	63	261	13.1
1975-76	Buffalo		56	67	40	174	3.1
1976-77	Buffalo		77	216	129	561	7.3
	Totals		523	1823	952	4598	8.8
ADAMS, GEORGE							
b. May 15, 1949 Ht. 6-6 Wt. 210 College—Gardner-Webb							
1972-73	San Diego	(ABA)	60	153(2)	65	373	6.2
1973-74	San Diego	(ABA)	80	253(1)	78	585	7.3
1974-75	San Diego	(ABA)	75	310(1)	73	694	9.3
	Totals		215	716(4)	216	1652	7.7
ADELMAN, RICK							
b. June 16, 1946 Ht. 6-1 Wt. 178 College—Loyola (Calif.)							
1968-69	San Diego		77	177	131	485	6.3
1969-70	San Diego		35	96	68	260	7.4
1970-71	Portland		81	378	267	1023	12.6
1971-72	Portland		80	329	151	809	10.1
1972-73	Portland		76	214	73	501	6.6
1973-74	Chicago		55	64	54	182	3.3
1974-75	Chi-NO-KC.-O		58	123	73	319	5.5
	Totals		462	1381	817	3579	7.7
AITCH, MATT							
b. 1945 Ht. 6-7 Wt. 230 College—Michigan State							
1967-68	Indiana	(ABA)	45	100	52	252	5.6
AKIN, HENRY							
b. July 31, 1944 Ht. 6-10 Wt. 235 College—Morehead St.							
1966-67	New York		50	83	26	192	3.8
1967-68	Seattle		36	46	20	112	3.1
1968-69	Kentucky	(ABA)	2	1	2	4	2.0
	Totals		68	130	48	308	3.5

Yr.	Team		G	FG	FT	TP	Avg.
ALCORN, GARY							
b. Oct. 8, 1936 Ht. 6-9 Wt. 225 College—Fresno State							
1960-61 Los Angeles			19	12	7	31	1.6
ALLEN, BILL							
b. 1945 Ht. 6-8 Wt. 205 College—New Mexico St.							
1967-68 Anaheim	(ABA)		38	120(2)	58	300	7.9
ALLEN, BOB							
b. July 17, 1946 Ht. 6-9 Wt. 205 College—Marshall							
1968-69 San Francisco			27	14	20	48	1.8
ALLEN, LUCIUS							
b. Sept. 26, 1947 Ht. 6-2 Wt. 175 College—UCLA							
1969-70 Seattle			81	306	182	794	9.8
1970-71 Milwaukee			61	178	77	433	7.1
1971-72 Milwaukee			80	441	198	1080	13.5
1972-73 Milwaukee			80	547	143	1237	15.5
1973-74 Milwaukee			72	526	216	1268	17.6
1974-75 Mil.-L.A.			66	511	238	1260	19.1
1975-76 Los Angeles			76	461	197	1119	14.7
1976-77 Los Angeles			78	472	195	1139	14.6
1977-78 Kansas City			77	373	174	920	11.9
1978-79 Kansas City			31	69	19	157	5.1
	Totals		702	3884	1639	9407	13.4
ALLEN, WILLIE							
Ht. 6-6 Wt. 230 College—Miami (Fla.)							
1971-72 Floridians	(ABA)		7	4	5	13	1.9
ALLISON, ODIS							
b. Oct. 2, 1949 Ht. 6-6 Wt. 195 College—Nev.-Las V.							
1971-72 Golden State			36	17	33	67	1.9
ANDEREGG, ROBERT							
b. Aug. 24, 1937 Ht. 6-3 Wt. 200 College—Mich. State							
1959-60 New York			33	55	23	133	4.0
ANDERSON, ANDY							
b. Feb. 6, 1945 Ht. 6-2 Wt. 185 College—Canisius							
1967-68 Oakland	(ABA)		77	279(9)	163	730	9.5
1968-69 Oak.-Miami	(ABA)		36	123	98	344	9.6
	Totals		113	402(9)	261	1074	9.5
ANDERSON, CLIFF							
b. Sept. 7, 1944 Ht. 6-4 Wt. 200 College—St. Joseph's (Pa.)							
1967-68 Los Angeles			18	7	12	26	1.4
1968-69 Los Angeles	(ABA)		35	44	47	135	3.9
1969-70 Denver			3	2	2	6	2.0
1970-71 Cleve.-Phila.			28	20	46	86	3.1
	Totals		84	73	107	253	3.0
ANDERSON, DAN							
b. Feb. 15, 1943 Ht. 6-10 Wt. 230 College—Augsburg							
1967-68 New Jersey	(ABA)		78	463	223	1149	14.7
1968-69 N.Y.-Ky.-Minn.	(ABA)		62	220	118	558	9.0
	Total		140	683	341	1707	12.2

Yr.	Team		G	FG	FT	TP	Avg.
ANDERSON, DAN							
b. Jan. 1, 1951 Ht. 6-2 Wt. 185 College—USC							
1974-75 Portland			43	47	26	120	2.8
1975-76 Portland			52	88	51	227	4.4
	Totals		95	135	77	347	3.7
ANDERSON, JEROME							
b. October 9, 1953 Ht. 6-5 Wt. 195 College—W. Va.							
1975-76 Boston			22	25	11	61	2.8
1976-77 Indiana			27	26	14	66	2.4
	Totals		49	51	25	127	2.6
ANDERSON, KIM							
b. May 12, 1955 Ht. 6-7 Wt. 200 College—Missouri							
1978-79 Portland			21	24	15	63	3.0
ANDERZUNAS, WALLY							
b. Jan. 11, 1946 Ht. 6-7 Wt. 220 College—Creighton							
1969-70 Cincinnati			44	65	29	159	3.6
ANIELAK, DON							
b. 1932 Ht. 6-7½ Wt. 192 College—Southwest Missouri							
1954-55 New York			1	0	3	3	3.0
ARCENEAUX, STACEY (Robert L. Stacey)							
b. Feb. 17, 1936 Ht. 6-4½ Wt. 220 College—Iowa St.							
1961-62 St. Louis			7	22	6	50	7.1
ARD, JIM							
b. Sept. 19, 1948 Ht. 6-9 Wt. 215 College—Cincinnati							
1970-71 New York	(ABA)		73	174	79	427	5.9
1971-72 New York	(ABA)		71	159(2)	77	397	5.6
1972-73 New York	(ABA)		42	53	34	140	3.3
1973-74 Memphis	(ABA)		27	66(2)	40	174	6.4
1974-75 Boston			59	89	48	226	3.8
1975-76 Boston			81	107	71	285	3.5
1976-77 Boston			63	96	49	241	3.8
1977-78 Bos.-Chic.			15	8	3	19	1.3
	Totals		431	752(4)	401	1909	4.4
ARIZIN, PAUL							
b. April 9, 1928 Ht. 6-4 Wt. 200 College—Villanova							
1950-51 Philadelphia			65	352	417	1121	17.2
1951-52 Philadelphia			66	548	578	1674	25.4
1954-55 Philadelphia			72	529	454	1512	21.0
1955-56 Philadelphia			72	617	507	1741	24.2
1956-57 Philadelphia			71	613	591	1817	25.6
1957-58 Philadelphia			68	483	440	1406	20.7
1958-59 Philadelphia			70	632	587	1851	26.4
1959-60 Philadelphia			72	593	420	1606	22.3
160-61 Philadelphia			79	650	532	1832	23.2
1961-62 Philadelphia			78	611	484	1706	21.9
	Totals		713	5628	5010	16266	22.8
ARMSTRONG, PAUL (Curly)							
b. Nov. 1, 1918 Ht. 5-11 Wt. 170 College—Indiana							
1941-42 Ft. Wayne	(NL)		24	69	60	198	8.3
1942-43 Ft. Wayne	(NL)		23	67	49	183	8.0

Yr.	Team		G	FG	FT	TP	Avg.
1945-46	Ft. Wayne	(NL)	6	3	1	7	1.2
1946-47	Ft. Wayne	(NL)	44	127	134	388	8.8
1947-48	Ft. Wayne		53	148	139	435	8.2
1948-49	Ft. Wayne		52	131	118	380	7.3
1949-50	Ft. Wayne		63	144	170	458	7.3
1950-51	Ft. Wayne		38	72	58	202	5.3
	Totals		303	761	729	2251	7.1

ARMSTRONG, ROBERT
b. June 17, 1933 Ht. 6-8 Wt. 230 College—Mich. State

Yr.	Team	G	FG	FT	TP	Avg.
1956-57	Philadelphia	19	11	6	28	1.5

ARMSTRONG, TATE
b. Oct. 5, 1955 Ht. 6-3 Wt. 175 College—Duke

Yr.	Team	G	FG	FT	TP	Avg.
1977-78	Chicago	66	131	22	284	4.3
1978-79	Chicago	26	28	10	66	2.5
	Totals	92	159	32	350	3.8

ARMSTRONG, WARREN
See Jabali, Warren

ARNELLE, JESSE
b. Dec. 30, 1933 Ht. 6-5 Wt. 220 College—Penn State

Yr.	Team	G	FG	FT	TP	Avg.
1955-56	Ft. Wayne	31	52	43	147	4.7

ARNETTE, JAY
b. Dec. 19, 1938 Ht. 6-2 Wt. 175 College—Texas

Yr.	Team	G	FG	FT	TP	Avg.
1963-64	Cincinnati	48	71	42	184	3.8
1964-65	Cincinnati	63	91	56	238	3.8
1965-66	Cincinnati	3	1	0	2	0.7
	Totals	114	163	98	424	3.7

ARNZEN, BOB
b. Nov. 3, 1947 Ht. 6-6 Wt. 215 College—Notre Dame

Yr.	Team		G	FG	FT	TP	Avg.
1969-70	New York	(ABA)	13	19	2	40	3.1
1970-71	Cincinnati		55	128	45	301	5.5
1972-73	Indiana	(ABA)	23	20	6	46	2.0
1973-74	Indiana	(ABA)	20	24(1)	7	56	2.8
	Totals		111	191(1)	60	443	4.0

ARTHURS, JOHN
b. Aug. 15, 1947 Ht. 6-4 Wt. 185 College—Tulane

Yr.	Team	G	FG	FT	TP	Avg.
1969-70	Milwaukee	11	12	11	35	3.2

ASMONGA, DON
b. 1925 Ht. 6-2 Wt. 185 College—Alliance

Yr.	Team	G	FG	FT	TP	Avg.
1953-54	Baltimore	7	2	1	5	0.7

ATHA, RICHARD
b. Sept. 21, 1931 Ht. 6-2 Wt. 195 College—Indiana St.

Yr.	Team	G	FG	FT	TP	Avg.
1955-56	New York	25	36	21	93	3.7
1957-58	Detroit	18	17	10	44	2.4
	Totals	43	53	31	137	3.2

ATTLES, ALVIN
b. Nov. 7, 1936 Ht. 6-2 Wt. 175 College—No. Car. A&T

Yr.	Team	G	FG	FT	TP	Avg.
1960-61	Philadelphia	77	222	97	541	7.0
1961-62	Philadelphia	75	343	158	844	11.2
1962-63	San Francisco	71	301	133	735	10.4
1963-64	San Francisco	70	289	185	763	10.9
1964-65	San Francisco	73	254	171	679	9.3
1965-66	San Francisco	79	364	154	882	11.2
1966-67	San Francisco	70	212	88	512	7.3
1967-68	San Francisco	67	252	150	654	9.8
1968-69	San Francisco	51	162	95	419	8.2
1969-70	San Francisco	45	78	75	231	5.1
1970-71	San Francisco	34	22	24	68	2.0
	Totals	712	2499	1330	6328	8.9

AUBUCHON, CHET (Aubie)
b. May 8, 1916 Ht. 5-10 Wt. 145 College—Mich. State

Yr.	Team	G	FG	FT	TP	Avg.
1946-47	Detroit	30	23	19	65	2.2

AUSTIN, JOHN
b. Aug. 31, 1944 Ht. 6-0 Wt. 175 College—Boston College

Yr.	Team		G	FG	FT	TP	Avg.
1966-67	Baltimore		4	5	13	23	5.9
1967-68	New Jersey	(ABA)	41	108	101	317	7.7
	Totals		45	113	114	340	7.6

AVERITT, WILLIAM (Bird)
b. July 22, 1952 Ht. 6-2 Wt. 175 College—Pepperdine

Yr.	Team		G	FG	FT	TP	Avg.
1973-74	San Antonio	(ABA)	74	343(9)	156	851	11.5
1974-75	Kentucky	(ABA)	84	422(7)	249	1100	13.1
1975-76	Kentucky	(ABA)	78	546(40)	266	1398	17.9
1976-77	Buffalo		75	234	121	589	7.9
1977-78	N.J.-Buff.		55	198	100	496	9.0
	Totals		366	1743(56)	892	4434	12.1

BACH, JOHN
b. July 10, 1924 Ht. 6-2 Wt. 180 College—Rochester and Fordham

Yr.	Team	G	FG	FT	TP	Avg.
1948-49	Boston	34	34	51	119	3.5

BACON, W. HENRY
Ht. 6-3 Wt. 205 College—Louisville

Yr.	Team		G	FG	FT	TP	Avg.
1972-73	San Diego	(ABA)	47	60(2)	44	166	3.5

BAECHTOLD, JIM
b. Dec. 9, 1927 Ht. 6-4 Wt. 205 College—Eastern Ky.

Yr.	Team	G	FG	FT	TP	Avg.
1952-53	Baltimore	64	242	177	661	10.3
1953-54	New York	70	170	134	474	6.8
1954-55	New York	72	362	279	1003	13.9
1955-56	New York	70	268	233	769	11.0
1956-57	New York	45	75	66	216	4.8
	Totals	321	1117	889	3123	9.7

BAILEY, GUS
b. Feb. 18, 1951 Ht. 6-5 Wt. 185 College—Texas-El Paso

Yr.	Team	G	FG	FT	TP	Avg.
1974-75	Houston	47	51	20	122	2.6
1975-76	Houston	30	28	14	70	2.3
1977-78	New Orleans	48	59	37	155	3.2
1978-79	New Orleans	2	2	0	4	2.0
1979-80	Washington	20	16(1)	5	38	1.9
	Totals	147	156(1)	76	389	2.6

BAKER, JIMMIE
b. Dec. 25, 1953 Ht. 6-9 Wt. 220 College—Nevada-Las Vegas/Hawaii

Yr.	Team		G	FG	FT	TP	Avg.
1975-76	Kentucky	(ABA)	5	3	0	6	1.2

Yr.	Team		G	FG	FT	TP	Avg.

BAKER, NORMAN
Ht. 6-2 Wt. 180 College—None

Yr.	Team	G	FG	FT	TP	Avg.
1946-47 Chicago		4	0	0	0	0.0

BALTIMORE, HERSCHEL
b. June 21, 1921 Ht. 6-4 Wt. 195 College—Penn St.

1946-47 St. Louis		58	53	32	138	2.4

BANKS, WALKER
Ht. 6-10 Wt. 205 College—Western Kentucky

1970-71 Pittsburgh	(ABA)	16	17	7	41	2.6

BARBER, JOHN
b. June 27, 1927 Ht. 6-6 Wt. 210 College—L.A. State

1956-57 St. Louis		5	2	3	7	1.4

BARKER, CLIFF
b. Jan. 15, 1921 Ht. 6-2 Wt. 185 College—Kentucky

1949-50 Indianapolis		49	102	75	279	5.7
1950-51 Indianapolis		56	51	50	152	2.7
1951-52 Indianapolis		44	48	30	126	2.9
	Totals	149	201	155	557	3.7

BARKSDALE, DON
b. March 31, 1923 Ht. 6-6 Wt. 200 College—UCLA

1951-52 Baltimore		62	272	237	781	12.6
1952-53 Baltimore		65	321	257	899	13.8
1953-54 Boston		63	156	149	461	7.3
1954-55 Boston		72	267	220	754	10.5
	Totals	262	1016	863	2895	11.0

BARNES, HARRY
b. July 25, 1945 Ht. 6-3 Wt. 205 College—Northeastern

1968-69 San Diego		22	18	7	43	2.0

BARNES, JIM (Bad News)
b. April 13, 1941 Ht. 6-8 Wt. 240 College—Tex. West.

1964-65 New York		75	454	251	1159	15.5
1965-66 N.Y.-Balt.		73	348	212	908	12.4
1966-67 Los Angeles		80	217	128	562	7.0
1967-68 L.A.-Chicago		79	221	133	575	7.3
1968-69 Chi.-Bos.		59	115	75	305	5.2
1969-70 Boston		77	178	95	451	5.9
1970-71 Baltimore		11	15	7	37	3.4
	Totals	454	1548	901	3997	8.8

BARNES, MARVIN
b. July 27, 1952 Ht. 6-9 Wt. 225 College—Providence

1974-75 St. Louis	(ABA)	77	777	295	1849	24.0
1975-76 St. Louis	(ABA)	67	681(3)	251	1616	24.1
1976-77 Detroit		53	202	106	510	9.6
1977-78 Det.-Buff.		60	279	128	686	11.4
1978-79 Boston		38	133	43	309	8.1
1979-80 San Diego		20	24	16	64	3.2
	Totals	315	2096(3)	839	5034	16.0

BARNETT, JIM
b. July 7, 1944 Ht. 6-4 Wt. 180 College—Oregon

1966-67 Boston		48	78	42	198	4.1
1967-68 San Diego		47	179	84	442	9.4
1968-69 San Diego		80	465	233	1163	14.5
1969-70 San Diego		80	450	289	1189	14.9
1970-71 Portland		78	559	326	1444	18.5
1971-72 Golden State		80	374	244	992	12.4
1972-73 Golden State		82	394	183	971	11.8
1973-74 Golden State		77	350	184	884	11.5
1974-75 N.O.-N.Y.		73	285	199	769	10.5
1975-76 New York		71	164	90	418	5.9
1976-77 Philadelphia		16	28	10	66	4.1
	Totals	732	3326	1884	8536	11.7

BARNETT, NATE
b. Jan. 29, 1953 Ht. 6-4 Wt. 180 College—Akron

1975-76 Indiana	(ABA)	12	12	3	27	2.3

BARNETT, RICHARD (Dick)
b. Oct. 2, 1936 Ht. 6-4 Wt. 190 College—Tenn. State

1959-60 Syracuse		75	289	128	706	12.4
1960-61 Syracuse		78	540	240	1320	16.9
1962-63 Los Angeles		80	547	343	1437	18.0
1963-64 Los Angeles		78	541	351	1433	18.4
1964-65 Los Angeles		74	375	270	1020	13.8
1965-66 New York		75	631	467	1729	23.1
1966-67 New York		67	454	231	1139	17.0
1967-68 New York		81	559	343	1461	18.0
1968-69 New York		82	565	312	1442	17.6
1969-70 New York		82	494	232	1220	14.9
1970-71 New York		82	540	193	1273	15.5
1971-72 New York		79	401	162	964	12.2
1972-73 New York		51	88	16	192	3.8
1973-74 New York		5	10	2	22	4.4
	Totals	971	6034	3290	15358	15.8

BARNHILL, JOHN (Rabbit)
b. March 30, 1938 Ht. 6-1 Wt. 180 College—Tenn. State

1962-63 St. Louis		77	360	181	901	11.7
1963-64 St. Louis		74	208	70	486	6.6
1964-65 St. Louis		41	121	45	287	7.0
1965-66 St. L.-Det.		76	243	113	599	7.9
1966-67 Baltimore		53	187	66	440	8.3
1967-68 San Diego		75	295	154	744	9.9
1968-69 Baltimore		30	76	39	191	6.4
1969-70 Indiana	(ABA)	77	325(71)	158	879	11.4
1970-71 Ind.-Den.	(ABA)	67	181(32)	96	490	7.3
1971-72 Indiana	(ABA)	19	28(4)	8	68	3.6
	Totals	589	2024(107)	930	5085	8.6

BARNHILL, NORTON
b. July 15, 1953 Ht. 6-4 Wt. 205 College—Wash. St.

1976-77 Seattle		4	2	0	4	1.0

BARNHORST, LEO
b. May 17, 1924 Ht. 6-4 Wt. 195 College—Notre Dame

1949-50 Chicago		67	174	90	438	6.5
1950-51 Indianapolis		68	232	82	546	8.0
1951-52 Indianapolis		66	349	122	820	12.4
1952-53 Indianapolis		71	402	163	967	13.6
1953-54 Balt.-Ft. W.		72	199	63	461	6.4
	Totals	344	1356	520	3232	9.4

Yr.	Team		G	FG	FT	TP	Avg.
BARR, JOHN E.							
b. Aug. 18, 1918 Ht. 6-3 Wt. 205 College—Penn State							
1946-47 St. Louis			58	124	47	295	5.1
BARR, MIKE							
b. Oct. 9, 1950 Ht. 6-3 Wt. 180 College—Duquesne							
1972-73 Virginia	(ABA)		79	289(1)	141	720	9.1
1973-74 Virginia	(ABA)		45	82(2)	33	199	4.4
1974-75 St. Louis	(ABA)		54	136	28	300	5.6
1975-76 St. Louis	(ABA)		56	124(6)	46	300	5.4
1976-77 Kansas City			73	122	41	285	3.9
	Totals		307	753(9)	289	1804	5.9
BARR, THOMAS (Moe)							
b. June 19, 1944 Ht. 6-4 Wt. 195 College—Duquesne							
1970-71 Cincinnati			31	25	11	61	2.0
BARRETT, ERNIE							
b. Dec. 27, 1929 Ht. 6-3 Wt. 180 College—Kan. State							
1953-54 Boston			59	60	14	134	2.3
1955-56 Boston			72	207	93	507	7.0
	Totals		131	267	107	641	4.9
BARRETT, MICHAEL							
b. Sept. 5, 1943 Ht. 6-2 Wt. 160 College—W. Va. Tech							
1969-70 Washington	(ABA)		84	479(62)	232	1252	14.9
1970-71 Virginia	(ABA)		84	458(28)	208	1152	13.7
1972-73 San Diego	(ABA)		19	37(4)	18	96	5.1
	Totals		187	974(94)	458	2500	13.4
BARRY, RICHARD (Rick)							
b. March 28, 1944 Ht. 6-7 Wt. 205 College—Miami (Fl.)							
1965-66 San Francisco			80	745	569	2059	25.7
1966-67 San Francisco			78	1011	753	2775	35.6
1968-69 Oakland	(ABA)		35	392(3)	403	1190	34.0
1969-70 Washington	(ABA)		52	517(8)	400	1442	27.7
1970-71 New York	(ABA)		59	632(19)	451	1734	29.4
1971-72 New York	(ABA)		80	902(73)	641	2518	31.5
1972-73 Golden State			82	737	358	1832	22.3
1973-74 Golden State			80	796	417	2009	25.1
1974-75 Golden State			80	1028	394	2450	30.6
1975-76 Golden State			81	707	287	1701	21.0
1976-77 Golden State			79	682	359	1723	21.8
1977-78 Golden State			82	760	378	1898	23.1
1978-79 Houston			80	461	160	1082	13.5
1979-80 Houston			72	325(73)	143	866	12.0
	Totals		1020	9695(176)	5713	25279	24.8
BARTELS, ED							
b. Oct. 8, 1925 Ht. 6-5 Wt. 195 College—No. Car. St.							
1949-50 Den.-N.Y.			15	22	19	63	4.2
1950-51 Washington			17	24	24	72	4.2
	Totals		32	46	43	135	4.2
BARTOLOME, VIC							
b. Sept. 29, 1948 Ht. 7-0 Wt. 230 College—Oreg. State							
1971-72 Golden State			38	15	4	34	0.9
BASKERVILLE, JERRY							
b. Nov. 10, 1951 Ht. 6-7 Wt. 190 College—Temple							
1975-76 Philadelphia			21	8	10	26	1.2

Yr.	Team		G	FG	FT	TP	Avg.
BASSETT, E. TIMOTHY (Tim)							
b. April 1, 1951 Ht. 6-8 Wt. 225 College—Georgia							
1973-74 San Diego	(ABA)		82	233	99	565	6.9
1974-75 San Diego	(ABA)		72	244(3)	82	573	8.0
1975-76 New York	(ABA)		84	173(1)	58	405	4.8
1976-77 N.Y. Nets			76	293	101	687	9.0
1977-78 New Jersey			65	149	50	348	5.4
1978-79 New Jersey			82	116	89	321	3.9
1979-80 N.J.-S.Ant.			12	12	10	34	2.8
	Totals		473	1220(4)	489	2933	6.2
BATTS, LLOYD							
b. May 9, 1951 Ht. 6-4 Wt. 185 College—Cincinnati							
1974-75 Virginia	(ABA)		58	289(42)	58	598	10.3
BAUM, JOHN							
b. June 19, 1946 Ht. 6-5 Wt. 200 College—Temple							
1969-70 Chicago			3	1	0	6	2.0
1970-71 Chicago			62	123	40	286	4.6
1971-72 New York	(ABA)		44	103	41	247	5.6
1972-73 New York	(ABA)		75	221	107	549	7.3
1973-74 Mem.-Ind.	(ABA)		60	180	50	410	6.8
	Totals		244	630	238	1498	6.1
BAUMHOLTZ, FRANK							
b. Oct. 7, 1919 Ht. 5-10 Wt. 170 College—Ohio Univ.							
1945-46 Youngstown	(NL)		26	99	76	274	10.5
1946-47 Cleveland			45	255	121	631	14.0
	Totals		71	354	197	905	12.7
BAYLOR, ELGIN							
b. Sept. 16, 1934 Ht. 6-5 Wt. 225 College—Seattle							
1958-59 Minneapolis			70	605	532	1742	24.9
1959-60 Minneapolis			70	755	564	2074	29.6
1960-61 Los Angeles			73	931	676	2538	34.8
1961-62 Los Angeles			48	680	476	1836	38.2
1962-63 Los Angeles			80	1029	661	2719	34.0
1963-64 Los Angeles			78	756	471	1983	25.4
1964-65 Los Angeles			74	763	483	2009	27.1
1965-66 Los Angeles			65	415	249	1079	16.6
1966-67 Los Angeles			70	711	440	1862	26.6
1967-68 Los Angeles			77	757	488	2002	26.0
1968-69 Los Angeles			76	730	421	1881	24.8
1969-70 Los Angeles			54	511	276	1298	24.0
1970-71 Los Angeles			2	8	4	20	10.0
1971-72 Los Angeles			9	42	22	106	11.8
	Totals		846	8693	5763	23149	27.4
BAYNE, HOWARD							
Ht. 6-6 Wt. 235 College—Tennessee							
1967-68 Kentucky	(ABA)		69	130(1)	77	338	4.9
BEACH, ED							
b. Jan. 25, 1929 Ht. 6-3 Wt. 200 College—West Va.							
1950-51 Minn.-Tri-Cit.			12	8	6	22	1.8
BEARD, ALBERT (Al)							
Ht. 6-9½ College—Norfolk State							
1967-68 New Jersey	(ABA)		12	12	6	30	2.5

Yr.	Team		G	FG	FT	TP	Avg.

BEARD, ALFRED (Butch)
b. May 4, 1947 Ht. 6-3 Wt. 185 College—Louisville

Yr.	Team		G	FG	FT	TP	Avg.
1969-70	Atlanta		72	183	135	501	7.0
1970-71	Cleveland		(Military Service)				
1971-72	Cleveland		68	394	260	1048	15.4
1972-73	Seattle		73	191	100	482	6.6
1973-74	Golden State		79	316	173	805	10.2
1974-75	Golden State		82	408	232	1048	12.8
1975-76	Cleve.-N.Y.		75	228	144	600	8.0
1976-77	N.Y. Knicks		70	148	75	371	5.3
1977-78	New York		79	308	129	745	9.4
1978-79	New York		7	11	0	22	3.1
	Totals		605	2187	1248	5622	9.3

BEARD, RALPH
b. Dec. 2, 1927 Ht. 5-10 Wt. 176 College—Kentucky

Yr.	Team		G	FG	FT	TP	Avg.
1949-50	Indianapolis		60	340	215	895	14.9
1950-51	Indianapolis		66	409	293	1111	16.8
	Totals		126	749	508	2006	15.9

BEASLEY, CHARLES
b. Sept. 23, 1945 Ht. 6-5 Wt. 190 College—SMU

Yr.	Team		G	FG	FT	TP	Avg.
1967-68	Dallas	(ABA)	78	374(3)	285	1036	13.3
1968-69	Dallas	(ABA)	75	220(1)	161	602	8.0
1969-70	Dallas	(ABA)	80	292(19)	231	834	10.4
1970-71	Fla.-Tex.	(ABA)	48	57(7)	43	164	3.4
	Totals		281	943(30)	720	2636	9.4

BEASLEY, JOHN MICHAEL
b. Feb. 5, 1944 Ht. 6-9 Wt. 225 College—Texas A&M

Yr.	Team		G	FG	FT	TP	Avg.
1967-68	Dallas	(ABA)	77	622	271	1515	19.7
1968-69	Dallas	(ABA)	78	585(3)	332	1505	19.3
1969-70	Dallas	(ABA)	84	626(3)	284	1539	18.3
1970-71	Texas	(ABA)	83	532(16)	236	1316	15.8
1971-72	Dall.-Utah	(ABA)	70	132(8)	61	333	4.8
1972-73	Utah	(ABA)	71	214(29)	62	519	7.3
1973-74	Utah	(ABA)	43	75(22)	10	182	4.2
	Totals		506	2786(81)	1256	6909	13.7

BEATY, ZELMO (Big Z)
b. Oct. 25, 1939 Ht. 6-9 Wt. 235 College—Prairie View

Yr.	Team		G	FG	FT	TP	Avg.
1962-63	St. Louis		80	297	220	814	10.2
1963-64	St. Louis		59	287	200	774	13.1
1964-65	St. Louis		80	505	341	1351	16.9
1965-66	St. Louis		80	616	424	1656	20.7
1966-67	St. Louis		48	328	197	853	17.8
1967-68	St. Louis		82	539	455	1733	21.1
1968-69	Atlanta		72	588	370	1546	21.5
1970-71	Utah	(ABA)	76	661(2)	418	1742	22.9
1971-72	Utah	(ABA)	84	729	522	1980	23.6
1972-73	Utah	(ABA)	82	521	306	1348	16.4
1973-74	Utah	(ABA)	77	417	194	1028	13.4
1974-75	Los Angeles		69	136	108	380	5.5
	Totals		889	5724(2)	3755	15205	17.1

BECK, BYRON
b. Jan. 25, 1945 Ht. 6-9 Wt. 240 College—Denver

Yr.	Team		G	FG	FT	TP	Avg.
1967-68	Denver	(ABA)	71	275	119	669	9.4
1968-69	Denver	(ABA)	71	423(2)	182	1030	14.5
1969-70	Denver	(ABA)	79	440	137	1017	12.9
1970-71	Denver	(ABA)	84	490(4)	158	1142	13.6
1971-72	Denver	(ABA)	66	337	140	814	12.3
1972-73	Denver	(ABA)	77	466(2)	158	1092	14.2
1973-74	Denver	(ABA)	82	425	120	970	11.8
1974-75	Denver	(ABA)	84	384	81	849	10.1
1975-76	Denver	(ABA)	80	334(5)	97	770	9.6
1976-77	Denver		53	107	36	250	4.7
	Totals		747	3681(13)	1228	8603	11.5

BECK, ERNEST
b. Dec. 11, 1931 Ht. 6-4 Wt. 190 College—Pennsylvania

Yr.	Team		G	FG	FT	TP	Avg.
1953-54	Philadelphia		15	39	34	112	7.5
1954-55	Philadelphia		(Military Service)				
1955-56	Philadelphia		67	136	76	348	5.2
1956-57	Philadelphia		72	195	111	501	7.0
1957-58	Philadelphia		71	272	170	714	10.1
1958-59	Philadelphia		70	163	43	369	5.3
1959-60	Philadelphia		66	114	27	255	3.9
	Totals		361	919	461	2299	6.4

BECKER, ARTHUR C.
b. Jan. 12, 1942 Ht. 6-8 Wt. 210 College—Arizona St.

Yr.	Team		G	FG	FT	TP	Avg.
1967-68	Houston	(ABA)	76	563(4)	297	1427	18.8
1968-69	Houston	(ABA)	78	423	200	1046	13.4
1969-70	Indiana	(ABA)	82	309	111	729	8.9
1970-71	Ind.-Den.	(ABA)	80	370(5)	135	880	11.0
1971-72	Denver	(ABA)	84	435	165	1035	12.3
1972-73	N.Y.-Dal.	(ABA	14	16	11	43	3.1
	Totals		414	2116(9)	919	5160	12.5

BECKER, MORRIS (Moe)
b. Feb. 24, 1917 Ht. 6-1 Wt. 185 College—Duquesne

Yr.	Team		G	FG	FT	TP	Avg.
1944-45	Cleveland	(NL)	1	0	0	0	0.0
1945-46	Youngstown	(NL)	30	115	40	270	9.0
1946-47	Pitt.-Bos.-Det.		43	70	22	162	3.8
	Totals		74	185	62	432	5.8

BEDELL, ROBERT GEORGE
b. June 26, 1944 Ht. 6-8 Wt. 205 College—Stanford

Yr.	Team		G	FG	FT	TP	Avg.
1967-68	Anaheim	(ABA)	76	325	142	792	10.4
1968-69	Dallas	(ABA)	42	92	48	232	5.5
1969-70	Dallas	(ABA)	80	285(2)	207	779	9.7
1970-71	Texas	(ABA)	71	176(9)	93	454	6.4
	Totals		269	878(11)	490	2257	8.4

BEENDERS, HENRY (Hank)
b. June 2, 1916 Ht. 6-6 Wt. 185 College—Long Island U.

Yr.	Team		G	FG	FT	TP	Avg.
1946-47	Providence		58	266	181	713	12.3
1974-78	Prov.-Phila.		45	76	51	203	4.5
1948-49	Boston		8	6	7	19	2.4
	Totals		111	348	239	935	8.4

BEHAGEN, RON
b. Jan. 19, 1951 Ht. 6-9 Wt. 185 College—Minnesota

Yr.	Team		G	FG	FT	TP	Avg.
1973-74	Kansas City		80	357	162	876	11.0
1974-75	Kansas City		81	333	199	865	10.7
1975-76	New Orleans		66	308	144	760	11.5
1976-77	New Orleans		60	213	90	516	8.6
1977-78	Hou.-Art.-Ind.		80	346	179	871	10.9
1978-79	Det.-N.Y.-K.C.		15	28	10	66	4.4
1979-80	Washington		6	9	5	23	3.8
	Totals		388	1594	789	3977	10.3

Yr.	Team	G	FG	FT	TP	Avg.

BEHNKE, ELMER
b. Feb. 3, 1929 Ht. 6-7 Wt. 210 College—Bradley

| 1951-52 Milwaukee | | 4 | 6 | 4 | 16 | 4.0 |

BELL, DENNIS
b. June 2, 1951 Ht. 6-5 Wt. 225 College—Drake

1973-74 New York		1	0	0	0	0.0
1974-75 New York		52	68	20	156	3.0
1975-76 New York		10	8	3	19	1.9
	Totals	63	76	23	175	2.5

BELL, WILLIAM H. (Whitey)
b. Sept. 13, 1932 Ht. 6-0 Wt. 181 College—N.C. State

1959-60 New York		31	70	28	168	5.4
1960-61 New York		5	7	1	15	3.0
	Totals	36	77	29	183	5.1

BELLAMY, WALTER (Bells)
b. July 24, 1939 Ht. 6-10½ Wt. 245 College—Indiana

1961-62 Chicago		79	973	549	2495	31.6
1962-63 Chicago		80	840	553	2233	27.9
1963-64 Baltimore		80	811	537	2159	27.0
1964-65 Baltimore		80	733	515	1981	24.8
1965-66 Balt.-N.Y.		80	695	430	1820	22.8
1966-67 New York		79	565	369	1499	19.0
1967-68 New York		82	511	350	1372	16.7
1968-69 N.Y.-Detroit		88	563	401	1527	17.4
1969-70 Det.-Atlanta		79	351	215	917	11.6
1970-71 Atlanta		82	433	336	1202	14.7
1971-72 Atlanta		82	593	340	1526	18.6
1972-73 Atlanta		74	455	283	1193	16.1
1973-74 Atlanta		77	389	233	1011	13.1
1974-75 New Orleans		1	2	2	6	6.0
	Totals	1043	7914	5113	20941	20.1

BEMORAS, IRV
b. Nov. 18, 1930 Ht. 6-3 Wt. 187 College—Illinois

1953-54 Milwaukee		69	185	139	509	7.4
1956-57 St. Louis		62	124	70	318	5.1
	Totals	131	309	209	827	6.3

BENBOW, LEON
b. July 23, 1952 Ht. 6-4 Wt. 185 College—Jacksonville

1974-75 Chicago		39	35	15	85	2.2
1975-76 Chicago		76	219	105	543	7.1
	Totals	115	254	120	628	5.4

BENNETT, WILLIS (Spider)
b. Aug. 4, 1943 Ht. 6-3 Wt. 190 College—Winston-Salem

| 1968-69 Dallas-Hou. | (ABA) | 59 | 147(6) | 140 | 440 | 7.5 |

BERCE, EUGENE
b. Nov. 22, 1926 Ht. 5-11 Wt. 175 College—Marquette

1948-49 Oshkosh	(NL)	58	120	101	341	5.9
1949-50 Tri-Cities		3	5	0	10	3.3
	Totals	61	125	101	351	5.8

BERGEN, GARY
b. 1933 Ht. 6-8 Wt. 212 College—Utah

| 1956-57 New York | | 6 | 3 | 2 | 8 | 1.3 |

BERGH, LARRY
b. April 2, 1945 Ht. 6-8 Wt. 215 College—Tuskegee

| 1969-70 Pittsburgh | (ABA) | 20 | 49 | 23 | 121 | 6.1 |

BESHORE, DELMAR
b. Nov. 29, 1956 Ht. 6-1 Wt. 165 College—Calif. (Pa.)

1978-79 Milwaukee		1	0	0	0	0.0
1979-80 Chicago		68	88(10)	58	244	3.6
	Totals	69	88(10)	58	244	3.5

BIALOSUKNIA, WES
b. June 8, 1945 Ht. 6-2 Wt. 185 College—Connecticut

| 1967-68 Oakland | (ABA) | 70 | 238(29) | 103 | 608 | 8.7 |

BIANCHI, ALFRED (Al)
b. March 26, 1932 Ht. 6-3 Wt. 185 College—Bowling Green

1956-57 Syracuse		68	199	165	563	8.3
1957-58 Syracuse		69	215	140	570	8.3
1958-59 Syracuse		72	285	149	719	10.0
1959-60 Syracuse		69	215	112	542	7.8
1960-61 Syracuse		52	118	60	296	5.7
1961-62 Syracuse		80	336	154	826	10.3
1962-63 Syracuse		61	202	120	524	8.6
1963-64 Philadelphia		78	257	109	623	8.0
1964-65 Philadelphia		60	175	54	404	6.7
1965-66 Philadelphia		78	214	66	494	6.3
	Totals	687	2216	1129	5561	8.1

BIASETTI, HENRY
b. Jan. 14, 1925 Ht. 6-0 Wt. 180 College—Assumption (Ont.)

| 1946-47 Toronto | | 6 | 2 | 2 | 6 | 1.0 |

BIEDENBACH, EDWARD
b. Aug. 12, 1945 Ht. 6-1 Wt. 175 College—N.C. State

| 1968-69 Phoenix | | 7 | 0 | 4 | 4 | 0.6 |

BIELKE, DON
Ht. 6-8 Wt. 240 College—Valparaiso

| 1955-56 Ft. Wayne | | 7 | 5 | 4 | 14 | 2.0 |

BIGELOW, BOB
b. Dec. 26, 1953 Ht. 6-7 Wt. 215 College—Pennsylvania

1975-76 Kansas City		31	16	24	56	1.8
1976-77 Kansas City		29	35	15	85	2.9
1977-78 KC-Bost.		5	4	0	8	1.6
1978-79 San Diego		29	36	13	85	2.9
	Totals	94	91	52	234	2.5

BILLINGY, LIONEL
b. 1952 Ht. 6-9 Wt. 215 College—Duquesne

| 1974-75 Virginia | (ABA) | 46 | 150 | 93 | 393 | 8.5 |

Yr.	Team	G	FG	FT	TP	Avg.

BING, DAVE
b. Nov. 24, 1943 Ht. 6-3 Wt. 180 College—Syracuse

Yr.	Team	G	FG	FT	TP	Avg.
1966-67	Detroit	80	664	273	1601	20.0
1967-68	Detroit	79	835	472	2142	27.1
1968-69	Detroit	77	678	444	1800	23.4
1969-70	Detroit	70	575	454	1604	22.9
1970-71	Detroit	82	799	615	2213	27.0
1971-72	Detroit	45	369	278	1016	22.6
1972-73	Detroit	82	692	456	1840	22.4
1973-74	Detroit	81	582	356	1520	18.0
1974-75	Detroit	79	578	343	1499	19.0
1975-76	Washington	82	497	332	1326	16.2
1976-77	Washington	64	271	136	678	10.6
1977-78	Boston	80	422	244	1088	13.6
	Totals	901	6962	4403	18327	20.3

BIRD, JERRY
b. 1934 Ht. 6-6 Wt. 215 College—Kentucky

Yr.	Team	G	FG	FT	TP	Avg.
1958-59	New York	11	12	1	25	2.3

BISHOP, GALE
b. June 9, 1922 Ht. 6-3 Wt. 195 College—Wash. State

Yr.	Team	G	FG	FT	TP	Avg.
1948-49	Philadelphia	56	170	127	467	8.3

BLACK, CHARLES (Hawk)
b. June 15, 1921 Ht. 6-5 Wt. 200 College—Kansas

Yr.	Team		G	FG	FT	TP	Avg.
1947-48	Anderson	(NL)	58	148	149	445	7.7
1948-49	Ft. W.-Ind.		58	203	161	567	9.8
1949-50	Ft. W.-Andsn.		65	226	209	661	10.2
1951-52	Milwaukee		13	6	5	17	1.3
	Totals		194	583	524	1690	8.7

BLACK, TOM
b. July 9, 1941 Ht. 6-10½ Wt. 234 College—Wisconsin/S. Dakota St.

Yr.	Team	G	FG	FT	TP	Avg.
1970-71	Sea.-Cin.	71	121	57	299	4.2

BLANEY, GEORGE
b. Nov. 12, 1939 Ht. 6-1 Wt. 175 College—Holy Cross

Yr.	Team	G	FG	FT	TP	Avg.
1961-62	New York	36	54	9	117	3.3

BLEVINS, LEON
b. June 25, 1926 Ht. 6-2 Wt. 160 College—Arizona

Yr.	Team	G	FG	FT	TP	Avg.
1950-51	Indiananpolis	3	1	0	2	0.7

BLOCK, JOHN
b. April 16, 1944 Ht. 6-9 Wt. 207 College—USC

Yr.	Team	G	FG	FT	TP	Avg.
1966-67	Los Angeles	22	20	24	64	2.9
1967-68	San Diego	52	366	316	1048	20.2
1968-69	San Diego	78	448	299	1195	15.3
1969-70	San Diego	82	453	287	1193	14.5
1970-71	San Diego	73	245	212	702	9.6
1971-72	Milwaukee	79	233	206	672	8.5
1972-73	Phila.-K.C.-O.	73	391	300	1082	14.8
1973-74	K.C.-Omaha	82	275	164	714	8.7
1974-75	N.O.-Chi	54	159	114	432	8.0
1975-76	Chicago	2	2	0	4	2.0
	Totals	597	2592	1922	7106	11.9

BLOOM, MEYER (Mike)
b. Jan. 14, 1915 Ht. 6-6 Wt. 190 College—Temple

Yr.	Team	G	FG	FT	TP	Avg.
1947-48	Balt.-Boston	48	174	160	508	10.6
1948-49	Minn.-Chic.	45	35	56	126	2.8
	Totals	93	209	216	634	6.8

BOBB, NELSON
b. Feb. 25, 1924 Ht. 6-0 Wt. 170 College—Temple

Yr.	Team	G	FG	FT	TP	Avg.
1949-50	Philadelphia	57	80	82	242	4.2
1950-51	Philadelphia	53	52	44	148	2.8
1951-52	Philadelphia	62	110	99	319	5.1
1952-53	Philadelphia	55	119	105	343	6.2
	Totals	227	361	330	1052	4.6

BOCKHORN, ARLEN (Bucky)
b. July 8, 1933 Ht. 6-4 Wt. 200 College—Dayton

Yr.	Team	G	FG	FT	TP	Avg.
1958-59	Cincinnati	71	294	130	726	10.2
1959-60	Cincinnati	75	323	145	791	10.5
1960-61	Cincinnati	79	420	152	992	12.6
1961-62	Cincinnati	80	531	198	1260	15.7
1962-63	Cincinnati	80	375	183	933	11.7
1963-64	Cincinnati	70	242	96	580	8.3
1964-65	Cincinnati	19	60	28	148	7.8
	Totals	474	2245	940	5430	11.5

BOERWINKLE, THOMAS
b. Aug. 23, 1945 Ht. 7-0 Wt. 265 College—Tennessee

Yr.	Team	G	FG	FT	TP	Avg.
1968-69	Chicago	80	318	145	781	9.8
1969-70	Chicago	81	348	150	846	10.4
1970-71	Chicago	82	357	168	882	10.8
1971-72	Chicago	80	219	118	556	7.0
1972-73	Chicago	8	9	12	30	3.8
1973-74	Chicago	46	58	42	158	3.4
1974-75	Chicago	80	132	73	337	4.2
1975-76	Chicago	74	265	118	648	8.8
1976-77	Chicago	82	134	34	302	3.7
1977-78	Chicago	22	23	10	56	2.5
	Totals	635	1863	870	4596	7.2

BOLGER, BILL
b. Aug. 21, 1931 Ht. 6-5 Wt. 205 College—Georgetown

Yr.	Team	G	FG	FT	TP	Avg.
1953-54	Baltimore	20	24	8	56	2.8

BOLSTORFF, DOUG
b. Oct. 29, 1931 Ht. 6-4 Wt. 195 College—Minnesota

Yr.	Team	G	FG	FT	TP	Avg.
1957-58	Detroit	3	2	0	4	1.3

BOND, PHIL
b. July 27, 1954 Ht. 6-2 Wt. 175 College—Louisville

Yr.	Team	G	FG	FT	TP	Avg.
1977-78	Houston	7	2	0	4	0.6

BONHAM, RON
b. May 31, 1942 Ht. 6-5 Wt. 200 College—Cincinnati

Yr.	Team		G	FG	FT	TP	Avg.
1964-65	Boston		37	91	92	274	7.4
1965-66	Boston		39	76	52	204	5.2
1967-68	Indiana	(ABA)	42	80	85	245	5.8
	Totals		118	247	229	723	6.1

Yr.	Team	G	FG	FT	TP	Avg.

BON SALLE, GEORGE
b. July 1, 1935 Ht. 6-8 Wt. 220 College—Illinois

Yr.	Team	G	FG	FT	TP	Avg.
1961-62	Chicago	3	2	0	4	1.3

BOOKER, HAL (Butch)
Ht. 6-10 Wt. 230 College—Cheyney State

Yr.	Team		G	FG	FT	TP	Avg.
1969-70	Miami	(ABA)	12	30	10	70	5.8

BOOZER, ROBERT (Bullet Bob)
b. April 26, 1937 Ht. 6-8 Wt. 215 College—Kan. State

Yr.	Team	G	FG	FT	TP	Avg.
1960-61	Cincinnati	79	250	166	666	8.4
1961-62	Cincinnati	79	410	263	1083	13.7
1962-63	Cincinnati	79	440	252	1132	14.3
1963-64	Cinn.-N.Y.	81	468	272	1208	14.9
1964-65	New York	80	424	288	1136	14.2
1965-66	Los Angeles	78	365	225	955	12.2
1966-67	Chicago	80	538	360	1436	18.0
1967-68	Chicago	77	622	411	1655	21.5
1968-69	Chicago	79	661	394	1716	21.7
1969-70	Seattle	82	493	263	1249	15.2
1970-71	Milwaukee	80	290	148	728	9.1
	Total	874	4961	3042	12964	14.8

BORNHEIMER, JACOB (Jake)
b. June 29, 1927 Ht. 6-5 Wt. 205 College—Muhlenberg

Yr.	Team	G	FG	FT	TP	Avg.
1948-49	Philadelphia	15	34	20	88	5.9
1949-50	Philadelphia	60	88	78	254	4.2
	Totals	75	122	98	342	4.6

BORSAVAGE, COSTIC (Ike)
b. July 25, 1924 Ht. 6-8 Wt. 220 College—Temple

Yr.	Team	G	FG	FT	TP	Avg.
1950-51	Philadelphia	24	26	12	64	2.7

BORYLA, VINCE
b. March 11, 1927 Ht. 6-5 Wt. 210 College—Notre Dame/Denver

Yr.	Team	G	FG	FT	TP	Avg.
1949-50	New York	59	204	204	612	10.4
1950-51	New York	66	352	278	982	14.9
1951-52	New York	42	202	96	500	11.9
1952-53	New York	66	254	165	673	10.2
1953-54	New York	52	175	70	420	8.1
	Totals	285	1187	813	3187	11.2

BOSTIC, JIM
b. Jan. 28, 1953 Ht. 6-7 Wt. 225 College—New Mexico State

Yr.	Team	G	FG	FT	TP	Avg.
1977-78	Detroit	4	12	2	26	6.5

BOSTON, LAWRENCE
b. May 18, 1856 Ht. 6-8 Wt. 225 College—Vincennes and Maryland

Yr.	Team	G	FG	FT	TP	Avg.
1979-80	Washington	13	24	8	56	4.3

BOSWELL, TOM
b. Oct. 2, 1953 Ht. 6-8 Wt. 215 College—S.C. St./So.Car.

Yr.	Team	G	FG	FT	TP	Avg.
1975-76	Boston	35	41	14	96	2.7
1976-77	Boston	70	175	96	446	6.4
1977-78	Boston	65	185	93	463	7.1
1978-79	Denver	79	321	198	840	10.6
1979-80	Denv.-Utah	79	346(5)	206	903	11.4
	Totals	328	1068(5)	607	2748	8.4

BOVEN, DON
b. March 6, 1925 Ht. 6-4 Wt. 210 College—West. Mich.

Yr.	Team	G	FG	FT	TP	Avg.
1949-50	Waterloo	62	208	240	656	10.6
1951-52	Milwaukee	66	200	256	656	9.9
1952-53	Milw.-Ft.W.	67	153	145	451	6.7
	Totals	195	561	641	1763	9.0

BOWENS, TOM
b. July 7, 1940 Ht. 6-8 Wt. 220 College—Grambling

Yr.	Team		G	FG	FT	TP	Avg.
1967-68	Denver	(ABA)	67	177(1)	55	410	6.1
1968-69	New York	(ABA)	76	186	83	455	6.0
1969-70	New Orleans	(ABA)	68	110	47	267	3.9
	Totals		211	473(1)	185	1132	5.4

BOWLING, ORB
b. Mar. 21, 1939 Ht. 6-10 Wt. 215 College—Tennessee

Yr.	Team		G	FG	FT	TP	Avg.
1967-68	Kentucky	(ABA)	11	9	3	21	1.9

BOWMAN, NATE
b. March 19, 1943 Ht. 6-10 Wt. 230 College—Wichita St.

Yr.	Team		G	FG	FT	TP	Avg.
1966-67	Chicago		9	8	6	22	2.4
1967-68	New York		42	52	10	114	2.7
1968-69	New York		67	82	29	193	2.9
1969-70	New York		81	98	41	237	2.9
1970-71	Buffalo		44	58	20	136	3.1
1971-72	Pittsburgh	(ABA)	18	19	5	43	2.4
	Totals		261	317	111	745	2.9

BOYD, FRED
b. June 13, 1950 Ht. 6-2 Wt. 180 College—Oregon State

Yr.	Team	G	FG	FT	TP	Avg.
1972-73	Philadelphia	82	362	136	860	10.5
1973-74	Philadelphia	73	286	141	713	9.5
1974-75	Philadelphia	66	205	55	465	7.0
1975-76	Phila.-N.O.	36	74	29	177	4.9
1976-77	New Orleans	47	194	79	467	9.9
1977-78	New Orleans	21	44	14	102	4.9
1978-79	Detroit	5	3	0	6	1.2
	Totals	330	1168	454	2790	8.5

BOYD, KEN
b. March 25, 1952 Ht. 6-5 Wt. 195 College—Bos. Univ.

Yr.	Team	G	FG	FT	TP	Avg.
1974-75	New Orleans	6	7	5	19	3.2

BOYKOFF, HARRY (Big Hesh)
b. July 24, 1922 Ht. 6-10 Wt. 227 College—St. John's (N.Y.)

Yr.	Team		G	FG	FT	TP	Avg.
1947-48	Toledo	(NL)	59	225	124	574	9.7
1948-49	Waterloo	(NL)	61	293	191	777	12.7
1949-50	Waterloo		61	288	203	779	12.8
1950-51	Bos.-Tri. C.		48	126	74	326	6.8
	Totals		229	932	592	2456	10.7

BRACEY, STEVE
b. August 1, 1950 Ht. 6-1 Wt. 185 College—Tulsa

Yr.	Team	G	FG	FT	TP	Avg.
1972-73	Atlanta	70	192	73	457	6.5
1973-74	Atlanta	75	241	69	551	7.3
1974-75	Golden State	42	54	25	133	3.2
	Totals	187	487	167	1141	6.1

Yr.	Team		G	FG	FT	TP	Avg.

BRADDS, GARY (Tex)
b. July 26, 1942 Ht. 6-8 Wt. 210 College—Ohio State

Yr.	Team		G	FG	FT	TP	Avg.
1964-65	Baltimore		41	46	45	137	3.3
1965-66	Baltimore		3	2	3	7	2.3
1967-68	Oakland	(ABA)	49	199	221	619	12.6
1968-69	Oakland	(ABA)	75	517(1)	364	1399	18.7
1969-70	Washington	(ABA)	60	292	217	801	13.4
1970-71	Car.-Dall.	(ABA)	26	52	39	143	5.5
	Totals		254	1108(1)	889	3106	12.2

BRADLEY, ALONZO
b. Oct. 16, 1953 Ht. 6-7 Wt. 195 College—Texas Southern

Yr.	Team	G	FG	FT	TP	Avg.
1977-78	Houston	43	130	43	303	7.0
1978-79	Houston	34	37	22	96	2.8
1979-80	Houston	22	17(1)	6	41	1.9
	Totals	99	184(1)	71	440	4.4

BRADLEY, BILL
b. July 28, 1943 Ht. 6-5 Wt. 205 College—Princeton

Yr.	Team	G	FG	FT	TP	Avg.
1967-68	New York	45	142	76	360	8.0
1968-69	New York	82	407	206	1020	12.4
1969-70	New York	67	413	145	971	14.5
1970-71	New York	78	413	144	970	12.4
1971-72	New York	78	504	169	1177	15.1
1972-73	New York	82	575	169	1319	16.1
1973-74	New York	82	502	146	1150	14.0
1974-75	New York	79	452	144	1048	13.3
1975-76	New York	82	392	130	914	11.1
1976-77	N.Y. Knicks	67	127	34	288	4.3
	Totals	742	3927	1363	9217	12.4

BRADLEY, BILL
Ht. 5-11 Wt. 167 College—Tennessee

Yr.	Team		G	FG	FT	TP	Avg.
1967-68	Kentucky	(ABA)	58	82(3)	51	218	3.8

BRADLEY, JIM
b. March 16, 1952 Ht. 6-8 Wt. 215 College—Northern Ill.

Yr.	Team		G	FG	FT	TP	Avg.
1973-74	Kentucky	(ABA)	35	130	31	291	8.3
1974-75	Kentucky	(ABA)	56	144	76	364	6.5
1975-76	Denver	(ABA)	7	15	2	32	4.6
	Totals		98	289	109	687	6.5

BRADLEY, JOE
b. 1928 Ht. 6-3 Wt. 175 College—Oklahoma State

Yr.	Team	G	FG	FT	TP	Avg.
1949-50	Chicago	46	36	15	87	1.9

BRANNUM, ROBERT (Beeb)
b. May 28, 1925 Ht. 6-5½ Wt. 215 College—Kentucky/Mich. St.

Yr.	Team		G	FG	FT	TP	Avg.
1948-49	Sheboygan	(NL)	64	169	169	507	7.9
1949-50	Sheboygan		59	234	245	713	12.1
1951-52	Boston		66	149	107	405	6.1
1952-53	Boston		71	188	110	486	6.8
1953-54	Boston		71	140	129	409	5.8
1954-55	Boston		71	176	90	442	6.2
	Totals		402	1056	850	2962	7.4

Yr.	Team		G	FG	FT	TP	Avg.

BRANSON, JESSEE
b. Jan. 7, 1942 Ht. 6-7 Wt. 200 College—Elon

Yr.	Team		G	FG	FT	TP	Avg.
1965-66	Philadelphia		5	1	3	5	1.0
1967-68	New Orleans	(ABA)	78	376(2)	332	1086	13.9
	Totals		83	377(2)	335	1091	13.1

BRASCO, JIM
b. Feb. 3, 1931 Ht. 6-1 Wt. 170 College—N.Y.U.

Yr.	Team	G	FG	FT	TP	Avg.
1952-53	Syr.-Milw.	30	36	38	110	3.7

BRAUN, CARL
b. Sept. 25, 1927 Ht. 6-5 Wt. 180 College—Colgate

Yr.	Team	G	FG	FT	TP	Avg.
1947-48	New York	47	276	119	671	14.3
1948-49	New York	57	299	212	810	14.2
1949-50	New York	67	373	285	1031	15.4
1952-53	New York	70	323	331	977	14.0
1953-54	New York	72	354	354	1062	14.8
1954-55	New York	71	400	274	1074	15.1
1955-56	New York	72	396	320	1112	15.4
1956-57	New York	72	378	245	1001	13.9
1957-58	New York	71	426	321	1173	16.5
1958-59	New York	72	287	180	754	10.5
1959-60	New York	54	285	129	699	12.9
1960-61	New York	15	37	11	85	5.7
1961-62	Boston	48	78	20	176	3.6
	Totals	788	3912	2801	10625	13.5

BRENNAN, PETER
b. Sept. 23, 1936 Ht. 6-6 Wt. 205 College—N. Carolina

Yr.	Team	G	FG	FT	TP	Avg.
1958-59	New York	16	13	14	40	2.5

BRENNAN, THOMAS
Ht. 6-4 Wt. 200 College—Villanova

Yr.	Team	G	FG	FT	TP	Avg.
1954-55	Philadelphia	11	5	0	10	0.9

BRIAN, FRANK (Flash)
b. May 1, 1923 Ht. 6-1½ Wt. 180 College—La. State

Yr.	Team		G	FG	FT	TP	Avg.
1947-48	Anderson	(NL)	59	248	155	651	11.0
1948-49	Anderson		64	216	201	633	9.9
1949-50	Anderson		64	368	402	1138	17.8
1950-51	Tri-Cities		68	363	418	1144	16.8
1951-52	Ft. Wayne		66	342	367	1051	15.9
1952-53	Ft. Wayne		68	245	236	726	10.7
1953-54	Ft. Wayne		64	132	137	401	6.3
1954-55	Ft. Wayne		71	237	217	691	9.7
1955-56	Ft. Wayne		37	78	72	228	6.2
	Totals		561	2229	2205	6663	11.9

BRIDGES, BILL
b. April 4, 1939 Ht. 6-6½ Wt. 228 College—Kansas

Yr.	Team	G	FG	FT	TP	Avg.
1962-63	St. Louis	27	66	32	164	6.1
1963-64	St. Louis	80	268	146	682	8.5
1964-65	St. Louis	79	362	186	910	11.5
1965-66	St. Louis	78	377	257	1011	13.0
1966-67	St. Louis	79	503	367	1373	17.4
1967-68	St. Louis	82	466	347	1279	15.6
1968-69	Atlanta	80	351	239	941	11.8
1969-70	Atlanta	82	443	331	1217	14.8
1970-71	Atlanta	82	382	211	975	11.9
1971-72	Atl.-Phila.	78	379	222	980	12.6

Yr.	Team		G	FG	FT	TP	Avg.
1972-73	Phil.-L.A.		82	333	179	845	10.3
1973-74	Los Angeles		65	216	116	548	8.4
1974-75	L.A.-G.S.		32	35	17	87	2.7
	Totals		926	4181	2650	11012	11.9

BRIGHTMAN, ALBERT
b. 1922 Ht. 6-2 Wt. 195 College—Morris Harvey

1946-47	Boston		58	223	121	567	9.8

BRINDLEY, AUDLEY
b. Dec. 31, 1923 Ht. 6-4 Wt. 175 College—Dartmouth
d. Nov. 19, 1958

1946-47	New York		12	14	6	34	2.8

BRISKER, JOHN
b. June 15, 1947 Ht. 6-5 Wt. 210 College—Toledo

1969-70	Pittsburgh	(ABA)	77	627(34)	329	1617	21.0
1970-71	Pittsburgh	(ABA)	79	898(89)	430	2315	29.3
1971-72	Pittsburgh	(ABA)	49	563(43)	248	1417	28.9
1972-73	Seattle		70	352	194	898	12.8
1973-74	Seattle		35	178	82	438	12.5
1974-75	Seattle		21	60	42	162	7.7
	Totals		331	2678(166)	1325	6847	20.7

BRITT, TYRONE
Ht. 6-4 Wt. 190 College—North Carolina College

1967-68	San Diego		11	13	2	28	2.5

BRITT, WAYMAN
b. Aug. 31, 1952 Ht. 6-2 Wt. 185 College—Michigan

1977-78	Detroit		7	3	3	9	1.3

BROKAW, GARY
b. Jan. 11, 1954 Ht. 6-4 Wt. 180 College—Notre Dame

1974-75	Milwaukee		73	234	126	594	8.1
1975-76	Milwaukee		75	237	159	633	8.4
1976-77	Milwaukee		80	242	163	647	8.1
1977-78	Mil.-Cle.-Buff.		13	18	18	54	4.2
	Totals		241	731	466	1928	8.0

BROOKFIELD, PRICE
b. May 11, 1920 Ht. 6-4½ Wt. 185 College—W. Texas St./Iowa State

1946-47	Chicago	(NL)	42	82	24	188	4.5
1947-48	Anderson	(NL)	49	82	27	191	3.9
1948-49	Indianapolis		54	176	90	442	8.2
1949-50	Rochester		7	11	12	34	4.9
	Totals		152	351	153	855	5.6

BROOKINS, CLARENCE
b. 1946 Ht. 6-4 Wt. 190 College—Temple

1970-71	Miami	(ABA)	8	8	5	21	2.6

BROWN, BOB
b. 1925 Ht. 6-4½ Wt. 205 College—Miami (Ohio)

1948-49	Providence		20	37	34	108	5.4
1949-50	Denver		62	276	172	724	11.7
	Totals		82	313	206	832	10.1

BROWN, DARRELL
b. Mar. 14, 1923 Ht. 6-2 Wt. 175 College—Humboldt St.

1948-49	Baltimore		3	2	0	4	1.3

BROWN, GEORGE
b. Oct. 30, 1935 Ht. 6-6 Wt. 190 College—Wayne (Mi.)

1957-58	Minneapolis		1	0	1	1	1.0

BROWN, HAROLD (Brownie)
b. Oct. 2, 1923 Ht. 6-0 Wt. 155 College—Evansville

1946-47	Detroit		54	95	74	264	4.9

BROWN, JOHN
b. Dec. 14, 1951 Ht. 6-7 Wt. 220 College—Missouri

1973-74	Atlanta		77	277	163	717	9.3
1974-75	Atlanta		73	315	185	815	11.2
1975-76	Atlanta		75	215	162	592	7.9
1976-77	Atlanta		77	160	121	441	5.7
1977-78	Atlanta		75	192	165	549	7.3
1978-79	Chicago		77	152	84	388	5.0
1979-80	Utah-Atl.		32	37	38	112	3.5
	Totals		486	1348	918	3614	7.4

BROWN, LARRY
b. Sept. 14, 1940 Ht. 5-9 Wt. 160 College—No. Carolina

1967-68	New Orleans	(ABA)	78	330(19)	366	1045	13.4
1968-69	Oakland	(ABA)	77	308(8)	301	925	12.0
1969-70	Washington	(ABA)	82	376(10)	362	1124	13.7
1970-71	Vir.-Denv.	(ABA)	63	127(6)	186	446	7.1
1971-72	Denver	(ABA)	76	243(5)	198	689	9.1
	Totals		376	1384(48)	1413	4229	11.2

BROWN, LEON (Stretch)
b. Oct. 12, 1919 Ht. 6-3 Wt. 190 College—Wyoming

1946-47	Cleveland		5	3	0	6	1.2

BROWN, ROGER
b. May 22, 1942 Ht. 6-5 Wt. 207 College—Dayton

1967-68	Indiana	(ABA)	76	544(14)	390	1492	19.6
1968-69	Indiana	(ABA)	75	563(5)	442	1573	21.0
1969-70	Indiana	(ABA)	84	719(40)	457	1935	23.1
1970-71	Indiana	(ABA)	82	610(63)	407	1690	20.6
1971-72	Indiana	(ABA)	78	532(57)	323	1444	18.5
1972-73	Indiana	(ABA)	72	332(42)	203	909	12.6
1973-74	Indiana	(ABA)	82	379(56)	155	969	11.8
1974-75	Mem-Ut-Ind.	(ABA)	56	181(35)	89	486	8.7
1975-76	Denver	(ABA)	37	28(2)	16	74	2.0
	Totals		642	3888(314)	2482	10572	16.5

BROWN, ROGER
b. Feb. 23, 1950 Ht. 6-11 Wt. 230 College—Kansas

1972-73	Los Angeles		1	0	1	1	1.0
1972-73	Carolina	(ABA)	62	59	28	146	2.4
1973-74	S.A.-Vir.	(ABA)	63	98	34	230	3.7
1974-75	Denver	(ABA)	37	28(2)	16	74	2.0
1975-76	Detroit		29	29	14	72	2.5
1976-77	Detroit		43	21	18	60	1.4
1979-80	Chicago		4	1	0	2	0.5
	Totals		239	236(2)	111	585	2.4

Yr.	Team	G	FG	FT	TP	Avg.

BROWN, STANLEY
b. 1929 Ht. 6-3 Wt. 200

Yr.	Team	G	FG	FT	TP	Avg.
1947-48	Philadelphia	19	19	12	50	2.6
1951-52	Philadelphia	15	22	10	54	3.6
	Totals	34	41	22	104	3.1

BROWNE, JAMES
b. 1930 Ht. 6-10 Wt. 235

Yr.	Team	G	FG	FT	TP	Avg.
1948-49	Chicago	4	1	1	3	0.8
1949-50	Denver	31	17	13	47	1.5
	Totals	35	18	14	50	1.4

BRUNKHORST, BRIAN (Bronk)
b. June 12, 1945 Ht. 6-6 Wt. 210 College—Marquette

Yr.	Team		G	FG	FT	TP	Avg.
1968-69	Los Angeles	(ABA)	3	6	13	25	8.3

BRUNS, GEORGE
b. Aug. 30, 1946 Ht. 6-0 Wt. 160 College—Manhattan

Yr.	Team		G	FG	FT	TP	Avg.
1972-73	New York	(ABA)	13	31(2)	22	86	6.6

BRYANT, EMMETTE
b. Nov. 4, 1938 Ht. 6-1 Wt. 175 College—DePaul

Yr.	Team	G	FG	FT	TP	Avg.
1964-65	New York	77	145	87	377	4.9
1965-66	New York	71	212	74	498	7.0
1966-67	New York	63	236	74	546	8.7
1967-68	New York	77	112	59	283	3.7
1968-69	Boston	80	197	65	459	5.7
1969-70	Boston	71	210	135	555	7.8
1970-71	Buffalo	73	228	151	727	10.0
1971-72	Buffalo	54	101	75	277	5.1
	Totals	566	1501	720	3722	6.6

BUCCI, GEORGE
b. July 9, 1953 Ht. 6-3 Wt. 202 College—Manhattan

Yr.	Team		G	FG	FT	TP	Avg.
1975-76	New York	(ABA)	33	50	28	128	3.9

BUCKHALTER, JOSEPH
b. Aug. 1, 1937 Ht. 6-7 Wt. 210 College—Manhattan

Yr.	Team	G	FG	FT	TP	Avg.
1961-62	Cincinnati	63	153	67	373	5.9
1962-63	Cincinnati	2	0	2	2	1.0
	Totals	65	153	69	375	5.8

BUCKNER, CLEVELAND
b. Aug. 17, 1938 Ht. 6-9 Wt. 210 College—Jackson St.

Yr.	Team	G	FG	FT	TP	Avg.
1961-62	New York	62	158	83	399	6.4
1962-63	New York	6	5	2	12	2.0
	Totals	68	163	85	411	6.0

BUDD, DAVID
b. Oct. 28, 1938 Ht. 6-6 Wt. 210 College—Wake Forest

Yr.	Team	G	FG	FT	TP	Avg.
1960-61	New York	61	156	87	399	6.5
1961-62	New York	79	188	138	514	6.5
1962-63	New York	78	294	151	739	9.5
1963-64	New York	73	128	84	340	4.7
1964-65	New York	62	196	121	513	8.3
	Totals	353	962	581	2505	7.1

BUDKO, WALTER
b. June 30, 1925 Ht. 6-5 Wt. 220 College—Columbia

Yr.	Team	G	FG	FT	TP	Avg.
1948-49	Baltimore	60	224	244	692	11.5
1949-50	Baltimore	66	198	199	595	9.0
1950-51	Baltimore	64	165	166	496	7.8
1951-52	Philadelphia	63	97	60	254	4.0
	Totals	253	684	669	2037	8.1

BUNCE, LARRY
b. July 29, 1945 Ht. 7-0 Wt. 245 College—Utah State

Yr.	Team		G	FG	FT	TP	Avg.
1967-68	Anaheim	(ABA)	71	300	256	856	12.1
1968-69	Den.-Dal.-Hou.	(ABA)	58	86	114	286	4.9
	Totals		129	386	370	1142	8.9

BUNCH, GREG
b. May 15, 1956 Ht. 6-6 Wt. 190 College—Cal. St.-Fullerton

Yr.	Team	G	FG	FT	TP	Avg.
1978-79	New York	12	9	10	28	2.3

BUNT, DICK
b. July 13, 1930 Ht. 6-0 Wt. 170 College—N.Y.U.

Yr.	Team	G	FG	FT	TP	Avg.
1952-53	N.Y.-Balt.	26	29	34	92	3.5

BUNTIN, WILLIAM
b. May 5, 1942 Ht. 6-7 Wt. 250 College—Michigan
d. May 9, 1968

Yr.	Team	G	FG	FT	TP	Avg.
1965-66	Detroit	41	118	88	324	7.7

BUNTING, BILL
b. Aug. 26, 1947 Ht. 6-8 Wt. 200 College—No. Carolina

Yr.	Team		G	FG	FT	TP	Avg.
1969-70	Carolina	(ABA)	57	96	79	271	4.8
1970-71	N.Y.-Vir.	(ABA)	72	114	104	332	4.6
1971-72	Virginia	(ABA)	16	4	12	20	1.3
	Totals		145	214	195	623	4.3

BURDEN, LUTHER (Ticky)
b. Feb. 28, 1953 Ht. 6-2 Wt. 190 College—Utah

Yr.	Team		G	FG	FT	TP	Avg.
1975-76	Virginia	(ABA)	71	561(8)	283	1413	19.9
1976-77	N.Y. Knicks		61	148	51	347	5.7
1977-78	New York		2	1	0	2	1.0
	Totals		134	710(8)	334	1762	13.1

BURMASTER, JACK
b. Dec. 23, 1926 Ht. 6-3 Wt. 190 College—Illinois

Yr.	Team		G	FG	FT	TP	Avg.
1948-49	Oshkosh	(NL)	64	140	80	360	5.6
1949-50	Sheboygan		61	237	124	598	9.8
	Totals		125	377	204	958	7.7

BURNS, JIM
b. Sept. 21, 1945 Ht. 6-3½ Wt. 195 College—Northwestern

Yr.	Team		G	FG	FT	TP	Avg.
1967-68	Chicago		3	2	0	4	1.3
1967-68	Dallas	(ABA)	33	52	51	155	4.7
	Totals		36	54	51	159	4.4

BURRIS, ART
b. Apr. 7, 1924 Ht. 6-5 Wt. 220 College—Tennessee

Yr.	Team	G	FG	FT	TP	Avg.
1950-51	Ft. Wayne	33	28	21	77	2.3
1951-52	Ft. W.-Milw.	41	42	26	110	2.7
	Totals	74	70	47	187	2.5

Yr.	Team	G	FG	FT	TP	Avg.

BURROW, ROBERT
b. June 29, 1934 Ht. 6-7 Wt. 230 College—Kentucky

Yr.	Team		G	FG	FT	TP	Avg.
1956-57	Rochester		67	137	130	404	6.0
1957-58	Minnesota		14	22	11	55	3.9
	Totals		81	159	141	459	5.7

BURTON, ED
b. Aug. 13, 1939 Ht. 6-6½ Wt. 225 College—Michigan St.

Yr.	Team		G	FG	FT	TP	Avg.
1961-62	New York		8	7	1	15	1.9
1964-65	St. Louis		7	7	4	18	2.6
	Totals		15	14	5	33	2.2

BUSTION, DAVE
b. Aug. 30, 1949 Ht. 6-8 Wt. 215 College—Denver

Yr.	Team		G	FG	FT	TP	Avg.
1972-73	Denver	(ABA)	47	58	42	158	3.4

BUTCHER, DONNIS (Donnie)
b. Feb. 8, 1936 Ht. 6-3 Wt. 200 College—Pikeville

Yr.	Team		G	FG	FT	TP	Avg.
1961-62	New York		47	48	42	138	2.9
1962-63	New York		68	172	131	475	7.0
1963-64	N.Y.-Det.		78	202	159	563	7.2
1964-65	Detroit		71	143	126	412	5.8
1965-66	Detroit		15	45	18	108	7.2
	Totals		279	610	476	1696	6.1

BUTLER, ELBERT (Al)
b. July 9, 1938 Ht. 6-2 Wt. 175 College—Niagara

Yr.	Team		G	FG	FT	TP	Avg.
1961-62	Boston-N.Y.		59	350	131	831	14.1
1962-63	New York		74	297	144	738	10.0
1963-64	New York		76	260	138	658	8.7
1964-65	Baltimore		25	24	11	59	2.4
	Totals		234	931	424	2286	9.8

BUTLER, MIKE
b. Oct. 22, 1946 Ht. 6-2 Wt. 175 College—Memphis St.

Yr.	Team		G	FG	FT	TP	Avg.
1968-69	New Orleans	(ABA)	77	207(50)	112	576	7.5
1969-70	New Orleans	(ABA)	83	298(87)	135	818	9.9
1970-71	Utah	(ABA)	71	271(32)	153	727	10.2
1971-72	Utah	(ABA)	14	14(3)	6	37	2.6
	Totals		245	790(172)	406	2158	8.8

BYRD, WALT
Ht. 6-7 Wt. 205 College—Temple

Yr.	Team		G	FG	FT	TP	Avg.
1969-70	Miami	(ABA)	22	14	5	33	1.5

BYRNES, THOMAS
b. Feb. 19, 1923 Ht. 6-3 Wt. 175 College—Seton Hall

Yr.	Team		G	FG	FT	TP	Avg.
1946-47	New York		60	175	103	453	7.6
1947-48	New York		47	117	65	299	6.4
1948-49	N.Y.-Indiana		57	160	92	412	7.2
1949-50	Baltimore		53	120	87	327	6.2
1950-51	Balt.-Wash.-Tri C.		48	83	55	221	4.6
	Totals		265	655	402	1712	6.5

BYTZURA, MICHAEL
b. June 18, 1922 Ht. 6-3 Wt. 175 College—Duquesne/LIU

Yr.	Team		G	FG	FT	TP	Avg.
1944-45	Cleveland	(NL)	30	113	35	261	8.7
1945-46	Cleveland	(NL)	33	78	35	191	5.8
1946-47	Pittsburgh		60	87	36	210	3.5
	Totals		123	278	106	662	5.4

CABLE, BARNEY
b. July 29, 1935 Ht. 6-7 Wt. 200 College—Bradley

Yr.	Team		G	FG	FT	TP	Avg.
1958-59	Detroit		31	43	23	109	3.5
1959-60	Syracuse		57	109	44	262	4.6
1960-61	Syracuse		75	266	73	605	8.1
1961-62	Chi.-St. Louis		67	305	118	728	10.9
1962-63	St. Louis-Chi.		62	173	62	408	6.6
1963-64	Baltimore		71	116	28	260	3.7
	Totals		363	1012	348	2372	6.5

CALABRESE, GERRY
b. Feb. 4, 1925 Ht. 6-1 Wt. 175 College—St. John's

Yr.	Team		G	FG	FT	TP	Avg.
1950-51	Syracuse		46	70	61	201	4.4
1951-52	Syracuse		58	109	73	291	5.0
	Totals		104	179	134	492	4.7

CALDWELL, JIM
b. Jan. 28, 1943 Ht. 6-10 Wt. 240 College—Georgia Tech

Yr.	Team		G	FG	FT	TP	Avg.
1967-68	New York		2	0	0	0	0.0
1967-68	N.J.-Ky.	(ABA)	70	223(1)	99	546	7.8
1968-69	Kentucky	(ABA)	65	167(1)	87	422	6.5
	Totals		137	390(2)	186	968	7.1

CALDWELL, JOE (Pogo)
b. Nov. 1, 1941 Ht. 6-5 Wt. 195 College—Ariz. State

Yr.	Team		G	FG	FT	TP	Avg.
1964-65	Detroit		66	290	129	709	10.7
1965-66	Det.-St. Louis		79	411	179	1001	12.7
1966-67	St. Louis		81	458	200	1116	13.8
1967-68	St. Louis		79	564	165	1293	16.4
1968-69	Atlanta		81	561	159	1281	15.8
1969-70	Atlanta		82	674	379	1727	21.1
1970-71	Carolina	(ABA)	72	685(6)	302	1678	23.3
1971-72	Carolina	(ABA)	61	434(5)	159	1032	16.9
1972-73	Carolina	(ABA)	77	555(1)	172	1283	14.4
1973-74	Carolina	(ABA)	79	502(3)	128	1135	14.6
1974-75	St. Louis	(ABA)	25	161(3)	39	364	17.5
	Totals		782	5315(18)	2011	12619	16.1

CALHOUN, DAVID (Corky)
b. No. 1, 1950 Ht. 6-7 Wt. 210 College—Pennsylvania

Yr.	Team		G	FG	FT	TP	Avg.
1972-73	Phoenix		82	211	71	493	6.0
1973-74	Phoenix		77	268	98	634	8.2
1974-75	Pho.-L.A.		70	132	58	322	4.6
1975-76	Los Angeles		76	172	65	409	5.4
1976-77	Portland		70	85	66	236	3.4
1977-78	Portland		79	175	66	416	5.3
1978-79	Indiana		81	153	72	378	4.7
1979-80	Indiana		7	4	0	8	1.1
	Totals		542	1200	496	2896	5.3

Yr.	Team		G	FG	FT	TP	Avg.

CALHOUN, WILLIAM
b. 1927 Ht. 6-3 Wt. 180

Yr.	Team		G	FG	FT	TP	Avg.
1947-48	Rochester	(NL)	43	31	18	80	1.9
1948-49	Rochester		56	146	75	367	6.6
1949-50	Rochester		62	207	146	560	9.0
1950-51	Rochester		66	175	161	511	7.7
1951-52	Baltimore		55	129	125	383	7.0
1952-53	Syra.-Milw.		62	180	211	571	9.2
1953-54	Milwaukee		72	190	214	594	8.3
1954-55	Milwaukee		69	144	166	454	6.6
	Totals		485	1202	1116	3520	7.3

CALLAHAN, THOMAS
b. 1921 Ht. 6-1 Wt. 180 College—Notre Dame/Rockhurst

Yr.	Team	G	FG	FT	TP	Avg.
1946-47	Providence	13	6	5	17	1.3

CALVERLEY, ERNEST
b. Jan. 30, 1924 Ht. 5-10 Wt. 155 College—Rhode Is.

Yr.	Team	G	FG	FT	TP	Avg.
1946-47	Providence	59	323	199	845	14.3
1947-48	Providence	47	226	107	559	11.9
1948-49	Providence	59	218	121	557	9.4
	Totals	165	767	427	1961	11.9

CANNON, LARRY
b. April 12, 1947 Ht. 6-5 Wt. 195 College—LaSalle

Yr.	Team		G	FG	FT	TP	Avg.
1969-70	Miami	(ABA)	57	253(8)	158	672	11.8
1970-71	Denver	(ABA)	80	751(18)	606	2126	26.6
1971-72	Memphis-Ind.	(ABA)	54	228(3)	164	623	11.5
1972-73	Indiana	(ABA)		(Injured)			
1973-74	Indiana	(ABA)	3	3	1	7	2.3
1973-74	Philadelphia	(ABA)	19	49	19	117	6.2
	Totals		213	1284(29)	948	3545	16.6

CARD, FRANK
b. Dec. 28, 1944 Ht. 6-7 Wt. 195 College—S.C. State

Yr.	Team		G	FG	FT	TP	Avg.
1968-69	Minnesota	(ABA)	76	222(1)	146	591	7.8
1969-70	Washington	(ABA)	74	351(1)	178	881	11.9
1970-71	Virginia-Car.	(ABA)	70	303(1)	196	803	11.5
1971-72	Car.-Den.	(ABA)	82	235	130	600	7.3
1972-73	Denver	(ABA)	4	6	9	21	5.3
	Totals		306	1117(3)	659	2896	9.5

CARL, HOWARD
b. June 7, 1938 Ht. 5-9½ Wt. 160 College—Illinois/DePaul

Yr.	Team	G	FG	FT	TP	Avg.
1961-62	Chicago	31	67	36	170	5.5

CARLISLE, CHESTER
b. Nov. 2, 1916 Ht. 6-5 Wt. 195 College—California

Yr.	Team	G	FG	FT	TP	Avg.
1946-47	Chicago	51	100	56	256	5.0

CARLOS, DON
b. March 3, 1944 Ht. 6-4½ Wt. 210 College—Otterbein

Yr.	Team		G	FG	FT	TP	Avg.
1968-69	Houston	(ABA)	56	207	214	628	11.2

CARLSON, AL
b. Sept. 17, 1951 Ht. 6-11 Wt. 235 College—S. California

Yr.	Team	G	FG	FT	TP	Avg.
1975-76	Seattle	28	27	18	72	2.6

CARLSON, DON (Swede)
b. March 20, 1920 Ht. 6-0 Wt. 170 College—Minnesota

Yr.	Team		G	FG	FT	TP	Avg.
1946-47	Chicago		59	272	86	630	10.7
1947-48	Minneapolis	(NL)	58	205	65	475	8.2
1948-49	Minneapolis		55	211	86	508	9.2
1949-50	Minneapolis		57	99	69	267	4.7
1950-51	Washington		9	17	8	42	4.7
	Totals		238	804	314	1922	8.1

CARNEY, BOB
b. Aug. 3, 1932 Ht. 6-3 Wt. 172 College—Bradley

Yr.	Team	G	FG	FT	TP	Avg.
1954-55	Minneapolis	19	24	21	69	3.6

CARPENTER, ROBERT
b. Nov. 6, 1917 Ht. 6-5 Wt. 200 College—East Texas

Yr.	Team		G	FG	FT	TP	Avg.
1940-41	Oshkosh	(NL)	24	40	41	121	5.0
1945-46	Oshkosh	(NL)	34	186	101	473	13.9
1946-47	Oshkosh	(NL)	44	199	115	513	11.7
1947-48	Oshkosh	(NL)	60	211	160	582	9.7
1948-49	Ham-Osh.	(NL)	47	160	131	451	9.6
1949-50	Ft. Wayne		66	212	190	614	9.3
1950-51	F.W.-Tri-C.		56	109	105	323	5.8
	Totals		331	1117	843	3077	9.3

CARRIER, J. DAREL
b. Oct. 26, 1940 Ht. 6-3 Wt. 185 College—Western Ky.

Yr.	Team		G	FG	FT	TP	Avg.
1967-68	Kentucky	(ABA)	77	643(84)	395	1765	22.0
1968-69	Kentucky	(ABA)	73	559(125)	447	1690	23.2
1969-70	Kentucky	(ABA)	77	610(107)	454	1781	23.1
1970-71	Kentucky	(ABA)	84	505(63)	327	1380	16.4
1971-72	Ken.-Mem.	(ABA)	23	117(16)	76	326	14.2
	Totals		334	2434(395)	1699	6942	20.8

CARRINGTON, BOB
b. July 3, 1953 Ht. 6-6 Wt. 195 College—Boston College

Yr.	Team	G	FG	FT	TP	Avg.
1977-78	N.J.-Ind.	72	253	130	636	8.8
1979-80	San Diego	10	15	6	36	3.6
	Totals	82	268	136	672	8.2

CARTER, FRED
b. Feb. 14, 1945 Ht. 6-3 Wt. 185 College—Mt. St. Mary's

Yr.	Team	G	FG	FT	TP	Avg.
1969-70	Baltimore	76	157	80	394	5.2
1970-71	Baltimore	77	340	119	799	10.4
1971-72	Balt.-Phila.	79	446	182	1074	13.6
1972-73	Philadelphia	81	679	259	1617	20.0
1973-74	Philadelphia	78	706	254	1666	21.4
1974-75	Philadelphia	77	715	256	1686	21.9
1975-76	Philadelphia	82	665	219	1549	18.9
1976-77	Phila.-Milw.	61	209	68	486	8.0
	Totals	611	3917	1437	9271	15.2

CARTER, GEORGE
b. Jan. 18, 1944 Ht. 6-5 Wt. 218 College—St. Bonaventure

Yr.	Team		G	FG	FT	TP	Avg.
1967-68	Detroit		1	1	1	3	3.0
1969-70	Washington	ABA	67	397(7)	167	968	14.4
1970-71	Virginia	(ABA)	81	594	346	1534	18.9
1971-72	Pitt.-Car.	(ABA)	75	538	388	1464	19.5
1972-73	New York	(ABA)	83	569	440	1578	19.3
1973-74	Virginia	(ABA)	80	561(32)	392	1546	18.4
1974-75	Memphis	(ABA)	82	590(10)	318	1508	18.4
1975-76	Utah	(ABA)	10	25	32	82	8.2
	Totals		479	3275(49)	2084	8683	18.0

Yr.	Team		G	FG	FT	TP	Avg.
CARTER, JOHN (Jake)							
b. July 25, 1924 Ht. 6-5 Wt. 195 College—East Texas							
1948-49 Hammond	(NL)		62	133	188	454	7.3
1949-50 Den.-And.			24	23	36	82	3.4
	Totals		86	156	224	536	6.2
CARTER, RON							
b. Aug. 31, 1956 Ht. 6-5 Wt. 190 College-VMI							
1978-79 Los Angeles			46	54	36	144	3.1
1979-80 Indiana			13	15	2	32	2.5
	Totals		59	69	38	176	3.0
CARTY, JAY							
b. July 4, 1941 Ht. 6-8 Wt. 230 College—Oregon St.							
1968-69 Los Angeles			28	34	8	76	2.7
CASH, CORNELIUS							
b. March 3, 1952 Ht. 6-8 Wt. 220 College—Bowling Green							
1976-77 Detroit			6	9	3	21	3.5
CASH, SAM							
b. 1950 Ht. 6-8 Wt. 230 College—Riverside							
1972-73 Memphis	(ABA)		7	4	12	20	2.9
CATLETT, SID							
b. April 8, 1948 Ht. 6-8 Wt. 230 College—Notre Dame							
1971-72 Cincinnati			9	2	2	6	0.7
CERVI, ALFRED (Digger)							
b. Feb. 12, 1917 Ht. 5-11½ Wt. 185							
1937-38 Buffalo	(NL)		9	19	6	44	4.9
1945-46 Rochester	(NL)		28	112	76	300	10.7
1946-47 Rochester	(NL)		44	228	176	632	14.4
1947-48 Rochester	(NL)		49	234	187	655	13.4
1948-49 Syracuse	(NL)		57	204	287	695	12.2
1949-50 Syracuse			56	143	287	573	10.2
1950-51 Syracuse			53	132	194	458	8.6
1951-52 Syracuse			55	99	219	417	7.6
1952-53 Syracuse			38	31	81	143	3.8
	Totals		389	1202	1513	3917	10.1
CHAMBERLAIN, BILL							
b. Dec. 16, 1949 Ht. 6-6 Wt. 205 College—No. Carolina							
1972-73 Ken.-Mem.	(ABA)		50	112(2)	36	262	5.2
1973-74 Phoenix			28	57	39	153	5.5
	Totals		78	169(2)	75	415	5.3
CHAMBERLAIN, WILT							
b. Aug. 21, 1936 Ht. 7-1 Wt. 275 College—Kansas							
1959-60 Philadelphia			72	1065	577	2707	37.6
1960-61 Philadelphia			79	1251	531	3033	38.4
1961-62 Philadelphia			80	1597	835	4029	50.4
1962-63 San Francisco			80	1463	660	3586	44.8
1963-64 San Francisco			80	1204	540	2948	36.9
1964-65 S.F.-Phila.			73	1063	408	2534	34.7
1965-66 Philadelphia			79	1074	501	2649	33.5
1966-67 Philadelphia			81	785	386	1956	24.1
1967-68 Philadelphia			82	819	354	1992	24.3
1968-69 Los Angeles			81	641	382	1664	20.5
1969-70 Los Angeles			12	129	70	328	27.3
1970-71 Los Angeles			82	668	360	1696	20.7
1971-72 Los Angeles			82	496	221	1213	14.8
1972-73 Los Angeles			82	426	232	1084	13.2
	Totals		1045	12681	6057	31419	30.1
CHAMBERS, JERRY							
b. July 18, 1943 Ht. 6-5 Wt. 186 College—Utah							
1966-67 Los Angeles			69	224	68	516	7.5
1969-70 Phoenix			79	283	91	657	8.3
1970-71 Atlanta			65	237	106	580	8.9
1971-72 Buffalo			26	78	22	178	6.8
	Totals		239	822	287	1931	8.1
CHANEY, JOHN							
b. Feb. 29, 1920 Ht. 6-3 Wt. 190 College—La. State							
1946-47 Syracuse	(NL)		42	138	86	362	8.6
1947-48 Syracuse	(NL)		40	107	80	294	7.4
1948-49 Syracuse	(NL)		57	79	65	223	3.9
1949-50 Tri C.-Sheb.			16	25	20	70	4.4
	Totals		155	349	251	949	6.1
CHANEY, DON (Duck)							
b. March 22, 1946 Ht. 6-5 Wt. 210 College—Houston							
1968-69 Boston			20	36	8	80	4.0
1969-70 Boston			63	115	82	312	5.0
1970-71 Boston			81	348	234	930	11.5
1971-72 Boston			79	373	197	943	11.9
1972-73 Boston			79	414	210	1038	13.1
1973-74 Boston			81	348	149	845	10.4
1974-75 Boston			82	321	133	775	9.5
1975-76 St. Louis	(ABA)		48	191(1)	64	447	9.3
1976-77 Los Angeles			81	213	70	496	6.1
1977-78 L.A.-Bost.			51	104	38	246	4.8
1978-79 Boston			65	174	36	384	5.9
1979-80 Boston			60	67(1)	32	167	2.8
	Totals		790	2704(2)	1253	6663	8.4
CHAPMAN, WAYNE							
b. June 15, 1945 Ht. 6-6 Wt. 190 College—Western Ky.							
1968-69 Kentucky	(ABA)		48	68(4)	54	194	4.0
1969-70 Kentucky	(ABA)		82	261(8)	134	664	8.1
1970-71 Den.-Ind.	(ABA)		69	214(15)	113	556	8.1
1971-72 Indiana	(ABA)		7	7(1)	3	18	2.6
	Totals		206	550(28)	304	1432	7.0
CHAPPELL, LEONARD							
b. Jan. 31, 1941 Ht. 6-8 Wt. 240 College—Wake Forest							
1962-63 Syracuse			80	281	148	710	8.9
1963-64 Phila.-N.Y.			79	531	288	1350	17.1
1964-65 New York			43	145	68	358	8.3
1965-66 New York			46	100	46	246	5.3
1966-67 Chicago-Cinn.			73	132	53	317	4.3
1967-68 Cinn.-Detroit			68	235	138	608	8.9
1968-69 Milwaukee			80	459	250	1168	14.6
1969-70 Milwaukee			75	243	135	621	8.3
1970-71 Cleve.-Atl.			48	86	71	243	5.1
1971-72 Dallas	(ABA)		79	231	144	606	7.7
	Totals		671	2443	1341	6227	9.3

Yr.	Team	G	FG	FT	TP	Avg.
CHARLES, KEN						
b. July 10, 1951 Ht. 6-3 Wt. 180 College—Fordham						
1973-74 Buffalo		59	88	53	229	3.9
1974-75 Buffalo		79	240	120	600	7.6
1975-76 Buffalo		81	328	161	817	10.1
1976-77 Atlanta		82	354	205	913	11.1
1977-78 Atlanta		21	73	42	188	9.0
	Totals	322	1083	581	2747	8.5
CHOLLET, LEROY						
b. March 5, 1925 Ht. 6-2 Wt. 190 College—Canisius						
1949-50 Syracuse		49	61	35	157	3.2
1950-51 Syracuse		14	6	12	24	1.7
	Totals	63	67	47	181	2.9
CHRIST, FRED						
b. 1930 Ht. 6-4 Wt. 210 College—Fordham						
1954-55 New York		6	5	10	20	3.3
CHRISTENSEN, CAL						
b. June 6, 1927 Ht. 6-5 Wt. 210 College—Toledo						
1950-51 Tri-Cities		67	134	175	443	6.6
1951-52 Milwaukee		24	29	30	88	3.7
1952-53 Rochester		59	72	68	212	3.6
1953-54 Rochester		70	137	138	412	5.9
1954-55 Rochester		71	114	124	352	5.0
	Totals	291	486	535	1507	5.2
CHRISTIAN, BOB						
b. May 11, 1944 Ht. 7-0 Wt. 245 College—Grambling						
1969-70 N.Y.-Dallas (ABA)		2	1	0	2	1.0
1970-71 Atlanta		54	55	40	150	2.8
1971-72 Atlanta		56	66	44	176	3.1
1972-73 Atlanta		55	85	60	230	4.2
1973-74 Phoenix		81	140	106	386	4.8
	Totals	248	347	250	944	3.8
CHUBIN, STEVE (Chube)						
b. Feb. 8, 1944 Ht. 6-2 Wt. 200 College—Rhode Island						
1967-68 Anaheim (ABA)		77	439(2)	518	1398	18.2
1968-69 L.A.-Min.-Ind.-N.Y. (ABA)		77	344(3)	386	1077	14.0
1969-70 Pittsburgh (ABA)		72	127(5)	170	429	6.0
	Totals	226	910(10)	1074	2904	12.8
CLARK, ARCHIE						
b. July 15, 1941 Ht. 6-2 Wt. 175 College—Minnesota						
1966-67 Los Angeles		76	331	136	798	10.5
1967-68 Los Angeles		81	628	356	1612	19.9
1968-69 Philadelphia		82	444	219	1107	13.5
1969-70 Philadelphia		76	594	311	1499	19.7
1970-71 Philadelphia		82	662	422	1746	21.3
1971-72 Phila.-Balt.		77	712	514	1938	25.2
1972-73 Baltimore		39	302	111	715	18.3
1973-74 Capital		56	315	103	733	13.1
1974-75 Seattle		77	455	161	1071	13.9
1975-76 Detroit		79	250	100	600	7.6
	Totals	725	4693	2433	11819	16.3

Yr.	Team	G	FG	FT	TP	Avg.
CLARK, DICK						
b. Jan. 5, 1944 Ht. 6-4 Wt. 195 College—Eastern Ky.						
1967-68 Minnesota (ABA)		26	46	48	140	5.4
1968-69 Houston (ABA)		32	64(1)	89	218	6.8
	Totals	58	110(1)	137	358	6.2
CLAWSON, JOHN						
b. May 15, 1944 Ht. 6-4 Wt. 200 College—Michigan						
1968-69 Oakland (ABA)		70	147	37	331	4.7
CLEAMONS, JIM						
b. Sept. 13, 1949 Ht. 6-3½ Wt. 185 College—Ohio State						
1971-72 Los Angeles		38	35	28	98	2.6
1972-73 Cleveland		80	192	75	459	5.7
1973-74 Cleveland		81	236	93	565	7.0
1974-75 Cleveland		74	369	144	882	11.9
1975-76 Cleveland		82	413	174	1000	12.2
1976-77 Cleveland		60	257	112	626	10.4
1977-78 New York		79	215	81	511	6.5
1978-79 New York		79	311	130	752	9.5
1979-80 N.Y.-Wash.		79	214(7)	84	519	6.6
	Totals	652	2242(7)	921	5412	8.3
CLEMENS, BARRY						
b. May 1, 1942 Ht. 6-7 Wt. 210 College—Ohio Wesleyan						
1965-66 New York		70	161	54	376	5.4
1966-67 Chicago		60	186	68	440	7.3
1967-68 Chicago		78	301	123	725	9.3
1968-69 Chicago		75	235	82	552	7.4
1969-70 Seattle		78	270	111	651	8.3
1970-71 Seattle		78	247	83	577	7.4
1971-72 Seattle		82	252	76	580	7.1
1972-73 Cleveland		72	209	53	471	6.5
1973-74 Cleveland		71	163	62	388	5.5
1974-75 Portland		77	168	45	381	4.9
1975-76 Portland		49	70	31	171	3.5
	Totals	790	2262	788	5312	6.7
CLIFTON, NATHANIEL (Sweetwater)						
b. Oct. 13, 1922 Ht. 6-7 Wt. 225 College—Xavier (La.)						
1950-51 New York		65	211	140	562	8.6
1951-52 New York		62	244	170	658	10.6
1952-53 New York		70	272	200	744	10.6
1953-54 New York		72	257	174	688	9.6
1954-55 New York		72	360	224	944	13.1
1955-56 New York		64	213	135	561	8.8
1956-57 New York		71	308	146	762	10.7
1957-58 Detroit		68	217	91	525	7.7
	Totals	544	2082	1280	5444	10.0
CLOSS, WILLIAM						
b. Jan. 8, 1922 Ht. 6-6 Wt. 205 College—Rice						
1946-47 Indianapolis (NL)		44	119	34	272	6.2
1947-48 Indianapolis (NL)		55	162	72	396	7.2
1948-49 Anderson (NL)		64	203	110	516	8.1
1949-50 Anderson (NL)		64	283	186	752	11.8
1950-51 Philadelphia		65	202	166	570	8.8
1951-52 Ft. Wayne		57	120	107	347	6.1
	Totals	349	1089	675	2853	8.2

Yr.	Team		G	FG	FT	TP	Avg.
CLOYD, PAUL							

b. June 13, 1920 Ht. 6-2 Wt. 180 College—Wisconsin

Yr.	Team		G	FG	FT	TP	Avg.
1947-48 Sheboygan	(NL)		60	213	129	555	9.3
1948-49 Sheboygan	(NL)		56	119	98	336	6.0
1949-50 Balt.-Waterloo			7	7	5	19	2.7
	Totals		123	339	232	910	7.3

CLUGGISH, ROBERT

b. 1918 Ht. 6-10 Wt. 235 College—Kentucky

1946-47 New York		54	93	52	238	6.3

CLYDE, BEN

b. June 10, 1951 Ht. 6-7 Wt. 198 College—Florida State

1974-75 Boston		25	31	7	69	2.8

COLEMAN, E. C.

b. Sept. 25, 1950 Ht. 6-8 Wt. 225 College—Houston Baptist

1973-74 Houston		58	128	47	303	5.2
1974-75 New Orleans		77	253	116	622	8.1
1975-76 New Orleans		67	216	59	491	7.3
1976-77 New Orleans		77	290	82	662	8.6
1977-78 Golden State		72	212	40	464	6.4
1978-79 Houston		6	5	1	11	1.8
	Totals	357	1104	345	2553	7.2

COLEMAN, JACK

b. May 23, 1924 Ht. 6-7 Wt. 230 College—Louisville

1949-50 Rochester		68	250	90	590	8.7
1950-51 Rochester		67	315	134	764	11.4
1951-52 Rochester		66	308	120	736	11.2
1952-53 Rochester		70	314	135	763	10.9
1953-54 Rochester		71	289	108	686	9.7
1954-55 Rochester		72	400	124	924	12.8
1955-56 Roch.-St. L.		75	390	177	957	12.8
1956-57 St. Louis		72	316	123	755	10.5
1957-58 St. Louis		72	231	84	546	7.6
	Totals	633	2813	1095	6721	10.6

COLLINS, JIMMY

b. Nov. 24, 1946 Ht. 6-2 Wt. 175 College—N. Mex. St.

1970-71 Chicago		55	92	35	219	4.0
1971-72 Chicago		19	26	10	62	3.3
	Totals	74	118	45	281	3.8

COLONE, JOE (Bells)

b. Jan. 23, 1926 Ht. 6-5 Wt. 210

1948-49 New York		16	35	13	83	5.5

COMBS, GLEN COURTNEY

b. Oct. 30, 1946 Ht. 6-2 Wt. 185 College—Virginia Tech

1968-69 Dallas	(ABA)	72	364(84)	300	1112	15.4
1969-70 Dallas	(ABA)	84	640(130)	458	1868	22.2
1970-71 Tex-Utah	(ABA)	86	610(77)	448	1745	20.3
1971-72 Utah	(ABA)	84	483(103)	319	1388	16.5
1972-73 Utah	(ABA)	50	228(51)	154	661	13.2
1973-74 Utah-Mem.	(ABA)	76	304(52)	156	816	10.7
1974-75 Virginia	(ABA)	13	23(6)	24	76	5.9
	Totals	465	2652(503)	1859	7666	16.5

COMEAUX, JOHN

b. Sept. 5, 1943 Ht. 6-5 Wt. 193 College—Grambling

1967-68 New Orleans	(ABA)	23	27	23	77	3.3

COMLEY, LARRY

b. Aug. 17, 1939 Ht. 6-5½ Wt. 210 College—Kansas State

1963-64 Baltimore		11	8	9	25	2.3

CONGDON, JEFF

b. Oct. 17, 1943 Ht. 6-2 Wt. 180 College—Brigham Young

1967-68 Ana.-Denv.	(ABA)	64	150(13)	49	362	5.7
1968-69 Denver	(ABA)	59	107(5)	69	288	4.9
1969-70 Denver	(ABA)	83	299(63)	151	812	9.8
1970-71 Utah-NY	(ABA)	80	178(18)	79	453	5.7
1971-72 Dallas	(ABA)	20	30(3)	17	80	4.0
	Totals	306	764(102)	365	1995	6.5

CONLEY, GENE

b. Nov. 10, 1930 Ht. 6-8 Wt. 255 College—Washington St.

1952-53 Boston		39	35	18	88	2.3
1958-59 Boston		50	86	37	209	4.2
1959-60 Boston		71	201	76	478	6.7
1960-61 Boston		75	183	106	472	6.3
1962-63 New York		70	254	122	630	9.0
1963-64 New York		46	74	44	192	4.2
	Totals	351	833	403	2069	5.9

CONLEY, LARRY

Ht. 6-3 Wt. 175 College—Kentucky

1967-68 Kentucky	(ABA)	1	1	0	2	2.0

CONLIN, EDWARD

b. Sept. 2, 1933 Ht. 6-6 Wt. 200 College—Fordham

1955-56 Syracuse		66	211	121	543	8.2
1956-57 Syracuse		71	335	283	953	13.4
1957-58 Syracuse		60	343	215	901	15.0
1958-59 Syr.-Detroit		72	329	197	855	11.9
1959-60 Detroit		70	300	181	781	11.2
1960-61 Philadelphia		76	216	104	536	7.1
1961-62 Philadelphia		70	128	66	322	4.6
	Totals	485	1862	1167	4891	10.1

CONNORS, KEVIN (Chuck)

b. April 10, 1921 Ht. 6-7 Wt. 205 College—Seton Hall

1945-46 Rochester	(NL)	14	11	6	28	2.0
1946-47 Boston		49	94	39	227	4.6
1947-48 Boston		4	5	2	12	3.0
	Totals	67	110	47	267	4.0

COOK, BERT

b. April 26, 1929 Ht. 6-3 Wt. 186 College—Utah State

1954-55 New York		37	42	34	118	3.2

COOK, NORM

b. March 21, 1955 Ht. 6-8 Wt. 210 College—Kansas

1976-77 Boston		25	27	9	63	2.5
1977-78 Denver		2	1	0	2	1.0
	Totals	27	28	9	65	2.4

Yr.	Team		G	FG	FT	TP	Avg.

COOK, ROBERT (Cookie)
b. 1923 Ht. 5-10½ Wt. 155 College—Wisconsin

Yr.	Team		G	FG	FT	TP	Avg.
1948-49	Sheboygan	(NL)	64	172	98	442	6.9
1949-50	Sheboygan		51	222	143	587	11.5
	Totals		115	394	241	1029	8.9

COOKE, JOE
b. Aug. 14, 1948 Ht. 6-3 Wt. 175 College—Indiana

Yr.	Team	G	FG	FT	TP	Avg.
1970-71	Cleveland	73	134	48	316	4.3

COOPER, CHARLES (Chuck)
b. 1927 Ht. 6-5 Wt. 215 College—Duquesne

Yr.	Team	G	FG	FT	TP	Avg.
1950-51	Boston	66	207	201	615	9.3
1951-52	Boston	66	197	149	543	8.2
1952-53	Boston	70	157	144	458	6.5
1953-54	Boston	70	78	78	234	3.3
1954-55	Milwaukee	70	193	187	573	8.2
1955-56	St. L.-Ft. W.	67	101	100	302	4.5
	Totals	409	933	859	2725	6.7

COPELAND, HOLLIS
b. Dec. 20, 1955 Ht. 6-6 Wt. 180 College—Rutgers

Yr.	Team	G	FG	FT	TP	Avg.
1979-80	New York	75	182	63	427	5.7

CORLEY, KENNETH
Ht. 6-5 Wt. 220 College—Oklahoma St. Teachers

Yr.	Team	G	FG	FT	TP	Avg.
1946-47	Cleveland	3	0	0	0	0.0

CORLEY, RAY
b. Jan. 1, 1928 Ht. 6-0 Wt. 180 College—Notre Dame/Georgetown

Yr.	Team	G	FG	FT	TP	Avg.
1949-50	Syracuse	60	117	75	309	5.2
1950-51	Balt.-Tri.-C.	18	29	16	74	4.1
1952-53	Ft. Wayne	8	3	5	11	1.4
	Totals	86	149	96	394	4.6

COSTELLO, LARRY
b. July 2, 1931 Ht. 6-1 Wt. 188 College—Niagara

Yr.	Team	G	FG	FT	TP	Avg.
1954-55	Philadelphia	19	46	26	118	6.2
1956-57	Philadelphia	72	186	175	547	7.6
1957-58	Syracuse	72	378	320	1076	14.9
1958-59	Syracuse	70	414	280	1108	15.8
1959-60	Syracuse	71	372	249	993	14.0
1960-61	Syracuse	75	407	270	1084	14.5
1961-62	Syracuse	63	310	247	867	13.7
1962-63	Syracuse	78	285	288	858	11.0
1963-64	Philadelphia	45	191	147	529	11.8
1964-65	Philadelphia	64	309	243	861	13.5
1966-67	Philadelphia	49	130	120	380	7.8
1967-68	Philadelphia	28	67	67	201	7.2
	Totals	706	3095	2432	8622	12.2

COTTON, JOHN
b. Oct. 15, 1924 Ht. 6-7 Wt. 205 College—Wyoming

Yr.	Team		G	FG	FT	TP	Avg.
1946-47	Chicago	(NL)	3	1	2	4	1.3
1948-49	Denver	(NL)	57	71	67	209	3.7
1949-50	Denver		54	97	82	276	5.1
	Totals		114	169	151	489	4.3

COUGHRAN, JOHN
b. Sept. 12, 1951 Ht. 6-8 Wt. 230 College—California

Yr.	Team	G	FG	FT	TP	Avg.
1979-80	Golden State	24	29(2)	8	68	2.8

COUNTS, MEL
b. Oct. 16, 1941 Ht. 7-0 Wt. 230 College—Oregon St.

Yr.	Team	G	FG	FT	TP	Avg.
1964-65	Boston	54	100	58	258	4.7
1965-66	Boston	67	221	120	562	8.4
1966-67	Balt.-L.A.	56	177	69	423	7.6
1967-68	Los Angeles	82	384	190	958	11.7
1968-69	Los Angeles	77	390	178	958	12.4
1969-70	Los Angeles	81	434	156	1024	12.6
1970-71	Phoenix	80	365	149	879	11.0
1971-72	Phoenix	76	147	101	395	5.2
1972-73	Phil.-L.A.	66	132	39	303	4.6
1973-74	Los Angeles	45	61	24	146	3.2
1974-75	New Orleans	75	217	86	520	6.9
1975-76	New Orleans	30	37	16	90	3.0
	Totals	789	2665	1186	6516	8.3

COURTIN, STEVE
b. Sept. 21, 1942 Ht. 6-1 Wt. 188 College—St. Joseph's (Pa.)

Yr.	Team	G	FG	FT	TP	Avg.
1964-65	Philadelphia	24	42	17	101	4.2

COUSY, BOB
b. Aug. 9, 1928 Ht. 6-1 Wt. 175 College—Holy Cross

Yr.	Team	G	FG	FT	TP	Avg.
1950-51	Boston	69	401	276	1078	15.6
1951-52	Boston	66	512	409	1433	21.7
1952-53	Boston	71	464	479	1407	19.8
1953-54	Boston	72	486	411	1383	19.2
1954-55	Boston	71	522	460	1504	21.2
1955-56	Boston	72	440	476	1356	18.8
1956-57	Boston	64	478	363	1319	20.6
1957-58	Boston	65	445	277	1167	18.0
1958-59	Boston	65	484	329	1297	20.0
1959-60	Boston	75	568	319	1455	19.4
1960-61	Boston	76	513	352	1378	18.1
1961-62	Boston	75	462	251	1175	15.7
1962-63	Boston	76	392	219	1003	13.2
1969-70	Cincinnati	7	1	3	5	0.7
	Totals	924	6168	4624	16960	18.4

COWENS, DAVE
b. Oct. 25, 1948 Ht. 6-9 Wt. 230 College—Florida State

Yr.	Team	G	FG	FT	TP	Avg.
1970-71	Boston	81	550	273	1373	17.0
1971-72	Boston	79	657	175	1489	18.8
1972-73	Boston	82	740	204	1684	20.5
1973-74	Boston	80	645	226	1518	19.0
1974-75	Boston	65	569	191	1329	20.4
1975-76	Boston	78	611	157	1379	17.7
1976-77	Boston	50	328	162	818	16.4
1977-78	Boston	77	598	239	1435	18.6
1978-79	Boston	68	488	151	1127	16.6
1979-80	Boston	66	422(1)	95	940	14.2
	Totals	726	5608(1)	1875	13092	18.0

COX, JOHN
b. Nov. 1, 1936 Ht. 6-4 Wt. 180 College—Kentucky

Yr.	Team	G	FG	FT	TP	Avg.
1962-63	Chicago	73	239	95	573	7.8

COX, WESLEY
b. Jan. 27, 1955 Ht. 6-6 Wt. 215 College—Louisville

Yr.	Team	G	FG	FT	TP	Avg.
1977-78	Golden State	43	69	58	196	4.6
1978-79	Golden State	31	53	40	146	4.7
	Totals	74	122	98	342	4.6

Yr.	Team		G	FG	FT	TP	Avg.
CRAWFORD, FRED							
b. Dec. 23, 1941 Ht. 6-4 Wt. 190 College—St. Bonaventure							
1966-67	New York		19	44	24	112	5.9
1967-68	N.Y.-L.A.		69	224	111	559	8.1
1968-69	Los Angeles		81	211	83	505	6.2
1969-70	Milwaukee		77	243	101	587	7.6
1970-71	Buffalo-Phila.		51	110	48	268	5.3
	Totals		297	832	367	2031	6.8
CREIGHTON, JIM							
b. April 18, 1950 Ht. 6-8 Wt. 200 College—Colorado							
1975-76	Atlanta		32	12	7	31	1.0
CRISLER, HERBERT							
Ht. 6-3 Wt. 215							
1946-47	Boston		4	2	2	6	1.5
CRITCHFIELD, RUSS							
b. June 27, 1946 Ht. 5-10 Wt. 150 College—California							
1968-69	Oakland	(ABA)	47	53	55	161	3.4
CROCKER, DILLARD							
b. 1925 Ht. 6-4 Wt. 205 College—Western Michigan							
1948-49	Det.-And.	(NL)	51	101	95	297	5.8
1948-49	Ft. Wayne		2	1	4	6	3.0
1949-50	Denver		53	245	233	723	13.6
1951-52	Ind.-Milw.		38	98	97	293	7.7
1952-53	Milwaukee		61	100	130	330	5.4
	Totals		205	545	559	1649	8.0
CROFT, BOBBY							
Ht. 6-10 Wt. 200 College—Tennessee							
1970-71	Ky.-Texas	(ABA)	62	126	73	325	5.2
CROSBY, TERRY							
b. Jan. 4, 1957 Ht. 6-4 Wt. 195 College—Tennessee							
1979-80	Kansas City		4	2	2	6	1.5
CROSS, PETE							
b. March 28, 1948 Ht. 6-9 Wt. 231 College—San Francisco							
d. Jan. 2, 1977							
1970-71	Seattle		79	245	140	630	8.0
1971-72	Seattle		74	152	103	407	5.5
1972-73	K.C.-O.-Sea.		29	6	8	20	0.7
	Totals		182	403	251	1057	5.8
CROSSIN, FRANCIS (Chink)							
b. June 4, 1924 Ht. 6-1 Wt. 165 College—Pennsylvania							
d. Jan. 1981							
1947-48	Philadelphia		39	29	13	71	1.8
1948-49	Philadelphia		44	74	26	174	3.0
1949-50	Philadelphia		64	185	79	449	7.0
	Totals		147	288	118	694	4.7
CROW, BILL							
1967-68	Anaheim	(ABA)	1	1	1	3	3.0
CROW, MARK							
b. Oct. 22, 1954 Ht. 6-7 Wt. 210 College—Duke							
1977-78	New Jersey		15	35	14	84	5.6

Yr.	Team		G	FG	FT	TP	Avg.
CUETO, AL							
b. Aug. 2, 1946 Ht. 6-8 Wt. 230 College—Tulsa							
1969-70	Miami	(ABA)	78	182(5)	102	471	6.0
1970-71	Memphis	(ABA)	71	134	55	323	4.6
	Totals		149	316(5)	157	794	5.3
CUNNINGHAM, BILLY							
b. June 3, 1943 Ht. 6-6 Wt. 220 College—North Carolina							
1965-66	Philadelphia		80	431	281	1143	14.3
1966-67	Philadelphia		81	556	383	1495	18.5
1967-68	Philadelphia		74	516	368	1400	19.0
1968-69	Philadelphia		82	739	556	2034	24.8
1969-70	Philadelphia		81	802	510	2114	26.1
1970-71	Philadelphia		81	702	455	1859	23.0
1971-72	Philadelphia		75	658	428	1744	23.3
1972-73	Carolina	(ABA)	84	771(14)	472	2028	24.1
1973-74	Carolina	(ABA)	32	253(1)	149	656	20.5
1974-75	Philadelphia		80	609	345	1563	19.5
1975-76	Philadelphia		20	103	68	274	13.7
	Totals		770	6140(15)	4015	16310	21.2
CUNNINGHAM, DICK							
b. July 11, 1946 Ht. 6-10 Wt. 240 College—Murray State							
1968-69	Milwaukee		77	141	69	351	4.6
1969-70	Milwaukee		60	52	22	126	2.1
1970-71	Milwaukee		76	81	39	201	2.6
1971-72	Houston		63	67	37	171	2.7
1972-73	Milwaukee		74	64	29	157	2.1
1973-74	Milwaukee		8	3	0	6	0.8
1974-75	Milwaukee		2	0	0	0	0.0
	Totals		360	408	196	1012	2.8
CURE, ARMAND							
b. Aug. 7, 1919 Ht. 6-1 Wt. 198 College—Rhode Island							
1946-47	Providence		12	4	2	10	0.8
CURRAN, FRANCIS							
b. Sept. 19, 1925 Ht. 6-0 Wt. 175 College—Notre Dame							
1947-48	Toledo	(NL)	58	120	119	377	6.5
1948-49	Rochester		57	61	85	207	3.6
1949-50	Rochester		66	98	199	395	6.0
	Totals		181	288	403	979	5.4
DABICH, MIKE (Dabbo)							
b. Dec. 27, 1942 Ht. 7-0 Wt. 255 College—N.M. State							
1967-68	Oakland-Dal.	(ABA)	10	8	4	20	2.0
DAHLER, ED							
b. Jan. 31, 1926 Ht. 6-5 Wt. 190 College—Duquesne							
1951-52	Philadelphia		14	14	7	35	2.5
DALLMAR, HOWARD							
b. May 24, 1922 Ht. 6-4 Wt. 202 College—Stanford/Pennsylvania							
1946-47	Philadelphia		60	199	130	528	8.8
1947-48	Philadelphia		48	215	157	587	12.2
1948-49	Philadelphia		38	105	83	293	7.7
	Totals		146	519	370	1408	9.6

Yr.	Team		G	FG	FT	TP	Avg.
DAMPIER, LOUIE							
b. Nov. 20, 1944 Ht. 6-0 Wt. 170 College—Kentucky							
1967-68	Kentucky	(ABA)	72	620(38)	209	1487	20.7
1968-69	Kentucky	(ABA)	78	713(199)	308	1933	24.8
1969-70	Kentucky	(ABA)	82	643(198)	447	2131	25.9
1970-71	Kentucky	(ABA)	84	566(103)	320	1555	18.5
1971-72	Kentucky	(ABA)	83	487(84)	281	1319	15.9
1972-73	Kentucky	(ABA)	80	515(54)	262	1346	16.8
1973-74	Kentucky	(ABA)	84	603(48)	238	1492	17.8
1974-75	Kentucky	(ABA)	83	598(38)	161	1395	16.8
1975-76	Kentucky	(ABA)	82	455(32)	126	1068	13.0
1976-77	San Antonio		80	233	64	530	6.6
1977-78	San Antonio		82	336	76	748	9.1
1978-79	San Antonio		70	123	29	275	3.9
	Totals		960	5982(794)	2521	15279	15.9
DANIELS, MEL							
b. July 20, 1944 Ht. 6-9 Wt. 220 College—N.M.							
1967-68	Minnesota	(ABA)	78	669(1)	390	1729	22.3
1968-69	Indiana	(ABA)	76	712	400	1824	24.0
1969-70	Indiana	(ABA)	83	613	330	1556	18.8
1970-71	Indiana	(ABA)	82	698(1)	326	1723	21.0
1971-72	Indiana	(ABA)	79	598	317	1513	19.2
1972-73	Indiana	(ABA)	81	587(1)	322	1497	18.5
1973-74	Indiana	(ABA)	76	478	211	1167	15.4
1974-75	Memphis	(ABA)	71	290	116	696	9.8
1976-77	N.Y. Nets		11	13	13	39	3.5
	Totals		637	4658(3)	2425	11744	18.4
D'ANTONI, MIKE							
b. May 8, 1951 Ht. 6-3 Wt. 190 College—Marshall							
1973-74	K.C.-O.		52	107	33	247	4.8
1974-75	K.C.-O.		67	69	28	166	2.5
1975-76	Kansas City		9	7	2	16	1.8
1975-76	St. Louis	(ABA)	50	77	19	173	3.5
1976-77	San Antonio		2	1	1	3	1.5
	Totals		180	261	83	605	3.4
DARCEY, PETER							
b. March 3, 1930 Ht. 6-7 Wt. 235 College—Okla. A&M							
1952-53	Milwaukee		12	3	5	11	0.9
DARDEN, JAMES							
b. June 19, 1922 Ht. 6-1 Wt. 170 College—Wyoming/Denver							
1948-49	Denver	(NL)	57	107	193	587	10.3
1949-50	Denver		26	78	55	211	4.3
	Totals		83	275	248	798	9.6
DARDEN, OLIVER							
b. July 28, 1944 Ht. 6-7 Wt. 240 College—Michigan							
1967-68	Indiana	(ABA)	77	371	180	922	12.0
1968-69	N.Y.-Ky.	(ABA)	77	318(1)	178	815	10.6
1969-70	Ky.-Ind.	(ABA)	69	126(1)	57	310	4.5
	Totals		223	815(2)	415	2047	9.2
DARK, JESSE							
b. Sept. 2, 1951 Ht. 6-5 Wt. 210 College—Va. Com.							
1974-75	New York		47	74	22	170	3.6
DARNELL, RICK							
b. 1953 Ht. 6-10 Wt. 215 College—San Jose State							
1975-76	Virginia	(ABA)	11	11	4	26	2.4

Yr.	Team		G	FG	FT	TP	Avg.
DARROW, JAMES							
b. Sept. 25, 1937 Ht. 5-10¾ Wt. 170 College—Bowling Green							
1961-62	St. Louis		5	3	6	12	2.4
DAUGHTRY, MACK							
Ht. 6-3 Wt. 175 College—Albany State (Ga.)							
1970-71	Carolina	(ABA)	4	4	5	13	3.3
DAVIES, BOB							
b. Jan. 15, 1920 Ht. 6-1 Wt. 175 College—Seton Hall							
1945-46	Rochester	(NL)	27	86	70	242	9.0
1946-47	Rochester	(NL)	32	166	130	462	14.4
1947-48	Rochester	(NL)	48	176	120	472	9.8
1948-49	Rochester		60	317	270	904	15.1
1949-50	Rochester		64	317	261	895	14.0
1950-51	Rochester		63	326	303	955	15.2
1951-52	Rochester		65	379	294	1052	16.2
1952-53	Rochester		66	339	351	1029	15.6
1953-54	Rochester		72	288	311	887	12.3
1954-55	Rochester		72	326	220	872	12.1
	Totals		569	2720	2330	7770	13.7
DAVIS, AUBREY							
b. 1923 Ht. 6-2 Wt. 175 College—Oklahoma Baptist							
1946-47	St. Louis		59	107	73	287	4.9
1948-49	Hammond	(NL)	8	3	3	9	1.1
	Totals		67	110	76	296	4.4
DAVIS, BOB							
b. April 2, 1950 Ht. 6-7 Wt. 215 College—Weber State							
1972-73	Portland		9	6	4	16	1.8
DAVIS, CHARLIE							
b. Sept. 7, 1949 Ht. 6-2 Wt. 160 College—Wake Forest							
1971-72	Cleveland		61	229	142	600	9.8
1972-73	Cleve.-Port.		75	263	130	656	8.7
1973-74	Portland		8	14	3	31	3.9
	Totals		144	506	275	1287	8.9
DAVIS, DWIGHT							
b. Oct. 28, 1949 Ht. 6-8 Wt. 220 College—Houston							
1972-73	Cleveland		81	293	176	762	9.4
1973-74	Cleveland		76	376	197	949	12.5
1974-75	Cleveland		78	295	176	766	9.8
1975-76	Golden State		72	111	78	300	4.2
1976-77	Golden State		33	55	49	159	4.8
	Totals		340	1130	676	2936	8.6
DAVIS, HARRY							
b. Jan. 27, 1956 Ht. 6-7 Wt. 220 College—Florida State							
1978-79	Cleveland		40	66	30	162	4.1
1979-80	San Antonio		4	6	1	13	3.3
	Totals		44	72	31	175	4.0
DAVIS, JAMES							
b. 1933 Ht. 6-7 Wt. 220 College—St. John's (N.Y.)							
1955-56	Rochester		3	0	2	2	0.7

Yr.	Team	G	FG	FT	TP	Avg.

DAVIS, JIM
b. Dec. 18, 1941 Ht. 6-9½ Wt. 235 College—Colorado

Yr.	Team	G	FG	FT	TP	Avg.
1967-68	St. Louis	50	61	25	147	2.9
1968-69	Atlanta	78	265	154	684	8.8
1969-70	Atlanta	82	438	240	1116	13.6
1970-71	Atlanta	82	241	195	677	8.3
1971-72	Atl.-Hou.-Det.	75	147	100	394	5.3
1972-73	Detroit	73	131	72	334	4.6
1973-74	Detroit	78	117	90	324	4.2
1974-75	Detroit	79	118	85	321	4.1
	Totals	597	1518	961	3997	6.7

DAVIS, LEE
b. Oct. 11, 1945 Ht. 6-8 Wt. 240 College—N.C. College

Yr.	Team		G	FG	FT	TP	Avg.
1968-69	New Orleans	(ABA)	65	88(1)	45	222	3.4
1969-70	New Orleans	(ABA)	16	16	8	40	2.5
1970-71	Memphis	(ABA)	75	197	63	457	6.1
1971-72	Memphis	(ABA)	58	101(1)	25	228	3.9
1972-73	Memphis	(ABA)	78	453	131	1037	13.3
1973-74	Memphis	(ABA)	79	266(1)	98	631	8.0
1974-75	San Diego	(ABA)	75	387(4)	113	891	11.9
1975-76	San Diego	(ABA)	7	2	1	5	0.7
	Totals		453	1510(7)	484	3511	7.8

DAVIS, MEL
b. Oct. 28, 1949 Ht. 6-8 Wt. 220 College—St. John's

Yr.	Team	G	FG	FT	TP	Avg.
1973-74	New York	30	33	12	78	2.6
1974-75	New York	62	154	48	356	5.7
1975-76	New York	42	76	22	174	4.1
1976-77	NYK-NYN	56	168	64	400	7.1
	Totals	190	431	146	1008	5.3

DAVIS, MICKEY
b. June 15, 1950 Ht. 6-7 Wt. 215 College—Duquesne

Yr.	Team		G	FG	FT	TP	Avg.
1971-72	Pittsburgh	(ABA)	23	25	14	64	2.8
1972-73	Milwaukee		74	152	76	380	5.1
1973-74	Milwaukee		73	169	93	431	5.9
1974-75	Milwaukee		75	174	78	426	5.7
1975-76	Milwaukee		45	55	50	160	3.6
1976-77	Milwaukee		19	29	23	81	4.3
	Totals		309	604	334	1542	5.0

DAVIS, MIKE
b. July 26, 1946 Ht. 6-3 Wt. 185 College—Va. Union

Yr.	Team		G	FG	FT	TP	Avg.
1969-70	Baltimore		56	260	149	669	11.9
1970-71	Buffalo		73	317	199	833	11.4
1971-72	Buffalo		62	213	138	564	9.1
1972-73	Baltimore		13	50	23	123	9.5
1972-73	Memphis	(ABA)	38	93(6)	62	254	6.7
	Totals		242	933(6)	571	2443	10.1

DAVIS, RALPH
b. Sept. 7, 1938 Ht. 6-4 Wt. 180 College—Cincinnati

Yr.	Team	G	FG	FT	TP	Avg.
1960-61	Cincinnati	73	181	34	396	5.4
1961-62	Chicago	77	364	71	799	10.4
	Totals	150	545	105	1195	8.0

DAVIS, RON
b. May 1, 1954 Ht. 6-6 Wt. 195 College—Washington St.

Yr.	Team	G	FG	FT	TP	Avg.
1976-77	Atlanta	7	8	4	20	2.9

DAVIS, WALTER (Buddy)
b. Jan. 5, 1931 Ht. 6-8 Wt. 205 College—Texas A&M

Yr.	Team	G	FG	FT	TP	Avg.
1953-54	Philadelphia	68	167	65	399	5.9
1954-55	Philadelphia	61	70	35	175	2.9
1955-56	Philadelphia	70	123	77	323	4.6
1956-57	Philadelphia	65	178	74	430	6.6
1957-58	Phila.-St. L.	61	85	61	231	3.8
	Totals	325	623	312	1558	4.8

DAVIS, WARREN
b. June 30, 1943 Ht. 6-6 Wt. 213 College—N.C. A&T

Yr.	Team		G	FG	FT	TP	Avg.
1967-68	Anaheim	(ABA)	54	343(1)	229	916	17.0
1968-69	Los Angeles	(ABA)	78	356	282	994	12.7
1969-70	L.A.-Pitt.	(ABA)	80	428(1)	304	1161	14.5
1970-71	Florida	(ABA)	76	308	209	825	10.9
1971-72	Car.-Mem.	(ABA)	86	337	207	881	10.2
1972-73	Memphis	(ABA)	73	250	172	672	9.2
	Totals		447	2022(2)	1403	5449	12.2

DAVIS, WILLIAM
b. Oct. 3, 1921 Ht. 6-3 Wt. 215 College—Notre Dame

Yr.	Team	G	FG	FT	TP	Avg.
1946-47	Chicago	47	35	14	84	1.8

DAVIS, WILLIE
b. 1946 Ht. 6-8½ Wt. 234 College—North Texas State

Yr.	Team		G	FG	FT	TP	Avg.
1970-71	Dallas	(ABA)	8	7	4	18	2.3

DAWKINS, PAUL
b. June 10, 1957 Ht. 6-5 Wt. 190 College—No. Illinois

Yr.	Team	G	FG	FT	TP	Avg.
1979-80	Utah	57	141(1)	33	316	5.5

DAWSON, JAMES
Ht. 6-0 College—Illinois

Yr.	Team		G	FG	FT	TP	Avg.
1967-68	Indiana	(ABA)	21	46(1)	25	118	5.6

DEANE, GREG
b. Dec. 6, 1957 Ht. 6-4 Wt. 190 College—Utah

Yr.	Team	G	FG	FT	TP	Avg.
1979-80	Utah	7	2(1)	5	10	1.4

DeANGELIS, BILLY
b. 1946 Ht. 6-1 Wt. 180 College—St. Joseph's

Yr.	Team		G	FG	FT	TP	Avg.
1970-71	New York	(ABA)	8	3	4	10	1.3

DeBUSSCHERE, DAVE
b. Oct. 16, 1940 Ht. 6-6 Wt. 220 College—Detroit

Yr.	Team	G	FG	FT	TP	Avg.
1962-63	Detroit	80	406	206	1018	12.7
1963-64	Detroit	15	52	25	129	8.6
1964-65	Detroit	79	508	306	1322	16.7
1965-66	Detroit	79	524	249	1297	16.4
1966-67	Detroit	78	531	361	1423	18.2
1967-68	Detroit	80	573	289	1435	17.9
1968-69	Det.-N.Y.	76	506	229	1241	16.3
1969-70	New York	79	488	176	1152	14.6
1970-71	New York	81	523	217	1263	15.6
1971-72	New York	80	520	193	1233	15.4
1972-73	New York	77	532	194	1258	16.3
1973-74	New York	71	559	164	1282	18.1
	Totals	875	5722	2609	14053	16.1

Yr.	Team		G	FG	FT	TP	Avg.

DEE, DON
b. 1943 Ht. 6-8 Wt. 210 College—St. Louis and St. Mary of the Plains

Yr.	Team		G	FG	FT	TP	Avg.
1968-69	Indiana	(ABA)	58	138	56	332	5.7

DEES, ARCHIE
b. Feb. 22, 1936 Ht. 6-8 Wt. 205 College—Indiana

Yr.	Team	G	FG	FT	TP	Avg.
1958-59	Cincinnati	68	200	159	559	8.2
1959-60	Detroit	73	271	165	707	9.7
1960-61	Detroit	28	53	39	145	5.2
1961-62	Chi.-St. Louis	21	51	35	137	6.5
	Totals	190	575	398	1548	8.1

DEHNERT, ROBERT (Red)
b. 1924 Ht. 6-3 Wt. 178 College—St. John's

Yr.	Team	G	FG	FT	TP	Avg.
1946-47	Providence	10	6	2	14	1.4

DeLONG, NATE
b. 1928 Ht. 6-6½ Wt. 220 College—River Falls

Yr.	Team	G	FG	FT	TP	Avg.
1951-52	Milwaukee	17	20	24	64	3.8

DEMPSEY, GEORGE
b. July 19, 1929 Ht. 6-3 Wt. 192 College—King's (N.Y.)

Yr.	Team	G	FG	FT	TP	Avg.
1954-55	Philadelphia	48	127	98	352	7.3
1955-56	Philadelphia	72	126	88	340	4.7
1956-57	Philadelphia	71	134	55	323	4.5
1957-58	Philadelphia	67	112	70	294	5.1
	Totals	258	499	311	1309	5.1

DENNING, BLAINE
Ht. 6-2 Wt. 175 College—Lawrence Tech

Yr.	Team	G	FG	FT	TP	Avg.
1952-53	Baltimore	1	2	1	5	5.0

DENTON, RANDY
b. Feb. 18, 1949 Ht. 6-10 Wt. 245 College—Duke

Yr.	Team		G	FG	FT	TP	Avg.
1971-72	Car.-Mem.	(ABA)	81	430	135	995	12.3
1972-73	Memphis	(ABA)	66	472(3)	177	1124	17.0
1973-74	Memphis	(ABA)	79	447	156	1050	13.3
1974-75	Utah	(ABA)	75	300	92	692	9.2
1975-76	Utah-St. L.	(ABA)	67	283	83	649	9.7
1976-77	Atlanta		45	103	33	239	5.3
	Totals		413	2035(3)	676	4749	11.5

DePRE, JOE
b. Dec. 19, 1947 Ht. 6-3½ Wt. 185 College—St. John's

Yr.	Team		G	FG	FT	TP	Avg.
1970-71	New York	(ABA)	72	250	132	632	8.8
1971-72	New York	(ABA)	46	79(2)	34	194	4.3
	Totals		118	329(2)	166	826	7.0

DERLINE, ROD
b. March 11, 1952 Ht. 6-4 Wt. 175 College—Seattle

Yr.	Team	G	FG	FT	TP	Avg.
1974-75	Seattle	58	142	43	327	5.6
1975-76	Seattle	49	73	45	191	3.9
	Totals	107	215	88	518	4.8

DEUTSCH, DAVE
b. May 13, 1945 Ht. 6-1 Wt. 170 College—Rochester

Yr.	Team	G	FG	FT	TP	Avg.
1966-67	New York	19	6	9	21	1.1

DEVLIN, WALTER (Corky)
b. Dec. 21, 1931 Ht. 6-5 Wt. 195 College—G. Washington

Yr.	Team	G	FG	FT	TP	Avg.
1955-56	Fort Wayne	69	200	146	546	7.9
1956-57	Fort Wayne	71	190	97	477	6.7
1957-58	Minneapolis	70	170	133	473	6.8
	Totals	210	560	376	1496	7.1

DeZONIE, HANK
b. Feb. 12, 1942 Ht. 6-6 Wt. 215 College—Clark (Ga.)

Yr.	Team		G	FG	FT	TP	Avg.
1948-49	Dayton	(NL)	18	90	44	224	12.4
1950-51	Tri-Cities		5	6	5	17	3.4
	Totals		23	96	49	241	10.5

DICKERSON, HENRY
b. Nov. 27, 1951 Ht. 6-4 Wt. 190 College—Morris-Harvey

Yr.	Team	G	FG	FT	TP	Avg.
1975-76	Detroit	17	9	10	28	1.6
1976-77	Atlanta	6	6	5	17	2.9
	Totals	23	15	15	45	2.0

DICKEY, CLYDE
b. Dec. 14, 1951 Ht. 6-3 Wt. 185 College—Boston Coll.

Yr.	Team		G	FG	FT	TP	Avg.
1974-75	Utah	(ABA)	57	66(2)	16	150	2.6

DICKEY, DERRICK
b. March 20, 1951 Ht. 6-7 Wt. 218 College—Cincinnati

Yr.	Team	G	FG	FT	TP	Avg.
1973-74	Golden State	66	115	51	281	4.3
1974-75	Golden State	80	274	66	614	7.7
1975-76	Golden State	79	220	62	502	6.4
1976-77	Golden State	49	158	45	361	7.4
1977-78	G.S.-Chi.	47	87	30	204	4.3
	Totals	321	854	254	1962	6.1

DICKEY, DICK
b. Oct. 26, 1926 Ht. 6-1 Wt. 175 College—N. Carolina St.

Yr.	Team	G	FG	FT	TP	Avg.
1951-52	Boston	45	40	47	127	2.8

DICKSON, JOHN
b. Nov. 18, 1945 Ht. 6-10 Wt. 240 College—Ariz. State

Yr.	Team		G	FG	FT	TP	Avg.
1967-68	New Orleans	(ABA)	21	14	8	36	1.7

DIERKING, CONNIE
b. Oct. 2, 1936 Ht. 6-10 Wt. 222 College—Cincinnati

Yr.	Team	G	FG	FT	TP	Avg.
1958-59	Syracuse	64	105	83	293	3.6
1959-60	Syracuse	71	192	108	492	6.9
1963-64	Philadelphia	76	191	114	496	6.5
1964-65	Phil.-San. Fr.	68	218	100	536	7.9
1965-66	Cincinnati	57	134	50	318	5.6
1966-67	Cincinnati	77	291	134	716	9.3
1967-68	Cincinnati	81	544	237	1325	16.4
1968-69	Cincinnati	82	546	243	1335	16.3
1969-70	Cincinnati	76	521	230	1272	16.7
1970-71	Cin.-Phila.	54	125	61	311	5.8
	Totals	706	2867	1360	7094	10.0

DI GREGORIO, ERNIE
b. Jan. 15, 1951 Ht. 6-0 Wt. 180 College—Providence

Yr.	Team	G	FG	FT	TP	Avg.
1973-74	Buffalo	81	530	174	1234	15.2
1974-75	Buffalo	31	103	35	241	7.8

Yr.	Team		G	FG	FT	TP	Avg.
1975-76	Buffalo		67	182	86	450	6.7
1976-77	Buffalo		81	365	138	868	10.7
1977-78	L.A.-Bos.		52	88	28	204	3.9
	Totals		312	1268	461	2997	9.6

DILL, CRAIG
b. 1945 Ht. 6-11 Wt. 220 College—Michigan

1967-68	Pittsburgh	(ABA)	65	187	71	445	6.8

DILLARD, DAVE

1975-76	Utah	(ABA)	3	1	2	4	1.3

DILLE, ROBERT (Oscar)
b. July 2, 1917 Ht. 6-3 Wt. 200 College—Valparaiso

1940-41	Hammond	(NL)	3	8	3	19	6.3
1946-47	Detroit		57	111	74	296	5.2
	Totals		60	119	77	315	5.3

DILLON, JOHN (Hooks)
b. Jan. 8, 1924 Ht. 6-3 Wt. 180 College—Kentucky/N. Carolina

1949-50	Washington		22	10	16	36	1.6

DINKINS, JACKIE
b. Jan. 22, 1950 Ht. 6-5 Wt. 210 College—Voorhees

1971-72	Chicago		18	17	11	45	2.5

DINNELL, HARRY
b. 1941 Ht. 6-4 Wt. 200 College—Pepperdine

1967-68	Anaheim	(ABA)	11	6	7	19	1.7

DINWIDDIE, BILL
b. 1943 Ht. 6-7 Wt. 220 College—New Mexico Highlands

1967-68	Cincinnati		67	141	62	344	5.1
1968-69	Cincinnati		69	124	45	293	4.2
1970-71	Boston		61	123	54	300	4.9
1971-72	Milwaukee		23	16	5	37	1.6
	Totals		220	404	166	974	4.4

DISCHINGER, TERRY
b. Nov. 21, 1940 Ht. 6-7 Wt. 189 College—Purdue

1962-63	Chicago		57	525	402	1452	25.5
1963-64	Baltimore		80	604	454	1662	20.8
1964-65	Detroit		80	568	320	1456	18.2
1967-68	Detroit		78	394	237	1025	13.1
1968-69	Detroit		75	264	130	658	8.8
1969-70	Detroit		75	342	174	858	11.4
1970-71	Detroit		65	304	161	769	11.8
1971-72	Detroit		79	295	156	746	9.4
1972-73	Portland		63	161	64	386	6.1
	Totals		652	3457	2098	9012	13.8

DIUTE, FRED
Ht. 6-3 Wt. 210 College—St. Bonaventure

1954-55	Milwaukee		7	2	7	11	1.6

DODD, EARL
Ht. 6-5 College—Northeast Missouri

1949-50	Denver		9	6	3	15	1.7

DOLHON, JOE
b. 1928 Ht. 6-0 Wt. 175 College—New York University
d. Jan. 1981

1949-50	Baltimore		64	143	157	443	6.9
1950-51	Baltimore		11	15	9	39	3.5
	Totals		75	158	166	482	6.4

DOLL, ROBERT
b. Aug. 10, 1919 Ht. 6-5 Wt. 195 College—Colorado
d. Sept. 18, 1959

1946-47	St. Louis		60	194	134	522	8.7
1947-48	St. Louis		42	174	98	446	10.6
1948-49	Denver	(NL)	9	16	13	45	5.0
1948-49	Boston		47	145	80	370	7.9
1949-50	Boston		47	120	75	315	6.7
	Totals		205	649	400	1698	8.3

DONHAM, BOB
b. Oct. 11, 1926 Ht. 6-2 Wt. 190 College—Ohio State

1950-51	Boston		68	151	114	416	6.1
1951-52	Boston		66	201	149	551	8.3
1952-53	Boston		71	169	113	451	6.4
1953-54	Boston		68	141	118	400	5.9
	Totals		273	662	494	1818	6.7

DONOVAN, HARRY
b. Sept. 10, 1926 Ht. 6-2 Wt. 190 College—Muhlenberg

1949-50	New York		45	90	73	253	5.6

DORSEY, RON
b. Oct. 10, 1948 Ht. 6-4 Wt. 200 College—Tenn. State

1971-72	Carolina	(ABA)	1	2	0	4	4.0

DOVE, LLOYD (Sonny)
b. Aug. 16, 1945 Ht. 6-8 Wt. 198 College—St. John's (N.Y.)

1967-68	Detroit		28	22	12	56	2.0
1968-69	Detroit		29	47	24	118	4.1
1969-70	New York	(ABA)	80	456(2)	140	1154	14.4
1970-71	New York	(ABA)	83	467(4)	186	1124	13.5
1971-72	New York	(ABA)	2	2	2	6	3.0
	Totals		222	994(6)	264	2458	11.1

DOVER, JERRY
b. Oct. 16, 1949 Ht. 5-7 Wt. 155 College—LeMoyne

1971-72	Memphis	(ABA)	4	3(2)	0	8	2.0

DOWNEY, BILL
b. 1923 Ht. 6-6 Wt. 210 College—Marquette

1947-48	Providence		3	0	0	0	0.0

DOWNING, STEVE
b. Sept. 9, 1950 Ht. 6-8 Wt. 225 College—Indiana

1973-74	Boston		24	21	22	64	2.7
1974-75	Boston		3	0	0	0	0.0
	Totals		27	21	22	64	2.4

DOYLE, DANIEL
b. Feb. 6, 1940 Ht. 6-8 Wt. 200 College—Belmont Abbey

1962-63	Detroit		4	6	4	16	4.0

Yr.	Team		G	FG	FT	TP	Avg.

DRISCOLL, TERRY
b. Aug. 28, 1947 Ht. 6-7 Wt. 215 College—Boston College

1970-71	Detroit		69	132	108	372	5.4
1971-72	Baltimore		40	40	27	107	2.7
1972-73	Balt.-Milw.		60	140	43	323	5.4
1973-74	Milwaukee		64	88	30	206	4.3
1974-75	Milwaukee		11	3	1	7	0.6
1974-75	St. Louis	(ABA)	30	46	20	112	3.7
	Totals		274	449	229	1127	4.1

DUCKETT, RICHARD
b. March 25, 1933 Ht. 6-1 Wt. 185 College—St. John's (N.Y.)

| 1957-58 | Cincinnati | | 34 | 54 | 24 | 132 | 3.9 |

DUDLEY, CHARLES
b. March 5, 1950 Ht. 6-2 Wt. 180 College—Washington

1972-73	Seattle		12	10	14	34	2.8
1974-75	Golden State		67	102	70	274	4.1
1975-76	Golden State		82	182	157	521	6.4
1976-77	Golden State		79	220	129	569	7.2
1977-78	Golden State		78	127	138	392	5.0
1978-79	Chicago		43	45	28	118	2.7
	Totals		361	686	536	1908	5.3

DUFFY, ROBERT
b. July 5, 1922 Ht. 6-4 Wt. 175 College—Tulane

| 1946-47 | Chic.-Bost. | | 17 | 7 | 5 | 19 | 1.1 |

DUFFY, ROBERT
b. Sept. 26, 1940 Ht. 6-3 Wt. 185 College—Colgate

1962-63	St. Louis		42	66	22	154	3.7
1963-64	St.L.-N.Y.-Det.		48	94	44	232	4.8
1964-65	Detroit		4	4	6	14	3.5
	Totals		94	164	72	400	4.3

DUKES, WALTER
b. June 23, 1930 Ht. 7-0 Wt. 220 College—Seton Hall

1955-56	New York		60	149	167	465	7.8
1956-57	Minneapolis		71	228	264	720	10.1
1957-58	Detroit		72	278	247	803	11.2
1958-59	Detroit		72	318	297	933	13.0
1959-60	Detroit		66	314	376	1004	15.2
1960-61	Detroit		73	286	281	853	11.7
1961-62	Detroit		77	256	208	720	9.3
1962-63	Detroit		62	83	101	267	4.3
	Totals		553	1912	1941	5765	10.4

DUMAS, RICH
College—Northeastern Oklahoma

| 1968-69 | Houston | (ABA) | 1 | 1 | 0 | 2 | 2.0 |

DUNCAN, ANDREW
b. 1923 Ht. 6-6 Wt. 195 College—Kentucky and William & Mary

1947-48	Rochester	(NL)	60	200	119	519	8.7
1948-49	Rochester		55	162	83	407	7.4
1949-50	Rochester		67	125	60	310	4.6
1950-51	Boston		14	7	15	29	2.1
	Totals		196	494	277	1265	6.5

Yr.	Team		G	FG	FT	TP	Avg.

DUNN, PAT
b. March 17, 1931 Ht. 6-2 Wt. 170 College—Utah State

| 1957-58 | Philadelphia | | 28 | 28 | 14 | 70 | 2.5 |

DURHAM, JARRETT
Ht. 6-5 Wt. 188 College—Duquesne

| 1971-72 | New York | (ABA) | 1 | 0 | 0 | 0 | 0.0 |

DURRETT, KEN
b. Dec. 8, 1948 Ht. 6-8 Wt. 190 College—LaSalle

1971-72	Cincinnati		19	31	21	83	4.4
1972-73	K.C.-Omaha		8	8	6	22	2.8
1973-74	K.C.-Omaha		45	86	42	214	4.8
1974-75	K.C.-O.-Phila.		48	67	31	165	3.4
	Totals		120	192	100	484	4.0

DUVAL, DENNIS
b. March 31, 1952 Ht. 6-3 Wt. 175 College—Syracuse

1974-75	Washington		37	24	12	60	1.6
1975-76	Atlanta		13	15	6	36	2.8
	Totals		50	39	18	96	1.9

DWAN, JACK
b. May 3, 1921 Ht. 6-4 Wt. 200 College—Loyola (Ill.)

1947-48	Minneapolis	(NL)	55	128	50	306	5.5
1948-49	Minneapolis		60	121	34	276	4.6
	Totals		115	249	84	582	5.1

DYKER, GENE
b. Feb. 17, 1930 Ht. 6-6 Wt. 225 College—DePaul

| 1953-54 | Milwaukee | | 11 | 6 | 4 | 16 | 1.5 |

EAKINS, JIM
b. May 24, 1946 Ht. 6-11 Wt. 215 College—Brig. Young

1968-69	Oakland	(ABA)	78	351	309	1011	13.0
1969-70	Washington	(ABA)	82	181	166	528	6.4
1970-71	Virginia	(ABA)	84	332	242	906	10.8
1971-72	Virginia	(ABA)	84	371	288	1030	12.3
1973-74	Virginia	(ABA)	84	445	339	1229	14.6
1974-75	Utah	(ABA)	84	380	291	1051	12.5
1975-76	Utah-Va.-NY	(ABA)	73	215	198	628	8.6
1976-77	Kansas City		82	151	188	490	6.0
1977-78	S.A.-Mil.		33	44	50	138	4.2
	Totals		684	2470	2071	7011	10.3

EARLE, EDWIN (Ed)
b. April 28, 1927 Ht. 6-3 Wt. 190 College—Loyola (Ill.)

| 1953-54 | Syracuse | | 2 | 1 | 2 | 4 | 2.0 |

EBBEN, WILLIAM
b. Oct. 7, 1935 Ht. 6-4 Wt. 200 College—Detroit

| 1957-58 | Detroit | | 8 | 6 | 3 | 15 | 1.9 |

EBERHARD, AL
b. May 10, 1952 Ht. 6-6 Wt. 225 College—Missouri

| 1974-75 | Detroit | | 34 | 31 | 17 | 79 | 2.3 |
| 1975-76 | Detroit | | 81 | 283 | 191 | 757 | 9.3 |

Yr.	Team		G	FG	FT	TP	Avg.
1976-77	Detroit		68	181	109	471	6.9
1977-78	Detroit		37	71	41	183	4.9
		Totals	220	566	358	1490	6.8

EBRON, ROY

b. Aug. 31, 1951 Ht. 6-9 Wt. 225 College—Southwest Louisiana

Yr.	Team		G	FG	FT	TP	Avg.
1973-74	Utah	(ABA)	40	103	43	249	6.2

EDDLEMAN, DWIGHT (Dike)

b. Dec. 27, 1922 Ht. 6-3 Wt. 189 College—Illinois

Yr.	Team		G	FG	FT	TP	Avg.
1949-50	Tri-Cities		64	332	162	826	12.9
1950-51	Tri-Cities		68	398	244	1040	15.3
1951-52	Milw.-Ft. W.		65	269	202	740	11.4
1952-53	Ft. Wayne		69	241	134	616	8.9
		Totals	266	1240	742	3222	12.1

EDGE, CHARLIE

b. Feb. 27, 1950 Ht. 6-6 Wt. 210 College—Lemoyne-Owen

Yr.	Team		G	FG	FT	TP	Avg.
1973-74	Memphis	(ABA)	78	324(12)	124	784	9.6
1974-75	Indiana	(ABA)	77	195	63	453	5.9
		Totals	155	519(12)	187	1237	8.0

EDMONDS, BOBBY JOE

b. March 8, 1941 Ht. 6-7 Wt. 220 College—Tenn. St.

Yr.	Team		G	FG	FT	TP	Avg.
1967-68	Indiana	(ABA)	72	213(1)	150	577	8.0
1969-70	Indiana	(ABA)	3	1	1	3	1.0
		Totals	75	214(1)	151	580	7.7

EGAN, JOHN

b. Jan. 31, 1939 Ht. 6-0 Wt. 180 College—Providence

Yr.	Team		G	FG	FT	TP	Avg.
1962-62	Detroit		58	128	64	320	5.5
1962-63	Detroit		46	110	53	273	5.9
1963-64	Det.-N.Y.		66	334	193	861	13.0
1964-65	New York		74	258	162	678	9.2
1965-66	N.Y.-Balt.		76	259	173	691	9.1
1966-67	Baltimore		71	267	185	719	10.1
1967-68	Baltimore		67	163	142	468	7.0
1968-69	Los Angeles		82	246	204	696	8.5
1969-70	Los Angeles		72	215	99	529	7.3
1970-71	Cleve.-S.D.		62	67	42	176	2.8
1971-72	Houston		38	42	26	110	2.9
		Totals	712	2089	1343	5521	7.8

EGGLESTON, LONNIE

b. June 8, 1918 Ht. 6-0½ Wt. 170 College—Okla. A&M

Yr.	Team		G	FG	FT	TP	Avg.
1948-49	St. Louis		2	1	2	4	2.0

EHLERS, EDWIN (Bulbs)

b. 1924 Ht. 6-3 Wt. 198 College—Purdue

Yr.	Team		G	FG	FT	TP	Avg.
1947-48	Boston		40	104	78	286	7.2
1948-49	Boston		59	182	150	514	8.7
		Totals	99	286	228	800	8.1

EICHHORST, RICHARD

b. Oct. 21, 1933 Ht. 6-3 Wt. 200 College—Southeast Missouri

Yr.	Team		G	FG	FT	TP	Avg.
1961-62	St. Louis		1	1	0	2	2.0

ELIASON, ROBERT

Ht. 6-2 College—Hamline

Yr.	Team		G	FG	FT	TP	Avg.
1946-47	Boston		1	0	0	0	0.0

ELLEFSON, RAY

b. Nov. 18, 1922 Ht. 6-8 Wt. 230 College—Okla. A&M/Colo.

Yr.	Team		G	FG	FT	TP	Avg.
1948-49	Minneapolis		3	1	0	2	0.7
1948-49	Waterloo	(NL)	7	4	8	16	2.3
1950-51	N.Y.-Balt.		3	0	4	4	1.3
		Totals	13	5	12	22	1.7

ELLIS, ALEX (Boo)

b. Feb. 11, 1936 Ht. 6-5 Wt. 185 College—Niagara

Yr.	Team		G	FG	FT	TP	Avg.
1958-59	Minneapolis		72	163	102	428	5.9
1959-60	Minneapolis		46	64	51	179	3.9
		Totals	118	227	153	607	5.1

ELLIS, BO

b. Aug. 8, 1954 Ht. 6-9 Wt. 195 College—Marquette

Yr.	Team		G	FG	FT	TP	Avg.
1977-78	Denver		78	133	72	338	4.3
1978-79	Denver		42	42	29	113	2.7
1979-80	Denver		48	61	40	162	3.4
		Totals	168	236	141	613	3.6

ELLIS, JOSEPH

b. May 3, 1944 Ht. 6-6 Wt. 175 College—San Francisco

Yr.	Team		G	FG	FT	TP	Avg.
1966-67	San Francisco		41	67	19	153	3.7
1967-68	San Francisco		51	111	32	254	5.0
1968-69	San Francisco		74	371	147	889	12.0
1969-70	San Francisco		76	501	200	1202	15.8
1970-71	San Francisco		80	356	151	863	10.8
1971-72	Golden State		78	280	95	655	8.4
1972-73	Golden State		74	199	69	467	6.3
1973-74	Golden State		50	61	18	140	2.8
		Totals	524	1946	731	4623	8.8

ELLIS, LEROY

b. March 10, 1940 Ht. 6-10 Wt. 210 College—St. John's (N.Y.)

Yr.	Team		G	FG	FT	TP	Avg.
1962-63	Los Angeles		80	222	133	577	7.2
1963-64	Los Angeles		78	200	112	512	6.6
1964-65	Los Angeles		80	311	198	820	10.3
1965-66	Los Angeles		80	393	186	972	12.2
1966-67	Baltimore		81	496	211	1203	14.9
1967-68	Baltimore		78	380	207	967	12.4
1968-69	Baltimore		80	229	117	575	7.2
1969-70	Baltimore		72	194	86	474	6.6
1970-71	Portland		74	485	209	1179	15.9
1971-72	Los Angeles		74	138	66	342	4.6
1972-73	L.A.-Phil.		79	421	129	971	12.3
1973-74	Philadelphia		81	326	147	799	9.9
1974-75	Philadelphia		82	287	72	646	7.9
1975-76	Philadelphia		29	61	17	139	4.8
		Totals	1048	4143	1890	10176	9.7

ELSTON, DARRELL

b. Aug. 15, 1952 Ht. 6-4 Wt. 205 College—N.C.

Yr.	Team		G	FG	FT	TP	Avg.
1974-75	Virginia	(ABA)	72	250(3)	93	596	8.3
1976-77	Indiana		5	2	1	5	1.0
		Totals	77	252(3)	94	601	7.8

Yr.	Team		G	FG	FT	TP	Avg.

EMBRY, WAYNE (Goose)
b. March 26, 1937 Ht. 6-8 Wt. 255 College—Miami (Ohio)

Yr.	Team	G	FG	FT	TP	Avg.
1958-59	Cincinnati	66	272	206	750	11.4
1959-60	Cincinnati	73	303	167	773	10.6
1960-61	Cincinnati	79	458	221	1137	14.4
1961-62	Cincinnati	75	564	356	1484	19.8
1962-63	Cincinnati	76	534	343	1411	18.6
1963-64	Cincinnati	80	556	271	1383	17.3
1964-65	Cincinnati	74	352	239	943	12.7
1965-66	Cincinnati	80	232	141	605	7.6
1966-67	Boston	72	147	82	376	5.2
1967-68	Boston	78	193	109	495	6.3
1968-69	Milwaukee	78	382	259	1023	13.1
	Totals	831	3993	2394	10380	12.5

ENDRESS, NED
b. March 2, 1918 Ht. 6-2 Wt. 200 College—Akron

Yr.	Team		G	FG	FT	TP	Avg.
1943-44	Cleveland	(NL)	16	25	15	65	4.1
1944-45	Cleveland	(NL)	29	62	46	170	5.9
1945-46	Cleveland	(NL)	22	58	36	152	6.9
1946-47	Cleveland		16	3	8	14	0.9
	Totals		83	148	105	401	4.8

ENGLISH, CLAUDE
b. Dec. 26, 1946 Ht. 6-4 Wt. 190 College—Rhode Island

Yr.	Team	G	FG	FT	TP	Avg.
1970-71	Portland	18	11	5	27	1.5

ENGLISH, SCOTT
b. Oct. 20, 1950 Ht. 6-6 Wt. 205 College—North Carolina

Yr.	Team		G	FG	FT	TP	Avg.
1972-73	Phoenix		29	36	21	93	3.2
1973-74	Virginia	(ABA)	5	3	4	10	2.0
1974-75	San Diego	(ABA)	71	210(1)	69	490	6.9
	Totals		105	249(1)	94	593	5.6

ENGLUND, GENE
b. Oct. 21, 1917 Ht. 6-5 Wt. 205 College—Wisconsin

Yr.	Team		G	FG	FT	TP	Avg.
1941-42	Oshkosh	(NL)	22	61	42	164	7.5
1942-43	Oshkosh	(NL)	17	41	48	130	7.6
1943-44	Oshkosh	(NL)	2	9	5	23	11.5
1945-46	Oshkosh	(NL)	33	78	64	220	6.7
1946-47	Oshkosh	(NL)	43	176	105	479	11.1
1947-48	Oshkosh	(NL)	58	246	242	734	12.7
1948-49	Oshkosh		63	284	282	850	13.5
1949-50	Bos.-Tri C.		46	104	152	360	7.8
	Totals		284	1010	940	2960	10.4

EPPS, RAY
b. Aug. 20, 1956 Ht. 6-6 Wt. 195 College—Norfolk St.

Yr.	Team	G	FG	FT	TP	Avg.
1978-79	Golden State	13	10	6	26	2.0

ERIAS, BALTICO (Bo)
b. July 30, 1932 Ht. 6-3½ Wt. 220 College—Niagara

Yr.	Team	G	FG	FT	TP	Avg.
1957-58	Minneapolis	18	59	30	148	8.2

ERICKSON, KEITH
b. April 19, 1944 Ht. 6-5 Wt. 195 College—UCLA

Yr.	Team	G	FG	FT	TP	Avg.
1965-66	San Francisco	65	95	43	233	3.6
1966-67	Chicago	76	235	117	587	7.7
1967-68	Chicago	78	377	194	948	12.2
1968-69	Los Angeles	77	264	120	648	8.4
1969-70	Los Angeles	68	258	91	607	8.9
1970-71	Los Angeles	73	369	85	823	11.3
1971-72	Los Angeles	15	40	6	86	5.7
1972-73	Los Angeles	76	299	89	687	9.0
1973-74	Phoenix	66	393	177	963	14.6
1974-75	Phoenix	49	237	130	604	12.3
1975-76	Phoenix	74	305	134	744	10.1
1976-77	Phoenix	50	142	37	321	6.4
	Totals	767	3014	1223	7251	9.5

ESKRIDGE, JACK
b. Jan. 21, 1924 Ht. 6-5 Wt. 200 College—Kansas

Yr.	Team	G	FG	FT	TP	Avg.
1948-49	Chi.-Ind.	23	25	14	64	2.8

EVANS, BILL
Ht. 6-0 Wt. 170 College—Boston College

Yr.	Team		G	FG	FT	TP	Avg.
1969-70	New York	(ABA)	53	32	38	102	1.9

EVANS, BOB
b. May 31, 1925 Ht. 6-2 Wt. 175 College—Indiana/Butler

Yr.	Team	G	FG	FT	TP	Avg.
1949-50	Indianapolis	47	56	30	142	3.0

EVANS, EARL
b. Nov. 11, 1955 Ht. 6-88 Wt. 202 College—USC/Nev.-L.V.

Yr.	Team	G	FG	FT	TP	Avg.
1979-80	Detroit	36	63(7)	24	157	4.4

EZERSKY, JOHN
b. 1921 Ht. 6-3 Wt. 175 College—St. John's

Yr.	Team		G	FG	FT	TP	Avg.
1947-48	Tri-Cities	(NL)	5	9	5	23	4.6
1947-48	Providence		25	95	63	253	10.1
1948-49	Prov.-Bos.-Balt.		56	128	109	365	6.5
1949-50	Balt.-Boston		54	143	127	413	7.6
	Totals		140	375	304	1054	7.5

FABEL, JOSEPH
Ht. 6-1 Wt. 190 College—Pittsburgh

Yr.	Team		G	FG	FT	TP	Avg.
1938-39	Pittsburgh	(NL)	1	3	0	6	6.0
1946-47	Pittsburgh		30	25	13	63	2.1
	Totals		31	28	13	69	2.2

FAIRCHILD, JOHN
b. April 28 1943 Ht. 6-7½ Wt. 205 College—Brigham Young

Yr.	Team		G	FG	FT	TP	Avg.
1965-66	Los Angeles		30	23	14	60	2.0
1967-68	Anaheim	(ABA)	62	271(1)	135	678	10.9
1968-69	Den.-Ind.	(ABA)	63	113(10)	89	325	5.2
1969-70	Ind.-Ky.	(ABA)	10	7(3)	5	22	2.2
	Totals		165	414(14)	243	1085	6.6

FARBMAN, PHILIP
b. 1924 Ht. 6-4 Wt. 185 College—CCNY

Yr.	Team	G	FG	FT	TP	Avg.
1948-49	Phil.-Bos.	48	50	55	155	3.2

FARLEY, RICHARD
b. April 13, 1932 Ht. 6-4 Wt. 190 College—Indiana
d. Oct. 1, 1969

Yr.	Team	G	FG	FT	TP	Avg.
1954-55	Syracuse	69	136	136	408	5.9
1955-56	Syracuse	72	168	143	479	6 6
	Totals	141	304	279	887	6.1

Yr.	Team	G	FG	FT	TP	Avg.

FARMER, MIKE
b. Sept. 26, 1936 Ht. 6-7 Wt. 210 College—San Francisco

Yr.	Team	G	FG	FT	TP	Avg.
1958-59	New York	72	176	83	435	6.0
1959-60	New York	67	212	70	494	7.4
1960-61	N.Y.-Cinn.	59	180	69	429	7.3
1962-63	St. Louis	80	239	117	595	7.4
1963-64	St. Louis	76	178	68	424	5.6
1964-65	St. Louis	60	167	75	409	6.8
	Totals	414	1152	482	2786	6.7

FAUGHT, ROBERT
b. Sept. 2, 1921 Ht. 6-5 Wt. 185 College—Notre Dame

Yr.	Team	G	FG	FT	TP	Avg.
1946-47	Cleveland	51	141	61	343	6.7

FEDOR, DAVID
b. Dec. 10, 1940 Ht. 6-6 Wt. 192 College—Florida State

Yr.	Team	G	FG	FT	TP	Avg.
1962-63	San Francisco	7	3	0	6	0.9

FEERICK, BOB
b. Jan. 2, 1920 Ht. 6-3 Wt. 190 College—Santa Clara
d. June 8, 1976

Yr.	Team		G	FG	FT	TP	Avg.
1945-46	Oshkosh	(NL)	21	81	36	198	9.4
1946-47	Washington		55	364	198	926	16.8
1947-48	Washington		48	293	189	775	16.1
1948-49	Washington		58	248	256	752	13.0
1949-50	Washington		60	172	139	483	8.1
	Totals		242	1158	818	3134	13.0

FEHER, RAYMOND (Butch)
b. May 19, 1954 Ht. 6-4 Wt. 185 College—Vanderbilt

Yr.	Team	G	FG	FT	TP	Avg.
1976-77	Phoenix	48	86	76	248	5.2

FEIEREISEL, RON
b. Aug. 6, 1931 Ht. 6-3 Wt. 185 College—DePaul

Yr.	Team	G	FG	FT	TP	Avg.
1955-56	Minneapolis	10	8	14	30	3.0

FEIGENBAUM, GEORGE
b. July 2, 1929 Ht. 6-1 Wt. 185 College—LIU/Kentucky

Yr.	Team	G	FG	FT	TP	Avg.
1949-59	Baltimore	12	14	8	36	3.0
1952-53	Milwaukee	5	4	8	16	3.2
	Totals	17	18	16	52	3.1

FELIX, RAY
b. Dec. 10, 1930 Ht. 6-11 Wt. 220 College—LIU

Yr.	Team	G	FG	FT	TP	Avg.
1953-54	Baltimore	72	410	449	1269	17.6
1954-55	New York	72	364	310	1038	14.4
1955-56	New York	72	277	331	885	12.3
1956-57	New York	72	295	277	867	12.0
1957-58	New York	72	304	271	879	12.2
1958-59	New York	72	260	229	749	10.4
1959-60	N.Y.-Minn.	47	136	70	342	7.3
1960-61	Los Angeles	78	189	135	513	6.6
1961-62	Los Angeles	80	171	90	432	5.4
	Totals	637	2406	2162	6974	10.9

FENDLEY, JAKE
b. June 12, 1929 Ht. 6-1 Wt. 180 College—Northwestern

Yr.	Team	G	FG	FT	TP	Avg.
1951-52	Ft. Wayne	58	54	75	183	3.2
1952-53	Ft. Wayne	45	32	40	104	2.3
	Totals	103	86	115	287	2.8

FENLEY, WILLIAM
b. Feb. 8, 1922 Ht. 6-3½ Wt. 190 College—Manhattan

Yr.	Team	G	FG	FT	TP	Avg.
1946-47	Boston	23	31	23	85	3.7

FERRARI, ALBERT
b. July 6, 1933 Ht. 6-4 Wt. 190 College—Michigan State

Yr.	Team	G	FG	FT	TP	Avg.
1955-56	St. Louis	68	191	164	546	8.0
1958-59	St. Louis	72	134	145	413	5.7
1959-60	St. Louis	71	216	176	608	8.6
1960-61	St. Louis	63	117	95	329	5.2
1961-62	St. Louis	79	208	175	591	7.5
1962-63	Chicago	18	12	14	38	2.1
	Totals	371	878	769	2525	6.8

FERRIN, ARNOLD
b. July 29, 1925 Ht. 6-4 Wt. 180 College—Utah

Yr.	Team	G	FG	FT	TP	Avg.
1948-49	Minneapolis	47	130	85	345	7.3
1949-50	Minneapolis	63	132	76	340	5.4
1950-51	Minneapolis	68	119	114	352	5.2
	Totals	178	381	275	1037	5.8

FERRY, ROBERT
b. May 31, 1937 Ht. 6-8 Wt. 230 College—St. Louis

Yr.	Team	G	FG	FT	TP	Avg.
1959-60	St. Louis	62	144	76	364	5.9
1960-61	Detroit	79	350	189	889	11.3
1961-62	Detroit	80	411	286	1108	13.8
1962-63	Detroit	79	426	220	1072	13.6
1963-64	Detroit	74	298	186	782	10.6
1964-65	Baltimore	77	143	122	408	5.3
1965-66	Baltimore	66	188	105	481	7.3
1966-67	Baltimore	51	132	70	334	6.5
1967-68	Baltimore	59	128	73	329	5.6
1968-69	Baltimore	7	5	3	13	1.0
	Totals	634	2225	1330	5780	9.1

FEUTSCH, HERMAN (Dutch)
b. July 6, 1921 Ht. 6-0 Wt. 170 College—UCLA

Yr.	Team		G	FG	FT	TP	Avg.
1945-46	Cleveland	(NL)	27	82	61	225	8.3
1947-48	Baltimore		42	42	25	109	2.6
	Totals		69	124	86	334	4.8

FIELDS, BOBBY
b. Oct. 20, 1949 Ht. 6-3 Wt. 175 College—LaSalle

Yr.	Team		G	FG	FT	TP	Avg.
1971-72	Utah	(ABA)	22	22(2)	8	54	2.5

FILIPEK, RON
b. Feb. 5, 1944 Ht. 6-5 Wt. 210 College—Tennessee Tech

Yr.	Team	G	FG	FT	TP	Avg.
1967-68	Philadelphia	19	18	7	43	2.3

FILLMORE, GREG
b. March 7, 1947 Ht. 7-1 Wt. 250 College—Cheyney State

Yr.	Team	G	FG	FT	TP	Avg.
1970-71	New York	39	45	13	103	2.6
1971-72	New York	10	7	1	15	1.5
	Totals	49	52	14	118	2.4

FINCH, LARRY
b. Feb. 16, 1951 Ht. 6-2 Wt. 195 College—Memphis St.

Yr.	Team		G	FG	FT	TP	Avg.
1973-74	Memphis	(ABA)	65	164(7)	108	443	6.8
1974-75	Memphis	(ABA)	64	284(20)	115	663	10.5
	Totals		129	448(27)	223	1106	8.6

Yr.	Team		G	FG	FT	TP	Avg.

FINKEL, HENRY
b. April 20, 1942 Ht. 7-0 Wt. 240 College—Dayton

Yr.	Team		G	FG	FT	TP	Avg.
1966-67	Los Angeles		27	17	7	41	1.5
1967-68	San Diego		53	242	131	615	11.6
1968-69	San Diego		35	49	31	129	3.7
1969-70	Boston		80	310	156	776	9.7
1970-71	Boston		80	214	93	521	6.5
1971-72	Boston		78	103	43	249	3.2
1972-73	Boston		76	78	28	184	2.4
1973-74	Boston		60	60	28	148	2.5
1974-75	Boston		62	52	23	127	2.0
	Totals		551	1125	540	2790	5.1

FINN, DANIEL
b. May 27, 1928 Ht. 6-1 Wt. 185 College—St. John's (NY)

Yr.	Team	G	FG	FT	TP	Avg.
1952-53	Philadelphia	31	135	99	369	11.9
1953-54	Philadelphia	68	170	126	466	6.9
1954-55	Philadelphia	43	77	53	207	4.8
	Totals	142	382	278	1042	7.3

FISHER, RICK
b. Oct. 27, 1948 Ht. 6-5 Wt. 220 College—Colorado St.

Yr.	Team		G	FG	FT	TP	Avg.
1971-72	Utah-Fla.	(ABA)	12	18	1	37	3.1

FITZGERALD, RICHARD
b. 1921 Ht. 6-5 Wt. 175

Yr.	Team	G	FG	FT	TP	Avg.
1946-47	Toronto	60	118	41	277	4.6
1947-48	Providence	1	0	0	0	0.0
	Totals	61	118	41	277	4.5

FITZGERALD, ROBERT
b. March 14, 1923 Ht. 6-5 Wt. 190 College—Seton Hall and Fordham

Yr.	Team		G	FG	FT	TP	Avg.
1945-46	Rochester	(NL)	10	9	15	33	3.3
1946-47	Tor.-N.Y.		50	70	81	221	4.4
1947-48	Syracuse	(NL)	1	0	0	0	0.0
1948-49	Rochester		18	6	7	19	1.1
	Totals		79	85	103	273	3.5

FLEISHMAN, JERRY
b. Feb. 14, 1922 Ht. 6-2 Wt. 190 College—N.Y.U.

Yr.	Team	G	FG	FT	TP	Avg.
1946-47	Philadelphia	59	97	69	263	4.5
1947-48	Philadelphia	46	119	95	333	7.2
1948-49	Philadelphia	59	123	77	323	5.5
1949-50	Philadelphia	65	102	93	297	4.6
1952-53	Phila.-N.Y.	33	100	96	296	9.0
	Totals	262	541	430	1512	5.8

FLEMING, AL
b. April 5, 1954 Ht. 6-7 Wt. 215 College—Arizona

Yr.	Team	G	FG	FT	TP	Avg.
1977-78	Seattle	20	15	10	40	2.0

FLEMING, EDWARD
b. July 25, 1933 Ht. 6-3 Wt. 190 College—Niagara

Yr.	Team	G	FG	FT	TP	Avg.
1955-56	Rochester	71	306	277	889	12.5
1956-57	Rochester	51	109	139	357	7.0
1957-58	Minneapolis	72	226	181	633	8.8
1958-59	Minneapolis	71	162	137	461	6.5
1959-60	Minneapolis	27	59	53	171	6.3
	Totals	292	862	787	2511	8.6

FLYNN, MIKE
b. July 3, 1953 Ht. 6-3 Wt. 190 College—Kentucky

Yr.	Team		G	FG	FT	TP	Avg.
1975-76	Indiana	(ABA)	67	166(25)	64	421	6.3
1976-77	Indiana		73	250	101	601	8.2
1977-78	Indiana		71	120	55	295	4.2
	Totals		211	536(25)	220	1317	6.2

FOGLE, LARRY
b. March 19, 1953 Ht. 6-5 Wt. 210 College—Canisius

Yr.	Team	G	FG	FT	TP	Avg.
1975-76	New York	2	1	0	2	1.0

FOLEY, JACK (The Shot)
b. Nov. 17, 1940 Ht. 6-5 Wt. 185 College—Holy Cross

Yr.	Team	G	FG	FT	TP	Avg.
1962-63	Boston-N.Y.	11	20	13	53	4.8

FONTAINE, LEVI
b. Nov. 1, 1948 Ht. 6-4 Wt. 190 College—Maryland State

Yr.	Team	G	FG	FT	TP	Avg.
1970-71	San Francisco	35	53	28	134	3.8

FORD, BOB
b. Jan. 26, 1950 Ht. 6-7 Wt. 228 College—Purdue

Yr.	Team		G	FG	FT	TP	Avg.
1972-73	Memphis	(ABA)	9	5	4	14	1.6

FORD, JAKE
b. April 29, 1946 Ht. 6-3 Wt. 181 College—Maryland St.

Yr.	Team	G	FG	FT	TP	Avg.
1970-71	Seattle	5	9	16	34	6.8
1971-72	Seattle	26	33	26	92	3.5
	Totals	31	42	42	126	4.1

FORMAN, DON
b. Jan. 17, 1926 Ht. 6-1 Wt. 175 College—N.Y.U.

Yr.	Team	G	FG	FT	TP	Avg.
1948-49	Minneapolis	44	68	43	179	4.1

FORREST, BAYARD
b. July 8, 1954 Ht. 6-10 Wt. 235 College-Grand Canyon

Yr.	Team	G	FG	FT	TP	Avg.
1977-78	Phoenix	64	111	49	271	4.2
1978-79	Phoenix	75	118	62	298	4.0
1979-80	Phoenix		(Injured)			
	Totals	139	229	111	569	4.1

FOSTER, FRED
b. March 18, 1946 Ht. 6-5 Wt. 210 College—Miami (Ohio)

Yr.	Team	G	FG	FT	TP	Avg.
1968-69	Cincinnati	56	74	43	191	3.4
1969-70	Cincinnati	73	461	176	1098	15.0
1970-71	Cincinnati	67	148	73	369	5.5
1971-72	Philadelphia	74	347	185	879	11.9
1972-73	Detroit	63	243	61	547	8.7
1973-74	Cleveland	58	112	54	278	4.8
1974-75	Cleveland	73	217	69	503	6.9
1975-76	Buffalo	59	99	30	228	3.9
	Totals	523	1701	691	4093	7.8

FOSTER, JIMMY
b. Dec. 16, 1951 Ht. 6-1 Wt. 175 College—Connecticut

Yr.	Team		G	FG	FT	TP	Avg.
1974-75	St. Louis	(ABA)	41	78	27	183	4.5
1975-76	Denver	(ABA)	48	54(1)	39	148	3.1
	Totals		89	132(1)	66	331	3.7

Yr.	Team	G	FG	FT	TP	Avg.
FOUST, LARRY						
b. June 24, 1928 Ht. 6-9 Wt. 250 College—LaSalle						
1950-51 Ft. Wayne		68	327	261	915	13.5
1951-52 Ft. Wayne		66	390	267	1047	15.9
1952-53 Ft. Wayne		67	311	336	958	14.3
1953-54 Ft. Wayne		72	376	338	1090	15.1
1954-55 Ft. Wayne		70	398	393	1189	17.0
1955-56 Ft. Wayne		72	367	432	1166	16.2
1956-57 Ft. Wayne		61	243	273	759	12.4
1957-58 Minneapolis		72	391	428	1210	16.8
1958-59 Minneapolis		72	301	280	882	12.3
1959-60 Minn.-St. L.		72	312	253	877	12.2
1960-61 St. Louis		68	194	164	552	8.1
1961-62 St. Louis		57	204	145	553	9.7
Totals		817	3814	3570	11198	13.7
FOWLER, CALVIN						
b. 1940 Ht. 6-0½ Wt. 175 College—St. Francis (Pa.)						
1969-70 Carolina	(ABA)	78	131(7)	74	343	4.4
FOWLER, JERRY						
b. 1926 Ht. 6-8 Wt. 236 College—Missouri						
1951-52 Milwaukee		6	4	1	9	1.5
FOX, HAROLD						
b. Aug. 29, 1949 Ht. 6-2 Wt. 175 College—Jacksonville						
1972-73 Buffalo		10	12	7	31	3.1
FOX, JIM						
b. May 7, 1943 Ht. 6-10 Wt. 230 College—S. Carolina						
1967-68 Cin.-Detroit		55	66	66	198	3.6
1968-69 Det.-Phoenix		76	318	191	827	10.9
1969-70 Phoenix		81	413	218	1044	12.9
1970-71 Chicago		82	280	239	799	9.7
1971-72 Chi.-Cin.		81	354	227	935	11.5
1972-73 Seattle		74	316	214	846	11.4
1973-74 Seattle		78	322	241	885	11.3
1974-75 Seattle		75	253	170	676	9.0
1975-76 Milwaukee		70	105	62	272	3.9
1976-77 N.Y. Nets		71	184	95	463	6.5
Totals		743	2611	1723	6945	9.3
FRANKEL, NAT						
b. 1914 Ht. 6-2 Wt. 195						
1939-40 Detroit	(NL)	27	73	55	201	7.4
1946-47 Pittsburgh		6	4	8	16	2.7
Totals		33	77	63	217	6.6
FRANKLIN, BILL						
b. Oct. 19, 1949 Ht. 6-7 Wt. 225 College—Purdue						
1973-74 Virginia	(ABA)	73	218(2)	107	545	7.5
1974-75 San Antonio	(ABA)	24	32	15	79	3.3
1975-76 San Antonio	(ABA)	10	12	9	33	3.3
Totals		107	262(2)	131	657	6.1
FRANZ, RON						
b. Oct. 20, 1945 Ht. 6-7 Wt. 207 College—Kansas						
1967-68 Oakland	(ABA)	74	354(25)	197	930	12.6
1968-69 New Orleans	(ABA)	73	381(11)	286	1059	14.5

Yr.	Team	G	FG	FT	TP	Avg.
1969-70 New Orleans	(ABA)	55	231(7)	163	632	11.5
1979-71 Floridians	(ABA)	67	309(7)	188	813	12.1
1971-72 Floridians	(ABA)	74	342(2)	171	857	11.6
1972-73 Mem.-Dal.	(ABA)	60	148(1)	145	442	7.4
Totals		403	1765(53)	1150	4733	11.7
FRAZIER, WALT (Clyde)						
b. Mar. 29, 1945 Ht. 6-4 Wt. 202 College—Southern Illinois						
1967-68 New York		74	256	154	666	9.0
1968-69 New York		80	531	341	1403	17.5
1969-70 New York		77	600	409	1609	20.9
1970-71 New York		80	651	434	1736	21.7
1971-72 New York		77	669	450	1788	23.2
1972-73 New York		78	681	286	1648	21.1
1973-74 New York		80	674	295	1643	20.5
1974-75 New York		78	672	331	1675	21.5
1975-76 New York		59	470	186	1126	19.1
1076-77 N.Y. Knicks		76	532	259	1323	17.4
1077-78 Cleveland		51	336	153	825	16.2
1978-79 Cleveland		12	54	21	129	10.8
1979-80 Cleveland		3	4	2	10	3.3
Totals		825	6130	3321	15581	18.9
FRAZIER, WILBERT						
b. Aug. 24, 1942 Ht. 6-7 Wt. 210 College—Grambling						
1965-66 San Francisco		2	0	1	1	0.5
1967-68 Houston	(ABA)	76	358(1)	228	945	12.4
1968-69 New York	(ABA)	75	217	120	554	7.4
Totals		153	575(1)	349	1500	9.8
FREEMAN, DON						
b. July 18, 1944 Ht. 6-3 Wt. 185 College—Illinois						
1967-68 Minnesota	(ABA)	69	414	296	1124	16.3
1968-69 Miami	(ABA)	78	651(2)	420	1724	22.1
1969-70 Miami	(ABA)	79	766(5)	626	2173	27.4
1970-71 Utah-Tex.	(ABA)	66	596	367	1559	23.6
1971-72 Dallas	(ABA)	72	628(2)	475	1733	24.1
1972-73 Indiana	(ABA)	77	412(2)	277	1103	14.3
1973-74 Indiana	(ABA)	66	383	177	943	14.3
1974-75 San Antonio	(ABA)	77	453	289	1195	15.5
1975-76 Los Angeles		64	263	163	689	10.8
Totals		648	4566(11)	3090	12233	18.9
FREEMAN, GARY						
b. July 25, 1948 Ht. 6-9 Wt. 208 College—Oregon State						
1970-71 Milw.-Cleve.		52	69	29	167	3.2
FREEMAN, ROD						
b. May 11, 1950 Ht. 6-7 Wt. 225 College—Vanderbilt						
1973-74 Philadelphia		35	39	28	106	3.0
FREY, FRIDO						
b. Oct. 26, 1921 Ht. 6-2 Wt. 195 College—St. John's/L.I.U.						
1946-47 New York		23	28	32	88	3.8
FRIEND, LARRY						
b. April 14, 1935 Ht. 6-4 Wt. 186 College—California						
1957-58 New York		44	74	27	175	4.0

Yr.	Team		G	FG	FT	TP	Avg.

FRINK, PAT
b. Feb. 18, 1945 Ht. 6-4 Wt. 195 College—Colorado

Yr.	Team		G	FG	FT	TP	Avg.
1968-69 Cincinnati			48	50	23	123	2.6

FRITSCHE, JAMES
b. Dec. 10, 1931 Ht. 6-8 Wt. 210 College—Hamline

Yr.	Team		G	FG	FT	TP	Avg.
1953-54 Minn.-Balt.			68	116	49	281	4.1
1954-55 Ft. Wayne			16	16	13	45	2.8
	Totals		84	132	62	326	3.9

FRYER, BERNIE
b. Dec. 25, 1949 Ht. 6-3 Wt. 185 College—Brigham Young

Yr.	Team		G	FG	FT	TP	Avg.
1973-74 Portland			80	226	107	559	7.0
1974-75 New Orleans			31	47	33	127	4.1
1974-75 St. Louis	(ABA)		9	24	22	70	7.8
	Totals		120	297	162	756	6.3

FUCARINO, FRANK
b. July 24, 1920 Ht. 6-2 Wt. 175 College—L.I.U.

Yr.	Team		G	FG	FT	TP	Avg.
1946-47 Toronto			28	53	34	140	5.0

FULKS, JOSEPH (Jumpin' Joe)
b. Oct. 26, 1921 Ht. 6-5 Wt. 190 College—Murray State
d. March 21, 1976

Yr.	Team		G	FG	FT	TP	Avg.
1946-47 Philadelphia			60	475	439	1389	23.2
1947-48 Philadelphia			43	326	297	949	22.1
1948-49 Philadelphia			60	529	502	1560	26.0
1949-50 Philadelphia			68	336	293	965	14.2
1950-51 Philadelphia			66	429	378	1236	18.7
1951-52 Philadelphia			61	336	250	922	15.1
1952-53 Philadelphia			70	332	168	832	11.9
1953-54 Philadelphia			61	61	28	150	2.5
	Totals		489	2824	2355	8003	16.4

FULLER, CARL
b. Jan. 10, 1946 Ht. 6-9 Wt. 225 College—Bethune-Cookman

Yr.	Team		G	FG	FT	TP	Avg.
1970-71 Floridians	(ABA)		70	170	72	412	5.9
1971-72 Fla.-Mem.	(ABA)		6	6	9	21	2.5
	Totals		76	176	81	433	5.7

FURLOW, TERRY
b. Oct. 8, 1954 Ht. 6-5 Wt. 200 College—Michigan State
d. May 23, 1980

Yr.	Team		G	FG	FT	TP	Avg.
1976-77 Phiadelphia			32	34	16	84	2.6
1977-78 Cleveland			53	192	88	472	8.9
1978-79 Cleve.-Atl.			78	388	163	939	12.0
1979-80 Atl.-Utah			76	430(24)	171	1055	13.9
	Totals		239	1044(24)	438	2550	10.7

GABOR, WILLIAM (Bullet)
b. May 13, 1922 Ht. 5-11½ Wt. 180 College—Syracuse

Yr.	Team		G	FG	FT	TP	Avg.
1948-49 Syracuse	(NL)		55	113	124	350	6.4
1949-50 Syracuse			56	226	157	609	10.9
1950-51 Syracuse			61	255	179	689	11.3
1951-52 Syracuse			57	173	142	488	8.6
1952-53 Syracuse			69	215	217	647	9.4
1953-54 Syracuse			61	204	139	547	9.0
1954-55 Syracuse			3	7	3	17	5.7
	Totals		362	1193	961	3347	9.2

GAINER, ELMER
b. 1919 Ht. 6-6 Wt. 195 College—DePaul

Yr.	Team		G	FG	FT	TP	Avg.
1941-42 Fort Wayne	(NL)		24	36	28	100	4.2
1943-44 Sheboygan	(NL)		22	15	20	50	2.3
1944-45 Chicago	(NL)		29	44	38	126	4.3
1945-46 Chicago			5	2	2	6	1.2
1946-47 Anderson			43	77	59	213	5.0
1947-48 Baltimore	(NL)		5	1	3	5	1.0
1948-49 Waterloo	(NL)		36	33	30	96	2.7
1949-50 Waterloo			15	9	6	24	1.6
	Totals		179	217	186	620	3.5

GAINES, BILL
College—East Texas State

Yr.	Team		G	FG	FT	TP	Avg.
1968-69 Houston	(ABA)		1	1	0	2	2.0

GAINES, DAVE
b. 1941 Ht. 6-1 Wt. 170 College—LeMoyne

Yr.	Team		G	FG	FT	TP	Avg.
1967-68 Kentucky	(ABA)		3	4(1)	1	10	3.3

GALLATIN, HARRY (The Horse)
b. April 26, 1928 Ht. 6-6 Wt. 215 College—Northeast Mo.

Yr.	Team		G	FG	FT	TP	Avg.
1948-49 New York			52	157	120	434	8.3
1949-50 New York			68	263	277	803	11.8
1950-51 New York			66	293	259	845	12.8
1951-52 New York			66	233	275	741	11.2
1952-53 New York			70	282	301	865	12.4
1953-54 New York			72	258	433	949	13.2
1954-55 New York			72	330	393	1053	14.6
1955-56 New York			72	322	358	1002	13.9
1956-57 New York			72	332	415	1079	15.0
1957-58 Detroit			72	340	392	1072	14.9
	Totals		682	2810	3223	8843	13.0

GAMBEE, DAVE
b. April 16, 1937 Ht. 6-6 Wt. 215 College—Oregon State

Yr.	Team		G	FG	FT	TP	Avg.
1958-59 St. Louis			2	1	0	2	1.0
1959-60 St. L.-Cin.			61	117	69	303	5.0
1960-61 Syracuse			79	397	291	1085	13.7
1961-62 Syracuse			80	477	384	1338	16.7
1962-63 Syracuse			60	235	199	669	11.2
1963-64 Philadelphia			41	149	151	449	11.0
1964-65 Philadelphia			80	356	299	1011	12.6
1965-66 Philadelphia			72	168	159	495	6.9
1966-67 Philadelphia			63	150	107	407	6.5
1967-68 San Diego			80	375	321	1071	13.4
1968-69 Milw.-Det.			59	210	159	579	9.8
1969-70 San Francisco			73	185	156	526	7.2
	Totals		750	2820	2295	7935	10.6

GANTT, ROBERT
b. 1923 Ht. 6-4 Wt. 205 College—Duke

Yr.	Team		G	FG	FT	TP	Avg.
1946-47 Washington			23	29	13	71	3.1
1947-48 Sheboygan	(NL)		6	4	3	11	1.8
	Totals		29	33	16	82	2.8

GARDNER, CHARLES
Ht. 6-8 Wt. 205 College—Colorado

Yr.	Team		G	FG	FT	TP	Avg.
1967-68 Denver	(ABA)		42	71	56	197	4.7

Yr.	Team	G	FG	FT	TP	Avg.

GARDNER, EARL
b. 1926 Ht. 6-3 Wt. 200 College—DePaul

Yr.	Team	G	FG	FT	TP	Avg.
1948-49	Minneapolis	50	38	13	89	1.8

GARDNER, KEN
b. Sept. 20, 1949 Ht. 6-5 Wt. 205 College—Utah

1975-76	Utah	(ABA)	9	6	2	14	1.6

GARDNER, VERN
b. May 14, 1925 Ht. 6-5 Wt. 200 College—Utah

1949-50	Philadelphia	63	313	227	853	13.5
1950-51	Philadelphia	61	129	69	327	5.4
1951-52	Philadelphia	27	72	15	159	5.9
	Totals	151	514	311	1339	8.9

GARFINKEL, JACK (Dutch)
b. June 13, 1918 Ht. 6-0 Wt. 190 College—St. John's

1945-46	Rochester	(NL)	18	14	6	34	1.9
1946-47	Rochester	(NL)	10	5	3	13	1.3
1946-47	Boston		40	81	17	179	4.5
1947-48	Boston		43	114	35	263	6.1
1948-49	Boston		9	12	10	34	3.8
	Totals		120	226	71	523	4.4

GARLAND, GARY
b. Oct. 12, 1957 Ht. 6-4 Wt. 180 College—DePaul

1979-80	Denver	78	155(6)	18	334	4.3

GARMAKER, DICK
b. Oct. 29, 1932 Ht. 6-3½ Wt. 206 College—Minnesota

1955-56	Minneapolis	68	138	112	388	5.7
1956-57	Minneapolis	72	406	365	1177	16.3
1957-58	Minneapolis	68	390	314	1094	16.1
1958-59	Minneapolis	72	350	284	984	13.7
1959-60	Minn.-N.Y.	70	323	203	849	12.1
1960-61	New York	71	415	275	1105	15.6
	Totals	421	2022	1553	5597	13.3

GARNER, BILL
b. 1940 Ht. 6-10 Wt. 220 College—Portland

1967-68	Anaheim	(ABA)	53	28	25	81	1.5

GARRETT, ELDO (Dick)
b. Jan. 31, 1947 Ht. 6-3 Wt. 185 College—Southern Ill.

1969-70	Los Angeles	73	354	138	846	11.6
1970-71	Buffalo	75	373	218	964	12.9
1971-72	Buffalo	73	325	136	786	10.8
1972-73	Buffalo	78	341	96	778	10.0
1973-74	N.Y.-Mil.	40	43	15	101	2.5
	Totals	339	1436	603	3475	10.3

GARRETT, ROWLAND
b. July 16, 1950 Ht. 6-6 Wt. 212 College—Florida State

1972-73	Chicago	35	52	21	125	3.6
1973-74	Chicago	41	68	21	157	3.8
1974-75	Chicago	70	228	77	533	7.6
1975-76	Chi.-Cleve.	55	108	53	269	4.9
1976-77	Cleve.-Milw.	62	106	41	253	4.1
	Totals	263	562	213	1337	5.1

GARVIN, JIM
b. Feb. 5, 1950 Ht. 6-7 Wt. 200 College—Boston U.

1973-74	Boston	6	1	0	2	0.3

GATES, FRANK (Needle)
b. April 12, 1920 Ht. 6-0 Wt. 167 College—S. Houston St.

1946-47	And.-F.W.	(NL)	32	68	30	166	5.2
1948-49	Anderson	(NL)	64	150	78	378	5.9
1949-50	Anderson		64	113	61	287	4.5
	Totals		160	331	169	831	5.2

GAYDA, EDWARD
b. May 11, 1927 Ht. 6-4 Wt. 210 College—Washington St.

1950-51	Tri-Cities	14	18	18	54	3.9

GEORGE, JACK
b. Nov. 13, 1928 Ht. 6-3 Wt. 190 College—LaSalle

1953-54	Philadelphia	71	259	157	675	9.5
1954-55	Philadelphia	68	291	192	774	11.4
1955-56	Philadelphia	72	352	296	1000	13.9
1956-57	Philadelphia	67	253	200	706	10.5
1957-58	Philadelphia	72	232	178	642	8.9
1958-59	Phil.-N.Y.	71	233	153	619	8.7
1959-60	New York	69	250	155	655	9.5
1960-61	New York	16	31	20	82	5.1
	Totals	506	1901	1351	5153	10.2

GETCHELL, GORHAM
b. Aug. 14, 1920 Ht. 6-6 Wt. 215 College—Temple

1946-47	Pittsburgh	16	0	5	5	0.3

GIANELLI, JOHN
b. June 10, 1950 Ht. 6-10 Wt. 220 College—Pacific

1972-73	New York	52	79	23	181	3.5
1973-74	New York	70	208	92	508	7.3
1974-75	New York	80	343	135	821	10.3
1975-76	New York	82	325	114	764	9.3
1976-77	NYK-Buf.	76	257	90	604	7.9
1977-78	Milwaukee	82	307	79	693	8.5
1978-79	Milwaukee	82	256	72	584	7.1
1979-80	Utah	17	23	9	55	3.2
	Totals	541	1798	614	4210	7.8

GIBBS, DICK
b. Dec. 20, 1948 Ht. 6-5 Wt. 210 College—Texas El Paso

1971-72	Houston	64	90	55	235	3.7
1972-73	Hou.-K.C.-O.	76	80	47	207	3.1
1973-74	Seattle	71	302	162	766	10.8
1974-75	Washington	59	74	48	196	3.3
1975-76	Buffalo	72	129	77	335	4.7
	Totals	333	675	389	1739	5.2

GIBSON, DEE (Gibby)
b. 1923 Ht. 5-11 Wt. 175 College—Western Kentucky

1948-49	Tri-Cities	(NL)	64	94	113	301	4.7
1949-50	Tri-Cities		44	77	127	281	6.4
	Totals		108	171	240	582	5.4

GIBSON, MEL
b. Dec. 30, 1940 Ht. 6-3 Wt. 180 College—W. Carolina

1963-64	Los Angeles	9	6	1	13	1.4

Yr.	Team		G	FG	FT	TP	Avg.
GIBSON, WARD (Hoot)							
b. Dec. 6, 1921 Ht. 6-5 Wt. 215 College—Creighton							
1948-49 Den.-Tri-C.	(NL)		62	291	223	805	12.8
1949-50 Bos.-Wat.			32	67	42	176	5.5
	Totals		94	358	265	981	10.4
GILLESPIE, JACK							
b. 1947 Ht. 6-9 Wt. 230 College—Montana State							
1969-70 New York	(ABA)	2	0		2	2	1.0
GILLETTE, GENE							
b. 1922 Ht. 6-2 Wt. 201 College—St. Mary's (Calif.)							
1946-47 Washington		14	1		6	8	0.6
GILLIAM, HERM							
b. May 5, 1946 Ht. 6-3 Wt. 190 College—Purdue							
1969-70 Cincinnati		57	179	68	426	7.5
1970-71 Buffalo		80	378	142	898	11.2
1971-72 Atlanta		82	345	145	835	10.2
1972-73 Atlanta		76	471	123	1065	14.0
1973-74 Atlanta		62	384	106	874	14.1
1974-75 Atlanta		60	314	94	722	12.0
1975-76 Seattle		81	299	90	688	8.5
1976-77 Portland		80	326	92	744	9.3
	Totals		578	2696	860	6252	10.8
GILMORE, WALT							
b. Feb. 27, 1947 Ht. 6-6 Wt. 235 College—Fort Valley St.							
1970-71 Portland		27	23	12	58	2.1
GILMUR, CHARLES							
b. Aug. 13, 1922 Ht. 6-4 Wt. 225 College—Washington							
1946-47 Chicago		51	76	26	178	3.5
1947-48 Chicago		48	181	97	459	9.6
1948-49 Chicago		56	110	66	286	5.1
1949-50 Chi.-Wash.		68	127	164	418	6.1
1950-51 Washington		16	17	17	51	3.2
	Totals		239	511	370	1392	5.8
GIVENS, JACK							
b. Sept. 21, 1956 Ht. 6-5 Wt. 205 College—Kentucky							
1978-79 Atlanta		74	234	102	570	7.7
1979-80 Atlanta		82	182	106	470	5.7
	Totals		156	416	208	1040	6.7
GLAMACK, GEORGE (Blind Bomber)							
b. June 17, 1919 Ht. 6-9 Wt. 230 College—N. Carolina							
1941-42 Akron	(NL)	24	87	82	256	10.7
1945-46 Rochester	(NL)	34	151	115	417	12.3
1946-47 Rochester		44	141	90	372	8.5
1947-48 Indianapolis	(NL)	57	215	162	592	10.4
1948-49 Indianapolis		11	30	42	102	9.3
1948-49 Hammond	(NL)	43	169	163	501	11.7
	Totals		213	793	654	2240	10.5
GLICK, NORMIE							
b. Nov. 10, 1927 Ht. 6-7 Wt. 190 College—Loyola (Calif.)							
1949-50 Minneapolis		1	1	0	2	2.0

Yr.	Team		G	FG	FT	TP	Avg.
GLOVER, CLARENCE							
b. Nov. 1, 1947 Ht. 6-8 Wt. 210 College—W. Kentucky							
1971-72 Boston		25	25	15	65	2.6
GOLA, TOM							
b. Jan. 13, 1933 Ht. 6-6 Wt. 205 College—LaSalle							
1955-56 Philadelphia		68	244	244	732	10.8
1957-58 Philadelphia		59	295	223	813	13.8
1958-59 Philadelphia		64	310	281	901	14.1
1959-60 Philadelphia		75	426	270	1122	15.0
1960-61 Philadelphia		74	420	210	1050	14.2
1961-62 Philadelphia		60	322	176	820	13.7
1962-63 S.F.-N.Y.		73	363	170	896	12.3
1963-64 New York		74	258	154	670	9.1
1964-65 New York		77	204	133	541	7.0
1965-66 New York		74	122	82	326	4.4
	Totals		698	2964	1943	7871	11.3
GOLDFADEN, BEN							
b. Sept. 6, 1913 Ht. 6-3 Wt. 185 College—G. Washington							
1946-47 Washington		2	0		2	2	1.0
GOODRICH, GAIL							
b. April 23, 1943 Ht. 6-1 Wt. 170 College—UCLA							
1965-66 Los Angeles		65	203	103	509	7.8
1966-67 Los Angeles		77	352	253	957	12.4
1967-68 Los Angeles		79	395	302	1092	13.8
1968-69 Phoenix		81	718	495	1031	23.8
1969-70 Phoenix		81	568	488	1624	20.0
1970-71 Los Angeles		79	558	264	1380	17.5
1971-72 Los Angeles		82	826	475	2127	25.9
1972-73 Los Angeles		76	750	314	1814	23.9
1973-74 Los Angeles		82	784	508	2076	25.3
1974-75 Los Angeles		72	656	318	1630	22.6
1975-76 Los Angeles		75	583	293	1459	19.5
1976-77 New Orleans		27	136	68	340	12.6
1977-78 New Orleans		81	520	264	1304	16.1
1978-79 New Orleans		74	382	174	938	12.7
	Totals		1031	7431	4319	19181	18.6
GOODWIN, WILFRED (Pop)							
b. 1921 Ht. 6-2 Wt. 203							
1945-46 Sheboygan	(NL)	2	1	1	3	1.5
1946-47 Providence		55	98	60	256	4.7
1947-48 Providence		24	36	19	91	3.8
	Totals		81	135	80	350	4.3
GORDON, PAUL							
b. April 8, 1927 Ht. 6-3 Wt. 195 College—Notre Dame							
1949-50 Baltimore		4	0	3	3	0.8
GOTTLIEB, LEO							
b. 1920 Ht. 5-11 Wt. 180							
1946-47 New York		57	149	36	334	5.9
1947-48 New York		27	59	13	131	4.9
	Totals		84	208	49	465	5.5

Yr.	Team		G	FG	FT	TP	Avg.

GOVAN, GERALD
b. Jan. 2, 1942 Ht. 6-10 Wt. 220 College—St. Mary of Plains

Yr.	Team		G	FG	FT	TP	Avg.
1967-68	New Orleans	(ABA)	78	156(1)	79	392	5.0
1968-69	New Orleans	(ABA)	77	211(1)	134	567	7.2
1969-70	New Orleans	(ABA)	84	422(1)	208	1053	12.5
1970-71	Memphis	(ABA)	84	296(1)	119	712	8.6
1971-72	Memphis	(ABA)	83	277	162	716	8.6
1972-73	Utah	(ABA)	84	229	81	539	6.4
1973-74	Utah	(ABA)	83	255	73	583	7.0
1974-75	Utah	(ABA)	84	239(1)	83	562	6.7
1975-76	Virginia	(ABA)	24	57	23	137	5.7
	Totals		681	2142(5)	962	5251	7.7

GOVEDARICA, BATO
b. 1928 Ht. 5-11 Wt. 185 College—DePaul

Yr.	Team	G	FG	FT	TP	Avg.
1953-54	Syracuse	23	25	25	75	3.3

GRABOSKI, JOE (Grabbo)
b. Jan. 15, 1930 Ht. 6-8 Wt. 230

Yr.	Team	G	FG	FT	TP	Avg.
1948-49	Chicago	45	54	17	125	2.8
1949-50	Chicago	57	75	53	203	3.6
1951-52	Indianapolis	66	320	264	904	13.7
1952-53	Indianapolis	69	272	350	894	13.0
1953-54	Philadelphia	71	354	236	944	13.3
1954-55	Philadelphia	70	373	208	954	13.6
1955-56	Philadelphia	72	397	240	1034	14.4
1956-57	Philadelphia	72	390	252	1032	14.3
1957-58	Philadelphia	72	341	227	909	12.6
1958-59	Philadelphia	72	394	270	1058	14.7
1959-60	Philadelphia	73	217	131	565	7.7
1960-61	Philadelphia	68	169	127	465	6.8
1961-62	St.L.-Chi.-Syr.	38	77	39	193	5.1
	Totals	845	3433	2414	9280	11.0

GRAHAM, CAL
Ht. 6-2½ Wt. 195 College—Gannon

Yr.	Team		G	FG	FT	TP	Avg.
1967-68	Pittsburgh	(ABA)	8	4	5	13	1.6

GRAHAM, MAL
b. Feb. 23, 1945 Ht. 6-1 Wt. 185 College—N.Y.U.

Yr.	Team	G	FG	FT	TP	Avg.
1967-68	Boston	48	117	56	290	6.0
1968-69	Boston	22	13	11	37	1.7
	Totals	70	130	67	327	4.7

GRANT, HARRY (Bud)
b. May 20, 1927 Ht. 6-3 Wt. 193 College—Minnesota

Yr.	Team	G	FG	FT	TP	Avg.
1949-50	Minneapolis	35	42	7	91	2.6
1950-51	Minneapolis	61	53	52	158	2.6
	Totals	96	95	59	249	2.6

GRANT, TRAVIS
b. Jan. 1, 1950 Ht. 6-7 Wt. 215 College—Kentucky State

Yr.	Team		G	FG	FT	TP	Avg.
1972-73	Los Angeles		33	51	23	125	3.8
1973-74	Los Angeles		3	1	1	3	1.0
1973-74	San Diego	(ABA)	56	357(1)	141	856	15.3
1974-75	San Diego	(ABA)	53	576(1)	182	1335	25.2
1975-76	Ken.-Ind.	(ABA)	56	198	52	448	8.0
	Totals		201	1183(2)	399	2767	13.8

GRATE, DON
b. Aug. 27, 1922 Ht. 6-2½ Wt. 185 College—Ohio State

Yr.	Team		G	FG	FT	TP	Avg.
1947-48	Indianapolis	(NL)	11	14	3	31	2.8
1949-50	Sheboygan		2	1	2	4	2.0
	Totals		13	15	5	35	2.7

GRAY, GARY
b. 1945 Ht. 6-1 Wt. 185 College—Oklahoma City

Yr.	Team	G	FG	FT	TP	Avg.
1967-68	Cincinnati	44	49	7	105	2.4

GRAY, LEONARD
b. Dec. 19, 1951 Ht. 6-8 Wt. 240 Coll.—Kansas and Long Beach St.

Yr.	Team	G	FG	FT	TP	Avg.
1974-75	Seattle	75	378	104	860	11.5
1975-76	Seattle	66	394	126	914	13.8
1976-77	Sea.-Wash.	83	258	118	634	7.6
	Totals	224	1030	348	2408	10.8

GRAY, WYNDOL
b. March 20, 1922 Ht. 6-1 Wt. 175 College—Harvard/Bowling Green

Yr.	Team	G	FG	FT	TP	Avg.
1946-47	Boston	55	139	72	350	6.4
1947-48	Prov.-St. L.	12	6	1	13	1.1
	Totals	67	145	73	363	5.4

GREACEN, BOB
b. Sept. 15, 1947 Ht. 6-7 Wt. 210 College—Rutgers

Yr.	Team		G	FG	FT	TP	Avg.
1969-70	Milwaukee		41	44	18	106	2.6
1970-71	Milwaukee		2	1	3	5	2.5
1971-72	New York	(ABA)	4	1	0	2	0.5
	Totals		47	46	21	113	2.4

GREEN, JOHN
b. Dec. 8, 1933 Ht. 6-5 Wt. 200 College—Michigan State

Yr.	Team	G	FG	FT	TP	Avg.
1959-60	New York	69	209	63	481	7.0
1960-61	New York	78	326	145	797	10.2
1961-62	New York	80	507	261	1275	16.1
1962-63	New York	80	582	280	1444	18.1
1963-64	New York	80	482	195	1159	14.5
1964-65	New York	78	346	165	857	11.0
1965-66	N.Y.-Balt.	79	358	202	918	11.6
1966-67	Baltimore	61	203	96	502	8.2
1967-68	S.D.-Phil.	77	310	139	759	10.0
1968-69	Philadelphia	74	146	57	349	4.7
1969-70	Cincinnati	78	481	254	1216	15.6
1970-71	Cincinnati	75	502	248	1252	16.7
1971-72	Cincinnati	82	331	141	803	9.8
1972-73	K.C.-Omaha	66	190	89	469	7.1
	Totals	1057	4973	2335	12281	11.6

GREEN, LAMAR
b. March 22, 1947 Ht. 6-7 Wt. 210 College—Morehead St.

Yr.	Team		G	FG	FT	TP	Avg.
1979-70	Phoenix		58	101	41	243	4.2
1970-71	Phoenix		68	167	64	398	5.9
1971-72	Phoenix		67	133	66	332	5.0
1972-73	Phoenix		80	224	89	537	6.7
1973-74	Phoenix		72	129	38	296	4.1
1974-75	Virginia	(ABA)	51	115	40	270	5.3
1974-75	New Orleans		15	24	9	57	3.8
	Totals		462	893	347	2133	4.6

Yr.	Team		G	FG	FT	TP	Avg.

GREEN, LUTHER
b. Nov. 13, 1946 Ht. 6-7 Wt. 190 College—L.I.U.

1969-70 New York	(ABA)	59	114	55	283	4.8
1970-71 New York	(ABA)	26	40	18	98	3.8
Totals		85	154	73	381	4.5

GREEN, MIKE
b. Aug. 6, 1951 Ht. 6-10 Wt. 200 College— La. Tech

1973-74 Denver	(ABA)	79	367(1)	169	904	11.4
1974-75 Denver	(ABA)	81	593	225	1411	17.4
1975-76 Virginia	(ABA)	54	385	154	924	17.1
1976-77 Seattle		76	290	166	746	9.8
1977-78 Sea.-S.A.		72	238	107	583	8.1
1978-79 San Antonio		76	235	101	571	7.5
1979-80 Kansas City		21	69	24	162	7.7
Totals		459	2176	946	5301	11.5

GREEN, SIHUGO
b. Aug. 20, 1934 Ht. 6-2 Wt 185 College—Duquesne

1956-57 Rochester	13	50	49	149	11.5
1957-58 Cincinnati	(Military Service)				
1958-59 Cin.-St. L.	46	146	104	396	8.6
1959-60 St. Louis	70	159	111	429	6.1
1960-61 St. Louis	76	263	174	700	9.2
1961-62 St. L.-Chi.	71	341	218	900	12.7
1962-63 Chicago	73	322	209	853	11.7
1963-64 Baltimore	75	287	198	772	10.3
1964-65 Baltimore	70	152	101	405	5.8
1965-66 Boston	10	12	8	32	3.2
Totals	504	1732	1172	4636	9.2

GREEN, STEVE
b. Oct. 4, 1953 Ht. 6-7 Wt. 220 College—Indiana

1975-76 Utah-St. L.	(ABA)	52	195	84	474	9.1
1976-77 Indiana		70	183	84	450	6.4
1977-78 Indiana		44	56	39	151	3.4
1978-79 Indiana		39	42	20	104	2.7
Totals		205	476	227	1179	5.8

GREEN, TOMMY
b. April 8, 1956 Ht. 6-2 Wt. 185 College—Southern

1978-79 New Orleans	59	92	48	232	3.9

GREENSPAN, GERALD (Jerry)
b. Nov. 22, 1941 Ht. 6-5 Wt. 195 College—Maryland

1963-64 Philadelphia	20	32	34	98	4.9
1964-65 Philadelphia	5	8	8	24	4.8
Totals	25	40	42	122	4.9

GREER, HAL
b. June 26, 1936 Ht. 6-2 Wt. 176 College—Marshall

1958-59 Syracuse	68	308	137	753	11.1
1959-60 Syracuse	70	388	148	924	13.2
1960-61 Syracuse	79	623	305	1551	19.6
1961-62 Syracuse	71	644	331	1619	22.8
1962-63 Syracuse	80	600	362	1562	19.5
1963-64 Philadelphia	80	715	435	1865	23.3
1964-65 Philadelphia	70	539	335	1413	20.2
1965-66 Philadelphia	80	703	413	1819	22.7
1966-67 Philadelphia	80	699	367	1765	22.1
1967-68 Philadelphia	82	777	422	1976	24.1
1968-69 Philadelphia	82	732	432	1896	23.1
1969-70 Philadelphia	80	705	352	1762	22.0
1970-71 Philadelphia	81	591	326	1508	18.6
1971-72 Philadelphia	81	389	181	959	11.8
1972-73 Philadelphia	38	91	32	214	5.6
Totals	1122	8504	4578	21586	19.2

GREGOR, GARY
b. Aug. 13, 1945 Ht. 6-7 Wt. 235 College—South Carolina

1968-69 Phoenix		80	400	85	885	11.1
1969-70 Atlanta		81	286	88	660	8.1
1970-71 Portland		44	181	59	421	9.6
1971-72 Portland		82	399	114	912	11.1
1972-73 Milwaukee		9	11	5	27	3.0
1972-73 New York	(ABA)	40	99(1)	32	231	5.8
1973-74 New York	(ABA)	25	40(2)	9	91	3.6
Totals		361	1416(3)	392	3227	8.9

GREKIN, NORMAN
b. June 22, 1930 Ht. 6-5 Wt. 180 College—LaSalle

1953-54 Philadelphia	1	0	0	0	0.0

GREY, DENNIS
b. Aug. 26, 1947 Ht. 6-8 Wt. 215 College—Calif. Western

1968-69 Los Angeles	(ABA)	58	184	157	525	9.1
1969-70 New York	(ABA)	4	6	6	18	4.5
Totals		62	190	163	543	8.8

GRIFFIN, GREG
b. Sept. 6, 1952 Ht. 6-7 Wt. 190 College—Idaho St.

1977-78 Phoenix	36	61	23	145	4.0

GRIGSBY, CHUCK
b. 1930 Ht. 6-5 Wt. 190 College—Dayton

1954-55 New York	7	7	2	16	2.3

GRIMSHAW, GEORGE (Woodie)
b. Sept. 24, 1919 Ht. 6-1 Wt. 185 College—Brown

1946-47 Providence	21	20	21	61	2.9

GROAT, DICK
b. Nov. 4, 1930 Ht. 6-1 Wt. 185 College—Duke

1952-53 Ft. Wayne	26	100	109	309	11.9

GROSSO, MIKE
b. Sept. 7, 1947 Ht. 6-9 Wt. 232 College—Louisville

1971-72 Pittsburgh	(ABA)	25	45	13	103	4.1

GROTE, JERRY
b. Dec. 28, 1940 Ht. 6-4 Wt. 216 College—Loyola (Calif.)

1964-65 Los Angeles	11	6	2	14	1.3

GROZA, ALEX
b. Oct. 7, 1926 Ht. 6-7 Wt. 218 College—Kentucky

1949-50 Indianapolis	64	521	454	1496	23.4
1950-51 Indianapolis	66	492	445	1429	21.7
Totals	130	1013	899	2925	22.5

Yr.	Team	G	FG	FT	TP	Avg.

GRUBAR, DICK
b. July 26, 1947 Ht. 6-4 Wt. 184 College—North Carolina

Yr.	Team	G	FG	FT	TP	Avg.
1969-70 Indiana (ABA)	2	2	0	4	2.0

GUARILIA, GENE
b. Sept. 13, 1927 Ht. 6-5 Wt. 220 College— Potomac St./G. Wash.

Yr.	Team	G	FG	FT	TP	Avg.
1959-60 Boston	48	58	29	145	3.0
1960-61 Boston	25	38	3	79	3.2
1961-62 Boston	46	61	41	163	3.5
1962-63 Boston	11	11	4	26	2.4
Totals	130	168	77	413	3.2

GUERIN, RICHIE
b. May 29, 1932 Ht. 6-4 Wt. 210 College—Iona

Yr.	Team	G	FG	FT	TP	Avg.
1956-57 New York	72	257	181	695	9.7
1957-58 New York	63	344	353	1041	16.5
1958-59 New York	71	443	405	1291	18.2
1959-60 New York	74	579	457	1615	21.8
1960-61 New York	79	612	496	1720	21.8
1961-62 New York	78	839	625	2303	29.5
1962-63 New York	79	596	509	1701	21.5
1963-64 N.Y.-St. L.	80	351	347	1049	13.1
1964-65 St. Louis	57	295	231	821	14.4
1965-66 St. Louis	80	414	362	1190	14.9
1966-67 St. Louis	79	394	304	1092	13.8
1968-69 Atlanta	27	47	57	151	5.6
1969-70 Atlanta	8	3	1	7	0.9
Totals	847	5174	4328	14676	17.3

GUNTHER, COULBY
b. Feb. 5, 1924 Ht. 6-4 Wt. 190 College—Brown

Yr.	Team	G	FG	FT	TP	Avg.
1946-47 Pittsburgh	52	254	226	734	14.1
1948-49 St. Louis	32	57	45	159	5.0
Totals	84	311	271	893	10.6

GUNTHER, DAVID
b. July 22, 1937 Ht. 6-7 Wt. 220 College—Iowa

Yr.	Team	G	FG	FT	TP	Avg.
1962-63 San Francisco	1	1	0	2	2.0

GUOKAS, ALBERT (Gook)
b. Aug. 7, 1925 Ht. 6-5½ Wt. 200 College—St. Joseph's (Pa.)

Yr.	Team	G	FG	FT	TP	Avg.
1948-49 Denver (NL)	60	146	81	373	6.2
1949-50 Den.-Phil.	57	93	28	214	3.8
Totals	117	239	109	587	5.0

GUOKAS, JR., MATT
b. Feb. 25, 1944 Ht. 6-5 Wt. 175 College—St. Joseph's (Pa.)

Yr.	Team	G	FG	FT	TP	Avg.
1966-67 Philadelphia	69	79	49	207	3.0
1967-68 Philadelphia	82	190	118	498	6.1
1968-69 Philadelphia	72	92	54	238	3.3
1969-70 Philadelphia	80	189	106	484	6.1
1970-71 Phila.-Chi.	79	206	101	513	6.5
1971-72 Cincinnati	61	191	64	446	7.3
1972-73 K.C.-Omaha	79	322	74	718	9.1
1973-74 K.C.-O.-Hou.-Buff.	75	195	39	429	5.7
1974-75 Chicago	82	255	78	588	7.2
1975-76 Chi.-K.C.	56	73	18	164	2.9
Totals	735	1792	701	4285	5.8

GUOKAS, SR., MATT
b. Nov. 11, 1915 Ht. 6-3 Wt. 195 College—St. Joseph's (Pa.)

Yr.	Team	G	FG	FT	TP	Avg.
1946-47 Philadelphia	47	28	26	82	1.7

HACKETT, RUDY
b. May 10, 1953 Ht. 6-9 Wt. 215 College—Syracuse

Yr.	Team	G	FG	FT	TP	Avg.
1975-76 St. Louis (ABA)	22	55	31	141	6.4
1976-77 N.Y. Nets-Ind.	6	3	8	14	2.3
Totals	28	58	39	155	5.5

HADNOT, JIM
b. Jan. 15, 1940 Ht. 6-10 Wt. 237 College—Providence

Yr.	Team	G	FG	FT	TP	Avg.
1967-68 Oakland (ABA)	77	488	368	1344	17.5

HAGAN, CLIFF
b. Dec. 9, 1931 Ht. 6-4 Wt. 215 College—Kentucky

Yr.	Team	G	FG	FT	TP	Avg.
1956-57 St. Louis	67	134	100	368	5.5
1957-58 St. Louis	70	503	385	1391	19.9
1958-59 St. Louis	72	646	415	1707	23.7
1959-60 St. Louis	75	719	421	1859	24.8
1960-61 St. Louis	78	661	383	1705	21.9
1961-62 St. Louis	77	701	362	1764	22.9
1962-63 St. Louis	79	491	244	1226	15.5
1963-64 St. Louis	77	572	269	1413	18.4
1964-65 St. Louis	77	393	214	1000	13.0
1965-66 St. Louis	74	419	176	1014	13.7
1967-68 Dallas (ABA)	56	371	277	1019	18.2
1968-69 Dallas (ABA)	35	132	123	387	11.1
1969-70 Dallas (ABA)	3	8	1	17	5.7
Totals	840	5750	3370	14870	17.7

HAGAN, THOMAS MEDARD
b. Jan. 29, 1947 Ht. 6-4 Wt. 185 College—Vanderbilt

Yr.	Team	G	FG	FT	TP	Avg.
1969-70 Dallas (ABA)	24	37(7)	22	103	4.3
1970-71 Texas (ABA)	45	98(12)	43	251	5.6
Totals	69	135(19)	65	354	5.1

HAHN, BOB
b. Aug. 25, 1925 Ht. 6-10 Wt. 240 College—N. Carolina St.

Yr.	Team	G	FG	FT	TP	Avg.
1949-50 Chicago	10	4	2	10	1.0

HAIRSTON, AL
b. Dec. 11, 1945 Ht. 6-1 Wt. 170 College—Bowling Green

Yr.	Team	G	FG	FT	TP	Avg.
1968-69 Seattle	39	38	8	84	2.2
1969-70 Seattle	3	3	1	7	2.3
Totals	42	41	9	91	2.2

HAIRSTON, HAROLD (Happy)
b. May 31, 1942 Ht. 6-7 Wt. 225 College—N.Y.U.

Yr.	Team	G	FG	FT	TP	Avg.
1964-65 Cincinnati	61	131	110	372	6.1
1965-66 Cincinnati	72	398	220	1016	14.1
1966-67 Cincinnati	79	461	252	1174	14.9
1967-68 Cinn.-Detroit	74	481	365	1327	17.9
1968-69 Detroit	81	530	404	1464	18.1
1969-70 Det.-L.A.	70	483	326	1292	18.5
1970-71 Los Angeles	80	574	337	1485	18.6
1971-72 Los Angeles	80	368	311	1047	13.1
1972-73 Los Angeles	28	158	140	456	16.3
1973-74 Los Angeles	77	385	343	1113	14.5
1974-75 Los Angeles	74	271	217	759	10.3
Totals	776	4240	3025	11505	14.8

Yr.	Team		G	FG	FT	TP	Avg.

HAIRSTON, LINDSAY
b. Dec. 8, 1951 Ht. 6-8 Wt. 190 College—Michigan St.

Yr.	Team		G	FG	FT	TP	Avg.
1975-76	Detroit		47	104	65	273	5.8

HALBERT, CHARLES (Chuck)
b. Feb. 27, 1919 Ht. 6-9½ Wt. 225 College—West Texas

1946-47	Chicago		61	280	213	773	12.7
1947-48	Chi.-Phila.		46	156	140	452	9.8
1948-49	Bos.-Prov.		60	202	214	618	10.3
1949-50	Washington		68	108	112	328	4.8
1950-51	Wash.-Balt.		68	164	172	500	7.4
	Totals		303	910	851	2671	8.8

HALBROOK, HARVEY WADE (Swede)
b. Jan. 30, 1933 Ht. 7-3 Wt. 235 College—Oregon State

1960-61	Syracuse		79	155	76	386	4.9
1961-62	Syracuse		64	152	96	400	6.2
	Totals		143	307	172	786	5.5

HALE, BRUCE
b. Aug. 31, 1918 Ht. 6-1 Wt. 170 College—Santa Clara

1946-47	Chicago	(NL)	41	156	116	428	10.4
1947-48	Indianapolis	(NL)	48	196	155	547	11.4
1948-49	Ind.-Ft. W.		52	187	172	546	10.5
1949-50	Indianapolis		64	217	223	657	10.3
1950-51	Indianapolis		26	40	14	94	3.6
	Totals		231	796	680	2272	9.8

HALE, HAL
b. Sept. 21, 1945 Ht. 6-1 Wt. 185 College—Utah State

| 1967-68 | Houston | (ABA) | 72 | 133(35) | 60 | 361 | 5.0 |

HALIMON, SHALER
b. March 30, 1945 Ht. 6-6 Wt. 199 College—Utah State

1968-69	Philadelphia		50	88	10	186	3.7
1969-70	Chicago		38	96	49	241	6.3
1970-71	Chi.-Port.		81	301	107	709	8.8
1971-72	Atlanta		1	0	0	0	0.0
1971-72	Dallas	(ABA)	55	123	62	308	5.6
1972-73	Dallas	(ABA)	29	59(1)	23	142	4.9
	Totals		254	667(1)	251	1586	6.2

HALLIBURTON, JEFF
b. July 3, 1949 Ht. 6-5 Wt. 199 College—Drake

1971-72	Atlanta		37	61	25	147	4.0
1972-73	Atl.-Phil.		55	172	71	415	7.5
	Totals		92	233	96	562	6.1

HAMILTON, DALE
b. Aug. 16, 1919 Ht. 6-1 Wt. 198 College—Franklin

1939-40	Hammond	(NL)	7	5	1	11	1.6
1941-42	Ft. Wayne	(NL)	16	10	16	36	2.3
1942-43	Ft. Wayne	(NL)	18	8	1	17	0.9
1943-44	Ft. Wayne	(NL)	11	2	0	4	0.4
1944-45	Ft. Wayne	(NL)	2	0	0	0	0.0
1946-47	Toledo	(NL)	44	114	67	295	6.7
1947-48	Toledo	(NL)	53	93	62	248	4.7
1948-49	Waterloo	(NL)	62	78	94	250	4.0
1949-50	Waterloo		14	8	9	25	1.8
	Totals		227	318	250	886	3.9

HAMILTON, DENNIS
b. May 8, 1944 Ht. 6-8 Wt. 210 College—Arizona State

Yr.	Team		G	FG	FT	TP	Avg.
1967-68	Los Angeles		44	54	13	121	2.8
1968-69	Atlanta		25	37	2	76	3.0
	Totals		69	91	15	197	2.9

HAMILTON, JOE
b. July 5, 1948 Ht. 5-10 Wt. 175 College—N. Texas State

1970-71	Texas	(ABA)	84	500(85)	233	1318	15.7
1971-72	Dallas	(ABA)	82	317(46)	201	881	10.7
1972-73	Dallas	(ABA)	83	370(66)	209	1015	12.2
1973-74	S.A.-Ken.	(ABA)	73	331(37)	117	816	11.2
1974-75	Kentucky	(ABA)	9	15(3)	5	38	4.2
	Totals		331	1533(237)	765	4068	12.3

HAMILTON, RALPH (Ham)
b. June 10, 1921 Ht. 6-1 Wt. 188 College—Indiana

1947-48	Ft. Wayne		49	143	101	387	7.9
1948-49	Ft. W.-Ind.		48	114	61	289	6.0
	Totals		97	257	162	676	7.0

HAMILTON, STEVE
b. Nov. 30, 1934 Ht. 6-7 Wt. 190 College—Morehead St.

1958-59	Minneapolis		67	109	74	292	4.4
1959-60	Minneapolis		15	29	18	76	5.1
	Totals		82	138	92	368	4.5

HAMMOND, JULIAN
b. May 7, 1943 Ht. 6-5 Wt. 205 College—Tulsa

1967-68	Denver	(ABA)	74	224	143	591	8.0
1968-69	Denver	(ABA)	78	329	165	823	10.6
1969-70	Denver	(ABA)	69	329	169	827	10.0
1970-71	Denver	(ABA)	83	435	273	1143	13.8
1971-72	Denver	(ABA)	25	66	31	163	6.5
	Totals		329	1383	781	3547	10.8

HAMOOD, JOE
Ht. 6-0 College—Houston

| 1967-68 | Houston | (ABA) | 76 | 274(16) | 186 | 750 | 9.9 |

HANKINS, CECIL
b. Jan. 6, 1922 Ht. 6-1 Wt. 175 College—Oklahoma A&M

1946-47	St. Louis		55	117	90	324	5.9
1947-48	Boston		25	23	24	70	2.8
1947-48	Sheboygan	(NL)	1	0	1	1	1.0
	Totals		81	140	115	395	4.9

HANKINSON, PHIL
b. July 26, 1951 Ht. 6-8 Wt. 195 College—Pennsylvania

1973-74	Boston		28	50	10	110	3.9
1974-75	Boston		3	6	0	12	4.0
	Totals		31	56	10	122	3.9

HANNUM, ALEX
b. July 19, 1923 Ht. 6-7 Wt. 225 College—So. California

1948-49	Oshkosh	(NL)	64	126	113	365	5.7
1949-50	Syracuse		64	177	128	482	7.5
1950-51	Syracuse		63	182	107	471	7.5
1951-52	Balt.-Roch.		66	170	98	438	6.6

Yr.	Team	G	FG	FT	TP	Avg.
1952-53	Rochester	68	129	88	346	5.1
1953-54	Rochester	72	175	102	452	6.3
1954-55	Milwaukee	53	126	61	313	5.9
1955-56	St. Louis	71	146	93	385	5.4
1956-57	Ft. W.-St. Lo.	59	77	37	191	3.2
	Totals	580	1308	827	3443	5.9

HANRAHAN, DON
b. Feb. 6, 1929 Ht. 6-7 Wt. 200 College—Loyola (Ill.)

Yr.	Team	G	FG	FT	TP	Avg.
1952-53	Indianapolis	18	11	11	33	1.8

HANS, ROLLEN
b. 1930 Ht. 6-2 Wt. 210 College—Long Island U.

Yr.	Team	G	FG	FT	TP	Avg.
1953-54	Baltimore	67	191	101	483	7.2
1954-55	Baltimore	13	30	13	73	5.6
	Totals	80	221	114	556	7.0

HANSEN, GLENN
b. April 21, 1952 Ht. 6-4 Wt. 205 College—Ut. S. & LSU

Yr.	Team	G	FG	FT	TP	Avg.
1975-76	Kansas City	66	173	85	431	6.5
1976-77	Kansas City	41	67	23	157	3.8
1977-78	Chi.-K.C.	5	0	0	0	0.0
1978-79	Seattle	15	29	18	76	5.1
	Totals	127	269	126	664	5.2

HARDING, REGGIE
b. May 4, 1942 Ht. 7-0 Wt. 255

Yr.	Team		G	FG	FT	TP	Avg.
1963-64	Detroit		39	184	61	429	11.0
1964-65	Detroit		78	405	128	938	12.0
1966-67	Detroit		74	172	63	407	5.5
1967-68	Chicago		14	24	17	65	4.6
1967-68	Indiana	(ABA)	25	142	52	336	13.4
	Totals		230	927	321	2175	9.5

HARDNETT, CHARLES
b. Sept. 13, 1938 Ht. 6-8 Wt. 225 College—Grambling

Yr.	Team	G	FG	FT	TP	Avg.
1962-63	Chicago	78	301	225	827	10.6
1963-64	Baltimore	67	107	84	298	4.4
1964-65	Baltimore	20	25	23	73	3.7
	Totals	165	433	332	1198	7.3

HARDY, DARRELL
Ht. 6-7 College—Baylor

Yr.	Team		G	FG	FT	TP	Avg.
1967-68	Houston	(ABA)	17	32	25	89	5.2

HARDY, JAMES
b. Dec. 1, 1956 Ht. 6-8 Wt. 220 College—San Fran.

Yr.	Team	G	FG	FT	TP	Avg.
1978-79	New Orleans	68	196	61	453	6.7
1979-80	Utah	76	184(1)	51	420	5.5
	Totals	144	380(1)	112	873	6.1

HARGE, IRA
b. March 14, 1941 Ht. 6-9 Wt. 225 Coll.—Bowling Green/New Mexico

Yr.	Team		G	FG	FT	TP	Avg.
1967-68	Pitt.-Oak.	(ABA)	82	311	202	824	10.0
1968-69	Oakland	(ABA)	78	269	123	661	8.5
1969-70	Washington	(ABA)	84	415	196	1026	12.2
1970-71	Car.-Fla.	(ABA)	82	460(2)	197	1119	13.7
1971-72	Fla.-Utah	(ABA)	84	314	104	732	8.7
1972-73	Utah-Car.	(ABA)	17	14	6	34	2.0
	Totals		427	1783(2)	828	4396	10.3

Yr.	Team		G	FG	FT	TP	Avg.
HARGIS, JOHN (Shotgun)							
b. Aug. 20, 1920 Ht. 6-2 Wt. 185 College—Texas							
1947-48	Anderson	(NL)	59	235	172	642	10.9
1948-49	Anderson	(NL)	57	169	106	444	7.8
1949-50	Anderson		60	223	197	643	10.7
1950-51	Ft. W.-Tri-C.		14	25	17	67	4.8
	Totals		190	652	492	1796	9.5

HARKNESS, JERRY
b. May 7, 1940 Ht. 6-2 Wt. 175 College—Loyola (Ill.)

Yr.	Team		G	FG	FT	TP	Avg.
1963-64	New York		5	13	3	29	5.8
1967-68	Indiana	(ABA)	71	172(1)	152	497	7.0
1968-69	Indiana	(ABA)	10	31	30	92	9.2
	Totals		86	216(1)	185	618	7.2

HARLICKA, JULES (Skip)
b. Oct. 14, 1946 Ht. 6-1½ Wt. 185 College—S. Carolina

Yr.	Team	G	FG	FT	TP	Avg.
1968-69	Atlanta	26	41	24	106	4.1

HARRIS, ART
b. Jan. 13, 1947 Ht. 6-4 Wt. 186 College—Stanford

Yr.	Team	G	FG	FT	TP	Avg.
1968-69	Seattle	80	416	161	993	12.4
1969-70	Seattle-Phoe.	81	285	86	656	8.1
1970-71	Phoenix	56	199	69	467	8.3
1971-72	Phoenix	21	23	9	55	2.6
	Totals	238	923	325	2171	9.1

HARRIS, BERNIE
b. Nov. 26, 1950 Ht. 6-10 Wt. 200 College—Va. Com.

Yr.	Team	G	FG	FT	TP	Avg.
1974-75	Buffalo	11	2	1	5	0.5

HARRIS, BILLY
b. Nov. 12, 1951 Ht. 6-2 Wt. 190 College—No. Illinois

Yr.	Team		G	FG	FT	TP	Avg.
1974-75	San Diego	(ABA)	76	264(16)	65	609	8.0

HARRIS, BOB
b. Mar. 16, 1927 Ht. 6-7 Wt. 195 College—Murray St./Oklahoma St.

Yr.	Team	G	FG	FT	TP	Avg.
1949-50	Ft. Wayne	62	168	140	476	7.7
1950-51	Ft. W.-Boston	56	98	86	282	5.0
1951-52	Boston	66	190	134	514	7.8
1952-53	Boston	70	192	133	517	7.4
1953-54	Boston	71	156	108	420	5.9
	Totals	325	804	601	2209	6.8

HARRIS, CHRIS
b. Aug. 11, 1933 Ht. 6-3 Wt. 190 College—Dayton

Yr.	Team	G	FG	FT	TP	Avg.
1955-56	St. L.-Roch.	41	37	27	101	2.5

HARRISON, BOB
b. Aug. 12, 1927 Ht. 6-1 Wt. 190 College—Michigan

Yr.	Team	G	FG	FT	TP	Avg.
1949-50	Minneapolis	66	125	50	300	4.6
1950-51	Minneapolis	68	150	101	401	5.9
1951-52	Minneapolis	65	156	89	401	6.2
1952-53	Minneapolis	70	195	107	497	7.1
1953-54	Minn.-Milw.	64	144	94	382	6.0
1954-55	Milwaukee	72	299	126	724	10.1
1955-56	St. Louis	72	260	97	617	8.6
1956-57	Syracuse	66	243	93	579	8.8
1957-58	Syracuse	72	210	97	517	7.2
	Totals	615	1782	854	4418	7.2

Yr.	Team		G	FG	FT	TP	Avg.

HASKINS, CLEM
b. Aug. 11, 1944 Ht. 6-2 Wt. 195 College—W. Kentucky

Yr.	Team	G	FG	FT	TP	Avg.
1967-68 Chicago		76	273	133	679	8.9
1968-69 Chicago		79	537	282	1356	17.2
1969-70 Chicago		82	668	332	1668	20.3
1970-71 Phoenix		82	562	338	1462	17.8
1971-72 Phoenix		79	509	220	1238	15.7
1972-73 Phoenix		77	339	130	808	10.5
1973-74 Phoenix		81	364	171	899	11.1
1974-75 Washington		70	115	53	283	4.0
1975-76 Washington		55	148	54	350	6.4
Totals		681	3515	1713	8743	12.8

HASSETT, WILLIAM
b. Oct. 21, 1921 Ht. 6-1 Wt. 180 Coll.—Georgetown and Notre Dame

Yr.	Team		G	FG	FT	TP	Avg.
1946-47 Tri-Cities	(NL)	27	73	66	212	7.9
1947-48 Tri-Cities	(NL)	56	199	203	601	10.7
1948-49 Tri-Cities	(NL)	64	125	106	356	5.6
1949-50 Tri-C.-Minn.		60	84	104	272	4.5
1950-51 Baltimore		30	45	40	130	4.3
Totals		237	526	519	1571	6.6

HATTON, VERNON
b. Jan. 13, 1936 Ht. 6-3 Wt. 195 College—Kentucky

Yr.	Team	G	FG	FT	TP	Avg.
1958-59 Cin.-Phila.	64	149	77	375	5.9
1959-60 Philadelphia	67	127	53	307	4.6
1960-61 Philadelphia	54	97	46	240	4.4
1961-62 Ch.-St. Louis	40	112	98	322	8.1
Totals	225	485	274	1244	5.5

HAVLICEK, JOHN (Hondo)
b. April 8, 1940 Ht. 6-5 Wt. 205 College—Ohio State

Yr.	Team	G	FG	FT	TP	Avg.
1962-63 Boston	80	483	174	1140	14.3
1963-64 Boston	80	640	315	1595	19.9
1964-65 Boston	75	570	235	1375	18.3
1965-66 Boston	71	530	274	1334	18.8
1966-67 Boston	81	684	365	1733	21.4
1967-68 Boston	82	666	368	1700	20.7
1968-69 Boston	82	692	387	1771	21.6
1969-70 Boston	81	736	488	1960	24.2
1970-71 Boston	81	892	554	2338	28.9
1971-72 Boston	82	897	458	2252	27.5
1972-73 Boston	80	766	370	1902	23.8
1973-74 Boston	76	685	346	1716	22.6
1974-75 Boston	82	642	289	1573	19.2
1975-76 Boston	76	504	281	1289	17.0
1976-77 Boston	79	580	235	1395	17.7
1977-78 Boston	82	546	230	1322	16.1
Totals	1270	10513	5369	26395	20.8

HAWKINS, CONNIE
b. July 17, 1942 Ht. 6-8 Wt. 215 College—Iowa

Yr.	Team		G	FG	FT	TP	Avg.
1967-68 Pittsburgh	(ABA)	70	635(2)	603	1875	26.8
1968-69 Minnesota	(ABA)	47	496(3)	425	1420	30.2
1969-70 Phoenix		81	709	577	1995	24.6
1970-71 Phoenix		71	512	457	1481	20.9
1971-72 Phoenix		76	571	456	1598	21.0
1972-73 Phoenix		75	441	322	1204	16.1
1973-74 Phoe.-L.A.		79	404	191	999	12.6
1974-75 Los Angeles		43	139	68	346	8.0
1975-76 Atlanta		74	237	136	610	8.2
Totals		616	4144(5)	3235	11528	18.7

HAWKINS, MARSHALL
b. Aug. 3, 1924 Ht. 6-3 Wt. 210 College—Tennessee

Yr.	Team		G	FG	FT	TP	Avg.
1948-49 Oshkosh	(NL)	64	200	116	516	8.1
1949-50 Indianapolis		39	55	42	152	3.9
Totals		103	255	158	668	6.5

HAWKINS, ROBERT (Bubbles)
b. June 30, 1954 Ht. 6-4 Wt. 190 College—Illinois St.

Yr.	Team	G	FG	FT	TP	Avg.
1975-76 Golden State	32	53	20	126	3.9
1976-77 N.Y. Nets	52	406	194	1006	19.3
1977-78 New Jersey	15	69	25	163	10.9
1978-79 Detroit	4	6	6	18	4.5
Totals	103	534	245	1313	12.7

HAWKINS, THOMAS (Hawk)
b. Dec. 22, 1936 Ht. 6-5 Wt. 210 College—Notre Dame

Yr.	Team	G	FG	FT	TP	Avg.
1959-60 Minneapolis	69	220	106	546	7.9
1960-61 Los Angeles	78	310	140	760	9.7
1961-62 Los Angeles	79	289	143	721	9.1
1962-63 Cincinnati	79	299	147	745	9.4
1963-64 Cincinnati	73	256	113	625	8.6
1964-65 Cincinnati	79	220	116	556	7.0
1965-66 Cincinnati	79	273	116	662	8.4
1966-67 Los Angeles	76	275	82	632	8.3
1967-68 Los Angeles	78	389	125	903	11.6
1968-69 Los Angeles	74	230	62	522	7.1
Totals	764	2761	1150	6672	8.7

HAWTHORNE, NATE
b. Jan. 15, 1950 Ht. 6-4 Wt. 190 College—S. Illinois

Yr.	Team	G	FG	FT	TP	Avg.
1973-74 Los Angeles	33	38	30	106	3.2
1974-75 Phoenix	50	118	61	297	5.9
1975-76 Phoenix	79	182	115	479	6.1
Totals	162	338	206	882	5.4

HAYES, JIM
b. Feb. 18, 1948 Ht. 6-3 Wt. 200 College—Boston Univ.

Yr.	Team		G	FG	FT	TP	Avg.
1970-71 New York	(ABA)	47	46	52	144	3.1

HAYWOOD, SPENCER
b. April 22, 1949 Ht. 6-8 Wt. 225 College—Detroit

Yr.	Team		G	FG	FT	TP	Avg.
1969-70 Denver	(ABA)	84	986	547	2519	30.0
1970-71 Seattle		33	260	160	680	20.6
1971-72 Seattle		73	717	480	1914	26.2
1972-73 Seattle		77	889	473	2251	29.2
1973-74 Seattle		75	694	373	1761	23.5
1974-75 Seattle		68	608	309	1525	22.4
1975-76 New York		78	605	339	1549	19.9
1976-77 N.Y. Knicks		31	202	109	513	16.5
1977-78 New York		67	412	96	920	13.7
1978-79 N.Y.-N.O.		68	595	231	1421	20.9
1979-80 Los Angeles		76	288(1)	159	736	9.7
Totals		730	6256(1)	3276	15789	21.6

HAZEN, JOHN
b. 1927 Ht. 6-2 Wt. 172 College—Indiana State

Yr.	Team	G	FG	FT	TP	Avg.
1948-49 Boston	6	6	6	18	3.0

HAZZARD, WALT
(See Abdul-Rahmad, Mahdi)

Yr.	Team	G	FG	FT	TP	Avg.
HEANEY, BRIAN						
b. Sept. 3, 1946 Ht. 6-2 Wt. 180 College—Acadia						
1969-70 Baltimore		14	13	2	28	2.0
HEDDERICK, HERMAN						
b. Jan. 1, 1930 Ht. 6-5 Wt. 170 College—Canisius						
1954-55 New York		5	2	0	4	0.8
HEINSOHN, TOM						
b. Aug. 26, 1934 Ht. 6-7 Wt. 218 College—Holy Cross						
1956-57 Boston		72	446	271	1163	16.2
1957-58 Boston		69	468	294	1230	17.8
1958-59 Boston		66	465	312	1242	18.8
1959-60 Boston		75	673	283	1629	21.7
1960-61 Boston		74	627	325	1579	21.3
1961-62 Boston		78	692	358	1742	22.3
1962-63 Boston		77	550	340	1440	18.7
1963-64 Boston		76	487	283	1257	16.5
1964-65 Boston		67	365	182	912	13.6
	Totals	654	4773	2648	12194	18.6
HEMRIC, DIXON (Dick)						
b. Aug. 29, 1933 Ht. 6-6 Wt. 220 College—Wake Forest						
1955-56 Boston		71	161	177	499	7.0
1956-57 Boston		67	109	146	364	5.4
	Totals	138	270	323	863	6.3
HENNESSEY, LAWRENCE						
b. May 20, 1929 Ht. 6-3 Wt. 185 College—Villanova						
1955-56 Philadelphia		53	85	26	196	3.7
1956-57 Syracuse		21	56	23	135	6.4
	Totals	74	141	49	331	4.5
HENRIKSEN, DON						
b. Oct. 10, 1929 Ht. 6-7 Wt. 225 College—California						
1952-53 Baltimore		68	199	176	574	8.4
1954-55 Rochester		70	139	137	415	5.9
	Totals	138	338	313	989	7.2
HENRY, AL						
b. Feb. 9, 1949 Ht. 6-9 Wt. 190 College—Wisconsin						
1970-71 Philadelphia		6	1	5	7	1.2
1971-72 Philadelphia		43	68	51	187	4.3
	Totals	49	69	56	194	4.0
HENRY, WILLIAM (Big Bill)						
b. Dec. 27, 1924 Ht. 6-9 Wt. 215 College—Rice						
1948-49 Ft. Wayne		32	96	125	317	9.9
1949-50 Ft. W.-Tri.-C.		63	89	118	296	4.7
	Totals	95	185	243	613	6.5
HENTZ, CHARLIE						
b. Sept. 13, 1947 Ht. 6-6 Wt. 235 College—Ark. A.M.&N.						
1970-71 Pittsburgh	(ABA)	57	142	57	341	6.0
HERMAN, BILL						
b. May 17, 1924 Ht. 6-3 Wt. 170 College—Mt. Union						
1949-50 Denver		13	25	6	56	4.3

Yr.	Team	G	FG	FT	TP	Avg.
HERMSEN, CLARENCE (Kleggie)						
b. March 12, 1923 Ht. 6-9 Wt. 235 College—Minnesota						
1943-44 Sheboygan	(NL)	12	3	5	11	0.9
1945-46 Sheboygan	(NL)	21	19	17	55	2.6
1946-47 Cleve.-Tor.		32	113	71	297	9.3
1947-48 Baltimore		48	212	151	575	12.0
1948-49 Washington		60	248	212	708	11.8
1949-50 Chicago		67	196	153	545	8.1
1950-51 Tri-Cities-Bos.		71	189	155	533	7.5
1952-53 Bos.-Ind.		10	4	3	11	1.1
	Totals	321	984	767	2735	8.5
HERN, BEN						
1967-68 Denver	(ABA)	1	0	2	2	2.0
HERTZBERG, SIDNEY (Sonny)						
b. July 29, 1922 Ht. 5-10 Wt. 195 College—CCNY						
1946-47 New York		59	201	113	515	8.7
1947-48 N.Y.-Wash.		41	110	58	278	6.8
1948-49 Washington		60	154	134	442	7.4
1949-50 Boston		68	275	143	693	10.2
1951-51 Boston		65	206	223	635	9.8
	Totals	293	946	671	2563	8.7
HESTER, DAN						
Ht. 6-8 Wt. 210 College—Louisiana State						
1970-71 Denver-Ky.	(ABA)	42	97(5)	49	248	5.9
HETZEL, FRED						
b. July 21, 1942 Ht. 6-8 Wt. 230 College—Davidson						
1965-66 San Francisco		56	160	63	383	6.8
1966-67 San Francisco		77	373	192	938	12.2
1967-68 San Francisco		77	533	395	1461	19.0
1968-69 Milw.-Cin.		84	456	299	1211	14.4
1969-70 Philadelphia		63	156	71	383	6.1
1970-71 Los Angeles		59	111	60	282	4.8
	Totals	416	1789	1080	4658	11.2
HEWITT, BILL						
b. Aug. 8, 1944 Ht. 6-7 Wt. 210 College—S. California						
1968-69 Los Angeles		75	239	61	539	7.2
1969-70 L.A.-Det.		65	110	54	274	4.2
1970-71 Detroit		62	203	69	475	7.7
1971-72 Detroit		68	131	41	303	4.5
1972-73 Buffalo		73	152	41	345	4.7
1974-75 Chicago		18	56	14	126	7.0
	Totals	361	891	280	2062	5.7
HEWSON, JACK						
b. Sept. 7, 1924 Ht. 6-6 Wt. 195 College—Temple						
1947-48 Boston		24	22	21	65	2.7
HEYMAN, ARTHUR						
b. June 24, 1941 Ht. 6-5 Wt. 205 College—Duke						
1963-64 New York		75	432	289	1153	15.4
1964-65 New York		55	114	88	316	5.7
1965-66 Cinn.-Phila.		17	18	14	50	2.9
1967-68 N.J.-Pitt.	(ABA)	73	457(35)	400	1349	18.5
1968-69 Minnesota	(ABA)	71	350(37)	285	1022	14.4
1969-70 Pitt.-Miami	(ABA)	19	47	46	140	7.4
	Totals	310	1418(72)	1122	4030	13.0

Yr.	Team		G	FG	FT	TP	Avg.

HICKEY, MATTHEW (Nat)
b. Jan. 30, 1902 Ht. 5-11½ Wt. 180

Yr.	Team		G	FG	FT	TP	Avg.
1944-45	Pittsburgh	(NL)	2	3	2	8	4.0
1945-46	Indianapolis	(NL)	13	30	13	73	5.6
1946-47	Buf.-Tri-C.	(NL)	8	9	6	24	3.0
1947-48	Tri-Cities	(NL)	3	1	1	3	1.0
1947-48	Providence		1	0	0	0	0.0
	Totals		27	43	22	108	4.0

HICKS, PHIL
b. Jan. 31, 1953 Ht. 6-7 Wt. 205 College—Tulane

Yr.	Team	G	FG	FT	TP	Avg.
1976-77	Hou.-Chi.	37	41	11	93	2.5
1978-79	Denver	20	18	3	39	2.0
	Totals	57	59	14	132	2.3

HIGGINS, BILL
b. Nov. 12, 1951 Ht. 6-2 Wt. 185 College—Northern Ill.

Yr.	Team		G	FG	FT	TP	Avg.
1974-75	Virginia	(ABA)	15	61(1)	15	138	9.2

HIGGINS, EARLE
Ht. 6-8 Wt. 200 College—Eastern Michigan

Yr.	Team		G	FG	FT	TP	Avg.
1970-71	Indiana	(ABA)	53	104(3)	20	231	4.4
1971-72	Indiana	(ABA)	0	0	0	0	0.0
	Totals		53	104(3)	20	231	4.4

HIGHTOWER, WAYNE
b. Jan. 14, 1940 Ht. 6-8½ Wt. 192 College—Kansas

Yr.	Team		G	FG	FT	TP	Avg.
1962-63	San Francisco		66	192	105	489	7.4
1963-64	San Francisco		79	393	260	1046	13.2
1964-65	S.F.-Balt.		75	196	195	587	7.8
1965-66	Baltimore		24	63	57	183	7.6
1966-67	Balt.-Detroit		72	195	153	543	7.5
1967-68	Denver	(ABA)	74	431	420	1282	17.3
1968-69	Denver	(ABA)	67	311	311	933	13.9
1969-70	Los Angeles	(ABA)	27	180	129	489	18.1
1970-71	Utah-Tex.	(ABA)	68	339	268	946	13.9
1971-72	Carolina	(ABA)	13	20	30	70	5.4
	Totals		565	2320	1928	6568	11.6

HILL, CLEO
b. May 24, 1938 Ht. 6-1 Wt. 185 College—Winston-Salem State

Yr.	Team	G	FG	FT	TP	Avg.
1961-62	St. Louis	58	110	106	326	5.6

HILL, GARY
b. Oct. 7, 1941 Ht. 6-4 Wt. 185 College—Ok. City

Yr.	Team	G	FG	FT	TP	Avg.
1963-64	San Francisco	66	145	51	341	5.2
1964-65	S.F.-Balt.	12	10	7	27	2.3
	Totals	78	155	58	368	4.7

HILL, SIMMIE
Ht. 6-7 Wt. 235 College—West Texas State

Yr.	Team		G	FG	FT	TP	Avg.
1969-70	L.A.-Miami	(ABA)	53	297(5)	126	725	13.7
1971-72	Dallas	(ABA)	70	281(4)	129	695	9.9
1972-73	San Diego	(ABA)	69	315(27)	103	760	11.0
1973-74	San Antonio	(ABA)	60	112	45	269	4.5
	Totals		252	1005(36)	403	2449	9.7

HILLHOUSE, ARTHUR
b. June 12, 1916 Ht. 6-7 Wt. 220 College—L.I. Univ.

Yr.	Team	G	FG	FT	TP	Avg.
1946-47	Philadelphia	60	120	120	360	6.0
1947-48	Philadelphia	11	14	30	58	5.3
	Totals	71	134	150	418	5.9

HILLMAN, DARNELL
b. Aug. 8, 1949 Ht. 6-9 Wt. 215 College—San Jose St.

Yr.	Team		G	FG	FT	TP	Avg.
1971-72	Indiana	(ABA)	73	200(1)	114	515	7.1
1972-73	Indiana	(ABA)	84	328	148	804	9.6
1973-74	Indiana	(ABA)	83	328(3)	99	758	9.1
1974-75	Indiana	(ABA)	81	486	152	1124	13.9
1975-76	Indiana	(ABA)	74	375(1)	243	994	13.4
1976-77	Indiana		82	359	161	879	10.7
1977-78	N.J.-Den.		78	340	167	847	10.9
1978-79	Kansas City		78	211	125	547	7.0
1979-80	Golden State		49	82	34	198	4.0
	Totals		682	2709(5)	1243	6666	9.8

HILTON, FRED
b. Jan. 15, 1948 Ht. 6-3 Wt. 185 College—Grambling

Yr.	Team	G	FG	FT	TP	Avg.
1971-72	Buffalo	61	309	90	708	11.6
1972-73	Buffalo	59	191	41	423	7.2
	Totals	120	400	131	1131	9.4

HIRSCH, MEL
b. July 31, 1921 Ht. 5-8 Wt. 165 College—Bklyn Coll.

Yr.	Team	G	FG	FT	TP	Avg.
1946-47	Boston	13	9	1	19	1.5

HITCH, LEW
b. July 16, 1929 Ht. 6-8 Wt. 200 College—Kansas St.

Yr.	Team	G	FG	FT	TP	Avg.
1951-52	Minneapolis	61	77	63	217	3.6
1952-53	Minneapolis	70	89	83	261	3.7
1953-54	Milwaukee	72	221	133	575	8.0
1954-55	Milwaukee	74	167	115	449	6.1
1955-56	Milw.-Minn.	69	94	100	288	4.2
1956-57	Minn.-Phila.	68	111	63	285	4.2
	Totals	414	759	557	2075	5.0

HOEFER, CHARLES (Dutch)
b. 1922 Ht. 5-9 Wt. 158 College—Queens

Yr.	Team	G	FG	FT	TP	Avg.
1946-47	Tor.-Bos.	58	130	91	351	6.1
1947-48	Boston	7	3	4	10	1.4
	Totals	65	133	95	361	5.6

HOFFMAN, PAUL (Bear)
b. April 12, 1922 Ht. 6-2 Wt. 205 College—Purdue

Yr.	Team	G	FG	FT	TP	Avg.
1947-48	Baltimore	37	142	104	388	10.5
1949-50	Baltimore	60	312	242	866	14.4
1950-51	Baltimore	41	127	105	359	8.8
1952-53	Baltimore	69	240	224	704	10.2
1953-54	Baltimore	72	253	217	723	10.0
1954-55	Balt.-N.Y.-Phila.	38	65	64	194	5.1
	Totals	317	1139	956	3234	10.2

HOGSETT, BOB
b. Jan. 29, 1941 Ht. 6-7½ Wt. 230 College—Tennessee

Yr.	Team		G	FG	FT	TP	Avg.
1966-67	Detroit		7	5	6	16	2.3
1968-69	Pittsburgh	(ABA)	13	7	7	21	1.6
	Totals		20	12	13	37	1.9

Yr.	Team	G	FG	FT	TP	Avg.
HOGUE, PAUL (Duke)						
b. April 28, 1940 Ht. 6-9 Wt. 240 College—Cincinnati						
1962-63	New York	50	152	79	383	7.7
1963-64	N.Y.-Balt.	15	12	2	26	1.7
	Totals	65	164	81	409	6.3
HOLCOMB, DOUGLAS						
b. Feb. 9, 1925 Ht. 6-4 Wt. 200 College—Wisconsin						
1948-49	Baltimore	3	3	9	15	5.0
HOLLAND, JOE						
b. Sept. 26, 1925 Ht. 6-4 Wt. 185 College—Berea and Kentucky						
1949-50	Indianapolis	64	145	98	388	6.1
1950-51	Indianapolis	67	196	78	470	7.0
1951-52	Indianapolis	55	93	40	226	4.1
	Totals	186	434	216	1084	5.8
HOLLAND, WILBUR						
b. Nov. 8, 1951 Ht. 6-0 Wt. 175 College—New Orleans						
1975-76	Atlanta	33	85	22	192	5.8
1976-77	Chicago	79	509	158	1176	14.9
1977-78	Chicago	82	569	223	1361	16.6
1978-79	Chicago	82	445	141	1031	12.6
	Totals	276	1608	544	3760	13.6
HOLLIS, ESSIE						
b. May 16, 1955 Ht. 6-6 Wt. 195 College—St. Bonaventure						
1978-79	Detroit	25	30	9	69	2.8
HOLMAN, DENNY						
b. Oct. 8, 1945 Ht. 6-3 Wt. 175 College—Southern Methodist						
1967-68	Dallas (ABA)	46	55(4)	62	176	3.8
HOLSTEIN, JIM						
b. Sept. 24, 1930 Ht. 6-3 Wt. 180 College—Cincinnati						
1952-53	Minneapolis	66	98	70	266	4.0
1953-54	Minneapolis	70	88	64	240	3.4
1954-55	Minneapolis	62	107	67	281	4.5
1955-56	Ft. Wayne	27	24	24	72	2.7
	Totals	225	317	225	859	3.3
HOLT, ALVIN W. (A.W.)						
b. Aug. 26, 1946 Ht. 6-7½ Wt. 210 College—Jackson St.						
1970-71	Chicago	6	1	2	4	0.7
HOLUB, RICHARD						
b. Oct. 29, 1921 Ht. 6-6 Wt. 205 College—L.I.U.						
1947-48	New York	48	195	114	504	10.5
HOLUP, JOSEPH						
b. Feb. 26, 1934 Ht. 6-6 Wt. 215 College—G. Washington						
1956-57	Syracuse	71	160	204	524	7.4
1957-58	Syr.-Det.	53	91	71	253	4.8
	Totals	124	251	275	777	6.3
HOLZMAN, WILLIAM (Red)						
b. Aug. 10, 1920 Ht. 5-10 Wt. 175 College—Baltimore/CCNY						
1945-46	Rochester (NL)	34	143	77	363	10.7
1946-47	Rochester (NL)	44	227	74	528	12.0

Yr.	Team	G	FG	FT	TP	Avg.
1947-48	Rochester (NL)	60	246	117	609	10.2
1948-49	Rochester	60	225	96	546	9.1
1949-50	Rochester	68	206	144	556	8.2
1950-51	Rochester	68	183	130	496	7.3
1951-52	Rochester	65	104	61	269	4.1
1952-53	Rochester	46	38	27	103	2.2
1953-54	Milwaukee	51	74	48	196	3.8
	Totals	496	1446	774	3666	7.4
HOOPER, BOBBY						
b. Dec. 22, 1946 Ht. 6-0 Wt. 180 College—Dayton						
1968-69	Indiana (ABA)	54	107(4)	53	271	5.0
HOOSER, CARROLL						
b. 1943 Ht. 6-7 Wt. 230 College—Southern Methodist						
1967-68	Dallas (ABA)	56	128(1)	59	316	5.6
HOOVER, THOMAS						
b. Jan. 23, 1941 Ht. 6-10 Wt. 240 College—Villanova						
1963-64	New York	59	102	81	285	4.8
1964-65	New York	24	13	8	34	1.4
1966-67	St. Louis	17	13	5	31	1.8
1967-68	Denver (ABA)	70	161(4)	128	454	6.5
1968-69	Hou.-Minn.-N.Y.(ABA)	53	191	125	507	9.6
	Totals	223	480(4)	347	1311	5.9
HOPKINS, ROBERT						
b. Nov. 3, 1934 Ht. 6-8 Wt. 205 College—Grambling						
1956-57	Syracuse	62	130	94	354	5.7
1957-58	Syracuse	69	221	123	565	8.2
1958-59	Syracuse	67	246	176	668	10.0
1959-60	Syracuse	75	257	136	650	8.7
	Totals	273	854	529	2237	8.2
HORAN, JOHN						
b. Nov. 24, 1932 Ht. 6-8 Wt. 190 College—Dayton						
1955-56	Minneapolis	19	12	10	34	1.8
HORN, RON						
b. May 24, 1938 Ht. 6-7 Wt. 225 College—Indiana						
1961-62	St. Louis	3	1	1	3	1.0
1962-63	Los Angeles	28	27	20	74	2.6
	Totals	31	28	21	77	2.5
HOSKET, WILMER (Bill)						
b. Dec. 20, 1946 Ht. 6-8 Wt. 225 College—Ohio State						
1968-69	New York	50	53	24	130	2.6
1969-70	New York	36	46	26	118	3.3
1970-71	Buffalo	13	47	11	105	8.1
1971-72	Buffalo	44	89	42	220	5.0
	Totals	143	235	103	573	4.0
HOUBREGS, BOB (Houby)						
b. March 12, 1932 Ht. 6-8 Wt. 225 College—Washington						
1953-54	Milw.-Balt.	70	209	190	608	8.7
1954-55	Balt.-Bos.-Ft. W.	64	148	129	425	6.6
1955-56	Ft. Wayne	70	247	283	777	11.1
1956-57	Ft. Wayne	60	253	167	673	11.2
1957-58	Detroit	17	49	30	128	7.5
	Totals	281	906	799	2611	9.3

Yr.	Team	G	FG	FT	TP	Avg.

HOWARD, GREGG
b. Jan. 8, 1948 Ht. 6-9 Wt. 215 College—New Mexico

Yr.	Team	G	FG	FT	TP	Avg.
1970-71	Phoenix	44	68	37	173	3.9
1971-72	Cleveland	48	50	39	139	2.9
	Totals	92	118	76	312	3.4

HOWARD, MAURICE (Mo)
b. Aug. 25, 1954 Ht. 6-2 Wt. 175 College—Maryland

Yr.	Team	G	FG	FT	TP	Avg.
1976-77	Clev.-N.O.	32	64	24	152	4.8

HOWARD, OTIS
b. Nov. 6, 1956 Ht. 6-7 Wt. 220 College—Austin Peay

Yr.	Team	G	FG	FT	TP	Avg.
1978-79	Milw.-Detr.	14	24	11	59	4.2

HOWELL, BAILEY
b. Jan. 20, 1937 Ht. 6-7 Wt. 220 College—Miss. State

Yr.	Team	G	FG	FT	TP	Avg.
1959-60	Detroit	75	510	312	1332	17.8
1960-61	Detroit	77	607	601	1815	23.4
1961-62	Detroit	79	553	470	1576	19.9
1962-63	Detroit	79	637	519	1793	22.7
1963-64	Detroit	77	598	470	1666	21.6
1964-65	Baltimore	80	515	504	1534	19.2
1965-66	Baltimore	79	481	402	1364	17.3
1966-67	Boston	81	636	349	1621	20.0
1967-68	Boston	82	643	335	1621	19.8
1968-69	Boston	78	612	313	1537	19.7
1969-70	Boston	82	399	235	1033	12.6
1970-71	Philadelphia	82	324	230	878	10.7
	Totals	951	6515	4740	17770	18.7

HUBBARD, ROBERT
b. Dec. 27, 1922 Ht. 6-6 Wt. 215 College—Springfield

Yr.	Team		G	FG	FT	TP	Avg.
1947-48	Tri-Cities	(NL)	20	27	22	76	3.8
1947-48	Providence		28	58	36	152	5.4
1948-49	Providence		34	25	22	72	2.1
	Totals		82	110	80	300	3.7

HUDSON, LOU
b. July 11, 1944 Ht. 6-5 Wt. 220 College—Minnesota

Yr.	Team	G	FG	FT	TP	Avg.
1966-67	St. Louis	80	620	231	1471	18.4
1967-68	St. Louis	46	227	120	574	12.5
1968-69	Atlanta	81	716	338	1770	21.9
1969-70	Atlanta	80	830	371	2031	25.4
1970-71	Atlanta	76	829	381	2039	26.8
1971-72	Atlanta	77	775	349	1899	24.7
1972-73	Atlanta	75	816	397	2029	27.1
1973-74	Atlanta	65	678	295	1651	25.4
1974-75	Atlanta	11	97	48	242	22.0
1975-76	Atlanta	81	569	237	1375	17.0
1976-77	Atlanta	58	413	142	968	16.7
1977-78	Los Angeles	82	493	137	1123	13.7
1978-79	Los Angeles	78	329	110	768	9.8
	Totals	890	7392	3156	17940	20.2

HUMMER, JOHN
b. May 4, 1948 Ht. 6-9 Wt. 230 College—Princeton

Yr.	Team	G	FG	FT	TP	Avg.
1970-71	Buffalo	81	339	225	913	11.3
1971-72	Buffalo	55	113	58	284	5.2
1972-73	Buffalo	66	206	115	527	8.0

Yr.	Team		G	FG	FT	TP	Avg.
1973-74	Chi.-Sea.		53	144	59	347	6.5
1974-75	Seattle		43	41	14	96	2.2
1975-76	Seattle		29	32	17	81	2.8
	Totals		327	875	488	2248	6.9

HUNDLEY, RODNEY (Hot Rod)
b. Oct. 26, 1934 Ht. 6-4 Wt. 185 College—West Virginia

Yr.	Team	G	FG	FT	TP	Avg.
1957-58	Minneapolis	65	174	104	452	7.0
1958-59	Minneapolis	71	259	164	682	9.6
1959-60	Minneapolis	73	365	203	933	12.8
1960-61	Los Angeles	79	323	223	869	11.0
1961-62	Los Angeles	79	173	83	429	5.4
1962-63	Los Angeles	65	88	84	250	4.0
	Totals	432	1382	861	3625	8.4

HUNTER, LESLIE (Big Game)
b. Aug. 16, 1942 Ht. 6-7 Wt. 212 College—Loyola (Ill.)

Yr.	Team		G	FG	FT	TP	Avg.
1964-65	Baltimore		24	18	6	42	1.8
1967-68	Minnesota	(ABA)	75	513(2)	290	1318	17.6
1968-69	Miami	(ABA)	77	476	335	1287	16.7
1969-70	New York	(ABA)	79	486(6)	317	1295	16.0
1970-71	Kentucky	(ABA)	80	288(10)	159	745	9.3
1971-72	Kentucky	(ABA)	70	183(5)	101	472	6.7
	Totals		405	1964(23)	1208	5159	12.7

HURLEY, ROY
b. 1922 Ht. 6-2½ Wt. 170 College—Indiana/Murray St.

Yr.	Team		G	FG	FT	TP	Avg.
1945-46	Indianapolis	(NL)	30	76	24	176	5.9
1946-47	Toronto		46	100	39	239	5.2
1947-48	Tri-C.-Syra.	(NL)	16	19	13	51	3.2
	Totals		92	195	76	466	5.1

HUSTON, PAUL
b. June 2, 1925 Ht. 6-3 Wt. 175 College—Ohio State

Yr.	Team	G	FG	FT	TP	Avg.
1947-48	Chicago	46	51	62	164	3.6

HUTCHINS, MEL (Hutch)
b. Nov. 22, 1928 Ht. 6-6 Wt. 205 College—Brigham Young

Yr.	Team	G	FG	FT	TP	Avg.
1951-52	Milwaukee	66	231	145	607	9.2
1952-53	Milwaukee	71	319	193	831	11.7
1953-54	Ft. Wayne	72	295	151	741	10.3
1954-55	Ft. Wayne	72	341	182	864	12.0
1955-56	Ft. Wayne	66	325	142	792	12.0
1956-57	Ft. Wayne	72	369	152	890	12.4
1957-58	New York	18	51	24	126	7.0
	Totals	437	1931	989	4851	11.1

HUTTON, JOE
b. Oct. 6, 1928 Ht. 6-1 Wt. 170 College—Hamline

Yr.	Team	G	FG	FT	TP	Avg.
1950-51	Minneapolis	60	59	29	147	2.5
1951-52	Minneapolis	60	53	49	155	2.6
	Totals	120	112	78	302	2.5

HYDER, GREG
b. June 21, 1948 Ht. 6-6 Wt. 215 Coll.—East. N.M.

Yr.	Team	G	FG	FT	TP	Avg.
1970-71	Cincinnati	77	183	51	417	5.4

Yr.	Team	G	FG	FT	TP	Avg.

IMHOFF, DARRALL
b. Oct. 11, 1938 Ht. 6-10 Wt. 220 College—California

Yr.	Team	G	FG	FT	TP	Avg.
1960-61	New York	62	122	49	293	4.7
1961-62	New York	76	186	80	452	5.9
1962-63	Detroit	45	48	24	120	2.7
1963-64	Detroit	58	104	69	277	4.8
1964-65	Los Angeles	76	145	88	378	4.8
1965-66	Los Angeles	77	151	77	379	4.9
1966-67	Los Angeles	81	370	127	867	10.7
1967-68	Los Angeles	82	293	177	763	9.3
1968-69	Philadelphia	82	279	194	752	9.2
1696-70	Philadelphia	79	430	215	1075	13.6
1970-71	Cincinnati	34	119	37	275	8.1
1971-72	Cin.-Port.	49	52	24	128	2.6
	Totals	801	2299	1161	5759	7.2

INGLESBY, TOM
b. Feb. 12, 1951 Ht. 6-3 Wt. 185 College—Villanova

Yr.	Team		G	FG	FT	TP	Avg.
1973-74	Atlanta		48	50	29	129	2.7
1974-75	St. Louis	(ABA)	22	43(3)	20	109	5.0
	Totals		70	93(3)	49	238	3.4

INGRAM, McCOY
b. Aug. 31, 1931 Ht. 6-0 Wt. 210 College—Jackson State

Yr.	Team	G	FG	FT	TP	Avg.
1957-58	Minneapolis	24	27	13	67	2.8

INNIGER, ERV
b. Jan. 16, 1945 Ht. 6-4 Wt. 190 College—Indiana

Yr.	Team		G	FG	FT	TP	Avg.
1967-68	Minnesota	(ABA)	75	345(5)	99	794	10.6
1968-69	Miami	(ABA)	34	73(3)	21	170	5.0
	Totals		109	418(8)	120	964	8.8

IRVINE, GEORGE
b. Feb. 1, 1948 Ht. 6-6 Wt. 200 College—Washington

Yr.	Team		G	FG	FT	TP	Avg.
1970-71	Virginia	(ABA)	34	83(2)	26	194	5.7
1971-72	Virginia	(ABA)	75	200(3)	54	457	6.1
1972-73	Virginia	(ABA)	79	424(7)	169	1024	13.0
1973-74	Virginia	(ABA)	75	254(12)	120	640	8.5
1974-75	Virginia	(ABA)	59	311(13)	139	774	13.1
1975-76	Denver	(ABA)	3	2	0	4	1.3
	Totals		325	1274(37)	508	3093	9.5

IVERSON, WILLIE
b. Oct. 8, 1945 Ht. 6-0 Wt. 180 College—Central Michigan

Yr.	Team		G	FG	FT	TP	Avg.
1968-69	Miami	(ABA)	28	50	36	136	4.9

IVORY, ELVIN
b. July 2, 1948 Ht. 6-8 Wt. 215 College—S. Louisiana

Yr.	Team		G	FG	FT	TP	Avg.
1968-69	Los Angeles	(ABA)	20	38(1)	11	88	4.4

JABALI, WARREN (Warren Armstrong)
b. Aug. 29, 1946 Ht. 6-2 Wt. 200 College—Wichita State

Yr.	Team		G	FG	FT	TP	Avg.
1968-69	Oakland	(ABA)	71	573(11)	373	1520	21.5
1969-70	Washington	(ABA)	40	342(19)	210	913	22.8
1970-71	Indiana	(ABA)	62	227(47)	180	681	11.0
1971-72	Floridians	(ABA)	81	569(102)	375	1615	19.9
1972-73	Denver	(ABA)	82	441(36)	480	1398	17.1
1973-74	Denver	(ABA)	49	257(45)	220	779	15.9
1974-75	San Diego	(ABA)	62	254(62)	179	749	12.1
	Totals		447	2663(322)	2017	7665	17.1

JACKSON, AL
b. July 29, 1943 Ht. 6-1½ Wt. 185 College—Wilberforce

Yr.	Team	G	FG	FT	TP	Avg.
1967-68	Cincinnati	2	0	0	0	0.0

JACKSON, GREG
b. Aug. 2, 1952 Ht. 6-0 Wt. 185 College—Guilford

Yr.	Team	G	FG	FT	TP	Avg.
1974-75	N.Y.-Phoe.	49	73	36	182	3.7

JACKSON, LUCIOUS (Luke)
b. Oct. 31, 1941 Ht. 6-9 Wt. 240 College—Pan American

Yr.	Team	G	FG	FT	TP	Avg.
1964-65	Philadelphia	76	419	288	1126	14.8
1965-66	Philadelphia	79	246	158	650	8.2
1966-67	Philadelphia	81	386	198	970	12.0
1967-68	Philadelphia	82	401	166	968	11.8
1968-69	Philadelphia	25	145	69	359	14.4
1969-70	Philadelphia	37	71	60	202	5.5
1970-71	Philadelphia	79	199	131	529	6.7
1971-72	Philadelphia	63	137	92	366	5.8
	Totals	522	2004	1162	5170	9.9

JACKSON, MERV
b. Aug. 15, 1946 Ht. 6-3 Wt. 175 College—Utah

Yr.	Team		G	FG	FT	TP	Avg.
1968-69	Los Angeles	(ABA)	71	423(19)	249	1114	15.7
1969-70	Los Angeles	(ABA)	52	169(16)	92	446	8.6
1970-71	Utah	(ABA)	65	351(7)	192	901	13.8
1971-72	Utah	(ABA)	52	185(5)	92	467	9.0
1972-73	Memphis	(ABA)	22	34(4)	28	100	4.5
	Totals		262	1162(51)	653	3028	11.5

JACKSON, MIKE
b. July 31, 1949 Ht. 6-7 Wt. 230 College—California State

Yr.	Team		G	FG	FT	TP	Avg.
1972-73	Utah	(ABA)	30	36	28	100	3.3
1973-74	Utah-Mem.	(ABA)	72	247(3)	110	607	8.4
1974-75	Virginia	(ABA)	82	382(1)	232	997	12.2
1975-76	Virginia	(ABA)	80	390	199	979	12.2
	Totals		264	1055(4)	569	2683	10.2

JACKSON, PHIL
b. Sept. 17, 1945 Ht. 6-8 Wt. 220 College—No. Dakota

Yr.	Team	G	FG	FT	TP	Avg.
1967-68	New York	75	182	99	463	6.2
1968-69	New York	47	126	80	332	7.1
1970-71	New York	71	118	95	331	4.7
1971-72	New York	80	205	167	577	7.2
1972-73	New York	80	245	154	644	8.1
1973-74	New York	82	361	191	913	11.1
1974-75	New York	78	324	193	841	10.8
1975-76	New York	80	185	110	480	6.0
1976-77	N.Y. Knicks	76	102	51	255	2.4
1977-78	New York	63	55	43	153	2.4
1978-79	New Jersey	59	144	86	374	6.3
1979-80	New Jersey	16	29	7	65	4.1
	Totals	807	2076	1276	5428	6.7

JACKSON, TONY
b. Nov. 7, 1940 Ht. 6-4 Wt. 200 College—St. John's

Yr.	Team		G	FG	FT	TP	Avg.
1967-68	New Jersey	(ABA)	74	449(91)	450	1439	19.5
1968-69	N.Y.-Minn.-Hou.	(ABA)	64	210(32)	299	751	11.7
	Totals		138	659(123)	749	2190	15.9

Yr.	Team		G	FG	FT	TP	Avg.

JACKSON, WARDELL
b. July 18, 1951 Ht. 6-7 Wt. 200 College—Ohio State

Yr.	Team	G	FG	FT	TP	Avg.
1974-75 Seattle		56	96	51	243	4.3

JACOBS, FRED
b. Dec. 2, 1922 Ht. 6-3 Wt. 175 College—Denver

Yr.	Team	G	FG	FT	TP	Avg.
1946-47 St. Louis		18	19	12	50	2.8

JAMES, AARON
b. Oct. 5, 1952 Ht. 6-8 Wt. 210 College—Grambling

Yr.	Team	G	FG	FT	TP	Avg.
1974-75 New Orleans	76	370	147	887	11.7
1975-76 New Orleans	75	262	153	677	9.0
1976-77 New Orleans	52	238	89	565	10.9
1977-78 New Orleans	80	428	117	973	12.2
1978-79 New Orleans	73	311	105	727	10.0
Totals	356	1609	611	3829	10.8

JAMES, BILLY
b. 1951 Ht. 6-3 Wt. 185 College—Marshall

Yr.	Team		G	FG	FT	TP	Avg.
1973-74 Kentucky	(ABA)	1	1	0	2	2.0

JAMES, GENE (Goose)
b. Feb. 15, 1925 Ht. 6-4½ Wt. 180 College—Marshall

Yr.	Team	G	FG	FT	TP	Avg.
1948-49 New York	11	18	6	42	3.8
1949-50 New York	29	19	14	52	1.8
1950-51 N.Y.-Balt.	48	79	44	202	4.2
Totals	88	116	64	296	3.4

JANISCH, JOHN
b. March 15, 1920 Ht. 6-3 Wt. 200 College—Valparaiso

Yr.	Team		G	FG	FT	TP	Avg.
1946-47 Detroit		60	283	131	697	11.6
1947-48 Boston-Prov.		10	14	9	37	3.7
1947-48 Flint	(NL)	36	36	21	93	2.6
Totals		106	333	161	827	7.8

JANOTTA, HOWARD
b. Oct. 19, 1924 Ht. 6-3 Wt. 185 College—Seton Hall

Yr.	Team	G	FG	FT	TP	Avg.
1949-50 Baltimore	9	9	13	31	3.4

JAROS, ANTHONY
b. Feb. 22, 1920 Ht. 6-3 Wt. 185 College—Minnesota

Yr.	Team		G	FG	FT	TP	Avg.
1946-47 Chicago		59	177	128	482	8.2
1947-48 Minneapolis	(NL)	58	95	83	273	4.7
1948-49 Minneapolis		59	132	79	343	5.8
1949-50 Minneapolis		61	84	72	240	3.9
1950-51 Minneapolis		63	88	65	241	3.8
Totals		300	576	427	1579	5.3

JARVIS, JIM
b. March 3, 1943 Ht. 6-1 Wt. 175 College—Oregon State

Yr.	Team		G	FG	FT	TP	Avg.
1967-68 Pittsburgh	(ABA)	63	132(12)	53	329	5.2
1968-69 Minn.-L.A.	(ABA)	62	147(19)	86	399	6.4
Totals		125	279(31)	139	728	5.8

JEANNETTE, HARRY (Buddy)
b. Sept. 15, 1917 Ht. 5-11 Wt. 175 Coll.—Washington and Jefferson

Yr.	Team		G	FG	FT	TP	Avg.
1938-39 War.-Cleve.	(NL)	26	54	65	173	6.7
1939-40 Detroit	(NL)	25	45	52	142	5.7
1940-41 Detroit	(NL)	23	75	54	204	8.9

Yr.	Team		G	FG	FT	TP	Avg.
1942-43 Sheboygan	(NL)	4	24	14	62	15.5
1943-44 Fort Wayne	(NL)	22	68	48	184	8.4
1944-45 Fort Wayne	(NL)	27	85	82	252	9.3
1945-46 Fort Wayne	(NL)	34	99	105	303	8.9
1947-48 Baltimore		46	150	191	491	10.7
1948-49 Baltimore		56	73	167	313	5.6
1949-50 Baltimore		37	42	109	193	5.2
Totals		300	715	887	2317	7.7

JETER, HAL
College—Drake

Yr.	Team		G	FG	FT	TP	Avg.
1969-70 Washington	(ABA)	5	1	0	2	0.4

JOHNSON, ANDY
b. Nov. 3, 1931 Ht. 6-5 Wt. 215 College—Portland

Yr.	Team	G	FG	FT	TP	Avg.
1958-59 Philadelphia	67	174	115	463	6.9
1959-60 Philadelphia	75	245	125	615	8.2
1960-61 Philadelphia	79	299	157	755	9.6
1961-62 Chicago	71	365	284	1014	14.3
Totals	292	1083	681	2847	9.8

JOHNSON, ARNITZ (Arnie)
b. May 17, 1920 Ht. 6-5 Wt. 240 College—Bemidji State

Yr.	Team		G	FG	FT	TP	Avg.
1946-47 Rochester	(NL)	32	68	68	204	6.4
1947-48 Rochester	(NL)	57	101	97	299	5.2
1948-49 Rochester		60	156	199	511	8.5
1949-50 Rochester		68	149	200	498	7.3
1950-51 Rochester		68	185	269	639	9.4
1951-52 Rochester		66	178	301	657	10.0
1952-53 Rochester		70	140	303	583	8.3
Totals		421	977	1437	3391	8.1

JOHNSON, CHARLES
B. March 31, 1949 Ht. 6-0 Wt. 170 College—California

Yr.	Team	G	FG	FT	TP	Avg.
1972-73 Golden State	70	171	33	375	5.4
1973-74 Golden State	59	194	38	426	7.2
1974-75 Golden State	79	394	75	863	10.9
1975-76 Golden State	81	342	60	744	9.2
1976-77 Golden State	79	255	49	559	7.1
1977-78 Golden State	71	237	49	523	7.4
1978-79 Washington	82	342	67	751	9.2
Totals	521	1935	371	4241	8.1

JOHNSON, ED
b. June 17, 1944 Ht. 6-9 Wt. 205 College—Tennessee St.

Yr.	Team		G	FG	FT	TP	Avg.
1968-69 Los Angeles	(ABA)	58	263	156	682	11.8
1969-70 New York	(ABA)	74	405(1)	226	1037	14.0
1970-71 N.Y.-Tex.	(ABA)	34	119	82	320	9.4
Totals		166	787(1)	464	2039	12.3

JOHNSON, GEORGE
b. June 19, 1947 Ht. 6-11 Wt. 255 College—Stephen F. Austin

Yr.	Team		G	FG	FT	TP	Avg.
1970-71 Baltimore		24	41	11	93	3.9
1971-72 Dallas	(ABA)	67	128	61	317	4.7
Totals		91	169	72	410	4.5

JOHNSON, GUS (Honeycomb)
b. Dec. 13, 1938 Ht. 6-6 Wt. 235 College—Idaho

Yr.	Team	G	FG	FT	TP	Avg.
1963-64 Baltimore	78	571	210	1352	17.3
1964-65 Baltimore	76	577	261	1415	18.6

Yr.	Team		G	FG	FT	TP	Avg.
1965-66	Baltimore		42	273	131	677	16.1
1966-67	Baltimore		73	620	271	1511	20.7
1967-68	Baltimore		60	482	180	1144	19.0
1968-69	Baltimore		49	359	160	878	17.9
1969-70	Baltimore		78	578	197	1353	17.3
1970-71	Baltimore		66	494	214	1202	18.2
1971-72	Baltimore		39	103	43	249	6.4
1972-73	Phoenix		20	69	25	163	8.2
1972-73	Indiana	(ABA)	50	132(4)	31	299	6.0
	Totals		631	4258(4)	1723	10243	16.2

JOHNSON, HAROLD
b. Jan. 20, 1920 Ht. 6-6 Wt. 240 College—Indiana State

1946-47	Detroit		27	4	7	15	0.6

JOHNSON, LARRY
b. Nov. 28, 1954 Ht. 6-3 Wt. 205 College—Kentucky

1977-78	Buffalo		4	3	0	6	1.5

JOHNSON, LYNBERT (Cheese)
b. Sept. 7, 1957 Ht. 6-6 Wt. 195 College—Wichita St.

1979-80	Golden State		9	12	3	27	3.0

JOHNSON, NEIL
b. April 14, 1943 Ht. 6-7 Wt. 220 College—Tulsa/Creighton

1966-67	New York		51	59	57	175	3.4
1967-68	New York		43	44	23	111	2.6
1968-69	Phoenix		80	177	110	464	5.8
1969-70	Phoenix		28	20	8	48	1.4
1970-71	Virginia	(ABA)	78	398	194	990	12.7
1971-72	Virginia	(ABA)	31	128(1)	65	322	10.4
1972-73	Virginia	(ABA)	69	210	103	523	7.6
	Totals		380	1036(1)	560	2633	6.9

JOHNSON, RALPH (Boag)
b. Dec. 6, 1921 Ht. 5-11 Wt. 170 College—Huntington

1947-48	Anderson	(NL)	57	84	31	199	3.5
1948-49	Anderson	(NL)	64	218	85	521	8.1
1949-50	And.-Ft. W.		67	243	104	590	8.8
1950-51	Ft. Wayne		68	235	114	584	8.6
1951-52	Ft. Wayne		66	211	101	523	7.9
1952-53	Ft. Wayne		3	3	2	8	2.7
	Totals		325	994	437	2425	7.5

JOHNSON, RICH
b. Dec. 18, 1946 Ht. 6-9 Wt. 210 College—Grambling

1968-69	Boston		31	29	11	69	2.2
1969-70	Boston		65	167	46	380	5.8
1970-71	Boston		1	4	0	8	8.0
	Totals		97	200	57	457	4.7

JOHNSON, RONALD
b. July 20, 1938 Ht. 6-8 Wt. 215 College—Minnesota

1960-61	Detroit-L.A.		14	13	11	37	2.6

JOHNSON, STEWART
b. Aug. 19, 1944 Ht. 6-9 Wt. 225 College—Murray State

1967-68	Kent.-N.J.	(ABA)	72	255(25)	69	604	8.4
1968-69	N.Y.-Hous.	(ABA)	78	616(64)	199	1495	19.2

Yr.	Team		G	FG	FT	TP	Avg.
1969-70	Pittsburgh	(ABA)	81	544(15)	137	1240	15.3
1970-71	Pittsburgh	(ABA)	84	593(12)	144	1342	15.9
1971-72	Pitt.-Car.	(ABA)	67	368(16)	73	825	12.3
1972-73	San Diego	(ABA)	80	769(37)	195	1770	22.1
1973-74	San Diego	(ABA)	84	716(59)	199	1690	20.1
1974-75	S.D.-Mem.	(ABA)	81	664(40)	63	1431	17.7
1975-76	S.D.-S.A.	(ABA)	20	61(1)	18	141	7.1
	Totals		647	4586(269)	1097	10538	16.3

JOHNSTON, NEIL
b. Feb. 4, 1929 Ht. 6-8 Wt. 215 College—Ohio State

1951-52	Philadelphia		64	141	100	382	6.0
1952-53	Philadelphia		70	504	556	1564	22.3
1953-54	Philadelphia		72	591	577	1759	24.4
1954-55	Philadelphia		72	521	589	1631	22.7
1955-56	Philadelphia		70	499	549	1547	22.1
1956-57	Philadelphia		69	520	535	1575	22.8
1957-58	Philadelphia		71	473	442	1388	19.5
1958-59	Philadelphia		28	54	69	177	6.3
	Totals		516	3303	3417	10023	19.4

JOLLIFF, HOWARD
b. July 20, 1938 Ht. 6-7 Wt. 218 College—Ohio Univ.

1970-61	Los Angeles		46	46	11	103	2.2
1961-62	Los Angeles		64	104	41	249	3.9
1962-63	Los Angeles		28	15	6	36	1.3
	Totals		138	165	58	388	2.8

JONES, JAKE
b. May 9, 1949 Ht. 6-3 Wt. 180 College—Assumption

1971-72	Philadelphia		17	28	20	76	4.5

JONES, JAMES
b. Jan. 1, 1945 Ht. 6-4 Wt. 188 College—Grambling

1967-68	New Orleans	(ABA)	78	551(2)	360	1464	18.8
1968-69	New Orleans	(ABA)	77	764(1)	521	2050	26.6
1969-70	New Orleans	(ABA)	70	533(2)	380	1448	20.7
1970-71	Memphis	(ABA)	80	593(4)	374	1564	19.5
1971-72	Utah	(ABA)	78	462(2)	282	1207	15.5
1972-73	Utah	(ABA)	80	496	345	1337	16.7
1973-74	Utah	(ABA)	83	583	229	1395	16.8
1974-75	Washington		73	237	103	577	7.1
1975-76	Washington		64	153	72	378	5.9
1976-77	Washington		3	2	2	6	2.0
	Totals		686	4374(10)	2668	11426	16.7

JONES, J. COLLIS
b. July 3, 1949 Ht. 6-7 Wt. 205 College—Notre Dame

1971-72	Dallas	(ABA)	78	163(1)	98	425	5.5
1972-73	Dallas	(ABA)	81	357	227	941	11.6
1973-74	Kentucky	(ABA)	58	102	51	255	4.4
1974-75	Memphis	(ABA)	81	333(5)	134	805	9.9
1975-76	Ken.-St. L.	(ABA)	76	423	140	986	13.0
	Totals		374	1378(6)	650	3412	9.1

JONES, JOHN
b. March 12, 1943 Ht. 6-7½ Wt. 205 College—L.A. St.

1967-68	Boston		51	86	42	214	4.2
1968-69	Kentucky	(ABA)	29	81	41	203	7.0
	Totals		80	167	83	417	5.2

Yr.	Team	G	FG	FT	TP	Avg.

JONES, K. C.
b. May 25, 1932 Ht. 6-1 Wt. 202 College—San Francisco

Yr.	Team	G	FG	FT	TP	Avg.
1958-59	Boston	49	65	41	171	3.5
1959-60	Boston	74	169	128	466	6.3
1960-61	Boston	78	203	186	592	7.6
1961-62	Boston	79	289	145	723	9.1
1962-63	Boston	79	230	112	572	7.2
1963-64	Boston	80	283	88	654	8.2
1964-65	Boston	78	253	143	649	8.3
1965-66	Boston	80	240	209	689	8.6
1966-67	Boston	78	182	119	483	6.2
	Totals	675	1914	1171	4999	7.4

JONES, RICH WESLEY
b. Dec. 27, 1946 Ht. 6-8 Wt. 230 Coll.—Illinois and Memphis St.

Yr.	Team		G	FG	FT	TP	Avg.
1969-70	Dallas	(ABA)	2	9	10	28	14.0
1970-71	Texas	(ABA)	79	371(33)	175	950	12.0
1971-72	Dallas	(ABA)	82	475(14)	212	1176	14.3
1972-73	Dallas	(ABA)	67	564(43)	324	1495	22.3
1973-74	San Antonio	(ABA)	78	410(13)	180	1219	15.6
1974-75	San Antonio	(ABA)	83	649(13)	287	1598	19.3
1975-76	New York	(ABA)	83	441(15)	199	1096	13.2
1976-77	N.Y. Net		34	134	92	360	10.6
	Totals		508	3153(131)	1485	7922	15.6

JONES, ROBIN (Major)
b. Feb. 2, 1954 Ht. 6-9 Wt. 215 College—Albany St. (Ga.)

Yr.	Team	G	FG	FT	TP	Avg.
1976-77	Portland	63	139	66	344	5.5
1977-78	Houston	12	11	4	26	2.2
	Totals	75	150	70	370	4.9

JONES, RYAN (Nick)
b. March 28, 1945 Ht. 6-2 Wt. 191 College—Oregon

Yr.	Team		G	FG	FT	TP	Avg.
1967-68	San Diego		42	86	55	227	5.4
1968-69	Dallas-Miami	(ABA)	7	9	2	20	2.9
1970-71	San Francisco		81	225	111	561	6.9
1971-72	Golden State		65	82	51	215	3.3
1972-73	Dallas	(ABA)	3	3	2	8	2.7
	Totals		198	405	221	1031	5.2

JONES, SAM
b. June 24, 1933 Ht. 6-4 Wt. 205 College—N. Car. Col.

Yr.	Team	G	FG	FT	TP	Avg.
1957-58	Boston	56	100	60	260	4.6
1958-59	Boston	71	305	151	761	10.7
1959-60	Boston	74	355	168	878	11.9
1960-61	Boston	78	474	210	1158	14.8
1961-62	Boston	78	589	239	1417	18.2
1962-63	Boston	76	621	257	1499	19.7
1963-64	Boston	76	612	249	1473	19.4
1964-65	Boston	80	821	428	2070	25.9
1965-66	Boston	68	626	325	1577	23.2
1966-67	Boston	72	638	318	1594	22.1
1967-68	Boston	73	621	311	1553	21.3
1968-69	Boston	70	496	148	1140	16.3
	Totals	872	6258	2864	15380	17.6

JONES, STEVE
b. Oct. 17, 1942 Ht. 6-5 Wt. 205 College—Oregon

Yr.	Team		G	FG	FT	TP	Avg.
1967-68	Oakland	(ABA)	76	278(23)	186	765	10.1
1968-69	New Orleans	(ABA)	78	576(52)	348	1552	19.9
1969-70	New Orleans	(ABA)	84	689(15)	412	1805	21.5

Yr.	Team		G	FG	FT	TP	Avg.
1970-71	Memphis	(ABA)	83	732(40)	332	1836	22.1
1971-72	Dallas	(ABA)	84	572(26)	367	1537	18.3
1972-73	Dal.-Car.	(ABA)	80	430(13)	200	1073	13.4
1973-74	Car.-Den.	(ABA)	86	400(13)	128	941	10.9
1974-75	St. Louis	(ABA)	69	287(4)	171	749	10.9
1975-76	Portland		64	168	78	414	6.5
	Totals		704	4132(186)	2222	10672	15.2

JONES, WALI
b. Feb. 14, 1942 Ht. 6-2 Wt. 180 College—Villanova

Yr.	Team		G	FG	FT	TP	Avg.
1964-65	Baltimore		77	154	99	407	5.3
1965-66	Philadelphia		80	296	128	720	9.0
1966-67	Philadelphia		81	423	223	1069	13.2
1967-68	Philadelphia		77	413	159	985	12.8
1968-69	Philadelphia		81	432	207	1071	13.2
1969-70	Philadelphia		78	366	190	922	11.8
1970-71	Philadelphia		41	168	79	415	10.1
1971-72	Milwaukee		48	144	74	362	7.5
1972-73	Milwaukee		27	59	16	134	5.0
1974-75	Utah	(ABA)	71	212(6)	102	532	7.5
1975-76	Det.-Phil.		17	23	9	55	3.2
	Totals		678	2690(6)	1286	6672	9.8

JONES, WALLACE (Wah Wah)
b. July 14, 1926 Ht. 6-4 Wt. 225 College—Kentucky

Yr.	Team	G	FG	FT	TP	Avg.
1949-50	Indianapolis	60	264	223	751	12.5
1950-51	Indianapolis	22	93	61	247	11.2
1951-52	Indianapolis	58	164	102	430	7.4
	Totals	140	521	386	1428	10.2

JONES, WALTER (Larry)
b. Sept. 22, 1941 Ht. 6-2½ Wt. 180 College—Toledo

Yr.	Team		G	FG	FT	TP	Avg.
1964-65	Philadelphia		23	47	37	131	5.7
1967-68	Denver	(ABA)	76	602(8)	530	1742	22.9
1968-69	Denver	(ABA)	75	759(24)	591	2133	28.4
1969-70	Denver	(ABA)	75	625(41)	579	1870	24.9
1970-71	Floridians	(ABA)	84	764(45)	471	2044	24.3
1971-72	Floridians	(ABA)	66	423(18)	300	1164	17.6
1972-73	Utah-Dal.	(ABA)	80	240(16)	202	698	8.7
1973-74	Philadelphia		72	263	197	723	10.0
	Totals		551	3723(152)	2710	9782	20.4

JONES, WILBERT
b. Feb. 27, 1947 Ht. 6-8 Wt. 205 College—Albany St. (Ga.)

Yr.	Team		G	FG	FT	TP	Avg.
1969-70	Miami	(ABA)	74	243(2)	118	606	8.2
1970-71	Memphis	(ABA)	84	391(1)	174	957	11.4
1971-72	Memphis	(ABA)	84	506(2)	240	1254	14.9
1972-73	Memphis	(ABA)	76	344(1)	146	835	11.0
1973-74	Memphis	(ABA)	81	453(3)	163	1072	13.2
1974-75	Kentucky	(ABA)	84	458	139	1055	12.6
1975-76	Kentucky	(ABA)	83	483(3)	158	1127	13.6
1976-77	Indiana		80	438	166	1042	13.0
1977-78	Buffalo		79	226	84	536	6.8
	Totals		725	3542(12)	1388	8484	11.7

JONES, WILLIE (The Bird)
b. June 29, 1936 Ht. 6-3½ Wt. 185 College—Northwestern

Yr.	Team	G	FG	FT	TP	Avg.
1960-61	Detroit	35	78	40	196	5.6
1961-62	Detroit	69	177	64	418	6.0
1962-63	Detroit	79	305	118	728	9.2
1963-64	Detroit	77	265	100	630	8.2
1964-65	Detroit	12	21	2	44	3.7
	Totals	272	846	324	2016	7.4

Yr.	Team	G	FG	FT	TP	Avg.

JORDAN, CHARLES
b. Jan. 31, 1954 Ht. 6-8 Wt. 220 College—Canisius

Yr.	Team		G	FG	FT	TP	Avg.
1975-76 Indiana	(ABA)		71	162(2)	43	369	5.2

JORDON, PHIL
b. Sept. 12, 1933 Ht. 6-10 Wt. 205 College—Whitworth
d. June 7, 1965

Yr.	Team	G	FG	FT	TP	Avg.
1956-57	New York	9	18	8	44	4.9
1957-58	Detroit	58	193	64	450	7.8
1958-59	Detroit	72	399	231	1029	14.3
1959-60	Cincinnati	75	381	242	1004	13.4
1960-61	Cin.-N.Y.	79	360	208	928	11.7
1961-62	New York	76	403	96	902	11.9
1962-63	St. Louis	73	211	56	478	6.5
	Totals	442	1965	905	4835	10.9

JORGENSEN, JOHN
b. Dec. 28, 1921 Ht. 6-2 Wt. 185 College—DePaul
d. Jan. 19, 1973

Yr.	Team		G	FG	FT	TP	Avg.
1947-48 Chicago-Balt.			3	4	1	9	3.0
1947-48 Minneapolis	(NL)		38	37	27	101	2.7
1948-49 Minneapolis			48	41	24	106	2.2
	Totals		89	82	52	216	2.4

JORGENSEN, NOBLE (Jorgy)
b. May 18, 1925 Ht. 6-9 Wt. 230 College—Iowa/Westminster

Yr.	Team		G	FG	FT	TP	Avg.
1946-47 Pittsburgh			15	25	16	66	4.4
1948-49 Sheboygan	(NL)		63	218	194	630	10.0
1949-50 Sheboygan			54	218	268	704	13.0
1950-51 Tri-Cities-Syr.			63	223	182	628	10.0
1951-52 Syracuse			66	190	149	529	8.0
1952-53 Syracuse			70	145	146	436	6.2
	Totals		331	1019	955	2993	9.0

JORGENSEN, ROGER
b. Sept. 2, 1920 Ht. 6-5 Wt. 200 College—Ohio State

Yr.	Team	G	FG	FT	TP	Avg.
1946-47 Pittsburgh	28	14	13	41	1.5

JOYCE, KEVIN
b. June 27, 1951 Ht. 6-3 Wt. 190 College—South Carolina

Yr.	Team		G	FG	FT	TP	Avg.
1973-74 Indiana	(ABA)		56	171(5)	64	411	7.3
1974-75 Indiana	(ABA)		81	530(8)	142	1210	14.9
1975-76 S.D.-Ken.	(ABA)		43	114(2)	55	285	6.6
	Totals		180	815(15)	261	1906	10.6

JOYNER, HARRY (Butch)
b. Apr. 26, 1945 Ht. 6-5 Wt. 200 College—Indiana

Yr.	Team		G	FG	FT	TP	Avg.
1968-69 Indiana	(ABA)		2	0	0	0	0.0

KACHAN, ED
b. Sept. 15, 1925 Ht. 6-2 Wt. 175 College—DePaul

Yr.	Team	G	FG	FT	TP	Avg.
1948-49 Chi.-Minn.	52	38	36	112	2.2

KAFTAN, GEORGE
b. Feb. 22, 1928 Ht. 6-3 Wt. 190 College—Holy Cross

Yr.	Team	G	FG	FT	TP	Avg.
1948-49 Boston	21	116	72	304	14.5
1949-50 Boston	55	199	136	534	9.7
1950-51 New York	61	111	78	300	4.9
1951-52 New York	52	115	92	322	6.2
1952-53 Baltimore	23	45	44	134	5.8
Totals	212	586	422	1594	7.5

KALAFAT, ED
b. Oct. 13, 1932 Ht. 6-6 Wt. 245 College—Minnesota

Yr.	Team	G	FG	FT	TP	Avg.
1954-55 Minneapolis	72	118	111	347	4.8
1955-56 Minneapolis	72	194	186	574	8.0
1956-57 Minneapolis	65	178	197	553	8.5
Totals	209	490	494	1474	7.1

KAPLOWITZ, RALPH (Kappy)
b. May 18, 1919 Ht. 6-2 Wt. 170 College—N.Y.U.

Yr.	Team	G	FG	FT	TP	Avg.
1946-47 N.Y.-Phila.	57	146	111	403	7.1
1947-48 Philadelphia	48	71	47	189	3.9
Totals	105	217	158	592	5.6

KAPPEN, ANTHONY
b. April 13, 1919 Ht. 5-10 Wt. 165

Yr.	Team	G	FG	FT	TP	Avg.
1946-47 Pitt.-Boston	59	128	128	384	6.5

KARL, GEORGE
b. May 12, 1951 Ht. 6-2 Wt. 185 College—No. Carolina

Yr.	Team		G	FG	FT	TP	Avg.
1973-74 San Antonio	(ABA)		74	236(8)	94	574	7.7
1974-75 San Antonio	(ABA)		82	261(4)	137	663	8.1
1975-76 San Antonio	(ABA)		75	150	81	381	5.1
1976-77 San Antonio			29	25	29	79	2.7
1977-78 San Antonio			4	2	2	6	1.5
	Totals		264	475(12)	343	1703	6.5

KASID, EDWARD
b. Aug. 13, 1923 Ht. 5-11 Wt. 185

Yr.	Team	G	FG	FT	TP	Avg.
1946-47 Toronto	8	6	0	12	1.5

KATKAVECK, LEO
b. April 17, 1923 Ht. 6-0 Wt. 185 College—No. Carolina St.

Yr.	Team	G	FG	FT	TP	Avg.
1948-49 Washington	53	84	53	221	4.2
1949-50 Balt.-Wash.	54	101	34	236	4.4
Totals	107	185	87	457	4.3

KAUFFMAN, BOB
b. July 13, 1946 Ht. 6-8 Wt. 240 College—Guilford

Yr.	Team	G	FG	FT	TP	Avg.
1968-69 Seattle	82	219	203	641	7.8
1969-70 Chicago	64	94	88	276	4.3
1970-71 Buffalo	78	616	359	1591	20.4
1971-72 Buffalo	77	558	341	1457	18.9
1972-73 Buffalo	77	535	280	1350	17.5
1973-74 Buffalo	74	171	107	449	6.1
1974-75 Atlanta	73	113	59	285	3.9
Totals	525	2306	1437	6049	11.5

KAUTZ, WILBERT (Wibs)
b. Sept. 7, 1915 Ht. 6-0 Wt. 180 College—Loyola (Ill.)

Yr.	Team		G	FG	FT	TP	Avg.
1939-40 Chicago	(NL)		28	105	63	273	9.8
1940-41 Chicago	(NL)		21	94	39	227	10.8
1941-42 Chicago	(NL)		20	85	40	210	10.5
1946-47 Chicago			50	107	39	253	5.1
	Totals		119	391	181	963	8.1

KEARNS, MICHAEL
Ht. 6-2 Wt. 178 College—Princeton

Yr.	Team	G	FG	FT	TP	Avg.
1954-55 Philadelphia	6	0	1	1	0.2

Yr.	Team		G	FG	FT	TP	Avg.

KEARNS, THOMAS
b. Oct. 6, 1936 Ht. 5-11 Wt. 185 College—North Carolina

Yr.	Team		G	FG	FT	TP	Avg.
1958-59	Syracuse		1	1	0	2	2.0

KELLER, BILL
b. Aug. 30, 1947 Ht. 5-10 Wt. 180 College—Purdue

1969-70	Indiana	(ABA)	82	252(42)	164	710	8.7
1970-71	Indiana	(ABA)	83	417(84)	267	1185	14.3
1971-72	Indiana	(ABA)	76	264(56)	153	737	9.7
1972-73	Indiana	(ABA)	83	421(71)	234	1147	13.8
1973-74	Indiana	(ABA)	75	279(50)	107	715	9.5
1974-75	Indiana	(ABA)	79	397(80)	113	987	12.5
1975-76	Indiana	(ABA)	78	410(123)	164	1107	14.2
	Totals		556	2440(506)	1202	6588	11.8

KELLER, GARY
b. June 13, 1944 Ht. 6-9 Wt. 220 College—Florida

1967-68	Minnesota	(ABA)	69	184	139	507	7.4
1968-69	Miami	(ABA)	53	78	72	228	4.3
	Totals		122	262	211	735	6.0

KELLER, KENNETH
b. 1922 Ht. 6-1 Wt. 180 College—St. John's (N.Y.)

1946-47	Wash.-Prov.		28	10	2	22	0.8

KELLEY, GERARD (Jerry)
b. 1922 Ht. 6-2 Wt. 172 College—Marshall

1946-47	Boston		43	91	74	256	6.0
1947-48	Providence		3	3	0	6	2.0
	Totals		46	94	74	262	5.7

KELLY, ARVESTA
b. Nov. 20, 1945 Ht. 6-3 Wt. 175 College—Lincoln (Mo.)

1967-68	Pittsburgh	(ABA)	16	26(3)	8	63	3.9
1968-69	Minnesota	(ABA)	68	155(25)	63	398	5.9
1969-70	Pittsburgh	(ABA)	70	384(21)	168	957	13.6
1970-71	Car.-Pitt.	(ABA)	22	20	18	58	2.6
1971-72	Pitt.-Ind.	(ABA)	12	13(1)	3	30	2.5
	Totals		188	598(50)	260	1506	8.0

KELLY, TOM
b. March 5, 1924 Ht. 6-2 Wt. 172 College—N.Y.U.

1948-49	Boston		27	73	45	191	7.1

KELSO, BEN
b. April 11, 1949 Ht. 6-3 Wt. 195 College—Cen. Michigan

1973-74	Detroit		46	35	15	85	1.8

KENDRICK, FRANK
b. Nov. 11, 1951 Ht. 6-6 Wt. 198 College—Purdue

1974-75	Golden State		24	31	18	80	3.3

KENNEDY, EUGENE (Goo)
b. Aug. 23, 1949 Ht. 6-6 Wt. 205 College—Texas Christian

1971-72	Dallas	(ABA)	65	234	88	556	8.6
1972-73	Dallas	(ABA)	70	365	148	878	12.5
1973-74	San Antonio	(ABA)	76	194	60	448	5.9
1974-75	St. Louis	(ABA)	74	281(1)	129	692	9.4
1975-76	Utah	(ABA)	16	38	9	85	5.9
1976-77	Houston		32	31	3	65	2.0
	Totals		333	1143(1)	437	2724	8.2

KENNEDY, JOE
b. Jan. 12, 1947 Ht. 6-6 Wt. 210 College—Duke

1968-69	Seattle		72	174	98	446	6.2
1969-70	Seattle		14	3	2	8	0.6
	Totals		86	177	100	454	5.3

KENNEDY, WILLIAM (Pickles)
b. May 17, 1938 Ht. 5-11 Wt. 180 College—Temple

1960-61	Philadelphia		7	4	4	12	1.7

KENVILLE, BILL (The Kid)
b. Dec. 1, 1930 Ht. 6-2 Wt. 190 College—St. Bonaventure

1953-54	Syracuse		72	149	136	434	6.0
1954-55	Syracuse		70	172	154	498	7.1
1955-56	Syracuse		72	170	195	535	7.4
1956-57	Ft. Wayne		71	204	174	582	8.2
1957-58	Detroit		35	106	46	248	7.4
1959-60	Detroit		25	47	33	127	5.1
	Totals		345	848	738	2434	7.1

KERR, JOHN (Red)
b. Aug. 17, 1932 Ht. 6-9 Wt. 230 College—Illinois

1954-55	Syracuse		72	301	152	754	10.5
1955-56	Syracuse		72	377	207	961	13.3
1956-57	Syracuse		72	333	225	891	12.4
1957-58	Syracuse		72	407	280	1094	15.2
1958-59	Syracuse		72	502	281	1285	17.8
1959-60	Syracuse		75	436	233	1105	14.7
1960-61	Syracuse		79	419	218	1056	13.4
1961-62	Syracuse		80	541	222	1304	16.3
1962-63	Syracuse		80	507	241	1255	15.7
1963-64	Philadelphia		80	536	268	1340	16.8
1964-65	Philadelphia		80	264	126	654	8.2
1965-66	Baltimore		71	286	209	781	11.0
	Totals		905	4909	2662	12480	13.8

KERRIS, JACK
b. Jan. 30, 1925 Ht. 6-6 Wt. 215 College—Loyola (Ill.)

1949-50	Tri. C.-Ft. W.		68	157	169	483	7.1
1950-51	Ft. Wayne		68	255	201	711	10.5
1951-52	Ft. Wayne		66	186	217	589	8.9
1952-53	Ft. W.-Balt.		69	93	88	274	4.0
	Totals		271	691	675	2057	7.6

KERWIN, TOM
Ht. 6-7 Wt. 210 College—Centenary

1967-68	Pittsburgh	(ABA)	13	7	0	14	1.1

KEYE, JULIUS
b. July 5, 1946 Ht. 6-10 Wt. 225 College—Alcorn A & M

1969-70	Denver	(ABA)	77	245	116	606	7.9
1970-71	Denver	(ABA)	83	505	212	1222	14.7
1971-72	Denver	(ABA)	84	192	108	492	5.9
1972-73	Denver	(ABA)	83	163(3)	130	459	5.5
1973-74	Denver	(ABA)	79	147(1)	57	352	4.5
1974-75	Memphis	(ABA)	12	12	36	30	2.5
	Totals		418	1264(4)	629	3161	7.6

KIFFIN, IRV
b. Aug. 8, 1951 Ht. 6-9 Wt. 225 Coll.—Va. Union/Oklahoma Baptist

1979-80	San Antonio		26	32	18	82	3.2

Yr.	Team	G	FG	FT	TP	Avg.

KILEY, JACK
b. 1930 Ht. 6-1 Wt. 170 College—Syracuse

Yr.	Team	G	FG	FT	TP	Avg.
1951-52	Ft. Wayne	47	44	30	118	2.5
1952-53	Ft. Wayne	6	2	2	6	1.0
	Totals	53	46	32	124	2.3

KILLUM, EARNEST
b. June 11, 1948 Ht. 6-3 Wt. 180 College—Stetson

Yr.	Team	G	FG	FT	TP	Avg.
1970-71	Los Angeles	4	0	1	1	0.3

KILPATRICK, CARL
b. May 16, 1956 Ht. 6-10 Wt. 230 College—N.E. Louisiana

Yr.	Team	G	FG	FT	TP	Avg.
1979-80	Utah	2	1	1	3	1.5

KIMBALL, THOMAS (Toby)
b. Sept. 23, 1942 Ht. 6-8 Wt. 220 College—Connecticut

Yr.	Team	G	FG	FT	TP	Avg.
1966-67	Boston	38	35	27	97	2.6
1967-68	San Diego	81	354	181	889	11.0
1968-69	San Diego	76	239	117	595	7.8
1969-70	San Diego	77	218	107	543	7.1
1970-71	San Diego	80	111	51	273	3.4
1971-72	Milwaukee	74	107	44	258	3.4
	Totals	426	1064	527	2655	6.2

KING, DANIEL
b. Jan. 7, 1931 Ht. 6-6 Wt. 220 College—W. Kentucky

Yr.	Team	G	FG	FT	TP	Avg.
1954-55	Baltimore	12	7	5	19	1.6

KING, GEORGE
b. Aug. 16, 1928 Ht. 6-0 Wt. 185 College—Morris Harvey

Yr.	Team	G	FG	FT	TP	Avg.
1951-52	Syracuse	66	235	188	658	10.0
1952-53	Syracuse	71	255	284	794	11.2
1953-54	Syracuse	72	280	257	817	11.3
1954-55	Syracuse	67	228	140	596	8.9
1955-56	Syracuse	72	284	176	744	10.3
1957-58	Cincinnati	63	235	140	610	9.7
	Totals	411	1517	1185	4219	10.3

KING, JAMES (Country)
b. Feb. 7, 1941 Ht. 6-2 Wt. 175 College—Tulsa

Yr.	Team	G	FG	FT	TP	Avg.
1963-64	Los Angeles	60	84	66	234	3.9
1964-65	Los Angeles	77	184	118	486	6.3
1965-66	Los Angeles	76	238	94	570	7.5
1966-67	San Francisco	67	286	174	746	11.1
1967-68	San Francisco	54	340	217	897	16.6
1968-69	San Francisco	46	137	78	352	7.7
1969-70	S.F.-Cin.	34	53	33	139	4.1
1970-71	Chicago	55	100	64	264	4.8
1971-72	Chicago	73	162	89	413	5.7
	Totals	542	1584	933	4101	7.6

KING, LOYD
b. May 29, 1949 Ht. 6-2 Wt. 180 College—Virginia Tech

Yr.	Team		G	FG	FT	TP	Avg.
1971-72	Memphis	(ABA)	74	185(21)	96	487	6.6
1972-73	Memphis	(ABA)	10	6	7	19	1.9
	Totals		84	191(21)	103	506	6.0

KING, MAURICE (Maury)
b. March 12, 1935 Ht. 6-3 Wt. 195 College—Kansas

Yr.	Team	G	FG	FT	TP	Avg.
1959-60	Boston	1	5	0	10	10.0
1962-63	Chicago	37	94	28	216	5.8
	Totals	38	99	28	226	5.9

KING, RON
b. 1951 Ht. 6-4 Wt. 195 College—Florida State

Yr.	Team		G	FG	FT	TP	Avg.
1973-74	Kentucky	(ABA)	9	24(2)	14	64	7.1

KING, THOMAS
b. Jan. 23, 1926 Ht. 6-1 Wt. 165 College—Michigan

Yr.	Team	G	FG	FT	TP	Avg.
1946-47	Detroit	58	97	101	295	5.1

KINNEY, ROBERT (Hi-Pocket)
b. Sept. 16, 1920 Ht. 6-6½ Wt. 215 College—Rice

Yr.	Team		G	FG	FT	TP	Avg.
1945-46	Fort Wayne	(NL)	13	16	2	34	2.6
1946-47	Fort Wayne	(NL)	44	102	42	246	5.6
1947-48	Fort Wayne	(NL)	58	149	92	390	6.7
1948-49	Ft. W.-Boston		58	161	136	458	7.9
1949-50	Boston		60	233	201	667	11.1
	Totals		233	661	473	1795	7.7

KIRK, WALTON (Junior)
b. Sept. 3, 1924 Ht. 6-3 Wt. 173 College—Illinois

Yr.	Team		G	FG	FT	TP	Avg.
1947-48	Fort Wayne	(NL)	45	62	44	168	3.7
1948-49	Ft. W.-Ind.		49	140	167	447	9.1
1949-50	And.-Tri-C.		58	97	155	349	6.0
1951-52	Milwaukee		11	28	55	111	10.1
	Totals		163	327	421	1075	6.6

KIRKLAND, WILBUR
Ht. 6-7 Wt. 191 College—Cheyney State

Yr.	Team		G	FG	FT	TP	Avg.
1969-70	Pittsburgh	(ABA)	2	3	0	6	3.0

KISSANE, JIM
b. Aug. 17, 1946 Ht. 6-7 Wt. 210 College—Boston Coll.

Yr.	Team		G	FG	FT	TP	Avg.
1968-69	Minnesota	(ABA)	2	2	2	6	3.0

KISTLER, DOUGLAS
b. March 21, 1938 Ht. 6-9 Wt. 210 College—Duke
d. Feb. 29, 1980

Yr.	Team	G	FG	FT	TP	Avg.
1961-62	New York	5	3	2	8	1.6

KLIER, LEO (Crystal)
b. May 21, 1923 Ht. 6-2 Wt. 170 College—Notre Dame

Yr.	Team		G	FG	FT	TP	Avg.
1946-47	Indianapolis	(NL)	44	162	93	417	9.5
1947-48	Indianapolis	(NL)	56	227	152	606	10.8
1948-49	Ft. Wayne		47	125	97	347	7.4
1949-50	Ft. Wayne		66	157	141	455	6.9
	Totals		213	671	483	1825	8.6

KLOTZ, LOUIS HERMAN (Red)
b. Oct. 21, 1921 Ht. 5-7 Wt. 150 College—Villanova

Yr.	Team	G	FG	FT	TP	Avg.
1947-48	Baltimore	11	7	1	15	1.4

KLUEH, DUANE
b. Jan. 6, 1926 Ht. 6-3 Wt. 175 College—Indiana State

Yr.	Team	G	FG	FT	TP	Avg.
1949-50	Den.-Ft. W.	52	159	157	475	9.1
1950-51	Ft. Wayne	61	157	135	449	7.4
	Totals	113	316	292	924	8.2

KLUTTZ, LONNIE
b. Sept. 13, 1945 Ht. 6-7 Wt. 220 College—N. Car. A & T

Yr.	Team		G	FG	FT	TP	Avg.
1970-71	Carolina	(ABA)	3	0	0	0	0.0

Yr.	Team		G	FG	FT	TP	Avg.
KNIGHT, BOB							
b. 1931 Ht. 6-2 Wt. 185							
1954-55	New York		2	3	1	7	3.5
KNIGHT, RON							
b. Aug. 4, 1947 Ht. 6-7 Wt. 220 College—Los Angeles St.							
1970-71	Portland		52	99	19	217	4.2
1971-72	Portland		49	112	31	255	5.2
	Totals		101	211	50	472	4.7
KNOREK, LEONARD (Lee)							
b. July 15, 1921 Ht. 6-7 Wt. 215 College—Denison and Detroit							
1946-47	New York		22	62	47	171	7.8
1947-48	New York		48	99	61	259	5.4
1948-49	New York		60	156	131	443	7.4
1949-50	Baltimore		1	0	0	0	0.0
	Totals		131	317	239	873	6.7
KNOSTMAN, RICHARD							
b. Aug. 9, 1931 Ht. 6-6 Wt. 215 College—Kansas State							
1953-54	Syracuse		5	3	7	13	2.6
KNOWLES, RODNEY							
b. Feb. 27, 1946 Ht. 6-9 Wt. 215 College—Davidson							
1968-69	Phoenix		8	4	1	9	1.1
1968-69	New York	(ABA)	1	0	0	0	0.0
	Totals		9	4	1	9	1.0
KOJIS, DON							
b. Jan. 15, 1939 Ht. 6-3 Wt. 215 College—Marquette							
1963-64	Baltimore		78	203	82	488	6.3
1964-65	Detroit		65	180	62	422	6.5
1965-66	Detroit		60	182	76	440	7.3
1966-67	Chicago		78	329	134	792	10.2
1967-68	San Diego		69	530	300	1360	19.7
1968-69	San Diego		81	687	446	1820	22.5
1969-70	San Diego		56	338	181	857	15.3
1970-71	Seattle		79	454	249	1157	14.6
1971-72	Seattle		81	322	188	832	11.4
1972-73	K.C.-Omaha		77	276	106	658	8.5
1973-74	K.C.-Omaha		77	400	210	1010	13.1
1974-75	Kansas City		77	46	20	112	5.3
	Totals		814	3947	2054	9948	12.2
KOMENICH, MILO (Miles)							
b. June 23, 1920 Ht. 6-7 Wt. 220 College—Wyoming							
1946-47	Fort Wayne	(NL)	36	50	23	123	3.4
1947-48	Ft. W.-And.	(NL)	50	127	44	298	6.0
1948-49	Anderson	(NL)	64	243	124	610	9.5
1949-50	Anderson		64	244	146	634	9.9
	Totals		214	664	337	1665	7.8
KOMIVES, HOWARD (Butch)							
b. May 9, 1941 Ht. 6-1 Wt. 185 College—Bowling Green							
1964-65	New York		80	381	212	974	12.2
1965-66	New York		80	436	241	1113	13.9
1966-67	New York		65	402	217	1021	15.7
1967-68	New York		78	233	132	598	7.7
1968-69	N.Y.-Det.		85	379	211	969	11.4
1969-70	Detroit		82	363	190	916	11.2

Yr.	Team		G	FG	FT	TP	Avg.
1970-71	Detroit		82	275	121	671	8.2
1971-72	Detroit		79	262	164	688	8.7
1972-73	Buffalo		67	163	85	411	6.1
1973-74	K.C.-Omaha		44	78	33	189	4.3
	Totals		742	2972	1606	7550	10.2
KONDLA, TOM							
b. Nov. 30, 1946 Ht. 6-8 Wt. 225 College—Minnesota							
1968-69	Minn.-Hou.	(ABA)	42	58	22	138	3.3
KOPER, HERBERT (Bud)							
b. Aug. 9, 1942 Ht. 6-6 Wt. 210 College—Oklahoma City							
1964-65	San Francisco		56	106	35	247	4.4
KOSKI, TONY							
Ht. 6-8½ Wt. 215 College—Providence							
1968-69	New York	(ABA)	5	2	2	6	1.2
KOSMALSKI, LEN							
b. Nov. 29, 1951 Ht. 7-0 Wt. 245 College—Tennessee							
1974-75	K.C.-O.		67	33	24	90	1.3
1975-76	Kansas City		9	8	4	20	2.2
	Totals		76	41	28	110	1.4
KOSTECKA, ANDY							
b. Feb. 10, 1921 Ht. 6-3 Wt. 203 College—Georgetown							
1948-49	Indianapolis		21	46	43	135	6.4
KOTTMAN, HAROLD							
b. Aug. 22, 1922 Ht. 6-8 Wt. 220 College—Cal. Stockton							
1946-47	Boston		53	59	47	165	3.1
KOZELKO, TOM							
b. July 1, 1951 Ht. 6-8 Wt. 220 College—Toledo							
1973-74	Capital		49	59	23	141	2.9
1974-75	Washington		73	60	31	151	2.1
1975-76	Washington		67	48	19	115	1.7
	Totals		189	167	73	407	2.2
KOZLICKI, RON							
b. Dec. 12, 1944 Ht. 6-7 Wt. 215 College—Northwestern							
1967-68	Indiana	(ABA)	37	41(6)	21	109	2.9
KRAMER, ARVID							
b. Oct. 2, 1956 Ht. 6-9 Wt. 220 College—Augustana							
1979-80	Denver		8	7	2	16	2.0
KRAMER, BARRY							
b. Nov. 10, 1942 Ht. 6-4 Wt. 200 College—N.Y.U.							
1964-65	SF.-N.Y.		52	63	60	186	3.6
1969-70	New York	(ABA)	7	10	7	27	3.9
	Totals		59	73	67	213	3.6
KRAMER, STEVE							
Ht. 6-5 Wt. 200 College—Brigham Young							
1967-68	Anaheim	(ABA)	50	218(1)	129	566	11.3
1968-69	Houston	(ABA)	23	113	95	321	14.0
1969-70	Carolina	(ABA)	51	49	63	161	3.3
	Totals		124	380(1)	287	1048	8.5

Yr.	Team	G	FG	FT	TP	Avg.

KRAUS, DANIEL
b. 1923 Ht. 6-0 Wt. 195 College—Georgetown

Yr.	Team	G	FG	FT	TP	Avg.
1948-49	Baltimore	13	5	11	21	1.6

KRAUTBLATT, HERB
b. Nov. 19, 1926 Ht. 6-1 Wt. 190 College—Rider

1948-49	Baltimore	10	4	5	13	1.3

KREBS, JAMES
b. Sept. 8, 1935 Ht. 6-8 Wt. 230 College—S. Methodist

Yr.	Team	G	FG	FT	TP	Avg.
1957-58	Minneapolis	68	199	135	533	7.8
1958-59	Minneapolis	72	271	92	634	8.8
1959-60	Minneapolis	75	237	98	572	7.6
1960-61	Los Angeles	75	275	79	629	8.4
1961-62	Los Angeles	78	312	156	780	10.0
1962-63	Los Angeles	79	272	115	659	8.3
1963-64	Los Angeles	68	134	65	333	4.9
	Totals	515	1700	740	4140	8.0

KRON, TOMMY
b. Feb. 28, 1943 Ht. 6-5 Wt. 200 College—Kentucky

Yr.	Team		G	FG	FT	TP	Avg.
1966-67	St. Louis		33	27	13	67	2.0
1967-68	Seattle		76	277	184	738	9.7
1968-69	Seattle		76	146	96	388	5.1
1969-70	Kentucky	(ABA)	40	55(7)	41	158	4.0
	Totals		225	505(7)	334	1351	6.0

KROPP, TOM
b. Feb. 12, 1953 Ht. 6-3 Wt. 205 College—Kearney State

Yr.	Team	G	FG	FT	TP	Avg.
1975-76	Washington	25	7	5	19	0.8
1976-77	Chicago	53	73	28	174	3.3
	Totals	78	80	33	193	2.5

KUBERSKI, STEVE
b. Nov. 6, 1947 Ht. 6-8 Wt. 215 College—Illinois and Bradley

Yr.	Team	G	FG	FT	TP	Avg.
1969-70	Boston	51	130	64	324	6.4
1970-71	Boston	82	313	133	759	9.3
1971-72	Boston	71	185	80	450	6.3
1972-73	Boston	78	140	65	345	4.4
1973-74	Boston	78	157	86	400	5.1
1974-75	Milwaukee	59	62	44	168	2.8
1975-76	Buf.-Bos.	70	135	71	341	4.9
1976-77	Boston	76	131	63	325	4.3
1977-78	Boston	3	1	0	2	0.7
	Totals	568	1254	606	3114	5.5

KUBIAK, LEO
b. Dec. 25, 1927 Ht. 5-11 Wt. 175 College—Bowling Green

Yr.	Team		G	FG	FT	TP	Avg.
1948-49	Waterloo	(NL)	62	177	108	462	7.5
1949-50	Waterloo		62	259	192	710	11.5
	Totals		124	436	300	1172	9.5

KUDELKA, FRANK (Apples)
b. 1925 Ht. 6-2 Wt. 193 St. Mary's (Calif.)

Yr.	Team	G	FG	FT	TP	Avg.
1949-50	Chicago	65	172	89	433	6.7
1950-51	Wash.-Bos.	62	179	83	441	7.1
1951-52	Baltimore	65	204	198	606	9.3
1952-53	Balt.-Phila.	36	59	44	162	4.5
	Totals	228	614	414	1642	7.2

KUESTER, JOHN
b. Feb. 6, 1955 Ht. 6-3 Wt. 182 College—North Carolina

Yr.	Team	G	FG	FT	TP	Avg.
1977-78	K.C.	78	145	87	377	4.8
1978-79	Denver	33	15	13	45	1.4
1979-80	Indiana	24	12	5	29	1.2
	Totals	135	173	105	451	3.3

KUKA, RAPHAEL (Ray)
b. Feb. 17, 1922 Ht. 6-3 Wt. 200 College—Montana St. and Notre Dame

Yr.	Team	G	FG	FT	TP	Avg.
1947-48	New York	44	89	50	228	5.2
1948-49	New York	8	10	5	25	3.1
	Totals	52	99	55	253	4.9

KUNZE, TERRY
b. 1943 Ht. 6-4 Wt. 210 College—Minnesota

Yr.	Team		G	FG	FT	TP	Avg.
1967-68	Minnesota	(ABA)	46	83(5)	59	230	5.0

KUPEC, CHARLES J. (C.J.)
b. Jan. 16, 1953 Ht. 6-6 Wt. 220 College—Michigan

Yr.	Team	G	FG	FT	TP	Avg.
1975-76	Los Angeles	16	10	7	27	1.7
1976-77	Los Angeles	82	153	78	384	4.7
1977-78	Houston	49	84	27	195	4.0
	Totals	147	247	112	606	4.1

LACEFIELD, REGGIE
b. April 10, 1945 Ht. 6-6 Wt. 230 College—W. Michigan

Yr.	Team		G	FG	FT	TP	Avg.
1968-69	Kentucky	(ABA)	8	11	2	24	3.0

LACEY, EDGAR
b. Aug. 2, 1944 Ht. 6-6 Wt. 190 College—UCLA

Yr.	Team		G	FG	FT	TP	Avg.
1968-69	Los Angeles	(ABA)	46	98	38	234	5.1

LACKEY, BOB
b. April 4, 1949 Ht. 6-6 Wt. 210 College—Marquette

Yr.	Team		G	FG	FT	TP	Avg.
1972-73	New York	(ABA)	68	153(2)	99	407	6.0
1973-74	New York	(ABA)	3	3	0	6	2.0
	Totals		71	156(2)	99	413	5.8

LaCOUR, FRED
b. Feb. 7, 1938 Ht. 6-5 Wt. 210 College—San Francisco

Yr.	Team	G	FG	FT	TP	Avg.
1960-61	St. Louis	55	123	63	309	5.6
1961-62	St. Louis	73	230	106	566	7.7
1962-63	San Francisco	16	28	9	65	4.1
	Totals	144	381	178	940	6.5

LADNER, WENDELL
b. Oct. 6, 1948 Ht. 6-5 Wt. 220 College—So. Mississippi
d. June 24, 1975

Yr.	Team		G	FG	FT	TP	Avg.
1970-71	Memphis	(ABA)	77	572(8)	154	1306	17.0
1971-72	Mem.-Car.	(ABA)	82	491(61)	122	1165	14.2
1972-73	Mem.-Ken.	(ABA)	52	146(12)	55	359	6.9
1973-74	Ken.-N.Y.	(ABA)	64	244(24)	29	541	8.5
1974-75	New York	(ABA)	25	45(7)	6	103	4.1
	Totals		300	1498(112)	366	3474	11.6

Yr.	Team		G	FG	FT	TP	Avg.

LALICH, PETER
b. June 23, 1920 Ht. 6-2 Wt. 190 College—Ohio Univ.

Yr.	Team		G	FG	FT	TP	Avg.
1942-43	Sheboygan	(NL)	1	0	0	0	0.0
1943-44	Cleveland	(NL)	17	44	21	109	6.4
1944-45	Pittsburgh	(NL)	9	8	4	20	2.2
1945-46	Youngstown		11	2	3	7	0.6
1946-47	Cleveland		1	0	0	0	0.0
	Totals		39	54	28	136	3.5

LAMAR, DWIGHT (Bo)
b. April 7, 1951 Ht. 6-1 Wt. 180 College—S.W. Louisiana

Yr.	Team		G	FG	FT	TP	Avg.
1973-74	San Diego	(ABA)	84	686(69)	272	1713	20.4
1974-75	San Diego	(ABA)	77	667(25)	247	1606	20.9
1975-76	S.D.-Ind.	(ABA)	41	277(24)	79	657	16.0
1976-77	Los Angeles		71	228	46	502	7.1
	Totals		273	1858(118)	644	4478	16.4

LANTZ, STU
b. July 13, 1946 Ht. 6-3 Wt. 175 College—Nebraska

Yr.	Team	G	FG	FT	TP	Avg.
1968-69	San Diego	73	220	129	569	7.8
1969-70	San Diego	82	455	278	1188	14.5
1970-71	San Diego	82	585	519	1689	20.6
1971-72	Houston	81	557	387	1501	18.5
1972-73	Detroit	51	185	120	490	9.6
1973-74	Detroit	50	154	139	447	8.9
1974-75	N.O.-L.A.	75	228	192	648	8.6
1975-76	Los Angeles	53	85	80	250	4.7
	Totals	547	2469	1844	6782	12.4

LARESE, YORK
b. July 18, 1938 Ht. 6-4 Wt. 183 College—North Carolina

Yr.	Team	G	FG	FT	TP	Avg.
1961-62	Chi.-Phila.	59	122	58	302	5.1

LaRUSSO, RUDY
b. Nov. 11, 1937 Ht. 6-8 Wt. 220 College—Dartmouth

Yr.	Team	G	FG	FT	TP	Avg.
1959-60	Minneapolis	71	355	265	975	13.7
1960-61	Los Angeles	79	416	323	1155	14.6
1961-62	Los Angeles	80	516	342	1374	17.1
1962-63	Los Angeles	74	321	282	924	12.5
1963-64	Los Angeles	79	337	298	972	12.3
1964-65	Los Angeles	78	381	321	1083	13.9
1965-66	Los Angeles	77	410	350	1170	15.2
1966-67	Los Angeles	45	211	156	578	12.8
1967-68	San Francisco	79	602	522	1726	21.8
1968-69	San Francisco	75	553	444	1550	20.7
	Totals	737	4102	3303	11507	15.6

LASKOWSKI, JOHN
b. June 7, 1953 Ht. 6-6 Wt. 190 College—Indiana

Yr.	Team	G	FG	FT	TP	Avg.
1975-76	Chicago	71	284	87	655	9.2
1976-77	Chicago	47	75	27	177	3.8
	Totals	118	359	114	832	7.1

LATTIN, DAVID (Big Daddy)
b. Dec. 23, 1943 Ht. 6-7 Wt. 230 College—Texas Western

Yr.	Team		G	FG	FT	TP	Avg.
1967-68	San Francisco		44	37	23	97	2.2
1968-69	Phoenix		68	150	109	419	6.2
1970-71	Pittsburgh	(ABA)	71	177	108	462	6.5
1971-72	Pittsburgh	(ABA)	64	329	148	806	12.6
1972-73	Memphis	(ABA)	16	48	34	130	8.1
	Totals		263	741	422	1914	7.3

LAUREL, RICH
b. July 11, 1954 Ht. 6-7 Wt. 195 College—Hofstra

Yr.	Team	G	FG	FT	TP	Avg.
1977-78	Milwaukee	10	10	4	24	2.4

LAURIE, HARRY
b. Nov. 2, 1944 Ht. 6-1 Wt. 178 College—Loyola (Ill.) and St. Peter's

Yr.	Team		G	FG	FT	TP	Avg.
1968-69	Pittsburgh	(ABA)	9	3	7	13	1.4

LAUTENBACH, WALTER
b. Nov. 17, 1922 Ht. 6-2 Wt. 190 College—Wisconsin

Yr.	Team		G	FG	FT	TP	Avg.
1947-48	Oshkosh	(NL)	60	159	36	354	5.9
1948-49	Oshkosh	(NL)	61	104	26	234	3.8
1949-50	Sheboygan		55	100	38	238	4.3
	Totals		176	363	100	826	4.7

LAVELLI, TONY
b. July 11, 1926 Ht. 6-3 Wt. 185 College—Yale

Yr.	Team	G	FG	FT	TP	Avg.
1949-50	Boston	56	162	168	492	8.8
1950-51	Bos.-N.Y.	30	32	35	99	3.3
	Totals	86	194	203	591	6.9

LAVOY, BOB
b. June 29, 1926 Ht. 6-7 Wt. 185 College—W. Kentucky

Yr.	Team	G	FG	FT	TP	Avg.
1950-51	Indianapolis	63	221	84	526	8.3
1951-52	Indianapolis	63	240	168	648	10.3
1952-53	Indianapolis	70	225	168	618	8.8
1953-54	Milw.-Syra.	68	135	94	364	5.4
	Totals	264	821	514	2156	8.2

LAYTON, DENNIS (Mo)
b. Dec. 24, 1948 Ht. 6-1 Wt. 180 College—So. California

Yr.	Team		G	FG	FT	TP	Avg.
1971-72	Phoenix		80	304	122	730	9.1
1972-73	Phoenix		65	187	90	464	7.1
1973-74	Portland		22	55	14	124	5.6
1973-74	Memphis	(ABA)	3	8	3	19	6.3
1976-77	N.Y. Knicks		56	134	58	326	5.8
1977-78	San Antonio		41	85	12	182	4.4
	Totals		267	773	299	1845	6.9

LEAKS, EMMANUEL (Manny)
b. Nov. 27, 1945 Ht. 6-8 Wt. 235 College—Niagara

Yr.	Team		G	FG	FT	TP	Avg.
1968-69	KY.-N.Y.-Dal.	(ABA)	78	299	160	758	9.7
1969-70	Dallas	(ABA)	84	636	305	1577	18.7
1970-71	Tex.-N.Y.	(ABA)	80	510	279	1299	16.2
1971-72	N.Y.-Utah-Fla.	(ABA)	69	240	74	554	8.0
1972-73	Philadelphia		82	377	144	898	11.0
1973-74	Capital		53	79	58	216	4.1
	Totals		446	2141	1020	5302	11.9

LEAR, HAL (King)
b. Jan. 31, 1935 Ht. 6-0 Wt. 163 College—Temple

Yr.	Team	G	FG	FT	TP	Avg.
1956-57	Philadelphia	3	2	0	4	1.3

LEE, ALFRED (Butch)
b. Dec. 5, 1956 Ht. 6-0 Wt. 185 College—Marquette

Yr.	Team	G	FG	FT	TP	Avg.
1978-79	Atl.-Cleve.	82	290	175	755	9.2
1979-80	Cleve.-L.A.	14	6	6	18	1.3
	Totals	96	296	181	773	8.1

LEE, CLYDE
b. March 14, 1944 Ht. 6-10 Wt. 205 College—Vanderbilt

Yr.	Team	G	FG	FT	TP	Avg.
1966-67	San Francisco	74	205	105	515	7.0
1967-68	San Francisco	82	373	229	975	11.9
1968-69	San Francisco	65	268	160	696	10.7
1969-70	San Francisco	82	362	178	902	11.0
1970-71	San Francisco	82	194	111	499	6.1
1971-72	Golden State	78	256	120	632	8.1
1972-73	Golden State	66	170	74	414	6.3
1973-74	Golden State	54	129	62	320	5.9
1974-75	Atl.-Phila.	80	176	119	471	5.9
1975-76	Philadelphia	79	123	63	309	3.9
	Totals	742	2256	1221	5733	7.7

LEE, DAVE
b. March 31, 1942 Ht. 6-7½ Wt. 225 College—San Francisco

Yr.	Team		G	FG	FT	TP	Avg.
1967-68	Oakland	(ABA)	54	125(2)	120	372	6.9
1968-69	New Orleans	(ABA)	4	1	0	2	0.6
	Totals		58	126(2)	120	374	6.4

LEE, GEORGE
b. Nov. 23, 1936 Ht. 6-4 Wt. 200 College—Michigan

Yr.	Team	G	FG	FT	TP	Avg.
1960-61	Detroit	74	310	276	896	12.1
1961-62	Detroit	75	179	213	571	7.6
1962-63	San Francisco	64	149	152	450	7.0
1963-64	San Francisco	54	64	47	175	3.2
1964-65	San Francisco	19	27	38	92	4.8
1966-67	San Francisco	1	3	6	12	12.0
1967-68	San Francisco	10	8	17	33	3.3
	Totals	297	740	749	2229	7.5

LEE, RUSSELL
b. Jan. 27, 1950 Ht. 6-5 Wt. 185 College—Marshall

Yr.	Team	G	FG	FT	TP	Avg.
1972-73	Milwaukee	46	49	32	130	2.8
1973-74	Milwaukee	36	38	11	87	2.4
1974-75	New Orleans	15	29	7	65	4.3
	Totals	97	116	50	282	2.9

LEEDE, ED
b. July 17, 1927 Ht. 6-3 Wt. 185 College—Dartmouth

Yr.	Team	G	FG	FT	TP	Avg.
1949-50	Boston	64	174	223	571	8.9
1950-51	Boston	57	119	140	378	6.6
	Totals	121	293	363	949	7.8

LEFKOWITZ, HENRY
b. Aug. 31, 1923 Ht. 6-2 Wt. 190 College—West. Reserve

Yr.	Team	G	FG	FT	TP	Avg.
1946-47	Cleveland	24	22	7	51	2.1

LEHMANN, GEORGE
b. May 1, 1942 Ht. 6-3 Wt. 190 College—Campbell

Yr.	Team		G	FG	FT	TP	Avg.
1967-68	St. Louis		55	59	35	153	2.8
1968-69	Atl.-L.A.	(ABA)	43	238(48)	140	664	15.4
1969-70	L.A.-N.Y.-Mia.	(ABA)	81	318(92)	180	908	11.2
1970-71	Carolina	(ABA)	83	535(154)	214	1438	17.3
1971-72	Car.-Mem.	(ABA)	53	303(71)	169	846	16.0
1972-73	Memphis	(ABA)	28	95(26)	61	277	9.9
1973-74	Memphis	(ABA)	33	68(18)	18	172	5.2
	Totals		376	1616(409)	817	4458	11.9

LENTZ, LARRY
b. Feb. 23, 1945 Ht. 6-6 Wt. 200 College—Houston

Yr.	Team		G	FG	FT	TP	Avg.
1967-68	Houston	(ABA)	78	343	147	833	10.7
1968-69	Hou.-N.Y.	(ABA)	70	135	76	346	4.9
	Totals		148	478	223	1179	8.0

LEONARD, ROBERT (Slick)
b. July 17, 1932 Ht. 6-3 Wt. 185 College—Indiana

Yr.	Team	G	FG	FT	TP	Avg.
1956-57	Minneapolis	72	303	186	792	11.0
1957-58	Minneapolis	66	266	205	737	11.2
1958-59	Minneapolis	58	206	120	532	9.2
1959-60	Minneapolis	73	231	136	598	8.2
1960-61	Los Ang.	55	61	71	193	3.5
1961-62	Chicago	70	423	279	1125	16.1
1962-63	Chicago	32	84	59	227	7.1
	Totals	426	1574	1056	4204	9.9

LEVANE, ANDREW (Fuzzy)
b. April 11, 1920 Ht. 6-2 Wt. 190 College—St. John's (N.Y.)

Yr.	Team		G	FG	FT	TP	Avg.
1945-46	Rochester	(NL)	22	52	8	112	5.1
1946-47	Rochester	(NL)	39	133	49	315	8.1
1947-48	Rochester	(NL)	54	147	45	339	6.3
1948-49	Rochester		36	55	13	123	3.4
1949-50	Syracuse		60	139	54	332	5.5
1952-53	Milwaukee		7	3	2	8	1.1
	Totals		218	529	171	1229	5.6

LEWIS, BOB
b. March 20, 1945 Ht. 6-3 Wt. 185 College—N.C.

Yr.	Team	G	FG	FT	TP	Avg.
1967-68	San Francisco	41	59	61	179	4.4
1968-69	San Francisco	62	113	83	309	5.0
1969-70	San Francisco	73	213	100	526	7.2
1970-71	Cleveland	79	179	109	467	5.9
	Totals	255	564	353	1481	5.8

LEWIS, FRED
b. Jan. 6, 1921 Ht. 6-2 Wt. 195 College—LIU/E. Kentucky

Yr.	Team		G	FG	FT	TP	Avg.
1946-47	Sheboygan	(NL)	44	230	125	585	13.3
1947-48	Sheb.-Ind.	(NL)	44	169	101	439	10.0
1948-49	Ind.-Balt.		61	272	138	682	11.2
1949-50	Balt.-Phila.		34	46	25	117	3.4
	Totals		183	717	389	1823	10.0

LEWIS, FRED
b. Jan. 7, 1943 Ht. 6-0 Wt. 180 College—Arizona State

Yr.	Team		G	FG	FT	TP	Avg.
1966-67	Cincinnati		32	60	29	149	4.7
1967-68	Indiana	(ABA)	76	542(16)	465	1565	20.6
1968-69	Indiana	(ABA)	78	572(22)	419	1585	20.3
1969-70	Indiana	(ABA)	81	448(47)	383	1326	16.4
1970-71	Indiana	(ABA)	81	547(59)	372	1525	18.8
1971-72	Indiana	(ABA)	77	405(31)	341	1182	15.4
1972-73	Indiana	(ABA)	72	375(38)	287	1075	14.9
1973-74	Indiana	(ABA)	78	290(13)	182	775	9.9
1974-75	Mem.-St. L.	(ABA)	69	579(18)	355	1531	22.2
1975-76	St. Louis	(ABA)	74	403(31)	259	1096	14.8
1976-77	Indiana		32	81	62	224	7.0
	Totals		750	4302(275)	3154	12033	16.0

Yr.	Team		G	FG	FT	TP	Avg.

LEWIS, GRADY
b. March 25, 1917 Ht. 6-7 Wt. 215 College—Southwestern/Okla.

Yr.	Team		G	FG	FT	TP	Avg.
1946-47	Detroit		60	106	75	287	4.8
1947-48	St. L.-Balt.		45	114	87	315	7.0
1948-49	St. Louis		34	53	42	148	4.4
	Totals		139	273	204	750	5.4

LEWIS, MIKE
b. March 12, 1946 Ht. 6-8 Wt. 225 College—Duke

Yr.	Team		G	FG	FT	TP	Avg.
1968-69	Ind.-Minn.	(ABA)	76	247	153	647	8.5
1969-70	Pittsburgh	(ABA)	78	499	269	1267	16.2
1970-71	Pittsburgh	(ABA)	83	420	235	1075	12.9
1971-72	Pittsburgh	(ABA)	82	385	165	935	11.4
1972-73	Carolina	(ABA)	15	59	33	151	10.1
1973-74	Carolina	(ABA)	3	3	0	6	2.0
	Totals		337	1613	855	4081	12.1

LIEBOWITZ, BARRY
Ht. 6-2 Wt. 105 College Long Island University

Yr.	Team		G	FG	FT	TP	Avg.
1967-68	N.J.-Oak.	(ABA)	82	323	248	894	10.9

LIGON, BILL
b. May 19, 1952 Ht. 6-4 Wt. 180 College—Vanderbilt

Yr.	Team		G	FG	FT	TP	Avg.
1974-75	Detroit		38	55	16	126	3.3

LIGON, JIM (Goose)
b. Feb. 22, 1944 Ht. 6-7 Wt. 215

Yr.	Team		G	FG	FT	TP	Avg.
1967-68	Kentucky	(ABA)	78	428(1)	405	1262	16.2
1968-69	Kentucky	(ABA)	75	391(1)	337	1120	14.9
1969-70	Kentucky	(ABA)	84	507	287	1301	15.5
1970-71	Kentucky	(ABA)	84	429	214	1072	12.8
1971-72	Ky.-Pitt.	(ABA)	82	213(1)	141	568	6.9
1972-73	Virginia	(ABA)	12	58	28	144	12.0
1973-74	Virginia	(ABA)	19	37	19	93	4.9
	Totals		434	2063(3)	1431	5560	12.8

LITTLE, SAM
College—Delta State

Yr.	Team		G	FG	FT	TP	Avg.
1969-70	Kentucky	(ABA)	3	2	1	5	1.7

LITTLES, GENE
b. June 29, 1943 Ht. 6-1 Wt. 185 College—High Point

Yr.	Team		G	FG	FT	TP	Avg.
1969-70	Carolina	(ABA)	82	414	197	1025	12.5
1970-71	Carolina	(ABA)	70	223(4)	117	567	8.1
1971-72	Carolina	(ABA)	69	280(7)	178	745	10.8
1972-73	Carolina	(ABA)	84	310(8)	179	807	9.6
1973-74	Carolina	(ABA)	84	294(4)	115	707	8.4
1974-75	Kentucky	(ABA)	61	85(2)	43	215	3.5
	Totals		450	1606(25)	829	4066	9.0

LIVINGSTONE, RONALD
b. Oct. 9, 1925 Ht. 6-10 Wt. 220 College—Wyoming/St. Mary's

Yr.	Team		G	FG	FT	TP	Avg.
1949-50	Balt.-Phila.		54	163	122	448	8.3
1950-51	Philadelphia		63	104	76	284	4.5
	Totals		117	267	198	732	6.3

LLOYD, CHUCK
Ht. 6-8 Wt. 220 College—Yankton

Yr.	Team		G	FG	FT	TP	Avg.
1970-71	Carolina	(ABA)	14	23	20	66	4.7

LLOYD, EARL (Big Cat)
b. April 3, 1928 Ht. 6-6 Wt. 220 College—W. Va. State

Yr.	Team		G	FG	FT	TP	Avg.
1950-51	Washington		7	16	11	43	6.1
1952-53	Syracuse		64	156	160	472	7.4
1953-54	Syracuse		72	249	156	654	9.1
1954-55	Syracuse		72	286	159	731	10.2
1955-56	Syracuse		72	213	186	612	8.5
1956-57	Syracuse		72	256	134	646	9.0
1957-58	Syracuse		61	119	79	317	5.2
1958-59	Detroit		72	234	137	605	8.4
1959-60	Detroit		68	237	128	602	8.8
	Totals		560	1766	1150	4682	8.4

LLOYD, ROBERT
b. Jan. 3, 1946 Ht. 6-2 Wt. 185 College—Rutgers

Yr.	Team		G	FG	FT	TP	Avg.
1967-68	New Jersey	(ABA)	58	147(3)	170	467	8.1
1968-69	New York	(ABA)	67	215(12)	218	660	9.9
	Totals		125	362(15)	388	1127	9.0

LOCHMANN, REINHOLD D. (Riney)
b. May 26, 1944 Ht. 6-6 Wt. 215 College—Kansas

Yr.	Team		G	FG	FT	TP	Avg.
1967-68	Dallas	(ABA)	63	108(1)	49	266	4.2
1968-69	Dallas	(ABA)	60	115(1)	60	291	4.9
1969-70	Dallas	(ABA)	47	73(3)	25	174	3.7
	Totals		170	296(5)	134	731	4.3

LOCHMUELLER, ROBERT
b. June 5, 1927 Ht. 6-5 Wt. 185 College—Louisville

Yr.	Team		G	FG	FT	TP	Avg.
1952-53	Syracuse		62	79	74	232	3.7

LOFGRAN, DON
b. Nov. 18, 1928 Ht. 6-6 Wt. 200 College—San Fran.
d. June, 1976

Yr.	Team		G	FG	FT	TP	Avg.
1950-51	Syracuse-Ind.		61	79	79	237	3.9
1951-52	Indianapolis		63	149	156	454	7.2
1952-53	Philadelphia		64	173	126	472	7.4
1953-54	Milwaukee		21	35	32	102	4.9
	Totals		209	436	393	1265	6.1

LOGAN, HENRY
b. March 14, 1946 Ht. 6-0 Wt. 185 College—Western Carolina

Yr.	Team		G	FG	FT	TP	Avg.
1968-69	Oakland	(ABA)	76	339(1)	268	947	12.5
1969-70	Washington	(ABA)	32	110	91	311	9.7
	Totals		108	449(1)	359	1258	11.6

LOGAN, JOHN
b. Jan. 1, 1921 Ht. 6-2 Wt. 175 College—Indiana

Yr.	Team		G	FG	FT	TP	Avg.
1946-47	St. Louis		61	290	190	770	12.6
1947-48	St. Louis		48	221	202	644	13.4
1948-49	St. Louis		57	282	239	803	14.1
1949-50	St. Louis		62	251	253	755	12.2
1950-51	Tri-Cities		29	81	62	224	7.7
	Totals		257	1125	946	3196	12.4

LONG, PAUL
b. Feb. 8, 1944 Ht. 6-2 Wt. 180 College—Wake Forest

Yr.	Team		G	FG	FT	TP	Avg.
1967-68	Detroit		16	23	11	57	3.6
1968-69	Kentucky	(ABA)	9	9	17	35	3.9
1969-70	Detroit		25	28	27	83	3.3
1970-71	Buffalo		30	57	20	134	4.5
	Totals		80	117	75	309	3.9

Yr.	Team		G	FG	FT	TP	Avg.

LONG, WILLIE
b. March 1, 1950 Ht. 6-8 Wt. 235 College—New Mexico

Yr.	Team		G	FG	FT	TP	Avg.
1971-72	Floridians	(ABA)	75	336	206	878	11.7
1972-73	Denver	(ABA)	56	183	138	504	12.6
1973-74	Denver	(ABA)	82	383	270	1036	11.4
	Totals		213	902	614	2418	11.4

LOSCUTOFF, JAMES (Jungle Jim)
b. Feb. 4, 1930 Ht. 6-5 Wt. 230 College—Oregon

Yr.	Team	G	FG	FT	TP	Avg.
1955-56	Boston	71	226	139	591	8.3
1956-57	Boston	70	306	132	744	10.6
1957-58	Boston	5	11	1	23	4.6
1958-59	Boston	66	242	62	546	8.3
1959-60	Boston	28	66	22	154	5.5
1960-61	Boston	76	154	50	358	4.7
1961-62	Boston	79	188	45	421	5.3
1962-63	Boston	64	94	22	210	3.3
1963-64	Boston	53	56	18	130	2.5
	Totals	512	1343	491	3177	6.2

LOTT, PLUMMER
b. Dec. 11, 1945 Ht. 6-5 Wt. 210 College—Seattle

Yr.	Team	G	FG	FT	TP	Avg.
1967-68	Seattle	44	46	19	111	2.5
1968-69	Seattle	23	17	2	36	1.6
	Totals	67	63	21	147	2.2

LOUGHERY, KEVIN (Murph)
b. March 28, 1940 Ht. 6-3 Wt. 190 College—St. John's (N.Y.)

Yr.	Team	G	FG	FT	TP	Avg.
1962-63	Detroit	57	146	71	363	6.4
1963-64	Det.-Balt.	66	236	126	598	9.1
1964-65	Baltimore	80	406	212	1024	12.8
1965-66	Baltimore	74	526	297	1349	18.2
1966-67	Baltimore	76	520	340	1380	18.2
1967-68	Baltimore	77	458	305	1221	15.9
1968-69	Baltimore	80	717	372	1806	22.6
1969-70	Baltimore	55	477	253	1207	21.9
1970-71	Baltimore	82	481	275	1237	15.1
1971-72	Balt.-Phila.	76	341	263	945	12.4
	Totals	723	4308	2514	11130	15.4

LOVE, BOB
b. Dec. 8, 1942 Ht. 6-8 Wt. 215 College—Southern U.

Yr.	Team	G	FG	FT	TP	Avg.
1966-67	Cincinnati	66	173	93	439	6.7
1967-68	Cincinnati	72	193	78	464	6.4
1968-69	Mil.-Chi.	49	108	71	287	5.9
1969-70	Chicago	82	640	442	1722	21.0
1970-71	Chicago	81	765	513	2043	25.2
1971-72	Chicago	79	819	399	2037	25.8
1972-73	Chicago	82	774	347	1895	23.1
1973-74	Chicago	82	731	323	1785	21.8
1974-75	Chicago	61	539	264	1342	22.0
1975-76	Chicago	76	543	362	1448	19.1
1976-77	Chi.-N.Y.N.-Sea.	59	162	109	433	7.3
	Totals	789	5447	3001	13895	17.6

LOVE, STAN
b. April 9, 1949 Ht. 6-9 Wt. 215 College—Oregon

Yr.	Team	G	FG	FT	TP	Avg.
1971-72	Baltimore	74	242	103	587	7.9
1972-73	Baltimore	72	190	79	459	6.4
1973-74	Los Angeles	51	119	49	287	5.6
1974-75	Los Angeles	30	85	47	217	7.2
	Totals	227	636	278	1550	6.8

LOVELLETTE, CLYDE
b. Sept. 7, 1929 Ht. 6-9 Wt. 235 College—Kansas

Yr.	Team	G	FG	FT	TP	Avg.
1953-54	Minneapolis	72	237	114	588	8.2
1954-55	Minneapolis	70	519	273	1311	18.7
1955-56	Minneapolis	71	594	338	1526	21.5
1956-57	Minneapolis	69	574	286	1434	20.8
1957-58	Cincinnati	71	679	301	1659	23.4
1958-59	St. Louis	70	402	205	1009	14.4
1959-60	St. Louis	68	550	316	1416	20.8
1960-61	St. Louis	67	599	273	1471	22.0
1961-62	St. Louis	40	341	155	837	20.9
1962-63	Boston	61	161	73	395	6.5
1963-64	Boston	45	128	45	301	6.7
	Totals	704	4784	2379	11947	17.0

LOWERY, CHARLES
b. Nov. 12, 1949 Ht. 6-3 Wt. 185 College—Puget Sound

Yr.	Team	G	FG	FT	TP	Avg.
1971-72	Milwaukee	20	17	11	45	2.3

LUCAS, ALBERT (Lukey)
b. July 4, 1922 Ht. 6-3 Wt. 195 College—Fordham

Yr.	Team		G	FG	FT	TP	Avg.
1944-45	Sheboygan	(NL)	26	57	36	150	5.8
1945-46	Sheboygan	(NL)	32	75	24	174	5.4
1946-47	Sheboygan	(NL)	42	87	32	206	4.9
1947-48	Sheboygan	(NL)	58	98	39	235	4.1
1948-49	Boston		2	1	0	2	1.0
	Totals		160	318	131	767	4.8

LUCAS, JERRY (Luke)
b. March 30, 1940 Ht. 6-8 Wt. 230 College—Ohio State

Yr.	Team	G	FG	FT	TP	Avg.
1963-64	Cincinnati	79	545	310	1400	17.7
1964-65	Cincinnati	66	558	298	1414	21.4
1965-66	Cincinnati	79	690	317	1697	21.5
1966-67	Cincinnati	81	577	284	1438	17.8
1967-68	Cincinnati	82	707	346	1760	21.4
1968-69	Cincinnati	74	555	247	1357	18.3
1969-70	Cin.-S.F.	67	405	200	1010	15.1
1970-71	San Fran.	80	623	289	1535	19.2
1971-72	New York	77	543	197	1283	16.7
1972-73	New York	71	312	80	704	9.9
1973-74	New York	73	194	67	455	6.2
	Totals	829	5709	2635	14053	17.0

LUCKENBILL, TED
b. July 27, 1939 Ht. 6-6 Wt. 205 College—Houston

Yr.	Team	G	FG	FT	TP	Avg.
1961-62	Phila.	67	43	49	135	2.0
1962-63	San Fran.	20	26	9	61	3.1
	Totals	87	79	58	196	2.3

LUISI, JAMES
b. 1930 Ht. 6-2 Wt. 180 College—St. Francis (N.Y.)

Yr.	Team	G	FG	FT	TP	Avg.
1953-54	Baltimore	31	31	27	89	2.9

LUJACK, ALOYSIUS (Al)
b. Oct. 5, 1921 Ht. 6-3 Wt. 220 College—Georgetown

Yr.	Team	G	FG	FT	TP	Avg.
1946-47	Washington	5	1	2	4	0.8

LUMPKIN, PHIL
b. Dec. 20, 1951 Ht. 6-0 Wt. 167 College—Miami (Ohio)

Yr.	Team	G	FG	FT	TP	Avg.
1974-75	Portland	48	86	30	202	4.2
1975-76	Phoenix	34	22	26	70	2.1
	Totals	82	108	56	272	3.3

Yr.	Team	G	FG	FT	TP	Avg.
LUMPP, RAY						
b. July 11, 1923 Ht. 6-1 Wt. 178 College—N.Y.U.						
1948-49 Ind.-N.Y.		61	279	219	777	12.7
1949-50 New York		58	91	86	268	4.6
1950-51 New York		64	153	124	430	6.7
1951-52 New York		62	184	90	458	7.4
1952-53 N.Y.-Balt.		55	188	153	529	9.6
Totals		300	895	672	2462	8.2
LYNAM, R. B.						
Ht. 6-1 Wt. 200 College—Oklahoma Baptist						
1967-68 Denver	(ABA)	7	5	7	17	2.4
LYNN, LONNIE						
b. 1944 Ht. 6-7½ Wt. 215 College—Wilberforce						
1969-70 Den.-Pitt.	(ABA)	52	112	36	260	5.0
LYNN, MIKE						
b. Nov. 25, 1945 Ht. 6-7 Wt. 215 College—UCLA						
1969-70 Los Angeles		44	44	31	119	2.7
1970-71 Buffalo		5	2	3	7	1.4
Totals		49	46	34	126	2.6
MACALUSO, MIKE						
b. July 20, 1951 Ht. 6-5 Wt. 210 College—Canisius						
1973-74 Buffalo		30	19	10	48	1.6
MACAULEY, EDWARD (Easy Ed)						
b. March 22, 1928 Ht. 6-8 Wt. 190 College—St. Louis						
1949-50 St. Louis		67	351	379	1081	16.1
1950-51 Boston		68	459	466	1384	20.4
1951-52 Boston		66	384	496	1264	19.2
1952-53 Boston		69	451	500	1402	20.3
1953-54 Boston		71	462	420	1344	18.9
1954-55 Boston		71	403	442	1248	17.6
1955-56 Boston		71	420	400	1240	17.5
1956-57 St. Louis		72	414	359	1187	16.5
1957-58 St. Louis		72	376	267	1019	14.2
1958-59 St. Louis		14	22	21	65	4.6
Totals		641	3742	3750	11234	17.5
MacGILVRAY, RONNIE						
b. July 20, 1930 Ht. 6-2 Wt. 185 College—St. John's (N.Y.)						
1954-55 Milwaukee		6	2	4	8	1.3
MACKNOWSKI, JOHN (Whitey)						
b. Jan. 7, 1923 Ht. 6-0 Wt. 185 College—Seton Hall						
1948-49 Syracuse	(NL)	62	146	128	420	6.8
1949-50 Syracuse		59	154	131	439	7.4
1950-51 Syracuse		58	131	122	384	6.6
Totals		179	431	381	1243	6.9
MADDOX, JACK						
Ht. 6-3½ Wt. 190 College—West Texas						
1946-47 Oshkosh	(NL)	43	102	33	237	5.5
1947-48 Oshkosh	(NL)	60	146	59	351	5.9
1948-49 Hammond	(NL)	17	39	18	96	5.6
1948-49 Indianapolis		1	0	0	0	0.0
Totals		121	287	110	684	5.7

Yr.	Team	G	FG	FT	TP	Avg.
MAGER, NORM						
b. March 23, 1926 Ht. 6-5 Wt. 185 College—St. John's/CCNY						
1950-51 Baltimore		22	32	37	101	4.6
MAHAFFEY, RANDY						
b. Sept. 28, 1945 Ht. 6-7 Wt. 210 College—Clemson						
1967-68 Kentucky	(ABA)	75	373	281	1027	13.7
1968-69 Ky.-N.Y.	(ABA)	79	351	232	934	11.8
1969-70 Carolina	(ABA)	84	367	194	928	11.0
1970-71 Carolina	(ABA)	83	385	156	926	11.7
Totals		321	1476	863	3815	11.9
MAHNKEN, JOHN						
b. June 16, 1922 Ht. 6-8 Wt. 220 College—Georgetown						
1945-46 Rochester	(NL)	16	50	23	123	7.7
1946-47 Washington		60	223	111	557	9.3
1947-48 Washington		48	131	54	316	6.6
1948-49 Balt -Ind.-Ft. W.		57	215	104	534	9.4
1949-50 Ft.W.-Tri-C.-Bos.		62	132	77	341	5.5
1950-51 Bos.-Ind.		58	111	45	267	4.6
1951-52 Boston		60	78	26	182	3.0
1952-53 Boston		69	76	39	191	2.8
Totals		430	1016	479	2511	5.8
MAHONEY, BRIAN						
b. 1948 Ht. 6-3 Wt. 175 College—Manhattan						
1972-73 New York	(ABA)	19	17	24	58	3.1
MAHONEY, FRANCIS (Mo)						
b. Nov. 20, 1927 Ht. 6-0 Wt. 205 College—Brown						
1952-53 Boston		6	4	4	12	2.0
1953-54 Baltimore		2	0	0	0	0.0
Totals		8	4	4	12	1.5
MALAMED, LIONEL						
b. Nov. 15, 1924 Ht. 5-9 Wt. 150 College—CCNY						
1948-49 Ind.-Roch.		44	97	64	258	5.9
MALOVIC, STEVE						
b. July 21, 1956 Ht. 6-10 Wt. 230 Coll.—USC/San Diego State						
1979-80 Wsh.-SD-Det.		39	31	18	80	2.1
MALOY, MIKE						
b. May 10, 1949 Ht. 6-7 Wt. 215 College—Davidson						
1970-71 Virginia	(ABA)	55	149	98	396	7.2
1971-72 Virginia	(ABA)	7	12	2	26	3.7
1972-73 Dallas	(ABA)	9	7	6	20	2.2
Totals		71	168	106	442	6.2
MANAKAS, TED						
b. Feb. 22, 1951 Ht. 6-2 Wt. 180 College—Princeton						
1973-74 K.C.-Omaha		5	4	4	12	2.4
MANDIC, JOHN						
b. Oct. 3, 1919 Ht. 6-4 Wt. 205 College—Oreg. State						
1947-48 Rochester	(NL)	33	32	13	77	2.3
1948-49 Indianapolis		56	97	75	269	4.8
1949-50 Wash.-Balt.		25	22	22	66	2.6
Totals		114	151	110	412	3.6

Yr.	Team		G	FG	FT	TP	Avg.

MANGIAPANE, FRANK
b. Aug. 25, 1925 Ht. 5-10 Wt. 195 College—NYU

Yr.	Team		G	FG	FT	TP	Avg.
1946-47	New York		6	2	1	5	0.8

MANNING, ED
b. Jan. 2, 1944 Ht. 6-7½ Wt. 215 College—Jackson State

1967-68	Baltimore		71	112	60	284	4.0
1968-69	Baltimore		63	129	35	293	4.7
1969-70	Balt.-Chi.		67	119	42	280	4.2
1970-71	Portland		79	243	75	561	7.1
1971-72	Carolina	(ABA)	77	228	95	551	7.2
1972-73	Carolina	(ABA)	83	263	64	590	7.1
1973-74	Carolina	(ABA)	82	297(1)	86	681	8.3
1974-75	New York	(ABA)	70	103	35	241	3.4
	Totals		591	1494(1)	492	3481	5.9

MANNING, GUY
b. Feb. 4, 1944 Ht. 6-6½ Wt. 205 College—Prairie View

1967-68	Houston	(ABA)	59	206(2)	115	529	9.0
1968-69	Houston	(ABA)	14	27	21	75	5.4
	Totals		73	233(2)	136	604	8.3

MANTIS, NICHOLAS
b. Dec. 7, 1935 Ht. 6-3 Wt. 190 College—Northwestern

1959-60	Minneapolis		10	10	1	21	2.1
1962-63	St. L.-Chi.		42	94	27	215	5.1
	Totals		52	104	28	236	4.5

MARAVICH, PETE
b. June 22, 1948 Ht. 6-5 Wt. 200 College—Louisiana St.

1970-71	Atlanta		81	738	404	1880	23.2
1971-72	Atlanta		66	460	355	1275	19.3
1972-73	Atlanta		79	789	485	2063	26.1
1973-74	Atlanta		76	819	469	2107	27.7
1974-75	New Orleans		79	655	390	1700	21.5
1975-76	New Orleans		62	604	396	1604	25.9
1976-77	New Orleans		73	886	501	2273	31.1
1977-78	New Orleans		50	556	240	1352	27.0
1978-79	New Orleans		49	436	233	1105	22.6
1979-80	Utah-Bost.		43	244(10)	91	589	13.7
	Totals		658	6187(10)	3564	15948	24.2

MARAVICH, PRESS
b. Aug. 20, 1920 Ht. 6-0 Wt. 185 College—Davis & Elkins

1945-46	Youngstown	(NL)	31	70	34	174	5.6
1946-47	Pittsburgh		51	102	30	234	4.6
	Totals		82	172	64	408	5.0

MARIASCHIN, SAUL
b. Sept. 1, 1924 Ht. 5-11 Wt. 165 College—Harvard

| 1947-48 | Boston | | 43 | 125 | 83 | 333 | 7.7 |

MARIN, JACK
b. Oct. 12, 1944 Ht. 6-6½ Wt. 200 College—Duke

1966-67	Baltimore		74	283	145	711	9.6
1967-68	Baltimore		82	429	250	1108	13.5
1968-69	Baltimore		82	505	292	1302	15.9
1969-70	Baltimore		82	666	286	1618	19.7
1970-71	Baltimore		82	626	290	1542	18.8
1971-72	Baltimore		78	690	356	1736	22.3
1972-73	Houston		81	624	248	1496	18.5

Yr.	Team	G	FG	FT	TP	Avg.
1973-74	Hou.-Buf.	74	355	153	863	11.7
1974-75	Buffalo	81	380	193	953	11.8
1975-76	Buf.-Chi.	79	343	161	847	10.7
1976-77	Chicago	54	167	31	365	6.8
	Totals	849	5068	2405	12541	14.8

MARLATT, HARVEY
b. Aug. 26, 1948 Ht. 6-3 Wt. 185 College—Eastern Mich.

1970-71	Detroit	23	25	15	65	2.8
1971-72	Detroit	31	60	36	156	5.0
1972-73	Detroit	7	2	0	4	0.6
	Totals	61	87	51	225	3.7

MARSH, JIM
b. Apr. 26, 1946 Ht. 6-7 Wt. 215 College—USC

| 1971-72 | Portland | 39 | 39 | 41 | 119 | 3.1 |

MARSH, ERIC (Ricky)
b. March 10, 1954 Ht. 6-3 Wt. 200 College—Nebraska and Manhattan

| 1977-78 | Gold. St. | 60 | 123 | 23 | 269 | 4.5 |

MARSHALL, THOMAS
b. Jan. 6, 1931 Ht. 6-4 Wt. 215 College—Western Ky.

1956-57	Rochester	40	56	47	159	4.0
1957-58	Det.-Cinn.	38	52	48	152	4.0
	Totals	78	108	95	311	4.0

MARSHALL, VESTER
b. Dec. 22, 1948 Ht. 6-7 Wt. 200 College—Oklahoma

| 1973-74 | Seattle | 13 | 7 | 3 | 17 | 1.3 |

MARTIN, DONALD (Dino)
b. 1920 Ht. 5-8 Wt. 160 College—Georgetown

1946-47	Providence	60	311	111	733	12.3
1947-48	Providence	32	46	9	101	3.2
	Totals	92	357	120	834	9.1

MARTIN, JAMES D.
b. May 25, 1920 Ht. 6-7 Wt. 210 College—Central Mo.

1946-47	St. Louis	54	89	13	191	3.5
1947-48	St. Louis	39	35	15	85	2.2
1948-49	St. L.-Balt.	44	52	30	134	3.0
	Totals	137	176	58	410	3.0

MARTIN, LARUE
b. March 30, 1950 Ht. 6-11 Wt. 208 College—Loyola (Ill.)

1972-73	Portland	77	145	50	340	4.4
1973-74	Portland	50	101	42	244	4.9
1974-75	Portland	81	236	99	571	7.0
1975-76	Portland	63	109	57	275	4.4
	Totals	271	591	248	1430	5.3

MARTIN, PHIL
Ht. 6-3 Wt. 190 College—Toledo

| 1954-55 | Milwaukee | 7 | 5 | 2 | 12 | 1.7 |

MARTIN, RONALD (Whitey)
b. April 11, 1939 Ht. 6-2 Wt. 185 College—St. Bonaventure

| 1961-62 | New York | 66 | 95 | 37 | 227 | 3.4 |

Yr.	Team	G	FG	FT	TP	Avg.

MARTIN, SLATER (Dugie)
b. Oct. 22, 1925 Ht. 5-10 Wt. 170 College—Texas

Yr.	Team	G	FG	FT	TP	Avg.
1949-50	Minneapolis	67	106	59	271	4.0
1950-51	Minneapolis	68	227	121	575	3.5
1951-52	Minneapolis	66	237	142	616	9.3
1952-53	Minneapolis	70	260	224	744	10.6
1953-54	Minneapolis	69	254	176	684	9.9
1954-55	Minneapolis	72	350	276	976	13.6
1955-56	Minneapolis	72	309	329	947	13.2
1956-57	N.Y.-St. L.	66	244	230	718	10.9
1957-58	St. Louis	60	258	206	722	12.0
1958-59	St. Louis	71	245	197	687	9.4
1959-60	St. Louis	64	142	113	397	6.2
	Totals	745	2632	2073	7337	9.8

MASINO, AL
b. 1928 Ht. 5-11 Wt. 174 College—Canisius

Yr.	Team	G	FG	FT	TP	Avg.
1952-53	Milwaukee	72	134	128	396	5.5
1953-54	Roch.-Syra.	27	26	30	82	3.0
	Totals	99	160	158	478	4.8

MAST, EDDIE
b. Oct. 3, 1948 Ht. 6-9 Wt. 220 College—Temple

Yr.	Team	G	FG	FT	TP	Avg.
1970-71	New York	30	25	11	61	2.0
1971-72	New York	40	39	25	103	2.6
1972-73	Atlanta	42	50	19	119	2.8
	Totals	112	114	55	283	2.5

MATHIS, JOHN
b. July 14, 1943 Ht. 6-6½ Wt. 220 College—Savannah St.

Yr.	Team		G	FG	FT	TP	Avg.
1967-68	New Jersey	(ABA)	51	69	35	173	3.4

MAUGHAN, ARIEL (Ace)
b. April 23, 1923 Ht. 6-4 Wt. 190 College—Utah State

Yr.	Team	G	FG	FT	TP	Avg.
1946-47	Detroit	59	224	84	532	9.0
1947-48	Prov.-St. L.	42	76	32	184	4.4
1948-49	St. Louis	55	206	184	596	10.8
1949-50	St. Louis	68	160	157	477	7.0
1950-51	Washington	35	78	101	257	7.3
	Totals	259	744	558	2046	7.9

MAY, DON
b. Jan. 3, 1946 Ht. 6-4 Wt. 220 College—Dayton

Yr.	Team	G	FG	FT	TP	Avg.
1968-69	New York	48	81	42	204	4.3
1969-70	New York	37	39	18	96	2.6
1970-71	Buffalo	76	629	277	1535	20.2
1971-72	Atlanta	75	234	126	594	7.9
1972-73	Atl.-Phoe.	58	189	75	453	7.8
1973-74	Philadelphia	56	152	89	393	7.0
1974-75	Kansas City	29	27	10	64	2.2
	Totals	379	1351	637	3339	8.8

MAYES, CLYDE
b. March 17, 1953 Ht. 6-7 Wt. 230 College—Furman

Yr.	Team	G	FG	FT	TP	Avg.
1975-76	Milwaukee	65	114	56	284	4.4
1976-77	Ind.-Buf.-Port.	9	5	3	13	1.4
	Totals	74	119	59	297	4.0

MAYFIELD, KEN
b. May 11, 1948 Ht. 6-2 Wt. 185 College—Tuskegee

Yr.	Team	G	FG	FT	TP	Avg.
1975-76	New York	13	17	3	37	2.8

MAZZA, MATT
b. Sept. 23, 1923 Ht. 6-3 Wt. 210 College—Mich. State

Yr.	Team	G	FG	FT	TP	Avg.
1949-50	Sheboygan	26	33	32	98	3.8

McBRIDE, KEN
Ht. 6-3 Wt. 190 College—Maryland State

Yr.	Team	G	FG	FT	TP	Avg.
1954-55	Milwaukee	12	48	21	117	9.8

McCANN, BRENDAN
b. July 5, 1935 Ht. 6-2 Wt. 178 College—St. Bonaventure

Yr.	Team	G	FG	FT	TP	Avg.
1957-58	New York	36	22	25	69	1.9
1958-59	New York	1	0	0	0	0.0
1959-60	New York	4	1	4	6	1.5
	Totals	41	23	29	75	1.8

McCARRON, MICHAEL
b. March 2, 1922 Ht. 5-11 Wt. 180 College—Seton Hall

Yr.	Team	G	FG	FT	TP	Avg.
1946-47	Toronto	60	236	177	649	10.8
1949-50	Balt.-St. L.	8	3	3	9	1.1
	Totals	68	239	180	658	9.7

McCARTER, WILLIE
b. July 26, 1946 Ht. 6-3 Wt. 175 College—Drake

Yr.	Team	G	FG	FT	TP	Avg.
1969-70	Los Angeles	40	132	43	307	7.7
1970-71	Los Angeles	76	247	46	540	7.1
1971-72	Portland	39	103	37	243	6.2
	Totals	155	482	126	1090	7.0

McCARTHY, JOHN
b. April 25, 1934 Ht. 6-1 Wt. 185 College—Canisius

Yr.	Team	G	FG	FT	TP	Avg.
1956-57	Rochester	72	173	130	476	6.6
1958-59	Cincinnati	47	245	116	606	12.9
1959-60	St. Louis	75	240	149	629	8.4
1960-61	St. Louis	79	266	122	654	8.3
1961-62	St. Louis	15	18	12	48	3.2
1963-64	Boston	28	16	5	37	1.3
	Totals	316	958	534	2450	7.8

McCARTY, HOWARD
b. 1919 Ht. 6-2 Wt. 190 College—Wayne State
d. 1973

Yr.	Team		G	FG	FT	TP	Avg.
1945-46	Cleveland	(NL)	13	40	13	93	7.2
1946-47	Detroit	(NL)	16	46	29	121	7.6
1946-47	Detroit		19	10	1	21	1.1
	Totals		48	96	43	235	4.9

McCLAIN, TED
b. Aug. 30, 1947 Ht. 6-3 Wt. 190 College—Tenn. State

Yr.	Team		G	FG	FT	TP	Avg.
1971-72	Carolina	(ABA)	64	148(13)	110	419	6.6
1972-73	Carolina	(ABA)	84	325(8)	145	803	9.6
1973-74	Carolina	(ABA)	84	423(2)	251	1099	13.1
1974-75	Kentucky	(ABA)	72	256(1)	104	617	8.6
1975-76	Kent.-N.Y.	(ABA)	73	267(3)	136	673	9.2
1976-77	Denver		72	245	99	589	8.2
1977-78	Buff.-Phil.		70	123	57	303	4.3
1978-79	Phoenix		36	62	42	166	4.6
	Totals		555	1849(27)	944	4669	8.4

McCLOSKEY, JACK
b. 1926 Ht. 6-2 Wt. 192 College—Pennsylvania

Yr.	Team	G	FG	FT	TP	Avg.
1952-53	Philadelphia	1	3	0	6	6.0

Yr.	Team	G	FG	FT	TP	Avg.

McCONATHY, JOHN
b. Apr. 9, 1930 Ht. 6-5 Wt. 195 College—Northwest Louisiana

Yr.	Team	G	FG	FT	TP	Avg.
1951-52	Milwaukee	11	4	6	14	1.3

McCONNELL, BUCKY
Ht. 5-10 Wt. 170 College—Marshall

Yr.	Team	G	FG	FT	TP	Avg.
1952-53	Milwaukee	14	27	14	68	4.9

McCRACKEN, PAUL
b. Sept. 11, 1950 Ht. 6-4 Wt. 180 College—Northridge St.

Yr.	Team	G	FG	FT	TP	Avg.
1972-73	Houston	24	44	23	111	4.6
1973-74	Houston	4	1	0	2	0.5
1976-77	Chicago	9	18	11	47	5.2
	Totals	37	63	34	160	4.3

McDANIELS, JIM
b. April 2, 1948 Ht. 7-0 Wt. 225 College—W. Kentucky

Yr.	Team		G	FG	FT	TP	Avg.
1971-72	Carolina	(ABA)	58	659	234	1552	26.8
1971-72	Seattle		12	51	11	113	9.4
1972-73	Seattle		68	154	70	378	5.6
1973-74	Seattle		27	63	23	149	5.5
1975-76	Los Angeles		35	41	9	91	2.6
1975-76	Kentucky	(ABA)	29	78	23	179	6.2
1977-78	Buffalo		42	100	36	236	5.6
	Totals		271	1146	406	2698	9.9

McDONALD, GLENN
b. March 18, 1952 Ht. 6-6 Wt. 190 College—Long Beach St.

Yr.	Team	G	FG	FT	TP	Avg.
1974-75	Boston	62	70	28	168	2.7
1975-76	Boston	75	191	40	422	5.6
1976-77	Milwaukee	9	8	3	19	2.1
	Totals	146	269	71	609	4.2

McDONALD, ROD
b. April 9, 1945 Ht. 6-6 Wt. 205 College—Whitworth

Yr.	Team		G	FG	FT	TP	Avg.
1970-71	Utah	(ABA)	29	50(2)	15	117	4.0
1971-72	Utah	(ABA)	33	34	27	95	2.9
1972-73	Utah	(ABA)	25	27(1)	15	70	2.8
	Totals		87	111(3)	57	282	3.2

McFARLAND, PAT
b. Dec. 7, 1951 Ht. 6-5 Wt. 185 College—St. Joseph's

Yr.	Team	G	FG	FT	TP	Avg.
1973-74	Denver	67	159(8)	35	361	5.4
1974-75	Denver	70	200(2)	52	454	6.5
1975-76	San Diego	11	55(1)	21	132	12.0
	Totals	148	414(11)	108	947	6.4

McGAHA, MEL
b. Sept. 26, 1926 Ht. 6-1 Wt. 190 College—Arkansas

Yr.	Team	G	FG	FT	TP	Avg.
1948-49	New York	51	62	52	176	3.5

McGILL, BILL (The Hill)
b. Sept. 16, 1939 Ht. 6-9½ Wt. 225 College—Utah

Yr.	Team		G	FG	FT	TP	Avg.
1962-63	Chicago		61	181	80	442	7.2
1963-64	Balt.-N.Y.		74	456	204	1116	15.1
1964-65	St. L.-L.A.		24	21	13	55	2.3
1968-69	Denver	(ABA)	78	411	180	1002	12.8
1969-70	L.A.-Dallas	(ABA)	59	201	77	479	8.1
	Totals		296	1270	554	3094	10.5

McGLOCKLIN, JON
b. June 10, 1943 Ht. 6-5 Wt. 205 College—Indiana

Yr.	Team	G	FG	FT	TP	Avg.
1965-66	Cincinnati	72	153	62	368	5.1
1966-67	Cincinnati	60	217	74	508	8.5
1967-68	San Diego	65	316	156	788	12.1
1968-69	Milwaukee	80	662	246	1570	19.6
1969-70	Milwaukee	82	639	169	1447	17.6
1970-71	Milwaukee	82	574	144	1292	15.8
1971-72	Milwaukee	80	374	109	857	10.7
1972-73	Milwaukee	80	351	63	765	9.6
1973-74	Milwaukee	79	329	72	730	9.2
1974-75	Milwaukee	79	323	63	709	9.0
1975-76	Milwaukee	33	63	9	135	4.1
	Totals	792	4001	1167	9169	11.6

McGREGOR, GIL
b. June 14, 1949 Ht. 6-8 Wt. 240 College—Wake Forest

Yr.	Team	G	FG	FT	TP	Avg.
1971-72	Cincinnati	42	66	39	171	4.1

McGRIFF, ELTON (Mac)
b. Aug. 21, 1942 Ht. 6-9 Wt. 230 College—Creighton

Yr.	Team		G	FG	FT	TP	Avg.
1967-68	Dallas	(ABA)	20	49	33	131	6.6
1968-69	Dal.-N.O.-Ky.	(ABA)	36	75	57	207	5.8
	Totals		56	124	90	338	6.0

McGUIRE, AL
b. Sept. 7, 1928 Ht. 6-2 Wt. 180 College—St. John's (N.Y.)

Yr.	Team	G	FG	FT	TP	Avg.
1951-52	New York	59	72	64	208	3.5
1952-53	New York	58	112	128	352	6.1
1953-54	New York	64	58	58	174	2.7
1954-55	Baltimore	10	9	5	23	2.3
	Totals	191	251	255	757	4.0

McGUIRE, ALLIE
b. July 10, 1951 Ht. 6-3 Wt. 175 College—Marquette

Yr.	Team	G	FG	FT	TP	Avg.
1973-74	New York	2	2	0	4	2.0

McGUIRE, RICHARD (Tricky Dick)
b. Jan. 25, 1926 Ht. 6-0 Wt. 180 College—St. John's/Dartmouth

Yr.	Team	G	FG	FT	TP	Avg.
1949-50	New York	68	190	204	584	8.6
1950-51	New York	64	179	179	537	8.4
1951-52	New York	64	204	183	591	9.2
1952-53	New York	61	142	153	437	7.2
1953-54	New York	68	201	220	622	9.1
1954-55	New York	71	226	195	647	9.1
1955-56	New York	62	152	121	425	6.9
1956-57	New York	72	140	105	385	5.3
1957-58	Detroit	69	203	150	556	8.1
1958-59	Detroit	71	232	191	655	9.2
1959-60	Detroit	68	179	124	482	7.1
	Totals	738	2048	1825	5921	8.0

McHARTLEY, MAURICE (Mo)
b. Aug. 1, 1942 Ht. 6-3 Wt. 200 College—No. Carolina A & T

Yr.	Team		G	FG	FT	TP	Avg.
1967-68	Dallas	(ABA)	58	330(3)	225	888	15.3
1968-69	N.Y.-Mia.	(ABA)	76	390(6)	263	1049	13.8
1969-70	Mia-Pit-Dall	(ABA)	55	155(6)	98	414	7.5
	Totals		189	875(15)	586	2351	12.4

Yr.	Team	G	FG	FT	TP	Avg.

McINTOSH, KENNEDY
b. Jan. 21, 1949 Ht. 6-7 Wt. 225 College—Eastern Mich.

Yr.	Team	G	FG	FT	TP	Avg.
1971-72	Chicago	43	57	21	135	3.1

McINTYRE, BOB
b. Jan. 23, 1944 Ht. 6-7 Wt. 215 College—St. John's

Yr.	Team		G	FG	FT	TP	Avg.
1967-68	New Jersey	(ABA)	21	70	34	174	8.3

McKEE, GERALD
b. Aug. 4, 1946 Ht. 6-3 Wt. 190 College—Ohio Univ.

Yr.	Team		G	FG	FT	TP	Avg.
1969-70	Indiana	(ABA)	1	0	0	0	0.0

McKENZIE, STAN
b. Oct. 6, 1944 Ht. 6-5 Wt. 210 College—NYU

Yr.	Team	G	FG	FT	TP	Avg.
1967-68	Baltimore	50	73	58	204	4.1
1968-69	Phoenix	80	264	219	747	9.3
1969-70	Phoenix	58	81	58	220	3.8
1970-71	Portland	82	398	331	1127	13.7
1971-72	Portland	82	410	315	1135	13.8
1972-73	Port.-Hou.	33	48	30	126	3.8
1973-74	Houston	11	7	6	20	1.8
	Totals	396	1281	1017	3579	9.0

McKINNEY, HORACE (Bones)
b. Jan. 1, 1919 Ht. 6-6 Wt. 187 College—No. Car./No. Car. St.

Yr.	Team	G	FG	FT	TP	Avg.
1946-47	Washington	58	275	145	695	12.0
1947-48	Washington	43	182	121	485	11.3
1948-49	Washington	57	263	197	723	12.7
1949-50	Washington	53	187	118	492	9.3
1950-51	Wash.-Bos.	44	102	58	262	6.0
1951-52	Boston	63	136	65	337	5.3
	Totals	318	1145	704	2994	9.4

McLEMORE, McCOY
b. April 3, 1942 Ht. 6-7 Wt. 230 College—Drake

Yr.	Team	G	FG	FT	TP	Avg.
1964-65	San Fran.	78	244	157	645	8.3
1965-66	San Fran.	80	225	142	592	7.4
1966-67	Chicago	79	258	210	726	9.2
1967-68	Chicago	76	374	215	963	12.7
1968-69	Pho.-Det.	81	282	169	733	9.0
1969-70	Detroit	73	233	119	585	8.0
1970-71	Cleve.-Mil.	86	303	204	810	9.4
1971-72	Mil.-Hou.	27	28	20	76	2.8
	Totals	580	1947	1236	5130	8.8

McLEOD, GEORGE
b. 1932 Ht. 6-5 Wt. 200 College—Texas Christian

Yr.	Team	G	FG	FT	TP	Avg.
1952-53	Baltimore	10	2	8	12	1.2

McMAHON, JACK
b. Dec. 3, 1928 Ht. 6-1 Wt. 185 College—St. John's (N.Y.)

Yr.	Team	G	FG	FT	TP	Avg.
1952-53	Rochester	70	176	155	507	7.2
1953-54	Rochester	71	250	211	711	10.0
1954-55	Rochester	72	251	143	645	9.0
1955-56	Roch.-St. L.	70	202	110	514	7.3
1956-57	St. Louis	72	239	142	620	8.6
1957-58	St. Louis	72	216	134	566	7.9
1958-59	St. Louis	72	248	96	592	8.2
1959-60	St. Louis	25	33	16	82	3.3
	Totals	524	1615	1007	4237	8.1

McMILLIAN, JIM
b. March 11, 1948 Ht. 6-5 Wt. 225 College—Columbia

Yr.	Team	G	FG	FT	TP	Avg.
1970-71	Los Angeles	81	289	100	678	8.4
1971-72	Los Angeles	80	642	219	1503	18.8
1972-73	Los Angeles	81	655	223	1533	18.9
1973-74	Buffalo	82	600	325	1525	18.6
1974-75	Buffalo	62	347	194	888	14.3
1975-76	Buffalo	74	492	188	1172	15.8
1976-77	N.Y. Knicks	67	298	67	663	9.9
1977-78	New York	81	288	115	691	8.5
1978-79	Portland	23	33	17	83	3.6
	Totals	631	3644	1448	8736	13.8

McMILLON, SHELLIE
b. March 11, 1936 Ht. 6-5 Wt. 205 College—Bradley
d. July 11, 1980

Yr.	Team	G	FG	FT	TP	Avg.
1958-59	Detroit	48	127	55	309	6.4
1959-60	Detroit	75	267	132	666	8.9
1960-61	Detroit	78	322	140	784	10.1
1961-62	Det.-St. L.	62	265	108	638	10.3
	Totals	263	981	435	2397	9.1

McMULLAN, MALCOLM
b. Aug. 23, 1927 Ht. 6-5 Wt. 210 College—Xavier (Ohio) and Kentucky

Yr.	Team	G	FG	FT	TP	Avg.
1949-50	Indianapolis	58	123	77	323	5.6
1950-51	Indianapolis	51	78	48	204	4.0
	Totals	109	201	125	527	4.8

McNABB, CHESTER
b. 1921 Ht. 6-2 Wt. 200 College—West Texas

Yr.	Team	G	FG	FT	TP	Avg.
1947-48	Baltimore	2	0	0	0	0.0

McNAMEE, JOE
b. 1927 Ht. 6-6 Wt. 210 College—San Francisco

Yr.	Team	G	FG	FT	TP	Avg.
1950-51	Rochester	60	48	27	123	2.1
1951-52	Roch.-Balt.	58	68	30	166	2.9
	Totals	118	116	57	289	2.4

McNEILL, LARRY
b. Jan. 31, 1951 Ht. 6-9 Wt. 195 College—Marquette

Yr.	Team	G	FG	FT	TP	Avg.
1973-74	K.C.-Omaha	54	106	99	311	5.8
1974-75	K.C.-Omaha	80	296	189	781	9.8
1975-76	K.C.-Omaha	82	295	207	797	9.7
1976-77	NYN-G.S.	24	47	52	146	6.1
1977-78	G.S.-Buff.	46	162	145	469	10.2
1978-79	Detroit	11	9	11	29	2.6
	Totals	297	915	703	2533	8.5

McNEILL, ROBERT
b. Oct. 22, 1938 Ht. 6-1 Wt. 180 College—St. Joseph's (Pa.)

Yr.	Team	G	FG	FT	TP	Avg.
1960-61	New York	75	166	105	437	5.8
1961-62	Phila.-L.A.	50	56	26	138	2.8
	Totals	125	222	131	575	4.6

McNULTY, CARL
b. Feb. 14, 1930 Ht. 6-3 Wt. 185 College—Purdue

Yr.	Team	G	FG	FT	TP	Avg.
1954-55	Milwaukee	1	1	0	2	2.0

Yr.	Team		G	FG	FT	TP	Avg.

McPIPE, ROY
b. May 5, 1950 Ht. 6-3 Wt. 205 College—Eastern Montana.

Yr.	Team		G	FG	FT	TP	Avg.
1974-75 Utah		(ABA)	5	8(2)	3	21	4.2

McREYNOLDS, THALES
b. June 8, 1943 Ht. 6-3 Wt. 185 College—Miles

| 1965-66 Baltimore | | | 5 | 1 | 1 | 3 | 0.6 |

McWILLIAMS, ERIC
b. April 18, 1950 Ht. 6-8 Wt. 200 College—Long Beach St.

| 1972-73 Houston | | | 44 | 34 | 18 | 86 | 2.0 |

MEARNS, GEORGE
b. April 18, 1922 Ht. 6-3 Wt. 175 College—Rhode Is.

1946-47 Providence			57	128	126	382	6.7
1947-48 Providence			24	23	15	61	2.5
Totals			81	151	141	443	5.5

MEELY, CLIFF
b. July 10, 1947 Ht. 6-8 Wt. 215 College—Colorado

1971-72 Houston			77	315	133	763	9.9
1972-73 Houston			82	268	92	628	7.7
1973-74 Houston			77	330	90	750	9.7
1974-75 Houston			48	156	68	380	7.9
1975-76 Hou.-L.A.			34	52	33	137	4.0
Totals			318	1121	416	2658	8.4

MEHEN, RICHARD
b. May 20, 1922 Ht. 6-6 Wt. 195 College—Tennessee

1947-48 Toledo		(NL)	57	151	85	387	6.8
1948-49 Waterloo		(NL)	62	315	211	841	13.6
1949-50 Waterloo			62	347	198	892	14.4
1950-51 Balt.-Bos.-Ft. W.			66	192	90	474	7.2
1951-52 Milwaukee			65	293	117	703	10.8
Totals			312	1298	701	3297	10.6

MEINEKE, DON (Monk)
b. Oct. 30, 1930 Ht. 6-7 Wt. 210 College—Dayton

1952-53 Ft. Wayne			68	240	245	725	10.7
1953-54 Ft. Wayne			71	135	136	406	5.7
1954-55 Ft. Wayne			68	136	119	391	5.8
1955-56 Rochester			69	154	181	489	7.1
1957-58 Cincinnati			67	125	77	327	4.9
Totals			343	790	758	2338	6.8

MEINHOLD, CARL (Red)
b. 1925 Ht. 6-2 Wt. 185 College—Long Island Univ.

1947-48 Baltimore			48	108	37	253	5.3
1948-49 Chi.-Prov.			50	101	61	263	5.2
Totals			98	209	98	516	5.3

MELCHIONNI, BILL
b. Oct. 19, 1944 Ht. 6-1 Wt. 165 College—Villanova

1966-67 Philadelphia			71	138	39	315	4.4
1967-68 Philadelphia			71	146	33	325	4.6
1969-70 New York		(ABA)	80	479(5)	255	1218	15.2
1970-71 New York		(ABA)	81	561(2)	301	1425	17.5
1971-72 New York		(ABA)	80	672(2)	336	1682	21.0
1972-73 New York		(ABA)	61	291(6)	163	751	12.3
1973-74 New York		(ABA)	56	116(5)	59	296	5.3
1974-75 New York		(ABA)	77	201(8)	62	472	6.1
Totals			577	2604(28)	1248	6484	11.2

MELCHIONNI, GARY
b. Jan. 19, 1951 Ht. 6-2 Wt. 187 College—Duke

1973-74 Phoenix			69	202	92	496	7.2
1974-75 Phoenix			68	232	114	578	8.5
Totals			137	434	206	1074	7.8

MELVIN, EDWARD
b. Feb. 13, 1916 Ht. 5-9 Wt. 170 College—Duquesne

| 1946-47 Pittsburgh | | | 57 | 99 | 83 | 281 | 4.9 |

MEMINGER, DEAN
b. May 13, 1948 Ht. 6-1 Wt. 175 College—Marquette

1971-72 New York			78	139	79	357	4.6
1972-73 New York			80	188	81	457	5.7
1973-74 New York			78	274	103	651	8.3
1974-75 Atlanta			80	233	168	634	7.9
1975-76 Atlanta			68	155	100	410	6.0
1976-77 N.Y. Knicks			32	15	13	43	1.3
Totals			416	1004	544	2552	6.1

MENCEL, CHUCK
b. April 21, 1933 Ht. 6-0 Wt. 168 College—Minnesota

1955-56 Minneapolis			69	120	78	318	4.6
1956-57 Minneapolis			72	243	179	665	9.2
Totals			141	363	257	983	7.0

MENKE, KEN (Angles)
b. 1922 Ht. 6-0 Wt. 168 College—Illinois

1947-48 Ft. Wayne		(NL)	44	39	45	123	2.8
1949-50 Waterloo			6	6	3	15	2.5
Totals			50	45	48	138	2.8

MENYARD, DEWITT
Ht. 6-10 Wt. 210 College—Utah

| 1967-68 Houston | | (ABA) | 71 | 256 | 131 | 643 | 9.1 |

MERIWETHER, PORTER
b. March 16, 1940 Ht. 6-2 Wt. 180 College—Tenn. St.

| 1962-63 Syracuse | | | 31 | 48 | 23 | 119 | 3.8 |

MESCHERY, TOM
b. Oct. 26, 1938 Ht. 6-6 Wt. 215 College—St. Mary's (Calif.)

1961-62 Philadelphia			80	375	216	966	12.1
1962-63 San Fran.			64	397	228	1022	16.0
1963-64 San Fran.			80	436	207	1079	13.5
1964-65 San Fran.			79	361	278	1000	12.2
1965-66 San Fran.			80	401	224	1026	12.8
1966-67 San Fran.			72	293	175	761	10.6
1967-68 Seattle			82	473	244	1190	14.5
1968-69 Seattle			82	462	220	1144	14.0
1969-70 Seattle			80	394	196	984	12.3
1970-71 Seattle			79	285	162	732	9.3
Totals			778	3877	2150	9904	12.7

Yr.	Team		G	FG	FT	TP	Avg.

MEYER, BILL
Ht. 6-3 Wt. 195 College—Hiram

Yr.	Team		G	FG	FT	TP	Avg.
1967-68 Pittsburgh	(ABA)		7	10	2	22	3.1

MEYERS, DAVID
b. April 21, 1953 Ht. 6-8 Wt. 215 College—UCLA

Yr.	Team	G	FG	FT	TP	Avg.
1975-76 Milwaukee		72	198	135	531	7.4
1976-77 Milwaukee		50	179	127	485	9.7
1977-78 Milwaukee		80	432	314	1178	14.7
1978-79 Milwaukee			(Injured)			
1979-80 Milwaukee		79	399(1)	156	955	12.1
Totals		281	1108(1)	732	3149	11.2

MIASEK, STAN
b. 1924 Ht. 6-5 Wt. 210

Yr.	Team	G	FG	FT	TP	Avg.
1946-47 Detroit		60	331	233	895	14.9
1947-48 Chicago		48	263	190	716	14.9
1948-49 Chicago		58	169	113	451	7.8
1949-50 Chicago		68	176	146	498	7.3
1951-52 Baltimore		66	258	263	779	11.8
1952-53 Balt.-Milw.		65	178	156	512	7.9
Totals		365	1375	1101	3851	10.6

MIHALIK, ZIGMUND (Red)
Ht. 6-0 Wt. 180

Yr.	Team		G	FG	FT	TP	Avg.
1946-47 Pittsburgh			7	3	0	6	0.9
1946-47 Youngstown	(NL)		31	41	12	94	3.0
Totals			38	44	12	100	2.6

MIKAN, EDWARD
b. Oct. 20, 1925 Ht. 6-8 Wt. 230 College—DePaul

Yr.	Team	G	FG	FT	TP	Avg.
1948-49 Chicago		60	229	136	594	9.9
1949-50 Chi.-Roch.		65	89	92	270	4.2
1950-51 Roch.-Wash.-Phila.		61	193	137	523	8.6
1951-52 Philadelphia		66	202	116	520	7.9
1952-53 Phila.-Ind.		62	78	79	235	3.8
1953-54 Boston		9	8	5	21	2.3
Totals		323	799	565	2163	6.7

MIKAN, GEORGE
b. June 18, 1924 Ht. 6-10 Wt. 245 College—DePaul

Yr.	Team		G	FG	FT	TP	Avg.
1946-47 Chicago	(NL)		25	147	119	413	16.5
1947-48 Minneapolis	(NL)		56	406	383	1195	21.3
1948-49 Minneapolis			60	583	532	1698	28.3
1949-50 Minneapolis			68	649	567	1865	27.4
1950-51 Minneapolis			68	678	576	1932	28.4
1951-52 Minneapolis			64	545	433	1523	23.8
1952-53 Minneapolis			70	500	442	1442	20.6
1953-54 Minneapolis			72	441	424	1306	18.1
1955-56 Minneapolis			37	148	94	390	10.5
Totals			520	4097	3570	11764	22.6

MIKAN, LARRY
b. April 8, 1948 Ht. 6-7 Wt. 215 College—Minnesota

Yr.	Team	G	FG	FT	TP	Avg.
1970-71 Cleveland		53	62	34	158	3.0

MIKKELSEN, VERN
b. Oct. 21, 1928 Ht. 6-7 Wt. 230 College—Hamline

Yr.	Team	G	FG	FT	TP	Avg.
1949-50 Minneapolis		68	288	215	791	11.6
1950-51 Minneapolis		64	359	186	904	14.1

Yr.	Team	G	FG	FT	TP	Avg.
1951-52 Minneapolis	66	363	283	1009	15.3
1952-53 Minneapolis	70	378	291	1047	15.0
1953-54 Minneapolis	72	288	221	797	11.1
1954-55 Minneapolis	71	440	447	1327	18.7
1955-56 Minneapolis	72	317	328	962	13.4
1956-57 Minneapolis	72	322	342	986	13.7
1957-58 Minneapolis	72	439	370	1248	17.3
1958-59 Minneapolis	72	353	286	992	13.8
Totals	699	3547	2969	10063	14.4

MIKSIS, AL
b. Feb. 2, 1928 Ht. 6-7 Wt. 210 College—Eastern Ill.

Yr.	Team	G	FG	FT	TP	Avg.
1949-50 Waterloo	8	5	17	27	3.4

MILES, EDDIE
b. July 5, 1940 Ht. 6-4 Wt. 196 College—Seattle

Yr.	Team	G	FG	FT	TP	Avg.
1963-64 Detroit	60	131	62	324	5.4
1964-65 Detroit	76	439	166	1044	13.7
1965-66 Detroit	80	634	298	1566	19.6
1966-67 Detroit	81	582	261	1425	17.6
1967-68 Detroit	76	561	282	1404	18.5
1968-69 Detroit	80	441	182	1064	13.3
1969-70 Det.-Balt.	47	238	133	609	13.0
1970-71 Baltimore	63	252	118	622	9.9
1971-72 New York	42	23	16	62	1.5
Totals	605	3301	1518	8120	13.4

MILITZOK, NAT
b. 1923 Ht. 6-3 Wt. 195 College—CCNY, Hofstra and Cornell

Yr.	Team	G	FG	FT	TP	Avg.
1946-47 N.Y.-Toronto	56	90	64	244	4.4

MILLER, EDWIN (Ed)
b. June 18, 1931 Ht. 6-8 Wt. 225 College—Syracuse

Yr.	Team	G	FG	FT	TP	Avg.
1952-53 Milw.-Balt.	70	273	187	733	10.5
1953-54 Baltimore	72	244	231	719	10.0
Totals	142	517	418	1452	10.2

MILLER, HARRY
b. July 28, 1923 Ht. 6-4 Wt. 230 College—Seton Hall and No. Carolina

Yr.	Team	G	FG	FT	TP	Avg.
1946-47 Toronto	53	58	36	152	2.9

MILLER, JAY
b. July 19, 1943 Ht. 6-5 Wt. 210 College—Notre Dame

Yr.	Team		G	FG	FT	TP	Avg.
1967-68 St. Louis			8	8	4	20	2.5
1968-69 Milwaukee			3	2	5	9	3.0
1968-69 L.A.-Ind.	(ABA)		52	147	127	421	8.1
1969-70 Indiana	(ABA)		52	75	41	191	3.7
1970-71 Indiana	(ABA)		2	4	0	8	4.0
Totals			117	236	177	649	5.5

MILLER, LARRY (Mills)
b. April 4, 1946 Ht. 6-4 Wt. 210 College—No. Carolina

Yr.	Team		G	FG	FT	TP	Avg.
1968-69 Los Angeles	(ABA)		78	463(42)	340	1328	17.0
1969-70 L.A.-Car.	(ABA)		80	317(15)	223	872	10.9
1970-71 Carolina	(ABA)		77	364(13)	197	938	12.2
1971-72 Carolina	(ABA)		83	562(12)	393	1529	18.4
1972-73 San Diego	(ABA)		83	450	306	1206	14.5
1973-74 S.D.-Virg.	(ABA)		80	281	151	713	8.9
1974-75 Utah	(ABA)		5	3	3	9	1.8
Totals			486	2450(82)	1613	6595	13.6

Yr.	Team		G	FG	FT	TP	Avg.

MILLER, WALTER
b. July 30, 1915 Ht. 6-2 Wt. 191 College—Duquesne

Yr.	Team		G	FG	FT	TP	Avg.
1937-38	Pittsburgh	(NL)	9	18	10	46	5.1
1938-39	Pittsburgh	(NL)	19	52	44	148	7.8
1945-46	Youngstown	(NL)	10	4	5	13	1.3
1946-47	Pittsburgh		12	7	9	23	1.9
	Totals		50	81	68	230	4.6

MILLER, WILLIAM
b. Nov. 23, 1924 Ht. 6-3 Wt. 190 College—N.C.

Yr.	Team	G	FG	FT	TP	Avg.
1948-49	Chi.-St. L.	28	21	11	53	1.9

MILLS, JOHN
b. Sept. 7, 1919 Ht. 6-8 Wt. 210 College—Western Ky.

Yr.	Team		G	FG	FT	TP	Avg.
1944-45	Cleveland	(NL)	29	29	42	100	3.4
1945-46	Cleveland	(NL)	19	13	25	51	2.7
1946-47	Pittsburgh		47	55	71	181	3.9
	Totals		95	97	138	332	3.5

MINOR, DAVAGE (Dave)
b. Feb. 23, 1922 Ht. 6-2 Wt. 185 College—Toledo and UCLA

Yr.	Team	G	FG	FT	TP	Avg.
1951-52	Baltimore	57	185	101	471	8.3
1952-53	Balt.-Milw.	59	154	98	406	6.9
	Totals	116	339	199	877	7.6

MINOR, MARK
b. May 14, 1950 Ht. 6-6 Wt. 215 College—Ohio State

Yr.	Team	G	FG	FT	TP	Avg.
1972-73	Boston	4	1	3	5	1.3

MISAKA, WAT
b. Dec. 21, 1923 Ht. 5-7 Wt. 150 College—Utah

Yr.	Team	G	FG	FT	TP	Avg.
1947-48	New York	3	3	1	7	2.3

MITCHELL, LELAND
b. Feb. 22, 1941 Ht. 6-4 Wt. 210 College—Miss. State

Yr.	Team		G	FG	FT	TP	Avg.
1967-68	New Orleans	(ABA)	78	122(21)	56	321	4.1

MITCHELL, MURRAY
b. March 19, 1923 Ht. 6-6 College—Sam Houston

Yr.	Team	G	FG	FT	TP	Avg.
1949-50	Anderson	2	1	0	2	1.0

MLKVY, BILL
b. Jan. 19, 1931 Ht. 6-4 Wt. 190 College—Temple

Yr.	Team	G	FG	FT	TP	Avg.
1952-53	Philadelphia	31	75	31	181	5.8

MODZELEWSKI, STANLEY (Stutz)
See Stutz, Stan

MOE, DOUG
b. Sept. 21, 1938 Ht. 6-5 Wt. 220 College—No. Carolina

Yr.	Team		G	FG	FT	TP	Avg.
1967-68	New Orleans	(ABA)	78	665(3)	551	1884	24.2
1968-69	Oakland	(ABA)	75	529(5)	360	1423	19.0
1969-70	Carolina	(ABA)	80	535(8)	304	1382	17.2
1970-71	Virginia	(ABA)	78	397(2)	221	1017	13.0
1971-72	Virginia	(ABA)	67	175(1)	104	455	6.8
	Totals		378	2301(19)	1540	6161	16.3

MOFFETT, LARRY
b. Nov. 5, 1954 Ht. 6-8 Wt. 210 College—Nevada Las Vegas

Yr.	Team	G	FG	FT	TP	Avg.
1977-78	Houston	20	5	6	16	0.8

MOGUS, LEO
b. April 13, 1921 Ht. 6-4 Wt. 205 College—Youngstown

Yr.	Team		G	FG	FT	TP	Avg.
1945-46	Youngstown	(NL)	16	61	66	188	11.8
1946-47	Cleve.-Tor.		58	259	235	753	13.0
1948-49	Balt.-Ft. W.-Ind.		52	172	177	521	10.0
1949-50	Philadelphia		64	172	218	562	8.8
1950-51	Philadelphia		57	43	53	139	2.4
	Totals		247	707	749	2163	8.8

MOLINAS, JACK
b. 1932 Ht. 6-6 Wt. 200 College—Columbia
d. Aug. 3, 1975

Yr.	Team	G	FG	FT	TP	Avg.
1953-54	Ft. Wayne	29	108	134	350	12.1

MOLIS, WAYNE
b. April 17, 1943 Ht. 6-8 Wt. 230 College—Lewis

Yr.	Team		G	FG	FT	TP	Avg.
1966-67	New York		13	19	7	45	3.5
1967-68	Oakland	(ABA)	5	5	4	14	2.8
	Totals		18	24	11	59	3.3

MONEY, ERIC
b. Feb. 6, 1956 Ht. 6-0 Wt. 170 College—Arizona

Yr.	Team	G	FG	FT	TP	Avg.
1974-75	Detroit	66	144	31	319	4.8
1975-76	Detroit	80	449	145	1043	13.0
1976-77	Detroit	73	329	90	748	10.2
1977-78	Detroit	76	600	214	1414	18.6
1978-79	N.J.-Phil.	69	444	170	1058	15.3
1979-80	Phil.-Detr.	61	273	83	629	10.3
	Totals	425	2239	733	5211	12.3

MONROE, V. EARL (The Pearl)
b. Nov. 21, 1944 Ht. 6-3 Wt. 180 College—Winston-Salem

Yr.	Team	G	FG	FT	TP	Avg.
1967-68	Baltimore	82	742	507	1991	24.3
1968-69	Baltimore	80	809	447	2065	25.8
1969-70	Baltimore	82	695	532	1922	23.4
1970-71	Baltimore	81	663	406	1732	21.4
1971-72	Balt.-N.Y.	63	287	175	749	11.9
1972-73	New York	75	496	171	1163	15.5
1973-74	New York	41	240	93	573	14.0
1974-75	New York	78	668	297	1633	20.9
1975-76	New York	76	647	280	1574	20.7
1976-77	N.Y. Knicks	77	613	307	1533	19.9
1977-78	New York	76	556	242	1354	17.8
1978-79	New York	64	329	129	787	12.3
1979-80	New York	51	161	56	378	7.4
	Totals	926	6906	3642	17454	18.8

MONTGOMERY, HOWARD
b. Aug. 22, 1940 Ht. 6-4½ Wt. 220 College—Pan American

Yr.	Team	G	FG	FT	TP	Avg.
1962-63	San Fran.	20	65	14	144	7.2

MOONEY, JAMES
b. 1927 Ht. 6-5 Wt. 215 College—Villanova

Yr.	Team	G	FG	FT	TP	Avg.
1952-53	Balt.-Phil.	18	54	27	135	7.5

Yr.	Team		G	FG	FT	TP	Avg.

MOORE, GENE
b. July 29, 1945 Ht. 6-9 Wt. 240 College—St. Louis U.

Yr.	Team		G	FG	FT	TP	Avg.
1968-69	Kentucky	(ABA)	76	417	204	1038	13.7
1969-70	Kentucky	(ABA)	83	630(2)	209	1471	17.7
1970-71	Texas	(ABA)	84	467(2)	189	1125	13.4
1971-72	Dal.-N.Y.	(ABA)	77	253(1)	89	596	7.7
1972-73	San Diego	(ABA)	83	400(4)	180	984	11.9
1973-74	San Diego	(ABA)	49	154(1)	41	350	7.1
1974-75	St. Louis	(ABA)	13	13	4	30	2.3
	Totals		465	2334(10)	916	5594	12.0

MOORE, JACKIE
b. Sept. 24, 1932 Ht. 6-5 Wt. 182 College—LaSalle

Yr.	Team	G	FG	FT	TP	Avg.
1954-55	Syra.-Milw.-Phila.	23	44	22	110	4.8
1955-56	Philadelphia	54	50	32	132	2.4
1956-57	Philadelphia	57	43	37	123	2.2
	Totals	134	137	91	365	2.7

MOORE, LARRY
Ht. 6-7

Yr.	Team		G	FG	FT	TP	Avg.
1967-68	Anaheim	(ABA)	12	8	11	27	2.3

MOORE, OTTO
b. Aug. 27, 1946 Ht. 6-11 Wt. 205 Coll.—Pan American

Yr.	Team	G	FG	FT	TP	Avg.
1968-69	Detroit	74	241	88	570	7.7
1969-70	Detroit	81	383	194	960	11.9
1970-71	Detroit	82	310	121	741	9.0
1971-72	Phoenix	81	260	94	614	7.6
1972-73	Houston	82	418	127	963	11.7
1973-74	Hou.-K.C.-O.	78	120	39	279	3.6
1974-75	Det.-N.O.	42	118	46	282	6.7
1975-76	New Orleans	81	293	144	730	9.0
1976-77	New Orleans	81	193	91	477	5.9
	Totals	682	2336	944	5616	8.2

MOORE, RICHIE
b. 1945 Ht. 6-2 Wt. 190 College—Villanova and Hiram Scott

Yr.	Team		G	FG	FT	TP	Avg.
1967-68	Denver	(ABA)	18	24	21	69	3.8

MORELAND, JACK
b. March 11, 1938 Ht. 6-7 Wt. 215 College—La. Tech.
d. Dec. 19, 1971

Yr.	Team		G	FG	FT	TP	Avg.
1960-61	Detroit		64	191	86	468	7.3
1961-62	Detroit		74	205	139	549	7.4
1962-63	Detroit		78	271	145	687	8.8
1963-64	Detroit		78	272	164	708	9.1
1964-65	Detroit		54	103	66	272	5.0
1967-68	New Orleans	(ABA)	76	459(2)	192	1112	14.6
1968-69	New Orleans	(ABA)	78	468(2)	221	1159	14.9
1969-70	New Orleans	(ABA)	80	317(2)	139	775	9.2
	Totals		582	2286(6)	1152	5730	9.8

MORGAN, REX
b. Oct. 27, 1948 Ht. 6-5 Wt. 190 College—Jacksonville

Yr.	Team	G	FG	FT	TP	Avg.
1970-71	Boston	34	41	35	117	3.4
1971-72	Boston	28	16	23	55	2.0
	Totals	62	57	58	172	2.8

MORGENTHALER, ELMORE
b. 1925 Ht. 6-9 Wt. 230 College—Boston College/N. Mexico St.

Yr.	Team	G	FG	FT	TP	Avg.
1946-47	Providence	11	4	7	15	1.4
1948-49	Philadelphia	20	15	12	42	2.1
	Totals	31	19	19	57	1.8

MORRIS, G. MAX
b. March 14, 1925 Ht. 6-2 Wt. 195 College—Northwestern

Yr.	Team		G	FG	FT	TP	Avg.
1946-47	Chicago	(NL)	33	44	33	121	3.7
1947-48	Sheboygan	(NL)	39	132	132	396	10.2
1948-49	Sheboygan	(NL)	41	70	68	208	5.1
1949-50	Sheboygan		62	252	277	781	12.6
	Totals		175	498	510	1506	8.6

MORRISON, DWIGHT (Red)
b. 1931 Ht. 6-8 Wt. 225 College—Idaho

Yr.	Team	G	FG	FT	TP	Avg.
1954-55	Boston	71	120	72	312	4.4
1955-56	Boston	71	89	44	222	3.1
1957-58	St. Louis	13	9	3	21	1.6
	Totals	155	218	119	555	3.6

MORRISON, JOHN
b. 1945 Ht. 6-2 Wt. 190 College—Canisius

Yr.	Team		G	FG	FT	TP	Avg.
1967-68	Denver	(ABA)	9	10(1)	6	27	3.0

MOSLEY, GLENN
b. Dec. 26, 1955 Ht. 6-8 Wt. 195 College—Seton Hall

Yr.	Team	G	FG	FT	TP	Avg.
1977-78	Philadelphia	6	5	3	13	2.2
1978-79	San Antonio	26	31	23	85	3.3
	Totals	32	36	26	98	3.1

MOUNT, RICK
b. Jan. 5, 1947 Ht. 6-4 Wt. 185 College—Purdue

Yr.	Team		G	FG	FT	TP	Avg.
1970-71	Indiana	(ABA)	66	149(23)	116	437	6.6
1971-72	Indiana	(ABA)	78	420(57)	216	1113	14.3
1972-73	Kentucky	(ABA)	61	369(9)	159	906	14.9
1973-74	Ken.-Utah	(ABA)	52	179(12)	59	429	8.3
1974-75	Memphis	(ABA)	26	181(20)	63	445	17.1
	Totals		283	1298(121)	613	3330	11.8

MRAZOVICH, CHARLES
b. Feb. 26, 1924 Ht. 6-5 Wt. 185 College—Eastern Ky.

Yr.	Team	G	FG	FT	TP	Avg.
1950-51	Indianapolis	23	24	28	76	3.3

MUELLER, ERWIN
b. March 12, 1944 Ht. 6-8 Wt. 230 College—San Fran.

Yr.	Team		G	FG	FT	TP	Avg.
1966-67	Chicago		80	422	171	1015	12.7
1967-68	Chi.-L.A.		74	223	107	553	7.5
1968-69	Chi.-Sea.		78	144	89	377	4.8
1969-70	Sea.-Det.		78	300	189	789	10.1
1970-71	Detroit		52	126	60	312	6.0
1971-72	Detroit		42	68	43	179	4.3
1972-73	Detroit		21	9	5	23	1.1
1972-73	Virginia	(ABA)	17	17	3	37	2.2
1973-74	Memphis	(ABA)	3	0	2	2	0.7
	Totals		445	1309	669	3287	7.4

MULLANEY, JOE
b. Nov. 17, 1925 Ht. 6-0 Wt. 165 College—Holy Cross

Yr.	Team	G	FG	FT	TP	Avg.
1949-50	Boston	37	9	12	30	0.8

Yr.	Team		G	FG	FT	TP	Avg.

MULLENS, ROBERT
b. Nov. 1, 1922 Ht. 6-1 Wt. 175 College—Fordham

Yr.	Team	G	FG	FT	TP	Avg.
1946-47 N.Y.-Toronto		54	125	64	314	5.8

MULLINS, JEFF (Pork Chop)
b. March 18, 1942 Ht. 6-4 Wt. 190 College—Duke

Yr.	Team	G	FG	FT	TP	Avg.
1964-65 St. Louis		44	87	41	215	4.9
1965-66 St. Louis		44	113	29	255	5.8
1966-67 San Fran.		77	421	150	992	12.9
1967-68 San Fran.		79	610	273	1493	18.9
1968-69 San Fran.		78	697	381	1775	22.8
1969-70 San Fran.		74	656	320	1632	22.1
1970-71 San Fran.		75	630	302	1562	20.8
1971-72 Golden St.		80	685	350	1720	21.5
1972-73 Golden St.		81	651	143	1445	17.8
1973-74 Golden St.		77	541	168	1250	16.2
1974-75 Golden St.		66	234	71	539	8.2
1975-76 Golden St.		29	58	23	139	4.8
	Totals	804	5383	2251	13017	16.2

MUNROE, GEORGE
b. Jan. 5, 1922 Ht. 5-11½ Wt. 170 College—Dartmouth

Yr.	Team	G	FG	FT	TP	Avg.
1946-47 St. Louis		59	164	86	414	7.0
1947-48 Boston		21	27	17	71	3.4
	Totals	80	191	103	485	6.1

MURPHY, ALLEN
b. July 15, 1952 Ht. 6-5 Wt. 190 College—Louisville

Yr.	Team		G	FG	FT	TP	Avg.
1975-76 Kentucky	(ABA)		29	43	27	113	3.9

MURPHY, JOHN
b. 1923 Ht. 6-2 Wt. 175 College—Manhattan and John Marshall

Yr.	Team	G	FG	FT	TP	Avg.
1946-47 N.Y.-Phila.		20	11	10	32	1.6

MURPHY, RICHARD
b. 1921 Ht. 6-1 Wt. 180 College—Manhattan
d. Oct. 22, 1973

Yr.	Team	G	FG	FT	TP	Avg.
1946-47 N.Y.-Boston		31	15	4	34	1.1

MURRAY, KEN
b. April 20, 1928 Ht. 6-2 Wt. 195 College—St. Bonaventure

Yr.	Team	G	FG	FT	TP	Avg.
1950-51 Balt.-Ft. W.		66	301	248	850	12.9
1953-54 Ft. Wayne		49	53	43	149	3.0
1954-55 Balt.-Phila.		66	187	98	472	7.2
	Totals	181	541	389	1471	8.1

MURRELL, WILLIE
b. Sept. 13, 1941 Ht. 6-6½ Wt. 225 College—E. Okla./Kans. St.

Yr.	Team		G	FG	FT	TP	Avg.
1967-68 Denver	(ABA)	71	498(3)	166	1165	16.4
1968-69 Miami	(ABA)	75	476(4)	191	1147	15.3
1969-70 Kentucky	(ABA)	35	48(4)	18	118	3.4
	Totals		181	1022(11)	375	2430	13.4

MURREY, DORIE
b. Sept. 7, 1943 Ht. 6-8 Wt. 215 College—Detroit

Yr.	Team	G	FG	FT	TP	Avg.
1966-67 Detroit		35	33	32	98	2.8
1967-68 Seattle		81	211	168	590	7.3
1968-69 Seattle		38	75	62	212	5.6
1969-70 Seattle		81	153	136	442	5.5
1970-71 Port.-Balt.		71	78	75	231	3.3
1971-72 Baltimore		51	43	24	110	2.2
	Totals	357	593	497	1683	4.7

MUSI, ANGELO
b. July 25, 1918 Ht. 5-9 Wt. 145 College—Temple

Yr.	Team	G	FG	FT	TP	Avg.
1946-47 Phila.		60	230	102	562	9.4
1947-48 Phila.		43	134	51	319	7.4
1948-49 Phila.		58	194	90	478	8.2
	Totals	161	558	243	1359	8.4

NABER, ROBERT
b. Sept. 3, 1929 Ht. 6-3 Wt. 185 College—Louisville

Yr.	Team	G	FG	FT	TP	Avg.
1952-53 Indianapolis		4	0	1	1	0.3

NACHAMKIN, BORIS
Ht. 6-6 Wt. 210 College—New York University

Yr.	Team	G	FG	FT	TP	Avg.
1954-55 Rochester		6	6	8	20	3.3

NAGEL, JERRY
b. May 18, 1928 Ht. 6-0½ Wt. 190 College—Loyola (Ill.)

Yr.	Team	G	FG	FT	TP	Avg.
1949-50 Ft. Wayne		14	6	1	13	0.9

NAGY, FRITZ
b. Jan. 3, 1924 Ht. 6-2 Wt. 185 College—Akron

Yr.	Team		G	FG	FT	TP	Avg.
1947-48 Indianapolis	(NL)	39	42	42	126	3.2
1948-49 Indianapolis		50	94	65	253	5.1
	Totals		89	136	107	379	4.3

NAPOLITANO, PAUL
b. 1922 Ht. 6-2 Wt. 185 College—San Francisco

Yr.	Team		G	FG	FT	TP	Avg.
1947-48 Minneapolis	(NL)	52	72	11	155	3.0
1948-49 Indianapolis		1	0	0	0	0.0
	Totals		53	72	11	155	2.9

NASH, BOB
b. Aug. 24, 1950 Ht. 6-8 Wt. 204 College—Hawaii

Yr.	Team		G	FG	FT	TP	Avg.
1972-73 Detroit		36	16	11	43	1.2
1973-74 Detroit		35	41	24	106	3.0
1974-75 San Diego	(ABA)	17	27	13	67	3.9
1977-78 Kansas City		66	157	50	364	5.5
1978-79 Kansas City		82	227	69	523	6.4
	Totals		236	468	167	1103	4.0

NASH, CHARLES (Cotton)
b. July 24, 1942 Ht. 6-5 Wt. 225 College—Kentucky

Yr.	Team		G	FG	FT	TP	Avg.
1964-65 L.A.-S.F.		45	47	43	137	3.0
1967-68 Kentucky	(ABA)	39	106	121	333	8.5
	Totals		84	153	164	470	5.6

NAULLS, WILLIE
b. Oct. 7, 1934 Ht. 6-6 Wt. 225 College—UCLA

Yr.	Team	G	FG	FT	TP	Avg.
1956-57 St. L.-N.Y.		71	293	132	718	10.1
1957-58 New York		68	472	284	1228	18.1
1958-59 New York		68	405	258	1068	15.7
1959-60 New York		65	551	286	1388	21.3
1960-61 New York		79	737	372	1846	23.4
1961-62 New York		75	747	383	1877	25.0
1962-63 N.Y.-S.F.		70	370	166	906	12.7
1963-64 Boston		78	321	125	767	9.8
1964-65 Boston		71	302	143	747	10.5
1965-66 Boston		71	328	104	760	10.7
	Totals	716	4526	2253	11305	15.8

Yr.	Team		G	FG	FT	TP	Avg.

NEAL, EBBERLE (Jim)
b. 1930 Ht. 6-11 Wt. 235 College—Wofford

Yr.	Team		G	FG	FT	TP	Avg.
1953-54	Syracuse		67	117	78	312	4.7
1954-55	Baltimore		13	12	15	39	3.3
	Totals		80	129	93	351	4.4

NEAL, LLOYD
b. Dec. 10, 1950 Ht. 6-7 Wt. 225 College—Tenn. State

Yr.	Team	G	FG	FT	TP	Avg.
1972-73	Portland	82	455	187	1097	13.4
1973-74	Portland	80	246	117	609	7.6
1974-75	Portland	82	409	189	1007	12.3
1975-76	Portland	68	435	186	1056	15.5
1976-77	Portland	58	160	77	397	6.8
1977-78	Portland	61	272	127	671	11.0
1978-79	Portland	4	4	1	9	2.3
	Totals	435	1981	884	4846	11.1

NEGRATTI, ALBERT
b. 1922 Ht. 6-3½ Wt. 200 College—Seton Hall

Yr.	Team		G	FG	FT	TP	Avg.
1945-46	Rochester	(NL)	16	19	10	48	3.0
1946-47	Rochester	(NL)	33	15	14	44	1.3
1946-47	Washington		11	13	5	31	2.8
	Totals		60	47	29	123	2.1

NELSON, BARRY
b. Sept. 19, 1949 Ht. 6-10 Wt. 230 College—Duquesne

Yr.	Team	G	FG	FT	TP	Avg.
1971-72	Milwaukee	28	15	5	35	1.3

NELSON, DON
b. May 15, 1940 Ht. 6-6 Wt. 210 College—Iowa

Yr.	Team	G	FG	FT	TP	Avg.
1962-63	Chicago	63	129	161	419	6.7
1963-64	Los Angeles	80	135	149	419	5.2
1964-65	Los Angeles	39	36	20	92	2.4
1965-66	Boston	75	271	223	765	10.2
1966-67	Boston	79	227	141	595	7.5
1967-68	Boston	82	312	195	819	10.0
1968-69	Boston	82	374	201	949	11.6
1969-70	Boston	82	461	337	1259	15.4
1970-71	Boston	82	412	317	1141	13.9
1971-72	Boston	82	389	356	1134	13.8
1972-73	Boston	72	309	159	777	10.8
1973-74	Boston	82	364	215	943	11.5
1974-75	Boston	79	423	263	1109	14.0
1975-76	Boston	75	175	127	477	6.4
	Totals	1053	4017	2864	10898	10.3

NELSON, LOUIE
b. May 28, 1951 Ht. 6-3 Wt. 190 College—Washington

Yr.	Team	G	FG	FT	TP	Avg.
1973-74	Capital	49	93	53	239	4.9
1974-75	New Orleans	72	307	192	806	11.2
1975-76	New Orleans	66	327	169	823	12.5
1976-77	San Antonio	4	7	4	18	4.5
1977-78	K.C.-N.J.	33	85	57	227	6.9
	Totals	224	819	475	2113	9.4

NEMELKA, DICK
b. Oct. 1, 1943 Ht. 6-0 Wt. 175 College—Brigham Young

Yr.	Team		G	FG	FT	TP	Avg.
1970-71	Utah	(ABA)	39	82(20)	32	216	5.5

NETOLICKY, BOB (Neto)
b. Aug. 2, 1942 Ht. 6-9 Wt. 225 College—Drake

Yr.	Team		G	FG	FT	TP	Avg.
1967-68	Indiana	(ABA)	71	468	220	1156	16.3
1968-69	Indiana	(ABA)	78	583	306	1472	18.9
1969-70	Indiana	(ABA)	82	673(2)	343	1691	20.6
1970-71	Indiana	(ABA)	82	651(2)	237	1541	18.8
1971-72	Indiana	(ABA)	83	522(4)	202	1250	15.1
1972-73	Dallas	(ABA)	84	650	269	1569	18.7
1973-74	S.A.-Ind.	(ABA)	75	314(7)	106	736	9.8
1974-75	Indiana	(ABA)	59	189(2)	62	442	7.5
1975-76	Indiana	(ABA)	4	8	3	19	4.8
	Totals		618	4058(12)	1748	9876	16.0

NEUMANN, JOHNNY
b. Sept. 11, 1951 Ht. 6-6 Wt. 200 College—Mississippi

Yr.	Team		G	FG	FT	TP	Avg.
1971-72	Memphis	(ABA)	77	545(26)	293	1409	18.3
1972-73	Memphis	(ABA)	79	605(9)	338	1548	19.5
1973-74	Mem.-Utah	(ABA)	87	482(18)	166	1148	13.2
1974-75	Vir.-Ind.	(ABA)	52	186(21)	52	445	8.6
1975-76	Vir.-Ken.	(ABA)	77	393(71)	151	1008	13.1
1976-77	Buff.-L.A.		63	161	59	381	6.0
1977-78	Indiana		20	35	13	83	4.2
	Totals		455	2407(145)	1063	6022	13.2

NEUMANN, PAUL
b. Jan. 30, 1938 Ht. 6-1 Wt. 175 College—Stanford

Yr.	Team	G	FG	FT	TP	Avg.
1961-62	Syracuse	79	172	133	477	6.0
1962-63	Syracuse	80	237	181	655	8.2
1963-64	Phila.	74	324	210	858	11.6
1964-65	Phila.-S.F.	76	365	234	964	12.7
1965-66	San Fran.	66	343	265	951	14.4
1966-67	San Fran.	78	386	312	1084	13.9
	Totals	453	1827	1335	4989	11.0

NEWMARK, DAVE
b. Sept. 11, 1946 Ht. 7-0 Wt. 240 College—Columbia

Yr.	Team		G	FG	FT	TP	Avg.
1968-69	Chicago		81	185	86	456	5.6
1969-70	Atlanta		64	127	59	313	4.9
1970-71	Carolina	(ABA)	31	100	34	234	7.6
	Totals		176	412	179	1003	5.7

NEWTON, BILL
b. Dec. 22, 1950 Ht. 6-9 Wt. 220 College—Indiana

Yr.	Team		G	FG	FT	TP	Avg.
1972-73	Indiana	(ABA)	24	24(1)	9	58	2.4
1973-74	Indiana	(ABA)	11	7	1	15	1.4
	Totals		35	31(1)	10	73	2.1

NICHOLS, JACK
b. April 9, 1926 Ht. 6-7 Wt. 230 College—Washington

Yr.	Team	G	FG	FT	TP	Avg.
1948-49	Washington	34	153	92	398	11.7
1949-50	Wash.-Tri-C.	67	310	259	879	13.1
1950-51	Tri-Cities	5	18	10	46	9.2
1952-53	Milwaukee	69	425	240	1090	15.8
1953-54	Mil.-Boston	75	163	113	439	5.9
1954-55	Boston	64	249	138	636	9.9
1955-56	Boston	60	330	200	860	14.3
1956-57	Boston	61	195	108	498	8.2
1957-58	Boston	69	170	59	399	5.8
	Totals	504	2013	1219	5245	10.4

Yr.	Team		G	FG	FT	TP	Avg.

NIEMANN, RICH

b. July 2, 1946 Ht. 6-0 Wt. 245 College—St. Louis Univ.

Yr.	Team		G	FG	FT	TP	Avg.
1968-69	Det.-Mil.		34	44	19	107	3.1
1969-70	Boston		6	2	2	6	1.0
1969-70	Carolina	(ABA)	63	285	141	711	11.3
1970-71	Floridians	(ABA)	51	121	43	285	5.6
1971-72	Dallas	(ABA)	33	48	25	121	3.7
	Totals		187	500	230	1230	6.6

NIEMIERA, RICHARD

b. May 26, 1926 Ht. 6-1 Wt. 165 College—Notre Dame

Yr.	Team		G	FG	FT	TP	Avg.
1946-47	Ft. Wayne	(NL)	13	28	17	73	5.6
1947-48	Ft. Wayne	(NL)	59	118	97	333	5.6
1948-49	Ft. Wayne		55	115	132	362	6.6
1949-50	Ft. W.-And.		60	110	104	324	5.4
	Totals		187	371	350	1092	5.8

NOBLE, CHUCK

b. July 24, 1931 Ht. 6-4 Wt. 195 College—Louisville

Yr.	Team	G	FG	FT	TP	Avg.
1955-56	Ft. Wayne	72	270	146	686	9.5
1956-57	Ft. Wayne	54	200	76	476	8.8
1957-58	Detroit	61	199	56	454	7.4
1958-59	Detroit	65	189	83	461	7.1
1959-60	Detroit	58	276	101	653	11.3
1960-61	Detroit	75	196	82	474	6.3
1961-62	Detroit	26	32	8	72	2.8
	Totals	411	1362	552	3276	8.0

NOEL, PAUL

b. Aug. 8, 1924 Ht. 6-4 Wt. 185 College—Kentucky

Yr.	Team	G	FG	FT	TP	Avg.
1947-48	New York	29	40	19	99	3.4
1948-49	New York	47	70	37	177	3.8
1949-50	New York	65	98	53	249	3.8
1950-51	Rochester	52	49	32	130	2.5
1951-52	Rochester	8	2	2	6	0.8
	Totals	201	259	143	661	3.3

NOLAN, JIM

Ht. 6-8 Wt. 210 College—Georgia Tech

Yr.	Team	G	FG	FT	TP	Avg.
1949-50	Philadelphia	5	4	0	8	1.6

NOLEN, PAUL

b. June 9, 1927 Ht. 6-10 Wt. 215 College—Texas Tech

Yr.	Team	G	FG	FT	TP	Avg.
1953-54	Baltimore	1	0	0	0	0.0

NORDMANN, ROBERT (Bevo)

b. Dec. 11, 1939 Ht. 6-10 Wt. 225 College—St. Louis

Yr.	Team	G	FG	FT	TP	Avg.
1961-62	Cincinnati	58	51	29	131	2.2
1962-63	St. L.-N.Y.	53	156	59	371	7.0
1963-64	N.Y.-St. L.	19	27	9	63	3.3
1964-65	Boston	3	3	0	6	2.2
	Totals	133	237	97	571	4.3

NORLANDER, JOHN

b. March 5, 1921 Ht. 6-3 Wt. 180 College—Hamline/Maryland St.

Yr.	Team	G	FG	FT	TP	Avg.
1946-47	Washington	60	223	180	626	10.4
1947-48	Washington	48	167	135	469	9.8
1948-49	Washington	60	164	116	444	7.4
1949-50	Washington	40	99	53	251	6.3
1950-51	Washington	9	6	9	21	2.3
	Totals	217	659	493	1811	8.3

NORMAN, CONIEL

b. Sept. 24, 1953 Ht. 6-3 Wt. 176 College—Arizona

Yr.	Team	G	FG	FT	TP	Avg.
1974-75	Philadelphia	12	23	2	48	4.0
1975-76	Philadelphia	65	183	20	386	5.9
1978-79	San Diego	22	71	19	161	7.3
	Totals	99	277	41	595	6.0

NORRIS, SYLVESTER

b. Feb. 18, 1957 Ht. 6-11 Wt. 220 College—Jackson State

Yr.	Team	G	FG	FT	TP	Avg.
1979-80	San Antonio	17	18	4	40	2.4

NORWOOD, WILLIE

b. Aug. 8, 1947 Ht. 6-7 Wt. 220 College—Alcorn A & M

Yr.	Team	G	FG	FT	TP	Avg.
1971-72	Detroit	78	222	140	584	7.5
1972-73	Detroit	79	249	154	652	8.3
1973-74	Detroit	74	247	95	589	8.0
1974-75	Detroit	24	64	31	159	6.6
1975-76	Seattle	64	146	152	444	6.9
1976-77	Seattle	76	216	151	583	7.7
1977-78	Sea.-Port.	35	74	50	198	5.7
	Totals	430	1218	773	3209	7.5

NOSTRAND, GEORGE

b. April 5, 1924 Ht. 6-8 Wt. 197 College—High Point and Wyoming

Yr.	Team	G	FG	FT	TP	Avg.
1946-47	Clev.-Tor.	61	192	98	482	7.9
1947-48	Providence	45	196	129	521	11.6
1948-49	Prov.-Boston	60	212	165	589	9.8
1949-50	Bos.-Tri. C.-Chi.	55	78	56	212	3.9
	Totals	221	678	448	1804	8.2

NOSZKA, STANLEY

b. Sept. 19, 1920 Ht. 6-1 Wt. 185 College—Duquesne

Yr.	Team		G	FG	FT	TP	Avg.
1945-46	Youngstown	(NL)	2	0	1	1	0.5
1946-47	Pittsburgh		48	199	109	507	8.6
1947-48	Boston		22	27	24	78	3.5
1948-49	Boston		30	30	15	75	2.5
	Totals		102	256	149	661	6.5

NOVAK, MICHAEL

b. April 23, 1915 Ht. 6-9 Wt. 220 College—Loyola (Ill.)

Yr.	Team		G	FG	FT	TP	Avg.
1939-40	Chicago	(NL)	28	113	65	293	10.5
1940-41	Chicago	(NL)	23	56	34	146	6.3
1941-42	Chicago	(NL)	19	58	31	147	7.7
1942-43	Chicago	(NL)	18	50	35	135	7.5
1943-44	Sheboygan	(NL)	22	39	14	92	4.2
1944-45	Sheboygan	(NL)	27	88	57	233	8.6
1945-46	Sheboygan	(NL)	34	111	88	310	9.1
1946-47	Syracuse	(NL)	36	153	73	379	10.5
1947-48	Syracuse	(NL)	60	211	124	546	9.1
1948-49	Rochester		60	124	72	320	5.3
1949-50	Roch.-Phila.		60	37	25	99	1.7
1953-54	Syracuse		5	0	1	1	0.2
	Totals		392	1041	619	2701	6.9

NOWELL, MEL

b. Dec. 27, 1939 Ht. 6-2 Wt. 174 College—Ohio State

Yr.	Team		G	FG	FT	TP	Avg.
1962-63	Chicago		39	92	48	232	5.9
1967-68	New Jersey	(ABA)	76	273(9)	176	731	9.6
	Totals		115	365(9)	224	963	8.4

Yr.	Team		G	FG	FT	TP	Avg.
O'BOYLE, JOHN							
b. March 7, 1928 Ht. 6-2 Wt. 186 College—Colo. State							
1952-53 Milwaukee			5	8	5	21	4.2
O'BRIEN, JIM							
b. April 9, 1950 Ht. 6-3 Wt. 170 College—Boston Coll.							
1971-72 Pitt.-Ky.	(ABA)		84	173(7)	65	418	5.0
1972-73 Kentucky	(ABA)		68	126	68	320	4.7
1973-74 Ken.-S.D.	(ABA)		72	211(7)	79	508	7.1
1974-75 San Diego	(ABA)		79	210(4)	125	549	7.0
	Totals		302	720(18)	337	1795	5.9
O'BRIEN, JIM							
b. Nov. 7, 1951 Ht. 6-7 Wt. 200 College—Maryland							
1973-74 New York	(ABA)		11	15	9	39	3.6
1974-75 Memphis	(ABA)		47	88(6)	47	229	4.9
	Totals		58	103(6)	56	268	4.6
O'BRIEN, RALPH (Buckshot)							
b. April 28, 1928 Ht. 5-9 Wt. 160 College—Butler							
1951-52 Indianapolis			64	228	122	578	9.0
1952-53 Ind.-Balt.			55	96	78	270	4.9
	Totals		119	324	200	858	7.1
O'BRIEN, ROBERT							
b. Jan. 26, 1927 Ht. 6-4½ Wt. 190 College—Kansas and Pepperdine							
1947-48 Philadelphia			22	17	15	49	2.2
1948-49 Phila.-St. L.			24	10	12	32	1.3
	Totals		46	27	27	81	1.8
O'CONNELL, DERMOTT							
b. April 13, 1928 Ht. 6-0 Wt. 174 College—Holy Cross							
1948-49 Boston			21	87	30	204	9.7
1949-50 Bos.-St. Louis			61	111	47	269	4.4
	Totals		82	198	77	473	5.8
O'DONNELL, ANDY							
b. March 10, 1925 Ht. 6-1 Wt. 180 College—Loyola (Md.)							
1949-50 Baltimore			25	38	14	90	3.6
OGDEN, BUD							
b. Dec. 19, 1946 Ht. 6-6 Wt. 215 College—Santa Clara							
1969-70 Philadelphia			47	82	27	191	4.1
1970-71 Philadelphia			27	24	18	66	2.4
	Totals		74	106	45	257	3.5
OGDEN, RALPH							
b. Jan 25, 1948 Ht. 6-5 Wt. 205 College—Santa Clara							
1970-71 San Francisco			32	17	8	42	1.3
O'GRADY, FRANCIS							
b. Jan. 19, 1920 Ht. 5-11 Wt. 160 College—Georgetown							
1946-47 Washington			55	55	38	148	2.7
1947-48 Washington			44	67	36	170	3.9
1948-49 St. L.-Prov.			47	85	49	219	4.7
	Totals		146	207	123	537	3.7

Yr.	Team		G	FG	FT	TP	Avg.
O'HANLON, FRAN							
b. 1948 Ht. 6-1 Wt. 175 College—Villanova							
1970-71 Floridians	(ABA)		14	8	6	22	1.6
OHL, DON							
b. April 18, 1936 Ht. 6-3 Wt. 190 College—Illinois							
1960-61 Detroit			79	427	200	1054	13.1
1961-62 Detroit			77	555	201	1311	17.0
1962-63 Detroit			80	636	275	1547	19.3
1963-64 Detroit			71	500	225	1225	17.3
1964-65 Baltimore			77	568	284	1420	18.4
1965-66 Baltimore			73	593	316	1502	20.6
1966-67 Baltimore			58	452	276	1180	20.3
1967-68 Balt.-St. L.			70	393	197	983	14.0
1968-69 Atlanta			76	385	147	917	12.1
1969-70 Atlanta			66	176	58	410	6.2
	Totals		727	4685	2179	11549	15.9
O'KEEFE, RICHARD							
b. Sept. 29, 1923 Ht. 6-2 Wt. 185 College—Santa Clara							
1947-48 Washington			37	63	30	156	4.2
1948-49 Washington			50	70	51	191	3.8
1949-50 Washington			68	162	150	474	7.0
1950-51 Washington			17	21	25	67	3.9
	Totals		172	316	256	888	5.2
O'KEEFE, THOMAS							
b. July 16, 1926 Ht. 6-2 Wt. 185 College—N. Dame/Georgetown							
1950-51 Balt.-Wash.			6	10	3	23	3.8
OLDHAM, JOHN							
b. June 22, 1923 H. 6-3 Wt. 185 College—W. Kentucky							
1949-50 Ft. Wayne			59	127	103	357	6.1
1950-51 Ft. Wayne			68	199	171	569	8.4
	Totals		127	326	274	926	7.3
OLEYNICK, FRANK							
b. Feb. 20, 1955 Ht. 6-3 Wt. 190 College—Seattle							
1975-76 Seattle			52	127	53	307	5.9
1976-77 Seattle			50	81	39	201	4.0
	Totals		102	208	92	508	5.0
OLIVE, JOHN							
b. March 1, 1955 Ht. 6-7 Wt. 215 College—Villanova							
1978-79 San Diego			34	13	18	44	1.3
1979-80 San Diego			1	0	0	0	0.0
	Totals		35	13	18	44	1.3
OLLRICH, GENE (Moe)							
b. June 30, 1922 Ht. 5-11 Wt. 160 College—Drake							
1949-50 Waterloo			14	17	10	44	3.1
OLSEN, ENOCH (Bud)							
b. July 25, 1940 Ht. 6-8 Wt. 220 College—Louisville							
1962-63 Cincinnati			52	43	27	113	2.2
1963-64 Cincinnati			49	85	32	202	4.1
1964-65 Cincinnati			79	224	144	592	7.5
1965-66 Cin.-S.F.			59	81	39	201	3.4
1966-67 San Francisco			40	75	23	173	4.3

Yr.	Team		G	FG	FT	TP	Avg.
1967-68	Seattle		73	130	17	277	3.8
1968-69	Bos.-Det.		17	15	4	34	2.0
1969-70	Kentucky	(ABA)	84	158(1)	26	343	4.1
	Totals		453	811(1)	312	1935	4.3

O'MALLEY, V. GRADY
b. April 25, 1948 Ht. 6-5 Wt. 205 College—Manhattan

Yr.	Team	G	FG	FT	TP	Avg.
1969-70	Atlanta	24	21	8	50	2.1

O'NEIL, MIKE
b. 1927 Ht. 6-3 Wt. 210 College—California

Yr.	Team	G	FG	FT	TP	Avg.
1952-53	Milwaukee	4	4	4	12	3.0

ORMS, BARRY
b. May 2, 1946 Ht. 6-3 Wt. 190 College—St. Louis Un.

Yr.	Team		G	FG	FT	TP	Avg.
1968-69	Baltimore		64	76	29	181	2.8
1969-70	Ind.-Pitt.	(ABA)	77	272(5)	152	701	9.1
	Totals		141	348(5)	181	882	6.2

ORR, JOHN
b. 1927 Ht. 6-3 College—Beloit and St. Benedict

Yr.	Team	G	FG	FT	TP	Avg.
1949-50	St. L.-Waterloo	34	40	12	92	2.7

OSBORNE, CHARLES
b. Jan. 21, 1939 Ht. 6-6 Wt. 210 College—W. Kentucky

Yr.	Team	G	FG	FT	TP	Avg.
1961-62	Syracuse	4	1	3	5	1.3

O'SHEA, KEVIN
b. July 10, 1925 Ht. 6-2 Wt. 175 College—Notre Dame

Yr.	Team	G	FG	FT	TP	Avg.
1950-51	Minneapolis	63	87	97	271	4.3
1951-52	Mil.-Balt.	65	153	144	450	6.9
1952-53	Baltimore	46	71	48	190	4.1
	Totals	174	311	289	911	5.2

O'SHIELDS, GARLAND (Mule)
b. May 23, 1921 Ht. 6-1 Wt. 195 College—Tennessee

Yr.	Team		G	FG	FT	TP	Avg.
1946-47	Chicago		9	2	0	4	0.4
1947-48	Syracuse	(NL)	5	3	3	9	1.8
	Totals		14	5	3	13	0.9

OSTERKORN, WALLY
b. July 6, 1928 Ht. 6-5 Wt. 215 College—Illinois

Yr.	Team	G	FG	FT	TP	Avg.
1951-52	Syracuse	66	145	199	489	7.4
1952-53	Syracuse	49	85	106	276	5.6
1953-54	Syracuse	70	203	209	615	8.8
1954-55	Syracuse	19	20	16	56	2.9
	Totals	204	453	530	1436	7.0

OTTEN, DON
b. April 18, 1921 Ht. 6-11 Wt. 250 College—Bowling Green

Yr.	Team		G	FG	FT	TP	Avg.
1946-47	Buf.-Tri-C.	(NL)	44	200	169	569	12.9
1947-48	Tri-Cities	(NL)	60	282	260	824	13.7
1948-49	Tri-Cities		64	301	297	899	14.0
1949-50	Tri C.-Wash.		64	242	341	825	12.9
1950-51	Wsh.-Bal.-Ft. W.		67	162	246	570	8.5
1951-52	Ft. W.-Mil.		64	222	323	767	12.0
1952-53	Milwaukee		24	34	64	132	5.5
	Totals		387	1443	1700	4586	11.9

OTTEN, MAC
b. Dec. 16, 1925 Ht. 6-7 Wt. 220 College—Bowling Green

Yr.	Team	G	FG	FT	TP	Avg.
1949-50	Tri C.-St. L.	59	51	40	142	2.4

OVERTON, CLAUDELL (Claude)
b. Dec. 16, 1927 Ht. 6-2 Wt. 195 College—East Central Oklahoma

Yr.	Team	G	FG	FT	TP	Avg.
1952-53	Philadelphia	15	19	20	58	3.9

OWENS, EDDIE
b. Dec. 26, 1953 Ht. 6-7 Wt. 210 College—Nev. L. Vegas

Yr.	Team	G	FG	FT	TP	Avg.
1977-78	Buffalo	8	9	3	21	2.6

OWENS, JAMES (Red)
b. Sept. 2, 1925 Ht. 6-3 Wt. 185 College—Baylor

Yr.	Team	G	FG	FT	TP	Avg.
1949-50	Tri C.-And.	61	86	68	240	3.9
1951-52	Balt.-Milw.	29	83	64	230	7.9
	Totals	90	169	132	470	5.2

OWENS, JIM
b. May 1, 1950 Ht. 6-5 Wt. 200 College—Arizona St.

Yr.	Team	G	FG	FT	TP	Avg.
1973-74	Phoenix	17	21	11	53	3.1
1974-75	Phoenix	41	56	12	124	3.0
	Totals	58	77	23	177	3.1

PACE, JOE
b. Dec. 18, 1953 Ht. 6-10 Wt. 220 College—Coppin St.

Yr.	Team	G	FG	FT	TP	Avg.
1976-77	Washington	30	24	16	64	2.1
1977-78	Washington	49	67	57	191	3.9
	Totals	79	91	73	255	3.2

PACK, WAYNE
b. July 5, 1950 Ht. 6-0 Wt. 165 College—Tennessee Tech

Yr.	Team		G	FG	FT	TP	Avg.
1974-75	Indiana	(ABA)	21	28(5)	10	61	2.9

PAGETT, DANA
b. March 29, 1949 Ht. 6-2 Wt. 180 College—So. California

Yr.	Team		G	FG	FT	TP	Avg.
1971-72	Virginia	(ABA)	5	1(1)	2	5	1.0

PAINE, FRED
b. Dec. 7, 1925 Ht. 6-5 Wt. 210 College—Westminster (Pa.)

Yr.	Team	G	FG	FT	TP	Avg.
1948-49	Providence	3	3	1	7	2.3

PALAZZI, TOGO
b. Aug. 8, 1932 Ht. 6-4 Wt. 205 College—Holy Cross

Yr.	Team	G	FG	FT	TP	Avg.
1954-55	Boston	53	101	45	247	4.7
1955-56	Boston	63	145	85	375	6.0
1956-57	Bos.-Syracuse	63	210	136	556	8.8
1957-58	Syracuse	67	228	123	579	8.6
1958-59	Syracuse	71	240	115	595	8.4
1959-60	Syracuse	7	13	4	30	4.3
	Totals	324	937	508	2382	7.4

PALMER, ERROL
Ht. 6-5 Wt. 195 College—DePaul

Yr.	Team		G	FG	FT	TP	Avg.
1967-68	Minnesota	(ABA)	63	165	170	500	7.9

Yr.	Team	G	FG	FT	TP	Avg.

PALMER, JAMES
b. June 8, 1933 Ht. 6-8 Wt. 224 College—Dayton

Yr.	Team	G	FG	FT	TP	Avg.
1958-59	Cincinnati	67	256	178	690	10.3
1959-60	Cin.-N.Y.	74	246	119	611	8.3
1960-61	New York	56	125	44	294	5.3
	Totals	197	627	341	1595	8.1

PALMER, JOHN (Bud)
b. Sept. 14, 1921 Ht. 6-4 Wt. 180 College—Princeton

Yr.	Team	G	FG	FT	TP	Avg.
1946-47	New York	42	160	81	401	9.5
1947-48	New York	48	224	174	622	13.0
1948-49	New York	58	240	234	714	12.3
	Totals	148	624	489	1737	11.7

PARHAM, ESTES (Easy)
b. Dec. 27, 1921 Ht. 6-3 Wt. 200 College—Texas Wesleyan

Yr.	Team	G	FG	FT	TP	Avg.
1948-49	St. Louis	60	124	96	344	5.7
1949-50	St. Louis	66	137	88	362	5.5
1950-51	Philadelphia	7	3	4	10	1.4
	Totals	133	264	188	716	5.4

PARK, MEDFORD (Med)
b. April 11, 1933 Ht. 6-2 Wt. 205 College—Missouri

Yr.	Team	G	FG	FT	TP	Avg.
1955-56	St. Louis	40	53	44	150	3.8
1956-57	St. Louis	66	118	108	344	5.2
1957-58	St. Louis	71	133	118	384	5.4
1958-59	St. L.-Cin.	62	145	115	405	6.5
1959-60	Cincinnati	74	226	189	641	8.7
	Totals	313	675	574	1924	6.1

PARKHILL, BARRY
b. May 10, 1951 Ht. 6-4 Wt. 185 College—Virginia

Yr.	Team		G	FG	FT	TP	Avg.
1973-74	Virginia	(ABA)	60	115(3)	50	283	4.7
1974-75	Virginia	(ABA)	78	266	75	607	7.8
1975-76	St. Louis	(ABA)	35	37(1)	5	80	2.3
	Totals		173	418(4)	130	970	5.6

PARKINSON, JACK
b. March 4, 1924 Ht. 6-0 Wt. 174 College—Kentucky

Yr.	Team	G	FG	FT	TP	Avg.
1949-50	Indianapolis	4	1	1	3	0.8

PARKS, CHARLEY
Ht. 6-5 Wt. 210 College—Idaho State

Yr.	Team		G	FG	FT	TP	Avg.
1968-69	Denver	(ABA)	2	0	0	0	0.0

PARKS, RICH
b. October 26, 1943 Ht. 6-7 Wt. 235 College—Tulsa and St. Louis U.

Yr.	Team		G	FG	FT	TP	Avg.
1967-68	Pittsburgh	(ABA)	40	59(1)	12	131	3.3

PARR, JACK
b. March 13, 1936 Ht. 6-9 Wt. 222 College—Kansas St.

Yr.	Team	G	FG	FT	TP	Avg.
1958-59	Cincinnati	66	109	44	262	4.0

PARRACK, DOYLE
b. Dec. 6, 1921 Ht. 6-0 Wt. 165 College—Oklahoma A&M

Yr.	Team	G	FG	FT	TP	Avg.
1946-47	Chicago	58	110	52	272	4.7

PARSLEY, CHARLES
Ht. 6-2 Wt. 175 College—Western Kentucky

Yr.	Team	G	FG	FT	TP	Avg.
1948-49	Philadelphia	9	8	6	22	2.4

PASSAGLIA, MARTIN
b. Apr. 22, 1919 Ht. 6-1 Wt. 195 College—Santa Clara

Yr.	Team	G	FG	FT	TP	Avg.
1946-47	Washington	43	51	18	120	2.8
1948-49	Indianapolis	19	14	3	31	1.6
	Totals	62	65	21	151	2.4

PASTUSHOK, GEORGE
b. 1922 Ht. 6-1 Wt. 195 College—St. John's (N.Y.)

Yr.	Team	G	FG	FT	TP	Avg.
1946-47	Providence	39	48	25	121	3.1

PATRICK, STANLEY
b. May 5, 1922 Ht. 6-3 Wt. 215 College—Santa Clara and Illinois

Yr.	Team		G	FG	FT	TP	Avg.
1944-45	Chicago	(NL)	28	187	84	458	16.4
1945-46	Chicago	(NL)	33	123	66	312	9.5
1946-47	Chicago	(NL)	42	72	36	180	4.3
1947-48	Flint	(NL)	48	149	90	388	8.1
1948-49	Hammond	(NL)	61	150	127	427	7.0
1949-50	Wat.-Sheboygan		53	116	89	321	6.1
	Totals		265	797	492	2086	7.9

PATTERSON, GEORGE
b. Nov. 26, 1939 Ht. 6-8 Wt. 240 College—Toledo

Yr.	Team	G	FG	FT	TP	Avg.
1967-68	Detroit	59	44	32	120	2.0

PATTERSON, STEVE
b. June 24, 1948 Ht. 6-9 Wt. 225 College—UCLA

Yr.	Team	G	FG	FT	TP	Avg.
1971-72	Cleveland	65	94	23	211	3.2
1972-73	Cleveland	62	71	34	176	2.8
1973-74	Cleveland	76	262	69	593	7.8
1974-75	Cleveland	81	161	48	370	4.6
1975-76	Cleve.-Chi.	66	84	34	202	3.1
	Totals	350	672	208	1552	4.4

PATTERSON, TOMMY
b. Oct. 15, 1948 Ht. 6-6 Wt. 220 College—Ouachita Baptist

Yr.	Team	G	FG	FT	TP	Avg.
1972-73	Baltimore	23	21	13	55	2.4
1973-74	Capital	2	0	1	1	0.5
	Totals	25	21	14	56	2.2

PATTERSON, WORTHINGTON (Worthy)
b. June 17, 1931 Ht. 6-2 Wt. 175 College—Connecticut

Yr.	Team	G	FG	FT	TP	Avg.
1957-58	St. Louis	4	3	1	7	1.8

PAULK, CHARLES
b. June 14, 1944 Ht. 6-9 Wt. 219 College—Tulsa/N.E. Okla. St.

Yr.	Team	G	FG	FT	TP	Avg.
1968-69	Milwaukee	17	19	13	51	3.0
1970-71	Cincinnati	68	274	79	627	9.2
1971-72	Chic.-N.Y.	28	16	8	40	1.4
	Totals	113	309	100	718	6.4

PAULSON, GERALD (Jerry)
b. July 21, 1935 Ht. 6-2 Wt. 187 College—Manhattan

Yr.	Team	G	FG	FT	TP	Avg.
1957-58	Cincinnati	6	8	4	20	3.3

Yr.	Team	G	FG	FT	TP	Avg.

PAXSON, JAMES
b. Dec. 19, 1932 Ht. 6-6 Wt. 200 College—Dayton

Yr.	Team	G	FG	FT	TP	Avg.
1956-57	Minneapolis	71	138	170	446	6.3
1957-58	Cincinnati	67	225	209	659	9.8
	Totals	138	363	379	1105	8.0

PAYAK, JOHN
b. Nov. 20, 1926 Ht. 6-4 Wt. 180 College—Bowling Green

1949-50	Phila.-Waterloo	52	98	121	317	6.1
1952-53	Milwaukee	68	128	180	436	6.4
	Totals	120	226	301	753	6.3

PAYNE, TOM
b. Nov. 19, 1950 Ht. 6-2 Wt. 240 College—Kentucky

1971-72	Atlanta	29	45	29	119	4.1

PAYTON, MEL
b. 1927 Ht. 6-4 Wt. 185 College—Tulane

1951-52	Philadelphia	45	54	21	129	2.9
1952-53	Indianapolis	66	173	120	466	7.1
	Totals	111	227	141	595	5.4

PEARCY, GEORGE (Wig)
b. July 2, 1919 Ht. 6-1 Wt. 165 College—Indiana State

1946-47	Detroit	37	31	32	94	2.5

PEARCY, HENRY
b. 1922 Ht. 6-1 Wt. 170 College—Indiana State

1946-47	Detroit	29	24	25	73	2.5

PECK, WILEY
b. Sept. 15, 1957 Ht. 6-7 Wt. 220 College—Mississippi State

1979-80	San Antonio	52	73	34	180	3.5

PEEK, RICH
b. 1945 Ht. 6-11 Wt. 230 College—Louisiana Tech

1967-68	Dallas	(ABA)	51	101	35	237	4.6

PEEPLES, GEORGE
b. Oct. 30, 1943 Ht. 6-8 Wt. 205 College—Iowa

1967-68	Indiana	(ABA)	65	138	115	391	6.0
1968-69	Indiana	(ABA)	64	122	101	345	5.4
1969-70	Carolina	(ABA)	83	279	209	767	9.2
1970-71	Carolina	(ABA)	82	377	202	956	11.7
1971-72	Dallas	(ABA)	6	11	7	29	4.8
1972-73	Indiana	(ABA)	9	4	6	14	1.6
	Totals		309	931	640	2502	8.1

PELKINGTON, JOHN
b. 1916 Ht. 6-6 Wt. 220 College—Manhattan

1940-41	Akron	(NL)	24	57	70	184	7.7
1942-43	Ft. Wayne	(NL)	23	83	70	236	10.3
1943-44	Ft. Wayne	(NL)	20	46	40	132	6.6
1944-45	Ft. Wayne	(NL)	30	85	76	246	8.2
1945-46	Ft. Wayne	(NL)	33	94	76	264	8.0
1946-47	Ft. Wayne	(NL)	42	129	125	383	9.1
1947-48	Ft. Wayne	(NL)	54	174	156	504	9.3
1948-49	Ft. W.-Balt.		54	193	211	597	11.1
	Totals		280	861	824	2546	9.1

PENDER, JERRY
b. 1951 Ht. 6-3 Wt. 185 College—Fresno State

1973-74	San Diego	(ABA)	11	8(1)	10	27	2.5

PERKINS, WARREN
b. Feb. 2, 1924 Ht. 6-3 Wt. 190 College—Tulane

1949-50	Tri-Cities	60	128	115	371	6.2
1950-51	Tri-Cities	66	135	126	396	6.0
	Totals	126	263	241	767	6.1

PERRY, AULCIE
b. July 3, 1950 Ht. 6-11 Wt. 215 College—Bethune-Cookman

1974-75	Virginia	(ABA)	21	81	19	181	8.6

PERRY, CURTIS
b. Sept. 13, 1948 Ht. 6-7 Wt. 220 College—Southwest Mo.

1970-71	San Diego	18	21	11	53	2.9
1971-72	Hou.-Mil.	75	181	76	438	5.8
1972-73	Milwaukee	67	265	83	613	9.1
1973-74	Milwaukee	81	325	78	728	9.0
1974-75	Phoenix	79	437	184	1058	13.4
1975-76	Phoenix	71	386	175	947	13.3
1976-77	Phoenix	44	179	112	470	10.7
1977-78	Phoenix	45	110	51	271	6.0
	Totals	480	1904	770	4578	9.5

PERRY, RON
b. Dec. 29, 1943 Ht. 6-3 Wt. 190 College—Virginia Tech

1967-68	Minnesota	(ABA)	67	339(62)	118	858	12.8
1968-69	Mia.-N.Y.-Ind.	(ABA)	74	402(67)	212	1083	14.6
1969-70	Car.-N.O.	(ABA)	46	104(10)	69	287	6.2
	Totals		187	845(139)	399	2228	11.9

PETERSEN, LOY
b. July 26, 1945 Ht. 6-5 Wt. 205 College—Oreg. St.

1968-69	Chicago	38	44	19	107	2.8
1969-70	Chicago	31	33	26	92	3.0
	Totals	69	77	45	199	2.9

PETERSON, EDWARD
b. 1925 Ht. 6-9 Wt. 230 College—Cornell

1948-49	Syracuse	(NL)	63	165	104	434	6.9
1949-50	Syracuse		62	167	111	445	7.2
1950-51	Syr.-Tri-Cities		53	130	99	359	6.8
	Totals		178	462	314	1238	7.0

PETERSON, MEL
b. March 23, 1938 Ht. 6-4½ Wt. 185 College—Wheaton

1963-64	Baltimore		2	1	0	2	1.0
1967-68	Oakland	(ABA)	77	323(9)	76	731	9.5
1968-69	Oakland	(ABA)	51	132	12	276	5.4
1969-70	Los Angeles	(ABA)	4	10	3	23	5.8
	Totals		134	466(9)	91	1032	7.7

PETERSON, ROBERT
b. 1932 Ht. 6-5 Wt. 210 College—Oregon

1953-54	Balt.-Milw.	8	3	9	15	1.9
1954-55	New York	37	62	30	154	4.2
1955-56	New York	58	121	68	310	5.3
	Totals	103	186	107	479	4.7

Yr.	Team		G	FG	FT	TP	Avg.

PETRIE, GEOFFREY
b. April 17, 1948 Ht. 6-4 Wt. 190 College—Princeton

Yr.	Team	G	FG	FT	TP	Avg.
1970-71 Portland		82	784	463	2031	24.8
1971-72 Portland		60	465	202	1132	18.9
1972-73 Portland		79	836	298	1970	24.9
1973-74 Portland		73	740	291	1771	24.3
1974-75 Portland		80	602	261	1465	18.3
1975-76 Portland		72	543	277	1363	18.9
1976-77 Atlanta		(Injured)				
Totals		446	3970	1792	9732	21.8

PETTIT, BOB
b. Dec. 12, 1932 Ht. 6-9 Wt. 215 College—La. State

Yr.	Team	G	FG	FT	TP	Avg.
1954-55 Milwaukee	72	520	426	1466	20.4
1955-56 St. Louis	72	646	557	1849	25.7
1956-57 St. Louis	71	613	529	1755	24.7
1957-58 St. Louis	70	581	557	1719	24.6
1958-59 St. Louis	72	719	667	2105	29.2
1959-60 St. Louis	72	669	544	1882	26.1
1960-61 St. Louis	76	769	582	2120	27.9
1961-62 St. Louis	78	867	695	2429	31.1
1962-63 St. Louis	79	778	685	2241	28.4
1963-64 St. Louis	80	791	608	2190	27.4
1964-65 St. Louis	50	396	332	1124	22.5
Totals	792	7349	6182	20880	26.4

PETTWAY, JERRY
b. Feb. 13, 1944 Ht. 6-3 Wt. 185 College—Northwood

Yr.	Team		G	FG	FT	TP	Avg.
1967-68 Houston	(ABA)	76	289(16)	119	713	9.4
1968-69 Houston	(ABA)	11	37	5	79	7.2
Totals		87	326(16)	124	792	9.1

PHELAN, JACK
b. Nov. 6, 1925 Ht. 6-5 College—DePaul

Yr.	Team	G	FG	FT	TP	Avg.
1949-50 Waterloo-Sheboygan	55	87	52	226	4.1

PHELAN, JIM
b. 1929 Ht. 6-1 Wt. 175 College—LaSalle

Yr.	Team	G	FG	FT	TP	Avg.
1953-54 Philadelphia	4	0	3	3	0.8

PHILLIP, ANDY
b. March 7, 1922 Ht. 6-2 Wt. 195 College—Illinois

Yr.	Team	G	FG	FT	TP	Avg.
1947-48 Chicago	32	143	60	346	10.8
1948-49 Chicago	60	285	148	718	12.0
1949-50 Chicago	65	284	190	758	11.2
1950-51 Philadelphia	66	275	190	740	11.2
1951-52 Philadelphia	66	279	232	790	12.0
1952-53 Phila.-Ft. W.	70	250	222	722	10.3
1953-54 Ft. Wayne	71	255	241	751	10.6
1954-55 Ft. Wayne	64	202	213	617	9.6
1955-56 Ft. Wayne	70	148	112	408	5.8
1956-57 Boston	67	105	88	298	4.4
1957-58 Boston	70	97	42	236	3.4
Totals	701	2323	1738	6384	9.1

PHILLIPS, GARY
b. Dec. 7, 1939 Ht. 6-3 Wt. 189 College—Houston

Yr.	Team	G	FG	FT	TP	Avg.
1961-62 Boston	72	110	50	270	3.7
1962-63 San Fran.	75	256	97	609	8.1
1963-64 San Fran.	66	256	146	658	10.0
1964-65 San Fran.	73	198	120	516	7.1
1965-66 San Fran.	67	106	54	266	4.0
Totals	353	926	467	2319	6.6

PHILLIPS, GENE
b. Oct. 25, 1948 Ht. 6-4 Wt. 180 College—Southern Methodist

Yr.	Team		G	FG	FT	TP	Avg.
1971-72 Dallas	(ABA)	28	30(7)	11	78	2.8
1972-73 Dallas	(ABA)	3	0	0	0	0.0
Totals		31	30(7)	11	78	2.5

PIATKOWSKI, WALT
b. June 11, 1945 Ht. 6-8 Wt. 225 College—Bowling Green

Yr.	Team		G	FG	FT	TP	Avg.
1968-69 Denver	(ABA)	77	399(27)	117	942	12.2
1969-70 Denver	(ABA)	75	215(11)	76	517	6.9
1971-72 Floridians	(ABA)	6	3	0	6	1.0
Totals		158	617(38)	193	1465	9.3

PILCH, JOHN
b. July 11, 1925 Ht. 6-3 Wt. 185 College—Wyoming

Yr.	Team	G	FG	FT	TP	Avg.
1951-52 Minneapolis	9	1	3	5	0.6

PIONTEK, DAVID
b. Aug. 27, 1934 Ht. 6-6 Wt. 230 College—Xavier (Ohio)

Yr.	Team	G	FG	FT	TP	Avg.
1956-57 Rochester	71	257	122	636	9.0
1957-58 Cincinnati	71	150	95	395	5.6
1958-59 Cincinnati	72	305	156	766	10.6
1959-60 Cinn.-St. Lou.	77	292	129	713	9.3
1960-61 St. Louis	29	46	16	110	3.8
1961-62 Chicago	45	83	39	205	4.5
1962-63 Cincinnati	48	60	10	130	2.6
Totals	413	1194	567	2955	7.2

POLLARD, JIM
b. July 9, 1922 Ht. 6-3½ Wt. 190 College—Stanford

Yr.	Team		G	FG	FT	TP	Avg.
1947-48 Minneapolis	(NL)	59	310	140	760	12.9
1948-49 Minneapolis		53	314	156	784	14.8
1949-50 Minneapolis		66	394	185	973	14.7
1950-51 Minneapolis		54	256	117	629	11.6
1951-52 Minneapolis		65	411	183	1005	15.5
1952-53 Minneapolis		66	333	193	859	13.0
1953-54 Minneapolis		71	326	179	831	11.7
1954-55 Minneapolis		63	265	151	681	10.8
Totals		497	2609	1304	6522	13.1

POLSON, RALPH
b. 1930 Ht. 6-7½ Wt. 205 College—Whitworth

Yr.	Team	G	FG	FT	TP	Avg.
1952-53 N.Y.-Phila.	49	65	61	191	3.9

PONDEXTER, CLIFTON
b. Sept. 15, 1954 Ht. 6-9 Wt. 235 College—Long Beach St.

Yr.	Team	G	FG	FT	TP	Avg.
1975-76 Chicago	75	156	122	434	5.8
1976-77 Chicago	78	107	42	256	3.3
1977-78 Chicago	44	37	14	88	2.0
Totals	197	300	178	778	3.9

PORTER, HOWARD
b. Aug. 31, 1948 Ht. 6-8 Wt. 220 College—Villanova

Yr.	Team	G	FG	FT	TP	Avg.
1971-72 Chicago	67	171	59	401	6.0
1972-73 Chicago	43	98	22	218	5.1

Yr.	Team		G	FG	FT	TP	Avg.
1973-74	Chicago		73	296	92	684	9.4
1974-75	N.Y.-Det.		58	201	66	468	8.1
1975-76	Detroit		75	298	73	669	8.9
1976-77	Detroit		78	465	103	1033	13.2
1977-78	Det.-N.J.		63	309	124	742	11.8
	Totals		457	1838	539	4215	9.2

PORTER, WILLIE
b. July 3, 1942 Ht. 6-7 Wt. 205 College—Tennessee State

Yr.	Team		G	FG	FT	TP	Avg.
1967-68	Oak.-Pitt.	(ABA)	56	225	199	649	11.6
1968-69	Minn.-Hou.	(ABA)	13	28	17	73	5.6
	Totals		69	253	216	722	10.5

PORTMAN, BOB
b. March 22, 1947 Ht. 6-5 Wt. 200 College—Creighton

Yr.	Team	G	FG	FT	TP	Avg.
1969-70	San Francisco	60	177	66	420	7.0
1970-71	San Francisco	68	221	77	519	7.6
1971-72	Golden State	61	89	53	231	3.9
1972-73	Golden State	32	32	20	84	2.6
	Totals	221	519	216	1254	5.7

POSTLEY, JOHN
Ht. 6-5 College—Bethune-Cookman

Yr.	Team		G	FG	FT	TP	Avg.
1967-68	Pittsburgh	(ABA)	1	1	0	2	2.0

POWELL, CINCINNATUS (Cincy)
b. Feb. 25, 1942 Ht. 6-7 Wt. 227 College—Portland

Yr.	Team		G	FG	FT	TP	Avg.
1967-68	Dallas	(ABA)	77	533(1)	343	1410	18.3
1968-69	Dallas	(ABA)	75	555(2)	342	1454	19.4
1969-70	Dallas	(ABA)	76	562(2)	402	1528	20.1
1970-71	Kentucky	(ABA)	81	578(4)	302	1462	18.1
1971-72	Kentucky	(ABA)	65	430(4)	185	1049	16.1
1972-73	Utah	(ABA)	83	423(3)	167	1016	12.2
1973-74	Virginia	(ABA)	82	528(10)	209	1275	15.6
1974-75	Virginia	(ABA)	60	214(5)	119	552	9.2
	Totals		599	3823(31)	2069	9746	16.3

PRADD, MARLBERT (Mal)
b. Nov. 17, 1944 Ht. 6-3 Wt. 170 College—Dillard

Yr.	Team		G	FG	FT	TP	Avg.
1967-68	New Orleans	(ABA)	29	27	20	74	2.6
1968-69	New Orleans	(ABA)	50	81(3)	93	258	5.2
	Totals		79	108(3)	113	332	4.2

PRATT, MIKE
b. Aug. 4, 1948 Ht. 6-4 Wt. 205 College—Kentucky

Yr.	Team		G	FG	FT	TP	Avg.
1970-71	Kentucky	(ABA)	78	173(3)	91	440	5.6
1971-72	Kentucky	(ABA)	65	133(16)	84	366	5.6
	Totals		143	306(19)	175	806	5.6

PREVIS, STEVE
b. Feb. 9, 1950 Ht. 6-3 Wt. 183 College—North Carolina

Yr.	Team		G	FG	FT	TP	Avg.
1972-73	Carolina	(ABA)	30	23(1)	8	55	1.8

PRICE, MIKE
b. Sept. 11, 1948 Ht. 6-3 Wt. 200 College—Illinois

Yr.	Team		G	FG	FT	TP	Avg.
1970-71	New York		56	30	24	84	1.5
1971-72	New York		6	5	9	19	3.2
1971-72	Indiana	(ABA)	4	3	0	6	1.5
	Totals		66	38	33	109	1.7

PRICE, JIM
b. Nov. 27, 1949 Ht. 6-3 Wt. 195 College—Louisville

Yr.	Team	G	FG	FT	TP	Avg.
1972-73	Los Angeles	59	158	60	376	6.4
1973-74	Los Angeles	82	538	187	1263	15.4
1974-75	L.A.-Mil.	50	317	169	803	16.1
1975-76	Milwaukee	80	398	141	937	11.7
1976-77	Mil.-Buf.-Den.	81	253	83	589	7.3
1977-78	Den.-Detroit	83	294	135	723	8.7
1978-79	Los Angeles	75	171	55	397	5.3
	Totals	510	2129	830	5088	9.9

PRIDDY, ROBERT
b. 1930 Ht. 6-3 Wt. 190 College—New Mexico A&M

Yr.	Team	G	FG	FT	TP	Avg.
1952-53	Baltimore	16	14	8	36	2.3

PRITCHARD, JOHN
b. 1927 Ht. 6-9 Wt. 220 College—Drake

Yr.	Team	G	FG	FT	TP	Avg.
1949-50	Waterloo	7	9	4	22	3.1

PUGH, LESLIE
b. Sept. 18, 1923 Ht. 6-7 Wt. 195 College—Ohio State

Yr.	Team	G	FG	FT	TP	Avg.
1948-49	Providence	60	168	125	461	7.7
1949-50	Baltimore	56	68	115	251	4.5
	Totals	116	236	240	712	6.1

PUGH, ROY
b. 1923 Ht. 6-6 Wt. 210 College—Southern Methodist

Yr.	Team		G	FG	FT	TP	Avg.
1947-48	Indianapolis	(NL)	4	1	2	4	1.0
1948-49	Ft. W.-Ind.-Phil.		23	13	6	32	1.4
	Totals		27	14	8	36	1.3

PUTMAN, J. DONALD
b. Nov. 13, 1922 Ht. 6-1 Wt. 170 College—Colo. and Denver

Yr.	Team	G	FG	FT	TP	Avg.
1946-47	St. Louis	58	156	68	380	6.6
1947-48	St. Louis	42	105	57	267	6.4
1948-49	St. Louis	59	98	52	248	4.2
1949-50	St. Louis	57	51	33	135	2.4
	Totals	216	410	210	1030	4.8

QUICK, BOB
b. March 5, 1946 Ht. 6-5 Wt. 215 College—Xavier (O.)

Yr.	Team		G	FG	FT	TP	Avg.
1968-69	Baltimore		28	30	27	87	3.1
1969-70	Balt.-Det.		34	63	49	175	5.1
1970-71	Detroit		56	155	138	448	8.0
1971-72	Detroit		18	39	34	112	6.2
1971-72	Dallas	(ABA)	6	8	10	26	4.3
	Totals		142	295	258	848	6.0

RACKLEY, LUTHER
b. June 11, 1946 Ht. 6-10 Wt. 220 College—Xavier (O.)

Yr.	Team		G	FG	FT	TP	Avg.
1969-70	Cincinnati		66	190	124	504	7.6
1970-71	Cleveland		74	219	121	559	7.6
1971-72	Cleve.-N.Y.		71	103	50	256	3.6
1972-73	Memphis	(ABA)	57	170	78	418	7.3
1972-73	New York		1	0	0	0	0.0
1973-74	Philadelphia		9	5	8	18	2.0
	Totals		278	687	381	1755	6.3

Yr.	Team		G	FG	FT	TP	Avg.

RADER, HOWARD
b. Mar. 29, 1921 Ht. 6-1 Wt. 190 College—Long Island University

Yr.	Team		G	FG	FT	TP	Avg.
1946-47	Buf.-Tri-C.	(NL)	41	76	43	195	4.8
1947-48	Tri-Cities	(NL)	45	44	29	117	2.6
1948-49	Baltimore		13	7	3	17	1.3
	Totals		99	127	75	329	3.3

RADFORD, WAYNE
b. May 29, 1956 Ht. 6-3 Wt. 205 College—Indiana

Yr.	Team	G	FG	FT	TP	Avg.
1978-79	Indiana	52	83	36	202	3.9

RADOVICH, FRANK
b. March 3, 1938 Ht. 6-8 Wt. 235 College—Indiana

Yr.	Team	G	FG	FT	TP	Avg.
1961-62	Philadelphia	37	37	13	87	2.4

RADOVICH, GEORGE (Moe)
b. 1930 Ht. 6-0 Wt. 160 College—Wyoming

Yr.	Team	G	FG	FT	TP	Avg.
1952-53	Philadelphia	4	5	4	14	3.5

RADZISZEWSKI, RAY
b. March 1, 1935 Ht. 6-5 Wt. 210 College—St. Joseph's (Pa.)

Yr.	Team	G	FG	FT	TP	Avg.
1957-58	Philadelphia	1	0	0	0	0.0

RAGELIS, RAY
b. 1929 Ht. 6-4 Wt. 205 College—Northwestern

Yr.	Team	G	FG	FT	TP	Avg.
1951-52	Rochester	51	25	18	68	1.3

RAIKEN, SHERWIN
b. Oct. 29, 1928 Ht. 6-2 Wt. 185 College—Villanova

Yr.	Team	G	FG	FT	TP	Avg.
1952-53	New York	6	3	3	9	1.5

RAMSEY, CAL
b. July 13, 1937 Ht. 6-4 Wt. 200 College—N.Y. Univ.

Yr.	Team	G	FG	FT	TP	Avg.
1959-60	St. L.-N.Y.	11	39	19	97	8.8
1960-61	Syracuse	2	2	2	6	3.0
	Totals	13	41	21	103	7.9

RAMSEY, FRANK
b. July 13, 1931 Ht. 6-3 Wt. 190 College—Kentucky

Yr.	Team	G	FG	FT	TP	Avg.
1954-55	Boston	64	236	243	715	11.2
1956-57	Boston	35	137	144	418	11.9
1957-58	Boston	69	377	383	1137	16.5
1958-59	Boston	72	383	341	1107	15.4
1959-60	Boston	73	422	273	1117	15.3
1960-61	Boston	79	448	295	1191	15.1
1961-62	Boston	79	436	334	1206	15.3
1962-63	Boston	77	284	271	839	10.9
1963-64	Boston	75	226	196	648	8.6
	Totals	623	2949	2480	8378	13.4

RAMSEY, RAY
b. 1921 Ht. 6-2 Wt. 166 College—Bradley

Yr.	Team		G	FG	FT	TP	Avg.
1947-48	Tri-Cities	(NL)	2	0	0	0	0.0
1948-49	Baltimore		2	0	2	2	1.0
	Totals		4	0	2	2	0.5

RANZINO, SAM
b. June 21, 1927 Ht. 6-1 Wt. 185 College—N.C. State

Yr.	Team	G	FG	FT	TP	Avg.
1951-52	Rochester	39	30	26	86	2.2

RASCOE, BOBBY
b. July 22, 1940 Ht. 6-4 Wt. 205 College—Western Kentucky

Yr.	Team		G	FG	FT	TP	Avg.
1967-68	Kentucky	(ABA)	77	245	190	680	8.8
1968-69	Kentucky	(ABA)	78	201(3)	129	534	6.8
1969-70	Kentucky	(ABA)	4	4	6	14	3.5
	Totals		159	450(3)	325	1228	7.7

RATKOVICZ, GEORGE
b. Nov. 13, 1922 Ht. 6-7 Wt. 225

Yr.	Team		G	FG	FT	TP	Avg.
1941-42	Chicago	(NL)	13	9	14	32	2.5
1945-46	Chicago	(NL)	33	80	66	226	6.8
1946-47	Chicago	(NL)	37	43	26	112	3.0
1947-48	Rochester	(NL)	53	79	76	234	4.4
1948-49	Tri-Cities	(NL)	64	109	106	324	5.1
1949-50	Syracuse		62	162	211	535	8.6
1950-51	Syracuse		66	264	321	849	12.9
1951-52	Syracuse		66	165	163	493	7.5
1952-53	Balt.-Milw.		71	208	262	678	9.5
1953-54	Milwaukee		69	197	176	570	8.3
1954-55	Milwaukee		9	3	10	16	1.8
	Totals		543	1319	1431	4069	7.5

RATLEFF, ED
b. March 29, 1950 Ht. 6-6 Wt. 195 College—Long Beach St.

Yr.	Team	G	FG	FT	TP	Avg.
1973-74	Houston	81	254	103	611	7.5
1974-75	Houston	80	392	157	941	11.8
1975-76	Houston	72	314	168	796	11.1
1976-77	Houston	37	70	26	166	4.5
1977-78	Houston	68	130	39	299	4.4
	Totals	338	1160	493	2813	8.3

RATLIFF, MIKE
b. June 7, 1951 Ht. 6-10 Wt. 230 College—Eau Claire State

Yr.	Team	G	FG	FT	TP	Avg.
1972-73	K.C.-Omaha	58	98	45	241	4.2
1973-74	K.C.-Omaha	2	0	0	0	0.0
	Totals	60	98	45	241	4.0

RAY, DON (Duck)
b. July 8, 1921 Ht. 6-6 Wt. 190 College—Western Kentucky

Yr.	Team		G	FG	FT	TP	Avg.
1948-49	Tri-Cities	(NL)	46	123	80	326	7.1
1949-50	Tri-Cities		61	130	104	364	6.0
	Totals		107	253	184	690	6.4

RAY, JAMES
b. Jan. 12, 1934 Ht. 6-1 Wt. 180 College—Toledo

Yr.	Team	G	FG	FT	TP	Avg.
1956-57	Syracuse	4	2	3	7	1.8
1959-60	Syracuse	4	1	0	2	0.5
	Totals	8	3	3	9	1.1

RAYL, JIM
b. June 21, 1941 Ht. 6-2 Wt. 180 College—Indiana

Yr.	Team		G	FG	FT	TP	Avg.
1967-68	Indiana	(ABA)	74	317(57)	195	886	12.0
1968-69	Indiana	(ABA)	27	72(34)	61	239	8.9
	Totals		101	389(91)	256	1125	11.1

RAYMOND, CRAIG
b. April 5, 1945 Ht. 6-11 Wt. 235 College—Brigham Young

Yr.	Team		G	FG	FT	TP	Avg.
1968-69	Philadelphia		27	22	11	55	2.0
1969-70	Pitt.-L.A.	(ABA)	80	386	190	962	12.0
1970-71	Memphis	(ABA)	56	142	67	351	6.3

Yr.	Team		G	FG	FT	TP	Avg.
1971-72	Mem.-Fla.	(ABA)	64	104	48	256	4.0
1972-73	S.D.-Ind.	(ABA)	14	12	10	34	2.4
	Totals		241	666	326	1658	6.9

REA, CONNIE
b. 1931 Ht. 6-3 Wt. 175 College—Centenary

Yr.	Team	G	FG	FT	TP	Avg.
1953-54	Baltimore	20	9	5	23	1.2

REAVES, JOE
b. May 27, 1950 Ht. 6-6 Wt. 220 College—Bethel

Yr.	Team		G	FG	FT	TP	Avg.
1973-74	Phoenix		7	6	4	16	2.3
1973-74	Memphis	(ABA)	12	30	4	64	5.3
	Totals		19	36	8	80	4.2

REDDOUT, FRANK
Ht. 6-5 Wt. 195 College—Syracuse

Yr.	Team	G	FG	FT	TP	Avg.
1953-54	Rochester	7	5	3	13	1.9

REDMOND, MARLON
b. April 15, 1955 Ht. 6-6 Wt. 188 College—San Fran.

Yr.	Team	G	FG	FT	TP	Avg.
1978-79	K.C.-Phil.	53	163	31	357	6.7
1979-80	Kansas City	24	59	24	142	5.9
	Totals	77	222	55	499	6.5

REED, HUBERT (Hub)
b. Oct. 4, 1936 Ht. 6-9 Wt. 220 College—Okla. City

Yr.	Team	G	FG	FT	TP	Avg.
1958-59	St. Louis	65	136	53	325	5.0
1959-60	St. L.-Cinc.	71	270	134	674	9.5
1960-61	Cincinnati	75	156	85	397	5.3
1961-62	Cincinnati	80	203	60	466	5.8
1962-63	Cincinnati	80	199	74	472	5.9
1963-64	Los Angeles	46	33	10	76	1.7
1964-65	Detroit	62	84	40	208	3.4
	Totals	479	1081	456	2618	5.5

REED, RON
b. Nov. 2, 1942 Ht. 6-2 Wt. 205 College—Notre Dame

Yr.	Team	G	FG	FT	TP	Avg.
1965-66	Detroit	57	186	54	426	7.5
1966-67	Detroit	62	223	79	525	8.5
	Totals	119	409	133	951	8.0

REED, WILLIS
b. June 25, 1942 Ht. 6-10 Wt. 235 College—Grambling

Yr.	Team	G	FG	FT	TP	Avg.
1964-65	New York	80	629	302	1560	19.5
1965-66	New York	76	438	302	1178	15.5
1966-67	New York	78	635	358	1628	20.9
1967-68	New York	81	659	367	1685	20.8
1968-69	New York	82	704	325	1733	21.1
1969-70	New York	81	702	351	1755	21.7
1970-71	New York	73	614	299	1527	20.9
1971-72	New York	11	60	27	147	13.4
1972-73	New York	69	334	92	760	11.0
1973-74	New York	19	84	42	210	11.1
	Totals	650	4859	2465	12183	18.7

REGAN, RICHIE
b. Nov. 30, 1930 Ht. 6-2 Wt. 180 College—Seton Hall

Yr.	Team	G	FG	FT	TP	Avg.
1955-56	Rochester	72	240	85	565	7.8
1956-57	Rochester	71	257	182	696	9.8
1957-58	Cincinnati	72	202	120	524	7.3
	Totals	215	699	387	1785	8.3

REHFELDT, DON
b. Jan. 7, 1927 Ht. 6-6 Wt. 210 College—Wisconsin

Yr.	Team	G	FG	FT	TP	Avg.
1950-51	Baltimore	59	164	103	431	8.6
1951-52	Balt.-Milw.	39	99	63	261	6.7
	Totals	98	263	166	692	7.1

REID, JIM
b. Aug. 3, 1945 Ht. 6-6 Wt. 210 College—Winston-Salem State

Yr.	Team	G	FG	FT	TP	Avg.
1967-68	Philadelphia	6	10	1	21	3.5

REISER, JOSEPH (Chick)
b. Dec. 17, 1914 Ht. 5-11 Wt. 165 College—NY University

Yr.	Team		G	FG	FT	TP	Avg.
1943-44	Ft. Wayne	(NL)	22	28	25	81	3.7
1944-45	Ft. Wayne	(NL)	30	82	53	217	7.2
1945-46	Ft. Wayne	(NL)	34	90	53	233	6.9
1946-47	Ft. Wayne	(NL)	44	153	104	410	9.3
1947-48	Baltimore		47	202	137	541	11.5
1948-49	Baltimore		57	219	188	626	11.0
1949-50	Washington		67	197	212	606	9.0
	Totals		301	971	772	2714	9.0

RENNICKE, JOHN
b. Aug. 11, 1929 Ht. 6-2 Wt. 185 College—Drake

Yr.	Team	G	FG	FT	TP	Avg.
1951-52	Milwaukee	6	4	3	11	1.8

RENSBERGER, ROBERT
b. 1920 Ht. 6-2 Wt. 170 College—Notre Dame

Yr.	Team	G	FG	FT	TP	Avg.
1946-47	Chicago	3	0	0	0	0.0

REYNOLDS, GEORGE
b. Nov. 23, 1947 Ht. 6-4 Wt. 195 College—Houston

Yr.	Team	G	FG	FT	TP	Avg.
1969-70	Detroit	10	8	5	21	2.1

RHINE, KENDALL
b. Feb. 13, 1943 Ht. 6-10 Wt. 240 College—Rice

Yr.	Team		G	FG	FT	TP	Avg.
1967-68	Kentucky	(ABA)	52	50	27	127	2.4
1968-69	Houston	(ABA)	73	255	149	659	9.0
	Totals		125	305	176	786	6.3

RHODES, GENE
b. Sept. 2, 1927 Ht. 6-1 Wt. 170 College—Western Ky.

Yr.	Team	G	FG	FT	TP	Avg.
1952-53	Indianapolis	65	109	119	337	5.2

RICHTER, JOHN
b. March 12, 1937 Ht. 6-9 Wt. 225 College—N.C. State

Yr.	Team	G	FG	FT	TP	Avg.
1959-60	Boston	66	113	59	285	4.3

RICKETTS, DICK
b. Dec. 4, 1933 Ht. 6-7 Wt. 220 College—Duquesne

Yr.	Team	G	FG	FT	TP	Avg.
1955-56	St. L.-Rchstr	68	235	138	608	8.9
1956-57	Rochester	72	299	206	804	11.2
1957-58	Cincinnati	72	215	132	562	7.8
	Totals	212	749	476	1974	9.3

RIDGLE, JACKIE
b. Feb. 13, 1948 Ht. 6-4 Wt. 195 College—California

Yr.	Team	G	FG	FT	TP	Avg.
1971-72	Cleveland	32	19	19	57	1.8

Yr.	Team		G	FG	FT	TP	Avg.

RIEBE, MEL (Mouse)
b. July 12, 1916 Ht. 5-11½ Wt. 180

Yr.	Team		G	FG	FT	TP	Avg.
1943-44	Cleveland	(NL)	18	113	97	323	17.9
1944-45	Cleveland	(NL)	30	223	161	607	20.2
1945-46	Cleveland	(NL)	5	23	26	72	14.4
1946-47	Cleveland		55	276	111	663	12.1
1947-48	Boston		48	202	85	489	10.2
1948-49	Bos.-Prov.		43	172	79	423	9.8
	Totals		199	1009	559	2577	12.9

RIEDY, BOB
b. Aug. 26, 1945 Ht. 6-6 Wt. 215 College—Duke

Yr.	Team		G	FG	FT	TP	Avg.
1967-68	Houston	(ABA)	23	45	41	131	5.7

RIFFEY, JAMES
b. 1924 Ht. 6-4 Wt. 200 College—Tulane

Yr.	Team	G	FG	FT	TP	Avg.
1950-51	Ft. Wayne	35	65	20	150	4.3

RIKER, TOM
b. Feb. 28, 1950 Wt. 6-10 Wt. 225 College—S. Carolina

Yr.	Team	G	FG	FT	TP	Avg.
1972-73	New York	14	10	15	35	2.5
1973-74	New York	17	13	12	38	2.2
1974-75	New York	51	53	46	152	3.0
	Totals	82	76	73	225	2.7

RILEY, BOB
b. July 6, 1948 Ht. 6-9 Wt. 235 College—Mt. St. Mary's

Yr.	Team	G	FG	FT	TP	Avg.
1970-71	Atlanta	7	4	5	13	1.9

RILEY, PAT
b. March 20, 1945 Ht. 6-4 Wt. 205 College—Kentucky

Yr.	Team	G	FG	FT	TP	Avg.
1967-68	San Diego	80	250	128	628	7.9
1968-69	San Diego	56	202	90	494	8.8
1969-70	San Diego	36	75	40	190	5.3
1970-71	Los Angeles	54	105	56	266	4.9
1971-72	Los Angeles	67	197	55	449	6.7
1972-73	Los Angeles	55	167	65	339	7.3
1973-74	Los Angeles	72	287	110	684	9.5
1974-75	Los Angeles	46	219	69	507	11.0
1975-76	L.A.-Phoe.	62	117	55	289	4.7
	Totals	528	1619	668	3906	7.4

RILEY, RON
b. Nov. 11, 1950 Ht. 6-8 Wt. 200 College—USC

Yr.	Team	G	FG	FT	TP	Avg.
1972-73	K.C.-O.	74	273	79	625	8.4
1973-74	K.C.-O.-Hou.	48	81	24	186	3.9
1974-75	Houston	77	196	71	463	6.0
1975-76	Houston	65	115	38	268	4.1
	Totals	264	665	212	1542	5.8

RINALDI, RICH
b. Aug. 3, 1949 Ht. 6-3 Wt. 195 College—St. Peter's

Yr.	Team		G	FG	FT	TP	Avg.
1971-72	Baltimore		39	42	20	104	2.7
1972-73	Baltimore		33	116	48	280	8.5
1973-74	Capital		7	3	3	9	1.3
1973-74	New York	(ABA)	5	4	4	12	2.4
	Totals		84	165	75	405	4.8

RIORDAN, MIKE
b. July 9, 1945 Ht. 6-4 Wt. 200 College—Providence

Yr.	Team	G	FG	FT	TP	Avg.
1968-69	New York	54	49	28	126	2.3
1969-70	New York	81	255	114	624	7.7
1970-71	New York	82	162	67	391	4.8
1971-72	N.Y.-Balt.	58	233	84	550	9.5
1972-73	Baltimore	82	652	179	1483	18.1
1973-74	Capital	81	577	136	1290	15.9
1974-75	Washington	74	520	98	1138	15.4
1975-76	Washington	78	291	71	653	8.4
1976-77	Washington	49	34	11	79	1.6
	Totals	639	2773	788	6334	9.9

RISEN, ARNOLD (Stilts)
b. Oct. 9, 1924 Ht. 6-9 Wt. 200 College—Ohio State

Yr.	Team		G	FG	FT	TP	Avg.
1945-46	Indianapolis	(NL)	18	77	65	219	12.2
1946-47	Indianapolis	(NL)	44	204	174	582	13.2
1947-48	Ind.-Roch.	(NL)	61	282	241	805	13.1
1948-49	Rochester		60	345	305	995	16.6
1949-50	Rochester		62	206	213	625	10.1
1950-51	Rochester		66	377	323	1077	16.3
1951-52	Rochester		66	365	302	1032	15.6
1952-53	Rochester		68	295	294	884	13.0
1953-54	Rochester		72	321	307	949	11.6
1954-55	Rochester		69	259	279	797	11.6
1955-56	Boston		68	189	170	548	8.1
1956-57	Boston		43	119	106	344	8.0
1957-58	Boston		63	134	114	382	6.1
	Totals		760	3173	2893	9239	12.2

RITTER, GOEBEL (Tex)
b. 1924 Ht. 6-2 Wt. 185 College—Eastern Kentucky

Yr.	Team	G	FG	FT	TP	Avg.
1948-49	New York	55	123	91	337	6.1
1949-50	New York	62	100	125	325	5.2
1950-51	New York	34	39	49	127	3.7
	Totals	151	262	265	789	5.2

ROBBINS, AUSTIN (Red)
b. Sept. 30, 1944 Ht. 6-8 Wt. 200 College—Tennessee

Yr.	Team		G	FG	FT	TP	Avg.
1967-68	New Orleans	(ABA)	73	448(2)	245	1143	15.7
1968-69	New Orleans	(ABA)	76	456(7)	291	1210	15.9
1969-70	New Orleans	(ABA)	82	525(7)	285	1342	16.4
1970-71	Utah	(ABA)	82	396(11)	227	1030	12.6
1971-72	Utah	(ABA)	78	379(29)	167	954	12.2
1972-73	San Diego	(ABA)	58	218(9)	131	576	9.9
1973-74	S.D.-Kent.	(ABA)	80	276(1)	116	669	8.4
1974-75	Kent.-Virg.	(ABA)	57	307(3)	162	779	13.7
	Totals		586	3005(69)	1624	7703	13.1

ROBBINS, LEE ROY
b. 1923 Ht. 6-3 Wt. 175 College—Colorado
d. Apr. 8, 1968

Yr.	Team	G	FG	FT	TP	Avg.
1947-48	Providence	31	72	51	195	6.3
1948-49	Providence	16	9	11	29	1.8
	Totals	47	81	62	224	4.8

ROBERTS, JOSEPH
b. May 18, 1936 Ht. 6-6 Wt. 214 College—Ohio State

Yr.	Team	G	FG	FT	TP	Avg.
1960-61	Syracuse	68	130	62	322	4.7
1961-62	Syracuse	80	243	129	615	7.7

Yr.	Team		G	FG	FT	TP	Avg.
1962-63	Syracuse		33	73	35	181	5.5
1967-68	Kentucky	(ABA)	37	54(1)	28	137	3.7
		Totals	218	500(1)	254	1255	5.8

ROBERTS, MARV
b. Jan. 29, 1950 Ht. 6-8 Wt. 220 College—Utah State

1971-72	Denver	(ABA)	68	217(1)	86	521	7.7
1972-73	Denver	(ABA)	77	374(1)	201	950	12.3
1973-74	Den.-Cav.	(ABA)	74	266(1)	129	662	9.0
1974-75	Kentucky	(ABA)	83	201	127	529	6.4
1975-76	Ken.-Vir.	(ABA)	72	259	107	625	8.7
1976-77	Los Angeles		28	27	4	58	2.1
		Totals	402	1344(3)	654	3345	8.3

ROBERTS, WILLIAM
b. 1925 Ht. 6-9 Wt. 210 College—Wyoming

1948-49	Chi.-Bos.-St. L.		50	89	44	222	4.4
1949-50	St. Louis		67	77	28	182	2.7
		Totals	117	166	72	404	3.5

ROBERTSON, OSCAR (The Big O)
b. Nov. 24, 1938 Ht. 6-5 Wt. 205 College—Cincinnati

1960-61	Cincinnati	71	756	653	2165	30.5
1961-62	Cincinnati	79	866	700	2432	30.8
1962-63	Cincinnati	80	825	614	2264	28.3
1963-64	Cincinnati	79	840	800	2480	31.4
1964-65	Cincinnati	75	807	665	2279	30.4
1965-66	Cincinnati	76	818	742	2378	31.3
1966-67	Cincinnati	79	838	736	2412	30.5
1967-68	Cincinnati	65	660	576	1896	29.2
1968-69	Cincinnati	79	656	643	1955	24.7
1969-70	Cincinnati	69	647	454	1748	25.3
1970-71	Milwaukee	81	592	385	1569	19.4
1971-72	Milwaukee	64	419	276	1114	17.4
1972-73	Milwaukee	73	446	238	1130	15.5
1973-74	Milwaukee	70	338	212	888	12.7
	Totals	1040	9508	7694	26710	25.7

ROBERTSON, TONY
b. Jan. 1, 1956 Ht. 6-4 Wt. 195 College—West Virginia

1977-78	Atlanta	63	168	37	373	5.9
1978-79	Golden State	12	15	6	36	3.0
	Totals	75	183	43	409	5.5

ROBINSON, FLYNN
b. April 28, 1941 Ht. 6-1 Wt. 190 College—Wyoming

1966-67	Cincinnati		76	274	120	668	8.8
1967-68	Cinn.-Chicago		75	444	288	1176	15.7
1968-69	Chi.-Mil.		83	625	412	1662	20.0
1969-70	Milwaukee		81	663	439	1765	21.8
1970-71	Cincinnati		71	374	195	943	13.3
1971-72	Los Angeles		64	262	111	635	9.9
1972-73	L.A.-Balt.		44	133	32	298	6.8
1973-74	San Diego	(ABA)	49	185(8)	52	430	8.8
		Totals	543	2960(8)	1649	7577	14.0

ROBINSON, JACKIE
b. May 20, 1955 Ht. 6-6 Wt. 206 College—Nev.-Las Vegas

1978-79	Seattle	12	19	8	46	3.8
1979-80	Detroit	7	9	9	27	3.9
	Totals	19	28	17	73	3.8

Yr.	Team		G	FG	FT	TP	Avg.
ROBINSON, RONNIE							

b. Mar. 9, 1951 Ht. 6-8 Wt. 220 College—Memphis State

1973-74	Utah-Mem.	(ABA)	62	174	49	397	6.4
1974-75	Memphis	(ABA)	10	18	4	40	4.0
		Totals	72	192	53	437	6.1

ROBINSON, SAM
b. Apr. 1, 1948 Ht. 6-7 Wt. 200 College—Long Beach State

1970-71	Floridians	(ABA)	83	405(4)	103	917	11.5
1971-72	Floridians	(ABA)	51	126	54	306	6.0
		Totals	134	531(4)	157	1223	9.1

ROBINSON, WILL
b. 1949 Ht. 6-2 Wt. 175 College—West Virginia

1973-74	Memphis	(ABA)	45	166	57	389	8.6

ROCHA, EPHRAIM (Red)
b. Sept. 18, 1923 Ht. 6-9 Wt. 185 College—Oreg. State

1947-48	St. Louis	48	232	147	611	12.8
1948-49	St. Louis	58	223	162	608	10.5
1949-50	St. Louis	65	275	220	770	11.8
1950-51	Baltimore	64	297	242	836	13.1
1951-52	Syracuse	66	300	254	854	12.9
1952-53	Syracuse	69	268	234	770	11.2
1954-55	Syracuse	72	295	222	812	11.3
1955-56	Syracuse	72	250	220	720	10.0
1956-57	Ft. Wayne	72	136	109	381	5.3
	Totals	586	2276	1810	6362	10.9

ROCK, GENE
b. Nov. 4, 1921 Ht. 5-9½ Wt. 155 College—Southern California

1947-48	Chicago	11	4	2	10	0.9

ROCKER, JACK
b. Aug. 12, 1922 Ht. 6-5 Wt. 185 College—California

1947-48	Minn.	(NL)	5	2	0	4	0.8
1947-48	Phila.		9	8	1	17	1.9
		Totals	14	10	1	21	1.5

RODGERS, GUY
b. Sept. 1, 1935 Ht. 6-0 Wt. 185 College—Temple

1958-59	Philadelphia	45	211	61	483	10.7
1959-60	Philadelphia	68	338	111	787	11.6
1960-61	Philadelphia	78	397	206	1000	12.8
1961-62	Philadelphia	80	267	121	655	8.2
1962-63	San Fran.	79	445	208	1098	14.1
1963-64	San Fran.	79	337	198	872	11.0
1964-65	San Fran.	79	465	223	1153	14.6
1965-66	San Fran.	79	586	296	1468	18.6
1966-67	Chicago	81	538	383	1459	18.0
1967-68	Chi.-Cin.	78	148	107	403	5.2
1968-69	Milwaukee	81	325	184	834	10.3
1969-70	Milwaukee	64	68	67	203	3.2
	Totals	891	4125	2165	10415	11.7

ROGERS, HARRY
b. 1953 Ht. 6-7 Wt. 195 College—St. Louis

1975-76	St. Louis	(ABA)	18	60	17	137	7.6

Yr.	Team		G	FG	FT	TP	Avg.
ROGERS, MARSHALL							
b. Aug. 27, 1953 Ht. 6-1 Wt. 190 College—Pan American							
1976-77 Golden State			26	43	14	100	3.8
ROGERS, WILLIE DANIEL							
b. Sept. 11, 1945 Ht. 6-3 Wt. 195 College—Oklahoma							
1968-69 Denver	(ABA)		40	27	31	85	2.1
ROGES, ALBERT							
b. 1931 Ht. 6-4 Wt. 200 College—Long Island Univ.							
1953-54 Baltimore			67	220	130	570	8.5
1954-55 Balt.-Ft. W.			17	23	15	61	3.6
	Totals		84	243	145	631	7.5
ROHLOFF, KEN							
b. April 18, 1939 Ht. 6-0 Wt. 195 College—N.C. State							
1963-64 St. Louis			2	0	0	0	0.0
ROLLINS, KEN							
b. Sept. 14, 1923 Ht. 6-0 Wt. 168 College—Kentucky							
1948-49 Chicago			59	144	77	365	6.2
1949-50 Chicago			66	144	66	354	5.4
1952-53 Boston			43	38	22	98	2.3
	Totals		168	326	165	817	4.9
ROLLINS, PHILIP							
b. Jan. 19, 1934 Ht. 6-2 Wt. 190 College—Louisville							
1958-59 Phila.-Cin.			44	83	63	229	5.2
1959-60 Cincinnati			72	158	77	393	5.5
1960-61 Cin.-St. L.-N.Y.			61	105	56	266	4.4
	Totals		177	346	196	888	5.0
ROOK, JERRY							
Ht. 6-5 Wt. 220 College—Arkansas State							
1969-70 New Orleans	(ABA)		28	37	11	85	3.0
ROSENBERG, ALEXANDER (Petey)							
b. April 7, 1918 Ht. 5-10 Wt. 165 College—St. Joseph's (Pa.)							
1946-47 Philadelphia			51	60	30	150	2.9
ROSENBLUTH, LEONARD							
b. Jan. 22, 1933 Ht. 6-5 Wt. 200 College—N.C. State							
1957-58 Philadelphia			53	91	53	235	4.4
1958-59 Philadelphia			29	43	21	107	3.7
	Totals		82	134	74	342	4.2
ROSENSTEIN, HENRY							
b. 1920 Ht. 6-4 Wt. 185 College—CCNY							
1946-47 New York			31	38	57	133	4.3
1947-48 Providence			29	81	87	249	8.6
	Totals		60	119	144	382	6.4
ROSENTHAL, RICHARD							
Ht. 6-5 Wt. 205 College—Notre Dame							
1954-55 Ft. Wayne			67	197	130	524	7.8
1956-57 Ft. Wayne			18	21	9	51	2.8
	Totals		85	218	139	575	6.8

Yr.	Team		G	FG	FT	TP	Avg.
ROTHENBERG, IRWIN (Irv)							
b. Dec. 31, 1922 Ht. 6-8 Wt. 215 College—L.I.U.							
1946-47 Cleveland			29	36	30	102	3.5
1947-48 Balt.-St. L.Wash.			49	103	87	293	6.0
1948-49 New York			53	101	112	314	5.9
	Totals		131	240	229	709	5.4
ROTTNER, MARVIN (Mickey)							
b. Mar. 23, 1919 Ht. 5-10 Wt. 185 College—Loyola (Ill.)							
1945-46 Sheboygan	(NL)		5	10	0	20	4.0
1946-47 Chicago			56	190	43	423	7.6
1947-48 Chicago			44	53	11	117	2.7
	Totals		105	253	54	560	5.3
ROUX, GIFFORD							
b. June 28, 1923 Ht. 6-5 Wt. 195 College—Kansas							
1946-47 St. Louis			60	142	70	354	5.9
1947-48 St. Louis			46	68	40	176	3.8
1948-49 St. L.-Prov.			45	29	29	87	1.9
	Totals		151	239	139	617	4.1
ROWE, CURTIS							
b. July 2, 1949 Ht. 6-7 Wt. 225 College—UCLA							
1971-72 Detroit			82	369	192	930	11.2
1972-73 Detroit			81	547	210	1304	16.1
1973-74 Detroit			82	380	118	878	10.7
1974-75 Detroit			82	422	171	1015	12.4
1975-76 Detroit			80	514	252	1280	16.0
1976-77 Boston			79	315	170	800	10.1
1977-78 Boston			51	123	66	312	6.1
1978-79 Boston			53	151	52	354	6.7
	Totals		590	2821	1231	6873	11.6
ROYALS, REGGIE							
b. Sept. 18, 1954 Ht. 6-11 Wt. 220 College—Florida State							
1974-75 San Diego	(ABA)		2	2	0	4	2.0
ROYER, BOB							
b. 1927 Ht. 5-10 Wt. 155 College—K.C. and Ind. State							
d. May 30, 1973							
1949-50 Denver			42	78	41	197	4.7
RUDD, JOHN							
b. Aug. 7, 1955 Ht. 6-7 Wt. 230 College—McNeese St.							
1978-79 New York			58	59	66	184	3.2
RUDOMETKIN, JOHN							
b. June 6, 1940 Ht. 6-6 Wt. 205 College—USC							
1962-63 New York			56	108	73	289	5.2
1963-64 New York			52	154	87	395	7.6
1964-65 N.Y.-S.F.			23	52	34	138	6.0
	Totals		131	314	194	822	6.3
RUFFNER, PAUL							
b. Oct. 15, 1948 Ht. 6-10 Wt. 225 College—Brigham Young							
1970-71 Chicago			10	15	4	34	3.4
1971-72 Pittsburgh	(ABA)		79	182	84	448	5.7
1973-74 Buffalo			20	11	8	30	1.5
1974-75 Buffalo			22	22	1	45	2.0
	Totals		131	230	97	557	4.3

Yr.	Team		G	FG	FT	TP	Avg.

RUKLICK, JOSEPH
b. Aug. 3, 1938 Ht. 6-9 Wt. 220 College—Northwestern

Yr.	Team	G	FG	FT	TP	Avg.
1959-60	Philadelphia	39	85	26	196	5.0
1960-61	Philadelphia	29	43	8	94	3.2
1961-62	Philadelphia	46	48	12	108	1.8
	Totals	114	176	46	398	3.5

RULE, BOB
b. June 29, 1944 Ht. 6-9 Wt. 220 College—Colo. St.

Yr.	Team	G	FG	FT	TP	Avg.
1967-68	Seattle	82	568	348	1484	18.1
1968-69	Seattle	82	776	413	1965	24.0
1969-70	Seattle	80	789	387	1965	24.6
1970-71	Seattle	4	47	25	119	29.8
1971-72	Sea.-Phil.	76	461	226	1148	15.1
1972-73	Phila.-Cleve.	52	60	20	140	2.7
1973-74	Cleveland	26	76	34	186	7.2
1974-75	Milwaukee	1	0	0	0	0.0
	Totals	403	2777	1453	7007	17.4

RULLO, GENEROSO (Jerry)
b. 1923 Ht. 5-10 Wt. 165 College—Temple

Yr.	Team	G	FG	FT	TP	Avg.
1946-47	Philadelphia	50	52	23	127	2.5
1947-48	Baltimore	2	0	0	0	0.0
1948-49	Philadelphia	39	53	31	137	3.5
1949-50	Philadelphia	4	3	1	7	1.8
	Totals	95	108	55	271	2.9

RUSSELL, BILL
b. Feb. 12, 1934 Ht. 6-9½ Wt. 220 College—San Francisco

Yr.	Team	G	FG	FT	TP	Avg.
1956-57	Boston	48	277	152	706	14.7
1957-58	Boston	69	456	230	1142	16.6
1958-59	Boston	70	456	256	1168	16.7
1959-60	Boston	74	555	240	1350	18.2
1960-61	Boston	78	532	258	1322	16.9
1961-62	Boston	76	575	286	1436	18.9
1962-63	Boston	78	511	287	1309	16.8
1963-64	Boston	78	466	236	1168	15.0
1964-65	Boston	78	429	244	1102	14.1
1965-66	Boston	78	391	223	1005	12.9
1966-67	Boston	81	395	285	1075	13.4
1967-68	Boston	78	365	247	977	12.5
1968-69	Boston	77	279	204	762	9.9
	Totals	963	5687	3148	14522	15.1

RUSSELL, CAZZIE
b. June 7, 1944 Ht. 6-5½ Wt. 218 College—Michigan

Yr.	Team	G	FG	FT	TP	Avg.
1966-67	New York	77	344	179	867	11.3
1967-68	New York	82	551	282	1384	16.9
1968-69	New York	50	362	191	915	18.3
1969-70	New York	78	385	124	894	11.5
1970-71	New York	57	216	92	524	9.2
1971-72	Golden State	79	689	315	1693	21.4
1972-73	Golden State	80	541	172	1254	15.7
1973-74	Golden State	82	738	208	1684	20.5
1974-75	Los Angeles	40	264	101	629	15.7
1975-76	Los Angeles	74	371	132	874	11.8
1976-77	Los Angeles	82	578	188	1344	16.4
1977-78	Chicago	36	133	49	315	8.8
	Totals	817	5172	2033	12377	15.1

RUSSELL, FRANK
b. April 17, 1949 Ht. 6-3 Wt. 180 College—Detroit

Yr.	Team	G	FG	FT	TP	Avg.
1972-73	Chicago	23	29	16	74	3.2

RUSSELL, PIERRE
b. Dec. 13, 1949 Ht. 6-4 Wt. 190 College—Kansas

Yr.	Team		G	FG	FT	TP	Avg.
1971-72	Kentucky	(ABA)	51	65	16	146	2.9
1972-73	Kentucky	(ABA)	59	119(2)	49	289	4.9
	Totals		110	184(2)	65	435	4.0

RUSSELL, RUBIN
b. 1945 Ht. 6-3 Wt. 180 College—North Texas State

Yr.	Team		G	FG	FT	TP	Avg.
1967-68	Dallas-Ky.	(ABA)	26	56(4)	25	141	5.4

SADOWSKI, EDWARD (Big Ed)
b. July 11, 1917 Ht. 6-5 Wt. 240 College—Seton Hall

Yr.	Team		G	FG	FT	TP	Avg.
1940-41	Detroit	(NL)	24	95	66	256	10.7
1944-45	Ft. Wayne	(NL)	1	4	2	10	10.0
1945-46	Ft. Wayne	(NL)	34	122	82	326	9.6
1946-47	Tor.-Cleve.		53	329	219	877	16.5
1947-48	Boston		47	308	294	910	19.4
1948-49	Philadelphia		60	340	240	920	15.3
1949-50	Phila.-Balt.		69	299	274	872	12.6
	Totals		288	1497	1177	4171	14.5

SAILORS, KEN
b. Jan. 14, 1922 Ht. 5-10 Wt. 197 College—Wyoming

Yr.	Team	G	FG	FT	TP	Avg.
1946-47	Cleveland	58	229	119	577	9.9
1947-48	Chi.-Phila.-Prov.	44	207	110	524	11.9
1948-49	Providence	57	309	281	899	15.8
1949-50	Denver	57	329	329	987	17.3
1950-51	Bos.-Balt.	60	181	131	493	8.2
	Totals	276	1255	970	3480	12.6

SALVADORI, ALBERT (Al)
b. May 6, 1945 Ht. 6-9½ Wt. 220 College—South Carolina

Yr.	Team		G	FG	FT	TP	Avg.
1967-68	Oakland	(ABA)	17	21(1)	11	54	3.2

SANDERS, AL
b. 1950 Ht. 6-7 Wt. 240 College—Louisiana State

Yr.	Team		G	FG	FT	TP	Avg.
1972-73	Virginia	(ABA)	4	2	4	8	2.0

SANDERS, THOMAS (Satch)
b. Nov. 8, 1938 Ht. 6-6 Wt. 210 College—N.Y. Univ.

Yr.	Team	G	FG	FT	TP	Avg.
1960-61	Boston	68	148	67	363	5.3
1961-62	Boston	80	350	197	897	11.2
1962-63	Boston	80	339	186	864	10.8
1963-64	Boston	80	349	213	911	11.4
1964-65	Boston	80	374	193	941	11.8
1965-66	Boston	72	349	211	909	12.6
1966-67	Boston	81	323	178	824	10.2
1967-68	Boston	78	296	200	792	10.2
1968-69	Boston	82	364	187	915	11.2
1969-70	Boston	57	246	161	653	11.5
1970-71	Boston	17	16	7	39	2.3
1971-72	Boston	82	215	111	541	6.6
1972-73	Boston	59	47	23	117	2.0
	Totals	916	3416	1934	8766	9.6

SANFORD, RON
b. June 11, 1946 Ht. 6-9 Wt. 215 College—New Mexico

Yr.	Team		G	FG	FT	TP	Avg.
1971-72	Dallas	(ABA)	1	0	0	0	0.0

Yr.	Team	G	FG	FT	TP	Avg.

SANTINI, ROBERT
b. Feb. 17, 1935 Ht. 6-5 Wt. 190 College—Iona

Yr.	Team	G	FG	FT	TP	Avg.
1955-56 New York		4	5	1	11	2.8

SAUL, FRANK (Pep)
b. Feb. 16, 1924 Ht. 6-2 Wt. 185 College—Seton Hall

Yr.	Team	G	FG	FT	TP	Avg.
1949-50 Rochester		49	74	34	182	3.7
1950-51 Rochester		65	105	72	282	4.3
1951-52 Balt.-Minn.		64	157	119	433	6.8
1952-53 Minneapolis		70	187	142	516	7.4
1953-54 Minneapolis		71	162	128	452	6.4
1954-55 Milwaukee		65	96	95	287	4.4
Totals		384	781	590	2152	5.6

SAULDSBERRY, WOODY
b. July 11, 1934 Ht. 6-7 Wt. 220 College—Tex. Southern

Yr.	Team	G	FG	FT	TP	Avg.
1957-58 Philadelphia		71	389	134	912	12.8
1958-59 Philadelphia		72	501	110	1112	15.4
1959-60 Philadelphia		71	325	55	705	9.9
1960-61 St. Louis		68	230	56	516	7.6
1961-62 St. L.-Chic.		63	298	79	675	10.7
1962-63 Chi.-St. L.		77	366	107	839	10.9
1965-66 Boston		39	80	11	171	4.4
Totals		461	2189	552	4930	10.7

SAULTERS, GLYNN
b. Feb. 10, 1945 Ht. 6-2 Wt. 175 College—Western L.A.

Yr.	Team	G	FG	FT	TP	Avg.
1968-69 New Orleans (ABA)		22	22	15	59	2.7

SAUNDERS, FRED
b. June 13, 1951 Ht. 6-7 Wt. 210 College—Syracuse

Yr.	Team	G	FG	FT	TP	Avg.
1974-75 Phoenix		69	176	66	418	6.1
1975-76 Phoenix		17	28	6	62	3.6
1976-77 Boston		68	184	35	403	5.9
1977-78 Bos.-N.O.		56	99	26	224	4.0
Totals		210	487	133	1107	5.3

SAVAGE, DON
b. April 9, 1929 Ht. 6-3 Wt. 205 College—LeMoyne (N.Y.)

Yr.	Team	G	FG	FT	TP	Avg.
1951-52 Syracuse		12	9	18	36	3.0
1956-57 Syracuse		5	6	6	18	3.6
Totals		17	15	24	54	3.2

SAWYER, ALAN
b. 1928 Ht. 6-5 Wt. 195 College—UCLA

Yr.	Team	G	FG	FT	TP	Avg.
1950-51 Washington		33	87	43	217	6.6

SCHADE, FRANK
b. Jan. 22, 1950 Ht. 6-1 Wt. 170 College—Eau Claire St.

Yr.	Team	G	FG	FT	TP	Avg.
1972-73 K.C.-O.		9	2	6	10	1.1

SCHADLER, BERNARD (Ben)
b. March 9, 1924 Ht. 6-2 Wt. 185 College—Northwestern

Yr.	Team	G	FG	FT	TP	Avg.
1947-48 Chicago		37	23	10	56	1.5
1948-49 Det.-Wat. (NL)		53	150	58	358	6.8
Totals		90	173	68	414	4.6

SCHAEFFER, BILLY
b. Dec. 11, 1951 Ht. 6-5 Wt. 200 College—St. John's

Yr.	Team	G	FG	FT	TP	Avg.
1973-74 New York (ABA)		59	171(2)	41	385	6.5
1974-75 New York (ABA)		27	61(2)	15	139	5.2
1975-76 N.Y.-Vir. (ABA)		51	114(2)	48	278	5.5
Totals		137	346(6)	104	802	5.9

SCHAEFER, HERMAN
b. 1919 Ht. 6-0 Wt. 175 College—Indiana

Yr.	Team	G	FG	FT	TP	Avg.
1941-42 Ft. Wayne (NL)		24	85	37	207	8.6
1942-43 Ft. Wayne (NL)		21	36	12	84	4.0
1945-46 Ft. Wayne (NL)		15	10	3	23	1.5
1946-47 Indianapolis)NL)		44	147	65	359	8.2
1947-48 Ind.-Minn. (NL)		57	110	78	298	5.2
1948-49 Minneapolis		58	214	174	602	10.4
1949-50 Minneapolis		65	122	86	330	5.1
Totals		284	724	455	1903	6.7

SCHAFER, ROBERT
Ht. 6-3 Wt. 195 College—Villanova

Yr.	Team	G	FG	FT	TP	Avg.
1955-56 Phila.-St. L.		54	81	63	224	4.1
1956-57 Syracuse		11	19	11	49	4.5
Totals		65	100	73	273	4.2

SCHARNUS, BEN (Whitey)
b. Jan. 6, 1918 Ht. 6-2 Wt. 173 College—Seton Hall

Yr.	Team	G	FG	FT	TP	Avg.
1946-47 Cleveland		51	33	37	103	2.0
1948-49 Providence		1	0	0	0	0.0
Totals		52	33	37	103	2.0

SCHATZMAN, MARVIN
b. 1926 Ht. 6-5 Wt. 200 College—St. Louis

Yr.	Team	G	FG	FT	TP	Avg.
1949-50 Baltimore		34	43	29	115	3.4

SCHAUS, FRED
b. June 30, 1925 Ht. 6-5 Wt. 210 College—West Va.

Yr.	Team	G	FG	FT	TP	Avg.
1949-50 Ft. Wayne		68	351	270	972	14.3
1950-51 Ft. Wayne		68	312	404	1028	15.1
1951-52 Ft. Wayne		62	281	310	872	14.1
1952-53 Ft. Wayne		69	240	243	723	10.5
1953-54 Ft. W.-N.Y.		67	161	153	475	7.1
Totals		334	1345	1380	4070	12.2

SCHAYES, DOLPH
b. May 19, 1928 Ht. 6-8 Wt. 220 College—N.Y. Univ.

Yr.	Team	G	FG	FT	TP	Avg.
1948-49 Syracuse (NL)		63	271	267	809	12.8
1949-50 Syracuse		64	348	376	1072	16.8
1950-51 Syracuse		66	332	457	1121	17.0
1951-52 Syracuse		63	263	342	868	13.8
1952-53 Syracuse		71	375	512	1262	17.8
1953-54 Syracuse		72	370	488	1228	17.1
1954-55 Syracuse		72	422	489	1333	18.5
1955-56 Syracuse		72	465	542	1472	20.4
1956-57 Syracuse		72	496	625	1617	22.5
1957-58 Syracuse		72	581	629	1791	24.9
1958-59 Syracuse		72	504	526	1534	21.3
1959-60 Syracuse		75	578	533	1689	22.5
1960-61 Syracuse		79	594	680	1868	23.6
1961-62 Syracuse		56	268	286	822	14.7
1962-63 Syracuse		66	223	181	627	9.5
1963-64 Philadelphia		24	44	46	134	5.6
Totals		1059	6134	6979	19247	18.2

Yr.	Team	G	FG	FT	TP	Avg.
SCHECTMAN, OSCAR (Ossie)						
b. 1919 Ht. 6-0½ Wt. 175 College—Long Island Univ.						
1946-47 New York		54	162	111	435	8.1
SCHELLHASE, DAVE						
b. Oct. 14, 1944 Ht. 6-3½ Wt. 205 College—Purdue						
1966-67 Chicago		31	40	14	94	3.0
1967-68 Chicago		42	47	20	114	2.7
Totals		73	87	34	208	2.8
SCHERER, HERB						
b. Dec. 21, 1929 Ht. 6-9 Wt. 215 College—LIU						
1950-51 Tri-Cities		20	24	20	68	3.4
1951-52 New York		12	19	9	47	3.9
Totals		32	43	29	115	3.6
SCHLUETER, DALE						
b. Nov. 12, 1945 Ht. 6-10 Wt. 226 College—Col. State						
1968-69 San Francisco		31	68	45	181	5.8
1969-70 San Francisco		63	82	60	224	3.6
1970-71 Portland		80	257	143	657	8.2
1971-72 Portland		81	353	241	974	11.7
1972-73 Philadelphia		78	166	86	418	5.4
1973-74 Atlanta		57	63	38	164	2.9
1974-75 Buffalo		76	92	84	268	3.5
1975-76 Buffalo		71	61	54	176	2.5
1976-77 Phoenix		39	26	18	70	1.8
1977-78 Portland		10	8	9	25	2.5
Totals		586	1176	778	3130	5.3
SCHNELLBACHER, OTTO						
b. April 15, 1923 Ht. 6-5 Wt. 185 College—Kansas						
1948-49 Prov.-St. L.		43	93	89	275	6.4
SCHNITTKER, RICHARD						
b. May 27, 1928 Ht. 6-5 Wt. 205 College—Ohio State						
1950-51 Washington		29	85	123	293	10.1
1953-54 Minneapolis		71	122	86	330	4.6
1954-55 Minneapolis		72	226	298	750	10.4
1955-56 Minneapolis		72	254	304	812	11.3
1956-57 Minneapolis		70	113	160	386	5.5
1957-58 Minneapolis		50	128	201	457	9.1
Totals		364	928	1172	3028	8.3
SCHOLZ, DAVE						
b. April 12, 1948 Ht. 6-8 Wt. 220 College—Illinois						
1969-70 Philadelphia		1	1	0	2	2.0
SCHOON, MILTON						
b. Feb. 25, 1922 Ht. 6-9 Wt. 230 College—Valparaiso						
1946-47 Detroit		41	43	34	120	2.9
1947-48 Flint	(NL)	55	114	120	348	6.3
1948-49 Sheboygan	(NL)	57	81	109	271	4.8
1949-50 Sheboygan	(NL)	62	150	196	496	8.0
Totals		215	388	459	1235	5.7
SCHULTZ, HOWARD (Stretch)						
b. July 3, 1922 Ht. 6-8 Wt. 220 College—Hamline						
1946-47 Anderson	(NL)	41	155	147	457	11.1
1947-48 Anderson	(NL)	60	213	179	605	10.1
1948-49 Anderson	(NL)	64	176	186	538	8.4

Yr.	Team		G	FG	FT	TP	Avg.
1949-50 And.-Ft. W.			67	179	196	554	8.3
1951-52 Minneapolis			66	89	90	268	4.1
1952-53 Minneapolis			40	24	43	91	2.3
Totals			338	836	841	2513	7.4
SCHULZ, RICHARD							
b. Jan. 3, 1917 Ht. 6-2 Wt. 205							
1942-43 Sheboygan	(NL)		1	0	0	0	0.0
1943-44 Sheboygan	(NL)		20	18	10	46	2.3
1944-45 Sheboygan	(NL)		29	86	71	243	8.4
1945-46 Sheboygan	(NL)		29	56	66	178	6.1
1946-47 Cleve.-Tor.			57	130	94	354	6.2
1947-48 Baltimore			48	133	117	383	8.0
1948-49 Washington			50	65	65	195	3.9
1949-50 Wsh.-Tri-C.-She.			50	63	83	209	4.2
Totals			284	551	506	1608	5.7
SCHURIG, ROGER							
b. April 3, 1942 Ht. 6-3 Wt. 185 College—Vanderbilt							
1967-68 Houston	(ABA)		21	35(3)	27	100	4.8
SCOLARI, FRED							
b. March 1, 1922 Ht. 5-10 Wt. 180 College—San Francisco							
1946-47 Washington			58	291	146	728	12.6
1947-48 Washington			47	229	131	589	12.5
1948-49 Washington			48	196	146	538	11.2
1949-50 Washington			66	312	236	860	13.0
1950-51 Wash.-Syr.			66	302	279	883	13.4
1951-52 Baltimore			64	290	353	933	14.6
1952-53 Balt.-Ft. W.			62	277	276	830	13.4
1953-54 Ft. Wayne			64	159	144	462	7.2
1954-55 Boston			59	76	39	191	3.2
Totals			534	2132	1750	6014	11.3
SCOTT, CHARLIE							
b. Dec. 15,1948 Ht. 6-5 Wt. 175 College—No. Carolina							
1970-71 Virginia	(ABA)		84	852(16)	456	2276	27.1
1971-72 Virginia	(ABA)		73	985(29)	525	2524	34.6
1971-72 Phoenix			6	48	17	113	18.8
1972-73 Phoenix			81	806	436	2048	25.3
1973-74 Phoenix			52	538	246	1322	25.4
1974-75 Phoenix			69	703	274	1680	24.3
1975-76 Boston			82	588	267	1443	17.6
1976-77 Boston			43	326	129	781	18.2
1977-78 Bos.-L.A.			79	435	194	1064	13.5
1978-79 Denver			79	393	161	947	12.0
1979-80 Denver			69	276(2)	85	639	9.3
Totals			717	6000(47)	2790	14837	20.7
SCOTT, RAY (Chink)							
b. July 12, 1938 Ht. 6-9 Wt. 215 College—Portland							
1961-62 Detroit			75	370	255	995	13.3
1962-63 Detroit			76	460	308	1228	16.2
1963-64 Detroit			80	539	328	1406	17.6
1964-65 Detroit			66	402	220	1024	15.5
1965-66 Detroit			79	544	323	1411	17.9
1966-67 Det-Baltimore			72	458	256	1172	16.3
1967-68 Baltimore			81	490	348	1328	16.4
1968-69 Baltimore			82	386	195	967	11.8
1969-70 Baltimore			73	257	139	653	8.9
1970-71 Virginia	(ABA)		72	420(1)	187	1028	14.3
1971-72 Virginia	(ABA)		55	163(2)	89	417	7.6
Totals			811	4489(3)	2648	11629	14.3

Yr.	Team		G	FG	FT	TP	Avg.
SCOTT, WILLIE							
b. 1947 Ht. 6-5 Wt. 210 College—Alabama State							
1969-70 Dallas	(ABA)		8	6	1	13	1.6
SCRANTON, PAUL							
Ht. 6-5 Wt. 230 College—Cal. Poly-Pomona							
1967-68 Anaheim	(ABA)		5	4	1	9	1.8
SEALS, BRUCE							
b. June 18, 1953 Ht. 6-9 Wt. 210 College—Xavier							
1973-74 Utah	(ABA)		78	229(19)	68	545	7.0
1974-75 Utah	(ABA)		35	60	20	140	4.0
1975-76 Seattle			81	388	181	957	11.8
1976-77 Seattle			81	378	138	894	11.0
1977-78 Seattle			73	230	111	571	7.8
	Totals		348	1285(19)	518	3107	8.9
SEARCY, EDWIN							
Ht. 6-7 College—St. John's							
1975-76 Boston			4	2	2	6	1.5
SEARS, KEN (Big Cat)							
b. Aug. 17, 1933 Ht. 6-9 Wt. 200 College—Santa Clara							
1955-56 New York			70	319	258	896	12.8
1956-57 New York			72	343	383	1069	14.8
1957-58 New York			72	445	452	1342	18.6
1958-59 New York			71	491	506	1488	21.0
1959-60 New York			64	412	363	1187	18.5
1960-61 New York			52	241	268	750	14.4
1962-63 NY-San Fran.			77	161	131	453	5.9
1963-64 San Fran.			51	53	64	170	3.3
	Totals		529	2465	2425	7355	13.9
SEE, WAYNE							
b. 1925 Ht. 6-3 Wt. 190 College—Arizona State at Flagstaff							
1949-50 Waterloo			61	113	94	320	5.2
SELBO, GLEN							
b. 1926 Ht. 6-3 Wt. 195 College—Wisconsin							
1947-48 Oshkosh	(NL)		59	157	62	376	6.4
1948-49 Oshkosh	(NL)		60	119	77	315	5.3
1949-50 Sheboygan			13	10	22	42	3.2
	Totals		132	286	161	733	5.6
SELLERS, PHIL							
b. Nov. 20, 1953 Ht. 6-4 Wt. 195 College—Rutgers							
1976-77 Detroit			44	73	52	198	4.5
SELTZ, ROLLIE							
b. Jan. 25, 1924 Ht. 5-10½ Wt. 170 College—Hamline							
1946-47 Anderson	(NL)		41	123	104	350	8.5
1947-48 Anderson	(NL)		59	118	90	326	5.5
1948-49 Waterloo	(NL)		62	188	127	503	8.1
1949-50 Anderson			34	93	80	266	7.8
	Totals		196	522	401	1445	7.4
SELVAGE, LES							
Ht. 6-1 Wt. 175 College—Kirksville State							
1967-68 Anaheim	(ABA)		78	371(147)	206	1095	14.0
1969-70 Los Angeles	(ABA)		4	4	0	8	2.0
	Totals		82	375(147)	206	1103	13.5

Yr.	Team		G	FG	FT	TP	Avg.
SELVY, FRANK							
b. Nov. 9, 1932 Ht. 6-2½ Wt. 180 College—Furman							
1954-55 Balt.-Milw.			71	452	444	1348	19.0
1955-56 St. Louis			17	67	53	187	11.0
1957-58 St. L.-Minn.			38	44	47	135	3.6
1958-59 New York			68	233	201	667	9.8
1959-60 Syr.-Minn.			62	205	153	563	9.1
1960-61 Los Angeles			77	311	210	832	10.8
1961-62 Los Angeles			79	433	298	1164	14.7
1962-63 Los Angeles			80	317	192	826	10.3
1963-64 Los Angeles			73	160	78	398	5.5
	Totals		565	2222	1676	6120	10.8
SEMINOFF, JAMES							
b. Sept. 1, 1922 Ht. 6-2 Wt. 190 College—Southern California							
1946-47 Chicago			60	184	71	439	7.3
1947-48 Chicago			48	113	73	299	6.3
1948-49 Boston			58	153	151	457	7.9
1949-50 Boston			65	85	142	312	4.8
	Totals		231	535	437	1507	6.5
SENESKY, GEORGE							
b. April 4, 1922 Ht. 6-2 Wt. 180 College—St. Joseph's (Pa.)							
1946-47 Philadelphia			58	142	82	366	6.3
1947-48 Philadelphia			47	158	98	414	8.8
1948-49 Philadelphia			60	138	111	387	6.4
1949-50 Philadelphia			68	227	157	611	9.0
1950-51 Philadelphia			65	249	181	679	10.4
1951-52 Philadelphia			57	164	146	474	8.3
1952-53 Philadelphia			69	160	93	413	6.0
1953-54 Philadelphia			58	41	29	111	1.9
	Totals		482	1279	897	3455	7.2
SEYMOUR, PAUL							
b. Jan. 30, 1928 Ht. 6-2 Wt. 180 College—Toledo							
1946-47 Toledo	(NL)		33	41	17	99	3.0
1947-48 Baltimore			22	27	22	76	3.5
1947-48 Syracuse	(NL)		30	79	47	205	6.8
1948-49 Syracuse	(NL)		63	120	70	310	4.9
1949-50 Syracuse			62	175	126	476	7.7
1950-51 Syracuse			51	125	117	367	7.2
1951-52 Syracuse			66	206	186	598	9.1
1952-53 Syracuse			67	306	340	952	14.2
1953-54 Syracuse			71	316	299	931	13.1
1954-55 Syracuse			72	375	300	1050	14.6
1955-56 Syracuse			57	227	188	642	11.3
1956-57 Syracuse			65	143	101	387	6.0
1957-58 Syracuse			64	107	53	267	4.2
1958-59 Syracuse			21	32	26	90	4.3
1959-60 Syracuse			4	0	0	0	0.0
	Totals		748	2279	1892	6450	8.6
SHABACK, NICHOLAS							
b. 1919 Ht. 5-11 Wt. 182							
1946-47 Cleveland			53	102	38	242	4.6
SHACKELFORD, R. LYNN							
b. Aug. 27, 1947 Ht. 6-5 Wt. 195 College—UCLA							
1969-70 Miami	(ABA)		22	22(4)	10	58	2.6

Yr.	Team	G	FG	FT	TP	Avg.
SHAEFFER, CARL						
b. 1925 Ht. 6-3½ Wt. 185 College—Alabama						
1949-50 Indianapolis		43	59	32	150	3.5
1950-51 Indianapolis		10	6	3	15	1.5
	Totals	53	65	35	165	3.1
SHAFFER, LEE						
b. Feb. 23, 1939 Ht. 6-7 Wt. 220 College—No. Carolina						
1961-62 Syracuse		75	514	239	1267	16.9
1962-63 Syracuse		80	597	294	1488	18.6
1963-64 Philadelphia		41	217	102	536	13.1
	Totals	196	1328	635	3291	16.8
SHANNON, EARL						
b. Nov. 23, 1921 Ht. 5-11 Wt. 170 College—Rhode Island						
1946-47 Providence		57	245	197	687	12.1
1947-48 Providence		45	123	116	362	8.0
1948-49 Prov.-Bos.		32	34	39	107	3.3
	Totals	134	402	352	1156	8.6
SHANNON, HOWARD						
b. June 10, 1923 Ht. 6-2 Wt. 175 College—Kans. St./N. Tex. St.						
1948-49 Providence		55	292	152	736	13.1
1949-50 Boston		67	222	143	587	8.8
	Totals	122	514	295	1323	10.8
SHARE, CHARLIE						
b. March 14, 1927 Ht. 6-11 Wt. 235 College—Bowling Gr.						
1951-52 Ft. Wayne		63	76	96	248	3.9
1952-53 Ft. Wayne		67	91	172	354	5.3
1953-54 Ft. W.-Milw.		68	188	188	564	8.3
1954-55 Milwaukee		69	235	351	821	11.9
1955-56 St. Louis		72	315	346	976	13.6
1956-57 St. Louis		72	235	269	739	10.3
1957-58 St. Louis		72	216	190	622	8.6
1958-59 St. Louis		72	147	139	433	6.6
	Totals	555	1503	1751	4757	8.6
SHARMAN, BILL						
b. May 25, 1926 Ht. 6-1 Wt. 190 College—So. California						
1950-51 Washington		31	141	96	378	12.2
1951-52 Boston		63	244	183	671	10.7
1952-53 Boston		71	403	341	1147	16.2
1953-54 Boston		72	412	331	1155	16.0
1954-55 Boston		68	453	347	1253	18.4
1955-56 Boston		72	538	358	1434	19.9
1956-57 Boston		67	516	381	1413	21.1
1957-58 Boston		63	550	302	1402	22.3
1958-59 Boston		72	562	342	1466	20.4
1959-60 Boston		71	559	252	1370	19.3
1960-61 Boston		60	383	210	976	16.3
	Totals	710	4761	3143	12665	17.8
SHAVLIK, RON						
b. Dec. 4, 1933 Ht. 6-8 Wt. 200 College—No. Carolina St.						
1956-57 New York		7	4	2	10	1.4
1957-58 New York		1	0	0	0	0.0
	Totals	8	4	2	10	1.3

Yr.	Team		G	FG	FT	TP	Avg.
SHEA, ROBERT							
b. 1924 Ht. 6-2 Wt. 194 College—Rhode Island							
1946-47 Providence			43	37	19	93	2.2
SHEFFIELD, FRED							
b. Nov. 5, 1923 Ht. 6-2 Wt. 165 College—Utah							
1946-47 Philadelphia			22	29	16	74	3.4
SHEPHERD, BILLY							
b. Nov. 18, 1949 Ht. 5-10 Wt. 165 College—Butler							
1972-73 Virginia	(ABA)		16	7(4)	9	27	1.7
1973-74 San Diego	(ABA)		84	200(65)	42	507	6.0
1974-75 Memphis	(ABA)		69	161(60)	52	434	6.3
	Totals		169	368(129)	103	968	5.7
SHEPPARD, STEVE							
b. March 21, 1954 Ht. 6-6 Wt. 220 College—Maryland							
1977-78 Chicago			64	119	37	275	4.3
1978-79 Chi.-Det.			42	36	20	92	2.2
	Totals		106	155	57	367	3.5
SHIPP, CHARLES							
b. Dec. 3, 1913 Ht. 6-1 Wt. 205							
1937-38 Akron	(NL)		16	38	14	90	5.6
1938-39 Akron	(NL)		24	59	24	142	5.9
1939-40 Oshkosh	(NL)		28	74	26	174	6.2
1940-41 Oshkosh	(NL)		22	46	21	113	5.1
1941-42 Oshkosh	(NL)		24	70	38	178	7.4
1942-43 Oshkosh	(NL)		23	52	36	140	6.1
1943-44 Oshkosh	(NL)		20	57	36	150	7.5
1944-45 Ft. Wayne	(NL)		30	31	16	78	2.6
1945-46 Ft. Wayne	(NL)		34	42	14	98	2.9
1946-47 Ft. W.-And.	(NL)		44	89	58	236	5.4
1947-48 Anderson	(NL)		55	103	63	269	4.9
1948-49 Waterloo	(NL)		56	104	59	267	4.8
1949-50 Waterloo			23	35	37	107	4.7
	Totals		399	800	442	2042	5.1
SHORT, EUGENE							
b. Aug. 7, 1953 Ht. 6-7 Wt. 200 College—Jackson State							
1975-76 Sea.-N.Y.			34	32	20	84	2.5
SHRIDER, DICK							
b. 1923 Ht. 6-2 Wt. 190 College—Ohio University							
1948-49 Detroit	(NL)		3	3	3	9	3.0
1948-49 New York			4	0	1	1	0.3
	Totals		7	3	4	10	1.4
SHUE, GENE							
b. Dec. 18, 1931 Ht. 6-2 Wt. 175 College—Maryland							
1954-55 Phila.-N.Y.			62	100	59	259	4.2
1955-56 New York			72	240	181	661	9.2
1956-57 Ft. Wayne			72	273	241	787	10.9
1957-58 Detroit			63	353	276	982	15.6
1958-59 Detroit			72	464	338	1266	17.6
1959-60 Detroit			75	620	472	1712	22.8
1960-61 Detroit			78	650	465	1765	22.6
1961-62 Detroit			80	580	362	1522	19.0
1962-63 New York			78	354	208	916	11.7
1963-64 Baltimore			48	81	36	198	3.1
	Totals		700	3715	2638	10068	14.4

Yr.	Team		G	FG	FT	TP	Avg.

SIBERT, SAM
b. Feb. 11, 1949 Ht. 6-7 Wt. 215 College—Kentucky St.

| 1972-73 K.C.-Omaha | | | 5 | 4 | 4 | 12 | 2.4 |

SIBLEY, MARK
b. Nov. 13, 1950 Ht. 6-2 Wt. 175 College—Northwestern

| 1973-74 Portland | | | 28 | 20 | 6 | 46 | 1.6 |

SIDLE, DON
b. June 21, 1946 Ht. 6-9 Wt. 215 College—Oklahoma

1968-69 Miami	(ABA)		77	304	321	929	12.1
1969-70 Miami	(ABA)		84	639(1)	469	1748	20.8
1970-71 Den.-Ind.	(ABA)		84	425(2)	241	1093	12.0
1971-72 Ind.-Mem.	(ABA)		69	175(1)	124	475	6.9
	Totals		314	1543(4)	1155	4245	13.5

SIEGFRIED, LARRY
b. May 22, 1939 Ht. 6-4 Wt. 192 College—Ohio State

1963-64 Boston			31	35	31	101	3.3
1964-65 Boston			72	173	109	455	6.3
1965-66 Boston			71	349	274	972	13.7
1966-67 Boston			73	368	294	1030	14.1
1967-68 Boston			62	261	236	758	12.2
1968-69 Boston			79	392	336	1120	14.2
1969-70 Boston			78	382	220	984	12.6
1970-71 San Diego			53	146	130	422	8.0
1971-72 Hou.-Atl.			31	43	32	118	3.8
	Totals		550	2149	1662	5960	10.8

SIEWERT, RALPH (Sky)
Ht. 7-1 Wt. 230 College—North Dakota State

| 1946-47 St. Louis-Tor. | | | 21 | 6 | 8 | 20 | 1.0 |

SILAS, PAUL
b. July 12, 1943 Ht. 6-7 Wt. 235 College—Creighton

1964-65 St. Louis			79	140	83	363	4.6
1965-66 St. Louis			46	70	35	175	3.8
1966-67 St. Louis			76	207	113	527	6.9
1967-68 St. Louis			82	399	299	1097	13.4
1968-69 Atlanta			79	241	204	686	8.7
1969-70 Phoenix			78	373	250	996	12.8
1970-71 Phoenix			81	338	285	961	11.9
1971-72 Phoenix			80	485	433	1403	17.5
1972-73 Boston			80	400	266	1066	13.3
1973-74 Boston			82	340	264	944	11.5
1974-75 Boston			82	312	244	868	10.6
1975-76 Boston			81	315	236	866	10.7
1976-77 Denver			81	206	170	582	7.2
1977-78 Seattle			82	184	109	477	5.8
1978-79 Seattle			82	170	116	456	5.6
1979-80 Seattle			82	113	89	315	3.8
	Totals		1253	4293	3196	11782	9.4

SILLIMAN, MIKE
b. May 4, 1944 Ht. 6-6 Wt. 225 College—U.S. Mil. Acad.

| 1970-71 Buffalo | | | 36 | 36 | 19 | 91 | 2.5 |

SIMMONS, CONNIE
b. March 15, 1925 Ht. 6-8 Wt. 225

1946-47 Boston			60	246	128	620	10.3
1947-48 Bos.-Balt.			45	162	62	386	8.6
1948-49 Baltimore			60	299	181	779	13.0
1949-50 New York			60	241	198	680	11.3
1950-51 New York			66	229	146	604	9.2
1951-52 New York			66	227	175	629	9.5
1952-53 New York			65	240	249	729	11.2
1953-54 New York			72	255	210	720	10.0
1954-55 Balt.-Syra.			36	137	72	346	9.6
1955-56 Rochester			68	144	78	366	5.4
	Totals		598	2180	1499	5859	9.8

SIMMONS, GRANT
Ht. 6-3 Wt. 190 College—Nebraska

1967-68 Denver	(ABA)		78	292(1)	208	793	10.2
1968-69 Denver	(ABA)		17	22(1)	20	65	3.8
	Totals		95	314(2)	228	858	9.0

SIMMONS, JOHN
b. July 7, 1924 Ht. 6-1 Wt. 184 College—New York University

| 1946-47 Boston | | | 60 | 120 | 78 | 318 | 5.3 |

SIMON, WALT
b. Dec. 1, 1941 Ht. 6-6 Wt. 200 College—Benedict

1967-68 New Jersey	(ABA)		78	433(1)	169	1036	13.3
1968-69 New York	(ABA)		68	570(6)	290	1436	21.1
1969-70 New York	(ABA)		81	454(1)	178	1162	14.4
1970-71 Kentucky	(ABA)		83	274(1)	100	649	7.8
1971-72 Kentucky	(ABA)		67	243(1)	109	596	8.9
1972-73 Kentucky	(ABA)		83	432(3)	143	1010	12.2
1973-74 Kentucky	(ABA)		80	233(2)	57	525	6.6
	Totals		549	2639(15)	1121	6414	11.9

SIMPSON, RALPH
b. Aug. 10, 1949 Ht. 6-5 Wt. 200 College—Michigan St.

1970-71 Denver	(ABA)		81	460(17)	215	1152	14.2
1971-72 Denver	(ABA)		84	920(3)	457	2300	27.4
1972-73 Denver	(ABA)		81	732(5)	421	1890	23.3
1973-74 Denver	(ABA)		75	597(2)	208	1404	18.7
1974-75 Denver	(ABA)		82	694(1)	303	1692	20.6
1975-76 Denver	(ABA)		84	619(4)	273	1515	18.0
1976-77 Detroit			77	356	138	850	11.0
1977-78 Det.-Denv.			64	216	85	517	8.1
1978-79 Phil.-N.J.			69	174	76	424	6.2
1979-80 New Jersey			8	18	5	41	5.1
	Totals		705	4786(32)	2181	11785	16.7

SIMS, DOUG
b. June 29, 1943 Ht. 6-7 Wt. 195 College—Kent State

| 1968-69 Cincinnati | | | 4 | 2 | 0 | 4 | 1.0 |

SIMS, ROBERT
b. Oct. 9, 1938 Ht. 6-5 Wt. 220 College—Pepperdine

1961-62 L.A.-St. Louis			65	193	123	509	7.8
1967-68 Anaheim	(ABA)		2	2	4	8	4.0
	Totals		67	195	127	517	7.7

SIMS, SCOTT
b. April 18, 1955 Ht. 6-1 Wt. 170 College—Missouri

| 1977-78 San Antonio | | | 12 | 10 | 10 | 30 | 2.5 |

Yr.	Team		G	FG	FT	TP	Avg.
SINICOLA, EMILIO (Zeke)							
b. 1930 Ht. 5-10 Wt. 165 College—Niagara							
1951-52	Ft. Wayne		3	1	0	2	0.7
1953-54	Ft. Wayne		9	4	3	11	1.2
	Totals		12	5	3	13	1.1
SKINNER, AL							
b. June 16, 1952 Ht. 6-4 Wt. 195 College—Massachusetts							
1974-75	New York	(ABA)	51	129(1)	72	333	6.5
1975-76	New York	(ABA)	83	330(2)	203	865	10.4
1976-77	N.Y. Nets		79	382	231	995	12.6
1977-78	N.J.-Detr.		77	222	162	606	7.9
1978-79	N.J.-Phil.		45	91	99	281	6.2
1979-80	Philadelphia		2	1	0	2	1.0
	Totals		337	1156(3)	767	3082	9.1
SKINNER, TALVIN							
b. Sept. 10, 1952 Ht. 6-5 Wt. 210 College—Md. East. Shore							
1974-75	Seattle		73	142	63	347	4.8
1975-76	Seattle		72	132	49	313	4.3
	Totals		145	274	112	660	4.6
SKOOG, MEYER (Whitey)							
b. Nov. 2, 1926 Ht. 5-11 Wt. 180 College—Minnesota							
1951-52	Minneapolis		35	102	30	234	6.7
1952-53	Minneapolis		68	102	46	250	3.7
1953-54	Minneapolis		71	212	72	496	7.0
1954-55	Minneapolis		72	330	125	785	10.9
1955-56	Minneapolis		72	340	155	835	11.0
1956-57	Minneapolis		23	78	44	200	8.7
	Totals		341	1164	472	2800	8.2
SLADE, JEFFREY							
b. March 1, 1941 Ht. 6-6 Wt. 220 College—Kenyon							
1962-63	Chicago		3	2	0	4	1.3
SLAUGHTER, JIM							
b. 1928 Ht. 6-11 Wt. 212 College—South Carolina							
1951-52	Baltimore		28	53	41	147	5.3
SLOAN, JERRY (Spider)							
b. March 28, 1942 Ht. 6-6 Wt. 195 College—Evansville							
1965-66	Baltimore		59	120	98	338	5.7
1966-67	Chicago		80	525	340	1390	17.4
1967-68	Chicago		77	369	289	1027	13.3
1968-69	Chicago		78	488	333	1309	16.8
1969-70	Chicago		53	310	207	827	15.6
1970-71	Chicago		80	592	278	1462	18.3
1971-72	Chicago		82	535	258	1328	16.2
1972-73	Chicago		69	301	94	696	10.1
1973-74	Chicago		77	412	194	1018	13.2
1974-75	Chicago		78	380	193	953	12.2
1975-76	Chicago		22	84	55	223	10.1
	Totals		755	4116	2339	10571	14.0
SMAWLEY, BELUS							
b. 1921 Ht. 6-1½ Wt. 195 College—Appalachian State							
1946-47	St. Louis		22	113	36	262	11.9
1947-48	St. Louis		48	212	111	535	11.2
1948-49	St. Louis		59	352	210	914	15.5

Yr.	Team		G	FG	FT	TP	Avg.
1949-50	St. Louis		61	287	260	834	13.7
1950-51	Syr.-Balt.		60	252	227	731	12.2
	Totals		250	1216	844	3276	13.1
SMILEY, JACK (Smiles)							
b. Dec. 22, 1922 Ht. 6-3 Wt. 190 College—Illinois							
1947-48	Ft. Wayne	(NL)	60	105	90	300	5.0
1948-49	Ft. Wayne		59	141	112	394	6.7
1949-50	And.-Waterloo		59	98	136	332	5.6
	Totals		178	344	338	1026	5.8
SMITH, ADRIAN (Odie)							
b. Oct. 5, 1936 Ht. 6-1 Wt. 180 College—Kentucky							
1961-62	Cincinnati		80	202	172	576	7.2
1962-63	Cincinnati		79	241	223	705	8.9
1963-64	Cincinnati		66	234	154	622	9.4
1964-65	Cincinnati		80	463	284	1210	15.1
1965-66	Cincinnati		80	531	408	1470	18.4
1966-67	Cincinnati		81	502	343	1347	16.6
1967-68	Cincinnati		82	480	320	1280	15.6
1968-69	Cincinnati		73	243	217	703	9.6
1969-70	Cin.-S.F.		77	153	152	458	5.9
1970-71	San Francisco		21	38	35	111	5.3
1971-72	Virginia	(ABA)	53	87(2)	92	268	5.1
	Totals		772	3174(2)	2400	8750	11.3
SMITH, ALAN							
b. Jan. 15, 1947 Ht. 6-1 Wt. 185 College—Bradley							
1971-72	Denver	(ABA)	83	292(32)	153	769	9.3
1972-73	Denver	(ABA)	83	315(17)	272	919	11.1
1973-74	Denver	(ABA)	76	311(22)	187	831	10.9
1974-75	Utah	(ABA)	80	225(34)	157	641	8.0
1975-76	Utah	(ABA)	15	42(6)	48	138	9.2
	Totals		337	1185(111)	817	3298	9.8
SMITH, BILL							
b. Feb. 14, 1949 Ht. 6-0½ Wt. 220 College—Syracuse							
1971-72	Portland		22	72	38	182	8.3
1972-73	Portland		8	9	5	23	2.9
	Totals		30	81	43	205	6.8
SMITH, BOBBY (Bingo)							
b. Feb. 26, 1946 Ht. 6-5 Wt. 212 College—Tulsa							
1969-70	San Diego		75	242	66	550	7.3
1970-71	Cleveland		77	495	178	1168	15.2
1971-72	Cleveland		82	527	178	1232	15.0
1972-73	Cleveland		73	268	64	600	8.2
1973-74	Cleveland		82	536	139	1211	14.8
1974-75	Cleveland		82	585	132	1302	15.9
1975-76	Cleveland		81	495	111	1101	13.6
1976-77	Cleveland		81	513	148	1174	14.5
1977-78	Cleveland		82	369	108	846	10.3
1978-79	Cleveland		72	361	83	805	11.2
1979-80	Clev.-S.D.		78	385(23)	100	893	11.4
	Totals		865	4776(23)	1307	10882	12.6
SMITH, DELBERT (Deb)							
b. Jan. 7, 1920 Ht. 6-3 Wt. 180 College—Utah							
1946-47	St. Louis		48	32	9	73	1.5

Yr.	Team		G	FG	FT	TP	Avg.

SMITH, DON
b. 1920 Ht. 6-2 Wt. 190 College—Minnesota

Yr.	Team		G	FG	FT	TP	Avg.
1942-43	Oshkosh	(NL)	13	22	15	59	4.5
1945-46	Oshkosh	(NL)	9	1	6	8	0.9
1946-47	Osh.-Ind.	(NL)	12	5	5	15	1.3
1947-48	Minneapolis	(NL)	57	69	62	200	3.5
1948-49	Minneapolis		8	2	2	6	0.8
	Totals		99	99	90	288	2.9

SMITH, DON
b. Oct. 10, 1951 Ht. 6-0 Wt. 160 College—Dayton

Yr.	Team	G	FG	FT	TP	Avg.
1974-75	Philadelphia	54	131	21	283	5.2

SMITH, EDWARD
b. July 5, 1929 Ht. 6-6 Wt. 195 College—Harvard

Yr.	Team	G	FG	FT	TP	Avg.
1953 54	New York	11	11	6	28	2.5

SMITH, GARFIELD
b. Nov. 18, 1945 Ht. 6-9 Wt. 235 College—Eastern Ky.

Yr.	Team		G	FG	FT	TP	Avg.
1970-71	Boston		37	42	22	106	2.9
1971-72	Boston		26	28	6	62	2.4
1972-73	San Diego	(ABA)	71	116	28	260	3.7
	Totals		134	186	56	428	3.2

SMITH, GREG
b. Jan. 28, 1947 Ht. 6-5 Wt. 195 College—W. Kentucky

Yr.	Team	G	FG	FT	TP	Avg.
1968-69	Milwaukee	79	276	91	643	8.1
1969-70	Milwaukee	82	339	125	803	9.8
1970-71	Milwaukee	82	409	141	959	11.7
1971-72	Mil.-Hou.	82	309	111	729	8.9
1972-73	Hou.-Port.	76	234	75	543	7.1
1973-74	Portland	67	99	48	246	3.7
1974-75	Portland	55	71	32	174	3.2
1975-76	Portland	1	0	0	0	0.0
	Totals	524	1737	623	4097	7.8

SMITH, JOHN, JR.
b. May 24, 1944 Ht. 7-0 Wt. 235 College—Southern Colorado

Yr.	Team		G	FG	FT	TP	Avg.
1968-69	Dallas	(ABA)	77	246	116	608	7.9
1969-70	Dal.-Pitt-N.Y.	(ABA)	70	105	56	266	3.8
	Totals		147	351	172	847	5.9

SMITH, KEN
b. July 12, 1953 Ht. 6-7 Wt. 185 College—Tulsa

Yr.	Team		G	FG	FT	TP	Avg.
1975-76	San Antonio	(ABA)	19	34(1)	13	82	4.3

SMITH, PETE
b. 1950 Ht. 6-6 Wt. 205 College—Valdosta State

Yr.	Team		G	FG	FT	TP	Avg.
1972-73	San Diego	(ABA)	5	2	0	4	0.8

SMITH, ROBERT
b. Aug. 20, 1937 Ht. 6-4 Wt. 190 College—West Virginia

Yr.	Team	G	FG	FT	TP	Avg.
1959-60	Minneapolis	10	13	11	37	3.7
1961-62	Los Angeles	3	0	0	0	0.0
	Totals	13	13	11	37	2.8

SMITH, SAM
b. Jan. 27, 1944 Ht. 6-7 Wt. 230 College—Louisville/Kent. Wesl.

Yr.	Team		G	FG	FT	TP	Avg.
1967-68	Minnesota	(ABA)	77	284(2)	185	755	9.8
1968-69	Kentucky	(ABA)	62	173(1)	114	461	7.4
1969-70	Kentucky	(ABA)	81	307(1)	163	778	9.6
1970-71	Ky.-Utah	(ABA)	35	39(1)	24	103	2.5
	Totals		255	803(5)	486	2097	8.2

SMITH, SAM
b. Jan. 8, 1955 Ht. 6-4 Wt. 200 College—Nevada Las Vegas

Yr.	Team	G	FG	FT	TP	Avg.
1978-79	Milwaukee	16	19	18	56	3.5
1979-80	Chicago	30	97(8)	57	259	8.6
	Totals	46	116(8)	75	315	6.8

SMITH, THOMAS
b. 1929 Ht. 6-1 Wt. 165 College—St. Peter's

Yr.	Team	G	FG	FT	TP	Avg.
1951-52	New York	1	0	4	4	4.0

SMITH, WILLIAM
b. April 26, 1939 Ht. 6-5 Wt. 190 College—St. Peter's

Yr.	Team	G	FG	FT	TP	Avg.
1961-62	New York	9	8	7	23	2.6

SMITH, WILLIE
b. Oct. 26, 1953 Ht. 6-3 Wt. 190 College—Missouri

Yr.	Team	G	FG	FT	TP	Avg.
1976-77	Chicago	2	0	0	0	0.0
1977-78	Indiana	1	0	0	0	0.0
1978-79	Portland	13	23	12	58	4.5
1979-80	Cleveland	62	121(17)	40	299	4.8
	Totals	78	144(17)	52	357	4.6

SMYTH, JOSEPH
b. 1929 Ht. 6-3½ Wt. 215 College—Niagara

Yr.	Team	G	FG	FT	TP	Avg.
1953-54	Baltimore	40	48	35	131	3.3

SNYDER, DICK
b. Feb. 1, 1944 Ht. 6-5 Wt. 210 College—Davidson

Yr.	Team	G	FG	FT	TP	Avg.
1966-67	St. Louis	54	144	46	334	6.2
1967-68	St. Louis	75	257	129	643	8.6
1968-69	Phoenix	81	399	185	983	12.1
1969-70	Pho.-Sea.	82	456	169	1081	13.2
1970-71	Seattle	82	645	302	1592	19.4
1971-72	Seattle	73	496	218	1210	16.6
1972-73	Seattle	82	473	186	1132	13.8
1973-74	Seattle	74	572	194	1338	18.1
1974-75	Cleveland	82	498	165	1161	14.2
1975-76	Cleveland	82	441	155	1037	12.6
1976-77	Cleveland	82	316	127	759	9.3
1977-78	Cleveland	58	112	56	280	4.8
1978-79	Seattle	56	81	43	205	3.7
	Totals	963	4890	1975	11755	12.2

SOBEK, GEORGE (Chips)
b. Feb. 10, 1920 Ht. 6-0½ Wt. 180 College—Notre Dame

Yr.	Team		G	FG	FT	TP	Avg.
1945-46	Indianapolis	(NL)	1	2	1	5	5.0
1946-47	Toledo		42	186	179	551	13.1
1947-48	Toledo	(NL)	48	118	124	360	7.5
1948-49	Hammond	(NL)	57	143	232	518	9.1
1949-50	Sheboygan		60	95	156	346	5.8
	Totals		208	544	692	1780	8.6

Yr.	Team	G	FG	FT	TP	Avg.

SOBIESZCZYK, RON (Sobie)
b. Sept. 21, 1934 Ht. 6-3 Wt. 195 College—DePaul

Yr.	Team	G	FG	FT	TP	Avg.
1956-57	New York	71	166	152	484	6.8
1957-58	New York	55	217	196	630	11.5
1958-59	New York	50	144	112	400	8.0
1959-60	N.Y.-Minn.	16	37	31	105	6.6
	Totals	192	564	491	1619	8.4

SOJOURNER, MIKE
b. Oct. 16, 1953 Ht. 6-9 Wt. 225 College—Utah

Yr.	Team	G	FG	FT	TP	Avg.
1974-75	Atlanta	73	378	95	851	11.7
1975-76	Atlanta	67	248	80	576	8.6
1976-77	Atlanta	51	95	41	231	4.5
	Totals	191	721	216	1658	8.7

SOJOURNER, WILLARD (Willie)
b. Sept. 10, 1948 Ht. 6-8 Wt. 225 College—Weber State

Yr.	Team		G	FG	FT	TP	Avg.
1971-72	Virginia	(ABA)	84	222	124	568	6.8
1972-73	Virginia	(ABA)	64	199	84	482	7.5
1973-74	New York	(ABA)	82	202	54	458	5.6
1974-75	New York	(ABA)	79	155(1)	49	360	4.6
	Totals		309	778(1)	311	1868	6.0

SOMERSET, WILLARD (Willie)
b. March 17, 1942 Ht. 5-10 Wt. 150 College—Duquesne

Yr.	Team		G	FG	FT	TP	Avg.
1965-66	Baltimore		8	18	9	45	5.6
1967-68	Houston	(ABA)	61	467(33)	359	1326	21.7
1968-69	Hous-N.Y.	(ABA)	74	619(36)	484	1758	23.8
	Totals		143	1104(69)	852	3129	21.9

SORENSON, DAVE
b. July 8, 1948 Ht. 6-8 Wt. 227 College—Ohio State

Yr.	Team	G	FG	FT	TP	Avg.
1970-71	Cleveland	79	353	229	890	11.3
1971-72	Cleveland	76	213	106	532	7.0
1972-73	Cleve.-Phila.	58	124	64	312	5.4
	Totals	213	690	354	1734	8.1

SOVRAN, GINO
Ht. 6-2 Wt. 175 College—Assumption (Ont.)

Yr.	Team	G	FG	FT	TP	Avg.
1946-47	Toronto	6	5	1	11	1.8

SPAIN, KEN
b. Oct. 6, 1946 Ht. 6-9 Wt. 235 College—Houston

Yr.	Team		G	FG	FT	TP	Avg.
1970-71	Pittsburgh	(ABA)	11	8	8	24	2.2

SPARKS, DAN
b. April 17, 1945 Ht. 6-8 Wt. 200 College—Vincennes and Weber State

Yr.	Team		G	FG	FT	TP	Avg.
1968-69	Miami	(ABA)	64	153	113	419	6.5
1969-70	Miami	(ABA)	3	7	5	19	6.3
	Totals		67	160	118	438	6.5

SPARROW, GUY
b. Nov. 2, 1932 Ht. 6-6 Wt. 218 College—Detroit

Yr.	Team	G	FG	FT	TP	Avg.
1957-58	New York	72	318	165	801	11.1
1958-59	N.Y.-Phila.	67	129	78	336	5.0
1959-60	Philadelphia	11	14	2	30	2.7
	Totals	150	461	245	1167	7.8

SPEARS, MARION (Odie)
b. June 26, 1925 Ht. 6-5 Wt. 205 College—W. Kentucky

Yr.	Team	G	FG	FT	TP	Avg.
1948-49	Chicago	57	200	131	531	9.3
1949-50	Chicago	57	227	158	712	12.5
1951-52	Rochester	66	225	116	566	8.6
1952-53	Rochester	62	198	199	595	9.6
1953-54	Rochester	72	184	183	551	7.7
1954-55	Rochester	71	226	220	672	9.5
1955-56	Ft. Wayne	72	166	159	491	6.8
1956-57	Ft. W.-St. Lou.	11	12	19	43	3.9
	Totals	468	1488	1185	4161	8.8

SPECTOR, ARTHUR (Speed)
b. Oct. 17, 1920 Ht. 6-4 Wt. 200 College—Villanova

Yr.	Team	G	FG	FT	TP	Avg.
1946-47	Boston	55	123	83	329	6.0
1947-48	Boston	48	67	60	194	4.0
1948-49	Boston	59	130	64	324	5.5
1949-50	Boston	7	2	1	5	0.7
	Totals	169	322	208	852	5.0

SPICER, LOU
b. 1923 Ht. 6-2 Wt. 195 College—Syracuse

Yr.	Team	G	FG	FT	TP	Avg.
1946-47	Providence	4	0	1	1	0.3

SPITZER, CRAIG
Ht. 7-0 Wt. 220 College—Tulane

Yr.	Team	G	FG	FT	TP	Avg.
1967-68	Chicago	10	8	2	18	1.8

SPOELSTRA, ART
b. Sept. 11, 1932 Ht. 6-9 Wt. 220 College—W. Kentucky

Yr.	Team	G	FG	FT	TP	Avg.
1954-55	Rochester	70	159	108	426	6.1
1955-56	Rochester	72	226	163	615	8.5
1956-57	Rochester	69	217	88	522	7.6
1957-58	Minn.-N.Y.	67	161	127	449	6.7
	Totals	278	763	486	2012	7.2

SPRAGGINS, BRUCE
b. 1940 Ht. 6-5 Wt. 190 College—Virginia Union

Yr.	Team		G	FG	FT	TP	Avg.
1967-68	New Jersey	(ABA)	70	306(2)	238	852	12.2

SPRINGER, JIM
b. 1924 Ht. 6-9 Wt. 235 College—Canterbury

Yr.	Team		G	FG	FT	TP	Avg.
1947-48	And.-Ind.	(NL)	25	12	25	49	2.0
1948-49	Indianapolis		2	0	1	1	0.5
	Totals		27	12	26	50	1.9

SPRUILL, JIM
Ht. 6-2½ Wt. 225 College—Rice

Yr.	Team	G	FG	FT	TP	Avg.
1948-49	Indianapolis	1	1	0	2	2.0

STACOM, KEVIN
b. Sept. 4, 1951 Ht. 6-3 Wt. 185 College—Providence

Yr.	Team	G	FG	FT	TP	Avg.
1974-75	Boston	61	72	29	173	2.8
1975-76	Boston	77	170	68	408	5.3
1976-77	Boston	79	179	46	404	5.1
1977-78	Boston	55	206	54	466	8.5
1978-79	Ind.-Bos.	68	128	44	300	4.4
	Totals	340	755	241	1751	5.2

Yr.	Team		G	FG	FT	TP	Avg.

STAGGS, ERV
Ht. 6-6 Wt. 195 College—North Carolina A & T

Yr.	Team		G	FG	FT	TP	Avg.
1969-70 Miami	(ABA)	53	189(2)	73	453	8.5

STALLWORTH, ISAAC (Bud)
b. Jan. 18, 1950 Ht. 6-5 Wt. 190 College—Kansas

1972-73 Seattle		77	198	86	482	6.3
1973-74 Seattle		67	188	48	424	6.3
1974-75 New Orleans		73	298	125	721	9.9
1975-76 New Orleans		56	211	85	507	9.1
1976-77 New Orleans		40	126	17	269	6.7
Totals		313	1021	361	2403	7.7

STALLWORTH, DAVID (The Rave)
b. Dec. 20, 1941 Ht. 6-7 Wt. 200 College—Wichita State

1965-66 New York		80	373	258	1004	12.6
1966-67 New York		76	380	229	989	13.0
1969-70 New York		82	239	161	639	7.8
1970-71 New York		81	295	169	759	9.4
1971-72 N.Y.-Balt.		78	336	152	824	10.6
1972-73 Baltimore		73	180	78	438	6.0
1973-74 Capital		45	75	47	197	4.4
1974-75 New York		7	5	0	10	1.4
Totals		522	1883	1094	4860	9.3

STANCZAK, EDMUND (Moose)
b. Aug. 15, 1921 Ht. 6-1½ Wt. 205

1946-47 Anderson	(NL)	44	142	118	402	9.1
1947-48 Anderson	(NL)	55	73	61	207	3.8
1948-49 Anderson	(NL)	64	191	202	584	9.1
1949-50 Anderson		57	159	203	521	9.1
1950-51 Boston		17	11	35	57	3.4
Totals		237	576	619	1771	7.5

STARR, KEITH
b. March 14, 1954 Ht. 6-7 Wt. 200 College—Pittsburgh

1976-77 Chicago		17	6	2	14	0.8

STAVERMAN, LARRY
b. Oct. 11, 1936 Ht. 6-7 Wt. 205 College—Villa Madonna

1958-59 Cincinnati		57	101	45	247	4.3
1959-60 Cincinnati		49	70	47	187	3.8
1960-61 Cincinnati		66	111	79	301	4.6
1962-63 Chicago		33	94	49	237	7.2
1963-64 Bt.-Det.-Cinn.		60	98	69	265	4.4
Totals		265	474	289	1237	4.7

STEELE, LARRY
b. May 5, 1949 Ht. 6-5 Wt. 180 College—Kentucky

1971-72 Portland		72	148	70	366	5.1
1972-73 Portland		66	159	71	389	5.9
1973-74 Portland		81	325	135	785	9.7
1974-75 Portland		76	265	122	652	8.6
1975-76 Portland		81	322	154	798	9.9
1976-77 Portland		81	326	183	835	10.3
1977-78 Portland		65	210	100	520	8.0
1978-79 Portland		72	203	112	518	7.2
1979-80 Portland		16	62	22	146	9.1
Totals		610	2020	969	5009	8.2

STEPHENS, JACK
b. May 18, 1933 Ht. 6-3 Wt. 185 College—Notre Dame

1955-56 St. Louis		72	248	247	743	10.3

STEVENS, WAYNE
b. June 19, 1936 Ht. 6-3½ Wt. 185 College—Cincinnati

1959-60 Cincinnati		8	3	7	13	1.6

STEWART, DENNIS
b. April 11, 1947 Ht. 6-6 Wt. 220 College—Michigan

1970-71 Baltimore		2	1	2	4	2.0
1970-71 Floridians	(ABA)	10	14	5	36	3.6
Totals		12	15	7	40	3.3

STEWART, NORMAN
b. Jan. 20, 1935 Ht. 6-5 Wt. 205 College—Missouri

1956-57 St. Louis		5	4	2	10	2.0

STITH, SAM
b. July 22, 1937 Ht. 6-2 Wt. 185 College—St. Bonaventure

1961-62 New York		32	59	23	141	4.4

STITH, THOMAS
b. Jan. 21, 1939 Ht. 6-5 Wt. 210 College—St. Bonaventure

1962-63 New York		25	37	3	77	3.1

STOKES, MAURICE (Mo)
b. June 17, 1933 Ht. 6-7 Wt. 240 College—St. Francis (Pa.)
d. Apr. 6, 1970

1955-56 Rochester		67	403	319	1125	16.8
1956-57 Rochester		72	434	256	1124	15.6
1957-58 Cincinnati		63	414	238	1066	16.9
Totals		202	1251	813	3315	16.4

STOLKEY, ARTHUR
b. Oct. 23, 1920 Ht. 6-1 Wt. 180 College—Detroit

1946-47 Detroit		23	36	30	102	4.4

STOLL, RANDY
Ht. 6-7 Wt. 235 College—Washington State

1967-68 Anaheim	(ABA)	25	66	10	142	5.7

STONE, GEORGE (Radar)
b. Feb. 9, 1946 Ht. 6-7 Wt. 195 College—Marshall

1968-69 Los Angeles	(ABA)	74	437(28)	261	1163	15.7
1969-70 Los Angeles	(ABA)	83	512(65)	239	1328	16.0
1970-71 Utah	(ABA)	78	373(50)	121	917	11.8
1971-72 Utah-Car.	(ABA)	24	49(1)	25	124	4.5
Totals		259	1371(144)	646	3532	13.6

STOVALL, PAUL
b. Aug. 16, 1948 Ht. 6-5 Wt. 225 College—Arizona State
d. Jan. 9, 1978

1972-73 Phoenix		25	26	24	76	3.0
1973-74 San Diego	(ABA)	13	36	28	100	7.7
Totals		38	62	52	176	4.6

Yr.	Team		G	FG	FT	TP	Avg.

STRAWDER, JOSEPH
b. Sept. 21, 1940 Ht. 6-10 Wt. 235 College—Bradley

Yr.	Team		G	FG	FT	TP	Avg.
1965-66	Detroit		79	250	176	676	8.6
1966-67	Detroit		79	281	188	750	9.4
1967-68	Detroit		73	206	139	551	7.5
	Totals		231	737	503	1977	8.6

STRICKER, BILL
b. Jan. 22, 1948 Ht. 6-9 Wt. 210 College—Pacific

Yr.	Team		G	FG	FT	TP	Avg.
1970-71	Portland		1	2	0	4	4.0

STRICKLAND, ROGER (The Rifle)
b. Sept. 4, 1940 Ht. 6-5 Wt. 200 College—Jacksonville

Yr.	Team		G	FG	FT	TP	Avg.
1963-64	Baltimore		1	1	0	2	2.0

STROUD, WILLIAM D. (Red)
b. May 2, 1941 Ht. 6-1 Wt. 160 College—Mississippi State

Yr.	Team		G	FG	FT	TP	Avg.
1967-68	New Orleans	(ABA)	7	5(1)	9	20	2.9

STUMP, EUGENE
b. Nov. 13, 1923 Ht. 6-2½ Wt. 185 College—DePaul

Yr.	Team		G	FG	FT	TP	Avg.
1947-48	Boston		43	59	24	142	3.3
1948-49	Boston		56	193	92	478	8.5
1949-50	Minn.-Waterloo		49	63	37	163	3.3
	Totals		148	315	153	783	5.3

STUTZ, STAN (Stanley Modzelewski)
b. April 14, 1920 Ht. 5-11 Wt. 175 College—Rhode Is.

Yr.	Team		G	FG	FT	TP	Avg.
1946-47	New York		60	172	133	477	8.0
1947-48	New York		47	109	113	331	7.0
1948-49	Baltimore		59	121	131	373	6.3
	Totals		166	402	377	1181	7.1

SUITER, GARY
b. Jan. 18, 1945 Ht. 6-9 Wt. 235 College—Midwestern

Yr.	Team		G	FG	FT	TP	Avg.
1970-71	Cleveland		30	19	4	42	1.4

SUNDERLAGE, DON
b. Dec. 20, 1929 Ht. 6-1 Wt. 180 College—Illinois

Yr.	Team		G	FG	FT	TP	Avg.
1953-54	Milwaukee		68	254	252	760	11.2
1954-55	Minneapolis		45	33	48	114	2.5
	Totals		113	287	300	874	7.7

SURHOFF, RICHARD
b. 1932 Ht. 6-4 Wt. 210 College—L.I. Univ./J. Marshall

Yr.	Team		G	FG	FT	TP	Avg.
1952-53	New York		26	13	19	45	1.7
1953-54	Milwaukee		32	43	47	133	4.2
	Totals		58	56	66	178	3.1

SUTOR, GEORGE
b. Sept. 14, 1943 Ht. 6-8 Wt. 240 College—LaSalle

Yr.	Team		G	FG	FT	TP	Avg.
1967-68	Kentucky	(ABA)	1	0	0	0	0.0
1968-69	Minnesota	(ABA)	64	139	71	349	5.5
1969-70	Car.-Mia.	(ABA)	14	12	7	31	2.2
	Totals		79	151	78	380	4.8

SWAGERTY, KEITH
b. Oct. 30, 1945 Ht. 6-7 Wt. 235 College—Pacific

Yr.	Team		G	FG	FT	TP	Avg.
1968-69	Houston	(ABA)	77	362	256	980	12.7
1969-70	Kentucky	(ABA)	3	2	3	7	2.3
	Totals		80	364	259	987	12.3

SWAIN, BENNIE
b. Dec. 16, 1933 Ht. 6-8 Wt. 222 College—Texas Southern

Yr.	Team		G	FG	FT	TP	Avg.
1958-59	Boston		58	99	67	265	4.6

SWANSON, NORMAN
b. Oct. 4, 1930 Ht. 6-6 Wt. 212 College—Detroit

Yr.	Team		G	FG	FT	TP	Avg.
1953-54	Rochester		63	31	38	100	1.6

SWARTZ, DAN
b. Dec. 23, 1934 Ht. 6-4 Wt. 215 College—Morehead St.

Yr.	Team		G	FG	FT	TP	Avg.
1962-63	Boston		39	57	61	175	4.5

SWIFT, HARLEY (Skeeter)
b. June 19, 1946 Ht. 6-3 Wt. 210 College—Middle Tennessee

Yr.	Team		G	FG	FT	TP	Avg.
1969-70	New Orleans	(ABA)	66	215(38)	139	607	9.2
1970-71	Mem.-Pitt.	(ABA)	80	402(39)	206	1049	13.1
1971-72	Pittsburgh	(ABA)	79	401(33)	224	1059	13.4
1972-73	Dallas	(ABA)	42	177(19)	128	501	11.9
1973-74	San Antonio	(ABA)	16	23(1)	16	63	3.9
	Totals		283	1218(130)	713	3279	11.6

SYDNOR, WALLACE (Buck)
b. Sept. 19, 1921 Ht. 5-10 Wt. 175 College—W. Kentucky

Yr.	Team		G	FG	FT	TP	Avg.
1946-47	Chicago		15	5	5	15	1.0

SZCZERBIAK, WALT
b. Aug. 21, 1949 Ht. 6-6 Wt. 210 College—Geo. Washington

Yr.	Team		G	FG	FT	TP	Avg.
1971-72	Pittsburgh	(ABA)	53	149	35	333	6.3

TANENBAUM, SIDNEY
b. Oct. 8, 1925 Ht. 6-0 Wt. 160 College—N.Y. University

Yr.	Team		G	FG	FT	TP	Avg.
1947-48	New York		24	90	62	242	10.1
1948-49	N.Y.-Balt.		46	146	99	391	8.5
	Totals		70	236	161	633	9.0

TART, LEVERN DONIHUE (Doc)
b. June 1, 1942 Ht. 6-3 Wt. 195 College—Bradley

Yr.	Team		G	FG	FT	TP	Avg.
1967-68	Oak.-N.J.	(ABA)	73	633(1)	451	1718	22.5
1968-69	N.Y.-Hou.-Den.	(ABA)	61	274	193	741	12.2
1969-70	New York	(ABA)	80	756(11)	412	1935	24.1
1970-71	N.Y.-Tex.	(ABA)	60	357(10)	198	922	15.4
	Totals		274	2020(22)	1254	5316	19.4

TATUM, EARL
b. July 26, 1953 Ht. 6-4½ Wt. 185 College—Marquette

Yr.	Team		G	FG	FT	TP	Avg.
1976-77	Los Angeles		68	283	72	638	9.4
1977-78	L.A.-Ind.		82	510	153	1173	14.3
1978-79	Bos.-Det.		79	280	52	612	7.7
1979-80	Cleveland		33	36(2)	11	85	2.6
	Totals		262	1109(2)	288	2508	9.6

Yr.	Team		G	FG	FT	TP	Avg.
TAYLOR, FRED							
b. Feb. 5, 1948 Ht. 6-5 Wt. 187 College—Pan American							
1970-71 Phoenix			54	110	78	298	5.5
1971-72 Pho.-Cin.			34	36	15	87	2.6
	Totals		88	146	93	385	4.3
TAYLOR, OLLIE							
b. March 7, 1947 Ht. 6-2 Wt. 194 College—Houston							
1970-71 New York	(ABA)		80	251(5)	187	694	8.7
1971-72 New York	(ABA)		82	245	218	708	8.6
1972-73 San Diego	(ABA)		69	325(11)	286	947	13.7
1973-74 N.Y.-Car.	(ABA)		31	65(2)	58	190	6.1
	Totals		262	886(18)	749	2539	9.7
TAYLOR, ROLAND (Fatty)							
b. March 13, 1946 Ht. 6-0 Wt. 175 College—LaSalle							
1969-70 Washington	(ABA)		83	243(1)	178	665	8.0
1970-71 Virginia	(ABA)		84	180(4)	175	539	6.4
1971-72 Virginia	(ABA)		84	306(1)	164	777	9.3
1972-73 Virginia	(ABA)		78	316(3)	150	785	10.1
1973-74 Virginia	(ABA)		80	292(3)	185	772	9.7
1974-75 Denver	(ABA)		76	251(6)	129	637	8.4
1975-76 Virginia	(ABA)		76	243(11)	125	622	8.2
1976-77 Denver			79	132	37	301	3.8
	Totals		640	1963(29)	1143	5098	8.0
TAYLOR, RON							
b. Nov. 21, 1946 Ht. 7-1 Wt. 265 College—USC							
1969-70 Wash.-N.Y.	(ABA)		75	156	57	369	4.9
1970-71 Virginia	(ABA)		1	1	0	2	2.0
1971-72 Pittsburgh	(ABA)		1	0	0	0	0.0
	Totals		77	157	57	371	4.8
TEMPLE, COLLIS							
b. Nov. 8, 1952 Ht. 6-8 Wt. 220 College—LSU							
1974-75 San Antonio	(ABA)		24	17	8	42	1.8
TERRELL, IRA							
b. June 19, 1954 Ht. 6-8 Wt. 205 College—SMU							
1976-77 Phoenix			78	277	111	665	8.5
1978-79 N.O.-Port.			49	93	35	221	4.5
	Totals		127	370	146	886	7.0
TERRY, CHUCK							
b. Sept. 27, 1950 Ht. 6-6 Wt. 215 College—Long Beach St.							
1972-73 Milwaukee			67	55	17	127	1.9
1973-74 Milwaukee			7	4	0	8	1.1
1973-74 San Antonio	(ABA)		61	132(1)	36	301	4.9
1974-75 San Antonio	(ABA)		79	148(3)	39	338	4.3
1975-76 New York	(ABA)		66	96(6)	22	220	3.3
1976-77 N.Y. Nets			61	128	48	304	5.0
	Totals		341	563(10)	162	1298	3.8
TERRY, CLAUDE							
b. Jan. 12, 1950 Ht. 6-5 Wt. 195 College—Stanford							
1972-73 Denver	(ABA)		68	120(10)	74	324	4.8
1973-74 Denver	(ABA)		60	113(14)	60	300	5.0
1974-75 Denver	(ABA)		70	193(10)	70	466	6.7
1975-76 Denver	(ABA)		79	232(13)	80	557	7.1

Yr.	Team		G	FG	FT	TP	Avg.
1976-77 Buff.-Atla.			45	96	36	228	5.1
1977-78 Atlanta			27	25	9	59	2.2
	Totals		349	779(47)	329	1934	5.5
THACKER, TOM (Tack)							
b. Nov. 2, 1939 Ht. 6-2 Wt. 170 College—Cincinnati							
1963-64 Cincinnati			48	53	26	132	2.8
1964-65 Cincinnati			55	56	23	135	2.5
1965-66 Cincinnati			50	84	15	183	3.7
1967-68 Boston			65	114	43	271	4.2
1968-69 Indiana	(ABA)		18	40	18	98	5.4
1969-70 Indiana	(ABA)		70	70(10)	38	188	2.7
1970-71 Indiana	(ABA)		8	6	1	13	1.6
	Totals		314	423(10)	164	1020	3.2
THEARD, FLOYD							
b. Sept. 5, 1944 Ht. 6-1 Wt. 170 College—Kentucky State							
1969-70 Denver	(ABA)		25	39	18	96	3.8
THIEBEN, WILLIAM							
Ht. 6-7 Wt. 215 College—Hofstra							
1956-57 Ft. Wayne			58	90	57	237	4.1
1957-58 Detroit			27	42	16	100	3.7
	Totals		85	132	73	337	4.0
THIGPEN, JUSTUS							
College—Weber State							
1969-70 Pittsburgh	(ABA)		3	5	1	11	3.7
THOMAS, JOE							
b. March 9, 1948 Ht. 6-5 Wt. 205 College—Marquette							
1970-71 Phoenix			39	23	9	55	1.4
THOMAS, RON							
b. Nov. 19, 1950 Ht. 6-6 Wt. 215 College—Louisville							
1972-73 Kentucky	(ABA)		31	62	21	145	4.7
1973-74 Kentucky	(ABA)		71	128(1)	37	294	4.1
1974-75 Kentucky	(ABA)		79	190(1)	58	439	4.3
1975-76 Kentucky	(ABA)		83	134(1)	55	324	3.9
	Totals		264	514(3)	171	1202	4.5
THOMAS, TERRY							
b. Aug. 20, 1953 Ht. 6-8 Wt. 220 College—Detroit							
1975-76 Detroit			28	28	21	77	2.8
THOMAS, WILLIS							
Ht. 6-2 Wt. 185 College—Harbor Junior College							
1967-68 Den.-Ana.	(ABA)		62	243	69	555	9.0
THOMPSON, GEORGE							
b. Nov. 29, 1947 Ht. 6-2 Wt. 215 College—Marquette							
1969-70 Pittsburgh	(ABA)		54	259(7)	176	701	12.9
1970-71 Pittsburgh	(ABA)		82	575(23)	347	1520	18.5
1971-72 Pittsburgh	(ABA)		70	696(41)	455	1888	27.0
1972-73 Memphis	(ABA)		80	579(20)	549	1727	21.6
1973-74 Memphis	(ABA)		78	539(10)	410	1498	19.2
1974-75 Milwaukee			73	306	168	780	10.7
	Totals		437	2954(101)	2105	8114	18.6

Yr.	Team		G	FG	FT	TP	Avg.

THOMPSON, JACK
Ht. 6-1 Wt. 185 College—South Carolina

Yr.	Team		G	FG	FT	TP	Avg.
1968-69 Indiana		(ABA)	2	1	0	2	1.0

THOMPSON, JOHN
b. Sept. 2, 1941 Ht. 6-10 Wt. 230 College—Providence

Yr.	Team	G	FG	FT	TP	Avg.
1964-65 Boston		64	84	62	230	3.6
1965-66 Boston		10	14	4	32	3.2
	Totals	74	98	66	262	3.5

THOREN, DUANE (Skip)
b. April 5, 1943 Ht. 6-10 Wt. 230 College—Illinois

Yr.	Team		G	FG	FT	TP	Avg.
1967-68 Minnesota		(ABA)	63	206	102	514	8.2
1968-69 Miami		(ABA)	78	532	241	1305	16.7
1969-70 Miami		(ABA)	29	164	92	420	14.5
	Totals		170	902	435	2239	13.2

THORN, ROD
b. May 23, 1941 Ht. 6-4 Wt. 195 College—W. Virginia

Yr.	Team	G	FG	FT	TP	Avg.
1963-64 Baltimore		75	411	258	1080	14.4
1964-65 Detroit		74	320	176	816	11.0
1965-66 Det.-St. Lou.		73	306	168	780	10.7
1966-67 St. Louis		67	233	125	591	8.8
1967-68 Seattle		66	377	252	1006	15.2
1968-69 Seattle		29	131	71	333	11.5
1969-70 Seattle		19	20	15	55	2.9
1970-71 Seattle		63	141	69	351	5.6
	Totals	466	1939	1134	5012	10.8

THORTON, DALLAS
b. Sept. 1, 1946 Ht. 6-4 Wt. 190 College—Kentucky Wesleyan

Yr.	Team		G	FG	FT	TP	Avg.
1968-69 Miami		(ABA)	45	108(2)	79	297	6.6
1969-70 Miami		(ABA)	5	15	14	44	8.8
	Totals		50	123(2)	93	341	6.8

THURMOND, NATE
b. July 25, 1941 Ht. 6-11 Wt. 225 College—Bowling Green

Yr.	Team	G	FG	FT	TP	Avg.
1963-64 San Francisco		76	219	95	533	7.0
1964-65 San Francisco		77	519	235	1273	16.5
1965-66 San Francisco		73	454	280	1188	16.3
1966-67 San Francisco		65	467	280	1214	18.7
1967-68 San Francisco		51	382	282	1046	20.5
1968-69 San Francisco		71	571	382	1524	21.5
1969-70 San Francisco		43	341	261	943	21.9
1970-71 San Francisco		82	623	395	1641	20.0
1971-72 Golden St.		78	628	417	1673	21.4
1972-73 Golden St.		79	517	315	1349	17.1
1973-74 Golden St.		62	308	191	807	13.0
1974-75 Chicago		80	250	132	632	7.9
1975-76 Chi.-Cleve.		78	142	62	346	4.4
1976-77 Cleveland		49	100	68	268	5.5
	Totals	964	5521	3395	14437	15.0

THURSTON, MEL
Ht. 6-0 Wt. 175 College—Canisius

Yr.	Team		G	FG	FT	TP	Avg.
1946-47 Buf.-Tri-C.		(NL)	39	39	36	114	2.9
1947-48 Tri-Cities		(NL)	34	36	38	110	3.2
1947-48 Providence			14	32	14	78	5.6
	Totals		87	107	88	302	3.5

TIDRICK, HOWARD (Hal)
b. 1919 Ht. 6-1 Wt. 190 College—Washington & Jefferson

Yr.	Team		G	FG	FT	TP	Avg.
1944-45 Sheboygan		(NL)	1	0	0	0	0.0
1946-47 Toledo		(NL)	44	232	115	579	13.2
1947-48 Toledo		(NL)	59	267	189	723	12.3
1948-49 Ind.-Balt.			61	194	164	552	9.0
	Totals		165	693	468	1854	11.2

TIEMAN, DANIEL
b. Nov. 30, 1940 Ht. 6-0 Wt. 185 College—Villa Madonna

Yr.	Team	G	FG	FT	TP	Avg.
1962-63 Cincinnati		29	15	4	34	1.2

TINGLE, JACK
b. 1925 Ht. 6-4 Wt. 205 College—Kentucky

Yr.	Team	G	FG	FT	TP	Avg.
1947-48 Washington		37	36	17	89	2.4
1948-49 Minneapolis		2	1	0	2	1.0
	Totals	39	37	17	91	2.3

TINSLEY, GEORGE
b. Sept. 19, 1946 Ht. 6-5 Wt. 205 College—Kentucky Wesleyan

Yr.	Team		G	FG	FT	TP	Avg.
1969-70 Wash.-Ky.		(ABA)	77	173(1)	159	506	6.6
1971-72 Floridians		(ABA)	51	70(5)	46	191	3.8
	Totals		128	243(6)	205	697	5.4

TODOROVICH, MARKO (Mike)
b. June 11, 1923 Ht. 6-5 Wt. 229 College—Notre Dame/Wyoming

Yr.	Team		G	FG	FT	TP	Avg.
1947-48 Sheboygan		(NL)	60	277	223	777	13.0
1948-49 Sheboygan		(NL)	60	239	170	648	10.8
1949-50 St. L.-Tri-C.			65	263	266	792	12.2
1950-51 Tri-Cities			66	221	211	653	9.9
	Totals		251	1000	870	2870	11.4

TOLSON, DEAN
b. Nov. 25, 1951 Ht. 6-8 Wt. 190 College—Arkansas

Yr.	Team	G	FG	FT	TP	Avg.
1974-75 Seattle		19	16	11	43	2.3
1976-77 Seattle		60	137	85	359	6.0
1977-78 Seattle		1	0	0	0	0.0
	Totals	80	153	96	402	5.1

TONKOVICH, ANDY
b. Nov. 1, 1922 Ht. 6-1 Wt. 185 College—Marshall

Yr.	Team	G	FG	FT	TP	Avg.
1948-49 Providence		17	19	6	44	2.6

TOOMAY, JOHN
b. Aug. 9, 1922 Ht. 6-6 Wt. 215 College—College of Pacific

Yr.	Team	G	FG	FT	TP	Avg.
1947-48 Chic.-Prov.		23	61	60	182	7.9
1948-49 Balt.-Wash.		36	32	36	100	2.8
1949-50 Denver		62	204	186	594	9.6
	Totals	121	297	282	876	7.2

TOONE, BERNARD
b. July 14, 1956 Ht. 6-9 Wt. 210 College—Marquette

Yr.	Team	G	FG	FT	TP	Avg.
1979-80 Philadelphia		23	23(1)	8	55	2.4

Yr.	Team		G	FG	FT	TP	Avg.

TORGOFF, IRVING
b. 1917 Ht. 6-2 Wt. 192 College—Long Island University

Yr.	Team		G	FG	FT	TP	Avg.
1939-40 Detroit		(NL)	26	64	43	171	6.6
1946-47 Washington			58	187	116	490	8.4
1947-48 Washington			47	111	117	339	7.2
1948-49 Balt.-Phila.			42	59	50	168	4.0
	Totals		173	421	326	1168	6.8

TORMOHLEN, EUGENE
b. May 12, 1937 Ht. 6-9 Wt. 245 College—Tennessee

Yr.	Team	G	FG	FT	TP	Avg.
1962-63 St. Louis		7	5	2	12	1.7
1963-64 St. Louis		51	94	22	210	4.1
1965-66 St. Louis		71	144	54	342	4.8
1966-67 St. Louis		63	172	50	394	6.3
1967-68 St. Louis		77	98	33	229	3.0
1969-70 Atlanta		2	2	0	4	2.0
	Totals	271	515	161	1191	4.4

TOSHEFF, BILL
b. June 2, 1926 Ht. 6-1 Wt. 175 College—Indiana

Yr.	Team	G	FG	FT	TP	Avg.
1951-52 Indianapolis		65	213	182	608	9.4
1952-53 Indianapolis		67	253	253	759	11.3
1953-54 Milwaukee		71	168	156	492	6.9
	Totals	203	634	591	1859	9.2

TOUGH, ROBERT (Red)
b. Aug. 28, 1920 Ht. 6-0 Wt. 185 College—St. John's (N.Y.)

Yr.	Team		G	FG	FT	TP	Avg.
1945-46 Ft. Wayne		(NL)	5	12	5	29	5.8
1946-47 Ft. Wayne		(NL)	44	124	55	303	6.9
1947-48 Ft. Wayne		(NL)	60	129	48	306	5.1
1948-49 Ft. Wayne			53	183	100	466	8.8
1949-50 Balt.-Waterloo			29	43	37	123	4.2
	Totals		191	491	245	1227	6.4

TOWE, MONTE
b. Sept. 27, 1953 Ht. 5-7 Wt. 150 College—N.C. State

Yr.	Team		G	FG	FT	TP	Avg.
1975-76 Denver		(ABA)	64	72(9)	36	189	3.0
1976-77 Denver			51	56	18	130	2.5
	Totals		115	128(9)	54	319	2.8

TOWERY, CARLISLE (Blackie)
b. June 20, 1920 Ht. 6-4½ Wt. 210 College—Western Kentucky

Yr.	Team		G	FG	FT	TP	Avg.
1941-42 Ft. Wayne		(NL)	24	64	35	163	6.8
1942-43 Ft. Wayne		(NL)	23	53	33	139	6.0
1943-44 Ft. Wayne		(NL)	22	48	33	129	5.9
1944-45 Ft. Wayne		(NL)	1	0	1	1	1.0
1946-47 Ft. Wayne		(NL)	41	100	80	280	6.8
1947-48 Ft. Wayne		(NL)	59	139	129	407	6.9
1948-49 Ft. W.-Ind.			60	203	195	601	10.0
1949-50 Baltimore			68	222	153	597	8.8
	Totals		298	829	659	2317	7.8

TOWNSEND, RAYMOND
b. Dec. 20, 1955 Ht. 6-3 Wt. 175 College—UCLA

Yr.	Team		G	FG	FT	TP	Avg.
1978-79 Golden State			127	127	50	304	4.7
1979-80 Golden State			75	171(4)	60	406	5.4
	Total		140	298(4)	110	710	5.1

TRAPP, GEORGE
b. July 11, 1948 Ht. 6-8½ Wt. 200 College—Long Beach St.

Yr.	Team	G	FG	FT	TP	Avg.
1971-72 Atlanta		60	144	105	393	6.6
1972-73 Atlanta		77	359	150	868	11.3
1973-74 Detroit		82	333	99	765	9.3
1974-75 Detroit		78	288	99	675	8.7
1975-76 Detroit		76	278	63	619	8.1
1976-77 Detroit		6	15	3	33	5.5
	Totals	379	1417	519	3353	8.8

TRAPP, JOHN Q.
b. Oct. 2, 1945 Ht. 6-7 Wt. 215 College—Nevada Southern

Yr.	Team		G	FG	FT	TP	Avg.
1968-69 San Diego			25	29	19	77	3.1
1969-70 San Diego			70	185	72	442	6.3
1970-71 San Diego			82	322	142	786	9.6
1971-72 Los Angeles			58	139	51	329	5.7
1972-73 L.A.-Phila.			44	171	90	432	9.8
1972-73 Denver		(ABA)	25	54	19	127	5.1
	Totals		304	900	393	2193	7.2

TRESVANT, JOHN
b. Nov. 6, 1939 Ht. 6-7 Wt. 215 College—Seattle

Yr.	Team	G	FG	FT	TP	Avg.
1964-65 St. Louis		4	4	6	14	3.5
1965-66 St. L.-Det.		61	171	142	484	7.9
1966-67 Detroit		68	256	164	676	9.9
1967-68 Det.-Cin.		85	396	250	1042	12.3
1968-69 Cin.-Sea.		77	380	202	962	12.5
1969-70 Sea.-L.A.		69	264	206	734	10.6
1970-71 L.A.-Balt.		75	202	146	550	7.3
1971-72 Baltimore		65	162	121	445	6.8
1972-73 Baltimore		55	85	41	211	3.8
	Totals	559	1920	1278	5118	9.2

TRIPTOW, RICHARD (Tiptoe)
b. Nov. 3, 1922 Ht. 6-0 Wt. 170 College—DePaul

Yr.	Team		G	FG	FT	TP	Avg.
1944-45 Chicago		(NL)	30	113	73	299	10.0
1945-46 Chicago		(NL)	34	68	85	221	6.5
1946-47 Chicago		(NL)	44	59	60	178	4.0
1947-48 Tri-C.-Ft. W.		(NL)	57	92	87	271	4.8
1948-49 Ft. Wayne			55	116	102	334	6.1
1949-50 Baltimore			4	0	2	2	0.5
	Totals		224	448	409	1305	5.8

TRUITT, ANSLEY
b. Aug. 24, 1950 Ht. 6-9 Wt. 215 College—California

Yr.	Team		G	FG	FT	TP	Avg.
1972-73 Dallas		(ABA)	16	18	3	39	2.4

TSCHOGL, JOHN
b. April 25, 1950 Ht. 6-6 Wt. 206 College—Santa Barbara

Yr.	Team	G	FG	FT	TP	Avg.
1972-73 Atlanta		10	14	2	30	3.0
1973-74 Atlanta		64	59	10	128	2.0
1974-75 Philadelphia		39	53	13	119	3.1
	Totals	113	126	25	277	2.5

TSIOROPOULOS, LOUIS
b. Aug. 31, 1930 Ht. 6-5 Wt. 195 College—Kentucky

Yr.	Team	G	FG	FT	TP	Avg.
1956-57 Boston		52	79	69	227	4.4
1957-58 Boston		70	198	142	538	7.7
1958-59 Boston		35	60	25	145	4.1
	Totals	157	337	236	910	5.8

Yr.	Team		G	FG	FT	TP	Avg.

TUCKER, AL
b. Feb. 24, 1943 Ht. 6-8 Wt. 190 College—Okla. Baptist

Yr.	Team		G	FG	FT	TP	Avg.
1967-68	Seattle		81	437	186	1060	13.1
1968-69	Sea.-Cin.		84	361	158	880	10.5
1969-70	Chi.-Balt.		61	146	70	362	5.9
1970-71	Baltimore		31	52	25	129	4.2
1970-71	Florida	(ABA)	14	66(3)	34	169	12.1
1971-72	Floridians	(ABA)	81	377(30)	157	941	11.6
	Totals		352	1439(33)	630	3541	10.1

TUCKER, JAMES
b. Dec. 11, 1932 Ht. 6-7½ Wt. 185 College—Duquesne

Yr.	Team	G	FG	FT	TP	Avg.
1954-55	Syracuse	20	39	27	105	5.3
1955-56	Syracuse	70	101	66	268	3.8
1956-57	Syracuse	9	17	0	34	3.8
	Totals	99	157	93	407	4.1

TURNER, GARY
College—Texas Christian

Yr.	Team		G	FG	FT	TP	Avg.
1967-68	Houston	(ABA)	2	2	2	6	3.0

TURNER, HERSCHEL
Ht. 6-2 Wt. 195 College—Nebraska

Yr.	Team		G	FG	FT	TP	Avg.
1967-68	Pitt.-Ana.	(ABA)	41	51(6)	23	131	3.2

TURNER, JACK
b. June 29, 1930 Ht. 6-4 Wt. 170 College—W. Kentucky

Yr.	Team	G	FG	FT	TP	Avg.
1954-55	New York	65	111	60	282	4.3

TURNER, JOHN
b. June 5, 1939 Ht. 6-5 Wt. 200 College—Louisville

Yr.	Team	G	FG	FT	TP	Avg.
1961-62	Chicago	42	84	32	200	4.8

TURNER, WILLIAM
b. Feb. 18, 1944 Ht. 6-7 Wt. 220 College—Akron

Yr.	Team	G	FG	FT	TP	Avg.
1967-68	San Fran.	42	68	36	172	4.1
1968-69	San Fran.	79	222	175	619	7.8
1969-70	S.F.-Cin.	72	197	123	517	7.2
1970-71	San Fran.	18	26	13	65	3.6
1971-72	Golden St.	62	71	40	182	2.9
	Totals	273	584	387	1555	5.7

TWYMAN, JACK
b. May 11, 1934 Ht. 6-6 Wt. 210 College—Cincinnati

Yr.	Team	G	FG	FT	TP	Avg.
1955-56	Rochester	72	417	204	1038	14.4
1956-57	Rochester	72	449	276	1174	16.3
1957-58	Cincinnati	72	465	307	1237	17.2
1958-59	Cincinnati	72	710	437	1857	25.8
1959-60	Cincinnati	75	870	598	2338	31.2
1960-61	Cincinnati	79	796	405	1997	25.3
1961-62	Cincinnati	80	739	353	1831	22.9
1962-63	Cincinnati	80	641	304	1586	19.8
1963-64	Cincinnati	68	447	189	1083	19.9
1964-65	Cincinnati	80	479	198	1156	14.5
1965-66	Cincinnati	73	224	95	543	7.4
	Totals	823	6237	3366	15840	19.2

Yr.	Team		G	FG	FT	TP	Avg.

TYRA, CHARLES
b. Aug. 16, 1935 Ht. 6-8 Wt. 235 College—Louisville

Yr.	Team	G	FG	FT	TP	Avg.
1957-58	New York	68	175	150	500	7.4
1958-59	New York	69	240	129	609	8.8
1959-60	New York	74	406	133	945	12.8
1960-61	New York	59	199	120	518	8.8
1961-62	Chicago	78	193	133	519	6.6
	Totals	348	1213	665	3091	8.9

UPLINGER, HAL
b. 1920 Ht. 6-4 Wt. 185 College—Long Island University

Yr.	Team	G	FG	FT	TP	Avg.
1953-54	Baltimore	23	33	20	86	3.7

VACENDAK, STEVE
b. Aug. 15, 1944 Ht. 6-1½ Wt. 185 College—Duke

Yr.	Team		G	FG	FT	TP	Avg.
1967-68	Pittsburgh	(ABA)	9	13	10	36	4.0
1968-69	Minnesota	(ABA)	60	288(2)	167	745	12.4
1969-70	Pitt.-Miami	(ABA)	14	15	13	43	3.1
	Totals		83	316(2)	190	824	9.9

VALLELY, JOHN
b. Oct. 3, 1948 Ht. 6-3 Wt. 185 College—UCLA

Yr.	Team	G	FG	FT	TP	Avg.
1970-71	Atlanta	51	73	45	191	3.7
1971-72	Atl.-Hou.	49	69	30	168	3.4
	Totals	100	142	75	359	3.6

VAN ARSDALE, RICHARD
b. Feb. 22, 1943 Ht. 6-4½ Wt. 210 College—Indiana

Yr.	Team	G	FG	FT	TP	Avg.
1965-66	New York	79	359	251	969	12.3
1966-67	New York	79	410	371	1191	15.1
1967-68	New York	78	316	227	859	11.0
1968-69	Phoenix	80	612	454	1678	21.0
1969-70	Phoenix	77	592	459	1643	21.3
1970-71	Phoenix	81	609	553	1771	21.9
1971-72	Phoenix	82	545	529	1619	19.7
1972-73	Phoenix	81	532	426	1490	18.4
1973-74	Phoenix	78	514	361	1389	17.8
1974-75	Phoenix	70	421	282	1124	16.1
1975-76	Phoenix	58	276	195	747	12.9
1976-77	Phoenix	78	227	145	599	7.7
	Totals	921	5413	4253	15079	16.4

VAN ARSDALE, THOMAS
b. Feb. 22, 1943 Ht. 6-5 Wt. 215 College—Indiana

Yr.	Team	G	FG	FT	TP	Avg.
1965-66	Detroit	79	312	209	833	10.5
1966-67	Detroit	79	347	272	966	12.2
1967-68	Det.-Cin.	77	211	188	610	7.9
1968-69	Cincinnati	77	547	398	1492	19.4
1969-70	Cincinnati	71	620	381	1621	22.8
1970-71	Cincinnati	82	749	377	1875	22.9
1971-72	Cincinnati	73	550	299	1399	19.2
1972-73	K.C.-O.-Phila.	79	445	250	1140	14.4
1973-74	Philadelphia	78	614	298	1526	19.6
1974-75	Phil.-Atl.	82	593	322	1508	18.4
1975-76	Atlanta	75	346	126	818	10.9
1976-77	Phoenix	77	171	102	444	5.8
	Totals	929	5505	3222	14232	15.3

Yr.	Team		G	FG	FT	TP	Avg.

VAN BREDA KOLFF, WILLIAM (Butch)
b. Oct. 28, 1922 Ht. 6-3 Wt. 185 College—Princeton/NYU

Yr.	Team	G	FG	FT	TP	Avg.
1946-47 New York		16	7	11	25	1.6
1947-48 New York		44	53	74	180	4.1
1948-49 New York		59	127	161	415	7.0
1949-50 New York		56	55	96	206	3.7
	Totals	175	242	342	826	4.7

VANCE, ELLIS (Gene)
b. Feb. 25, 1923 Ht. 6-3 Wt. 196 College—Illinois

Yr.	Team	G	FG	FT	TP	Avg.
1947-48 Chicago		48	163	76	402	8.4
1948-49 Chicago		56	222	131	575	10.3
1949-50 Tri-Cities		35	110	86	306	8.7
1950-51 Tri-Cities		28	44	43	131	4.7
1951-52 Milwaukee		7	7	9	23	3.3
	Totals	174	546	345	1437	8.3

VANDEWEGHE, ERNIE
b. Sept. 12, 1926 Ht. 6-3 Wt. 195 College—Colgate

Yr.	Team	G	FG	FT	TP	Avg.
1949-50 New York		42	164	93	421	10.0
1950-51 New York		44	135	68	338	7.7
1951-52 New York		57	200	124	524	9.2
1952-53 New York		61	272	187	731	12.0
1953-54 New York		15	37	25	99	6.6
1955-56 New York		5	10	2	22	4.4
	Totals	224	818	499	2135	9.5

VAN LIER, NORM
b. Apr. 1, 1947 Ht. 6-2 Wt. 175 College—St. Francis (Pa.)

Yr.	Team	G	FG	FT	TP	Avg.
1969-70 Cincinnati		81	302	166	770	9.5
1970-71 Cincinnati		82	478	359	1315	16.0
1971-72 Cin.-Chi.		79	334	237	905	11.5
1972-73 Chicago		80	474	166	1114	13.9
1973-74 Chicago		80	427	288	1142	14.3
1974-75 Chicago		70	407	236	1050	15.0
1975-76 Chicago		76	361	235	957	12.6
1976-77 Chicago		82	300	238	838	10.2
1977-78 Chicago		78	200	172	572	7.3
1978-79 Milwaukee		38	30	47	107	2.8
	Totals	746	3313	2144	8770	11.8

VAN ZANT, DENNIS
b. June 1, 1952 Ht. 6-9 Wt. 210 College—Azusa Pacific

Yr.	Team	G	FG	FT	TP	Avg.
1975-76 San Antonio		1	0	2	2	2.0

VAUGHN, CHARLES (Chico)
b. eb. 19, 1940 Ht. 6-3 Wt. 215 College—So. Illinois

Yr.	Team		G	FG	FT	TP	Avg.
1962-63 St. Louis			77	295	188	778	10.1
1963-64 St. Louis			68	238	107	583	8.6
1964-65 St. Louis			75	344	182	870	11.6
1965-66 St. L-Detr.			56	182	106	470	8.4
1966-67 Detroit			51	85	50	220	4.3
1967-68 Pittsburgh	(ABA)		74	512(137)	308	1469	19.9
1968-69 Minnesota	(ABA)		69	415(145)	253	1228	17.8
1969-70 Pittsburgh	(ABA)		21	66(24)	48	204	9.7
	Totals		491	2137(306)	1242	5822	11.9

VAUGHN, DAVID
b. June 4, 1952 Ht. 7-0 Wt. 220 College—U.N.L.V./Oral Rbts.

Yr.	Team		G	FG	FT	TP	Avg.
1974-75 Virginia	(ABA)		83	422	125	969	11.7
1975-76 Virginia	(ABA)		10	12	5	29	2.9
	Totals		93	434	130	998	10.7

VAUGHN, VIRGIL
Ht. 6-4 Wt. 205 College—Kentucky Wesleyan

Yr.	Team		G	FG	FT	TP	Avg.
1946-47 Boston			17	15	15	45	2.6
1947-48 Syracuse	(NL)		11	29	5	63	5.7
	Totals		28	44	20	108	3.9

VERGA, ROBERT BRUCE
b. Sept. 7, 1945 Ht. 6-1 Wt. 190 College—Duke

Yr.	Team		G	FG	FT	TP	Avg.
1967-68 Dallas	(ABA)		31	280(13)	162	735	23.7
1968-69 Den-NY-Hou	(ABA)		63	416(19)	336	1187	18.8
1969-70 Carolina	(ABA)		82	867(66)	458	2258	27.5
1970-71 Carolina	(ABA)		75	550(10)	302	1412	18.8
1971-72 Car.-Pitt.	(ABA)		70	459(19)	285	1222	17.5
1973-74 Portland			21	42	20	104	5.0
	Totals		342	2614(127)	1563	6915	20.2

VIRDEN, CLAUDE
b. Nov. 25, 1947 Ht. 6-6 Wt. 200 College—Murray State

Yr.	Team		G	FG	FT	TP	Avg.
1972-73 Kentucky	(ABA)		31	130	46	306	9.9

VOLKER, FLOYD
b. June 21, 1921 Ht. 6-4 Wt. 205 College—Wyoming

Yr.	Team		G	FG	FT	TP	Avg.
1947-48 Oshkosh	(NL)		57	102	31	235	4.1
1948-49 Oshkosh	(NL)		64	166	78	410	6.4
1949-50 Ind.-Denver			54	613	71	397	7.4
	Totals		175	431	180	1042	6.0

VON NIEDA, STANLEY (Whitey)
b. 1923 Ht. 6-1 Wt. 175 College—Penn State

Yr.	Team		G	FG	FT	TP	Avg.
1947-48 Tri-Cities	(NL)		60	276	174	726	12.1
1948-49 Tri-Cities	(NL)		64	247	147	641	10.0
1949-50 Tri-C.-Balt.			59	120	73	313	5.3
	Totals		183	643	394	1680	9.2

WAGER, CLINT
b. 1921 Ht. 6-6 Wt. 230 College—St. Mary's (Minn.)

Yr.	Team		G	FG	FT	TP	Avg.
1943-44 Oshkosh	(NL)		22	79	72	230	10.4
1944-45 Oshkosh	(NL)		27	70	28	168	6.2
1945-46 Oshkosh	(NL)		34	68	31	167	4.9
1946-47 Oshkosh	(NL)		44	68	50	186	4.2
1947-48 Oshkosh	(NL)		59	90	56	236	4.0
1948-49 Hammond	(NL)		61	125	82	332	5.4
1949-50 Ft. Wayne			63	57	29	143	2.3
	Totals		310	557	348	1462	4.7

WAGNER, DAN
b. 1923 Ht. 6-0 Wt. 170 College—Texas

Yr.	Team		G	FG	FT	TP	Avg.
1947-48 Flint	(NL)		50	96	59	251	5.0
1948-49 Sheboygan	(NL)		62	111	109	331	5.3
1949-50 Sheboygan			11	19	31	69	6.3
	Totals		123	226	199	651	5.3

WAGNER, PHIL
b. Dec. 18, 1945 Ht. 6-2 Wt. 190 College—Georgia Tech

Yr.	Team		G	FG	FT	TP	Avg.
1968-69 Indiana	(ABA)		12	11(1)	13	36	3.0

WAKEFIELD, ANDRE
b. Jan. 11, 1955 Ht. 6-3 Wt. 176 College—So. Idaho/Loyola (Chi.)

Yr.	Team	G	FG	FT	TP	Avg.
1978-79 Chic.-Detr.		73	62	48	172	2.4
1979-80 Utah		8	6	3	15	1.9
	Totals	81	68	51	187	2.3

Yr.	Team	G	FG	FT	TP	Avg.

WALK, NEAL
b. July 29, 1948 Ht. 6-10 Wt. 250 College—Florida

Yr.	Team	G	FG	FT	TP	Avg.
1969-70	Phoenix	82	257	155	669	8.2
1970-71	Phoenix	82	426	205	1057	12.9
1971-72	Phoenix	81	506	256	1268	15.7
1972-73	Phoenix	81	678	279	1635	20.2
1973-74	Phoenix	82	573	235	1381	16.8
1974-75	N.O.-N.Y.	67	198	86	482	7.2
1975-76	New York	82	262	79	603	7.4
1976-77	N.Y. Knicks	11	28	6	62	5.6
	Totals	568	2928	1301	7157	12.6

WALKER, ANDY
b. March 25, 1955 Ht. 6-4 Wt. 190 College—Niagara

Yr.	Team	G	FG	FT	TP	Avg.
1976-77	New Orleans	40	72	36	180	4.5

WALKER, BRADY
b. March 15, 1921 Ht. 6-6 Wt. 205 College—Brigham Young

Yr.	Team	G	FG	FT	TP	Avg.
1948-49	Providence	59	202	87	491	8.3
1949-50	Boston	68	218	72	508	7.5
1950-51	Bos.-Balt.	66	164	72	400	6.1
1951-52	Baltimore	35	89	26	204	5.8
	Totals	228	673	257	1603	7.0

WALKER, CHESTER (Chet)
b. Feb. 22, 1940 Ht. 6-6½ Wt. 210 College—Bradley

Yr.	Team	G	FG	FT	TP	Avg.
1962-63	Syracuse	78	352	253	957	12.3
1963-64	Philadelphia	76	492	330	1314	17.3
1964-65	Philadelphia	79	377	288	1042	13.2
1965-66	Philadelphia	80	443	335	1221	15.3
1966-67	Philadelphia	81	561	445	1567	19.3
1967-68	Philadelphia	82	539	387	1465	17.9
1968-69	Philadelphia	82	554	369	1477	18.0
1969-70	Chicago	78	596	483	1675	21.5
1970-71	Chicago	81	650	480	1780	22.0
1971-72	Chicago	78	619	481	1719	22.0
1972-73	Chicago	79	597	376	1570	19.9
1973-74	Chicago	82	572	439	1583	19.3
1974-75	Chicago	76	524	413	1461	19.2
	Totals	1032	6876	5079	18831	18.2

WALKER, HORACE
b. April 17, 1938 Ht. 6-3½ Wt. 210 College—Mich. St.

Yr.	Team	G	FG	FT	TP	Avg.
1961-62	Chicago	64	147	139	433	6.8

WALKER, JIM
b. April 8, 1944 Ht. 6-3 Wt. 205 College—Providence

Yr.	Team	G	FG	FT	TP	Avg.
1967-68	Detroit	81	289	134	712	8.8
1968-69	Detroit	69	312	182	806	11.7
1969-70	Detroit	81	666	355	1687	20.8
1970-71	Detroit	79	524	344	1392	17.6
1971-72	Detroit	78	634	397	1665	21.3
1972-73	Houston	81	605	244	1454	18.0
1973-74	Hou.-K.C.-O.	75	582	273	1437	19.2
1974-75	K.C.-Omaha	81	553	247	1353	16.7
1975-76	Kansas City	73	459	231	1149	15.7
	Totals	698	4624	2407	11655	16.7

WALKER, PHIL
b. March 20, 1956 Ht. 6-3 Wt. 190 College—Millersville (Pa.)

Yr.	Team	G	FG	FT	TP	Avg.
1977-78	Washington	40	57	64	178	4.5

WALLACE, MICHAEL (Red)
b. July 12, 1918 Ht. 6-1 Wt. 185 College—Scranton

Yr.	Team	G	FG	FT	TP	Avg.
1946-47	Bos.-Toronto	61	225	106	556	9.1

WALLER, DWIGHT
b. Oct. 5, 1945 Ht. 6-7 Wt. 230 College—Tennessee State

Yr.	Team		G	FG	FT	TP	Avg.
1968-69	Atlanta		11	2	3	7	0.6
1971-72	Denver	(ABA)	2	2	0	4	2.0
	Totals		13	4	3	11	0.8

WALSH, JAMES
b. Aug. 29, 1931 Ht. 6-4 Wt. 195 College—Stanford
d. March 4, 1976

Yr.	Team	G	FG	FT	TP	Avg.
1957-58	Philadelphia	10	5	10	20	2.0

WALTHER, PAUL (Lefty)
b. 1927 Ht. 6-2 Wt. 160 College—Tennessee

Yr.	Team	G	FG	FT	TP	Avg.
1949-50	Minn.-Ind.	53	114	63	291	5.5
1950-51	Indianapolis	63	213	145	571	9.1
1951-52	Indianapolis	55	220	231	671	12.2
1952-53	Indianapolis	67	227	264	718	10.7
1953-54	Philadelphia	64	138	145	421	6.6
1954-55	Ft. Wayne.	68	56	54	166	2.4
	Totals	370	968	902	2838	7.7

WALTHOUR, ISAAC (Rabbit)
b. 1929 Ht. 5-11 Wt. 163

Yr.	Team	G	FG	FT	TP	Avg.
1953-54	Milwaukee	4	1	0	2	0.5

WALTON, BILL
b. Nov. 5, 1952 Ht. 6-11 Wt. 255 College—UCLA

Yr.	Team	G	FG	FT	TP	Avg.
1974-75	Portland	35	177	94	448	12.8
1975-76	Portland	51	345	133	823	16.1
1976-77	Portland	65	491	228	1210	18.6
1977-78	Portland	8	461	177	1097	18.9
1978-79	Portland		(Injured)			
1979-80	San Diego	14	81	32	194	13.9
	Totals	223	1554	664	3772	16.9

WANZER, ROBERT (Bobby)
b. June 4, 1921 Ht. 6-0 Wt. 172 College—Seton Hall

Yr.	Team		G	FG	FT	TP	Avg.
1947-48	Rochester	(NL)	40	55	57	167	4.2
1948-49	Rochester		60	202	209	613	10.2
1949-50	Rochester		67	254	283	791	11.8
1950-51	Rochester		68	252	232	736	10.8
1951-52	Rochester		66	328	377	1033	15.7
1952-53	Rochester		70	318	384	1020	14.6
1953-54	Rochester		72	322	314	958	13.3
1954-55	Rochester		72	324	294	942	13.1
1955-56	Rochester		72	245	259	749	10.4
1956-57	Rochester		21	23	36	82	3.9
	Totals		608	2323	2445	7091	11.7

WARBINGTON, PERRY
b. Sept. 7, 1952 Ht. 6-2 Wt. 166 College—Georgia Southern

Yr.	Team	G	FG	FT	TP	Avg.
1974-75	Philadelphia	5	4	2	10	2.0

Yr.	Team		G	FG	FT	TP	Avg.

WARD, GERRY
b. Sept. 6, 1941 Ht. 6-4 Wt. 200 College— Boston College

Yr.	Team		G	FG	FT	TP	Avg.
1963-64	St. Louis		24	16	11	43	1.8
1964-65	Boston		3	2	1	5	1.7
1965-66	Philadelphia		66	67	39	173	2.6
1966-67	Chicago		76	117	87	321	4.2
	Totals		169	202	138	542	3.2

WARD, HENRY
b. Jan. 30, 1952 Ht. 6-4 Wt. 195 College—Jackson State

Yr.	Team		G	FG	FT	TP	Avg.
1975-76	San Antonio	(ABA)	61	154(6)	16	330	5.4
1976-77	San Antonio		27	34	15	83	3.1
	Totals		88	188(6)	31	413	4.7

WARE, JIM
b. May 2, 1944 Ht. 6-7½ Wt. 210 College—Oklahoma City

Yr.	Team		G	FG	FT	TP	Avg.
1966-67	Cincinnati		33	30	10	70	2.1
1967-68	San Diogo		30	25	23	73	2.4
1968-69	Dallas	(ABA)	1	3	1	7	7.0
	Totals		64	58	34	150	2.3

WARLEY, BEN
b. Sept. 4, 1936 Ht. 6-6 Wt. 200 College—Tennessee State

Yr.	Team		G	FG	FT	TP	Avg.
1962-63	Syracuse		26	50	25	125	4.8
1963-64	Philadelphia		79	215	220	650	8.2
1964-65	Philadelphia		64	94	124	312	4.8
1965-66	Phil.-Balt.		57	116	64	296	5.2
1966-67	Baltimore		62	125	134	384	6.2
1967-68	Anaheim	(ABA)	71	435(52)	313	1235	17.4
1968-69	Los Angeles	(ABA)	35	172(31)	116	491	14.0
1969-70	Denver	(ABA)	42	60(15)	58	193	4.6
	Totals		436	1267(98)	1054	3686	8.5

WARLICK, ROBERT
b. March 20, 1941 Ht. 6-5 Wt. 205 College—Pepperdine

Yr.	Team		G	FG	FT	TP	Avg.
1965-66	Detroit		10	11	2	24	2.3
1966-67	San Fran.		12	15	6	36	3.0
1967-68	San Fran.		69	257	97	611	8.9
1968-69	Mil.-Phoe.		66	213	87	513	7.8
	Totals		157	496	192	1184	7.5

WARNER, CORNELL
b. Aug. 12, 1948 Ht. 6-9 Wt. 220 College—Jackson State

Yr.	Team		G	FG	FT	TP	Avg.
1970-71	Buffalo		65	156	79	391	6.0
1971-72	Buffalo		62	162	58	382	6.2
1972-73	Buf.-Cleve.		72	174	59	407	5.7
1973-74	Cleve.-Mil.		72	174	85	433	6.0
1974-75	Milwaukee		79	248	106	602	7.6
1975-76	Los Angeles		81	251	89	591	7.3
1976-77	Los Angeles		14	25	4	54	3.9
	Totals		445	1190	480	2860	6.4

WARREN, BOB (Colonel)
b. July 17, 1946 Ht. 6-5 Wt. 190 College—Vanderbilt

Yr.	Team		G	FG	FT	TP	Avg.
1968-69	Los Angeles	(ABA)	76	285(31)	297	898	11.8
1969-70	Los Angeles	(ABA)	72	266(25)	176	733	10.2
1970-71	Memphis	(ABA)	46	146(21)	107	420	9.2
1971-72	Mem.-Caro.	(ABA)	75	313(11)	213	850	11.3
1972-73	Car-Dal-Utah	(ABA)	77	244(5)	236	729	9.5
1973-74	Utah-S.A.	(ABA)	59	110	63	283	4.8
1974-75	San Antonio	(ABA)	71	127(2)	77	333	4.7
	Totals		473	1491(95)	1169	4246	9.0

WARREN, JOHN
b. July 7, 1947 Ht. 6-3 Wt. 180 College—St. John's

Yr.	Team		G	FG	FT	TP	Avg.
1969-70	New York		44	44	24	112	2.5
1970-71	Cleveland		82	380	180	940	11.5
1971-72	Cleveland		68	144	49	337	5.0
1972-73	Cleveland		40	54	18	126	3.2
1973-74	Cleveland		69	132	35	299	4.3
	Totals		303	754	306	1814	6.0

WASHINGTON, BOBBY
b. July 11, 1947 Ht. 6-0 Wt. 175 College—Eastern Kentucky

Yr.	Team		G	FG	FT	TP	Avg.
1969-70	Kentucky	(ABA)	2	0	0	0	0.0
1970-71	Cleveland		47	123	104	350	7.4
1971-72	Cleveland		69	123	104	350	5.1
	Totals		118	246	208	700	5.9

WASHINGTON, DON
b. April 22, 1952 Ht. 6-8 Wt. 210 College—N. Carolina

Yr.	Team		G	FG	FT	TP	Avg.
1974-75	Denver	(ABA)	50	79	38	196	3.9
1975-76	Utah	(ABA)	6	12	0	24	4.0
	Totals		56	91	38	220	3.9

WASHINGTON, JAMES
b. July 1, 1943 Ht. 6-7 Wt. 215 College—Villanova

Yr.	Team		G	FG	FT	TP	Avg.
1965-66	St. Louis		65	158	68	384	5.9
1966-67	Chicago		77	252	88	592	7.7
1967-68	Chicago		82	418	187	1023	12.5
1968-69	Chicago		80	440	241	1121	14.0
1969-70	Philadelphia		79	401	204	1006	12.7
1970-71	Philadelphia		78	395	259	1049	13.4
1971-72	Phil.-Atl.		84	393	256	1042	12.4
1972-73	Atlanta		75	308	163	779	10.4
1973-74	Atlanta		73	297	134	728	10.0
1974-75	Atl.-Buf.		80	191	62	444	5.6
	Totals		773	3253	1662	8168	10.6

WASHINGTON, STAN
b. Jan. 23, 1952 Ht. 6-4 Wt. 190 College—San Diego

Yr.	Team		G	FG	FT	TP	Avg.
1974-75	Washington		1	0	0	0	0.0

WASHINGTON, TOM (Trooper)
b. April 21, 1944 Ht. 6-7 Wt. 225 College—Cheney State

Yr.	Team		G	FG	FT	TP	Avg.
1967-68	Pittsburgh	(ABA)	63	312(2)	106	732	11.6
1968-69	Minnesota	(ABA)	69	421	190	1032	15.0
1969-70	Pitt.-L.A.	(ABA)	81	320(4)	155	799	9.8
1970-71	Floridians	(ABA)	57	216	102	534	9.3
1971-72	New York	(ABA)	80	387	107	881	11.0
1972-73	New York	(ABA)	76	229	63	521	6.9
	Totals		426	1885(6)	723	4499	10.6

WASHINGTON, WILSON
b. Aug. 3, 1955 Ht. 6-9 Wt. 227 College—Old Dominion

Yr.	Team		G	FG	FT	TP	Avg.
1977-78	Phil.-N.J.		38	100	29	229	6.0
1978-79	New Jersey		62	218	66	502	8.1
	Totals		100	318	95	731	7.3

WATSON, BOB
b. March 22, 1930 Ht. 6-0 Wt. 162 College—Kentucky

Yr.	Team		G	FG	FT	TP	Avg.
1954-55	Milwaukee		63	72	31	175	2.8

Yr.	Team		G	FG	FT	TP	Avg.
WATTS, DON (Slick)							
b. July 21, 1951 Ht. 6-1 Wt. 175 College—Xavier							
1973-74	Seattle		62	198	100	496	8.0
1974-75	Seattle		82	232	93	557	6.8
1975-76	Seattle		82	433	199	1065	13.0
1976-77	Seattle		79	428	172	1028	13.0
1977-78	Sea.-N.O.		71	219	92	530	7.5
1978-79	Houston		61	92	41	225	3.7
	Totals		437	1602	697	3901	8.9
WATTS, RONALD							
b. May 21, 1943 Ht. 6-6 Wt. 210 College—Wake Forest							
1965-66	Boston		1	1	0	2	2.0
1966-67	Boston		27	11	16	38	1.4
	Totals		28	12	16	40	1.4
WATTS, SAM							
Ht. 6-3 Wt. 185 College—Great Falls							
1970-71	Pittsburgh	(ABA)	54	109(14)	49	281	5.2
WEATHERSPOON, NICK							
b. July 20, 1950 Ht. 6-7 Wt. 197 College—Illinois							
1973-74	Capital		65	199	96	494	7.6
1974-75	Washington		82	256	103	615	7.5
1975-76	Washington		64	218	96	532	8.3
1976-77	Wash.-Sea.		62	310	91	711	11.5
1977-78	Chicago		41	86	37	209	5.1
1978-79	San Diego		82	479	176	1134	13.8
1979-80	San Diego		57	164	63	391	6.9
	Totals		453	1712	662	4086	9.0
WEBB, JEFF							
b. July 6, 1948 Ht. 6-4 Wt. 170 College—Kansas State							
1970-71	Milwaukee		29	27	11	65	2.2
1971-72	Mil.-Phoe.		46	40	16	96	2.1
	Totals		75	67	27	161	2.1
WEBER, FOREST (Jake)							
b. March 18, 1918 Ht. 6-6 Wt. 225 College—Purdue							
1945-46	Indianapolis	(NL)	5	7	4	18	3.6
1946-47	N.Y.-Prov.		50	59	55	173	3.5
	Totals		55	66	59	191	3.5
WEBSTER, ELNARDO							
b. March 6, 1948 Ht. 6-5 Wt. 195 College—St. Peter's							
1971-72	N.Y.-Mem.	(ABA)	19	50(1)	21	122	6.4
WEHR, DICK							
b. 1925 Ht. 6-4 Wt. 180 College—Rice and Indiana							
1948-49	Indianapolis		9	5	2	12	1.3
WEISS, ROBERT							
b. May 7, 1942 Ht. 6-2 Wt. 180 College—Penn State							
1956-66	Philadelphia		7	3	0	6	0.9
1966-67	Philadelphia		6	5	2	12	2.0
1967-68	Seattle		82	295	213	803	9.8
1968-69	Mil.-Chi.		77	189	128	506	6.6
1969-70	Chicago		82	365	213	943	11.5
1970-71	Chicago		82	278	226	782	9.5

Yr.	Team		G	FG	FT	TP	Avg.
1971-72	Chicago		82	358	212	928	11.3
1972-73	Chicago		82	279	159	717	8.7
1973-74	Chicago		79	263	142	668	8.5
1974-75	Buffalo		76	102	54	258	3.4
1975-76	Buffalo		66	89	35	213	3.2
1976-77	Washington		62	62	29	153	2.5
	Totals		783	2288	1413	5989	7.6
WEITZMAN, RICH							
b. April 30, 1946 Ht. 6-2 Wt. 185 College—Northeastern							
1967-68	Boston		25	12	9	33	1.3
WELLS, OWEN							
b. Dec. 9, 1950 Ht. 6-7 Wt. 200 College—Detroit							
1974-75	Houston		33	42	15	99	3.0
WELLS, RALPH							
b. Sept. 3, 1940 Ht. 6-1 Wt. 180 College—Northwestern							
1962-63	Chicago		3	1	0	2	0.7
WERTIS, RAY							
b. 1922 Ht. 5-11 Wt. 175 College—St. John's (N.Y.)							
1946-47	Clevel.-Tor.		61	79	56	214	3.5
1947-48	Providence		7	13	6	32	4.6
	Totals		68	92	62	246	3.6
WESLEY, WALT							
b. April 25, 1945 Ht. 6-11 Wt. 230 College—Kansas							
1966-67	Cincinnati		64	131	52	314	4.9
1967-68	Cincinnati		66	188	76	452	6.8
1968-69	Cincinnati		82	245	134	624	7.6
1969-70	Chicago		72	270	145	685	9.5
1970-71	Cleveland		82	565	325	1455	17.7
1971-72	Cleveland		82	412	196	1020	12.4
1972-73	Cleve.-Phoe.		57	77	26	180	3.2
1973-74	Capital		39	71	26	168	4.3
1974-75	Phil.-Mil.		45	42	16	100	2.2
1975-76	Los Angeles		1	1	2	4	4.0
	Totals		590	2002	998	5002	8.5
WEST, JERRY							
b. May 28, 1938 Ht. 6-3 Wt. 175 College—W. Virginia							
1960-61	Los Angeles		79	529	331	1389	17.6
1961-62	Los Angeles		75	799	712	2310	30.8
1962-63	Los Angeles		55	559	371	1489	26.6
1963-64	Los Angeles		72	740	584	2064	28.7
1964-65	Los Angeles		74	822	648	2292	31.0
1965-66	Los Angeles		79	818	840	2476	31.4
1966-67	Los Angeles		66	645	602	1892	28.7
1967-68	Los Angeles		51	476	391	1343	26.3
1968-69	Los Angeles		61	545	490	1580	25.9
1969-70	Los Angeles		74	831	647	2309	31.2
1970-71	Los Angeles		69	667	525	1859	26.9
1971-72	Los Angeles		77	735	515	1985	25.8
1972-73	Los Angeles		69	618	339	1575	22.8
1973-74	Los Angeles		31	232	165	629	20.3
	Totals		932	9016	7160	25192	27.0
WEST, ROLAND							
Ht. 6-4 Wt. 178 College—Cincinnati							
1967-68	Baltimore		4	2	0	4	1.0

Yr.	Team	G	FG	FT	TP	Avg.
WESTBROOK, DEXTER						
b. 1943 Ht. 6-8 Wt. 190 College—Providence						
1967-68 N.J.-Pitt. (ABA)		12	19	10	48	4.0
WETZEL, JOHN						
b. Oct. 22, 1944 Ht. 6-5 Wt. 185 College—VPI						
1967-68 Los Angeles		38	52	35	139	3.7
1970-71 Phoenix		70	124	83	331	4.7
1971-72 Phoenix		51	31	24	86	1.7
1972-73 Atlanta		28	42	14	98	3.5
1973-74 Atlanta		70	107	41	255	3.6
1974-75 Atlanta		63	87	68	242	3.8
1975-76 Phoenix		37	22	20	64	1.7
Totals		357	465	285	1215	3.4
WHITE, HERB						
b. June 15, 1948 Ht. 6-2 Wt. 195 College—Georgia						
1970-71 Atlanta		38	34	22	90	2.4
WHITE, HUBIE						
b. Jan. 26, 1940 Ht. 6-4 Wt. 205 College—Villanova						
1962-63 San Francisco		29	40	12	92	3.2
1963-64 Philadelphia		23	31	17	79	3.4
1969-70 Miami (ABA)		54	146(7)	62	361	6.7
1970-71 Pittsburgh (ABA)		14	17(2)	10	46	3.3
Totals		120	234(9)	101	578	4.8
WHITE, JOSEPH (Jo Jo)						
b. Nov. 16, 1946 Ht. 6-3 Wt. 190 College—Kansas						
1969-70 Boston		60	309	111	729	12.2
1970-71 Boston		75	693	215	1601	21.3
1971-72 Boston		79	770	285	1825	23.1
1972-73 Boston		82	717	178	1612	19.7
1973-74 Boston		82	649	190	1488	18.1
1974-75 Boston		82	658	186	1502	18.3
1975-76 Boston		82	670	212	1552	18.9
1976-77 Boston		82	638	333	1609	19.6
1977-78 Boston		46	289	103	681	14.8
1978-79 Bost.-G.S.		76	404	139	947	12.5
1979-80 Golden State		78	336(1)	97	770	9.9
1980-81 Kansas City		13	36	11	83	6.4
Totals		837	6169(1)	2052	14399	17.2
WHITNEY, HENRY (Hank)						
b. April 28, 1939 Ht. 6-7 Wt. 235 College—Iowa State						
1967-68 New Jersey (ABA)		37	217	157	591	16.0
1968-69 N.Y.-Hous. (ABA)		49	131	89	351	7.2
1969-70 Carolina (ABA)		59	170	57	397	6.7
Totals		145	518	303	1339	9.2
WHITTAKER, LUCIAN (Skippy)						
Ht. 6-1 Wt. 185 College—Kentucky						
1954-55 Boston		3	1	0	2	0.7
WIDBY, G. RONALD						
b. Mar. 9, 1945 Ht. 6-4 Wt. 210 College—Tennessee						
1967-68 New Orleans (ABA)		20	27	4	58	2.9

Yr.	Team	G	FG	FT	TP	Avg.
WIER, MURRAY						
b. Dec. 12, 1926 Ht. 5-9 Wt. 155 College—Iowa						
1948-49 Tri-Cities (NL)		60	80	79	239	4.0
1949-50 Tri-Cities		56	157	115	429	7.7
Totals		116	237	194	668	5.8
WIESENHAHN, ROBERT						
b. Dec. 22, 1938 Ht. 6-4 Wt. 215 College—Cincinnati						
1961-62 Cincinnati		60	51	17	119	2.0
WILBURN, KEN						
b. June 8, 1944 Ht. 6-6 Wt. 195 College—Cen. State (Ohio)						
1967-68 Chicago		3	5	1	11	3.3
1968-69 Chicago		4	3	1	7	1.8
1968-69 Minn.-N.Y.-Den. (ABA)		47	76	38	190	4.0
Totals		54	84	40	208	3.9
WILCUTT, D. C.						
b. March 25, 1923 Ht. 6-2 Wt. 165 College—St. Louis						
1948-49 St. Louis		22	18	15	51	2.3
1949-50 St. Louis		37	24	29	77	2.1
Totals		59	42	44	128	2.2
WILEY, EUGENE						
b. Nov. 12, 1937 Ht. 6-10 Wt. 210 College—Wichita						
1962-63 Los Angeles		75	109	23	241	3.2
1963-64 Los Angeles		77	144	45	333	4.3
1964-65 Los Angeles		80	175	56	406	5.1
1965-66 Los Angeles		67	123	43	289	4.3
1967-68 Oak.-Dal. (ABA)		9	7	4	18	2.0
Totals		308	558	171	1287	4.2
WILFONG, WIN						
b. Mar. 18, 1932 Ht. 6-2 Wt. 185 College—Mem. St./Missouri						
1957-58 St. Louis		71	196	163	555	7.8
1958-59 St. Louis		63	99	62	260	4.1
1959-60 Cincinnati		72	283	161	727	10.1
1960-61 Cincinnati		62	109	75	293	4.7
Totals		268	687	461	1835	6.8
WILKENS, LEN						
b. Oct. 28, 1937 Ht. 6-1 Wt. 185 College—Providence						
1960-61 St. Louis		75	335	220	890	11.9
1961-62 St. Louis		20	140	84	364	18.2
1962-63 St. Louis		75	333	222	888	11.8
1963-64 St. Louis		78	334	270	938	12.0
1964-65 St. Louis		78	434	416	1284	16.5
1965-66 St. Louis		69	411	422	1244	18.0
1966-67 St. Louis		78	448	459	1355	17.4
1967-68 St. Louis		82	546	546	1638	20.0
1968-69 Seattle		82	644	547	1835	22.4
1969-70 Seattle		75	448	438	1334	17.8
1970-71 Seattle		71	471	461	1403	19.8
1971-72 Seattle		80	479	480	1438	18.0
1972-73 Cleveland		75	572	394	1538	20.5
1973-74 Cleveland		74	462	289	1213	16.4
1974-75 Portland		65	134	152	420	6.5
Totals		1077	6189	5394	17772	16.5

Yr.	Team		G	FG	FT	TP	Avg.

WILLIAMS, AL

b. 1948 Ht. 6-6 Wt. 215 College—Drake

1970-71 Kentucky	(ABA)	11	19	5	43	3.9

WILLIAMS, ART (Hambone)

b. Sept. 29, 1939 Ht. 6-2 Wt. 180 College—California Poly

Yr.	Team		G	FG	FT	TP	Avg.
1967-68 San Diego		79	265	113	643	8.1
1968-69 San Diego		79	227	105	559	7.1
1969-70 San Diego		80	189	88	466	5.8
1970-71 Boston		74	150	60	360	4.9
1971-72 Boston		81	161	90	412	5.1
1972-73 Boston		81	110	43	263	3.2
1973-74 Boston		67	73	27	173	2.6
1974-75 San Diego	(ABA)	7	8	0	16	2.3
Totals		548	1183	526	2892	5.3

WILLIAMS, BERNIE

b. Dec. 30, 1945 Ht. 6-3 Wt. 175 College—LaSalle

1969-70 San Diego		72	251	96	598	8.3
1970-71 San Diego		56	112	68	292	5.2
1971-72 Virginia	(ABA)	78	349(18)	113	829	10.6
1972-73 Virginia	(ABA)	71	356(10)	166	888	12.5
1973-74 Virginia	(ABA)	6	6(1)	2	15	2.5
Totals		283	1074(29)	445	2622	9.3

WILLIAMS, CHARLES

b. Sept. 5, 1943 Ht. 6-0 Wt. 195 College—Seattle

1967-68 Pittsburgh	(ABA)	78	642(51)	290	1625	20.8
1968-69 Minnesota	(ABA)	66	484(66)	203	1237	18.7
1969-70 Pittsburgh	(ABA)	26	193(16)	104	506	19.4
1970-71 Pitt.-Mem.	(ABA)	88	501(33)	204	1239	14.1
1971-72 Memphis	(ABA)	82	480(41)	294	1295	15.8
1972-73 Mem.-Utah	(ABA)	32	37(3)	41	118	3.7
Totals		372	2337(210)	1136	6020	16.2

WILLIAMS, CHUCK

b. June 6, 1946 Ht. 6-2 Wt. 175 College—Colorado

1970-71 Pittsburgh	(ABA)	83	268(1)	249	786	9.5
1971-72 Denver	(ABA)	84	263	205	731	8.7
1972-73 San Diego	(ABA)	83	488(1)	493	1470	17.7
1973-74 S.D.-Ken.	(ABA)	90	405(4)	299	1113	12.4
1974-75 Memphis	(ABA)	81	476(10)	212	1174	14.5
1975-76 Denver	(ABA)	79	339	188	866	11.0
1976-77 Denv.-Buff.		65	78	68	224	3.4
1977-78 Buffalo		73	208	114	530	7.3
Totals		638	2525(16)	1828	6894	10.8

WILLIAMS, CHUCKIE

b. Dec. 31, 1953 Ht. 6-3 Wt. 180 College—Kansas State

1976-77 Cleveland		22	14	9	37	1.7

WILLIAMS, CLIFF

b. April 15, 1945 Ht. 6-3 Wt. 180 College—Bowling Green

1968-69 Detroit		3	2	0	4	1.3

WILLIAMS, DONALD (Duck)

b.. Aug. 2, 1956 Ht. 6-2 Wt. 180 College—Notre Dame

1979-80 Utah		77	232	42	506	6.6

WILLIAMS, EARL

b. March 24, 1951 Ht. 6-7 Wt. 230 College—Winston-Salem

Yr.	Team		G	FG	FT	TP	Avg.
1974-75 Phoenix		79	163	45	371	4.7
1975-76 Detroit		46	73	22	168	3.7
1976-77 N.Y. Nets		1	0	3	3	3.0
1978-79 Boston		20	54	14	122	6.1
Totals		146	290	84	664	4.5

WILLIAMS, JAMES (Fly)

b. Feb. 18, 1953 Ht. 6-5 Wt. 200 College—Austin Peay

1974-75 St. Louis	(ABA)	71	297(2)	69	665	9.4

WILLIAMS, GENE

b. April 1, 1947 Ht. 6-7 Wt. 235 College—Kansas State

1969-70 Kentucky	(ABA)	1	0	0	0	0.0

WILLIAMS, HENRY

b. April 28, 1952 Ht. 6-5 Wt. 210 College—Jacksonville

1974-75 Utah	(ABA)	40	76(3)	18	173	4.3

WILLIAMS, MILT

b. Nov. 22, 1945 Ht. 6-2½ Wt. 185 College—Lincoln and Campbell

1970-71 New York		5	1	2	4	0.8
1971-72 Atlanta		10	23	21	67	6.7
1973-74 Seattle		53	62	41	165	3.1
1974-75 St. Louis	(ABA)	4	11	0	22	5.5
Totals		72	97	64	258	3.6

WILLIAMS, NATE

b. May 2, 1950 Ht. 6-5 Wt. 225 College—Utah State

1971-72 Cincinnati		81	418	127	963	11.9
1972-73 K.C.-O.		80	417	106	940	11.8
1973-74 K.C.-O.		82	538	193	1269	15.5
1974-75 K.C.-O.-N.O.		85	474	181	1129	13.3
1975-76 New Orleans		81	421	197	1039	12.8
1976-77 New Orleans		79	414	146	974	12.3
1977-78 N.O.-G. State		73	312	101	725	9.9
1978-79 Golden State		81	284	102	670	8.3
Totals		642	3278	1153	7709	12.0

WILLIAMS, ROBERT

b. May 12, 1931 Ht. 6-6 Wt. 230 College—Florida A & M

1955-56 Minneapolis		20	21	24	66	3.3
1956-57 Minneapolis		4	1	2	4	1.0
Totals		24	22	26	70	2.9

WILLIAMS, RON (Fritz)

b. Sept. 24, 1944 Ht. 6-3 Wt. 190 College—W. Virginia

1968-69 San Fran.		75	238	109	585	7.8
1969-70 San Fran.		80	452	277	1181	14.8
1970-71 San Fran.		82	426	331	1183	14.4
1971-72 Golden St.		80	291	195	777	9.7
1972-73 Golden St.		73	180	75	435	6.0
1973-74 Milwaukee		71	192	60	444	6.3
1974-75 Milwaukee		46	62	24	148	3.2
1975-76 Los Angeles		9	17	10	44	4.9
Totals		516	1858	1081	4797	9.3

Yr.	Team		G	FG	FT	TP	Avg.
WILLIAMS, SAM							
b. Jan. 22, 1945 Ht. 6-3 Wt. 180 College—Iowa							
1968-69 Milwaukee			55	78	72	228	4.1
1969-70 Milwaukee			11	11	5	27	2.5
	Totals		66	89	77	255	3.9
WILLIAMS, WARD							
b. June 26, 1923 Ht. 6-4 Wt. 195 College—Indiana							
1948-49 Ft. Wayne			53	61	93	215	4.1
WILLIAMS, WILLIE							
b. July 28, 1946 Ht. 6-7 Wt. 198 College—Florida State							
1970-71 Bos.-Cin.			25	10	3	23	0.9
WILLIFORD, VANN							
b. Jan. 26, 1948 Ht. 6-6 Wt. 195 College—N. Carolina St.							
1970-71 Carolina	(ABA)		38	62(3)	21	148	3.9
WILSON, BOB							
b. 1927 Ht. 6-4 Wt. 185 College—West Virginia State							
1951-52 Milwaukee			63	79	78	236	3.7
WILSON, BOBBY							
Ht. 6-8 Wt. 215 College—Kansas							
1967-68 Dallas	(ABA)		69	226(1`	163	616	8.9
WILSON, BOBBY							
b. Jan. 15, 1951 Ht. 6-3 Wt. 180 College—Wichita St.							
1974-75 Chicago			48	115	46	276	5.8
1975-76 Chicago			58	197	43	437	7.5
1976-77 Boston			25	19	11	49	2.0
1977-78 Indiana			12	14	2	30	2.5
	Totals		143	345	102	792	5.5
WILSON, GEORGE							
b. May 9, 1942 Ht. 6-8 Wt. 225 College—Cincinnati							
1964-65 Cincinnati			39	41	9	91	2.3
1965-66 Cincinnati			47	54	27	135	2.9
1966-67 Cin.-Chicago			55	85	58	228	4.1
1967-68 Seattle			77	179	109	467	6.1
1968-69 Phoe.-Phil.			79	272	153	697	8.8
1969-70 Philadelphia			67	118	122	358	5.3
1970-71 Buffalo			46	92	56	240	5.2
	Totals		410	841	534	2216	5.4
WILSON, ISAIAH (Bunny)							
b. May 31, 1948 Ht. 6-2½ Wt. 175 College—Baltimore							
1971-72 Detroit			48	63	41	167	3.5
1972-73 Memphis	(ABA)		30	68(3)	51	190	6.3
	Totals		78	131(3)	92	357	4.6
WILSON, JASPER							
b. July 12, 1947 Ht. 6-6 Wt. 200 College—Southern Univ.							
1968-69 New Orleans	(ABA)		66	128(5)	82	343	5.2
1969-70 New Orleans	(ABA)		4	8(1)	6	23	5.8
	Totals		70	136(6)	88	366	5.2

Yr.	Team		G	FG	FT	TP	Avg.
WILSON, JIM							
Ht. 5-10 Wt. 175 College—Cheney State							
1970-71 Pittsburgh	(ABA)		6	1	4	6	1.0
WILSON, RICK							
b. Feb. 7, 1956 Ht. 6-5 Wt. 200 College—Louisville							
1978-79 Atlanta			61	81	24	186	3.0
1979-80 Atlanta			5	2	4	8	1.6
	Totals		66	83	28	194	2.9
WILSON, STEVE							
b. Oct. 16, 1948 Ht. 6-5 Wt. 185 College—Hanover							
1970-71 Denver	(ABA)		39	52(8)	22	134	3.4
1971-72 Denver	(ABA)		9	5	4	14	1.7
	Totals		48	57(8)	26	148	3.1
WILSON, THOMAS (Bubba)							
b. Aug. 7, 1955 Ht. 6-3 Wt. 175 College—Western Carolina							
1979-80 Golden State			16	7	3	17	1.1
WINDIS, TONY							
b. Jan. 27, 1933 Ht. 6-1 Wt. 160 College—Wyoming							
1959-60 Detroit			9	16	4	36	4.0
WINDSOR, JOHN							
b. April 3, 1940 Ht. 6-8 Wt. 215 College—Stanford							
1963-64 San Fran.			10	9	7	25	2.5
WINFIELD, LEE							
b. Feb. 4, 1947 Ht. 6-2 Wt. 175 College—No. Texas St.							
1969-70 Seattle			64	138	87	363	5.7
1970-71 Seattle			79	334	162	830	10.5
1971-72 Seattle			81	343	175	861	10.6
1972-73 Seattle			53	143	62	348	6.6
1973-74 Buffalo			36	37	33	107	3.0
1974-75 Buffalo			68	164	49	377	5.5
1975-76 Kansas City			22	32	9	73	3.3
	Totals		403	1191	579	2959	7.3
WINGO, HARTHORNE							
b. Sept. 9, 1948 Ht. 6-8 Wt. 210 College—Friendship J.C.							
1972-73 New York			11	9	2	20	1.5
1973-74 New York			60	82	48	212	3.5
1974-75 New York			82	233	141	607	7.4
1975-76 New York			57	72	40	184	3.2
	Totals		212	396	231	1023	4.8
WINKLER, MARV							
b. Feb. 18, 1948 Ht. 6-1 Wt. 175 College—SW Louisiana							
1970-71 Milwaukee			3	3	2	8	2.7
1971-72 Indiana	(ABA)		20	15(2)	8	40	2.0
	Totals		23	18(2)	10	48	2.1
WISE, SKIP							
b. July 25, 1955 Ht. 6-3 Wt. 180 College—Clemson							
1975-76 San Antonio	(ABA)		2	2	0	4	2.0

Yr. Team		G	FG	FT	TP	Avg.

WISE, WILLIE
b. March 3, 1947 Ht. 6-6 Wt. 215 College—Drake

Yr. Team		G	FG	FT	TP	Avg.
1969-70 Los Angeles	(ABA)	82	483(4)	278	1248	15.2
1970-71 Utah	(ABA)	82	491(5)	312	1299	15.8
1971-72 Utah	(ABA)	83	743(6)	459	1951	23.2
1972-73 Utah	(ABA)	83	672(3)	476	1823	22.0
1973-74 Utah	(ABA)	82	714(2)	396	1826	22.3
1974-75 Virginia	(ABA)	16	128(1)	77	331	20.9
1975-76 Virginia	(ABA)	46	247	135	629	13.7
1976-77 Denver		75	237	142	616	8.2
1977-78 Seattle		2	0	1	1	0.5
Totals		552	3715(21)	2276	9727	17.6

WITTE, LUKE
b. Oct. 19, 1950 Ht. 7-0 Wt. 240 College—Ohio State

Yr. Team		G	FG	FT	TP	Avg.
1973-74 Cleveland		57	105	46	256	4.5
1974-75 Cleveland		39	33	19	85	2.2
1975-76 Cleveland		22	11	9	31	1.4
Totals		118	149	74	372	3.2

WITTMAN, GREG
b. May 10, 1947 Ht. 6-8 Wt. 210 College—W. Carolina

Yr. Team		G	FG	FT	TP	Avg.
1969-70 Denver	(ABA)	50	80(4)	32	196	4.0
1970-71 Tex.-Fla.	(ABA)	10	6	4	16	1.6
Totals		60	86(4)	36	212	3.5

WOHL, DAVE
b. Nov. 2, 1949 Ht. 6-2 Wt. 185 College—Pennsylvania

Yr. Team		G	FG	FT	TP	Avg.
1971-72 Philadelphia		79	243	156	642	8.1
1972-73 Port.-Buf.		78	254	103	611	7.8
1973-74 Buf.-Hou.		67	121	75	317	4.7
1974-75 Houston		75	203	79	485	6.5
1975-76 Houston		50	66	38	170	3.1
1976-77 Hou.-NYN		51	116	61	293	5.7
1977-78 New Jersey		10	12	11	35	3.5
Totals		410	1015	523	2553	6.2

WOODS, BOB
b. 1927 Ht. 5-10½ College—Northern Illinois

Yr. Team		G	FG	FT	TP	Avg.
1949-50 Sheboygan		6	3	1	7	1.2

WOODS, TOMMY
Ht. 6-7 Wt. 215 College—East Tennessee State

Yr. Team		G	FG	FT	TP	Avg.
1967-68 Kentucky	(ABA)	18	14	14	42	2.3

WOOLLARD, BOB
Ht. 6-10 College—Wake Forest

Yr. Team		G	FG	FT	TP	Avg.
1969-70 Miami	(ABA)	20	32	20	84	4.2

WORKMAN, MARK
b. March 10, 1930 Ht. 6-9 Wt. 217 College—W. Virginia

Yr. Team		G	FG	FT	TP	Avg.
1952-53 Milw.-Phila.		65	130	70	330	5.1
1953-54 Baltimore		14	25	6	56	4.0
Totals		79	155	76	386	4.9

WORKMAN, TOM
b. Nov. 14, 1944 Ht. 6-7 Wt. 230 College—Seattle

Yr. Team		G	FG	FT	TP	Avg.
1967-68 St. Louis-Balt.		20	19	18	56	2.8
1968-69 Baltimore		21	22	9	53	2.5
1969-70 Detroit		2	0	0	0	0.0
1969-70 Los Angeles	(ABA)	26	116(1)	77	310	11.9
1970-71 Utah-Den.	(ABA)	56	133(3)	86	355	6.3
Totals		125	290(4)	190	774	6.2

WORSLEY, WILLIE
b. Nov. 13, 1945 Ht. 5-10 Wt. 175 College—Texas-El Paso

Yr. Team		G	FG	FT	TP	Avg.
1968-69 New York	(ABA)	24	36(10)	63	145	6.0

WRIGHT, HOWARD
Ht. 6-3 Wt. 185 College—Austin Peay

Yr. Team		G	FG	FT	TP	Avg.
1970-71 Kentucky	(ABA)	52	94(9)	40	237	4.6
1971-72 Kentucky	(ABA)	1	0	0	0	0.0
Totals		53	94(9)	40	237	4.5

WRIGHT, JOBY
b. Sept. 5, 1950 Ht. 6-8 Wt. 222 College—Indiana

Yr. Team		G	FG	FT	TP	Avg.
1972-73 Seattle		77	133	37	303	3.9
1973-74 Memphis	(ABA)	3	5	2	12	4.0
1975-76 S.D.-Vir.	(ABA)	23	50	21	121	5.3
Totals		108	188	60	436	4.2

WRIGHT, LAWRENCE (Lonnie)
b. Jan. 23, 1944 Ht. 6-2 Wt. 205 College—Colorado State

Yr. Team		G	FG	FT	TP	Avg.
1967-68 Denver	(ABA)	38	146(2)	79	373	9.8
1968-69 Denver	(ABA)	69	453(19)	205	1130	16.4
1969-70 Denver	(ABA)	79	393(54)	121	961	12.2
1970-71 Den.-Fla.	(ABA)	72	199(17)	93	508	7.1
1971-72 Floridians	(ABA)	77	252(19)	95	618	8.0
Totals		335	1443(111)	593	3590	10.7

WRIGHT, LEROY
b. May 6, 1938 Ht. 6-9 Wt. 215 College—Pacific

Yr. Team		G	FG	FT	TP	Avg.
1967-68 Pittsburgh	(ABA)	17	24	9	57	3.4
1968-69 Minnesota	(ABA)	10	4	0	8	0.8
Totals		27	28	9	65	2.4

WUYCIK, DENNIS
b. Mar. 29, 1950 Ht. 6-6 Wt. 215 College—North Carolina

Yr. Team		G	FG	FT	TP	Avg.
1972-73 Carolina	(ABA)	83	151	75	377	4.5
1973-74 Carolina	(ABA)	49	88(1)	51	228	4.7
1974-75 St. Louis	(ABA)	25	34	11	79	3.2
Totals		157	273(1)	137	684	4.4

YATES, BARRY
b. Jan. 30, 1946 Ht. 6-7 Wt. 215 College—Nebraska/Maryland

Yr. Team		G	FG	FT	TP	Avg.
1971-72 Philadelphia		24	31	7	69	2.9

YATES, WAYNE
b. Nov. 7, 1937 Ht. 6-8 Wt. 235 College—Memphis St.

Yr. Team		G	FG	FT	TP	Avg.
1961-62 Los Angeles		37	31	10	72	1.9

Yr.	Team	G	FG	FT	TP	Avg.
YARDLEY, GEORGE						
b. Nov. 3, 1928 Ht. 6-5 Wt. 195 College—Stanford						
1953-54 Ft. Wayne		63	209	146	564	9.0
1954-55 Ft. Wayne		60	363	310	1036	17.3
1955-56 Ft. Wayne		71	434	365	1233	17.4
1956-57 Ft. Wayne		72	522	503	1547	21.5
1957-58 Detroit		72	673	655	2001	27.8
1958-59 Det.-Syr.		61	446	317	1209	19.8
1959-60 Syracuse		73	546	381	1473	20.2
	Totals	472	3193	2677	9063	19.2
YELVERTON, CHARLIE						
b. Dec. 5, 1948 Ht. 6-2 Wt. 190 College—Fordham						
1971-72 Portland		69	206	133	545	7.9
ZASLOFSKY, MAX (Slats)						
b. Dec. 7, 1925 Ht. 6-2 Wt. 170 College—Chicago/St. John's						
1946-47 Chicago		61	336	205	877	14.4
1947-48 Chicago		48	373	261	1007	21.0
1948-49 Chicago		58	425	347	1197	20.6
1949-50 Chicago		68	397	321	1115	16.4
1950-51 New York		66	302	231	835	12.7
1951-52 New York		66	322	287	93′	14.1
1952-53 New York		29	123	98	344	11.9
1953-54 Balt.-Mil.-Ft. W.		65	278	255	811	12.5
1954-55 Ft. Wayne		70	269	247	785	11.2
1955-56 Ft. Wayne		9	29	30	88	9.8
	Totals	540	2854	2282	7990	14.8
ZAWOLUK, ROBERT (Zeke)						
b. Dec. 13, 1930 Ht. 6-7 Wt. 215 College—St. John's (N.Y.)						
1952-53 Indianapolis		41	55	77	187	4.6
1953-54 Philadelphia		71	203	186	592	8.3
1954-55 Philadelphia		67	138	155	431	6.4
	Totals	179	396	418	1210	6.8

Yr.	Team	G	FG	FT	TP	Avg.
ZELLER, DAVID						
b. June 8, 1939 Ht. 6-1½ Wt. 175 College—Miami (Ohio)						
1961-62 Cincinnati		61	36	18	90	1.5
ZELLER, GARY						
b. Nov. 20, 1947 Ht. 6-3 Wt. 205 College—Drake						
1970-71 Baltimore		50	34	15	83	1.7
1971-72 Balt.-N.Y.	(ABA)	40	90	26	206	5.2
	Totals	90	124	41	289	3.2
ZELLER, HARRY (Hank)						
b. 1919 Ht. 6-4 Wt. 210 College—Pittsburgh						
1946-47 Pittsburgh		48	120	122	362	7.5
ZENO, TONY						
b. Oct. 1, 1957 Ht. 6-8 Wt. 210 College—Arizona State						
1979-80 Indiana		8	6	2	14	1.8
ZOPF, BILL						
b. June 7, 1948 Ht. 6-1 Wt. 170 College—Duquesne						
1970-71 Milwaukee		53	49	20	118	2.2
ZUNIC, MATT						
b. Sept. 12, 1919 Ht. 6-7 Wt. 195 College—George Washington						
1947-48 Flint	(NL)	57	123	85	331	5.8
1948-49 Washington		56	98	77	273	4.9
	Totals	113	221	162	604	5.3

Index

All persons who appear in the encyclopedia are indexed with the exception of those whose names appear only in the All-Time Player Directory or only in lists of college drafts, all-time records, box scores or acknowledgments. **Boldface numerals** and **color insert** denote references to photo captions.